PEARSON ALWAYS LEARNING

Margaret L. Lial • Diana L. Hestwood

Prealgebra

Second Custom Edition for
Mercer County Community College—Trenton

Taken from:
Prealgebra, Fifth Edition
by Margaret L. Lial and Diana L. Hestwood

Cover Art: Courtesy of Pearson Learning Solutions.

Taken from:

Prealgebra, Fifth Edition
by Margaret L. Lial and Diana L. Hestwood
Copyright © 2014, 2010, 2006 by Pearson Education, Inc.
New York, New York 10013

This special edition published in cooperation with Pearson Learning Solutions.

Pearson Learning Solutions, 501 Boylston Street, Suite 900, Boston, MA 02116
A Pearson Education Company
www.pearsoned.com

Printed in the United States of America

1 2 3 4 5 6 7 8 9 10 V0UD 19 18 17 16 15

0002000102719146673

SL

ISBN 10: 1-323-10349-X
ISBN 13: 978-1-323-10349-4

This book is dedicated to Margaret L. Lial

Always passionate about mathematics and teaching,

Always a valued colleague, a mentor, and a friend,

Always in our memory.

This book is also dedicated to my husband, Earl Orf, who is the wind beneath my wings, and to my students at Minneapolis Community and Technical College, from whom I have learned so much.

Diana Hestwood

Contents

Preface

The fifth edition of *Prealgebra* continues our ongoing commitment to provide the best possible text and supplements package that will help instructors teach and students succeed. To that end, we have addressed the diverse needs of today's students by creating a tightly coordinated text and technology package that includes integrated activities to help students improve their study skills, an attractive design, updated applications and graphs, helpful features, and careful explanations of concepts. We've also expanded the supplements and study aids. We've revamped the video series into a complete Lial Video Library with expanded video coverage and new, easier navigation. And we've added the new Lial MyWorkBook. We have also responded to the suggestions of users and reviewers and have added many new examples and exercises based on their feedback.

The text is designed for mathematics students who are new to algebra, are relearning the algebra they studied in the past, or are anxious about their ability to learn algebra. The text interweaves just-in-time arithmetic review and geometry topics, as appropriate, into the algebraic themes of integers, variables and expressions, equations, solving application problems, positive and negative fractions and decimals, proportions, percents, measurement, graphing, and polynomials. The emphasis is on building a solid understanding of the foundations of algebra. This is accomplished by tying the content to students' experiences and previous knowledge, explaining important terminology in everyday English, showing *why* things work the way they do, and providing carefully sequenced exercises. This text is part of a series that also includes the following books:

* *Essential Mathematics,* Fourth Edition, by Lial and Salzman

* *Basic College Mathematics,* Ninth Edition, by Lial, Salzman, and Hestwood

* *Introductory Algebra,* Tenth Edition, by Lial, Hornsby, and McGinnis

* *Intermediate Algebra,* Tenth Edition, by Lial, Hornsby, and McGinnis

* *Introductory and Intermediate Algebra,* Fifth Edition, by Lial, Hornsby, and McGinnis

* *Prealgebra and Introductory Algebra,* Fourth Edition, by Lial, Hestwood, Hornsby, and McGinnis

* *Developmental Mathematics: Basic Mathematics and Algebra,* Third Edition, by Lial, Hornsby, McGinnis, Salzman, and Hestwood

WHAT'S NEW IN THIS EDITION

The scope and sequence of topics in *Prealgebra* has stood the test of time and rates highly with our reviewers. Therefore, you will find the table of contents intact, making the transition to the new edition easier.

▶ *Examples and Exercises*   Throughout the text, examples and exercises have been adjusted or replaced to reflect current data and practices. Applications have been updated and cover a wider variety of topics, such as the fields of technology, ecology, and health sciences.

▶ *Guided Solutions*   Selected exercises in the margins and in the exercise sets, marked with a GS icon, now show the first few solution steps. This provides guidance to students as they start learning a new concept or procedure and gets them off to a successful start. (See p. 168 margin, and p. 249, Exercises 15–16.)

▶ *Concept Checks*   The Concept Checks at the beginning of each exercise set assure students that they have necessary background skills or information to proceed. Concept Checks later in the exercise sets help students summarize and consolidate their learning by writing explanations, correcting common errors, and practicing mathematical processes. (See pp. 327 and 330.)

▶ *Vocabulary Tips*   Many students at this level of mathematics do not have strong reading skills. The vocabulary tips included in the margins throughout the book help them to learn the meaning of root words and prefixes commonly used in mathematics vocabulary (for example, *equ-, centi, tri-*), distinguish the mathematical meaning from the common usage of particular words (such as *volume, average*), and provide tips for remembering the difference between often-confused terms (such as the commutative and associative properties of addition on p. 25).

▶ *Teaching Tips*   Although the mathematical content in this text is familiar to instructors, they may not have experience in teaching the material to adult students. The Teaching Tips, printed in the margins of the Annotated Instructor's Edition, provide helpful comments from colleagues with successful experience at this level. Common trouble spots are noted, with suggestions for improving student understanding. (See pp. 540 and 541.) Simple, but effective, hands-on activities are also included. (See p. 297.)

▶ *Study Skills*   Thirteen carefully designed study skills activities provide opportunities for students to practice proven strategies for learning mathematics. Poor study skills and behaviors are major factors in low success rates in mathematics courses. Research shows that a few generic tips sprinkled here and there are not enough to help students change their study behaviors. Because students need specific instruction in study skills, we have contextualized them, integrating them into the text material. Topics include note taking, homework, study cards, math anxiety, test preparation, test taking, preparing for a final exam, and more. (See pp. 65–66, 105–106, and 152–153.) Most are located within the first few chapters so that students can use the skills throughout the course. (See the Contents for titles and locations.) The first activity, "Your Brain *Can* Learn Mathematics," explains how the brain actually learns and remembers so that students understand why the study skills will help them succeed in the course.

▶ *Lial Video Library*   The Lial Video Library, available in MyMathLab and on the Video Resources DVD, provides students with a wealth of video resources to help them navigate the road to success. All video resources in the library include optional captions in English and Spanish. The Lial Video Library includes Section Lecture Videos, Solutions Clips, Quick Review Lectures, and Chapter Test Prep Videos. The Chapter Test Prep Videos are also available on YouTube (searchable using author name and book title), or by scanning the QR code on the inside back cover for easy access.

▶ *MyWorkBook*   This new workbook provides Guided Examples and corresponding Now Try Exercises for each text objective. The extra practice exercises for every section of the text, with ample space for students to show their work, are correlated to Examples, Lecture Videos, and Exercise Solution Clips, to give students the help they need to successfully complete problems. Additionally, MyWorkBook lists the learning objectives and key vocabulary terms for every text section, along with vocabulary practice problems.

HALLMARK FEATURES

We believe students and instructors will welcome these familiar hallmark features.

▶ *Chapter Openers*   The new and engaging Chapter Openers portray real life situations making math relevant for students. (See Chapter 2, p. 93.)

▶ *Real-Life Applications*   We are always on the lookout for interesting data to use in real-life applications. As a result, we have included many new or updated examples and exercises throughout the text that focus on real-life applications of mathematics. Students are often asked to find data in a table, chart, graph, or advertisement. (See pp. 439 and 440.) These applied problems provide an up-to-date flavor that will appeal to and motivate students.

▶ *Figures and Photos*   Today's students are more visually oriented than ever. Thus, we have made a concerted effort to include mathematical figures, diagrams, tables, and graphs whenever possible. (See pp. 642 and 655.) Many of the graphs use a style similar to that seen by students in today's print and electronic media. Photos have been incorporated to enhance applications in examples and exercises. (See pp. 183 and 184.)

▶ *Emphasis on Problem Solving*   Chapter 3 introduces students to our six-step process for solving application problems algebraically: *Read, Assign a Variable, Write an Equation, Solve, State the Answer,* and *Check.* Devoting an entire chapter to this process allows students to build a strong foundation for problem solving, which is then reinforced through specific problem-solving examples in Chapters 4, 5, 6, 7, and 8. (See p. 188.)

▶ *Learning Objectives*   Each section begins with clearly stated, numbered objectives, and the material within sections is keyed to these objectives so that students know exactly what concepts are covered. (See p. 322.)

▶ *Pointers*   More pointers have been added to examples to provide students with important on-the-spot reminders and warnings about common pitfalls. (See pp. 111 and 463.)

▶ *Cautions and Notes*   These color-coded and boxed comments, one of the most popular features of previous editions, warn students about common errors and emphasize important ideas throughout the exposition. (See pp. 334–335.) Cautions are highlighted in yellow and Notes are highlighted with blue tabs.

▶ *Calculator Tips*   These optional tips, marked with a red calculator icon, offer helpful information and instruction for students using calculators in the course. (See p. 349.)

▶ *Margin Problems*   Margin problems, with answers immediately available on the bottom of the page, are found in every section of the text. (See pp. 14–15.) This key feature allows students to immediately practice the material covered in the examples in preparation for the exercise sets.

▶ *Ample and Varied Exercise Sets*   The text contains a wealth of exercises to provide students with opportunities to practice, apply, connect, and extend the skills they are learning. Numerous illustrations, tables, graphs, and photos help students visualize the problems they are solving. Problem types include skill building, writing, estimation, and calculator exercises, as well as applications and correct-the-error problems. In the Annotated Instructor's Edition of the text, the writing exercises are marked with an icon 🖉 so that instructors may assign these problems at their discretion. Exercises suitable for calculator work are marked in both the student and instructor editions with a calculator icon ▦ . (See pp. 586–587.) Students can watch an instructor work through the complete solution for all exercises marked with a Play Button icon ▶ on the Videos on DVD or in MyMathLab.

▶ *Relating Concepts Exercises*   These help students tie concepts together and develop higher level problem-solving skills as they compare and contrast ideas, identify and describe patterns, and extend concepts to new situations. (See pp. 133, 263, and 354.) These exercises make great collaborative activities for pairs or small groups of students.

▶ *Solutions*   Solutions to selected section exercises are included in the back of the book (following the Answers section). This provides students with easily accessible step-by-step help in solving the exercises that are most commonly missed. Solutions are provided for the exercises marked with a square of blue color around the exercise number, for example, **15.**

▶ *Summary Exercises*   All chapters now include this helpful mid-chapter review. These exercises provide students with the all-important *mixed* practice they need at these critical points in their skill development. (See pp. 185–186.)

▶ *Ample Opportunity for Review*   Each chapter ends with a Chapter Summary featuring: Key Terms with definitions and helpful graphics, New Formulas, New Symbols, Test Your Word Power, and a Quick Review of each section's content with additional examples. Also included is a comprehensive set of Chapter Review Exercises keyed to individual sections, a set of Mixed Review Exercises, and a Chapter Test. Students can watch an instructor work out the full solutions to the Chapter Test problems in the Chapter Test Prep Videos. Beginning with Chapter 2, each chapter concludes with a set of Cumulative Review Exercises. (See pp. 307–320.)

▶ *Test Your Word Power*   This feature, incorporated into each Chapter Summary, helps students understand and master mathematical vocabulary. Key terms from the chapter are presented along with three possible definitions in a multiple-choice format. Answers and examples illustrating each term are provided. (See p. 308.)

STUDENT SUPPLEMENTS

Student's Solutions Manual

- By Jeffery A. Cole, Anoka-Ramsey Community College
- Provides detailed solutions to the odd-numbered section-level exercises and to all margin, Relating Concepts, Summary, Chapter Review, Chapter Test, and Cumulative Review Exercises
  ISBNs: 0-321-84554-4, 978-0-321-84554-2

NEW MyWorkBook

- Provides Guided Examples and corresponding Now Try Exercises for each text objective
- Refers students to correlated Examples, Lecture Videos, and Exercise Solution Clips
- Includes extra practice exercises for every section of the text with ample space for students to show their work
- Lists the learning objectives and key vocabulary terms for every text section, along with vocabulary practice problems
  ISBNs: 0-321-84522-6, 978-0-321-84522-1

NEW Lial Video Library

The Lial Video Library, available in MyMathLab and on the Video Resources DVD, provides students with a wealth of video resources to help them navigate the road to success! All video resources in the library include optional captions in English and Spanish. The Lial Video Library includes the following resources:

- **Section Lecture Videos** offer a new navigation menu that allows students to easily focus on the key examples and exercises that they need to review in each section.
- **Solutions Clips** show an instructor working through the complete solutions to selected exercises from the text. Exercises with a solution clip are marked in the text and e-book with a Play Button icon ●.
- **Quick Review Lectures** provide a short summary lecture of each key concept from the Quick Reviews at the end of every chapter in the text.
- **The Chapter Test Prep Videos** provide step-by-step solutions to all exercises from the Chapter Tests. These videos provide guidance and support when students need it the most: the night before an exam. The Chapter Test Prep Videos are also available on YouTube (searchable using author name and book title), or by scanning the QR code on the inside back cover for easy access.

INSTRUCTOR SUPPLEMENTS

Annotated Instructor's Edition

- Provides answers to all text exercises in color next to the corresponding problems
- Icons identify writing ✎ and calculator ▦ exercises
  ISBNs: 0-321-84511-0, 978-0-321-84511-5

Instructor's Solutions Manual (Download only)

- By Jeffery A. Cole, Anoka-Ramsey Community College
- Provides complete solutions to all exercises in the text
- Available for download at www.pearsonhighered.com
  ISBNs: 0-321-84510-2, 978-0-321-84510-8

Instructor's Resource Manual with Tests and Mini-Lectures (Download only)

- Contains a test bank with two diagnostic pretests, six free-response and two multiple-choice test forms per chapter, and two final exams
- Contains a mini-lecture for each section of the text with objectives, key examples, and teaching tips
- Includes a correlation guide from the fourth to the fifth edition and phonetic spellings for all key terms in the text
- Includes resources to help both new and adjunct faculty with course preparation and classroom management, by offering helpful teaching tips correlated to the sections of the text
- Available for download at www.pearsonhighered.com
  ISBNs: 0-321-84515-3, 978-0-321-84515-3

ADDITIONAL MEDIA SUPPLEMENTS

MyMathLab® **MyMathLab® Online Course (access code required)**
MyMathLab delivers **proven results** in helping individual students succeed. It provides **engaging experiences** that personalize, stimulate, and measure learning for each student. And, it comes from a **trusted partner** with educational expertise and an eye on the future.

To learn more about how MyMathLab combines proven learning applications with powerful assessment, visit **www.mymathlab.com** or contact your Pearson representative.

MyMathLab® Ready to Go Course (access code required)

These new Ready to Go courses provide students with all the same great MyMathLab features that they are used to but make it easier for instructors to get started. Each course includes pre-assigned homework and quizzes to make creating a course even simpler.

Ask your Pearson representative about the details for this particular course or to see a copy of this course.

MyMathLab® Plus/MyStatLab™ Plus

MyLabsPlus combines proven results and engaging experiences from MyMathLab® and MyStatLab™ with convenient management tools and a dedicated services team. Designed to support growing math and statistics programs, it includes additional features such as:

- **Batch Enrollment:** Schools can create the login name and password for every student and instructor, so everyone can be ready to start class on the first day. Automation of this process is also possible through integration with the school's Student Information System.
- **Login from your campus portal:** Instructors and their students can link directly from their campus portal into the MyLabsPlus courses. A Pearson service team works with the institution to create a single sign-on experience for instructors and students.
- **Advanced Reporting:** MyLabsPlus's advanced reporting enables instructors to review and analyze students' strengths and weaknesses by tracking their performance on tests, assignments, and tutorials. Administrators can review grades and assignments across all courses on a MyLabsPlus campus for a broad overview of program performance.
- **24/7 Support:** Students and instructors receive 24/7 support, 365 days a year, by email or online chat.

MyLabsPlus is available to qualified adopters. For more information, visit our website at *www.mylabsplus.com* or contact your Pearson representative.

MathXL® Online Course (access code required)

MathXL® is the homework and assessment engine that runs MyMathLab. (MyMathLab is MathXL plus a learning management system.)

With MathXL, instructors can:

- Create, edit, and assign online homework and tests using algorithmically-generated exercises correlated at the objective level to the textbook.
- Create and assign their own online exercises and import TestGen tests for added flexibility.
- Maintain records of all student work tracked in MathXL's online gradebook.

With MathXL, students can:

- Take chapter tests in MathXL and receive personalized study plans and/or personalized homework assignments based on their test results.
- Use the study plan and/or the homework to link directly to tutorial exercises for the objectives they need to study.
- Access supplemental animations and video clips directly from selected exercises.

MathXL is available to qualified adopters. For more information, visit our website at *www.mathxl.com*, or contact your Pearson representative.

TestGen®

TestGen® (*www.pearsoned.com/testgen*) enables instructors to build, edit, print, and administer tests using a computerized bank of questions developed to cover all the objectives of the text. TestGen is algorithmically based, allowing instructors to create multiple but equivalent versions of the same question or test with the click of a button. Instructors can also modify test bank questions or add new questions. The software and testbank are available for download from Pearson Education's online catalog.

PowerPoint® Lecture Slides

- Present key concepts and definitions from the text
- Available for download at *www.pearsonhighered.com* or in MyMathLab

ACKNOWLEDGMENTS

The comments, criticisms, and suggestions of users, nonusers, instructors, and students have positively shaped this textbook over the years, and we are most grateful for the many responses we have received. The feedback gathered for this revision of the text was particularly helpful, and we especially wish to thank the following individuals who provided invaluable suggestions for this and the previous edition:

Carla Ainsworth, *Salt Lake Community College*
Vickie Aldrich, *Dona Ana Community College*
Barbara Brown, *Anoka-Ramsey Community College*
Kim Brown, *Tarrant County College—Northeast Campus*
Hien Bui, *Hillsborough Community College*
John Close, *Salt Lake Community College*
Jane Cuellar, *Taft College*
Ky Davis, *Zane State College*
Patricia Donovan, *San Joaquin Delta College*
Randy Gallaher, *Lewis and Clark Community College*
Nancy Graham, *Rose State College*
Lynn Hargrove, *Sierra College*
Susan Kautz, *Lone Star College Cy-Fair*
Nancy Ketchum, *Moberly Area Community College*
Lou Ann Mahaney, *Tarrant County College—Northeast Campus*
Susan Martin, *Diablo Valley College*
Pam Miller, *Phoenix College*

Elizabeth Morrison, *Valencia College—West Campus*
Faith Peters, *Broward College*
Sara Pries, *Sierra College*
Brooke Quinlan, *Hillsborough Community College—Dale Mabry Campus*
Manoj Raghunandanan, *Temple University*
Janalyn Richards, *Idaho State University*
Heather Roth, *Nova Southeastern University*
Julia Simms, *Southern Illinois University—Edwardsville*
Sounny Slitine, *Palo Alto College*
Marie E. St. James, *St. Clair County Community College*
Sharon Testone, *Onondaga Community College*
Shae Thompson, *Montana State University*
Joe Timpe, *Tarrant County College*
Cheryl Wilcox, *Diablo Valley College*
Kevin Yokoyama, *College of the Redwoods*
Karl Zilm, *Lewis and Clark Community College*

Our sincere thanks go to the dedicated individuals at Pearson who have worked hard to make this revision a success: Maureen O'Connor, Kathy Manley, Barbara Atkinson, Michelle Renda, Rachel Ross, Kari Heen, Christine Whitlock, Lauren Morse, Stephanie Green, and Rachel Haskell. We are also grateful to Marilyn Dwyer and Carol Merrigan of Cenveo/Nesbitt Graphics for their excellent production work; Bonnie Boehme, for supplying her copyediting expertise; Beth Anderson, for her fine photo research; Lucie Haskins, for producing a useful Index; Jeff Cole, for writing the Solutions Manuals; and Sara Van Asten and Perian Herring for their accuracy checking.

Special thanks go to Janis M. Cimperman, Associate Professor of Mathematics at St. Cloud State University, for her careful review of the new material and features in the book.

Linda Russell developed and wrote all the Study Skills activities, made the text more readable for developmental-level students, wrote all of the vocabulary tips, and provided much-needed help during the production phase. Her many years of experience with students at this level was invaluable.

The ultimate measure of this textbook's success is whether it helps students master algebra skills, develop problem-solving techniques, and increase their confidence in learning and using mathematics. In order for us, as authors, to know what to keep and what to improve for the next edition, we need to hear from you, the instructor, and you, the student. Please tell us what you like and where you need additional help by sending an e-mail to *math@pearson.com*. We appreciate your feedback!

Diana L. Hestwood

1 Introduction to Algebra: Integers

In this chapter, you'll see how we use both *positive* and *negative* numbers. For example, we use them to report temperatures, check our bank account balance, and interpret medical test results.

Study Skills
YOUR BRAIN *CAN* LEARN MATHEMATICS

OBJECTIVES

1. Describe how practice fosters dendrite growth.
2. Explain the effect of anxiety on the brain.

Your brain knows how to learn, just as your lungs know how to breathe; however, there are important things you can do to maximize your brain's ability to do its work. This short introduction will help you choose effective strategies for learning mathematics. This is a simplified explanation of a complex process.

Your brain's outer layer is called the **neocortex**, which is where higher level thinking, language, reasoning, and purposeful behavior occur. The neocortex has about 100 billion (100,000,000,000) brain cells called **neurons.**

Learning Something New

▶ As you learn something new, threadlike branches grow out of each neuron. These branches are called **dendrites.**

▶ When the dendrite from one neuron grows close enough to the dendrite from another neuron, a connection is made. There is a small gap at the connection point called a **synapse.** One dendrite sends an electrical signal across the gap to another dendrite.

▶ *Learning = growth and connecting of dendrites.*

Remembering New Skills

▶ When you practice a skill just once or twice, the connections between neurons are very weak. If you do not practice the skill again, the dendrites at the connection points wither and die back. You have forgotten the new skill!

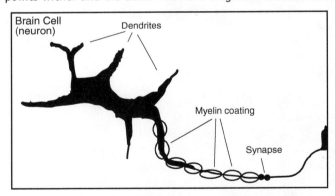

A neuron with several dendrites: one dendrite has developed a myelin coating through repeated practice.

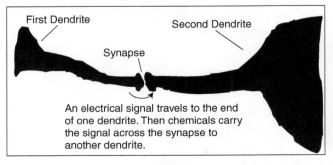

A close-up view of the connection (synapse) between two dendrites.

▶ If you practice a new skill many times, the dendrites for that skill become coated with a fatty protein called **myelin.** Each time one dendrite sends a signal to another dendrite, the myelin coating becomes thicker and smoother, allowing the signals to move faster and with less interference. Thinking can now occur more quickly and easily, and *you will remember the skill for a long time* because the dendrite connections are very strong.

Become An Effective Student

▶ You grow dendrites specifically for the thing you are studying. If you practice dividing fractions, you will grow specialized dendrites just for dividing fractions. If you *watch other people* solve fraction problems, *you will grow dendrites for watching, not for solving.* So, be sure you are actively learning and practicing.

▶ If you practice something the *wrong* way, you will develop strong dendrite connections for doing it the wrong way! So, as you study, check frequently that you are getting correct answers.

▶ As you study a new topic that is related to things you already know, you will grow new dendrites, but your brain will also send signals throughout the network of dendrites for the related topics. In this way, you build a complex **neural network** that allows you to apply concepts, see differences and similarities between ideas, and understand relationships between concepts.

In the first few chapters of this textbook you will find "brain friendly" activities that are designed to help you grow and develop your own reliable neural networks for mathematics. Since you must grow your own dendrites (no one can grow them for you), these activities show you how to

▶ develop new dendrites,

▶ strengthen existing ones, and

▶ encourage the myelin coating to become thicker so signals are sent with less effort.

When you incorporate the activities into your regular study routine, you will discover that you understand better, remember longer, and forget less.

Also remember that *it does take time for dendrites to grow.* Trying to cram in several new concepts and skills at the last minute is not possible. Your dendrites simply can't grow that quickly. You can't expect to develop huge muscles by lifting weights for just one evening before a body building competition! In the same way, practice the study techniques *throughout the course* to facilitate strong growth of dendrites.

When Anxiety Strikes

If you are under stress or feeling anxious, such as during a test, your body secretes **adrenaline** into your system. Adrenaline in the brain blocks connections between neurons. In other words, you can't think! If you've ever experienced "blanking out" on a test, you know what adrenaline does. You'll learn several solutions to that problem in later activities.

Start Your Course Right!

▶ Attend all class sessions (especially the first one).

▶ Gather the necessary supplies.

▶ Carefully read the syllabus for the course, and ask questions if you don't understand.

1.1 Place Value

OBJECTIVES

1. Identify whole numbers.
2. Identify the place value of a digit through hundred-trillions.
3. Write a whole number in words or digits.

Make a Strong Start!
Before you start **Chapter 1**, go to the beginning of **Chapter R** and take the **Whole Numbers Computation Pretest**. Based on your test results, work the appropriate sections of **Chapter R** to refresh your skills and then begin **Chapter 1**.

VOCABULARY TIP

Value The meaning of the word "value" in mathematics is slightly different than in everyday use. In math, "value" refers to "how much" or "a quantity." You will see the word "value" in many places in this textbook.

Answers

About $11\frac{1}{2}$ days to receive a million dollars; nearly 32 *years* to receive a billion dollars; about 31,700 *years* to receive a trillion dollars.

It would be nice to earn millions of dollars like some of our favorite entertainers or sports stars. But how much is a million? If you received $1 every second, 24 hours a day, day after day, how many days would it take for you to receive a million dollars? How long to receive a billion dollars? Or a trillion dollars? Make some guesses and write them here.

It would take _____ to receive a million dollars.

It would take _____ to receive a billion dollars.

It would take _____ to receive a trillion dollars.

The answers are at the bottom left of the page. Later in this chapter, you'll find out how to calculate the answers.

OBJECTIVE ▶ ① **Identify whole numbers.** First we have to be able to write the number that represents *one million*. We can write *one* as 1. How do we make it 1 *million?* Our number system is a **place value system.** That means that the location, or place, in which a number is written gives it a different value. Using money as an example, you can see that

$1 is one dollar.

$10 is ten dollars.

$100 is one hundred dollars.

$1000 is one thousand dollars.

Each time the 1 moved to the left one place, it was worth *ten times* as much. Can you keep moving it to the left? Yes, as many times as you like.

The chart below shows the *value* of each *place*. In other words, you write the 1 in the correct place to represent the number you want to express. It is important to memorize the place value names shown on the chart.

Whole Number Place Value Chart

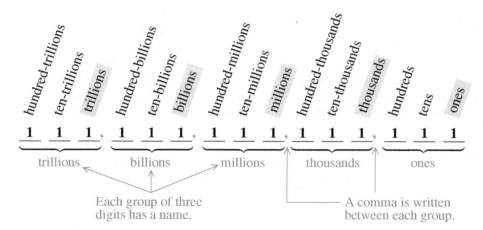

If there had been more room on this page, we could have continued to the left with quadrillions, quintillions, sextillions, septillions, octillions, and more.

Of course, we can use other *digits* besides 1. In our decimal system of writing numbers, we can use these ten **digits:** 0, 1, 2, 3, 4, 5, 6, 7, 8, and 9. In this section we will use the digits to write **whole numbers.**

These are whole numbers.

| 0 | 8 | 37 | 100 | 24,014 |

These are *not* whole numbers.

$$-6 \qquad \frac{3}{4} \qquad 7.528 \qquad 0.3 \qquad 5\frac{2}{3}$$

EXAMPLE 1 Identifying Whole Numbers

Circle the whole numbers in this list.

> Zero **is** a whole number.

$$75 \qquad -4 \qquad 300 \qquad 1.5 \qquad \frac{5}{8} \qquad 0 \qquad 0.666 \qquad 7\frac{1}{2} \qquad 2$$

 Whole numbers *do* include zero. If we started a list of *all* the whole numbers, it would look like this: 0, 1, 2, 3, 4, 5, . . . with the three dots indicating that the list goes on and on. So the whole numbers in this example are: 75, 300, 0, and 2.

········· Work Problem **1** at the Side. ▶

OBJECTIVE ▶ **2** **Identify the place value of a digit through hundred-trillions.** The estimated world population in 2010 was 6,853,049,416 people. There are two 6s in this number but the value of each 6 is very different. The 6 on the right is in the ones place, so its value is simply 6. But the 6 on the left is worth a great deal more because of the *place* where it is written. Looking back at the place value chart, we see that this 6 is in the billions place, so its value is *6 billion*.

$$6,853,049,416 \text{ people in the world}$$

   ↑   ↑

Value of   Value of
6 billion   *6 ones*

EXAMPLE 2 Identifying Place Value

Identify the place value of each 4 in the number of people in the world.

$$6,853,049,416$$

Ten-thousands place ─┘ └─ Hundreds place

········· Work Problem **2** at the Side. ▶

OBJECTIVE ▶ **3** **Write a whole number in words or digits.** To write a whole number in words, or to say it aloud, begin at the left. Write or say the number in each group of three, followed by the name for that group. When you get to the ones group, do *not* include the group name. Hyphens (dashes) are used whenever you write a number from 21 to 99, like twenty–one thousand, or thirty–seven million, or ninety–four billion.

EXAMPLE 3 Writing Numbers in Words

(a) Write 6,058,120 in words.
    Start at the left.

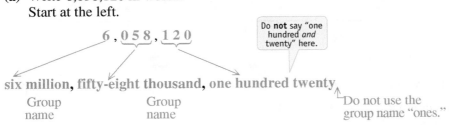

> Do **not** say "one hundred *and* twenty" here.

six million, fifty-eight thousand, one hundred twenty

Group name   Group name   Do not use the group name "ones."

········· **Continued on Next Page**

---

1 Circle the whole numbers. (*Hint:* There are five whole numbers.)

0.8	−14	502
$\frac{7}{9}$	3	$\frac{3}{2}$
14	0	$6\frac{4}{5}$
9.082	$-\frac{8}{3}$	60,005

VOCABULARY TIP

Place value Think of the number 3333. Each "3" has a different value, even though it is the same digit. The **place** where the 3 is located determines its value: three thousands, three hundreds, three tens, and three ones.

2 Identify the place value of the digit 8 in each number. Use the place value chart on the previous page if you need help.

(a) 45,628,665

(b) 800,503,622

(c) 428,000,000,000

(d) 2,385,071

Answers

1. 502; 3; 14; 0; 60,005
2. **(a)** thousands   **(b)** hundred-millions
    (c) billions   **(d)** ten-thousands

3 Write these numbers in words.

(a) 23,605

twenty-three _____,

six hundred _____

(b) 400,033,007

(c) 193,080,102,000,000

4 Write each number using digits.

(a) Eighteen million, two thousand, three hundred five

___ ___ ___ , ___ ___ ___ , ___ ___ ___

millions,   thousands,   ones

(b) Two hundred billion, fifty million, six hundred sixteen

(c) Five trillion, forty-two billion, nine million

(d) Three hundred six million, seven hundred thousand, nine hundred fifty-nine

Answers

3. **(a)** twenty-three *thousand*, six hundred <u>five</u>
   (b) four hundred *million*, thirty-three *thousand*, seven
   (c) one hundred ninety-three *trillion*, eighty *billion*, one hundred two *million*
4. **(a)** 18,002,305   **(b)** 200,050,000,616
   (c) 5,042,009,000,000   **(d)** 306,700,959

(b) Write 50,588,000,040,000 in words.
Start at the left.

$50,588,000,040,000$

fifty trillion, five hundred eighty-eight billion, forty thousand

No millions and no ones in this number

Group name   Group name   Group name

Notice the hyphen (dash) in eighty-eight.

CAUTION

You often hear people say "and" when reading a group of three digits. For example, you may hear 120 as "one hundred **and** twenty," but this is **not** correct. The word **and** is used when reading a **decimal point,** which we do not have here. The correct wording for 120 is "one hundred twenty." (See **Example 3(a)** at the bottom of the previous page.)

◀ **Work Problem 3 at the Side.**

When you read or hear a number and want to write it in digits, look for the group names: trillion, billion, million, and thousand. Write the number in each group, followed by a comma. Do *not* put a comma at the end of the ones group.

EXAMPLE 4   **Writing Numbers in Digits**

Write each number using digits.

(a) Five hundred sixteen thousand, nine

The first group name is *thousand,* so you need to fill *two groups* of three digits: thousands and ones.

$5\ 1\ 6\,,\ 0\ 0\ 9$

Write 009 in the ones group. If you wrote 900 it would be 9 *hundred.*

thousands | ones

comma between groups

The number is 516,009.

(b) Seventy-seven billion, thirty thousand, five hundred

The first group name is *billion,* so you need to fill *four groups* of three digits: billions, millions, thousands, and ones.

$0\ 7\ 7\,,\ 0\ 0\ 0\,,\ 0\ 3\ 0\,,\ 5\ 0\ 0$

billions   millions   thousands   ones

There are no millions, so fill the millions group with zeros.

When writing the number, you can omit the leading 0 in the billions group.

The number is 77,000,030,500.

◀ **Work Problem 4 at the Side.**

1.1 Exercises

MyMathLab®

Download the MyDashBoard App

CONCEPT CHECK *In Exercises 1–4, decide whether each statement is* true *or* false. *If a statement is* false, *fix it.*

1. The digits we can use to write numbers are

1, 2, 3, 4, 5, 6, 7, 8, and 9.

2. All of these numbers are whole numbers.

16,565   2   0   400

3. None of these numbers are whole numbers.

$\dfrac{7}{10}$ -21 0.03 $1\dfrac{1}{2}$

4. Each 7 in this number has the same value.

1,372,075

Circle the whole numbers. **See Example 1.**

5.   15 $8\dfrac{3}{4}$ 0   3.781

83,001 -8 $\dfrac{7}{16}$ $\dfrac{9}{5}$

6. 33.7 -5 457 $\dfrac{8}{5}$

0   6 $1\dfrac{3}{4}$ -14.1

7. 5.8 -6 7 $\dfrac{5}{4}$

$\dfrac{1}{10}$ 362,049   0.1 $7\dfrac{7}{8}$

8. 75,039 $\dfrac{1}{3}$ -87 6.49

-0.5 $2\dfrac{7}{10}$ $\dfrac{15}{8}$ 4

Identify the place value of the digit 2 in each number. **See Example 2.**

9. 61,284

10. 82,110

11. 284,100

12. 823,415

13. 725,837,166

14. 442,653,199

15. 253,045,701,000

16. 823,000,419,567

CONCEPT CHECK *In Exercises 17–18, name the place value for each 0 in the number, going from left to right.*

17. 302,016,450,098,570

18. 810,704,069,809,035

In Exercises 19–30, write each number in words. ***See Example 3.***

19. 8421

eight _____, four _____ twenty-_____

20. 1936

one _____, nine _____ thirty-_____

21. 46,205

22. 75,089

23. 3,064,801

24. 7,900,408

25. 840,111,003

26. 304,008,401

27. 51,006,888,321

28. 99,046,733,214

29. 3,000,712,000,000

30. 50,918,000,000,600

In Exercises 31–40, write each number using digits. ***See Example 4.***

31. Forty-six thousand, eight hundred five

___ ___ ___ , ___ ___ ___ ___
thousands   ones

32. Seventy-nine thousand, forty-six

___ ___ ___ , ___ ___ ___ ___
thousands   ones

33. Five million, six hundred thousand, eighty-two

34. One million, thirty thousand, five

35. Two hundred seventy-one million, nine hundred thousand

36. Three hundred eleven million, four hundred

37. Twelve billion, four hundred seventeen million, six hundred twenty-five thousand, three hundred ten

38. Seventy-five billion, eight hundred sixty-nine million, four hundred eighty-eight thousand, five hundred six

39. Six hundred trillion, seventy-one million, four hundred

40. Four hundred forty trillion, thirty-six thousand, one hundred two

In Exercises 41–52, if the number is given in digits, write it in words. If the number is given in words, write it in digits. **See Examples 3 and 4.** *(Source: World Almanac and Book of Facts, Statistical Abstract of the United States,* Associated Press, *Top Ten of Everything.)*

41. In the United States, 6041 couples get married every day.

42. The New Year's Eve ball that drops at midnight on December 31 in Times Square, New York, has 9576 energy-efficient bulbs.

43. The movie *Avatar* took in a total of seven hundred sixty million, three hundred nine thousand dollars in ticket sales in the United States.

44. The movie *Toy Story 3* took in one hundred ten million, three hundred seven thousand, two hundred dollars in ticket sales during its first weekend in U.S. movie theaters.

45. Every year in the United States, there are 1,056,720,000 take-out food orders.

46. The man who founded Facebook, Mark Zuckerberg, was worth $13,500,000,000 when he was 26 years old.

47. Play Station 2, first released in the year 2000, has sold one hundred forty-one million, seven hundred units.

48. The biggest employer in the United States is Walmart, with two million, one hundred thousand employees.

49. Dunkin' Donuts sells nearly 6,400,000 doughnuts every day. That's 2,336,000,000 doughnuts in one year!

50. The Hostess company bakeries are able to make 60,000 Twinkies every hour. That adds up to 525,600,000 Twinkies per year.

51. Americans sit in traffic jams for a total of four billion, two hundred million hours each year.

52. It is estimated that American drivers waste two billion, nine hundred million gallons of fuel yearly while sitting in traffic.

Relating Concepts (Exercises 53–56) For Individual or Group Work

Use your knowledge of place value to **work Exercises 53–56 in order.**

53. Here is a group of digits: 6, 0, 9, 1, 5, 0, 7, 1. Using each of these digits exactly once, arrange them to make the largest possible whole number and the smallest possible whole number. Then write each number in words.

54. Write these numbers in digits and in words.

(a) Your house number or apartment building number

(b) Your phone number, including the area code

(c) The approximate cost of your tuition and books for this quarter or semester

(d) Your zip code

Now tell how you *usually* say each of the numbers in parts (a)–(d) above. Why do you think we ignore the rules when saying these numbers in everyday situations?

55. Look again at the Whole Number Place Value Chart at the beginning of this section. As you move to the left, each place is worth *ten* times as much as the previous place. Computers work on a *binary* system, where each place is worth *two* times as much as the previous place. Complete this place value chart based on 2s.

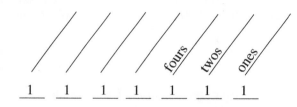

| 1 | 1 | 1 | 1 | 1 | 1 | 1 |

The *only* digits you may use in the binary system are 0 and 1. Here is an example.

$$6 = 110 \text{ in binary}$$

one 4 + one 2 + zero 1s = 4 + 2 + 0 = 6

Now try writing some numbers using the 2s (binary) place value chart.

(a) 5 = _____

(b) 10 = _____

(c) 15 = _____

56. (a) Explain in your own words why our number system is called a *place value system*. Include an example as part of your explanation.

(b) Find information on the Roman numeral system. Write these numbers using Roman numerals.

8 = _____   38 = _____

275 = _____   3322 = _____

(c) Explain why the Roman system is *not* a place value system. What are the disadvantages of the Roman system?

Study Skills
USING YOUR TEXTBOOK

Be sure to read *Your Brain **Can** Learn Mathematics* (pages 2–3) before this activity. You'll find out how your brain learns and remembers.

Your textbook can be very helpful. Find out what it has to offer. First, let's look at some general features that will help in all chapters.

OBJECTIVES

1 Explain the meaning of text features such as section numbering, objectives, margin exercises.

2 Locate the Answers, Solutions, and Index sections.

Table of Contents

Look on page v in the very front of the book for the Table of Contents. Before you start Chapter 1, you'll want to look at Chapter R, Whole Numbers Review, near the end of the book.

On page x in the Preface is a list of supplementary resources for students. If you are interested in any of these, ask your instructor if they are available.

Section Numbering

Each chapter is divided into sections, and each section has a number, such as 1.3 or 3.5. Your instructor will use these numbers to assign homework.

Chapter 3 $\longrightarrow$ **3.5** $\longleftarrow$ Section 5 within Chapter 3

Chapter Features

There are four features to pay special attention to as you work in your book.

▶ **Objectives.** Each section lists the objectives in the upper corner of the first page. The objectives are listed again as each one is introduced. An objective tells you *what you will be able to do after you complete the section*. An excellent way to check your learning is to go back to the list of objectives when you are finished with a section and ask yourself if you can do them all.

▶ **Margin exercises.** The exercises in the shaded margins of the pages in your textbook give you immediate practice. **This is a perfect way to get your dendrites growing right away!** Often you will be given the first few steps to help you start solving margin exercises. The answers are given at the bottom of the page, so you can check yourself easily.

▶ **Cautions, Pointers, Notes, and Calculator Tips.**

- **Caution!** A yellow box is a comment about a common error that students make, or a common trouble spot you will want to avoid.

- **Pointers** are little "clouds" next to worked examples. They point to specific places where common mistakes are made and give on-the-spot reminders.

- Look for the specially marked **Note** boxes with blue tabs. They contain hints, explanations, or interesting side comments about a topic.

- A small picture of a red calculator ▦ appears several places. In the main part of the chapter, the icon means that there is a **Calculator Tip,** which helps you learn more about using your calculator. A calculator in an Exercise section is a recommendation to use your calculator to work that exercise.

▶ **Vocabulary Tips** appear in the margins to help you learn the language of mathematics. Use them to create study cards for terminology that is new to you.

List a page number from Chapter 1 for each of these features:

A *Caution* appears on page _____.

A *Pointer* appears on page _____.

A *Note* appears on page _____.
A *Calculator Tip* appears on page _____.

Study Skills

Continued from page 11

How will you make good use of the
features at the end of each chapter?

_____

_____

_____

*Flag the Answers section
with a sticky note or other
device, so that you can turn
to it quickly.*

Why Are These Features
Brain Friendly?

The textbook authors included text
features that make it easier for you
to understand the mathematics.
**Your brain naturally seeks orga-
nization and predictability.** When
you pay attention to the regular
features of your textbook, you are
allowing your brain to get familiar
with all of the helpful tips, suggestions, and explanations that your
book has to offer. You will make the
best possible use of your textbook.

End-of-Chapter Features

Go back to the Table of Contents again. What is listed at the end of each chapter?

▶ **Chapter Summary** Turn to page 79 to find the Summary for Chapter 1. It lists
the chapter's **Key Terms** (arranged in the order that they appear in the chapter)
and **New Symbols** and/or **New Formulas.** Then, **Test Your Word Power** checks
your understanding of the math vocabulary. Next is a **Quick Review** section. It
lists each topic in the chapter and shows a worked example, with tips.

▶ **Review Exercises** Use these exercises as a way to check your understanding
of all the concepts in the chapter. You can practice every type of problem. If
you get stuck, the numbers in the dark blue rectangles tell you which section
of the chapter to go back to for more explanations. Make sure you do the
Mixed Review Exercises to practice for tests.

▶ **Chapter Test** Plan to take the test as a practice exam. That way you can be sure you
really know how to work all types of problems without looking back at the chapter.

▶ **Cumulative Review (starting with Chapter 2)** These exercises help you
maintain the skills you've learned in all previous chapters. Practicing previous
skills throughout the course will be a big help on the final exam.

Answers

How do you find out if you've worked the exercises correctly? Your textbook provides many of the answers. Throughout each chapter you should work the sample
problems in the **margins.** The answers for those are at the **bottom of each page**
in the margin area.

For homework, you can find the answers to all of the **odd-numbered section
exercises** in the **Answers to Selected Exercises** section near the end of your textbook.
Also, *all* of the answers are given for the Chapter Review Exercises and Chapter Tests.
Check your textbook now, and find the page on which the Answers section begins.

Solutions

The **Solutions** section near the end of the book shows how to solve some of the
harder odd-numbered exercises step by step. In the exercise sets, look for the
problem numbers with a square of blue shading around them. These are the ones
that have a solution in the back of the book.

Index

The **Index** is the last thing in your textbook. All of the topics, vocabulary, and
concepts are listed in alphabetical order in the Index. For example, look up the
words below. Go to the page or pages listed and find each word. Write down the
page that introduces or defines each one. There may be several subheadings
listed under the main word, or several page numbers listed. Usually, the *first*
place that a word appears in the textbook is where it is introduced and defined.
So, the earliest page number is a good place to start.

Commutative property of multiplication is defined on page _____.

Factors of numbers are defined on page _____.

Rounding of mixed numbers is explained on page _____.

1.2 Introduction to Integers

OBJECTIVES

1. Write positive and negative numbers used in everyday situations.
2. Graph numbers on a number line.
3. Use the < and > symbols to compare integers.
4. Find the absolute value of integers.

OBJECTIVE ▶ 1 Write positive and negative numbers used in everyday situations. The whole numbers in the previous section were either 0 or greater than 0. Numbers *greater* than 0 are called *positive numbers*. But many everyday situations involve numbers that are *less* than 0, called *negative numbers*. Here are a few examples.

At midnight the temperature dropped to 4 degrees *below* zero.

−4 degrees

Jean had $30 in her checking account. She wrote a check for $40.75. We say she is now $10.75 "in the hole," or $10.75 "in the red," or *overdrawn* by $10.75.

−$10.75

The Packers football team *gained* 6 yards on the first play. On the second play they *lost* 9 yards. We can write these results using a positive number and a negative number.

+6 yards   and   **−9 yards**

A plane took off from the airport and climbed to 20,000 feet *above* sea level. We can write this using a positive number.

+20,000 feet

A scuba diver swam down to $25\frac{1}{2}$ feet *below* the surface. We can write this using a negative number.

−$25\frac{1}{2}$ feet

Note

To write a negative number, put a negative sign (a dash) in front of it: −10. Notice that the negative sign looks exactly like the subtraction sign, as in 5 − 3 = 2. The negative sign and subtraction sign do *not* mean the same thing. See the example below.

−10 means negative 10   14 − 10 means 14 minus 10

Positive numbers can be written two ways:

1. Write a positive sign in front of the number: +2 is *positive 2.*

2. Do not write any sign. For example, 16 is assumed to be *positive 16.*

1 Write each negative number with a negative sign. Write each positive number in two ways.

(a) The temperature is $5\frac{1}{2}$ degrees below zero.

(b) Cameron lost 12 pounds on a diet.

(c) I deposited $210.35 in my bank account.

(d) I made too many charges, so my account is overdrawn by $65.

(e) The submarine dived to 100 feet below the surface of the sea.

(f) In this round of the card game, I won 50 points.

VOCABULARY TIPS

Graphs show information in the form of a drawing. A number line is one type of graph.

Graph integers by putting a dot at the correct place on a number line. Negative numbers are to the **left** of zero on a number line. Positive numbers are to the right of zero.

2 Graph each set of numbers.

(a) −2   (b) 2   (c) 0

(d) −4   (e) 4

(f) $-3\frac{1}{2}$ (g) 1   (h) −1   (i) 3

Answers

1. (a) $-5\frac{1}{2}$ degrees   (b) −12 pounds
   (c) $210.35 or +$210.35   (d) −$65
   (e) −100 feet   (f) 50 points or +50 points

2.

| EXAMPLE 1 | Writing Positive and Negative Numbers |

Write each negative number with a negative sign. Write each positive number in two ways.

(a) The river rose to 8 feet above flood stage.

$$+8 \text{ feet} \quad \text{or} \quad 8 \text{ feet}$$

       ↑   ↑

   Positive sign   No sign

(b) Michael lost $500 in the stock market.

$$-\$500$$

     ↑

  Negative sign

◀ **Work Problem 1 at the Side.**

OBJECTIVE ▶ 2 Graph numbers on a number line. Mathematicians often use a **number line** to show how numbers relate to each other. A number line is like a thermometer turned sideways. *Zero* is the dividing point between the positive and negative numbers.

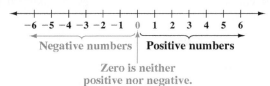

Zero is neither positive nor negative.

The number line could be shown with positive numbers on the left side of 0 instead of the right side. But it helps if everyone draws it the same way, as shown above. This method will also match what you do when graphing points and lines in **Chapter 9.**

| EXAMPLE 2 | Graphing Numbers on a Number Line |

Graph each number on the number line.

(a) −5   (b) 3   (c) $1\frac{1}{2}$ (d) 0   (e) −1

Draw a dot at the correct location for each number.

> 0 separates negative numbers from positive numbers.

◀ **Work Problem 2 at the Side.**

OBJECTIVE ▶ 3 Use the < and > symbols to compare integers. In **Chapters 4 and 5** you will work with fractions and decimals. For the rest of this chapter, you will work only with *integers*. A list of **integers** can be written like this:

$$\ldots, -6, -5, -4, -3, -2, -1, 0, 1, 2, 3, 4, 5, 6, \ldots$$

The dots show that the list goes on forever in both directions.

We can use the number line to compare two integers.

When comparing 1 and 4,
1 is to the *left* of 4.
1 is *less than* 4.
Use < to mean "is less than."

1   <   4

1 is less than 4

When comparing 0 and −3,
0 is to the *right* of −3.
0 is *greater than* −3.
Use > to mean "is greater than."

0   >   −3

0 is greater than −3

Note

One way to remember which symbol to use is that the "smaller end of the symbol" points to the "smaller number" (the number that is less).

1 < 4   0 > −3

Smaller number ⌐⌐ Smaller end   Smaller end ⌐ ⌐ Smaller number
of symbol   of symbol

EXAMPLE 3   **Comparing Integers, Using the < and > Symbols**

Write < or > between each pair of integers to make a true statement.

(a) 0 ____ 2

     0 is to the *left* of 2 on the number line,
     so 0 is *less than* 2. Write 0 < 2.

> The smaller end of the symbol points to the smaller number.

(b) −1 ____ −4

     1 is to the *right* of −4, so 1 is *greater than* −4. Write 1 > −4.

(c) −4 ____ −2

     −4 is to the *left* of −2, so −4 is *less than* −2. Write −4 < −2.

··························· **Work Problem ❸ at the Side.** ▶

OBJECTIVE ❹ Find the absolute value of integers. In order to graph a number on the number line, you need to ask two things:

1. Which *direction* is it from 0? It can be in a positive direction or a negative direction. You can tell the direction by looking for a positive sign (or no sign, which means positive) or a negative sign.

2. How *far* is it from 0? The distance from 0 is the *absolute value* of a number.

---

❸ Write < or > between each pair of integers to make a true statement.

(a) 5 ____ 4

     5 is to the *right* of 4
     on the number line, so
     5 *is greater than* 4.

(b) 0 ____ 2

(c) −3 ____ −2

(d) −1 ____ −4

(e) 2 ____ −2

(f) −5 ____ 1

Answers

3. (a) >   (b) <   (c) <   (d) >
    (e) >   (f) <

VOCABULARY TIP

> *and* < The lesser of two numbers is the one **farther to the left** on a number line. To use < or >, recall that the **point** on the symbol points to the **lesser** number. For example, −5 < 2 reads "negative five is less than two" and −5 is **to the left** of 2 on the number line.

4 Find each absolute value.

(a) $|13|$

How far away is 13 from 0 on the number line?

(b) $|-7|$

How far away is -7 from 0 on the number line?

(c) $|0|$

(d) $|-350|$

(e) $|6000|$

Absolute Value

The **absolute value** of a number is its distance from 0 on the number line. *Absolute value* is indicated by two vertical bars. For example,

$|6|$ is read "the absolute value of 6."

The absolute value of a number will *always* be positive (or 0), because it is the *distance* from 0. A distance is never negative. (You wouldn't say that your living room is -16 feet long.) So absolute value concerns only *how far away* the number is from 0; we don't care which direction it is from 0.

EXAMPLE 4   **Finding Absolute Values**

Find each absolute value.

(a) $|4|$ The distance from 0 to 4 on the number line is 4 spaces. So, $|4| = 4$.

(b) $|-4|$ The distance from 0 to -4 on the number line is also 4 spaces. So, $|-4| = 4$.

Absolute value is always positive (or 0), never negative.

(c) $|0|$ $|0| = 0$ because the distance from 0 to 0 on the number line is 0 spaces.

◀ **Work Problem** **4** **at the Side.**

Answers

4. **(a)** 13   **(b)** 7   **(c)** 0   **(d)** 350   **(e)** 6000

1.2 Exercises

  FOR EXTRA HELP   Download the MyDashBoard App   ▶ MyMathLab®

CONCEPT CHECK *Write a positive or negative number for each situation.* **See Example 1.**

1. Mount Everest, the tallest mountain in the world, rises 29,035 feet **above** sea level. The word "above" indicates a *positive* number.

2. The bottom of Lake Baikal in Siberia, Russia, is 5314 feet **below** the surface of the water. The word "below" indicates a *negative* number.

Depth below surface

3. ▶ The coldest temperature ever recorded on Earth is 128.6 degrees below zero in Antarctica. (*Source: Fact Finder.*)

4. Normal body temperature is 98.6 degrees Fahrenheit, although it varies slightly for some people. (*Source:* Mayo Clinic *Health Letter.*)

5. During the first three plays of the football game, the Trojans lost a total of 18 yards.

6. The Jets gained 25 yards on a pass play.

7. ▶ Angelique won $100 in a prize drawing at the shopping mall.

8. Derice overdrew his bank account by $37.

9. Keith lost $6\frac{1}{2}$ pounds while he was sick with the flu.

10. The mice in an experiment gained $2\frac{1}{2}$ ounces.

Graph each set of numbers. **See Example 2.**

11. ▶ $-3, 3, 0, -5$

12. $-2, 2, 0, 5$

13. $-1, 4, -2, 5$

14. $3, -4, 1, -5$

CONCEPT CHECK *Write each statement in words.*

15. **(a)** $0 < 5$

(b) $-10 > -17$

16. **(a)** $3 > -7$

(b) $12 < 22$

Write < or > between each pair of numbers to make a true statement.
See Example 3.

17. 10 ____ 2

18. 6 ____ 0

19. −1 ____ 0

20. −3 ____ −1

21. −10 ____ 2

22. −9 ____ 7

23. −3 ____ −6

24. 0 ____ −1

25. −10 ____ −2

26. −1 ____ −5

27. 0 ____ −8

28. 6 ____ −4

29. 10 ____ −2

30. −2 ____ 1

31. −4 ____ 4

32. 9 ____ −9

Find each absolute value. *See Example 4.*

33. $|15|$

34. $|10|$

35. $|-3|$

36. $|-8|$

37. $|0|$

38. $|100|$

39. $|200|$

40. $|-99|$

41. $|-75|$

42. $|-6320|$

43. $|-8042|$

44. $|0|$

Relating Concepts (Exercises 45–48) For Individual or Group Work

A special type of X-ray, called a DEXA test, is a quick way to screen patients for osteoporosis (brittle bone disease). Use the information on the Patient Report Form to **work Exercises 45–48 in order.**

Patient Report Form

Your T score measures your bone density compared to that of a young, healthy woman when peak bone mass is achieved.

T Score	Interpretation
Above 0	Above normal
0 to −1	Normal
Below −1	You may be at risk; further discussion with your health care provider is recommended.

Source: Health Partners, Inc.

45. Here are the T scores for four patients. Draw a number line and graph the four scores.

Patient A: −1.5   Patient C: −1
Patient B: 0.5   Patient D: 0

46. List the patients' scores in order from lowest to highest.

47. What is the interpretation of each patient's score?

Taking a DEXA test of a patient's spine.

48. **(a)** What could happen if patient A did not understand the importance of a negative sign?

(b) For which patient does the sign of the score make no difference? Explain your answer.

Study Skills
HOMEWORK: HOW, WHY, AND WHEN

I t is best for your brain if you keep up with the reading and homework in your math class. Remember that the more times you work with the information, the more dendrites you grow! So, give yourself every opportunity to read, work problems, and review your mathematics.

You have two choices for reading your math textbook. Read the short descriptions below and decide which will be best for you.

Preview before Class; Read Carefully after Class

Maddy learns best by listening to her teacher explain things. She "gets it" when she sees the instructor work problems on the board. She likes to ask questions in class and put the information in her notes. She has learned that it helps if she has *previewed* the section and read the definitions of new vocabulary before the lecture, so she knows generally what to expect in class. *But after the class instruction,* when Maddy gets home, she finds that she can understand the math textbook easily. She remembers what her teacher said, and she can double-check her notes if she gets confused. So, Maddy does her **careful** reading of the section in her text **after** hearing the classroom lecture on the topic.

Read Carefully before Class

De'Lore, on the other hand, feels he learns well by reading on his own. He prefers to read the section, learn the new vocabulary, and try working the example problems before coming to class. That way, he already knows what the teacher is going to talk about. Then, he can follow the teacher's examples more easily. It is also easier for him to take notes in class. De'Lore likes to have his questions answered right away, which he can do if he has already read the chapter section. So, De'Lore **carefully** reads the section in his text **before** he hears the classroom lecture on the topic.

Notice that there is **no one right way** to work with your textbook. You always must figure out what works best for you. Note also that both Maddy and De'Lore work with one section at a time. **The key is that you read the textbook regularly!** The rest of this activity will give you some ideas of how to make the most of your reading.

Try the following steps as you **read** your math textbook.

▶ Pay attention to every word, even small ones.
"15 divided **by** 3" is **not** the same as "15 divided **into** 3."

$$3\overline{)15} = 5 \qquad\qquad 15\overline{)3.0} = 0.2$$

One little word makes a difference in how you solve a problem!

▶ Read slowly. Read only one section—or even part of a section—at a time. You may even need to read some sentences two or three times. This is what **all** math students must do to succeed. Mathematics textbooks require a different type of reading than most other subjects. You must read every word carefully and accurately so you don't miss any important details.

▶ Do the sample problems in the margins **as you go.** Check them right away. The answers are at the bottom of the page.

▶ If your mind wanders, work problems on separate paper and write explanations in your own words.

Why Are These Reading Techniques Brain Friendly?

The steps at the left encourage you to be **actively working with the material** in your text. Your brain **grows dendrites when it is doing something.**

These methods require you to **try several different techniques,** not just the same thing over and over. Your brain loves variety!
Also, the techniques allow you to take small breaks in your learning. Those **rest periods are crucial for good dendrite growth.**

Study Skills

Continued from page 19

Why Are These Homework Suggestions Brain Friendly?

Your brain will grow dendrites as you study the worked examples in the text and try doing them yourself on separate paper. So, when you see similar problems in the homework, you will already have dendrites to work from.

Giving yourself a practice test by trying to remember the steps (without looking at your card) is an excellent way to reinforce what you are learning.

Correcting errors right away is how you learn and reinforce the correct procedures. It is hard to unlearn a mistake, so always check to see that you are on the right track!

▶ Make study cards as you read each section. Make cards for new vocabulary, rules, procedures, formulas, and sample problems.

▶ **NOW,** you are ready to do your homework assignment!

Now Try This

Which steps for reading this book will be most helpful for you?

1 _____

2 _____

3 _____

Homework

Teachers assign homework so you can grow your own dendrites (learn the material) and then coat the dendrites with myelin through practice (remember the material). In learning, you get good at what you practice. So, completing homework every day will strengthen your neural network and prepare you for exams.

If you have read each section in your textbook according to the steps above, you will probably encounter few difficulties with the exercises in the homework. Here are some additional suggestions that will help you succeed with the homework.

▶ If you **have trouble with a problem,** find a similar worked example in the section. Pay attention to *every line* of the worked example to see how to get from step to step. Work it yourself too, on separate paper; don't just look at it.

▶ If it is **hard to remember the steps** to follow for certain procedures, write the steps on a separate card. Then write a short explanation of each step. Keep the card nearby while you do the exercises, but try *not* to look at it.

▶ If you **aren't sure you are working the assigned exercises correctly,** choose two or three odd-numbered problems that are a similar type and work them. Then check the answers in the Answers section at the back of your book to see if you are doing them correctly. If you aren't, go back to the section in the text and review the examples and find out how to correct your errors. When you are sure you understand, try the assigned problems again.

▶ **Make sure you do some homework every day,** even if the math class does not meet each day!

Now Try This

What are your biggest homework concerns?
List your two main concerns and a **brain friendly solution** for each one.

1 Concern: _____

　　 Solution: _____

2 Concern: _____

　　 Solution: _____

1.3 Adding Integers

OBJECTIVE **1** **Add integers.** Numbers that you are adding are called **addends,** and the result is called the **sum.** You can add integers while watching a football game. On each play, you can use a *positive* integer to stand for the yards *gained* by your team, and a *negative* integer for yards *lost*. Zero indicates no gain or loss. For example,

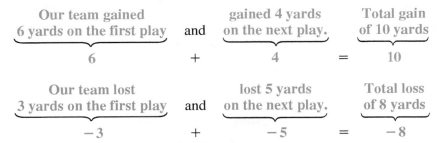

A drawing of a football field can help you add integers. Notice how similar the drawing is to a number line. Zero marks your team's starting point.

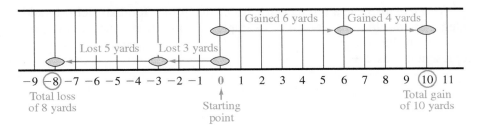

EXAMPLE 1 **Using a Number Line to Add Integers**

Use a number line to find $-5 + (-4)$.

Think of the number line as a football field. Your team starts at 0. On the first play it lost 5 yards. On the next play it lost 4 yards. The total loss is 9 yards.

$$-5 + (-4) = -9$$

·········· **Work Problem** **1** **at the Side.** ▶

Do you see a pattern in the margin problems you just did? The first two sums are -4 and 4. They are the same, *except for the sign*. The same is true for the next two sums, -11 and 11, and for the last two sums, -10 and 10. This pattern leads to a rule for adding two integers when the signs are the same.

Adding Two Integers with the Same Sign

Step 1 *Add* the absolute values of the numbers.

Step 2 Use the *common sign* as the sign of the sum. If both numbers are positive, the sum is positive. If both numbers are negative, the sum is negative.

OBJECTIVES

1 Add integers.
2 Identify properties of addition.

1 Find each sum. Use the number line to help you.

(a) $-2 + (-2)$

(b) $2 + 2$

(c) $-10 + (-1)$

(d) $10 + 1$

(e) $-3 + (-7)$

(f) $3 + 7$

Answers
1. (a) -4 **(b)** 4 **(c)** -11 **(d)** 11
(e) -10 **(f)** 10

2 Find each sum.

(a) $-6 + (-6)$

Both negative, so the sum is negative.

(b) $9 + 7$

Both positive, so the sum is positive.

(c) $-5 + (-10)$

(d) $-12 + (-4)$

(e) $13 + 2$

EXAMPLE 2	Adding Two Integers with the Same Sign

Add.

(a) $-8 + (-7)$

Step 1 *Add* the absolute values.
$$|-8| = 8 \qquad \text{and} \qquad |-7| = 7$$
Add $8 + 7$ to get 15.

Step 2 Use the *common sign* as the sign of the sum. Both numbers are negative, so the sum is negative.

$$-8 + (-7) = -15$$

Both negative   Sum is negative.

(b) $3 + 6 = 9$

In *Step 1*, when both numbers are positive, their absolute values are also positive, so we only need to show *Step 2*.

Both positive   Sum is positive.

◀ **Work Problem 2** at the Side.

You can also use a number line (or drawing of a football field) to add integers with *different* signs. For example, suppose that your team gained 2 yards on the first play and then lost 7 yards on the next play. We can represent this as $2 + (-7)$.

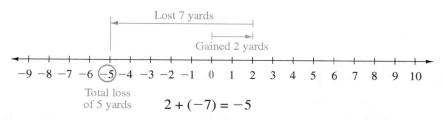

Lost 7 yards

Gained 2 yards

Total loss of 5 yards

$$2 + (-7) = -5$$

Or, try this one. On the first play your team gained 10 yards, but then it lost 4 yards on the next play. We can represent this as $10 + (-4)$.

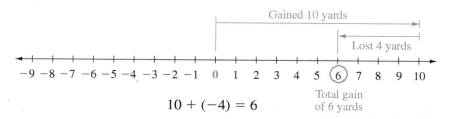

Gained 10 yards

Lost 4 yards

$$10 + (-4) = 6$$

Total gain of 6 yards

These examples illustrate the rule for adding two integers with unlike, or different, signs.

Adding Two Integers with Unlike Signs

Step 1 *Subtract* the lesser absolute value from the greater absolute value.

Step 2 Use the sign of the number with the *greater absolute value* as the sign of the sum.

EXAMPLE 3   Adding Two Integers with Unlike Signs

Add.

(a) $-8 + 3$

Step 1 $|-8| = 8$ and $|3| = 3$

Subtract $8 - 3$ to get 5.

Step 2 -8 has the *greater absolute value* and is negative, so the sum is also negative.

$$-8 + 3 = -5$$

(b) $-5 + 11$

Step 1 $|-5| = 5$ and $|11| = 11$

Subtract $11 - 5$ to get 6.

Step 2   11 has the *greater absolute value* and is positive, so the sum is also positive.

$$-5 + 11 = +6 \quad \text{or} \quad 6$$

················· **Work Problem ❸ at the Side.** ▶

EXAMPLE 4   Adding Several Integers

A football team has to gain at least 10 yards during four plays in order to keep the ball. Suppose that your college team lost 6 yards on the first play, gained 8 yards on the second play, lost 2 yards on the third play, and gained 7 yards on the fourth play. Did the team gain enough to keep the ball?

When you're adding several integers, work from left to right.

1st play	2nd play		3rd play		4th play

-6 yards $+$ 8 yards $\; + \; (-2$ yards$) + 7$ yards   First add $-6 + 8$.

2 yards $\qquad\quad + \; (-2$ yards$) + 7$ yards   Add $2 + (-2)$.

0 yards $\qquad\qquad\quad\; + 7$ yards   Add $0 + 7$.

7 yards

The team gained 7 yards, which are *not* enough yards to keep the ball.

················· **Work Problem ❹ at the Side.** ▶

OBJECTIVE ▶ ②   Identify properties of addition. In our football model for adding integers, we said that 0 indicated no gain or loss, that is, no change in the position of the ball. This example illustrates one of the *properties of addition*. The properties of addition apply to all addition problems, regardless of the specific numbers you use.

Addition Property of 0

Adding 0 to any number leaves the number unchanged.

Some examples are shown below.

$$0 + 6 = 6 \qquad -25 + 0 = -25 \qquad 72{,}399 + 0 = 72{,}399$$
$$0 + (-100) = -100$$

---

❸ Find each sum.

ɢs (a) $-3 + 7$

$|-3| = $ _____   and $|7| = $ _____.

Subtract $7 - 3$ to get _____.

The sum is positive because 7 has the greater absolute value and is positive.

$-3 + 7 = $ _____

(b) $6 + (-12)$

(c) $12 + (-7)$

(d) $-10 + 2$

(e) $5 + (-9)$

❹ Write an addition problem and solve it for each situation.

(a) The temperature was -15 degrees this morning. It rose 21 degrees during the day, then dropped 10 degrees. What is the new temperature?

(b) Andrew had $60 in his bank account. First he deposited an $85 tax refund in his account. Then he used his debit card to pay $20 for gas and $75 for groceries. What is the balance in his account?

Answers

3. (a) $|-3| = 3$ and $|7| = 7$; $7 - 3$ is 4; 4
   (b) -6 **(c)** 5   **(d)** -8 **(e)** -4
4. (a) $-15 + 21 + (-10) = -4$ degrees
   (b) $60 + 85 + (-20) + (-75) = 50

5 Rewrite each sum using the commutative property of addition. Check that the sum is unchanged.

(GS) **(a)** $175 + 25 = $ __25__ + ____

Both sums are ____.

(b) $7 + (-37) = $ ____ + ____

Both sums are ____.

(c) $-16 + 16 = $ ____ + (____)

Both sums are ____.

(d) $-9 + (-41) = $ ____ + (____)

Both sums are ____.

Another property of addition is that you can change the *order* of the addends and still get the same sum. For example,

Gaining 2 yards, then losing 7 yards, gives a result of -5 yards.

Losing 7 yards, then gaining 2 yards, also gives a result of -5 yards.

Commutative Property of Addition

Changing the *order* of two addends does *not* change the sum.

Here are some examples.

$$84 + 2 = 2 + 84 \qquad \qquad -10 + 6 = 6 + (-10)$$

Both sums are 86. $\qquad$ Both sums are -4.

EXAMPLE 5 **Using the Commutative Property of Addition**

Rewrite each sum, using the **commutative property of addition.** Check that the sum is unchanged.

(a) $65 + 35$

$$\underbrace{65 + 35}_{100} = \underbrace{35 + 65}_{100}$$

Both sums are 100, so the sum is unchanged.

> Adding two numbers in a different order does *not* change the sum.

(b) $-20 + (-30)$

$$\underbrace{-20 + (-30)}_{-50} = \underbrace{-30 + (-20)}_{-50}$$

Both sums are -50, so the sum is unchanged.

◀ **Work Problem** **5** at the Side.

When there are three addends, parentheses may be used to tell you which pair of numbers to add first, as shown below.

$\underbrace{(3 + 4)} + 2$ $\quad$ First add $3 + 4$. $\qquad$ $3 + \underbrace{(4 + 2)}$ $\quad$ First add $4 + 2$.

$\underbrace{7 \quad + 2}$ $\quad$ Then add $7 + 2$. $\qquad$ $3 + \quad 6$ $\quad$ Then add $3 + 6$.

9 $\qquad\qquad\qquad\qquad\qquad$ 9

Both sums are 9. This example illustrates another property of addition.

Associative Property of Addition

Changing the *grouping* of addends does *not* change the sum.

Some examples are shown below.

$\underbrace{(-5 + 5)} + 8 = -5 + \underbrace{(5 + 8)}$ $\qquad$ $3 + \underbrace{(4 + 6)} = \underbrace{(3 + 4)} + 6$

$\underbrace{0 \quad + 8} = -5 + \quad 13$ $\qquad$ $3 + \quad 10 \quad = \quad 7 \quad + 6$

$8 \quad = \quad 8$ $\qquad\qquad\qquad$ $13 \quad = \quad 13$

Both sums are 8. $\qquad\qquad$ Both sums are 13.

Answers

5. **(a)** $175 + 25 = 25 + 175; 200$
  (b) $7 + (-37) = -37 + 7; -30$
  (c) $-16 + 16 = 16 + (-16); 0$
  (d) $-9 + (-41) = -41 + (-9); -50$

We can use the associative property to make addition problems easier. Notice in the first example in the green box at the bottom of the previous page that it is easier to group $-5 + 5$ (which is 0) and then add 8. In the second example in the box, it is helpful to group $4 + 6$ because the sum is 10, and it is easy to work with multiples of 10. (See **Chapter R** for more on multiples of 10.)

(See **Chapter R** for more on multiples of 10.)

EXAMPLE 6 Using the Associative Property of Addition

In each addition problem, pick out the two addends that would be easiest to add. Write parentheses around those addends. Then find the sum.

(a) $-9 + 9 + 6$

Group $-9 + 9$ because the sum is 0.

$$(-9 + 9) + 6$$

> Use the associative property to add the easiest numbers first.

$$\underbrace{0} + 6$$
$$6$$

(b) $-25 + 17 + 3$

Group $17 + 3$ because the sum is 20, which is a multiple of 10.

$$-25 + \underbrace{(17 + 3)}$$
$$-25 + \quad 20$$
$$-5$$

Note

When using the associative property to make the addition of a group of numbers easier:

1. Look for two numbers whose sum is 0.

2. Look for two numbers whose sum is a multiple of 10 (the sum ends in 0, such as 10, 20, 30, or -100, -200, etc.).

If neither of these occurs, look for two numbers that are easier for you to add. For example, in $98 + 43 + 5$, you may find that adding $43 + 5$ is easier than adding $98 + 43$.

················ **Work Problem 6 at the Side.** ▶

---

6 In each problem, find the two addends that would be easiest to add. Then find the sum.

(a) $-12 + 12 + (-19)$

(b) $31 + (-75) + 75$

(c) $1 + 9 + (-16)$

(d) $-38 + 5 + 25$

Answers

6. (a) $\underbrace{(-12 + 12)} + (-19)$
$\quad \underbrace{0} \quad + (-19)$
$\quad\quad -19$

(b) $31 + \underbrace{(-75 + 75)}$
$\quad 31 + \quad \underbrace{0}$
$\quad\quad 31$

(c) $\underbrace{(1 + 9)} + (-16)$
$\quad \underbrace{10} \quad + (-16)$
$\quad\quad -6$

(d) $-38 + \underbrace{(5 + 25)}$
$\quad -38 + \quad \underbrace{30}$
$\quad\quad -8$

1.3 Exercises FOR EXTRA HELP   MyMathLab®

Add by using the number line. **See Example 1.**

1. $-2 + 5$

2. $-3 + 4$

3. $-5 + (-2)$

4. $-2 + (-2)$

5. $3 + (-4)$

6. $5 + (-1)$

Add. **See Example 2.**

7. (a) $-5 + (-5)$

(b) $5 + 5$

8. (a) $-9 + (-9)$

(b) $9 + 9$

9. (a) $7 + 5$

(b) $-7 + (-5)$

10. (a) $3 + 6$

(b) $-3 + (-6)$

11. (a) $-25 + (-25)$

(b) $25 + 25$

12. (a) $-30 + (-30)$

(b) $30 + 30$

13. (a) $48 + 110$

(b) $-48 + (-110)$

14. (a) $235 + 21$

(b) $-235 + (-21)$

15. CONCEPT CHECK   What pattern do you see in your answers to **Exercises 7–14?** Explain why this pattern occurs.

16. CONCEPT CHECK   In your own words, explain how to add two integers that have the same sign.

Add. See Example 3.

17. (a) $-6 + 8$

   (b) $6 + (-8)$

18. (a) $-3 + 7$

   (b) $3 + (-7)$

19. (a) $-9 + 2$

   (b) $9 + (-2)$

20. (a) $-8 + 7$

   (b) $8 + (-7)$

21. (a) $20 + (-25)$

   (b) $-20 + 25$

22. (a) $30 + (-40)$

   (b) $-30 + 40$

23. (a) $200 + (-50)$

   (b) $-200 + 50$

24. (a) $150 + (-100)$

   (b) $-150 + 100$

25. CONCEPT CHECK What pattern do you see in your answers to **Exercises 17–24?** Explain why this pattern occurs.

26. CONCEPT CHECK In your own words, explain how to add two integers that have different signs.

Add. See Examples 2–4.

27. $-8 + 5$

28. $-3 + 2$

29. $-1 + 8$

30. $-4 + 10$

31. $-2 + (-5)$

32. $-7 + (-3)$

33. $6 + (-5)$

34. $11 + (-3)$

35. $4 + (-12)$

36. $9 + (-10)$

37. $-10 + (-10)$

38. $-5 + (-20)$

39. $-17 + 0$

40. $0 + (-11)$

41. $1 + (-23)$

42. $13 + (-1)$

43. $\underbrace{-2 + (-12)}_{-14} + (-5)$

$\underbrace{ + (-5)}$

_____

44. $\underbrace{-16 + (-1)}_{-17} + (-3)$

$\underbrace{ + (-3)}$

_____

45. $8 + 6 + (-8)$

46. $-5 + 2 + 5$

47. $-7 + 6 + (-4)$

48. $-9 + 8 + (-2)$

49. $-3 + (-11) + 14$

50. $15 + (-7) + (-8)$

51. $10 + (-6) + (-3) + 4$

52. $2 + (-1) + (-9) + 12$

53. $-7 + 28 + (-56) + 3$

54. $4 + (-37) + 29 + (-5)$

Write an addition problem for each situation and find the sum.

55. The football team gained 13 yards on the first play and lost 17 yards on the second play. How many yards did the team gain or lose in all?

56. At penguin breeding grounds on Antarctic islands, temperatures routinely drop to $-15\,°C$. Temperatures in the interior of the continent may drop another $60\,°C$ below that. What is the temperature in the interior?

57. Nick's bank account was overdrawn by $62. He deposited $50 in his account. What is the balance in his account?

58. Cynthia had $100 in her checking account. She wrote a check for $73 and was charged $27 for overdrawing her account last month. What is her account balance?

59. $88 was stolen from Jay's car. He got $35 of it back. What was his net loss?

60. Marion lost 4 pounds in April, gained 2 pounds in May, and gained 3 pounds in June. What was her net gain or loss in weight?

61. Use the score sheet to find each player's point total after three rounds in a card game.

	Jeff	Terry
Round 1	Lost 20 pts	Won 42 pts
Round 2	Won 75 pts	Lost 15 pts
Round 3	Lost 55 pts	Won 20 pts

62. Use the information in the table on flood water depths to find the new flood level for each river.

	Red River	Mississippi
Monday	Rose 8 ft	Rose 4 ft
Tuesday	Fell 3 ft	Rose 7 ft
Wednesday	Fell 5 ft	Fell 13 ft

The table below shows the number of pounds gained or lost by several health club members during a four-month period. A negative number indicates a loss of pounds. A positive number indicates a gain. Find the net gain or loss for each member at the end of the four months.

	Member	Month 1	Month 2	Month 3	Month 4	Net gain or loss
63.	Angela	−2	0	5	−5	
64.	Syshe	−1	2	−6	0	
65.	Brittany	3	−2	−2	3	
66.	Nicole	1	1	−4	2	

Rewrite each sum, using the commutative property of addition. Show that the sum is unchanged. **See Example 5.**

67. $-18 + (-5) =$ _____ $+$ _____

Both sums are _____ .

68. $-12 + 20 =$ _____ $+$ _____

Both sums are _____ .

69. $-4 + 15 =$ _____ $+$ _____

Both sums are _____ .

70. $17 + 1 =$ _____ $+$ _____

Both sums are _____ .

In each addition problem, find the two addends that would be easiest to add. Then find the sum. **See Example 6.**

71. $6 + (-14) + 14$ *Hint:* Find two addends whose sum is 0.

72. $-9 + 9 + (-8)$

73. $14 + 6 + (-7)$

74. $-18 + 3 + 7$

75. Make up three of your own examples that illustrate the addition property of 0.

76. Make up three of your own examples that illustrate the associative property of addition. Show that the sum is unchanged.

Find each sum.

77. $-7081 + 2965$

78. $-1398 + 3802$

79. $-179 + (-61) + 8926$

80. $36 + (-6215) + 428$

81. $86 + (-99,000) + 0 + 2837$

82. $-16,719 + 0 + 8878 + (-14)$

1.4 Subtracting Integers

OBJECTIVES

1. Find the opposite of an integer.
2. Subtract integers.
3. Combine adding and subtracting of integers.

VOCABULARY TIP

Opposite Just as your left hand is the **opposite** of your right hand, if two numbers are **opposite**, they are on **opposite sides of zero** and have **opposite signs**. So, if one number is positive (like +6), then the opposite will be negative (−6).

1 Find the opposite (additive inverse) of each number. Show that the sum of the number and its opposite is 0.

(a) 5

The opposite of 5 is ____.

5 + (____) = 0

(b) 48

(c) 0

(d) −1

(e) −24

Answers

1. **(a)** −5; 5 + (−5) = 0
   (b) −48; 48 + (−48) = 0
   (c) 0; 0 + 0 = 0   **(d)** 1; −1 + 1 = 0
   (e) 24; −24 + 24 = 0

OBJECTIVE **1** **Find the opposite of an integer.** Look at how the integers match up on this number line.

Each integer is matched with its *opposite*. **Opposites** are the same *distance* from 0 on the number line but are on *opposite sides* of 0.

$$+2 \text{ is the opposite of } -2 \quad \text{and} \quad -2 \text{ is the opposite of } +2$$

When you add opposites, the sum is always 0. The opposite of a number is also called its *additive inverse*.

$$2 + (-2) = 0 \quad \text{and} \quad -2 + 2 = 0$$

EXAMPLE 1 **Finding the Opposites of Integers**

Find the opposite (additive inverse) of each number. Show that the sum of the number and its opposite is 0.

> The sum of opposites is 0.

(a) 6   The opposite of 6 is −6   and   6 + (−6) = 0

(b) −10   The opposite of −10 is 10   and   −10 + 10 = 0

(c) 0   The opposite of 0 is 0   and   0 + 0 = 0

◀ **Work Problem** **1** **at the Side.**

OBJECTIVE **2** **Subtract integers.** Now that you know how to add integers and how to find opposites, you can subtract integers. Every subtraction problem has the same answer as a related addition problem. The examples below illustrate how to change subtraction problems into addition problems.

$$6 - 2 = 4 \quad \text{Same answer}$$
$$6 + (-2) = 4$$

$$8 - 3 = 5 \quad \text{Same answer}$$
$$8 + (-3) = 5$$

Subtracting Two Integers

To subtract two numbers, *add* the first number to the *opposite* of the second number. Remember to change *two* things:

Step 1   Make one pencil stroke to change the subtraction symbol to an addition symbol.

Step 2   Make a second pencil stroke to change the *second* number to its *opposite*. If the second number is positive, change it to negative. If the second number is negative, change it to positive.

CAUTION

When changing a subtraction problem to an addition problem, do *not* make any change in the *first* number. The pattern is

1st number − 2nd number = 1st number + opposite of 2nd number.

Subtracting Two Integers

Make *two* pencil strokes to change each subtraction problem into an addition problem. Then find the sum.

Change 10 to −10.

> Do **not** change 4.
> Change 10 to −10.

(a) $4 - 10 = 4 + (-10) = -6$

Change subtraction to addition.

Change −6 to +6.

> Do **not** change −9.
> Change −6 to +6.

(b) $-9 - (-6) = -9 + (+6) = -3$

Change subtraction to addition.

Change −5 to +5.

(c) $3 - (-5) = 3 + (+5) = 8$ Make *two* pencil strokes.

Change subtraction to addition.

> Do **not** change
> the first number
> when subtracting.

Change 9 to −9.

(d) $-2 - 9 = -2 + (-9) = -11$ Make *two* pencil strokes.

Change subtraction to addition.

·········· **Work Problem ➋ at the Side.** ▶

OBJECTIVE ▶ ❸ **Combine adding and subtracting of integers.** When adding and subtracting more than two signed numbers, first change all subtractions to adding the opposite. Then add from left to right.

EXAMPLE 3   **Combining Addition and Subtraction**

Simplify by completing all the calculations.

$-5 - \quad 10 - \quad 12 + 1$ Change all subtractions to adding the opposite.
                                Change 10 to −10. Change 12 to −12.

$-5 + (-10) + (-12) + 1$ Add from left to right. First add $-5 + (-10)$.

$\quad -15 \quad + (-12) + 1$ Then add $-15 + (-12)$.

$\qquad -27 \qquad + 1$ Finally, add $-27 + 1$.

$\qquad\qquad -26$

·········· **Work Problem ➌ at the Side.** ▶

▦ **Calculator Tip**

Use the *change of sign* key ⊕/⊖, or the negative sign key ⊝, on a *scientific* calculator to enter negative numbers. To enter -5, press ⑤ ⊕/⊖, or ⊝ 5 (check the instructions). To enter $+5$, just press ⑤. For **Example 3** above, press these keys.

5 ⊕/⊖ ⊖ 10 ⊖ 12 ⊕ 1 ⊜   The answer is -26.

-5 Subtract.

❷ Subtract by changing subtraction to adding the opposite. (Make *two* pencil strokes.)

🅖🅢 **(a)** $-6 - 5$
$\qquad -6 + (-5) = \underline{\quad}$

🅖🅢 **(b)** $3 - (-10)$
$\qquad 3 + \underline{\quad} = \underline{\quad}$

(c) $-8 - (-2)$

(d) $0 - 10$

(e) $-4 - (-12)$

(f) $9 - 7$

❸ Simplify.

🅖🅢 **(a)** $6 - 7 + (-3)$
$\qquad 6 + (\underline{\quad}) + (-3)$
$\qquad\quad \underbrace{-1} \quad + (-3)$
$\qquad\qquad \underline{\quad}$

(b) $-2 + (-3) - (-5)$

(c) $7 - 7 - 7$

(d) $-3 - 9 + 4 - (-20)$

Answers

2. **(a)** -11 **(b)** $3 + 10 = 13$ **(c)** -6
   (d) -10 **(e)** 8 **(f)** 2
3. **(a)** $6 + (-7) + (-3)$; $-1 + (-3)$; -4
   (b) 0 **(c)** -7 **(d)** 12

1.4   Exercises

Find the opposite (additive inverse) of each number. Show that the sum of the number and its opposite is 0. **See Example 1.**

1. 6

2. −3

3. −13

4. 0

5. CONCEPT CHECK Find, correct, and explain the mistake made in this subtraction.

$$\begin{array}{c} -6 - 6 \\ \downarrow \ \downarrow \\ -6 + 6 = 0 \end{array}$$

6. CONCEPT CHECK Find, correct, and explain the mistake made in this subtraction.

$$\begin{array}{c} -7 - \ \ 5 \\ \downarrow \ \ \ \downarrow \\ +7 + (-5) = 2 \end{array}$$

Subtract by changing subtraction to addition. **See Example 2.**

7. 19 − 5
$$19 + (-5) = \underline{\quad}$$

8. 24 − 11
$$24 + (-11) = \underline{\quad}$$

9. 10 − 12

10. 1 − 8

11. 7 − 19

12. 2 − 17

13. −15 − 10

14. −10 − 4

15. −9 − 14

16. −3 − 11

17. −3 − (−8)
$$-3 + (\underline{\quad}) = \underline{\quad}$$

18. −1 − (−4)
$$-1 + (\underline{\quad}) = \underline{\quad}$$

19. 6 − (−14)

20. 8 − (−1)

21. 1 − (−10)

22. 6 − (−1)

23. −30 − 30

24. −25 − 25

25. −16 − (−16)

26. −20 − (−20)

27. 13 − 13

28. 19 − 19

29. 0 − 6

30. 0 − 12

31. (a) 3 − (−5)
(b) 3 − 5
(c) −3 − (−5)
(d) −3 − 5

32. (a) 9 − 6
(b) −9 − 6
(c) 9 − (−6)
(d) −9 − (−6)

33. (a) 4 − 7
(b) 4 − (−7)
(c) −4 − 7
(d) −4 − (−7)

34. (a) 8 − (−2)
(b) −8 − (−2)
(c) 8 − 2
(d) −8 − 2

Simplify. **See Example 3.**

35. −2 − 2 − 2
$$\begin{array}{c} -2 + (-2) + (-2) \\ \underbrace{-4} \ \ + (-2) = \underline{\quad} \end{array}$$

36. −8 − 4 − 8
$$\begin{array}{c} -8 + (-4) + (-8) \\ \underbrace{-12} \ \ + (-8) = \underline{\quad} \end{array}$$

37. 9 − 6 − 3 − 5

38. 12 − 7 − 5 − 4

39. 3 − (−3) − 10 − (−7)

40. 1 − 9 − (−2) − (−6)

41. −2 + (−11) − (−3)

42. −5 − (−2) + (−6)

43. 4 − (−13) + (−5)

44. 6 − (−1) + (−10)

45. 6 + 0 − 12 + 1

46. −10 − 4 + 0 + 18

This windchill table shows how wind increases a person's heat loss. For example, find the temperature of 15 °F along the top of the table. Then find a wind speed of 20 mph along the left side of the table. The column and row intersect at −2 °F, the "windchill temperature." The actual temperature is 15 °F but the wind makes it feel like −2 °F. The difference between the actual temperature and the windchill temperature is
$15 - (-2) = 15 + (+2) = 17$ *degrees difference.*

Use the table to find the windchill temperatures in Exercises 47–48. Then write and solve a subtraction problem to calculate actual temperature minus windchill temperature.

WINDCHILL
Temperature (degrees Fahrenheit)

Calm	40	35	30	25	20	15	10	5	0	−5	−10	−15	−20	−25	−30
5	36	31	25	19	13	7	1	−6	−11	−16	−22	−28	−34	−40	−46
10	34	27	21	15	9	3	−4	−10	−16	−22	−28	−35	−41	−47	−53
15	32	25	19	13	6	0	−7	−13	−19	−26	−32	−39	−45	−51	−58
20	30	24	17	11	4	−2	−9	−15	−22	−29	−35	−42	−48	−55	−61
25	29	23	16	9	3	−4	−11	−17	−24	−31	−37	−44	−51	−58	−64
30	28	22	15	8	1	−5	−12	−19	−26	−33	−39	−46	−53	−60	−67
35	28	21	14	7	0	−7	−14	−21	−27	−34	−41	−48	−55	−62	−69
40	27	20	13	6	−1	−8	−15	−22	−29	−36	−43	−50	−57	−64	−71

Wind Speed (miles per hour)

Shaded area: Frostbite occurs in 15 minutes or less.

Source: National Weather Service

47. (a) 30 °F; 10 mph wind

 (b) 15 °F; 15 mph wind

 (c) 5 °F; 25 mph wind

 (d) −10 °F; 35 mph wind

48. (a) 40 °F; 20 mph wind

 (b) 20 °F; 35 mph wind

 (c) 10 °F; 15 mph wind

 (d) −5 °F; 30 mph wind

Simplify. Begin each exercise by working inside the absolute value bars or the parentheses.

49. $-2 + (-11) + |-2|$

50. $5 - |-3| + 3$

51. $0 - |-7 + 2|$

52. $|1 - 8| - |0|$

53. $-3 - (-2 + 4) + (-5)$

54. $5 - 8 - (6 - 7) + 1$

Relating Concepts (Exercises 55–56) For Individual or Group Work

Use your knowledge of the properties of addition to **work Exercises 55 and 56 in order.**

55. Look for a pattern in these pairs of subtractions.

$-3 - 5 \ \ = \_\_\_$ $-4 - (-3) = \_\_\_$

$5 - (-3) = \_\_\_$ $-3 - (-4) = \_\_\_$

Explain what happens when you try to apply the commutative property to subtraction.

56. Recall the addition property of 0. Can 0 be used in a subtraction problem without changing the other number? Explain what happens and give several examples. (*Hint:* Think about *order* in a subtraction problem.)

1.5 Problem Solving: Rounding and Estimating

OBJECTIVES

1 Locate the place to which a number is to be rounded.

2 Round integers.

3 Use front end rounding to estimate answers in addition and subtraction.

One way to get a rough check on an answer is to *round* the numbers in the problem. **Rounding** a number means finding a number that is close to the original number, but easier to work with.

For example, a superintendent of schools in a large city might be discussing the need to build new schools. In making her point, it probably would not be necessary to say that the school district has 152,807 students— it probably would be sufficient to say that there are about 153,000 students, or even 150,000 students.

OBJECTIVE ▶ 1 Locate the place to which a number is to be rounded. The first step in rounding a number is to locate the *place to which the number is to be rounded.*

EXAMPLE 1 Finding the Place to Which a Number Is to Be Rounded

Locate and draw a line under the place to which each number is to be rounded. Then answer the question.

(a) Round −23 to the nearest ten. Is −23 closer to −2̲0 or −3̲0?

-23 is closer to -20
Tens place

(b) Round $381 to the nearest hundred. Is it closer to $3̲00 or $4̲00?

$381 is closer to $400
Hundreds place

(c) Round −54,702 to the nearest thousand. Is it closer to −54̲,000 or −55̲,000?

$-54,702$ is closer to $-55,000$

Thousands place ⌐

◀ **Work Problem 1 at the Side.**

---

1 Locate and draw a line under the place to which the number is to be rounded. Then answer the question.

(a) −74̲6 (nearest ten)
↑——Tens place
Is it closer to −740 or −750? _____

(b) 2412 (nearest thousand)
Is it closer to 2000 or 3000? _____

(c) −89,5̲12 (nearest hundred)
Is it closer to −89,500 or −89,600? _____

(d) 546,325 (nearest ten-thousand)
Is it closer to 540,000 or 550,000? _____

OBJECTIVE ▶ 2 Round integers. Use these steps to round integers.

Rounding an Integer

Step 1 Locate the *place* to which the number is to be rounded. Draw a line under that place.

Step 2 Look only at the next digit to the right of the one you underlined. If the next digit is *5 or more, increase* the underlined digit by 1. If the next digit is *4 or less,* do *not* change the digit in the underlined place.

Step 3 Change all digits to the right of the underlined place to zeros.

CAUTION

If you are rounding a negative number, be careful to write the negative sign in front of the rounded number. For example, −79 rounds to −80.

Answers

1. **(a)** −746 is closer to −750
(b) 2412 is closer to 2000
(c) −89,512 is closer to −89,500
(d) 546,325 is closer to 550,000

EXAMPLE 2	**Using the Rounding Rule for 4 or Less**

Round 349 to the nearest hundred.

Step 1   Locate the place to which the number is being rounded. Draw a line under that place.

349
⌐— Hundreds place

Step 2   Because the next digit to the right of the underlined place is 4, which is *4 or less,* do *not* change the digit in the underlined place.

┌— Next digit is *4 or less.*
349
└— 3 remains 3.

Step 3   Change all digits to the right of the underlined place to zeros.

349 rounded to the nearest hundred is 300

—— Leave 3 as 3. ——

> Think of money.
> $349 is closer to
> $300 than to $400.

In other words, 349 is closer to 300 than to 400.

·············· Work Problem ❷ at the Side. ▶

EXAMPLE 3	**Using the Rounding Rule for 5 or More**

Round 36,833 to the nearest thousand.

Step 1   Find the place to which the number is to be rounded. Draw a line under that place.

36,833
└— Thousands place

Step 2   Because the next digit to the right of the underlined place is 8, which is *5 or more,* add 1 to the underlined place.

┌— Next digit is *5 or more.*
36,833
└— Change 6 to 7.

Step 3   Change all digits to the right of the underlined place to zeros.

—— Change to 0. ——
36,833 rounded to the nearest thousand is 37,000
—— Change 6 to 7. ——

In other words, 36,833 is closer to 37,000 than to 36,000.

·············· Work Problem ❸ at the Side. ▶

❷ Round to the nearest ten.

(a)
┌— Next digit is *4 or less.*
34
⊤
└— Tens place

34 rounds to _____.
└Leave 3 as 3.⌐

(b) −61

(c) −683

(d) 1792

❸ Round to the nearest thousand.

(a)
┌— Next digit is *5 or more.*
1725
⊤
└— Thousands place

┌— Change to 0.
1725 rounds to _____.
⊤
└— Change 1 to 2.

(b) −6511

(c) 58,829

(d) −83,904

Answers

2. (a) 30 **(b)** −60 **(c)** −680 **(d)** 1790
3. (a) 2000 **(b)** −7000 **(c)** 59,000
    (d) −84,000

❹ Round as indicated.

(a) −6036 to the nearest ten

GS (b) 34,968 to the nearest hundred

┌─Next digit is *5 or more.*
34,968
└── Change 9 to 10 and regroup 1 into thousands place.
└── 4 + regrouped 1 is 5

So 34,968 rounds to _____.

(c) −73,077 to the nearest thousand

GS (d) 9852 to the nearest thousand

┌─ Next digit is *5 or more.*
9852
└── Change 9 to 10; write 0 and regroup 1 into ten-thousands place.
10852

So 9852 rounds to _____.

(e) 85,949 to the nearest hundred

(f) 40,387 to the nearest thousand

EXAMPLE 4   Using the Rules for Rounding

(a) Round −2382 to the nearest ten.

Step 1   −2382
                └── Tens place

Step 2   The next digit to the right is 2, which is *4 or less.*

┌─ Next digit is *4 or less.*
−2382
└── Leave 8 as 8.

Step 3   −2382 rounds to −2380
┌─Change to 0.─┐
└── Leave 8 as 8.──┘

> Remember to write the negative sign.

−2382 rounded to the nearest ten is −2380.

(b) Round 13,961 to the nearest hundred.

Step 1   13,961
              └── Hundreds place

Step 2   The next digit to the right is 6, which is *5 or more.*

┌─ Next digit is *5 or more.*
13,961
└── Change 9 to 10; write 0 and regroup 1 into thousands place.
└── 3 + regrouped 1 = 4

Step 3   13,961 rounds to 14,000
┌─Change to 0.─┐
└── Change 39 to 40.

> $13,961 is closer to $14,000 than to $13,900.

13,961 rounded to the nearest hundred is 14,000.

Note

In *Step 2* above, when you added 1 to the hundreds place, notice that the first three digits increased from 139 to 140.

13,961 rounded to 14,000

◀ **Work Problem ❹ at the Side.**

Answers

4. (a) −6040   (b) 35,000   (c) −73,000
    (d) 10,000   (e) 85,900   (f) 40,000

| EXAMPLE 5 | **Rounding Large Numbers** |

(a) Round −37,892 to the nearest ten-thousand.

Step 1 −37,892

Ten-thousands place

Step 2 The next digit to the right is 7, which is *5 or more*.

Next digit is *5 or more*.

−37,892

Change 3 to 4.

Step 3 −37,892 rounds to −40,000
Change to 0.
Change 3 to 4.

Remember to write the negative sign.

−37,892 rounded to the nearest ten-thousand is −40,000.

(b) Round 528,498,675 to the nearest million.

Step 1 528,498,675

Millions place

Step 2 528,498,675
Next digit is *4 or less*.
Leave 8 as 8.

Step 3 528,498,675 rounds to 528,000,000
Change to 0.
Leave 8 as 8.

528,498,675 rounded to the nearest million is 528,000,000.

················· **Work Problem ❺ at the Side. ▶**

OBJECTIVE ▶ ❸ Use front end rounding to estimate answers in addition and subtraction. In many everyday situations, we can round numbers and **estimate** the answer to a problem. For example, suppose that you're thinking about buying a sofa for $988 and a chair for $209. You can round the prices and estimate the total cost as $1000 + $200 ≈ $1200. The ≈ symbol means "approximately equal to." The estimated total of $1200 is close enough to help you decide whether you can afford both items. Of course, when it comes time to pay the bill, you'll want the *exact* total of $988 + $209 = $1197.

	Sofa		**Chair**			
$988	+	$209	=	$1197	← Exact cost
Rounds to		Rounds to		
$1000	+	$200	=	$1200	← Estimated cost

❺ Round as indicated.

(a) −14,679 to the nearest ten-thousand

(b) 724,518,715 to the nearest million

GS **(c)** −49,900,700 to the nearest million

Next digit is *5 or more*.
−49,900,700
Millions place

−49,900,700
Change 9 to 10; write 0 and regroup 1 into ten-millions place.
4 + regrouped 1 is 5.

−49,900,700 rounds to

_____.

(d) 306,779,000 to the nearest hundred-million

6 Use front end rounding to round each number.

(a) −94

(b) 508

(c) −2522

(d) 9700

(e) 61,888

(f) −963,369

In **front end rounding,** each number is rounded to the highest possible place, so all the digits become 0 except the first digit. Once the numbers have lots of zeros, working with them is easy. Front end rounding is often used to estimate answers.

EXAMPLE 6   Using Front End Rounding

Use front end rounding to round each number.

(a) −216

Round to the highest possible place, that is, the leftmost digit. In this case, the leftmost digit, 2, is in the hundreds place, so round to the nearest hundred.

The rounded number is −200. Notice that all the digits in the rounded number are 0, except the first digit. Also, remember to write the negative sign.

(b) 97,203

The leftmost digit, 9, is in the ten-thousands place, so round to the nearest ten-thousand.

The rounded number is 100,000. Notice that all the digits in the rounded number are 0, except the first digit.

◀ Work Problem **6** at the Side.

EXAMPLE 7   Using Front End Rounding to Estimate an Answer

Use front end rounding to estimate an answer. Then find the exact answer.

Meisha's paycheck showed gross pay of $823. It also listed deductions of $291. What is her net pay after deductions?

Estimate: Use front end rounding to round $823 and $291.

┌─Next digit is *4 or less.*   ┌─Next digit is *5 or more.*
↓   ↓
$823 rounds to $800 $291 rounds to $300
↑   ↑
└─Leave 8 as 8.─┘   └─Change 2 to 3.─┘

Use the rounded numbers and subtract to *estimate* Meisha's net pay.

$$\$800 - \$300 = \$500 \leftarrow \text{Estimate}$$

Exact: Use the original numbers and subtract to find the *exact* amount.

$$\$823 - \$291 = \$532 \leftarrow \text{Exact}$$

Meisha's paycheck will show the *exact* amount of $532. Because $532 is fairly close to the *estimate* of $500, Meisha can quickly see that the amount shown on her paycheck probably is correct. She might also use the estimate when talking to a friend, saying, "My net pay is about $500."

Continued on Next Page

Answers

6. (a) −90 (b) 500 (c) −3000
  (d) 10,000 (e) 60,000 (f) −1,000,000

CAUTION

Always *estimate* the answer first. Then, when you find the *exact* answer, check that it is close to the estimate. If your exact answer is very far off, rework the problem because you probably made an error.

▦ **Calculator Tip**

It's easy to press the wrong key when using a calculator. If you use front end rounding and estimate the answer *before* entering the numbers, you can catch many such mistakes. For example, a student thought that he entered **Example 7** from the previous page correctly.

823 ⊖ 291 ⊜ [**1114**]

Front end rounding gives an estimated answer of $800 - 300 = 500$, which is very different from 1114. Can you figure out which key the student pressed incorrectly?

Answer: The student pressed ⊕ instead of ⊖.

················· **Work Problem 7 at the Side.** ▶

7 Use front end rounding to
GS estimate an answer. Then find the exact answer.

Pao Xiong is a bookkeeper for a small business. The company bank account is overdrawn by $3881. He deposits $2090. What is the balance in the account?

Estimate: Use front end rounding.

$-\$4000 + \underline{\hspace{1.5cm}} = \underline{\hspace{1.5cm}}$

Exact:

1.5 Exercises

  MyMathLab®

CONCEPT CHECK *For each number in Exercises 1 and 2, underline the digit to which you are rounding. Then explain the next step in rounding the number.*

1. (a) Round 3702 to the nearest ten.

2. (a) Round 65,081 to the nearest hundred.

(b) Round 908,546 to the nearest thousand.

(b) Round 723,900 to the nearest ten-thousand.

Round each number to the indicated place. **See Examples 1–5.**

3. 625 to the nearest ten

4. 206 to the nearest ten

5. −1083 to the nearest ten

6. −2439 to the nearest ten

7. 7862 to the nearest hundred

8. 6746 to the nearest hundred

9. −86,813 to the nearest hundred

10. −17,211 to the nearest hundred

11. 42,495 to the nearest hundred

12. 18,273 to the nearest hundred

13. −5996 to the nearest hundred

14. −8451 to the nearest hundred

15. −78,499 to the nearest thousand

16. −14,314 to the nearest thousand

17. 5847 to the nearest thousand

18. 49,706 to the nearest thousand

19. 595,008 to the nearest ten-thousand

┌─Next digit is *5 or more.*
↓
595,008
↑
└─Change 9 to 10; write 0 and
    regroup 1 into hundred-thousands place.

20. 725,182 to the nearest ten-thousand

┌─Next digit is *5 or more.*
↓
725,182
↑
└─Change 2 to 3; digits to the
    right become zeros.

21. −8,906,422 to the nearest million

22. −13,713,409 to the nearest million

23. 139,610,000 to the nearest million

24. 609,845,500 to the nearest million

25. 19,951,880,500 to the nearest hundred-million

26. 5,993,505,000 to the nearest hundred-million

27. 8,608,200,000 to the nearest billion

28. 703,750,678,005 to the nearest billion

29. CONCEPT CHECK Explain in your own words how to do front end rounding. Also show two examples of numbers and how you round them.

30. CONCEPT CHECK Describe two situations in your own life when you might use rounded numbers. Describe two situations in which exact numbers are important.

Use front end rounding to round each number. ***See Example 6.***

31. Tyrone's truck shows this number on the odometer.

32. Ezra bought a used car with this odometer reading.

33. From summer to winter the average temperature drops 56 degrees.

34. The flood waters fell 42 inches yesterday.

35. Jan earned $9942 working part time.

36. Carol deposited $285 in her bank account.

37. People in the United States spend 53,500,000,000 minutes per month on Facebook.
(*Source: Huffington Post.*)

38. 104,100,000 U.S. households have cable TV.
(*Source:* Nielsen Media Research.)

39. The population of Alaska is 698,473 people, and the population of California is 36,961,664 people.
(*Source:* U.S. Census Bureau.)

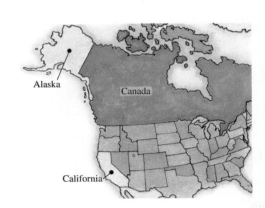

40. Within forty years, it is estimated that the U.S. population will be 439,010,000 people and Canada's population will be 41,135,648 people.
(*Source:* U.S. Census Bureau.)

First, use front end rounding to estimate each answer. Then find the exact answer.
*In Exercises 49–54, change subtraction to adding the opposite. **See Example 7.***

41. $-42 + 89$

Estimate: $-40 + 90 = 50$

Exact:

42. $-66 + 25$

Estimate: $-70 + 30 = 40$

Exact:

43. $16 + (-97)$

Estimate:

Exact:

44. $58 + (-19)$

Estimate:

Exact:

45. $-273 + (-399)$

Estimate:

Exact:

46. $-311 + (-582)$

Estimate:

Exact:

47. $3081 + 6826$

Estimate:

Exact:

48. $4904 + 1181$

Estimate:

Exact:

49. $23 - 81$

Estimate:

Exact:

50. $72 - 84$

Estimate:

Exact:

51. $-39 - 39$

Estimate:

Exact:

52. $-91 - 91$

Estimate:

Exact:

53. $-106 + 34 - (-72)$

Estimate:

Exact:

54. $52 - (-87) - 139$

Estimate:

Exact:

First use front end rounding to estimate the answer to each application problem. Then find the exact answer. ***See Example 7.***

55. The community has raised $52,882 for the homeless shelter. If the goal is $78,650, how much more needs to be collected?

Estimate:

Exact:

56. A truck weighs 9250 pounds when empty. After being loaded with firewood, it weighs 21,375 pounds. What is the weight of the firewood?

Estimate:

Exact:

57. Dorene Cox decided to establish a monthly budget. She plans to spend $845 for rent, $325 for food, $365 for child care, $182 for transportation, $240 for other expenses, and put the remainder in savings. If her monthly take-home pay is $2120, find her monthly savings.

Estimate:

Exact:

58. Jared Ueda had $2874 in his bank account. He used his debit card to pay $308 for auto repairs, $580 for a laptop computer, and $778 for tuition. Find the amount remaining in his account.

Estimate:

Exact:

59. In a laboratory experiment, a mixture started at a temperature of −102 degrees. First the temperature was raised 37 degrees and then raised 52 degrees. What was the final temperature?

Estimate:

Exact:

60. A scuba diver was photographing fish at 65 feet below the surface of the ocean. She swam up 24 feet and then swam down 49 feet. What was her final depth?

Estimate:

Exact:

61. The White House in Washington, D.C., has 132 rooms, 412 doors, and 147 windows. What is the total number of doors and windows? (*Source: Scholastic Book of World Records.*)

Estimate:

Exact:

62. There are 33,000 McDonald's restaurants throughout the world in 119 different countries. Burger King has 12,500 restaurants in 69 countries. How many restaurants do the two companies have together? (*Source:* mcdonalds.com and bk.com)

Estimate:

Exact:

1.6 Multiplying Integers

OBJECTIVES

1. Use a raised dot or parentheses to express multiplication.
2. Multiply integers.
3. Identify properties of multiplication.
4. Estimate answers to application problems involving multiplication.

VOCABULARY TIPS

Factor In everyday language, a factor influences the result, or outcome of something. In math, factors are the numbers being multiplied in a multiplication problem, **resulting** in the product.

Product Think of a product as the **result** that you get when you multiply numbers together.

---

❶ Rewrite each multiplication in three different ways using a dot or parentheses. Also identify the factors and the product.

Ⓖ **(a)** 100×6

$100(6)$

_____
        ↘ Write it two
_____ ↗ more ways.

The factors are 100 and ____.

The product is ____.

(b) 7×12

Answers

1. **(a)** $100 \cdot 6$ or $(100)(6)$;
   The factors are 100 and 6;
   the product is 600.
   (b) $7 \cdot 12$ or $7(12)$ or $(7)(12)$
   The factors are 7 and 12;
   the product is 84.

OBJECTIVE ❶ **Use a raised dot or parentheses to express multiplication.** In arithmetic we usually use "×" when writing multiplication problems. But in algebra, we use a raised dot or parentheses to show multiplication. The numbers being multiplied are called **factors** and the answer is called the **product.**

Arithmetic —————————— **Algebra** ——————————

$3 \times 5 = 15$ $3 \cdot 5 = 15$ or $3(5) = 15$ or $(3)(5) = 15$

Factors Product   Factors Product   Factors Product   Factors Product

---

EXAMPLE 1 **Expressing Multiplication in Algebra**

Rewrite each multiplication in three different ways, using a dot or parentheses. Also identify the factors and the product.

(a) 10×7

Raised dot
        ↓
Rewrite it as $10 \cdot 7$ or $10(7)$ or $(10)(7)$

The factors are 10 and 7. The product is 70.

(b) 4×80

Rewrite it as $4 \cdot 80$ or $4(80)$ or $(4)(80)$

The factors are 4 and 80. The product is 320.

·· ◀ **Work Problem** ❶ **at the Side.**

Note

Parentheses are used to show several different things in algebra. When we discussed the associative property of addition earlier in this chapter, we used parentheses as shown below.

$\underbrace{(-9 + 9)} + 6 \leftarrow$ Parentheses show which numbers to add first.
$\underbrace{0 \quad + 6}$
6

Now we are using parentheses to indicate multiplication, as in 3(5) or (3)(5).

OBJECTIVE ❷ **Multiply integers.** Suppose that our football team gained 5 yards on the first play, gained 5 yards again on the second play, and gained 5 yards again on the third play. We can add to find the result.

$$5 \text{ yards} + 5 \text{ yards} + 5 \text{ yards} = 15 \text{ yards}$$

A quick way to add the same number several times is to multiply.

$\underbrace{\text{Our team made 3 plays}}$ and $\underbrace{\text{gained 5 yards each time.}}$ $\underbrace{\text{Our team gained a total of 15 yards,}}$

$\qquad 3 \qquad \cdot \qquad 5 \qquad = \qquad 15$

When multiplying two integers, first multiply the absolute values. Then attach a positive sign or negative sign to the product according to the rules below.

Multiplying Two Integers

If two factors have *different signs,* the product is *negative.*
For example,

$$-2 \cdot 6 = -12 \quad \text{and} \quad 4 \cdot (-5) = -20$$

If two factors have the *same sign,* the product is *positive.* For example,

$$7 \cdot 3 = 21 \quad \text{and} \quad -3 \cdot (-10) = 30$$

There are several ways to illustrate these rules. First we'll continue with football. Remember, you are interested in the results for *our* team. We will designate our team with a positive sign and their team with a negative sign.

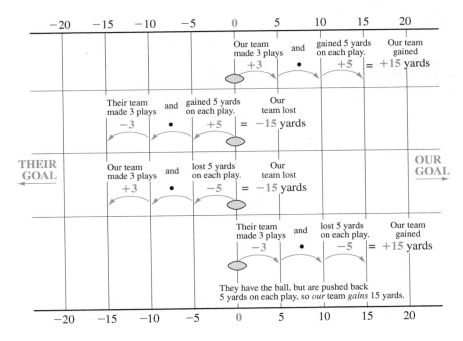

Here is a summary of the football examples.

When two factors have the *same* sign, the product is *positive.*

Both positive

$$3 \cdot 5 = 15 \quad \text{Product is positive.}$$

Two factors with *matching* signs give a *positive* product.

$$-3 \cdot (-5) = 15$$

Both negative

When two factors have *different* signs, the product is *negative.*

$$-3 \cdot 5 = -15 \quad \text{Product is negative.}$$

Two factors with *different* signs give a *negative* product.

$$3 \cdot (-5) = -15$$

2 Multiply.

GS (a) $7(-2)$

The factors have **different** signs, so the product is **negative.**

$7(-2) =$ _____

(b) $-5 \cdot (-5)$

(c) $-1(14)$

(d) $10 \cdot 6$

(e) $(-4)(-9)$

There is another way to look at these multiplication rules. In mathematics, the rules or patterns must always be consistent.

Look for a pattern in this list of products.

$$4 \cdot 2 = 8$$
$$3 \cdot 2 = 6$$

Blue numbers decrease by 1.　　$2 \cdot 2 = 4$　Red numbers *decrease* by 2.

$$1 \cdot 2 = 2$$
$$0 \cdot 2 = 0$$
$$-1 \cdot 2 = ?$$

To keep the red pattern going, replace the ? with a number that is 2 *less than* 0, which is −2.

So, $-1 \cdot 2 = -2$. This pattern illustrates that the product of two numbers with *different* signs is *negative.*

Look for a pattern in this list of products.

$$4 \cdot (-2) = -8$$
$$3 \cdot (-2) = -6$$

Blue numbers decrease by 1.　　$2 \cdot (-2) = -4$　Red numbers *increase* by 2.

$$1 \cdot (-2) = -2$$
$$0 \cdot (-2) = 0$$
$$-1 \cdot (-2) = ?$$

To keep the red pattern going, replace the ? with a number that is 2 *more than* 0, which is +2.

So, $-1 \cdot (-2) = +2$. This pattern illustrates that the product of two numbers with the *same* sign is *positive.*

EXAMPLE 2 **Multiplying Two Integers**

(a) $-2 \cdot 8 = -16$　　The factors have *different signs*, so the product is *negative.*

Positive
Negative

(b) $-10(-6) = 60$　　The factors have the *same sign*, so the product is *positive.*

Both negative

(c) $(9)(-11) = -99$　　The factors have *different signs*, so the product is *negative.*

Negative
Positive

◀ **Work Problem** **2** **at the Side.**

Sometimes there are more than two factors in a multiplication problem. If there are parentheses around two of the factors, multiply them first. If there aren't any parentheses, start at the left and work with two factors at a time.

EXAMPLE 3 **Multiplying Several Factors**

(a) $-3 \cdot (4 \cdot 5)$

$-3 \cdot \quad 20$

-60

Parentheses tell you to multiply $4 \cdot 5$ first. The factors have the *same* signs, so the product is *positive.*

Then multiply $-3 \cdot 20$. The factors have *different* signs, so the product is *negative.*

(b) $-2 \cdot (-2) \cdot (-2)$

$\quad 4 \quad \cdot (-2)$

$\quad\quad -8$

There is no work to do inside parentheses, so multiply $-2 \cdot (-2)$ first. The factors have the *same* sign, so the product is *positive.*

Then multiply $4 \cdot (-2)$. The factors have *different* signs, so the product is *negative.*

Continued on Next Page

Answers

2. (a) −14　(b) 25　(c) −14
(d) 60　(e) 36

CAUTION

In **Example 3(b)** on the previous page, you may be tempted to think that the final product will be *positive* because all the factors have the *same* sign. Be careful to **work with two factors at a time** and keep track of the sign at each step.

· Work Problem ❸ at the Side. ▶

OBJECTIVE ❸ **Identify properties of multiplication.** Addition involving 0 is unusual because adding 0 does *not* change the number. For example, $7 + 0$ is still 7. (See the section on adding integers.) But what happens in multiplication? Let's use our football team as an example.

Our team made 3 plays	and	didn't gain or lose yards on any play.		Altogether our team didn't gain or lose any yards.
3	•	0	=	0

This example illustrates one of the properties of multiplication.

Multiplication Property of 0

Multiplying any number by 0 gives a product of 0.
Some examples are shown below.

$$-16 \cdot 0 = 0 \qquad (0)(5) = 0 \qquad 32{,}977(0) = 0$$

So, can you multiply a number by something that will *not* change the number?

$$6 \cdot \,? = 6 \qquad -12(?) = -12 \qquad (?)(5876) = 5876$$

The number 1 can replace the *?* in each example. This illustrates another property of multiplication.

Multiplication Property of 1

Multiplying a number by 1 leaves the number unchanged.
Some examples are shown below.

$$6 \cdot 1 = 6 \qquad -12(1) = -12 \qquad (1)(5876) = 5876$$

EXAMPLE 4 Using Properties of Multiplication

Multiply. Then name the property illustrated by each example.

(a) $(0)(-48) = 0$ — Illustrates the **multiplication property of 0.**

(b) $615(1) = 615$ — Illustrates the **multiplication property of 1.**

· Work Problem ❹ at the Side. ▶

---

❸ Multiply.

GS **(a)** $-5 \cdot \underbrace{(10 \cdot 2)}$

$$-5 \cdot (\underline{\quad})$$
$$(\underline{\quad})$$

(b) $-1 \cdot 8 \cdot (-5)$

GS **(c)** $\underbrace{-3(-2)}(-4)$

$$(\underline{\quad})(-4)$$
$$(\underline{\quad})$$

(d) $-2(7)(-3)$

(e) $(-1)(-1)(-1)$

❹ Multiply. Then name the property illustrated by each example.

(a) $819 \cdot 0$

(b) $1(-90)$

(c) $25 \cdot 1$

(d) $(0)(-75)$

Answers

3. **(a)** $-5 \cdot (20); -100$ **(b)** 40
  (c) $(6)(-4); -24$ **(d)** 42 **(e)** -1
4. **(a)** 0; multiplication property of 0
  (b) -90; multiplication property of 1
  (c) 25; multiplication property of 1
  (d) 0; multiplication property of 0

5 Show that the product is unchanged and name the property that is illustrated in each case.

(a) $(3 \cdot 3) \cdot 2 = 3 \cdot (3 \cdot 2)$

$\underline{\hspace{1cm}} \cdot 2 = 3 \cdot \underline{\hspace{1cm}}$

$\underline{\hspace{1cm}} = \underline{\hspace{1cm}}$

This illustrates the

_____ property

of multiplication.

(b) $11 \cdot 8 = 8 \cdot 11$

(c) $2 \cdot (-15) = -15 \cdot 2$

(d) $-4 \cdot (2 \cdot 5) = (-4 \cdot 2) \cdot 5$

When adding, we said that changing the order of the addends did not change the sum (commutative property of addition). We also found that changing the *grouping* of addends did not change the sum (associative property of addition). These same ideas apply to multiplication.

Commutative Property of Multiplication

Changing the **order** of two factors does not change the product.
For example,

$$2 \cdot 5 = 5 \cdot 2 \qquad \text{and} \qquad -4 \cdot 6 = 6 \cdot (-4)$$

Associative Property of Multiplication

Changing the **grouping** of factors does not change the product.
For example,

$$9 \cdot (3 \cdot 2) = (9 \cdot 3) \cdot 2$$

EXAMPLE 5 Using the Commutative and Associative Properties

Show that the product is unchanged and name the property that is illustrated in each case.

(a) $-7 \cdot (-4) = -4 \cdot (-7)$ — Multiplying two numbers in a different order does *not* change the product.

$28 \qquad = \qquad 28$ Both products are 28.

This example illustrates the **commutative property of multiplication.**

(b) $5 \cdot (10 \cdot 2) = (5 \cdot 10) \cdot 2$ — Use the associative property to multiply the easiest numbers first.

$5 \cdot \quad 20 \quad = \quad 50 \quad \cdot 2$

$100 \qquad = \qquad 100$ Both products are 100.

This example illustrates the **associative property of multiplication.**

◀ **Work Problem 5 at the Side.**

Now we look at a property that involves multiplication and addition.

Distributive Property

Multiplication *distributes* over addition. An example is shown below.

$$3(6 + 2) = 3 \cdot 6 + 3 \cdot 2$$

What is the **distributive property** really saying? Notice that there is an understood multiplication symbol between the 3 and the parentheses. To "distribute" the 3 means to multiply 3 times each number inside the parentheses.

$3(6 + 2)$

This is understood to be *multiplying* by 3. → $3 \cdot (6 + 2)$

Using the distributive property,

$3 \cdot (6 + 2)$ can be rewritten as $3 \cdot 6 + 3 \cdot 2$

Answers

5. **(a)** $9 \cdot 2 = 3 \cdot 6$; $18 = 18$;
associative property of multiplication
(b) $88 = 88$; commutative property of multiplication
(c) $-30 = -30$; commutative property of multiplication
(d) $-4 \cdot 10 = -8 \cdot 5$; $-40 = -40$;
associative property of multiplication

EXAMPLE 6 Using the Distributive Property

Rewrite each product, using the distributive property. Show that the result is unchanged.

(a) $4(3 + 7)$

> Careful! Multiply *both* numbers by 4.

$$4(\underbrace{3 + 7}) = \underbrace{4 \cdot 3} + \underbrace{4 \cdot 7}$$
$$\underbrace{4(10)} = \underbrace{12} + \underbrace{28}$$
$$40 = 40 \qquad \text{Both results are 40.}$$

(b) $-2(-5 + 1)$

> Multiple *both* numbers by −2.

$$-2(\underbrace{-5 + 1}) = \underbrace{(-2) \cdot (-5)} + \underbrace{(-2) \cdot (1)}$$
$$\underbrace{-2(-4)} = \underbrace{(10)} + \underbrace{(-2)}$$
$$8 = 8 \qquad \text{Both results are 8.}$$

························ **Work Problem 6 at the Side.** ▶

OBJECTIVE 4 Estimate answers to application problems involving multiplication. Front end rounding can be used to estimate answers in multiplication, just as we did when adding and subtracting (see the previous section). Once the numbers have been rounded so that there are lots of zeros, we can use the multiplication shortcut described in **Chapter R.** As a brief review, look at the pattern in these examples.

$-3 \cdot 2$ is -6

$$-30 \cdot 200 = -6000$$

Total of three zeros   Write three zeros after the −6.

$-2 \cdot (-5)$ is 10

$$-2000 \cdot (-5000) = 10,000,000$$

Total of six zeros   Write six zeros after the 10.

EXAMPLE 7 Using Front End Rounding to Estimate an Answer

Use front end rounding to estimate an answer. Then find the exact answer.

Last year Video Land had to replace 392 defective DVDs at a cost of $19 each. How much money was lost on defective DVDs? (*Hint:* Because it's a loss, use a negative number for the cost.)

Estimate: Use front end rounding: 392 rounds to 400 and −$19 rounds to −$20. Use the rounded numbers and multiply to estimate the total amount of money lost.

$4 \cdot (-2)$ is -8

$$400 \cdot (-\$20) = -\$8000 \qquad \text{Estimate}$$

Total of three zeros   Write three zeros after the −8.

Exact: $392 \cdot (-\$19) = -\$7448$

Because the exact answer of −$7448 is fairly close to the estimate of −$8000, you can see that −$7448 probably is correct. Video Land could also use the estimate to report, "We lost about $8000 on defective DVDs last year."

························ **Work Problem 7 at the Side.** ▶

---

6 Rewrite each product, using the distributive property. Show that the result is unchanged.

GS (a) $3(\underbrace{8 + 7}) = \underbrace{3 \cdot 8} + \underline{\quad} \cdot 7$

$\underbrace{3(\underline{\quad})} = \underline{\quad} + \underline{\quad}$

$\underline{\quad} = \underline{\quad}$

(b) $10(-6 + 9)$

(c) $-6(4 + 4)$

7 Use front end rounding to estimate an answer. Then find the exact answer.

An average of 27,095 baseball fans attended each of the 81 home games during the season. What was the total home game attendance for the season?

Estimate:

Exact:

Answers

6. (a) $3(8 + 7) = 3 \cdot 8 + 3 \cdot 7$;
$3(15) = 24 + 21$; $45 = 45$;
both results are 45.
(b) $10(-6) + 10(9)$; both results are 30.
(c) $-6 \cdot 4 + (-6) \cdot 4$; both results are −48.
7. (a) *Estimate:* $30,000 \cdot 80 = 2,400,000$ fans
(b) *Exact:* $27,095 \cdot 81 = 2,194,695$ fans

1.6 Exercises

FOR EXTRA HELP

 Download the MyDashBoard App

MyMathLab®

CONCEPT CHECK *Watch for patterns as you work Exercises 1–4.*

1. (a) $9 \cdot 7$

(b) $-9 \cdot (-7)$

(c) $-9 \cdot 7$

(d) $9 \cdot (-7)$

2. (a) $-6 \cdot 9$

(b) $6 \cdot (-9)$

(c) $-6 \cdot (-9)$

(d) $6 \cdot 9$

3. (a) $7(-8)$

(b) $-7(8)$

(c) $7(8)$

(d) $-7(-8)$

4. (a) $8(6)$

(b) $-8(-6)$

(c) $-8(6)$

(d) $8(-6)$

Multiply. See Examples 1–4.

5. $-5 \cdot 7$

6. $-10 \cdot 2$

7. $(-5)(9)$

8. $(-9)(4)$

9. $3(-6)$

10. $8(-9)$

11. $10(-5)$

12. $5(-11)$

13. $(-1)(40)$

14. $(75)(-1)$

15. $-56 \cdot 1$

16. $1 \cdot (-87)$

17. $-8(-4)$

18. $-3(-9)$

19. $11 \cdot 7$

20. $4 \cdot 25$

21. $25 \cdot 0$

22. $0 \cdot 30$

23. $-19(-7)$

24. $-21(-3)$

25. $-13(-1)$

26. $-1(-31)$

27. $(0)(-25)$

28. $(-50)(0)$

29. $\underbrace{-4 \cdot (-6)}_{24} \cdot 2$
$\underbrace{ \cdot 2}$
____

30. $\underbrace{-9 \cdot 3}_{-27} \cdot (-3)$
$\underbrace{ \cdot (-3)}$
____

31. $(-4)(-2)(-7)$

32. $(-6)(-2)(-3)$

33. $5(-8)(4)$

34. $5(4)(-6)$

Write an integer in each blank to make a true statement.

35. $(-3)(\underline{}) = -15$

36. $6 \cdot (\underline{}) = -24$

37. $\underline{} \cdot 10 = -30$

38. $(\underline{})(-4) = 16$

39. $-17 = 17(\underline{})$

40. $29 = -29(\underline{})$

41. $(\underline{})(-350) = 0$

42. $\underline{} \cdot 99 = 99$

43. $5 \cdot (-4) \cdot \underline{} = -100$

44. $\underline{} \cdot 2 \cdot (-2) = -24$

45. $(\underline{})(-5)(-2) = -40$

46. $(-3)(\underline{})(-3) = -27$

47. In your own words, explain the difference between the commutative and associative properties of multiplication. Show an example of each.

48. A student did this multiplication.

$$(-3) \cdot (-3) \cdot (-3) = 27$$

He knew that $3 \cdot 3 \cdot 3$ is 27. Since all the factors have the same sign, he made the product positive. Do you agree with his reasoning? Explain.

Rewrite each multiplication, using the stated property. Show that the result is unchanged. **See Examples 5 and 6.**

49. Distributive property
▶ $9(-3 + 5)$

50. Distributive property
$-6(4 + 5)$

51. Commutative property
▶ $25 \cdot 8$

52. Commutative property
$-7 \cdot (-11)$

53. Associative property
▶ $-3 \cdot (2 \cdot 5)$

54. Associative property
$(5 \cdot 5) \cdot 10$

First use front end rounding to estimate the answer to each application problem. Then find the exact answer. **See Example 7.**

55. Alliette receives $324 per week for doing child care in her home. How much income will she have for an entire year? There are 52 weeks in a year.

Estimate:

Exact:

56. Enrollment at our community college has increased by 875 students each of the last four semesters. What is the total increase?

Estimate:

Exact:

57. A new computer software store had losses of $9950 during each month of its first year. What was the total loss for the year?

Estimate:

Exact:

58. A cell phone company estimates that it is losing 95 customers each week. How many customers will it lose in a year?

Estimate:

Exact:

59. Tuition at the state university is $182 per credit for undergraduates. How much tuition will Wei Chen pay for 13 credits?

Estimate:

Exact:

60. Pat ate a dozen crackers as a snack. Each cracker had 17 calories. How many calories did Pat eat?

Estimate:

Exact:

61. There are 24 hours in one day. How many hours are in one year (365 days)?

Estimate:

Exact:

62. There are 5280 feet in one mile. How many feet are in 17 miles?

Estimate:

Exact:

Simplify.

63. $-8 \cdot |-8 \cdot 8|$

$-8 \cdot \quad |-64|$

$-8 \cdot \quad 64$

_____

64. $-7 \cdot |7| \cdot |-7|$

$-7 \cdot 7 \cdot \quad 7$

$-49 \quad \cdot \quad 7$

_____

65. $(-37)(-1)(85)(0)$

66. $-1(9732)(-1)(-1)$

67. $|6 - 7| \cdot (-355,299)$

68. $987 \cdot (-65,432) \cdot |9 - 9|$

*Each of these application problems requires several steps and may involve
addition and subtraction as well as multiplication.*

69. Each of Maurice's four cats needed a $24 rabies
shot and a $29 shot to prevent respiratory infections.
There was also one $35 office visit charge. What
was the total amount of Maurice's bill?

70. Chantele has three children. Her older daughter had
a throat culture taken at the clinic today. Her baby
needed two prescription medicines and her son
received two immunization shots. The co-pay
amounts were a $22 office charge for each child,
$20 for the throat culture, and $12 for each
prescription medicine. There was no co-pay for the
shots. How much did Chantele pay?

71. There is a 3-degree drop in temperature for every
thousand feet that an airplane climbs into the sky. If
the temperature on the ground is 50 degrees, what
will be the temperature when the plane reaches an
altitude of 24,000 feet? (*Source:* Lands' End.)

72. An unmanned research submarine descends to
150 feet below the surface of the ocean. Then it
continues to go deeper, taking a water sample every
25 feet. What is its depth when it takes the
15th sample?

73. In Ms. Zubero's algebra class, there are six tests of
100 points each, eight quizzes of six points each,
and 20 homework assignments of five points each.
There are also four "bonus points" on each test.
What is the total number of possible points?

74. In Mr. Jackson's prealgebra class, there are three
group projects worth 25 points each, five 100-point
tests, a 150-point final exam, and seven quizzes
worth 12 points each. Find the total number of
possible points.

Relating Concepts (Exercises 75–76) For Individual or Group Work

*Look for patterns as you **work Exercises 75 and 76 in order.***

75. Write three numerical examples for each of these
situations:

(a) A positive number multiplied by -1

(b) A negative number multiplied by -1

Now write a rule that explains what happens when
you multiply a signed number by -1.

76. Do these multiplications.

$$-2 \cdot (-2) = \underline{\hspace{1cm}}$$
$$-2 \cdot (-2) \cdot (-2) = \underline{\hspace{1cm}}$$
$$-2 \cdot (-2) \cdot (-2) \cdot (-2) = \underline{\hspace{1cm}}$$
$$-2 \cdot (-2) \cdot (-2) \cdot (-2) \cdot (-2) = \underline{\hspace{1cm}}$$

Describe the pattern in the products. Then find the
next three products without multiplying all the -2s.

1.7 Dividing Integers

OBJECTIVES

1. Divide integers.
2. Identify properties of division.
3. Combine multiplying and dividing of integers.
4. Estimate answers to application problems involving division.
5. Interpret remainders in division application problems.

OBJECTIVE 1 Divide integers. In arithmetic, we usually use $\overline{)}$ to write division problems so that we can do them by hand. Calculator keys use the $\div$ symbol for division. In algebra, we usually show division by using a fraction bar, a slash mark, or the $\div$ symbol. The answer to a division problem is called the **quotient.**

Arithmetic

$$\text{Divisor} \rightarrow 2\overline{)16} \begin{array}{l} \leftarrow \text{Quotient} \\ \leftarrow \text{Dividend} \end{array} \quad 8 \leftarrow \text{Quotient}$$

Calculator and Algebra

$$\overset{\text{Dividend}}{\underset{\downarrow}{16}} \div \overset{\text{Divisor}}{\underset{\downarrow}{2}} = \underset{\underset{\text{Quotient}}{\uparrow}}{8}$$

$$\text{Dividend} \rightarrow \frac{16}{2} = \underset{\underset{\text{Quotient}}{\uparrow}}{8}$$
$$\text{Divisor} \rightarrow$$

For every division problem, we can write a related multiplication problem. (See **Chapter R.**) Because of this relationship, the sign rules for dividing integers are the same as the rules for multiplying integers. Examples:

> Signs are the **same**, so the quotient is **positive**.

$$\frac{16}{8} = 2 \quad \text{because} \quad (2)(8) = 16$$

$$\frac{-16}{-8} = 2 \quad \text{because} \quad (2)(-8) = -16$$

> Signs are **different**, so the quotient is **negative**.

$$\frac{-16}{8} = -2 \quad \text{because} \quad (-2)(8) = -16$$

$$\frac{16}{-8} = -2 \quad \text{because} \quad (-2)(-8) = 16$$

Dividing Two Integers

If two numbers have **different signs,** the quotient is **negative.**
Some examples are shown below.

$$\frac{-18}{3} = -6 \qquad \frac{40}{-5} = -8$$

If two numbers have the **same sign,** the quotient is **positive.**
Some examples are shown below.

$$\frac{-30}{-6} = 5 \qquad \frac{48}{8} = 6$$

---

① Divide.

GS (a) $\dfrac{40}{-8}$ The integers have **different signs**, so the quotient is **negative.**

(b) $\dfrac{49}{7}$

(c) $\dfrac{-32}{4}$

GS (d) $\dfrac{-10}{-10}$ The integers have the **same sign**, so the quotient is **positive.**

(e) $-81 \div 9$

(f) $-100 \div (-50)$

EXAMPLE 1 Dividing Two Integers

(a) $\dfrac{-20}{5}$ ← Numbers have *different* signs, so the quotient is *negative*. $\quad \dfrac{-20}{5} = -4$

(b) $\dfrac{-24}{-4}$ ← Numbers have the *same* sign, so the quotient is *positive*. $\quad \dfrac{-24}{-4} = 6$

> The sign rules for dividing and multiplying are the same.

(c) $60 \div (-2)$ Numbers have *different* signs, so the quotient is *negative*. $60 \div (-2) = -30$

◀ **Work Problem ① at the Side.**

Answers

1. (a) −5 **(b)** 7 **(c)** −8 **(d)** 1
(e) −9 **(f)** 2

OBJECTIVE ▶ 2 Identify properties of division. You have seen that 0 and 1 are used in special ways in addition and multiplication. This is also true in division.

Examples	Pattern (Division Property)
$\frac{5}{5}=1$ $\frac{-18}{-18}=1$ $\frac{-793}{-793}=1$	When a nonzero number is divided by itself, the quotient is 1.
$\frac{5}{1}=5$ $\frac{-18}{1}=-18$ $\frac{-793}{1}=-793$	When a number is divided by 1, the quotient is the number.
$\frac{0}{5}=0$ $\frac{0}{-18}=0$ $\frac{0}{-793}=0$	When 0 is divided by any other number (except 0), the quotient is 0.
$\frac{5}{0}$ is undefined. $\frac{-18}{0}$ is undefined.	Division by 0 is *undefined*. There is no answer.

The most surprising property is that division by 0 *cannot be done*. Let's review the reason for that by rewriting this division problem as a related multiplication problem.

$$\frac{-18}{0}=?\quad\text{can be written as the multiplication}\quad ?\cdot 0=-18$$

If you thought the answer to $\frac{-18}{0}$ should be 0, try replacing **?** with 0. It doesn't work in the related multiplication problem! Try replacing **?** with any number you like. The result in the related multiplication problem is always 0 instead of -18. That is how we know that *dividing by 0 cannot be done*. Mathematicians say that it is **undefined** and have agreed never to divide by 0.

EXAMPLE 2   Using the Properties of Division

Divide. Then state the property illustrated by each example.

(a) $\frac{-312}{-312}=1$ Any nonzero number divided by itself is 1.

(b) $\frac{75}{1}=75$ Any number divided by 1 is the number.

(c) $\frac{0}{19}=0$ Zero divided by any nonzero number is 0.

(d) $\frac{48}{0}$ is *undefined*.   Division by 0 is *undefined*.

> You *cannot* divide by 0. Write "undefined."

⊞ Calculator Tip

Try **Examples 2(c) and 2(d)** above on your calculator.

0 ⊕ 19 ⊜   Answer is 0.

48 ⊕ 0 ⊜   Calculator shows "Error" or "ERR" or "E" for error because it cannot divide by 0.

···· **Work Problem 2 at the Side.** ▶

2 Divide. Then state the property illustrated by each division.

GS (a) $\frac{-12}{0}=$ _____

   Hint: Division by 0 is _____.

(b) $\frac{0}{39}$

(c) $\frac{-9}{1}$

(d) $\frac{21}{21}$

Answers

2. (a) undefined; Division by 0 is undefined.
   (b) 0; 0 divided by any nonzero number is 0.
   (c) -9; any number divided by 1 is the number.
   (d) 1; any nonzero number divided by itself is 1.

❸ Simplify.

Ⓖ (a) $60 \div (-3)(-5)$

$$\underbrace{(\quad)}(-5)$$

$$\underline{\quad}$$

(b) $-6(-16 \div 8) \cdot 2$

(c) $-8(10) \div 4(-3) \div (-6)$

(d) $56 \div (-8) \div (-1)$

OBJECTIVE ❸ Combine multiplying and dividing of integers. When a problem involves both multiplying and dividing, first check to see if there are any parentheses. Do what is inside parentheses first. Then start at the left and work toward the right, using two numbers at a time.

| EXAMPLE 3 | Combining Multiplication and Division of Integers |

Simplify.

(a) $6(-10) \div \underbrace{(-3 \cdot 2)}$ Do operations inside parentheses first: $-3 \cdot 2$ is -6. The signs are *different*, so the product is *negative*.

$\underbrace{6(-10)} \div (-6)$ Start at the left: $6(-10)$ is -60. The signs are *different*, so the product is *negative*.

$\underbrace{-60 \div (-6)}$ Finally, $-60 \div (-6)$ is 10. The signs are the *same*, so the quotient is *positive*.

$\qquad 10$

(b) $\underbrace{-24 \div (-2)}(4) \div (-6)$ No operations inside parentheses, so start at the left: $-24 \div (-2)$ is 12. (*Same* signs, *positive* quotient.)

$\quad \longrightarrow \underbrace{12(4)} \div (-6)$ Next, $12(4)$ is 48. (*Same* signs, *positive* product.)

$\qquad \underbrace{48 \div (-6)}$ Finally, $48 \div (-6)$ is -8. (*Different* signs, *negative* quotient.)

$\qquad \quad -8$

(c) $\underbrace{-50 \div (-5)} \div (-2)$ No operations inside parentheses, so start at the left: $-50 \div (-5)$ is 10. (*Same* signs, *positive* quotient.)

$\underbrace{10 \div (-2)}$ Now, $10 \div (-2)$ is -5. (*Different* signs, *negative* quotient.)

$\qquad -5$

◀ **Work Problem ❸ at the Side.**

OBJECTIVE ❹ Estimate answers to application problems involving division. Front end rounding can be used to estimate answers in division just as you did when multiplying in the previous section. Once the numbers have been rounded so that there are lots of zeros, you can use the division shortcut described in **Chapter R.** As a brief review, look at the pattern in these examples.

$$4000 \div (-50) = 400 \div (-5) = -80$$

Drop one 0 from both
dividend and divisor.

$$-6000 \div (-3000) = -6 \div (-3) = 2$$

Drop three zeros from both
dividend and divisor.

Answers

3. (a) $(-20)(-5)$; 100 **(b)** 24 **(c)** -10
(d) 7

EXAMPLE 4 Estimating an Answer in Division

First use front end rounding to estimate an answer. Then find the exact answer.

During a 24-hour laboratory experiment, the temperature of a solution dropped 96 degrees. What was the average drop in temperature each hour?

Estimate: Use front end rounding: −96 degrees rounds to −100 degrees and 24 hours rounds to 20 hours. To estimate the average, divide the rounded number of degrees by the rounded number of hours.

$$-100 \text{ degrees} \div 20 \text{ hours} = -5 \text{ degrees each hour} \leftarrow \text{Estimate}$$

Exact: −96 degrees ÷ 24 hours = −4 degrees each hour ← Exact

Because the exact answer of −4 degrees is close to the estimate of −5 degrees, you can see that −4 degrees probably is correct.

> **Calculator Tip**
>
> The answer in **Example 4** above "came out even." In other words, the quotient was an integer. Suppose that the drop in temperature had been 97 degrees. Do the division on your calculator.
>
> 97 (+/−) (÷) 24 (=)   Calculator shows −4.041666667
> −97
>
> The quotient is *not* an integer. We will work with numbers like these in **Chapter 5,** Positive and Negative Decimals.

··········· **Work Problem 4 at the Side.** ▶

OBJECTIVE 5 Interpret remainders in division application problems.
In arithmetic, division problems often have a remainder, as shown below.

```
      14  R10
  25)360
      25
     110
     100
      10 ← Remainder
```

But what does **R10** really mean? Let's look at this same problem by using money amounts.

EXAMPLE 5 Interpreting Remainders in Division Applications

Divide; then interpret the remainder in each application.

(a) The math department at Lake Community College has $360 to buy scientific calculators for the math lab. If the calculators cost $25 each, how many can be purchased? How much money will be left over?

We can solve this problem by using the same division as shown above. But this time we can decide what the remainder really means.

```
                       14 ← Number of calculators purchased
Cost of one calculator → $25)$360 ← Budget
                       25
                      110
                      100
                      $10 ← Money left over
```

The remainder is the money that is left over.

The department can buy 14 calculators. There will be $10 left over.

··········· **Continued on Next Page**

5 Divide; then interpret the remainder in each of these applications.

(a) Chad and Martha are baking cookies for a fund-raiser. They baked 116 cookies and are putting them into packages of a dozen each. How many packages will they have for the fund-raiser? How many cookies will be left over for them to eat?

$$\left.\begin{array}{l}\text{Cookies}\\\text{in each}\\\text{package}\end{array}\right\}\overline{116}\leftarrow\left\{\begin{array}{l}\text{Total}\\\text{number}\\\text{of cookies}\end{array}\right.$$

← Packages

(b) Coreen is a dispatcher for a bus company. A group of 249 senior citizens is going to a baseball game. If the buses each hold 44 people, how many buses should she send to pick up the seniors?

Calculator Tip

You can use your calculator to solve **Example 5(a)** on the previous page. Recall that digits on the *right* side of the decimal point show *part* of one whole. You cannot order *part* of one calculator, so ignore those digits and use only the *whole number part* of the quotient.

$$360\ \boxed{\div}\ 25\ \boxed{=}\ =14.\cancel{4}$$

Write the whole number

$$\begin{array}{r}14\\25\overline{)360}\\\underline{350}\\10\end{array}$$

Number of calculators

Subtract $360-350$ to get the amount of money remaining. The remainder is $10.

Now use your calculator to find how much money was spent to buy 14 calculators.

$$\boxed{\text{ON/AC}}\ 14\ \boxed{\times}\ 25\ \boxed{=}\ 350\ \leftarrow\ \text{Cost of 14 calculators}$$

Clear 14.4 from calculator before multiplying by pressing $\boxed{\text{C}}$, $\boxed{\text{ON/C}}$, $\boxed{\text{ON/AC}}$, or $\boxed{\text{CLEAR}}$.

(b) Luke's son is going on a Scout camping trip. There are 135 Scouts. Luke is renting tents that sleep 6 people each. How many tents should he rent?

We again use division to solve the problem. There is a remainder, but this time it must be interpreted differently than in the calculator example.

$$\begin{array}{r}22\\6\overline{)135}\\\underline{12}\\15\\\underline{12}\\3\end{array}$$

22 ← Number of tents with 6 Scouts each

Each tent holds → 6)135 ← Total number of Scouts

22 tents is *not* enough for all the Scouts.

3 ← Scouts left over

If Luke rents 22 tents, 3 Scouts will have to sleep out in the rain. He must rent **23 tents** to accommodate all the Scouts. (One tent will have only 3 Scouts in it.)

◄ **Work Problem 5 at the Side.**

Answers

5. (a) $\begin{array}{r}9\\12\overline{)116}\\\underline{-108}\\8\end{array}$ 9 packages, with 8 cookies left over to eat

(b) 6 buses, because 5 buses would leave 29 seniors standing on the curb

1.7 Exercises

FOR EXTRA HELP

 Download the MyDashBoard App

MyMathLab®

CONCEPT CHECK   *Watch for patterns as you work Exercises 1–4.*

1. (a) $14 \div 2$

   (b) $-14 \div (-2)$

   (c) $14 \div (-2)$

   (d) $-14 \div 2$

2. (a) $-18 \div (-3)$

   (b) $18 \div 3$

   (c) $-18 \div 3$

   (d) $18 \div (-3)$

3. (a) $-42 \div 6$

   (b) $-42 \div (-6)$

   (c) $42 \div (-6)$

   (d) $42 \div 6$

4. (a) $45 \div 5$

   (b) $45 \div (-5)$

   (c) $-45 \div (-5)$

   (d) $-45 \div 5$

Divide. **See Examples 1 and 2.**

5. (a) $\dfrac{35}{35}$

   (b) $\dfrac{35}{1}$

   (c) $\dfrac{-13}{1}$

   (d) $\dfrac{-13}{-13}$

6. (a) $\dfrac{-23}{1}$

   (b) $\dfrac{-23}{-23}$

   (c) $\dfrac{17}{1}$

   (d) $\dfrac{17}{17}$

7. (a) $\dfrac{0}{50}$

   (b) $\dfrac{50}{0}$

   (c) $\dfrac{-11}{0}$

   (d) $\dfrac{0}{-11}$

8. (a) $\dfrac{-85}{0}$

   (b) $\dfrac{0}{-85}$

   (c) $\dfrac{6}{0}$

   (d) $\dfrac{0}{6}$

9. $\dfrac{-8}{2}$

10. $\dfrac{-14}{7}$

11. $\dfrac{21}{-7}$

12. $\dfrac{30}{-6}$

13. $\dfrac{-54}{-9}$

14. $\dfrac{-48}{-6}$

15. $\dfrac{55}{-5}$

16. $\dfrac{70}{-7}$

17. $\dfrac{-28}{0}$

18. $\dfrac{-40}{0}$

19. $\dfrac{14}{-1}$

20. $\dfrac{25}{-1}$

21. $\dfrac{-20}{-2}$

22. $\dfrac{-80}{-4}$

23. $\dfrac{-48}{-12}$

24. $\dfrac{-30}{-15}$

25. $\dfrac{-18}{18}$

26. $\dfrac{50}{-50}$

27. $\dfrac{0}{-9}$

28. $\dfrac{0}{-4}$

29. $\dfrac{-573}{-3}$

30. $\dfrac{-580}{-5}$

31. $\dfrac{163{,}672}{-328}$

32. $\dfrac{-69{,}496}{1022}$

*Simplify. **See Example 3.***

33. $-60 \div 10 \div (-3)$
$\underbrace{-60 \div 10} \div (-3)$
$\underbrace{-6 \div (-3)}$
_____

34. $36 \div (-4) \div 3$
$\underbrace{36 \div (-4)} \div 3$
$\underbrace{-9 \div 3}$
_____

35. $-64 \div (-8) \div (-2)$

36. $-72 \div (-9) \div (-4)$

37. $100 \div (-5)(-2)$

38. $-80 \div 4(-5)$

39. $48 \div 3 \cdot (-12 \div 4)$

40. $-2 \cdot (-3) \cdot (-7) \div 7$

41. $-5 \div (-5)(-10) \div (-2)$

42. $-9(4) \div (-36)(50)$

43. $64 \cdot 0 \div (-8)(10)$

44. $-88 \div (-8) \div (-11)(0)$

CONCEPT CHECK *Use your knowledge of the properties of multiplication and division as you work Exercises 45–50.*

45. Explain whether or not division is commutative like multiplication. Start by doing these two divisions on your calculator: $2 \div 1$ and $1 \div 2$.

46. Explain whether or not division is associative like multiplication. Start by doing these two divisions: $(12 \div 6) \div 2$ and $12 \div (6 \div 2)$.

47. Explain what is different and what is similar about multiplying and dividing two signed numbers.

48. In your own words, describe at least three division properties. Include examples to illustrate each property.

49. Write three numerical examples for each situation.
   (a) A negative number divided by -1

   (b) A positive number divided by -1

   Now write a rule that explains what happens when you divide a signed number by -1.

50. Explain why $\frac{0}{-3}$ and $\frac{-3}{0}$ do not give the same result.

Solve these application problems by using addition, subtraction, multiplication, or division. First use front end rounding to estimate the answer. Then find the exact answer. ***See Example 4.***

51. The greatest ocean depth is 35,836 feet below sea level. If an unmanned research sub dives to that depth in 17 equal steps, how far does it dive in each step? (*Source: The Top 10 of Everything.*)

Estimate: $-40,000 \div$ ____ = _____

Exact:

52. Our college enrollment dropped by 3245 students over the last 11 years. What was the average drop in enrollment each year?

Estimate: $-3000 \div$ ____ = _____

Exact:

53. When Ashwini discovered that her checking account was overdrawn by $238, she quickly transferred $450 from her savings to her checking account. What is the new balance in her checking account?

Estimate:

Exact:

54. Sarah lost 48 points during the first round of a card game. During the second round she won 191 points. How many points does she have now?

Estimate:

Exact:

55. The foggiest place in the United States is Cape Disappointment, Washington. It is foggy there an average of 106 days each year. How many days is it not foggy each year? (*Source:* National Weather Service.)

Estimate:

Exact:

56. The number of cell phone users in the United States in 1991 was 11 million. The number of users reached 327 million in 2011. What was the increase in the number of users during this 20-year period? (*Source: World Almanac and Book of Facts.*)

Estimate:

Exact:

57. A plane descended an average of 730 feet each minute during a 37-minute landing. How far did the plane descend during the landing?

Estimate:

Exact:

58. A discount store found that 174 items were lost to shoplifting last month. The average value of each item was $24. What was the total loss due to shoplifting?

Estimate:

Exact:

59. Mr. and Mrs. Martinez drove on the Interstate for five hours and traveled 315 miles. What was the average number of miles they drove each hour?

Estimate:

Exact:

60. Rochelle has a 48-month car loan for $15,072. How much is her monthly payment?

Estimate:

Exact:

Find the exact answer in Exercises 61–66. Solving these problems requires more than one step.

61. Clarence bowled four games and had scores of 143, 190, 162, and 177. What was his average score? (*Hint:* To find the average, add all the scores and divide by the number of scores.)

62. Sheila kept track of her grocery expenses for six weeks. The amounts she spent were $184, $111, $136, $110, $98, and $153. What was the average weekly cost of her groceries?

63. On the back of an oatmeal box, it says that one serving weighs 40 grams and that there are 13 servings in the box. On the front of the box, it says that the weight of the contents is 510 grams. What is the difference in the total weight on the front and the back of the box? (*Source:* Quaker Oats.)

64. A 2000-calorie-per-day diet recommends that you eat no more than 67 grams of fat. If each gram of fat is 9 calories, how many calories can you consume in other types of food? (*Source:* Nutrition.com)

65. Stephanie had $302 in her bank account. She made payments of $116 for day care and $548 for rent. She also deposited her $347 paycheck. What is the balance in her account?

66. Gary started a new checking account with a $500 deposit. The bank charged him $18 to print his checks. He also wrote a $193 check for car repairs and a $289 check to his credit card company. What is the balance in his account?

Divide; then interpret the remainder in each application. **See Example 5.**

67. A cellular phone company is offering 1000 free minutes of air time to new subscribers. How many hours of free time will a new subscriber receive?

68. Nikki is catering a large party. If one pie will serve eight guests, how many pies should she make for 100 guests?

69. Hurricane victims are being given temporary shelter in a hotel. Each room can hold five people. How many rooms are needed for 163 people?

70. A college received a $250,000 donation for scholarships. How many $3500 scholarships can be given to students?

Simplify:

71. $|-8| \div (-4) \cdot |-5| \cdot |1|$

72. $-6 \cdot |-3| \div |9| \cdot (-2)$

73. $-6(-8) \div (-5 + 5)$

74. $-9 \div (-9)(-9 \div 9) \div (12 - 13)$

75. Look back at page 4 of this chapter. You guessed how many days it would take to receive a million dollars if you got $1 each second. Here's how to use your calculator to get the answer. If you get $1 per second, it would take 1,000,000 seconds to receive $1,000,000. Press these keys.

| 1000000 | ÷ 60 | = 16666.66667 | ÷ 60 | = 277.7777778 | ÷ 24 | = 11.57407407 |

| There are 60 seconds in one minute. | About 16,667 minutes | There are 60 minutes in one hour. | About 278 hours | There are 24 hours in one day. | About $11\frac{1}{2}$ days (11.5 is equivalent to $11\frac{1}{2}$.) |

Notice that you do *not* have to re-enter the intermediate answers. When the answer 16666.66667 appears on your calculator display, just go ahead and enter ÷ 60.

Now use a *scientific* calculator to find how long it takes to receive a *billion* dollars. Start by entering 1000000000. Then follow the pattern shown above. You will need to do one more division step to get the number of years. (Assume that there are 365 days in one year.)

Summary Exercises *Operations with Integers*

Simplify each expression.

1. $2 - 8$

2. $(-16)(0)$

3. $-14 - (-7)$

4. $\dfrac{-42}{6}$

5. $-9(-7)$

6. $\dfrac{-12}{12}$

7. $(1)(-56)$

8. $1 + (-23)$

9. $5 - (-7)$

10. $-88 \div (-11)$

11. $-18 + 5$

12. $\dfrac{0}{-10}$

13. $-40 - (-40)$

14. $-17 + 0$

15. $8(-6)$

16. $-1 - 9$

17. $-5(10)$

18. $\dfrac{30}{0}$

19. $0 - 14$

20. $\dfrac{18}{-3}$

21. $-13 + 13$

22. $\dfrac{-16}{-1}$

23. $20 - 50$

24. $\dfrac{-7}{0}$

25. $(-4)(-6)(2)$

26. $-2 + (-12) + (-5)$

27. $-60 \div 10 \div (-3)$

28. $-8 - 4 - 8$

29. $64(0) \div (-8)$

30. $2 - (-5) + 9$

31. $-9 + 8 + (-2)$

32. $(-6)(-2)(-3)$

33. $8 + 6 + (-8)$

34. $9 - 0 - 16$

35. $-25 \div (-1) \div (-5)$

36. $1 - 32 + 0$

37. $-72 \div (-9) \div (-4)$

38. $-7 + 28 + (-56) + 3$

39. $9 - 6 - 3 - 5$

40. $-6(-8) \div (-5 - 7)$

41. $-1(9732)(-1)(-1)$

42. $-80 \div 4(-5)$

43. $-10 - 4 + 0 + 18$

44. $-7 \cdot |7| \cdot |-7|$

45. $5 - |-3| + 3$

46. $-2(-3)(7) \div (-7)$

47. $-3 - (-2 + 4) - 5$

48. $0 - |-7 + 2|$

49. CONCEPT CHECK   Describe what happens in each situation.

  (a) Zero is divided by a nonzero number.

  (b) Any number is multiplied by 0.

  (c) A nonzero number is divided by itself.

50. CONCEPT CHECK   Find, explain, and correct the errors in this student's work.

  (a) $\dfrac{15}{-15} = 0$

  (b) $\dfrac{8}{0} = 8$

  (c) $-10 \div (-2) \div (-5) = 1$

Study Skills
TAKING LECTURE NOTES

Study the set of sample math notes from the next section on exponents, and read the comments about them. Then try to incorporate the techniques into your own math note taking in class.

OBJECTIVES

1. Apply note taking strategies, such as writing problems as well as explanations.

2. Use appropriate abbreviations in notes.

▶ The **date and title** of the day's lecture topic are always at the top of every page. **Always begin a new day with a new page.**

▶ Note the **definitions** of base and exponent are written in parentheses—don't trust your memory!

▶ **Skipping lines** makes the notes easier to read.

▶ See how the **direction word** (*simplify*) is emphasized and explained.

▶ A **star marks an important concept.** This warns you to avoid future mistakes. **Note the underlining,** too, which highlights the importance.

▶ Notice the two columns, which allow for the example and its explanation to be close together. **Whenever you know you'll be given a series of steps to follow, try the two-column method.**

▶ Note the **braces and arrows,** which clearly show how the problem is set up to be simplified.

January 2   *Exponents*

Exponents used to show repeated multiplication.

$3 \cdot 3 \cdot 3 \cdot 3$ can be written 3^4 exponent (how many times it's multiplied)

base (the number being multiplied)

Read 3^2 as 3 to the 2nd power or 3 squared

3^3 as 3 to the 3rd power or 3 cubed

3^4 as 3 to the 4th power

etc.

Simplifying an expression with exponents

→ actually do the repeated multiplication

2^3 means $2 \cdot 2 \cdot 2$ and $2 \cdot 2 \cdot 2 = 8$

☆ Careful! 5^2 means $5 \cdot 5$ <u>NOT</u> $5 \cdot 2$

so $5^2 = 5 \cdot 5 = 25$ BUT $5^2 \neq 10$

Example	*Explanation*
Simplify $2^4 \cdot 3^2$	Exponents means <u>multiplication</u>.
$2 \cdot 2 \cdot 2 \cdot 2 \cdot 3 \cdot 3$	Use 2 as a factor 4 times. Use 3 as a factor 2 times.
$16 \cdot 9$	$2 \cdot 2 \cdot 2 \cdot 2$ is 16, $3 \cdot 3$ is 9 → $16 \cdot 9$ is 144
144	Simplified result is 144 (no exponents left)

Study Skills

Continued from page 65

Why Are These Notes Brain Friendly?

The notes are **easy to look at,** and you know that the brain responds to things that are visually pleasing. Other techniques that are visually memorable are the use of spacing (the two columns), stars, underlining, and circling. All of these methods **allow your brain to take note of important concepts and steps.**

The notes are also **systematic,** which means that they use certain techniques regularly. This way, your brain easily recognizes the topic of the day, the signals that show an important point, and the steps to follow for procedures. When you develop a system that you always use in your notes, your notes are easy to understand later when you are reviewing for a test.

Now Try This

Find one or two people in your math class to work with. Compare each other's lecture notes over a period of a week or so. Ask yourself the following questions as you examine the notes.

1 What are you doing in your notes to show the **main points** or larger concepts? (Such as underlining, boxing, using stars, capital letters, etc.)

2 In what ways do you **set off the explanations** for worked problems, examples, or smaller ideas (subpoints)? (Such as indenting, using arrows, circling or boxing)

3 What does **your instructor do** to show that he or she is moving from one idea to the next? (Such as saying "Next" or "Any questions," "Now," or erasing the board, etc.)

4 **How do you mark** that in your notes? (Such as skipping lines, using dashes or numbers, etc.)

5 What **explanations (in words) do you give yourself** in your notes, so when those new dendrites you grew in lecture are fading, you can read your notes and still remember the new concepts later when you try to do your homework?

6 What **did you learn** by examining your classmates' notes?

▶ _____

▶ _____

▶ _____

7 What **will you try** in your own note taking? List **four** techniques that you will use next time you take notes in math class.

▶ _____

▶ _____

▶ _____

▶ _____

1.8 Exponents and Order of Operations

OBJECTIVE **1** **Use exponents to write repeated factors.** An **exponent** is a quick way to write repeated multiplication. Here is an example.

$2 \cdot 2 \cdot 2 \cdot 2 \cdot 2$ can be written 2^5 ← Exponent
$\uparrow$
Base

The *base* is the number being multiplied over and over, and the exponent tells how many times to use the number as a factor. This is called *exponential notation* or *exponential form*.

To simplify 2^5, actually do the multiplication.

$$\underbrace{2^5}_{\text{Exponential form}} = \underbrace{2 \cdot 2 \cdot 2 \cdot 2 \cdot 2}_{\text{Factored form}} = \underset{\text{Simplified form}}{32}$$

Here are some more examples, using 2 as the base.

$2 = 2^1$	is read	"2 to the **first power**."
$2 \cdot 2 = 2^2$	is read	"2 to the **second power**" or, more commonly, "2 **squared**."
$2 \cdot 2 \cdot 2 = 2^3$	is read	"2 to the **third power**" or, more commonly, "2 **cubed**."
$2 \cdot 2 \cdot 2 \cdot 2 = 2^4$	is read	"2 to the **fourth power**."
$2 \cdot 2 \cdot 2 \cdot 2 \cdot 2 = 2^5$	is read	"2 to the **fifth power**."

and so on.

We usually don't write an exponent of 1, so if no exponent is shown, you can assume that it is 1. For example, 6 is actually 6^1, and 4 is actually 4^1.

EXAMPLE 1 **Using Exponents**

Complete this table.

Exponential Form	Factored Form	Simplified	Read as
(a) 5^3	$5 \cdot 5 \cdot 5$	125	5 cubed, or 5 to the third power
(b) 4^2	$(4)(4)$	16	4 squared, or 4 to the second power
(c) 7^1	7	7	7 to the first power

··· **Work Problem** **1** **at the Side.** ▶

OBJECTIVE **2** **Simplify expressions containing exponents.** Exponents are also used with signed numbers, as shown below.

$(-3)^2 = (-3)(-3) = 9$ The factors have the same sign, so the product is positive.

$(-4)^3 = \underbrace{(-4)(-4)}(-4)$ Multiply two numbers at a time.

$\underbrace{16}(-4)$ First, $(-4)(-4)$ is positive 16.

-64 Then, $16(-4)$ is -64.

OBJECTIVES

1 Use exponents to write repeated factors.

2 Simplify expressions containing exponents.

3 Use the order of operations.

4 Simplify expressions with fraction bars.

VOCABULARY TIP

Exponent "Ex" means "out." The exponent is the small, raised number sitting "outside" of another number or outside parentheses, such as 2^3 or $(-3)^2$ or $(1 - 5)^3$.

---

1 Write each multiplication using exponents. Indicate how to read the exponential form.

(a) $3 \cdot 3 \cdot 3 \cdot 3$

$3^{}$ ← exponent
$\uparrow$
base

Read it as 3 to the _____ power.

(b) $6 \cdot 6$

(c) 9

(d) $(2)(2)(2)(2)(2)(2)$

Answers

1. **(a)** 3^4; Read it as "3 to the fourth power."
  (b) 6^2 is read "6 squared" or "6 to the second power."
  (c) 9^1 is read "9 to the first power."
  (d) 2^6 is read "2 to the sixth power."

2 Simplify.

(a) $(-2)^3$

$$\underbrace{(-2)\,(-2)\,(-2)}$$
$$\longrightarrow \underbrace{(\underline{})\,(-2)}$$
$$\underline{}$$

(b) $(-6)^2$

(c) $2^4\,(-3)^2$

(d) $3^3\,(-4)^2$

Simplify exponents before you do other multiplications, as shown below. Notice that the exponent applies only to the *first* thing to its *left*.

Exponent applies only to the 2. ⟶ $2^3\,(5)\,(4^2)$ ⟵ Exponent applies only to the 4.

(2) (2) (2) is 8. ⟶ $8\,(5)\,(16)$ ⟵ (4) (4) is 16.

$$\underbrace{(40)\,(16)}$$
$$640$$

EXAMPLE 2 **Using Exponents with Negative Numbers**

Simplify.

(a) $(-5)^2 = (-5)\,(-5) = 25$

(b) $(-5)^3 = \underbrace{(-5)\,(-5)}\,(-5)$

> Be careful! Work with two factors at a time and watch the signs.

$$\longrightarrow \underbrace{(25)(-5)}$$
$$-125$$

(c) $(-2)^4 = (-2)\,(-2)\,(-2)\,(-2) = 16$

(d) $2^3(-3)^2 = \underbrace{(2)\,(2)\,(2)}\,\underbrace{(-3)\,(-3)}$

$$\longrightarrow (8)\,(9) \longleftarrow$$
$$72$$

📟 Calculator Tip

On a *scientific* calculator, use the exponent key $\boxed{y^x}$ (or $\boxed{\wedge}$) to enter exponents. To enter 5^8, press the following keys.

$$5 \quad \boxed{y^x} \quad 8 \quad \boxed{=} \qquad \text{Answer is 390,625.}$$
$$\uparrow \qquad\qquad \uparrow$$
$$\text{Base} \qquad \text{Exponent}$$

Be careful when using your calculator's exponent key with a negative number, such as $(-5)^3$. Different calculators use different keystrokes, so check the instruction manual, or experiment to see how your calculator works.

◀ **Work Problem 2 at the Side.**

OBJECTIVE 3 **Use the order of operations.** In earlier sections, you worked examples that mixed addition and subtraction or mixed multiplication and division. In those situations, you worked from left to right. **Example 3** below is a review.

EXAMPLE 3 **Working from Left to Right**

Simplify.

(a) $-8 - (-6) + (-11)$ Change all subtractions to adding the opposite.

$$-8 + \quad 6 \; + (-11)$$ Add from left to right. First add $-8 + 6$.

$$\underbrace{-2 \quad\; + (-11)}$$ Finally, add $-2 + (-11)$.
$$-13$$

Answers

2. **(a)** $(4)(-2); -8$
  (b) $(-6) \cdot (-6) = 36$
  (c) $16 \cdot 9 = 144$ **(d)** $27 \cdot 16 = 432$

Continued on Next Page

(b) $-15 \div (-3)(6)$ Do multiplications and divisions from left to right.

$$(5)(6)$$

$$30$$

· Work Problem **3** at the Side. ▶

Now we're ready to do problems that use a mix of the four operations, parentheses, and exponents. Let's start with a simple example: $4 + 2 \cdot 3$.

If we work from left to right

$$4 + 2 \cdot 3$$
$$6 \quad \cdot 3$$
$$18$$

If we multiply first

$$4 + 2 \cdot 3$$
$$4 + \quad 6$$
$$10$$

Which answer is correct?

To be sure that everyone gets the same answer to a problem like this, mathematicians have agreed to do things in a certain order. The following order of operations shows that multiplying is done ahead of adding, so *the correct answer is 10*.

Order of Operations

Step 1   Work inside *parentheses* or *other grouping symbols*.

Step 2   Simplify expressions with *exponents*.

Step 3   Do the remaining *multiplications and divisions* as they occur from left to right.

Step 4   Do the remaining *additions and subtractions* as they occur from left to right.

▦ **Calculator Tip**

Enter the example above in your calculator.

$$4 \;\oplus\; 2 \;\otimes\; 3 \;\ominus$$

Which answer do you get? If you have a scientific calculator, it automatically uses the order of operations and multiplies first to get the correct answer of 10. Some standard, four-function calculators may *not* have the order of operations built into them and will give the *incorrect* answer of 18.

3 Simplify.

(a) $-9 + (-15) - 3$

$$(\underline{\quad}) - 3$$

$$\underline{\quad}$$

(b) $-4 - 2 + (-6)$

(c) $3(-4) \div (-6)$

(d) $-18 \div 9(-4)$

$$(\underline{\quad})(-4)$$

4 Simplify.

(a) $8 + 6(14 \div 2)$

$$8 + \quad 6\,(7)$$

$$8 + \quad \underline{\quad}$$

$$\underline{\quad}$$

(b) $4(1) + 8(9 - 2)$

(c) $3(5 + 1) + 20 \div 4$

5 Simplify.

(a) $2 + 40 \div (-5 + 3)$

$$2 + 40 \div \quad (-2)$$

$$2 + \quad (\underline{\quad})$$

$$\underline{\quad}$$

(b) $-5(5) - (15 + 5)$

(c) $(-24 \div 2) + (15 - 3)$

(d) $-3(2 - 8) - 5(4 - 3)$

(e) $3(3) - (10 \cdot 3) \div 5$

(f) $6 - (2 + 7) \div (-4 + 1)$

| EXAMPLE 4 | Using the Order of Operations with Whole Numbers |

Simplify.

*Do **not** start by adding $9 + 3$.*

$9 + 3\,(20 - 4) \div 8$ — Work inside parentheses first: $20 - 4$ is 16. Bring down the other numbers and symbols that you haven't used.

$9 + \quad 3\,(16) \quad \div 8$ — Look for exponents: none. Move from left to right, looking for multiplying and dividing.

$9 + \quad 3\,(16) \quad \div 8$ — Yes, here is multiplying: $3(16)$ is 48.

$9 + \quad 48 \quad \div 8$ — Here is dividing: $48 \div 8$ is 6. There is no other multiplying or dividing, so look for adding and subtracting.

$9 + \quad 6$ — Add last: $9 + 6$ is 15.

$\quad 15$

◄ **Work Problem 4 at the Side.**

| EXAMPLE 5 | Using the Order of Operations with Integers |

Simplify.

(a) $-8 \div (7 - 5) - 9$ — Work inside parentheses first: $7 - 5$ is 2. Bring down the other numbers and symbols that you haven't used. Look for exponents: none.

$-8 \div \quad (2) \quad - 9$ — Move from left to right, looking for multiplying and dividing.

$-8 \div \quad (2) - \quad 9$ — Here is dividing: $-8 \div 2$ is -4. No other multiplying or dividing, so look for adding and subtracting.

$-4 \quad - \quad 9$ — Change subtracting to adding. Change 9 to its opposite.

$-4 \quad + (-9)$ — Add $-4 + (-9)$.

-13

*Do **not** start by adding $3 + 2$.*

(b) $3 + 2(6 - 8) \cdot (15 \div 3)$ — Work inside first set of parentheses. Change $6 - 8$ to $6 + (-8)$ to get -2.

$3 + 2\,(-2) \cdot (15 \div 3)$ — Work inside second set of parentheses: $15 \div 3$ is 5.

$3 + 2\,(-2) \cdot \quad 5$ — Multiply and divide from left to right. First multiply $2(-2)$ to get -4.

$3 + \quad (-4) \quad \cdot \quad 5$ — Then multiply $-4 \cdot 5$ to get -20.

$3 + \quad (-20)$ — Add last: $3 + (-20)$ is -17.

-17

◄ **Work Problem 5 at the Side.**

Answers

4. **(a)** $8 + 42; 50$ **(b)** 60 **(c)** 23
5. **(a)** $2 + (-20); -18$ **(b)** -45
   (c) 0 **(d)** 13 **(e)** 3 **(f)** 9

| EXAMPLE 6 | Using the Order of Operations with Exponents |

Simplify.

(a) $4^2 - (-3)^2$ — The only parentheses are around -3, but there is no work to do inside these parentheses.

$4^2 - (-3)^2$ — Simplify the exponents: $4^2 = (4)(4) = 16$, and $(-3)^2 = (-3)(-3) = 9$.

$16 - 9$ — There is no multiplying or dividing, so add and subtract: $16 - 9$ is 7.

7

(b) $(-4)^3 - (4 - 6)^2 (-3)$ — Work inside parentheses: $4 - 6$ becomes $4 + (-6)$, which is -2.

$(-4)^3 - (-2)^2 (-3)$ — Simplify the exponents next: $(-4)^3$ is $(-4)(-4)(-4) = -64$, and $(-2)^2$ is $(-2)(-2) = 4$.

$-64 - 4(-3)$ — Look for multiplying and dividing. Multiply $4(-3)$ to get -12.

$-64 - (-12)$ — Change subtraction to addition. Change -12 to its opposite.

$-64 + (12)$ — Add: $-64 + 12$ is -52.

-52

CAUTION

To help in remembering the order of operations, you may have memorized the letters **PEMDAS**, or the phrase "Please Excuse My Dear Aunt Sally."

| **P**lease | **E**xcuse | **M**y | **D**ear | **A**unt | **S**ally |

Parentheses; **E**xponents; **M**ultiply and **D**ivide; **A**dd and **S**ubtract

Be careful! Do **not** automatically do all multiplication before division. Multiplying and dividing are done *from left to right* (after parentheses and exponents).

· Work Problem **6** at the Side. ▶

---

6 Simplify.

(a) $2^3 - 3^2$

$\boxed{2 \cdot 2 \cdot 2}$ $\boxed{3 \cdot 3}$

(b) $6^2 \div (-4)(-3)$

(c) $(-4)^2 - 3^2 (5 - 2)$

(d) $(-3)^3 + (3 - 9)^2$

7 Simplify.

(GS) **(a)** $\dfrac{-3\,(2^3)}{-10-6+8}$

Numerator: $-3\underbrace{(2^3)}$

$\qquad -3(\underline{}) = \underline{}$

Denominator: $-10 - \quad 6 + 8$

$\qquad \underbrace{-10 + (-6)} + 8$

$\qquad\qquad \underline{} + 8 = \underline{}$

Numerator $\longrightarrow$
Denominator $\longrightarrow$ $\quad\overline{\underline{}}\ =$

(b) $\dfrac{(-10)\,(-5)}{-6 \div 3\,(5)}$

(c) $\dfrac{6 + 18 \div (-2)}{(1 - 10) \div 3}$

(d) $\dfrac{6^2 - 3^2\,(4)}{5 + (3 - 7)^2}$

OBJECTIVE **4** **Simplify expressions with fraction bars.** A fraction bar indicates division, as in $\dfrac{-6}{2}$, which means $-6 \div 2$. In the expression

$$\frac{-5 + 3^2}{16 - 7(2)}$$

the fraction bar also acts as a grouping symbol, like parentheses. It tells us to do the work in the numerator (above the bar) first. Then do the work in the denominator (below the bar). The last step is to divide the results.

$$\frac{-5 + 3^2}{16 - 7\,(2)} \longrightarrow \frac{-5 + 9}{16 - 14} \longrightarrow \frac{4}{2} \longrightarrow 4 \div 2 = 2$$

The final result is 2.

EXAMPLE 7 **Using the Order of Operations with Fraction Bars**

Simplify $\dfrac{-8 + 5(4 - 6)}{4 - 4^2 \div 8}$.

First do the work in the numerator.

Do **not** start by adding $-8 + 5$.	$-8 + 5\underbrace{(4 - 6)}$	Work inside the parentheses.
	$-8 + \underbrace{5(-2)}$	Multiply.
	$\underbrace{-8 + \quad (-10)}$	Add.

Numerator $\longrightarrow -18$

Now do the work in the denominator.

$4 - \underbrace{4^2} \div 8$ There are no parentheses; simplify the exponent.

$4 - \underbrace{16 \div 8}$ Divide.

$\underbrace{4 - \quad 2}$ Subtract.

Denominator $\longrightarrow 2$

The last step is the division.

Numerator $\longrightarrow$
Denominator $\longrightarrow$ $\dfrac{-18}{2} = -9$ Signs are **different**, so the quotient is **negative**.

◀ **Work Problem** **7** at the Side.

Answers

7. **(a)** Numerator: $-3\,(8) = -24$;
Denominator: $-16 + 8 = -8$;
$\dfrac{-24}{-8} = 3$

(b) $\dfrac{50}{-10} = -5$ **(c)** $\dfrac{-3}{-3} = 1$

(d) $\dfrac{0}{21} = 0$

1.8 Exercises

  MyMathLab®

CONCEPT CHECK *Complete this table.*

	Exponential Form	Factored Form	Simplified	Read as
1.	4^3		64	
2.	10^2		100	
3.		2 • 2 • 2 • 2 • 2 • 2 • 2		
4.		3 • 3 • 3 • 3 • 3		
5.		5 • 5 • 5 • 5		
6.		2 • 2 • 2 • 2 • 2 • 2		
7.				7 squared
8.				6 cubed
9.				10 to the first power
10.				4 to the fourth power

Simplify. See Examples 1 and 2.

11. (a) 10^1

   (b) 10^2

   (c) 10^3

   (d) 10^4

12. (a) 5^1

   (b) 5^2

   (c) 5^3

   (d) 5^4

13. (a) 4^1

   (b) 4^2

   (c) 4^3

   (d) 4^4

14. (a) 3^1

   (b) 3^2

   (c) 3^3

   (d) 3^4

15. 5^{10}

16. 4^9

17. 2^{12}

18. 3^{10}

19. $(-2)^2$

20. $(-4)^2$

21. $(-5)^2$

22. $(-10)^2$

23. $(-4)^3$

24. $(-2)^3$

25. $(-3)^4$

26. $(-2)^4$

27. $(-10)^3$

28. $(-5)^3$

29. 1^4

30. 1^5

31. $3^3 \cdot 2^2$ **32.** $4^2 \cdot 5^2$ **33.** $2^3 (-5)^2$ **34.** $3^2 (-2)^2$

35. $6^1 (-5)^3$ **36.** $7^1 (-4)^3$ **37.** $(-2)(-2)^4$ **38.** $-6(-6)^2$

39. CONCEPT CHECK   Simplify.

$(-2)^2 =$ _____ $(-2)^6 =$ _____
$(-2)^3 =$ _____ $(-2)^7 =$ _____
$(-2)^4 =$ _____ $(-2)^8 =$ _____
$(-2)^5 =$ _____ $(-2)^9 =$ _____

(a) Describe the pattern you see in the signs of the answers.

(b) What would be the sign of $(-2)^{15}$ and the sign of $(-2)^{24}$?

40. CONCEPT CHECK   Explain why it is important to have rules for the order of operations. Why do you think our "natural instinct" is to just work from left to right?

*Simplify. **See Examples 3–7.***

41. $12 \div 6(-3)$ Multiply and divide from left to right.
$\underbrace{\hspace{1cm}} (-3)$
$\underbrace{\hspace{2cm}}$
_____

42. $10 - 30 \div 2$ Divide before subtracting.
$10 - \underbrace{\hspace{1cm}}$
_____

43. $-1 + 15 - 7 - 7$

44. $9 + (-5) + 2(-2)$

45. $10 - 7^2$

46. $5 - 5^2$

47. $2 - (-5) + 3^2$

48. $6 - (-9) + 2^3$

49. $3 + 5(6 - 2)$

50. $4 + 3(8 - 3)$

51. $-7 + 6(8 - 14)$

52. $-3 + 5(9 - 12)$

53. $2(-3 + 5) - (9 - 12)$

54. $3(2 - 7) - (-5 + 1)$

55. $-5(7 - 13) \div (-10)$

56. $-4(9-17) \div (-8)$

57. $9 \div (-3)^2 + (-1)$

58. $-48 \div (-4)^2 + 3$

59. $2 - (-5)(-2)^3$

60. $1 - (-10)(-3)^3$

61. $-2(-7) + 3(9)$

62. $4(-2) + (-3)(-5)$

63. $30 \div (-5) - 36 \div (-9)$

64. $8 \div (-4) - 42 \div (-7)$

65. $2(5) - 3(4) + 5(3)$

66. $9(3) - 6(4) + 3(7)$

67. $4(3^2) + 7(3+9) - (-6)$

68. $5(4^2) - 6(1+4) - (-3)$

69. $(-4)^2 \cdot (7-9)^2 \div 2^3$

70. $(-5)^2 \cdot (9-17)^2 \div (-10)^2$

71. $\dfrac{-1 + 5^2 - (-3)}{-6 - 9 + 12}$

72. $\dfrac{-6 + 3^2 - (-7)}{7 - 9 - 3}$

73. $\dfrac{-2\left(4^2\right) - 4\left(6 - 2\right)}{-4\left(8 - 13\right) \div \left(-5\right)}$

74. $\dfrac{3\left(3^2\right) - 5\left(9 - 2\right)}{8\left(6 - 9\right) \div \left(-3\right)}$

75. $\dfrac{2^3 \cdot \left(-2 - 5\right) + 4\left(-1\right)}{4 + 5\left(-6 \cdot 2\right) + \left(5 \cdot 11\right)}$

76. $\dfrac{3^3 + 4\left(-1 - 2\right) - 25}{-4 + 4\left(3 \cdot 5\right) + \left(-6 \cdot 9\right)}$

77. $5^2\left(9 - 11\right)\left(-3\right)\left(-3\right)^3$

78. $4^2\left(13 - 17\right)\left(-2\right)\left(-2\right)^3$

79. $\left|-12\right| \div 4 + 2 \cdot \left|\left(-2\right)^3\right| \div 4$

80. $6 - \left|2 - 3 \cdot 4\right| + \left(-5\right)^2 \div 5^2$

81. $\dfrac{-9 + 18 \div \left(-3\right)\left(-6\right)}{32 - 4\left(12\right) \div 3\left(2\right)}$

82. $\dfrac{-20 - 15\left(-4\right) - \left(-40\right)}{14 + 27 \div 3\left(-2\right) - \left(-4\right)}$

Study Skills
REVIEWING A CHAPTER

This activity is really about **preparing for tests.** Some of the suggestions are ideas that you will learn to use a little later in the term, but get started trying them out now. Often, the first chapter in your math textbook will be review, so it is good to practice some of the study techniques on material that is not too challenging.

Chapter Reviewing Techniques

Use these **chapter reviewing techniques.**

▶ **Make a study card for each vocabulary word and concept.** Include a definition, an example, a sketch, and a page reference. Include the symbol or formula if there is one. See the *Using Study Cards* activity for a quick look at some sample study cards.

▶ **Go back to the section** to find more explanations or information about any new vocabulary, formulas, or symbols.

▶ **Use the Chapter Summary** to practice each type of problem. Do not expect the Summary to substitute for reading and working through the whole chapter! First, take the "Test Your Word Power" quiz to check your understanding of new vocabulary. The answers are at the end of the quiz. Then read the Quick Review. **Pay special attention to the blue headings.** Check the explanations for the solutions to problems given. Try to think about the **whole chapter.**

▶ **Study your lecture notes** to see what your instructor has emphasized in class. Then review that material in your text.

▶ **Do the Review Exercises.**
  ✓ Check your answers **after** you're done with each **section of exercises.**
  ✓ If you get stuck on a problem, **first** check the Chapter Summary. If that doesn't clear up your confusion, then check the section and your lecture notes.
  ✓ Pay attention to **direction words** for the problems, such as *simplify, round, solve,* and *estimate.*
  ✓ Make **study cards for especially difficult problems.**

▶ **Do the Mixed Review exercises.** This is a good check to see if you can still do the problems when they are in mixed-up order. **Check your answers carefully** in the Answers section in the back of your book. Are your answers **exact** and **complete?** Make sure you are **labeling** answers correctly, using the right **units.** For example, does your answer need to include $\$$, cm^2, ft, and so on?

Study Skills
Continued from page 77

Why Are These Review Activities Brain Friendly?

You have already become familiar with the features of your textbook. This activity requires you to make good use of them. Your **brain needs repetition** to strengthen dendrites and the connections between them. By following the steps outlined here, you will be re-inforcing the concepts, procedures, and skills you need to use for tests (and for the next chapters).

The combination of techniques provides repetition in different ways. That **promotes good branching of dendrites** instead of just relying on one branch or route to connect to the other dendrites. A thorough review of each chapter will **solidify your dendrite connections**. It will help you be sure that you understand the concepts **completely and accurately**. Also, taking the Chapter Test will **simulate the testing situation**, which gives you practice in test taking conditions.

▶ **Take the Chapter Test as if it is a real test.** If your instructor has skipped sections in the chapter, figure out which problems to skip on the test before you start.

- ✓ **Time yourself** just as you would for a real test.
- ✓ **Use a calculator or notes** just as you would be permitted to (or not) on a real test.
- ✓ **Take the test in one sitting,** just like a real test is given in one sitting.
- ✓ **Show all your work.** Practice showing your work just the way your instructor has asked you to show it.
- ✓ **Practice neatness.** Can someone else follow your steps?
- ✓ **Check your answers** in the back of the book.

Notice that reviewing a chapter will take some time. Remember that it takes time for dendrites to grow! You cannot grow a good network of dendrites by rushing through a review in one night. But if you use the suggestions over a few days or evenings, you will notice that you understand the material more thoroughly and remember it longer.

Now Try This

Follow the reviewing techniques listed above for your next test. For each technique, write a comment *about how it worked for you in the spaces below.*

1. **Make a study card for each vocabulary word and concept.**

2. **Go back to the section** to find more explanations or information.

3. **Take the Test Your Word Power quiz and use the Quick Review** to review each concept in the chapter.

4. **Study your lecture notes** to see what your instructor has emphasized in class.

5. **Do the Review Exercises,** following the specific suggestions on the previous page.

6. **Do the Mixed Review exercises.**

7. **Take the Chapter Test** as if it is a real test.

78

Chapter 1 *Summary*

Key Terms

1.1

place value system A place value system is a number system in which the location, or place, where a digit is written gives it a different value.

digits The 10 digits in our number system are 0, 1, 2, 3, 4, 5, 6, 7, 8, and 9.

whole numbers The whole numbers are 0, 1, 2, 3, 4, 5, . . .

1.2

number line A number line is like a thermometer turned sideways. It is used to show how numbers relate to each other.

integers Integers are the whole numbers and their opposites.

absolute value The absolute value of a number is its distance from 0 on the number line. Absolute value is indicated by two vertical bars and is always positive (or 0) but never negative.

1.3

addends In an addition problem, the numbers being added are called addends.

sum The answer to an addition problem is called the sum.

addition property of 0 Adding 0 to any number leaves the number unchanged.

commutative property of addition Changing the *order* of two addends does not change the sum.

associative property of addition Changing the *grouping* of addends does not change the sum.

1.4

opposite The opposite of a number is the same distance from 0 on the number line but on the opposite side of 0. It is also called the *additive inverse* because a number plus its opposite equals 0.

1.5

rounding Rounding a number means finding a number that is close to the original number but easier to work with.

estimate Use rounded numbers to get an approximate answer, or estimate.

front end rounding Front end rounding is rounding numbers to the highest possible place, so all the digits become 0 except the first digit.

1.6

factors In a multiplication problem, the numbers being multiplied are called factors.

product The answer to a multiplication problem is called the product.

multiplication property of 0 Multiplying any number by 0 gives a product of 0.

multiplication property of 1 Multiplying a number by 1 leaves the number unchanged.

commutative property of multiplication Changing the *order* of two factors does not change the product.

associative property of multiplication Changing the *grouping* of factors does not change the product.

distributive property Multiplication distributes over addition. For example, $3(6 + 2) = 3 \cdot 6 + 3 \cdot 2$.

1.7

quotient The answer to a division problem is called the quotient.

1.8

exponent An exponent tells how many times a number is used as a factor in repeated multiplication.

New Symbols

$<$		is less than
$>$		is greater than
$\lvert 6 \rvert$	and $\lvert -2 \rvert$	absolute value of 6; absolute value of -2
$\approx$		approximately equal to

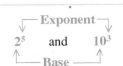

2^5 and 10^3 exponential form

Test Your Word Power

See how well you have learned the vocabulary in this chapter.

① In $(4)(-6) = -24$, the 4 and -6 are called
  A. products
  B. factors
  C. addends.

② A list of all the **whole numbers** is
  A. $1, 2, 3, 4, \ldots$
  B. $\ldots, -4, -3, -2, -1, 0, 1, 2, 3, \ldots$
  C. $0, 1, 2, 3, 4, \ldots$

③ The **absolute value** of a number is
  A. its distance from 0 on the number line
  B. always negative
  C. equal to 0.

④ An **exponent**
  A. tells how many times a number is added
  B. is the number being multiplied
  C. tells how many times a number is used as a factor.

⑤ The **opposite** of a number is
  A. never negative
  B. called the additive inverse
  C. called the absolute value.

⑥ **Front end rounding** is rounding numbers
  A. to the nearest thousand
  B. so there are no zeros
  C. to the highest possible place.

⑦ A list of all the **integers** is
  A. $1, 2, 3, 4, \ldots$
  B. $\ldots, -4, -3, -2, -1, 0, 1, 2, 3, \ldots$
  C. $0, 1, 2, 3, 4, \ldots$

⑧ The **associative property of multiplication** says that
  A. changing the order of two factors does not change the product
  B. multiplication distributes over addition
  C. changing the grouping of factors does not change the product.

Answers to Test Your Word Power

1. B; *Example:* In $7(10) = 70$, the factors are 7 and 10.

2. C; *Example:* $12, 0, 710$, and $89{,}475$ are all whole numbers.

3. A; *Example:* $|-3| = 3$ and $|3| = 3$ because both -3 and 3 are 3 steps away from 0 on the number line.

4. C; *Example:* In 2^5, the exponent is 5, which indicates that 2 is used as a factor 5 times, so $2^5 = 2 \cdot 2 \cdot 2 \cdot 2 \cdot 2 = 32$.

5. B; *Example:* The opposite of 5 is -5; it is the additive inverse because $5 + (-5) = 0$.

6. C; *Example:* Using front end rounding, round $48{,}299$ to the highest possible place, which is ten-thousands. So, $48{,}299$ rounds to $50{,}000$. All digits are 0 except the first digit.

7. B; *Example:* $-10, 0$, and 6 are all integers.

8. C; *Example:* $-4 \cdot (2 \cdot 3)$ can be rewritten as $(-4 \cdot 2) \cdot 3$; both products are -24.

Quick Review

Concepts	Examples

1.1 Reading and Writing Whole Numbers

Do not use the word *and* when reading whole numbers. Commas separate groups of three digits. The first few group names are ones, thousands, millions, billions, trillions.

Write $3, \underline{008}, \underline{160}$ in words.

three million, eight thousand, one hundred sixty

Write this number using digits:
twenty **billion**, sixty-five **thousand**, eighteen.

$$\underset{\text{billions}}{\underline{2 \ \ 0}}, \underset{\text{millions}}{\underline{0 \ \ 0 \ \ 0}}, \underset{\text{thousands}}{\underline{0 \ \ 6 \ \ 5}}, \underset{\text{ones}}{\underline{0 \ \ 1 \ \ 8}}$$

1.2 Graphing Numbers

Place a dot at the correct location on the number line.

Graph: **(a)** -4 **(b)** 0   **(c)** -1 **(d)** $\dfrac{1}{2}$ **(e)** 2

Concepts	Examples

1.2 Comparing Integers

When comparing two integers, the one that is farther to the left on the number line is less than the other.
Use the $<$ symbol for "is less than" and the $>$ symbol for "is greater than."

Write $<$ or $>$ between each pair of numbers to make a true statement.

$$-3 < -2 \qquad\qquad 0 > -4$$

−3 is less than −2 because −3 is to the *left* of −2 on the number line.

0 is greater than −4 because 0 is to the *right* of −4 on the number line.

1.2 Finding the Absolute Value of a Number

Find the distance on the number line from 0 to the number. The absolute value is always positive (or 0) but never negative.

Find each absolute value.

$|-5| = 5$ because −5 is 5 steps away from 0 on the number line.

$|3| = 3$ because 3 is 3 steps away from 0 on the number line.

1.3 Adding Two Integers

When both integers have the *same sign,* add the absolute values and use the common sign as the sign of the sum.

    When the integers have *different signs,* subtract the lesser absolute value from the greater absolute value. Use the sign of the number with the greater absolute value as the sign of the sum.

Add.

(a) $-6 + (-7)$ Integers have the *same sign.*

    Add the absolute values.

$$|-6| = 6 \quad \text{and} \quad |-7| = 7$$

Add $6 + 7 = 13$ and use the common sign as the sign of the sum: $-6 + (-7) = -13$.

(b) $-10 + 4$ Integers have *different signs.*

    Subtract the lesser absolute value from the greater.

$$|-10| = 10 \quad \text{and} \quad |4| = 4$$

Subtract $10 - 4 = 6$; the number with the greater absolute value is negative, so the sum is negative: $-10 + 4 = -6$.

1.3 Using Properties of Addition

Addition Property of 0: Adding 0 to any number leaves the number unchanged.

Commutative Property of Addition: Changing the *order* of two addends does not change the sum.

Associative Property of Addition: Changing the *grouping* of addends does not change the sum.

Name the property illustrated by each case.

(a) $-16 + 0 = -16$

(b) $4 + 10 = 10 + 4$ Both sums are 14.

(c) $2 + (6 + 1) = (2 + 6) + 1$ Both sums are 9.

(a) Addition property of 0

(b) Commutative property of addition

(c) Associative property of addition

Concepts	Examples

1.4 **Subtracting Two Integers**

To subtract two numbers, add the first number to the opposite of the second number.

Step 1 Make one pencil stroke to change the subtraction symbol to an addition symbol.

Step 2 Make a second pencil stroke to change the *second* number to its *opposite*.

Subtract.

(a) $7 - (-2)$ Change subtraction to addition.
      $\downarrow\ \downarrow\ \ \downarrow$ Change -2 to its opposite, $+2$.
      $\underbrace{7 + (+2)}$
          9

(b) $-9\ -\ \ 12$ Change subtraction to addition.
      $\downarrow\ \downarrow\ \ \ \ \downarrow$ Change 12 to its opposite, -12.
      $\underbrace{-9 + (-12)}$
          -21

1.5 **Rounding Integers**

Step 1 Draw a line under the place to which the number is to be rounded.

Step 2 Look only at the next digit to the right of the underlined place. If the next digit is *5 or more,* increase the underlined digit by 1. If the next digit is *4 or less,* do not change the digit in the underlined place.

Step 3 Change all digits to the right of the underlined place to zeros.

Round 36,833 to the nearest thousand.

Next digit
is *5 or more.*   Changed to 0
      $\downarrow$
      36,8<u>3</u>3   rounds to   37,000
      $\uparrow$ $\uparrow$
Thousands place   Change 6 to 7.

Round -3582 to the nearest ten.

Next digit
is *4 or less.*   Changed to 0
      $\downarrow$
      $-358\underline{2}$ rounds to $-358\underline{0}$
      $\uparrow$ $\uparrow$
Tens place   Leave 8 as 8.

1.5 **Front End Rounding**

Round to the highest possible place so that all the digits become 0 except the first digit.

Use front end rounding.

Next digit
is *5 or more.*   Changed to 0
  $\downarrow$
  <u>9</u>7,203   rounds to   100,000
  $\uparrow$ $\uparrow$
  Change 9 to 10. Regroup 1
  into hundred-thousands place.

1.5 **Estimating Answers in Addition and Subtraction**

Use front end rounding to round the numbers in a problem. Then add or subtract the rounded numbers to estimate the answer.

First use front end rounding to estimate the answer. Then find the exact answer.

The temperature was 48 degrees below zero. During the morning it rose 21 degrees. What was the new temperature?

Estimate: $-50 + 20 = -30$ degrees

Exact: $-48 + 21 = -27$ degrees

Concepts	Examples

1.6 Multiplying Two Integers

If two factors have *different signs*, the product is *negative*.

If two factors have the *same sign*, the product is *positive*.

Multiply.

(a) $-5(6) = -30$ — The factors have *different* signs, so the product is *negative*.

(b) $(-10)(-2) = 20$ — The factors have the *same* sign, so the product is *positive*.

1.6 Using Properties of Multiplication

Multiplication property of 0: Multiplying any number by 0 gives a product of 0.

Multiplication property of 1: Multiplying any number by 1 leaves the number unchanged.

Commutative property of multiplication: Changing the *order* of two factors does not change the product.

Associative property of multiplication: Changing the *grouping* of factors does not change the product.

Distributive property: Multiplication distributes over addition.

Name the property illustrated by each case.

(a) $-49 \cdot 0 = 0$

(b) $1(675) = 675$

(c) $(-8)(2) = (2)(-8)$ — Both products are -16.

(d) $(-3 \cdot 2) \cdot 4 = -3 \cdot (2 \cdot 4)$ — Both products are -24.

(e) $5(2 + 4) = 5 \cdot 2 + 5 \cdot 4$ — Both results are 30.

(a) Multiplication property of 0

(b) Multiplication property of 1

(c) Commutative property of multiplication

(d) Associative property of multiplication

(e) Distributive property

1.6 Estimating Answers in Multiplication

First use front end rounding. Then multiply the rounded numbers using a shortcut: Multiply the nonzero digits in each factor; count the total number of zeros in the two factors and write that number of zeros in the product.

First use front end rounding to estimate the answer. Then find the exact answer.

At a PTA fund-raiser, Lionel sold 96 photo albums at $22 each. How much money did he take in?

Estimate: $100 \cdot \$20 = \$2000$

Exact: $96 \cdot \$22 = \$2112$

1.7 Dividing Two Integers

Use the same sign rules for dividing two integers as for multiplying two integers.

If two numbers have *different signs*, the quotient is *negative*.

If two numbers have the *same sign*, the quotient is *positive*.

Divide.

$\dfrac{-24}{6} = -4$ — Numbers have *different* signs, so the quotient is *negative*.

$-72 \div (-8) = 9$ — Numbers have the *same* sign, so the quotient is *positive*.

$\dfrac{50}{-5} = -10$ — Numbers have *different* signs, so the quotient is *negative*.

1.7 Using Properties of Division

(a) When a nonzero number is divided by itself, the quotient is 1.

(b) When a number is divided by 1, the quotient is the number.

(c) When 0 is divided by any other number (except 0), the quotient is 0.

(d) Division by 0 is *undefined*. There is no answer.

State the property illustrated by each case.

(a) $\dfrac{-4}{-4} = 1$ **(b)** $\dfrac{65}{1} = 65$

(c) $\dfrac{0}{9} = 0$ **(d)** $\dfrac{-10}{0}$ is undefined.

The examples are in the same order as the properties listed at the left. Note that division is *not* commutative nor associative.

Concepts	Examples

1.7 **Estimating Answers in Division**

First use front end rounding. Then divide the rounded numbers, using a shortcut: Drop the same number of zeros in both the divisor and the dividend.

First use front end rounding to estimate the answer. Then find the exact answer.

Joan has one year to pay off a $1020 loan. What is her monthly payment?

Estimate: $1000 \div 10 = \$100$

Exact: $1020 \div 12 = \$85$

1.7 **Interpreting Remainders in Division**

In some situations the remainder tells you how much is left over. In other situations, you must increase the quotient by 1 in order to accommodate the "left over."

Divide; then interpret the remainder.

Each chemistry student needs 35 milliliters of acid for an experiment. How many students can be served from a bottle holding 500 milliliters of acid?

$$\begin{array}{r} 14 \\ 35\overline{)500} \\ 35 \\ \hline 150 \\ 140 \\ \hline 10 \end{array}$$

$14 \longrightarrow$ 14 students served

$10 \longrightarrow$ 10 milliliters of acid left over

1.8 **Using Exponents**

An exponent tells how many times a number is used as a factor in repeated multiplication. An exponent applies only to its base (the first thing to the left of the exponent).

Simplify.

Exponent

(a) $2^5 = 2 \cdot 2 \cdot 2 \cdot 2 \cdot 2 = 32$

(b) $(-3)^2 = (-3)(-3) = 9$

1.8 **Order of Operations**

Mathematicians have agreed to follow this order.

Step 1 Work inside parentheses or other grouping symbols.

Step 2 Simplify expressions with exponents.

Step 3 Do the remaining multiplications and divisions as they occur from left to right.

Step 4 Do the remaining additions and subtractions as they occur from left to right.

Simplify.

$(-2)^4 + 3(-4 + 2)$ Work inside parentheses.

$(-2)^4 + \quad 3(-2)$ Simplify exponents.

$16 \quad + \quad 3(-2)$ Multiply.

$16 \quad + \quad (-6)$ Add.

10

1.8 **Using the Order of Operations with Fraction Bars**

When there is a fraction bar, do all the work in the numerator. Then do all the work in the denominator. Finally, divide numerator by denominator.

Simplify.

$$\frac{-10 + 4^2 - 6}{2 + 3(1 - 4)} = \frac{-10 + 16 - 6}{2 + 3(-3)} = \frac{0}{-7} = 0$$

Chapter 1 *Review Exercises*

If you need help with any of these Review Exercises, look in the section indicated in the dark blue rectangles.

1.1 **1.** Circle the whole numbers: 86   2.831   −4   0 $\frac{2}{3}$ 35,600

Write these numbers in words.

2. 806

3. 319,012

4. 60,003,200

5. 15,749,000,000,006

Write these numbers using digits.

6. Five hundred four thousand, one hundred

7. Six hundred twenty million, eighty thousand

8. Ninety-nine billion, seven million, three hundred fifty-six

1.2 **9.** Graph these numbers: −3, 2, −5, 0.

Write < or > between each pair of numbers to make a true statement.

10. 0 _____ −4

11. −3 _____ −1

12. 2 _____ −2

13. −2 _____ 1

Find each absolute value.

14. $|-5|$

15. $|9|$

16. $|0|$

17. $|-125|$

1.3 *Add.*

18. −9 + 8

19. −8 + (−5)

20. 16 + (−19)

21. −4 + 4

22. 6 + (−5)

23. −12 + (−12)

24. 0 + (−7)

25. −16 + 19

26. 9 + (−4) + (−8) + 3

27. −11 + (−7) + 5 + (−4)

1.4 *Find the opposite (additive inverse) of each number. Show that the sum of the number and its opposite is 0.*

28. −5

29. 18

Subtract by changing subtraction to addition.

30. 5 − 12

31. 24 − 7

32. −12 − 4

33. 4 − (−9)

34. −12 − (−30)

35. −8 − 14

36. −6 − (−6)

37. −10 − 10

38. −8 − (−7)

39. 0 − 3

40. 1 − (−13)

41. 15 − 0

Simplify.

42. 3 − 12 − 7

43. −7 − (−3) + 7

44. 4 + (−2) − 0 − 10

45. −12 − 12 + 20 − (−4)

1.5 *Round each number as indicated.*

46. 205 to the nearest ten

47. 59,499 to the nearest thousand

48. 85,066,000 to the nearest million

49. −2963 to the nearest hundred

50. −7,063,885 to the nearest ten-thousand

51. 399,712 to the nearest thousand

Use front end rounding to round each number.

52. The combined weight loss of ten dieters was 197 pounds.

53. The land on the shore of the Dead Sea in the Middle East is 1388 feet below sea level. (*Source: Goode's World Atlas.*)

54. There were 2,095,006,000 Internet users in the world in 2011. (*Source:* Computer Industry Almanac.)

55. Within forty years, the Census Bureau predicts a world population of 9,502,000,000 people. (*Source:* U.S. Census Bureau.)

1.6 *Multiply.*

56. $-6(9)$ **57.** $(-7)(-8)$ **58.** $10(-10)$ **59.** $-45 \cdot 0$

60. $-1(-24)$ **61.** $17 \cdot 1$ **62.** $4(-12)$ **63.** $(-5)(-25)$

64. $-3(-4)(-3)$ **65.** $-5(2)(-5)$ **66.** $(-8)(-1)(-9)$

1.7 *Simplify.*

67. $\dfrac{-63}{-7}$ **68.** $\dfrac{70}{-10}$ **69.** $\dfrac{-15}{0}$ **70.** $-100 \div (-20)$

71. $18 \div (-1)$ **72.** $\dfrac{0}{12}$ **73.** $\dfrac{-30}{-2}$ **74.** $\dfrac{-35}{35}$

75. $-40 \div (-4) \div (-2)$ **76.** $-18 \div 3(-3)$ **77.** $0 \div (-10)(5) \div 5$

78. Divide; then interpret the remainder. It took 1250 hours to build the set for a new play. How many working days of eight hours each did it take to build the set?

1.8 *Simplify.*

79. 10^4 **80.** 2^5 **81.** 3^3 **82.** $(-4)^2$

83. $(-5)^3$ **84.** 8^1 **85.** $6^2 \cdot 3^2$ **86.** $5^2(-2)^3$

87. $-30 \div 6 - 4(5)$ **88.** $6 + 8(2 - 3)$ **89.** $16 \div 4^2 + (-6 + 9)^2$

90. $-3(4) - 2(5) + 3(-2)$ **91.** $\dfrac{-10 + 3^2 - (-9)}{3 - 10 - 1}$

92. $\dfrac{-1(1 - 3)^3 + 12 \div 4}{-5 + 24 \div 8 \cdot 2(6 - 6) + 5}$

Mixed Review Exercises*

Name the property illustrated by each case.

93. $-3 + (5 + 1) = (-3 + 5) + 1$ **94.** $-7(2) = 2(-7)$ **95.** $0 + 19 = 19$

96. $-42 \cdot 0 = 0$ **97.** $2(-6 + 4) = 2 \cdot (-6) + 2 \cdot 4$ **98.** $(-6 \cdot 3) \cdot 1 = -6 \cdot (3 \cdot 1)$

First use front end rounding to estimate each answer. Then find the exact answer.

99. Last year, 192 Elvis jukeboxes were sold at a price of $11,900 each. What was the total value of the jukeboxes?

Estimate:

Exact:

100. Chad had $185 in his checking account. He deposited his $428 paycheck and then wrote a $706 check for car repairs. What is the balance in his account?

Estimate:

Exact:

101. Georgia's hybrid car used 22 gallons of gas on her 880-mile vacation trip. What was the average number of miles she drove on each gallon of gas?

Estimate:

Exact:

102. When inventory was taken at Mathtronic Company, 19 calculators and 12 computer modems were missing. Each calculator is worth $39 and each modem is worth $85. What is the total value of the missing items?

Estimate:

Exact:

Elena Sanchez opened a shop that does alterations and designs custom clothing. Use the table of her income and expenses to answer Exercises 103–106.

Month	Income	Expenses	Profit or Loss
Jan.	$2400	− $3100	
Feb.	$1900	− $2000	
Mar.	$2500	− $1800	
Apr.	$2300	− $1400	
May	$1600	− $1600	
June	$1900	− $1200	

103. Complete the table by finding Elena's profit or loss for each month.

104. Which month had the greatest loss? Which month had the greatest profit?

105. What was Elena's average monthly income?

106. What was the average monthly amount of expenses?

*The order of exercises in this final group does not correspond to the order in which topics occur in the chapter. This random ordering should help you prepare for the chapter test in yet another way.

Chapter 1 Test

1. Write this number in words: 20,008,307

2. Write this number using digits: thirty billion, seven hundred thousand, five

3. Graph the numbers $3, -2, 0, -\dfrac{1}{2}$ on the number line below.

$$\text{-3 -2 -1 0 1 2 3}$$

4. Write $<$ or $>$ between each pair of numbers to make a true statement.

$$0 \underline{\hspace{0.5cm}} -3 \qquad -2 \underline{\hspace{0.5cm}} -1$$

5. Find each absolute value: $|10|$ and $|-14|$.

Add, subtract, multiply, or divide.

6. $3 - 9$

7. $-12 + 7$

8. $\dfrac{-28}{-4}$

9. $-1\,(40)$

10. $-5 - (-15)$

11. $(-8)(-8)$

12. $-25 + (-25)$

13. $\dfrac{17}{0}$

14. $-30 - 30$

15. $\dfrac{50}{-10}$

16. $5\,(-9)$

17. $0 - (-6)$

Simplify.

18. $-35 \div 7\,(-5)$

19. $-15 - (-8) + 7$

20. $3 - 7\,(-2) - 8$

21. $(-4)^2 \cdot 2^3$

22. $\dfrac{5^2 - 3^2}{(4)(-2)}$

23. $-2\,(-4 + 10) + 5\,(4)$

24. $-3 + (-7 - 10) + 4\,(6 - 10)$

25. Explain how an exponent is used. Include two examples, one using a positive number as the base and one using a negative number as the base.

26. Explain the commutative property of addition and the associative property of addition. Also give an example to illustrate each property.

Round each number as indicated.

27. 851 to the nearest hundred

28. 36,420,498,725
to the nearest million

29. 349,812 to the
nearest thousand

First use front end rounding to estimate each answer. Then find the exact answer.

30. Lorene had $184 in her checking account. She deposited her $293 paycheck and then wrote a $506 check for tuition. What is the balance in her account?

Estimate:

Exact:

31. Twenty-two people were in a weight loss program for a year. The total loss for the entire group of people was 1144 pounds. What was the average weight loss for each person?

Estimate:

Exact:

32. One kind of cereal has 220 calories in each serving. Another kind has 110 calories in each serving. During a month with 31 days, how many calories would you save by eating the second kind of cereal each morning for breakfast? (*Source:* General Mills and Post Cereals.)

Estimate:

Exact:

Write and solve a subtraction problem to answer this question.

33. On the planet Mars the average high temperature is $-10\ °F$ and the average low is $-100\ °F$. What is the difference between the high and low temperatures? (*Source:* NASA.)

Divide; then interpret the remainder.

34. Anthony has a part-time job as a shipping clerk. He is sending 1276 mathematics books to a college bookstore. Each shipping carton can safely hold 48 books. What is the minimum number of cartons he will need?

Study Skills
MANAGING YOUR TIME

Many college students find themselves juggling a difficult schedule and multiple responsibilities. Perhaps you are going to school, working part time, and managing family demands. Here are some tips to help you develop good time management skills and habits.

▶ **Read the syllabus for each class.** Check on class policies, such as attendance, late homework, and make-up tests. Find out how you are graded. Keep the syllabus in your notebook.

▶ **Make a semester or quarter calendar.** Put test dates and major due dates for *all* your classes on the same calendar. That way you will see which weeks are the really busy ones. Try using a different color pen for each class. Your brain responds well to the use of color. A semester calendar is on the next page.

▶ **Make a weekly schedule.** After you fill in your classes and other regular responsibilities (such as work, picking up kids from school, etc.), block off some study periods during the day that you can guarantee you will use for studying. Aim for 2 hours of study for each 1 hour you are in class.

▶ **Make "To Do" lists.** Then use them by crossing off the tasks as you complete them. You might even number them in the order they need to be done (most important ones first).

▶ **Break big assignments into smaller chunks.** They won't seem so big that way. Make deadlines for each small part so you stay on schedule.

▶ **Give yourself small breaks in your studying.** Do not try to study for hours at a time! Your brain needs rest between periods of learning. Try to give yourself a 10 minute break each hour or so. You will learn more and remember it longer.

▶ **If you get off schedule, just try to get back on schedule tomorrow.** We all slip from time to time. All is not lost! Make a new "to do" list and start doing the most important things first.

▶ **Get help when you need it.** Talk with your instructor during office hours. Also, most colleges have some kind of learning center, tutoring center, or counseling office. If you feel lost and overwhelmed, ask for help. Someone can help you decide what to do first and what to spend your time on right away.

What two or three of the suggestions above will you try this week? How do you think they will help you?

1. _____

2. _____

3. _____

Why Are These Techniques Brain Friendly?

Your brain appreciates some order. It enjoys a little routine, for example, choosing the same study time and place each day. You will find that you quickly settle in to your reading or homework.

Also, your brain **functions better when you are calm.** Too much rushing around at the last minute to get your homework and studying done sends hostile chemicals to your brain and makes it more difficult for you to learn and remember. So, a little planning can really pay off.

Building rest into your schedule is good for your brain. Remember, it takes time for dendrites to grow.

We've suggested using color on your calendars. This too, is brain friendly. Remember, your brain **likes pleasant colors and visual material** that are nice to look at. Messy and hard to read calendars will not be helpful, and you probably won't look at them often.

Study Skills

Continued from page 91

SEMESTER CALENDAR

WEEK	MON	TUES	WED	THUR	FRI	SAT	SUN
1							
2							
3							
4							
5							
6							
7							
8							
9							
10							
11							
12							
13							
14							
15							
16							

2 Understanding Variables and Solving Equations

As many as 50,000 thunderstorms occur worldwide in a single day, and an average of 300 people are struck by lightning each year in the United States. In this chapter, you'll see how you can use algebraic expressions to estimate your distance from a storm, the weight of a fish you caught, or the temperature on a summer day.

2.1 Introduction to Variables

OBJECTIVE ▶ **1** **Identify variables, constants, and expressions.** You probably know that algebra uses letters, especially the letter x. But why use letters when numbers are easier to understand? Here is an example.

Suppose you manage your college bookstore. When deciding how many books to order for a certain class, you first find out the class limit, that is, the maximum number of students allowed in the class. You will need at least that many books. But you decide to order 5 extra copies for emergencies.

Rule for ordering books: Order the class limit + 5 extra

How many books would you order for a prealgebra class with a limit of 25 students?

Class limit ⌐   ⌐ Extra

$25 + 5$ You would order 30 prealgebra books.

How many books would you order for a geometry class that allows 40 students to register?

Class limit ⌐   ⌐ Extra

$40 + 5$ You would order 45 geometry books.

You could set up a table to keep track of the number of books to order for various classes.

Class	Rule for Ordering Books: Class Limit + 5 Extra	Number of Books to Order
Prealgebra	25 + 5	30
Geometry	40 + 5	45
College algebra	35 + 5	40
Calculus 1	50 + 5	55

A shorthand way to write your rule is shown below.

$c + 5$

↑

The c stands for class limit.

You can't write your rule by using just numbers because the class limit varies, or changes, depending on which class you're talking about. So you use a letter, called a **variable,** to represent the part of the rule that varies. Notice the similarity in the words *varies* and *variable*. When part of a rule does *not* change, it is called a **constant.**

The variable, or the part of
the rule that varies or changes

↓

$c + 5$

↑

The constant, or the part of
the rule that does *not* change

$c + 5$ is called an **expression.** It expresses (tells) the rule for ordering books. You could use any letter you like for the variable part of the expression, such as $x + 5$, or $n + 5$, and so on. But one suggestion is to use a letter that reminds you of what it stands for. In this situation, the letter c reminds us of "class limit."

| EXAMPLE 1 | Writing an Expression and Identifying the Variable and Constant |

Write an expression for this rule. Identify the variable and the constant.

Order the class limit minus 10 books because some students will buy used books.

Variable

The variable can have different values. → $c - 10$ ← The constant does *not* change.

↑ Constant

···· **Work Problem ❶ at the Side.** ▶

| OBJECTIVE ❷ | **Evaluate variable expressions for given replacement values.** When you need to figure out how many books to order for a particular class, you use a specific value for the class limit, like 25 students in prealgebra. Then you **evaluate the expression,** that is, you follow the rule.

Ordering Books for a Prealgebra Class

$c + 5$ Expression (rule for ordering books) is $c + 5$.
↓   Replace c with 25, the class limit for prealgebra.
$25 + 5$ Follow the rule. Add $25 + 5$.
30   Order 30 prealgebra books.

| EXAMPLE 2 | Evaluating an Expression |

Use this rule for ordering books: Order the class limit minus 10. The expression is $c - 10$.

(a) Evaluate the expression when the class limit is 32.

$c - 10$ Replace c with 32.
↓
$32 - 10$ Follow the rule. Subtract $32 - 10$.
22   Order 22 books.

(b) Evaluate the expression when the class limit is 48.

$c - 10$ Replace c with 48.
↓
$48 - 10$ Follow the rule. Subtract $48 - 10$.
38   Order 38 books.

···· **Work Problem ❷ at the Side.** ▶

In any career you choose, there will be many useful "rules" that need to be written using variables (letters) because part of the rule changes depending on the situation. This is one reason algebra is such a powerful tool. Here is another example.

Suppose that you work in a landscaping business. You are putting a fence around a square-shaped garden. Each side of the garden is 6 feet long. How much fencing material should you bring for the job? You could add the lengths of the four sides.

6 feet + 6 feet + 6 feet + 6 feet = 24 feet of fencing

---

❶ Write an expression for this rule.
Ⓖⓢ Identify the variable and the constant.

Order the class limit plus 15 extra books because it is a very large class.

Variable
↳ $c +$ ____

The expression is _____.

The variable is _____.

The constant is _____.

❷ Use this expression for ordering books: $c + 3$.

Ⓖⓢ **(a)** Evaluate the expression when the class limit is 25.

$c + 3$
↓

____ $+ 3$

____

Order ____ books.

(b) Evaluate the expression when the class limit is 60.

Answers

1. $c + 15$. The expression is $c + 15$.
   The variable is c. The constant is 15.
2. (a) $25 + 3$; 28; order 28 books
   (b) $60 + 3$ is 63; order 63 books

3 **(a)** Evaluate the expression $4s$ when the length of one side of a square table is 3 feet.

(b) Evaluate the expression $4s$ when the length of one side of a square park is 7 miles.

Or, recall that multiplication is a quick way to do repeated addition. The square garden has 4 sides, so multiply by 4.

$$4 \cdot 6 \text{ feet} = 24 \text{ feet of fencing}$$

So the rule for calculating the amount of fencing for a square garden is:

$$4 \cdot \text{length of one side}$$

Other jobs may require fencing for larger or smaller square shapes. The following table shows how much fencing you will need.

Length of One Side of Square Shape	Expression (Rule) to Find Total Amount of Fencing: 4 • Length of One Side	Total Amount of Fencing Needed
6 feet	4 • 6 feet	24 feet
9 feet	4 • 9 feet	36 feet
10 feet	4 • 10 feet	40 feet
3 feet	4 • 3 feet	12 feet

The expression (rule) can be written in shorthand form as shown below.

Length of one side
↓
$$4 \cdot s$$
Coefficient ↗   ↖ Variable

The number part in a *multiplication* expression is called the numerical coefficient, or just the **coefficient.** We usually don't write multiplication dots in expressions, so we do the following.

$$4 \cdot s \quad \text{is written as} \quad 4s$$

You can use the expression $4s$ any time you need to know the *perimeter* of a square shape, that is, the total distance around all four sides of the square.

CAUTION

If an expression involves adding, subtracting, or dividing, then you **do** have to write $+$, $-$, or $\div$. It is *only* multiplication that is understood without writing an operation symbol.

$$4 + s \qquad 4 - s \qquad 4 \div s \qquad 4s$$
$$\uparrow \qquad\qquad \uparrow \qquad\qquad \uparrow \qquad\qquad \uparrow$$
Add s.   Subtract s.   Divide by s.   Multiply by s.

EXAMPLE 3   **Evaluating an Expression with Multiplication**

The expression (rule) for finding the perimeter of a square shape is $4s$. Evaluate the expression when the length of one side of a square parking lot is 30 yards.

$4s$ Replace s with 30 yards.
↓
$4 \cdot 30 \text{ yards}$ There is no operation symbol between the 4 and the s, so it is understood to be multiplication. 4 times 30 is 120.

120 yards ⟵ Total distance around the lot (perimeter) is 120 yards.

Answers

3. **(a)** 4 • 3 feet; 12 feet
(b) 4 • 7 miles; 28 miles

◄ **Work Problem ❸ at the Side.**

Some expressions (rules) involve several different steps. An expression for finding the approximate systolic blood pressure of a person of a certain age is shown below.

$$100 + \frac{a}{2} \leftarrow \text{Age of person (the variable)}$$

Remember that a fraction bar means division, so $\frac{a}{2}$ is the person's age divided by 2. You also need to remember the order of operations, which means doing division before addition.

EXAMPLE 4 **Evaluating an Expression with Several Steps**

Evaluate the expression $100 + \frac{a}{2}$ when the age of the person is 24.

$100 + \frac{a}{2}$ — Replace a with 24, the age of the person.

$100 + \frac{24}{2}$ — Follow the rule using the order of operations. First divide: $24 \div 2$ is 12.

$\underbrace{100 + 12}$ — Now add: $100 + 12$ is 112.

112 ——— The approximate systolic blood pressure is 112.

························· **Work Problem ④ at the Side.** ▶

🖩 Calculator Tip

If you like to fish, you can use an expression (rule) like the one below to find the approximate weight (in pounds) of a fish you catch. Measure the length of the fish (in inches) and then use the correct expression for that type of fish. For a northern pike, the weight expression is shown below.

Variable (length of fish) ⌐

$$\frac{l^3}{3600}$$

where l is the length of the fish in inches. (*Source: InFisherman.*)

To evaluate this expression for a fish that is 43 inches long, follow the rule by calculating as follows.

$\frac{43^3}{3600}$ Replace l with 43, the length of the fish in inches.

In the numerator, multiply $43 \cdot 43 \cdot 43$. Or, use the y^x or $\wedge$ key on a calculator. Then divide by 3600.

Enter 43 y^x 3 $\div$ 3600 $=$ Calculator shows 22.08527778
      ↑   ↑
    Base   Exponent

The fish weighs about 22 pounds.

Now use the expression to find the approximate weight of a northern pike that is 37 inches long. (Answer: about 14 pounds.)

(Continued)

④ Evaluate the expression $100 + \frac{a}{2}$ when the age of the person is 40.

Answer

4. $100 + \frac{40}{2}$ ← Replace a with 40.

$\underbrace{100 + 20}$

120 ← Approximate systolic blood pressure is 120.

5 **(a)** Use the expression for finding your average bowling score. Evaluate the expression if your total score for 4 games is 532.

$$\frac{t \rightarrow \underline{\qquad}}{g \rightarrow}$$

Your average score is _____ .

(b) Complete this table.

Value of x	Value of y	Expression x − y
16	10	16 − 10 is 6
100	5	
3	7	
8	0	

Notice that variables are used on your calculator keys. On the y^x key, y represents the base and x represents the exponent. You first evaluated y^x by entering 43 as the base and 3 as the exponent for the first fish. Then you evaluated y^x again by entering 37 as the base and 3 as the exponent for the second fish.

Some expressions (rules) involve several variables. For example, if you go bowling and want to know your average score, you can use this expression.

$$\frac{t}{g}$$

$t \leftarrow$ Total score for all games (variable)

$g \leftarrow$ Number of games (variable)

EXAMPLE 5 **Evaluating Expressions with Two Variables**

(a) Find your average score if you bowl three games and your total score for all three games is 378.

Use the expression (rule) for finding your average score.

Replace t with your total score of 378.

$$\frac{t}{g} \longrightarrow \frac{378}{3}$$

Replace g with 3, the number of games.

} Follow the rule. Divide 378 by 3 to get 126. Your average score is 126.

(b) Complete these tables to show how to evaluate each expression.

Value of X	Value of y	Expression (Rule) X + y
2	5	2 + 5 is 7
− 6	4	___ + ___ is ___
0	16	___ + ___ is ___

Value of X	Value of y	Expression (Rule) xy
2	5	2 • 5 is 10
− 6	4	___ • ___ is ___
0	16	___ • ___ is ___

The expression (rule) is to *add* the two variables. So the completed table is:

Value of X	Value of y	Expression (Rule) X + y
2	5	2 + 5 is 7
− 6	4	− 6 + 4 is −2
0	16	0 + 16 is 16

The expression (rule) is to *multiply* the two variables. We know that it's multiplication because there is no operation symbol between the x and y. So the completed table is:

Value of X	Value of y	Expression (Rule) xy
2	5	2 • 5 is 10
− 6	4	− 6 • 4 is −24
0	16	0 • 16 is 0

◀ **Work Problem 5 at the Side.**

Answers

5. (a) $\frac{532}{4}$; average score is 133.

(b) 100 − 5 is 95; 3 − 7 is −4; 8 − 0 is 8

OBJECTIVE ❸ **Write properties of operations using variables.** Now you can use variables as a shorthand way to express the properties you learned about in **Chapter 1.** We'll use the letters a and b to represent any two numbers.

<table>
<tr><td align="center">**Commutative Property
of Addition**</td><td align="center">**Commutative Property
of Multiplication**</td></tr>
<tr><td align="center">$a + b = b + a$</td><td align="center">$a \cdot b = b \cdot a$

or, $ab = ba$</td></tr>
</table>

To get specific examples, you can pick values for a and b. For example, if a is -3, replace every a with -3. If b is 5, replace every b with 5.

$$a + b = b + a$$
$$-3 + 5 = 5 + (-3)$$
$$2 \quad = \quad 2$$

Both sums are 2

$$ab = ba$$
$$-3 \cdot 5 = 5 \cdot (-3)$$
$$-15 \quad = \quad -15$$

Both products are -15

Of course, you could pick many different values for a and b, because the commutative "rule" will always work for adding *any* two numbers or multiplying *any* two numbers.

EXAMPLE 6 **Writing Properties of Operations Using Variables**

Use the variable b to state this property: When any number is divided by 1, the quotient is the number.

Use the letter b to represent any number.

$$\frac{b}{1} = b$$

························· **Work Problem ❻ at the Side.** ▶

OBJECTIVE ❹ **Use exponents with variables.** In **Chapter 1** we used an exponent as a quick way to write repeated multiplication. For example,

$$\underbrace{3 \cdot 3 \cdot 3 \cdot 3 \cdot 3}_{\text{3 is used as a factor 5 times.}} \quad \text{can be written} \quad 3^5 \leftarrow \text{Exponent}$$
$$\qquad\qquad\qquad\qquad\qquad\qquad\qquad \uparrow\text{\_\_\_\_ Base}$$

The meaning of an exponent is the same when a variable is the base.

$$\underbrace{c \cdot c \cdot c \cdot c \cdot c}_{\text{c is used as a factor 5 times.}} \quad \text{can be written} \quad c^5 \leftarrow \text{Exponent}$$
$$\qquad\qquad\qquad\qquad\qquad\qquad\qquad \uparrow\text{\_\_\_\_ Base}$$

m^2 means $m \cdot m$ Here m is used as a factor 2 times.

$x^4 y^3$ means $x^4 \cdot y^3$ or $\underbrace{x \cdot x \cdot x \cdot x}_{x^4} \cdot \underbrace{y \cdot y \cdot y}_{y^3}$

$7b^2$ means $7 \cdot b \cdot b$ The exponent applies *only* to b.

$-4xy^2 z$ means $-4 \cdot x \cdot y \cdot y \cdot z$ The exponent applies *only* to y.

---

❻ **(a)** Use the variable a to state this property: Multiplying any number by 0 gives a product of 0.

Any   times   zero
number   ↓   ↓
↓
a $\cdot$ ___ $=$ ___

(b) Use the variables a, b, and c to state the associative property of addition: Changing the grouping of addends does not change the sum.

7 Rewrite each expression without exponents.

(a) x^5

$$\underbrace{x \cdot \underline{} \cdot \underline{} \cdot \underline{} \cdot \underline{}}$$
x is used as a factor 5 times.

(b) $4a^2b^2$

$$4 \cdot \underline{} \cdot \underline{} \cdot \underline{} \cdot \underline{}$$

(c) $-10xy^3$

(d) s^4tu^2

8 Evaluate each expression.

(a) y^3 when y is -5

y^3 means $y \cdot y \cdot y$

$$\underbrace{(-5) \cdot (-5)} \cdot (-5)$$
$$\underbrace{\underline{} \cdot (-5)}$$
$$\underline{}$$

(b) r^2s^2 when r is 6 and s is 3

r^2s^2 means $r \cdot r \cdot s \cdot s$

$$6 \cdot \underline{} \cdot 3 \cdot \underline{}$$

(c) $10xy^2$ when x is 4 and y is -3

(d) $-3c^4$ when c is 2

EXAMPLE 7 **Understanding Exponents Used with Variables**

Rewrite each expression without exponents.

(a) y^6 can be written as $y \cdot y \cdot y \cdot y \cdot y \cdot y$

y is used as a factor 6 times.

(b) $12bc^3$ can be written as $12 \cdot b \cdot \underbrace{c \cdot c \cdot c}_{c^3}$

Coefficient is 12. — The exponent applies *only* to c.

(c) $-2m^2n^4$ can be written as $-2 \cdot \underbrace{m \cdot m}_{m^2} \cdot \underbrace{n \cdot n \cdot n \cdot n}_{n^4}$

Coefficient is -2.

◀ **Work Problem 7 at the Side.**

To evaluate an expression with exponents, multiply all the factors.

EXAMPLE 8 **Evaluating Expressions with Exponents**

Evaluate each expression.

(a) x^2 when x is -3

x^2 means $x \cdot x$ — Replace each x with -3.

$$\underbrace{(-3) \cdot (-3)}_{9}$$ Multiply -3 times -3.

So x^2 becomes $(-3)^2$, which is $(-3)(-3)$, or 9.

(b) x^3y when x is -4 and y is -10

x^3y means $x \cdot x \cdot x \cdot y$ — Replace x with -4, and replace y with -10.

Multiplying two negative factors gives a *positive* product.

$$\underbrace{-4 \cdot (-4)} \cdot (-4) \cdot (-10)$$ Multiply two factors at a time.

$$\underbrace{16 \quad \cdot (-4)} \cdot (-10)$$

$$\underbrace{-64 \quad\quad \cdot (-10)}$$

$$640$$

So x^3y becomes $(-4)^3(-10)$, which is $(-4)(-4)(-4)(-10)$, or 640.

(c) $-5ab^2$ when a is 5 and b is 3

$-5ab^2$ means $-5 \cdot a \cdot b \cdot b$ — Replace a with 5, and replace b with 3.

Multiplying two factors with *different* signs gives a *negative* product.

$$\underbrace{-5 \cdot 5} \cdot 3 \cdot 3$$ Multiply two factors at a time.

$$\underbrace{-25 \quad \cdot 3} \cdot 3$$

$$\underbrace{-75 \quad\quad \cdot 3}$$

$$-225$$

So $-5ab^2$ becomes $-5(5)(3)^2$, which is $-5(5)(3)(3)$, or -225.

Coefficient is -5.

◀ **Work Problem 8 at the Side.**

Answers

7. (a) $x \cdot x \cdot x \cdot x \cdot x$ **(b)** $4 \cdot a \cdot a \cdot b \cdot b$
   (c) $-10 \cdot x \cdot y \cdot y$
   (d) $s \cdot s \cdot s \cdot s \cdot t \cdot u \cdot u$
8. (a) $25 \cdot (-5)$; -125
   (b) $6 \cdot 6 \cdot 3 \cdot 3$ is 324.
   (c) $10(4)(-3)^2$ is 360.
   (d) $-3(2)^4$ is -48.

2.1 Exercises

 Download the MyDashBoard App

▶ MyMathLab®

CONCEPT CHECK *Identify the parts of each expression. Choose from these labels:* variable, constant, coefficient.

1. $c + 4$

c is the variable;

4 is the _____ .

2. $d + 6$

_____ is the variable;

6 is the constant.

3. $-3 + m$

4. $-4 + n$

5. $5h$

6. $3s$

7. $2c - 10$

8. $6b - 1$

9. $x - y$

10. xy

11. $-6g + 9$

12. $-10k + 15$

Evaluate each expression. ***See Examples 2–5.***

13. The expression (rule) for ordering robes for the graduation ceremony at West Community College is $g + 10$, where *g* is the number of graduates. Evaluate the expression when

(a) there are 654 graduates.

$g \;+\; 10$

$654 + 10$

_____ robes

(b) there are 208 graduates.

(c) there are 95 graduates.

14. Crickets chirp faster as the weather gets hotter. The expression (rule) for finding the approximate temperature (in degrees Fahrenheit) is $c + 37$ where *c* is the number of chirps made in 15 seconds by a field cricket. (*Source:* AccuWeather.com) Evaluate the expression when the cricket

(a) chirps 45 times.

$c + 37$

$45 + 37$

_____ degrees

(b) chirps 33 times.

(c) chirps 58 times.

15. The expression for finding the perimeter of a triangle with sides of equal length is $3s$, where *s* is the length of one side. Evaluate the expression when

(a) the length of one side is 11 inches.

(b) the length of one side is 3 feet.

s

16. The expression for finding the perimeter of a pentagon with sides of equal length is $5s$, where *s* is the length of one side. Evaluate the expression when

(a) the length of one side is 25 meters.

(b) the length of one side is 8 inches.

s

17. The expression for ordering brushes for an art class is $3c - 5$, where c is the class limit. Evaluate the expression when

   (a) the class limit is 12.

   (b) the class limit is 16.

18. The expression for ordering doughnuts for the office staff is $2n - 4$, where n is the number of people at work. Evaluate the expression when

   (a) there are 13 people at work.

   (b) there are 18 people at work.

19. The expression for figuring a student's average test score is $\frac{p}{t}$, where p is the total points earned on all the tests and t is the number of tests. Evaluate the expression when

   (a) 332 points were earned on 4 tests.

   (b) there were 7 tests and 637 points were earned.

20. The expression for deciding how many buses are needed for a group trip is $\frac{p}{b}$, where p is the total number of people and b is the number of people that one bus will hold. Evaluate the expression when

   (a) 176 people are going on a trip and one bus holds 44 people.

   (b) a bus holds 36 people and 72 people are going on a trip.

Complete each table by evaluating the expressions. ***See Example 5.***

21.

Value of x	Expression $x + x + x + x$	Expression $4x$
-2	$(-2) + (-2) + (-2) + (-2)$ is -8	$4 \cdot (-2)$ is -8
12		
0		
-5		

22.

Value of y	Expression $3y$	Expression $y + 2y$
-6	$3(-6)$ is -18	$-6 + 2(-6)$ is $-6 + (-12)$, or -18
10		
-3		
0		

23.

Value of x	Value of y	Expression $-2x + y$
3	7	$-2(3) + 7$ is $-6 + 7$, or 1
-4	5	
-6	-2	
0	-8	

24.

Value of x	Value of y	Expression $-2xy$
3	7	$-2 \cdot 3 \cdot 7$ is -42
-4	5	
-6	-2	
0	-8	

25. Explain the words *variable* and *expression*.

26. Explain the words *coefficient* and *constant*.

Use the variable b to express each of these properties. **See Example 6.**

27. Multiplying a number by 1 leaves the number unchanged.

28. Adding 0 to any number leaves the number unchanged.

29. Any number divided by 0 is undefined.

30. Multiplication distributes over addition. (Use *a*, *b*, and *c* as the variables.)

Rewrite each expression without exponents. **See Example 7.**

31. c^6

32. d^7

33. x^4y^3

34. c^2d^5

35. $-3a^3b$

36. $-8m^2n$

37. $9xy^2$

38. $5ab^4$

39. $-2c^5d$

40. $-4x^3y$

41. a^3bc^2

42. x^2yz^6

In Exercises 43–54, evaluate each expression when r is −3, s is 2, and t is −4. **See Example 8.**

43. t^2

44. r^2

45. rs^3

46. s^4t

47. $3rs$

48. $6st$

49. $-2s^2t^2$
▶

50. $-4rs^4$

51. $r^2s^5t^3$

52. $r^3s^4t^2$

53. $-10r^5s^7$

54. $-5s^6t^5$

Evaluate each expression when x is 4, y is −2, and z is −6.

55. $|xy| + |xyz|$

56. $x + |y^2| + |xz|$

57. $\dfrac{z^2}{-3y + z}$

58. $\dfrac{y^2}{x + 2y}$

Relating Concepts (Exercises 59–60) For Individual or Group Work

At the beginning of this chapter, we said there is an expression to estimate your distance from a thunderstorm. First, count the number of seconds from the time you see a lightning flash until you start to hear the thunder. Then, to estimate the distance (in miles), use the expression $\dfrac{s}{5}$, where s is the number of seconds.

*Use this expression as you **work Exercises 59 and 60 in order.** (The expression is based on the fact that the light from the lightning travels faster than the sound from the thunder.)*

59. Evaluate the thunderstorm expression for each number of seconds. How far away is the storm?

  (a) 15 seconds

  (b) 10 seconds

  (c) 5 seconds

60. Explain how you can use your answers from **Exercise 59** to:

  (a) Estimate the distance when the time is $2\frac{1}{2}$ seconds.

  (b) Find the number of seconds when the distance is $1\frac{1}{2}$ miles.

  (c) Find the number of seconds when the distance is $2\frac{1}{2}$ miles.

Study Skills
USING STUDY CARDS

OBJECTIVES

1. **Create study cards for all new terms.**
2. **Create study cards for new procedures.**

You may have used "flash cards" in other classes before. In math, study cards can be helpful, too. However, they are different because the main things to remember in math are *not* necessarily terms and definitions; they are *sets of steps to follow* to solve problems (and how to know which set of steps to follow) and *concepts about how math works* (principles). So, the cards will look different but will be just as useful.

In this two-part activity, you will find four types of study cards to use in math. Look carefully at what kinds of information to put on them and where to put it. Then use them the way you would any flash card:

▶ to quickly review when you have a few minutes,

▶ to do daily reviews,

▶ to review before a test.

Remember, the most helpful thing about study cards is making them. It is in the making of them that you have to do the kind of thinking that is most brain friendly and will improve your neural network of dendrites. After each card description you will find an assignment to try. It is marked "**NOW TRY THIS.**"

New Vocabulary Cards

For **new vocabulary cards,** put the word (spelled correctly) and the page number where it is found on the front of the card. On the back, write:

▶ the definition (in your own words if possible),

▶ an example, an exception (if there are any),

▶ any related words, and

▶ a sample problem (if appropriate).

variable   *page* ___   Front of Card

Definition: A letter representing a number that varies (changes) depending on the situation.

Example: $c + 5$ *where c represents the class limit which varies for different classes.*
variable   *constant*   *varies* ⟷ *variable*

– Use any letter you like: a, b, c, d, h, k, m, n, o, p, x, y, etc.
– Related words: constant, coefficient

Back of Card

Why Are Study Cards Brain Friendly?

- Making cards is **active.**
- Cards are **visually** appealing.
- **Repetition** is good for your brain.

For more details, see **Using Study Cards Revisited** following the next section.

Study Skills

Continued from page 105

Now Try This

List four new vocabulary words/concepts you need to learn right now. Make a card for each one.

_____   _____

_____   _____

Procedure ("Steps") Cards

For **procedure cards,** write the name of the procedure at the top on the front of the card. Then write each step **in words.** If you need to know abbreviations for some words, include them along with the whole words written out. On the back, put an example of the procedure, showing each step you need to take. You can review by looking at the front and practicing a new worked example, or by looking at the back and remembering what the procedure is called and what the steps are.

Front of Card

Evaluating an expression

Step 1: Replace each variable with the value you are given.

Step 2: Do the calculations, following the order of operations.

Back of Card

Example: Evaluate 3c – 5 when c is 20
     must be given the replacement value

$3c - 5$
$\downarrow$
$3(20)-5$ *Replace c with 20. Do the calculations.*

$60 - 5$ *Follow order of operations; multiply first, then subtract.*

55 *No variables in final answer.*

Now Try This

What procedure are you learning right now? Make a "steps" card for it.

Procedure: _____

2.2 Simplifying Expressions

OBJECTIVE ▶ 1 Combine like terms using the distributive property. In the previous section, the expression for ordering math textbooks was $c + 5$. This expression was simple and easy to use. Sometimes expressions are *not* written in the simplest possible way. For example:

OBJECTIVES
1 Combine like terms using the distributive property.
2 Simplify expressions.
3 Use the distributive property to multiply.

Evaluate this expression when c is 20.

$c + 5$ Replace c with 20.
$\downarrow$
$\underbrace{20 + 5}$ Add $20 + 5$.
25

Evaluate this expression when c is 20.

$$2c - 10 - c + 15 \quad \text{Replace } c \text{ with 20.}$$
$$2 \cdot 20 - 10 - 20 + 15 \quad \text{Multiply } 2 \cdot 20.$$
$$40 - 10 - 20 + 15 \quad \text{Change subtraction to adding the opposite.}$$
$$40 + (-10) + (-20) + 15 \quad \text{Add from left to right.}$$
$$\underbrace{30} \quad + (-20) + 15$$
$$\underbrace{10} \quad + 15$$
$$25$$

These two expressions are actually equivalent. When you evaluate them, the final result is the same, but it takes a lot more work when you use the righthand expression. Once you know how to *simplify expressions,* you can rewrite $2c - 10 - c + 15$ as $c + 5$.

The basic idea in **simplifying expressions** is to *combine,* or *add,* **like terms.** Each addend in an expression is a **term.** Here are two examples.

Separates the terms
$c + 5$
Two terms

Separates the terms
$6x^2 + (-2xy) + 8$
Three terms

In $6x^2 + (-2xy) + 8$, the 8 is the **constant term.** There are also two *variable terms* in the expression: $6x^2$ is a variable term, and $-2xy$ is a variable term. A **variable term** has a number part (coefficient) and a letter part (variable).

$6x^2$
Variable part is x^2
Coefficient is 6.

$-2xy$
Variable part is xy.
Coefficient is -2.

VOCABULARY TIPS

Constant term Think about the meaning of the words **constant** and **term.** A constant term is a type of term (or addend) that is a number, not a variable. An example is the number 5 in the expression $2x + 5$.

Variable term Think about the meaning of the words **variable** and **term.** A variable term is a type of term (or addend) that contains a variable. An example is the $2x$ in the expression $2x + 5$.

If no coefficient is shown, it is assumed to be 1. Remember from **Chapter 1** that multiplying any number by 1 does *not* change the number.

c can be written $1 \cdot c$ or just $1c$

Coefficient is understood to be 1.

Variable part is c.

Also, $-c$ can be written $-1 \cdot c$. The coefficient of $-c$ is understood to be -1.

Like Terms

Like terms are terms with exactly the same variable parts (the same letters and exponents). The coefficients do *not* have to match.

1 List the like terms in each expression. Then identify the coefficients of the like terms.

(a) $3b^2 + (-3b) + 3 + b^3 + b$

Like terms are $-3b$ and b.

Coefficients are _____ and

_____.

(b) $-4xy + 4x^2y + (-4xy^2) + (-4) + 4$

(c) $5r^2 + 2r + (-2r^2) + 5 + 5r^3$

(d) $-10 + (-x) + (-10x) + (-x^2) + (-10y)$

	Like Terms			Unlike Terms	
$5x$ and $3x$	Variable parts match; both are x.		$3x$ and $3x^2$	Variable parts do *not* match; exponents are different.	
$-6y^3$ and y^3	Variable parts match; both are y^3.		$-2x$ and $-2y$	Variable parts do *not* match; letters are different.	
$4a^2b$ and $5a^2b$	Variable parts match; both are a^2b.		a^3b and a^2b	Variable parts do *not* match; exponents are different.	
-8 and 4	There are no variable parts; numbers are like terms.		$-8c$ and 4	Variable parts do *not* match; one term has a variable part, but the other term does not.	

EXAMPLE 1 **Identifying Like Terms and Their Coefficients**

List the like terms in each expression. Then identify the coefficients of the like terms.

(a) $-5x + (-5x^2) + 3xy + x + (-5)$
The like terms are $-5x$ and x.
The coefficient of $-5x$ is -5, and the coefficient of x is understood to be 1.

(b) $2yz^2 + 2y^2z + (-3y^2z) + 2 + (-6yz)$
The like terms are $2y^2z$ and $-3y^2z$.
The coefficients are 2 and -3.

(c) $10ab + 12 + (-10a) + 12b + (-6)$
The like terms are 12 and -6.
The like terms are constants (there are no variable parts).

> Numbers alone (no variable parts) are like terms.

◀ **Work Problem 1** at the Side.

The distributive property (see **Chapter 1**) can be used "in reverse" to combine like terms. Here is an example.

$$\underbrace{3 \cdot x}_{3x} + \underbrace{4 \cdot x}_{4x} \quad \text{can be written as} \quad \underbrace{(3 + 4)}_{7} \cdot x$$

$$7 \cdot x$$

$$\underbrace{}_{7x}$$

> 7x is written in *simplified form.*

Thus, $3x + 4x$ can be written in *simplified form* as $7x$. To check that $3x + 4x$ is the same as $7x$, evaluate each expression when x is 2.

$$
\begin{array}{cc}
3x + \quad 4x & 7x \\
\downarrow \quad\quad \downarrow & \downarrow \\
3 \cdot 2 + 4 \cdot 2 & 7 \cdot 2 \\
\underbrace{6}_{} + \underbrace{8}_{} & 14 \\
14 &
\end{array}
$$

These expressions are equivalent, so both results are 14. But you can see how much easier it is to work with $7x$, the simplified expression.

Answers

1. (a) Coefficients are -3 and 1.
(b) -4 and 4; they are constants.
(c) $5r^2$ and $-2r^2$; the coefficients are 5 and -2.
(d) $-x$ and $-10x$; the coefficients are -1 and -10.

CAUTION

Notice that $3x + 4x$ is simplified to $7x$, **not** to ~~$7x^2$~~.

Variable part is unchanged.   Do *not* change x to x^2.

Combining Like Terms

Step 1 If there are any variable terms with no coefficient, write in the understood 1.

Step 2 If there are any subtractions, change each one to adding the opposite.

Step 3 Find *like* terms (the variable parts match).

Step 4 Add the coefficients (number parts) of like terms. ***The variable part stays the same.***

EXAMPLE 2   **Combining Like Terms**

Combine like terms.

(a) $2x + 4x + x$

$2x + 4x + x$ No coefficient; write understood 1.
There are no subtractions to change.

$2x + 4x + 1x$ Find like terms: $2x$, $4x$, and $1x$ are like terms.
Add the coefficients, $2 + 4 + 1$.

$(2 + 4 + 1)x$ The variable part, x, stays the same.

$7x$

Therefore, $2x + 4x + x$ can be written as $7x$. ⟨Do **not** write $7x^3$. Keep x as x.⟩

(b) $-3y^2 - 8y^2$

$-3y^2 - 8y^2$ Both coefficients are shown.
Change subtraction to adding the opposite.

$-3y^2 + (-8y^2)$ Find like terms: $-3y^2$ and $-8y^2$ are like terms.
Add the coefficients, $-3 + (-8)$.

$[-3 + (-8)]y^2$ Brackets show what to do first: $-3 + (-8)$ is -11.
The variable part, y^2, stays the same.

$-11y^2$ ⟨Do **not** write $-11y^4$. Keep y^2 as y^2.⟩

Therefore, $-3y^2 - 8y^2$ can be written as $-11y^2$.

···················· **Work Problem ❷ at the Side.** ▶

OBJECTIVE ❷ Simplify expressions. When simplifying expressions, be careful to combine only *like* terms—those having variable parts that match. You *cannot* combine terms if the variable parts are different.

---

❷ Combine like terms.

(a) $10b + 4b + 10b$

$(10 + 4 + 10)b$

$\underline{\quad}b$

(b) $y^3 + 8y^3$

(c) $-7n - n$

(d) $3c - 5c - 4c$

(e) $-9xy + xy$

(f) $-4p^2 - 3p^2 + 8p^2$

(g) $ab - ab$

Answers

2. **(a)** $24b$ **(b)** $9y^3$ **(c)** $-8n$ **(d)** $-6c$
   (e) $-8xy$ **(f)** $1p^2$, or just p^2
   (g) 0, because $1ab + (-1ab)$ is $0ab$, and 0 times anything is 0.

③ Simplify each expression by combining like terms.

(a) $3b^2 + 4d^2 + 7b^2$

Rewrite the expression so the like terms are next to each other.

$3b^2 + 7b^2 + 4d^2$

$(3 + 7)\,b^2 + 4d^2$

$\underline{\quad\quad}\,b^2 + \underline{\quad\quad}$

(b) $4a + b - 6a + b$

(c) $-6x + 5 + 6x + 2$

(d) $2y - 7 - y + 7$

(e) $-3x - 5 + 12 + 10x$

EXAMPLE 3 **Simplifying Expressions**

Simplify each expression by combining like terms.

(a) $6xy + 2y + 3xy$

The *like* terms are $6xy$ and $3xy$. We can use the **commutative property** to rewrite the expression so that the like terms are next to each other. This helps to organize our work.

$6xy + 3xy + 2y$ Combine *like* terms only.

$(6 + 3)\,xy + 2y$ Add the coefficients, $6 + 3$.
The variable part, xy, stays the same.

$9xy + 2y$ Keep writing $2y$, the term that was not combined; it is still part of the expression.

The simplified expression is $9xy + 2y$.   Remember to include $2y$ in your answer.

(b) Here is the expression from the first page in this section.

$2c - 10 - c + 15$ Write the understood 1 as the coefficient of c.

$2c - 10 - 1c + 15$ Change subtractions to adding the opposite.

$2c + (-10) + (-1c) + 15$ We can add in any order, so rewrite the expression so that like terms are next to each other.

$2c + (-1c) + (-10) + 15$ Combine $2c + (-1c)$.
Also combine $-10 + 15$.

$[2 + (-1)]\,c + 5$ Brackets show what to do first: $2 + (-1)$ is 1. The variable part, c, stays the same.

$1c + 5$

The simplified expression is $1c + 5$ or just $c + 5$

$1c$ is the same as c.

Note

In this book, when combining like terms we will usually write the variable terms in *alphabetical order*. A constant term (number only) will be written last. So, in **Examples 3(a) and 3(b)** above, the preferred and alternative ways of writing the expressions are as follows.

The simplified expression is $9xy + 2y$ (alphabetical order). However, by the commutative property of addition, $2y + 9xy$ is also correct.

The simplified expression is $c + 5$ (constant written last). However, by the commutative property of addition, $5 + c$ is also correct.

◀ **Work Problem ③ at the Side.**

We can use the **associative property of multiplication** to simplify an expression such as $4(3x)$.

$4(3x)$ can be written as $4 \cdot (3 \cdot x)$

Understood multiplications

Answers

3. **(a)** $10b^2 + 4d^2$ **(b)** $-2a + 2b$
(c) 7 **(d)** y **(e)** $7x + 7$

Using the associative property, we can regroup the factors.

$4 \cdot (3 \cdot x)$ can be written as $(4 \cdot 3) \cdot x$ To simplify, multiply $4 \cdot 3$.

$12 \cdot x$ Write $12 \cdot x$ without the multiplication dot.

$12x$

The simplified expression is $12x$.

EXAMPLE 4   **Simplifying Multiplication Expressions**

Simplify.

(a) $5(10y)$

Use the associative property.

$5 \cdot (10 \cdot y)$ can be written as $(5 \cdot 10) \cdot y$ Multiply $5 \cdot 10$.

$50 \cdot y$ Write $50 \cdot y$ without the multiplication dot.

$50y$

So, $5(10y)$ simplifies to $50y$.

(b) $-6(3b)$

Use the associative property.

$-6(3b)$ can be written as $(-6 \cdot 3)b$

$-18b$

So, $-6(3b)$ simplifies to $-18b$.

(c) $-4(-2x^2)$

Use the associative property.

> Brackets show what to do first: $-4 \cdot (-2)$ is 8.

$-4(-2x^2)$ can be written as $\left[-4 \cdot (-2)\right] x^2$

$8x^2$

So, $-4(-2x^2)$ simplifies to $8x^2$.

· **Work Problem ④ at the Side.** ▶

OBJECTIVE ▶ ③ Use the distributive property to multiply. The distributive property can also be used to simplify expressions such as $3(x + 5)$. You *cannot* add the terms inside the parentheses because x and 5 are *not* like terms. But notice the understood multiplication dot between the 3 and the parentheses.

$$3 (x + 5)$$
$$3 \cdot (x + 5)$$

Thus you can *distribute* multiplication over addition, as you did in **Chapter 1.** That is, multiply 3 times each term inside the parentheses.

$3 \cdot (x + 5)$ can be written as $3 \cdot x + 3 \cdot 5$

$3x + 15$

So, $3(x + 5)$ simplifies to $3x + 15$.

⌐— Stays as addition —⌐

④ Simplify.

(a) $7(4c)$ means $7 \cdot (4 \cdot c)$.

Using the associative property, it can be rewritten as

$(7 \cdot 4) \cdot c$

$\underline{} \cdot c$

$\underline{}$ Rewrite without the multiplication dot.

(b) $-3(5y^3)$

(c) $20(-2a)$

(d) $-10(-x)$

5 Simplify.

(a) $7(a + 10)$

$7(a + 10)$

$\underbrace{7 \cdot a} + \underbrace{7 \cdot 10}$

___ + ___

(b) $3(x - 3)$

$3(x - 3)$

$\underbrace{3 \cdot x} - \underbrace{3 \cdot 3}$

___ − ___

(c) $4(2y + 6)$

(d) $-5(3b + 2)$

(e) $-8(c + 4)$

EXAMPLE 5	Using the Distributive Property

Simplify.

(a) $5(3x + 2)$ can be written as $\quad 5 \cdot 3x + 5 \cdot 2$ ◁ Remember to multiply $5 \cdot 3x$ **and** $5 \cdot 2$.

$$5 \cdot 3 \cdot x + 10$$
$$\underbrace{15 \cdot x} + 10$$
$$15x + 10$$

So, $5(3x + 2)$ simplifies to $15x + 10$.

(b) $-2(4a + 3)$ can be written as $\quad -2 \cdot 4a + (-2) \cdot 3$

$$-2 \cdot 4 \cdot a + \quad (-6)$$
$$\underbrace{-8 \cdot a} + \quad (-6)$$
$$-8a \quad + \quad (-6)$$

Now we will use the definition of subtraction "in reverse" to rewrite $-8a + (-6)$.

Change -6 to its opposite, 6.

Write $-8a + (-6) \quad$ as $\quad -8a - 6$

Change addition to subtraction.

Think back to the way we changed subtraction to adding the opposite. Here we are "working backward." From now on, whenever addition is followed by a negative number, we will change it to subtracting a positive number.

$$-8a + (-6)$$
$$-8a - 6$$

Equivalent expressions

So, $-2(4a + 3)$ simplifies to $-8a - 6$.

(c) $6(y - 4)$

$6[y + (-4)]$ Change subtraction to adding the opposite.

$6[y + (-4)]$ Multiply 6 times each term inside the brackets.

$\underbrace{6 \cdot y} + \underbrace{6(-4)}$ Do the multiplications.

$6y + (-24)$ Use the definition of subtraction "in reverse." Change addition to subtraction.

$6y - 24$ Change -24 to its opposite, 24.

This is an example of how *multiplication distributes over subtraction*, in the same way that *multiplication distributes over addition* in **Example 5(a)** above. You can show fewer steps, like this:

$$6(y - 4) \quad \text{can be written as} \quad \underbrace{6 \cdot y} - \underbrace{6(4)}$$
$$6y \quad - \quad 24$$

So, $6(y - 4)$ simplifies to $6y - 24$.

◁ **Work Problem** **5** **at the Side.**

Sometimes you need to do several steps to simplify an expression.

EXAMPLE 6   Simplifying a More Complex Expression

Simplify: $8 + 3(x - 2)$

$8 + 3(x - 2)$ Do *not* add $8 + 3$. Use the distributive property first because multiplying is done *before* adding.

$8 + \underbrace{3 \cdot x} - \underbrace{3 \cdot 2}$ Do the multiplications.

$8 + \;\; 3x \;\; - \;\; 6$ Rewrite so that like terms are next to each other.

$3x + \underbrace{8 \;\; - \;\; 6}$ Subtract to find $8 - 6$ or change to adding $8 + (-6)$.

$3x + \;\;\;\; 2$

The simplified expression is $3x + 2$.

CAUTION

Do **not** add $8 + 3$ as the first step in **Example 6** above. Remember that the order of operations tells you to do multiplying *before* adding.

Working with Expressions

- An expression expresses, or tells, a rule for doing something.

- An expression is a combination of operations on variables and numbers. Here are some examples:

$$c + 5 \qquad\qquad 4s \qquad\qquad 100 + \frac{a}{2}$$

$$4 + 3x - 10 + x \qquad -8a^2b^3 \qquad 7 + 9(2y - 1)$$

- You can **evaluate an expression** by replacing each variable with specific numbers. Then do all possible calculations, following the order of operations. There are **no variables** in the final answer.

  For example, if x is 5, then **evaluating** the expression $4 + 3x - 10 + x$ becomes $4 + 3(5) - 10 + 5$, or 14.

- You can **simplify an expression** by combining (adding) all the like terms. When you simplify an expression, you write it in a simpler way.

  For example, the expression $4 + 3x - 10 + x$ **simplifies** to $4x - 6$.

- **IMPORTANT NOTE:** An expression **does not have an = sign in it.** The next section shows you equations, which **do** have = signs. You will learn how to **solve equations.** So look carefully at the directions for exercises. You can *evaluate* or *simplify* an expression, but only equations can be *solved.*

···· Work Problem **6** at the Side. ▶

---

6 Simplify.

(a) $-4 + 5(y + 1)$

$-4 + \underbrace{5 \cdot y} + \underbrace{5 \cdot 1}$

$-4 + \underline{\quad} + \underline{\quad}$

$\underset{\downarrow}{5y} \; \underbrace{- \, 4 + 5}$ Combine

$\underline{\qquad\qquad}$ like terms.

(b) $2(3w + 4) - 5$

(c) $5(6x - 2) + 3x$

(d) $21 + 7(a^2 - 3)$

(e) $-y + 3(2y + 5) - 18$

Answers

6. (a) $-4 + 5y + 5$; $5y + 1$ **(b)** $6w + 3$
    (c) $33x - 10$ **(d)** $7a^2$ **(e)** $5y - 3$

2.2 Exercises

  Download the MyDashBoard App MyMathLab®

CONCEPT CHECK   *Circle the like terms in each expression. Then identify the coefficients of the like terms.* **See Example 1.**

1. $2b^2 + 2b + 2b^3 + b^2 + 6$

The like terms are $2b^2$ and b^2.

The coefficient of $2b^2$ is _____ and

the coefficient of b^2 is understood to be _____.

2. $3x + x^3 + 3x^2 + 3 + 2x^3$

3. $-x^2y + (-xy) + 2xy + (-2xy^2)$

4. $ab^2 + (-a^2b) + 2ab + (-3a^2b)$

5. $7 + 7c + 3 + 7c^3 + (-4)$

6. $4d + (-5) + 1 + (-5d^2) + 4$

Simplify each expression. **See Example 2.**

7. $6r + 6r$

$(6 + 6)\, r$

_____ r

8. $4t + 10t$

$(4 + 10)\, t$

_____ t

9. $x^2 + 5x^2$

10. $9y^3 + y^3$

11. $p - 5p$

12. $n - 3n$

13. $-2a^3 - a^3$

14. $-10x^2 - x^2$

15. $c - c$

16. $b^2 - b^2$

17. $9xy + xy - 9xy$

18. $r^2s - 7r^2s + 7r^2s$

19. $5t^4 + 7t^4 - 6t^4$

20. $10mn - 9mn + 3mn$

21. $y^2 + y^2 + y^2 + y^2$

22. $a + a + a$

23. $-x - 6x - x$

24. $-y - y - 3y$

Simplify by combining like terms. Write each answer with the variables in alphabetical order and any constant term last. **See Example 3.**

25. $8a + 4b + 4a$

26. $6x + 5y + 4y$

27. $6 + 8 + 7rs$

28. $10 + 2c^2 + 15$

29. $a + ab^2 + ab^2$

30. $n + mn + n$

31. $6x + y - 8x + y$

32. $d + 3c - 7c + 3d$

33. $8b^2 - a^2 - b^2 + a^2$

34. $5ab - ab + 3a^2b - 4ab$

35. $-x^3 + 3x - 3x^2 + 2$

36. $a^2b - 2ab - ab^3 + 3a^3b$

37. $-9r + 6t - s - 5r + s + t - 6t + 5s - r$

38. $-x - 3y + 4z + x - z + 5y - 8x - y$

Simplify by using the associative property of multiplication. **See Example 4.**

39. $3(10a)$

40. $8(4b)$

41. $-4(2x^2)$

42. $-7(3b^3)$

43. $5(-4y^3)$

44. $2(-6x)$

45. $-9(-2cd)$

46. $-6(-4rs)$

47. $7(3a^2bc)$

48. $4(2xy^2z^2)$

49. $-12(-w)$

50. $-10(-k)$

Use the distributive property to simplify each expression. ***See Example 5.***

51. $6(b + 6)$

$6(b \ \ + 6)$

$\underbrace{6 \cdot b} + \underbrace{6 \cdot 6}$

___ + ___

52. $5(a + 3)$

$5(a \ \ + 3)$

$\underbrace{5 \cdot a} + \underbrace{5 \cdot 3}$

___ + ___

53. $7(x - 1)$

54. $4(y - 4)$

55. $3(7t + 1)$

56. $8(2c + 5)$

57. $-2(5r + 3)$

58. $-5(6z + 2)$

59. $-9(k + 4)$

60. $-3(p + 7)$

61. $50(m - 6)$

62. $25(n - 1)$

Simplify each expression. ***See Example 6.***

63. $10 + 2(4y + 3)$ Part of the work is done. Now finish it.

$10 + 2(4y + 3)$

$10 + \underbrace{2 \cdot 4} \cdot y + \underbrace{2 \cdot 3}$

64. $4 + 7(x^2 + 3)$ Part of the work is done. Now finish it.

$4 + 7(x^2 + 3)$

$4 + \underbrace{7 \cdot x^2} + \underbrace{7 \cdot 3}$

65. $6(a^2 - 2) + 15$

66. $5(b - 4) + 25$

67. $2 + 9(m - 4)$

68. $6 + 3(n - 8)$

69. $-5(k + 5) + 5k$

70. $-7(p + 2) + 7p$

71. $4(6x - 3) + 12$

72. $6(3y - 3) + 18$

73. $5 + 2(3n + 4) - n$

74. $8 + 8(4z + 5) - z$

75. $-p + 6(2p - 1) + 5$

76. $-k + 3(4k - 1) + 2$

77. Explain the difference between *simplifying* an expression and *evaluating* an expression.

78. Simplify each expression. Are the answers equivalent? Explain why or why not.

$$5(3x + 2) \qquad 5(2 + 3x)$$

79. Explain what makes two terms *like* terms. Include several examples in your explanation.

80. Explain how to combine like terms. Include an example in your explanation.

81. Explain and correct the error made by a student who simplified this expression.

$$\underbrace{-2x + 7x} + 8$$
$$5x^2 \quad + 8$$

82. Explain and correct the error made by a student who simplified this expression.

$$\underbrace{-10a + 6a} - \underset{\downarrow}{7} + 2$$
$$-4a \quad + \underbrace{(-7) + 2}$$
$$-4a \quad + \quad (-5)$$
$$4a - 5$$

Simplify.

83. $-4(3y) - 5 + 2(5y + 7)$

84. $6(-3x) - 9 + 3(-2x + 6)$

85. $-10 + 4(-3b + 3) + 2(6b - 1)$

86. $12 + 2(4a - 4) + 4(-2a - 1)$

87. $-5(-x + 2) + 8(-x) + 3(-2x - 2) + 16$

88. $-7(-y) + 6(y - 1) + 3(-2y) + 6 - y$

Study Skills

USING STUDY CARDS REVISITED

OBJECTIVES

1. Create study cards for difficult problems.
2. Create study cards of quiz problems.

This is the second part of the Study Cards activity. As you get further into a chapter, you can choose particular problems that will serve as a good test review. Here are two more types of study cards that will help you.

Tough Problem Cards

When you are doing your homework and find yourself saying, "This is really hard," or "I'm worried I'll make a mistake," make a **tough problem** study card! On the front, write out the procedure to work the type of problem *in words*. Include any special notes, like what *not* to do. On the back, work at least one example; make sure you label what you are doing.

Front of Card

Simplifying Expressions   *page*____

    Combine (add) <u>like</u> terms only.

    Like terms have variable parts that match.

    Use the distributive property if possible.

Back of Card

Example	*Simplify this expression.*	
$7 + 3(2n - 4)$	*Do <u>not</u> add 7 + 3!*
$7 + 3(2n - 4)$	*Use the distributive property.*
$7 + 3 \cdot 2n - 3 \cdot 4$	*Do the multiplications.*
$7 + 6n - 12$	*Rewrite so like terms are next to each other.*
$6n + 7 + (-12)$	*Change subtraction to adding the opposite.*
$6n + (-5)$	*Do <u>not</u> stop here!*
$6n - 5$	*Use definition of subtraction "in reverse."*

Now Try This

Choose three types of difficult problems or problems that have given you trouble, and work them out on study cards. Be sure to put the words for solving the problem on one side and the worked problem on the other side.

Practice Quiz Cards

Make up a few **quiz cards** for each type of problem you learn, and use them to prepare for a test. Choose two or three problems from the different sections of the chapter. Be sure you don't just choose the easiest problems! Put the problem

with the direction words (such as *solve, simplify, evaluate*) on the front, and work the problem on the back. If you like, put the page number from the text there, too. When you review, you work the problem on a separate paper, and check it by looking at the back.

Front of Card

Back of Card

Why Are Study Cards Brain Friendly?

▶ Making the study cards is an **active technique** that really gets your dendrites growing. You have to make decisions about what is most important and how to put it on the card. This kind of thinking is more in depth than just memorizing, and as a result, you will understand the concepts better and remember them longer.

▶ The cards are **visually appealing** (if you write neatly and use some color). Your brain responds to pleasant visual images, and again, you will remember longer and may even be able to "picture in your mind" how your cards look. This will help you during tests.

▶ Because study cards are small and portable, you can review them easily whenever you have a few minutes. Even while you're waiting for a bus or have a few minutes between classes you can take out your cards and read them to yourself. Your **brain really benefits from repetition;** each time you review your cards your dendrites are growing thicker and stronger. After a while, the information will become automatic and you will remember it for a long time.

Summary Exercises *Variables and Expressions*

CONCEPT CHECK *Identify the parts of each expression. Choose from these labels:*
variable, constant, coefficient.

1. $-10 - m$

2. $-8cd$

3. $6 + 4x$

4. The expression for finding the perimeter of an octagon with sides of equal length is $8s$. Evaluate the expression when

(**a**) the length of one side is 4 yards.

5. The expression for the total cost of a car is $d + mt$ where d is the down payment, m is the monthly payment, and t is the number of months you must make payments. Evaluate the expression when

(**a**) the down payment is \$3000 and you make 36 monthly payments of \$280.

(**b**) the length of one side is 15 inches.

(**b**) the down payment is \$1750 and you make 48 monthly payments of \$429.

CONCEPT CHECK *Rewrite each expression without exponents.*

6. ad^4

7. b^3cd

8. $-7ab^5c^2$

Evaluate each expression when w is 5, x is -2, y is -6, and z is 0.

9. w^4

10. $5xz$

11. yz^2

12. wxy

13. x^3

14. $-4wy$

15. $3xy^2$

16. w^2x^5

17. $-7wx^4y^3$

Simplify each expression.

18. $10b + 4b + 10b$

19. $-3x - 5 + 12 + 10x$

20. $-8(c + 4)$

21. $-9xy + 9xy$

22. $-4(-3c^2d)$

23. $3f - 5f - 4f$

24. $2(3w + 4)$

25. $-a - 6b - a$

26. $-10(-5x^3y^2)$

27. $5r^3 + 2r^2 - 2r^2 + 5r^3$

28. $21 + 7(h^2 - 3)$

29. $-3(m + 3) + 3m$

30. $-4(8y - 5) + 5$

31. $2 + 12(3x - 1)$

32. $-n + 5(4n - 2) + 11$

33. Explain and correct each error made by the student who simplified these expressions.

   (a) $6(n + 2)$

       $6n + 2$

   (b) $-5(-4a)$

       $-20a$

   (c) $\underbrace{3y + 2y}_{5y^2} - 10$

       $ - 10$

34. Explain and correct the error made by this student.

$$\underbrace{-8x + x}_{-7x} \underset{\downarrow}{-} \underset{\downarrow}{12} + 3$$
$$-7x + \underbrace{(-12) + 3}$$
$$-7x + (-9)$$
$$7x - 9$$

2.3 Solving Equations Using Addition

OBJECTIVES

1 Determine whether a given number is a solution of an equation.

2 Solve equations using the addition property of equality.

3 Simplify equations before using the addition property of equality.

Now you are ready for a look at the "heart" of algebra, writing and solving **equations.** *Writing* an equation is a way to show the relationship between what you *know* about a problem and what you *don't* know. Then, *solving* the equation is a way to figure out the part that you didn't know and answer your question.

The questions you can answer by writing and solving equations are as varied as the careers people choose. A zookeeper can solve an equation that answers the question of how long to incubate the egg of a particular tropical bird. A fitness instructor can solve an equation that answers the question of how hard a certain person should exercise for maximum benefit.

OBJECTIVE ▶ 1 **Determine whether a given number is a solution of an equation.** Let's start with the example from the beginning of this chapter: ordering textbooks for math classes. The expression we used to order books was $c + 5$, where c was the class limit (the maximum number of students allowed in the class). Suppose that 30 prealgebra books were ordered. What is the class limit for prealgebra? To answer this question, write an equation showing the relationship between what you know and what you don't know.

You don't know
the class limit.   You do know the total
                                        number of books ordered.

$$c + 5 = 30$$

You do know that 5 extra books were ordered.

Note

An equation has an equal sign. Notice the similarity in the words **equa**tion and **equal**. An *expression* does *not* have an equal sign.

The equal sign in an equation is like the balance point on a playground teeter-totter, or seesaw. To have a true equation, the two sides must balance.

These equations balance, so we can use the $=$ sign.

These equations do *not* balance, so we write $\neq$ to mean "is not equal to."

$$6 + 8 = 14$$

$$6 + 8 \neq 15$$

$$10 = 5 \cdot 2$$

$$10 \neq 4 \cdot 2$$

$$3 \cdot 2 = 5 + 1$$

$$4 + 5 \neq 5 \cdot 4$$

When an equation has a variable, we **solve the equation** by finding a number that can replace the variable and make the equation balance. For the example about ordering prealgebra textbooks:

$$c + 5 = 30$$

What number can replace c so that the equation balances?

Try replacing c with 15. $15 + 5 \neq 30$ Does *not* balance: 15 + 5 is only 20.

Try replacing c with 40. $40 + 5 \neq 30$ Does *not* balance: 40 + 5 is more than 30.

Try replacing c with 25. $25 + 5 = 30$ Balances: 25 + 5 is 30.

The solution is **25** because **25** is the *only* number that makes the equation balance. By solving the equation, you have answered the question about the class limit for prealgebra. The class limit is 25.

Note

Most of the equations that you will solve in this book have only one solution, that is, one number that makes the equation balance. In **Chapter 9,** and in other algebra courses, you will solve equations that have two or more solutions.

EXAMPLE 1 Identifying the Solution of an Equation

Which of these numbers, 70, 40, or 60, is the solution of the equation $c - 10 = 50$?

Replace c with each of the numbers. The one that makes the equation balance is the solution.

The solution is 60.

$70 - 10 \neq 50$ $40 - 10 \neq 50$ $60 - 10 = 50$

Does *not* balance: 70 − 10 is more than 50.

Does *not* balance: 40 − 10 is only 30.

Balances: 60 − 10 is 50.

The solution is 60 because, when c is 60, the equation balances.

························· Work Problem **1** at the Side. ▶

---

1 (a) Which of these numbers, 95, 65, 80, or 70, is the solution of the equation $c + 15 = 80$?

Try replacing c with 95.
$95 + 15 \neq 80$

Does **not** balance:
95 + 15 is more than 80.

Now try the other numbers. Which one makes the equation balance? ____

(b) Which of these numbers, 28, 20, 24, or 32, is the solution of the equation $28 = c - 4$?

OBJECTIVE **2** **Solve equations using the addition property of equality.** When solving the book-ordering equation, $c + 5 = 30$, you could just look at the equation and think, "What number, plus 5, would balance with 30?" You could easily see that c had to be 25. Not all equations can be solved this easily, so you'll need some tools for the harder ones. The first tool, called the **addition property of equality,** allows us to add the *same* number to *both* sides of an equation.

Addition Property of Equality

If $a = b$, then $a + c = b + c$.

In other words, you may add the *same* number to *both* sides of an equation and still keep it balanced.

Think of the teeter-totter. If there are 3 children of the same weight on each side, it will balance. If 2 more children climb onto the left side, the only way to keep the balance is to have 2 more children of the same weight climb onto the right side as well.

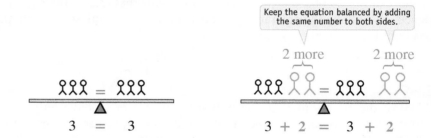

All the tools you will learn to use with equations have one goal.

Goal in Solving an Equation

The goal is to end up with the variable (the letter) on one side of the equal sign balancing a number on the other side.

We work on the original equation until we get:

$$\text{variable} = \text{number} \qquad \text{or} \qquad \text{number} = \text{variable}$$

Once we have arrived at that point, the number balancing the variable is the solution to the original equation.

EXAMPLE 2   Using the Addition Property of Equality

Solve each equation and check the solution.

(a) $c + 5 = 30$

   We want to get the variable, c, by itself on the left side of the equal sign. To do that, we add the *opposite* of 5, which is -5. Then $5 + (-5)$ will be 0.

$$c + 5 = 30$$

Add -5 to the left side. $\longrightarrow$ $\quad -5 \qquad -5 \quad \leftarrow$ To keep the balance, add -5 to the right side also.

$$c + 0 = 25 \quad \leftarrow 30 + (-5) \text{ is } 25.$$

$5 + (-5)$ is 0.

Recall that adding 0 to any number leaves the number unchanged, so $c + 0$ is c.

$$c + 0 = 25$$
$$c \;\;= 25$$

Because c *balances* with 25, the *solution* is 25.

Check the solution by replacing c with 25 in the *original equation*.

$$c + 5 = 30 \qquad \text{Original equation}$$
$$25 + 5 = 30 \qquad \text{Replace } c \text{ with 25.} \quad \boxed{\text{The solution is 25, \textbf{not} 30.}}$$
$$30 \;\;= 30 \;\checkmark \quad \text{Balances}$$

Because the equation balances when we use 25 to replace the variable, we know that **25 is the correct solution.** If it had *not* balanced, we would need to rework the problem, find our error, and correct it.

(b) $-5 = x - 3$

   We want the variable, x, by itself on the right side of the equal sign. (Remember, it doesn't matter which side of the equal sign the variable is on, just so it ends up by itself.) To see what number to add, we change the subtraction to adding the opposite.

$$-5 = x - 3 \qquad \text{Change subtraction to adding the opposite.}$$
$$-5 = x + (-3) \qquad \text{To get } x \text{ by itself on the right side, add the opposite of } -3, \text{ which is 3. Then } -3 + 3 \text{ is } 0.$$

To keep the balance, add 3 to the left side also. $-5 + 3$ is -2.
$$\quad 3 \qquad\qquad 3$$
$$-2 = x + 0 \qquad \text{Adding 0 to } x \text{ leaves } x \text{ unchanged.}$$
$$-2 = \quad x \qquad x \text{ balances with } -2, \text{ so } -2 \text{ is the solution.}$$

We check the solution by replacing x with -2 in the *original equation*. If the equation balances when we use -2, we know that it is the correct solution. If the equation does *not* balance when we use -2, we made an error and need to try solving the equation again.

Continued on Next Page

② Solve each equation and check each solution.

GS (a) $12 = y + 5$

To get y by itself, add the opposite of 5, which is -5. To keep the balance, add -5 to *both* sides.

$$12 = y + 5$$
$$\underline{-5 \qquad -5}$$
$$7 = y + \underline{\quad}$$
$$7 = \underline{\quad}$$

CHECK

$12 = y + 5$ Original equation
$12 = \overline{7 + 5}$ Replace y with 7.
$12 = \underline{\quad}$

Does it balance? ____
So the solution is ____.

(b) $b - 2 = -6$

CHECK

CHECK $-5 = x - 3$ Original equation
$-5 = -2 - 3$ Replace x with -2.
$-5 = \underbrace{-2 + (-3)}$ Change subtraction to adding the opposite.
$-5 = \qquad -5 \checkmark$ Balances; this means -2 is the correct solution.

When x is replaced with -2, the equation balances, so -2 **is the correct solution**.

> **CAUTION**
>
> When checking the solution to **Example 2(b)** above, we ended up with $-5 = -5$. Notice that -5 is *not* the solution. The solution is -2, the number used to replace x in the original equation.

◀ **Work Problem ②** at the Side.

OBJECTIVE ③ Simplify equations before using the addition property of equality. Sometimes you can simplify the expression on one or both sides of the equal sign. Doing so will make it easier to solve the equation.

EXAMPLE 3 **Simplifying before Solving Equations**

Solve each equation and check each solution.

(a) $y + 8 = 3 - 7$

You cannot simplify the left side because y and 8 are *not* like terms.

$y + 8 = 3 - 7$ Simplify the right side by changing subtraction to adding the opposite.
$y + 8 = \underbrace{3 + (-7)}$ Add $3 + (-7)$ to get -4

To get y by itself on the left side, add the opposite of 8, which is -8.

$8 + (-8)$ is 0.

$y + 8 = \qquad -4$ To keep the balance, add -8 to the right side also.
$\underline{\quad -8 \qquad -8}$
$\underbrace{y + 0} = \qquad -12$ $-4 + (-8)$ is -12.
$y = -12$

The solution is -12. Now check the solution.

CHECK $y + 8 = 3 - 7$ Go back to the *original* equation and replace y with -12.

Add $-12 + 8$. $\underbrace{-12 + 8} = 3 - 7$ Change $3 - 7$ to $3 + (-7)$.

$-4 = \underbrace{3 + (-7)}$ Add $3 + (-7)$ to get -4

$-4 = \qquad -4 \checkmark$ Balances; so -12 is the correct solution.

When y is replaced with -12, the equation balances, so -12 **is the correct solution** (**not** -4).

.... **Continued on Next Page**

Answers

2. **(a)** $7 = y + 0$; $7 = y$

CHECK $12 = y + 5$
$12 = \overline{7 + 5}$
Balances $12 = 12 \checkmark$
So the solution is 7.

(b) $b = -4$

CHECK $b - 2 = -6$
$\overline{-4 + (-2)} = -6$
Balances $-6 = -6 \checkmark$

(b) $-2 + 2 = -4b - 6 + 5b$

Simplify the left side by adding $-2 + 2$.

$$-2 + 2 = -4b - 6 + 5b$$

$$0 = -4b + (-6) + 5b \qquad \text{Simplify the right side by changing subtraction to adding the opposite.}$$

$$0 = \underbrace{-4b + 5b} + (-6) \qquad \text{Find like terms.}$$

$$0 = 1b + (-6) \qquad \text{Combine } -4b + 5b.$$

To keep the balance, add 6 to the left side also.

$$\underrightarrow{6} \qquad\qquad\qquad 6 \longleftarrow \text{To get } 1b \text{ by itself, add the opposite of } -6, \text{ which is } 6.$$

$$6 = 1b + 0$$

$$6 = \underbrace{1b} \qquad 1b \text{ is equivalent to } b.$$

$$6 = b$$

The solution is 6.

CHECK $\qquad -2 + 2 = -4b - 6 + 5b \qquad$ Go back to the *original* equation and replace each b with 6.

Add $-2 + 2$. $\quad \underbrace{-2 + 2} = -4 \cdot 6 - 6 + 5 \cdot 6 \qquad$ On the right side, do multiplications first.

$$0 = \underbrace{-24 + (-6)} + 30 \qquad \text{Change subtraction to adding the opposite.}$$

$$0 = \underbrace{-30 + 30} \qquad \text{Add from left to right.}$$

$$0 = 0 \checkmark \qquad \text{Balances}$$

When b is replaced with 6, the equation balances, so **6 is the correct solution** (**not** 0).

CAUTION

When checking a solution, always go back to the *original* equation. That way, you will catch any errors you made when simplifying each side of the equation.

· **Work Problem ❸ at the Side.** ▶

---

❸ Simplify each side of the equation when possible. Then solve the equation and check the solution.

ⓖ (a) $2 - 8 = k - 2$

$$2 + (-8) = k + (-2) \quad \text{Simplify.}$$

$$-6 = k + (-2)$$

$$+2 \qquad\qquad +2 \quad \text{Add } +2 \text{ to both sides.}$$

$$\underline{\qquad} = k + \underline{\qquad}$$

$$\underline{\qquad} = \underline{\qquad}$$

CHECK

$$2 - 8 = k - 2 \quad \text{Original equation}$$

$$2 - 8 = -4 - 2 \quad \text{Replace } k \text{ with } -4.$$

$$\underbrace{2 + (-8)} = \underbrace{-4 + (-2)}$$

$$\underline{\qquad} = \underline{\qquad}$$

Does it balance? _____
So the solution is _____.

(b) $4r + 1 - 3r = -8 + 11$

CHECK

Answers

3. (a) $-4 = k + 0; -4 = k$

CHECK $\quad 2 - 8 = k - 2$

$$\underbrace{2 + (-8)} = \underbrace{-4 + (-2)}$$

Balances $\quad -6 = -6 \checkmark$
So the solution is -4.

(b) $r = 2$

CHECK $\quad 4r + 1 - 3r = -8 + 11$

$$\underbrace{4 \cdot 2} + 1 - \underbrace{3 \cdot 2} = \underbrace{-8 + 11}$$

$$8 + 1 - 6 = 3$$

$$\underbrace{9 + (-6)} = 3$$

Balances $\quad\quad 3 = 3 \checkmark$

2.3 Exercises

FOR EXTRA HELP

 Download the MyDashBoard App

MyMathLab®

CONCEPT CHECK   *In each list of numbers, find the one that is a solution of the given equation. See Example 1.*

1. $n - 50 = 8$

58, 42, 60, 8

2. $r - 20 = 5$

5, 15, 30, 25

3. $-6 = y + 10$

$-4, -16, 16, -6$

4. $-4 = x + 13$

$-4, 17, -17, -9$

CONCEPT CHECK   *To solve each equation, state the number you would add to both sides of the equation. Then explain why you picked that number. Do **not** finish the solution.*

5. **(a)** $m - 8 = 1$

(b) $-7 = w + 5$

6. **(a)** $n + 2 = -9$

(b) $10 = b - 6$

Solve each equation and check each solution. See Example 2.

7. $p + 5 = 9$

$$
\begin{array}{rcl}
p + 5 &=& 9 \\
-5 & & -5 \\
\hline
p + 0 &=& 4 \\
\underline{} &=& \underline{}
\end{array}
$$

CHECK $p + 5 = 9$
↓

8. $a + 3 = 12$

$$
\begin{array}{rcl}
a + 3 &=& 12 \\
-3 & & -3 \\
\hline
a + 0 &=& 9 \\
\underline{} &=& \underline{}
\end{array}
$$

CHECK $a + 3 = 12$
↓

9. $8 = r - 2$

$$
\begin{array}{rcl}
8 &=& r + (-2) \\
+2 & & +2 \\
\hline
10 &=& r + 0 \\
\underline{} &=& \underline{}
\end{array}
$$

CHECK $8 = r - 2$
↓

10. $3 = b - 5$

$$
\begin{array}{rcl}
3 &=& b - 5 \\
+5 & & +5 \\
\hline
8 &=& b + 0 \\
\underline{} &=& \underline{}
\end{array}
$$

CHECK $3 = b - 5$
↓

11. $-5 = n + 3$

CHECK

12. $-1 = a + 8$

CHECK

13. $-4 + k = 14$

CHECK

14. $-9 + y = 7$

CHECK

15. $y - 6 = 0$

CHECK

16. $k - 15 = 0$

CHECK

17. $7 = r + 13$ CHECK

18. $12 = z + 19$ CHECK

19. $x - 12 = -12$ CHECK

20. $-3 = m - 3$ CHECK

21. $-5 = -2 + t$ CHECK

22. $-1 = -10 + w$ CHECK

A solution is given for each equation. Show how to check the solution. If the solution is correct, leave it. If the solution is not correct, solve the equation and check your new solution. **See Example 2.**

23. $z - 5 = 3$ CHECK $z - 5 = 3$
The solution is -2.

24. $x - 9 = 4$ CHECK $x - 9 = 4$
The solution is 13.

25. $7 + x = -11$ CHECK
The solution is -18.

26. $2 + k = -7$ CHECK
The solution is -5.

27. $-10 = -10 + b$ CHECK
The solution is 10.

28. $0 = -14 + a$ CHECK
The solution is 0.

Simplify each side of the equation when possible. Then solve the equation and check the solution. Show your work. ***See Example 3.***

29. $c - 4 = -8 + 10$ CHECK   **30.** $b - 8 = 10 - 6$ CHECK

31. $-1 + 4 = y - 2$ CHECK   **32.** $2 + 3 = k - 4$ CHECK

33. $10 + b = -14 - 6$ CHECK   **34.** $1 + w = -8 - 8$ CHECK

35. $t - 2 = 3 - 5$ CHECK   **36.** $p - 8 = -10 + 2$ CHECK

37. $10z - 9z = -15 + 8$ CHECK   **38.** $2r - r = 5 - 10$ CHECK

39. $-5w + 2 + 6w = -4 + 9$ CHECK   **40.** $-2t + 4 + 3t = 6 - 7$ CHECK

Solve each equation. Show your work. ***See Examples 2 and 3.***

41. $-3 - 3 = 4 - 3x + 4x$

42. $-5 - 5 = -2 - 6b + 7b$

43. $-3 + 7 - 4 = -2a + 3a$

44. $6 - 11 + 5 = -8c + 9c$

45. $y - 75 = -100$

46. $a - 200 = -100$

47. $-x + 3 + 2x = 18$

48. $-s + 2s - 4 = 13$

49. $82 = -31 + k$

50. $-5 = 72 + w$

51. $-2 + 11 = 2b - 9 - b$

52. $-6 + 7 = 2h - 1 - h$

53. $r - 6 = 7 - 10 - 8$

54. $m - 5 = 2 - 9 + 1$

55. $-14 = n + 91$

56. $66 = x - 28$

57. $-9 + 9 = 5 + h$

58. $18 - 18 = 6 + p$

59. CONCEPT CHECK   A student did this work when solving an equation. Do you agree that the solution is -7? Explain why or why not.

$$\underbrace{-8 + 1} = x + 7$$
$$-7 = x + 7$$
$$\underline{-7 \qquad -7}$$
$$-14 = x + 0$$
$$-14 = \underbrace{x}$$

CHECK

$$-8 + 1 = \quad \overset{\downarrow}{x} + 7$$
$$\underbrace{-8 + 1} = \underbrace{-14 + 7}$$
$$-7 = -7 \checkmark$$

Balances, so
-7 is the solution.

60. CONCEPT CHECK   A student did this work when solving an equation. Show how to check the solution. If the solution does not check, find and correct the errors.

$$-3 - 6 = n - 5$$
$$\underbrace{-3 + 6} = n - 5$$
$$3 = n - 5$$
$$\underline{-5 \qquad -5}$$
$$-2 = \underbrace{n + 0}$$
$$-2 = n$$

61. West Community College always orders 10 extra robes for the graduation ceremony. The college ordered 305 robes this year. Solving the equation $g + 10 = 305$ will give the number of graduates (g) this year. Solve the equation.

62. Refer to **Exercise 61.** The college ordered 278 robes last year. Solve the equation $g + 10 = 278$ to find the number of graduates last year.

63. The warmer the temperature, the faster a field cricket chirps. Solving the equation $92 = c + 37$ will give you the number of chirps (in 15 seconds) when the temperature is 92 degrees. Solve the equation.

64. Refer to **Exercise 63.** Solve the equation $77 = c + 37$ to find the number of times a field cricket chirps (in 15 seconds) when the temperature is 77 degrees.

65. During the summer months, Ernesto spends an average of only $45 per month on parking fees by riding his bike to work on nice days. This is $65 less per month than what he spends for parking in the winter. Solving the equation $p - 65 = 45$ will give you his monthly parking fees in the winter. Solve the equation.

66. By walking to work several times a week in the summer, Aimee spends an average of $56 less per month on parking fees. If she spends $98 per month on parking in the summer, solve the equation $p - 56 = 98$ to find her monthly parking fees in the winter.

Solve each equation. Show your work.

67. $-17 - 1 + 26 - 38 = -3 - m - 8 + 2m$

68. $19 - 38 - 9 + 11 = -t - 6 + 2t - 6$

69. $-6x + 2x + 6 + 5x = |0 - 9| - |-6 + 5|$

70. $-h - |-9 - 9| + 8h - 6h = -12 - |-5 + 0|$

Relating Concepts (Exercises 71–72) For Individual or Group Work

Use what you have learned about solving equations to ***work Exercises 71 and 72 in order.***

71. **(a)** Write two *different* equations that have -2 as the solution. Be sure that you have to use the *addition property of equality* to solve the equations. Show how to solve each equation. Use **Exercises 7 to 22** as models.

(b) Follow the directions in part (a), but this time write two equations that have 0 as the solution.

72. Not all equations have solutions that are integers. Try solving these equations.

(a) $x + 1 = 1\dfrac{1}{2}$

(b) $\dfrac{1}{4} = y - 1$

(c) $\$2.50 + n = \$3.35$

(d) Write two more equations that have fraction or decimal solutions.

2.4 Solving Equations Using Division

OBJECTIVE ▶ 1 Solve equations using the division property of equality.
Earlier in this chapter you worked with the expression for finding the perimeter of a square-shaped garden, that is, finding the total distance around all four sides of the garden:

$4s$, where s is the length of one side of the square

Suppose you know that 24 feet of fencing was used around a square-shaped garden. What was the length of one side of the garden? To answer this question, write an equation showing the relationship between what you know and what you don't know.

You don't know the length of one side.

You do know that — there are 4 sides.

You do know the perimeter.

$$4\,s = 24$$

To solve the equation, what number can replace s so that the equation balances? You can see that s is 6 feet.

$$4 \cdot 6 = 24$$

Balances:
4 · 6 is exactly 24.

The solution is 6 feet because 6 is the *only* number that makes the equation balance. You have answered the question about the length of one side: The length is 6 feet.

There is a tool that you can use to solve equations such as $4s = 24$ called the **division property of equality.** It allows you to *divide* both sides of an equation by the *same* number. (The only exception is that you cannot divide by 0.)

Division Property of Equality

If $a = b$, then $\dfrac{a}{c} = \dfrac{b}{c}$ as long as c is *not* 0.

In other words, you may divide both sides of an equation by the same nonzero number and still keep it balanced.

In the previous section, you saw that *adding* the same number to both sides of an equation kept it balanced. We could also have *subtracted* the same number from both sides because subtraction is defined as adding the opposite. Now we're saying that you can *divide* both sides by the same number. In **Chapter 4** we'll *multiply* both sides by the same number.

Equality Principle for Solving an Equation

As long as you do the *same* thing to *both* sides of an equation, the balance is maintained. (The only exception is that you cannot divide by 0.)

| EXAMPLE 1 | Using the Division Property of Equality |

Solve each equation and check each solution.

(a) $4s = 24$

As with any equation, the goal is to get the variable by itself on one side of the equal sign. On the left side we have $4s$, which means $4 \cdot s$. The variable is multiplied by 4. Division is the reverse of multiplication, so dividing by 4 can be used to "undo" multiplying by 4.

Divide $4s$ by 4. The fraction bar indicates division:
$4s \div 4$ is s.
$$\frac{4s}{4} = \frac{24}{4}$$
To keep the balance, divide the right side by 4 also: $24 \div 4$ is 6.

$$s = 6$$

So, as we already knew, 6 is the solution. We check the solution by replacing s with 6 in the original equation.

CHECK

$4s = 24$ Original equation

$4 \cdot 6 = 24$ Replace s with 6.

$24 = 24$ ✓   Balances

The solution is 6, not 24.

When s is replaced with 6, the equation balances, so **6 is the correct solution.**

(b) $42 = -6w$

On the right side of the equation, the variable is *multiplied* by -6. To undo the multiplication, *divide* by -6.

To keep the balance, divide by -6 on the left side also.
$$\frac{42}{-6} = \frac{-6w}{-6}$$
Use division to undo multiplication: $-6w \div (-6)$ is w.

$$-7 = w$$

The solution is -7.

CHECK

$42 = -6w$ Original equation

$42 = -6 \cdot (-7)$ Replace w with -7.

$42 = 42$ ✓   Balances

The solution is -7, not 42.

When w is replaced with -7, the equation balances, so -7 is the correct solution.

| CAUTION |

Be careful to divide both sides by the *same* number as the coefficient of the variable term. In **Example 1(b)** above, the coefficient of $-6w$ is -6, so divide both sides by -6. (Do **not** divide by the *opposite* of -6, which is 6. Use the opposite only when you're *adding* the same number to both sides.)

Work Problem **1** at the Side. ▶

---

1 Solve each equation and check each solution.

(a) $4s = 44$

$$\frac{4s}{4} = \frac{44}{4}$$ Divide both sides by 4.

$$s = \underline{\quad}$$

CHECK

$4s = 44$ Original equation

$4 \cdot \underline{\quad} = 44$ Replace s with $\underline{\quad}$.

$\underline{\quad} = 44$

Does it balance? $\underline{\quad}$

(b) $27 = -9p$

CHECK

(c) $-40 = -5x$

CHECK

(d) $7t = -70$

CHECK

Answers

1. (a) $s = 11$

CHECK $4s = 44$

$4 \cdot 11 = 44$ Replace s with 11.

Balances $44 = 44$ ✓

(b) $p = -3$

CHECK $27 = -9p$

$27 = -9 \cdot (-3)$

Balances $27 = 27$ ✓

(c) $x = 8$

CHECK $-40 = -5x$

$-40 = -5 \cdot 8$

Balances $-40 = -40$ ✓

(d) $t = -10$

CHECK $7t = -70$

$7 \cdot (-10) = -70$

Balances $-70 = -70$ ✓

2 Simplify each side of the equation when possible. Then solve the equation and check the solution.

(a) $-28 = -6n + 10n$

$-28 = \underbrace{-6n + 10n}$ Simplify the right side.

$-28 = \quad 4n$ Divide both sides by ____. Find the solution.

CHECK

$-28 = -6n + 10n$ Original equation

$-28 = \underbrace{-6 \cdot (-7)} + \underbrace{10 \cdot (-7)}$
$-28 = \quad (42) \quad + \quad (-70)$
$-28 = \quad \underline{\quad}$ Does it balance?

$\underline{\quad}$

(b) $p - 14p = -2 + 18 - 3$

CHECK

Answers

2. **(a)** $\dfrac{-28}{4} = \dfrac{4n}{4}; -7 = n$

   CHECK $-28 = -28$ ✓
   Balances
   (b) $p = -1$

   CHECK

EXAMPLE 2 **Simplifying before Solving Equations**

Solve each equation and check each solution.

(a) $4y - 7y = -12$

Simplify the left side by combining like terms.

$4y - \quad 7y \quad = -12$ The right side cannot be simplified.

Change subtraction to adding the opposite.

$\underbrace{4y + (-7y)} = -12$

Divide by the coefficient, which is -3.

$\dfrac{-3y}{-3} \quad = \dfrac{-12}{-3}$ To keep the balance, divide by -3 on the right side also.

$y \quad = \quad 4$ $-12 \div (-3)$ is 4.

The solution is 4.

CHECK

$4y - \quad 7y \quad = -12$ Go back to the *original* equation and replace each y with 4.

Do multiplications first.

$4 \cdot 4 - 7 \cdot 4 = -12$

$16 \quad - \quad 28 \quad = -12$

Change subtraction to adding the opposite.

$\underbrace{16 + (-28)} = -12$

$-12 \quad = -12$ ✓ Balances

When y is replaced with 4, the equation balances, so **4 is the correct solution.**

(b) $3 - 10 + 7 = h + 7h$

Change subtraction to adding the opposite.

$3 - \quad 10 \quad + 7 = h + 7h$ Write the understood 1 as the coefficient of h.

Add from left to right.

$\underbrace{3 + (-10)} + 7 = \underbrace{1h + 7h}$ Combine like terms on the right side.

$\underbrace{-7 \quad + 7} = \quad 8h$

To keep the balance, divide by 8 on the left side also.

$\dfrac{0}{8} \quad = \quad \dfrac{8h}{8}$ Divide by the coefficient, which is 8.

$0 \div 8$ is 0.

$0 \quad = \quad h$

The solution is 0.

CHECK

$3 - \quad 10 \quad + 7 = h + \quad 7h$ Go back to the *original* equation and replace each h with 0.

$3 + (-10) + 7 = 0 + 7 \cdot 0$

$\underbrace{-7 \quad + 7} = \underbrace{0 + \quad 0}$

$0 \quad = \quad 0$ ✓ Balances

When h is replaced with 0, the equation balances, so **0 is the correct solution.**

◀ **Work Problem 2** at the Side.

OBJECTIVE 3 **Solve equations such as** $-x = 5.$ **When solving equations, do *not* leave a negative sign in front of the variable.**

EXAMPLE 3 Solving an Equation of the Type $-x = 5$

Solve $-x = 5$ and check the solution.

It may look as if there is nothing more we can do to the equation $-x = 5$, but $-x$ is *not* the same as x. To see this, we write in the understood -1 as the coefficient of $-x$.

Coefficient is understood to be -1.

$$-x = 5 \qquad \text{can be written} \qquad -1x = 5$$

We want the coefficient of x to be positive 1, not -1. To accomplish that, we can divide both sides by the coefficient of x, which is -1.

$$\frac{-1x}{-1} = \frac{5}{-1} \qquad \text{Divide both sides by } -1.$$

On the left side, $-1 \div (-1)$ is 1. $\quad 1x = -5 \qquad$ On the right side, $5 \div (-1)$ is -5.

Now x is by itself on one side of the equal sign and has a coefficient of 1. The solution is -5.

CHECK $\qquad -x = 5 \qquad$ Go back to the *original* equation.

$-1x = 5 \qquad$ Write in the understood -1 as the coefficient of $-x$.

$-1 \cdot (-5) = 5 \qquad$ Replace x with -5. The solution is -5, **not** 5.

$\qquad 5 \quad = 5 \checkmark \qquad$ Balances

When x is replaced with -5, the equation balances, so -5 is the correct solution.

CAUTION

As the last step in solving an equation, do *not* leave a negative sign in front of a variable. For example, do *not* leave $-y = -8$. Write in the understood -1 as the coefficient, so that

$$-y = -8 \quad \text{is written as} \quad -1y = -8$$

Then divide both sides by -1 to get $y = 8$. The solution is 8.

········· Work Problem 3 at the Side. ▶

3 Solve each equation and check each solution.

(a) $-k = -12$

$-k = -12 \qquad$ can be written

$-1k = -12 \qquad$ Divide both sides by ____.

Find the solution.

CHECK

$-1k = -12$

$-1 \cdot 12 = -12$

____ $= -12 \qquad$ Does it balance? ____

(b) $7 = -t$

CHECK

(c) $-m = -20$

CHECK

Answers

3. (a) Divide both sides by -1; $k = 12$
CHECK $-12 = -12 \checkmark$
Balances
(b) $t = -7$
CHECK $7 = -1t$
$7 = -1 \cdot (-7)$
Balances $7 = 7 \checkmark$
(c) $m = 20$
CHECK $-1m = -20$
$-1 \cdot 20 = -20$
Balances $-20 = -20 \checkmark$

2.4 Exercises

FOR EXTRA HELP   MyMathLab®

CONCEPT CHECK *Solve each equation and check each solution.* ***See Example 1.***

1. $6z = 12$

GS Divide both sides by ____.

$\dfrac{6z}{6} = \dfrac{12}{6}$

$z = $ ____

CHECK $\quad 6z = 12$

$6 \cdot 2 = 12$

____ = ____

2. $8k = 24$

GS Divide both sides by ____.

$\dfrac{8k}{8} = \dfrac{24}{8}$

$k = $ ____

CHECK $\quad 8k = 24$

$8 \cdot 3 = 24$

____ = ____

3. $48 = 12r$

CHECK $\quad 48 = 12r$

4. $99 = 11m$

CHECK $\quad 99 = 11m$

5. $3y = 0$

CHECK

6. $5a = 0$

CHECK

Solve each equation. Show your work. ***See Example 1.***

7. $-7k = 70$

8. $-6y = 36$

9. $-54 = -9r$

10. $-36 = -4p$

11. $-25 = 5b$

12. $-70 = 10x$

Simplify where possible. Then solve each equation and check each solution.
See Example 2.

13. $2r = -7 + 13$

CHECK $\quad 2r = \underbrace{-7 + 13}$

14. $6y = 28 - 4$

CHECK $\quad 6y = \underbrace{28 - 4}$

15. $-12 = 5p - p$

CHECK

16. $20 = z - 11z$

CHECK

Solve each equation. Show your work. ***See Examples 1 and 2.***

17. $3 - 28 = 5a$

18. $-55 + 7 = 8n$

19. $x - 9x = 80$

20. $4c - c = -27$

21. $13 - 13 = 2w - w$

22. $-11 + 11 = 8t - 7t$

23. $3t + 9t = 20 - 10 + 26$

24. $6m + 6m = 40 + 20 - 12$

25. $0 = -9t$

26. $-10 = 10b$

27. $-14m + 8m = 6 - 60$

28. $7w - 14w = 1 - 50 + 49$

29. $100 - 96 = 31y - 35y$

30. $150 - 139 = 20x - 9x$

Use multiplication to simplify the side of the equation with the variable. Then solve each equation.

31. $3(2z) = -30$

32. $2(4k) = 16$

33. $50 = -5(5p)$

34. $60 = 4(-3a)$

35. $-2(-4k) = 56$

36. $-5(4r) = -80$

37. $-90 = -10(-3b)$

38. $-90 = -5(-2y)$

*Solve each equation. **See Example 3.***

39. $-x = 32$

40. $-c = 23$

41. $-2 = -w$

42. $-75 = -t$

43. $-n = -50$

44. $-x = -1$

45. $10 = -p$

46. $100 = -k$

47. Look again at the solutions to **Exercises 39–46.** Describe the pattern you see. Then write a rule for solving equations with a negative sign in front of the variable, such as $-x = 5$.

48. Write two *different* equations that have -4 as the solution. Be sure that you have to use the division property of equality to solve the equations. Show how to solve each equation.

49. CONCEPT CHECK Explain and correct the error made by a student who solved this equation.

$$3x = \underbrace{16 - 1}$$
$$\frac{3x}{-3} = \frac{15}{-3}$$
$$x = -5$$

50. CONCEPT CHECK Explain the division property of equality in your own words.

51. The perimeter of a triangle with sides of equal length is 3 times the length of one side (s). If the perimeter is 45 ft, solving the equation $3s = 45$ will give the length of one side. Solve the equation.

52. Refer to **Exercise 51.** If the perimeter of the triangle is 63 inches, solve the equation $3s = 63$ to find the length of one side.

53. The perimeter of a pentagon with sides of equal length is 5 times the length of one side (s). If the perimeter is 120 meters, solve the equation $120 = 5s$ to find the length of one side.

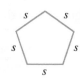

54. Refer to **Exercise 53.** If the pentagon has a perimeter of 335 yards, solving the equation $335 = 5s$ will give the length of one side. Solve the equation.

Solve each equation. Show your work.

55. $89 - 116 = -4(-4y) - 9(2y) + y$

56. $58 - 208 = -b + 8(-3b) + 5(-5b)$

57. $-37(14x) + 28(21x) = |72 - 72| + |-166 + 96|$

58. $6a - 10a - 3(2a) = |-25 - 25| - 5(8)$

2.5 Solving Equations with Several Steps

OBJECTIVES

1. Solve equations using the addition and division properties of equality.

2. Solve equations using the distributive, addition, and division properties.

1. Solve; check each solution.

GS (a) $2r + 7 = 13$

$$\underline{\begin{array}{rr} -7 = -7 \end{array}}\quad \begin{array}{l}\text{Add } -7 \text{ to}\\ \text{both sides.}\end{array}$$

$$\underbrace{2r + 0}_{2r} = \begin{array}{l} 6 \\ = 6 \end{array}$$

$$\frac{2r}{2} = \frac{6}{2}\quad \begin{array}{l}\text{Divide both}\\ \text{sides by 2.}\end{array}$$

$$r = \underline{\quad}$$

CHECK $2(3) + 7 = 13$ Replace r with 3.

$$\underbrace{6 + 7}_{\underline{\quad}} = 13$$
$$= 13$$

(b) $-10z - 9 = 11$

CHECK

OBJECTIVE 1 **Solve equations using the addition and division properties of equality.** To solve some equations, you need to use both the addition and division properties of equality. Here are the steps.

Solving an Equation Using the Addition and Division Properties

Step 1   *Add* the same amount to both sides of the equation so that the variable term (the variable and its coefficient) ends up by itself on one side of the equal sign.

Step 2   *Divide* both sides by the coefficient of the variable term to find the solution.

Step 3   *Check* the solution by going back to the *original* equation.

EXAMPLE 1   Solving an Equation with Several Steps

Solve this equation and check the solution: $5m + 1 = 16$.

Step 1   Get the variable term by itself on one side of the equal sign. The variable term is $5m$. Adding -1 to the left side of the equation will leave $5m$ by itself. To keep the balance, add -1 to the right side also.

$$5m + 1 = 16$$
$$\underline{\begin{array}{rr} -1 = -1 \end{array}}\quad\boxed{\begin{array}{l}\text{First } add \text{ the}\\ \text{same thing}\\ \text{to } both \text{ sides.}\end{array}}$$
$$\underbrace{5m + 0}_{5m} = \begin{array}{l} 15 \\ = 15 \end{array}$$

Step 2   Divide both sides by the coefficient of the variable term. In $5m$, the coefficient is 5, so divide both sides by 5.

$$\boxed{\begin{array}{l}Divide \text{ both}\\ \text{sides by the}\\ \text{coefficient.}\end{array}}\quad \frac{5m}{5} = \frac{15}{5}$$
$$m = 3$$

Step 3   Check the solution by going back to the *original* equation.

$$\boxed{\begin{array}{l}\text{The solution}\\ \text{is 3.}\end{array}}\quad \begin{array}{l} 5m + 1 = 16 \\ \downarrow \\ 5\underbrace{(3)} + 1 = 16 \\ \underbrace{15 + 1}_{16} = 16 \\ 16 = 16 \checkmark \end{array}\quad \begin{array}{l}\text{Use the } original \text{ equation}\\ \text{and replace } m \text{ with 3.}\end{array}$$

Balances

When m is replaced with 3, the equation balances, so 3 is the correct solution.

······◀ **Work Problem** 1 **at the Side.**

Answers

1. (a) $r = 3$
   CHECK $13 = 13 \checkmark$
   Balances
   (b) $z = -2$
   CHECK $-10(-2) - 9 = 11$
   $$\underbrace{20}_{\qquad} - 9 = 11$$
   Balances $\underbrace{11}_{} = 11 \checkmark$

So far, variable terms have appeared on just one side of the equal sign. But some equations start with variable terms on both sides. In that case, you can use the addition property of equality to add the same *variable term* to both sides of the equation, just as you have added the same *number* to both sides.

First decide whether to keep the variable term on the left side, or to keep the variable term on the right side. It doesn't matter which one you keep; just pick one side or the other. Then use the addition property to "get rid of" the variable term on the *other* side by adding its opposite.

EXAMPLE 2 Solving an Equation with Variable Terms on Both Sides

Solve this equation and check the solution: $2x - 2 = 5x - 11$.

First let's keep $2x$, the variable term on the *left* side. Then we need to "get rid of" $5x$ on the *right* side. Add the opposite of $5x$, which is $-5x$.

To keep the balance, add $-5x$ to the left side also. Write $-5x$ under $2x$, *not* under 2.

$$2x - 2 = 5x - 11$$
$$\underline{-5x \qquad = -5x}$$
$$-3x - 2 = 0 - 11$$
$$\downarrow \quad \downarrow \qquad \downarrow \quad \downarrow$$
$$-3x + (-2) = 0 + (-11)$$

Write $-5x$ under $5x$, *not* under 11.

$5x + (-5x)$ is $0x$, or 0.

Change subtractions to adding the opposite.

To get $-3x$ by itself, add 2 to both sides.

$$\underline{\qquad 2 \qquad\qquad 2 \qquad}$$
$$-3x + 0 = 0 + (-9)$$

Divide both sides by -3, the coefficient of the variable term.

$$\frac{-3x}{-3} = \frac{-9}{-3}$$
$$x = 3$$

> The solution is **3**.

Suppose that, in the first step, we decided to keep $5x$ on the *right* side and "get rid of" $2x$ on the *left* side. Let's see what happens.

$$2x - 2 = 5x - 11$$

Add $-2x$ to both sides.

$$\underline{-2x \qquad = -2x}$$
$$0 - 2 = 3x - 11$$
$$\downarrow \quad \downarrow \qquad \downarrow \quad \downarrow$$
$$0 + (-2) = 3x + (-11)$$

Change subtractions to adding the opposite.

$$\underline{\qquad 11 \qquad\qquad 11 \qquad}$$
$$0 + 9 = 3x + 0$$

To get $3x$ by itself, add 11 to both sides.

$$\frac{9}{3} = \frac{3x}{3}$$

Divide both sides by 3.

> The solution is **3**.

$$3 = x$$

The two solutions are the same. In both cases, x balances with 3.

Notice that we used the addition principle *twice:* once to "get rid of" the variable term $2x$ and once to "get rid of" the number -11. We could have done those steps in the reverse order without changing the result.

Note

More than one sequence of steps will work. The basic approach is:

- Simplify each side of the equation, if possible.
- Get the variable term by itself on one side of the equal sign and a number by itself on the other side.
- Divide both sides by the coefficient of the variable term.

························ **Work Problem ② at the Side.** ▶

② Solve each equation *two ways.* First keep the variable term on the *left* side when you solve. Then solve again, keeping the variable term on the *right* side. Compare the solutions.

(a) Keep variable on *left* side.

$$3y - 1 = 2y + 7$$
$$\underline{-2y \qquad\qquad -2y}$$
$$y - 1 = 0 + 7$$
$$\downarrow \quad \downarrow \qquad\qquad$$
$$y + (-1) = 7 \quad \text{Now find the}$$
$$\underline{\qquad +1 \qquad\qquad +1 \quad} \text{solution.}$$

Keep variable on *right* side.

$$3y - 1 = 2y + 7$$
$$\underline{-3y \qquad\qquad -3y}$$
$$0 - 1 = -1y + 7$$
$$\downarrow \quad \downarrow \qquad\qquad$$
$$0 + (-1) = -1y + 7$$
$$\underline{\qquad -7 \qquad\qquad -7 \quad}$$
$$0 + (-8) = -1y + 0 \quad \text{Now}$$
$$\underbrace{\qquad\qquad}_{-8} = \underbrace{\qquad}_{-1y} \quad \begin{array}{l}\text{find the}\\ \text{solution.}\end{array}$$

(b) $3p - 2 = p - 6$

$$3p - 2 = p - 6$$

---

3 Solve each equation.

(a) $-12 = 4(y - 1)$

$-12 = 4(y-1)$ Use the distributive property.

$-12 = \underbrace{4 \cdot y} - \underbrace{4 \cdot 1}$

$-12 = \quad 4y \quad - \quad 4$

$\qquad \downarrow \qquad \downarrow$

$-12 = \quad 4y \; + (-4)$ Add 4 to both

$\underline{+\; 4 \qquad\qquad\quad +4}$ sides.

$\;\;-8 = \quad 4y$ Divide both sides by ____ and find the solution.

(b) $5(m + 4) = 20$

(c) $6(t - 2) = 18$

OBJECTIVE ▶ 2 **Solve equations using the distributive, addition, and division properties.** If an equation contains parentheses, check to see whether you can use the distributive property to remove them.

EXAMPLE 3 Solving an Equation Using the Distributive Property

Solve this equation and check the solution: $-6 = 3(y - 2)$.

We can use the distributive property to simplify the right side of the equation. Recall that

$$3(y - 2) \quad \text{can be written as} \quad \underbrace{3 \cdot y - 3 \cdot 2}_{3y \;-\; 6}$$

So the original equation $-6 = 3(y - 2)$ becomes $-6 = 3y - 6$.

$-6 = 3y - \quad 6$ Change subtraction to adding the opposite.

$\qquad\qquad \downarrow \qquad \downarrow$

$-6 = 3y + (-6)$

$\qquad\qquad\qquad\qquad$ To get $3y$ by itself,

$\underline{\;6 \qquad\qquad\qquad 6\;}$ add 6 to both sides.

$\dfrac{0}{3} = \dfrac{3y}{3}$ Divide both sides by 3, the coefficient of $3y$.

$0 = y$

The solution is 0.

CHECK $-6 = 3(y - \quad 2)$ Go back to the *original* equation and replace y with 0.

$\qquad\qquad\qquad \downarrow$

$-6 = 3(0 - \quad 2)$ Follow the order of operations; work inside parentheses first.

$\qquad\qquad\quad \downarrow \qquad \downarrow$

$-6 = 3\big[\underbrace{0 + (-2)}\big]$ Change subtraction to addition. Brackets show what to do first: $0 + (-2)$ is -2.

$-6 = \quad \underbrace{3(-2)}$

$-6 = \qquad -6 \;\checkmark$ Balances

When y is replaced with 0, the equation balances, so **0 is the correct solution.**

◀ **Work Problem 3 at the Side.**

Here is a summary of all the steps you can use to solve an equation. Sometimes you will use only two or three steps, and sometimes you will need all five steps. (See the example on the next page.)

Solving an Equation

Step 1   If possible, use the *distributive property* to remove parentheses.

Step 2   *Combine* any like terms on the left side of the equation. *Combine* any like terms on the right side of the equation.

Step 3   *Add* the same amount to both sides of the equation so that the variable term ends up by itself on one side of the equal sign and a number is by itself on the other side. You may have to do this step more than once.

Step 4   *Divide* both sides by the coefficient of the variable term to find the solution.

Step 5   *Check* your solution by going back to the *original* equation. Replace the variable with your solution. Follow the order of operations to complete the calculations. If the two sides of the equation balance, your solution is correct.

Answers

3. **(a)** Divide both sides by 4; $\dfrac{-8}{4} = \dfrac{4y}{4}$; $-2 = y$

    (b) $m = 0$ **(c)** $t = 5$

EXAMPLE 4 Solving an Equation

Solve this equation and check the solution: $8 + 5(m + 2) = 6 + 2m$

Step 1 Use the distributive property on the left side.

$$8 + 5(m + 2) = 6 + 2m$$

Step 2 Combine like terms on the left side.

$$8 + 5m + 10 = 6 + 2m$$ No like terms on the right side

$$5m + 18 = 6 + 2m$$

Step 3 Add $-2m$ to both sides.

$$\frac{-2m \qquad\qquad -2m}{3m + 18 = 6 + 0}$$

$$3m + 18 = 6$$

Step 3 To get $3m$ by itself, add -18 to both sides.

$$\frac{-18 \qquad -18}{3m + 0 = -12}$$

Step 4 Divide both sides by 3, the coefficient of the variable term $3m$.

$$\frac{3m}{3} = \frac{-12}{3}$$

$$m = -4$$

The solution is -4.

Step 5 CHECK

$$8 + 5(m + 2) = 6 + 2m$$ Replace each m with -4.

$$8 + 5(-4 + 2) = 6 + 2(-4)$$

$$8 + \quad 5(-2) = 6 + (-8)$$

$$8 + \quad (-10) = \quad -2$$

$$-2 = \quad -2 \checkmark \text{ Balances}$$

When m is replaced with -4, the equation balances, so -4 **is the correct solution** (**not** -2).

··········· **Work Problem 4 at the Side.** ▶

---

4 Solve each equation and check each solution.

(a) $3(b + 7) = 2b - 1$

$$3(b + 7) = 2b - 1$$

$$3b + 21 = 2b + (-1)$$

$$\frac{-2b \qquad\qquad -2b}{b + 21 = 0 + (-1)}$$ Find the solution.

(b) $6 - 2n = 14 + 4(n - 5)$

Answers

4. (a) $b + 21 = -1$ **(b)** $n = 2$

$$\frac{-21 \quad -21}{b + 0 = -22}$$

$$b = -22$$

2.5 Exercises

CONCEPT CHECK *Solve each equation and check each solution.* ***See Example 1.***

1. $7p + 5 = 12$

$\underline{ -5 \quad -5}$

$\underbrace{7p + 0}_{} = 7$ Find the solution.

CHECK $\underbrace{7p}_{\downarrow\downarrow} + 5 = 12$

$\underbrace{7(1)}_{} + 5 = 12$

$\underbrace{7 + 5}_{} = 12$

$\underline{} = \underline{}$

2. $6k + 3 = 15$

$\underline{ -3 \quad -3}$

$\underbrace{6k + 0}_{} = 12$ Find the solution.

CHECK $\underbrace{6k}_{\downarrow\downarrow} + 3 = 15$

$\underbrace{6(2)}_{} + 3 = 15$

$\underbrace{12 + 3}_{} = 15$

$\underline{} = \underline{}$

3. $2 = 8y - 6$

$2 = 8y + (-6)$

$\underline{+6 +6}$

$8 = \underbrace{8y + 0}_{}$ Find the solution.

CHECK $2 = 8y - 6$

$\downarrow$

4. $10 = 11p - 12$

CHECK

5. $28 = -9a + 10$

CHECK

6. $-4k + 5 = 5$

CHECK

Solve each equation. Show your work. ***See Example 1.***

7. $-3m + 1 = 1$

8. $75 = -10w + 25$

9. $-5x - 4 = 16$

10. $-12b - 3 = 21$

*In Exercises 11–14, solve each equation **two** ways. First keep the variable term on the left side when you solve it. Then solve it again, keeping the variable term on the right side. Finally, check your solution. **See Example 2.***

11. $6p - 2 = 4p + 6$ $\qquad$ $6p - 2 = 4p + 6$ $\qquad$ CHECK $6p - 2 = 4p + 6$

12. $5y - 5 = 2y + 10$ $\qquad$ $5y - 5 = 2y + 10$ $\qquad$ CHECK $5y - 5 = 2y + 10$

13. $-2k - 6 = 6k + 10$ $\qquad$ $-2k - 6 = 6k + 10$ $\qquad$ CHECK

14. $5x + 4 = -3x - 4$ $\qquad$ $5x + 4 = -3x - 4$ $\qquad$ CHECK

First simplify where possible. Then solve each equation. Show your work.

15. $-18 + 7a = 2a + 3 + 4$ $\qquad$ **16.** $-10 + 5r = -7 - 12 - 1$ $\qquad$ **17.** $-3t = 8t$

18. $15z = -9z$

19. $4 + 16 - 2 = 2 - 2b$

20. $-9 + 2z = 9z - 1 + 13$

Use the distributive property to help you solve each equation. Show your work.
See Example 3.

21. $8(w - 2) = 32$

22. $9(b - 4) = 27$

23. $-10 = 2(y + 4)$

24. $-3 = 3(x + 6)$

25. $-4(t + 2) = 12$

26. $-5(k + 3) = 25$

27. $6(x - 5) = -30$

28. $7(r - 7) = -49$

29. $-12 = 12(h - 2)$

30. $-11 = 11(c - 3)$

31. $0 = -2(y + 2)$

32. $0 = -9(b + 1)$

Solve each equation. Show your work. See Example 4.

33. $6m + 18 = 0$

34. $8p - 40 = 0$

35. $6 = 9w - 12$

36. $8 = 8h + 24$

37. $5x = 3x + 10$

38. $7n = -2n - 36$

39. $2a + 11 = 8a - 7$

40. $r - 10 = 10r + 8$

41. $7 - 5b = 28 + 2b$

42. $1 - 8t = -9 - 3t$

43. $-20 + 2k = k - 4k$

44. $6y - y = -16 + y$

45. $10(c - 6) + 4 = 2 + c - 58$

46. $8(z + 7) - 6 = z + 60 - 10$

47. $-18 + 13y + 3 = 3(5y - 1) - 2$

48. $3 + 5h - 9 = 4(3h + 4) - 1$

49. $6 - 4n + 3n = 20 - 35$

50. $-19 + 8 = 6p - 7p - 5$

51. $6(c - 2) = 7(c - 6)$

52. $-3(5 + x) = 4(x - 2)$

53. $-5(2p + 2) - 7 = 3(2p + 5)$

54. $4(3m - 6) = 72 + 3(m - 8)$

55. $2(3b - 2) - 5b = 4(b - 1) + 8b$

56. $-3(w + 3) + 10 = -1(w + 14) + w$

57. CONCEPT CHECK   Solve $-2t - 10 = 3t + 5$. Show each step you take while solving it. Next to each step, write a sentence that explains what you did in that step. Be sure to tell when you used the addition property of equality and when you used the division property of equality.

58. CONCEPT CHECK   Explain the distributive property in your own words. Show two examples of using the distributive property to remove parentheses in an expression.

59. Here is one student's solution to an equation. Show how to check the solution. If the solution doesn't check, explain the error and correct it.

$$
\begin{array}{rcl}
-8 + 4a & = & 2a + 2 \\
\underline{-2a} & & \underline{-2a} \\
-10 + 4a & = & 0 + 2 \\
-10 + 4a & = & 2 \\
\underline{10} & & \underline{10} \\
0 + 4a & = & 12 \\
\dfrac{4a}{4} & = & \dfrac{12}{4} \\
a & = & 3
\end{array}
$$

60. Here is one student's solution to an equation. Show how to check the solution. If the solution doesn't check, explain the error and correct it.

$$
\begin{array}{rcl}
2(x + 4) & = & -16 \\
2x + 4 & = & -16 \\
\underline{-4} & & \underline{-4} \\
2x + 0 & = & -20 \\
\dfrac{2x}{2} & = & \dfrac{-20}{2} \\
x & = & -10
\end{array}
$$

Relating Concepts (Exercises 61–64)   For Individual or Group Work

Work Exercises 61–64 in order.

61. (a) Suppose that the sum of two numbers is negative and you know that one of the numbers is positive. What can you conclude about the other number?

(b) How can you tell, just by looking, that the solution to $x + 5 = -7$ must be a negative number? Recall your answer from part (a).

62. (a) Suppose that the sum of two numbers is positive and you know that one of the numbers is negative. What can you conclude about the other number?

(b) How can you tell, just by looking, that the solution to $-8 + d = 2$ must be a positive number? Recall your answer from part (a).

63. (a) Suppose the product of two numbers is negative and you know that one of the numbers is negative. What can you conclude about the other number?

(b) How can you tell, just by looking, that the solution to $-15n = -255$ must be positive?

64. (a) Suppose the product of two numbers is positive and you know that one of the numbers is negative. What can you conclude about the other number?

(b) How can you tell, just by looking, that the solution to $437 = -23y$ must be negative?

Study Skills
TIPS FOR TAKING MATH TESTS

OBJECTIVES

1 Apply suggestions to tests and quizzes.

2 Develop a set of "best practices" to apply while testing.

Improving Your Test Score

To Improve Your Test Score	Comments
Come prepared with a pencil, eraser, and calculator, if allowed. If you are easily distracted, sit away from high-traffic areas.	**Working in pencil lets you erase,** keeping your work neat and readable.
Scan the entire test, note the point value of different problems, and plan your time accordingly. Allow at least five minutes to check your work at the end of the testing time.	If you have 50 minutes to do 20 problems, $50 \div 20 = 2.5$ minutes per problem. **Spend less time on easy ones,** more time on problems with higher point values.
Read directions carefully, and circle any significant words. When you finish a problem, read the directions again to make sure you did what was asked.	**Pay attention to announcements** written on the board or made by your instructor. Ask if you don't understand. You don't want to get problems wrong because you misread the directions!
Show your work. Most math teachers give partial credit if some of the steps in your work are correct, even if the final answer is wrong. **Write neatly.** If you like to scribble when first working or checking a problem, do it on scratch paper.	**If your teacher can't read your writing, you won't get credit for it.** If you need more space to work, ask if you can use extra pieces of paper that you hand in with your test paper.
Check that the **answer to an application problem is reasonable,** makes sense, and includes the units. Read the problem again to make sure you've answered the question.	**Use common sense.** Can the father really be seven years old? Would a month's rent be $32,140? Label your answer: $, years, inches, etc.
To check for careless errors, you need to **rework the problem again, without looking at your previous work.** Cover up your work with a piece of scratch paper, and pretend you are doing the problem for the first time. Then compare the two answers.	If you just "look over" your work, your mind can make the same mistake again without noticing it. Reworking the problem from the beginning **forces you to rethink it.** If possible, use a different method to solve the problem the second time.

Reducing Anxiety

To Reduce Anxiety	Comments
Do not try to review up until the last minute before the test. Instead, go for a walk, do some deep breathing, and arrive just in time for the test. Ignore other students.	Listening to anxious classmates before the test **may cause you to panic.** Moderate exercise and deep breathing will calm your mind.

Reducing Anxiety (Continued)

To Reduce Anxiety	Comments
Do a "knowledge dump" as soon as you get the test. Write important notes to yourself in a corner of the test paper: formulas, or common errors you want to watch out for.	Writing down tips and things that you've memorized **lets you relax;** you won't have to worry about forgetting those things and can refer to them as needed.
Do the easy problems first to build confidence. If you feel your anxiety starting to build, *immediately* stop for a minute, close your eyes, and take several slow, deep breaths.	Greater confidence helps you **get the easier problems correct.** Anxiety causes shallow breathing, which leads to confusion and reduced concentration. Deep breathing calms you.
As you work on more difficult problems, **notice your "inner voice."** You may have negative thoughts such as, "I can't do it," or "Who cares about this test anyway." In your mind, yell "STOP" and take several deep, slow breaths. Or, replace the negative thought with a positive one.	Here are **examples of positive statements.** Try writing one of them on the top of your test paper. • I know I can do it. • I can do this one step at a time. • I've studied hard, and I'll do the best I can.
If you still can't solve a difficult problem when you come back to it the second time, **make a guess and do not change it.** In this situation, your first guess is your best bet. Do not change the answer just because you're a little unsure. **Change it only if you find an obvious mistake.**	If you are thinking about changing an answer, be sure you have a good reason for changing it. If you cannot find a specific error, leave your first answer alone. **When the tests are returned, check to see if changing answers helped or hurt you.**
Read the harder problems twice. Write down *anything* that might help solve the problem: a formula, a picture, etc. If you still can't get it, circle the problem and **come back to it later.** Do *not* erase any of the things you wrote down.	If you know even a *little* bit about the problem, write it down. The **answer may come to you** as you work on it, or you may get partial credit. Don't spend too long on any one problem. Your subconscious mind will work on the tough problem while you go on with the test.
Ignore students who finish early. Use the entire test time. *You do not get extra credit for finishing early.* Use the extra time to rework problems and correct careless errors.	Students who leave early are often the ones who didn't study or who are too anxious to continue working. If they bother you, **sit as far from the door as possible.**

Why Are These Suggestions Brain Friendly?

Several suggestions address anxiety. **Reducing anxiety** allows your brain to make the connections between dendrites; in other words, you can think clearly.

Remember that **your brain continues to work** on a difficult problem even if you skip it and go on to the next one. Your subconscious mind will come through for you if you are open to the idea!

Some of the suggestions ask you to **use your common sense.** Follow the directions, show your work, write neatly, and pay attention to whether your answers really make sense.

Chapter 2 *Summary*

Key Terms

2.1

variable A variable is a letter that represents a number that varies or changes, depending on the situation.

constant A constant is a number that is added or subtracted in an expression. It does not vary. For example, 5 is the constant in the expression $c + 5$.

expression An expression expresses, or tells, the rule for doing something. It is a combination of operations on variables and numbers. An expression does *not* have an equal sign.

evaluate the expression To evaluate an expression, replace each variable with specific values (numbers). Then do all possible calculations, following the order of operations. There are no variables in the final answer.

coefficient The number part in a multiplication expression is the coefficient. For example, 4 is the coefficient in the expression $4s$.

2.2

simplifying expressions To simplify an expression, write it in a simpler way by combining all the like terms.

term Each addend in an expression is a term.

constant term A constant term is a type of term that is just a number. In the expression $4x + 8$, the constant term is 8.

variable term A variable term has a number part (called the coefficient) multiplied by a variable part (a letter). In the expression $4x + 8$, the variable term is $4x$.

like terms Like terms are terms with exactly the same variable parts (the same letters and exponents). The coefficients may be different.

2.3

equations An equation has an equal sign. It shows the relationship between what is known about a problem and what isn't known. The left side of the equation has the same value as the right side, so the two sides balance.

solve the equation To solve an equation, find a number that can replace the variable and make the equation balance.

solution A solution of an equation is a number that can replace the variable and make the equation balance.

addition property of equality The addition property of equality states that adding the same quantity to both sides of an equation will keep it balanced.

check the solution To check the solution of an equation, go back to the *original* equation and replace the variable with the solution. If the equation balances, the solution is correct.

2.4

division property of equality The division property of equality states that dividing both sides of an equation by the same nonzero number will keep it balanced.

Test Your Word Power

See how well you have learned the vocabulary in this chapter. The answers are on the next page.

1 **A variable**
  A. can only be the letter x
  B. is never an addend in an expression
  C. represents a number that varies.

2 Which expression has 2 as a **coefficient?**
  A. x^2
  B. $2x$
  C. $2 - x$

3 Which expression has 4 as a **constant** term?
  A. $4y$
  B. y^4
  C. $4 + y$

4 Which expression has four **terms?**
  A. $2 + 3x = -6 + x$
  B. $2 + 3x - 6 + x$
  C. $(2)(3x)(-6)(x)$

5 **Like terms**
  A. have the same coefficients
  B. have the same solutions
  C. have the same variable parts.

6 To **simplify an expression,**
  A. combine all the like terms
  B. multiply the exponents
  C. add the same quantity to both sides.

Answers to Test Your Word Power

1. C; *Example:* In $c + 5$, the variable is c.

2. B; *Example:* $2y^3$ and $2n$ also have 2 as a coefficient.

3. C; *Example:* $-5a^2 + 4$ also has 4 as a constant term.

4. B; *Example:* $3y^2 - 6y + 2y - 5$ also has four terms. Choice (A) is an equation, not an expression; choice (C) is one term with four *factors*.

5. C; *Example:* $7n^2$ and $-3n^2$ are like terms.

6. A; *Example:* To simplify $4a - 9 + 6a$, combine $4a$ and $6a$ by adding the coefficients. The simplified expression is $10a - 9$.

Quick Review

Concepts

Examples

2.1 Evaluating Expressions

Replace each variable with the specified value. Then follow the order of operations to simplify the expression.

The expression for ordering textbooks for two prealgebra classes is $2c + 10$, where c is the class limit. Evaluate the expression when the class limit is 24.

$$2c + 10 \quad \text{Replace } c \text{ with 24.}$$
$$2 \cdot 24 + 10 \quad \text{Multiply first.}$$
$$48 \quad + 10 \quad \text{Add last.}$$
$$58 \quad \text{Order 58 books.}$$

2.1 Using Exponents with Variables

An exponent next to a variable tells how many times to use the variable as a factor in multiplication.

Rewrite $-6x^4$ without exponents.

$$-6x^4 \quad \text{can be written as} \quad -6 \cdot x \cdot x \cdot x \cdot x$$

Coefficient is -6 — x is used as a factor 4 times.

2.1 Evaluating Expressions with Exponents

Rewrite the expression without exponents, replace each variable with the specified value, and multiply all the factors.

Evaluate x^3y when x is -4 and y is 5.

x^3y means $x \cdot x \cdot x \cdot y$ — Replace x with -4 and y with 5.

$$(-4) \cdot (-4) \cdot (-4) \cdot 5 \quad \text{Multiply two factors at a time.}$$
$$16 \quad \cdot (-4) \cdot 5$$
$$-64 \quad \cdot 5$$
$$-320$$

2.2 Identifying Like Terms

Like terms have *exactly* the same letters and exponents. The coefficients may be different.

List the like terms in this expression. Then identify the coefficients of the like terms.

$$-3b + (-3b^2) + 3ab + b + 3$$

The like terms are $-3b$ and b. The coefficient of $-3b$ is -3, and the coefficient of b is understood to be 1.

Concepts	Examples

2.2 Combining Like Terms

Step 1 If there are any variable terms with no coefficient, write in the understood 1.

Step 2 Change any subtractions to adding the opposite.

Step 3 Find like terms.

Step 4 Add the coefficients of like terms, keeping the variable part the same.

Simplify $4x^2 - 10 + x^2 + 15$.

$$4x^2 - \quad 10 + \quad 1x^2 + 15 \quad \text{Write understood 1.}$$

$$4x^2 + (-10) + \quad 1x^2 + 15 \quad \begin{array}{l}\text{Change subtraction to}\\ \text{adding the opposite.}\end{array}$$

$$4x^2 + \quad 1x^2 + (-10) + 15 \quad \begin{array}{l}\text{Combine } 4x^2 + 1x^2.\\ \text{The variable part stays}\\ \text{the same.}\\ \text{Also combine } -10 + 15.\end{array}$$

$$(4 + 1)x^2 \quad + \quad 5$$

$$5x^2 \quad + \quad 5$$

The simplified expression is $5x^2 + 5$.

2.2 Simplifying Multiplication Expressions

Use the associative property to rewrite the expression so that the two number parts can be multiplied. The variable part stays the same.

Simplify: $-7(5k)$

Use the associative property of multiplication.

$$-7 \cdot (5 \cdot k) \text{ can be written as } (-7 \cdot 5) \cdot k$$

$$-35 \cdot k$$

$$-35k$$

The simplified expression is $-35k$.

2.2 Using the Distributive Property

Multiplication distributes over addition and over subtraction. Be careful to multiply *every* term inside the parentheses by the number outside the parentheses.

Simplify.

(a) $6(w - 4)$ can be written as $6 \cdot w - 6 \cdot 4$

$$6w \quad - \quad 24$$

The simplified expression is $6w - 24$.

(b) $-3(2b + 5)$ can be written as $-3 \cdot 2b + (-3) \cdot 5$

$$-6b \quad + \quad (-15)$$

Use the definition of subtraction "in reverse" to write $-6b + (-15)$ as $-6b - 15$.

The simplified expression is $-6b - 15$.

2.3 Solving and Checking Equations Using the Addition Property of Equality

If possible, *simplify* the expression on one or both sides of the equal sign.

Next, to get the variable by itself on one side of the equal sign, *add* the same number to both sides.

Finally, *check* the solution by going back to the original equation and replacing the variable with the solution. If the equation balances, the solution is correct.

Solve this equation and check the solution.

$$-5 + 8 = \quad 9 + r \quad \begin{array}{l}\text{Simplify the left side by}\\ \text{adding } -5 + 8.\end{array}$$

$$3 = \quad 9 + r \quad \begin{array}{l}\text{To get } r \text{ by itself, add the}\\ \text{opposite of 9, which is } -9,\\ \text{to both sides.}\end{array}$$

$$\underline{-9 \quad \quad -9}$$

$$-6 = \quad 0 + r$$

$$-6 = \quad r$$

The solution is -6. *(Continued)*

Concepts	Examples

2.3 Solving and Checking Equations Using the Addition Property of Equality *(Continued)*

CHECK $-5 + 8 = 9 + r$ — Use the original equation and replace r with -6.

$$-5 + 8 = 9 + (-6)$$

$$3 = 3 \checkmark \quad \text{Balances}$$

When r is replaced with -6, the equation balances, so -6 is the correct solution (**not** 3).

2.4 Solving and Checking Equations Using the Division Property of Equality

If possible, *simplify* the expression on one or both sides of the equal sign.

Next, to get the variable by itself on one side of the equal sign, *divide* both sides by the coefficient of the variable term.

Finally, *check* the solution by going back to the original equation and replacing the variable with the solution. If the equation balances, the solution is correct.

Solve this equation and check the solution.

Simplify the left side. Change subtraction to adding the opposite.
$$2h - 6h = 18 + 22 \quad \text{Simplify the right side; add } 18 + 22.$$
$$2h + (-6h) = 40$$
$$-4h = 40$$

Divide by -4, the coefficient of $-4h$.
$$\frac{-4h}{-4} = \frac{40}{-4} \quad \text{Also divide 40 by } -4 \text{ to keep the balance.}$$
$$h = -10$$

The solution is -10.

CHECK $2h - 6h = 18 + 22$ — Original equation; replace h with -10.
$$2(-10) - 6(-10) = 40$$
$$-20 - (-60) = 40$$
$$-20 + (+60)$$
$$40 = 40 \checkmark \quad \text{Balances}$$

When h is replaced with -10, the equation balances, so -10 is the correct solution (**not** 40).

2.4 Solving Equations Such as $-x = 5$

As the last step in solving an equation, do **not** leave a negative sign in front of the variable, such as $-x = 5$, because $-x$ is **not** the same as x. Divide both sides by -1, the understood coefficient of $-x$.

Solve this equation and check the solution.
$$9 = -n$$

Write the understood -1 as the coefficient of n.
$$9 = -n \quad \text{can be written as} \quad 9 = -1n$$

Now divide both sides by -1.
$$\frac{9}{-1} = \frac{-1n}{-1}$$
$$-9 = n$$

The solution is -9.

(Continued)

Concepts		Examples	

2.4 Solving Equations Such as $-x = 5$ (Continued)

CHECK
$$9 = -n \qquad \text{Original equation}$$
$$9 = -1n \qquad \text{Write understood } -1.$$
$$9 = -1(-9) \qquad \text{Replace } n \text{ with } -9.$$
$$9 = \quad 9 \checkmark \qquad \text{Balances}$$

When n is replaced with -9, the equation balances, so -9 is the correct solution (**not** 9).

2.5 Solving Equations with Several Steps

Solve this equation and check the solution.

Step 1 If possible, use the distributive property to remove parentheses.

Step 1
$$3 + 2(y + 8) = 5y + 4$$

Step 2 Combine any like terms on the left side of the equal sign. Combine any like terms on the right side of the equal sign.

Step 2
$$3 + 2y + 16 = 5y + 4$$
$$2y + 19 = 5y + 4$$

Step 3 Add the same amount to both sides of the equation so that the variable term ends up by itself on one side of the equal sign, and a number is by itself on the other side. You may have to do this step more than once.

Step 3
$$\underline{-2y \qquad\qquad -2y}$$
$$0 + 19 = 3y + 4$$

Step 3
$$\underline{\qquad -4 \qquad\qquad -4}$$
$$0 + 15 = 3y + 0$$

Step 4 Divide both sides by the coefficient of the variable term to find the solution.

Step 4
$$\frac{15}{3} = \frac{3y}{3}$$
$$5 = y$$

The solution is 5.

Step 5 Check the solution by going back to the original equation. Replace the variable with the solution. If the equation balances, the solution is correct.

CHECK
Step 5
$$3 + 2(y + 8) = 5y + 4 \qquad \text{Original equation}$$
$$3 + 2(5 + 8) = 5(5) + 4$$
$$3 + 2(13) = 25 + 4$$
$$3 + 26 = 29$$
$$29 = 29 \checkmark \qquad \text{Balances}$$

When y is replaced with 5, the equation balances, so 5 is the correct solution (**not** 29).

Chapter 2 *Review Exercises*

2.1

1. (a) Identify the variable, the coefficient, and the constant in this expression.

$$-3 + 4k$$

(b) Circle the expression that has 20 as the constant term and -9 as the coefficient.

$20m - 9$ $-9 + 20x$

$-9y + 20$ $20 + 9n$

2. The expression for ordering test tubes for a chemistry lab is $4c + 10$, where c is the class limit. Evaluate the expression when

(a) the class limit is 15.

(b) the class limit is 24.

3. Rewrite each expression without exponents.

(a) $x^2 y^4$

(b) $5ab^3$

4. Evaluate each expression when m is 2, n is -3, and p is 4.

(a) n^2 **(b)** n^3

(c) $-4mp^2$ **(d)** $5m^4 n^2$

2.2 *Simplify.*

5. $ab + ab^2 + 2ab$

6. $-3x + 2y - x - 7$

7. $-8(-2g^3)$

8. $4(3r^2 t)$

9. $5(k + 2)$

10. $-2(3b + 4)$

11. $3(2y - 4) + 12$

12. $-4 + 6(4x + 1) - 4x$

13. Write an expression with four terms that *cannot* be simplified.

2.3 *Solve each equation and check each solution.*

14. $16 + n = 5$ **CHECK** $16 + \quad n \quad = 5$

15. $-4 + 2 = 2a - 6 - a$ **CHECK**

$$-4 + 2 = 2a - \quad 6 \quad - \quad a$$

2.4 *Solve each equation. Show your work.*

16. $48 = -6m$

17. $k - 5k = -40$

18. $-17 + 11 + 6 = 7t$

19. $-2p + 5p = 3 - 21$ **20.** $-30 = 3(-5r)$ **21.** $12 = -h$

2.5 *Solve each equation. Show your work.*

22. $12w - 4 = 8w + 12$ **23.** $0 = -4(c + 2)$

24. Every Wednesday is "treat day" at the office. The person who brings the treats buys two treat items for each employee plus four extras. If Roger brings 34 doughnuts, solve the equation $34 = 2n + 4$ to find the number of employees.

Mixed Review Exercises

Solve each equation. Show your work.

25. $12 + 7a = 4a - 3$ **26.** $-2(p - 3) = -14$ **27.** $10y = 6y + 20$

28. $2m - 7m = 5 - 20$ **29.** $20 = 3x - 7$ **30.** $b + 6 = 3b - 8$

31. $z + 3 = 0$ **32.** $3(2n - 1) = 3(n + 3)$ **33.** $-4 + 46 = 7(-3t + 6)$

34. $6 + 10d - 19 = 2(3d + 4) - 1$ **35.** $-4(3b + 9) = 24 + 3(2b - 8)$

Chapter 2 Test

The Chapter Test Prep Videos with test solutions are available on DVD, in MyMathLab, and on YouTube — search "LialPrealgebra" and click on "Channels."

1. Identify the parts of this expression: $-7w + 6$ Choose from these labels: variable, constant, coefficient.

2. The expression for buying hot dogs for the company picnic is $3a + 2c$, where a is the number of adults and c is the number of children. Evaluate the expression when there are 45 adults and 21 children.

Rewrite each expression without exponents.

3. $x^5 y^3$

4. $4ab^4$

5. Evaluate $-2s^2 t$ when s is -5 and t is 4.

Simplify each expression.

6. $3w^3 - 8w^3 + w^3$

7. $xy - xy$

8. $-6c - 5 + 7c + 5$

9. $3m^2 - 3m + 3mn$

10. $-10(4b^2)$

11. $-5(-3k)$

12. $7(3t + 4)$

13. $-4(a + 6)$

14. $-8 + 6(x - 2) + 5$

15. $-9b - c - 3 + 9 + 2c$

Solve each equation and check each solution.

16. $-4 = x - 9$ **CHECK**

17. $-7w = 77$ **CHECK**

18. $-p = 14$ **CHECK**

19. $-15 = -3(a + 2)$ **CHECK**

Solve each equation. Show your work.

20. $6n + 8 - 5n = -4 + 4$

21. $5 - 20 = 2m - 3m$

22. $-2x + 2 = 5x + 9$

23. $3m - 5 = 7m - 13$

24. $2 + 7b - 44 = -3b + 12 + 9b$

25. $3c - 24 = 6(c - 4)$

26. Write an equation that requires the *addition* property of equality to solve it and has -4 as its solution. Then write a different equation that requires the *division* property of equality to solve it and has -4 as its solution. Show how to solve each equation.

Chapters 1–2 Cumulative Review Exercises

1. Write this number in words.
   306,000,004,210

2. Write this number, using digits.
   Eight hundred million, sixty-six thousand

3. Write $<$ or $>$ between each pair of numbers to make a true statement.

   (a) -3 _____ -10 (b) -1 _____ 0

4. Name the property illustrated by each example.

   (a) $-6 + 2 = 2 + (-6)$

   (b) $0 \cdot 25 = 0$

   (c) $5(-6 + 4) = 5 \cdot (-6) + 5 \cdot 4$

5. (a) Round 9047 to the nearest hundred.

   (b) Round 289,610 to the nearest thousand.

Simplify.

6. $0 - 8$

7. $|-6| + |4|$

8. $-3(-10)$

9. $(-5)^2$

10. $\dfrac{-42}{-6}$

11. $-19 + 19$

12. $(-4)^3$

13. $\dfrac{-14}{0}$

14. $-5 \cdot 12$

15. $-20 - 20$

16. $\dfrac{45}{-5}$

17. $-50 + 25$

18. $-10 + 6(4 - 7)$

19. $\dfrac{-20 - 3(-5) + 16}{(-4)^2 - 3^3}$

First use front end rounding to estimate the answer to each application problem. Then find the exact answer.

20. One Siberian tiger was tracked for 22 days while it was searching for food. It traveled 616 miles. What was the average distance it traveled each day?

    Estimate:

    Exact:

21. The temperature in Siberia got down to -48 degrees one night. The next day the temperature rose 23 degrees. What was the daytime temperature?

    Estimate:

    Exact:

22. Doug owned 52 shares of Mathtronic stock that had a total value of $2132. Yesterday the value of each share dropped $8. What are his shares worth now?

    Estimate:

    Exact:

23. Ikuko's monthly rent is $758 plus $45 for parking. How much will she spend for rent and parking in one year?

    Estimate:

    Exact:

24. Rewrite $-4ab^3c^2$ without exponents.

25. Evaluate $3xy^3$ when x is -5 and y is -2.

Simplify.

26. $3h - 7h + 5h$

27. $c^2d - c^2d$

28. $4n^2 - 4n + 6 - 8 + n^2$

29. $-10(3b^2)$

30. $7(4p - 4)$

31. $3 + 5(-2w^2 - 3) + w^2$

Solve each equation and check each solution.

32. $3x = x - 8$ **CHECK**

33. $-44 = -2 + 7y$ **CHECK**

34. $2k - 5k = -21$ **CHECK**

35. $m - 6 = -2m + 6$ **CHECK**

Solve each equation. Show your work.

36. $4 - 4x = 18 + 10x$

37. $18 = -r$

38. $-8b - 11 + 7b = b - 1$

39. $-2(t + 1) = 4(1 - 2t)$

40. $5 + 6y - 23 = 5(2y + 8) - 10$

3 Solving Application Problems

In this chapter, you'll apply your skills for solving equations to real-world situations. Some examples are using formulas for perimeter and area to solve problems about football fields, volleyball courts, gymnastics floor mats, hockey rinks, and camping tents.

3.1 Problem Solving: Perimeter

3.2 Problem Solving: Area

Summary Exercises *Perimeter and Area*

3.3 Solving Application Problems with One Unknown Quantity

Study Skills *Tips for Improving Test Scores*

3.1 Problem Solving: Perimeter

VOCABULARY TIP

Perimeter Remember, in **perimeter, peri** means "around," and **meter** means "measure." To find the perimeter, you measure around the outside edges of a flat shape. Write the perimeter using **linear units,** such as feet or yards; for example, 10 **ft** or 15 **yd.**

OBJECTIVE ① **Use the formula for perimeter of a square to find the perimeter or the length of one side.** If you have ever studied geometry, you probably used several different formulas such as $P = 2l + 2w$ and $A = lw$. A **formula** is just a shorthand way of writing a rule for solving a particular type of problem. A formula uses variables (letters) and it has an equal sign, so it is an equation. That means you can use the equation-solving techniques you learned in **Chapter 2** to work with formulas.

But let's start at the beginning. Geometry was developed centuries ago when people needed a way to measure land. The name *geometry* comes from the Greek *geo,* meaning earth, and *metron,* meaning measure. Today we still use geometry to measure land. It is also important in architecture, construction, navigation, art and design, physics, chemistry, and astronomy. You can use geometry at home when you buy carpet or wallpaper, hang a picture, or do home repairs. In this chapter you'll learn about two basic ideas, perimeter and area. Other geometry concepts will appear in later chapters.

In **Chapter 2,** you found the *perimeter* of a square garden.

Perimeter

The distance around the outside edges of any flat shape is called the **perimeter** of the shape.

To review, a **square** has four sides that are all the same length. Also, the sides meet to form *right angles,* which measure 90° (90 degrees). This means that the sides form "square corners." Two examples of squares are shown below.

To find the *perimeter* of a square, we can "unfold" the shape so the four sides lie end-to-end, as shown below.

Now we can see the total length of the four sides. The total length is the *perimeter* of the square. We can find the perimeter by adding.

$$\text{Perimeter} = 9\text{ ft} + 9\text{ ft} + 9\text{ ft} + 9\text{ ft} = 36\text{ ft}$$

A shorter way is to multiply the length of one side times 4, because all 4 sides are the same length.

Finding the Perimeter of a Square

Perimeter of a square = side + side + side + side

or $P = 4 \cdot \text{side}$

$P = 4s$

EXAMPLE 1 Finding the Perimeter of a Square

Find the perimeter of the square on the previous page that measures 9 ft on each side.

Use the formula for perimeter of a square, $P = 4s$. You know that for this particular square, the value of s is 9 ft.

$P = 4s$ Formula for perimeter of a square

$P = 4 \cdot 9 \text{ ft}$ Replace s with 9 ft. Multiply 4 times 9 ft.

$P = 36 \text{ ft}$ Write 36 ft; ft is the unit of measure.

The perimeter of the square is 36 ft. Notice that this answer matches the result we got by adding the four sides.

······ **Work Problem ❶ at the Side.** ▶

EXAMPLE 2 Finding the Length of One Side of a Square

If the perimeter of a square is 40 cm, find the length of one side. (Note: **cm** is the short way to write *centimeters*.)

Use the formula for perimeter of a square, $P = 4s$. This time you know that the value of P (the perimeter) is 40 cm.

$P = 4s$ Formula for perimeter of a square

$40 \text{ cm} = 4s$ Replace P with 40 cm.

$\dfrac{40 \text{ cm}}{4} = \dfrac{4s}{4}$ To get the variable by itself on the right side, divide both sides by 4.

$10 \text{ cm} = s$

The length of one side of the square is 10 cm.   ⟵ Write **cm** as part of your answer.

CHECK Check the solution by drawing a square and labeling the length of each side as 10 cm. The perimeter is $10 \text{ cm} + 10 \text{ cm} + 10 \text{ cm} + 10 \text{ cm} = 40 \text{ cm}.$

Matches the perimeter given in the problem.

······ **Work Problem ❷ at the Side.** ▶

OBJECTIVE ▶ ❷ Use the formula for perimeter of a rectangle to find the perimeter, the length, or the width. A **rectangle** is a figure with four sides that meet to form right angles, which measure 90°. Each set of opposite sides is parallel and congruent (has the same length). Three examples of rectangles are shown on the next page.

---

❶ Find the perimeter of each square, using the appropriate formula.

(GS) **(a)** The 20 in. square shown on the previous page

$P = 4s$

$P = 4 \cdot \underline{\hphantom{xx}} = \underline{\hphantom{xxxx}}$

(b) A square measuring 14 miles (14 mi) on each side (*Hint:* Draw a sketch of the square and label each side with its length.)

❷ Use the perimeter of each square and the appropriate formula to find the length of one side. Then check your solution by drawing a square, labeling each side, and finding the perimeter.

(GS) **(a)** Perimeter is 28 in.

$P = 4s$

$28 \text{ in.} = 4s$

$\dfrac{28 \text{ in.}}{4} = \dfrac{4s}{4}$

$\underline{\hphantom{xx}} = s$

(b) Perimeter is 100 ft.

Answers

1. **(a)** $P = 4 \cdot 20 \text{ in.} = 80 \text{ in.}$
   (b) $P = 56 \text{ miles}$

2. **(a)** $7 \text{ in.} = s$
   CHECK $P = 7 \text{ in.} + 7 \text{ in.} + 7 \text{ in.} + 7 \text{ in.} = 28 \text{ in.}$

   (b) $s = 25 \text{ ft}$
   CHECK $P = 25 \text{ ft} + 25 \text{ ft} + 25 \text{ ft} + 25 \text{ ft} = 100 \text{ ft}$

VOCABULARY TIP

Rect means "right." It reminds you that all the angles in a **rect**angle are "right" angles.

3 Find the perimeter of each rectangle using the appropriate formula. Check your solutions by adding the lengths of the four sides.

GS (a)

$P = 2l \qquad + 2w$

$P = 2 \cdot 17 \text{ cm} + 2 \cdot 10 \text{ cm}$

$P = \underline{\quad} + \underline{\quad}$

$P = \underline{\quad}$

CHECK

$P = \underline{\quad} + \underline{\quad} + \underline{\quad}$
$\qquad + \underline{\quad} = \underline{\quad}$

(b)

12 ft

25 ft

In a rectangle, if one right angle is shown, the other three angles are also right angles.

Each longer side of a rectangle is called the length (*l*) and each shorter side is called the width (*w*).

Look at the rectangle above with the lengths of the sides labeled. To find the perimeter (distance around), you could unfold the shape so the sides lie end-to-end. Then add the lengths of the sides.

$$P = 12 \text{ cm} + 7 \text{ cm} + 12 \text{ cm} + 7 \text{ cm} = 38 \text{ cm}$$

or $\quad P = 12 \text{ cm} + 12 \text{ cm} + 7 \text{ cm} + 7 \text{ cm} = 38 \text{ cm}$ Commutative property

Because the two long sides are both 12 cm, and the two short sides are both 7 cm, you can also use the formula below.

> **Finding the Perimeter of a Rectangle**
>
> Perimeter of a rectangle = length + length + width + width
>
> $$P = (2 \cdot \text{length}) + (2 \cdot \text{width})$$
> $$P = 2l + 2w$$

EXAMPLE 3 Finding the Perimeter of a Rectangle

Find the perimeter of this rectangle.

27 m

11 m   11 m

27 m

m is the short way to write *meters*.

The length is **27 m**, and the width is **11 m**.

$P = \quad 2l \quad + \quad 2w$ \qquad Replace *l* with 27 m and *w* with 11 m.

$P = 2 \cdot 27 \text{ m} + 2 \cdot 11 \text{ m}$ \qquad Do the multiplications first.

$P = \quad 54 \text{ m} \quad + \quad 22 \text{ m}$ \qquad Add last.

$P = 76 \text{ m}$

The perimeter of the rectangle (the distance you would walk around the outside edges of the rectangle) is 76 m.

CHECK To check the solution, add the lengths of the four sides.

$$P = 27 \text{ m} + 27 \text{ m} + 11 \text{ m} + 11 \text{ m}$$

$$P = 76 \text{ m} \leftarrow \text{Matches the solution above}$$

················· ◀ **Work Problem 3** at the Side.

Answers

3. **(a)** $P = 34 \text{ cm} + 20 \text{ cm}; P = 54 \text{ cm}$
   CHECK
   $P = 17 \text{ cm} + 17 \text{ cm} + 10 \text{ cm}$
   $\quad + 10 \text{ cm} = 54 \text{ cm}$

   (b) $P = 74 \text{ ft}$
   CHECK
   $25 \text{ ft} + 25 \text{ ft} + 12 \text{ ft} + 12 \text{ ft} = 74 \text{ ft}$

EXAMPLE 4 **Finding the Length or Width of a Rectangle**

If the perimeter of a rectangle is 20 ft and the width is 3 ft, find the length.

First draw a sketch of the rectangle and label the widths as 3 ft.

Then use the formula for perimeter of a rectangle, $P = 2l + 2w$. The value of P is 20 ft and the value of w is 3 ft.

$$P = 2l + 2w \qquad \text{Formula for perimeter of a rectangle}$$

$$20 \text{ ft} = 2l + \underbrace{2 \cdot 3 \text{ ft}} \qquad \begin{array}{l}\text{Replace } P \text{ with 20 ft and } w \text{ with 3 ft.}\\ \text{Simplify the right side by multiplying } 2 \cdot 3 \text{ ft.}\end{array}$$

$$20 \text{ ft} = 2l + 6 \text{ ft}$$

$$\frac{-6 \text{ ft} \qquad\qquad -6 \text{ ft}}{14 \text{ ft} = \underbrace{2l + 0}} \qquad \begin{array}{l}\text{To get } 2l \text{ by itself, add } -6 \text{ ft to both sides:}\\ 6 + (-6) \text{ is } 0.\end{array}$$

$$\frac{14 \text{ ft}}{2} = \frac{2l}{2} \qquad \text{To get } l \text{ by itself, divide both sides by 2.}$$

$$7 \text{ ft} = l$$

The length is 7 ft. ◁— Write **ft** as part of your answer.

CHECK To check the solution, put the length measurements on your sketch. Then add the four measurements.

$$P = 7 \text{ ft} + 7 \text{ ft} + 3 \text{ ft} + 3 \text{ ft}$$

$$P = 20 \text{ ft}$$

Matches the perimeter given in the original problem, so the solution checks.

························· **Work Problem ④ at the Side.** ▶

OBJECTIVE ▶ ③ Find the perimeter of parallelograms, triangles, and irregular shapes. A **parallelogram** is a four-sided figure in which opposite sides are both parallel and equal in length. Some examples are shown below. Notice that opposite sides have the same length.

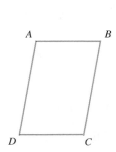

$\overline{AB}$ **parallel to** $\overline{DC}$ **and**

$\overline{AD}$ **parallel to** $\overline{BC}$

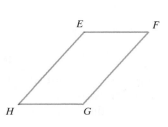

$\overline{EF}$ **parallel to** $\overline{HG}$ **and**

$\overline{EH}$ **parallel to** $\overline{FG}$

Perimeter is the distance around a flat shape, so the easiest way to find the perimeter of a parallelogram is to add the lengths of the four sides.

---

④ Use the perimeter of each rectangle and the appropriate formula to find the length or width. Draw a sketch of each rectangle and use it to check your solution.

GS (a) The perimeter of a rectangle is 36 in. and the width is 8 in. Find the length.

$$P = 2l + 2w$$

$$36 \text{ in.} = 2l + \underbrace{2 \cdot 8 \text{ in.}}$$

$$36 \text{ in.} = 2l + 16 \text{ in.}$$

$$\frac{-16 \text{ in.} \qquad\qquad -16 \text{ in.}}{20 \text{ in.} = 2l + \quad 0} \quad \begin{array}{l}\text{Find the}\\ \text{solution.}\end{array}$$

(b) A rectangle has a width of 4 cm. The perimeter is 32 cm. Find the length.

Answers

4. (a) $\dfrac{20 \text{ in.}}{2} = \dfrac{2l}{2}$; 10 in. = l

CHECK 10 in. + 10 in. + 8 in. + 8 in. = 36 in.

(b) $l = 12$ cm

CHECK 12 cm + 12 cm + 4 cm + 4 cm = 32 cm

5 Find the perimeter of each parallelogram.

(GS) (a)

27 m
15 m   15 m
27 m

$P = 27 \text{ m} + \underline{\quad} + \underline{\quad} + \underline{\quad} = \underline{\quad}$

(b)

5 ft
4 ft

VOCABULARY TIP

Tri- means "three". Just like a **tri**cycle has three wheels, a **tri**angle has three sides.

---

6 Find the perimeter of each triangle.

(GS) (a)

31 mm
25 mm   16 mm

$P = 31 \text{ mm} + \underline{\quad} + \underline{\quad}$

$P = \underline{\quad}$

(b) A triangle with sides that each measure 5 in.

7 How much fencing is needed to go around a flower bed with the measurements shown below?

6 m
2 m
5 m
4 m
3 m

Answers

5. (a) $P = 27 \text{ m} + 27 \text{ m} + 15 \text{ m} + 15 \text{ m} = 84 \text{ m}$
(b) $P = 18 \text{ ft}$
6. (a) $P = 31 \text{ mm} + 16 \text{ mm} + 25 \text{ mm} = 72 \text{ mm}$
(b) $P = 15 \text{ in.}$
7. 20 m of fencing are needed.

EXAMPLE 5   Finding the Perimeter of a Parallelogram

Find the perimeter of the middle parallelogram on the previous page.

$$P = 12 \text{ m} + 12 \text{ m} + 8 \text{ m} + 8 \text{ m}$$

$$P = 40 \text{ m}$$

◀ **Work Problem 5 at the Side.**

A **triangle** is a figure with exactly three sides. Some examples are shown below.

16 mm   34 mm

30 mm

mm is the short way to write *millimeters*.

To find the perimeter of a triangle (the distance around the edges), add the lengths of the three sides.

EXAMPLE 6   Finding the Perimeter of a Triangle

Find the perimeter of the triangle above on the right.
To find the perimeter, add the lengths of the sides.

$$P = 16 \text{ mm} + 30 \text{ mm} + 34 \text{ mm}$$

$$P = 80 \text{ mm}$$

◀ **Work Problem 6 at the Side.**

As with any other shape, you can find the perimeter of an irregular shape by adding the lengths of the sides.

EXAMPLE 7   Finding the Perimeter of an Irregular Shape

The ceiling of a room has the shape shown here.

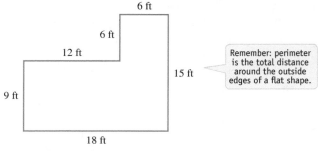

6 ft
6 ft
12 ft
15 ft
9 ft
18 ft

Remember: perimeter is the total distance around the outside edges of a flat shape.

Suppose you want to put a new wallpaper border along the top of all the walls. How much material do you need?
Find the perimeter of the room by adding the lengths of the sides.

$$P = 9 \text{ ft} + 12 \text{ ft} + 6 \text{ ft} + 6 \text{ ft} + 15 \text{ ft} + 18 \text{ ft}$$

$$P = 66 \text{ ft}$$

You need 66 ft of wallpaper border.

◀ **Work Problem 7 at the Side.**

3.1 Exercises

  MyMathLab®

Download the MyDashBoard App

1. CONCEPT CHECK Explain what is special about a square. Make a drawing of a square and label the length of each side.

2. CONCEPT CHECK Write the formula for finding the perimeter of a square. What do the letters in the formula stand for?

*Find the perimeter of each square, using the appropriate formula. **See Example 1**.*

3.

$P = 4s$

$P = 4 \cdot$ _____

$P =$ _____

4.

40 ft

40 ft   40 ft

40 ft

$P = 4s$

$P = 4 \cdot$ _____

$P =$ _____

5.

25 in.

25 in.

6.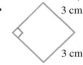

3 cm

3 cm

Draw a sketch of each square and label the lengths of the sides. Then find the perimeter. (Sketches may vary; show your sketches to your instructor.)

7. A square park measuring 1 mile on each side

8. A square garden measuring 4 meters on each side

9. A 22 mm square postage stamp

10. A 10 in. square piece of cardboard

*For the given perimeter of each square, find the length of one side using the appropriate formula. **See Example 2**.*

11. The perimeter is 120 ft.

$P = 4s$

$\dfrac{120 \text{ ft}}{4} = \dfrac{4s}{4}$

_____ $= s$

12. The perimeter is 52 cm.

$P = 4s$

$\dfrac{52 \text{ cm}}{4} = \dfrac{4s}{4}$

_____ $= s$

13. A square parking lot with a perimeter of 92 yards

14. A square building with a perimeter of 144 meters

15. A square closet with a perimeter of 8 ft

16. A square bedroom with a perimeter of 44 ft

17. CONCEPT CHECK Explain what is special about a rectangle. Make a drawing of a rectangle and label the length of each side.

18. CONCEPT CHECK Write the formula for finding the perimeter of a rectangle. What do the letters in the formula stand for?

Find the perimeter of each rectangle, using the appropriate formula. Check your solutions by adding the lengths of the four sides. ***See Example 3.***

19.

8 yd
6 yd   6 yd
8 yd

$P = 2l + 2w$

$P = 2 \cdot 8 \text{ yd} + 2 \cdot 6 \text{ yd}$

$P = \underline{\quad} + \underline{\quad}$

$P = \underline{\quad}$

20.

7 in.
18 in.   18 in.
7 in.

$P = 2l + 2w$

$P = 2 \cdot 18 \text{ in.} + 2 \cdot 7 \text{ in.}$

$P = \underline{\quad} + \underline{\quad}$

$P = \underline{\quad}$

21.

10 cm
25 cm

22.

15 mm
19 mm

Draw a sketch of each rectangle and label the lengths of the sides. Then find the perimeter by using the appropriate formula. (Sketches may vary; show your sketches to your instructor.)

23. A rectangular living room 20 ft long by 16 ft wide

24. A rectangular place mat 45 cm long by 30 cm wide

25. An 8 in. by 5 in. rectangular piece of paper

26. A 2 ft by 3 ft rectangular window

For each rectangle, you are given the perimeter and either the length or width. Find the unknown measurement using the appropriate formula. Check your solution by adding the lengths of the four sides. ***See Example 4.***

27. The perimeter is 30 cm and the width is 6 cm.

$$P = 2l + 2w$$
$$30 \text{ cm} = 2l + 2 \cdot 6 \text{ cm}$$
$$30 \text{ cm} = 2l + 12 \text{ cm}$$
$$\underline{-12 \text{ cm} = \qquad -12 \text{ cm}}$$ Find the solution.
$$18 \text{ cm} = 2l + 0$$

28. The perimeter is 48 yards and the length is 14 yards.

$$P = 2l + 2w$$
$$48 \text{ yd} = 2 \cdot 14 \text{ yd} + 2w$$
$$48 \text{ yd} = 28 \text{ yd} + 2w$$
$$\underline{-28 \text{ yd} \quad -28 \text{ yd}}$$ Find the solution.
$$20 \text{ yd} = 0 + 2w$$

29. The length is 4 miles and the perimeter is 10 miles.

30. The width is 8 meters and the perimeter is 34 meters.

31. A 6 ft long rectangular table has a perimeter of 16 ft.

32. A 13 in. wide rectangular picture frame has a perimeter of 56 in.

33. A rectangular door 1 meter wide has a perimeter of 6 meters.

|←1 m→|

34. A rectangular house 33 ft long has a perimeter of 118 ft.

33 ft

*In Exercises 35–44, find the perimeter of each shape. The figures in Exercises 35–36 are parallelograms. **See Examples 5–7.***

35.

100 ft
60 ft

36.
1000 ft
1240 ft

37.
26 mm
12 mm   16 mm

38.

9 yd   7 yd
11 yd

39.
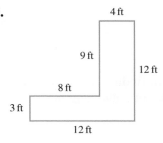
4 ft
9 ft
12 ft
8 ft
3 ft
12 ft

40.

7 m
3 m
5 m
12 m
9 m
2 m

41.

8 in.
18 in.
13 in.
8 in.
13 in.
18 in.

42.

13 ft
13 ft
12 ft
22 ft

43.

22 m
34 m
27 m
22 m
20 m

44.

87 cm
48 cm
41 cm
32 cm
44 cm
92 cm

For each shape, you are given the perimeter and the lengths of all sides except one.
Find the length of the unlabeled side.

45. The perimeter is 115 cm.

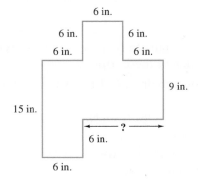
30 cm
10 cm
25 cm
10 cm
?

46. The perimeter is 63 in.
?
9 in.
20 in.   21 in.

47. The perimeter is 78 in.
6 in.
6 in.   6 in.
6 in.   6 in.
9 in.
15 in.
?
6 in.
6 in.

48. The perimeter is 196 ft.

12 ft
18 ft   20 ft
16 ft   10 ft
40 ft
32 ft
?

49. In an *equilateral* triangle, all sides have the same length.

   (a) Draw sketches of four different equilateral triangles, label the lengths of the sides, and find the perimeters.

   (b) Write a "shortcut" rule (a formula) for finding the perimeter of an equilateral triangle.

   (c) Will your formula work for other kinds of triangles that are not equilateral? Explain why or why not.

50. Be sure that you have done **Exercise 49** first.

   (a) Draw a sketch of a figure with five sides of equal length. Write a "shortcut" rule (a formula) for finding the perimeter of this shape.

   (b) Draw a sketch of a figure with six sides of equal length. Write a formula for finding the perimeter of the shape.

   (c) Write a formula for finding the perimeter of a shape with 10 sides of equal length.

   (d) Write a formula for finding the perimeter of a shape with n sides of equal length.

Relating Concepts (Exercises 51–54)   For Individual or Group Work

A formula that has many uses for drivers is d = rt, called the distance formula. If you are driving a car, then

        d is the *distance* you travel (how many miles),
        r is the *rate* (how fast you are driving in miles per hour),
        t is the *time* (how many hours you drive).

Use the distance formula as you **work Exercises 51–54 *in order.***

51. Suppose you are driving on an interstate highway at an average rate of 70 miles per hour. Use the distance formula to find out how far you will travel in

   (a) 2 hours.

   (b) 5 hours.

   (c) 8 hours.

52. An ice storm slows your driving rate to 35 miles per hour. Use the formula to find how far will you travel in

   (a) 2 hours.

   (b) 5 hours.

   (c) 8 hours.

   (d) Explain how to find each answer using the results from **Exercise 51** instead of the formula.

53. Use the distance formula to find out how many hours you would have to drive to travel the 3000 miles from Boston to San Francisco if your average rate is

   (a) 60 miles per hour.

   (b) 50 miles per hour.

   (c) 20 miles per hour (which was the speed limit 100 years ago).

54. Use the distance formula to find the average driving rate (speed) on each of these trips.

   (a) It took 11 hours to drive 671 miles from Atlanta to Chicago.

   (b) Sam drove 1539 miles from New York City to Dallas in 27 hours.

   (c) Carlita drove 16 hours to travel 1040 miles from Memphis to Denver.

3.2 Problem Solving: Area

OBJECTIVE ➤ ① Use the formula for area of a rectangle to find the area, the length, or the width.

OBJECTIVES

① Use the formula for area of a rectangle to find the area, the length, or the width.

② Use the formula for area of a square to find the area or the length of one side.

③ Use the formula for area of a parallelogram to find the area, the base, or the height.

④ Solve application problems involving perimeter and area of rectangles, squares, or parallelograms.

Understanding the Difference between Perimeter and Area

Perimeter is the *distance around the outside edges* of a flat shape. **Area** is the amount of *surface inside* a flat shape.

The *perimeter* of a rectangle is the distance around the *outside edges*. Recall that we unfolded a shape and laid the sides end-to-end so we could see the total distance. The *area* of a rectangle is the amount of surface *inside* the rectangle. We measure area by finding the number of squares of a certain size needed to cover the surface inside the rectangle. Think of covering the floor of a living room with carpet. Carpet is measured in square yards, that is, square pieces that measure 1 yard along each side. Here is a drawing of a rectangular living room floor.

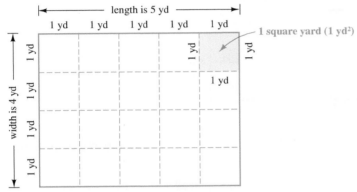

You can see from the drawing that it takes 20 squares to cover the floor. We say that the area of the floor is 20 *square yards*. A short way to write *square yards* is yd².

20 square yards   can be written as   20 yd²

To find the number of squares, you can count them, or you can multiply the number of squares in the length (5) times the number of squares in the width (4) to get 20. The formula is given below.

Finding the Area of a Rectangle

Area of a rectangle = length • width

$A = lw$

Use *square units* when measuring area, such as yd², in.², and so on.

VOCABULARY TIP

Area The **area** is the amount of surface **inside** a flat shape. Write the area using **square units,** such as square inches or square feet—for example, 10 **ft²** or 12 **in.²**

Squares of many sizes can be used to measure area.

For smaller areas, you might use the ones shown at the right.

1 square inch (1 in.²)

1 square centimeter (1 cm²)

1 square millimeter (1 mm²)

Actual-size drawings

1 Find the area of each rectangle, using the appropriate formula.

(a)

$$A = l \cdot w$$

$$A = 9 \text{ ft} \cdot 4 \text{ ft}$$

$$A = \underline{\qquad}$$

(b) A rectangle is 35 yd long and 20 yd wide. (First make a sketch of the rectangle and label the lengths of the sides.)

(c) A rectangular patio measures 3 m by 2 m. (First make a sketch of the patio and label the lengths of the sides.)

Answers

1. (a) $A = 36 \text{ ft}^2$
(b)
20 yd
35 yd
$A = 700 \text{ yd}^2$
(c)
2 m
3 m
$A = 6 \text{ m}^2$

Other sizes of squares that are often used to measure area are listed here, but they are too large to draw on this page.

1 square meter (1 m^2)
1 square kilometer (1 km^2)

1 square foot (1 ft^2)
1 square yard (1 yd^2)
1 square mile (1 mi^2)

CAUTION

The raised 2 in 4^2 means that you multiply $4 \cdot 4$ to get 16. The raised 2 in cm^2 or yd^2 is a short way to write the word "square." It means that you multiplied cm times cm to get cm^2, or yd times yd to get yd^2. Recall that a short way to write $x \cdot x$ is x^2. Similarly, $cm \cdot cm$ is cm^2. When you see 5 cm^2, say "five square centimeters." Do *not* multiply $5 \cdot 5$, because the exponent applies only to the *first* thing to its immediate left. The exponent applies to cm, *not* to the number.

EXAMPLE 1   **Finding the Area of Rectangles**

Find the area of each rectangle.

(a)

Each small square in this figure represents 1 square meter, written as 1 m^2. You could count all the squares to find the total area of 104 m^2.

The length of this rectangle is 13 m and the width is 8 m. Use the formula $A = lw$, which means $A = l \cdot w$.

$$A = \quad l \quad \cdot \quad w \qquad \text{Replace } l \text{ with 13 m and } w \text{ with 8 m.}$$

$$A = 13 \text{ m} \cdot 8 \text{ m} \qquad \text{Multiply 13 times 8 to get 104.}$$

$$A = 104 \text{ m}^2 \qquad \text{Multiply m times m to get m}^2.$$

The area of the rectangle is 104 m^2. If you count the number of squares in the sketch, you will also get 104 m^2. Each square in the sketch represents 1 m by 1 m, which is 1 square meter (1 m^2).

(b) A rectangle measuring 7 cm by 21 cm

First make a sketch of the rectangle. The length is 21 cm (the longer measurement) and the width is 7 cm. Then use the formula $A = lw$.

7 cm

21 cm

$$A = \quad l \quad \cdot \quad w \qquad \text{Replace } l \text{ with 21 cm and } w \text{ with 7 cm.}$$

$$A = 21 \text{ cm} \cdot 7 \text{ cm} \qquad \text{Multiply } 21 \cdot 7 \text{ to get 147.}$$

$$A = 147 \text{ cm}^2 \qquad \text{Multiply cm} \cdot \text{cm to get cm}^2.$$

The area of the rectangle is 147 cm^2.

◀ **Work Problem 1 at the Side.**

CAUTION

The units for *area* will always be *square* units (cm^2, m^2, yd^2, mi^2, and so on). The units for *perimeter* will always be *linear* units (cm, m, yd, mi, and so on), *not* square units.

EXAMPLE 2 **Finding the Length or Width of a Rectangle**

If the area of a rectangular rug is 12 yd² and
the length is 4 yd, find the width.
  Draw a sketch of the rug. Label the length as 4 yd.
  Use the formula for area of a rectangle, $A = lw$.

4 yd

$$A \quad = \quad l \quad \bullet \quad w$$

Replace A with 12 yd² and
replace l with 4 yd.

$$12 \text{ yd}^2 \; = 4 \text{ yd} \bullet w$$

To get w by itself, divide both sides by 4 yd.

$$\frac{12 \text{ yd} \bullet \text{yd}}{4 \text{ yd}} = \frac{4 \text{ yd} \bullet w}{4 \text{ yd}}$$

On the left side, rewrite yd² as yd • yd. Then $\dfrac{\text{yd}}{\text{yd}}$ is 1,
so they "cancel out."

On the right side, use division to "undo" multiplication:
4 yd • w ÷ 4 yd is w.

$$3 \text{ yd} \quad = \quad w$$

On the left side, 12 yd ÷ 4 is 3 yd.

The width of the rug is 3 yd.

CHECK To check the solution, put the width measurement on your sketch.
Then use the area formula.

$$A = \quad l \quad \bullet \quad w$$

$$A = 4 \text{ yd} \bullet 3 \text{ yd}$$

$$A = 12 \text{ yd}^2$$

3 yd

4 yd

An area of 12 yd² matches the information in the original problem.
So 3 yd is the correct width of the rug.

························ **Work Problem ❷ at the Side.** ▶

**OBJECTIVE ▶ ❷ Use the formula for area of a square to find the area or
the length of one side.** As with a rectangle, you can multiply length times
width to find the area (surface inside) of a square. Because the length and the
width are the same in a square, the formula is written as shown below.

Finding the Area of a Square

Area of a square = side • side

$$A = s \bullet s$$

$$A = s^2$$

Remember to use *square units* when measuring area.

EXAMPLE 3 **Finding the Area of a Square**

Find the area of a square highway sign that is 4 ft on each side.
  Use the formula for area of a square, $A = s^2$.

$$A = \quad s^2$$

Remember that s^2 means $s \bullet s$.

$$A = s \bullet s$$

Replace s with 4 ft.

$$A = 4 \text{ ft} \bullet 4 \text{ ft}$$

Multiply 4 • 4 to get 16.

> **Be careful!**
> s^2 is 4 • 4 or 16
> **(not 4 • 2).**

$$A = 16 \text{ ft}^2$$

Multiply ft • ft to get ft².

The area of the sign is 16 ft².

························· **Continued on Next Page** ▶

---

❷ Use the area of each rectangle
and the appropriate formula to
find the length or width. Draw a
sketch of each rectangle and use
it to check your solution.

GS **(a)** The area of a microscope
slide is 12 cm², and the
length is 6 cm. Find the
width.

$$A = l \bullet w$$

$$12 \text{ cm}^2 \; = 6 \text{ cm} \bullet w$$

$$\frac{12 \text{ cm} \bullet \text{cm}}{6 \text{ cm}} = \frac{6 \text{ cm} \bullet w}{6 \text{ cm}}$$

$$\underline{\hspace{2cm}} = w$$

(b) A child's play lot is 10 ft
wide and has an area of
160 ft². Find the length.

(c) A hallway floor is 31 m long
and has an area of 93 m².
Find the width of the floor.

Answers

2. (a) $w = 2$ cm

2 cm

6 cm

CHECK $A = 6 \text{ cm} \bullet 2 \text{ cm}$
      $A = 12 \text{ cm}^2$
Matches original problem

(b) $l = 16$ ft

10 ft

16 ft

CHECK $A = 16 \text{ ft} \bullet 10 \text{ ft}$
      $A = 160 \text{ ft}^2$
Matches original problem

(c) $w = 3$ m

3 m

31 m

CHECK $A = 31 \text{ m} \bullet 3 \text{ m}$
      $A = 93 \text{ m}^2$
Matches original problem

❸ Find the area of each square, using the appropriate formula. Make a sketch of each square.

(a) A 12 in. square piece of fabric

$$A = s^2$$

$$A = s \cdot s$$

$$A = 12 \text{ in.} \cdot 12 \text{ in.}$$

$$A = \underline{\qquad}$$

(b) A square township 7 miles on a side

(c) A square earring measuring 20 mm on each side

❹ Given the area of each square, find the length of one side by inspection.

(a) The area of a square-shaped nature center is 16 mi².

$$A = s^2$$ What number times itself gives 16?

$$16 \text{ mi}^2 = s \cdot s$$

$$16 \text{ mi}^2 = \underline{\qquad} \cdot \underline{\qquad}$$

So s is _____.

(b) A square floor with an area of 100 m²

(c) A square clock face with an area of 81 in.²

Answers

3. (a) $A = 144$ in.²
12 in.
12 in.

(b) $A = 49$ mi²
7 mi
7 mi

(c) $A = 400$ mm²
20 mm
20 mm

4. (a) $16 \text{ mi}^2 = 4 \text{ mi} \cdot 4 \text{ mi}$; s is 4 mi
(b) $s = 10$ m   **(c)** $s = 9$ in.

CAUTION

Be careful! s^2 means $s \cdot s$. It does **not** mean $s \cdot 2$. In this example s is 4 ft, so $(4 \text{ ft})^2$ is 4 ft $\cdot$ 4 ft = 16 ft². It is **not** 4 ft $\cdot$ 2 = 8 ft.

CHECK Check the solution by drawing a square and labeling each side as 4 ft. You can multiply length (4 ft) times width (4 ft), as you did for a rectangle. So the area is 4 ft $\cdot$ 4 ft, or 16 ft². This result matches the solution you got by using the formula $A = s^2$.

4 ft
4 ft

◀ **Work Problem ❸ at the Side.**

EXAMPLE 4 **Finding the Length of One Side of a Square**

If the area of a square township is 49 mi², what is the length of one side of the township?

Use the formula for area of a square, $A = s^2$. The value of A is 49 mi².

$A \quad = \quad s^2$ — Replace A with 49 mi².

$49 \text{ mi}^2 = \quad s^2$ — To get s by itself, we have to "undo" the squaring of s. This is called *finding the square root* (more on square roots in **Chapter 5**).

$49 \text{ mi}^2 = \quad s \cdot s$ — For now, solve by inspection. Ask, what number times itself gives 49?

$49 \text{ mi}^2 = 7 \text{ mi} \cdot 7 \text{ mi}$ — 7 $\cdot$ 7 is 49, so 7 mi $\cdot$ 7 mi is 49 mi².

The value of s is 7 mi, so the length of one side of the township is 7 mi. Notice how this result matches the information about the township in **Margin Problem 3(b).**

◀ **Work Problem ❹ at the Side.**

OBJECTIVE **❸** **Use the formula for area of a parallelogram to find the area, the base, or the height.** To find the area of a parallelogram, first draw a dashed line inside the figure, as shown here.

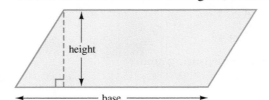
height
base

As an experiment, try this yourself by tracing this parallelogram onto a piece of paper.

The length of the dashed line is the *height* of the parallelogram. It forms a 90° angle (a right angle) with the base. The height is the shortest distance between the base and the opposite side.

Now cut off the triangle created on the left side of the parallelogram and move it to the right side, as shown on the next page.

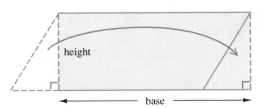

height

base

You have made the parallelogram into a rectangle. You can see that the area of the parallelogram and the rectangle are the same.

Equal areas
→ Area of the rectangle = length • width
→ Area of the parallelogram = base • height

Finding the Area of a Parallelogram

Area of a parallelogram = base • height
$$A = bh$$

Remember to use *square units* when measuring area.

EXAMPLE 5   Finding the Area of Parallelograms

Find the area of each parallelogram.

(a)

19 cm

24 cm

(b)

47 m

30 m   24 m   30 m

47 m

(a) The base is 24 cm and the height is 19 cm. The formula for the area of a parallelogram is $A = bh$.

$A = \quad b \quad • \quad h$ Replace b with 24 cm and h with 19 cm.

$A = $ **24 cm** • **19 cm**   Multiply 24 • 19 to get 456.

$A = 456 \text{ cm}^2$ Multiply cm • cm to get cm^2.

The area of the parallelogram is 456 cm^2.   `Write cm² as part of your answer.`

(b) Use the formula for area of a parallelogram, $A = bh$.

$A = \quad b \quad • \quad h$ Replace b with 47 m and h with 24 m.

$A = $ **47 m** • **24 m**   Multiply 47 • 24 to get 1128.

$A = 1128 \text{ m}^2$ Multiply m • m to get m^2.   `Write m² as part of your answer.`

Notice that the 30 m sides are *not* used in finding the area. But you would use them when finding the *perimeter* of the parallelogram.

· **Work Problem ❺ at the Side. ▶**

EXAMPLE 6   Finding the Base or Height of a Parallelogram

The area of a parallelogram is 24 ft^2 and the base is 6 ft. Find the height.

First draw a sketch of the parallelogram and label the base as 6 ft.

?

6 ft

· **Continued on Next Page**

---

❺ Find the area of each parallelogram.

⑤ₛ (a)

50 ft

44 ft   42 ft   44 ft

← 50 ft →

$A = b • h$

$A = 50 \text{ ft} • 42 \text{ ft}$

$A = $ _____

(b)

11 in.

18 in.   10 in.   18 in.

11 in.

(c) A parallelogram with base 8 cm and height 1 cm.

Answers

5. (a) $A = 2100 \text{ ft}^2$ **(b)** $A = 180 \text{ in.}^2$
   (c) $A = 8 \text{ cm}^2$

6 Use the area of each parallelogram and the appropriate formula to find the base or height. Draw a sketch of each parallelogram and use it to check your solution.

(a) The area of a parallelogram is 140 in.² and the base is 14 in. Find the height.

$$A = b \cdot h$$

$$140 \text{ in.}^2 = 14 \text{ in.} \cdot h$$

$$\frac{140 \text{ in} \cdot \text{in}}{14 \text{ in.}} = \frac{14 \text{ in.} \cdot h}{14 \text{ in.}}$$

$$\underline{\hspace{1.5cm}} = h$$

(b) A parallelogram has an area of 4 yd². The height is 1 yd. Find the base.

7 If sod costs $3 per square yard, how much will the neighbors in **Example 7** spend to cover the playground with grass?

Answers

6. (a) 10 in. $= h$

14 in.

CHECK $A = 14 \text{ in.} \cdot 10 \text{ in.}$
$A = 140 \text{ in.}^2$
Matches original problem

(b) $b = 4$ yd

1 yd — 4 yd

CHECK $A = 4 \text{ yd} \cdot 1 \text{ yd}$
$A = 4 \text{ yd}^2$
Matches original problem

7. $1056 (Find the area by multiplying
22 yd • 16 yd to get 352 yd². Then multiply
$3 • 352 to get $1056.)

Use the formula for the area of a parallelogram, $A = bh$. The value of A is 24 ft², and the value of b is 6 ft.

$$A = b \cdot h \qquad \text{Replace } A \text{ with 24 ft}^2 \text{ and } b \text{ with 6 ft.}$$

$$24 \text{ ft}^2 = 6 \text{ ft} \cdot h \qquad \text{To get } h \text{ by itself, divide both sides by 6 ft.}$$

$$\frac{24 \text{ ft} \cdot \text{ft}}{6 \text{ ft}} = \frac{6 \text{ ft} \cdot h}{6 \text{ ft}}$$

On the left side, rewrite ft² as ft • ft. Then $\frac{\text{ft}}{\text{ft}}$ is 1, so they "cancel out."
On the right side, use division to "undo" multiplication; 6 ft • h ÷ 6 ft is h.

$$4 \text{ ft} = h \qquad \text{On the left side, 24 ft} \div 6 \text{ is 4 ft.}$$

The height of the parallelogram is 4 ft.

CHECK To check the solution, put the height measurement on your sketch. Then use the area formula.

$$A = b \cdot h$$
$$A = 6 \text{ ft} \cdot 4 \text{ ft}$$
$$A = 24 \text{ ft}^2$$

An area of 24 ft² matches the information in the original problem. So 4 ft is the correct height of the parallelogram.

◀ **Work Problem 6** at the Side.

OBJECTIVE 4 **Solve application problems involving perimeter and area of rectangles, squares, or parallelograms.** When you are solving problems, first decide whether you need to find the perimeter or the area.

EXAMPLE 7 **Solving an Application Problem Involving Perimeter or Area**

A group of neighbors is fixing up a playground for their children. The rectangular lot is 22 yd by 16 yd. If chain-link fencing costs $6 per yard, how much will they spend to put a fence around the lot?

First draw a sketch of the rectangular lot and label the length and width. The fence will go around the edges of the lot, so you need to find the *perimeter* of the lot.

$$P = 2l + 2w \qquad \text{Formula for perimeter of a rectangle}$$

$$P = 2 \cdot 22 \text{ yd} + 2 \cdot 16 \text{ yd} \qquad \text{Replace } l \text{ with 22 yd and } w \text{ with 16 yd.}$$

$$P = 44 \text{ yd} + 32 \text{ yd}$$

$$P = 76 \text{ yd}$$

The perimeter of the lot is 76 yd, so the neighbors need to buy 76 yd of fencing. The cost of the fencing is $6 *per yard,* which means $6 *for 1 yard.* To find the cost for 76 yd, multiply $6 • 76. The neighbors will spend $456 on the fence.

◀ **Work Problem 7** at the Side.

3.2 Exercises

Download the MyDashBoard App

MyMathLab®

1. CONCEPT CHECK Write the formula for finding the area of a square. What do the letters in the formula stand for?

2. CONCEPT CHECK Write the formula for finding the area of a rectangle. What do the letters in the formula stand for?

CONCEPT CHECK *Perform each calculation.*

3. (a) 10^2 (b) $2 \cdot 10$

  (c) 25^2 (d) $25 \cdot 2$

4. (a) 8^2 (b) $2 \cdot 8$

  (c) 30^2 (d) $30 \cdot 2$

Find the area of each rectangle, square, or parallelogram using the appropriate formula.
See Examples 1, 3, and 5.

5.

7 ft

11 ft   11 ft

7ft

$A = l \cdot w$

$A = 11 \text{ ft} \cdot 7 \text{ ft}$

$A = \underline{}$

6.

15 yd

5 yd   5 yd

15 yd

$A = l \cdot w$

$A = 15 \text{ yd} \cdot 5 \text{ yd}$

$A = \underline{}$

7.

6 in.

$A = s^2$

$A = s \cdot s$

$A = \underline{} \cdot \underline{}$

$A = \underline{}$

8.

20 cm

$A = s^2$

$A = s \cdot s$

$A = \underline{} \cdot \underline{}$

$A = \underline{}$

9.

31 mm

31 mm

25 mm   31 mm

31 mm

$A = b \cdot h$

10.

21 m

20 m   13 m   20 m

21 m

$A = b \cdot h$

In Exercises 11–16, first draw a sketch of the shape and label the length and width or base and height. Then find the area. (Sketches may vary; show your sketches to your instructor.)

11. A rectangular calculator that measures 15 cm by 7 cm

12. A table 12 ft long by 3 ft wide

13. A parallelogram with height of 9 ft and base of 8 ft

14. A parallelogram measuring 18 mm on the base and 3 mm on the height

15. A fire burned a square-shaped forest 25 mi on a side.

16. A square piece of window glass 1 m on each side

In Exercises 17–22, use the area of each rectangle and either its length or width, and the appropriate formula, to find the other measurement. Draw a sketch of each rectangle and use it to check your solution. **See Example 2**. *(Sketches may vary; show your sketches to your instructor.)*

17. The area of a desk is 18 ft^2, and the width is 3 ft. Find its length.

$A = l \cdot w$

$18 \text{ ft}^2 = l \cdot 3 \text{ ft}$ Now divide both sides by 3 ft.

18. The area of a classroom is 630 ft^2, and the length is 30 ft. Find its width.

$A = \quad l \cdot w$

$630 \text{ ft}^2 = 30 \text{ ft} \cdot w$ Now divide both sides by 30 ft.

19. A parking lot is 90 yd long and has an area of 7200 yd^2. Find its width.

20. A playground is 60 yd wide and has an area of 6000 yd^2. Find its length.

21. A 154 in.^{2} photo has a width of 11 in. Find its length.

22. A 15 in.^{2} note card has a width of 3 in. Find its length.

Given the area of each square, find the length of one side by inspection. **See Example 4**.

23. A square floor has an area of 36 m^2.

$A = s^2$

$36 \text{ m}^2 = s \cdot s$

What number times itself gives 36? _____

So, $s =$ _____

24. A square stamp has an area of 9 cm^2.

$A = s^2$

$9 \text{ cm}^2 = s \cdot s$

What number times itself gives 9? _____

So, $s =$ _____

25. The area of a square sign is 4 ft^2.

26. The area of a square piece of metal is 64 in.^{2}.

Use the area of each parallelogram and either its base or height, and the appropriate formula, to find the other measurement. Draw a sketch of each parallelogram and use it to check your solution. **See Example 6**. *(Sketches may vary; show your sketches to your instructor.)*

27. The area is 500 cm^2, and the base is 25 cm. Find the height.

$A = b \cdot h$

$500 \text{ cm}^2 = 25 \text{ cm} \cdot h$ Now divide both sides by 25 cm.

28. The area is 1500 m^2, and the height is 30 m. Find the base.

$A = b \cdot h$

$1500 \text{ m}^2 = b \cdot 30 \text{ m}$ Now divide both sides by 30 m.

29. The height is 13 in. and the area is 221 in.^{2}. Find the base.

30. The base is 19 cm, and the area is 114 cm^2. Find the height.

31. The base is 9 m, and the area is 9 m^2. Find the height.

32. The area is 25 mm^2, and the height is 5 mm. Find the base.

CONCEPT CHECK   *Explain and correct the **two** errors made by students in Exercises 33 and 34.*

33.

25 cm   25 cm

24 cm

25 cm   25 cm

$P = 25 \text{ cm} + 24 \text{ cm} + 25 \text{ cm} + 25 \text{ cm} + 25 \text{ cm}$

$P = 124 \text{ cm}^2$

34.

7 ft

$A = s^2$

$A = 7 \text{ ft} \cdot 2$

$A = 14 \text{ ft}$

Name each figure and find its perimeter and area.

35.

45 in.

45 in.

36.

4 m

5 m   6 m

6 m

4 m

37.

12 cm

18 cm

18 cm   10 cm

12 cm

38.

100 yd

80 yd

Solve each application problem to find the perimeter, the area, or one of the side measurements. In Exercises 39–44, draw a sketch, including the appropriate measurements. See Example 7. (Sketches may vary; show sketches to your instructor.)

39. Gymnastic floor exercises are performed on a square mat that is 12 meters on a side. Find the perimeter and area of a mat. (*Source:* nist.gov)

40. A regulation volleyball court is 18 meters by 9 meters. Find the perimeter and area of a regulation court. (*Source:* nist.gov)

41. Tyra's kitchen is 4 m wide and 5 m long. She is pasting a decorative strip that costs $6 per meter around the top edge of all the walls. How much will she spend?

42. The Wang's family room measures 20 ft by 25 ft. They are covering the floor with square tiles that measure 1 ft on a side and cost $1 each. How much will they spend on tile?

43. Mr. and Mrs. Gomez are buying carpet for their square-shaped bedroom, which measures 5 yd along each wall. The carpet is $23 per square yard and padding and installation is another $6 per square yard. How much will they spend in all?

44. A page in this book measures about 27 cm from top to bottom and 21 cm from side to side. Find the perimeter and the area of the page.

45. A regulation football field is 100 yd long (excluding end zones) and has an area of 5300 yd². Find the width of the field. (*Source:* NFL.)

46. There are 14,790 ft² of ice on the rectangular playing area for a major league hockey game (excluding the area behind the goal lines). If the playing area is 85 ft wide, how long is it? (*Source:* NHL.)

47. The table below shows information on two rectangular tents for camping.

Tents	Coleman Family Dome	Eddie Bauer Dome Tent
Dimensions	13 ft × 13 ft	12 ft × 12 ft
Sleeps	8 campers	6 campers
Sale price	$127	$99

Source: Target.com

For the Coleman tent, find the perimeter, area, and number of square feet of floor space for each camper. Round to the nearest whole number if necessary.

48. Look at the table in **Exercise 47.** For the Eddie Bauer tent, find the perimeter, area, and number of square feet of floor space for each camper. Round to the nearest whole number if necessary.

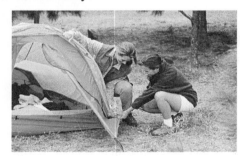

Relating Concepts (Exercises 49–52) For Individual or Group Work

Use your knowledge of perimeter and area to **work Exercises 49–52 in order.**

49. Suppose you have 12 ft of fencing to make a square or rectangular garden plot. Draw sketches of *all* the possible plots that use exactly 12 ft of fencing and label the lengths of the sides. Use only *whole number* lengths. (*Hint:* There are three possibilities.)

50. (a) Find the area of each plot in **Exercise 49.**

(b) Which plot has the greatest area?

51. Repeat **Exercise 49** using 16 ft of fencing. Be sure to draw *all* possible square or rectangular plots that have whole number lengths for the sides.

52. (a) Find the area of each plot in **Exercise 51.**

(b) Compare your results to those from **Exercise 50.** What do you notice about the plots with the greatest area?

Summary Exercises *Perimeter and Area*

Name each figure and find its perimeter and area using the appropriate formulas.

1.

2.

3.

4.

5.

6.

7.

8.

In Exercises 9–14, use the appropriate formula to find the unknown measurement. Draw a sketch of the figure and use it to check your solution. (Sketches may vary; show your instructor.)

9. A rectangle has a length of 7 ft and a perimeter of 16 ft. Find the width.

10. A parallelogram with an area of 5 yd^2 has a height of 1 yd. Find the base.

11. A square photograph has an area of 36 in.^{2}. Find the length of one side.

12. A sidewalk is 42 m long and has an area of 84 m². Find the width of the sidewalk.

13. The perimeter of a square map is 64 cm. What is the length of one side?

14. A rectangular patio is 9 ft wide and has a perimeter of 48 ft. What is the patio's length?

Solve each application problem using the appropriate formula. Show your work.

15. How much fencing is needed to enclose a triangular building site that measures 168 meters on each side?

16. Regulation soccer fields for teens and adults can measure 50 to 80 yards wide and 100 to 120 yards long, depending upon the age and skill level of the players. Find the difference in playing room between the smallest and largest fields.

17. A Toshiba laptop computer has a rectangular screen with a perimeter of 42 inches. The length of the screen is 12 inches. Find the width of the screen. (*Source:* Toshiba.)

18. Kari is decorating the cover of a square-shaped photo album that is 22 cm along each side. She is gluing braid along the edges of the front and back covers. How much braid will she need?

19. A school flag measures 3 feet by 5 feet. Find the amount of fabric needed to make seven flags, and the amount of binding needed to go around all the edges of all the flags.

20. The lobby floor of a new skyscraper is in the shape of a parallelogram, with an area of 3024 ft². If the base of the parallelogram measures 63 ft, what is its height?

3.3 Solving Application Problems with One Unknown Quantity

OBJECTIVES

OBJECTIVE ▶ 1 **Translate word phrases into algebraic expressions.** Earlier in this chapter, you worked with applications involving perimeter and area. You were able to use well-known rules (formulas) to write equations to solve. However, you will encounter many problems for which no formula is available. Then you need to analyze the problem and translate the words into an equation that fits the particular situation. We'll start by translating word phrases into algebraic expressions.

1 Translate word phrases into algebraic expressions.

2 Translate sentences into equations.

3 Solve application problems with one unknown quantity.

EXAMPLE 1   Translating Word Phrases into Algebraic Expressions

Write each phrase as an algebraic expression. Use x as the variable.

Words	Algebraic Expression	
A number plus 2	$x + 2$ or $2 + x$	
The sum of 8 and a number	$8 + x$ or $x + 8$	*Two* correct ways
5 more than a number	$x + 5$ or $5 + x$	to write each *addition*
-35 added to a number	$-35 + x$ or $x + (-35)$	expression
A number increased by 6	$x + 6$ or $6 + x$	
9 less than a number	$x - 9$	
A number subtracted from 3	$3 - x$	Only *one* correct
3 subtracted from a number	$x - 3$	way to write
7 fewer than a number	$x - 7$	each *subtraction*
A number decreased by 4	$x - 4$	expression
10 minus a number	$10 - x$	

> **CAUTION**
> Recall that addition can be done in any order, so $x + 2$ gives the same result as $2 + x$. This is *not* true in subtraction, so be careful. $10 - x$ does *not* give the same result as $x - 10$.

1 Write each phrase as an algebraic expression. Use x as the variable.

(a) 15 less than a number

(b) 12 more than a number

(c) A number increased by 13

(d) A number minus 8

(e) 10 plus a number

(f) A number subtracted from 6

(g) 6 subtracted from a number

·········· Work Problem **1** at the Side. ▶

EXAMPLE 2   Translating Word Phrases into Algebraic Expressions

Write each phrase as an algebraic expression. Use x as the variable.

Words	Algebraic Expression	
8 times a number	$8x$	
The product of 12 and a number	$12x$	
Double a number (meaning "2 times")	$2x$	
The quotient of -6 and a number	$\dfrac{-6}{x}$	Be careful when dividing! The order
A number divided by 10	$\dfrac{x}{10}$	of the numbers *does* matter.
15 subtracted from 4 times a number	$4x - 15$	
The result is	$=$	

2 Write each phrase as an algebraic expression. Use x as the variable.

(a) Double a number

(b) The product of -8 and a number

(c) The quotient of 15 and a number

(d) 5 times a number subtracted from 30

(e) A number divided by -9

Answers

1. (a) $x - 15$ **(b)** $x + 12$ or $12 + x$
(c) $x + 13$ or $13 + x$ **(d)** $x - 8$
(e) $10 + x$ or $x + 10$ **(f)** $6 - x$
(g) $x - 6$

2. (a) $2x$ **(b)** $-8x$ **(c)** $\dfrac{15}{x}$

(d) $30 - 5x$ (*not* $5x - 30$) **(e)** $\dfrac{x}{-9}$

·········· Work Problem **2** at the Side. ▶

❸ Translate each sentence into an equation and solve it. Check your solution by going back to the words in the original problem.

GS **(a)** If 3 times a number is added to 4, the result is 19. Find the number.

Let x represent the unknown number.

$$\underbrace{\begin{array}{c}3 \text{ times}\\ \text{a number}\end{array}}_{3x} \quad \underbrace{\begin{array}{c}\text{added}\\ \text{to}\end{array}}_{+} \quad \underset{\downarrow}{4} \quad \underbrace{\begin{array}{c}\text{result}\\ \text{is}\end{array}}_{=} \quad \underset{\downarrow}{19}$$

(b) If 7 is subtracted from 6 times a number, the result is −25. Find the number.

OBJECTIVE ▶ 2 Translate sentences into equations. The next example shows you how to translate a sentence into an equation that you can solve.

EXAMPLE 3 Translating a Sentence into an Equation

If 5 times a number is added to 11, the result is 26. Find the number.

Let x represent the unknown number. Use the information in the problem to write an equation.

$$\underbrace{5 \text{ times a number}}\ \underbrace{\text{added to}}\ \underset{\downarrow}{11}\ \underset{\downarrow}{\text{is}}\ \underset{\downarrow}{26}.$$
$$5x \qquad + \qquad 11 = 26$$

Next, solve the equation.

$$\begin{array}{rcl} 5x + 11 &=& 26 \\ -11 && -11 \\ \hline \underbrace{5x + 0} &=& 15 \\ \dfrac{5x}{5} &=& \dfrac{15}{5} \\ x &=& 3 \end{array}$$

To get $5x$ by itself, add -11 to both sides.

To get x by itself, divide both sides by 5.

The number is 3.

CHECK Go back to the words of the *original* problem.

$$\text{If } \underset{\downarrow}{5} \underset{\downarrow}{\text{ times}} \underbrace{\text{a number}}_{3} \underbrace{\text{ is added to}}_{+} \underbrace{11}_{11}, \underbrace{\text{the result is}}_{=} \underbrace{26}_{26}.$$
$$5 \quad \cdot \quad 3 \quad + \quad 11 \quad = \quad 26$$

Does $5 \cdot 3 + 11$ really equal 26? Yes, $5 \cdot 3 + 11 = 15 + 11 = 26$.

So 3 is the correct solution because it "works" when you put it back into the original problem.

◀ **Work Problem ❸ at the Side.**

OBJECTIVE ▶ 3 Solve application problems with one unknown quantity. Now you are ready to tackle application problems. Here are the steps.

Solving an Application Problem	
Step 1	**Read** the problem once to see what it is about. Read it carefully a second time. As you read, make a sketch or write word phrases that identify the known and the unknown parts of the problem.
Step 2(a)	If there is one unknown quantity, **assign a variable** to represent it. Write down what your variable represents.
Step 2(b)	If there is more than one unknown quantity, **assign a variable** to represent "the thing you know the least about." Then write variable expressions, using the same variable, to show the relationship of the other unknown quantities to the first one.
Step 3	**Write an equation,** using your sketch or word phrases as the guide.
Step 4	**Solve** the equation.
Step 5	**State the answer** to the question in the problem and label your answer.
Step 6	**Check** whether your answer fits all the facts given in the *original* statement of the problem. If it does, you are done. If it doesn't, start again at *Step 1*.

Answers

3. (a) $3x + 4 = 19$
$x = 5$

CHECK $\underbrace{3 \cdot 5} + 4$ does equal 19
$\underbrace{15\ + 4}$
19

(b) $6x - 7 = -25$
$x = -3$

CHECK $\underbrace{6 \cdot (-3)} - 7$ does equal -25
$\underbrace{-18\ + (-7)}$
-25

EXAMPLE 4 Solving an Application Problem with One Unknown Quantity

Heather put some money aside in an envelope for small household expenses. Yesterday she took out $20 for groceries. Today a friend paid back a loan and Heather put the $34 in the envelope. Now she has $43 in the envelope. How much was in the envelope at the start?

Step 1 **Read** the problem once. It is about money in an envelope. Read it a second time and write word phrases.

> Unknown: amount of money in the envelope at the start
> Known: took out $20; put in $34; ended up with $43

Step 2(a) There is only one unknown quantity, so **assign a variable** to represent it. Let m represent the money at the start.

Step 3 **Write an equation,** using the phrases you wrote as a guide.

Money at the start	Took out $20	Put in $34	Ended up with $43
m	$- \$20$	$+ \$34$	$= \$43$

Step 4 **Solve** the equation.

$$m - 20 + 34 = 43 \quad \text{Change subtraction to adding the opposite.}$$

$$m + (-20) + 34 = 43 \quad \text{Simplify the left side.}$$

$$\begin{array}{rcl} m + 14 & = & 43 \\ \underline{-14} & & \underline{-14} \end{array} \quad \begin{array}{l} \text{To get } m \text{ by itself.} \\ \text{add } -14 \text{ to both sides.} \end{array}$$

$$\begin{array}{rcl} m + 0 & = & 29 \\ m & = & 29 \end{array}$$

Step 5 **State the answer** to the question, "How much was in the envelope at the start?" There was $29 in the envelope.

Step 6 **Check** the solution by going back to the *original* problem and inserting the solution.

Started with $29 in the envelope

Took out $20, so $29 − $20 = $9 in the envelope

Put in $34, so $9 + $34 = $43

Now has $43 ←— Matches ——⌐

Because $29 "works" when you put it back into the original problem, you know it is the correct solution.

> If your answer does **not** work in the original problem, start again at *Step 1*.

·········· **Work Problem ④ at the Side.** ▶

---

④ Some people got on an empty bus at its first stop. At the second stop, 3 people got on. At the third stop, 5 more people got on. At the fourth stop, 10 people got off, but 4 people were still on the bus. How many people got on at the first stop? Show your work for each of the six problem-solving steps.

Step 1 **Read.**

Unknown: number of people who got on at first stop

Known: 3 got on; 5 got on; 10 got off; 4 people still on bus

Step 2(a) **Assign a variable.**

Let p be people who got on at first stop. (You may use any letter you like as the variable.)

Step 3 **Write an equation.**

$$p + \underline{} + \underline{} - \underline{} = \underline{}$$

Answer

4. *Step 3* **Write an equation.**
$$p + 3 + 5 - 10 = 4$$

Step 4 **Solve.**
$$p + 3 + 5 + (-10) = 4$$
$$\begin{array}{rcl} p + (-2) & = & 4 \\ \underline{+2} & & \underline{+2} \end{array}$$
$$\begin{array}{rcl} p + 0 & = & 6 \\ p & = & 6 \end{array}$$

Step 5 **State the answer.**
6 people got on at the first stop.

Step 6 **Check.**
6 got on at first stop
3 got on at 2nd stop: $\quad 6 + 3 = 9$
5 got on at 3rd stop: $\quad 9 + 5 = 14$
10 got off at 4th stop: $\quad 14 - 10 = 4$
4 people are left. ←— Matches ——⌐

5 Five donors each gave the same amount of money to a college to use for scholarships. From the money, scholarships of $1250, $900, and $850 were given to students; $250 was left. How much money did each donor give to the college? Show your work for each of the six problem-solving steps.

Step 1 **Read.**

Unknown: money given by each donor

Known: 5 donors; gave out $1250, $900, $850; $250 left

Step 2(a) **Assign a variable.**

Let m be each donor's money.

Step 3 **Write an equation.**

$5 \cdot m - \underline{\quad} - \underline{\quad} - \underline{\quad}$

$= \underline{\quad}$

Answer

5. *Step 3* **Write an equation.**
$5 \cdot m - \$1250 - \$900 - \$850 = \$250$

Step 4 **Solve.**
$5m + (-1250) + (-900) + (-850) = 250$

$$5m + \underbrace{\qquad (-3000) \qquad}_{} = 250$$
$$ \quad \underline{3000} \qquad\qquad \underline{3000}$$
$$5m + \qquad 0 \qquad\qquad = 3250$$

$$\underbrace{\frac{5m}{5}}_{} = \frac{3250}{5}$$
$$m = 650$$

Step 5 **State the answer.**
Each donor gave $650.

Step 6 **Check.**
5 donors each gave $650, so
$5 \cdot \$650 = \$3250$
Gave out $1250, $900, $850, so
$\$3250 - 1250 - 900 - 850 = \$250$
Had $250 left ⟵ Matches ⟶

EXAMPLE 5 **Solving an Application Problem with One Unknown Quantity**

Three friends each put in the same amount of money to buy a gift. After they spent $2 for a card and $31 for the gift, they had $6 left. How much money had each friend put in originally?

Step 1 **Read** the problem. It is about 3 friends buying a gift.

Unknown: amount of money each friend contributed
Known: 3 friends put in money; spent $2 and $31; had $6 left

Step 2(a) There is only one unknown quantity. **Assign a variable,** m, to represent the amount of money each friend contributed.

Step 3 **Write an equation.**

Number of friends	Amount each friend put in	Spent on card	Spent on gift	Left over
3 •	m	− $2	− $31	= $6

To see why this is multiplication, think of an example. If each friend put in $10, how much money would there be? 3 • $10, or $30

Step 4 **Solve.**

$3m - 2 - 31 = 6$ Change subtractions to adding the opposite.

$3m + \underbrace{(-2) + (-31)}_{} = 6$ Simplify the left side.

$$3m + \quad (-33) \quad = 6$$
$$\underline{\qquad\qquad 33 \qquad\qquad \underline{33}}$$
To get $3m$ by itself, add 33 to both sides.

$$\underbrace{3m + \qquad 0}_{} = 39$$

$$\frac{3m}{3} = \frac{39}{3}$$ To get m by itself, divide both sides by 3.

$$m = 13$$

> Write a **$** as part of your answer.

Step 5 **State the answer.** Each friend put in $13.

Step 6 **Check** the solution by putting it back into the *original* problem.

3 friends each put in $13, so 3 • $13 = $39.
Spent $2, spent $31, so $39 − $2 − $31 = $6
Had $6 left ⟵——— Matches ———⟶

$13 is the correct solution because it "works."

◄ **Work Problem 5 at the Side.**

| EXAMPLE 6 | Solving a More Complex Application Problem with One Unknown Quantity |

Michael has completed 5 less than three times as many lab experiments as David. If Michael has completed 13 experiments, how many experiments has David completed?

Step 1 **Read** the problem. It is about the number of experiments done by two students.

Unknown: number of experiments David did
Known: Michael did 5 less than 3 times the number David did; Michael did 13.

Step 2(a) **Assign a variable.** Let n represent the number of experiments David did.

Step 3 **Write an equation.**

| The number Michael did | is | 5 less than 3 times David's number. |
| 13 | = | $3n - 5$ |

> Be careful with subtraction!
> $5 - 3n$ is **not** the same as $3n - 5$.

Step 4 **Solve.**

$13 = 3n - 5$ Change subtraction to adding the opposite.

$13 = 3n + (-5)$

$\underline{5 5}$ To get $3n$ by itself, add 5 to both sides.

$18 = 3n + 0$

$\dfrac{18}{3} = \dfrac{3n}{3}$ To get n by itself, divide both sides by 3.

$6 = n$

Step 5 **State the answer.** David did 6 experiments.

Step 6 **Check** the solution by putting it back into the *original* problem.

3 times David's number $3 \cdot 6 = 18$

Less 5 $18 - 5 = 13$

Michael did 13. ⟵ Matches ⟶

The correct solution is: David did 6 experiments. ⟵

> Label your answer. Write *6 experiments*, **not** just 6.

·········· **Work Problem ⑥ at the Side.** ▶

---

⑥ Susan donated $10 more than twice what LuAnn donated. If Susan donated $22, how much did LuAnn donate?

Show your work for each of the six problem-solving steps.

Step 1 **Read.**

Unknown: LuAnn's donation

Known: Susan donated $10 more than twice what LuAnn donated; Susan donated $22.

Step 2(a) **Assign a variable.**

Let d be _____ donation.

3.3 Exercises

FOR EXTRA HELP

 Download the MyDashBoard App

MyMathLab®

CONCEPT CHECK *Write* true *or* false *for each statement. If a statement is false, correct it.*

1. (a) $14 - x$
means "14 subtracted from a number."

(b) $x - 7$
means "a number decreased by 7."

(c) $\dfrac{-20}{x}$
means "the product of -20 and a number."

2. (a) $3x - 6$
means "6 subtracted from 3 times a number."

(b) $18x$
means "the sum of 18 and a number."

(c) $\dfrac{x}{42}$
means "the quotient of 42 and a number."

Write an algebraic expression, using x as the variable. **See Examples 1 and 2.**

3. 14 plus a number

4. The sum of a number and -8

5. -5 added to a number

6. 16 more than a number

7. 20 minus a number

8. A number decreased by 25

9. 9 less than a number

10. A number subtracted from -7

11. -6 times a number

12. The product of -3 and a number

13. Double a number

14. A number times 10

15. A number divided by 2

16. 4 divided by a number

17. Twice a number added to 8

18. Five times a number plus 5

19. 10 fewer than seven times a number

20. 12 less than six times a number

21. The sum of twice a number and the number

22. Triple a number subtracted from the number

*Translate each sentence into an equation and solve it. Check your solution by going
back to the words in the original problem.* ***See Example 3***.

23. If four times a number is decreased by 2, the result
is 26. Find the number.

4 times a number	decreased by	2	result is	26

$$4n \quad - \quad 2 \quad = \quad 26$$

24. The sum of 8 and five times a number is 53. Find
the number.

$$8 \quad + \quad 5n \quad = \quad 53$$

25. If a number is added to twice the number, the result
is −15. What is the number?

26. If a number is subtracted from three times the
number, the result is −8. What is the number?

27. If the product of some number and 5 is increased
by 12, the result is seven times the number. Find
the number.

28. If eight times a number is subtracted from eleven
times the number, the result is −9. Find the number.

29. When three times a number is subtracted from 30,
the result is 2 plus the number. What is the number?

30. When twice a number is decreased by 8, the result
is the number increased by 7. Find the number.

Solve each application problem. Use the six problem-solving steps you learned in this section. See Examples 4–6.

31. Ricardo gained 15 pounds over the winter. He went on a diet and lost 28 pounds. Then he regained 5 pounds and weighed 177 pounds. How much did he weigh originally?

Let *w* be Ricardo's original weight.

32. Mr. Chee deposited $200 into his bank account. Then, after paying $43 for gas and $190 for his child's day care, the balance in his account was $67. How much was in his account before he made the deposit?

Let *m* be the original amount in the account.

33. There were 18 cookies in Magan's cookie jar. While she was busy in another room, her children ate some of the cookies. Magan bought three dozen cookies and added them to the jar. At that point she had 49 cookies in the jar. How many cookies did her children eat?

34. The Greens had a 20-pound bag of bird seed in their garage. Mice got into the bag and ate some of it. The Greens then bought an 8-pound bag of seed and put all the seed in a metal container. They now have 24 pounds of seed. How much did the mice eat?

35. A college bookstore ordered six boxes of red pens. The store sold 32 red pens last week and 35 red pens this week. Five pens were left on the shelf. How many pens were in each box?

36. A local charity received a donation of eight cartons filled with cans of soup. The charity gave out 100 cans of soup yesterday and 92 cans today before running out. How many cans were in each carton?

37. The 14 music club members each paid the same amount for dues. The club also earned $340 selling magazine subscriptions. They spent $575 to organize a jazz festival. Now their bank account, which started at $0, is overdrawn by $25. How much did each member pay in dues?

38. The manager of an apartment complex had 11 packages of lightbulbs on hand. He replaced 29 burned out bulbs in hallway lights and 7 bulbs in the party room. Eight bulbs were left. How many bulbs were in each package?

39. When 75 is subtracted from four times Tamu's age, the result is Tamu's age. How old is Tamu?

Let *a* be Tamu's age.

40. If three times Linda's age is decreased by 36, the result is twice Linda's age. How old is Linda?

Let *a* be Linda's age.

41. While shopping for clothes, Consuelo spent $3 less than twice what Brenda spent. Consuelo spent $81. How much did Brenda spend?

42. Dennis weighs 184 pounds. His weight is 2 pounds less than six times his child's weight. How much does his child weigh?

43. Paige bought five identical bags of candy for Halloween. Forty-eight children visited her home and she gave each child three pieces of candy. At the end of the night she still had one bag of candy. How many pieces of candy were in each bag?

44. A restaurant ordered four packages of paper napkins. Yesterday they used up one package, and today they used up 140 napkins. Two packages plus 60 napkins remain. How many napkins are in each package?

45. The recommended daily intake of vitamin C for an adult female is 8 mg more than four times the recommended amount for a young child. The amount for an adult female is 60 mg. How much should a young child receive? (*Source:* Food and Nutrition Board.)

46. A cheetah's sprinting speed is 61 miles per hour less than three times a zebra's running speed. A cheetah can sprint 68 miles per hour. Find the zebra's running speed. (*Source: Grolier Multimedia Encyclopedia.*)

Study Skills

TIPS FOR IMPROVING TEST SCORES

OBJECTIVES

1. Restate the importance of sleep and good nutrition as it affects learning.

2. Explain the effect of anxiety and stress on learning.

Many things besides studying can improve your test scores. You may not realize that eating the right foods, as well as getting enough exercise and sleep, can also improve your scores. Your brain (and therefore your ability to think) is affected by the condition of your whole body. So, part of your preparation for tests includes keeping yourself in good physical shape as well as spending time on the actual course material. Try these suggestions and see the difference.

Performance Health Tips

Performance Health Tips to Improve Your Test Score	Explanation
Get **seven to eight hours of sleep** the night before the exam. (It's helpful to get that much sleep *every* night.)	**Fatigue and exhaustion** reduce efficiency. They also cause poor memory and recall. If you didn't sleep much the night before a test, 20 minutes of relaxation or meditation can help. (Also see the comments below about eating carbohydrates to help you sleep.)
Eat a **small, high-energy meal** about two hours before the test. Start the meal with a small amount of protein such as fish, chicken, or nonfat yogurt. Include carbohydrates if you like, but no high-fat foods.	Just 3 to 4 ounces of protein increases the amount of a chemical in the brain called tyrosine, which **improves your alertness, accuracy, and motivation.** High-fat foods dull your mind and slow down your brain.
Drink plenty of water. Don't wait until you feel thirsty; your body is already dehydrated by the time you feel it.	Research suggests that staying well hydrated improves the electrochemical communications in your brain.
Give your brain the time it needs to grow dendrites!	**Cramming doesn't work;** your brain cannot grow dendrites that quickly. **Studying every day** using these study skills techniques is the way to give your brain the time it needs.

Anxiety Prevention Tips

To Prevent Anxiety	Explanation
Practice slow, deep breathing for five minutes each day. Then do a minute or two of deep breathing right before the test. Also, if you feel your anxiety building during the test, stop for a minute, close your eyes, and do some deep breathing.	When **test anxiety** hits, you breathe more quickly and shallowly, which causes hyperventilation. Symptoms may be confusion, inability to concentrate, shaking, dizziness, and more. Slow, deep breathing will **calm you and prevent panic.**

To Prevent Anxiety	Explanation
Do 15 to 20 minutes of *moderate exercise* (like walking) shortly before the test. Daily exercise is even better!	*Exercise reduces stress* and will help prevent "blanking out" on a test. Exercise also increases your alertness, clear thinking, and energy.
To help you sleep the night before the test, or any time you need to calm down, *eat high-carbohydrate foods* such as popcorn, bread, rice, crackers, muffins, bagels, pasta, corn, baked potatoes (not fries or chips), and cereals.	Carbohydrates increase the level of a chemical in the brain called serotonin, which has a *calming effect on the mind*. It reduces feelings of tension and stress and improves your ability to concentrate. You only need to eat a small amount, like half a bagel, to get this effect.
Before the test, *go easy on caffeinated beverages* such as coffee, tea, and soft drinks. Do not eat candy bars or other sugary snacks.	Extra caffeine can *make you jittery,* "hyper," and shaky for the test. It can increase the tendency to panic. Too much sugar causes negative emotional reactions in some people.

Now Try This

What will you do to improve your next test score? List the three or four tips you think will help you the most.

1 _____

2 _____

3 _____

4 _____

What changes will you have to make in order to try the tips you chose?

_____

_____

_____

_____

See *Tips for Taking Math Tests* **and** *Preparing for Your Final Exam* **for more ideas about managing anxiety.** (Check the Table of Contents to find their locations.)

Chapter 3 *Summary*

Key Terms

3.1

formula Formulas are well-known rules for solving common types of problems. They are written in a shorthand form that uses variables.

perimeter Perimeter is the distance around the outside edges of a flat shape. It is measured in linear units such as in., ft, yd, mm, cm, m, and so on.

square A square is a figure with four sides that are all the same length and meet to form right angles, which measure 90°. See example at the right.

20 in.

20 in.   20 in.

20 in.

rectangle A rectangle is a four-sided figure in which all sides meet to form right angles, which measure 90°. The opposite sides are the same length. See example at the right.

7 ft

3 ft   3 ft

7 ft

parallelogram A parallelogram is a four-sided figure in which opposite sides are both parallel and equal in length. See example at the right.

triangle A triangle is a figure with exactly three sides. See example at the right.

27 m

15 m   15 m

27 m

31 mm

25 mm   16 mm

3.2

area Area is the surface inside a two-dimensional (flat) shape. It is measured by determining the number of squares of a certain size needed to cover the surface inside the shape. Some of the commonly used units for measuring area are square inches (in.^{2}), square feet (ft^2), square yards (yd^2), square centimeters (cm^2), and square meters (m^2).

New Symbols

Right angle:
(90° angle)

Small square in the corner of a figure indicates a right angle.

Square units for measuring area: in.^{2} ft^2 yd^2 mi^2

mm^2 cm^2 m^2 km^2

New Formulas

Perimeter of a square: $P = 4s$

Perimeter of a rectangle: $P = 2l + 2w$

Area of a square: $A = s^2$

Area of a rectangle: $A = lw$

Area of a parallelogram: $A = bh$

Test Your Word Power

See how well you have learned the vocabulary in this chapter.

1 The **perimeter** of a flat shape is
   A. measured in square units
   B. found by adding the lengths of the sides
   C. found by multiplying length times width.

2 The **area** of a flat shape is
   A. found by adding length plus width
   B. measured in linear units
   C. measured in square units.

3 When working with a **square shape,**
   A. the perimeter formula is $P = s^2$
   B. the area formula is $A = \frac{1}{2} bh$
   C. all sides have the same length.

4 When working with a **rectangular shape,**
   A. the area formula is $A = lw$
   B. opposite sides have different lengths
   C. the perimeter formula is $P = bh$.

5 In **triangles**
   A. all the sides meet at 90° angles
   B. there are exactly three sides
   C. the area formula is $A = s^2$.

6 In *all* **parallelograms**
   A. there are exactly six sides
   B. all sides have the same length
   C. opposite sides are parallel and equal in length.

Answers to Test Your Word Power

1. B; *Example:* If a triangle has sides measuring 4 ft, 10 ft, and 8 ft, then $P = 4$ ft $+ 10$ ft $+ 8$ ft $= 22$ ft.

2. C; *Example:* Area is measured in square units such as in.^{2}, ft^2, yd^2, cm^2, and km^2.

3. C; *Example:* If one side of a square is 5 in. long, all the other sides are also 5 in. long.

4. A; *Example:* If the length of a rectangle is 12 cm and the width is 8 cm, then $A = 12$ cm $\cdot$ 8 cm $= 96$ cm^2.

5. B; *Examples:*

6. C; *Example:* In parallelogram *ABCD*, sides *AB* and *DC* are parallel and equal in length. Also, sides *AD* and *BC* are parallel and equal in length.

Quick Review

Concepts	Examples

3.1 Finding Perimeter

To find the perimeter of *any* flat shape with straight sides, add the lengths of the sides. Perimeter is measured in linear units (cm, m, ft, yd, and so on).

Or, for squares and rectangles, you can use the formulas shown below.

Find the perimeter of each figure.

$$P = 9 \text{ cm} + 11 \text{ cm} + 9 \text{ cm} + 11 \text{ cm}$$
$$P = 40 \text{ cm}$$

Perimeter of a square: $P = 4s$, where *s* is the length of one side.

$$P = 4s$$
$$P = 4 \cdot 8 \text{ in.}$$
$$P = 32 \text{ in.}$$

Perimeter of a rectangle: $P = 2l + 2w$, where *l* is the length and *w* is the width.

$$P = 2 \cdot l \ + 2 \cdot w$$
$$P = 2 \cdot 3 \text{ yd} + 2 \cdot 2 \text{ yd}$$
$$P = \ 6 \text{ yd} \ + \ 4 \text{ yd}$$
$$P = 10 \text{ yd}$$

Concepts	Examples

3.1 **Finding the Length of One Side of a Square**

If you know the perimeter of a square, use the formula $P = 4s$. Replace P with the value for the perimeter and solve the equation for s.

If the perimeter of a square room is 44 ft, find the length of one side.

$$P = 4s \quad \text{Replace } P \text{ with 44 ft.}$$

$$44 \text{ ft} = 4s$$

$$\frac{44 \text{ ft}}{4} = \frac{4s}{4} \quad \text{Divide both sides by 4.}$$

$$11 \text{ ft} = s$$

The length of one side is 11 ft.

CHECK   Check the solution by drawing a sketch of the room. The perimeter is 11 ft + 11 ft + 11 ft + 11 ft = 44 ft. The result matches the perimeter given in the problem.

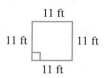

3.1 **Finding the Length or Width of a Rectangle**

If you know the perimeter of a rectangle and either its width or length, use the formula $P = 2l + 2w$. Replace P and either l or w with the values that you know. Then solve the equation.

The width of a rectangular rug is 8 ft. The perimeter is 36 ft. Find the length.

$$P = 2l + 2w \quad \text{Replace } P \text{ with 36 ft and } w \text{ with 8 ft.}$$

$$36 \text{ ft} = 2l + 2 \cdot 8 \text{ ft}$$

$$36 \text{ ft} = 2l + 16 \text{ ft}$$

$$\underline{-16 \text{ ft} \qquad -16 \text{ ft}} \quad \text{Add } -16 \text{ ft to both sides.}$$

$$20 \text{ ft} = 2l + 0$$

$$\frac{20 \text{ ft}}{2} = \frac{2l}{2} \quad \text{Divide both sides by 2.}$$

$$10 \text{ ft} = l \quad \text{The length is 10 ft.}$$

CHECK   To check the solution, draw a sketch of the rectangle and label the lengths of the sides. Then add the four measurements.

10 ft + 10 ft + 8 ft + 8 ft = 36 ft

The result matches the perimeter given in the problem.

Concepts	Examples

3.2 Finding Area

Use the appropriate formula. Remember to measure area in *square* units (cm^2, m^2, ft^2, yd^2, and so on).

Area of a rectangle: $A = lw$,
    where l is the length and w is the width.

Area of a square: $A = s^2$, which means $s \cdot s$,
    where s is the length of one side.

Area of a parallelogram: $A = bh$,
    where b is the base and h is the height.

Find the area of each figure.

$A = lw$
$A = 3\text{ m} \cdot 2\text{ m}$
$A = 6\text{ m}^2$

$A = s^2$
$A = s \cdot s$
$A = 8\text{ in.} \cdot 8\text{ in.}$
$A = 64\text{ in.}^2$

$A = bh$
$A = 4\text{ cm} \cdot 3\text{ cm}$
$A = 12\text{ cm}^2$

3.2 Finding the Unknown Length in a Rectangle or Parallelogram

If you know the area of a rectangle or parallelogram and one of the other measurements, use the appropriate area formula (see above). Replace A and one of the other variables with the values that you know. Then solve the equation.

The area of a parallelogram is 72 yd^2, and its height is 9 yd. Find the base.

Replace A with 72 yd^2 and h with 9 yd.

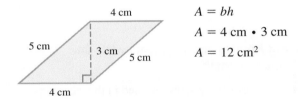

Divide both sides by 9 yd.

$$8\text{ yd} = b$$

The base of the parallelogram is 8 yd.

3.2 Finding the Length of One Side of a Square

If you know the area of a square, use the formula $A = s^2$. Replace A with the value that you know. Then solve the equation by asking, "What number, times itself, gives the value of A?"

A square ceiling has an area of 100 ft^2. What is the length of each side of the ceiling?

$A = s^2$ Replace A with 100 ft^2.

$100\text{ ft}^2 = s^2$ Rewrite s^2 as $s \cdot s$.

$100\text{ ft}^2 = s \cdot s$ Ask, "What number times itself gives 100?"

$100\text{ ft}^2 = 10\text{ ft} \cdot 10\text{ ft}$

The value of s is 10 ft, so each side of the ceiling is 10 ft long.

Concepts	Examples

3.3 Translating Sentences into Equations

Translate word phrases into symbols using x (or any other letter) as the variable. Then solve the equation. Check the solution by putting it back in the original problem.

If 10 is subtracted from three times a number, the result is 14. Find the number.

Let x represent the unknown number.

$$3x - 10 = 14 \qquad \text{Change subtraction to adding the opposite.}$$

$$3x + (-10) = 14$$
$$\underbrace{ \quad 10 \qquad 10}_{} \qquad \text{Add 10 to both sides.}$$
$$3x + \quad 0 = 24$$

$$\frac{3x}{3} = \frac{24}{3} \qquad \text{Divide both sides by 3.}$$

$$x = 8$$

The number is 8.

CHECK If 10 is subtracted from three times 8, do you get 14? Yes, $3 \cdot 8 - 10 = 24 - 10 = 14$.

3.3 Solving Application Problems with One Unknown Quantity

Use the six problem-solving steps outlined in this chapter. They are listed below in abbreviated form.

Denise had some money in her purse this morning. She gave $15 to her daughter and paid $4 to park in the lot at work. At that point she still had $27. How much was in her purse this morning?

Step 1 **Read** the problem and identify what is known and what is unknown.

Step 1 Unknown: money in purse this morning
Known: took out $15; took out $4; still had $27.

Step 2 **Assign a variable** to represent the unknown quantity.

Step 2 Let m represent the money in her purse this morning.

Step 3 **Write an equation.**

Step 3 $m - \$15 - \$4 = \$27$

Step 4 **Solve** the equation.

Step 4 $m - 15 - 4 = 27$

$$m + \underbrace{(-15) + (-4)}_{} = 27 \qquad \text{Change subtractions.}$$

$$m + (-19) = 27 \qquad \text{Combine like terms.}$$

$$\underline{\quad 19 \qquad\qquad 19} \qquad \text{Add 19 to both sides.}$$

$$m + 0 = 46$$

$$m = 46$$

Step 5 **State the answer.**

Step 5 She had $46 in her purse this morning.

Step 6 **Check** whether your answer fits all the facts given in the *original* statement of the problem.

Step 6 Started with $46.
Took out $15, so $46 − $15 = $31
Took out $4, so $31 − $4 = $27
Had $27 left ←— Matches —↗

Chapter 3 *Review Exercises*

3.1 *In Exercises 1–4, find the perimeter of each figure. Also, name each figure in Exercises 1–3.*

1.

28 cm

28 cm

2.

8 mi

3 mi

3.

14 yd

7 yd   5 yd   7 yd

14 yd

4.

44 m

26 m   14 m

20 m

24 m   12 m

In Exercises 5–7, use the appropriate formula to find the unknown measurement.

5. A square card table has a perimeter of 12 ft. Find the length of one side of the table.

6. A rectangular playground has a perimeter of 128 yd. Find its length if it is 31 yd wide.

7. A rectangular watercolor painting that is 21 in. long has a perimeter of 72 in. What is the width of the painting?

3.2 *In Exercises 8–10, draw a sketch of each shape with the appropriate measurements on it. Then find the area, using the appropriate formula. (Sketches may vary; show sketches to your instructor.)*

8. A tablecloth that measures 5 ft by 8 ft

9. A 25 m square dance floor

10. A parallelogram-shaped lot with a base of 16 yd and a height of 13 yd

In Exercises 11–13, use the appropriate formula to find the unknown measurement.

11. A rectangular patio that is 14 ft long has an area of 126 ft². Find its width.

12. A parallelogram has an area of 88 cm². If the base is 11 cm, what is the height?

13. The area of a square piece of land is 100 mi². What is the length of one side?

3.3 *Write each phrase as an algebraic expression. Use x as the variable.*

14. A number subtracted from 57

15. The sum of 15 and twice a number

16. The product of −9 and a number

Translate each sentence into an equation and solve it. Show your work.

17. The sum of four times a number and 6 is −30. What is the number?

18. When twice a number is subtracted from 10, the result is 4 plus the number. Find the number.

3.3–3.4 *Use the six problem-solving steps to solve each problem. Show your work.*

19. Grace wrote a $600 check for her rent. Then she deposited her $750 paycheck and a $75 tax refund into her account. The new balance was $309. How much was in her account before she wrote the rent check?

20. Yoku ordered four boxes of candles for his restaurant. One candle was put on each of the 25 tables. There were 23 candles left. How many candles were originally in each box?

21. $1000 in prize money is being split between Reggie and Donald. Donald should get $300 more than Reggie. How much will each man receive?

22. A rectangular photograph is twice as long as it is wide. The perimeter of the photograph is 84 cm. Find the length and the width of the photograph.

Mixed Review Exercises

Use the information in the advertisement and the appropriate formulas to solve Exercises 23–26. Show your work.

NOW ON SALE

Build Your Own Dog Pen

Kit #1 includes 20 feet of fencing.

Kit #2 includes 36 feet of fencing.

23. Anthony made a square dog pen using Kit #2.

(a) What was the length of each side of the pen?

(b) What was the area of the pen?

24. First draw sketches of two *different* rectangular dog pens that you could build using all the fencing in Kit #1. Label the lengths of the sides. Then find the area of each pen.

25. Timotha bought Kit #2. But she used some of the fencing around her garden, so she went back and bought Kit #1. Now she has 41 ft of fencing for a dog pen. How much fencing did she use around her garden? Use the six problem-solving steps.

26. Diana bought Kit #2. The pen she built had a length that was 2 ft more than the width. Find the length and width of the pen. Use the six problem-solving steps.

Chapter 3 Test **Test Prep** VIDEO

The Chapter Test Prep Videos with test solutions are available on DVD, in MyMathLab, and on YouTube — search "LialPrealgebra" and click on "Channels."

Find the perimeter of each shape.

1.

72 m
59 m   46 m   59 m
72 m

2.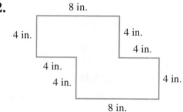

8 in.
4 in.   4 in.
               4 in.
4 in.
4 in.   4 in.
8 in.

3. A square wetland 3 miles on a side

4. A rectangular mirror that measures 2 ft by 4 ft

5.

50 cm
45 cm   15 cm

Find the area of each shape.

6.

27 mm
18 mm   18 mm
27 mm

7.

11 cm
10 cm
14 cm   14 cm
11 cm

8. A rectangular animal preserve is 55 mi wide and 68 mi long.

9. The floor of a square room measures 6 m on each side.

Solve Exercises 10–14 using the appropriate formulas. Show your work.

10. A square table has a perimeter of 12 ft. Find the length of one side.

11. The Mercado family has 34 ft of fencing to put around a garden plot. The plot is rectangular in shape. If it is 6 ft wide, find the length of the plot.

12. The area of a parallelogram is 65 in.^{2}, and the base is 13 in. What is the height of the parallelogram?

13. A rectangular postage stamp has a length of 4 cm and an area of 12 cm^2. Find its width.

14. A square bulletin board has an area of 16 ft². How long is each side of the bulletin board?

15. Explain the difference between ft and ft². For which types of problems might you use each of these units?

Translate each sentence into an equation and solve it. Show your work.

16. If 40 is added to four times a number, the result is zero. Find the number.

17. When 7 times a number is decreased by 23, the result is the number plus 7. What is the number?

Solve each application problem, using the six problem-solving steps.

18. Josephine had $43 in her wallet. Her son used some of it when he bought groceries. Josephine found $16 in her desk drawer and put it in her wallet. She counted $44 in the wallet. How much money did her son spend on groceries?

19. Ray is 39 years old. His age is 4 years more than five times his daughter's age. How old is his daughter?

20. A board is 118 cm long. Karin cut it into two pieces, with one piece 4 cm longer than the other. Find the length of both pieces.

21. The perimeter of a rectangular building is 420 ft. The length is four times as long as the width. Find the length and the width. Draw a sketch to help you solve this problem.

22. Marcella and her husband, Tim, spent a total of 19 hours redecorating their living room. Tim spent 3 hours less time than Marcella. How long did each person work on the room?

Chapters 1–3 *Cumulative Review Exercises*

1. Write this number in words.

4,000,206,300

2. Write this number, using digits.

seventy million, five thousand, four hundred eighty-nine

3. Write $<$ or $>$ between each pair of numbers to make a true statement.

-7 ____ -1 0 ____ -5

4. Name the property illustrated by each equation.

(a) $1(97) = 97$

5. (a) Round 3795 to the nearest ten.

(b) $-10 + 0 = -10$

(b) Round 493,662 to the nearest ten-thousand.

(c) $(3 \cdot 7) \cdot 6 = 3 \cdot (7 \cdot 6)$

Simplify.

6. $-12 - 12$

7. $-3(-9)$

8. $|7| - |-10|$

9. $-40 \div 2 \cdot 5$

10. $3 - 8 + 10$

11. $\dfrac{0}{-6}$

12. $-8 + 5(2 - 3)$

13. $(-3)^2 + 4^2$

14. $4 - 3(-6 \div 3) + 7(0 - 6)$

15. $\dfrac{4 - 2^3 + 5^2 - 3(-2)}{-1(3) - 6(-2) - 9}$

16. Rewrite $10w^2xy^4$ without exponents.

17. Evaluate $-6cd^3$ when c is 5 and d is -2.

Simplify.

18. $-4k + k + 5k$

19. $m^2 + 2m + 2m^2$

20. $xy^3 - xy^3$

21. $5(-4a)$

22. $-8 + x + 5 - 2x^2 - x$

23. $-3(4n + 3) + 10$

Solve each equation and check each solution.

24. $6 - 20 = 2x - 9x$ **CHECK**

25. $-5y = y + 6$ **CHECK**

Solve each equation. Show your work.

26. $3b - 9 = 19 - 4b$

27. $-16 - h + 2 = h - 10$

28. $-5(2x + 4) = 3x - 20$

29. $6 + 4(a + 8) = -8a + 5 + a$

Find the perimeter and area of each shape. The figure in Exercise 30 is a parallelogram.

30.

11 in.

18 in.

12 in.

31. A square plaza is 15 m on a side.

32. A rectangular piece of plywood is 4 ft wide and 8 ft long.

Translate each sentence into an equation and solve it. Show your work.

33. When -50 is added to five times a number, the result is 0. What is the number?

34. When three times a number is subtracted from 10, the result is two times the number. Find the number.

Solve each application problem, using the six problem-solving steps.

35. Some people were waiting in line at the bank. Three people made deposits and left. Six more people got in line. Then two more people were helped, but five people were still in line. How many were in the line originally?

36. Twelve soccer players each paid the same amount toward a team trip. Expenses for the trip were $2200, and now the team bank account, which started at $0, is overdrawn by $40. How much did each player originally pay?

37. A group of 192 students was divided into two smaller groups. One smaller group was three times the size of the other. How many students were in each smaller group?

38. A rectangular swimming pool is 14 ft longer than it is wide. If the perimeter of the pool is 92 ft, find the length and the width.

Math in the Media

To estimate the number of words in a child's vocabulary, a pediatrician may use this formula.

$$V = 60A - 900$$

where V is the number of vocabulary words and A is the age of the child in months.

Source: *Pediatrics.*

Use the formula to estimate the *age* of each child.

1. The child's vocabulary is 180 words.

2. The child's vocabulary is 1440 words.

3. The child's vocabulary is 60 words.

4. Describe *in words* what you were doing as you found each child's age.

5. Find the child's age if the child's vocabulary is 0 words.

6. Refer to **Problem 5** above. *Without solving an equation,* are there any other ages at which children would have a vocabulary of 0 words?

7. Is the formula useful for all ages of children? Explain your answer.

4 Rational Numbers: Positive and Negative Fractions

In this chapter, you'll see how fractions are used when measuring things for remodeling projects, cooking, sewing, medical jobs, or any time you want to talk about part of a whole thing.

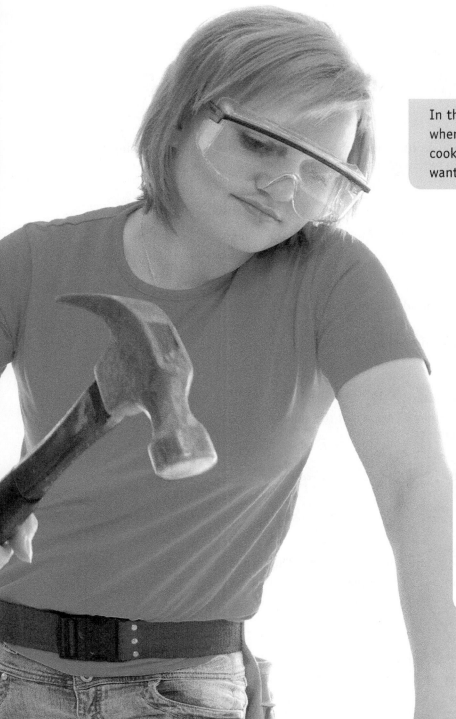

4.1 Introduction to Signed Fractions

OBJECTIVES

1. Use a fraction to name part of a whole.
2. Identify numerators, denominators, proper fractions, and improper fractions.
3. Graph positive and negative fractions on a number line.
4. Find the absolute value of a fraction.
5. Write equivalent fractions.

VOCABULARY TIP

Fract- means "to break." Take a whole and "break" it into equal-sized parts. Each part is a **fraction** of the whole.

1 Write fractions for the shaded portion and the unshaded portion of each figure.

 (a)

Number of shaded parts → ___3___

Number of equal parts ⟶

Number of **un**shaded parts → _____

Number of equal parts ⟶

(b)

(c)

Answers

1. (a) $\frac{3}{5}; \frac{2}{5}$ (b) $\frac{1}{6}; \frac{5}{6}$ (c) $\frac{7}{8}; \frac{1}{8}$

OBJECTIVE **1** **Use a fraction to name part of a whole.** In **Chapters 1–3** you worked with integers. Recall that a list of the integers can be written as follows.

$$\dots, -6, -5, -4, -3, -2, -1, 0, 1, 2, 3, 4, 5, 6, \dots$$

The dots show that the list goes on forever in both directions.

Now we will work with *fractions*.

Fractions

A **fraction** is a number of the form $\frac{a}{b}$ where a and b are integers and b is not 0.

One use for fractions is situations in which we need a number that is between two integers. Here is an example.

$\frac{2}{3}$ cup

A recipe uses $\frac{2}{3}$ cup of milk.

$\frac{2}{3}$ is between 0 and 1.

$\frac{2}{3}$ is a fraction because it is of the form $\frac{a}{b}$ and 2 and 3 are integers.

The number $\frac{2}{3}$ is a fraction that represents 2 of 3 equal parts. In this example, the cup is divided into 3 equal parts and we use enough milk to fill 2 of the parts.

We read $\frac{2}{3}$ as "two-thirds."

EXAMPLE 1 **Using Fractions to Represent Part of One Whole**

Use fractions to represent the shaded portion and the unshaded portion of each figure.

(a)

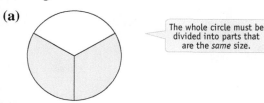

The whole circle must be divided into parts that are the *same* size.

The figure has 3 equal parts. The 2 shaded parts are represented by the fraction $\frac{2}{3}$. The *un*shaded part is $\frac{1}{3}$ of the figure.

(b)

The figure has 7 equal parts. The 4 shaded parts are represented by the fraction $\frac{4}{7}$. The *un*shaded part is $\frac{3}{7}$ of the figure.

◀ Work Problem **1** at the Side.

Fractions can also be used to represent more than one whole object.

EXAMPLE 2 **Using Fractions to Represent More Than One Whole**

Use a fraction to represent the shaded parts.

(a) $\frac{1}{4}$ $\frac{1}{4}$ $\frac{1}{4}$ $\frac{1}{4}$ $\quad$ $\frac{1}{4}$

1

An area equal to 5 of the $\frac{1}{4}$ parts is shaded, so $\frac{5}{4}$ is shaded.

(b)

$\frac{1}{3}\{$ $\quad\Big\}1$

An area equal to 5 of the $\frac{1}{3}$ parts is shaded, so $\frac{5}{3}$ is shaded.

·············· Work Problem **2** at the Side. ▶

OBJECTIVE ▶ **2** **Identify numerators, denominators, proper fractions, and improper fractions.** In the fraction $\frac{2}{3}$, the number 2 is the *numerator* and 3 is the *denominator*. The bar between the numerator and the denominator is the *fraction bar*.

$$\text{Fraction bar} \to \frac{2}{3} \begin{array}{l} \leftarrow \text{Numerator} \\ \leftarrow \text{Denominator} \end{array}$$

> **Numerator and Denominator**
>
> The **denominator** of a fraction shows the number of equal parts in the whole, and the **numerator** shows how many parts are being considered.

> **Note**
>
> Recall that a fraction bar, —, is a symbol for division and division by 0 is *undefined*. Therefore a fraction with a denominator of 0 is also *undefined*.

EXAMPLE 3 **Identifying Numerators and Denominators**

Identify the numerator and denominator in each fraction. Then state the number of equal parts in the whole.

(a) $\frac{5}{9}$ $\quad$ $\frac{5}{9}$ $\begin{array}{l} \leftarrow \text{Numerator} \\ \leftarrow \text{Denominator} \end{array}$

9 equal parts in the whole

(b) $\frac{11}{7}$ $\quad$ $\frac{11}{7}$ $\begin{array}{l} \leftarrow \text{Numerator} \\ \leftarrow \text{Denominator} \end{array}$

7 equal parts in the whole

·············· Work Problem **3** at the Side. ▶

Fractions are sometimes called *proper* or *improper* fractions.

> **Proper and Improper Fractions**
>
> If the numerator of a fraction is *less* than the denominator, the fraction is a **proper fraction.** A proper fraction is less than 1.
>
> If the numerator is *greater than or equal to* the denominator, the fraction is an **improper fraction.** An improper fraction is greater than or equal to 1.

---

2 Write fractions for the shaded portions.

(a)

(b)

3 Identify the numerator and the denominator. Draw a picture with shaded parts to show each fraction. Your drawings may vary, but they should have the correct number of shaded parts.

(a) $\frac{2}{3}$

(b) $\frac{1}{4}$

(c) $\frac{8}{5}$

(d) $\frac{5}{2}$

Answers

2. **(a)** $\frac{8}{7}$ **(b)** $\frac{7}{4}$

3. **(a)** N: 2; D: 3

(b) N: 1; D: 4

(c) N: 8; D: 5

(d) N: 5; D: 2

4 From this group of fractions:

$$\frac{3}{4} \quad \frac{8}{7} \quad \frac{5}{7} \quad \frac{6}{6} \quad \frac{1}{2} \quad \frac{2}{1}$$

GS **(a)** list all proper fractions.

Hint: In a proper fraction, the numerator is *less* than the denominator.

Proper Fractions			Improper Fractions		
$\dfrac{1}{2}$	$\dfrac{5}{11}$	$\dfrac{35}{36}$	$\dfrac{9}{7}$	$\dfrac{126}{125}$	$\dfrac{7}{7}$

EXAMPLE 4 **Classifying Types of Fractions**

(a) Identify all proper fractions in this list.

$$\frac{3}{4} \quad \frac{5}{9} \quad \frac{17}{5} \quad \frac{9}{7} \quad \frac{3}{3} \quad \frac{12}{25} \quad \frac{1}{9} \quad \frac{5}{3}$$

Proper fractions have a numerator that is *less* than the denominator. The proper fractions in the list are shown below.

$$\frac{3}{4} \leftarrow \text{3 is less than 4.} \qquad \frac{5}{9} \quad \frac{12}{25} \quad \frac{1}{9}$$

(b) Identify all improper fractions in the list in part (a).

Improper fractions have a numerator that is *equal to or greater* than the denominator. The improper fractions in the list are shown below.

$$\frac{17}{5} \leftarrow \text{17 is greater than 5.} \qquad \frac{9}{7} \quad \frac{3}{3} \quad \frac{5}{3}$$

· ◄ **Work Problem 4 at the Side.**

CAUTION

So far, you have seen only positive fractions. For negative fractions, the negative sign will be written in front of the fraction bar: for example, $-\frac{3}{4}$. As with integers, the negative sign tells you that a fraction is *less than 0*; it is to the *left* of 0 on the number line. When there is *no* sign in front of a fraction, the fraction is assumed to be positive. For example, $\frac{3}{4}$ is assumed to be $+\frac{3}{4}$. It is to the *right* of 0 on the number line.

When the negative sign might be confused with the symbol for subtraction, we will write parentheses around the negative number. Here is an example.

$$3 - \left(-\tfrac{1}{2}\right) \quad \text{means} \quad 3 \text{ minus } \left(\text{negative } \tfrac{1}{2}\right)$$

(b) list all improper fractions.

OBJECTIVE ▶ 3 **Graph positive and negative fractions on a number line.**

Sometimes we need *negative* numbers that are between two integers. For example, $-\frac{3}{4}$ is between 0 and -1. Graphing numbers on a number line helps us see the difference between $\frac{3}{4}$ and $-\frac{3}{4}$. Both represent 3 out of 4 equal parts, but they are in opposite directions from 0 on the number line. For $\frac{3}{4}$, divide the distance from 0 to 1 into 4 equal parts. Then start at 0, count over 3 parts, and make a dot. For $-\frac{3}{4}$, repeat the same process between 0 and -1.

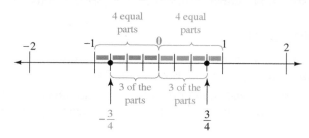

Answers

4. (a) $\dfrac{3}{4}, \dfrac{5}{7}, \dfrac{1}{2}$ **(b)** $\dfrac{8}{7}, \dfrac{6}{6}, \dfrac{2}{1}$

| EXAMPLE 5 | Graphing Positive and Negative Fractions |

Graph each fraction on the number line.

(a) $\dfrac{2}{5}$

There is *no* sign in front of $\frac{2}{5}$, so it is *positive*. Because $\frac{2}{5}$ is between 0 and 1, we divide that space into 5 equal parts. Then we start at 0 and count to the right 2 parts.

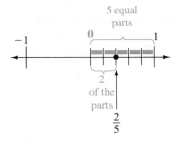

(b) $-\dfrac{4}{5}$

The fraction is *negative,* so it is between 0 and -1. We divide that space into 5 equal parts. Then we start at 0 and count to the left 4 parts.

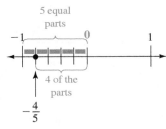

························· **Work Problem ⑤ at the Side.** ▶

| OBJECTIVE ▶ ④ | **Find the absolute value of a fraction.** In **Chapter 1** we said that the *absolute value* of a number was its distance from 0 on the number line. Two vertical bars indicate absolute value, as shown below.

$$\left|-\frac{3}{4}\right| \text{ is read "the absolute value of negative three-fourths."}$$

As with integers, the absolute value of fractions will *always* be positive (or 0) because it is the *distance* from 0 on the number line.

| EXAMPLE 6 | Finding the Absolute Value of Fractions |

Find each absolute value: $\left|\dfrac{1}{2}\right|$ and $\left|-\dfrac{1}{2}\right|$.

The distance from 0 to $\dfrac{1}{2}$ on the number line is $\dfrac{1}{2}$ space, so $\left|\dfrac{1}{2}\right| = \dfrac{1}{2}$.

The distance from 0 to $-\dfrac{1}{2}$ is also $\dfrac{1}{2}$ space, so $\left|-\dfrac{1}{2}\right| = \dfrac{1}{2}$.

························· **Work Problem ⑥ at the Side.** ▶

---

⑤ Graph each fraction on the number line.

(GS) (a) $\dfrac{2}{4}$ A *positive* fraction is to the *right* of 0.

(b) $\dfrac{1}{2}$

(c) $-\dfrac{2}{3}$

⑥ Find each absolute value.

(a) $\left|-\dfrac{3}{4}\right|$ **(b)** $\left|\dfrac{5}{8}\right|$

(c) $|0|$

Answers

5. (a)

(b)

(c)

6. (a) $\dfrac{3}{4}$ **(b)** $\dfrac{5}{8}$ **(c)** 0

OBJECTIVE ▶ 5 Write equivalent fractions. You may have noticed in **Margin Problems 5(a) and 5(b)** on the previous page that $\frac{2}{4}$ and $\frac{1}{2}$ were at the same point on the number line. Both of them were halfway between 0 and 1. There are actually *many* different names for this point. We illustrate some of them below.

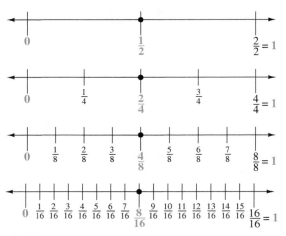

That is, $\frac{8}{16} = \frac{4}{8} = \frac{2}{4} = \frac{1}{2}$. If you have used a standard ruler with inches divided into sixteenths, you probably already noticed that these distances are the same. Although the fractions look different, they all name the same point that is halfway between 0 and 1. In other words, they have the same value. We say that they are *equivalent fractions*.

Equivalent Fractions

Fractions that represent the same number (the same point on a number line) are **equivalent fractions.**

Drawing number lines is tedious, so we usually find equivalent fractions by multiplying or dividing both the numerator and the denominator by the same number. We can use some of the fractions that we just graphed to illustrate this method.

$$\frac{1}{2} = \frac{1 \cdot 2}{2 \cdot 2} = \frac{2}{4} \qquad\qquad \frac{8}{16} = \frac{8 \div 4}{16 \div 4} = \frac{2}{4}$$

Multiply both numerator and denominator by 2.

Divide both numerator and denominator by 4.

Writing Equivalent Fractions

If a, b, and c are numbers (and b and c are not 0), then:

$$\frac{a}{b} = \frac{a \cdot c}{b \cdot c} \qquad \text{or} \qquad \frac{a}{b} = \frac{a \div c}{b \div c}$$

In other words, if the numerator and denominator of a fraction are multiplied or divide by the *same* nonzero number, the result is an *equivalent* fraction.

EXAMPLE 7 Writing Equivalent Fractions

(a) Write $-\dfrac{1}{2}$ as an equivalent fraction with a denominator of 16.

In other words, $-\dfrac{1}{2} = -\dfrac{?}{16}$.

The original denominator is 2. *Multiplying* 2 times 8 gives 16, the new denominator. To write an equivalent fraction, multiply *both* the numerator and denominator by 8.

$$-\dfrac{1}{2} = -\dfrac{1 \cdot 8}{2 \cdot 8} = -\dfrac{8}{16}$$

> Multiply numerator and denominator by the *same* number.

Keep the negative sign.

So, $-\dfrac{1}{2}$ is equivalent to $-\dfrac{8}{16}$.

(b) Write $\dfrac{12}{15}$ as an equivalent fraction with a denominator of 5.

In other words, $\dfrac{12}{15} = \dfrac{?}{5}$.

The original denominator is 15. *Dividing* 15 by 3 gives 5, the new denominator. To write an equivalent fraction, divide *both* the numerator and denominator by 3.

$$\dfrac{12}{15} = \dfrac{12 \div 3}{15 \div 3} = \dfrac{4}{5}$$

> Divide numerator and denominator by the *same* number.

So, $\dfrac{12}{15}$ is equivalent to $\dfrac{4}{5}$.

·········· **Work Problem 7 at the Side.** ▶

Look back at the set of four number lines on the previous page. Notice that there are many different names for 1.

$$\dfrac{2}{2} = 1 \qquad \dfrac{4}{4} = 1 \qquad \dfrac{8}{8} = 1 \qquad \dfrac{16}{16} = 1$$

Because a fraction bar is a symbol for division, you can think of $\dfrac{2}{2}$ as $2 \div 2$, which equals 1. Similarly, $\dfrac{4}{4}$ is $4 \div 4$, which also is 1, and so on. These examples illustrate one of the division properties from **Chapter 1.**

Division Properties

If a is any number (except 0), then $\dfrac{a}{a} = 1$. In other words, when a nonzero number is divided by itself, the result is 1.

For example: $\quad \dfrac{6}{6} = 1 \quad$ and $\quad \dfrac{-4}{-4} = 1$

Also recall that when any number is divided by 1, the result is the number. That is, $\dfrac{a}{1} = a$.

For example: $\quad \dfrac{6}{1} = 6 \quad$ and $\quad -\dfrac{12}{1} = -12$

---

7 (a) Write $\dfrac{2}{5}$ as an equivalent fraction with a denominator of 20.

$$\dfrac{2}{5} = \dfrac{?}{20}$$

The original denominator is 5. *Multiplying* 5 times ____ gives 20, the new denominator.

$$\dfrac{2}{5} = \dfrac{2 \cdot \underline{}}{5 \cdot \underline{}} = \dfrac{\underline{}}{20}$$

(b) Write $-\dfrac{21}{28}$ as an equivalent fraction with a denominator of 4.

8 Simplify each fraction by dividing the numerator by the denominator.

(a) $\dfrac{10}{10}$

Think of $\frac{10}{10}$ as $10 \div 10$.

The result is _____.

So $\frac{10}{10} =$ _____.

(b) $-\dfrac{3}{1}$

(c) $\dfrac{8}{2}$

(d) $-\dfrac{25}{5}$

EXAMPLE 8 **Using Division to Simplify Fractions**

Simplify each fraction by dividing the numerator by the denominator.

(a) $\dfrac{5}{5}$ Think of $\dfrac{5}{5}$ as $5 \div 5$. The result is 1, so $\dfrac{5}{5} = 1$.

> A fraction bar is a symbol for division.

(b) $-\dfrac{12}{4}$ Think of $-\dfrac{12}{4}$ as $-12 \div 4$. The result is -3, so $-\dfrac{12}{4} = -3$.

Keep the negative sign.

(c) $\dfrac{6}{1}$ Think of $\dfrac{6}{1}$ as $6 \div 1$. The result is 6, so $\dfrac{6}{1} = 6$.

◀ **Work Problem 8 at the Side.**

Note

The title of this chapter is "Rational Numbers: Positive and Negative Fractions." *Rational numbers* are numbers that can be written in the form $\dfrac{a}{b}$, where a and b are integers and b is not 0. In **Example 8(c)** above, you saw that an integer can be written in the form $\dfrac{a}{b}$ (6 can be written as $\frac{6}{1}$).

So rational numbers include all the integers and all the fractions. In **Chapter 5** you'll work with rational numbers that are in decimal form.

4.1 Exercises

 FOR EXTRA HELP

 Download the MyDashBoard App

▶ MyMathLab®

CONCEPT CHECK *Circle the correct word or phrase to answer the question.*

1. **(a)** When using fractions, the whole must be cut into ⟨ parts of equal size. / an odd number of parts.

   (b) Which number in a fraction tells how many equal parts are in the whole? ⟨ denominator / numerator

2. **(a)** Which number in a fraction tells how many equal parts are being considered? ⟨ numerator / denominator

   (b) In a fraction, what separates the numerator from the denominator? ⟨ an integer / a fraction bar

Write the fractions that represent the shaded and unshaded portions of each figure.
See Examples 1 and 2.

3.

Number of shaded parts → __
Number of equal parts → __

4.

Number of shaded parts → __
Number of equal parts → __

5.

6.

7.

8.

9.

10.

11. What fraction of these coins are dimes? What fraction are pennies? What fraction are nickels?

12. What fraction of these recording artists are men? What fraction are women? What fraction are wearing something red?

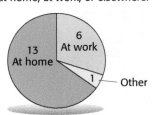

The circle graph shows the results of a survey on where women would like to have flowers delivered on Valentine's Day. Use the graph to answer Exercises 13–14.

13. **(a)** What fraction of the women would like flowers delivered at work?

   (b) Delivered at home or at work?

14. **(a)** What fraction picked a location other than home or work?

   (b) What fraction picked at home or other?

DELIVERING FLOWERS ON VALENTINE'S DAY

Out of every 20 women surveyed, the number who would like flowers delivered at home, at work, or elsewhere.

13 At home
6 At work
1 — Other

Source: FTD, Inc.

CONCEPT CHECK *Identify the numerator and denominator in each fraction. Then state the number of equal parts in the whole. See Example 3.*

15. $\dfrac{3}{4}$

16. $\dfrac{5}{8}$

17. $\dfrac{12}{7}$

18. $\dfrac{8}{3}$

List the proper and improper fractions in each group of numbers. See Example 4.

	Proper	Improper

19. $\dfrac{8}{5}, \dfrac{1}{3}, \dfrac{5}{8}, \dfrac{6}{6}, \dfrac{12}{2}, \dfrac{7}{16}$ _____ _____

	Proper	Improper

20. $\dfrac{1}{6}, \dfrac{5}{8}, \dfrac{15}{14}, \dfrac{11}{9}, \dfrac{7}{7}, \dfrac{3}{4}$ _____ _____

Graph each pair of fractions on the number line. See Example 5.

21. $\dfrac{1}{4}, -\dfrac{1}{4}$

22. $-\dfrac{1}{3}, \dfrac{1}{3}$

23. $-\dfrac{3}{5}, \dfrac{3}{5}$

24. $\dfrac{5}{6}, -\dfrac{5}{6}$

25. $\dfrac{7}{8}, -\dfrac{7}{8}$

26. $-\dfrac{3}{4}, \dfrac{3}{4}$

CONCEPT CHECK *Write a positive or negative fraction to describe each situation.*

27. The baby lost $\frac{3}{4}$ pound in weight while she was sick.

28. Greta needed $\frac{1}{3}$ cup of brown sugar for the cookie recipe.

29. Barb Brown's driveway is $\frac{3}{10}$ mile long.

30. The oil level in my car is $\frac{1}{2}$ quart below normal.

Find each absolute value. See Example 6.

31. $\left| -\dfrac{2}{5} \right|$

32. $\left| -\dfrac{4}{4} \right|$

33. $|0|$

34. $\left| \dfrac{9}{10} \right|$

35. Rewrite each fraction as an equivalent fraction with a denominator of 24. *See Example 7.*

(a) $\dfrac{1}{2} = \dfrac{}{24}$

Multiplying 2 times _____ gives 24.

(b) $\dfrac{1}{3} = \text{—}$

(c) $\dfrac{2}{3} = \text{—}$

(d) $\dfrac{1}{4} = \text{—}$

(e) $\dfrac{3}{4} = \text{—}$

(f) $\dfrac{1}{6} = \text{—}$

(g) $\dfrac{5}{6} = \text{—}$

(h) $\dfrac{1}{8} = \text{—}$

(i) $\dfrac{3}{8} = \text{—}$

(j) $\dfrac{5}{8} = \text{—}$

36. Rewrite each fraction as an equivalent fraction with a denominator of 36.
See Example 7.

(a) $\dfrac{1}{2} = \dfrac{}{36}$
Multiplying
2 times ____
gives 36.

(b) $\dfrac{1}{3} = \text{—}$

(c) $\dfrac{2}{3} = \text{—}$

(d) $\dfrac{1}{4} = \text{—}$

(e) $\dfrac{3}{4} = \text{—}$

(f) $\dfrac{1}{6} = \text{—}$

(g) $\dfrac{5}{6} = \text{—}$

(h) $\dfrac{1}{9} = \text{—}$

(i) $\dfrac{4}{9} = \text{—}$

(j) $\dfrac{8}{9} = \text{—}$

37. Rewrite each fraction as an equivalent fraction with a denominator of 3.
See Example 7.

(a) $-\dfrac{2}{6} = -\dfrac{}{3}$

(b) $-\dfrac{4}{6} = \text{—}$

(c) $-\dfrac{12}{18} = \text{—}$

(d) $-\dfrac{6}{18} = \text{—}$

(e) $-\dfrac{200}{300} = \text{—}$

(f) Write two more fractions that are equivalent to $-\frac{1}{3}$ and two more fractions equivalent to $-\frac{2}{3}$.

38. Rewrite each fraction as an equivalent fraction with a denominator of 4.
See Example 7.

(a) $-\dfrac{2}{8} = -\dfrac{}{4}$

(b) $-\dfrac{6}{8} = \text{—}$

(c) $-\dfrac{15}{20} = \text{—}$

(d) $-\dfrac{50}{200} = \text{—}$

(e) $-\dfrac{150}{200} = \text{—}$

(f) Write two more fractions that are equivalent to $-\frac{1}{4}$ and two more fractions equivalent to $-\frac{3}{4}$.

39. CONCEPT CHECK Can you write $\frac{3}{5}$ as an equivalent fraction with a denominator of 18? Explain why or why not. If not, what denominators could you use instead of 18?

40. CONCEPT CHECK Can you write $\frac{3}{4}$ as an equivalent fraction with a denominator of 0? Explain why or why not.

Simplify each fraction by dividing the numerator by the denominator. See Example 8.

41. $\dfrac{10}{1}$ means $10 \div 1 = $ ____

42. $\dfrac{9}{9}$ means $9 \div 9 = $ ____

43. $-\dfrac{16}{16}$

44. $-\dfrac{7}{1}$

45. $-\dfrac{18}{3}$

46. $-\dfrac{40}{4}$

47. $\dfrac{24}{8}$

48. $\dfrac{42}{6}$

49. $\dfrac{14}{7}$

50. $\dfrac{8}{2}$

51. $-\dfrac{90}{10}$

52. $-\dfrac{45}{9}$

53. $\dfrac{150}{150}$

54. $\dfrac{55}{5}$

55. $-\dfrac{32}{4}$

56. $-\dfrac{200}{200}$

There are many correct ways to draw the answers for Exercises 57–64,
so ask your instructor to check your work.

57. Shade $\frac{3}{5}$ of this figure.
What fraction is
unshaded?

58. Shade $\frac{5}{6}$ of this figure.
What fraction is
unshaded?

59. Shade $\frac{3}{8}$ of this figure.
What fraction is
unshaded?

60. Shade $\frac{1}{3}$ of this figure.
What fraction is
unshaded?

61. Draw a group of figures. Make $\frac{1}{10}$ of the figures circles, $\frac{6}{10}$ of the figures squares, and $\frac{3}{10}$ of the figures triangles.

62. Write a group of capital letters. Make $\frac{4}{9}$ of the letters A's, $\frac{2}{9}$ of the letters B's, and $\frac{3}{9}$ of the letters C's.

63. Draw a group of punctuation marks. Make $\frac{5}{12}$ of them exclamation points, $\frac{1}{12}$ of them commas, $\frac{3}{12}$ of them periods, and add enough question marks to make a full $\frac{12}{12}$ in all. Then circle $\frac{2}{5}$ of the exclamation points.

64. Draw a group of symbols. Make $\frac{2}{15}$ of them addition symbols, $\frac{4}{15}$ of them subtraction symbols, $\frac{2}{15}$ of them division symbols, and add enough equal signs to make a full $\frac{15}{15}$ in all. Then circle $\frac{3}{4}$ of the subtraction symbols.

Relating Concepts (Exercises 65–68) For Individual or Group Work

*Use your calculator as you **work Exercises 65–68 in order.***

65. (a) Write $\frac{3}{8}$ as an equivalent fraction with a denominator of 3912.

(b) Explain how you solved part (a).

66. (a) Write $\frac{7}{9}$ as an equivalent fraction with a denominator of 5472.

(b) Explain how you solved part (a).

67. (a) Is $-\dfrac{697}{3485}$ equivalent to $-\dfrac{1}{2}$, $-\dfrac{1}{3}$, or $-\dfrac{1}{5}$?

(b) Explain how you solved part (a).

68. (a) Is $-\dfrac{817}{4902}$ equivalent to $-\dfrac{1}{4}$, $-\dfrac{1}{6}$, or $-\dfrac{1}{8}$?

(b) Explain how you solved part (a).

4.2 Writing Fractions in Lowest Terms

OBJECTIVE **1** **Identify fractions written in lowest terms.** You can see from these drawings that $\frac{1}{2}$ and $\frac{4}{8}$ are different names for the same amount of pizza.

$\frac{1}{2}$ of the pizza has pepperoni on it.

$\frac{4}{8}$ of the pizza has pepperoni on it.

You saw in the last section that $\frac{1}{2}$ and $\frac{4}{8}$ are equivalent fractions. But we say that the fraction $\frac{1}{2}$ is in *lowest terms* because the numerator and denominator have no *common factor* other than 1. That means that 1 is the only number that divides evenly into both 1 and 2. However, the fraction $\frac{4}{8}$ is *not* in lowest terms because its numerator and denominator have a common factor of 4. That means 4 will divide evenly into both 4 and 8.

Note

Recall that *factors* are numbers being multiplied to give a product. For example,

$1 \cdot 4 = 4$, so 1 and 4 are factors of 4.

$2 \cdot 4 = 8$, so 2 and 4 are factors of 8.

4 is a factor of both 4 and 8, so 4 is a *common factor* of those numbers.

Writing a Fraction in Lowest Terms

A fraction is written in **lowest terms** when the numerator and denominator have no common factor other than 1. Examples are $\frac{1}{3}, \frac{3}{4}, \frac{2}{5}$, and $\frac{7}{10}$.

When you work with fractions, always write the final answer in lowest terms.

EXAMPLE 1 **Identifying Fractions Written in Lowest Terms**

Are the following fractions in lowest terms? If not, find a common factor of the numerator and denominator (other than 1).

(a) $\frac{3}{8}$ — 3 and 8 have no common factor (other than 1).

The numerator and denominator have no common factor other than 1, so the fraction is in lowest terms.

(b) $\frac{21}{36}$ — Both 21 and 36 are divisible by 3.

The numerator and denominator have a common factor of 3, so the fraction is *not* in lowest terms.

·········· **Work Problem** **1** **at the Side.** ▶

1 Are the following fractions in lowest terms? If not, find a common factor of the numerator and denominator (other than 1).

GS **(a)** $\frac{2}{3}$ 2 and 3 have no common factor other than 1.

Is $\frac{2}{3}$ in lowest terms?

_____

(b) $-\frac{8}{10}$

(c) $-\frac{9}{11}$

(d) $\frac{15}{20}$

Answers

1. (a) Yes, $\frac{2}{3}$ is in lowest terms
(b) No; 2 is a common factor.
(c) yes **(d)** No; 5 is a common factor.

2 Divide by a common factor to write each fraction in lowest terms.

(GS) **(a)** $\dfrac{5}{10}$ What number is a common factor for 5 and 10? _____

$$\dfrac{5}{10} = \dfrac{5 \div \underline{}}{10 \div \underline{}} = \underline{}$$

(b) $\dfrac{9}{12}$

(c) $-\dfrac{24}{30}$

(d) $\dfrac{15}{40}$

(e) $-\dfrac{50}{90}$

Answers

2. **(a)** 5; $\dfrac{5 \div 5}{10 \div 5} = \dfrac{1}{2}$ **(b)** $\dfrac{3}{4}$ **(c)** $-\dfrac{4}{5}$

(d) $\dfrac{3}{8}$ **(e)** $-\dfrac{5}{9}$

OBJECTIVE ▶ **2** **Write a fraction in lowest terms using common factors.**
We will show you two methods for writing a fraction in lowest terms. The first method, dividing by a common factor, works best when the numerator and denominator are small numbers.

EXAMPLE 2 **Using Common Factors to Write Fractions in Lowest Terms**

Divide by a common factor to write each fraction in lowest terms.

(a) $\dfrac{20}{24}$

The *greatest* common factor of 20 and 24 is 4. Divide both numerator and denominator by 4.

$$\dfrac{20}{24} = \dfrac{20 \div 4}{24 \div 4} = \dfrac{5}{6} \quad \boxed{\text{Now the fraction is in lowest terms.}}$$

(b) $\dfrac{30}{50} = \dfrac{30 \div 10}{50 \div 10} = \dfrac{3}{5}$ Divide both numerator and denominator by 10.

(c) $-\dfrac{24}{42} = -\dfrac{24 \div 6}{42 \div 6} = -\dfrac{4}{7}$ Divide both numerator and denominator by 6. Keep the negative sign.

(d) $\dfrac{60}{72}$

Suppose we made an error and thought that 4 was the greatest common factor of 60 and 72. Dividing by 4 gives the following.

$$\dfrac{60}{72} = \dfrac{60 \div 4}{72 \div 4} = \dfrac{15}{18}$$

But $\frac{15}{18}$ is *not* in lowest terms because 15 and 18 have a common factor of 3. Therefore, divide the numerator and denominator by 3.

$$\dfrac{15}{18} = \dfrac{15 \div 3}{18 \div 3} = \dfrac{5}{6} \leftarrow \text{Lowest terms}$$

The fraction $\frac{60}{72}$ could have been written in lowest terms in one step by dividing by 12, the *greatest* common factor of 60 and 72.

$$\dfrac{60}{72} = \dfrac{60 \div 12}{72 \div 12} = \dfrac{5}{6} \quad \left\{ \begin{array}{l} \text{Same answer} \\ \text{as above} \end{array} \right.$$

Either way works. Just keep dividing until the fraction is in lowest terms.

This method of writing a fraction in lowest terms by dividing by a common factor is summarized below.

Dividing by a Common Factor to Write a Fraction in Lowest Terms

Step 1 Find the *greatest* number that will divide evenly into both the numerator and denominator. This number is a ***common factor.***

Step 2 ***Divide*** both numerator and denominator by the common factor.

Step 3 ***Check*** to see if the new numerator and denominator have any common factors (besides 1). If they do, repeat *Steps 2 and 3*. If the only common factor is 1, the fraction is in lowest terms.

◀ **Work Problem 2 at the Side.**

OBJECTIVE ▶ ❸ **Write a number as a product of prime factors.** In **Example 2(d)** on the previous page, the greatest common factor of 60 and 72 was difficult to see quickly. You can handle a problem like that by writing the numerator and denominator as a product of *prime numbers*.

Prime Numbers

A **prime number** is a natural number that has exactly *two different* factors, itself and 1. (Natural numbers are 1, 2, 3, 4, 5, and so on.)

The number 3 is a prime number because it can be divided evenly only by itself and 1. The number 8 is *not* a prime number. The number 8 is a *composite number* because it can be divided evenly by 2 and 4, as well as by itself and 1.

Composite Numbers

A number with a factor other than itself or 1 is called a **composite number.**

CAUTION

A prime number has *only two* different factors, itself and 1. The number 1 is *not* a prime number because it does not have *two different* factors; the only factor of 1 is 1. Therefore, 1 is *neither* prime nor composite.

EXAMPLE 3 **Finding Prime Numbers**

Label each number as *prime* or *composite* or *neither*.

$$1 \quad 2 \quad 5 \quad 10 \quad 11 \quad 15$$

First, 1 is *neither* prime nor composite. Next, 2, 5, and 11, are *prime*. Each of these numbers is divisible only by itself and 1.

The number 10 can be divided by 5 and 2, so it is *composite*. Also, 15 is a *composite* number because 15 can be divided by 5 and 3.

· **Work Problem** ❸ **at the Side.** ▶

For reference, here are the prime numbers smaller than 100.

2	3	5	7	11
13	17	19	23	29
31	37	41	43	47
53	59	61	67	71
73	79	83	89	97

CAUTION

All prime numbers are odd numbers except the number 2. Be careful though, because *not all odd numbers are prime numbers.* For example, 9, 15, and 21 are odd numbers but they are *not* prime numbers.

The *prime factorization* of a number can be especially useful when working with fractions.

Prime Factorization

A **prime factorization** of a number shows the number as the product of prime numbers.

❸ Label each number as *prime* or *composite* or *neither.*

1, 2, 3, 4, 7, 9, 13, 19, 25, 29

4 Find the prime factorization of each number using division.

(a) 8

Keep
dividing. $2\overline{)4}$ ← Divide 4 by 2.
Start
here. $\Big\} \rightarrow 2\overline{)8}$ ← Divide 8 by 2, the first prime.

$8 = \underline{\quad} \cdot \underline{\quad} \cdot \underline{\quad}$

(b) 42

(c) 90

(d) 100

(e) 81

EXAMPLE 4   **Factoring Using the Division Method**

(a) Find the prime factorization of 48. Start by dividing 48 by 2 and work your way up the chain of divisions.

1 ← Continue to divide until the quotient is 1
All the
divisors
are prime
factors. $3\overline{)3}$ ← Divide 3 by 3; quotient is 1
$2\overline{)6}$ ← Divide 6 by 2; quotient is 3
$2\overline{)12}$ ← Divide 12 by 2; quotient is 6
$2\overline{)24}$ ← Divide 24 by 2; quotient is 12
Start here
and work up. $2\overline{)48}$ ← Divide 48 by 2 (the first prime number); quotient is 24

Because all the factors (divisors) are prime, the prime factorization of 48 is

$$2 \cdot 2 \cdot 2 \cdot 2 \cdot 3$$

Check by multiplying the factors to see if the product is 48.
Yes, $2 \cdot 2 \cdot 2 \cdot 2 \cdot 3$ does equal 48.

Note

You may write the factors in any order because multiplication is commutative. So you could write the factorization of 48 as $3 \cdot 2 \cdot 2 \cdot 2 \cdot 2$. We will show the factors from least to greatest in our examples.

(b) Find the prime factorization of 225. Start by dividing 225 by 3.

1 ← Quotient is 1
All the
divisors
are prime
factors. $5\overline{)5}$ ← Divide 5 by 5
$5\overline{)25}$ ← 25 is not divisible by 3; use 5
$3\overline{)75}$ ← Divide 75 by 3; quotient is 25
Start here
and work up. $3\overline{)225}$ ← 225 is not divisible by 2 (first prime) so use 3 (next prime)

$225 = 3 \cdot 3 \cdot 5 \cdot 5$ CHECK: 3 · 3 is 9;
9 · 5 is 45; 45 · 5 is **225**

CAUTION

When you're using the division method of factoring, the last quotient is 1. Do **not** list 1 as a prime factor because 1 is not a prime number.

◀ Work Problem **4** at the Side.

Another method of factoring uses what is called a *factor tree*.

EXAMPLE 5   **Factoring Using a Factor Tree**

Find the prime factorization of each number.

(a) 60

Try to divide 60 by the first prime number, 2. The quotient is 30. Write the factors 2 and 30 under the 60. Circle the 2, because it is a prime.

60
② 30 60 = 2 · 30

Answers
4. (a) $2 \cdot 2 \cdot 2$ **(b)** $2 \cdot 3 \cdot 7$
(c) $2 \cdot 3 \cdot 3 \cdot 5$ **(d)** $2 \cdot 2 \cdot 5 \cdot 5$
(e) $3 \cdot 3 \cdot 3 \cdot 3$

Try dividing 30 by 2. The quotient is 15. Write the factors 2 and 15 under the 30.

Because 15 cannot be divided evenly by 2, try dividing 15 by the next prime number, 3. The quotient is 5. Write the factors 3 and 5 under the 15.

③ ⑤ ← Circle 3 and 5 because both are primes.

No uncircled factors remain, so you have found the prime factorization (the circled factors).

$$60 = 2 \cdot 2 \cdot 3 \cdot 5$$

CHECK: 2 • 2 is 4;
4 • 3 is 12; 12 • 5 is **60**

(b) 72

Divide 72 by 2, the first prime number.

72 ← Divide by 2; 72 = 2 • 36
② 36 ← Divide by 2 again; 36 = 2 • 18
② 18 ← Divide by 2 again; 18 = 2 • 9
② 9 ← Divide by 3; 9 = 3 • 3
③ ③

$$72 = 2 \cdot 2 \cdot 2 \cdot 3 \cdot 3$$

(c) 45

Because 45 cannot be divided evenly by 2, try dividing by the next prime, 3.

45 ← Divide by 3; 45 = 3 • 15
③ 15 ← Divide by 3 again; 15 = 3 • 5
③ ⑤

$$45 = 3 \cdot 3 \cdot 5$$

CHECK: 3 • 3 is 9;
9 • 5 is **45**.

Note

Here is a reminder about the quick way to see whether a number is *divisible* by 2, 3, or 5; in other words, there is no remainder when you do the division.

A number is divisible by 2 if the ones digit is 0, 2, 4, 6, or 8.
For example, 30, 512, 76, and 3018 are all divisible by 2.

A number is divisible by 3 if the *sum* of the digits is divisible by 3.
For example, 129 is divisible by 3 because $1 + 2 + 9 = 12$ and 12 is divisible by 3.

A number is divisible by 5 if the ones digit is 0 or 5.
For example, 85, 610, and 1725 are all divisible by 5.

See **Chapter R** near the end of this book for more information.

.... Work Problem **5** at the Side. ▶

5 Complete each factor tree and write the prime factorization.

(a) 28 ←—— Divide by 2;
28 = 2 • 14
② 14 ← Divide by 2 again;
○ ○   14 = 2 • _____

(b) 35
⑤ ○

(c) 90

Answers

5. (a) 28
② 14
② ⑦
28 = 2 • 2 • 7

(b) 35
⑤ ⑦
35 = 5 • 7

(c) 90
② 45
③ 15
③ ⑤
90 = 2 • 3 • 3 • 5

Calculator Tip

You can use your calculator to find the prime factorization of a number. Here is an example that uses 539.

Try dividing 539 by the first prime number, 2.

$\quad$ 539 ÷ 2 = **269.5** $\quad$ Does not divide evenly

Try dividing 539 by the next prime number, 3.

$\quad$ 539 ÷ 3 = **179.6666667** $\quad$ Does not divide evenly

Keep trying the next prime numbers until you find one that divides evenly.

$\quad$ 539 ÷ 5 = **107.8** $\quad$ Does not divide evenly

$\quad$ 539 ÷ 7 = **77** $\quad$ Divides evenly

Once you have found that 7 works, try using it again on the quotient 77.

$\quad$ 77 ÷ 7 = **11** $\quad$ Divides evenly

Because 11 is prime, you're finished. The prime factorization of 539 is 7 • 7 • 11.

Now try factoring 2431 using your calculator. (The answer is at the bottom left of this page.)

OBJECTIVE ④ **Write a fraction in lowest terms using prime factorization.**
Now you can use the second method for writing fractions in lowest terms: prime factorization. This is a good method to use when the numerator and denominator are larger numbers or include variables.

EXAMPLE 6 **Using Prime Factorization to Write Fractions in Lowest Terms**

(a) Write $\frac{20}{35}$ in lowest terms.

20 can be written as 2 • 2 • 5 ← Prime factors
35 can be written as 5 • 7 ← Prime factors

$$\frac{20}{35} = \frac{2 \cdot 2 \cdot 5}{5 \cdot 7}$$

The numerator and denominator have 5 as a common factor. Dividing both numerator and denominator by 5 will give an equivalent fraction.

Any number divided by itself is 1.

$$\frac{20}{35} = \frac{2 \cdot 2 \cdot 5}{5 \cdot 7} = \frac{2 \cdot 2 \cdot 5}{7 \cdot 5} = \frac{2 \cdot 2 \cdot \boxed{5 \div 5}}{7 \cdot \boxed{5 \div 5}} = \frac{2 \cdot 2 \cdot 1}{7 \cdot 1} = \frac{4}{7}$$

Multiplication is commutative.

$\frac{20}{35}$ is written in lowest terms as $\frac{4}{7}$.

To shorten the work, you may use slashes to indicate the divisions. For example, the work on $\frac{20}{35}$ can be shown as follows.

$$\frac{20}{35} = \frac{2 \cdot 2 \cdot \overset{1}{\cancel{5}}}{\underset{1}{\cancel{5}} \cdot 7} \quad \begin{array}{l} \text{Slashes indicate} \\ 5 \div 5, \text{ and} \\ \text{the result is 1.} \end{array}$$

(b) Write $\frac{60}{72}$ in lowest terms.

Use the prime factorizations of 60 and 72 from **Examples 5(a) and 5(b).**

$$\frac{60}{72} = \frac{2 \cdot 2 \cdot 3 \cdot 5}{2 \cdot 2 \cdot 2 \cdot 3 \cdot 3}$$

This time there are three common factors. Use slashes to show the three divisions.

$$\overset{\textbf{2} \div \textbf{2 is 1}}{} $$

2 ÷ 2 is 1 ⟶ ↓ ↓ ↓ ⟵ 3 ÷ 3 is 1

$$\frac{60}{72} = \frac{\overset{1}{\cancel{2}} \cdot \overset{1}{\cancel{2}} \cdot \overset{1}{\cancel{3}} \cdot 5}{\underset{1}{\cancel{2}} \cdot \underset{1}{\cancel{2}} \cdot 2 \cdot \underset{1}{\cancel{3}} \cdot 3} = \frac{5}{6} \quad \begin{array}{l} \leftarrow \text{Multiply } 1 \cdot 1 \cdot 1 \cdot 5 \text{ to get } 5 \\ \leftarrow \text{Multiply } 1 \cdot 1 \cdot 2 \cdot 1 \cdot 3 \text{ to get } 6 \end{array}$$

(c) $\dfrac{18}{90}$

$$\frac{18}{90} = \frac{\overset{1}{\cancel{2}} \cdot \overset{1}{\cancel{3}} \cdot \overset{1}{\cancel{3}}}{\underset{1}{\cancel{2}} \cdot \underset{1}{\cancel{3}} \cdot \underset{1}{\cancel{3}} \cdot 5} = \frac{1}{5} \quad \begin{array}{l} \leftarrow \text{Multiply } 1 \cdot 1 \cdot 1 \text{ to get } 1 \\ \leftarrow \text{Multiply } 1 \cdot 1 \cdot 1 \cdot 5 \text{ to get } 5 \end{array}$$

CAUTION

In **Example 6(c)** above, all factors of the numerator divided out. But $1 \cdot 1 \cdot 1$ is still 1, so the final answer is $\frac{1}{5}$ (**not** 5).

This method of using prime factorization to write a fraction in lowest terms is summarized below.

Using Prime Factorization to Write a Fraction in Lowest Terms
Step 1 Write the **prime factorization** of both numerator and denominator.
Step 2 Use slashes to show where you are **dividing** the numerator and denominator by any common factors.
Step 3 **Multiply** the factors in the numerator and in the denominator.

······· **Work Problem** ❻ **at the Side.** ▶

OBJECTIVE ▶ ❺ **Write a fraction with variables in lowest terms.**
Fractions may have variables in the numerator or denominator. Examples are shown below.

$$\frac{6}{2x} \qquad \frac{3xy}{9xy} \qquad \frac{4b^3}{8ab} \qquad \frac{7ab^2}{n^2}$$

You can use prime factorization to write these fractions in lowest terms.

---

❻ Use the method of prime factorization to write each fraction in lowest terms.

⑤ (a) $\dfrac{16}{48}$

$$\frac{16}{48} = \frac{2 \cdot 2 \cdot 2 \cdot 2}{2 \cdot 2 \cdot 2 \cdot 2 \cdot 3}$$

Divide out all the common factors.

$$= \underline{\quad\quad}$$

(b) $\dfrac{28}{60}$

(c) $\dfrac{74}{111}$

(d) $\dfrac{124}{340}$

7 Write each fraction in lowest terms.

GS (a) $\dfrac{5c}{15}$

$$\dfrac{5c}{15} = \dfrac{5 \cdot c}{3 \cdot 5} = \underline{\qquad}$$

Divide out all the common factors.

(b) $\dfrac{10x^2}{8x^2}$

(c) $\dfrac{9a^3}{11b^3}$

(d) $\dfrac{6m^2n}{9n^2}$

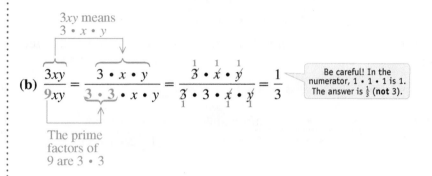

| EXAMPLE 7 | Writing Fractions with Variables in Lowest Terms |

Write each fraction in lowest terms.

(a) $\dfrac{6}{2x}$ ← Prime factors of 6 are 2 • 3
← $2x$ means 2 • x

$$\dfrac{6}{2x} = \dfrac{\overset{1}{\cancel{2}} \cdot 3}{\underset{1}{\cancel{2}} \cdot x} = \dfrac{3}{x} \begin{matrix} \leftarrow 1 \cdot 3 \text{ is } 3 \\ \leftarrow 1 \cdot x \text{ is } x \end{matrix}$$

$3xy$ means $3 \cdot x \cdot y$

(b) $\dfrac{3xy}{9xy} = \dfrac{3 \cdot x \cdot y}{3 \cdot 3 \cdot x \cdot y} = \dfrac{\overset{1}{\cancel{3}} \cdot \overset{1}{\cancel{x}} \cdot \overset{1}{\cancel{y}}}{\underset{1}{\cancel{3}} \cdot 3 \cdot \underset{1}{\cancel{x}} \cdot \underset{1}{\cancel{y}}} = \dfrac{1}{3}$

> Be careful! In the numerator, 1 • 1 • 1 is 1. The answer is $\frac{1}{3}$ (**not** 3).

The prime factors of 9 are 3 • 3

b^3 means $b \cdot b \cdot b$

(c) $\dfrac{4b^3}{8ab} = \dfrac{2 \cdot 2 \cdot b \cdot b \cdot b}{2 \cdot 2 \cdot 2 \cdot a \cdot b} = \dfrac{\overset{1}{\cancel{2}} \cdot \overset{1}{\cancel{2}} \cdot \overset{1}{\cancel{b}} \cdot b \cdot b}{\underset{1}{\cancel{2}} \cdot \underset{1}{\cancel{2}} \cdot 2 \cdot a \cdot \underset{1}{\cancel{b}}} = \dfrac{b^2}{2a} \begin{matrix} \leftarrow b \cdot b \text{ is } b^2 \\ \leftarrow 2 \cdot a \text{ is } 2a \end{matrix}$

The prime factors of 8 are 2 • 2 • 2

(d) $\dfrac{7ab^2}{n^2} = \dfrac{7 \cdot a \cdot b \cdot b}{n \cdot n}$

> There are no common factors.

$\dfrac{7ab^2}{n^2}$ is already in lowest terms.

◀ **Work Problem 7 at the Side.**

Answers

7. (a) $\dfrac{\overset{1}{\cancel{5}} \cdot c}{3 \cdot \underset{1}{\cancel{5}}} = \dfrac{1c}{3}$ or $\dfrac{c}{3}$

(b) $\dfrac{\overset{1}{\cancel{2}} \cdot 5 \cdot \overset{1}{\cancel{x}} \cdot \overset{1}{\cancel{x}}}{\underset{1}{\cancel{2}} \cdot 2 \cdot 2 \cdot \underset{1}{\cancel{x}} \cdot \underset{1}{\cancel{x}}} = \dfrac{5}{4}$

(c) already in lowest terms

(d) $\dfrac{2 \cdot \overset{1}{\cancel{3}} \cdot m \cdot m \cdot \overset{1}{\cancel{n}}}{\underset{1}{\cancel{3}} \cdot 3 \cdot n \cdot \underset{1}{\cancel{n}}} = \dfrac{2m^2}{3n}$

4.2 Exercises

  MyMathLab®

FOR EXTRA HELP

Download the MyDashBoard App

CONCEPT CHECK *Are the following fractions in lowest terms? If not, find a common factor of the numerator and denominator (other than 1).* **See Example 1.**

1. (a) $-\dfrac{3}{10}$ (b) $\dfrac{10}{15}$ (c) $\dfrac{9}{16}$ (d) $-\dfrac{4}{21}$ (e) $\dfrac{6}{9}$ (f) $-\dfrac{7}{28}$

2. (a) $\dfrac{10}{12}$ (b) $\dfrac{3}{18}$ (c) $-\dfrac{8}{15}$ (d) $-\dfrac{22}{33}$ (e) $\dfrac{2}{25}$ (f) $-\dfrac{14}{15}$

Write each fraction in lowest terms. Use the method of dividing by a common factor. **See Example 2.**

3. (a) $\dfrac{10}{15}$ (b) $\dfrac{6}{9}$ (c) $-\dfrac{7}{28}$ (d) $-\dfrac{25}{50}$ (e) $\dfrac{16}{18}$ (f) $-\dfrac{8}{20}$

4. (a) $\dfrac{10}{12}$ (b) $\dfrac{3}{18}$ (c) $-\dfrac{22}{33}$ (d) $\dfrac{12}{16}$ (e) $-\dfrac{15}{20}$ (f) $-\dfrac{9}{15}$

CONCEPT CHECK *Label each number as* prime *or* composite *or* neither. **See Example 3.**

5.   9   2   8   1   5   11   10   21

6.   12   3   7   6   1   15   13   25

Find the prime factorization of each number. **See Examples 4 and 5.**

7. GS
6 =

8. GS
12 =

9. 20

10. 30

11. 25

12. 18

13. 36

14. 56

15. (a) 44

(b) 88

16. (a) 45

(b) 135

17. (a) 75

(b) 68

(c) 189

18. (a) 80

(b) 64

(c) 385

Write each numerator and denominator as a product of prime factors. Then use the prime factorization to write the fraction in lowest terms. See Example 6.

19. $\dfrac{8}{16}$ $8 = 2 \cdot 2 \cdot 2$
$16 = 2 \cdot 2 \cdot 2 \cdot 2$

$\dfrac{8}{16} = \dfrac{\overset{1}{2} \cdot \overset{1}{2} \cdot \overset{1}{2}}{\underset{1}{2} \cdot \underset{1}{2} \cdot \underset{1}{2} \cdot 2} =$

20. $\dfrac{6}{8}$ $6 = 2 \cdot 3$
$8 = 2 \cdot 2 \cdot 2$

$\dfrac{6}{8} = \dfrac{\overset{1}{2} \cdot 3}{\underset{1}{2} \cdot 2 \cdot 2} =$

21. $\dfrac{32}{48}$

22. $\dfrac{9}{27}$

23. $\dfrac{14}{21}$

24. $\dfrac{20}{32}$

25. $\dfrac{36}{42}$

26. $\dfrac{22}{33}$

27. $\dfrac{50}{63}$

28. $\dfrac{72}{80}$

29. $\dfrac{27}{45}$

30. $\dfrac{36}{63}$

31. $\dfrac{12}{18}$

32. $\dfrac{63}{90}$

33. $\dfrac{35}{40}$

34. $\dfrac{36}{48}$

35. $\dfrac{90}{180}$

36. $\dfrac{16}{64}$

37. $\dfrac{210}{315}$

38. $\dfrac{96}{192}$

39. $\dfrac{429}{495}$

40. $\dfrac{135}{182}$

Write your answers to Exercises 41–46 in lowest terms.

41. There are 60 minutes in an hour. What fraction of an hour is

  (a) 15 minutes?   **(b)** 30 minutes?

  (c) 6 minutes?   **(d)** 60 minutes?

42. There are 24 hours in a day. What fraction of a day is

  (a) 8 hours?   **(b)** 18 hours?

  (c) 12 hours?   **(d)** 3 hours?

43. SueLynn's monthly income is $2400.

  (a) She spends $800 on rent. What fraction of her income is spent on rent?

  (b) She spends $400 on food. What fraction of her income is spent on food?

  (c) What fraction of her income is left for other expenses?

44. There are 15,000 students at Minneapolis Community and Technical College.

  (a) 10,500 of the students receive some form of financial aid. What fraction of the students receive financial aid?

  (b) 7500 of the students are women. What fraction are women?

  (c) What fraction of the students are men?

45. The pictograph below shows the number of hours spent on household chores each week by men and by women.

Of the typical 25 hours spent weekly on household chores, here is the amount of time spent by men and by women.

Men **10** hours   Women **15** hours

Source: U.S. Bureau of Labor Statistics.

What fraction of the time spent weekly on household chores is done by men? What fraction is done by women?

46. A survey asked adults how they think offices in the year 2021 will be different from offices today. The circle graph shows the number who gave each answer, out of every 100 adults in the survey.

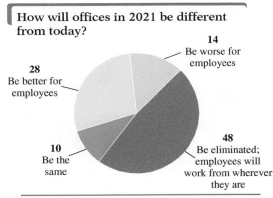

How will offices in 2021 be different from today?

28 Be better for employees

14 Be worse for employees

48 Be eliminated; employees will work from wherever they are

10 Be the same

Source: Monster.com survey.

What fraction of the adults gave each answer?

CONCEPT CHECK *Explain the error in each of these problems and correct it.*

47. $\dfrac{9}{36} = \dfrac{\cancel{3} \cdot \cancel{3}}{2 \cdot 2 \cdot \cancel{3} \cdot \cancel{3}} = 4$

48. $\dfrac{9}{16} = \dfrac{9 \div 3}{16 \div 4} = \dfrac{3}{4}$

Write each fraction in lowest terms. See **Example 7.**

49. $\dfrac{16c}{40}$ ▶

50. $\dfrac{36}{54a}$

51. $\dfrac{20x}{35x}$

52. $\dfrac{21n}{28n}$

53. $\dfrac{18r^2}{15rs}$

54. $\dfrac{18ab}{48b^2}$

55. $\dfrac{6m}{42mn^2}$

56. $\dfrac{10g^2}{90g^2h}$

57. $\dfrac{9x^2}{16y^2}$

58. $\dfrac{5rst}{8st}$

59. $\dfrac{7xz}{9xyz}$

60. $\dfrac{6a^3}{23b^3}$

61. $\dfrac{21k^3}{6k^2}$ ▶

62. $\dfrac{16x^3}{12x^4}$

63. $\dfrac{13a^2bc^3}{39a^2bc^3}$

64. $\dfrac{22m^3n^4}{55m^3n^4}$

65. $\dfrac{14c^2d}{14cd^2}$ ▶

66. $\dfrac{19rs}{19s^3}$

67. $\dfrac{210ab^3c}{35b^2c^2}$

68. $\dfrac{81w^4xy^2}{300wy^4}$

69. $\dfrac{25m^3rt^2}{36n^2s^3w^2}$

70. $\dfrac{42a^5b^4c^3}{7a^4b^3c^2}$

71. $\dfrac{33e^2fg^3}{11efg}$

72. $\dfrac{21xy^2z^3}{17ab^2c^3}$

4.3   Multiplying and Dividing Signed Fractions

OBJECTIVE ▶ 1   Multiply signed fractions. Suppose that you give $\frac{1}{3}$ of your candy bar to your friend Ann. Then Ann gives $\frac{1}{2}$ of her share to Tim. How much of the bar does Tim get to eat?

OBJECTIVES

1. Multiply signed fractions.
2. Multiply fractions that involve variables.
3. Divide signed fractions.
4. Divide fractions that involve variables.
5. Solve application problems involving multiplying and dividing fractions.

A sketch of the candy bar shows that Tim will get $\frac{1}{6}$ of the bar.

Tim's share is $\frac{1}{2}$ of $\frac{1}{3}$ candy bar. When used with fractions, the word **of** indicates multiplication.

$$\frac{1}{2} \text{ of } \frac{1}{3} \quad \text{means} \quad \frac{1}{2} \cdot \frac{1}{3}$$

Tim's share is $\frac{1}{6}$ bar, so $\frac{1}{2} \cdot \frac{1}{3} = \frac{1}{6}$.

This example illustrates the rule for multiplying fractions.

Multiplying Fractions

If a, b, c, and d are numbers (but b and d are not 0), then

$$\frac{a}{b} \cdot \frac{c}{d} = \frac{a \cdot c}{b \cdot d}$$

In other words, multiply the numerators and multiply the denominators.

When we apply this rule to find Tim's part of the candy bar, we get

$$\frac{1}{2} \cdot \frac{1}{3} = \frac{1 \cdot 1}{2 \cdot 3} = \frac{1}{6} \quad \begin{array}{l} \leftarrow \text{Multiply numerators.} \\ \leftarrow \text{Multiply denominators.} \end{array}$$

EXAMPLE 1   Multiplying Signed Fractions

Find each product.

(a) $-\dfrac{5}{8} \cdot -\dfrac{3}{4}$ Recall that the product of two negative numbers is a positive number.

Multiply the numerators and multiply the denominators.

$$-\frac{5}{8} \cdot -\frac{3}{4} = \frac{5 \cdot 3}{8 \cdot 4} = \frac{15}{32} \leftarrow \text{Lowest terms}$$

The product of two negative numbers is positive.

The answer is in lowest terms because 15 and 32 have no common factor other than 1.

······················· **Continued on Next Page**

1 Find each product.

(GS) (a) $-\dfrac{3}{4} \cdot \dfrac{1}{2}$

$$= -\dfrac{3 \cdot 1}{\overset{\wedge}{4 \cdot 2}\overset{\wedge}{}} = -\underline{\hspace{1cm}}$$

Product of a negative number and a positive number is negative.

(b) $\left(-\dfrac{2}{5}\right)\left(-\dfrac{2}{3}\right)$

The product of two negative numbers is _____.

(c) $\dfrac{3}{4}\left(\dfrac{3}{8}\right)$

(b) $\left(\dfrac{4}{7}\right)\left(-\dfrac{2}{5}\right) = -\dfrac{4 \cdot 2}{\overset{\wedge}{7 \cdot 5}} = -\dfrac{8}{\overset{\wedge}{35}}$ The product of a negative number and a positive number is negative.

◀ **Work Problem 1 at the Side.**

Sometimes the result won't be in lowest terms. For example, find $\dfrac{3}{10}$ of $\dfrac{5}{6}$.

$$\dfrac{3}{10} \text{ of } \dfrac{5}{6} \quad \text{means} \quad \dfrac{3}{10} \cdot \dfrac{5}{6} = \dfrac{3 \cdot 5}{10 \cdot 6} = \dfrac{15}{60} \quad \left\{ \begin{array}{l} \text{Not in lowest} \\ \text{terms} \end{array} \right.$$

Now write $\dfrac{15}{60}$ in lowest terms.

$$\dfrac{15}{60} = \dfrac{\overset{1}{3} \cdot \overset{1}{5}}{2 \cdot 2 \cdot 3 \cdot 5} = \dfrac{1}{4} \quad \leftarrow \text{Lowest terms}$$

You used prime factorization earlier in this chapter to write fractions in lowest terms. You can also use it when multiplying fractions. Writing the prime factors of the original fractions and dividing out common factors *before* multiplying usually saves time. If you divide out *all* the common factors, the result will automatically be in lowest terms. Let's see how that works when finding $\dfrac{3}{10}$ of $\dfrac{5}{6}$.

3 and 5 are already prime.

$$\dfrac{3}{10} \cdot \dfrac{5}{6} = \dfrac{3 \cdot 5}{2 \cdot 5 \cdot 2 \cdot 3} = \dfrac{\overset{1}{3} \cdot \overset{1}{5}}{2 \cdot \underset{1}{5} \cdot 2 \cdot \underset{1}{3}} = \dfrac{1}{4} \quad \left\{ \begin{array}{l} \text{Same result} \\ \text{as above} \end{array} \right.$$

Write 10 as $2 \cdot 5$

Write 6 as $2 \cdot 3$

Divide out the common factors.

> **CAUTION**
>
> When you are working with fractions, always write the final result in lowest terms. Visualizing $\dfrac{15}{60}$ is hard to do. But when $\dfrac{15}{60}$ is written as $\dfrac{1}{4}$, working with it is much easier. A fraction is *simplified* when it is written in lowest terms.

EXAMPLE 2 **Using Prime Factorization to Multiply Fractions**

(a) $-\dfrac{8}{5}\left(\dfrac{5}{12}\right)$

Multiplying a negative number times a positive number gives a negative product.

Write 8 as $2 \cdot 2 \cdot 2$

$$-\dfrac{8}{5}\left(\dfrac{5}{12}\right) = -\dfrac{2 \cdot 2 \cdot 2 \cdot 5}{5 \cdot 2 \cdot 2 \cdot 3} = -\dfrac{\overset{1}{2} \cdot \overset{1}{2} \cdot 2 \cdot \overset{1}{5}}{\underset{1}{5} \cdot \underset{1}{2} \cdot \underset{1}{2} \cdot 3} = -\dfrac{2}{\overset{\wedge}{3}} \quad \left\{ \begin{array}{l} \text{Lowest} \\ \text{terms} \end{array} \right.$$

5 is already prime.

Write 12 as $2 \cdot 2 \cdot 3$

Negative product

Continued on Next Page

(b) Find $\frac{2}{9}$ of $\frac{15}{16}$.

Recall that, when used with fractions, *of* indicates multiplication.

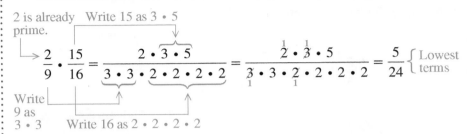

2 is already prime.

Write 15 as 3 • 5

$$\frac{2}{9} \cdot \frac{15}{16} = \frac{2 \cdot 3 \cdot 5}{3 \cdot 3 \cdot 2 \cdot 2 \cdot 2 \cdot 2} = \frac{\overset{1}{2} \cdot \overset{1}{3} \cdot 5}{\underset{1}{3} \cdot 3 \cdot \underset{1}{2} \cdot 2 \cdot 2 \cdot 2} = \frac{5}{24} \left\{ \begin{array}{l} \text{Lowest} \\ \text{terms} \end{array} \right.$$

Write 9 as 3 • 3

Write 16 as 2 • 2 • 2 • 2

Work Problem ➋ at the Side. ▶

🖩 Calculator Tip

If your calculator has a fraction key ⟨ab/c⟩, or ⟨Ab/c⟩, you can do calculations with fractions. You'll also need the change of sign key ⟨+/−⟩, or the negative sign key ⟨(−)⟩, to enter negative fractions, as you did to enter negative integers in **Chapter 1.**

Start by entering several different fractions. Clear your calculator after each one. Different calculator models may vary, so check your calculator's instructions.

To enter $\frac{3}{4}$, press 3 ⟨ab/c⟩ 4. The display will show **3⌐4**.

↑ Fraction bar

To enter $-\frac{9}{10}$, press ⟨(−)⟩ 9 ⟨ab/c⟩ 10. The display will show **−9⌐10**.

Let's check the result of **Example 2(a)** on the previous page: Multiply $-\frac{8}{5}\left(\frac{5}{12}\right)$ by pressing the following keys.

⟨(−)⟩ 8 ⟨ab/c⟩ 5 ⟨×⟩ 5 ⟨ab/c⟩ 12 ⟨=⟩   The display shows **−2/3**.

$-\frac{8}{5}$ $\frac{5}{12}$ $-\frac{2}{3}$

Now try **Example 2(b)** above: Find $\frac{2}{9}$ of $\frac{15}{16}$. (Did you get $\frac{5}{24}$?)

CAUTION

The fraction key on a calculator is useful for *checking* your work. But knowing the rules for fraction computation is important because you'll need them when fractions involve variables. (See **Example 4** on the next page).

➋ Use prime factorization to multiply these fractions.

(a) $\frac{15}{28}\left(-\frac{6}{5}\right)$ Product will be negative.

$$= -\frac{3 \cdot 5 \cdot 2 \cdot 3}{2 \cdot 2 \cdot 7 \cdot 5} = -\underline{}$$

Divide out the common factors.

(b) $\frac{12}{7} \cdot \frac{7}{24}$ Product will be _____.

(c) $\left(-\frac{11}{18}\right)\left(-\frac{9}{20}\right)$

Product will be _____.

Answers

2. **(a)** $-\dfrac{3 \cdot \overset{1}{\cancel{5}} \cdot \overset{1}{\cancel{2}} \cdot 3}{2 \cdot \underset{1}{\cancel{2}} \cdot 7 \cdot \underset{1}{\cancel{5}}} = -\dfrac{9}{14}$

(b) positive; $\dfrac{\overset{1}{\cancel{2}} \cdot \overset{1}{\cancel{2}} \cdot \overset{1}{\cancel{3}} \cdot \overset{1}{\cancel{7}}}{\underset{1}{\cancel{7}} \cdot \underset{1}{\cancel{2}} \cdot \underset{1}{\cancel{2}} \cdot 2 \cdot \underset{1}{\cancel{3}}} = \dfrac{1}{2}$

(c) positive; $\dfrac{11 \cdot \overset{1}{\cancel{3}} \cdot \overset{1}{\cancel{3}}}{2 \cdot \underset{1}{\cancel{3}} \cdot \underset{1}{\cancel{3}} \cdot 2 \cdot 2 \cdot 5} = \dfrac{11}{40}$

3 Use prime factorization to find these products.

GS (a) $\dfrac{3}{4}$ of 36

$$\dfrac{3}{4} \cdot \dfrac{36}{1} = \dfrac{3 \cdot 2 \cdot 2 \cdot 3 \cdot 3}{2 \cdot 2 \cdot 1}$$

$$= \underline{} =$$

(b) $-10 \cdot \dfrac{2}{5}$ Product will be _____ .

(c) $\left(-\dfrac{7}{8}\right)(-24)$ Product will be _____ .

4 Use prime factorization to find these products.

GS (a) $\dfrac{2c}{5} \cdot \dfrac{c}{4} = \dfrac{2 \cdot c \cdot c}{5 \cdot 2 \cdot 2}$ Divide out common factors.

$$= \underline{}$$

(b) $\left(\dfrac{m}{6}\right)\left(\dfrac{9}{m^2}\right)$

(c) $\left(\dfrac{w^2}{y}\right)\left(\dfrac{x^2 y}{w}\right)$

Answers

3. **(a)** $\dfrac{3 \cdot \overset{1}{\cancel{2}} \cdot \overset{1}{\cancel{2}} \cdot 3 \cdot 3}{\underset{1}{\cancel{2}} \cdot \underset{1}{\cancel{2}} \cdot 1} = \dfrac{27}{1} = 27$

(b) negative; $-\dfrac{2 \cdot \overset{1}{\cancel{5}} \cdot 2}{1 \cdot \underset{1}{\cancel{5}}} = -\dfrac{4}{1} = -4$

(c) positive; $\dfrac{7 \cdot \overset{1}{\cancel{2}} \cdot \overset{1}{\cancel{2}} \cdot \overset{1}{\cancel{2}} \cdot 3}{\underset{1}{\cancel{2}} \cdot \underset{1}{\cancel{2}} \cdot \underset{1}{\cancel{2}}} = \dfrac{21}{1} = 21$

4. **(a)** $\dfrac{\overset{1}{\cancel{2}} \cdot c \cdot c}{5 \cdot \underset{1}{\cancel{2}} \cdot 2} = \dfrac{c^2}{10}$

(b) $\dfrac{\overset{1}{\cancel{m}} \cdot \overset{1}{\cancel{3}} \cdot 3}{2 \cdot \underset{1}{\cancel{3}} \cdot \underset{1}{\cancel{m}} \cdot m} = \dfrac{3}{2m}$

(c) $\dfrac{\overset{1}{\cancel{w}} \cdot w \cdot x \cdot x \cdot \overset{1}{\cancel{y}}}{\underset{1}{\cancel{y}} \cdot \underset{1}{\cancel{w}}} = \dfrac{wx^2}{1} = wx^2$

EXAMPLE 3 **Multiplying a Fraction and an Integer**

Find $\dfrac{2}{3}$ of 6.

We can write 6 in fraction form as $\dfrac{6}{1}$. Recall that $\dfrac{6}{1}$ means $6 \div 1$, which is 6. So we can write any integer a as $\dfrac{a}{1}$.

$$\dfrac{2}{3} \text{ of 6 means } \dfrac{2}{3} \cdot \dfrac{6}{1} = \dfrac{2 \cdot 2 \cdot \overset{1}{\cancel{3}}}{\underset{1}{\cancel{3}} \cdot 1} = \dfrac{4}{1} = 4$$

$4 \div 1$ is 4.

◀ **Work Problem 3 at the Side.**

OBJECTIVE 2 **Multiply fractions that involve variables.** The multiplication method that uses prime factors also works when there are variables in the numerators and/or denominators of the fractions.

EXAMPLE 4 **Multiplying Fractions with Variables**

Find each product.

(a) $\dfrac{3x}{5} \cdot \dfrac{2}{9x}$

$3x$ means $3 \cdot x.$ $\dfrac{x}{x}$ is 1.

$$\dfrac{3x}{5} \cdot \dfrac{2}{9x} = \dfrac{3 \cdot x \cdot 2}{5 \cdot 3 \cdot 3 \cdot x} = \dfrac{\overset{1}{\cancel{3}} \cdot \overset{1}{\cancel{x}} \cdot 2}{5 \cdot \underset{1}{\cancel{3}} \cdot 3 \cdot \underset{1}{\cancel{x}}} = \dfrac{2}{15}$$

The prime factors of 9 are $3 \cdot 3$, so $9x$ is $3 \cdot 3 \cdot x$.

(b) $\left(\dfrac{3y}{4x}\right)\left(\dfrac{2x^2}{y}\right)$

$2x^2$ means $2 \cdot x \cdot x.$

$$\left(\dfrac{3y}{4x}\right)\left(\dfrac{2x^2}{y}\right) = \dfrac{3 \cdot y \cdot 2 \cdot x \cdot x}{2 \cdot 2 \cdot x \cdot y} = \dfrac{3 \cdot \overset{1}{\cancel{y}} \cdot \overset{1}{\cancel{2}} \cdot \overset{1}{\cancel{x}} \cdot x}{2 \cdot \underset{1}{\cancel{2}} \cdot \underset{1}{\cancel{x}} \cdot \underset{1}{\cancel{y}}} = \dfrac{3x}{2}$$

The prime factors of 4 are $2 \cdot 2$, so $4x$ is $2 \cdot 2 \cdot x$.

◀ **Work Problem 4 at the Side.**

OBJECTIVE 3 **Divide signed fractions.** To divide fractions, you will rewrite division problems as multiplication problems. For division, you will leave the first number (the dividend) as it is, but change the second number (the divisor) to its *reciprocal*.

Reciprocal of a Fraction

Two numbers are **reciprocals** of each other if their product is 1.

The reciprocal of the fraction $\dfrac{a}{b}$ is $\dfrac{b}{a}$ because

$$\frac{a}{b} \cdot \frac{b}{a} = \frac{\overset{1}{a} \cdot \overset{1}{b}}{\underset{1}{b} \cdot \underset{1}{a}} = \frac{1}{1} = 1$$

Notice that you "flip" or "invert" a fraction to find its reciprocal. Here are some examples.

VOCABULARY TIP

Vert- means "to turn." When you invert a fraction, you switch the position of the numerator and the denominator. For example, $\frac{1}{2}$ becomes $\frac{2}{1}$.

Number	Reciprocal	Reason
$\dfrac{1}{6}$	$\dfrac{6}{1}$	Because $\dfrac{1}{6} \cdot \dfrac{6}{1} = \dfrac{6}{6} = 1$
$-\dfrac{2}{5}$	$-\dfrac{5}{2}$	Because $\left(-\dfrac{2}{5}\right)\left(-\dfrac{5}{2}\right) = \dfrac{10}{10} = 1$
4 Think of 4 as $\frac{4}{1}$	$\dfrac{1}{4}$	Because $4 \cdot \dfrac{1}{4} = \dfrac{4}{1} \cdot \dfrac{1}{4} = \dfrac{4}{4} = 1$

Note

Every number has a reciprocal except 0. Why not 0? Recall that a number times its reciprocal equals 1. But that doesn't work for 0.

$$0 \cdot (\text{reciprocal}) \neq 1$$

↑——— Put any number here. When you multiply it by 0, you get 0, never 1.

Dividing Fractions

If a, b, c, and d are numbers (but b, c, and d are not 0), then we have the following.

$$\frac{a}{b} \div \frac{c}{d} = \frac{a}{b} \cdot \frac{d}{c}$$

Reciprocals

In other words, change division to multiplying by the reciprocal of the divisor.

Use this method to find the quotient for $\frac{2}{3} \div \frac{1}{6}$. Rewrite it as a multiplication problem and then use the steps for multiplying fractions.

Change division
to multiplication.

$$\frac{2}{3} \div \frac{1}{6} = \frac{2}{3} \cdot \frac{6}{1} = \frac{2 \cdot 2 \cdot \overset{1}{\cancel{3}}}{\underset{1}{\cancel{3}} \cdot 1} = \frac{4}{1} = 4$$

The reciprocal
of $\frac{1}{6}$ is $\frac{6}{1}$

Does it make sense that $\frac{2}{3} \div \frac{1}{6} = 4$? Let's compare dividing fractions to dividing whole numbers.

$15 \div 3$ is asking, "How many 3s are in 15?"

$\frac{2}{3} \div \frac{1}{6}$ is asking, "How many $\frac{1}{6}$s are in $\frac{2}{3}$?"

The figure below illustrates $\frac{2}{3} \div \frac{1}{6}$.

How many $\frac{1}{6}$s are in $\frac{2}{3}$?
There are 4 of the $\frac{1}{6}$ pieces in $\frac{2}{3}$.
So $\frac{2}{3} \div \frac{1}{6} = 4$.

As a final check on this method of dividing, try changing $15 \div 3$ into a multiplication problem. You know that the quotient should be 5.

$$15 \div 3 = 15 \cdot \frac{1}{3} = \frac{15}{1} \cdot \frac{1}{3} = \frac{\overset{1}{\cancel{3}} \cdot 5 \cdot 1}{1 \cdot \underset{1}{\cancel{3}}} = \frac{5}{1} = 5 \left\{ \begin{array}{l} \text{The quotient} \\ \text{we expected} \end{array} \right.$$

Reciprocals

So, you can see that *dividing* by a fraction is the same as *multiplying* by the *reciprocal* of the fraction.

EXAMPLE 5   Dividing Signed Fractions

Rewrite each division problem as a multiplication problem. Then multiply.

Do **not** change $\frac{3}{10}$.
Change the *divisor* $\left(\frac{4}{5}\right)$ to its reciprocal, $\frac{5}{4}$.

(a) $\dfrac{3}{10} \div \dfrac{4}{5} = \dfrac{3}{10} \cdot \dfrac{5}{4} = \dfrac{3 \cdot \overset{1}{\cancel{5}}}{2 \cdot \underset{1}{\cancel{5}} \cdot 2 \cdot 2} = \dfrac{3}{8}$

Reciprocals

Note

When multiplying fractions, you don't always have to factor the numerator and denominator completely into prime numbers. In **Example 5(a)** above, if you notice that 5 is a common factor of the numerator and denominator, you can write

$$\frac{3}{10} \cdot \frac{5}{4} = \frac{3 \cdot \overset{1}{\cancel{5}}}{2 \cdot \underset{1}{\cancel{5}} \cdot 4} = \frac{3}{8}$$

Factor 10 into $2 \cdot 5$ Leave 4 as it is.

If no common factors are obvious to you, then write out the complete prime factorization to help find the common factors.

Continued on Next Page

(b) $2 \div \left(-\dfrac{1}{3}\right)$

First notice that the numbers have different signs. In a division problem, different signs mean that the quotient is negative. Then write 2 in fraction form as $\frac{2}{1}$.

$$2 \div \left(-\dfrac{1}{3}\right) = \dfrac{2}{1} \cdot \left(-\dfrac{3}{1}\right) = -\dfrac{2 \cdot 3}{1 \cdot 1} = -\dfrac{6}{1} = -6$$

Reciprocals

Negative product

(c) $-\dfrac{3}{4} \div (-8) = -\dfrac{3}{4} \cdot \left(-\dfrac{1}{8}\right) = \dfrac{3 \cdot 1}{4 \cdot 8} = \dfrac{3}{32}$

Reciprocals

Both numbers in the problem were negative. When signs *match*, the quotient is *positive*.

No common factor to divide out

(d) $\dfrac{9}{16} \div 0$ Dividing by 0 **cannot** be done.

This is *undefined,* just as dividing by 0 was undefined for integers in **Chapter 1.** Recall that 0 does *not* have a reciprocal, so you can't change the division to multiplying by the reciprocal of the divisor.

(e) $0 \div \dfrac{9}{16} = 0 \cdot \dfrac{16}{9} = 0$ Recall that 0 divided by any nonzero number gives a result of 0.

Reciprocals

··········· **Work Problem ⑤ at the Side.** ▶

OBJECTIVE ▶ ④ **Divide fractions that involve variables.** The method for dividing fractions also works when there are variables in the numerators and/or denominators of the fractions.

EXAMPLE 6   **Dividing Fractions with Variables**

Divide. (Assume that none of the variables represent zero.)

(a) $\dfrac{x^2}{y} \div \dfrac{x}{3y} = \dfrac{x^2}{y} \cdot \dfrac{3y}{x} = \dfrac{x \cdot x \cdot 3 \cdot y}{y \cdot x} = \dfrac{3x}{1} = 3x$

Reciprocals

(b) $\dfrac{8b}{5} \div b^2 = \dfrac{8b}{5} \cdot \dfrac{1}{b^2} = \dfrac{8 \cdot b \cdot 1}{5 \cdot b \cdot b} = \dfrac{8}{5b}$

Think of b^2 as $\dfrac{b^2}{1}$ so the reciprocal is $\dfrac{1}{b^2}$.

··········· **Work Problem ⑥ at the Side.** ▶

---

⑤ Rewrite each division problem as a multiplication problem. Then multiply.

(a) $-\dfrac{3}{4} \div \dfrac{5}{8} = -\dfrac{3}{4} \cdot \dfrac{8}{5} =$

Reciprocals

$-\dfrac{3 \cdot 2 \cdot 4}{4 \cdot 5} = -\underline{\quad}$

(b) $0 \div \left(-\dfrac{7}{12}\right)$

(c) $\dfrac{5}{6} \div 10$

(d) $-9 \div \left(-\dfrac{9}{16}\right)$

(e) $\dfrac{2}{5} \div 0$

⑥ Divide. (Assume none of the variables represent zero.)

(a) $\dfrac{c^2d^2}{4} \div \dfrac{c^2d}{4} = \dfrac{c^2d^2}{4} \cdot \dfrac{4}{c^2d}$

$= \dfrac{c \cdot c \cdot d \cdot d \cdot 2 \cdot 2}{2 \cdot 2 \cdot c \cdot c \cdot d}$

$= \dfrac{\quad}{1} =$

(b) $\dfrac{20}{7h} \div \dfrac{5h}{7}$

(c) $\dfrac{n}{8} \div mn$

Answers

5. (a) $-\dfrac{6}{5}$ **(b)** $0 \cdot \left(-\dfrac{12}{7}\right) = 0$

  (c) $\dfrac{5}{6} \cdot \dfrac{1}{10} = \dfrac{5 \cdot 1}{6 \cdot 2 \cdot 5} = \dfrac{1}{12}$

  (d) $-\dfrac{9}{1} \cdot \left(-\dfrac{16}{9}\right) = \dfrac{9 \cdot 16}{1 \cdot 9} = \dfrac{16}{1} = 16$

  (e) undefined; can't be written as multiplication because 0 doesn't have a reciprocal

6. (a) $\dfrac{d}{1}; d$ **(b)** $\dfrac{4}{h^2}$ **(c)** $\dfrac{1}{8m}$

7 Look for indicator words or draw sketches to help you with these problems.

GS **(a)** How many times can a $\frac{2}{3}$-quart spray bottle be filled from an 18-quart bottle of window cleaner?

$$18 \div \frac{2}{3} = \underline{\quad} \cdot \underline{\quad}$$

18 qt   Window Cleaner

$\frac{2}{3}$ qt

GS **(b)** A retiring police officer will receive $\frac{5}{8}$ of her highest annual salary as retirement income. If her highest annual salary is $64,000, how much will she receive as retirement income?

$\dfrac{5}{8}$ of her highest salary

↓ ↓   ↓

$\dfrac{5}{8}$ • $\dfrac{\quad}{1}$

$= \dfrac{\quad}{\quad} =$

Answers

7. **(a)** $\dfrac{18}{1} \cdot \dfrac{3}{2} = \dfrac{\overset{1}{\cancel{2}} \cdot 9 \cdot 3}{1 \cdot \underset{1}{\cancel{2}}} = \dfrac{27}{1} = 27$

The bottle can be filled 27 times.

(b) $\dfrac{5}{8} \cdot \dfrac{64,000}{1} = \dfrac{5 \cdot \overset{1}{\cancel{8}} \cdot 8000}{\underset{1}{\cancel{8}} \cdot 1} = \dfrac{40,000}{1}$

$= 40,000$

The officer will receive $40,000.

OBJECTIVE **5** **Solve application problems involving multiplying and dividing fractions.** When you're solving application problems, some indicator words are used to suggest multiplication and some are used to suggest division.

INDICATOR WORDS FOR MULTIPLICATION	INDICATOR WORDS FOR DIVISION
product	per
double	each
triple	goes into
times	divided by
twice	divided into
of (when *of* follows a fraction)	divided equally

Look for these indicator words in the following examples. However, *you won't always find an indicator word*. Then, you need to think through the problem to decide what to do. Sometimes, drawing a sketch of the situation described in the problem will help you decide which operation to use.

EXAMPLE 7 Using Indicator Words and Sketches to Solve Application Problems

(a) Lois gives $\frac{1}{10}$ of her income to her church. Last month she earned $1980. How much of that did she give to her church?

Notice the word **of**. Because the word **of** *follows the fraction* $\frac{1}{10}$, it indicates multiplication.

$$\frac{1}{10} \quad \text{of} \quad 1980 = \frac{1}{10} \cdot \frac{1980}{1} = \frac{1 \cdot \overset{1}{\cancel{10}} \cdot 198}{\underset{1}{\cancel{10}} \cdot 1} = \frac{198}{1} = 198$$

Lois gave $198 to her church.

(b) The apparel design class is making infant snowsuits to give to a local shelter. A fabric store donated a 12 yd length of fabric for the project. If one snowsuit needs $\frac{2}{3}$ yd of fabric, how many suits can the class make?

The word **of** appears in the second sentence: "A fabric store donated a 12 yd length **of** fabric." But the word **of** does *not follow a fraction,* so it is *not* an indicator to multiply. Let's try a sketch. There is a piece of fabric 12 yd long. One snowsuit will use $\frac{2}{3}$ yd. The question is, how many $\frac{2}{3}$ yd pieces can be cut from the 12 yards?

←————12 yd of fabric————→

Cutting 12 yards into equal size pieces indicates division. How many $\frac{2}{3}$s are in 12?

$\frac{2}{3}$ yd

$$12 \div \frac{2}{3} = \frac{12}{1} \cdot \frac{3}{2} = \frac{\overset{1}{\cancel{2}} \cdot 6 \cdot 3}{1 \cdot \underset{1}{\cancel{2}}} = \frac{18}{1} = 18$$

Reciprocals

The class can make 18 snowsuits.

◀ **Work Problem** **7** at the Side.

4.3 Exercises

FOR EXTRA HELP

 Download the MyDashBoard App

MyMathLab®

CONCEPT CHECK *Circle the correct word or phrase to complete each statement.*

1. To multiply fractions, you should < divide / multiply

   the numerators and multiply the < denominators. / factors.

2. When you multiply two negative fractions, the product is < positive. / negative. When you multiply a positive fraction by a negative fraction, the product is < positive. / negative.

*Multiply. Write the products in lowest terms. See **Examples 1–4.***

3. $-\dfrac{3}{8} \cdot \dfrac{1}{2} = -\dfrac{3 \cdot 1}{8 \cdot 2} =$

4. $\left(\dfrac{2}{3}\right)\left(-\dfrac{5}{7}\right) = -\dfrac{2 \cdot 5}{3 \cdot 7} =$

5. $\left(-\dfrac{3}{8}\right)\left(-\dfrac{12}{5}\right)$

6. $\dfrac{4}{9} \cdot \dfrac{12}{7}$

7. $\dfrac{21}{30}\left(\dfrac{5}{7}\right)$

8. $\left(-\dfrac{6}{11}\right)\left(-\dfrac{22}{15}\right)$

9. $10\left(-\dfrac{3}{5}\right)$

10. $-20\left(\dfrac{3}{4}\right)$

11. $\dfrac{4}{9}$ of 81

12. $\dfrac{2}{3}$ of 48

13. $\left(\dfrac{3x}{4}\right)\left(\dfrac{5}{xy}\right)$

14. $\left(\dfrac{2}{5a^2}\right)\left(\dfrac{a}{8}\right)$

*Divide. Write the quotients in lowest terms. (Assume that none of the variables represent zero.) See **Examples 5 and 6.***

15. $\dfrac{1}{6} \div \dfrac{1}{3} = \dfrac{1}{6} \cdot \dfrac{3}{1} =$

    Reciprocals

16. $-\dfrac{1}{2} \div \dfrac{2}{3} = -\dfrac{1}{2} \cdot \dfrac{3}{2} =$

    Reciprocals

17. $-\dfrac{3}{4} \div \left(-\dfrac{5}{8}\right)$

18. $\dfrac{7}{10} \div \dfrac{2}{5}$

19. $6 \div \left(-\dfrac{2}{3}\right)$

20. $-7 \div \left(-\dfrac{1}{4}\right)$

21. $-\dfrac{2}{3} \div 4$

22. $\dfrac{5}{6} \div (-15)$

23. $\dfrac{11c}{5d} \div 3c$

24. $8x^2 \div \dfrac{4x}{7}$

25. $\dfrac{ab^2}{c} \div \dfrac{ab}{c}$

26. $\dfrac{mn}{6} \div \dfrac{n}{3m}$

CONCEPT CHECK *Explain and correct the error in each calculation in Exercises 27–30.*

27. (a) $\dfrac{3}{14} \cdot \dfrac{7}{9} = \dfrac{3 \cdot 7}{2 \cdot 7 \cdot 3 \cdot 3} = 6$

28. (a) $\dfrac{3}{4} \cdot \dfrac{8}{9} = \dfrac{3 \cdot 8}{4 \cdot 9} = \dfrac{24}{36}$

(b) $8 \cdot \dfrac{2}{3} = \dfrac{8}{1} \cdot \dfrac{3}{2} = \dfrac{2 \cdot 4 \cdot 3}{1 \cdot 2} = \dfrac{12}{1} = 12$

(b) $\dfrac{2}{5} \cdot \dfrac{3}{8} = \dfrac{2}{5} \cdot \dfrac{3}{8} = \dfrac{3}{10}$

29. (a) $\dfrac{2}{3} \div 4 = \dfrac{2}{3} \cdot \dfrac{4}{1} = \dfrac{2 \cdot 4}{3 \cdot 1} = \dfrac{8}{3}$

30. (a) $\dfrac{1}{2} \div 0 = 0$

(b) $\dfrac{5}{6} \div \dfrac{10}{9} = \dfrac{6}{5} \cdot \dfrac{10}{9} = \dfrac{2 \cdot \overset{1}{\cancel{3}} \cdot 2 \cdot \overset{1}{\cancel{5}}}{\underset{1}{\cancel{5}} \cdot \underset{1}{\cancel{3}} \cdot 3} = \dfrac{4}{3}$

(b) $\dfrac{\overset{1}{\cancel{3}}}{10} \div \dfrac{1}{\underset{1}{\cancel{3}}} = \dfrac{1}{10}$

*Find each product or quotient. Write all answers in lowest terms. **See Examples 1–6.***

31. $\dfrac{4}{5} \div 3 = \dfrac{4}{5} \cdot \dfrac{1}{3} =$

Reciprocals

32. $\left(-\dfrac{20}{21}\right)\left(-\dfrac{14}{15}\right) = \dfrac{2 \cdot 2 \cdot \overset{1}{\cancel{5}} \cdot 2 \cdot \overset{1}{\cancel{7}}}{3 \cdot \underset{1}{\cancel{7}} \cdot 3 \cdot \underset{1}{\cancel{5}}} =$

The product of two
negative numbers is positive.

33. $-\dfrac{3}{8}\left(\dfrac{3}{4}\right)$

34. $-\dfrac{8}{17} \div \dfrac{4}{5}$

35. $\dfrac{3}{5}$ of 35

36. $\dfrac{2}{3} \div (-6)$

37. $-9 \div \left(-\dfrac{3}{5}\right)$

38. $\dfrac{7}{8} \cdot \dfrac{25}{21}$

39. $\dfrac{12}{7} \div 0$

40. $\dfrac{5}{8}$ of (-48)

41. $\left(\dfrac{11}{2}\right)\left(-\dfrac{5}{6}\right)$

42. $\dfrac{3}{4} \div \dfrac{3}{16}$

43. $\dfrac{4}{7}$ of $14b$

44. $\dfrac{ab}{6} \div \dfrac{b}{9}$

45. $\dfrac{12}{5} \div 4d$

46. $\dfrac{18}{7} \div 2t$

47. $\dfrac{x^2}{y} \div \dfrac{w}{2y}$

48. $\dfrac{5}{6}$ of $18w$

*Solve each application problem. **See Example 7.***

49. Al is helping Tim make a mahogany lamp table for Jill's birthday. Find the area of the rectangular top of the table if it is $\frac{4}{5}$ yd long by $\frac{3}{8}$ yd wide.

50. A rectangular dog bed is $\frac{2}{3}$ yd by $\frac{5}{6}$ yd. Find its area.

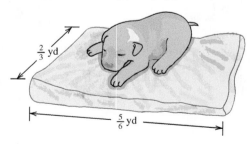

51. How many $\frac{1}{8}$-ounce eyedrop dispensers can be filled from a container that holds 10 ounces of eyedrops?

52. Ms. Shaffer has a piece of property with an area that is $\frac{9}{10}$ acre. She wishes to divide it into three equal parts for her children. How many acres of land will each child get?

53. Todd estimates that it will cost him $12,400 to attend a community college for one year. He thinks he can earn $\frac{3}{4}$ of the cost and borrow the balance. Find the amount he must earn and the amount he must borrow.

54. Joyce Chen wants to make children's vests to sell at a craft fair. Each vest requires $\frac{3}{4}$ yd of material. She has 36 yd of material. Find the number of vests she can make.

55. There are nearly 300 baseball players in the Baseball Hall of Fame. About one-fourth of these men played at infield positions (1st base, 2nd base, 3rd base, or short-stop). About how many infield players are in the Hall of Fame? (*Source:* National Baseball Hall of Fame.)

56. At the Garlic Festival Fun Run, $\frac{5}{12}$ of the runners are women. If there are 780 runners, how many are women? How many are men?

57. Pam Trizlia has a small pickup truck that can carry $\frac{2}{3}$ cord of firewood. Find the number of trips needed to deliver 6 cords of wood.

58. Parking lot A is $\frac{1}{4}$ mile long and $\frac{3}{16}$ mile wide, and parking lot B is $\frac{3}{8}$ mile long and $\frac{1}{8}$ mile wide. Which parking lot has the larger area?

59. An adult male alligator may weigh 400 pounds. A newly hatched alligator weighs only $\frac{1}{8}$ pound. The adult weighs how many times the hatchling? (*Source:* St. Marks NWR.)

60. A female alligator lays about 35 eggs in a nest of marsh grass and mud. But $\frac{4}{5}$ of the eggs or hatchlings will fall prey to raccoons, wading birds, or larger alligators. How many of the 35 eggs will hatch and survive? (*Source:* St. Marks NWR.)

A survey of 1600 students asked them where they got the money for college expenses. The circle graph shows what fraction of the students gave each answer. Use this information to work Exercises 61–64.

61. How many students in the survey borrowed money for college expenses?

62. What number of students used money from their parents' income/savings?

63. How many more students used their own income rather than money from relatives and friends?

64. How many fewer students used money that their parents borrowed rather than money they borrowed?

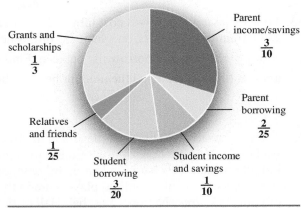

PAYING FOR COLLEGE

A survey of 1600 students shows where the money comes from:

Parent income/savings $\frac{3}{10}$

Grants and scholarships $\frac{1}{3}$

Parent borrowing $\frac{2}{25}$

Relatives and friends $\frac{1}{25}$

Student borrowing $\frac{3}{20}$

Student income and savings $\frac{1}{10}$

Source: Sallie Mae-Ipsos.

There are a total of about 175 million companion pets in the United States. This table shows the fraction of pets that are dogs, cats, birds, and horses. Use the table to answer Exercises 65–68.

COMPANION PETS IN THE UNITED STATES

Type of Pet	Fraction of All Pets
Dog	$\frac{2}{5}$
Cat	$\frac{12}{25}$
Bird	$\frac{3}{50}$
Horse	$\frac{1}{25}$

Source: American Veterinary Medical Association.

65. How many U.S. pets are horses?

66. How many U.S. pets are dogs?

67. How many dogs and cats are pets?

68. How many birds are pets?

69. Your friend missed class and is confused about how to divide fractions. Write a short explanation for your friend.

70. Mary spilled coffee on her math homework, and part of one problem is covered up.

$$\frac{3}{\blacksquare} \div \frac{4}{5}$$

She knows the answer given in the back of the book is $\frac{3}{4}$. Describe how to find the missing number.

4.4 Adding and Subtracting Signed Fractions

OBJECTIVE **1** **Add and subtract like fractions.** You probably remember learning something about "common denominators" in other math classes. When fractions have the *same* denominator, we say that they have a *common* denominator, which makes them **like fractions.** When fractions have different denominators, they are called **unlike fractions.** Here are examples.

Like Fractions	**Unlike Fractions**

$\dfrac{3}{4}$ and $-\dfrac{7}{4}$ $\dfrac{2}{9}$ and $\dfrac{2}{8}$

Common denominator   Different denominators

$\dfrac{6}{x}$ and $\dfrac{y}{x}$ $\dfrac{a^2}{3}$ and $\dfrac{3}{a}$

Common denominator   Different denominators

You can add or subtract fractions *only* when they have a common denominator. To see why, let's look at more pizzas.

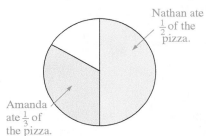

Nathan ate $\frac{1}{2}$ of the pizza.

Amanda ate $\frac{1}{3}$ of the pizza.

What fraction of the pizza has been eaten? We can't write a fraction until the pizza is cut into pieces of *equal* size. That's what the denominator of a fraction tells us: the number of *equal* size pieces in the pizza.

Now the pizza is cut into 6 *equal* pieces, and we can find out how much was eaten.

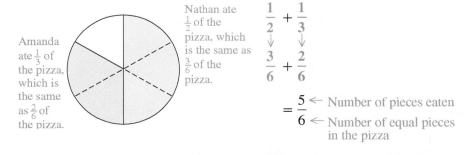

Amanda ate $\frac{1}{3}$ of the pizza, which is the same as $\frac{2}{6}$ of the pizza.

Nathan ate $\frac{1}{2}$ of the pizza, which is the same as $\frac{3}{6}$ of the pizza.

$$\dfrac{1}{2} + \dfrac{1}{3}$$
$$\downarrow \qquad \downarrow$$
$$\dfrac{3}{6} + \dfrac{2}{6}$$

$$= \dfrac{5}{6} \leftarrow \text{Number of pieces eaten}$$
$$\leftarrow \text{Number of equal pieces in the pizza}$$

Adding and Subtracting Like Fractions

You can add or subtract fractions **only** when they have a common denominator. If a, b, and c are numbers (and b is not 0), then

$$\dfrac{a}{b} + \dfrac{c}{b} = \dfrac{a+c}{b} \quad \text{and} \quad \dfrac{a}{b} - \dfrac{c}{b} = \dfrac{a-c}{b}$$

In other words, add or subtract the numerators and write the result over the common denominator. Then check to be sure that the answer is in lowest terms.

1 Write each sum or difference in lowest terms.

(a) $\dfrac{1}{6} + \dfrac{5}{6}$

$\dfrac{1}{6} + \dfrac{5}{6} = \dfrac{\underline{\quad} + \underline{\quad}}{6} = \dfrac{\underline{\quad}}{} =$

$\uparrow \quad \uparrow \qquad \uparrow \qquad \uparrow$

Common denominator

(b) $-\dfrac{11}{12} + \dfrac{5}{12}$

$-\dfrac{11}{12} + \dfrac{5}{12} = \dfrac{-11 + \underline{\quad}}{12}$

$= \dfrac{\underline{\quad}}{12} =$

Write your answer in lowest terms.

(c) $-\dfrac{2}{9} - \dfrac{3}{9}$

(d) $\dfrac{8}{ab} + \dfrac{3}{ab}$

Answers

1. (a) $\dfrac{1+5}{6} = \dfrac{6}{6} = 1$

   (b) $\dfrac{-11+5}{12} = \dfrac{-6}{12} = -\dfrac{1}{2}$

   (c) $-\dfrac{5}{9}$ (d) $\dfrac{11}{ab}$

EXAMPLE 1 **Adding and Subtracting Like Fractions**

Find each sum or difference.

(a) $\dfrac{1}{8} + \dfrac{3}{8}$

These are *like* fractions because they have a *common denominator of 8.* So they are ready to be added. Add the numerators and write the sum over the common denominator.

$\dfrac{1}{8} + \dfrac{3}{8} = \dfrac{1+3}{8} = \dfrac{4}{8}$ Now write $\frac{4}{8}$ in lowest terms. $\dfrac{4}{8} = \dfrac{\overset{1}{\cancel{2}} \cdot \overset{1}{\cancel{2}}}{\cancel{2} \cdot \cancel{2} \cdot 2} = \dfrac{1}{2}$

Common denominator

The sum, in lowest terms, is $\frac{1}{2}$.

CAUTION

Add **only** the numerators. **Do not add the denominators.** In **Example 1a** above we **kept the common denominator.**

$\dfrac{1}{8} + \dfrac{3}{8} = \dfrac{1+3}{8}$ **not** $\dfrac{1}{8} + \dfrac{3}{8} = \dfrac{1+3}{8+8} \cancel{=} \dfrac{4}{16}$ Incorrect

To help you understand why we add *only* the numerators, think of $\frac{1}{8}$ as $1\left(\frac{1}{8}\right)$ and $\frac{3}{8}$ as $3\left(\frac{1}{8}\right)$. Then we use the distributive property.

$\dfrac{1}{8} + \dfrac{3}{8} = \underbrace{1\left(\dfrac{1}{8}\right) + 3\left(\dfrac{1}{8}\right)} = \underbrace{(1+3)\left(\dfrac{1}{8}\right)} = 4\left(\dfrac{1}{8}\right) = \dfrac{4}{8} = \dfrac{1}{2}$

Use the distributive property.

Or think about a pie cut into 8 equal pieces. If you eat 1 piece and your friend eats 3 pieces, together you've eaten 4 of the 8 pieces or $\frac{4}{8}$ of the pie (**not** $\frac{4}{16}$ of the pie, which would be 4 out of 16 pieces).

(b) $-\dfrac{3}{5} + \dfrac{4}{5} = \dfrac{-3+4}{5} = \dfrac{1}{5}$ ← Lowest terms

Common denominator

Rewrite subtraction as adding the opposite.

(c) $\dfrac{3}{10} - \dfrac{7}{10} = \dfrac{3-7}{10} = \dfrac{3+(-7)}{10} = \dfrac{-4}{10}$ or $-\dfrac{4}{10}$

Common denominator

Now write $-\frac{4}{10}$ in lowest terms. $-\dfrac{4}{10} = -\dfrac{\overset{1}{\cancel{2}} \cdot 2}{\underset{1}{\cancel{2}} \cdot 5} = -\dfrac{2}{5}$

Always write fraction answers in lowest terms.

(d) $\dfrac{5}{x^2} - \dfrac{2}{x^2} = \dfrac{5-2}{x^2} = \dfrac{3}{x^2}$

Common denominator

◀ **Work Problem** **1** **at the Side.**

OBJECTIVE 2 **Find the lowest common denominator for unlike fractions.** When we first tried to add the pizza eaten by Nathan and Amanda, we could *not* do so because the pizza was *not cut into pieces of the same size*. So we rewrote $\frac{1}{2}$ and $\frac{1}{3}$ as equivalent fractions that both had 6 as the common denominator.

$$\frac{1}{2} = \frac{1 \cdot 3}{2 \cdot 3} = \frac{3}{6} \left. \right\}$$
$$\frac{1}{3} = \frac{1 \cdot 2}{3 \cdot 2} = \frac{2}{6} \left. \right\} \text{Common denominator of 6}$$

Then we could add the fractions, because the pizza was cut into pieces of *equal* size.

$$\frac{1}{2} + \frac{1}{3} = \frac{3}{6} + \frac{2}{6} = \frac{3 + 2}{6} = \frac{5}{6} \leftarrow \text{Lowest terms}$$

In other words, when you want to add or subtract unlike fractions, the first thing you must do is rewrite them so that they have a common denominator.

A Common Denominator for Unlike Fractions

To find a common denominator for two unlike fractions, find a number that is divisible by *both* of the original denominators.

For example, a common denominator for $\frac{1}{2}$ and $\frac{1}{3}$ is 6 because 2 goes into 6 evenly and 3 goes into 6 evenly.

Notice that 12 is also a common denominator for $\frac{1}{2}$ and $\frac{1}{3}$ because 2 and 3 both go into 12 evenly.

$$\frac{1}{2} = \frac{1 \cdot 6}{2 \cdot 6} = \frac{6}{12} \left. \right\}$$
$$\frac{1}{3} = \frac{1 \cdot 4}{3 \cdot 4} = \frac{4}{12} \left. \right\} \text{Common denominator of 12}$$

Now that the fractions have a common denominator, we can add them.

$$\frac{1}{2} + \frac{1}{3} = \frac{6}{12} + \frac{4}{12} = \frac{6 + 4}{12} = \frac{10}{12} \left\{ \begin{array}{l} \text{Not in} \\ \text{lowest} \\ \text{terms} \end{array} \right. \text{but } \frac{10}{12} = \frac{\overset{1}{\cancel{2}} \cdot 5}{\underset{1}{\cancel{2}} \cdot 6} = \frac{5}{6} \left\{ \begin{array}{l} \text{Same} \\ \text{result as} \\ \text{above} \end{array} \right.$$

Both 6 and 12 worked as common denominators for adding $\frac{1}{2}$ and $\frac{1}{3}$, but using the smaller number saved some work. You should always try to find the smallest common denominator. If you don't for some reason, you can still work the problem—but it may take you longer. You'll have to divide out some common factors at the end in order to write the answer in lowest terms.

Least Common Denominator (LCD)

The **least common denominator** (LCD) for two fractions is the *smallest* positive number divisible by both denominators of the original fractions.

For example, both 6 and 12 are common denominators for $\frac{1}{2}$ and $\frac{1}{3}$, but 6 is smaller, so it is the LCD.

2 Find the LCD for each pair of fractions by inspection.

(a) $\frac{3}{5}$ and $\frac{3}{10}$

10 is the larger denominator.

Is 10 divisible by 5? _____

So the LCD is _____.

(b) $\frac{1}{2}$ and $\frac{2}{5}$ LCD is _____.

(c) $\frac{3}{4}$ and $\frac{1}{6}$ LCD is _____.

(d) $\frac{5}{6}$ and $\frac{7}{18}$ LCD is _____.

3 Use prime factorization to find the LCD for each pair of fractions.

(a) $\frac{1}{10}$ and $\frac{13}{14}$ $10 = 2 \cdot 5$
$14 = 2 \cdot 7$

LCD = _____ • _____ • _____

LCD = _____

(b) $\frac{5}{12}$ and $\frac{17}{20}$

(c) $\frac{7}{15}$ and $\frac{7}{9}$

Answers

2. **(a)** yes; 10 **(b)** 10 **(c)** 12 **(d)** 18

3. **(a)** LCD = 2 • 5 • 7 = 70

(b) $12 = 2 \cdot 2 \cdot 3$
$20 = 2 \cdot 2 \cdot 5$ LCD = 2 • 2 • 3 • 5 = 60

(c) $15 = 3 \cdot 5$
$9 = 3 \cdot 3$ LCD = 3 • 3 • 5 = 45

There are several ways to find the LCD. When the original denominators are small numbers, you can often find the LCD by inspection. *Hint:* **Always check to see if the larger denominator will work as the LCD.**

EXAMPLE 2 **Finding the LCD by Inspection**

(a) Find the LCD for $\frac{2}{3}$ and $\frac{1}{9}$ by inspection.

Check to see if 9 (the larger denominator) will work as the LCD. Is 9 divisible by 3 (the other denominator)? Yes, so 9 is the LCD for $\frac{2}{3}$ and $\frac{1}{9}$.

(b) Find the LCD for $\frac{5}{8}$ and $\frac{5}{6}$ by inspection.

Check to see if 8 (the larger denominator) will work. No, 8 is not divisible by 6. So start checking numbers that are multiples of 8, that is, 16, 24, and 32. Notice that 24 will work because it is divisible by 8 and by 6. The LCD for $\frac{5}{8}$ and $\frac{5}{6}$ is 24.

◀ **Work Problem 2 at the Side.**

For large denominators, you can use prime factorization to find the LCD. Factor each denominator completely into prime numbers. Then use the factors to build the LCD.

EXAMPLE 3 **Using Prime Factors to Find the LCD**

(a) What is the LCD for $\frac{7}{12}$ and $\frac{13}{18}$?

Write 12 and 18 as the product of prime factors. Then use just enough prime factors in the LCD so you "cover" both 12 and 18.

$12 = 2 \cdot 2 \cdot 3$

$18 = 2 \cdot 3 \cdot 3$

LCD = 2 • 2 • 3 • 3 = 36

Check whether 36 is divisible by 12 (yes) and by 18 (yes). The LCD for $\frac{7}{12}$ and $\frac{13}{18}$ is 36.

CAUTION

When finding the LCD, notice that we did *not* have to repeat the factors that 12 and 18 have in common. If we had used *all* the 2s and 3s, we would get a common denominator, but not the *smallest* one.

(b) What is the LCD for $\frac{11}{15}$ and $\frac{9}{70}$?

$15 = 3 \cdot 5$

$70 = 2 \cdot 5 \cdot 7$

LCD = 3 • 5 • 2 • 7 = 210

Check whether 210 is divisible by 15 (yes) and divisible by 70 (yes). The LCD for $\frac{11}{15}$ and $\frac{9}{70}$ is 210.

◀ **Work Problem 3 at the Side.**

OBJECTIVE ▸ ③ **Add and subtract unlike fractions.** Here are the steps for adding or subtracting unlike fractions. The key idea is that you must rewrite the fractions so that they have a common denominator before you can add or subtract them.

Adding and Subtracting Unlike Fractions

Step 1 Find the LCD, the smallest number divisible by both denominators in the problem.

Step 2 Rewrite each original fraction as an equivalent fraction whose denominator is the LCD.

Step 3 Add or subtract the numerators of the like fractions. Keep the common denominator.

Step 4 Write the sum or difference in lowest terms.

EXAMPLE 4 **Adding and Subtracting Unlike Fractions**

Find each sum or difference.

(a) $\dfrac{1}{5} + \dfrac{3}{10}$ [First check to see if the larger denominator is the LCD.]

Step 1 The larger denominator (10) is the LCD.

Step 2 $\dfrac{1}{5} = \dfrac{1 \cdot 2}{5 \cdot 2} = \dfrac{2}{10} \leftarrow \text{LCD}$ and $\dfrac{3}{10}$ already has the LCD.

Step 3 Add the numerators. Write the sum over the common denominator.

$$\dfrac{1}{5} + \dfrac{3}{10} = \dfrac{2}{10} + \dfrac{3}{10} = \dfrac{2+3}{10} = \dfrac{5}{10}$$

Step 4 Write $\frac{5}{10}$ in lowest terms.

$$\dfrac{5}{10} = \dfrac{\overset{1}{\cancel{5}}}{2 \cdot \cancel{5}} = \dfrac{1}{2} \leftarrow \text{Lowest terms}$$

(b) $\dfrac{3}{4} - \dfrac{5}{6}$

Step 1 The LCD is 12.

Step 2 $\dfrac{3}{4} = \dfrac{3 \cdot 3}{4 \cdot 3} = \dfrac{9}{12} \leftarrow \text{LCD}$ and $\dfrac{5}{6} = \dfrac{5 \cdot 2}{6 \cdot 2} = \dfrac{10}{12} \leftarrow \text{LCD}$

Step 3 Subtract the numerators. Write the difference over the common denominator.

$9 + (-10)$ is -1

$$\dfrac{3}{4} - \dfrac{5}{6} = \dfrac{9}{12} - \dfrac{10}{12} = \dfrac{9-10}{12} = \dfrac{-1}{12} \quad \text{or} \quad -\dfrac{1}{12}$$

Step 4 $-\frac{1}{12}$ is in lowest terms.

⋯⋯⋯⋯⋯⋯⋯⋯⋯⋯⋯⋯⋯⋯⋯⋯⋯⋯⋯ **Continued on Next Page**

4 Find each sum or difference. Write all answers in lowest terms.

GS (a) $\dfrac{2}{3} + \dfrac{1}{6}$ 6 is the larger denominator. Is 6 divisible by 3? _____

The LCD is _____ .

$$\frac{2}{3} = \frac{2 \cdot \underline{\quad}}{3 \cdot \underline{\quad}} = \frac{\underline{\quad}}{6}$$

$\frac{1}{6}$ already has the LCD.

$$\frac{\underline{\quad}}{6} + \frac{1}{6} = \frac{\underline{\quad} + \underline{\quad}}{6} = \underline{\quad}$$

(b) $\dfrac{1}{12} - \dfrac{5}{6}$

(c) $3 - \dfrac{4}{5}$

(d) $-\dfrac{5}{12} + \dfrac{9}{16}$

Answers

4. **(a)** Yes; LCD is 6;

$\dfrac{2 \cdot 2}{3 \cdot 2} = \dfrac{4}{6}; \dfrac{4}{6} + \dfrac{1}{6} = \dfrac{4+1}{6} = \dfrac{5}{6}$

(b) $-\dfrac{3}{4}$ **(c)** $\dfrac{11}{5}$ **(d)** $\dfrac{7}{48}$

(c) $-\dfrac{5}{12} + \dfrac{5}{9}$

Step 1 Use prime factorization to find the LCD.

$$12 = 2 \cdot 2 \cdot 3$$

Factors of 12

$$LCD = 2 \cdot 2 \cdot 3 \cdot 3 = 36$$

$$9 = 3 \cdot 3$$

Factors of 9

Step 2 $-\dfrac{5}{12} = -\dfrac{5 \cdot 3}{12 \cdot 3} = -\dfrac{15}{36}$ and $\dfrac{5}{9} = \dfrac{5 \cdot 4}{9 \cdot 4} = \dfrac{20}{36}$

Step 3 Add the numerators. Keep the common denominator.

$$-\frac{5}{12} + \frac{5}{9} = -\frac{15}{36} + \frac{20}{36} = \frac{-15 + 20}{36} = \frac{5}{36}$$

Step 4 $\frac{5}{36}$ is in lowest terms.

(d) $4 - \dfrac{2}{3}$

Step 1 Think of 4 as $\frac{4}{1}$. The LCD for $\frac{4}{1}$ and $\frac{2}{3}$ is 3, the larger denominator.

Step 2 $\dfrac{4}{1} = \dfrac{4 \cdot 3}{1 \cdot 3} = \dfrac{12}{3}$ and $\dfrac{2}{3}$ already has the LCD.

Step 3 Subtract the numerators. Keep the common denominator.

$$\frac{4}{1} - \frac{2}{3} = \frac{12}{3} - \frac{2}{3} = \frac{12 - 2}{3} = \frac{10}{3}$$

Step 4 $\frac{10}{3}$ is in lowest terms.

◀ **Work Problem 4 at the Side.**

OBJECTIVE ▶ 4 Add and subtract unlike fractions that contain variables. We use the same steps to add or subtract unlike fractions with variables in the numerators or denominators.

EXAMPLE 5   Adding and Subtracting Unlike Fractions with Variables

Find each sum or difference.

(a) $\dfrac{1}{4} + \dfrac{b}{5}$

Step 1 The LCD is 20.

Step 2 $\dfrac{1}{4} = \dfrac{1 \cdot 5}{4 \cdot 5} = \dfrac{5}{20}$ and $\dfrac{b}{5} = \dfrac{b \cdot 4}{5 \cdot 4} = \dfrac{4b}{20}$

Continued on Next Page

Step 3 $\dfrac{1}{4} + \dfrac{b}{5} = \dfrac{5}{20} + \dfrac{4b}{20} = \dfrac{5 + 4b}{20}$ ← Add the numerators.
← Keep the common denominator.

Step 4 $\dfrac{5 + 4b}{20}$ is in lowest terms.

CAUTION

In *Step 4* above, we could **not** add $5 + 4b$ in the numerator of the answer because 5 and $4b$ are **not** like terms. We *could* add $5b + 4b$ but **not** $5 + 4b$.

Variable parts match.

(b) $\dfrac{2}{3} - \dfrac{6}{x}$

Step 1 The LCD is $3 \cdot x$, or $3x$.

Step 2 $\dfrac{2}{3} = \dfrac{2 \cdot x}{3 \cdot x} = \dfrac{2x}{3x}$ and $\dfrac{6}{x} = \dfrac{6 \cdot 3}{x \cdot 3} = \dfrac{18}{3x}$

Step 3 $\dfrac{2}{3} - \dfrac{6}{x} = \dfrac{2x}{3x} - \dfrac{18}{3x} = \dfrac{2x - 18}{3x}$ ← Subtract the numerators.
← Keep the common denominator.

Step 4 $\dfrac{2x - 18}{3x}$ is in lowest terms.

Note

Notice in **Example 5(b)** above that we found the LCD for $\frac{2}{3} - \frac{6}{x}$ by multiplying the two denominators. The LCD is $3 \cdot x$ or $3x$.

Multiplying the two denominators will *always* give you a common denominator, but it may not be the *least* common denominator. Here are more examples.

$\dfrac{1}{3} - \dfrac{2}{5}$ If you multiply the denominators, $3 \cdot 5 = 15$, and 15 is the LCD.

$\dfrac{5}{6} + \dfrac{3}{4}$ If you multiply the denominators, $6 \cdot 4 = 24$, and 24 will work. But you'll save some time by using the least common denominator, which is 12.

$\dfrac{7}{y} + \dfrac{a}{4}$ If you multiply the denominators, $y \cdot 4 = 4y$, and $4y$ is the LCD.

Work Problem ⑤ at the Side. ▶

⑤ Find each sum or difference.

(a) $\dfrac{5}{6} - \dfrac{h}{2}$ The LCD is 6.

$\dfrac{5}{6}$ already has the LCD.

$\dfrac{h}{2} = \dfrac{h \cdot \underline{\quad}}{2 \cdot \underline{\quad}} = \dfrac{\underline{\quad}}{6}$

$\dfrac{5}{6} - \dfrac{\underline{\quad}}{6} =$

Is the answer in lowest terms? _____

(b) $\dfrac{7}{t} + \dfrac{3}{5}$

(c) $\dfrac{4}{x} - \dfrac{8}{3}$

Answers

5. **(a)** $\dfrac{h \cdot 3}{2 \cdot 3} = \dfrac{3h}{6}$; $\dfrac{5}{6} - \dfrac{3h}{6} = \dfrac{5 - 3h}{6}$; yes

(b) $\dfrac{35 + 3t}{5t}$ **(c)** $\dfrac{12 - 8x}{3x}$

4.4 Exercises

CONCEPT CHECK *Circle the correct word or phrase to complete each statement.*

1. (a) When two fractions have the same denominator, they are called $\Big\langle$ fractions in lowest terms. / like fractions.

(b) Two fractions need to have a common denominator before you can $\Big\langle$ multiply them. / add them.

2. (a) If two fractions are unlike fractions, they have $\Big\langle$ different denominators. / different numerators.

(b) When adding two fractions with a common denominator $\Big\langle$ add only the denominators. / add only the numerators.

Find each sum or difference. Write all answers in lowest terms. ***See Examples 1–5.***

3. $\dfrac{3}{4} + \dfrac{1}{8}$ $\begin{cases} \text{The LCD is 8.} \\ \dfrac{3}{4} = \dfrac{3 \cdot 2}{4 \cdot 2} = \dfrac{6}{8} \end{cases}$

$\dfrac{6}{8} + \dfrac{1}{8} =$

4. $\dfrac{1}{3} + \dfrac{1}{2}$ $\begin{cases} \text{The LCD is 6.} \\ \dfrac{1}{3} = \dfrac{1 \cdot 2}{3 \cdot 2} = \dfrac{2}{6} \\ \dfrac{1}{2} = \dfrac{1 \cdot 3}{2 \cdot 3} = \dfrac{3}{6} \end{cases}$

$\dfrac{2}{6} + \dfrac{3}{6} =$

5. $-\dfrac{1}{14} + \left(-\dfrac{3}{7}\right)$

6. $-\dfrac{2}{9} + \dfrac{2}{3}$

7. $\dfrac{2}{3} - \dfrac{1}{6}$

8. $\dfrac{5}{12} - \dfrac{1}{4}$

9. $\dfrac{3}{8} - \dfrac{3}{5}$

10. $\dfrac{1}{3} - \dfrac{3}{5}$

11. $-\dfrac{5}{8} + \dfrac{1}{12}$

12. $-\dfrac{13}{16} + \dfrac{13}{16}$

13. $-\dfrac{7}{20} - \dfrac{5}{20}$

14. $-\dfrac{7}{9} - \dfrac{5}{6}$

15. $0 - \dfrac{7}{18}$

16. $-\dfrac{7}{8} + 3$

17. $2 - \dfrac{6}{7}$

18. $5 - \dfrac{2}{5}$

19. $-\dfrac{1}{2} + \dfrac{3}{24}$

20. $\dfrac{7}{10} + \dfrac{7}{15}$

21. $\dfrac{1}{5} + \dfrac{c}{3}$

22. $\dfrac{x}{4} + \dfrac{2}{3}$

23. $\dfrac{5}{m} - \dfrac{1}{2}$

Hint: The LCD is 2m.

24. $\dfrac{2}{9} - \dfrac{4}{y}$

Hint: The LCD is 9y.

25. $\dfrac{3}{b^2} + \dfrac{5}{b^2}$

26. $\dfrac{10}{xy} - \dfrac{7}{xy}$

27. $\dfrac{c}{7} + \dfrac{3}{b}$

28. $\dfrac{2}{x} - \dfrac{y}{5}$

29. $-\dfrac{4}{c^2} - \dfrac{d}{c}$

30. $-\dfrac{1}{n} + \dfrac{m}{n^2}$

31. $-\dfrac{11}{42} - \dfrac{11}{70}$

32. $\dfrac{7}{45} - \dfrac{7}{20}$

33. $\dfrac{b}{3} + \dfrac{4}{a^2}$

34. $\dfrac{16}{y^3} - \dfrac{x^2}{y^3}$

35. $-\dfrac{w}{10} + \dfrac{5}{w^2}$

36. $-\dfrac{r^2}{t^2} - \dfrac{8}{t^3}$

37. $\dfrac{m^4}{n^2} - 0$

38. $\dfrac{6c + 1}{h^3} + 0$

39. CONCEPT CHECK   Explain the error in each calculation and correct it.

(a) $\dfrac{3}{4} + \dfrac{2}{5} = \dfrac{3+2}{4+5} = \dfrac{5}{9}$

(b) $\dfrac{5}{6} - \dfrac{4}{9} = \dfrac{5}{18} - \dfrac{4}{18} = \dfrac{5-4}{18} = \dfrac{1}{18}$

40. CONCEPT CHECK   Explain the error in each calculation and correct it.

(a) $-\dfrac{1}{4} + \dfrac{7}{12} = -\dfrac{3}{12} + \dfrac{7}{12} = \dfrac{-3+7}{12} = \dfrac{4}{12}$

(b) $\dfrac{3}{10} - \dfrac{1}{4} = \dfrac{3-1}{10-4} = \dfrac{2}{6} = \dfrac{1}{3}$

Solve each application problem. Write all answers in lowest terms.

41. When assembling shelving units, Pam Phelps must use the proper type and size of hardware. Find the total length of the bolt shown.

$\frac{1}{5}$ in. $\frac{1}{3}$ in. $\frac{1}{4}$ in.

42. How much fencing will be needed to enclose this rectangular wildflower preserve?

$\frac{1}{6}$ mile

$\frac{1}{3}$ mile

43. LaSonya needs $\frac{1}{8}$ cup of milk for a muffin recipe and $\frac{1}{2}$ cup of milk to make pudding. She also needs $\frac{1}{3}$ cup of milk to make instant mashed potatoes. How much milk does she need in all?

44. A flower grower purchased $\frac{9}{10}$ acre of land one year and $\frac{3}{10}$ acre the next year. She then sold $\frac{7}{10}$ acre of land. How much land does she now have?

45. A group of foresters planted $\frac{5}{12}$ acre of seedlings in the morning and $\frac{11}{12}$ acre in the afternoon. The next day, $\frac{7}{12}$ acre of seedlings was destroyed by a brush fire. How many acres of seedlings remained?

46. Swiss cheese is full of holes. In the United States today, the holes must measure from $\frac{3}{8}$ inch to $\frac{13}{16}$ inch across the center. Before 2001, the holes had to measure between $\frac{11}{16}$ inch and $\frac{13}{16}$ inch across the center.

    (a) Before 2001, what was the difference in the measurements of the smaller and larger holes?

    (b) How much greater is the measurement of the smaller holes before 2001 than today?

The circle graph shows the fraction of U.S. workers who used various methods to learn about computers. Use the graph to answer Exercises 47–50.

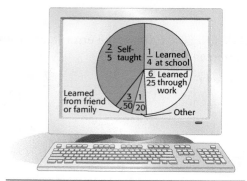

Ways To Learn Computers

$\frac{2}{5}$ Self-taught $\frac{1}{4}$ Learned at school $\frac{6}{25}$ Learned through work   Learned from friend or family $\frac{3}{50}$ $\frac{1}{20}$ Other

Source: John J. Heldrich Center for Workforce Development.

47. What fraction of workers are self-taught or learned from friends or family?

48. What fraction of workers learned at school or through work?

49. What is the difference in the fraction of workers who are self-taught and those who learned at work?

50. What is the difference in the fraction of workers who are self-taught and those who learned at school?

Use the photo to answer Exercises 51–52. A nut driver is like a screwdriver but is used to tighten nuts instead of screws. The ends of the drivers are sized from $\frac{3}{16}$ inch to $\frac{1}{2}$ inch to fit smaller or larger nuts. (The symbol " is for inches.)

HEAVY DUTY
7 PC. NUT DRIVER SET

$\frac{3}{16}"$ $\frac{1}{4}"$ $\frac{5}{16}"$ $\frac{11}{32}"$ $\frac{3}{8}"$ $\frac{7}{16}"$ $\frac{1}{2}"$

Source: Author's tool collection.

51. The rightmost driver fits a nut that is how much larger than the nut for the leftmost driver?

52. The nut size for the yellow-handled driver is how much less than the nut size for the blue-handled driver?

53. A hazardous waste dump site needs $\frac{7}{8}$ mile of security fencing. The site has four sides with three of the sides measuring $\frac{1}{4}$ mile, $\frac{1}{6}$ mile, and $\frac{3}{8}$ mile. Find the length of the fourth side.

54. Chakotay is fitting a turquoise stone into a bear claw pendant. Find the diameter of the hole in the pendant. (The diameter is the distance across the center of the hole.)

Relating Concepts (Exercises 55–56) For Individual or Group Work

*As you **work Exercises 55 and 56 in order**, think about the properties you learned when working with integers. Then explain what each pair of problems illustrates. (For a review of the properties, see the **Chapter 1 Summary**.)*

55. (a) $-\dfrac{2}{3} + \dfrac{3}{4} =$ ____ $\dfrac{3}{4} + \left(-\dfrac{2}{3}\right) =$ ____

56. (a) $-\dfrac{7}{12} + \dfrac{7}{12} =$ ____ $\dfrac{3}{5} + \left(-\dfrac{3}{5}\right) =$ ____

(b) $\dfrac{5}{6} - \dfrac{1}{2} =$ ____ $\dfrac{1}{2} - \dfrac{5}{6} =$ ____

(b) $-\dfrac{13}{16} \div \left(-\dfrac{13}{16}\right) =$ ____ $\dfrac{1}{8} \div \dfrac{1}{8} =$ ____

(c) $\left(-\dfrac{2}{3}\right)\left(\dfrac{9}{10}\right) =$ ____ $\left(\dfrac{9}{10}\right)\left(-\dfrac{2}{3}\right) =$ ____

(c) $\dfrac{5}{6} \cdot 1 =$ ____ $1\left(-\dfrac{17}{20}\right) =$ ____

(d) $\dfrac{2}{5} \div \dfrac{1}{15} =$ ____ $\dfrac{1}{15} \div \dfrac{2}{5} =$ ____

(d) $\left(-\dfrac{4}{5}\right)\left(-\dfrac{5}{4}\right) =$ ____ $7 \cdot \dfrac{1}{7} =$ ____

Study Skills
MAKING A MIND MAP

OBJECTIVES

1. **Create mind maps for appropriate concepts.**
2. **Visually show how concepts relate to each other using arrows or lines.**

Why Is Mapping Brain Friendly?

Remember that your brain grows dendrites when you are **actively thinking** about and working with information. Making a map requires you to think hard about **how to place the information, how to show connections** between parts of the map, and **how color will be useful.** It also takes a lot of thinking to fill in all related details and **show how those details connect to the larger concept.** All that thinking will let your brain grow a complex, many-branched neural network of interconnected dendrites. It is time well spent.

Mind mapping is a visual way to show information that you have learned. It is an excellent way to review. Mapping is flexible and can be personalized, which is helpful for your memory. Your brain likes to see things that are **pleasing** to look at, are **colorful,** and that **show connections** between ideas. Take advantage of that by creating maps that

▶ are easy to read,

▶ use color in a systematic way, and

▶ clearly show you how different concepts are related (using arrows or dotted lines, for example).

Directions for Making a Mind Map

Below are some general directions for making a map. After you read them, go to the next page and work on completing the map that has been started for you. It is from the two previous sections in this chapter.

▶ To begin a mind map, write the concept in the center of a piece of paper and either circle it or draw a box around it.

▶ Make a line out from the center concept, and draw a box large enough to write the definition of the concept.

▶ Think of the other aspects (subpoints) of the concept that you have learned, such as procedures to follow or formulas. Make a separate line and box connecting each subpoint to the center.

▶ From each of the new boxes, add the information you've learned. You can continue making new lines and boxes and circles, or you can list items below the new information.

▶ Use color to highlight the major points. For example, everything related to one subpoint might be the same color. That way you can easily see related ideas.

▶ You may also use arrows, underlining, or small drawings to help yourself remember.

Try This Fractions Mind Map

On a separate paper, make a map that summarizes computation with fractions. Follow the directions below. Use the starter map below.

▶ The longest rectangles are instructions for all four operations. (The first one starts "Rewrite all numbers as fractions . . . " and the second one is at the bottom of the map.)

▶ Notice the wavy dividing lines that separate the map into two sides.

▶ Your job is to complete the map by writing the steps used in multiplying fractions and the steps used in adding and subtracting fractions.

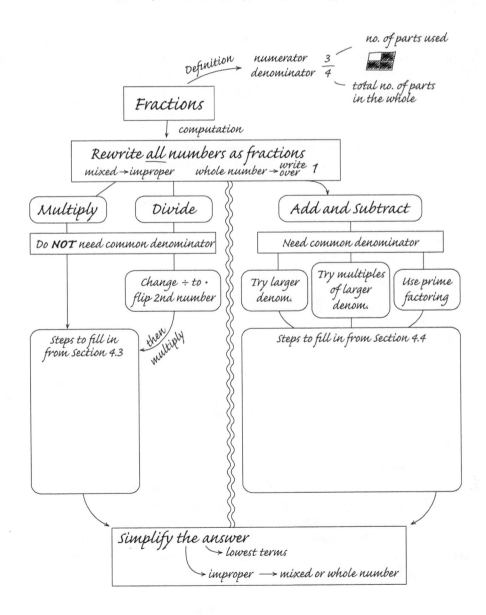

4.5 Problem Solving: Mixed Numbers and Estimating

OBJECTIVES

1. Identify mixed numbers and graph them on a number line.

2. Rewrite mixed numbers as improper fractions, or the reverse.

3. Estimate the answer and multiply or divide mixed numbers.

4. Estimate the answer and add or subtract mixed numbers.

5. Solve application problems containing mixed numbers.

OBJECTIVE 1 Identify mixed numbers and graph them on a number line. When a fraction and a whole number are written together, the result is a **mixed number.** For example, the mixed number

$$3\frac{1}{2} \quad \text{represents} \quad 3 + \frac{1}{2}$$

or 3 wholes and $\frac{1}{2}$ of a whole. Read $3\frac{1}{2}$ as "three and one half."

One common use of mixed numbers is to measure things. Examples are shown below.

Juan worked $5\frac{1}{2}$ hours.   The box weighs $2\frac{3}{4}$ pounds.

The park is $1\frac{7}{10}$ miles long.   Add $1\frac{2}{3}$ cups of flour.

EXAMPLE 1 Illustrating a Mixed Number with a Diagram and a Number Line

As this diagram shows, the mixed number $3\frac{1}{2}$ is equivalent to the improper fraction $\frac{7}{2}$.

$\frac{7}{2}$ ← Number of shaded parts
     ← Number of equal parts in each whole

We can also use a number line to show mixed numbers, as in this graph of $3\frac{1}{2}$ and $-3\frac{1}{2}$.

The number line shows the following.

$$3\frac{1}{2} \quad \text{is equivalent to} \quad \frac{7}{2}$$

$$-3\frac{1}{2} \quad \text{is equivalent to} \quad -\frac{7}{2}$$

Note

$3\frac{1}{2}$ represents $3 + \frac{1}{2}$.

$-3\frac{1}{2}$ represents $-3 + \left(-\frac{1}{2}\right)$, which can also be written as $-3 - \frac{1}{2}$.

In algebra we usually work with the improper fraction form of mixed numbers, especially for negative mixed numbers. However, positive mixed numbers are frequently used in daily life, so it's important to know how to work with them. For example, we usually say $3\frac{1}{2}$ inches rather than $\frac{7}{2}$ inches.

1 **(a)** Use this diagram to write $1\frac{2}{3}$ as an improper fraction.

(b) Now graph $1\frac{2}{3}$ and $-1\frac{2}{3}$ on this number line.

(c) Use this diagram to write $2\frac{1}{4}$ as an improper fraction.

(d) Now graph $2\frac{1}{4}$ and $-2\frac{1}{4}$ on this number line.

Answers

1. **(a)** $\frac{5}{3}$ **(b)**

(c) $\frac{9}{4}$ **(d)**

◀ **Work Problem 1 at the Side.**

OBJECTIVE ▶ ② **Rewrite mixed numbers as improper fractions, or the reverse.** You can use the following steps to write $3\frac{1}{2}$ as an improper fraction without drawing a diagram or a number line.

Step 1 Multiply 2 times 3 and add 1 to the product.

$$3\frac{1}{2} \qquad 2 \cdot 3 = 6 \qquad \text{Then } 6 + 1 = 7$$

Step 2 Use 7 (from *Step 1*) as the numerator and 2 as the denominator.

$$3\frac{1}{2} = \frac{7}{2} \leftarrow (2 \cdot 3) + 1$$

Same denominator

To see why this method works, recall that $3\frac{1}{2}$ represents $3 + \frac{1}{2}$. Let's add $3 + \frac{1}{2}$.

$$3 + \frac{1}{2} = \frac{3}{1} + \frac{1}{2} = \frac{6}{2} + \frac{1}{2} = \frac{6+1}{2} = \frac{7}{2} \quad \left\{ \begin{array}{l} \text{Same result} \\ \text{as above} \end{array} \right.$$

Common denominator

In summary, use the following steps to *write a mixed number as an improper fraction*.

Writing a Mixed Number as an Improper Fraction

Step 1 **Multiply** the denominator of the fraction times the whole number and **add** the numerator of the fraction to the product.

Step 2 Write the result of *Step 1* as the **numerator** and keep the original **denominator.**

EXAMPLE 2 **Writing a Mixed Number as an Improper Fraction**

Write $7\frac{2}{3}$ as an improper fraction (numerator greater than denominator).

Step 1 $7\frac{2}{3} \qquad 3 \cdot 7 = 21 \qquad \text{Then } 21 + 2 = 23$

Step 2 $7\frac{2}{3} = \frac{23}{3} \leftarrow (3 \cdot 7) + 2$

> Keep the same denominator.

Same denominator

······ **Work Problem ② at the Side.** ▶

---

② Write each mixed number as an equivalent improper fraction.

(a) $3\frac{2}{3}$

$$3\frac{2}{3} = \underline{\qquad} \leftarrow (3 \cdot 3) + 2$$

Same denominator

(b) $4\frac{7}{10}$

(c) $5\frac{3}{4}$

(d) $8\frac{5}{6}$

Answers

2. (a) $\frac{11}{3}$ (b) $\frac{47}{10}$ (c) $\frac{23}{4}$ (d) $\frac{53}{6}$

We used *multiplication* for the first step in writing a mixed number as an improper fraction. To work in *reverse*, writing an improper fraction as a mixed number, we will use *division*. Recall that the fraction bar is a symbol for division.

Writing an Improper Fraction as a Mixed Number

To write an *improper fraction* as a mixed number, divide the numerator by the denominator. The quotient is the whole number part (of the mixed number), the remainder is the numerator of the fraction part, and the denominator remains the same.

Always check to be sure that the fraction part of the mixed number is in lowest terms. Then the mixed number is in *simplest form*.

EXAMPLE 3 **Writing Improper Fractions as Mixed Numbers**

Write each improper fraction as an equivalent mixed number in simplest form.

(a) $\dfrac{17}{5}$

Divide 17 by 5.

$$
\begin{array}{r}
3 \quad \longleftarrow \text{Whole number part} \\
5\overline{)17} \\
\underline{15} \\
2 \quad \longleftarrow \text{Remainder}
\end{array}
$$

The quotient **3** is the whole number part of the mixed number. The remainder **2** is the numerator of the fraction, and the denominator stays as **5**.

$$
\frac{17}{5} = 3\frac{2}{5} \quad \longleftarrow \text{Remainder}
$$
$$
\longleftarrow \text{Same denominator}
$$

Let's look at a drawing of $\frac{17}{5}$ to check our work.

$\frac{5}{5} = 1$ (whole) $\frac{5}{5} = 1$ (whole) $\frac{5}{5} = 1$ (whole) $\frac{2}{5}$

Continued on Next Page

In other words,

$$\frac{17}{5} = \frac{5}{5} + \frac{5}{5} + \frac{5}{5} + \frac{2}{5}$$

$$= 1 + 1 + 1 + \frac{2}{5}$$

$$= 3 + \frac{2}{5}$$

$$= 3\frac{2}{5}$$

(b) $\frac{26}{4}$

Divide 26 by 4.

$$\begin{array}{r} 6 \\ 4)\overline{26} \\ 24 \\ \hline 2 \end{array} \quad \text{so} \quad \frac{26}{4} = 6\frac{2}{4} = 6\frac{1}{2} \quad \left\{ \begin{array}{l} \text{Simplest} \\ \text{form} \end{array} \right.$$

Write $\frac{2}{4}$ in lowest terms.

You could write $\frac{26}{4}$ in lowest terms first.

$$\frac{26}{4} = \frac{\overset{1}{2} \cdot 13}{\underset{1}{2} \cdot 2} = \frac{13}{2} \quad \text{Then} \quad \begin{array}{r} 6 \\ 2)\overline{13} \\ 12 \\ \hline 1 \end{array} \quad \text{so} \quad \frac{13}{2} = 6\frac{1}{2} \quad \left\{ \begin{array}{l} \text{Same result} \\ \text{as above} \end{array} \right.$$

···· **Work Problem ❸ at the Side.** ▶

OBJECTIVE ❸ Estimate the answer and multiply or divide mixed numbers. Rewrite mixed numbers as improper fractions. Then use the steps you learned earlier for multiplying and dividing. However, it's a good idea to estimate the answer before you start any other work.

EXAMPLE 4 Rounding Mixed Numbers to the Nearest Whole Number

To estimate answers, first round each mixed number to the *nearest whole number*. If the numerator is *half* of the denominator or *more*, round up the whole number part. If the numerator is *less* than half the denominator, leave the whole number as it is.

(a) Round $1\frac{5}{8}$ ← 5 is more than 4, ← Half of 8 is 4 $\quad 1\frac{5}{8}$ rounds up to 2

(b) Round $3\frac{2}{5}$ ← 2 is less than $2\frac{1}{2}$, ← Half of 5 is $2\frac{1}{2}$ $\quad 3\frac{2}{5}$ rounds to 3

···· **Work Problem ❹ at the Side.** ▶

❸ Write each improper fraction as an equivalent mixed number in simplest form.

(a) $\frac{7}{2}$ $\quad \begin{array}{r} 3 \\ 2)\overline{7} \\ 6 \\ \hline 1 \end{array}$ ← Whole number part ← Remainder

$\frac{7}{2} = 3$ ——— ← Remainder, Same denominator

(b) $\frac{14}{4}$

(c) $\frac{33}{5}$

(d) $\frac{58}{10}$

❹ Round each mixed number to the nearest whole number.

(a) $7\frac{3}{4}$ ← 3 is more than 2, ← Half of 4 is 2

$7\frac{3}{4}$ rounds up to ____.

(b) $6\frac{3}{8}$

(c) $4\frac{2}{3}$

(d) $1\frac{7}{10}$

(e) $3\frac{1}{2}$

(f) $5\frac{4}{9}$

Answers

3. (a) $3\frac{1}{2}$ (b) $3\frac{1}{2}$ (c) $6\frac{3}{5}$ (d) $5\frac{4}{5}$
4. (a) 8 (b) 6 (c) 5 (d) 2 (e) 4 (f) 5

⑤ First, round the numbers and estimate each answer. Then find the exact answer. Write exact answers in simplest form.

⊙ (a) $2\dfrac{1}{4}$ • $7\dfrac{1}{3}$

$$\downarrow \qquad \downarrow$$

$$\underline{\;2\;} \cdot \underline{\;7\;} = \underline{\qquad}$$
Estimate

Step 1 $2\dfrac{1}{4} = \dfrac{9}{4}$ and $7\dfrac{1}{3} = \dfrac{22}{3}$

$$\dfrac{9}{4} \cdot \dfrac{22}{3} = \dfrac{\overset{3}{\cancel{3}} \cdot 3 \cdot \overset{1}{\cancel{2}} \cdot 11}{\underset{1}{\cancel{2}} \cdot 2 \cdot \underset{1}{\cancel{3}}} =$$

(b) $\left(4\dfrac{1}{2}\right)\left(1\dfrac{2}{3}\right)$

$$\qquad \downarrow \qquad\quad \downarrow$$

$$(\underline{\quad})(\underline{\quad}) = \underline{\qquad}$$
Estimate

(c) $3\dfrac{3}{5}$ • $4\dfrac{4}{9}$

$$\downarrow \qquad\quad \downarrow$$

$$\underline{\qquad} \bullet \underline{\qquad} = \underline{\qquad}$$
Estimate

(d) $\left(3\dfrac{1}{5}\right)\left(5\dfrac{3}{8}\right)$

$$\quad \downarrow \qquad\quad \downarrow$$

$$(\underline{\quad}) \, (\underline{\quad}) = \underline{\qquad}$$
Estimate

Answers

5. **(a)** *Estimate:* $2 \cdot 7 = 14$; *Exact:* $\dfrac{33}{2} = 16\dfrac{1}{2}$

   (b) *Estimate:* $(5)(2) = 10$; *Exact:* $7\dfrac{1}{2}$

   (c) *Estimate:* $4 \cdot 4 = 16$; *Exact:* 16

   (d) *Estimate:* $(3)(5) = 15$; *Exact:* $17\dfrac{1}{5}$

Multiplying and Dividing Mixed Numbers

Step 1 **Rewrite** each mixed number as an improper fraction.

Step 2 **Multiply** or **divide** the improper fractions.

Step 3 Write the answer in lowest terms and change it to a mixed number or whole number when possible. This step gives you an answer that is in **simplest form.**

EXAMPLE 5 **Estimating the Answer and Multiplying Mixed Numbers**

First, round the numbers and estimate each answer. Then find the exact answer. Write exact answers in simplest form.

(a) $2\dfrac{1}{2}$ • $3\dfrac{1}{5}$

Estimate the answer by rounding the mixed numbers.

$$2\dfrac{1}{2} \text{ rounds to } 3 \qquad \text{and} \qquad 3\dfrac{1}{5} \text{ rounds to } 3$$

$$3 \cdot 3 = 9 \leftarrow \text{Estimated answer}$$

To find the exact answer, first rewrite each mixed number as an improper fraction.

$$\textit{Step 1} \qquad 2\dfrac{1}{2} = \dfrac{5}{2} \qquad \text{and} \qquad 3\dfrac{1}{5} = \dfrac{16}{5}$$

Next, multiply.

$$2\dfrac{1}{2} \cdot 3\dfrac{1}{5} = \dfrac{5}{2} \cdot \dfrac{16}{5} = \overset{\textit{Step 2}}{\dfrac{\overset{1}{\cancel{5}} \cdot \overset{1}{\cancel{2}} \cdot 8}{\underset{1}{\cancel{2}} \cdot \underset{1}{\cancel{5}}}} = \overset{\textit{Step 3}}{\dfrac{8}{1}} = 8 \;\begin{cases} \text{Simplest} \\ \text{form} \end{cases}$$

The estimate was 9, so an exact answer of 8 is reasonable.

> Estimating helps you catch errors.

(b) $\left(3\dfrac{5}{8}\right)\left(4\dfrac{4}{5}\right)$

First, round each mixed number and estimate the answer.

$$3\dfrac{5}{8} \text{ rounds to } 4 \qquad \text{and} \qquad 4\dfrac{4}{5} \text{ rounds to } 5$$

$$4 \cdot 5 = 20 \leftarrow \text{Estimated answer}$$

Now find the exact answer.

$$\left(3\dfrac{5}{8}\right)\left(4\dfrac{4}{5}\right) = \overset{\textit{Step 1}}{\left(\dfrac{29}{8}\right)\left(\dfrac{24}{5}\right)} = \overset{\textit{Step 2}}{\dfrac{29 \cdot 3 \cdot \overset{1}{\cancel{8}}}{\underset{1}{\cancel{8}} \cdot 5}} = \overset{\textit{Step 3}}{\dfrac{87}{5}} = 17\dfrac{2}{5} \;\begin{cases} \text{Simplest} \\ \text{form} \end{cases}$$

The estimate was 20, so an exact answer of $17\dfrac{2}{5}$ is reasonable.

◄ **Work Problem ⑤ at the Side.**

EXAMPLE 6 Estimating the Answer and Dividing Mixed Numbers

First, round the numbers and estimate each answer. Then find the exact answer. Write exact answers in simplest form.

(a) $3\frac{3}{5} \div 1\frac{1}{2}$

To estimate the answer, round each mixed number to the nearest whole number.

$$3\frac{3}{5} \quad \div \quad 1\frac{1}{2}$$
$$\text{Rounded}$$
$$4 \quad \div \quad 2 \quad = \quad 2 \leftarrow \text{Estimate}$$

To find the exact answer, first rewrite each mixed number as an improper fraction.

$$3\frac{3}{5} \div 1\frac{1}{2} = \frac{18}{5} \div \frac{3}{2}$$

> You do **not** need a common denominator when multiplying or dividing fractions.

Now rewrite the problem as multiplying by the reciprocal of $\frac{3}{2}$.

$$\frac{18}{5} \div \frac{3}{2} = \frac{18}{5} \cdot \frac{2}{3} = \frac{\overset{6}{3} \cdot 6 \cdot 2}{5 \cdot \underset{1}{3}} = \frac{12}{5} = 2\frac{2}{5} \quad \left\{ \begin{array}{l} \text{Simplest} \\ \text{form} \end{array} \right.$$
$$\text{Reciprocals}$$

The estimate was 2, so an exact answer of $2\frac{2}{5}$ is reasonable.

(b) $4\frac{3}{8} \div 5$

First, round the numbers and estimate the answer.

$$4\frac{3}{8} \quad \div \quad 5$$
$$\text{Rounded}$$
$$4 \quad \div \quad 5 \qquad \begin{array}{l} \text{Write } 4 \div 5 \text{ using} \\ \text{a fraction bar.} \end{array} \left. \right\} \frac{4}{5} \leftarrow \text{Estimate}$$

Now find the exact answer.

$$\text{Write 5 as } \frac{5}{1}$$

$$4\frac{3}{8} \div 5 = \frac{35}{8} \div \frac{5}{1} = \frac{35}{8} \cdot \frac{1}{5} = \frac{\overset{1}{5} \cdot 7 \cdot 1}{8 \cdot \underset{1}{5}} = \frac{7}{8} \quad \left\{ \begin{array}{l} \text{Simplest} \\ \text{form} \end{array} \right.$$
$$\text{Reciprocals}$$

The estimate was $\frac{4}{5}$, so an exact answer of $\frac{7}{8}$ is reasonable. They are both less than 1.

········· Work Problem **6** at the Side. ▶

6 First, round the numbers and estimate each answer. Then find the exact answer. Write exact answers in simplest form.

(a) $6\frac{1}{4} \div 3\frac{1}{3}$

$$\underline{\quad 6 \quad} \div \underline{\quad 3 \quad} = \underline{\quad\quad}$$
$$\textit{Estimate}$$

$$6\frac{1}{4} = \frac{\quad}{4} \quad \text{and} \quad 3\frac{1}{3} = \frac{\quad}{3}$$

$$\frac{25}{4} \div \frac{10}{3} = \frac{25}{4} \cdot \frac{3}{10} = \frac{\overset{1}{5} \cdot 5 \cdot 3}{4 \cdot 2 \cdot \underset{1}{5}} =$$
$$\text{Reciprocals}$$

Write $\frac{15}{8}$ in simplest form as _____ .

(b) $3\frac{3}{8} \div 2\frac{4}{7}$

$$\underline{\quad\quad} \div \underline{\quad\quad} = \underline{\quad\quad}$$
$$\textit{Estimate}$$

(c) $8 \div 5\frac{1}{3}$

$$\underline{\quad\quad} \div \underline{\quad\quad} = \underline{\quad\quad}$$
$$\textit{Estimate}$$

(d) $4\frac{1}{2} \div 6$

$$\underline{\quad\quad} \div \underline{\quad\quad} = \underline{\quad\quad}$$
$$\textit{Estimate}$$

Answers

6. **(a)** *Estimate:* $6 \div 3 = 2$; *Exact:* $\frac{25}{4}$; $\frac{10}{3}$; $1\frac{7}{8}$

(b) *Estimate:* $3 \div 3 = 1$; *Exact:* $1\frac{5}{16}$

(c) *Estimate:* $8 \div 5 = 1\frac{3}{5}$; *Exact:* $1\frac{1}{2}$

(d) *Estimate:* $5 \div 6 = \frac{5}{6}$; *Exact:* $\frac{3}{4}$

OBJECTIVE ▸ ④ **Estimate the answer and add or subtract mixed numbers.**
The steps you learned earlier for adding and subtracting fractions will also work for mixed numbers. Just rewrite the mixed numbers as equivalent improper fractions. Again, it is a good idea to estimate the answer before you start any other work.

EXAMPLE 7	Estimating the Answer and Adding or Subtracting Mixed Numbers

First, estimate each answer. Then add or subtract to find the exact answer. Write exact answers in simplest form.

(a) $2\frac{3}{8} + 3\frac{3}{4}$

To estimate the answer, round each mixed number to the nearest whole number.

$$2\frac{3}{8} + 3\frac{3}{4}$$
$$\downarrow \qquad \downarrow$$
$$2 + 4 \ = \ 6 \leftarrow \text{Estimate}$$

To find the exact answer, first rewrite each mixed number as an equivalent improper fraction.

$$2\frac{3}{8} + 3\frac{3}{4} = \frac{19}{8} + \frac{15}{4}$$

You **do** need a common denominator to add or subtract fractions.

You can't add fractions until they have a common denominator. The LCD for $\frac{19}{8}$ and $\frac{15}{4}$ is 8. Rewrite $\frac{15}{4}$ as an equivalent fraction with a denominator of 8.

$$\frac{19}{8} + \frac{15}{4} = \frac{19}{8} + \frac{30}{8} = \frac{19 + 30}{8} = \frac{49}{8} = 6\frac{1}{8} \quad \left\{ \begin{array}{l} \text{Simplest} \\ \text{form} \end{array} \right.$$

Common denominator

The estimate was 6, so an exact answer of $6\frac{1}{8}$ is reasonable.

(b) $4\frac{2}{3} - 2\frac{4}{5}$

Round each number and estimate the answer.

$$4\frac{2}{3} - 2\frac{4}{5}$$
$$\downarrow \qquad \downarrow$$
$$5 \ - \ 3 \ = \ 2 \leftarrow \text{Estimate}$$

To find the exact answer, rewrite the mixed numbers as improper fractions and subtract.

$$4\frac{2}{3} - 2\frac{4}{5} = \frac{14}{3} - \frac{14}{5} = \frac{70}{15} - \frac{42}{15} = \frac{70 - 42}{15} = \frac{28}{15} = 1\frac{13}{15} \quad \left\{ \begin{array}{l} \text{Simplest} \\ \text{form} \end{array} \right.$$

LCD is 15

The estimate was 2, so an exact answer of $1\frac{13}{15}$ is reasonable.

Continued on Next Page

(c) $5 - 1\frac{3}{8}$

$$5 - 1\frac{3}{8}$$
$$\downarrow \quad \downarrow$$
$$5 - 1 = 4 \leftarrow \text{Estimate}$$

Write 5 as $\frac{5}{1}$

$$5 - 1\frac{3}{8} = \frac{5}{1} - \frac{11}{8} = \frac{40}{8} - \frac{11}{8} = \frac{40 - 11}{8} = \frac{29}{8} = 3\frac{5}{8} \quad \left\{ \begin{array}{l} \text{Simplest} \\ \text{form} \end{array} \right.$$

LCD is 8

The estimate was 4, so an exact answer of $3\frac{5}{8}$ is reasonable.

················· **Work Problem 7 at the Side.** ▶

Note

In some situations the method of rewriting mixed numbers as improper fractions may result in very large numerators. Consider this example.

Last year Hue's child was $48\frac{3}{8}$ in. tall. This year the child is $51\frac{1}{4}$ in. tall. How much has the child grown?

First, estimate the answer by rounding each mixed number to the nearest whole number.

$$51\frac{1}{4} - 48\frac{3}{8}$$
$$\downarrow \qquad \downarrow$$
$$51 - 48 = 3 \text{ in.} \leftarrow \text{Estimate}$$

To find the exact answer, rewrite the mixed numbers as improper fractions.

Rewrite $\frac{205}{4}$ as $\frac{410}{8}$

$$51\frac{1}{4} - 48\frac{3}{8} = \frac{205}{4} - \frac{387}{8} = \frac{410}{8} - \frac{387}{8} = \frac{410 - 387}{8} = \frac{23}{8} = 2\frac{7}{8} \text{ in.}$$

LCD is 8

You can also use the fraction key $\boxed{a^{b/c}}$ on your *scientific* calculator to solve this problem. Either way the exact answer is $2\frac{7}{8}$ in., which is close to the estimate of 3 in.

Another efficient method for handling large mixed numbers is to rewrite them in decimal form. You will learn how to do that in **Chapter 5**.

OBJECTIVE ▶ **5** **Solve application problems containing mixed numbers.**
Rounding mixed numbers to the nearest whole number can also help you decide whether to solve an application problem by adding, subtracting, multiplying, or dividing.

---

7 First, round the numbers and estimate each answer. Then add or subtract to find the exact answer.

GS (a) $5\frac{1}{3} - 2\frac{5}{6}$
$$\downarrow \qquad \downarrow$$
$$\underline{} - \underline{} = \underline{}$$
$$\qquad\qquad\qquad \textit{Estimate}$$

$5\frac{1}{3} = \frac{16}{3}$ and $2\frac{5}{6} = \frac{17}{6}$

$$\frac{16}{3} - \frac{17}{6} = \frac{32}{6} - \frac{17}{6} = \frac{\underline{} - \underline{}}{6}$$

$$= \frac{\underline{}}{6} = \underline{} \qquad \begin{array}{l} \text{Write the answer} \\ \text{in simplest form.} \end{array}$$

(b) $\frac{3}{4} + 3\frac{1}{8}$
$$\downarrow \qquad \downarrow$$
$$\underline{} + \underline{} = \underline{}$$
$$\qquad\qquad\qquad \textit{Estimate}$$

(c) $6 - 3\frac{4}{5}$
$$\downarrow \qquad \downarrow$$
$$\underline{} - \underline{} = \underline{}$$
$$\qquad\qquad\qquad \textit{Estimate}$$

Answers

7. (a) *Estimate:* $5 - 3 = 2$;
   Exact: $\frac{32 - 17}{6} = \frac{15}{6} = 2\frac{3}{6} = 2\frac{1}{2}$

(b) *Estimate:* $1 + 3 = 4$; *Exact:* $3\frac{7}{8}$

(c) *Estimate:* $6 - 4 = 2$; *Exact:* $2\frac{1}{5}$

8 First, round the numbers and estimate the answer to each problem. Then find the exact answer.

(a) Richard's son grew $3\frac{5}{8}$ inches last year and $2\frac{1}{4}$ inches this year. How much has his height increased over the two years?

Estimate: $3\frac{5}{8}$ rounds to _____

$2\frac{1}{4}$ rounds to _____

Read the problem using the rounded numbers. Do you need to add, subtract, multiply, or divide? _____

Estimate is _____

Exact:

$3\frac{5}{8}$ is $\dfrac{}{8}$ and $2\frac{1}{4}$ is $\dfrac{}{4}$

Now find the exact answer.

(b) Ernestine used $2\frac{1}{2}$ packages of chocolate chips in her cookie recipe. Each package has $5\frac{1}{2}$ ounces of chips. How many ounces of chips did she use in the recipe?

Estimate:

Exact:

Answers

8. **(a)** *Estimate:* 4; 2; add; 4 + 2 = 6 inches;
Exact: $\frac{29}{8}$; $\frac{9}{4}$; $5\frac{7}{8}$ inches

(b) *Estimate:* 3 • 6 = 18 ounces;
Exact: $13\frac{3}{4}$ ounces

EXAMPLE 8 **Solving Application Problems with Mixed Numbers**

First, estimate the answer to each application problem. Then find the exact answer.

(a) Gary needs to haul $15\frac{3}{4}$ tons of sand to a construction site. His truck can carry $2\frac{1}{4}$ tons. How many trips will he need to make?

First, round each mixed number to the nearest whole number.

$15\frac{3}{4}$ rounds to **16** and $2\frac{1}{4}$ rounds to **2**

Now read the problem again, *using the rounded numbers.*
Gary needs to haul **16 tons** of sand to a construction site. His truck can carry **2 tons**. How many trips will he need to make?
Using the rounded numbers in the problem makes it easier to see that you need to *divide.*

$$16 \div 2 = 8 \text{ trips} \leftarrow \text{Estimate}$$

To find the exact answer, use the original mixed numbers and divide.

$$15\frac{3}{4} \div 2\frac{1}{4} = \frac{63}{4} \div \frac{9}{4} = \frac{63}{4} \cdot \frac{4}{9} = \frac{7 \cdot \overset{1}{9} \cdot \overset{1}{4}}{\underset{1}{4} \cdot \underset{1}{9}} = \frac{7}{1} = 7 \quad \begin{cases} \text{Simplest} \\ \text{form} \end{cases}$$

Gary needs to make 7 trips to haul all the sand. This result is close to the estimate of 8 trips.

(b) Zenitia worked $3\frac{5}{6}$ hours on Monday and $6\frac{1}{2}$ hours on Tuesday. How much longer did she work on Tuesday than on Monday?

First, round each mixed number to the nearest whole number.

$3\frac{5}{6}$ rounds to **4** and $6\frac{1}{2}$ rounds to **7**

Now read the problem again, *using the rounded numbers.*
Zenitia worked **4 hours** on Monday and **7 hours** on Tuesday. How much longer did she work on Tuesday than on Monday?
Using the rounded numbers in the problem makes it easier to see that you need to *subtract.*

$$7 - 4 = 3 \text{ hours} \leftarrow \text{Estimate}$$

To find the exact answer, use the original mixed numbers and subtract.

$$6\frac{1}{2} - 3\frac{5}{6} = \frac{13}{2} - \frac{23}{6} = \frac{39}{6} - \frac{23}{6} = \frac{39-23}{6} = \frac{16}{6} = 2\frac{4}{6} = 2\frac{2}{3}$$

LCD is 6

Zenitia worked $2\frac{2}{3}$ hours longer on Tuesday. This result is close to the estimate of 3 hours.

◀ **Work Problem 8 at the Side.**

4.5 Exercises

 Download the MyDashBoard App

 MyMathLab®

CONCEPT CHECK *Graph the mixed numbers or improper fractions on the number line.*
See Example 1.

1. Graph $2\frac{1}{3}$ and $-2\frac{1}{3}$.

Shade $2\frac{1}{3}$ of the circles.

2. Graph $1\frac{3}{4}$ and $-1\frac{3}{4}$.

Shade $1\frac{3}{4}$ of the rectangles.

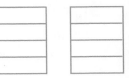

3. Graph $\frac{3}{2}$ and $-\frac{3}{2}$.

Shade $\frac{3}{2}$ of the squares.

4. Graph $\frac{11}{3}$ and $-\frac{11}{3}$.

Shade $\frac{11}{3}$ of the circles.

Write each mixed number as an improper fraction. **See Example 2.**

5. $4\frac{1}{2}$

6. $2\frac{1}{4}$

7. $-1\frac{3}{5}$

8. $-1\frac{5}{6}$

9. $2\frac{3}{8}$

10. $3\frac{4}{9}$

11. $-5\frac{7}{10}$

12. $-4\frac{5}{7}$

13. $10\frac{11}{15}$

14. $12\frac{9}{11}$

Write each improper fraction as a mixed number in simplest form. **See Example 3.**

15. $\frac{13}{3}$

16. $\frac{11}{2}$

17. $-\frac{10}{4}$

18. $-\frac{14}{5}$

19. $\frac{22}{6}$

20. $\frac{28}{8}$

21. $-\frac{51}{9}$

22. $-\frac{44}{10}$

23. $\frac{188}{16}$

24. $\frac{200}{15}$

First, round each mixed number to the nearest whole number and estimate the answer.
Then find the exact answer. Write exact answers in simplest form. **See Examples 4–7.**

25. *Exact:*
$2\frac{1}{4} \cdot 3\frac{1}{2} = \frac{9}{4} \cdot \frac{7}{2} =$
Estimate:
$\underline{\quad 2 \quad} \cdot \underline{\quad 4 \quad} = \underline{\qquad}$

26. *Exact:*
$\left(1\frac{1}{2}\right)\left(3\frac{3}{4}\right) = \frac{3}{2} \cdot \frac{15}{4} =$
Estimate:
$(\underline{\quad 2 \quad})(\underline{\qquad}) = \underline{\quad 8 \quad}$

27. *Exact:*
$3\frac{1}{4} \div 2\frac{5}{8}$
Estimate:
$\underline{\qquad} \div \underline{\qquad} = \underline{\qquad}$

28. *Exact:*
$2\frac{1}{4} \div 1\frac{1}{8}$
Estimate:
$\underline{\qquad} \div \underline{\qquad} = \underline{\qquad}$

29. *Exact:*
$3\frac{2}{3} + 1\frac{5}{6}$
Estimate:
$\underline{\qquad} + \underline{\qquad} = \underline{\qquad}$

30. *Exact:*
$4\frac{4}{5} + 2\frac{1}{3}$
Estimate:
$\underline{\qquad} + \underline{\qquad} = \underline{\qquad}$

31. *Exact:*

▶ $4\dfrac{1}{4} - \dfrac{7}{12}$

Estimate:

____ − ____ = ____

32. *Exact:*

$10\dfrac{1}{3} - 6\dfrac{5}{6}$

Estimate:

____ − ____ = ____

33. *Exact:*

$5\dfrac{2}{3} \div 6$

Estimate:

____ ÷ ____ = ____

34. *Exact:*

$1\dfrac{7}{8} \div 6\dfrac{1}{4}$

Estimate:

____ ÷ ____ = ____

35. *Exact:*

$8 - 1\dfrac{4}{5}$

Estimate:

____ − ____ = ____

36. *Exact:*

$7 - 3\dfrac{3}{10}$

Estimate:

____ − ____ = ____

Find the perimeter and the area of each square, rectangle, or parallelogram. Write all answers in simplest form.

37.

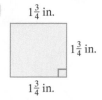

$1\frac{3}{4}$ in.

$1\frac{3}{4}$ in.

$1\frac{3}{4}$ in.

38.

$2\frac{1}{3}$ ft

$2\frac{1}{3}$ ft

39.

$3\frac{1}{4}$ yd

$6\frac{1}{2}$ yd

40.

$2\frac{3}{10}$ mi

$\frac{2}{5}$ mi

$\frac{2}{5}$ mi

$2\frac{3}{10}$ mi

41.

$2\frac{2}{3}$ ft

$3\frac{1}{4}$ ft

$3\frac{1}{4}$ ft   2 ft

$2\frac{2}{3}$ ft

42.

$5\frac{1}{2}$ in.

$2\frac{5}{8}$ in.   3 in.

$5\frac{1}{2}$ in.

First, estimate the answer to each application problem. Then find the exact answer. Write all answers in simplest form. ***See Example 8.***

43. A carpenter has two pieces of oak trim. One piece of trim is $12\frac{1}{2}$ ft long and the other is $8\frac{2}{3}$ ft long. How many feet of oak trim does he have in all?

Estimate:

Exact:

44. On Monday, $5\frac{3}{4}$ tons of cans were recycled, and on Tuesday, $9\frac{3}{5}$ tons were recycled. How many tons were recycled on these two days?

Estimate:

Exact:

45. The directions for mixing an insect spray say to use $1\frac{3}{4}$ ounces of chemical in each gallon of water. How many ounces of chemical should be mixed with $5\frac{1}{2}$ gallons of water?

Estimate:

Exact:

46. Shirley Cicero wants to make 16 holiday wreaths to sell at a craft fair. Each wreath requires $2\frac{1}{4}$ yd of ribbon. How many yards does she need in all?

Estimate:

Exact:

47. The Boy Scout troop has volunteered to pick up trash along a 4-mile stretch of highway. So far they have done $1\frac{7}{10}$ miles. How much do they have left to do?

Estimate:

Exact:

48. Marv bought a 10 yd length of Italian silk fabric. He used $3\frac{7}{8}$ yd to make a jacket. What length of fabric is left for other sewing projects?

Estimate:

Exact:

49. Suppose that a bridesmaid's floor-length dress requires a piece of material $3\frac{3}{4}$ yd in length. What length of material is needed to make dresses for five bridesmaids?

Estimate:

Exact:

50. A cookie recipe uses $\frac{2}{3}$ cup brown sugar. How much brown sugar is needed to make $2\frac{1}{2}$ times the original recipe?

Estimate:

Exact:

Solve each application problem. Write all answers in simplest form. Use the information on the Oregon state park sign for Exercises 51–54. The distances on the sign are in miles.

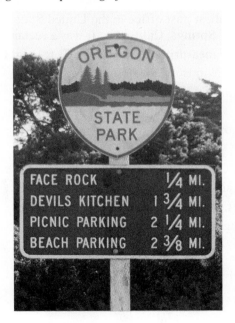

51. What is the distance from Devils Kitchen to the beach parking?

52. How far is it from Face Rock to the beach parking?

53. Suppose you bicycle from the park sign to the picnic parking, then bicycle back to Face Rock, and finally bicycle to the beach parking. How far will you have traveled?

54. If you drive back and forth from the sign to the picnic parking each day for a week, how many miles will you drive?

55. Find the length of the arrow shaft.

56. Find the length of the indented section on this board.

First, estimate the answer to each application problem. Then find the exact answer.

57. A craftsperson must attach a lead strip around all four sides of a rectangular stained glass window before it is installed. Find the length of lead stripping needed for the window shown.

$23\frac{3}{4}$ in.

$34\frac{1}{2}$ in.

Estimate:

Exact:

58. To complete a custom order, Zak Morten of Home Depot must find the number of inches of brass trim needed to go around the four sides of the lamp base plate shown. Find the length of brass trim needed.

$5\frac{1}{8}$ in.

$9\frac{7}{8}$ in.

Estimate:

Exact:

59. Alex bought a 126-ounce container of powdered laundry detergent. It takes $1\frac{1}{2}$ ounces of detergent to wash a load of clothes. How many loads can Alex wash?

Estimate:

Exact:

60. The smallest post office in the United States was in Wheeler Springs, California. It was a rectangular building measuring $5\frac{3}{4}$ ft wide by $7\frac{1}{3}$ ft long. Find the area of the post office floor.

Estimate:

Exact:

61. Claire and Deb create custom hat bands that people can put around the crowns of their hats. The finished bands are the lengths shown in the table. The strip of fabric for each band must include the finished length plus an extra $\frac{3}{4}$ in. for the seam.

Band Size	Finished Length
Small	$21\frac{7}{8}$ in.
Medium	$22\frac{5}{8}$ in.
Large	$23\frac{1}{2}$ in.

What length of fabric strip is needed to make 4 small bands, 5 medium bands, and 3 large bands, including the seam allowance?

Estimate:

Exact:

62. Three sides of a parking lot are $108\frac{1}{4}$ ft, $162\frac{3}{8}$ ft, and $143\frac{1}{2}$ ft. If the distance around the lot is $518\frac{3}{4}$ ft, find the length of the fourth side.

$108\frac{1}{4}$ ft

$162\frac{3}{8}$ ft

? ft

$143\frac{1}{2}$ ft

Estimate:

Exact:

Summary Exercises *Computation with Fractions*

1. Write fractions that represent the shaded and unshaded portion of each figure.

(a)

(b)

2. Graph $\frac{2}{3}$ and $-\frac{2}{3}$ on the number line.

3. Rewrite each fraction with the indicated denominator.

(a) $-\frac{4}{5} = -\frac{}{30}$

(b) $\frac{2}{7} = \frac{}{14}$

4. Simplify.

(a) $\frac{15}{15}$

(b) $-\frac{24}{6}$

(c) $\frac{9}{1}$

5. Write the prime factorization of each number.

(a) 72

(b) 105

6. Write each fraction in lowest terms.

(a) $\frac{24}{30}$

(b) $\frac{175}{200}$

Simplify.

7. $\left(-\frac{3}{4}\right)\left(-\frac{2}{3}\right)$

8. $-\frac{7}{8} + \frac{2}{3}$

9. $\frac{7}{16} + \frac{5}{8}$

10. $\frac{5}{8} \div \frac{3}{4}$

11. $\frac{2}{3} - \frac{4}{5}$

12. $\frac{7}{12}\left(-\frac{9}{14}\right)$

13. $-21 \div \left(-\frac{3}{8}\right)$

14. $\frac{7}{8} - \frac{5}{12}$

15. $-\frac{35}{45} \div \frac{10}{15}$

16. $-\frac{5}{6} - \frac{3}{4}$

17. $\frac{7}{12} + \frac{5}{6} + \frac{2}{3}$

18. $\frac{5}{8}$ of 56

First round the numbers and estimate each answer. Then find the exact answer.

19. *Exact:*

$4\frac{3}{4} + 2\frac{5}{6}$

Estimate:

____ + ____ = ____

20. *Exact:*

$2\frac{2}{9} \cdot 5\frac{1}{7}$

Estimate:

____ • ____ = ____

21. *Exact:*

$6 - 2\frac{7}{10}$

Estimate:

____ − ____ = ____

22. *Exact:*

$1\frac{3}{5} \div 3\frac{1}{2}$

Estimate:

____ ÷ ____ = _____

23. *Exact:*

$4\frac{2}{3} \div 1\frac{1}{6}$

Estimate:

____ ÷ ____ = ____

24. *Exact:*

$3\frac{5}{12} - \frac{3}{4}$

Estimate:

____ − ____ = ____

Solve each application problem. Write all answers in simplest form.

25. When installing cabinets, Cecil Feathers must be certain that the proper type and size of mounting screw is used.

(a) Find the total length of the screw shown.

(b) If the screw is put into a board that is $1\frac{3}{4}$ in. thick, how much of the screw will stick out the back of the board?

26. Find the perimeter and the area of this postage stamp.

27. A batch of cookies requires $\frac{3}{4}$ pound of chocolate chips. If you have nine pounds of chocolate chips, how many batches of cookies can you make?

28. The Municipal Utility District says that the cost of operating a large plasma television is $\frac{1}{5}$ ¢ per minute. Find the cost of operating the television for a half hour.

29. A survey asked 1500 adults if UFOs (unidentified flying objects) are real. The circle graph shows the fraction of the adults who gave each answer. How many adults gave each answer?

Out Of This World?
When asked in a survey if UFOs are real, respondents answered:

$\frac{3}{20}$ Not sure

$\frac{9}{20}$ Real

$\frac{2}{5}$ Imaginary

Source: Yankelovich Partners for *Life* magazine.

30. Find the diameter of the hole in the rectangular mounting bracket shown. (The diameter is the distance across the center of the hole.) Then find the perimeter of the bracket.

31. A travel size bottle of contact lens cleaning solution holds $\frac{1}{3}$ fluid ounce. How many bottles can be filled with $15\frac{1}{3}$ fluid ounces? (*Source:* Alcon Laboratories, Inc.)

32. The first experimental TV, built in 1928, had a tiny square screen that was only $1\frac{1}{2}$ in. on each side. Find the perimeter and area of the screen.

4.6 Exponents, Order of Operations, and Complex Fractions

OBJECTIVE ▶ ① **Simplify fractions with exponents.** We have used exponents as a quick way to write repeated multiplication of integers and variables. Here are two examples as a review.

$$\overset{\text{Exponent}}{(-3)^2} = \underbrace{(-3)(-3)}_{\text{Two factors of } -3} = 9 \qquad \text{and} \qquad \overset{\text{Exponent}}{x^3} = \underbrace{x \cdot x \cdot x}_{\text{Three factors of } x}$$

Base   Two factors of -3 Base   Three factors of x

The meaning of an exponent remains the same when a fraction is the base.

EXAMPLE 1   **Simplifying Fractions with Exponents**

Simplify.

(a) $\left(-\dfrac{1}{2}\right)^3$

The base is $-\dfrac{1}{2}$. The exponent indicates that there are three factors of $-\dfrac{1}{2}$.

$$\left(-\frac{1}{2}\right)^3 = \overbrace{\left(-\frac{1}{2}\right)\left(-\frac{1}{2}\right)\left(-\frac{1}{2}\right)}^{\text{Three factors of } -\frac{1}{2}} \quad \text{Multiply} \left(-\frac{1}{2}\right)\left(-\frac{1}{2}\right) \text{ to get } \frac{1}{4}.$$

> **Watch the signs!** Multiply *two* factors at a time.

$$= \underbrace{\frac{1}{4} \quad \left(-\frac{1}{2}\right)} \quad \text{Now multiply } \frac{1}{4}\left(-\frac{1}{2}\right) \text{ to get } -\frac{1}{8}.$$

$$= -\frac{1}{8} \quad \text{◀ The product is } negative.$$

(b) $\left(\dfrac{3}{4}\right)^2\left(\dfrac{2}{3}\right)^3$

Two factors of $\dfrac{3}{4}$

Three factors of $\dfrac{2}{3}$

$$\left(\frac{3}{4}\right)^2\left(\frac{2}{3}\right)^3 = \left(\frac{3}{4}\right)\left(\frac{3}{4}\right)\left(\frac{2}{3}\right)\left(\frac{2}{3}\right)\left(\frac{2}{3}\right)$$

$$= \frac{\overset{1}{\cancel{3}} \cdot \overset{1}{\cancel{3}} \cdot \overset{1}{\cancel{2}} \cdot \overset{1}{\cancel{2}} \cdot \overset{1}{\cancel{2}}}{\underset{1}{\cancel{2}} \cdot \underset{1}{\cancel{2}} \cdot \underset{1}{\cancel{2}} \cdot 2 \cdot \underset{1}{\cancel{3}} \cdot \underset{1}{\cancel{3}} \cdot 3} \quad \text{Divide out all common factors.}$$

$$= \frac{1}{6} \quad \text{◀ Remember the 1 in the numerator. The answer is } \tfrac{1}{6}, \textbf{ not } 6.$$

········· **Work Problem ①** at the Side. ▶

OBJECTIVE ▶ ② **Use the order of operations with fractions.** The order of operations that you used in **Chapter 1** for integers also applies to fractions.

OBJECTIVES

① **Simplify fractions with exponents.**

② **Use the order of operations with fractions.**

② **Simplify complex fractions.**

---

① Simplify.

GS (a) $\left(-\dfrac{3}{5}\right)^2$

$$\underbrace{\left(-\frac{3}{5}\right)\left(-\frac{3}{5}\right)}_{}$$

Two factors of $-\frac{3}{5}$

The product of two negative numbers is *positive*.

(b) $\left(\dfrac{1}{3}\right)^4$

(c) $\left(-\dfrac{2}{3}\right)^3\left(\dfrac{1}{2}\right)^2$

(d) $\left(-\dfrac{1}{2}\right)^2\left(\dfrac{1}{4}\right)^2$

Answers

1. (a) $\dfrac{9}{25}$ **(b)** $\dfrac{1}{81}$ **(c)** $-\dfrac{2}{27}$ **(d)** $\dfrac{1}{64}$

2 Simplify.

(a) $\dfrac{1}{3} - \dfrac{5}{9}\left(\dfrac{3}{4}\right)$

$\dfrac{1}{3} - \dfrac{}{}$ Multiply first.

$\dfrac{}{36} - \dfrac{}{36}$ Now subtract. The LCD is 36.

$\dfrac{-}{36}$

$-\dfrac{}{36}$ Now write the answer in lowest terms.

(b) $-\dfrac{3}{4} + \left(-\dfrac{1}{2}\right)^2 \div \dfrac{2}{3}$

(c) $\dfrac{12}{5} - \dfrac{1}{6}\left(3 - \dfrac{3}{5}\right)$

Answers

2. (a) $\dfrac{1}{3} - \dfrac{15}{36}; \dfrac{12}{36} - \dfrac{15}{36}; \dfrac{12-15}{36}; -\dfrac{3}{36}; -\dfrac{1}{12}$

    (b) $-\dfrac{3}{8}$ **(c)** 2

Order of Operations

Step 1 Work inside *parentheses* or *other grouping symbols.*

Step 2 Simplify expressions with *exponents.*

Step 3 Do the remaining *multiplications and divisions* as they occur from left to right.

Step 4 Do the remaining *additions and subtractions* as they occur from left to right.

EXAMPLE 2   **Using the Order of Operations with Fractions**

Simplify.

(a) $-\dfrac{1}{3} + \dfrac{1}{2}\left(\dfrac{4}{5}\right)$ There is no work to be done inside the parentheses. There are no exponents, so start with *Step 3*, multiplying and dividing.

$-\dfrac{1}{3} + \dfrac{1 \cdot 4}{2 \cdot 5}$ Multiply.   ⟨ Multiply $\frac{1}{2} \cdot \frac{4}{5}$ first. Do **not** start by adding $-\frac{1}{3} + \frac{1}{2}$.

$-\dfrac{1}{3} + \dfrac{4}{10}$ Now add. The LCD is 30. $-\dfrac{1}{3} = -\dfrac{10}{30}$ and $\dfrac{4}{10} = \dfrac{12}{30}$

$\dfrac{-10 + 12}{30}$ Add the numerators; keep the common denominator.

$\dfrac{2}{30}$ Write $\dfrac{2}{30}$ in lowest terms: $\dfrac{\overset{1}{\cancel{2}}}{\underset{1}{\cancel{2}} \cdot 15} = \dfrac{1}{15}$.

$\dfrac{1}{15}$ ⟵   The answer is in lowest terms.

(b) $-2 + \left(\dfrac{1}{4} - \dfrac{3}{2}\right)^2$ Work inside parentheses. The LCD for $\dfrac{1}{4}$ and $\dfrac{3}{2}$ is 4.

$-2 + \left(\dfrac{1 - 6}{4}\right)^2$ Rewrite $\dfrac{3}{2}$ as $\dfrac{6}{4}$ and subtract; $\dfrac{1}{4} - \dfrac{6}{4}$ is $\dfrac{1-6}{4}$

$-2 + \left(\dfrac{-5}{4}\right)^2$ Simplify the term with the exponent. Multiply $\left(-\dfrac{5}{4}\right)\left(-\dfrac{5}{4}\right)$. *Signs match,* so the product is *positive.*

$-2 + \left(\dfrac{25}{16}\right)$ Add last. Write -2 as $-\dfrac{2}{1}$.

$-\dfrac{2}{1} + \dfrac{25}{16}$ The LCD is 16. Rewrite $-\dfrac{2}{1}$ as $-\dfrac{32}{16}$.

$\dfrac{-32 + 25}{16}$ Add the numerators; keep the common denominator.

$-\dfrac{7}{16}$ ⟵   The answer is in lowest terms.

◀ **Work Problem ② at the Side.**

OBJECTIVE ▶ **3** **Simplify complex fractions.** We have used both the ÷ symbol and a fraction bar to indicate division. For example,

Indicates division → $\dfrac{6}{2}$ can be written as $6 \div 2$
↑ Indicates division

That means we could write $-\frac{4}{5} \div \left(-\frac{3}{10} \right)$ using a fraction bar instead of ÷.

$-\dfrac{4}{5} \div \left(-\dfrac{3}{10} \right)$ can be written as $\dfrac{-\dfrac{4}{5}}{-\dfrac{3}{10}}$ ← Indicates division
↑ Indicates division

The result looks a bit complicated, and its name reflects that fact. We call it a *complex fraction*.

Complex Fractions

A **complex fraction** is a fraction in which the numerator and/or the denominator contain one or more fractions.

To simplify a complex fraction, rewrite it in horizontal format using the ÷ symbol for division.

EXAMPLE 3 **Simplifying a Complex Fraction**

Simplify: **(a)** $\dfrac{-\dfrac{4}{5}}{-\dfrac{3}{10}}$ **(b)** $\dfrac{\left(\dfrac{2}{3} \right)^2}{6}$

(a) Rewrite the complex fraction using the ÷ symbol for division. Then follow the steps for dividing fractions.

$$\frac{-\dfrac{4}{5}}{-\dfrac{3}{10}} = -\frac{4}{5} \div -\frac{3}{10} = -\frac{4}{5} \cdot -\frac{10}{3} = \frac{4 \cdot 2 \cdot \overset{1}{\cancel{5}}}{\underset{1}{\cancel{5}} \cdot 3} = \frac{8}{3} \quad \text{or} \quad 2\frac{2}{3}$$

Reciprocals

> The quotient is *positive* because both numbers in the problem had the *same* sign (both were negative).

(b) Rewrite the complex fraction using the ÷ symbol for division. Then follow the order of operations.

$\left(\frac{2}{3} \right)\left(\frac{2}{3} \right)$ is $\frac{4}{9}$

$$\frac{\left(\dfrac{2}{3} \right)^2}{6} = \left(\frac{2}{3} \right)^2 \div 6 = \frac{4}{9} \div 6 = \frac{4}{9} \cdot \frac{1}{6} = \frac{\overset{1}{\cancel{2}} \cdot 2 \cdot 1}{9 \cdot \underset{1}{\cancel{2}} \cdot 3} = \frac{2}{27}$$

Reciprocals

······· **Work Problem 3** at the Side. ▶

---

3 Simplify.

GS (a) $\dfrac{-\dfrac{3}{5}}{\dfrac{9}{10}}$ Rewrite this complex fraction using the ÷ symbol.

$$-\frac{3}{5} \div \frac{9}{10} = -\frac{3}{5} \cdot \frac{10}{9}$$
↑ ↑
Reciprocals

$$= -\frac{3 \cdot \underline{\quad} \cdot \underline{\quad}}{5 \cdot \underline{\quad} \cdot \underline{\quad}} =$$

Divide out common factors.

(b) $\dfrac{6}{\dfrac{3}{4}}$ ← *Hint:* Write 6 as $\frac{6}{1}$.

(c) $\dfrac{-\dfrac{15}{16}}{-5}$

(d) $\dfrac{-3}{\left(-\dfrac{3}{4} \right)^2}$

Answers

3. **(a)** $-\dfrac{\overset{1}{\cancel{3}} \cdot 2 \cdot \overset{1}{\cancel{5}}}{\underset{1}{\cancel{5}} \cdot 3 \cdot \underset{1}{\cancel{3}}} = -\dfrac{2}{3}$ **(b)** 8 **(c)** $\dfrac{3}{16}$

(d) $-\dfrac{16}{3}$ or $-5\dfrac{1}{3}$

4.6 Exercises

  MyMathLab®

FOR EXTRA HELP

Download the MyDashBoard App

CONCEPT CHECK

CONCEPT CHECK

1. (a) What part of the expression $\left(-\frac{3}{8}\right)^2$ is called the base? _____

(b) What is the small raised "2" called? _____

(c) Circle the correct factored form.

$$\left(-\frac{3}{8}\right)(2) \quad \text{or} \quad \left(-\frac{3}{8}\right)\left(-\frac{3}{8}\right) \quad \text{or} \quad \left(-\frac{3}{8}\right)\left(-\frac{8}{3}\right)$$

CONCEPT CHECK

2. (a) When two factors are both negative numbers, is the product positive or negative? _____

(b) Circle all the multiplications that give a negative product.

$$5\left(-\frac{3}{10}\right) \quad \text{or} \quad \left(-\frac{1}{2}\right)(-8) \quad \text{or} \quad \left(-\frac{5}{6}\right)\left(\frac{3}{5}\right)$$

Simplify. ***See Example 1.***

3. $\left(-\frac{3}{4}\right)^2 = \left(-\frac{3}{4}\right)\left(-\frac{3}{4}\right)$

$= \underline{\quad}$ Signs match so the product is

_____.

4. $\left(-\frac{4}{5}\right)^2 = \left(-\frac{4}{5}\right)\left(-\frac{4}{5}\right)$

$= \underline{\quad}$ Signs match so the product is

_____.

5. $\left(\frac{2}{5}\right)^3$

6. $\left(\frac{1}{4}\right)^3$

7. $\left(-\frac{1}{3}\right)^3$

8. $\left(-\frac{3}{5}\right)^3$

9. $\left(\frac{1}{2}\right)^5$

10. $\left(\frac{1}{3}\right)^4$

11. $\left(\frac{7}{10}\right)^2$

12. $\left(\frac{8}{9}\right)^2$

13. $\left(-\frac{6}{5}\right)^2$

14. $\left(-\frac{8}{7}\right)^2$

15. $\frac{15}{16}\left(\frac{4}{5}\right)^3$

16. $-8\left(-\frac{3}{8}\right)^2$

17. $\left(\frac{1}{3}\right)^4\left(\frac{9}{10}\right)^2$

18. $\left(\dfrac{4}{5}\right)^2\left(\dfrac{1}{2}\right)^6$

19. $\left(-\dfrac{3}{2}\right)^3\left(-\dfrac{2}{3}\right)^2$

20. $\left(\dfrac{5}{6}\right)^2\left(-\dfrac{2}{5}\right)^3$

21. CONCEPT CHECK

(a) Evaluate this series of examples.

$$\left(-\dfrac{1}{2}\right)^2 = \underline{\hspace{1cm}}$$ $$\left(-\dfrac{1}{2}\right)^6 = \underline{\hspace{1cm}}$$

$$\left(-\dfrac{1}{2}\right)^3 = \underline{\hspace{1cm}}$$ $$\left(-\dfrac{1}{2}\right)^7 = \underline{\hspace{1cm}}$$

$$\left(-\dfrac{1}{2}\right)^4 = \underline{\hspace{1cm}}$$ $$\left(-\dfrac{1}{2}\right)^8 = \underline{\hspace{1cm}}$$

$$\left(-\dfrac{1}{2}\right)^5 = \underline{\hspace{1cm}}$$ $$\left(-\dfrac{1}{2}\right)^9 = \underline{\hspace{1cm}}$$

(b) Explain the pattern in the sign of the answers.

22. CONCEPT CHECK Several drops of ketchup fell on Ron's homework. Explain how he can figure out what number is covered by each drop. Be careful. More than one number may work.

(a) $\left(\blacksquare\right)^2 = \dfrac{4}{9}$

(b) $\left(\bullet\right)^3 = -\dfrac{1}{27}$

(c) $\left(\bullet\right)^4 = \dfrac{1}{16}$

Simplify. ***See Example 2.***

23. $\dfrac{1}{5} - 6\left(\dfrac{7}{10}\right)$ Multiply first!

$\dfrac{1}{5} - \underline{\hspace{1cm}}$ Now subtract. The LCD is 10.

$\dfrac{\overline{\hspace{0.8cm}}}{10} =$

24. $\dfrac{2}{9} - 4\left(\dfrac{5}{6}\right)$ Multiply first!

$\dfrac{2}{9} - \underline{\hspace{1cm}}$ Now subtract. The LCD is 18.

$\dfrac{\overline{\hspace{0.8cm}}}{18} =$

25. $\left(\dfrac{4}{3} \div \dfrac{8}{3}\right) + \left(-\dfrac{3}{4} \cdot \dfrac{1}{4}\right)$

26. $\left(-\dfrac{1}{3} \cdot \dfrac{3}{5}\right) + \left(\dfrac{3}{4} \div \dfrac{1}{4}\right)$

27. $-\dfrac{3}{10} \div \dfrac{3}{5}\left(-\dfrac{2}{3}\right)$

28. $5 \div \left(-\dfrac{10}{3}\right)\left(-\dfrac{4}{9}\right)$

29. $\dfrac{8}{3}\left(\dfrac{1}{4}-\dfrac{1}{2}\right)^{2}$

30. $\dfrac{1}{3}\left(\dfrac{4}{5}-\dfrac{3}{10}\right)^{3}$

31. $-\dfrac{3}{8}+\dfrac{2}{3}\left(-\dfrac{2}{3}+\dfrac{1}{6}\right)$

32. $\dfrac{1}{6}+4\left(\dfrac{2}{5}-\dfrac{7}{10}\right)$

33. $2\left(\dfrac{1}{3}\right)^{3}-\dfrac{2}{9}$

34. $8\left(-\dfrac{3}{4}\right)^{2}+\dfrac{3}{2}$

35. $\left(-\dfrac{2}{3}\right)^{3}\left(\dfrac{1}{8}-\dfrac{1}{2}\right)-\dfrac{2}{3}\left(\dfrac{1}{8}\right)$

36. $\left(\dfrac{3}{5}\right)^{2}\left(\dfrac{5}{9}-\dfrac{2}{3}\right)\div\left(-\dfrac{1}{5}\right)^{2}$

37. A square operation key on a calculator is $\frac{3}{8}$ inch on each side. What is the area of the key? Use the formula $A = s^{2}$. (*Source:* Texas Instruments.)

38. A square lot for sale in the country is $\frac{3}{10}$ mile on a side. Find the area of the lot by using the formula $A = s^{2}$.

$\frac{3}{10}$ mi

39. A rectangular parking lot at the megamall is $\frac{7}{10}$ mile long and $\frac{1}{4}$ mile wide. How much fencing is needed to enclose the lot? Use the formula $P = 2l + 2w$.

40. A rectangular computer chip is $\frac{7}{8}$ inch long and $\frac{5}{16}$ inch wide. An insulating strip must be put around all sides of the chip. Find the length of the strip. Use the formula $P = 2l + 2w$.

$\frac{5}{16}$ in.

$\frac{7}{8}$ in.

Simplify. See Example 3.

41. $\dfrac{-\dfrac{7}{9}}{-\dfrac{7}{36}}$ Rewrite using the ÷ symbol.

$$-\dfrac{7}{9} \div \left(-\dfrac{7}{36} \right) =$$

42. $\dfrac{\dfrac{15}{32}}{-\dfrac{5}{64}}$ Rewrite using the ÷ symbol.

$$\dfrac{15}{32} \div \left(-\dfrac{5}{64} \right) =$$

43. $\dfrac{\dfrac{-15}{6}}{5}$

44. $\dfrac{-6}{-\dfrac{5}{8}}$

45. $\dfrac{\dfrac{4}{7}}{8}$

46. $\dfrac{-\dfrac{11}{5}}{3}$

47. $\dfrac{-\dfrac{2}{3}}{-2\dfrac{2}{5}}$

48. $\dfrac{\dfrac{1}{2}}{3\dfrac{1}{3}}$

49. $\dfrac{-4\dfrac{1}{2}}{\left(\dfrac{3}{4} \right)^2}$

50. $\dfrac{1\dfrac{2}{3}}{\left(-\dfrac{1}{6} \right)^2}$

51. $\dfrac{\left(\dfrac{2}{5} \right)^2}{\left(-\dfrac{4}{3} \right)^2}$

52. $\dfrac{\left(-\dfrac{5}{6} \right)^2}{\left(\dfrac{1}{2} \right)^3}$

4.7 Problem Solving: Equations Containing Fractions

OBJECTIVE ▶ **1 Use the multiplication property of equality to solve equations containing fractions.** In **Chapter 2** you used the division property of equality to solve an equation such as $4s = 24$. The division property says that you may divide both sides of an equation by the same nonzero number and the equation will still be balanced. Now that you have some experience with fractions, let's look again at how the division property works.

$4s$ means $4 \cdot s$
$$4s = 24$$
$$\frac{4 \cdot s}{4} = \frac{24}{4} \qquad \text{Divide both sides by 4.}$$

Divide out the common factor of 4.
$$\frac{\overset{1}{\cancel{4}} \cdot s}{\underset{1}{\cancel{4}}} = 6$$
$$s = 6$$

Because multiplication and division are related to each other, we can also *multiply* both sides of an equation by the same nonzero number and keep it balanced.

Multiplication and Division Properties of Equality

The **multiplication property of equality** says, if $a = b$, then $a \cdot c = b \cdot c$

The **division property of equality** says, if $a = b$, then $\dfrac{a}{c} = \dfrac{b}{c}$ as long as c is not 0. In other words, you may multiply or divide both sides of an equation by the same nonzero number and it will still be balanced.

EXAMPLE 1 Using the Multiplication Property of Equality

Solve each equation and check each solution.

(a) $\dfrac{1}{2}b = 5$

We want the variable by itself on one side of the equal sign. In this example, we want $1b$, not $\frac{1}{2}b$, on the left side. (Recall that $1b$ is equivalent to b.)

Earlier in this chapter you learned that the product of a number and its reciprocal is 1. Thus, multiplying $\frac{1}{2}$ by $\frac{2}{1}$ will give the desired coefficient of 1.

$$\frac{1}{2}b = 5$$

$$\frac{2}{1}\left(\frac{1}{2}b\right) = \frac{2}{1}(5) \qquad \text{Multiply both sides by } \tfrac{2}{1} \text{ (the reciprocal of } \tfrac{1}{2}\text{).}$$

On the left side, use the associative property to regroup the factors.
$$\left(\frac{2}{1} \cdot \frac{1}{2}\right)b = \frac{2}{1}\left(\frac{5}{1}\right) \qquad \text{On the right side, 5 is equivalent to } \tfrac{5}{1}$$

$$\left(\frac{\overset{1}{\cancel{2}}}{1} \cdot \frac{1}{\underset{1}{\cancel{2}}}\right)b = \frac{10}{1}$$

$1b$ is equivalent to b.
$$1b = 10$$
$$b = 10$$

The solution is 10.

Continued on Next Page

Once you understand the process, you don't have to show every step. Here is a shorthand solution of the same problem.

$$\frac{1}{2}b = 5$$

$$\frac{\overset{1}{\cancel{2}}}{1}\left(\frac{1}{\underset{1}{\cancel{2}}}b\right) = \frac{2}{1}\left(\frac{5}{1}\right)$$

$$b = 10 \quad \boxed{\text{The solution is 10.}}$$

The solution is 10. Check the solution by going back to the *original* equation.

CHECK $\quad \frac{1}{2}b = 5 \qquad$ Replace *b* with 10 in the *original* equation.

$$\frac{1}{2}(10) = 5 \qquad \text{Multiply on the left side: } \frac{1}{2}(10)$$
$$\text{is } \frac{1}{2} \cdot \frac{10}{1} \quad \text{or} \quad \frac{1}{2} \cdot \frac{2 \cdot 5}{1}$$

$$\frac{1 \cdot \overset{1}{\cancel{2}} \cdot 5}{\underset{1}{\cancel{2}} \cdot 1} = 5$$

$$5 = 5 \checkmark \quad \text{Balances}$$

When *b* is 10, the equation balances, so **10** is the correct solution (*not* 5).

(b) $\qquad 12 = -\frac{3}{4}x$

$$12 = -\frac{3}{4}x \qquad \text{Multiply both sides by } -\frac{4}{3} \text{ (the reciprocal of } -\frac{3}{4}\text{).}$$
$$\text{The reciprocal of a negative number}$$
$$\text{is also negative.}$$

$$-\frac{4}{3}(12) = -\frac{\overset{1}{\cancel{4}}}{\underset{1}{\cancel{3}}}\left(-\frac{\overset{1}{\cancel{3}}}{\underset{1}{\cancel{4}}}x\right) \qquad \begin{array}{l} \text{On the left side } -\frac{4}{3}(12) \text{ is } -\frac{4}{3} \cdot \frac{12}{1} \\ \text{or } -\frac{4 \cdot \overset{1}{\cancel{3}} \cdot 4}{\underset{1}{\cancel{3}} \cdot 1} = -16 \end{array}$$

$$-16 = x \quad \boxed{\begin{array}{c}\text{The solution}\\\text{is } -16.\end{array}}$$

The solution is −16. Check the solution by going back to the *original* equation.

CHECK $\quad 12 = -\frac{3}{4}x \qquad$ Replace *x* with −16 in the *original* equation.

$$12 = -\frac{3}{4}(-16) \qquad \begin{array}{l}\text{The product of two negative}\\\text{numbers is positive.}\\ -\frac{3}{4}(-16) \text{ is } \frac{3}{4} \cdot \frac{16}{1} \text{ or } \frac{3}{4} \cdot \frac{4 \cdot 4}{1}\end{array}$$

$$12 = \frac{3 \cdot \overset{1}{\cancel{4}} \cdot 4}{\underset{1}{\cancel{4}} \cdot 1}$$

$$12 = 12 \checkmark \qquad \text{Balances} \quad \boxed{\begin{array}{c}\text{If the equation does \textbf{not} balance,}\\\text{your solution is wrong. Start over.}\end{array}}$$

When *x* is −16, the equation balances, so **−16** is the correct solution (*not* 12).

Continued on Next Page

1 Solve each equation. Check each solution.

(a) $\dfrac{1}{6}m = 3$ Multiply both sides by $\dfrac{6}{1}$ (reciprocal of $\dfrac{1}{6}$).

$$\dfrac{\overset{1}{\cancel{6}}}{1}\left(\dfrac{1}{\cancel{6}}m\right) = \dfrac{6}{1}\left(\dfrac{3}{1}\right)$$ Write 3 as $\dfrac{3}{1}$.

$$m = \underline{\quad}$$

CHECK

$$\dfrac{1}{6}\, m = 3$$ Replace m with ____.

$$\dfrac{1}{6}\left(\underline{\quad}\right) = 3$$

$$\underline{\quad} = 3$$ Does it balance?

(b) $\dfrac{3}{2}a = -9$

CHECK

(c) $\dfrac{3}{14} = -\dfrac{2}{7}x$

CHECK

Answers

1. **(a)** $m = 18$ Replace m with 18.

   CHECK $\dfrac{1}{6}m = 3$

   $$\dfrac{1}{6}(18) = 3$$

   Balances $3 = 3$ ✓

(b) $a = -6$ **CHECK** $\dfrac{3}{2}a = -9$

   $$\dfrac{3}{2}(-6) = -9$$

   Balances $-9 = -9$ ✓

(c) $x = -\dfrac{3}{4}$ **CHECK** $\dfrac{3}{14} = -\dfrac{2}{7}x$

   $$\dfrac{3}{14} = -\dfrac{2}{7}\left(-\dfrac{3}{4}\right)$$

   Balances $\dfrac{3}{14} = \dfrac{3}{14}$ ✓

(c) $-\dfrac{2}{5}n = -\dfrac{1}{3}$

$$-\dfrac{\overset{1}{\cancel{5}}}{\underset{1}{\cancel{2}}}\left(-\dfrac{2}{5}n\right) = \left(-\dfrac{5}{2}\right)\left(-\dfrac{1}{3}\right)$$ Multiply both sides by $-\dfrac{5}{2}$ (the reciprocal of $-\dfrac{2}{5}$).

$$n = \dfrac{5 \cdot 1}{2 \cdot 3}$$ The product of two negative numbers is positive.

$$n = \dfrac{5}{6}$$ The solution is $\dfrac{5}{6}$.

CHECK $-\dfrac{2}{5}n = -\dfrac{1}{3}$ Original equation

$$\left(-\dfrac{2}{5}\right)\left(\dfrac{5}{6}\right) = -\dfrac{1}{3}$$ Replace n with $\dfrac{5}{6}$

$$-\dfrac{\overset{1}{\cancel{2}} \cdot \overset{1}{\cancel{5}}}{\underset{1}{\cancel{5}} \cdot \underset{1}{2} \cdot 3} = -\dfrac{1}{3}$$ Multiply on the left side.

$$-\dfrac{1}{3} = -\dfrac{1}{3}$$ ✓   Balances

When n is $\dfrac{5}{6}$, the equation balances, so $\dfrac{5}{6}$ is the correct solution (**not** $-\dfrac{1}{3}$).

◄ **Work Problem ① at the Side.**

OBJECTIVE ▶ ② **Use both the addition and multiplication properties of equality to solve equations containing fractions.**

EXAMPLE 2   **Using the Addition and Multiplication Properties of Equality**

Solve each equation and check each solution.

(a) $\dfrac{1}{3}c + 5 = 7$

The first step is to get the variable term $\dfrac{1}{3}c$ by itself on the left side of the equal sign. Recall that to "get rid of" the 5 on the left side, add the opposite of 5, which is -5, to both sides.

$$\dfrac{1}{3}c + 5 = 7$$

$$\underline{\quad -5 \qquad -5\quad}$$ Add -5 to both sides.

$$\dfrac{1}{3}c + 0 = 2$$

$$\dfrac{1}{3}c = 2$$

$$\dfrac{\overset{1}{\cancel{3}}}{1}\left(\dfrac{1}{\cancel{3}}c\right) = \dfrac{3}{1}\left(\dfrac{2}{1}\right)$$ Multiply both sides by $\dfrac{3}{1}$ (the reciprocal of $\dfrac{1}{3}$).

$$c = 6$$ The solution is 6.

Continued on Next Page

The solution is 6. Check the solution by going back to the *original* equation.

CHECK $\dfrac{1}{3} c + 5 = 7$ Original equation

$\dfrac{1}{3} (6) + 5 = 7$ Replace c with 6.

$\underbrace{2} + 5 = 7$

$\underbrace{7} = 7$ ✓   Balances

When c is 6, the equation balances, so **6** is the correct solution (***not*** 7).

(b) $-3 = \dfrac{2}{3} y + 7$

To get the variable term $\frac{2}{3} y$ by itself on the right side, add -7 to both sides.

$$-3 = \dfrac{2}{3} y + 7$$

$$\underline{-7 \qquad -7}$$ Add -7 to both sides.

$$-10 = \dfrac{2}{3} y + 0$$

$$\dfrac{3}{2} (-10) = \dfrac{\overset{1}{\cancel{3}}}{\underset{1}{\cancel{2}}} \left(\dfrac{\overset{1}{\cancel{2}}}{\underset{1}{\cancel{3}}} y \right)$$ Multiply both sides by $\frac{3}{2}$ (the reciprocal of $\frac{2}{3}$).

$$-15 = y \quad \boxed{\text{The solution is } -15.}$$

CHECK $-3 = \dfrac{2}{3} y + 7$ Original equation

$-3 = \dfrac{2}{3} (-15) + 7$ Replace y with -15.

$-3 = \underbrace{-10} + 7$

$-3 = \underbrace{-3}$ ✓   Balances

When y is -15, the equation balances, so -15 is the correct solution (***not*** -3).

·········· **Work Problem ② at the Side.** ▶

OBJECTIVE ▶ ③ Solve application problems using equations containing fractions. Use the six problem-solving steps from **Chapter 3** to solve application problems.

---

② Solve each equation. Check each solution.

ᴳˢ (a) $18 = \dfrac{4}{5} x + 2$

$\underline{-2 \qquad\qquad -2}$ Add -2 to both sides.

$16 = \dfrac{4}{5} x + 0$

$16 = \dfrac{4}{5} x$ Multiply both sides by the reciprocal of $\frac{4}{5}$.

CHECK

(b) $\dfrac{1}{4} h - 5 = 1$

CHECK

(c) $\dfrac{4}{3} r + 4 = -8$

CHECK

Answers

2. **(a)** $\dfrac{5}{\underset{1}{\cancel{4}}} \left(\dfrac{\overset{4}{\cancel{16}}}{1} \right) = \dfrac{\overset{1}{\cancel{5}}}{\underset{1}{\cancel{4}}} \left(\dfrac{\overset{1}{\cancel{4}}}{\underset{1}{\cancel{5}}} x \right); 20 = x$

   CHECK $18 = \dfrac{4}{5} x + 2$

   $18 = \dfrac{4}{5} (20) + 2$

   $18 = 16 + 2$

   Balances $18 = 18$ ✓

(b) $h = 24$ CHECK $\dfrac{1}{4} h - 5 = 1$

   $\dfrac{1}{4} (24) - 5 = 1$

   $6 - 5 = 1$

   Balances $1 = 1$ ✓

(c) $r = -9$ CHECK $\dfrac{4}{3} r + 4 = -8$

   $\dfrac{4}{3} (-9) + 4 = -8$

   $-12 + 4 = -8$

   Balances $-8 = -8$ ✓

3 A woman's systolic blood pressure is 111. Find her age, using the expression for systolic blood pressure from **Example 3** and the six problem-solving steps. (Assume that the woman has normal blood pressure.)

Step 1

Unknown: woman's age

Known: blood pressure expression is $100 + \dfrac{age}{2}$; woman's pressure is 111.

Step 2 Let a represent the women's age.

Step 3 Write an equation.

$100 + \dfrac{age}{2}$ is blood pressure

$100 + \dfrac{a}{2} = $ _____

Answer

3. *Step 3* $100 + \dfrac{a}{2} = 111$

Step 4 $100 + \dfrac{a}{2} = 111$

$\phantom{100 + \dfrac{a}{2}} \begin{array}{r} -100 \quad -100 \\ \hline 0 + \dfrac{a}{2} = 11 \end{array}$

$\left(\dfrac{\cancel{2}}{1}\right)\left(\dfrac{1}{\cancel{2}}a\right) = \dfrac{2}{1}(11)$

$a = 22$

Step 5 The woman is 22 years old.

Step 6

Check. $100 + \dfrac{22}{2} = 100 + 11 = 111$

Woman's pressure is 111. $\longleftarrow$

 Matches

EXAMPLE 3 **Solving an Application Problem Using an Equation with Fractions**

The expression for finding an adult's approximate systolic blood pressure is $100 + \dfrac{age}{2}$. Suppose your adult friend's systolic blood pressure is 116 (and he has normal blood pressure). Find his age.

Step 1 **Read** the problem. It is about blood pressure and age.

Unknown: friend's age

Known: Blood pressure expression is $100 + \dfrac{age}{2}$; friend's pressure is 116.

Step 2 **Assign a variable.** Let a represent the friend's age.

Step 3 **Write an equation.**

$100 + \dfrac{age}{2}$ is blood pressure

$100 + \dfrac{a}{2} = 116$

Step 4 **Solve.** $100 + \dfrac{a}{2} = 116$

$\begin{array}{r} -100 \quad\quad -100 \\ \hline 0 + \dfrac{a}{2} = 16 \end{array}$ Add -100 to both sides.

$\dfrac{1}{2}a$ is equivalent to $\dfrac{a}{2}$ because $\dfrac{1}{2}a$ is $\dfrac{1}{2} \cdot \dfrac{a}{1}$

$\dfrac{a}{2} = 16$

$\dfrac{1}{2}a = 16$

$\dfrac{\cancel{2}}{1}\left(\dfrac{1}{\cancel{2}}a\right) = \dfrac{2}{1}(16)$ Multiply both sides by $\dfrac{2}{1}$ (the reciprocal of $\dfrac{1}{2}$).

$a = 32$

> Remember to write the units (years) in your answer.

Step 5 **State the answer.** Your friend is 32 years old.

Step 6 **Check** the solution by putting it back into the *original* problem.

Approximate systolic blood pressure is $100 + \dfrac{age}{2}$.

If the age is 32, then $100 + \dfrac{32}{2} = 100 + 16 = 116$.

Friend's blood pressure is 116. $\longleftarrow$ Matches

> Your answer must fit all the information in the original problem.

Age 32 is the correct solution because it "works" when you put it back into the original problem.

$\blacktriangleleft$ **Work Problem** **3** **at the Side.**

4.7 Exercises

FOR EXTRA HELP

 Download the MyDashBoard App

 MyMathLab®

CONCEPT CHECK

1. (a) To solve $\frac{2}{5}c = 6$, multiply both sides by which number? Circle your answer.

$$\frac{2}{5} \qquad \frac{1}{6} \qquad \frac{5}{2} \qquad \frac{6}{1}$$

(b) Explain why you picked that number.

CONCEPT CHECK

2. (a) To solve $12 = \frac{1}{4}x$, multiply both sides by which number? Circle your answer.

$$\frac{1}{12} \qquad \frac{1}{4} \qquad \frac{12}{1} \qquad \frac{4}{1}$$

(b) Explain why you picked that number.

Solve each equation and check each solution. ***See Examples 1 and 2.***

3. $\frac{1}{3}a = 10$ CHECK

GS

Multiply both sides by $\frac{3}{1}$, the reciprocal of $\frac{1}{3}$.

$$\frac{\overset{1}{\cancel{3}}}{1}\left(\frac{1}{\underset{1}{\cancel{3}}}a\right) = \frac{3}{1}\left(\frac{10}{1}\right)$$

$$a = \underline{\quad\quad}$$

4. $7 = \frac{1}{5}y$ CHECK

GS

Multiply both sides by $\frac{5}{1}$, the reciprocal of $\frac{1}{5}$.

$$\frac{5}{1}(7) = \frac{\overset{1}{\cancel{5}}}{1}\left(\frac{1}{\underset{1}{\cancel{5}}}y\right)$$

$$\underline{\quad\quad} = y$$

5. $-20 = \frac{5}{6}b$ CHECK

6. $-\frac{4}{9}w = 16$ CHECK

7. $-\frac{7}{2}c = -21$ CHECK

8. $-25 = \frac{5}{3}x$ CHECK

9. $\frac{3}{10} = -\frac{1}{4}d$ CHECK

10. $-\frac{7}{8}h = -\frac{1}{6}$ CHECK

11. $\frac{1}{6}n + 7 = 9$ CHECK

12. $3 + \frac{1}{4}p = 5$ CHECK

13. $-10 = \dfrac{5}{3}r + 5$ **CHECK**

Start by adding -5
to both sides.

14. $0 = 6 + \dfrac{3}{2}t$ **CHECK**

Start by adding -6
to both sides.

15. $\dfrac{3}{8}x - 9 = 0$ **CHECK**

16. $\dfrac{1}{3}s - 10 = -5$ **CHECK**

Solve each equation. Show your work.

17. $\underbrace{7 - 2} = \dfrac{1}{5}y - 4$ First simplify the left side.

$\underline{\quad\quad} = \dfrac{1}{5}y - 4$ Now add 4 to both sides.

Finish the work.

18. $0 - 8 = \dfrac{1}{10}k - 3$ First simplify the left side.

$\underbrace{0 + (-8)} = \dfrac{1}{10}k - 3$

$\underline{\quad\quad} = \dfrac{1}{10}k - 3$ Now add 3 to both sides.

Finish the work.

19. $4 + \dfrac{2}{3}n = -10 + 2$

20. $-\dfrac{2}{5}m - 3 = -9 + 0$

21. $3x + \dfrac{1}{2} = \dfrac{3}{4}$

22. $\dfrac{6}{21} = \dfrac{2}{7} - 6m$

23. $\dfrac{3}{10} = -4b - \dfrac{1}{5}$

24. $\dfrac{5}{6} = -3c - \dfrac{2}{3}$

25. $-1 - \dfrac{3}{8}n = 5 - 6$

26. $4y + \dfrac{1}{3} = \dfrac{7}{9}$

CONCEPT CHECK *Check the solution given for each equation in Exercises 27 and 28. If a solution doesn't check, show how to find the correct solution.*

27. (a) $\dfrac{1}{6}x + 1 = -2$

$x = 18$

(b) $-\dfrac{3}{2} = \dfrac{9}{4}k$

$k = -\dfrac{2}{3}$

28. (a) $-\dfrac{3}{4}y = -\dfrac{5}{8}$

$y = \dfrac{5}{6}$

(b) $16 = -\dfrac{7}{3}w + 2$

$w = 6$

In Exercises 29–34, find each person's age using the six problem-solving steps and this expression for approximate systolic blood pressure: $100 + \dfrac{\text{age}}{2}$. *Assume that all the people have normal blood pressure.* ***See Example 3.***

29. A man has systolic blood pressure of 109. How old is he?

30. A man has systolic blood pressure of 118. How old is he?

31. A woman has systolic blood pressure of 122. How old is she?

32. A woman has systolic blood pressure of 113. How old is she?

33. A woman with a systolic blood pressure of 128 is how old?

34. Find the age of a man who has a systolic blood pressure of 125.

Nails for home repair projects are classified by the "penny" system, which is a number that indicates the nail's length. The expression for finding the length of a nail, in inches, is $\dfrac{\text{penny size}}{4} + \dfrac{1}{2}$ *inch. In Exercises 35–38, find the penny size for each nail using this expression and the six problem-solving steps. (Source: Season by Season Home Maintenance.)*

35. The length of a common nail is 3 inches. What is its penny size?

36. The length of a drywall nail is 2 inches. Find the nail's penny size.

37. The length of a box nail is $2\frac{1}{2}$ inches. What penny size would you ask for when buying these nails?

38. The length of a finishing nail is $1\frac{1}{2}$ inches. What is its penny size?

Relating Concepts (Exercises 39–40) For Individual or Group Work

Use your skills in solving equations as you work Exercises 39 and 40 in order.

39. Write two different equations that have 8 as a solution. Write your equations with a fraction as the coefficient of the variable term. Use **Exercises 3–10** as models.

40. Write two different equations that have -12 as the solution. Write your equations with a fraction as the coefficient of the variable term. Use **Exercises 3–10** as models.

Study Skills
ANALYZING YOUR TEST RESULTS

OBJECTIVES

1. Determine the reason for errors.
2. Develop a plan to avoid test taking errors.
3. Review material to correct misunderstandings.

After taking a test, many students heave a big sigh of relief and try to forget it ever happened. Don't fall into this trap! An exam is a learning opportunity. It gives you clues about *what your instructor thinks is important,* what *concepts and skills are valued* in mathematics, and *if you are on the right track*.

Immediately After the Test
Jot down problems that caused you trouble. Find out how to solve them by checking your textbook, reviewing your notes, or asking your instructor or tutor (if available). You might see those same problems again on a final exam.

After the Test Is Returned
Find out what you got wrong and why you had points deducted. Write down the problem so you can learn how to do it correctly. Sometimes you have only a short time in class to review your test. *If you need more time,* ask your instructor if you can look at the test in his or her office.

Find Out Why You Made the Errors You Made
Here is a list of typical reasons for making errors on math tests.

1. You read the directions wrong.
2. You read the question wrong or skipped over something.
3. You made a computation error (maybe even an easy one).
4. Your answer is not accurate.
5. Your answer is not complete.
6. You labeled your answer wrong. For example, you labeled it "ft" and it should have been ft^2.
7. You didn't show your work.
8. *You didn't understand the concept.
9. *You were unable to go from words (in a word problem) to setting up the problem.
10. *You were unable to apply a procedure to a new situation.
11. You were so anxious that you made errors even when you knew the material.

The first seven errors are **test-taking errors.** They are easy to correct if you decide to carefully read test questions and directions, proofread or rework your problems, show all your work, and double check units and labels every time.

The three starred errors (*) are **test preparation errors.** Remember that to grow a complex neural network, you need to practice the kinds of problems that you will see on the tests. So, for example, if application problems are difficult for you, you must *do more application problems!* If you have practiced the study skills techniques, however, you are less likely to make these kinds of errors on tests because you will have a deeper understanding of course concepts and you will be able to remember them better.

The last error isn't really an error. **Anxiety** can play a big part in your test results. Go back to the *Preparing for Tests* activity and read the suggestions about exercise and deep breathing. Recall from the *Your Brain* Can *Learn Mathematics* activity that when you are anxious, your body produces adrenaline. The presence of *adrenaline in the brain blocks connections* between dendrites. If you can *reduce the adrenaline* in your system, you will be able to *think more clearly* during your test.

Study Skills

Continued from page 305

Just five minutes of brisk walking right before your test can help do that. Also, *practicing a relaxation technique while you do your homework* will make it more likely that you can benefit from using the technique during a test. *Deep breathing* is helpful because it gets *oxygen into your brain*. When you are anxious you tend to breathe more shallowly, which can make you feel confused and easily distracted.

Make a Plan for the Next Test

Make a plan for your next test based on your results from this test. You might review the Chapter Summary and work the problems in the Chapter Review Exercises or the Chapter Test. Ask your instructor or a tutor (if available) for more help if you are confused about any of the problems.

Now Try This

Below is a record sheet to track your progress in test taking. Use it to find out if you make particular kinds of errors. Then you can work specifically on correcting them. Just check in the box when you made one of the errors. If you take more than four tests, make your own grid on separate paper.

What will you do to avoid test taking errors?

_____

_____

_____

What will you do to avoid test preparation errors?

_____

_____

_____

What will you do to reduce anxiety?

_____

_____

_____

Test Taking Errors

Test #	Read directions wrong	Read question wrong	Computation error	Not exact or accurate	Not complete	Labeled wrong	Didn't show work
1							
2							
3							
4							

Test Preparation Errors

Test #	Didn't understand concept	Didn't set up problem correctly	Couldn't apply concept to new situation
1			
2			
3			
4			

Anxiety

Test #	Felt anxious *before* the exam	Felt anxious *during* the exam	Blanked out on questions	Got questions wrong that I knew how to do
1				
2				
3				
4				

Chapter 4 *Summary*

Key Terms

4.1

fraction A fraction is a number of the form $\frac{a}{b}$, where a and b are integers and b is not 0.

numerator The top number in a fraction is the numerator. It shows how many of the equal parts are being considered.

denominator The bottom number in a fraction is the denominator. It shows how many equal parts are in the whole.

proper fraction In a proper fraction, the numerator is less than the denominator. The fraction is less than 1.

improper fraction In an improper fraction, the numerator is greater than or equal to the denominator. The fraction is greater than or equal to 1.

equivalent fractions Equivalent fractions have the same value even though they look different. When graphed on a number line, they are names for the same point.

4.2

lowest terms A fraction is written in lowest terms when its numerator and denominator have no common factor other than 1.

prime number A prime number is a natural number that has exactly two different factors, itself and 1. The first few prime numbers are 2, 3, 5, 7, 11, 13, and 17.

composite number A composite number has at least one factor other than itself and 1. Examples are 4, 6, 9, and 10. The number 1 is neither prime nor composite.

prime factorization In a prime factorization, every factor is a prime number. For example, the prime factorization of 24 is $2 \cdot 2 \cdot 2 \cdot 3$.

4.3

reciprocal Two numbers are reciprocals of each other if their product is 1. The reciprocal of $\frac{a}{b}$ is $\frac{b}{a}$ because $\frac{a}{b} \cdot \frac{b}{a} = 1$.

4.4

like fractions Like fractions have the same denominator.

unlike fractions Unlike fractions have different denominators.

least common denominator The least common denominator (LCD) for two fractions is the smallest positive number that can be divided evenly by both denominators.

4.5

mixed number A mixed number is a fraction and a whole number written together. It represents the sum of the whole number and the fraction. For example, $5\frac{1}{3}$ represents $5 + \frac{1}{3}$.

4.6

complex fraction A complex fraction is a fraction in which the numerator and/or denominator contain one or more fractions.

4.7

multiplication property of equality The multiplication property of equality states that you may multiply both sides of an equation by the same nonzero number and it will still be balanced.

division property of equality The division property of equality states that you may divide both sides of an equation by the same nonzero number and it will still be balanced.

Test Your Word Power

See how well you have learned the vocabulary in this chapter.

① A **fraction** is in lowest terms if
  A. it has a value less than 1
  B. its numerator and denominator have no common factor other than 1
  C. it is rewritten as a mixed number.

② The **denominator** of a fraction
  A. is written above the fraction bar
  B. is a prime number
  C. shows how many equal parts are in the whole.

③ The **LCD** of two fractions is the
  A. smallest number divisible by both denominators
  B. largest factor common to both denominators
  C. smallest number divisible by both numerators.

④ Two numbers are **reciprocals** of each other if
  A. their sum is 0
  B. they are written in lowest terms
  C. their product is 1.

⑤ **Volume** is
  A. measured in square units
  B. the space inside a solid shape
  C. found by multiplying base times height.

⑥ A **mixed number**
  A. has a value equal to 1
  B. is the sum of a whole number and a fraction
  C. has a value less than 1.

⑦ A whole number is **prime** if
  A. it is divisible by itself and 1
  B. it can be divided by two
  C. it has exactly two different factors, itself and 1.

⑧ **Equivalent fractions**
  A. have the same denominators
  B. are written in lowest terms
  C. name the same point on a number line.

Answers to Test Your Word Power

1. B; *Example:* $\frac{2}{5}$ is in lowest terms, but $\frac{4}{10}$ is not.

2. C; *Example:* In $\frac{3}{4}$ the denominator, 4, shows that the whole is divided into 4 equal parts.

3. A; *Example:* The LCD of $\frac{1}{4}$ and $\frac{5}{6}$ is 12, because 12 is the smallest number that can be divided evenly by 4 and by 6.

4. C; *Example:* The reciprocal of $\frac{3}{8}$ is $\frac{8}{3}$ because $\frac{3}{8} \cdot \frac{8}{3} = \frac{24}{24} = 1$.

5. B; *Example:* The volume of a rectangular solid (box-like shape) is the space inside the box, measured in cubic units.

6. B; *Example:* The mixed number $2\frac{3}{4}$ represents $2 + \frac{3}{4}$.

7. C; *Example:* 7 is prime because it has *exactly* two different factors, 7 and 1.

8. C; *Example:* $\frac{1}{2}$ and $\frac{2}{4}$ are equivalent fractions because they both name the point halfway between 0 and 1.

Quick Review

Concepts	Examples

4.1 Understanding Fraction Terminology

The *numerator* is the top number. The *denominator* is the bottom number.

In a *proper fraction*, the numerator is less than the denominator, so the fraction is less than 1. In an *improper fraction*, the numerator is greater than or equal to the denominator, so the fraction is greater than or equal to 1.

Proper fractions

$$\frac{2}{3}, \frac{3}{4}, \frac{15}{16}, \frac{1}{8} \quad \substack{\leftarrow \text{Numerator} \\ \leftarrow \text{Denominator}}$$

Improper fractions

$$\frac{17}{8}, \frac{19}{12}, \frac{11}{2}, \frac{5}{3}, \frac{7}{7}$$

4.1 Writing Equivalent Fractions

Multiply or divide the numerator and denominator by the same nonzero number. The result is an equivalent fraction.

$$\frac{1}{2} = \frac{1 \cdot 8}{2 \cdot 8} = \frac{8}{16} \quad \leftarrow \text{Equivalent to } \tfrac{1}{2}$$

$$-\frac{12}{15} = -\frac{12 \div 3}{15 \div 3} = -\frac{4}{5} \quad \leftarrow \text{Equivalent to } -\tfrac{12}{15}$$

Concepts	Examples

4.2 Finding Prime Factorizations

A prime factorization of a number shows the number as the product of prime numbers. The first few prime numbers are 2, 3, 5, 7, 11, 13, and 17. You can use a division method or a factor tree to find the prime factorization.

Find the prime factorization of 24.

Division Method: Start at the bottom and work up.

$$\frac{1}{3)3} \quad \leftarrow \text{Continue to divide until the quotient is 1}$$
$$ \leftarrow \text{Divide 3 by 3; quotient is 1}$$
$$2)6 \quad \leftarrow \text{Divide 6 by 2; quotient is 3}$$
$$2)12 \quad \leftarrow \text{Divide 12 by 2; quotient is 6}$$

Start here; divide up. $2)24 \leftarrow$ Divide 24 by 2, the first prime; quotient is 12

$$24 = 2 \cdot 2 \cdot 2 \cdot 3$$

Factor Tree Method:

Circle each prime number.

$$24 = 2 \cdot 2 \cdot 2 \cdot 3$$

4.2 Writing Fractions in Lowest Terms

Write the prime factorization of both numerator and denominator. Divide out all common factors, using slashes to show the division. Multiply the factors in the numerator and in the denominator.

$$\frac{18}{90} = \frac{\overset{1}{\cancel{2}} \cdot \overset{1}{\cancel{3}} \cdot \overset{1}{\cancel{3}}}{\underset{1}{\cancel{2}} \cdot \underset{1}{\cancel{3}} \cdot \underset{1}{\cancel{3}} \cdot 5} = \frac{1}{5}$$

$$\frac{2b^3}{8ab} = \frac{\overset{1}{\cancel{2}} \cdot \overset{1}{\cancel{b}} \cdot b \cdot b}{\underset{1}{\cancel{2}} \cdot 2 \cdot 2 \cdot a \cdot \underset{1}{\cancel{b}}} = \frac{b^2}{4a}$$

4.3 Multiplying Fractions

Multiply the numerators and multiply the denominators. The product must be written in lowest terms. One way to do this is to write each original numerator and each original denominator as the product of primes and divide out any common factors before multiplying.

$$\left(-\frac{7}{10}\right)\left(\frac{5}{6}\right) = -\frac{7 \cdot \overset{1}{\cancel{5}}}{2 \cdot \underset{1}{\cancel{5}} \cdot 2 \cdot 3} = -\frac{7}{12}$$

$$\frac{3x^2}{5} \cdot \frac{2}{9x} = \frac{\overset{1}{\cancel{3}} \cdot \overset{1}{\cancel{x}} \cdot x \cdot 2}{5 \cdot \underset{1}{\cancel{3}} \cdot 3 \cdot \underset{1}{\cancel{x}}} = \frac{2x}{15}$$

4.3 Dividing Fractions

Rewrite the division problem as multiplying by the reciprocal of the divisor. In other words, the first number (dividend) stays the same and the second number (divisor) is changed to its reciprocal. Then use the steps for multiplying fractions. The quotient must be in lowest terms.

Division by 0 is undefined.

$$2 \div \left(-\frac{1}{3}\right) = \frac{2}{1} \cdot \left(-\frac{3}{1}\right) = -\frac{2 \cdot 3}{1 \cdot 1} = -6$$

Reciprocals

$$\frac{x^2}{y^2} \div \frac{x}{3y} = \frac{x^2}{y^2} \cdot \frac{3y}{x} = \frac{\overset{1}{\cancel{x}} \cdot x \cdot 3 \cdot \overset{1}{\cancel{y}}}{\underset{1}{\cancel{y}} \cdot y \cdot \underset{1}{\cancel{x}}} = \frac{3x}{y}$$

Reciprocals

Concepts	Examples

4.4 Adding and Subtracting Like Fractions

You can add or subtract fractions *only* when they have the *same* denominator. Add or subtract the numerators and write the result over the common denominator. Be sure that the final result is in lowest terms.

$$\frac{3}{10} - \frac{7}{10} = \frac{3-7}{10} = \frac{-4}{10} \quad \text{or} \quad -\frac{4}{10}$$

Now write $-\frac{4}{10}$ in lowest terms.

$$-\frac{4}{10} = -\frac{\overset{1}{2} \cdot 2}{\underset{1}{2} \cdot 5} = -\frac{2}{5} \left\{ \begin{array}{l} \text{Lowest} \\ \text{terms} \end{array} \right.$$

$$\frac{5}{a} + \frac{7}{a} = \frac{5+7}{a} = \frac{12}{a} \left\{ \begin{array}{l} \text{Lowest} \\ \text{terms} \end{array} \right.$$

4.4 Finding the Lowest Common Denominator (LCD)

Write the prime factorization of each denominator. Then use just enough prime factors in the LCD so you "cover" both denominators.

What is the LCD for $\frac{5}{12}$ and $\frac{5}{18}$?

Factors of 12

$$12 = 2 \cdot 2 \cdot 3$$
$$18 = 2 \cdot 3 \cdot 3$$
$$\text{LCD} = 2 \cdot 2 \cdot 3 \cdot 3 = 36$$

Factors of 18

The LCD for $\frac{5}{12}$ and $\frac{5}{18}$ is 36.

4.4 Adding and Subtracting Unlike Fractions

Find the LCD. Rewrite each original fraction as an equivalent fraction whose denominator is the LCD. Then add or subtract the numerators and keep the common denominator. Be sure that the final result is in lowest terms.

$$-\frac{5}{12} + \frac{7}{9}$$

The LCD is 36.

Rewrite: $\quad -\dfrac{5}{12} = -\dfrac{5 \cdot 3}{12 \cdot 3} = -\dfrac{15}{36}$

Rewrite: $\quad \dfrac{7}{9} = \dfrac{7 \cdot 4}{9 \cdot 4} = \dfrac{28}{36}$

Add: $\quad -\dfrac{15}{36} + \dfrac{28}{36} = \dfrac{-15 + 28}{36} = \dfrac{13}{36} \left\{ \begin{array}{l} \text{Lowest} \\ \text{terms} \end{array} \right.$

$$\frac{2}{3} - \frac{6}{x}$$

The LCD is $3 \cdot x$ or $3x$.

Rewrite: $\quad \dfrac{2}{3} = \dfrac{2 \cdot x}{3 \cdot x} = \dfrac{2x}{3x}$

Rewrite: $\quad \dfrac{6}{x} = \dfrac{6 \cdot 3}{x \cdot 3} = \dfrac{18}{3x}$

Subtract: $\quad \dfrac{2x}{3x} - \dfrac{18}{3x} = \dfrac{2x - 18}{3x} \left\{ \begin{array}{l} \text{Lowest} \\ \text{terms} \end{array} \right.$

Concepts	Examples

4.5 Mixed Numbers and Improper Fractions

Changing Mixed Numbers to Improper Fractions
Multiply the denominator by the whole number, add the numerator, and place the result over the original denominator.

Changing Improper Fractions to Mixed Numbers
Divide the numerator by the denominator and place the remainder over the original denominator.

Mixed to improper $\qquad 7\dfrac{2}{3} = \dfrac{23}{3} \leftarrow (3 \cdot 7) + 2$

Same denominator

Improper to mixed $\qquad \dfrac{17}{5} = 3\dfrac{2}{5}$

Same denominator

4.5 Multiplying Mixed Numbers

First, round the numbers and estimate the answer. Then follow these steps to find the exact answer.

Step 1 Rewrite each mixed number as an improper fraction.

Step 2 Multiply.

Step 3 Write the answer in lowest terms and change the answer to a mixed number if desired. Then the answer is in simplest form.

Estimate:

$$1\dfrac{3}{5} \quad \cdot \quad 3\dfrac{1}{3}$$

$$\downarrow \text{ Rounded } \downarrow$$

$$2 \quad \cdot \quad 3 = 6$$

Estimate

Exact:

$$1\dfrac{3}{5} \cdot 3\dfrac{1}{3} = \dfrac{8}{5} \cdot \dfrac{10}{3}$$

$$= \dfrac{8 \cdot 2 \cdot \overset{1}{\cancel{5}}}{\underset{1}{\cancel{5}} \cdot 3}$$

$$= \dfrac{16}{3} = 5\dfrac{1}{3} \leftarrow$$

Close to estimate

4.5 Dividing Mixed Numbers

First, round the numbers and estimate the answer. Then follow these steps to find the exact answer.

Step 1 Rewrite each mixed number as an improper fraction.

Step 2 Divide. (Rewrite as multiplication using the reciprocal of the divisor.)

Step 3 Write the answer in lowest terms and change the answer to a mixed number if desired. Then the answer is in simplest form.

Estimate:

$$3\dfrac{3}{4} \quad \div \quad 2\dfrac{2}{5}$$

$$\downarrow \text{ Rounded } \downarrow$$

$$4 \quad \div \quad 2 = 2$$

Estimate

Exact:

$$3\dfrac{3}{4} \div 2\dfrac{2}{5} = \dfrac{15}{4} \div \dfrac{12}{5}$$

Reciprocal of $\frac{12}{5}$ is $\frac{5}{12}$

$$= \dfrac{15}{4} \cdot \dfrac{5}{12}$$

$$= \dfrac{\overset{1}{\cancel{3}} \cdot 5 \cdot 5}{4 \cdot \underset{1}{\cancel{3}} \cdot 4}$$

$$= \dfrac{25}{16} = 1\dfrac{9}{16} \leftarrow$$

Close to estimate

4.5 Adding and Subtracting Mixed Numbers

First round the numbers and estimate the answer. Then rewrite the mixed numbers as improper fractions and follow the steps for adding and subtracting fractions. Write the answer in simplest form.

Estimate:

$$2\dfrac{3}{8} + 3\dfrac{3}{4}$$

$$\downarrow \qquad \downarrow$$

$$2 + 4 = 6 \leftarrow \text{Estimate}$$

Exact:

$$2\dfrac{3}{8} + 3\dfrac{3}{4} = \dfrac{19}{8} + \dfrac{15}{4} = \dfrac{19}{8} + \dfrac{30}{8} = \dfrac{19 + 30}{8}$$

$$= \dfrac{49}{8} = 6\dfrac{1}{8} \leftarrow \text{Close to estimate}$$

Concepts	**Examples**

4.6 Simplifying Fractions with Exponents

The meaning of an exponent is the same for fractions as it is for integers. An exponent is a way to write repeated multiplication.

$$\left(-\frac{2}{3}\right)^2 \quad \text{means} \quad \left(-\frac{2}{3}\right)\left(-\frac{2}{3}\right) = \frac{2 \cdot 2}{3 \cdot 3} = \frac{4}{9}$$

The product of two negative numbers is positive.

4.6 Order of Operations

The order of operations is the same for fractions as for integers.

1. Work inside *parentheses* or *other grouping symbols*.

2. Simplify expressions with *exponents*.

3. Do the remaining *multiplications and divisions* as they occur from left to right.

4. Do the remaining *additions and subtractions* as they occur from left to right.

Simplify.

$$-\frac{2}{3} + 3\left(\frac{1}{4}\right)^2$$
Cannot work inside parentheses. Apply the exponent: $\frac{1}{4} \cdot \frac{1}{4}$ is $\frac{1}{16}$

$$-\frac{2}{3} + 3\left(\frac{1}{16}\right)$$
Multiply next: $3\left(\frac{1}{16}\right)$ is $\frac{3}{1} \cdot \frac{1}{16} = \frac{3}{16}$

$$-\frac{2}{3} + \frac{3}{16}$$
Add last. The LCD is 48

$$-\frac{32}{48} + \frac{9}{48}$$
Rewrite $-\frac{2}{3}$ as $-\frac{32}{48}$
Rewrite $\frac{3}{16}$ as $\frac{9}{48}$

$$\frac{-32 + 9}{48}$$
Add the numerators. Keep the common denominator.

$$-\frac{23}{48}$$
The answer is in lowest terms.

4.6 Simplifying Complex Fractions

Recall that the fraction bar indicates division. Rewrite the complex fraction using the ÷ symbol for division. Then follow the steps for dividing fractions.

Simplify. $\dfrac{-\dfrac{4}{5}}{10}$

Rewrite as $-\dfrac{4}{5} \div 10.$

$$-\frac{4}{5} \div 10 = -\frac{4}{5} \cdot \frac{1}{10} = -\frac{\overset{1}{2} \cdot 2 \cdot 1}{5 \cdot 2 \cdot 5} = -\frac{2}{25}$$

Reciprocals

Concepts	Examples

4.7 Solving Equations Containing Fractions

Solve the equation. Check the solution.

$$\frac{1}{3}b + 6 = 10$$

$$\underline{\quad -6 \quad -6 \quad} \qquad \text{Add } -6 \text{ to both sides.}$$

$$\frac{1}{3}b + 0 = 4$$

$$\underbrace{\qquad\qquad}$$

$$\frac{1}{3}b = 4$$

Step 1 If necessary, add the same number to both sides of the equation so that the variable term is by itself on one side of the equal sign.

Step 2 Multiply both sides by the reciprocal of the coefficient of the variable term.

$$\frac{\cancel{3}^{1}}{1}\left(\frac{1}{\cancel{3}_{1}}b\right) = \frac{3}{1}(4) \qquad \begin{array}{l}\text{Multiply both sides by } \frac{3}{1}\\ \text{(the reciprocal of } \frac{1}{3}\text{).}\end{array}$$

$$b = 12 \qquad \text{The solution is 12.}$$

The solution is 12.

Step 3 To check your solution, go back to the *original* equation and replace the variable with your solution. If the equation balances, your solution is correct. If it does not balance, rework the problem.

CHECK $\quad \frac{1}{3}b + 6 = 10 \qquad$ Original equation

$$\frac{1}{3}(12) + 6 = 10 \qquad \text{Replace } b \text{ with 12.}$$

$$\underbrace{4}_{\quad} + 6 = 10$$

$$\underbrace{10}_{\quad} = 10 \checkmark \quad \text{Balances}$$

When b is 12, the equation balances, so 12 is the correct solution (**not** 10).

Chapter 4 Review Exercises

4.1 **1.** What fraction of these figures are squares? What fraction are circles?

2. Write fractions to represent the shaded and unshaded portions of this figure.

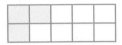

3. Graph $-\frac{1}{2}$ and $1\frac{1}{2}$ on the number line.

4. Simplify each fraction.

(a) $-\dfrac{20}{5}$ **(b)** $\dfrac{8}{1}$ **(c)** $-\dfrac{3}{3}$

4.2 *Write each fraction in lowest terms.*

5. $\dfrac{28}{32}$

6. $\dfrac{54}{90}$

7. $\dfrac{16}{25}$

8. $\dfrac{15x^2}{40x}$

9. $\dfrac{7a^3}{35a^3b}$

10. $\dfrac{12mn^2}{21m^3n}$

4.3 *Multiply or divide. Write all answers in lowest terms.*

11. $-\dfrac{3}{8} \div (-6)$

12. $\dfrac{2}{5}$ of (-30)

13. $\dfrac{4}{9}\left(\dfrac{2}{3}\right)$

14. $\left(\dfrac{7}{3x^3}\right)\left(\dfrac{x^2}{14}\right)$

15. $\dfrac{ab}{5} \div \dfrac{b}{10a}$

16. $\dfrac{18}{7} \div 3k$

4.4 *Add or subtract. Write all answers in lowest terms.*

17. $-\dfrac{5}{12} + \dfrac{5}{8}$

18. $\dfrac{2}{3} - \dfrac{4}{5}$

19. $4 - \dfrac{5}{6}$

20. $\dfrac{7}{9} + \dfrac{13}{18}$

21. $\dfrac{n}{5} + \dfrac{3}{4}$

22. $\dfrac{3}{10} - \dfrac{7}{y}$

4.5 *First, round each mixed number to the nearest whole number and estimate the answer. Then find the exact answer.*

23. *Exact:*

$$2\frac{1}{4} \div 1\frac{5}{8}$$

Estimate:

____ $\div$ ____ = ____

24. *Exact:*

$$7\frac{1}{3} - 4\frac{5}{6}$$

Estimate:

____ $-$ ____ = ____

25. *Exact:*

$$1\frac{3}{4} + 2\frac{3}{10}$$

Estimate:

____ $+$ ____ = ____

4.6 *Simplify.*

26. $\left(-\dfrac{3}{4}\right)^3$

27. $\left(\dfrac{2}{3}\right)^2\left(-\dfrac{1}{2}\right)^4$

28. $\dfrac{2}{5} + \dfrac{3}{10}(-4)$

29. $-\dfrac{5}{8} \div \left(-\dfrac{1}{2}\right)\left(\dfrac{14}{15}\right)$

30. $\dfrac{\frac{5}{8}}{\frac{1}{16}}$

31. $\dfrac{\frac{8}{9}}{-6}$

4.7 *Solve each equation. Show your work.*

32. $-12 = -\dfrac{3}{5}w$

33. $18 + \dfrac{6}{5}r = 0$

34. $3x - \dfrac{2}{3} = \dfrac{5}{6}$

Mixed Review Exercises

Solve each application problem.

38. A chili recipe that makes 10 servings uses $2\frac{1}{2}$ pounds of meat. How much meat will be in each serving? How much meat would be needed to make 30 servings?

39. Yanli worked as a math tutor for $4\frac{1}{2}$ hours on Monday, $2\frac{3}{4}$ hours on Tuesday, and $3\frac{2}{3}$ hours on Friday. How much longer did she work on Monday than on Friday? How many hours did she work in all?

40. There are 60 children in the day care center. If $\frac{1}{5}$ of the children are preschoolers, $\frac{2}{3}$ of the children are toddlers, and the rest are infants, find the number of children in each age group.

41. A rectangular city park is $\frac{3}{4}$ mile long and $\frac{3}{10}$ mile wide. Find the perimeter and area of the park.

1. Write fractions to represent the shaded and unshaded portions of the figure.

2. Graph $-\frac{2}{3}$ and $2\frac{1}{3}$ on the number line below.

Write each fraction in lowest terms.

3. $\dfrac{21}{84}$

4. $\dfrac{25}{54}$

5. $\dfrac{6a^2b}{9b^2}$

Add, subtract, multiply, or divide, as indicated. Write all answers in lowest terms.

6. $\dfrac{1}{6} + \dfrac{7}{10}$

7. $-\dfrac{3}{4} \div \dfrac{3}{8}$

8. $\dfrac{5}{8} - \dfrac{4}{5}$

9. $(-20)\left(-\dfrac{7}{10}\right)$

10. $\dfrac{\frac{4}{9}}{-6}$

11. $4 - \dfrac{7}{8}$

12. $-\dfrac{2}{9} + \dfrac{2}{3}$

13. $\dfrac{21}{24}\left(\dfrac{9}{14}\right)$

14. $\dfrac{12x}{7y} \div 3x$

15. $\dfrac{6}{n} - \dfrac{1}{4}$

16. $\dfrac{2}{3} + \dfrac{a}{5}$

17. $\left(\dfrac{5}{9b^2}\right)\left(\dfrac{b}{10}\right)$

18. Simplify.

$$\left(-\dfrac{1}{2}\right)^3\left(\dfrac{2}{3}\right)^2$$

19. Simplify.

$$\dfrac{1}{6} + 4\left(\dfrac{2}{5} - \dfrac{7}{10}\right)$$

First, round the numbers and estimate each answer. Then find the exact answer. Write exact answers in simplest form.

20. $4\dfrac{4}{5} \div 1\dfrac{1}{8}$ *Estimate:*   *Exact:*

21. $3\dfrac{2}{5} - 1\dfrac{9}{10}$ *Estimate:*   *Exact:*

Solve each equation. Show your work.

22. $7 = \dfrac{1}{5}d$

23. $-\dfrac{3}{10}t = \dfrac{9}{14}$

24. $0 = \dfrac{1}{4}b - 2$

25. $\dfrac{4}{3}x + 7 = -13$

Find the area of each triangle.

26.

27.

Name each solid and find its volume.

28.

29.

Solve each application problem. Show your work.

30. Ann-Marie Sargent is training for an upcoming wheelchair race. She rides $4\frac{5}{6}$ hours on Monday, $6\frac{2}{3}$ hours on Tuesday, and $3\frac{1}{4}$ hours on Wednesday. How many hours did she spend in all? How many more hours did she train on Tuesday than on Monday?

31. A new vaccine is synthesized at the rate of $2\frac{1}{2}$ ounces per day. How long will it take to synthesize $8\frac{3}{4}$ ounces?

32. There are 8448 students at the Metro Community College campus. If $\frac{7}{8}$ of the students work either full time or part time, find the total number of students who work.

Chapters 1–4 *Cumulative Review Exercises*

1. Write this number in words. 505,008,238

2. Write this number using digits.
thirty-five billion, six hundred million,
nine hundred sixteen

3. (a) Round 60,719 to the nearest hundred.

(b) Round 99,505 to the nearest thousand.

(c) Round 3206 to the nearest ten.

4. Name the property illustrated by each example.
(a) $-3 \cdot 6 = 6 \cdot (-3)$

(b) $(7 + 18) + 2 = 7 + (18 + 2)$

(c) $5(-10 + 7) = 5 \cdot (-10) + 5 \cdot 7$

Simplify.

5. $9(-6)$

6. $-10 - 10$

7. $\dfrac{-14}{0}$

8. $6 + 3(2 - 7)^2$

9. $|-8| + |2|$

10. $-8 + 24 \div 2$

11. $(-4)^2 - 2^5$

12. $\dfrac{-45 \div (-5)(3)}{-5 - 4(0 - 8)}$

13. $-3 \div \dfrac{3}{8}$

14. $-\dfrac{5}{6}\left(-42\right)$

15. $\left(\dfrac{5a^2}{12}\right)\left(\dfrac{18}{a}\right)$

16. $\dfrac{7}{x^2} \div \dfrac{7y^2}{3x}$

17. $\dfrac{3}{10} - \dfrac{5}{6}$

18. $-\dfrac{3}{8} + \dfrac{11}{16}$

19. $\dfrac{2}{3} - \dfrac{b}{7}$

20. $\dfrac{8}{5} + \dfrac{3}{n}$

21. $3\dfrac{1}{4} \div 2\dfrac{1}{4}$

22. $2\dfrac{2}{5} - 1\dfrac{3}{4}$

23. $\left(\dfrac{1}{2}\right)^3 (-2)^3$

24. $\dfrac{\dfrac{7}{12}}{-\dfrac{14}{15}}$

Solve each equation. Show your work.

25. $-5a + 2a = 12 - 15$

26. $y = -7y - 40$

27. $-10 = 6 + \dfrac{4}{9}k$

28. $20 + 5x = -2x - 8$

29. $3(-2m + 5) = -4m + 9 + m$

Name each figure and find its perimeter and area.

30.

$4\frac{1}{2}$ in. $4\frac{1}{2}$ in. $4\frac{1}{2}$ in. $4\frac{1}{2}$ in.

31.

$6\frac{1}{4}$ yd   5 yd $6\frac{1}{4}$ yd $7\frac{1}{2}$ yd

32.

24 mm   15 mm   12 mm   15 mm   24 mm

Solve each application problem using the six problem-solving steps.

33. Three new bags of birdseed each weighed the same amount. Sixteen pounds of seed were used from one bag and 25 pounds from another. There were still 79 pounds of seed left. How much did each bag weigh originally?

34. A rectangular parking lot is twice as long as it is wide. If the perimeter of the lot is 102 yd, find the length and width of the parking lot.

5 Rational Numbers: Positive and Negative Decimals

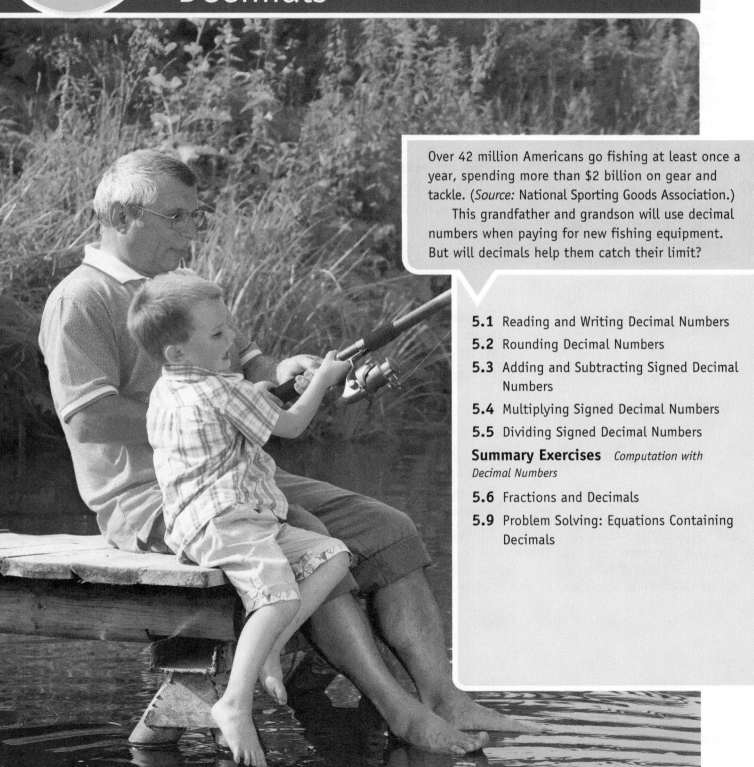

Over 42 million Americans go fishing at least once a year, spending more than $2 billion on gear and tackle. (*Source:* National Sporting Goods Association.)
This grandfather and grandson will use decimal numbers when paying for new fishing equipment. But will decimals help them catch their limit?

5.1 Reading and Writing Decimal Numbers

5.2 Rounding Decimal Numbers

5.3 Adding and Subtracting Signed Decimal Numbers

5.4 Multiplying Signed Decimal Numbers

5.5 Dividing Signed Decimal Numbers

Summary Exercises *Computation with Decimal Numbers*

5.6 Fractions and Decimals

5.9 Problem Solving: Equations Containing Decimals

5.1 Reading and Writing Decimal Numbers

OBJECTIVES

1. Write parts of a whole using decimals.
2. Identify the place value of a digit.
3. Read decimal numbers.
4. Write decimals as fractions or mixed numbers.

VOCABULARY TIP

Deci- The prefix **deci** means **tenth**. For example, a **deci**meter is one **tenth** of a meter.

---

1 There are 10 dimes in one dollar. Each dime is $\frac{1}{10}$ of a dollar. Write a fraction, a decimal, and the words that name the yellow shaded portion of each dollar.

(a)

(b)

(c)

In **Chapter 4**, you worked with rational numbers written in fraction form to represent parts of a whole. In this chapter, we will use rational numbers written as **decimals** to show parts of a whole. For example, our money system is based on decimals. One dollar is divided into 100 equivalent parts. One cent ($0.01) is one of the parts, and a dime ($0.10) is 10 of the parts.

OBJECTIVE ▶ **1** **Write parts of a whole using decimals.** Decimals are used when a whole is divided into 10 equivalent parts or into 100 or 1000 or 10,000 equivalent parts. In other words, decimals are fractions with denominators that are a power of 10. For example, the square at the right is cut into 10 equivalent parts. Written as a fraction, each part is $\frac{1}{10}$ of the whole. Written as a decimal, each part is **0.1**. Both $\frac{1}{10}$ and 0.1 are read as "*one tenth*."

One tenth of the square is shaded.

The dot in 0.1 is called the **decimal point.**

$$0.1$$
↑
Decimal point

The square at the right has **7** of its 10 parts shaded. Written as a *fraction,* $\frac{7}{10}$ of the square is shaded. Written as a *decimal,* **0.7** of the square is shaded. Both $\frac{7}{10}$ and 0.7 are read as "*seven tenths*."

Seven tenths of the square is shaded.

◀ **Work Problem 1 at the Side.**

Each square below is cut into 100 equivalent parts. Written as a fraction, each part is $\frac{1}{100}$ of the whole. Written as a decimal, each part is **0.01** of the whole. Both $\frac{1}{100}$ and 0.01 are read as "*one hundredth*."

Eighty-seven hundredths of the square is shaded.

The square above on the right has 87 of its 100 parts shaded. Written as a fraction, $\frac{87}{100}$ of the total area is shaded. Written as a decimal, **0.87** of the total area is shaded. Both $\frac{87}{100}$ and 0.87 are read as "*eighty-seven hundredths*."

Answers

1. (a) $\frac{1}{10}$; 0.1; one tenth

   (b) $\frac{3}{10}$; 0.3; three tenths

   (c) $\frac{9}{10}$; 0.9; nine tenths

Work Problem ② at the Side. ▶

The example below shows several numbers written as fractions, as decimals, and in words.

EXAMPLE 1 | **Using the Decimal Forms of Fractions**

Fraction	**Decimal**	**Read As**
(a) $\frac{4}{10}$	0.4	four tenths
(b) $-\frac{9}{100}$	-0.09	negative nine hundredths
(c) $\frac{71}{100}$	0.71	seventy-one hundredths
(d) $\frac{8}{1000}$	0.008	eight thousandths
(e) $-\frac{45}{1000}$	-0.045	negative forty-five thousandths
(f) $\frac{832}{1000}$	0.832	eight hundred thirty-two thousandths

········· Work Problem ③ at the Side. ▶

OBJECTIVE ▶ ② **Identify the place value of a digit.** The decimal point separates the *whole number part* from the *fractional part* in a decimal number. In the chart below, you see that the **place value** names for fractional parts are similar to those on the whole number side but end in "*ths*."

Decimal Place Value Chart

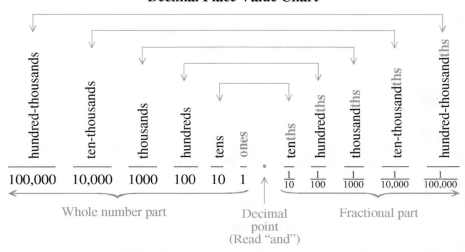

Note

Notice that the ones place is at the center of the place value chart above. There is no "oneths" place.

Also notice that each place is 10 times the value of the place to its right.

Finally, be sure to write a hyphen (dash) in ten–thousandths and hundred–thousandths.

---

② Write the portion of each square that is shaded as a fraction, as a decimal, and in words.

GS **(a)**

$\frac{3}{10} = 0.\underline{\hspace{1em}} = \underline{\hspace{2em}}$ tenths

(b)

③ Write each decimal as a fraction.

GS **(a)** $-0.7 = -\frac{7}{\underline{\hspace{1.5em}}}$

(b) 0.2

(c) -0.03

(d) 0.69

(e) 0.047

(f) -0.351

Answers

2. **(a)** 0.3; three tenths

   (b) $\frac{41}{100}$; 0.41; forty-one hundredths

3. **(a)** $-\frac{7}{10}$ **(b)** $\frac{2}{10}$ **(c)** $-\frac{3}{100}$

   (d) $\frac{69}{100}$ **(e)** $\frac{47}{1000}$ **(f)** $-\frac{351}{1000}$

4 Identify the place value of each digit.

(a) 971.54

(b) 0.4

(c) 5.60

(d) 0.0835

5 Tell how to read each decimal in words.

(a) 0.6   six _____

(b) 0.46   forty-six _____

(c) 0.05

(d) 0.409

(e) 0.0003

(f) 0.2703

(g) 0.088

Answers

4. (a) 9 7 1 . 5 4 (hundreds, tens, ones, tenths, hundredths) (b) 0 . 4 (ones, tenths)
(c) 5 . 6 0 (ones, tenths, hundredths) (d) 0 . 0 8 3 5 (ones, tenths, hundredths, thousandths, ten-thousandths)

5. (a) six tenths
(b) forty-six hundredths
(c) five hundredths
(d) four hundred nine thousandths
(e) three ten-thousandths
(f) two thousand seven hundred three ten-thousandths
(g) eighty-eight thousandths

> **CAUTION**
> If a number does *not* have a decimal point, it is an *integer*. An integer has no fractional part. If you want to show the decimal point in an integer, it is just to the **right** of the digit in the ones place. Here are three examples.
>
> 8 = 8.   306 = 306.   −42 = −42.
> ↑ Decimal point   ↑ Decimal point   ↑ Decimal point

EXAMPLE 2   Identifying the Place Value of a Digit

Identify the place value of each digit.

Notice the hyphen (dash) in ten-thousandths and in hundred-thousandths.

(a) 178.36   **(b)** 0.00935

1 7 8 . 3 6 (hundreds, tens, ones, tenths, hundredths)

0 . 0 0 9 3 5 (ones, tenths, hundredths, thousandths, ten-thousandths, hundred-thousandths)

Notice in **Example 2(b)** that we do *not* use commas on the right side of the decimal point.

◀ **Work Problem 4 at the Side.**

OBJECTIVE 3 Read decimal numbers. A decimal number is read according to its form as a fraction.

0.9 (ones, tenths)   We read 0.9 as "nine tenths" because 0.9 is the same as $\frac{9}{10}$. Notice that 0.9 ends in the tenths place.

0.02 (ones, tenths, hundredths)   We read 0.02 as "two hundredths" because 0.02 is the same as $\frac{2}{100}$. Notice that 0.02 ends in the hundredths place.

EXAMPLE 3   Reading Decimal Numbers

Tell how to read each decimal in words.

(a) 0.3   Because $0.3 = \frac{3}{10}$, read the decimal as: three tenths.

(b) 0.49   Read it as: forty-nine hundredths.

(c) 0.08   Read it as: eight hundredths.   *Think: $0.08 = \frac{8}{100}$ so write hundredths.*

(d) 0.918   Read it as: nine hundred eighteen thousandths.

(e) 0.0106   Read it as: one hundred six ten-thousandths.   *Think: $0.0106 = \frac{106}{10,000}$*

◀ **Work Problem 5 at the Side.**

Reading a Decimal Number

Step 1   Read any whole number part to the *left* of the decimal point as you normally would.

Step 2   Read the decimal point as "*and*."

Step 3   Read the part of the number to the *right* of the decimal point as if it were an ordinary whole number.

Step 4   Finish with the place value name of the rightmost digit; these names all end in "*ths*."

When there is *no whole number part*, use only *Steps 3 and 4*.

EXAMPLE 4   **Reading Decimal Numbers**

Read each decimal.

(a)

9 is in tenths place.

16.9

sixteen **and** nine **tenths**

Remember to say or write "and" when you see a decimal point.

16.9 is read "sixteen and nine tenths."

(b)

5 is in hundredths place.

482.35

four hundred eighty-two **and** thirty-five **hundredths**

482.35 is read "four hundred eighty-two and thirty-five hundredths."

3 is in thousandths place.

(c) 0.063 is "sixty-three **thousandths**." (No whole number part)

(d) 11.1085 is "eleven **and** one thousand eighty-five **ten-thousandths**."

CAUTION

Use "and" when reading a decimal point. A common mistake is to read the whole number 405 as "four hundred *and* five." But there is *no decimal point* shown in 405, so it is read "four hundred five."

························· Work Problem **6** at the Side. ▶

OBJECTIVE **4** **Write decimals as fractions or mixed numbers.** Knowing how to read decimals will help you when writing decimals as fractions or mixed numbers.

Writing a Decimal as a Fraction or Mixed Number

Step 1   The digits to the right of the decimal point are the numerator of the fraction.

Step 2   The denominator is 10 for tenths, 100 for hundredths, 1000 for thousandths, 10,000 for ten-thousandths, and so on.

Step 3   If the decimal has a whole number part, it is written as a mixed number with the same whole number part.

---

6 Tell how to read each decimal in words.

GS **(a)** 3.8 is read

three **and** eight _____

(b) 15.001

(c) 0.0073

(d) 764.309

Answers

6. (a) three and eight tenths
 (b) fifteen and one thousandth
 (c) seventy-three ten-thousandths
 (d) seven hundred sixty-four and three hundred nine thousandths

7 Write each decimal as a fraction or mixed number.

(a) 0.9 $\dfrac{9}{\underline{\hspace{1cm}}}$

(b) 12.21 $12\dfrac{21}{\underline{\hspace{1cm}}}$

(c) 0.101

(d) 0.007

(e) 1.3717

8 Write each decimal as a fraction or mixed number in lowest terms.

(a) 0.5   Write in lowest terms.

$$\frac{5}{10} = \frac{5 \div 5}{10 \div \underline{\hspace{0.6cm}}} = \frac{1}{\underline{\hspace{0.6cm}}}$$

(b) 12.6

$$12.6 = 12\frac{6}{10} = 12\frac{6 \div \underline{\hspace{0.6cm}}}{10 \div \underline{\hspace{0.6cm}}} =$$

(c) 0.85

(d) 3.05

(e) 0.225

(f) 420.0802

EXAMPLE 5   **Writing Decimals as Fractions or Mixed Numbers**

Write each decimal as a fraction or mixed number.

(a) 0.19

    The digits to the right of the decimal point, 19, are the numerator of the fraction. The denominator is 100 for hundredths because the rightmost digit is in the hundredths place.

$$0.19 = \frac{19}{100} \leftarrow 100 \text{ for hundredths}$$

Hundredths place

(b) 0.863

$$0.863 = \frac{863}{1000} \leftarrow 1000 \text{ for thousandths}$$

Thousandths place

(c) 4.0099

The whole number part stays the same.

$$4.0099 = 4\frac{99}{10,000} \leftarrow 10,000 \text{ for ten-thousandths}$$

Ten-thousandths place

◀ **Work Problem 7 at the Side.**

EXAMPLE 6   **Writing Decimals as Fractions or Mixed Numbers**

Write each decimal as a fraction or mixed number in lowest terms.

(a) $0.4 = \dfrac{4}{10} \leftarrow 10$ for tenths

Write $\dfrac{4}{10}$ in lowest terms. $\dfrac{4}{10} = \dfrac{4 \div 2}{10 \div 2} = \dfrac{2}{5} \leftarrow$ Lowest terms

(b) $0.75 = \dfrac{75}{100} = \dfrac{75 \div 25}{100 \div 25} = \dfrac{3}{4} \leftarrow$ Lowest terms

The whole number part stays the same.

(c) $18.105 = 18\dfrac{105}{1000} = 18\dfrac{105 \div 5}{1000 \div 5} = 18\dfrac{21}{200} \leftarrow$ Lowest terms

CAUTION

Always check that your fraction answers are in lowest terms.

◀ **Work Problem 8 at the Side.**

Answers

7. **(a)** $\dfrac{9}{10}$ **(b)** $12\dfrac{21}{100}$ **(c)** $\dfrac{101}{1000}$

   (d) $\dfrac{7}{1000}$ **(e)** $1\dfrac{3717}{10,000}$

8. **(a)** $\dfrac{5 \div 5}{10 \div 5} = \dfrac{1}{2}$ **(b)** $12\dfrac{6 \div 2}{10 \div 2} = 12\dfrac{3}{5}$

   (c) $\dfrac{17}{20}$ **(d)** $3\dfrac{1}{20}$ **(e)** $\dfrac{9}{40}$ **(f)** $420\dfrac{401}{5000}$

▦ Calculator Tip

In this book, we will write 0.45 instead of just .45, to emphasize that there is no whole number. Your *scientific* calculator shows these zeros also. Enter ⊙ ④ ⑤ ⊜ and notice that the display automatically shows 0.45 even though you did not press 0.

5.1 Exercises

FOR EXTRA HELP

 Download the MyDashBoard App

 MyMathLab®

CONCEPT CHECK *Circle the correct answer in Exercises 1–4.*

1. The number 11.084 has how many decimal places?
   2   3   5

2. The number 0.7185 has how many decimal places?
   4   5   1

3. In 22.85, the 8 means what?
   8 tenths   8 hundredths   8 ones

4. In 57.213, the 3 means what?
   3 thousandths   3 tenths   3 hundredths

Identify the digit that has the given place value. **See Example 2.**

5. 70.489
   tens
   ones
   tenths

6. 135.296
   ones
   tenths
   tens

7. 0.83472
   thousandths
   ten-thousandths
   tenths

8. 0.51968
   tenths
   ten-thousandths
   hundredths

9. 149.0832
   hundreds
   hundredths
   ones

10. 3458.712
    hundreds
    hundredths
    tenths

11. 6285.7125
    thousands
    thousandths
    hundredths

12. 5417.6832
    thousands
    thousandths
    ones

Write the decimal number that has the specified place values. **See Example 2.**

13. Fill in the blanks for the rest of this decimal number:

    0 ones, 5 hundredths, 1 ten, 4 hundreds, 2 tenths   __4__ __1__ __0__ . ____ ____

14. Fill in the blanks for the rest of this decimal number:

    7 tens, 9 tenths, 3 ones, 6 hundredths, 8 hundreds   __8__ __7__ __3__ . ____ ____

15. 3 thousandths, 4 hundredths, 6 ones, 2 ten-thousandths, 5 tenths

16. 8 ten-thousandths, 4 hundredths, 0 ones, 2 tenths, 6 thousandths

17. 4 hundredths, 4 hundreds, 0 tens, 0 tenths, 5 thousandths, 5 thousands, 6 ones

18. 7 tens, 7 tenths, 6 thousands, 6 thousandths, 3 hundreds, 3 hundredths, 2 ones

Write each decimal as a fraction or mixed number in lowest terms.
See Examples 5 and 6.

19. 0.7   **20.** 0.1   **21.** 13.4   **22.** 9.8

23. 0.35   **24.** 0.85   **25.** 0.66   **26.** 0.33

27. 10.17   **28.** 31.99   **29.** 0.06   **30.** 0.08

31. 0.205   **32.** 0.805   **33.** 5.002   **34.** 4.008

35. 0.686   **36.** 0.492

Tell how to read each decimal in words. **See Examples 1, 3, and 4.**

37. 0.5   **38.** 0.2

39. 0.78   **40.** 0.55

41. 0.105   **42.** 0.609

43. 12.04   **44.** 86.09

45. 1.075   **46.** 4.025

For Exercises 47–56, rewrite the words as a decimal number. **See Examples 3 and 4.**

47. Fill in the blanks to write six and seven tenths as a decimal number.

  ____.____

48. Fill in the blanks to write eight and twelve hundredths as a decimal number.

  ____.____ ____

49. Thirty-two hundredths

50. One hundred eleven thousandths

51. Four hundred twenty and eight thousandths

52. Two hundred and twenty-four thousandths

53. Seven hundred three ten-thousandths

54. Eight hundred and six hundredths

55. Seventy-five and thirty thousandths

56. Sixty and fifty hundredths

57. Anne read the number 4302 as "four thousand three hundred and two." Explain what is wrong with the way Anne read the number.

58. Jerry read the number 9.0106 as "nine and one hundred and six ten-thousandths." Explain the error he made.

The grandfather on the first page of this chapter needs to select the correct fishing line for his grandson's reel. Fishing line is sold according to how many pounds of "pull" the line can withstand before breaking. Use the table to answer Exercises 59–62. Write all fractions in lowest terms. (Note: The diameter of the fishing line is its thickness.)

FISHING LINE

Test Strength (pounds)	Average Diameter (inches)
4	0.008
8	0.010
12	0.013
14	0.014
17	0.015
20	0.016

Source: Berkley Outdoor Technologies Group.

The diameter is the distance across the end of the line (or its thickness).

59. Write the diameter of 8-pound test line in words and as a fraction.

60. Write the diameter of 17-pound test line in words and as a fraction.

61. What is the test strength of the line with a diameter of $\frac{13}{1000}$ inch?

62. What is the test strength of the line with a diameter of sixteen thousandths inch?

CONCEPT CHECK *Suppose your job is to take phone orders for precision parts. Use the table below. In Exercises 63–66, write the correct part number that matches what you hear the customer say over the phone. In Exercises 67–68, write the words you would say to the customer.*

Part Number	Size in Centimeters
3-A	0.06
3-B	0.26
3-C	0.6
3-D	0.86
4-A	1.006
4-B	1.026
4-C	1.06
4-D	1.6
4-E	1.602

63. "Please send the six tenths centimeter bolt."

Part number _____

64. "The part missing from our order was the one and six hundredths size."

Part number _____

65. "The size we need is one and six thousandths centimeters."

Part number _____

66. "Do you still stock the twenty-six hundredths centimeter bolt?"

Part number _____

67. "What size is part number 4-E?" Write your answer in words.

68. "What size is part number 4-B?" Write your answer in words.

Relating Concepts (Exercises 69–76) For Individual or Group Work

Use your knowledge of place value to **work Exercises 69–76 in order.**

69. Look back at the decimal place value chart earlier in this section. What do you think would be the names of the next four places to the *right* of hundred-thousandths? What information did you use to come up with these names?

70. A common mistake is to think that the first place to the right of the decimal point is "oneths" and the second place is "tenths." Why might someone make that mistake? How would you explain why there is no "oneths" place?

71. Use your answer from **Exercise 69** to write 0.72436955 in words.

72. Use your answer from **Exercise 69** to write 0.000678554 in words.

73. Write 8006.500001 in words.

74. Write 20,060.000505 in words.

75. Write this decimal using digits. three hundred two thousand forty ten-millionths

76. Write this decimal using digits. nine billion, eight hundred seventy-six million, five hundred forty-three thousand, two hundred ten and one hundred million two hundred thousand three hundred billionths

5.2 Rounding Decimal Numbers

In **Chapter 1** you learned how to round integers. For example, 89 rounded to the nearest ten is 90, and 8512 rounded to the nearest hundred is 8500.

OBJECTIVE **1** **Learn the rules for rounding decimals.** It is also important to be able to **round** decimals. For example, a store is selling 2 candy mints for $0.75 but you want only one mint. The price of each mint is $0.75 ÷ 2, which is $0.375, but you cannot pay part of a cent. Is $0.375 closer to $0.37 or to $0.38? Actually, it's exactly halfway between. When this happens in everyday situations, the rule is to round *up*. The store will charge you $0.38 for the mint.

OBJECTIVES

1 Learn the rules for rounding decimals.

2 Round decimals to any given place.

3 Round money amounts to the nearest cent or nearest dollar.

Rounding a Decimal Number

Step 1 Find the place to which the rounding is being done. Draw a "cut-off" line *after* that place to show that you are cutting off and dropping the rest of the digits.

Step 2 Look *only* at the *first* digit you are cutting off.

Step 3A If this digit is *4 or less,* the part of the number you are keeping *stays the same.*

Step 3B If this digit is *5 or more,* you must *round up* the part of the number you are keeping.

Step 4 You can use the ≈ symbol or the ≐ symbol to indicate that the rounded number is now an approximation (close, but *not exact*). Both symbols mean "is approximately equal to." (In this book we will use the ≈ symbol.)

CAUTION

Do *not* move the decimal point when rounding.

OBJECTIVE **2** **Round decimals to any given place.** These examples show you how to round decimals.

EXAMPLE 1 **Rounding a Decimal Number**

Round 14.39652 to the nearest thousandth. (Is it closer to 14.396 or to 14.397?)

Step 1 Draw a "cut-off" line after the thousandths place.

$$1\ 4\ .\ 3\ 9\ 6\ \big|\ 5\ 2$$

You are cutting off the 5 and 2
They will be dropped.

Thousandths

Step 2 Look *only* at the *first* digit you are cutting off. Ignore the other digits you are cutting off.

$$1\ 4\ .\ 3\ 9\ 6\ \big|\ 5\ 2$$

Look *only* at the 5
Ignore the 2

·········· **Continued on Next Page**

1 Round to the nearest thousandth.

(a) 0.33492

$$0.334 \mid 92$$
Thousandths ⤴   First digit cut is *5 or more.*

(b) 8.00851

(c) 265.42068

(d) 10.70180

Step 3   If the first digit you are cutting off is *5 or more*, round up the part of the number you are keeping.

$$
\begin{array}{r}
1\,4\,.\,3\,9\,6 \; \aleph \; 5\,2 \\
+\;\; 0\,.\,0\,0\,1 \\
\hline
1\,4\,.\,3\,9\,7
\end{array}
$$

First digit cut is *5 or more*, so round up by adding 1 thousandth to the part you are keeping.

So, 14.39652 rounded to the nearest thousandth is 14.397
You can write 14.39652 ≈ 14.397

> Rounding to **thousandths** means **three** decimal places.

CAUTION

When rounding integers in **Chapter 1**, you kept all the digits but changed some to zeros. With decimals, you cut off and *drop the extra digits*. In the example above, 14.39652 rounds to 14.397 (**not** 14.39700).

◀ **Work Problem 1 at the Side.**

In **Example 1** above, the rounded number 14.397 had *three decimal places*. **Decimal places** are the number of digits to the *right* of the decimal point. The first decimal place is tenths, the second is hundredths, the third is thousandths, and so on.

EXAMPLE 2   **Rounding Decimals to Different Places**

Round to the place indicated.

(a) Round 5.3496 to the nearest tenth. (Is it closer to 5.3 or to 5.4?)

Step 1   Draw a cut-off line after the tenths place.   ◁ **Tenths** is **one** decimal place.

$$5\,.\,3 \; \aleph \; 4\,9\,6$$
Tenths ⤴

You are cutting off the 4, 9, and 6

Step 2 $$5\,.\,3 \; \aleph \; 4\,\underline{9\,6}$$ Look *only* at the 4

Ignore these digits.

Step 3 $$\underline{5\,.\,3} \; \aleph \; 4\,9\,6$$ First digit cut is *4 or less*, so the part you are keeping stays the same.

$$5\,.\,3 \;\leftarrow \text{Stays the same}$$

5.3496 rounded to the nearest tenth is 5.3 (*one* decimal place for *tenths*). You can write 5.3496 ≈ 5.3

Notice: 5.3496 does **not** round to 5.3000 (which would be ten-thousandths instead of tenths).

(b) Round 0.69738 to the nearest hundredth. (Is it closer to 0.69 or to 0.70?)

Step 1 $$0\,.\,6\,9 \mid 7\,3\,8$$ Draw a cut-off line after the hundredths place.
Hundredths ⤴

Look *only* at the 7

Step 2 $$0\,.\,6\,9 \mid 7\,3\,8$$

Answers

1. **(a)** 0.335   **(b)** 8.009   **(c)** 265.421
    (d) 10.702

Continued on Next Page

Step 3   0.69|738   First digit cut is *5 or more*, so round up by adding 1 hundredth to the part you are keeping.

            1
      0.6 9 ← Keep this part.
    + 0.0 1 ← To round up, add 1 hundredth.
    ─────────
      0.7 0 ← 9 + 1 is 10; write 0 and regroup 1 to the tenths place.

So, 0.69738 rounded to the nearest hundredth is 0.70. Hundredths is *two* decimal places so you *must* write the 0 in the hundredths place. You can write 0.69738 ≈ 0.70

> **CAUTION**
>
> If a *rounded* number has a 0 in the rightmost place, you *must* keep the 0. As shown above, 0.69738 rounded to the nearest hundredth is 0.7**0**. Do *not* write 0.7, which is rounded to tenths instead of hundredths.

(c) Round 0.01806 to the nearest thousandth. (Is it closer to 0.018 or to 0.019?)

      0.018|06   First digit cut is *4 or less*, so the part you are keeping stays the same.
      0.018 ← Stays the same

> Rounding to *thousandths* means *three* decimal places.

So, 0.01806 rounded to the nearest thousandth is 0.018
You can write 0.01806 ≈ 0.018

(d) Round 57.976 to the nearest tenth. (Is it closer to 57.9 or to 58.0?)

      57.9|76   First digit cut is *5 or more*, so round up by adding 1 tenth to the part you are keeping.

         1
      57.9 ← Keep this part.
    + 0.1 ← To round up, add 1 tenth.
    ────────
      58.0 ← 9 + 1 is 10; write 0 and regroup 1 to the ones place.

> Be sure to write the 0 in the *tenths* place.

So, 57.976 rounded to the nearest tenth is 58.0. You can write 57.976 ≈ 58.**0**
You *must* write the 0 in the tenths place to show that the number was rounded to the nearest tenth.

> **CAUTION**
>
> Check that your rounded answer shows *exactly* the number of decimal places asked for in the problem. Be sure your answer shows *one decimal place* if you rounded to *tenths, two decimal places* for *hundredths, three decimal places* for *thousandths,* and so on.

··········· Work Problem **2** at the Side. ▶

OBJECTIVE ▶ **3** **Round money amounts to the nearest cent or nearest dollar.** When you are shopping in a store, money amounts are usually rounded to the nearest cent. There are 100 cents in a dollar.

$$\text{Each cent is } \frac{1}{100} \text{ of a dollar.}$$

Another way to write $\frac{1}{100}$ is 0.01. So rounding to the *nearest cent* is the same as rounding to the *nearest hundredth of a dollar.*

---

2 Round to the place indicated.

GS **(a)** 0.8988 to the nearest hundredth

      0.8 9|88   First digit cut is *5 or more*, so round up.
      0.8 9 ← Keep this part.
    + 0.0 1 ← To round up, add 1 hundredth.
    ─────────
      0. __ __

(b) 5.8903 to the nearest hundredth

(c) 11.0299 to the nearest thousandth

(d) 0.545 to the nearest tenth

Answers

2. (a) 0.90 **(b)** 5.89
    (c) 11.030 **(d)** 0.5

3 Round each money amount to the nearest cent.

(a) $14.595

$$\underbrace{\$14.\ 5\ 9}\ \Big|\ 5$$

First digit cut is *5 or more*, so round up.

$$\begin{array}{r} \$14.\ 5\ 9 \\ +\ 0.\ 0\ 1 \\ \hline \$14.\_\_\_ \end{array}$$

To round up, add 1 hundredth (1 cent).

You pay

(b) $578.0663

You pay _____.

(c) $0.849

You pay _____.

(d) $0.0548

You pay _____.

EXAMPLE 3 **Rounding to the Nearest Cent**

Round each money amount to the nearest cent.

(a) $2.4238 (Is it closer to $2.42 or to $2.43?)

$$\$2.42\ \Big|\ 38$$

First digit cut is *4 or less*, so the part you are keeping stays the same.

$2.42 ⟵ You pay $2.42

$2.4238 rounded to the nearest cent is $2.42.

> Rounding to the *nearest cent* is rounding to *hundredths*.

(b) $0.695 (Is it closer to $0.69 or to $0.70?)

$$\$0.69\ \Big|\ 5$$

5 or more; round up.

$$\begin{array}{r} \$0.69 \\ +\ \$0.01 \\ \hline \$0.70 \end{array}$$

To round up, add 1 hundredth (1 cent).
You pay $0.70

$0.695 rounded to the nearest cent is $0.70.

◀ **Work Problem 3 at the Side.**

Note

Some stores round *all* money amounts up to the next higher cent, even if the next digit is *4 or less*. In **Example 3(a)** above, some stores would round $2.4238 *up* to $2.43, even though it is closer to $2.42.

It is also common to round money amounts to the nearest dollar. For example, you can do that on your federal and state income tax returns to make the calculations easier.

EXAMPLE 4 **Rounding to the Nearest Dollar**

Round to the nearest dollar.

(a) $48.69 (Is it closer to $48 or to $49?)

Draw a cut-off line after the ones place.

$$\$48\ \Big|\ .69$$

First digit cut is *5 or more*, so round up by adding $1

$$\begin{array}{r} \$48 \\ +\ 1 \\ \hline \$49 \end{array}$$

> Write $49 not $49.00

$48.69 rounded to the nearest dollar is $49

CAUTION

$48.69 rounded to the nearest dollar is $49. Be careful to write the answer as **$49** to show that the rounding is to the *nearest dollar*. Writing $49.00 would show rounding to the *nearest cent*.

Answers

3. **(a)** $14.60 **(b)** $578.07 **(c)** $0.85
   (d) $0.05

Continued on Next Page

(b) $594.36 (Is it closer to $594 or to $595?)

Draw cut-off line after the ones place.

First digit cut is *4 or less,* so the part you are keeping stays the same.

$$\underbrace{\$594}\big|.36$$
$$\$594$$

Write $594 not $594.00

$594.36 rounded to the nearest dollar is $594

(c) $399.88 (Is it closer to $399 or to $400?)

5 or more, so round up by adding $1

$$\underbrace{\$399}\big|.88$$
$$\begin{array}{r}\$399 \\ +\quad 1 \\ \hline \$400\end{array}$$

You are rounding to the nearest whole number, so do *not* show any decimal places.

$399.88 rounded to the nearest dollar is $400

(d) $2689.50 (Is it closer to $2689 or to $2690?)

5 or more, so round up by adding $1

$$\underbrace{\$2689}\big|.50$$
$$\begin{array}{r}\$2689 \\ +\qquad 1 \\ \hline \$2690\end{array}$$

Careful! Write $2690 not $2690.00

$2689.50 rounded to the nearest dollar is $2690

Note

When rounding $2689.50 to the nearest dollar, above, notice that it is exactly halfway between $2689 and $2690. When this happens in everyday situations, the rule is to round *up*. (Scientists working with technical data may use a more complicated rule when rounding numbers that are exactly in the middle.)

(e) $0.61 (Is it closer to $0 or to $1?)

5 or more, so round up.

$$\$0\big|.61$$

$0.61 rounded to the nearest dollar is $1

Write $1 not $1.00

🖩 **Calculator Tip**

Accountants and other people who work with money amounts often set their calculators to automatically round to two decimal places (nearest cent) or to round to zero decimal places (nearest dollar). Your calculator may have this feature.

· **Work Problem ④ at the Side.** ▶

---

④ Round to the nearest dollar.

ⓖ (a) $29.10

$$\$2\,9\big|.1\,0$$

First digit cut is *4 or less,* so the part you keep stays the same.

_____

(b) $136.49

(c) $990.91

(d) $5999.88

(e) $49.60

(f) $0.55

(g) $1.08

Answers

4. (a) $29 **(b)** $136 **(c)** $991
(d) $6000 **(e)** $50 **(f)** $1 **(g)** $1

5.2 Exercises

 FOR EXTRA HELP   ▶   **MyMathLab®**

1. **CONCEPT CHECK**   Which digit would you look at when deciding how to round 4.8073 to the nearest tenth? _____

2. **CONCEPT CHECK**   Which digit would you look at when deciding how to round 875.639 to the nearest hundredth? _____

3. **CONCEPT CHECK**   Explain how to round 5.70961 to the nearest thousandth.

4. **CONCEPT CHECK**   Explain how to round 10.028 to the nearest tenth.

Round each number to the place indicated. ***See Examples 1 and 2.***

┌── First digit cut is *5 or more.*

5. 16.8│974 to the nearest tenth

┌── First digit cut is *5 or more.*

6. 193.84│5 to the nearest hundredth

┌── First digit cut is *4 or less*

7. 0.956│47 to the nearest thousandth

┌── First digit cut is *4 or less.*

8. 96.8158│4 to the nearest ten-thousandth

9. 0.799 to the nearest hundredth

10. 0.952 to the nearest tenth

11. 3.66062 to the nearest thousandth

12. 1.5074 to the nearest hundredth

13. 793.988 to the nearest tenth

14. 476.1196 to the nearest thousandth

15. 0.09804 to the nearest ten-thousandth

16. 176.004 to the nearest tenth

17. 9.0906 to the nearest hundredth

18. 30.1290 to the nearest thousandth

19. 82.000151 to the nearest ten-thousandth

20. 0.400594 to the nearest ten-thousandth

Nardos is grocery shopping. The store will round the amount she pays for each item to the nearest cent. Write the rounded amounts. ***See Example 3.***

21. Soup is three cans for $2.45, so one can is $0.81666. Nardos pays _____.

22. Orange juice is two cartons for $3.89, so one carton is $1.945. Nardos pays _____.

23. Facial tissue is four boxes for $4.89, so one box is $1.2225. Nardos pays _____.

24. Muffin mix is three packages for $1.99, so one package is $0.66333. Nardos pays _____.

25. Candy bars are six for $4.19, so one bar is $0.6983. Nardos pays _____.

26. Boxes of spaghetti are four for $4.39, so one box is $1.0975. Nardos pays _____.

As she gets ready to do her income tax return, Ms. Chen rounds each amount to the nearest dollar. Write the rounded amounts. ***See Example 4.***

27. Income from job, $48,649.60

28. Income from interest on bank account, $69.58

29. Donations to charity, $840.08

30. Federal withholding, $6064.49

Round each money amount as indicated. **See Examples 3 and 4.**

31. $499.98 to the nearest dollar

32. $9899.59 to the nearest dollar

33. $0.996 to the nearest cent

34. $0.09929 to the nearest cent

35. $999.73 to the nearest dollar

36. $9999.80 to the nearest dollar

The table lists speed records for various types of transportation. Use the table to answer Exercises 37–40.

Record	Speed (miles per hour)
Land speed record (specially built car)	763.04
Motorcycle speed record (conventional motorcycle)	252.662
Fastest rollercoaster	134.8
Fastest military jet	2193.167
Boeing 757-300 airplane (regular passenger service)	509
Indianapolis 500 auto race (fastest average winning speed)	185.981
Daytona 500 auto race (fastest average winning speed)	177.602

Source: *Guinness World Records* and *World Almanac and Book of Facts.*

37. Round these speed records to the nearest whole number.

(a) Motorcycle

(b) Rollercoaster

38. Round these speed records to the nearest hundredth.

(a) Daytona 500 average winning speed

(b) Indianapolis 500 average winning speed

39. Round these speed records to the nearest tenth.

(a) Indianapolis 500 average winning speed

(b) Land speed record

40. Round these speed records to the nearest hundred.

(a) military jet

(b) Boeing 757-300 airplane

Relating Concepts (Exercises 41–44)   For Individual or Group Work

Use your knowledge about rounding money amounts to **work Exercises 41–44 in order.**

41. Explain what happens when you round $0.499 to the nearest dollar. Why does this happen?

42. Look again at **Exercise 41.** How else could you round $0.499 that would be more helpful? What kind of guideline does this suggest about rounding to the nearest dollar?

43. Explain what happens when you round $0.0015 to the nearest cent. Why does this happen?

44. Suppose you want to know which of these amounts is less, so you round them both to the nearest cent.

$0.5968 $0.6014

Explain what happens. Describe what you could do instead of rounding to the nearest cent.

5.3 Adding and Subtracting Signed Decimal Numbers

OBJECTIVES

1. Add and subtract positive decimals.
2. Add and subtract negative decimals.
3. Estimate the answer when adding or subtracting decimals.

1 Find each sum.

(a) 2.86 + 7.09

$$\begin{array}{r} 2.86 \\ +7.09 \\ \hline \end{array}$$

⤶— Decimal points are lined up.

(b) 13.761 + 8.325

(c) 0.319 + 56.007 + 8.252

(d) 39.4 + 0.4 + 177.2

OBJECTIVE **1** **Add and subtract positive decimals.** When adding or subtracting *whole* numbers, you line up the numbers in columns so that you are adding ones to ones, tens to tens, and so on. A similar idea applies to adding or subtracting *decimal* numbers. With decimals, you line up the decimal points to be sure that you are adding tenths to tenths, hundredths to hundredths, and so on.

Adding and Subtracting Decimal Numbers

Step 1 Write the numbers in columns with the decimal points lined up.

Step 2 If necessary, write in zeros so both numbers have the same number of decimal places. Then add or subtract as if they were whole numbers.

Step 3 Line up the decimal point in the answer directly below the decimal points in the problem.

EXAMPLE 1 Adding Decimal Numbers

Find each sum.

(a) 16.92 and 48.34

Step 1 Write the numbers in columns with the decimal points lined up.

$$\begin{array}{r} \text{tens} \quad \text{ones} \quad \text{tenths} \quad \text{hundredths} \\ 1\,6\,.\,9\,2 \\ +\,4\,8\,.\,3\,4 \\ \hline \end{array}$$

↑———Decimal points are lined up.

Step 2 Add as if these were whole numbers.

$$\begin{array}{r} \overset{1\ 1}{16}.92 \\ +\ 48.34 \\ \hline \end{array}$$

Step 3
$$65.26$$

↑ Decimal point in answer is lined up under decimal points in problem.

(b) 5.897 + 4.632 + 12.174

Write the numbers in columns with the decimal points lined up. Then add.

$$\begin{array}{r} \overset{1\ 1}{5}.\overset{2\ 1}{897} \\ 4.632 \\ +\ 12.174 \\ \hline 22.703 \end{array}$$

When you rewrite the numbers in columns, be careful to line up the decimal points.

◀ Work Problem **1** at the Side.

In **Example 1(a)** above, both numbers had *two* decimal places (two digits to the right of the decimal point). In **Example 1(b),** all the numbers had *three decimal places* (three digits to the right of the decimal point). That made it easy to add tenths to tenths, hundredths to hundredths, and so on.

Answers

1. **(a)** 9.95 **(b)** 22.086 **(c)** 64.578
(d) 217.0

If the numbers of decimal places do *not* match, you can write in zeros as placeholders to make them match. This is shown in **Example 2** below.

EXAMPLE 2 **Writing Zeros as Placeholders before Adding**

Find each sum.

(a) 7.3 + 0.85

There are two decimal places in 0.85 (tenths and hundredths), so write a 0 in the hundredths place in 7.3 so that it has two decimal places also.

$$\begin{array}{r} 7.3\mathbf{0} \leftarrow \\ + \ 0.85 \\ \hline 8.15 \end{array} \begin{array}{l} \text{One 0 is} \\ \text{written in.} \end{array}$$

7.30   is equivalent to   7.3 because

$$7\frac{30}{100} \text{ in lowest terms is } 7\frac{3}{10}$$

(b) 6.42 + 9 + 2.576

Write in zeros so that all the addends have three decimal places. Notice how the whole number 9 is written with the decimal point on the *right* side. (If you put the decimal point on the *left* side of the 9, you would turn it into the decimal fraction 0.9.)

Write the decimal point on the *right* side of the 9.

$$\begin{array}{r} 6.42\mathbf{0} \leftarrow \text{One 0 is written in.} \\ 9.\mathbf{000} \leftarrow \text{9 is a whole number; decimal point} \\ \text{and three zeros are written in.} \\ + \ 2.576 \leftarrow \text{No zeros are needed.} \\ \hline 17.996 \end{array}$$

> **Note**
>
> Writing zeros to the right of a *decimal* number does *not* change the value of the number, as shown in **Example 2(a)** above.

·· **Work Problem ❷ at the Side.** ▶

EXAMPLE 3 **Subtracting Decimal Numbers**

Find each difference.

(a) 15.82 from 28.93

Step 1

$$\begin{array}{r} 28.93 \\ - \ 15.82 \end{array}$$

Line up decimal points. Then you will be subtracting hundredths from hundredths and tenths from tenths.

> Watch the order of the numbers when you see "from." Subtraction is **not** commutative like addition. So the number you are subtracting "from" goes first.

Step 2

$$\begin{array}{r} 28.93 \\ - \ 15.82 \\ \hline 13 \ 11 \end{array}$$

Both numbers have two decimal places; no need to write in zeros.
Subtract as if they were whole numbers.

Step 3

$$\begin{array}{r} 28.93 \\ - \ 15.82 \\ \hline 13.11 \end{array}$$

Decimal point in answer is lined up.

··· **Continued on Next Page**

---

❷ Find each sum.

(a) 6.54 + 9.8

$$\begin{array}{r} 6.5\ 4 \\ + \ 9.8\ \mathbf{0} \leftarrow \\ \hline \_\_ \ \_\_ . \_\_ \ \_\_ \end{array} \begin{array}{l} \text{One 0 is} \\ \text{written in.} \end{array}$$

(b) 0.831 + 222.2 + 10

(c) 8.64 + 39.115 + 3.0076

(d) 5 + 429.823 + 0.76

Answers

2. (a) 16.34 **(b)** 233.031 **(c)** 50.7626
(d) 435.583

3 Find each difference.

(a) 22.7 from 72.9

$$
\begin{array}{r}
7\ 2\ .\ 9 \\
-\ 2\ 2\ .\ 7 \\
\hline
\underline{\quad}\ \underline{\quad}\ .\ \underline{\quad}
\end{array}
$$

(b) 6.425 from 11.813

(c) $20.15 − $19.67

4 Find each difference.

(a) 18.651 from 25.3

(b) 5.816 − 4.98

(c) 40 less 3.66

(d) 1 − 0.325

Answers

3. (a) 50.2 (b) 5.388 (c) $0.48
4. (a) 6.649 (b) 0.836 (c) 36.34
   (d) 0.675

(b) 146.35 minus 58.98
Regrouping is needed here.

— Line up decimal points.

$$
\begin{array}{r}
{\scriptstyle 0\ 13\ 15\quad 12\ 15} \\
\cancel{1}\ 4\ \cancel{6}\ .\ \cancel{3}\ \cancel{5} \\
-\ 5\ 8\ .\ 9\ 8 \\
\hline
8\ 7\ .\ 3\ 7
\end{array}
$$

◀ **Work Problem 3 at the Side.**

EXAMPLE 4   **Writing Zeros as Placeholders before Subtracting**

Find each difference.

(a) 16.5 from 28.362
Use the same steps as in **Example 3** above. Remember to write in zeros so both numbers have three decimal places.

— Line up decimal points.

16.500 is equivalent to 16.5

$$
\begin{array}{r}
28.\overset{\downarrow}{3}62 \\
-\ 16.\mathbf{500} \leftarrow \text{Write two zeros.} \\
\hline
11.862 \leftarrow \text{Subtract as usual.}
\end{array}
$$

(b) 59.7 − 38.914

$$
\begin{array}{r}
59.\mathbf{700} \leftarrow \text{Write two zeros.} \\
-\ 38.914 \\
\hline
20.786 \leftarrow \text{Subtract as usual.}
\end{array}
$$

(c) 12 less 5.83

12.00 is equivalent to 12

$$
\begin{array}{r}
\mathbf{12.00} \leftarrow \text{Write a decimal point and two zeros.} \\
-\ 5.83 \\
\hline
6.17 \leftarrow \text{Subtract as usual.}
\end{array}
$$

◀ **Work Problem 4 at the Side.**

📖 **Calculator Tip**

If you are *adding* decimal numbers, you can enter them in any order on your calculator. Try these; jot down the answers.

9.82 ⊕ 1.86 ⊜ _____   1.86 ⊕ 9.82 ⊜ _____

The answers are the same because addition is *commutative*. But subtraction is *not* commutative. It *does* matter which number you enter first. Try these:

9.82 ⊖ 1.86 ⊜ _____   1.86 ⊖ 9.82 ⊜ _____

The answers are 7.96 and −7.96. As you know, positive numbers are *greater* than 0, but negative numbers are *less* than 0. So it is important to do subtraction in the correct order, particularly for your bank account!

OBJECTIVE **2** **Add and subtract negative decimals.** The rules that you used to add integers in **Chapter 1** will also work for positive and negative decimal numbers.

Adding Signed Numbers

To add two numbers with the *same* sign, add the absolute values of the numbers. Use the common sign as the sign of the sum.

To add two numbers with *unlike* signs, subtract the lesser absolute value from the greater absolute value. Use the sign of the number with the greater absolute value as the sign of the sum.

| EXAMPLE 5 | Adding Positive and Negative Decimal Numbers |

Find each sum.

(a) $-3.7 + (-16)$

Both addends are negative, so the sum will be negative. To begin, $|-3.7|$ is 3.7 and $|-16|$ is 16. Then add the absolute values.

$$\begin{array}{r} 3.7 \\ +\ 16.\underline{0} \\ \hline 19.7 \end{array} \leftarrow \text{Write a decimal point and one 0}$$

$$\underset{\underset{\text{Both negative}}{\uparrow}}{-}3.7 + (\underset{\uparrow}{-}16) = \underset{\underset{\text{Negative sum}}{\uparrow}}{-}19.7$$

Note

We will continue to write parentheses around negative numbers when the negative sign might be confused with other symbols. Thus in **Example 5(a)** above,

$-3.7 + (-16)$ means   **negative** 3.7   **plus**   **negative** 16

(b) $-5.23 + 0.792$

The addends have different signs. To begin, $|-5.23|$ is 5.23 and $|0.792|$ is 0.792. Then subtract the lesser absolute value from the greater.

$$\begin{array}{r} 5.23\underline{0} \\ -\ 0.792 \\ \hline 4.438 \end{array} \leftarrow \text{Write one 0}$$

$$\underset{\underset{\substack{\text{Number with} \\ \text{greater absolute} \\ \text{value is negative.}}}{\uparrow}}{-}5.23 + 0.792 = \underset{\underset{\substack{\text{Answer is} \\ \text{negative.}}}{\uparrow}}{-}4.438$$

·················· **Work Problem ❺ at the Side.** ▶

In **Chapter 1** you rewrote subtraction of integers as addition of the first number to the opposite of the second number. This same strategy works with positive and negative decimal numbers.

| EXAMPLE 6 | Subtracting Positive and Negative Decimal Numbers |

Find each difference.

(a) $4.3 - 12.73$

Rewrite subtraction as adding the opposite.

$$\underset{\downarrow}{4.3} \underset{\downarrow}{-} \underset{\downarrow}{12.73} \qquad \boxed{\begin{array}{l}\text{The opposite of}\\ 12.73 \text{ is } -12.73\end{array}}$$

$$4.3 + (-12.73)$$

-12.73 has the greater absolute value and is negative, so the answer will be negative.

$$4.3 + (-12.73) = \underset{\underset{\substack{\text{Answer is} \\ \text{negative.}}}{\uparrow}}{-}8.43 \qquad \begin{array}{l}\text{Subtract the absolute values.} \\ \quad 12.73 \\ \underline{-\ \ 4.30} \\ \quad\ 8.43 \end{array}$$

❺ Find each sum.

ⓖⓢ (a) $13.245 + (-18)$

$$|13.245| \text{ is } \underline{\hspace{1cm}}$$

$$|-18| \text{ is } \underline{\hspace{1cm}}$$

Now subtract the lesser absolute value from the greater.

$$\begin{array}{r} 1\ 8\ .\ 0\ 0\ 0 \\ -\ 1\ 3\ .\ 2\ 4\ 5 \\ \hline \underline{\hspace{0.3cm}}\ \underline{\hspace{0.3cm}}\ .\ \underline{\hspace{0.3cm}}\ \underline{\hspace{0.3cm}}\ \underline{\hspace{0.3cm}} \end{array} \begin{array}{l}\leftarrow \text{Write a}\\ \text{decimal point}\\ \text{and three 0s.}\end{array}$$

The number with the greater absolute value is negative,

so the answer is _____.

$$13.245 + (-18) = \underline{\hspace{1cm}}$$

(b) $-0.7 + (-0.33)$

(c) $-6.02 + 100.5$

·················· **Continued on Next Page**

6 Find each difference.

(a) $-0.37 - (-6)$

$\quad\quad\;\downarrow\quad\;\downarrow\quad$ Rewrite

$-0.37 + \;\;6\quad$ subtraction as adding the opposite.

(b) $5.8 - \quad 10.03$

$\quad\;\;\downarrow\quad\quad\quad\downarrow$

$5.8 + (-10.03)$

(c) $-312.72 - 65.7$

(d) $0.8 - (6 - 7.2)$ Work inside parentheses first.

(b) $-3.65 - (-4.8)$

Rewrite subtraction as adding the opposite.

$$-3.65 - (-4.8)$$
$$\quad\;\;\downarrow\quad\;\;\downarrow$$
$$-3.65 + 4.8$$

The opposite of -4.8 is 4.8

4.8 has the greater absolute value and is positive, so the answer will be positive.

$$-3.65 + 4.8 = 1.15 \quad\quad \text{Subtract the absolute values.}$$

$$\uparrow$$
Answer is positive.

$$\begin{array}{r} 4.80 \\ -3.65 \\ \hline 1.15 \end{array}$$

(c) $14.2 - \underbrace{(1.69 + 0.48)}$ Work inside parentheses first.

$\;\;14.2 - \quad (2.17)\quad$ Change subtraction to adding the opposite.

$\underbrace{14.2 + (-2.17)}$ 14.2 has the greater absolute value and is positive, so the answer will be positive.

$\quad\quad 12.03$

◄ **Work Problem 6 at the Side.**

OBJECTIVE 3 **Estimate the answer when adding or subtracting decimals.** A common error when working decimal problems by hand is to misplace the decimal point in the answer. Or, when using a calculator, you might press the wrong key. Using *front end rounding* to estimate the answer will help you avoid these mistakes. Start by rounding each number to the highest possible place (as you did in **Chapter 1**). Here are several examples. In the rounded numbers, only the leftmost digit is something other than 0.

3.25 rounds to 3		0.812 rounds to 1	
532.6 rounds to 500		26.397 rounds to 30	
7094.2 rounds to 7000		351.24 rounds to 400	

EXAMPLE 7 **Estimating Decimal Answers**

First, use front end rounding to round each number. Then add or subtract the rounded numbers to get an estimated answer. Finally, find the exact answer.

(a) Find the sum of 194.2 and 6.825

Estimate: *Exact:*

$$\begin{array}{r} 200 \\ + \;\;\;7 \\ \hline 207 \end{array} \begin{array}{c} \xleftarrow{\text{Rounds to}} \\ \xleftarrow{\text{Rounds to}} \end{array} \begin{array}{r} 194.200 \\ + \;\;6.825 \\ \hline 201.025 \end{array}$$

The estimate goes out to the hundreds place (three places to the *left* of the decimal point), and so does the exact answer. Therefore, the decimal point is probably in the correct place in the exact answer.

(b) Subtract $13.78 from $69.42

Estimate: *Exact:*

$$\begin{array}{r} \$70 \\ - \;\;10 \\ \hline \$60 \end{array} \begin{array}{c} \xleftarrow{\text{Rounds to}} \\ \xleftarrow{\text{Rounds to}} \end{array} \begin{array}{r} \$69.42 \\ - \;13.78 \\ \hline \$55.64 \end{array}$$

← Exact answer is close to estimate, so it is reasonable.

Answers

6. **(a)** 5.63 **(b)** -4.23 **(c)** -378.42 **(d)** 2

Continued on Next Page

(c) $-1.861 - 7.3$

Rewrite subtraction as adding the opposite. Then use front end rounding to get an estimated answer.

$$-1.861 \quad - \quad 7.3$$
$$\downarrow \qquad \downarrow$$
$$-1.861 \quad + \quad (-7.3)$$
$$\downarrow \qquad \downarrow$$
Rounded $\quad -2 \quad + \quad (-7) \; = \; -9 \leftarrow$ Estimate

To find the exact answer, add the absolute values.

$$1.861 \leftarrow \text{Absolute value of } -1.861$$
$$+ \, 7.300 \leftarrow \text{Absolute value of } -7.3 \text{ with two zeros written in}$$
$$\overline{9.161}$$

The answer will be negative because both numbers are negative.

$$-1.861 + (-7.3) = -9.161 \leftarrow \text{Exact}$$

The exact answer of -9.161 is reasonable because it is close to the estimated answer of -9.

· **Work Problem ⑦ at the Side.** ▶

⑦ Use front end rounding to estimate each answer. Then find the exact answer.

ᴳˢ **(a)** $2.83 + 5.009 + 76.1$

Estimate:		*Exact:*
3	$\longleftarrow$	2.830
5	$\longleftarrow$	5.009
$+ \, 80$	$\longleftarrow$	$+76.100$

(b) $19.28 less $1.53

Estimate: *Exact:*

(c) $11.365 - 38$

Estimate: *Exact:*

(d) $-214.6 + 300.72$

Estimate: *Exact:*

Answers

7. (a) *Estimate:* $3 + 5 + 80 = 88$;
    Exact: 83.939
  (b) *Estimate:* $20 - 2 = 18$;
    Exact: 17.75
  (c) *Estimate:* $10 + (-40) = -30$;
    Exact: -26.635
  (d) *Estimate:* $-200 + 300 = 100$;
    Exact: 86.12

5.3 Exercise

CONCEPT CHECK *Rewrite each addition in columns. Write in any decimal points or zeros, as needed. Do **not** complete the calculation.*

1. $6.42 + 10.163$

2. $7 + 9.204$

3. $20 - 9.1263$

4. $137.06 - 12$

Find each sum. See Examples 1 and 2.

5.
$$\begin{array}{r} 5.69 \\ 0.24 \\ + 11.79 \\ \hline \end{array}$$

6.
$$\begin{array}{r} 372.1 \\ 33.7 \\ + 42.3 \\ \hline \end{array}$$

7. $0.38 + 7 + 4.6$

8. $3.7 + 0.812 + 55$

9. $14.23 + 8 + 74.63 + 18.715 + 0.286$

10. $197.4 + 0.72 + 17.43 + 25 + 1.4$

11. $27.65 + 18.714 + 9.749 + 3.21$

12. $58.546 + 19.2 + 8.735 + 14.58$

13. CONCEPT CHECK Explain and correct the error when $0.72 + 6 + 39.5$ was added this way:
$$\begin{array}{r} 0.72 \\ 6 \\ + 39.50 \\ \hline 40.28 \end{array}$$

14. CONCEPT CHECK Explain and correct the error when $7.21 + 65 + 13.15$ was added this way:
$$\begin{array}{r} 7.21 \\ .65 \\ + 13.15 \\ \hline 21.01 \end{array}$$

15. CONCEPT CHECK Explain why 0.3 is equivalent to 0.3000.

16. CONCEPT CHECK Explain why 7 may be written as 7.0 but not as 0.7.

Find each difference. See Examples 3 and 4.

17. $90.5 - 0.8$

18. $303.72 - 0.68$

19. 0.4 less 0.291

20. 0.35 less 0.088

21. 6 minus 5.09
$$\begin{array}{r} 6.00 \\ - 5.09 \\ \hline \end{array}$$

22. 80 minus 16.3
$$\begin{array}{r} 80.0 \\ -16.3 \\ \hline \end{array}$$

23. Subtract 8.339 from 15

24. Subtract 0.08 from 44

25. Explain and correct the error that a student made when he subtracted 7.45 from 15.32 this way:
$$\begin{array}{r} 7.45 \\ - 15.32 \\ \hline 12.13 \end{array}$$

26. Explain the difference between saying "subtract 2.9 from 8" and saying "2.9 minus 8."

This drawing of a human skeleton shows the average length of the longest bones, in inches. Use the drawing to answer Exercises 27–30.

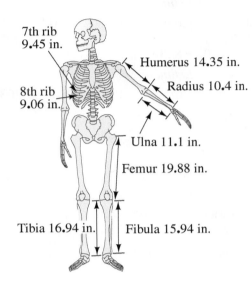

7th rib
9.45 in.

8th rib
9.06 in.

Humerus 14.35 in.

Radius 10.4 in.

Ulna 11.1 in.

Femur 19.88 in.

Tibia 16.94 in.   Fibula 15.94 in.

27. (a) What is the combined length of the humerus and radius bones?

(b) What is the difference in the lengths of these two bones?

28. (a) What is the total length of the femur and tibia bones?

(b) How much longer is the femur than the tibia?

29. (a) Find the sum of the lengths of the humerus, ulna, femur, and tibia.

(b) How much shorter is the 8th rib than the 7th rib?

30. (a) What is the difference in the lengths of the two bones in the lower arm?

(b) What is the difference in the lengths of the two bones in the lower leg?

Find each sum or difference. **See Examples 5 and 6.**

31. $24.008 + (-0.995)$

32. $0.77 + 3.06$

33. $-6.05 + (-39.7)$

34. $-6.409 + 8.224$

35. $0.9 - 7.59$

$0.9 + (-7.59)$

Change subtraction to adding the opposite.

36. $-489.7 - 38$

$-489.7 + (-38)$

Change subtraction to adding the opposite.

37. $-2 - 4.99$

38. $2.068 - (-32.7)$

39. $-5.009 + 0.73$

40. $-0.33 - 65$

41. $-1.7035 - (5 - 6.7)$

42. $60 + (-0.9345 + 1.4)$

43. $8000 - (8002.63 - 8)$

44. $-210 - (-0.7306 + 0.5)$

Use front end rounding to estimate each answer. The first two estimates are done for you. Then use your estimate to select the correct exact answer. Circle your choice. See Example 7.

45. 18 − 11.725

GS   *Estimate:* 20 − 10 = 10

     Exact: 29.725   6.275   −11.545

46. 20 − 1.37

GS   *Estimate:* 20 − 1 = 19

     Exact: −21.37   −1.863   18.63

47. −6.5 + 0.7

     Estimate:

     Exact: −5.8   7.2   −0.58

48. −9.67 + 3.09

     Estimate:

     Exact: −12.76   −6.58   6.58

49. −0.671 − 9

     Estimate:

     Exact: 1.571   8.329   −9.671

50. −803 − 0.6

     Estimate:

     Exact: −803.6   803.6   −203

51. 8.4 − (−50.83)

     Estimate:

     Exact: −42.43   −59.23   59.23

52. 14.98 − (−6.506)

     Estimate:

     Exact: −8.474   21.486   8.004

Use front end rounding to estimate each sum or difference. Then find the exact answer to each application problem. Use the information in the table for Exercises 53–56.

INTERNET USERS IN SELECTED COUNTRIES

Country	Number of Users
China	420 million
United States	239.9 million
Japan	99.14 million
India	81 million
Nigeria	43.98 million
Mexico	30.6 million
Canada	26.2 million
World total	1966.5 million

Source: internetworldstats.com.

53. How many fewer Internet users are there in Mexico than in India?

     Estimate:

     Exact:

54. How many more users are there in China than in Nigeria?

     Estimate:

     Exact:

55. How many Internet users are there in all the countries listed in the table?

     Estimate:

     Exact:

56. Using the exact answer from **Exercise 55,** calculate the number of worldwide Internet users in countries other than the ones in the table.

     Estimate:

     Exact:

57. The tallest known land mammal, a prehistoric ancestor of the rhino, was 6.4 m tall. Compare the rhino's height to the combined heights of these three NBA basketball players: Dirk Nowitzki at 2.13 meters, Kobe Bryant at 1.98 meters, and Kevin Love at 2.08 meters. Is their combined height greater or less than the rhino's height? By how much? (*Source:* NBA.com/players)

6.4 m

Estimate:

Exact:

58. Sammy works in a veterinarian's office. He weighed two kittens. One was 3.9 ounces and the other was 4.05 ounces. What was the difference in the weight of the two kittens?

     Estimate:

     Exact:

59. Steven One Feather gave the cashier a $20 bill to pay for $9.12 worth of groceries. How much change did he get?

     Estimate:

     Exact:

60. The cost of Julie's tennis racket, with tax, was $41.09. She gave the clerk two $20 bills and a $10 bill. What amount of change did Julie receive?

     Estimate:

     Exact:

When buying fishing equipment, the grandfather and grandson on the first page of this chapter brought along the store's sale insert from the Sunday paper. Use the information below on sale prices to answer Exercises 61–64. **When estimating, round prices to the nearest whole number (nearest dollar).**

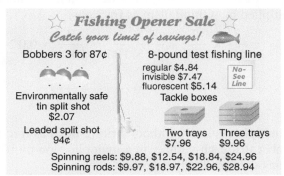

Source: Walmart.

61. What is the difference in price between the fluorescent and regular fishing line?

Estimate:

Exact:

62. How much more does the least expensive spinning rod cost than the least expensive spinning reel?

Estimate:

Exact:

63. Find the total cost of the second-highest-priced spinning reel, two packages of tin split shot, and a three-tray tackle box. Sales tax for all the items is $2.31.

Estimate:

Exact:

64. The grandfather bought three bobbers on sale. He also bought some SPF30 sunscreen for $7.53 and a flotation vest for $44.96. Sales tax was $3.74. How much did he spend in all?

Estimate:

Exact:

Olivia Sanchez kept track of her expenses for one month. Use her list to answer Exercises 65–68.

65. What were Olivia's total expenses for the month?

66. How much did Olivia pay for her cell phone, cable TV, and Internet access?

67. What was the difference in the amounts spent for groceries and for the car payment?

68. How much more did Olivia spend on rent than on all her car expenses?

Monthly Expenses	
Rent	$994
Car payment	$290.78
Car repairs, gas	$205
Cable TV	$49.95
Internet access	$29.95
Electricity	$40.80
Cell phone	$57.32
Groceries	$186.81
Entertainment	$97.75
Clothing, laundry	$107

Find the length of the dashed line in each rectangle or circle.

69.

0.91 cm   0.7 cm b

|← 3 cm →|

70.

z

1.002 meters   1.002 meters

|← 5 meters →|

71.

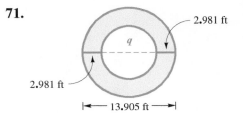

q

2.981 ft

2.981 ft

|← 13.905 ft →|

5.4 Multiplying Signed Decimal Numbers

OBJECTIVE 1 **Multiply positive and negative decimals.** The decimals 0.3 and 0.07 can be multiplied by writing them as fractions.

$$0.3 \times 0.07 = \frac{3}{10} \times \frac{7}{100} = \frac{3 \times 7}{10 \times 100} = \frac{21}{1000} = 0.021$$

1 decimal place + 2 decimal places → 3 decimal places

Can you see a way to multiply decimals without writing them as fractions? Use these steps. Remember that each number in a multiplication problem is called a *factor*, and the answer is called the *product*.

Multiplying Two Decimal Numbers

Step 1 Multiply the factors (the numbers being multiplied) as if they were whole numbers.

Step 2 Find the *total* number of decimal places in *both* factors.

Step 3 Write the decimal point in the product (the answer) so it has the same number of decimal places as the total from *Step 2*. You may need to write in extra zeros on the *left side* of the product in order to get the correct number of decimal places.

Step 4 If two factors have the *same sign,* the product is *positive*. If two factors have *different signs,* the product is *negative*.

Note

When multiplying decimals, you do *not* need to line up decimal points. (You *do* need to line up decimal points when adding or subtracting.)

EXAMPLE 1 **Multiplying Decimal Numbers**

Find the product of 8.34 and (-4.2)

Step 1 Multiply the numbers as if they were whole numbers.

$$
\begin{array}{r}
8.34 \\
\times\ 4.2 \\
\hline
1668 \\
3336\ \ \\
\hline
35028
\end{array}
$$

You do *not* have to line up decimal points when multiplying.

Step 2 Count the total number of decimal places in both factors.

$$
\begin{array}{r}
8.34 \\
\times\ 4.2 \\
\hline
1668 \\
3336\ \ \\
\hline
35028
\end{array}
$$

8.34 ← 2 decimal places
× 4.2 ← 1 decimal place
3 total decimal places

· **Continued on Next Page**

Step 3 Count over 3 places in the product and write the decimal point. Count from *right to left*.

$$
\begin{array}{r}
8.3\,4 \leftarrow \text{2 decimal places} \\
\times \quad 4.2 \leftarrow \text{1 decimal place} \\
\hline
1\,6\,6\,8 \quad \text{3 total decimal places} \\
3\,3\,3\,6 \quad \\
\hline
3\,5.0\,2\,8 \leftarrow \text{3 decimal places in product}
\end{array}
$$

Count over 3 places from right to left
to position the decimal point.

Step 4 The factors have *different* signs, so the product is *negative:* 8.34 times (-4.2) is -35.028

· **Work Problem ❶ at the Side.** ▶

EXAMPLE 2 **Writing Zeros as Placeholders in the Product**

Find the product: $(-0.042)(-0.03)$

Start by multiplying, then count decimal places.

$$
\begin{array}{r}
0.0\,4\,2 \leftarrow \text{3 decimal places} \\
\times \; 0.0\,3 \leftarrow \text{2 decimal places} \\
\hline
1\,2\,6 \leftarrow \text{5 decimal places needed in product}
\end{array}
$$

After multiplying, the answer has only three decimal places, but five are needed. So write two zeros on the *left* side of the answer.

$$
\begin{array}{r}
0.0\,4\,2 \\
\times \; 0.0\,3 \\
\hline
0\,0\,1\,2\,6 \\
\uparrow\;\uparrow
\end{array}
\qquad
\begin{array}{r}
0.0\,4\,2 \leftarrow \text{3 decimal places} \\
\times \; 0.0\,3 \leftarrow \text{2 decimal places} \\
\hline
.0\,0\,1\,2\,6 \leftarrow \text{5 decimal places}
\end{array}
$$

Write two zeros   Now count over 5 places
on *left* side of answer.   and write in the decimal point.

The final product is 0.00126, which has five decimal places. The product is positive because the factors have the *same* sign (both factors are negative).

· **Work Problem ❷ at the Side.** ▶

🖩 **Calculator Tip**

When working with money amounts, you may need to write a 0 in your answer. For example, try multiplying 3.54×5 on your calculator. Write down the result.

$$3.54 \;\otimes\; 5 \;\ominus\; \underline{\hspace{2cm}}$$

Notice that the result is 17.7, which is not the way to write a money amount. You have to write the 0 in the hundredths place: $17.70 is correct. The calculator does not show the "extra" 0 because:

$$17.70 \text{ or } 17\frac{70}{100} \quad \text{simplifies to} \quad 17\frac{7}{10} \text{ or } 17.7$$

So keep an eye on your calculator—it doesn't know when you're working with money amounts.

---

❶ Find each product.

(a) $-2.6(0.4)$

$$
\begin{array}{r}
2.6 \leftarrow \text{1 decimal place} \\
\times\; 0.4 \leftarrow \text{1 decimal place} \\
\hline
1\,0\,4 \leftarrow \text{2 decimal places}
\end{array}
$$

Write in the decimal point. Is the product positive or negative? _____

(b) $(45.2)(0.25)$

(c)
$$
\begin{array}{r}
0.104 \leftarrow \text{3 decimal places} \\
\times \quad\; 7 \leftarrow \text{0 decimal places} \\
\hline
\leftarrow \text{3 decimal places} \\
\text{in the product}
\end{array}
$$

(d) $(-3.18)^2$

Hint: Recall that squaring a number means multiplying the number by itself, so this is $(-3.18)(-3.18)$.

❷ Find each product.

(a) $0.04(-0.09)$

$$
\begin{array}{r}
0.04 \leftarrow \text{2 decimal places} \\
\times\; 0.09 \leftarrow \text{2 decimal places} \\
\hline
\leftarrow \text{4 decimal places}
\end{array}
$$

Is the product positive or negative? _____

(b) $(0.2)(0.008)$

(c) $(-0.063)(-0.04)$

(d) $(0.003)^2$

Answers

1. **(a)** Product is negative; -1.04
   (b) 11.300 or 11.3   **(c)** 0.728   **(d)** 10.1124
2. **(a)** Product is negative; -0.0036
   (b) 0.0016   **(c)** 0.00252   **(d)** 0.000009

3 First, use front end rounding to estimate the answer. Then find the exact answer.

(a) $(11.62)(4.01)$

Estimate:	Exact:
$10 \longleftarrow$	11.62
$\times\ 4 \longleftarrow$	$\times\ 4.01$

(b) $(-5.986)(-33)$

Estimate:　　　Exact:

(c) $8(\$4.35)$

Estimate:　　　Exact:

(d) $58.6(-17.4)$

Estimate:　　　Exact:

OBJECTIVE 2 **Estimate the answer when multiplying decimals.** If you are doing multiplication problems by hand, estimating the answer helps you check that the decimal point is in the right place. When you are using a calculator, estimating helps you catch an error like pressing the ÷ key instead of the × key.

EXAMPLE 3 **Estimating before Multiplying**

First, use front end rounding to estimate $(76.34)(12.5)$. Then find the exact answer.

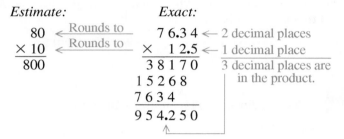

Estimate:	Exact:
$80 \xleftarrow{\text{Rounds to}}$	$76.3\,4 \leftarrow$ 2 decimal places
$\times\ 10 \xleftarrow{\text{Rounds to}}$	$\times\quad 1\,2.5 \leftarrow$ 1 decimal place
800	$3\,8\,1\,7\,0$　3 decimal places are
	$1\,5\,2\,6\,8$　　 in the product.
	$7\,6\,3\,4$
	$9\,5\,4.2\,5\,0$

Both the estimate and the exact answer go out to the hundreds place, so the decimal point in 954.250 is probably in the correct place.

◀ **Work Problem 3** at the Side.

Answers

3. **(a)** *Estimate:* $(10)(4) = 40$;
　　Exact: 46.5962
(b) *Estimate:* $(-6)(-30) = 180$;
　　Exact: 197.538
(c) *Estimate:* $8(\$4) = \$32$;
　　Exact: $34.80
(d) *Estimate:* $60(-20) = -1200$;
　　Exact: $-1019.64

5.4 Exercises Download the MyDashBoard App **MyMathLab®**

CONCEPT CHECK *Fill in the blanks for Exercises 1–4.*

1. In 4.2×3.46, how many decimal places will the product have? _____

2. In 8.071×2.79, how many decimal places will the product have? _____

3. In $(0.12)(0.03)$, how many zeros do you have to write in the product as placeholders? _____

4. In $(0.0006)(0.07)$, how many zeros do you have to write in the product as placeholders? _____

Find each product. See Example 1.

5. 0.042
$\times$ 3.2

6. 0.571
$\times$ 2.9

7. $-21.5(7.4)$

8. $-85.4(-3.5)$

9. $(-23.4)(-0.66)$

10. $0.896(-0.7)$

11. $51.88
$\times$ 665

12. $736.75
$\times$ 118

CONCEPT CHECK *Use the fact that $(72)(6) = 432$ to solve Exercises 13–18 by simply counting decimal places and writing the decimal point in the correct location. Be sure to indicate the sign of the product.*

13. $72(-0.6) =$ 4 3 2

14. $7.2(-6) =$ 4 3 2

15. $(7.2)(0.06) =$ 4 3 2

16. $(0.72)(0.6) =$ 4 3 2

17. $-0.72(-0.06) =$ 4 3 2

18. $-72(-0.0006) =$ 4 3 2

Find each product. See Example 2.

19. $(0.006)(0.0052)$

20. $(0.0052)(0.009)$

21. $(-0.003)^2$

22. $(0.0004)^2$

First, use front end rounding to estimate the answer. Then find the exact answer.
See Example 3.

23. The *Estimate* is already done. Now find the *Exact* answer.

Estimate: *Exact:*
   40 $\xleftarrow{\text{Rounds to}}$ 39.6
$\times$ 5 $\xleftarrow{\text{Rounds to}}$ $\times$ 4.8
  200

24. The *Estimate* is already done. Now find the *Exact* answer.

Estimate: *Exact:*
   20 $\xleftarrow{\text{Rounds to}}$ 18.7
$\times$ 2 $\xleftarrow{\text{Rounds to}}$ $\times$ 2.3
   40

25. *Estimate:*   *Exact:*
                   37.1
    $\times$ $\times$ 42

26. *Estimate:*   *Exact:*
                   5.08
    $\times$ $\times$ 71

27. *Estimate:*   *Exact:*
                   6.53
    $\times$ $\times$ 4.6

28. *Estimate:*   *Exact:*
                   7.51
    $\times$ $\times$ 8.2

29. *Estimate:*   *Exact:*
                   2.809
    $\times$ $\times$ 6.85

30. *Estimate:*   *Exact:*
                   73.52
    $\times$ $\times$ 22.34

Even with most of the problem missing, you can tell whether or not these answers are reasonable. Circle reasonable *or* unreasonable. *If the answer is unreasonable, move the decimal point or insert a decimal point to make the answer reasonable.*

31. How much was his car payment? $28.90

reasonable

unreasonable, should be _____

32. How many hours did she work today? 25 hours

reasonable

unreasonable, should be _____

33. How tall is her son? 60.5 inches

reasonable

unreasonable, should be _____

34. How much does he pay for rent now? $6.92

reasonable

unreasonable, should be _____

35. What is the price of one gallon of milk? $419

reasonable

unreasonable, should be _____

36. How long is the living room? 16.8 feet

reasonable

unreasonable, should be _____

37. How much did the baby weigh? 0.095 pound

reasonable

unreasonable, should be _____

38. What was the sale price of the jacket? $1.49

reasonable

unreasonable, should be _____

Solve each application problem. Round money answers to the nearest cent when necessary.

39. LaTasha worked 50.5 hours over the last two weeks. She earns $18.73 per hour. How much did she make?

40. Michael's time card shows 42.2 hours at $10.03 per hour. What are his earnings?

41. Sid needs a piece of canvas material 0.6 meter in length to make a carry-all bag that fits on his wheelchair. If canvas is $4.09 per meter, how much will Sid spend? (*Note:* $4.09 *per* meter means $4.09 for *one* meter.)

42. How much will Mrs. Nguyen pay for 3.5 yards of lace trim that costs $0.87 per yard?

43. Michelle filled the tank of her SUV with regular unleaded gas. Use the information shown on the pump to find how much she paid for gas.

GALLONS	PRICE PER GALLON	GALLONS	PRICE PER GALLON
10.329	$ 3.979	20.510	$ 3.759
SUPRA UNLEADED Minimum Octane Rating 90		UNLEADED REGULAR Minimum Octane Rating 87	

Source: Holiday.

44. Ground beef and chicken legs are on sale. Juma bought 1.7 pounds of legs. Use the information in the ad to find the amount she paid.

BIG ONE FOODS Sale

Ground Beef $2.09 per pound For juicy burgers

Chicken Legs $0.98 per pound

PRICES GOOD THROUGH SUNDAY!

45. Ms. Rolack is a real estate broker who helps people sell their homes. Her fee is 0.07 times the price of the home. What was her fee for selling a $289,500 home?

46. Josh Hamilton of the Texas Rangers baseball team had a batting average of 0.359 in the 2010 season. He went to bat 518 times. How many hits did he make? (*Hint:* Multiply the number of times at bat by his batting average.) Round to the nearest whole number.

Paper money in the United States has not always been the same size. Shown below are the measurements of bills printed before 1929 and the measurements from 1929 on. Use this information to answer Exercises 47–50. (Source: moneyfactory.com)

Before 1929
3.125 in.
7.4218 in.

From 1929 on
2.61 in.
6.14 in.

47. (a) Find the area of each bill, rounded to the nearest tenth. (*Hint:* Multiply to find area.)

(b) What is the difference in the rounded areas?

48. (a) Find the perimeter of each bill, to the nearest hundredth. (*Hint:* Add to find perimeter.)

(b) How much less is the perimeter of today's bills than the bills printed before 1929?

49. The thickness of one piece of today's paper money is 0.0043 inch.
(a) If you had a pile of 100 bills, how high would it be?

(b) How high would a pile of 1000 bills be?

50. (a) Use your answers from **Exercise 49** to find the number of bills in a pile that is 43 inches high.

(b) How much money would you have if the pile is all $20 bills?

51. Judy Lewis pays $48.96 per month for basic cable TV. The one-time installation fee was $89. How much will she pay for cable over two years? How much would she pay in two years for the deluxe cable package that costs $109.78 per month, plus the installation fee?

52. Chuck's car payment is $420.27 per month for four years. He also made a down payment of $5000 at the time he bought the car. How much will he pay altogether?

53. Barry bought 16.5 meters of rope at $0.47 per meter and three meters of wire at $1.05 per meter. How much change did he get from three $5 bills?

54. Susan bought a 46-inch LED Smart HDTV that cost $1249.97. She paid $66.59 per month for 24 months. How much could she have saved by paying for the HDTV when she bought it?

*Use the information below from the Look Smart online catalog to answer
Exercises 55–56. Disregard sales tax.*

Knit Shirt Ordering Information		
43–2A	short sleeved, solid colors	$14.75 each
43–2B	short sleeved, stripes	$16.75 each
43–3A	long sleeved, solid colors	$18.95 each
43–3B	long sleeved, stripes	$21.95 each
XXL size, add $2 per shirt.		
Monogram, $4.95 each. Gift box, $5 each.		

Total Price of Items (excluding monograms and gift boxes)	Shipping, Packing, and Handling
$0–25.00	$5.50
$25.01–75.00	$7.95
$75.01–125.005	$9.95
$125.01+	$11.95
Shipping to each additional address, add $4.25.	

43–2A 43–2B

43–3A 43–3B

55. (a) What is the total cost, including shipping, of sending three short-sleeved, solid-color shirts, size M, with monograms, in a gift box to your aunt for her birthday?

(b) How much did the monograms, gift box, and shipping add to the cost of your gift?

56. (a) Suppose you order one of each type of shirt for yourself, adding a monogram on each of the solid-color shirts. At the same time, you order three long-sleeved striped shirts, in the XXL size, shipped to your dad in a gift box. Find the total cost of your order.

(b) What is the difference in total cost (excluding shipping) between the shirts for yourself and the gift for your dad?

Relating Concepts (Exercises 57–58) For Individual or Group Work

*Look for patterns as you **work Exercises 57 and 58 in order.***

57. Do these multiplications:

$(5.96)(10) = $ _____ $(3.2)(10) = $ _____

$(0.476)(10) = $ _____ $(80.35)(10) = $ _____

$(722.6)(10) = $ _____ $(0.9)(10) = $ _____

What pattern do you see? Write a "rule" for multiplying by 10. What do you think the rule is for multiplying by 100? by 1000? Write the rules and try them out on the numbers above.

58. Do these multiplications:

$(59.6)(0.1) = $ _____ $(3.2)(0.1) = $ _____

$(0.476)(0.1) = $ _____ $(80.35)(0.1) = $ _____

$(65)(0.1) = $ _____ $(523)(0.1) = $ _____

What pattern do you see? Write a "rule" for multiplying by 0.1. What do you think the rule is for multiplying by 0.01? by 0.001? Write the rules and try them out on the numbers above.

5.5 Dividing Signed Decimal Numbers

There are two kinds of decimal division problems: those in which a decimal is divided by an integer, and those in which a number is divided by a decimal. First recall the parts of a division problem.

OBJECTIVES

1 Divide a decimal by an integer.

2 Divide a number by a decimal.

3 Estimate the answer when dividing decimals.

4 Use the order of operations with decimals.

$$\overset{8 \leftarrow \text{Quotient}}{\underset{\text{Divisor} \rightarrow}{2)\overline{16}} \leftarrow \text{Dividend}}$$

$$\overset{\text{Dividend}}{\underset{\text{Quotient}}{16 \div 2 = 8}} \overset{\text{Divisor}}{}$$

$$\underset{\text{Divisor} \rightarrow}{\overset{\text{Dividend} \rightarrow}{\frac{16}{2}}} = 8 \underset{\text{Quotient}}{}$$

OBJECTIVE 1 **Divide a decimal by an integer.** When the divisor is an integer, use these steps.

Dividing a Decimal Number by an Integer

Step 1 Write the decimal point in the quotient (answer) directly above the decimal point in the dividend.

Step 2 Divide as if both numbers were whole numbers.

Step 3 If both numbers have the *same sign*, the quotient is *positive*. If they have *different signs*, the quotient is *negative*.

EXAMPLE 1 Dividing Decimals by Integers

Find each quotient. Check the quotients by multiplying.

(a) $\underset{\text{Dividend}}{\underbrace{21.93}} \div \overset{\text{Divisor}}{(-3)}$

First consider $21.93 \div 3$. $\qquad 3)\overline{21.93}$

Decimal points lined up

Step 1 Write the decimal point in the quotient directly above the decimal point in the dividend.

$$3)\overline{21.93}$$

Step 2 Divide as if the numbers were whole numbers.

Check by multiplying the quotient times the divisor.

$$\begin{array}{r} 7.31 \\ 3)\overline{21.93} \end{array}$$

Matches, so 7.31 is correct.

CHECK

$$\begin{array}{r} 7.31 \\ \times \quad 3 \\ \hline 21.93 \end{array}$$

Step 3 The quotient is -7.31 because the numbers have *different* signs.

$$\underset{\text{Different signs}}{\underset{\uparrow}{21.93}} \div (-3) = \underset{\text{Negative quotient}}{\underset{\uparrow}{-7.31}}$$

Different signs, negative quotient.

Continued on Next Page

1 Divide. Check the quotients by multiplying.

(a) $4\overline{)93.6}$

$\begin{array}{r} 23.\_\_ \\ \underline{8} \\ 13 \\ \underline{12} \\ 1 \end{array}$

Finish the division. Then multiply the quotient by 4. If you get 93.6, the quotient is correct.

(b) $6\overline{)6.804}$

(c) $\dfrac{278.3}{11}$

(d) $-0.51835 \div 5$

Different signs; *negative* quotient

(e) $-213.45 \div (-15)$

Same sign; *positive* quotient

Answers

1. (a) 23.4;
CHECK $(23.4)(4) = 93.6$
(b) 1.134;
CHECK $(1.134)(6) = 6.804$
(c) 25.3;
CHECK $(25.3)(11) = 278.3$
(d) −0.10367;
CHECK $(-0.10367)(5) = -0.51835$
(e) 14.23;
CHECK $(14.23)(-15) = -213.45$

(b)

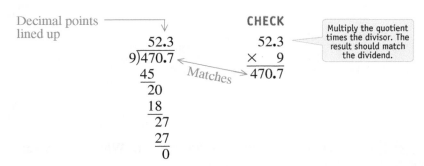

Write the decimal point in the quotient directly above the decimal point in the dividend. Then divide as if they were whole numbers.

Decimal points lined up

$\begin{array}{r} 52.3 \\ 9\overline{)470.7} \\ \underline{45} \\ 20 \\ \underline{18} \\ 27 \\ \underline{27} \\ 0 \end{array}$ Matches

CHECK

$\begin{array}{r} 52.3 \\ \times \quad 9 \\ \hline 470.7 \end{array}$

Multiply the quotient times the divisor. The result should match the dividend.

The quotient is **52.3** and is *positive* because both numbers have the *same* sign.

◀ **Work Problem 1** at the Side.

EXAMPLE 2 Writing Extra Zeros to Complete a Division

Divide 1.5 by 8. Use multiplying to check the quotient.

Keep dividing until the remainder is 0, or until the digits in the quotient begin to repeat in a pattern. In **Example 1(b)** above, you ended up with a remainder of 0. But sometimes you run out of digits in the dividend before that happens. If so, write extra zeros on the right side of the dividend so you can continue dividing.

$\begin{array}{r} 0.1 \\ 8\overline{)1.5} \\ \underline{8} \\ 7 \end{array}$ ← All digits have been used.

← Remainder is not yet 0.

Write a 0 after the 5 in the dividend so you can continue dividing. Keep writing more zeros in the dividend if needed. Recall that writing zeros to the *right* of a decimal number does **not** change its value.

CHECK

$\begin{array}{r} 0.1875 \\ \times \qquad 8 \\ \hline 1.5000 \end{array}$

Use multiplication to check the quotient.

Matches dividend, so 0.1875 is correct.

0 ← Stop dividing when the remainder is 0.

CAUTION

Notice that in decimals the dividend might *not* be the *greater* number. In **Example 2** above, the dividend is 1.5, which is *less* than 8.

⋯⋯⋯⋯⋯⋯⋯⋯⋯⋯⋯⋯⋯⋯⋯⋯⋯⋯ **Continued on Next Page**

▦ **Calculator Tip**

When *multiplying* numbers, you can enter them in any order because multiplication is commutative. But division is *not* commutative. It *does* matter which number you enter first. Try **Example 2** on the previous page both ways; jot down your answers.

1.5 ⊘ 8 ⊜ _____   8 ⊘ 1.5 ⊜ _____

Notice that the first answer, 0.1875, matches the result from **Example 2**. But the second answer is much different: 5.333333333. Be careful to enter the dividend first.

··· **Work Problem ❷ at the Side.** ▶

In the next example the remainder is never 0, even if we keep dividing.

EXAMPLE 3   **Rounding a Decimal Quotient**

Divide 4.7 by 3. Round the quotient to the nearest thousandth.

Write extra zeros in the dividend so that you can continue dividing.

$$
\begin{array}{r}
1.5\,6\,6\,6 \\
3\overline{)4.7\,0\,0\,0} \quad \leftarrow\text{Three zeros added so far} \\
\underline{3} \\
1\,7 \\
\underline{1\,5} \\
2\,0 \\
\underline{1\,8} \\
2\,0 \\
\underline{1\,8} \\
2\,0 \\
\underline{1\,8} \\
2 \quad \leftarrow\text{Remainder is still not 0.}
\end{array}
$$

Notice that the digit 6 in the quotient is repeating. It will continue to do so. The remainder will *never be 0*. There are two ways to show that an answer is a **repeating decimal** that goes on forever. You can write three dots after the answer, or you can write a bar above the digits that repeat (in this case, the 6).

1.5$\underbrace{666}$ ...   or   1.5$\overline{6}$ ← Bar above repeating digit
      Three dots

CAUTION

Do not use *both* the dots *and* the bar at the same time. Use three dots *or* the bar.

When repeating decimals occur, write the quotient according to the directions in the problem. In this example, to round to thousandths, divide out one *more* place, to ten-thousandths.

4.7 ÷ 3 = 1.5666...   rounds to   1.567 ← Nearest **thousandth** is **three** decimal places.

Check the answer by multiplying 1.567 by 3. Because 1.567 is a rounded answer, the check will *not* give exactly 4.7, but it should be very close.

(1.567)(3) = 4.701 ← Does not equal exactly 4.7 because 1.567 was rounded

··· **Continued on Next Page**

❷ Divide. Check the quotients by multiplying.

ᴳˢ **(a)** $\dfrac{6.4}{5}$ → $5\overline{)6\,.\,4\,\,0}$

Finish the division.

(b) $30.87 \div (-14)$

(c) $\dfrac{-259.5}{-30}$

(d) $0.3 \div 8$

Answers

2. **(a)** 1.28;
   CHECK (1.28)(5) = 6.40 or 6.4
   (b) −2.205;
   CHECK (−2.205)(−14) = 30.870
        or 30.87
   (c) 8.65;
   CHECK (8.65)(−30) = −259.50
        or −259.5
   (d) 0.0375;
   CHECK (0.0375)(8) = 0.3000 or 0.3

❸ Divide. Round quotients to the 🖩 nearest thousandth. If it is a repeating decimal, also write the answer using a bar. Check your answers by multiplying.

ᴳˢ (a) $13\overline{)267.01}$

Use your calculator.

$267.01 \div 13 \approx$ _____

Is the quotient a repeating decimal? _____

So round your answer to the nearest thousandth. _____

(b) $6\overline{)20.5}$

(c) $\dfrac{10.22}{9}$

(d) $16.15 \div 3$

(e) $116.3 \div 11$

CAUTION

When checking quotients that you've rounded, the check will *not* match the dividend exactly, but it should be very close.

················◀ **Work Problem ❸ at the Side.**

OBJECTIVE ▶ ❷ Divide a number by a decimal. To divide by a *decimal* divisor, first change the divisor to a whole number. Then divide as before. To see how this is done, write the problem in fraction form. Here is an example.

$$1.2\overline{)6.36} \quad \text{can be written} \quad \frac{6.36}{1.2}$$

In **Chapter 4** you learned that multiplying the numerator and denominator by the same number gives an equivalent fraction. We want the divisor (1.2) to be a whole number. Multiplying by 10 will accomplish that.

$$\text{Decimal divisor} \rightarrow \frac{6.36}{1.2} = \frac{(6.36)(10)}{(1.2)(10)} = \frac{63.6}{12} \leftarrow \text{Whole number divisor}$$

The short way to multiply by 10 is to move the decimal point *one place* to the *right* in both the divisor and the dividend.

$$1.2\overline{)6.36} \quad \text{is equivalent to} \quad 12\overline{)63.6}$$

Note

Moving the decimal points the ***same*** number of places to the right in ***both*** the divisor and dividend will ***not*** change the answer.

Dividing by a Decimal Number

Step 1 Count the number of decimal places in the divisor and move the decimal point that many places to the *right*. (This changes the divisor to a whole number.)

Step 2 Move the decimal point in the dividend the *same* number of places to the *right*. (Write in extra zeros if needed.)

Step 3 Write the decimal point in the quotient directly above the decimal point in the dividend. Then divide as usual.

Step 4 If both numbers have the *same sign,* the quotient is *positive.* If they have *different signs,* the quotient is *negative.*

Answers

3. (a) 20.5392; no repeating digits visible on calculator; 20.539 (rounded)
   CHECK $(20.539)(13) = 267.007$
(b) 3.417; $3.41\overline{6}$;
   CHECK $(3.417)(6) = 20.502$
(c) 1.136; $1.13\overline{5}$;
   CHECK $(1.136)(9) = 10.224$
(d) 5.383; $5.38\overline{3}$;
   CHECK $(5.383)(3) = 16.149$
(e) 10.573; $10.5\overline{72}$;
   CHECK $(10.573)(11) = 116.303$

EXAMPLE 4   **Dividing by Decimal Numbers**

(a) $\dfrac{27.69}{0.003}$

Move the decimal point in the divisor *three* places to the *right* so that 0.003 becomes the whole number 3. In order to move the decimal point in the dividend the same number of places, write in an extra 0.

Move decimal points in divisor and dividend. Then line up decimal point in the quotient.

Moving decimal point three places is the same as multiplying by 1000

$$9230.$$
$$3\overline{)27690.}$$
Divide as usual.

(b) Divide -5 by -4.2 and round the quotient to the nearest hundredth.

First consider $5 \div 4.2$. Move the decimal point in the divisor one place to the right so that 4.2 becomes the whole number 42. The decimal point in the dividend starts on the right side of 5 and is also moved one place to the right.

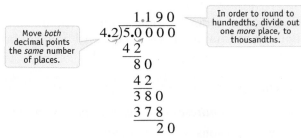

Move *both* decimal points the *same* number of places.

In order to round to hundredths, divide out one *more* place, to thousandths.

Rounding the quotient to the nearest hundredth gives 1.19. The quotient is *positive* because both the divisor and dividend have the *same* sign (both are negative).

$$-5 \div (-4.2) \approx 1.19$$

Same sign — Positive quotient

··· **Work Problem ④ at the Side.** ▶

OBJECTIVE ③ **Estimate the answer when dividing decimals.** Estimating the answer to a division problem helps you catch errors. Compare the estimate to your exact answer. If they are very different, do the division again.

④ Divide. If the quotient does not come out even, round to the nearest hundredth.

(a) $0.2\overline{)1.04}$

(b) $0.06\overline{)1.8072}$

(c) $0.005\overline{)32}$

(d) $-8.1 \div 0.025$

(e) $\dfrac{7}{1.3}$

(f) $-5.3091 \div (-6.2)$

Answers

4. **(a)** 5.2 **(b)** 30.12 **(c)** 6400
(d) -324 **(e)** 5.38 (rounded)
(f) 0.86 (rounded)

5 Decide whether each answer is reasonable by using front end rounding to estimate the answer. If the exact answer is *not* reasonable, find and correct the error.

GS **(a)** $42.75 \div 3.8 = 1.125$

Estimate: $40 \div 4 = 10$

Answer of 1.125 is **not** reasonable. Rework.

$3.8\overline{)42.75}$

(b) $807.1 \div 1.76 = 458.580$ to nearest thousandth

Estimate:

(c) $48.63 \div 52 = 93.519$ to nearest thousandth

Estimate:

(d) $9.0584 \div 2.68 = 0.338$

Estimate:

Answers

5. (a) Exact answer should be 11.25
   (b) Estimate is $800 \div 2 = 400$; exact answer is reasonable.
   (c) Estimate is $50 \div 50 = 1$; exact answer is not reasonable, should be 0.935
   (d) Estimate is $9 \div 3 = 3$; exact answer is not reasonable, should be 3.38

EXAMPLE 5 **Estimating before Dividing**

First, use front end rounding to estimate the answer. Then divide to find the exact answer.

$$580.44 \div 2.8$$

Here is how one student solved this problem. She rounded 580.44 to 600 and 2.8 to 3 to estimate the answer.

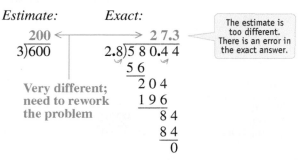

Estimate:

$$\begin{array}{r} 200 \\ 3\overline{)600} \end{array}$$

Very different; need to rework the problem

Exact:

$$\begin{array}{r} 27.3 \\ 2.8\overline{)580.44} \\ 56 \\ \hline 204 \\ 196 \\ \hline 84 \\ 84 \\ \hline 0 \end{array}$$

The estimate is too different. There is an error in the exact answer.

Notice that the estimate, which is in the hundreds, is very different from the exact answer, which is only in the tens. This tells the student that she needs to rework the problem. Can you find the error?
(The exact answer should be 207.3, which fits with the estimate of 200.)

◀ **Work Problem 5 at the Side.**

OBJECTIVE ▶ 4 **Use the order of operations with decimals.** Use the order of operations from **Chapter 1** when a decimal problem involves more than one operation.

Order of Operations

Step 1 Work inside *parentheses* or *other grouping symbols.*

Step 2 Simplify expressions with *exponents.*

Step 3 Do the remaining *multiplications and divisions* as they occur from left to right.

Step 4 Do the remaining *additions and subtractions* as they occur from left to right.

EXAMPLE 6 **Using the Order of Operations**

Simplify by using the order of operations.

(a) $2.5 + \underbrace{(-6.3)^2} + 9.62$ Apply the exponent: $(-6.3)(-6.3)$ is 39.69

$\underbrace{2.5 + 39.69} + 9.62$ Add from left to right.

$\underbrace{42.19 \qquad + 9.62}$

51.81

(b) $1.82 + \underbrace{(5.2 - 6.7)}(5.8)$ Work inside parentheses.

$1.82 + \underbrace{(-1.5) \ (5.8)}$ Multiply next.

$1.82 + \underbrace{(-8.7)}$ Add last.

-6.88

························· **Continued on Next Page**

(c) $\underbrace{3.7^2} - 1.8 \div 5(1.5)$ Apply the exponent.

$13.69 - \underbrace{1.8 \div 5}(1.5)$ Multiply and divide from *left to right*, so first divide 1.8 by 5

$13.69 - \underbrace{0.36\,(1.5)}$ Multiply 0.36 by 1.5   Careful! Do **not** subtract yet.

$13.69 - \underbrace{\quad 0.54 \quad}$ Subtract last.

$\underbrace{\qquad\qquad 13.15}$

·········· **Work Problem 6 at the Side.** ▶

🖩 Calculator Tip

You may want to use a calculator to check your work. Most calculators that have parentheses keys can handle calculations like those in **Example 6(b)** on the previous page just by entering the numbers in the order given. For example, the keystrokes for **Example 6(b)** are:

Parentheses

1.82 ⊕ ⦅ 5.2 ⊖ 6.7 ⦆ ⊗ 5.8 ⊜   Answer is -6.88

Standard, four-function calculators generally do *not* give the correct answer if you enter the numbers in the order given. Check the instruction manual that came with your calculator or look it up online. See if your model has the rules for order of operations built into it. For a quick check, try entering this problem:

2 ⊕ 2 ⊗ 2 ⊜

If the result is 6, the calculator follows the order of operations. If the result is 8, it does *not* have the rules built into it. Use the space below to explain how this test works.

Answer: The test works because a calculator that follows the order of operations will automatically do the multiplication first. If the calculator does *not* have the rules built into it, it will work from left to right.

Following Order of Operations	**Working from Left to Right**
$2 + \underbrace{2 \times 2}$ Multiply before adding.	$\underbrace{2 + 2} \times 2$
$\underbrace{2 + \quad 4}$	$\underbrace{4 \quad \times 2}$
$6 \leftarrow$ Correct	$8 \leftarrow$ Incorrect

---

6 Simplify. The blue brace shows you where to start.

(a) $-4.6 - 0.79 + \underbrace{1.5^2}$

(b) $\underbrace{3.64 \div 1.3}(3.6)$

(c) $0.08 + 0.6\underbrace{(2.99 - 3)}$

(d) $10.85 - \underbrace{2.3(5.2)} \div 3.2$

Answers

6. (a) -3.14 **(b)** 10.08 **(c)** 0.074
    (d) 7.1125

5.5 Exercises

  Download the MyDashBoard App MyMathLab®

1. **CONCEPT CHECK** Which problem below has a whole number for the divisor? Circle it and then rewrite the problem using the $\overline{)}$ symbol.

   Divide 0.25 by 0.05

   $25 \div 0.5$

   $25.5 \div 5$

2. **CONCEPT CHECK** Which problem below has a whole number for the divisor? Circle it and then rewrite the problem using the $\overline{)}$ symbol.

   $0.423 \div 0.07$

   $42.3 \div 7$

   Divide 423 by 0.7

3. **CONCEPT CHECK** In $2.2\overline{)8.24}$ how do you make 2.2 a whole number, and how does that change 8.24? Use arrows to show how to move the decimal points.

4. **CONCEPT CHECK** In $5.1\overline{)10.5}$ how do you make 5.1 a whole number, and how does that change 10.5? Use arrows to show how to move the decimal points.

Find each quotient. **See Examples 1, 2, and 4.**

5. $27.3 \div (-7)$

6. $-50.4 \div 8$

7. $\dfrac{4.23}{9}$

8. $\dfrac{1.62}{6}$

9. $-20.01 \div (-0.05)$

10. $-16.04 \div (-0.08)$

11. $1.5\overline{)54.0}$

12. $2.4\overline{)132.0}$

CONCEPT CHECK *Use the fact that $108 \div 18 = 6$ to work Exercises 13–20 simply by moving decimal points.* **See Examples 1, 2, and 4.**

13. $1.8\overline{)0.108}$

14. $18\overline{)10.8}$

15. $0.018\overline{)108}$

16. $0.18\overline{)1.08}$

17. $0.18\overline{)10.8}$

18. $0.18\overline{)108}$

19. $18\overline{)0.0108}$

20. $1.8\overline{)0.0108}$

Divide. Round quotients to the nearest hundredth when necessary. **See Examples 3 and 4.**

21. $4.6\overline{)116.38}$

22. $2.6\overline{)4.992}$

23. $\dfrac{-3.1}{-0.006}$

24. $\dfrac{-1.7}{0.09}$

Divide. Round quotients to the nearest thousandth. **See Examples 3 and 4.**

25. $-240.8 \div 9$

26. $-76.43 \div (-7)$

27. $0.034\overline{)342.81}$

28. $0.043\overline{)1748.4}$

Decide whether each answer is reasonable *or* unreasonable *by using front end rounding to estimate the answer. If the exact answer is not reasonable, find and correct the error.* **See Example 5.**

29. $37.8 \div 8 = 47.25$

   Estimate:

30. $345.6 \div 3 = 11.52$

   Estimate:

31. $54.6 \div 48.1 \approx 1.135$

Estimate:

32. $2428.8 \div 4.8 = 56$

Estimate:

33. $307.02 \div 5.1 = 6.2$

Estimate:

34. $395.415 \div 5.05 = 78.3$

Estimate:

Solve each application problem. Round money answers to the nearest cent when necessary.

35. Rob has discovered that his daughter's favorite brand of tights are on sale. He decided to buy one pair as a surprise for her. How much did he pay?

36. The bookstore has a special price on notepads. How much did Randall pay for one notepad?

37. It will take 21 months for Aimee to pay off her credit card balance of $1408.68. How much is she paying each month?

38. Marcella Anderson bought a 2.6 meter length of microfiber woven suede fabric for $33.77. How much did she pay per meter? (Cost per meter means the cost for *one* meter.)

39. Darren Jackson earned $476.80 for 40 hours of work. Find his earnings per hour. (Earnings *per* hour means how much he earned for *one* hour.)

40. Adrian Webb bought 108 patio blocks to build a backyard patio. He paid $237.60. Find the cost per block.

41. It took 12.3 gallons of gas to fill the gas tank of Kim's car. She had driven 344.1 miles since her last fill-up. How many miles per gallon did she get? Round to the nearest tenth.

42. Mr. Rodriquez pays $53.19 each month to Household Finance. How many months will it take him to pay off $1436.13?

43. Soup is on sale at six cans for $3.25, or you can purchase individual cans for $0.57. How much will you save per can if you buy six cans? Round to the nearest cent.

44. Nadia's diet says she can eat 3.5 ounces of chicken nuggets. The package weighs 10.5 ounces and contains 15 nuggets. How many nuggets can Nadia eat?

*Use the table of world records for the women's longest long jump (through the year 2010)
to answer Exercises 45–50. To find an average, add up the values you are interested in and
then divide the sum by the number of values. Round your answers to the nearest hundredth.*

Athlete	Country	Year	Length (meters)
Galina Christyakova	USSR	1988	7.52
Jackie Joyner-Kersee	U.S.	1994	7.49
Heike Drechsler	Germany	1992	7.48
Jackie Joyner-Kersee	U.S.	1987	7.45
Jackie Joyner-Kersee	U.S.	1988	7.40
Jackie Joyner-Kersee	U.S.	1991	7.32
Jackie Joyner-Kersee	U.S.	1996	7.20
Chioma Ajunwa	Nigeria	1996	7.12
Fiona May	Italy	2000	7.09
Tatyana Lebedeva	Russia	2004	7.07

Source: CNNSI.com

45. Find the average length of the long jumps made by Jackie Joyner-Kersee.

46. Find the average length of all the long jumps listed in the table.

47. How much longer was the fifth-longest jump than the sixth-longest jump?

48. If the first-place athlete made five jumps of the same length, what would be the total distance jumped?

49. What was the total length jumped by the top three athletes in the table?

50. How much less was the last-place jump than the next-to-last-place jump?

51. For $2.2^2 + (9.5 - 3.1)$ list what you would do, in the correct order, to simplify the expression.

First _____

_____

Second _____

_____

Third _____

52. For $60.41 - (0.4 + 5.07)(3)$ list what you would do, in the correct order, to simplify the expression.

First _____

_____

Second _____

_____

Third _____

*Simplify. **See Example 6.***

53. $7.2 - 5.2 + 3.5^2$

54. $6.2 + 4.3^2 - 9.72$

55. $38.6 + 11.6(10.4 - 13.4)$

56. $2.25 - 1.06(0.85 - 3.95)$

57. $-8.68 - 4.6(10.4) \div 6.4$

58. $25.1 + 11.4 \div 7.5(-3.75)$

59. $33 - 3.2(0.68 + 9) + (-1.3)^2$

60. $0.6 + (-1.89 + 0.11) \div 0.004(0.5)$

61. In 2010, the U.S. Treasury printed about 26,000,000 pieces of paper money each day. The printing presses run 24 hours a day. How many pieces of money are printed, to the nearest whole number:

26,000,000 pieces of paper money are printed each day. (*Source:* moneyfactory.com)

  (a) each hour

  (b) each minute

  (c) each second

62. Mach 1 is the speed of sound. Dividing a vehicle's speed by the speed of sound gives its speed on the Mach scale. In 1997, a specially built car with two 110,000-horsepower engines broke the world land speed record by traveling 763.035 miles per hour. The speed of sound changes slightly with the weather. That day it was 748.11 miles per hour. What was the car's Mach speed, to the nearest hundredth? (*Source:* Associated Press.)

General Mills will give a school 10¢ for each box top logo from its cereals and other products. A school can earn up to $10,000 per year. Use this information to answer Exercises 63–66. Round answers to the nearest whole number. (*Source:* General Mills.)

63. How many box tops would a school need to collect in one year to earn the maximum amount?

64. (Complete **Exercise 63** first.) If a school has 550 children, how many box tops would each child need to collect to reach the maximum?

65. How many box tops would need to be collected during each of the 38 weeks in the school year to reach the maximum amount?

66. How many box tops would each of the 550 children need to collect during each of the 38 weeks of school to reach the maximum amount?

Relating Concepts (Exercises 67–68)

*Look for patterns as you **work Exercises 67 and 68 below.***

67. Do these division problems.

  $3.77 \div 10 =$ _____ $9.1 \div 10 =$ _____

  $0.886 \div 10 =$ _____ $30.19 \div 10 =$ _____

  $406.5 \div 10 =$ _____ $6625.7 \div 10 =$ _____

  (a) What pattern do you see? Write a "rule" for dividing by 10. What do you think the rule is for dividing by 100? by 1000? Write the rules and try them out on the numbers above.

  (b) Compare your rules to the ones you wrote in the **previous section** for **Exercise 57.**

68. Do these division problems.

  $40.2 \div 0.1 =$ _____ $7.1 \div 0.1 =$ _____

  $0.339 \div 0.1 =$ _____ $15.77 \div 0.1 =$ _____

  $46 \div 0.1 =$ _____ $873 \div 0.1 =$ _____

  (a) What pattern do you see? Write a "rule" for dividing by 0.1. What do you think the rule is for dividing by 0.01? by 0.001? Write the rules and try them out on the numbers above.

  (b) Compare your rules to the ones you wrote in the **previous section** for **Exercise 58.**

Summary Exercises *Computation with Decimal Numbers*

CONCEPT CHECK *Write each decimal as a fraction or mixed number in lowest terms.*

1. 0.8

2. 6.004

3. 0.35

Write each decimal in words.

4. 94.5

5. 2.0003

6. 0.706

Write each decimal in numbers.

7. five hundredths

8. three hundred nine ten-thousandths

9. ten and seven tenths

Round to the place indicated.

10. 6.1873 to the nearest hundredth

11. 0.95 to the nearest tenth

12. 0.42025 to the nearest thousandth

13. $0.893 to the nearest cent

14. $3.0017 to the nearest cent

15. $99.64 to the nearest dollar

Simplify.

16. $-0.27(3.5)$

17. $50 - 0.3801$

18. $0.35 \div (-0.007)$

19. $\dfrac{-90.18}{-6}$

20. $(0.004)(1.22)$

21. $1.55 - 3.7$

22. $-0.95 + 10.005$

23. $3.6 + 0.718 + 9 + 5.0829$

24. $32.305 - 40 + 0.7$

25. $-8.9 + 4^2 \div (-0.02)$

26. $(-0.18 + 2.5) + 4(-0.05)$

27. $0.64 \div 16.3$ Round your answer to the nearest hundredth.

Find the perimeter of each figure.

28.

19.75 in.

6.3 in.   6.3 in.

19.75 in.

29.

2 meters   1 meter

0.9 meter

1.7 meters

1.18 meters   0.86 meter

2.095 meters

Solve each application problem.

30. At a bakery, Sue Chee bought $7.42 worth of muffins and $10.09 worth of croissants for a staff party and a $0.69 cookie for herself. How much change did she receive from two $10 bills?

31. A craft cooperative paid $60.32 for enough fabric to make eight baby blankets for their store. They sold the blankets for $18.95 each. How much profit was made on the blankets?

The table below shows information on two tents for camping. Use the table to answer Exercises 32 and 33.

Tents	Coleman Family Dome	Eddie Bauer Dome Tent
Dimensions	13 ft × 13 ft	12 ft × 12 ft
Sleeps	8 campers	6 campers
Sale price	$127	$99

Source: Target.com

32. For the Coleman tent, find:
   (a) the area of the tent floor

   (b) the cost per square foot of floor space, to the nearest cent.

33. Find the same information for the Eddie Bauer tent as you did for the Coleman tent.

Use the information in the table to answer Exercises 34–36.

Animal	Average Weight of Animal (ounces)	Average Weight of Food Eaten Each Day (ounces)
Hamster	3.5	0.4
Queen bee	0.004	?
Hummingbird	?	0.07

Source: NCTM News Bulletin.

34. (a) In how many days will a hamster eat enough food to equal its body weight? Round to the nearest whole number of days.

   (b) If a 140-pound woman ate her body weight of food in the same number of days as the hamster, how much would she eat each day? Round to the nearest tenth.

35. While laying eggs, a queen bee eats eighty times her weight each day. Use this information to fill in one of the missing values in the table.

36. A hummingbird's body weight is about 1.6 times the weight of its daily food intake. Find its body weight.

5.6 Fractions and Decimals

1. Rewrite each fraction so you could do the division by hand. Do **not** complete the division.

GS (a) $\dfrac{1}{9}$ is written $9\overline{)}$

(b) $\dfrac{2}{3}$ is written $\overline{)}$

(c) $\dfrac{5}{4}$ is written $\overline{)}$

(d) $\dfrac{3}{10}$ is written $\overline{)}$

(e) $\dfrac{21}{16}$ is written $\overline{)}$

(f) $\dfrac{1}{50}$ is written $\overline{)}$

Answers

1. (a) $9\overline{)1}$ (b) $3\overline{)2}$ (c) $4\overline{)5}$ (d) $10\overline{)3}$
   (e) $16\overline{)21}$ (f) $50\overline{)1}$

Writing fractions as equivalent decimals can help you do calculations or compare the size of two numbers more easily.

OBJECTIVE ▶ 1 Write fractions as equivalent decimals. Recall from **Chapter 1** that a fraction is one way to show division. For example, $\dfrac{3}{4}$ means $3 \div 4$. If you are doing the division by hand, write it as $4\overline{)3}$. When you do the division, the result is 0.75, the decimal equivalent of $\dfrac{3}{4}$.

Writing a Fraction as an Equivalent Decimal
Step 1   Divide the numerator of the fraction by the denominator.
Step 2   If necessary, round the answer to the place indicated.

◀ **Work Problem 1 at the Side.**

EXAMPLE 1   **Writing Fractions or Mixed Numbers as Decimals**

(a) Write $\dfrac{1}{8}$ as a decimal.

$\dfrac{1}{8}$ means $1 \div 8$. Write it as $8\overline{)1}$. The decimal point in the dividend is on the *right* side of the 1. Write extra zeros in the dividend so you can continue dividing until the remainder is 0.

Decimal points lined up

$$\dfrac{1}{8} \longrightarrow 1 \div 8 \longrightarrow 8\overline{)1} \longrightarrow \begin{array}{r} 0.125 \\ 8\overline{)1.000} \\ \underline{8} \\ 20 \\ \underline{16} \\ 40 \\ \underline{40} \\ 0 \end{array}$$

← Three extra zeros needed

Be careful to divide $8\overline{)1}$, **not** $1\overline{)8}$

← Remainder is 0

Therefore, $\dfrac{1}{8} = 0.125$

To check, write 0.125 as a fraction, then write it in lowest terms.

$$0.125 = \dfrac{125}{1000} \quad \text{In lowest terms:} \quad \dfrac{125 \div 125}{1000 \div 125} = \dfrac{1}{8} \left\{ \begin{array}{l} \text{Original} \\ \text{fraction} \end{array} \right.$$

▦ **Calculator Tip**

When using your calculator to write fractions as decimals, enter the numbers from the top down. Remember that the *order* in which you enter the numbers *does* matter in division. **Example 1(a)** above works like this:

$\dfrac{1}{8}$ ↓ Top down   Enter 1 ⊝ 8 ⊜   Answer is 0.125

What happens if you enter 8 ⊝ 1 ⊜? Do you see why that cannot possibly be correct? (Answer: $8 \div 1 = 8$. A proper fraction like $\dfrac{1}{8}$ *cannot* be equivalent to a whole number.)

············· **Continued on Next Page**

(b) Write $2\frac{3}{4}$ as a decimal.

One method is to divide 3 by 4 to get 0.75 for the fraction part. Then add the whole number part to 0.75.

$$\frac{3}{4} \rightarrow \begin{array}{r} 0.75 \\ 4\overline{)3.00} \\ \underline{2\,8} \\ 20 \\ \underline{20} \\ 0 \end{array}$$

$$\begin{array}{r} 2.00 \leftarrow \text{Whole number part} \\ +\ 0.75 \leftarrow \text{Fraction part} \\ \hline 2.75 \end{array}$$

So, $2\frac{3}{4} = 2.75$ **CHECK** $2.75 = 2\frac{75}{100} = 2\frac{3}{4} \leftarrow$ Lowest terms

Whole number parts match.

A second method is to write $2\frac{3}{4}$ as an improper fraction before dividing numerator by denominator.

$$2\frac{3}{4} = \frac{11}{4}$$

$$\frac{11}{4} \rightarrow 11 \div 4 \rightarrow 4\overline{)11} \rightarrow \begin{array}{r} 2.7\,5 \\ 4\overline{)11.0\,0} \\ \underline{8} \\ 3\,0 \\ \underline{2\,8} \\ 2\,0 \\ \underline{2\,0} \\ 0 \end{array} \leftarrow \text{Two extra zeros needed}$$

Whole number parts match.

So, $2\frac{3}{4} = 2.75$

$\frac{3}{4}$ is equivalent to $\frac{75}{100}$ or 0.75

························· Work Problem **2** at the Side. ▶

EXAMPLE 2   Writing a Fraction as a Decimal with Rounding

Write $\frac{2}{3}$ as a decimal and round to the nearest thousandth.

$\frac{2}{3}$ means $2 \div 3$. To round to thousandths, divide out one *more* place, to ten-thousandths.

$$\frac{2}{3} \rightarrow 2 \div 3 \rightarrow 3\overline{)2} \rightarrow \begin{array}{r} 0.6666 \\ 3\overline{)2.0000} \\ \underline{1\,8} \\ 20 \\ \underline{18} \\ 20 \\ \underline{18} \\ 20 \\ \underline{18} \\ 2 \end{array} \leftarrow \left\{ \begin{array}{l} \text{Four zeros needed} \\ \text{for ten-thousandths} \end{array} \right.$$

Be careful to divide $3\overline{)2}$, **not** $2\overline{)3}$

Written as a repeating decimal, $\frac{2}{3} = 0.\overline{6} \leftarrow$ Bar above repeating digit

Rounded to the nearest thousandth, $\frac{2}{3} \approx 0.667$

························· **Continued on Next Page**

---

2 Write each fraction or mixed number as a decimal.

(a) $\frac{1}{4} \rightarrow \begin{array}{r} 0.\underline{}\,\underline{} \\ 4\overline{)1.\ 0\ 0} \end{array}$ Finish the division.

(b) $2\frac{1}{2} = \frac{5}{2} \rightarrow 2\overline{)5.0}$

(c) $\frac{5}{8}$

(d) $4\frac{3}{5}$

(e) $\frac{7}{8}$

Answers

2. **(a)** 0.25   **(b)** 2.5   **(c)** 0.625
    (d) 4.6   **(e)** 0.875

❸ Write as decimals. Round to the nearest thousandth.

(a) $\dfrac{1}{3}$

(b) $2\dfrac{7}{9} = \dfrac{25}{9} = 25 \div 9$

Now use your calculator to do the division. Round the answer to the nearest thousandth.

(c) $\dfrac{10}{11}$

(d) $\dfrac{3}{7}$

(e) $3\dfrac{5}{6}$

Answers

3. **(a)** $\dfrac{1}{3} \approx 0.333$ **(b)** $2\dfrac{7}{9} \approx 2.778$

(c) $\dfrac{10}{11} \approx 0.909$ **(d)** $\dfrac{3}{7} \approx 0.429$

(e) $3\dfrac{5}{6} \approx 3.833$

▦ **Calculator Tip**

Try **Example 2** on your calculator. Enter 2 ÷ 3. Which answer do you get?

| **0.666666667** | or | **0.666666666** |

Many scientific calculators will show a 7 as the last digit. Because the 6s keep on repeating forever, the calculator automatically rounds in the last decimal place it has room to show. If you have a 10-digit display space, the calculator is rounding as shown below.

0.6666666666 (11 digits)   rounds to   0.666666667

Next digit is *5 or more*, so 6 rounds to 7

Other calculators, especially standard, four-function ones, may *not* round. They cut off, or *truncate,* the extra digits. Such a calculator would show 0.6666666 in the display.

Would this difference in calculators show up when changing $\frac{1}{3}$ to a decimal? Why not? (Answer: The repeating digit is a 3, which is *4 or less,* so it stays as a 3 whether it's rounded or not.)

◀ **Work Problem ❸ at the Side.**

OBJECTIVE ➤ 2 Compare the size of fractions and decimals. You can use a number line to compare fractions and decimals. For example, the number line below shows the space between 0 and 1. The locations of some commonly used fractions are marked, along with their decimal equivalents.

The next number line shows the locations of some commonly used fractions between 0 and 1 that are equivalent to repeating decimals. The decimal equivalents use a bar above repeating digits.

EXAMPLE 3 **Using a Number Line to Compare Numbers**

Use the number lines above to decide whether to write >, <, or = in the blank between each pair of numbers.

(a) 0.6875 _____ 0.625

You learned in **Chapter 1** that the number farther to the right on the number line is the greater number. On the first number line, 0.6875 is to the *right* of 0.625, so use the > symbol.

0.6875 is greater than 0.625   can be written as   0.6875 > 0.625

The larger end of the > symbol faces the greater number.

Continued on Next Page

(b) $\frac{3}{4}$ _____ 0.75

On the first number line, $\frac{3}{4}$ and 0.75 are at the same point on the number line. They are equivalent, so use the = symbol.

$$\frac{3}{4} = 0.75$$

(c) 0.5 _____ 0.$\overline{5}$

On the second number line, 0.5 is to the *left* of 0.$\overline{5}$ (which is actually 0.555 ...), so use the < symbol.

0.5 is less than 0.$\overline{5}$ can be written as   0.5 < 0.$\overline{5}$

> The smaller end of the < symbol points to the lesser number.

(d) $\frac{2}{6}$ _____ 0.$\overline{3}$

Write $\frac{2}{6}$ in lowest terms as $\frac{1}{3}$.
On the second number line you can see that $\frac{1}{3}$ and 0.$\overline{3}$ are equivalent.

$$\frac{1}{3} = 0.\overline{3}$$

························ **Work Problem ④ at the Side.** ▶

You can also compare fractions by first writing each one as a decimal.

EXAMPLE 4   **Arranging Numbers in Order**

Write each group of numbers in order, from least to greatest.

(a) 0.49   0.487   0.4903

It is easier to compare decimals if they are all tenths, or all hundredths, and so on. Because 0.4903 has four decimal places (ten-thousandths), write zeros to the right of 0.49 and 0.487 so they also have four decimal places. Recall that writing zeros to the right of a decimal number does *not* change its value. Then find the least and greatest number of ten-thousandths.

0.49 = 0.4900 = **4900** ten-thousandths ← 4900 is in the middle.
0.487 = 0.4870 = **4870** ten-thousandths ← 4870 is the least.
0.4903 = **4903** ten-thousandths ← 4903 is the greatest.

From least to greatest, the correct order is shown below.
0.487   0.49   0.4903

(b) $2\frac{5}{8}$ 2.63   2.6

Write $2\frac{5}{8}$ as $\frac{21}{8}$ and divide $8\overline{)21}$ to get the decimal form, 2.625. Then, because 2.625 has three decimal places, write zeros so all the numbers have three decimal places.

$2\frac{5}{8}$ = 2.625 = 2 and **625** thousandths ← 625 is in the middle.
2.63 = 2.630 = 2 and **630** thousandths ← 630 is the greatest.
2.6 = 2.600 = 2 and **600** thousandths ← 600 is the least.

From least to greatest, the correct order is shown below.
2.6 $2\frac{5}{8}$ 2.63

························ **Work Problem ⑤ at the Side.** ▶

---

④ Use the number lines on the previous page to help you decide whether to write <, >, or = in each blank.

(a) 0.4375 _____ 0.5

(b) 0.75 _____ 0.6875

(c) 0.625 _____ 0.0625

(d) $\frac{2}{8}$ _____ 0.375

(e) 0.8$\overline{3}$ _____ $\frac{5}{6}$

(f) $\frac{1}{2}$ _____ 0.$\overline{5}$

(g) 0.$\overline{1}$ _____ 0.1$\overline{6}$

(h) $\frac{8}{9}$ _____ 0.$\overline{8}$

(i) 0.$\overline{7}$ _____ $\frac{4}{6}$

(j) $\frac{1}{4}$ _____ 0.25

⑤ Arrange each group in order from least to greatest.

(a) 0.7, 0.703, 0.7029

(b) 6.39, 6.309, 6.401, 6.4

(c) 1.085, $1\frac{3}{4}$, 0.9

(d) $\frac{1}{4}, \frac{2}{5}, \frac{3}{7}$, 0.428

Answers

4. (a) <   (b) >   (c) >   (d) <   (e) =
  (f) <   (g) <   (h) =   (i) >   (j) =
5. (a) 0.7, 0.7029, 0.703
  (b) 6.309, 6.39, 6.4, 6.401
  (c) 0.9, 1.085, $1\frac{3}{4}$ (d) $\frac{1}{4}, \frac{2}{5}$, 0.428, $\frac{3}{7}$

5.6 Exercises

  MyMathLab®

FOR EXTRA HELP

Download the MyDashBoard App

CONCEPT CHECK *In Exercises 1 and 2, circle all the divisions that are correctly set up to convert the given fraction to a decimal. If a division is* **not** *set up correctly, fix it.*

1. (a) $\frac{2}{5} \rightarrow 2\overline{)5}$ **(b)** $\frac{1}{7} \rightarrow 7\overline{)1}$ **(c)** $\frac{3}{8} \rightarrow 8\overline{)3}$ **2. (a)** $\frac{4}{9} \rightarrow 9\overline{)4}$ **(b)** $\frac{1}{3} \rightarrow 1\overline{)3}$ **(c)** $\frac{5}{6} \rightarrow 6\overline{)5}$

CONCEPT CHECK *In Exercises 3 and 4, show the correct division set-up for converting the given fraction to a decimal. Place the decimal points in the dividend and quotient. Then write the first digit in the quotient. Finally, explain what you will do next in order to continue dividing.*

3. $\frac{3}{4} \rightarrow$

4. $\frac{1}{8} \rightarrow$

CONCEPT CHECK *In Exercises 5 and 6, write* greater than *or* less than *between each pair of numbers.*

5. (a) $\frac{2}{5}$ is _____ 0.5

   (b) $\frac{3}{4}$ is _____ 0.6

   (c) 0.2 is _____ $\frac{5}{8}$

6. (a) 0.1 is _____ $\frac{1}{5}$

   (b) $\frac{2}{3}$ is _____ 0.5

   (c) 0.7 is _____ $\frac{1}{2}$

Write each fraction or mixed number as a decimal. Round to the nearest thousandth when necessary. **See Examples 1 and 2.**

7. $\frac{1}{2} \rightarrow 2\overline{)1.0}^{0.\_}$

8. $\frac{1}{4} \rightarrow 4\overline{)1.0\ 0}^{0.\_\ \_}$

9. $\frac{3}{4}$

10. $\frac{1}{10}$

11. $\frac{3}{10}$

12. $\frac{7}{10}$

13. $\frac{9}{10}$

14. $\frac{4}{5}$

15. $\frac{3}{5}$

16. $\frac{2}{5}$

17. $\frac{7}{8}$

18. $\frac{3}{8}$

19. $2\frac{1}{4}$

20. $1\frac{1}{2}$

21. $14\frac{7}{10}$

22. $23\frac{3}{5}$

23. $3\frac{5}{8}$

24. $2\frac{7}{8}$

25. $6\frac{1}{3}$

26. $5\frac{2}{3}$

27. $\frac{5}{6}$

28. $\frac{1}{6}$

29. $1\frac{8}{9}$

30. $5\frac{4}{7}$

Find the decimal or fraction equivalent for each number. Write fractions in lowest terms.

	Fraction	Decimal		Fraction	Decimal
31.	_____	0.4	**32.**	_____	0.75
33.	_____	0.625	**34.**	_____	0.111
35.	_____	0.35	**36.**	_____	0.9
37.	$\frac{7}{20}$	_____	**38.**	$\frac{1}{40}$	_____
39.	_____	0.04	**40.**	_____	0.52
41.	$\frac{1}{5}$	_____	**42.**	$\frac{1}{8}$	_____
43.	_____	0.09	**44.**	_____	0.02

Solve each application problem.

45. The average length of a newborn baby is 20.8 inches. Charlene's baby is 20.08 inches long. Is her baby longer or shorter than the average? By how much?

46. The patient in room 830 is supposed to get 8.3 milligrams of medicine. She was actually given 8.03 milligrams. Did she get too much or too little medicine? What was the difference?

47. Ginny Brown hoped her crops would get $3\frac{3}{4}$ inches of rain this month. The newspaper said the area received 3.8 inches of rain. Was that more or less than Ginny hoped for? By how much?

48. The rats in a medical experiment gained $\frac{3}{8}$ ounce. They were expected to gain 0.3 ounce. Was their actual gain more or less than expected? By how much?

49. The label on the bottle of vitamins says that each capsule contains 0.5 gram of calcium. When checked, each capsule had 0.505 gram of calcium. Was there too much or too little calcium? What was the difference?

50. The glass mirror of the Hubble telescope had to be repaired in space because it would not focus properly. The problem was that the mirror's outer edge had a thickness of 0.6248 cm when it was supposed to be 0.625 cm. Was the edge too thick or too thin? By how much? (*Source:* NASA.)

51. Precision Medical Parts makes an artificial heart valve that must measure between 0.998 centimeter and 1.002 centimeters. Circle the lengths that are acceptable.

1.01 cm   0.9991 cm   1.0007 cm   0.99 cm

52. The white rats in a medical experiment must start out weighing between 2.95 ounces and 3.05 ounces. Circle the weights that can be used.

3.0 ounces   2.995 ounces   3.055 ounces

3.005 ounces

Use the number lines above Example 3 in the text to decide whether to write >, <, *or = between each pair of numbers.* **See Example 3.**

53. (a) 0.3125 _____ 0.375   **(b)** $\dfrac{6}{8}$ _____ 0.75   **(c)** $0.\overline{8}$ _____ $0.8\overline{3}$ **(d)** 0.5 _____ $\dfrac{5}{9}$

54. (a) 0.125 _____ 0.0625   **(b)** $\dfrac{4}{9}$ _____ $\dfrac{3}{6}$ **(c)** 1.0 _____ $\dfrac{4}{4}$ **(d)** $\dfrac{1}{6}$ _____ $0.\overline{1}$

Arrange each group of numbers in order from least to greatest. **See Example 4.**

55. 0.54, 0.5455, 0.5399

56. 0.76, 0.7, 0.7006

57. 5.8, 5.79, 5.0079, 5.804

58. 12.99, 12.5, 13.0001, 12.77

59. 0.628, 0.62812, 0.609, 0.6009

60. 0.27, 0.281, 0.296, 0.3

61. 5.8751, 4.876, 2.8902, 3.88

62. 0.98, 0.89, 0.904, 0.9

63. 0.043, 0.051, 0.006, $\dfrac{1}{20}$

64. 0.629, $\dfrac{5}{8}$, 0.65, $\dfrac{7}{10}$

65. $\dfrac{3}{8}, \dfrac{2}{5}$, 0.37, 0.4001

66. 0.1501, 0.25, $\dfrac{1}{10}, \dfrac{1}{5}$

CONCEPT CHECK *Four boxes of fishing line are in a sale bin. The thicker the line, the stronger it is. The diameter of the fishing line is its thickness. Use the information on the boxes to answer Exercises 67–68.*

67. (a) Which color box has the strongest line? The weakest line?

   (b) What is the difference in line diameter between the weakest and strongest lines?

68. (a) Which color box has the line that is $\frac{1}{125}$ inch in diameter?

   (b) What is the difference in line diameter between the blue and purple boxes?

Some rulers for technical drawings show each inch divided into tenths. Use this scale drawing for Exercises 69–74. Change the measurements on the drawing to decimals and round them to the nearest tenth of an inch.

69. Length **(a)** is _____

70. Length **(b)** is _____

71. Length **(c)** is _____

72. Length **(d)** is _____

73. Length **(e)** is _____

74. Length **(f)** is _____

Relating Concepts (Exercises 75–78) For Individual or Group Work

*Use your knowledge of fractions and decimals as you **work Exercises 75–78 in order.***

75. (a) Explain how you can tell that Keith made an error *just by looking at his final answer*. Here is his work.

$$\frac{5}{9} \quad 5\overline{)9.0}^{\,1.8} \quad \text{so} \quad \frac{5}{9} = 1.8$$

   (b) Show the correct way to change $\frac{5}{9}$ to a decimal. Explain why your answer makes sense.

76. (a) How can you prove to Sandra that $2\frac{7}{20}$ is *not* equivalent to 2.035? Here is her work.

$$2\frac{7}{20} \quad 20\overline{)7.00}^{\,0.35} \quad \text{so} \quad 2\frac{7}{20} = 2.035$$

   (b) What is the correct answer? Show how to prove it.

77. Ving knows that $\frac{3}{8} = 0.375$. How can he write $1\frac{3}{8}$ as a decimal *without* having to do a division? How can he write $3\frac{3}{8}$ as a decimal? $295\frac{3}{8}$ as a decimal? Explain your answer.

78. Iris has a shortcut for writing mixed numbers as decimals.

$$2\frac{7}{10} = 2.7 \qquad 1\frac{13}{100} = 1.13$$

Does her shortcut work for all mixed numbers? Explain when it works and why it works.

5.9 Problem Solving: Equations Containing Decimals

OBJECTIVE ▸ 1 Solve equations containing decimals using the addition property of equality. In **Chapter 2** you used the addition property of equality to solve an equation like $c + 5 = 30$. The addition property says that you can add the *same* number to *both* sides of an equation and still keep it balanced. You can also use this property when an equation contains decimal numbers.

OBJECTIVES

1 Solve equations containing decimals using the addition property of equality.

2 Solve equations containing decimals using the division property of equality.

3 Solve equations containing decimals using both properties of equality.

4 Solve application problems involving equations with decimals.

EXAMPLE 1   Using the Addition Property of Equality

Solve each equation and check each solution.

(a) $w + 2.9 = -0.6$

The first step is to get the variable term (w) by itself on the left side of the equal sign. Use the addition property to "get rid of" the 2.9 on the left side by adding its opposite, -2.9, to both sides.

$$w + 2.9 = -0.6$$
$$\underline{\quad -2.9 \quad -2.9 \quad} \quad \text{Add } -2.9 \text{ to both sides.}$$
$$\underbrace{w + 0}_{w} = -3.5$$
$$w = -3.5$$

The solution is -3.5. To check the solution, go back to the *original* equation.

CHECK $w + 2.9 = -0.6$ Original equation
$$\underbrace{-3.5 + 2.9}_{-0.6} = -0.6 \quad \text{Replace } w \text{ with } -3.5$$
$$-0.6 = -0.6 ✓ \quad \text{Balances}$$

When w is replaced with -3.5, the equation balances, so -3.5 is the correct solution (**not** -0.6).

(b) $7 = -4.3 + x$

To get x by itself on the right side of the equal sign, add 4.3 to both sides.

$$7 = -4.3 + x$$
$$\underline{+4.3 \quad +4.3 \quad} \quad \text{Add 4.3 to both sides.}$$
$$11.3 = \underbrace{0 + x}$$
$$11.3 = x$$

The solution is 11.3. To check the solution, go back to the *original* equation.

CHECK $7 = -4.3 + x$ Original equation
$$7 = \underbrace{-4.3 + 11.3} \quad \text{Replace } x \text{ with } 11.3 \quad \boxed{\text{The solution is 11.3 (not 7).}}$$
$$7 = 7 \quad ✓ \text{ Balances}$$

When x is replaced with 11.3, the equation balances, so 11.3 is the correct solution (**not** 7).

································ **Work Problem 1 at the Side.** ▶

---

1 Solve each equation and check each solution.

GS (a) $8.1 = h + 9$ **CHECK**
$$\underline{-9 \qquad -9}$$
$$-0.9 = \underbrace{h + 0}$$
$$\underline{\quad\quad} = \underline{\quad\quad}$$

(b) $-0.75 + y = 0$ **CHECK**

(c) $c - 6.8 = -4.8$ **CHECK**

Answers

1. **(a)** $-0.9 = h$ **CHECK** $8.1 = h + 9$
$$8.1 = \underbrace{-0.9 + 9}$$
Balances $8.1 = 8.1 ✓$

(b) $y = 0.75$ **CHECK** $-0.75 + y = 0$
$$-0.75 + 0.75 = 0$$
Balances $0 = 0 ✓$

(c) $c = 2$ **CHECK** $c - 6.8 = -4.8$
$$\underbrace{2 - 6.8} = -4.8$$
Balances $-4.8 = -4.8 ✓$

② Solve each equation and check each solution.

GS (a) $-3y = -0.63$

$$\frac{\overset{1}{\cancel{-3}} \cdot y}{\underset{1}{\cancel{-3}}} = \frac{-0.63}{-3}$$

Divide both sides by -3.

$$y = \underline{\hspace{1cm}}$$

Same sign, positive quotient.

CHECK

$$-3y = -0.63$$
$$\downarrow$$
$$-3(\underline{\hspace{0.8cm}}) = -0.63$$
$$\underline{\hspace{1cm}} = -0.63$$

(b) $2.25r = -18$

CHECK

(c) $1.7 = 0.5n$

CHECK

Answers

2. **(a)** $y = 0.21$ **CHECK** $\quad -3y = -0.63$
$$\downarrow$$
$$-3(0.21) = -0.63$$
Balances $\quad -0.63 = -0.63$ ✓

(b) $r = -8$ **CHECK** $\quad 2.25r = -18$
$$\downarrow$$
$$2.25(-8) = -18$$
Balances $\quad -18 = -18$ ✓

(c) $n = 3.4$ **CHECK** $1.7 = 0.5n$
$$\downarrow$$
$$1.7 = 0.5(3.4)$$
Balances $\quad 1.7 = 1.7$ ✓

OBJECTIVE ▶ ② Solve equations containing decimals using the division property of equality. You can also use the division property of equality (from **Chapter 2**) when an equation contains decimals.

EXAMPLE 2   Using the Division Property of Equality

Solve each equation and check each solution.

(a) $5x = 12.4$

On the left side of the equation, the variable is multiplied by 5. To undo the multiplication, divide both sides by 5.

$5x$ means $5 \cdot x$ → $\quad 5x = 12.4$

$$\frac{5 \cdot x}{5} = \frac{12.4}{5}$$ Divide both sides by 5

On the left side, divide out the common factor of 5

$$\frac{\overset{1}{\cancel{5}} \cdot x}{\underset{1}{\cancel{5}}} = 2.48$$ On the right side, $12.4 \div 5$ is 2.48

$$x = 2.48$$

The solution is 2.48. To check the solution, go back to the original equation.

CHECK $\quad 5x = 12.4$ Original equation
$$\downarrow$$
$$5(2.48) = 12.4$$ Replace x with 2.48 ◁ The solution is 2.48 (**not** 12.4)
$$12.4 = 12.4 ✓$$ Balances

When x is replaced with 2.48, the equation balances, so 2.48 is the correct solution (**not** 12.4).

(b) $-9.3 = 1.5t$

Signs are different, so quotient is negative.

$$\frac{-9.3}{1.5} = \frac{\overset{1}{\cancel{1.5}}t}{\underset{1}{\cancel{1.5}}}$$ Divide both sides by the coefficient of the variable term, 1.5

$$-6.2 = t$$

The solution is -6.2. To check the solution, go back to the original equation.

CHECK $\quad -9.3 = 1.5t$ Original equation

$$-9.3 = 1.5(-6.2)$$ Replace t with -6.2
$$-9.3 = -9.3 ✓$$ Balances

When t is replaced with -6.2, the equation balances, so -6.2 is the correct solution (**not** -9.3).

◀ **Work Problem ②** at the Side.

OBJECTIVE ▶ ③ Solve equations containing decimals using both properties of equality. Sometimes you need to use both the addition and division properties to solve an equation, as shown in **Example 3**.

EXAMPLE 3 **Solving Equations with Several Steps**

(a) $2.5b + 0.35 = -2.65$

The first step is to get the variable term, $2.5b$, by itself on the left side of the equal sign.

$$2.5b + 0.35 = -2.65$$
$$\underline{\quad -0.35 \quad -0.35} \quad \text{Add } -0.35 \text{ to both sides.}$$
$$\underbrace{2.5b + \quad 0} = -3.00$$
$$\quad\quad 2.5b \quad = -3$$

The next step is to divide both sides by the coefficient of the variable term. In $2.5b$, the coefficient is 2.5.

$$\frac{\overset{1}{2.\cancel{5}}b}{\underset{1}{2.\cancel{5}}} = \frac{-3}{2.5} \quad \begin{array}{l}\text{On the right side, signs do}\\ \textit{not} \text{ match, so the quotient}\\ \text{is } \textit{negative.}\end{array}$$
$$b = -1.2$$

The solution is -1.2. To check the solution, go back to the original equation.

CHECK
$$2.5b + 0.35 = -2.65 \quad \text{Original equation}$$
$$2.5(-1.2) + 0.35 = -2.65 \quad \text{Replace } b \text{ with } -1.2$$
$$\underbrace{-3} + 0.35 = -2.65$$
$$-2.65 = -2.65 \checkmark \quad \begin{array}{l}\text{Balances, so } -1.2 \text{ is the}\\ \text{correct solution.}\end{array}$$

(b) $5x - 0.98 = 2x + 0.4$

There is a variable term on both sides of the equation. You can choose to keep the variable term on the left side, or to keep the variable term on the right side. Either way will work. Just pick the left side or the right side.

Suppose that you decide to keep the variable term, $5x$, on the left side. Use the addition property to "get rid of" $2x$ on the right side by adding its opposite, $-2x$, to both sides.

$$5x - 0.98 = 2x + 0.4$$
$$\underline{-2x \quad\quad -2x} \quad \text{Add } -2x \text{ to both sides.}$$

Change subtraction to adding the opposite.
$$3x - 0.98 = \underbrace{0 + 0.4}$$
$$3x + (-0.98) = 0.4$$
$$\underline{\quad +0.98 \quad +0.98} \quad \text{Add } 0.98 \text{ to both sides.}$$
$$\underbrace{3x + \quad 0} = 1.38$$

$$\frac{\overset{1}{\cancel{3}}x}{\underset{1}{\cancel{3}}} = \frac{1.38}{3} \quad \text{Divide both sides by 3}$$
$$x = 0.46$$

The solution is 0.46. To check the solution, go back to the original equation.

CHECK
$$5x - 0.98 = 2x + 0.4 \quad \text{Original equation}$$
$$5(0.46) - 0.98 = 2(0.46) + 0.4 \quad \text{Replace } x \text{ with } 0.46$$
$$\underbrace{2.3} - 0.98 = \underbrace{0.92} + 0.4$$
$$1.32 = 1.32 \checkmark \quad \begin{array}{l}\text{Balances, so } 0.46 \text{ is}\\ \text{the correct solution.}\end{array}$$

· Work Problem **3** at the Side. ▶

---

3 Solve each equation and check each solution.

(a)
$$4 = 0.2c - 2.6$$
$$\underline{+ 2.6 \quad\quad +2.6}$$
$$6.6 = 0.2c + 0$$

$$\frac{6.6}{0.2} = \frac{\overset{1}{0.\cancel{2}}c}{\underset{1}{0.\cancel{2}}}$$
$$\underline{\quad\quad} = c$$

CHECK

(b) $3.1k - 4 = 0.5k + 13.42$

CHECK

(c) $-2y + 3 = 3y - 6$

CHECK

Answers

3. (a) $33 = c$ **CHECK** $4 = 0.2c - 2.6$
$$4 = 0.2(33) - 2.6$$
$$4 = \underbrace{6.6} - 2.6$$
$$\text{Balances } 4 = 4 \checkmark$$

(b) $k = 6.7$ **CHECK**
$$3.1k - 4 = 0.5k + 13.42$$
$$3.1(6.7) - 4 = 0.5(6.7) + 13.42$$
$$\underbrace{20.77} - 4 = \underbrace{3.35} + 13.42$$
$$\text{Balances } 16.77 = 16.77 \checkmark$$

(c) $y = 1.8$ **CHECK**
$$-2y + 3 = 3y - 6$$
$$-2(1.8) + 3 = 3(1.8) - 6$$
$$\underbrace{-3.6} + 3 = \underbrace{5.4} - 6$$
$$\text{Balances } -0.6 = -0.6 \checkmark$$

④ GS Maria found a cheaper calling card. The new card charges a $1 connection fee and $0.06 per minute. How many minutes long was a call that cost $4? Use the six problem-solving steps.

Step 1 Cost of a call

Unknown: number of minutes the call lasted

Known: Costs are $0.06 per minute plus $____ connection fee.

Step 2 Only one unknown; let m be the number of minutes.

Step 3 Write an equation.

OBJECTIVE ④ Solve application problems involving equations with decimals. Use the six problem-solving steps from **Chapter 3**.

EXAMPLE 4 Solving an Application Problem

Many international calling cards add a connection fee to the cost of each call. The card that Maria uses to call her sister's cell phone in Mexico charges $0.084 per minute plus a $1.25 connection fee for each call. The cost of the call Maria made today to her sister was $5.03. How many minutes did the call last?

Step 1 **Read** the problem. It is about the cost of a call to Mexico.

Unknown: number of minutes the call lasted

Known: Costs are $0.084 per minute plus $1.25 connection fee; total cost was $5.03.

Step 2 **Assign a variable:** There is only one unknown, so let m be the number of minutes.

Step 3 **Write an equation.**

Cost per minute		Number of minutes		Connection fee		Total cost
0.084	•	m	+	1.25	=	5.03

Step 4 **Solve** the equation.

$$0.084m + 1.25 = 5.03$$
$$\underline{\quad\quad -1.25 \quad -1.25} \quad \text{Add } -1.25 \text{ to both sides.}$$
$$0.084m + 0 = 3.78$$

$$\frac{0.084m}{0.084} = \frac{3.78}{0.084} \quad \text{Divide both sides by 0.084}$$

$$m = 45$$

> Write **minutes** as part of your answer.

Step 5 **State the answer.** The call lasted 45 minutes.

Step 6 **Check** the solution by putting it back into the original problem.

$0.084 per minute times 45 minutes = $3.78

$3.78 plus $1.25 connection fee = $5.03

Cost of the call was $5.03. ← Matches ↑

Because 45 minutes "works" when you put it back into the *original* problem, it is the correct solution.

> If your answer does **not** work in the original problem, start again at *Step 1*.

◄ **Work Problem ④ at the Side.**

Answer

4. *Step 1:* $1 connection fee
Step 3: $0.06m + 1 = 4$
Step 4: Add -1 to both sides; divide both sides by 0.06
Step 5: The call lasted 50 minutes.
Step 6: $0.06 per minute times 50 minutes = $3.00, or $3.
Then, $3 + $1 = $4

Maria's call ↑
cost $4. ← Matches

5.9 Exercises

  MyMathLab®

1. CONCEPT CHECK When solving this equation, state the number you would add to both sides. Then explain why you picked that number.

$$-0.3 = x - 6.2$$

2. CONCEPT CHECK When solving this equation, state the number you would divide both sides by. Then explain why you picked that number.

$$-4.5y = 2.25$$

*Solve each equation and check each solution. **See Examples 1 and 2.***

3. $-20.6 + n = -22$ CHECK

$$\underline{+20.6 \qquad +20.6}$$
$$\underbrace{0 \ + n} = \underline{\quad}$$
$$\underline{\quad} = \underline{\quad}$$

4. $g - 5 = \ \ 6.03$ CHECK

$$\underline{\quad +5 \qquad +5}$$
$$\underbrace{g + 0} = \underline{\quad}$$
$$\underline{\quad} = \underline{\quad}$$

5. $0 = b - 0.008$ CHECK

6. $0.18 + m = -4.5$ CHECK

7. $2.03 = 7a$ CHECK

8. $-6.2c = 0$ CHECK

9. $0.8p = -96$ CHECK

10. $-10.16 = -4r$ CHECK

11. $-3.3t = -2.31$ CHECK

12. $8.3w = -49.8$ CHECK

*Solve each equation. Show your work. **See Example 3.***

13. Finish the work.

$$7.5x + 0.15 = -6$$
$$\underline{\qquad -0.15 \quad -0.15}$$

14. Finish the work.

$$0.8 = 0.2y + 3.4$$
$$\underline{-3.4 \qquad -3.4}$$

15. $-7.38 = 2.05z - 7.38$

16. $6.2h - 0.4 = 2.7$

17. $-0.9 = 0.2 - 0.01h$

18. $3 = -0.3 - 2.2m$

19. $3c + 10 = 6c + 8.65$

20. $2.1b + 5 = 1.6b + 10$

21. $0.8w - 0.4 = -6 + w$

22. $7r + 9.64 = -2.32 + 5r$ **23.** $-10.9 + 0.5p = 0.9p + 5.3$ **24.** $0.7x - 4.38 = x - 2.16$

Solve each application problem using the six problem-solving steps. **See Example 4.**

25. Most adult medication doses are for a person weighing 150 pounds. For a 45-pound child, the adult dose should be multiplied by 0.3. If the child's dose of a decongestant is 9 milligrams, what is the adult dose?

26. For a 30-pound child, an adult dose of medication should be multiplied by 0.2. If the child's dose of a cough suppressant is 3 milliliters, find the adult dose.

27. A storm blew down many trees. Several neighbors rented a chain saw for $275.80 and helped each other cut up and stack the wood. The rental company charges $65.95 per day plus a $12 sharpening fee. How many days was the saw rented? (*Source:* Central Rental.)

28. A 20-inch chain saw can be rented for $29.95 for the first two hours, and $9 for each additional hour. Steve's rental charge was $56.95. How many hours did he rent the saw? (*Source:* Central Rental.)

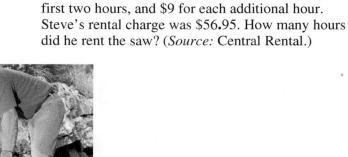

Relating Concepts (Exercises 29–32)   For Individual or Group Work

When doing aerobic exercises, it is important to increase your heart rate (the number of beats per minute) so that you get the maximum benefit from the exercise. But you don't want your heart rate to be so fast that it is dangerous. Here is an expression for finding a safe maximum heart rate for a healthy person with no heart disease: $0.7(220 - a)$, *where a is the person's age.* **Work Exercises 29–32 in order:** *Write an equation and solve it to find each person's age. Assume all the people are healthy.*

29. How old is a person who has a maximum safe heart rate of 140 beats per minute? *Hint:* Use the distributive property to simplify $0.7(220 - a)$.

30. How old is a person who has a maximum safe heart rate of 126 beats per minute?

31. If a person's maximum safe heart rate is 134 (rounded to the nearest whole number), how old is the person, to the nearest whole year?

32. If a person's maximum safe heart rate is 117 (rounded to the nearest whole number), how old is the person, to the nearest whole year?

Chapter 5 *Summary*

Key Terms

5.1

decimals Decimals, like fractions, are used to show parts of a whole.

decimal point A decimal point is the dot that is used to separate the whole number part from the fractional part of a decimal number.

place value Place value is the value assigned to each place to the right or left of the decimal point. Whole numbers, such as ones and tens, are to the *left* of the decimal point. Fractional parts, such as tenths and hundredths, are to the *right* of the decimal point.

5.2

round To round is to "cut off" a number after a certain place, such as to round to the nearest hundredth. The rounded number is less accurate than the original number. You can use the symbol " $\approx$ " to mean "is approximately equal to."

decimal places Decimal places are the number of digits to the *right* of the decimal point; for example, 6.37 has two decimal places, and 4.706 has three decimal places.

5.5

repeating decimal A repeating decimal is a decimal number with one or more digits that repeat forever; it never ends. For example, in 0.1666..., the digit 6 continues to repeat. Use three dots to indicate that it is a repeating decimal. Or write the number with a bar above the repeating digits, as in 0.1$\overline{6}$. (Use the dots or the bar, but not both.)

Test Your Word Power

See how well you have learned the vocabulary in this chapter.

① **Decimal numbers** are like fractions in that they both
   A. must be written in lowest terms
   B. have decimal points
   C. represent parts of a whole.

② **Decimal places** refer to
   A. digits to the left of the decimal point
   B. digits to the right of the decimal point
   C. the number of zeros in a decimal number.

③ The **hypotenuse** is
   A. the long base in a rectangle
   B. the height in a parallelogram
   C. the longest side in a right triangle.

④ The **decimal point**
   A. separates the whole number part from the fractional part
   B. is always moved when finding a quotient
   C. is at the far left side of a whole number.

⑤ The number **0.3̄** is an example of
   A. a repeating decimal
   B. a rounded number
   C. a truncated number.

⑥ π is the ratio of
   A. the diameter to the radius of a circle
   B. the circumference to the diameter of a circle
   C. the diameter to the circumference of a circle.

⑦ The **median** for a set of values is
   A. the mathematical average
   B. the value that occurs most often
   C. the middle value when the values are listed from least to greatest.

⑧ The **circumference** of a circle is
   A. the perimeter of the circle
   B. found using the expression πr^2
   C. the distance across the circle.

Answers to Test Your Word Power

1. C; *Example:* For 0.7, the whole is cut into ten parts, and you are interested in 7 of the parts.

2. B; *Examples:* The number 6.87 has two decimal places; 0.309 has three decimal places.

3. C; *Example:* In triangle *ABC*, side *AC* (the red side) is the hypotenuse.

4. A; *Example:* In 5.42, the decimal point separates the whole number part, 5 ones, from the decimal part, 42 hundredths.

5. A; *Example:* The bar above the 3 in 0.3̄ indicates that the 3 repeats forever.

6. B; *Example:* The ratio of a circumference of 12.57 cm to a diameter of 4 cm is $\dfrac{12.57}{4} \approx 3.14$ (rounded).

7. C; *Example:* For this set of prices—$4, $3, $7, $2, $5, $6, $7—the median is $5.

8. A; *Example:* If the radius of a circle is 4 ft, then $C \approx 2 \cdot 3.14 \cdot 4 \approx 25.1$ ft. So the distance around the circle is about 25.1 ft.

Quick Review

Concepts	Examples

5.1 Reading and Writing Decimals

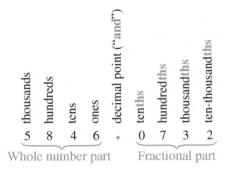

thousands	hundreds	tens	ones	decimal point ("and")	tenths	hundredths	thousandths	ten-thousandths
5	8	4	6	•	0	7	3	2

Whole number part   Fractional part

Write each decimal in words.

> 8 is in hundredths place.

15.38

fifteen **and** thirty-eight **hundredths**

> 3 is in ten-thousandths place.

0.0103

one hundred three **ten-thousandths**

5.1 Writing Decimals as Fractions

The digits to the right of the decimal point are the numerator. The place value of the rightmost digit determines the denominator.

Always write the fraction in lowest terms.

Write 0.45 as a fraction in lowest terms.

The numerator is 45. The rightmost digit, 5, is in the hundredths place, so the denominator is 100. Then write the fraction in lowest terms.

$$\frac{45}{100} = \frac{45 \div 5}{100 \div 5} = \frac{9}{20} \longleftarrow \text{Lowest terms}$$

5.2 Rounding Decimals

Find the place to which you are rounding. Draw a cut-off line to the right of that place; the rest of the digits will be dropped. Look *only* at the first digit being cut. If it is *4 or less,* the part you are keeping stays the same. If it is *5 or more,* the part you are keeping rounds up. Do not move the decimal point when rounding. Use the sign " ≈ " to mean "is approximately equal to."

Round 0.17952 to the nearest thousandth.

First digit cut is *5 or more* so round up.

0.179 | 52

0.179 ⟵ Keep this part.
+ 0.001 ⟵ To round up, add 1 thousandth.
0.180

0.17952 rounds to 0.180
Write 0.17952 ≈ 0.180

5.3 Adding Positive and Negative Decimals

Estimate the answer by using front end rounding: round each number to the highest possible place.

    To find the exact answer, line up the decimal points. If needed, write in zeros as placeholders. Add or subtract the absolute values as if they were whole numbers. Line up the decimal point in the answer.

    If the numbers have the same sign, use the common sign as the sign of the sum. If the numbers have different signs, the sign of the sum is the sign of the number with the greater absolute value.

Find the sum.
5.68 + 785.3 + 12 + 2.007

Estimate:	*Exact:*	
6 ⟵	5 . 680	Use zeros as
800 ⟵	785 . 300	placeholders so
10 ⟵	12 . 000	all numbers have
+ 2 ⟵	+ 2 . 007	three decimal
818	804 . 987	places.

Line up decimal points.

The estimate and exact answer are both in hundreds, so the decimal point is probably in the correct place.

Concepts	Examples

5.3 Subtracting Positive and Negative Decimals

Rewrite subtracting as adding the opposite of the second number. Then follow the rules for adding positive and negative decimals.

Subtract.

$$4.2 - \quad 12.91$$
$$\downarrow \qquad \downarrow$$
$$4.2 + (-12.91)$$

$|4.2|$ is 4.2 and $|-12.91|$ is 12.91.
Subtract $12.91 - 4.2$ to get 8.71.
Because -12.91 has the greater absolute value and is negative, the answer will be negative.

$$4.2 + (-12.91) = -8.71$$

5.4 Multiplying Positive and Negative Decimals

Step 1 Multiply as you would for whole numbers.

Step 2 Count the total number of decimal places in both factors.

Step 3 Write the decimal point in the answer so it has the same number of decimal places as the total from *Step 2*. You may need to write extra zeros on the left side of the product in order to get enough decimal places in the answer.

Step 4 If two factors have the *same sign*, the product is *positive*. If two factors have *different signs,* the product is negative.

Multiply $(0.169)(-0.21)$

$$
\begin{array}{r}
0.169 \leftarrow 3 \text{ decimal places} \\
\times \ \ 0.21 \leftarrow 2 \text{ decimal places} \\
\hline
169 \qquad 5 \text{ total decimal places} \\
338 \qquad\qquad \\
\hline
.03549 \leftarrow 5 \text{ decimal places in product}
\end{array}
$$

Write in a 0 so you can count over 5 decimal places.
The factors have *different* signs, so the product is *negative.*

$$(0.169)(-0.21) = -0.03549$$

5.5 Dividing by a Decimal

Step 1 Change the divisor to a whole number by moving the decimal point to the right.

Step 2 Move the decimal point in the dividend the same number of places to the right.

Step 3 Write the decimal point in the quotient directly above the decimal point in the dividend. Then divide as with whole numbers.

Step 4 If the numbers have the *same sign,* the quotient is *positive*. If they have *different signs,* the quotient is *negative.*

Divide -52.8 by -0.75.
First consider $52.8 \div 0.75$.

$$
\begin{array}{r}
70.4 \\
0.75{\overline{\smash{\big)}\,52.800}} \\
\underline{525} \\
300 \\
\underline{300} \\
0
\end{array}
$$

Move decimal point two places to the right in divisor and dividend.

Write zeros in the dividend so you can move the decimal point and continue dividing until the remainder is 0.

The quotient is positive because both the divisor and dividend were negative (same signs means positive quotient).

5.6 Writing Fractions as Decimals

Divide the numerator by the denominator. If necessary, round to the place indicated.

Write $\frac{1}{8}$ as a decimal.

$\frac{1}{8}$ means $1 \div 8$. Write it as $8{\overline{\smash{\big)}\,1}}$.
The decimal point is on the right side of 1.

$$
\begin{array}{r}
0.125 \\
8{\overline{\smash{\big)}\,1.000}} \\
\underline{8} \\
20 \\
\underline{16} \\
40 \\
\underline{40} \\
0
\end{array}
$$

$\leftarrow$ Write the decimal point and three zeros so you can continue dividing.

Therefore, $\frac{1}{8}$ is equivalent to 0.125.

Concepts	Examples

5.6 Comparing the Size of Fractions and Decimals

Step 1 Write any fractions as decimals.

Step 2 Write zeros so that all the numbers being compared have the same number of decimal places.

Step 3 Use < to mean "is less than," > to mean "is greater than," or list the numbers from least to greatest.

Arrange in order from least to greatest.

$$0.505 \quad \frac{1}{2} \quad 0.55$$

$0.505 = 505$ thousandths ← 505 is in the middle.

$\dfrac{1}{2} = 0.5 = 0.500 = 500$ thousandths ← 500 is least.

$0.55 = 0.550 = 550$ thousandths ← 550 is greatest.

(least) $\quad \dfrac{1}{2} \quad 0.505 \quad 0.55 \quad$ (greatest)

Concepts	Examples

5.9 Solving Equations Containing Decimals

Step 1 Use the addition property of equality to get the variable term by itself on one side of the equal sign.

Step 2 Divide both sides by the coefficient of the variable term to find the solution.

Step 3 Check the solution by going back to the *original* equation. Replace the variable with the solution. If the equation balances, the solution is correct.

Solve the equation and check the solution.

$$4.5x + 0.7 = -5.15$$
$$\frac{-0.7 \qquad -0.7}{4.5x + 0} = \frac{}{-5.85} \qquad \text{Add } -0.7 \text{ to both sides.}$$

$$\frac{\overset{1}{4.5x}}{\underset{1}{4.5}} = \frac{-5.85}{4.5} \qquad \text{Divide both sides by 4.5}$$

$$x = -1.3$$

The solution is -1.3. To check the solution, go back to the original equation.

CHECK $4.5x + 0.7 = -5.15$ Original equation

$4.5(-1.3) + 0.7 = -5.15$ Replace x with -1.3

$-5.85 \quad + 0.7 = -5.15$

$-5.15 \quad = -5.15$ ✓ Balances

When x is replaced with -1.3, the equation balances, so -1.3 is the correct solution (***not*** -5.15).

Chapter 5   Review Exercises

5.1 *Name the digit that has the given place value.*

1. 243.059

tenths

hundredths

2. 0.6817

ones

tenths

3. $5824.39

hundreds

hundredths

4. 896.503

tenths

tens

5. 20.73861

tenths

ten-thousandths

Write each decimal as a fraction or mixed number in lowest terms.

6. 0.5

7. 0.75

8. 4.05

9. 0.875

10. 0.027

11. 27.8

Write each decimal in words.

12. 0.8

13. 400.29

14. 12.007

15. 0.0306

Write each decimal in numbers.

16. Eight and three tenths

17. Two hundred five thousandths

18. Seventy and sixty-six ten-thousandths

19. Thirty hundredths

5.2 *Round to the place indicated.*

20. 275.635 to the nearest tenth

21. 72.789 to the nearest hundredth

22. 0.1604 to the nearest thousandth

23. 0.0905 to the nearest thousandth

24. 0.98 to the nearest tenth

Round each money amount to the nearest cent.

25. $15.8333

26. $0.698

27. $17,625.7906

Round each income or expense item to the nearest dollar.

28. The income from the pancake breakfast was $350.48.

29. Each member paid $129.50 in dues.

30. The refreshments cost $99.61.

31. The bank charges were $29.37.

5.3 *Find each sum or difference.*

32. $0.4 - 6.07$

33. $-20 + 19.97$

34. $-1.35 + 7.229$

35. $0.005 + (3 - 9.44)$

First, use front end rounding to estimate each answer. Then find the exact answer.

36. Americans' favorite recreational activity is exercise walking. About 95.8 million people go walking at least once during the year. Swimming is third with 51.9 million people, and camping is fourth with 44.7 million people. How many more people go walking than camping? (*Source:* nsga.org)

Estimate:

Exact:

37. Today, Jasmin had $406 in her bank account. She paid $315.53 to the day care center and $74.67 for groceries. What is the new balance in her account?

Estimate:

Exact:

38. Joey spent $1.59 for toothpaste, $5.33 for vitamins, and $18.94 for a toaster. He gave the clerk three $10 bills. How much change did he get?

Estimate:

Exact:

39. Roseanne is training for a wheelchair race. She raced 2.3 kilometers on Monday, 4 kilometers on Wednesday, and 5.25 kilometers on Friday. How far did she race altogether?

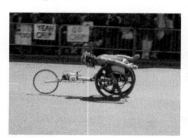

Estimate:

Exact:

5.4 *First, use front end rounding to estimate each answer. Then find the exact answer.*

40. *Estimate:*

$$\times \underline{}$$

Exact:
$$\begin{array}{r} 6.138 \\ \times \ \ 3.7 \\ \hline \end{array}$$

41. *Estimate:*

$$\times \underline{}$$

Exact:
$$\begin{array}{r} 42.9 \\ \times \ 3.3 \\ \hline \end{array}$$

Find each product.

42. $(-5.6)(-0.002)$

43. $(0.071)(-0.005)$

5.5 *Decide if each answer is* reasonable *or* unreasonable *by rounding the numbers and estimating the answer. If the exact answer is not reasonable, find and correct the error.*

44. $706.2 \div 12 = 58.85$

Estimate:

45. $26.6 \div 2.8 = 0.95$

Estimate:

Divide. Round quotients to the nearest thousandth when necessary.

46. $3\overline{)43.4}$

47. $\dfrac{-72}{-0.06}$

48. $-0.00048 \div 0.0012$

5.4–5.5 *Solve each application problem.*

49. Adrienne worked 46.5 hours this week. Her hourly wage is $14.24 for the first 40 hours and 1.5 times that rate over 40 hours. Find her total earnings to the nearest dollar.

50. A book of 12 tickets costs $59.89 at the State Fair midway. What is the cost per ticket, to the nearest cent?

51. Stock in Math Tronic sells for $3.75 per share. Kenneth is thinking of investing $500. How many whole shares could he buy?

52. Grapes are on sale at $2.29 per pound. How much will Ms. Lee pay for 3.5 pounds of grapes, to the nearest cent?

Simplify.

53. $3.5^2 + 8.7(-1.95)$

54. $11 - 3.06 \div (3.95 - 0.35)$

5.6 *Write each fraction as a decimal. Round to the nearest thousandth when necessary.*

55. $3\dfrac{4}{5}$

56. $\dfrac{16}{25}$

57. $1\dfrac{7}{8}$

58. $\dfrac{1}{9}$

Arrange each group of numbers in order from least to greatest.

59. 3.68, 3.806, 3.6008

60. 0.215, 0.22, 0.209, 0.2102

61. $0.17, \dfrac{3}{20}, \dfrac{1}{8}, 0.159$

5.9 *Solve each equation. Show your work.*

72. $-0.1 = b - 0.35$

73. $-3.8x = 0$

74. $6.8 + 0.4n = 1.6$

75. $-0.375 + 1.75a = 2a$

76. $0.3y - 5.4 = 2.7 + 0.8y$

Mixed Review Exercises

Simplify.

85. $89.19 + 0.075 + 310.6 + 5$

86. $72.8(-3.5)$

87. $1648.3 \div 0.46$ Round to thousandths.

88. $30 - 0.9102$

89. $(4.38)(0.007)$

90. $0.005\overline{)0.047}$

91. $72.105 + 8.2 - 95.37$

92. $\dfrac{-81.36}{9}$

93. $(0.6 - 1.22) + 4.8(-3.15)$

94. $0.455(18)$

95. $(-1.6)(-0.58)$

96. $0.218\overline{)7.63}$ 🖩

97. $-21.059 - 20.8$

98. $18.3 - 3^2 \div 0.5$

Use the information in the ad to solve Exercises 99–103. Round money answers to the nearest cent. (Disregard any sales tax.)

Grand Opening Sale!
Save on Clothing for the Entire Family

Jeans for Teens
only $19.95 each
women's sizes $24.99

Athletic Shoes
regularly priced
$89.99 to $149.50
NOW just $71 to $119.60

Men's socks NOW 3 pairs for $8.99
Children's socks 6 pairs for $5

Hurry in — *TWO DAYS ONLY*

99. How much would one pair of men's socks cost?

100. How much more would one pair of men's socks cost than one pair of children's socks?

101. How much would Fernando pay for a dozen pairs of men's socks?

102. How much would Akiko pay for five pairs of teen jeans and four pairs of women's jeans?

103. What is the difference between the cheapest sale price for athletic shoes and the highest regular price?

Solve each equation. Show your work.

104. $4.62 = -6.6y$

105. $1.05x - 2.5 = 0.8x + 5$

Solve each application problem. Round answers to the nearest tenth when necessary.

106. 🖩 A circular table has a diameter of 5 ft. What length of rubber strip is needed to go around the edge of the table? What is the area of the tabletop?

107. Jerry missed one math test, so his test scores are 82, 0, 78, 93, 85. Find his mean and median scores.

108. 🖩 LaRae drove 16 miles south, then made a 90° right turn and drove 12 miles west. How far is she, in a straight line, from her starting point?

109. 🖩 A juice can that is 7 in. tall has a diameter of 3 in. What is the volume of the can?

Write each decimal as a fraction or mixed number in lowest terms.

1. 18.4

2. 0.075

Write each decimal in words.

3. 60.007

4. 0.0208

First, use front end rounding to round each number and estimate the answer. Then find the exact answer.

5. $7.6 + 82.0128 + 39.59$

Estimate:

Exact:

6. $-5.79(1.2)$

Estimate:

Exact:

7. $-79.1 - 3.602$

Estimate:

Exact:

8. $-20.04 \div (-4.8)$

Estimate:

Exact:

Find the exact answer.

9. $670 - 0.996$

10. $0.15\overline{)72}$

11. $(-0.006)(-0.007)$

Solve each application problem.

12. Pat bought 6.5 ft of decorative gold chain to hang a light over her dining table. She paid $24.64. What was the cost per foot, to the nearest cent?

13. Davida ran a race in 3.059 minutes. Angela ran the race in 3.5 minutes. Who won? By how much?

14. Mr. Yamamoto bought 1.85 pounds of cheese at $2.89 per pound. What was the total amount he paid, to the nearest cent?

Solve each equation. Show your work.

15. $-5.9 = y + 0.25$

16. $-4.2x = 1.47$

17. $3a - 22.7 = 10$

18. $-0.8n + 1.88 = 2n - 6.1$

19. Arrange in order from least to greatest:

$0.44, 0.451, \dfrac{9}{20}, 0.4506$

20. Simplify: $6.3^2 - 5.9 + 3.4(-0.5)$

21. Find the mean number of books loaned: 52, 61, 68, 69, 73, 75, 79, 84, 91, 98.

22. Find the mode for hot tub temperatures (Fahrenheit) of 96°, 104°, 103°, 104°, 103°, 104°, 91°, 74°, 103°.

23. Find the weighted mean.

Cost	Frequency
$ 6	7
$10	3
$11	4
$14	2
$19	3
$24	1

24. Find the median cost of an online textbook: $54.50, $48, $39.75, $89, $56.25, $49.30, $46.90, $51.80.

 Find the unknown lengths. Round your answers to the nearest tenth when necessary.

25.

?

6 cm

7 cm

26.

11 ft

?

20 ft

Use 3.14 as the approximate value for π and round your answers to the nearest tenth when necessary.

27. Find the radius.

25 in.

28. Find the circumference.

0.9 km

29. Find the area.

16.2 cm

30. Find the volume.

18 ft

5 ft

31. Find the surface area of the solid in **Problem 30.**

Chapters 1–5   *Cumulative Review Exercises*

1. Write these numbers in words.
   (a) 45.0203

   (b) 30,000,650,008

2. Write these numbers using digits.
   (a) One hundred sixty million, five hundred

   (b) Seventy-five thousandths

Round each number as indicated.

3. 46,908 to the nearest hundred

4. 6.197 to the nearest hundredth

5. 0.66148 to the nearest thousandth

6. 9951 to the nearest hundred

Simplify.

7. $-5 - 8$

8. $-0.003(0.02)$

9. $\dfrac{-7}{0}$

10. $8 + 4(2 - 5)^2$

11. $-\dfrac{3}{8}(-48)$

12. $|4| - |-10|$

13. $0.721 + 55.9$

14. $3\dfrac{1}{3} - 1\dfrac{5}{6}$

15. $\left(\dfrac{3}{b^2}\right)\left(\dfrac{b}{8}\right)$

16. $12 - 0.853$

17. $\dfrac{3}{10} - \dfrac{3}{4}$

18. $\dfrac{\frac{5}{16}}{-10}$

19. $-3.75 \div (-2.9)$
   Round answer to the nearest tenth.

20. $\dfrac{x}{2} + \dfrac{3}{5}$

21. $5 \div \left(-\dfrac{5}{8}\right)$

22. $2^5 - 4^3$

23. $\dfrac{-36 \div (-2)}{-6 - 4(0 - 6)}$

24. $(0.8)^2 - 3.2 + 4(-0.8)$

25. $\dfrac{3}{4} \div \dfrac{3}{10}\left(\dfrac{1}{4} + \dfrac{2}{3}\right)$

The ages (in years) of the students in a math class are: 19, 23, 24, 19, 20, 29, 26, 35, 20, 22, 26, 23, 25, 26, 20, 30. *Use this data for Exercises 26–28.*

26. Find the mean age, to the nearest tenth.

27. Find the median age.

28. Find the mode.

Solve each equation. Show your work.

29. $3h - 4h = 16 - 12$
30. $-2x = x - 15$
31. $20 = 6r - 45.4$

32. $-3(y + 4) = 7y + 8$
33. $-0.8 + 1.4n = 2 + 0.7n$

Find the unknown length, perimeter, area, or volume. Use 3.14 *as the approximate value of* π *and round answers to the nearest tenth.*

34. Find the perimeter and the area.

35. Find the circumference and the area.

36. Find the length of the third side and the area.

37. Find the volume and surface area.

First, use front end rounding to estimate each answer. Then find the exact answer.

38. Lameck had three $20 bills. He spent $47.96 on gasoline and $0.87 for a candy bar at the convenience store. How much money does he have left?

Estimate:

Exact:

39. Toshihiro bought $2\frac{1}{3}$ yards of cotton fabric and $3\frac{7}{8}$ yards of wool fabric. How many yards of fabric did he buy in all?

Estimate:

Exact:

40. Paulette bought 2.7 pounds of strawberries for $6.18. What was the cost per pound, to the nearest cent?

Estimate:

Exact:

41. Carter Community College received a $78,000 grant from a local hospital to help students pay tuition for nursing classes. How much money could be given to each of 107 students? Round to the nearest dollar.

Estimate:

Exact:

Solve each application problem using the six problem-solving steps. Show your work.

42. A $30,000 scholarship is being divided between two students so that one student receives three times as much as the other. How much will each student receive?

43. The perimeter of a rectangular game board is 48 in. The length is 4 in. more than the width. Find the length and width of the game board.

6 Ratio, Proportion, and Line/Angle/Triangle Relationships

Nine out of every ten American teens and adults have a cell phone. Worldwide, about 2 out of 3 people use a cell phone! In this chapter, you will use unit rates to find the best deal on cell phone service plans and on international calling cards.

6.1 Ratios

OBJECTIVES

1. Write ratios as fractions.
2. Solve ratio problems involving decimals or mixed numbers.
3. Solve ratio problems after converting units.

VOCABULARY TIP

Ratio A **ratio** compares two quantities that have the **same** units. For example, if you are comparing two lengths, both measurements must be in feet, or both in yards, and so on. In a ratio, the common units divide out.

A **ratio** compares two quantities. You can compare two numbers, such as 8 and 4, or two measurements that have the *same* type of units, such as 3 days and 12 days. (*Rates* compare measurements with different types of units and are covered in the next section.)

Ratios can help you see important relationships. For example, if the ratio of your monthly expenses to your monthly income is 10 to 9, then you are spending $10 for every $9 you earn and going deeper into debt.

OBJECTIVE ▶ 1 Write ratios as fractions. A ratio can be written in three ways.

Writing a Ratio

The ratio of $7 to $3 can be written as follows.

$$7 \text{ to } 3 \quad \text{or} \quad 7{:}3 \quad \text{or} \quad \frac{7}{3} \leftarrow \text{Fraction bar indicates "to."}$$

"＂:＂" indicates "to."

Writing a ratio as a fraction is the most common method, and the one we will use here. All three ways are read, "the ratio of 7 to 3." The word to separates the quantities being compared.

Writing a Ratio as a Fraction

Order is important when you're writing a ratio. The quantity mentioned first is the numerator. The quantity mentioned second is the denominator. For example:

The ratio of 5 to 12   is written $\dfrac{5}{12}$

EXAMPLE 1   **Writing Ratios**

Ancestors of the Pueblo Indians built multistory apartment towns in New Mexico about 1100 years ago. A room might measure 14 feet long, 11 feet wide, and 15 feet high.

Continued on Next Page

Write each ratio as a fraction, using the room measurements.

(a) Ratio of length to width

> Do **not** rewrite the ratio as $1\frac{3}{11}$.

The ratio of **length to width** is $\dfrac{14 \text{ feet}}{11 \text{ feet}} = \dfrac{14}{11}$

Numerator (mentioned first)   Denominator (mentioned second)

You can divide out common *units* just as you divided out common *factors* when writing fractions in lowest terms. (See **Chapter 4.**) However, do *not* rewrite the fraction as a mixed number. Keep it as the ratio of 14 to 11.

(b) The ratio of width to height is $\dfrac{11 \text{ feet}}{15 \text{ feet}} = \dfrac{11}{15}$

> Divide out the common units (ft).

> **CAUTION**
>
> Remember, the *order* of the numbers is important in a ratio. Look for the words "ratio of a to b." Write the ratio as $\dfrac{a}{b}$, **not** $\dfrac{b}{a}$. The quantity mentioned first is the numerator.

·· Work Problem ❶ at the Side. ▶

You can write a ratio in *lowest terms*, just as you do with any fraction.

EXAMPLE 2 **Writing Ratios in Lowest Terms**

Write each ratio as a fraction in lowest terms.

(a) 60 days of sun to 20 days of rain

The ratio is $\dfrac{60 \text{ days}}{20 \text{ days}}$. Divide out the common units. Then write this ratio in lowest terms by dividing the numerator and the denominator by 20.

$$\dfrac{60 \text{ days}}{20 \text{ days}} = \dfrac{60}{20} = \dfrac{60 \div 20}{20 \div 20} = \dfrac{3}{1} \left. \begin{cases} \\ \end{cases} \right. \text{Ratio in lowest terms}$$

So, the ratio of 60 days to 20 days is 3 to 1, or, written as a fraction, $\dfrac{3}{1}$. In other words, for every 3 days of sun, there is 1 day of rain.

> **CAUTION**
>
> In the fractions chapter (**Chapter 4**), you would have rewritten $\dfrac{3}{1}$ as 3. But a *ratio* compares **two** quantities, so you need to keep both parts of the ratio and write it as $\dfrac{3}{1}$.

(b) 50 ounces of medicine to 120 ounces of water

The ratio is $\dfrac{50 \text{ ounces}}{120 \text{ ounces}}$. Divide out the common units. Then divide the numerator and the denominator by 10.

$$\dfrac{50 \text{ ounces}}{120 \text{ ounces}} = \dfrac{50}{120} = \dfrac{50 \div 10}{120 \div 10} = \dfrac{5}{12} \left. \begin{cases} \\ \end{cases} \right. \text{Ratio in lowest terms}$$

So, the ratio of 50 ounces to 120 ounces is $\dfrac{5}{12}$. In other words, for every 5 ounces of medicine, there is 12 ounces of water.

·· Continued on Next Page

---

❶ Shane spent $14 on meat, $5 on milk, and $7 on fresh fruit. Write the following ratios as fractions.

 (a) The ratio of amount spent on fruit to amount spent on milk

 Spent on fruit → $\dfrac{}{5}$ ← Spent on milk

 (b) The ratio of amount spent on milk to amount spent on meat

 (c) The ratio of amount spent on meat to amount spent on milk

Answers

1. (a) $\dfrac{7}{5}$ (b) $\dfrac{5}{14}$ (c) $\dfrac{14}{5}$

2 Write each ratio as a fraction in lowest terms.

(a) 9 hours to 12 hours

$$\frac{9 \text{ hours}}{12 \text{ hours}} = \frac{9}{12} = \frac{9 \div 3}{12 \div 3} = \underline{\hspace{1cm}}$$

(b) 100 meters to 50 meters

(c) The ratio of width to length for this rectangle

Length
48 ft

Width
24 ft

3 Write each ratio as a ratio of whole numbers in lowest terms.

(a) The price of Tamar's favorite brand of lipstick increased from $5.50 to $9.00. Find the ratio of the increase in price to the original price.

(b) Last week, Lance worked 4.5 hours each day. This week he cut back to 3 hours each day. Find the ratio of the decrease in hours to the original number of hours.

Answers

2. (a) $\frac{3}{4}$ (b) $\frac{2}{1}$ (c) $\frac{1}{2}$

3. (a) $\dfrac{(3.50)(100)}{(5.50)(100)} = \dfrac{350 \div 50}{550 \div 50} = \dfrac{7}{11}$

(b) $\dfrac{(1.5)(10)}{(4.5)(10)} = \dfrac{15 \div 15}{45 \div 15} = \dfrac{1}{3}$

(c) 15 people in a large van to 6 people in a small van

The ratio is $\dfrac{15}{6} = \dfrac{15 \div 3}{6 \div 3} = \dfrac{5}{2}$ ← {Ratio in lowest terms}

Note

Although $\frac{5}{2} = 2\frac{1}{2}$, ratios are *not* written as mixed numbers. Nevertheless, in **Example 2(c)** above, the ratio $\frac{5}{2}$ does mean the large van holds $2\frac{1}{2}$ times as many people as the small van.

◀ **Work Problem 2 at the Side.**

OBJECTIVE 2 Solve ratio problems involving decimals or mixed numbers.
Sometimes a ratio compares two decimal numbers or two fractions. It is easier to understand if we rewrite the ratio as a ratio of two whole numbers.

EXAMPLE 3 Using Decimal Numbers in a Ratio

The price of a Sunday newspaper increased from $1.50 to $1.75. Find the ratio of the <u>increase in price</u> to <u>the original price</u>.
    The words <u>increase in price</u> are mentioned first, so the increase will be the numerator. How much did the price go up? Use subtraction.

new price − original price = increase

$1.75 − $1.50 = $0.25

{Subtract first to find how much the price went up.}

The words <u>original price</u> are mentioned second, so the original price of $1.50 is the denominator.
    The ratio of <u>increase in price</u> to <u>original price</u> is shown below.

$\dfrac{0.25}{1.50}$ ← increase in price
      ← original price

Now rewrite the ratio as a ratio of whole numbers. Recall that if you multiply both the numerator and denominator of a fraction by the same number, you get an equivalent fraction. The decimals in this example are hundredths, so multiply by 100 to get whole numbers. (If the decimals are tenths, multiply by 10. If thousandths, multiply by 1000.) Then write the ratio in lowest terms.

$$\frac{0.25}{1.50} = \frac{(0.25)(100)}{(1.50)(100)} = \frac{25}{150} = \frac{25 \div 25}{150 \div 25} = \frac{1}{6}$$ ← {Ratio in lowest terms}

Ratio as two whole numbers

◀ **Work Problem 3 at the Side.**

EXAMPLE 4 Using Mixed Numbers in Ratios

Write each ratio as a comparison of whole numbers in lowest terms.

(a) 2 days to $2\frac{1}{4}$ days
    Write the ratio as follows. Divide out the common units.

$$\frac{2 \text{ days}}{2\frac{1}{4} \text{ days}} = \frac{2}{2\frac{1}{4}}$$

············ **Continued on Next Page**

Next, write 2 as $\frac{2}{1}$ and $2\frac{1}{4}$ as the improper fraction $\frac{9}{4}$.

Think: 4 · 2 is 8
and 8 + 1 = 9 so
$2\frac{1}{4} = \frac{9}{4}$

$$\frac{2}{2\frac{1}{4}} = \frac{\frac{2}{1}}{\frac{9}{4}}$$

Now rewrite the problem in horizontal format, using the "÷" symbol for division. Finally, multiply by the reciprocal of the divisor, as you did in **Chapter 4.**

$$\frac{\frac{2}{1}}{\frac{9}{4}} = \frac{2}{1} \div \frac{9}{4} = \frac{2}{1} \cdot \frac{4}{9} = \frac{8}{9} \quad \left\{ \begin{array}{l} \text{Ratio in} \\ \text{lowest terms} \end{array} \right.$$

Reciprocals

The ratio, in lowest terms, is $\frac{8}{9}$.

(b) $3\frac{1}{4}$ to $1\frac{1}{2}$

Write the ratio as $\dfrac{3\frac{1}{4}}{1\frac{1}{2}}$. Then write $3\frac{1}{4}$ and $1\frac{1}{2}$ as improper fractions.

Think: 4 · 3 = 12
and 12 + 1 = 13
so $3\frac{1}{4} = \frac{13}{4}$.

$$3\frac{1}{4} = \frac{13}{4} \quad \text{and} \quad 1\frac{1}{2} = \frac{3}{2}$$

Think: 2 · 1 = 2
and 2 + 1 = 3
so $1\frac{1}{2} = \frac{3}{2}$

The ratio is shown below.

$$\frac{3\frac{1}{4}}{1\frac{1}{2}} = \frac{\frac{13}{4}}{\frac{3}{2}}$$

Rewrite as a division problem in horizontal format, using the "÷" symbol. Then multiply by the reciprocal of the divisor.

$$\frac{13}{4} \div \frac{3}{2} = \frac{13}{4} \cdot \frac{2}{3} = \frac{13 \cdot \overset{1}{2}}{\underset{1}{2} \cdot 2 \cdot 3} = \frac{13}{6} \quad \left\{ \begin{array}{l} \text{Ratio in} \\ \text{lowest terms} \end{array} \right.$$

Reciprocals

Note

We can also work **Examples 4(a) and 4(b)** above by using decimals.

(a) $2\frac{1}{4}$ is equivalent to 2.25, so we have the ratio shown below.

$$\frac{2}{2\frac{1}{4}} = \frac{2}{2.25} = \frac{(2)(100)}{(2.25)(100)} = \frac{200}{225} = \frac{200 \div 25}{225 \div 25} = \frac{8}{9} \leftarrow \text{Same result}$$

(b) $3\frac{1}{4}$ is equivalent to 3.25 and $1\frac{1}{2}$ is equivalent to 1.5.

$$\frac{3\frac{1}{4}}{1\frac{1}{2}} = \frac{3.25}{1.5} = \frac{(3.25)(100)}{(1.5)(100)} = \frac{325}{150} = \frac{325 \div 25}{150 \div 25} = \frac{13}{6} \leftarrow \text{Same result}$$

This method would *not* work for fractions that are repeating decimals, such as $\frac{1}{3}$ or $\frac{5}{6}$.

$\cdots\cdots$ **Work Problem 4 at the Side.** ▶

---

4 Write each ratio as a ratio of whole numbers in lowest terms.

(a) $3\frac{1}{2}$ to 4

$$\frac{3\frac{1}{2}}{4} = \frac{\frac{7}{2}}{\frac{4}{1}}$$

$$= \frac{7}{2} \div \frac{4}{1} = \frac{7}{2} \cdot \frac{1}{4}$$

Reciprocals

$$= \underline{\quad\quad}$$

(b) $5\frac{5}{8}$ pounds to $3\frac{3}{4}$ pounds

(c) $3\frac{1}{3}$ inches to $\frac{5}{6}$ inch

Answers

4. (a) $\frac{7}{8}$ (b) $\frac{3}{2}$ (c) $\frac{4}{1}$

5 Write each ratio as a fraction in lowest terms. (*Hint:* Recall that it is usually easier to write the ratio using the smaller measurement unit.)

GS **(a)** 9 inches to 6 feet

Change 6 ft to inches

$$6 \cdot 12 \text{ in.} = \underline{\hspace{1cm}} \text{ in.}$$

$$\frac{9 \text{ in.}}{6 \text{ ft}} = \frac{9 \text{ in.}}{\underline{\hspace{0.7cm}} \text{ in.}} = \frac{9 \div \underline{\hspace{0.5cm}}}{\underline{\hspace{0.5cm}} \div \underline{\hspace{0.5cm}}}$$

$$= \frac{}{\underline{\hspace{1cm}}}$$

(b) 2 days to 8 hours

(c) 7 yards to 14 feet

(d) 3 quarts to 3 gallons

(e) 25 minutes to 2 hours

(f) 4 pounds to 12 ounces

Answers

5. **(a)** 72 in.; $\frac{9 \text{ in.}}{72 \text{ in.}} = \frac{9 \div 9}{72 \div 9} = \frac{1}{8}$ **(b)** $\frac{6}{1}$

(c) $\frac{3}{2}$ **(d)** $\frac{1}{4}$ **(e)** $\frac{5}{24}$ **(f)** $\frac{16}{3}$

OBJECTIVE **3** **Solve ratio problems after converting units.** When a ratio compares measurements, both measurements must be in the *same* units. For example, *feet* must be compared to *feet, hours* to *hours,* and so on.

EXAMPLE 5 **Ratio Applications Using Measurement**

(a) Write the ratio of the length of the shorter board on the left to the length of the longer board on the right. Compare in inches.

$$|\leftarrow 2 \text{ ft} \rightarrow| \quad |\leftarrow 30 \text{ in.} \rightarrow|$$

First, express 2 feet in inches. Because 1 foot has 12 inches, 2 feet is

$$2 \cdot 12 \text{ inches} = 24 \text{ inches}$$

The length of the board on the left is 24 inches, so the ratio of the lengths is shown below. The common units divide out.

> Once the units match, you can divide them out.

$$\frac{2 \text{ ft}}{30 \text{ in.}} = \frac{24 \text{ inches}}{30 \text{ inches}} = \frac{24}{30}$$

Write the ratio in lowest terms.

$$\frac{24}{30} = \frac{24 \div 6}{30 \div 6} = \frac{4}{5} \quad \begin{cases} \text{Ratio in} \\ \text{lowest terms} \end{cases}$$

The shorter board on the left is $\frac{4}{5}$ the length of the longer board on the right.

Note

Notice in the example above that we wrote the ratio using the smaller unit (inches are smaller than feet). Using the smaller unit will help you avoid working with fractions.

(b) Write the ratio of 28 days to 3 weeks.

It is usually easier to write the ratio using the smaller measurement so compare in *days* because days are shorter than weeks.

First express 3 weeks in days. Because 1 week has 7 days, 3 weeks is

$$3 \cdot 7 \text{ days} = 21 \text{ days}$$

The ratio in days is shown below.

$$\frac{28 \text{ days}}{3 \text{ weeks}} = \frac{28 \text{ days}}{21 \text{ days}} = \frac{28}{21} = \frac{28 \div 7}{21 \div 7} = \frac{4}{3} \quad \begin{cases} \text{Ratio in} \\ \text{lowest terms} \end{cases}$$

Use the table below to help set up ratios that compare measurements.

Measurement Comparisons	
Length	**Weight**
12 inches = 1 foot	16 ounces = 1 pound
3 feet = 1 yard	2000 pounds = 1 ton
5280 feet = 1 mile	**Time**
Capacity (Volume)	60 seconds = 1 minute
2 cups = 1 pint	60 minutes = 1 hour
2 pints = 1 quart	24 hours = 1 day
4 quarts = 1 gallon	7 days = 1 week

◀ Work Problem **5** at the Side.

6.1 Exercises

   MyMathLab®

1. **CONCEPT CHECK** What is a ratio? Write an explanation. Then make up an example of a ratio.

2. **CONCEPT CHECK** Both quantities in a ratio have the same units. That means you can do what to the units?

3. **CONCEPT CHECK** To rewrite the ratio $\frac{80}{20}$ in lowest terms, divide both the numerator and the denominator by _____. What is the ratio in lowest terms?

4. **CONCEPT CHECK** To rewrite the ratio $\frac{20}{75}$ in lowest terms, divide both the numerator and the denominator by _____. What is the ratio in lowest terms?

Write each ratio as a fraction in lowest terms. ***See Examples 1 and 2.***

5. 8 days to 9 days

6. $11 to $15

7. $100 to $50

8. 35¢ to 7¢

9. 30 minutes to 90 minutes

10. 9 pounds to 36 pounds

Write each ratio as a ratio of whole numbers in lowest terms. ***See Examples 3 and 4.***

11. $4.50 to $3.50

12. $0.08 to $0.06

13. $1\frac{1}{4}$ to $1\frac{1}{2}$

14. $2\frac{1}{3}$ to $2\frac{2}{3}$

15. **CONCEPT CHECK** When writing the ratio of 20 ounces to 3 pounds as a fraction in lowest terms, is it easier to use ounces or pounds? _____ Explain why.

16. **CONCEPT CHECK** When writing the ratio of 4 days to 36 hours as a fraction in lowest terms, would it be easier to use days or hours? _____ Explain why.

Write each ratio as a fraction in lowest terms. For help, use the table of measurement comparisons on the previous page. ***See Example 5.***

17. 4 feet to 30 inches

First convert 4 ft to inches.
4 • 12 in. = _____ in.

18. 8 feet to 4 yards

First convert 4 yd to feet.
4 • 3 ft = _____ ft.

19. 5 minutes to 1 hour

20. 3 pounds to 6 ounces

21. 5 gallons to 5 quarts

22. 3 cups to 3 pints

The table shows the number of greeting cards that Americans buy for various occasions. Use the information to answer Exercises 23–26. Write each ratio as a fraction in lowest terms.

Holiday/Event	Cards Sold
Valentine's Day	150 million
Mother's Day	130 million
Father's Day	95 million
Graduation	60 million
Halloween	20 million
Thanksgiving	10 million

Source: Hallmark Cards.

23. Find the ratio of Thanksgiving cards to graduation cards.

24. Find the ratio of Halloween cards to Mother's Day cards.

25. Find the ratio of Valentine's Day cards to Thanksgiving cards.

26. Find the ratio of Mother's Day cards to Father's Day cards.

The bar graph shows worldwide sales of the most popular songs of all time. Use the graph to complete Exercises 27–28. Write each ratio as a fraction in lowest terms.

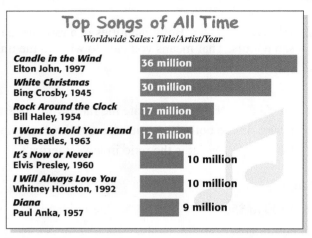

Top Songs of All Time
Worldwide Sales: Title/Artist/Year

Candle in the Wind Elton John, 1997	36 million
White Christmas Bing Crosby, 1945	30 million
Rock Around the Clock Bill Haley, 1954	17 million
I Want to Hold Your Hand The Beatles, 1963	12 million
It's Now or Never Elvis Presley, 1960	10 million
I Will Always Love You Whitney Houston, 1992	10 million
Diana Paul Anka, 1957	9 million

Source: The Music Information Database, songfacts.com

27. Sales of which two songs give a ratio of $\frac{3}{1}$? There may be more than one correct answer.

28. Sales of which two songs give a ratio of $\frac{5}{6}$? There may be more than one correct answer.

*For each figure in Exercises 29–32, find the ratio of the length of the longest side to the length of the shortest side. Write each ratio as a fraction in lowest terms. **See Examples 2–4.***

29.

1.8 meters

0.3 meter   0.3 meter

1.8 meters

30.
0.09 in.

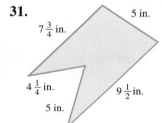

0.12 in.   0.12 in.

0.09 in.

31.

$7\frac{3}{4}$ in.   5 in.

$4\frac{1}{4}$ in. $9\frac{1}{2}$ in.

5 in.

32.
$3\frac{1}{4}$ ft

$5\frac{3}{4}$ ft $6\frac{3}{4}$ ft

$1\frac{3}{4}$ ft

$1\frac{1}{2}$ ft

Write each ratio as a fraction in lowest terms.

33. The price of automobile engine oil has gone from $10 to $12.50 for the 5 quarts needed for an oil change. Find the ratio of the increase in price to the original price.

34. The price of an antibiotic decreased from $8.80 to $5.60 for 10 tablets. Find the ratio of the decrease in price to the original price.

35. The first time a movie was made in Minnesota, the cast and crew spent $59\frac{1}{2}$ days filming winter scenes. The next year, another movie was filmed in $8\frac{3}{4}$ weeks. Find the ratio of the first movie's filming time to the second movie's time. Compare in weeks.

36. The percheron, a large draft horse, measures about $5\frac{3}{4}$ feet at the shoulder. The prehistoric ancestor of the horse measured only $15\frac{3}{4}$ inches at the shoulder. Find the ratio of the percheron's height to its prehistoric ancestor's height. Compare in inches. (*Source: Eyewitness Books: Horse.*)

$5\frac{3}{4}$ ft $15\frac{3}{4}$ in.

6.2 Rates

A *ratio* compares two measurements with the **same** units, such as 9 <u>feet</u> to 12 <u>feet</u> (both length measurements). But many of the comparisons we make use measurements with **different** units, such as shown here.

160 <u>dollars</u> for 8 <u>hours</u> (money to time)

450 <u>miles</u> on 15 <u>gallons</u> (distance to capacity)

This type of comparison is called a **rate.**

OBJECTIVE ▶ 1 Write rates as fractions. Suppose that yesterday you hiked 14 <u>miles</u> in 4 <u>hours</u>. The *rate* at which you hiked can be written as a fraction in lowest terms.

$$\frac{14 \text{ miles}}{4 \text{ hours}} = \frac{14 \text{ miles} \div 2}{4 \text{ hours} \div 2} = \frac{7 \text{ miles}}{2 \text{ hours}} \leftarrow \text{Rate in lowest terms}$$

In a rate, you often find one of these words separating the quantities you are comparing.

in   for   on   per   from

> **CAUTION**
> When writing a rate, always include the units, such as miles, hours, dollars, and so on. Because the units in a rate are different, the units do *not* divide out.

EXAMPLE 1 Writing Rates in Lowest Terms

Write each rate as a fraction in lowest terms.

(a) 5 gallons of chemical for $60

$$\frac{5 \text{ gallons} \div 5}{60 \text{ dollars} \div 5} = \frac{1 \text{ gallon}}{12 \text{ dollars}}$$ The units are different; you **cannot** divide them out.

(b) $4500 wages in 10 weeks

$$\frac{4500 \text{ dollars} \div 10}{10 \text{ weeks} \div 10} = \frac{450 \text{ dollars}}{1 \text{ week}}$$

(c) 2225 miles on 75 gallons of gas

$$\frac{2225 \text{ miles} \div 25}{75 \text{ gallons} \div 25} = \frac{89 \text{ miles}}{3 \text{ gallons}}$$

Be sure to write the units in a *rate*: dollars, miles, gallons, etc.

········· **Work Problem 1 at the Side. ▶**

OBJECTIVE ▶ 2 Find unit rates. When the *denominator* of a rate is 1, it is called a **unit rate.** We use unit rates frequently. For example, you earn $12.75 for *1 hour* of work. This unit rate is written:

$12.75 **per** hour   or $12.75 / hour.

Use **per** or a / mark when writing unit rates.

VOCABULARY TIP

Ratio vs. Rate **Ratios** compare two quantities that have the **same** units, so the units divide out. But **rates** compare two quantities with **different** units, so you must write the units in a rate.

---

1 Write each rate as a fraction in lowest terms.

(a) $6 for 30 packets

$$\frac{\$6}{30 \text{ packets}} = \frac{\$\underline{}}{\underline{} \text{ packets}}$$

To write the rate in lowest terms, divide both numerator and denominator by _____.

(b) 500 miles in 10 hours

(c) 4 teachers for 90 students

(d) 1270 bushels from 30 acres

Answers

1. **(a)** $\frac{\$1}{5 \text{ packets}}$; divide numerator and denominator by 6.
   (b) $\frac{50 \text{ miles}}{1 \text{ hour}}$ **(c)** $\frac{2 \text{ teachers}}{45 \text{ students}}$
   (d) $\frac{127 \text{ bushels}}{3 \text{ acres}}$

VOCABULARY TIP

Per means "for each." For example, if your car gets 30 miles **per** gallon, it gets 30 miles *for each gallon* of gas. Use **per** or a slash mark, like this: 30 miles/gallon.

2 Find each unit rate.

(a) $4.35 for 3 pounds of cheese

$$\frac{\$4.35}{3 \text{ pounds}} \leftarrow \begin{array}{l}\text{Fraction bar}\\ \text{indicates}\\ \text{division.}\end{array}$$

$$\overset{1.}{3)4.35} \quad \begin{array}{l}\text{Finish the}\\ \text{division.}\end{array}$$

(b) 304 miles on 9.5 gallons of gas

(c) $850 in 5 days

(d) 24-pound turkey for 15 people

EXAMPLE 2 Finding Unit Rates

Find each unit rate.

(a) 337.5 miles on 13.5 gallons of gas
Write the rate as a fraction.

$$\frac{337.5 \text{ miles}}{13.5 \text{ gallons}} \leftarrow \text{The fraction bar indicates division.}$$

Divide 337.5 by 13.5 to find the unit rate.

$$\overset{2\,5.}{13.5)337.5}$$

$$\frac{337.5 \text{ miles} \div 13.5}{13.5 \text{ gallons} \div 13.5} = \frac{25 \text{ miles}}{1 \text{ gallon}} \quad \begin{array}{l}\text{Be sure to write}\\ \textbf{miles} \text{ and } \textbf{gallons}\\ \text{in your answer.}\end{array}$$

The unit rate is 25 miles **per** gallon, or 25 miles/gallon.

(b) 549 miles in 18 hours

$$\frac{549 \text{ miles}}{18 \text{ hours}} \quad \text{Divide.} \quad \overset{30.5}{18)549.0}$$

The unit rate is 30.5 miles **per** hour, or 30.5 miles/hour.

(c) $810 in 6 days

$$\frac{810 \text{ dollars}}{6 \text{ days}} \quad \text{Divide.} \quad \overset{135}{6)810} \quad \begin{array}{l}\text{Use } per \text{ or a}\\ slash \text{ mark}\\ \text{to write}\\ \text{unit rates.}\end{array}$$

The unit rate is $135 **per** day, or $135/day.

◀ **Work Problem 2 at the Side.**

OBJECTIVE 3 **Find the best buy based on cost per unit.** When shopping for groceries, household supplies, and health and beauty items, you will find many different brands and package sizes. You can save money by finding the lowest *cost per unit*.

Cost per Unit

Cost per unit is a rate that tells how much you pay for *one* item or *one* unit. Examples are $3.95 per gallon, $47 per shirt, and $2.98 per pound.

EXAMPLE 3 Determining the Best Buy

The local store charges the following prices for pancake syrup. Find the best buy.

Answers

2. (a) $1.45/pound **(b)** 32 miles/gallon
   (c) $170/day **(d)** 1.6 pounds/person

Continued on Next Page

The best buy is the container with the *lowest* cost per unit. All the containers are measured in *ounces* (oz), so you first need to find the *cost per ounce* for each one. Divide the price of the container by the number of ounces in it. Round to the nearest thousandth if necessary.

Let the *order* of the *words* help you set up the rate.

cost ⟶ $1.28
per (means divide) → ⟶ ——————
ounce ⟶ 12 ounces

Size	Cost per Unit (Rounded)
12 ounces	$\dfrac{\$1.28}{12\ \text{ounces}} \approx \$0.107$ per ounce (highest)
24 ounces	$\dfrac{\$1.81}{24\ \text{ounces}} \approx \$0.075$ per ounce (lowest)
36 ounces	$\dfrac{\$2.73}{36\ \text{ounces}} \approx \$0.076$ per ounce

The lowest cost per ounce is $0.075, so the 24-ounce container is the best buy.

Note

Earlier we rounded money amounts to the nearest hundredth (nearest cent). But when comparing unit costs, rounding to the nearest thousandth helps you see the difference between very similar unit costs. Notice that the 24-ounce and 36-ounce syrup containers above both round to $0.08 per ounce if we round to hundredths.

··········· **Work Problem ③ at the Side.** ▶

▦ Calculator Tip

When using a calculator to find unit prices, remember that division is *not* commutative. In **Example 3** above you wanted to find cost per ounce. Let the *order* of the *words* help you enter the numbers in the correct order.

cost   per   ounce
↓   ↓   ↓
Enter   Per means   Enter
the cost.   divide.   number
                       of ounces.
↓   ↓   ↓
$2.73   ÷   36   =   0.076 (rounded)

If you reversed the order and entered 36 ÷ 2.73 =, the result is the number of *ounces* per *dollar*. How could you use that information to find the best buy? (*Answer:* The best buy would be the greatest number of ounces per dollar.)

Finding the best buy is sometimes a complicated process. Things that affect the cost per unit can include "cents off" coupons and differences in how much use you'll get out of each unit.

③ Find the best buy (lowest cost per unit) for each purchase.

(a) 2 quarts for $3.25
3 quarts for $4.95
4 quarts for $6.48

Divide to find each unit cost.

cost → $3.25
per → ——————— = $____ per quart
quart → 2 quarts

Now find the other two unit costs. Then compare. The *lowest* unit cost is the best buy. Circle it.

(b) 6 cans of cola for $1.99
12 cans of cola for $3.49
24 cans of cola for $7

4 Solve each problem.

(a) Some batteries claim to last longer than others. If you believe these claims, which brand is the best buy?

Four-pack of AA-size batteries for $2.79

One AA-size battery for $1.19; lasts twice as long

(b) Which tube of toothpaste is the best buy? You have a coupon for 85¢ off Brand C and a coupon for 50¢ off Brand D.

Brand C is $3.89 for 6 ounces.

Brand D is $1.89 for 2.5 ounces.

EXAMPLE 4	Solving Best Buy Applications

Solve each application problem.

(a) There are many brands of liquid laundry detergent. If you feel they all do a good job of cleaning your clothes, you can base your purchase on cost per unit. But some brands are "concentrated" so you can use less detergent for each load of clothes. The labels from two bottles are shown below. Which of the choices is the best buy?

To find Sudzy's unit cost, divide $3.99 by 64 ounces, not 50 ounces. Read the label. You're getting as many clothes washed as if you bought 64 ounces. Similarly, to find White-O's unit cost, divide $9.89 by 256 ounces (twice 128 ounces, or 2 • 128 ounces = 256 ounces).

$$\text{Sudzy} \quad \frac{\$3.99}{64 \text{ ounces}} \approx \$0.062 \text{ per ounce}$$

$$\text{White-O} \quad \frac{\$9.89}{256 \text{ ounces}} \approx \$0.039 \text{ per ounce}$$

> The best buy is the *lower* cost per ounce.

White-O has the lower cost per ounce and is the best buy. (However, if you try it and it doesn't get out all the stains, Sudzy may be worth the extra cost.)

(b) "Cents-off" coupons also affect the best buy. Suppose you are looking at these choices for "extra-strength" pain reliever. Both brands have the same amount of pain reliever in each tablet.

Brand X is $2.29 for 50 tablets.

Brand Y is $10.75 for 200 tablets.

You have a 40¢ coupon for Brand X and a 75¢ coupon for Brand Y. Which choice is the best buy?

To find the best buy, first subtract the coupon amounts, then divide to find the lowest cost per ounce.

Brand X costs $2.29 − $0.40 = $1.89

$$\frac{\$1.89}{50 \text{ tablets}} \approx \$0.038 \text{ per tablet}$$

Brand Y costs $10.75 − $0.75 = $10.00

> Look for the *lower* cost per tablet.

$$\frac{\$10.00}{200 \text{ tablets}} = \$0.05 \text{ per tablet}$$

Brand X has the lower cost per tablet and is the best buy.

◄ **Work Problem 4 at the Side.**

6.2 Exercises

  MyMathLab®

Download the MyDashBoard App

Write each rate as a fraction in lowest terms. **See Example 1.**

1. 15 feet in 35 seconds

2. 100 miles in 30 hours

3. 25 letters in 5 minutes

4. 68 pills for 17 people

5. 72 miles on 4 gallons

6. 132 miles on 8 gallons

7. CONCEPT CHECK   To find a unit rate, do you add, subtract, multiply, or divide? _____ Show the correct set-up to find this unit rate: $5.85 for 3 boxes.

8. CONCEPT CHECK   Circle the correct answer. When finding this unit rate, 15 hospital rooms for 3 nurses, the final answer will be:

5 to 1   5 rooms for 1 nurse   5 nurses for 1 room

Find each unit rate. **See Example 2.**

9. $60 in 5 hours

10. $2500 in 20 days

11. 7.5 pounds for 6 people

12. 44 bushels from 8 trees

13. $413.20 for 4 days

14. $74.25 for 9 hours

Earl kept the following record of the gas he bought for his car. For each entry, find the number of miles he traveled and the unit rate. Round your answers to the nearest tenth.

	Date	Odometer at Start	Odometer at End	Miles Traveled	Gallons Purchased	Miles per Gallon
15.	2/4	27,432.3	27,758.2		15.5	
16.	2/9	27,758.2	28,058.1		13.4	
17.	2/16	28,058.1	28,396.7		16.2	
18.	2/20	28,396.7	28,704.5		13.3	

Source: Author's car records.

Find the best buy (based on the cost per unit) for each item. Round to the nearest thousandth, if necessary. **See Example 3.** (*Source:* Cub Foods, Target, Rainbow Foods.)

19. Black pepper

20. Shampoo

21. Cereal
▶ 12 ounces for $2.49
   14 ounces for $2.89
   18 ounces for $3.96

22. Soup (same size cans)
2 cans for $2.18
3 cans for $3.57
5 cans for $5.29

23. Chunky peanut butter
▶ 12 ounces for $1.29
🖩 18 ounces for $1.79
   28 ounces for $3.39
   40 ounces for $4.39

24. Baked beans
🖩 8 ounces for $0.59
   16 ounces for $0.99
   21 ounces for $1.29
   28 ounces for $1.89

25. Suppose you are choosing between two brands of chicken noodle soup. Brand A is $0.88 per can and Brand B is $0.98 per can. The cans are the same size, but Brand B has more chunks of chicken in it. Which soup is the best buy? Explain your choice.

26. A small bag of potatoes costs $0.19 per pound. A large bag costs $0.15 per pound. But there are only two people in your family, so half the large bag would probably spoil before you used it up. Which bag is the best buy? Explain.

Solve each application problem. **See Examples 2–4.**

27. Makesha lost 10.5 pounds in six weeks. What was her rate of loss in pounds per week?

The rate is $\dfrac{10.5 \text{ pounds}}{6 \text{ weeks}}$ Divide: $6\overline{)10.5}$

28. Enrique's taco recipe uses three pounds of meat to feed 10 people. Give the rate in pounds per person.

The rate is $\dfrac{3 \text{ pounds}}{10 \text{ people}}$ Divide: $10\overline{)3.0}$

29. Russ works 7 hours to earn $85.82. What is his pay rate per hour?

30. Find the cost of 1 gallon of Hawaiian Punch beverage if 18 gallons for a graduation party cost $55.62.

The table lists information about three long-distance calling cards. The connection fee is charged each time you make a call, no matter how long the call lasts. Use the information in the table to answer Exercises 31–34. Round answers to the nearest thousandth when necessary.

LONG-DISTANCE CALLING CARDS (U.S.)

Card Name	Cost per Minute	Connection Fee
Penny Saver	$0.005	$0.39
Most Minutes	$0.0025	$0.49
USA Card	$0.01	$0.25

Source: noblecom.com

31. (a) Find the *actual* total cost, including the connection charge, for a five-minute call using each card.

(b) Find the cost per minute for this call using each card and select the best buy.

32. (a) Find the *actual* total cost, including the connection charge, for a 90-minute call using each card.

(b) Find the cost per minute for this call using each card and select the best buy.

33. Find the *actual* total cost and the per minute cost for a 30-minute call using each card. What do you see when you compare the unit rates for this call?

34. All the cards round calls up to the next full minute.

(a) Suppose you call the wrong number. How much would you pay for this 40-*second* call on each card?

(b) How much would you save on this call by using the USA card instead of Most Minutes?

35. If you believe the claims that some batteries last longer, which is the best buy?

36. Which is the best buy, assuming these laundry detergents both clean equally well?

37. Three brands of cornflakes are available. Brand G is priced at $2.39 for 10 ounces. Brand K is $3.99 for 20.3 ounces and Brand P is $3.39 for 16.5 ounces. You have a coupon for 50¢ off Brand P and a coupon for 60¢ off Brand G. Which cereal is the best buy based on cost per unit?

38. Two brands of facial tissue are available. Brand K is priced at $5 for three boxes of 175 tissues each. Brand S is priced at $1.29 per box of 125 tissues. You have a coupon for 20¢ off one box of Brand S and a coupon for 45¢ off one box of Brand K. How can you get the best buy on one box of tissue?

Relating Concepts (Exercises 39–43) For Individual or Group Work

On the first page of this chapter, we said that unit rates can help you get the best deal on cell phone service. Use the information in the table to **work Exercises 39–43** in order. Round all money answers to the nearest cent.

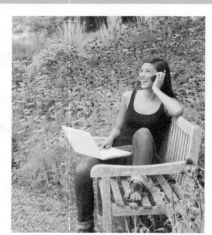

CELL PHONE PLANS

Plan	Anytime Minutes	Monthly Charge*	Cost per Minute (to nearest cent)	Overage†
A	450	$39.95		45¢
B	900	$59.95		40¢

Source: Verizon.com

* Does not include taxes or special fees.
† Cost per extra minute if you use more minutes than your plan covers.

39. Find the cost per minute for each plan. Round your answers to the nearest cent and write them in the table above. Which plan is the better buy based on cost per minute?

40. In a 30-day month, what is the average number of minutes you can use your phone each day on:

(a) Plan A

(b) Plan B

41. Suppose you are on Plan A. Last month you used 2 more minutes each day than the average number of minutes you calculated in **Exercise 40.** Find the new cost per minute for last month. (Assume 30 days in last month.)

42. Suppose you are on Plan B. Last month you used 3 more minutes each day than the average number of minutes you calculated in **Exercise 40.** Find the new cost per minute for last month. (Assume 30 days in last month.)

43. The company also offers Plan C with unlimited minutes for $69.95 per month. If you had Plan C, find the cost per minute for the situations described in **Exercises 41 and 42.**

6.3 Proportions

OBJECTIVE ① Write proportions. A **proportion** states that two ratios (or rates) are equal. Here is an example.

$$\frac{\$20}{4 \text{ hours}} = \frac{\$40}{8 \text{ hours}}$$

This is a proportion that says the rate $\frac{\$20}{4 \text{ hours}}$ is equal to the rate $\frac{\$40}{8 \text{ hours}}$. As the amount of money doubles, the number of hours also doubles. This proportion is read:

20 dollars **is to** 4 hours **as** 40 dollars **is to** 8 hours

EXAMPLE 1 Writing Proportions

Write each proportion.

(a) 6 feet is to 11 feet **as** 18 feet is to 33 feet.

$$\frac{6 \text{ feet}}{11 \text{ feet}} = \frac{18 \text{ feet}}{33 \text{ feet}} \quad \text{so} \quad \frac{6}{11} = \frac{18}{33}$$ The common units (feet) divide out and are not written.

(b) $9 is to 6 liters **as** $3 is to 2 liters.

$$\frac{\$9}{6 \text{ liters}} = \frac{\$3}{2 \text{ liters}}$$ The units are **different**, so you must write them in the proportion.

········· **Work Problem ① at the Side.** ▶

OBJECTIVE ② Determine whether proportions are true or false. There are two ways to see whether a proportion is true. One way is to *write both of the ratios in lowest terms.*

EXAMPLE 2 Writing Both Ratios in Lowest Terms

Determine whether each proportion is true or false by writing both ratios in lowest terms.

(a) $\frac{5}{9} = \frac{18}{27}$

Write each ratio in lowest terms.

$$\frac{5}{9} \leftarrow \text{Already in lowest terms} \qquad \frac{18 \div 9}{27 \div 9} = \frac{2}{3} \leftarrow \text{Lowest terms}$$

Because $\frac{5}{9}$ is *not* equal to $\frac{2}{3}$, the proportion is *false*. The ratios are *not* proportional.

(b) $\frac{16}{12} = \frac{28}{21}$

Write each ratio in lowest terms. Both ratios are in lowest terms.

$$\frac{16 \div 4}{12 \div 4} = \frac{4}{3} \quad \text{and} \quad \frac{28 \div 7}{21 \div 7} = \frac{4}{3}$$

Both ratios are equal to $\frac{4}{3}$, so the proportion is *true*. The ratios are proportional.

········· **Work Problem ② at the Side.** ▶

OBJECTIVES

① Write proportions.
② Determine whether proportions are true or false.
③ Find the unknown number in a proportion.

① Write each proportion.

(a) $7 is to 3 cans as $28 is to 12 cans.

$$\frac{\$7}{3 \text{ cans}} = \underline{}$$ Complete the proportion.

(b) 9 meters is to 16 meters as 18 meters is to 32 meters.

(c) 5 is to 7 as 35 is to 49.

(d) 10 is to 30 as 60 is to 180.

② Determine whether each proportion is true or false by writing both ratios in lowest terms.

(a) $\frac{6}{12} = \frac{15}{30}$

(b) $\frac{20}{24} = \frac{3}{4}$

(c) $\frac{25}{40} = \frac{30}{48}$

(d) $\frac{35}{45} = \frac{12}{18}$

Answers

1. **(a)** $\frac{\$7}{3 \text{ cans}} = \frac{\$28}{12 \text{ cans}}$ **(b)** $\frac{9}{16} = \frac{18}{32}$

   (c) $\frac{5}{7} = \frac{35}{49}$ **(d)** $\frac{10}{30} = \frac{60}{180}$

2. **(a)** $\frac{1}{2} = \frac{1}{2}$; true **(b)** $\frac{5}{6} \neq \frac{3}{4}$; false

   (c) $\frac{5}{8} = \frac{5}{8}$; true **(d)** $\frac{7}{9} \neq \frac{2}{3}$; false

A second way to see whether a proportion is true is to find *cross products*.

Using Cross Products to Determine Whether a Proportion Is True

To see whether a proportion is true, first multiply along one diagonal, then multiply along the other diagonal, as shown here.

$$5 \cdot 4 = 20$$

$$\frac{2}{5} = \frac{4}{10}$$

Cross products are equal.

$$2 \cdot 10 = 20$$

In this case the **cross products** are both 20. When cross products are *equal*, the proportion is *true*. If the cross products are *unequal*, the proportion is *false*.

Note

Why does the cross products test work? It is based on rewriting both fractions with a common denominator of 5 • 10 or 50. (We do not search for the *lowest* common denominator. We simply use the product of the two given denominators.)

$$\frac{2 \cdot 10}{5 \cdot 10} = \frac{20}{50} \quad \text{and} \quad \frac{4 \cdot 5}{10 \cdot 5} = \frac{20}{50}$$

We see that $\frac{2}{5}$ and $\frac{4}{10}$ are equivalent because both can be rewritten as $\frac{20}{50}$. The cross products test takes a shortcut by comparing only the two numerators $(20 = 20)$.

EXAMPLE 3   **Using Cross Products**

Use cross products to see whether each proportion is true or false.

(a) $\dfrac{3}{5} = \dfrac{12}{20}$ Multiply along one diagonal and then multiply along the other diagonal.

$$5 \cdot 12 = 60$$

$$\frac{3}{5} = \frac{12}{20}$$

Equal

When cross products are equal, the proportion is true.

$$3 \cdot 20 = 60$$

The cross products are *equal,* so the proportion is *true*.

CAUTION

Use cross products *only* when working with *proportions*. Do **not** use cross products when multiplying fractions, adding fractions, or writing fractions in lowest terms.

· **Continued on Next Page**

(b) $\dfrac{2\frac{1}{3}}{3\frac{1}{3}} = \dfrac{9}{16}$ Find the cross products.

> Write $3\frac{1}{3}$ as $\frac{10}{3}$ and write 9 as $\frac{9}{1}$.

$$3\frac{1}{3} \cdot 9 = \dfrac{10}{\cancel{3}} \cdot \dfrac{\overset{3}{\cancel{9}}}{1} = \dfrac{30}{1} = 30 \leftarrow$$

$$\dfrac{2\frac{1}{3}}{3\frac{1}{3}} \bowtie \dfrac{9}{16}$$

Unequal; proportion is false.

$$2\frac{1}{3} \cdot 16 = \dfrac{7}{3} \cdot \dfrac{16}{1} = \dfrac{112}{3} = 37\frac{1}{3} \leftarrow$$

The cross products are *unequal,* so the proportion is *false.*

Note

The numbers in a proportion do *not* have to be whole numbers. They may be fractions, mixed numbers, decimal numbers, and so on.

··· Work Problem ❸ at the Side. ▶

OBJECTIVE ❸ **Find the unknown number in a proportion.** Four numbers are used in a proportion. If any three of these numbers are known, the fourth can be found. For example, find the unknown number that will make this proportion true.

$$\dfrac{3}{5} = \dfrac{x}{40}$$

The variable x represents the unknown number. First find the cross products.

$$\dfrac{3}{5} \bowtie \dfrac{x}{40}$$

$5 \cdot x$ ⎫
⎬ Cross products
$3 \cdot 40$ ⎭

To make the proportion true, the cross products must be equal. This gives us the following equation.

$$\underbrace{5 \cdot x}_{5x} = \underbrace{3 \cdot 40}_{120}$$

Recall from **Chapter 2** that we can solve an equation of this type by dividing both sides by the coefficient of the variable term. In this case, the coefficient of $5x$ is 5.

$$\dfrac{5x}{5} = \dfrac{120}{5} \quad \leftarrow \text{Divide both sides by 5.}$$

On the left side, divide out the common factor of 5; slashes indicate the division.

$$\dfrac{\cancel{5}^{1} \cdot x}{\cancel{5}_{1}} = 24 \qquad \text{On the right side, divide 120 by 5 to get 24.}$$

$$x = 24$$

---

❸ Find the cross products to see whether each proportion is true or false.

$(9)(10) = \underline{\quad}$

GS (a) $\dfrac{5}{9} = \dfrac{10}{18}$

$(5)(18) = \underline{\quad}$

(b) $\dfrac{32}{15} = \dfrac{16}{8}$

(c) $\dfrac{10}{17} = \dfrac{20}{34}$

$(6)(5) = \underline{\quad}$

GS (d) $\dfrac{2.4}{6} = \dfrac{5}{12}$

$(2.4)(12) = \underline{\quad}$

(e) $\dfrac{3}{4.25} = \dfrac{24}{34}$

(f) $\dfrac{1\frac{1}{6}}{2\frac{1}{3}} = \dfrac{4}{8}$

Answers

3. **(a)** $(9)(10) = 90$; $(5)(18) = 90$; true
 (b) $240 \neq 256$; false
 (c) $340 = 340$; true
 (d) $(6)(5) = 30$; $(2.4)(12) = 28.8$; false
 (e) $102 = 102$; true
 (f) $9\frac{1}{3} = 9\frac{1}{3}$; true

The unknown number in the proportion is 24. The complete proportion is shown below.

$$\frac{3}{5} = \frac{24}{40} \leftarrow x \text{ is } 24.$$

Check by finding the cross products. If they are equal, you solved the problem correctly. If they are unequal, rework the problem.

$$5 \cdot 24 = 120 \leftarrow$$
$$\frac{3}{5} = \frac{24}{40}$$
Equal; proportion is true.
$$3 \cdot 40 = 120 \leftarrow$$

The solution is 24, not 120.

The cross products are equal, so the solution, $x = 24$, is correct.

> **CAUTION**
>
> The solution is 24, which is the unknown number in the proportion. 120 is **not** the solution; it is the cross product you get when *checking* the solution.

Solve a proportion for an unknown number by using the following steps.

> **Solving a Proportion to Find an Unknown Number**
>
> **Step 1** Find the cross products.
>
> **Step 2** Show that the cross products are equal.
>
> **Step 3** Divide both sides of the equation by the coefficient of the variable term.
>
> **Step 4** Check by writing the solution in the *original* proportion and finding the cross products.

EXAMPLE 4 **Solving Proportions**

Find the unknown number in each proportion. Round answers to the nearest hundredth when necessary.

(a) $\dfrac{16}{x} = \dfrac{32}{20}$ You can write $\frac{32}{20}$ in lowest terms as $\frac{8}{5}$

Recall that ratios can be rewritten in lowest terms. If desired, you can do that *before* finding the cross products. In this example, write $\frac{32}{20}$ in lowest terms as $\frac{8}{5}$, which gives the proportion $\dfrac{16}{x} = \dfrac{8}{5}$.

$$x \cdot 8 \leftarrow$$
Step 1 $\qquad\qquad \dfrac{16}{x} = \dfrac{8}{5}$ Find the cross products.
$$16 \cdot 5 \leftarrow$$

························ **Continued on Next Page**

Step 2 $x \cdot 8 = \underbrace{16 \cdot 5}$ Show that the cross products are equal.

$x \cdot 8 = \quad 80$

Step 3 $\dfrac{x \cdot \overset{1}{8}}{\underset{1}{8}} = \dfrac{80}{8}$ ← Divide both sides by 8.

$x = 10$ ← Find x. (No rounding is necessary.)

Step 4 Write the solution in the *original* proportion and check by finding the cross products.

$10 \cdot 32 = 320$ ←

x is 10 → $\dfrac{16}{10} = \dfrac{32}{20}$ Equal; proportion is true.

$16 \cdot 20 = 320$ ←

The cross products are equal, so **10** is the correct solution.   The solution is 10, not 320.

> **Note**
>
> It is not necessary to write the ratios in lowest terms before solving. However, if you do, you will have smaller numbers to work with.

(b) $\dfrac{7}{12} = \dfrac{15}{x}$

Step 1 $\dfrac{7}{12} = \dfrac{15}{x}$

$12 \cdot 15 = 180$ ←   Find the cross products.

$7 \cdot x$ ←

Step 2 $7 \cdot x = 180$ ← Show that cross products are equal.

Step 3 $\dfrac{\overset{1}{7} \cdot x}{\underset{1}{7}} = \dfrac{180}{7}$ ← Divide both sides by 7.

The rounded solution is 25.71

$x \approx 25.71$ ← Rounded to nearest hundredth

When the division does not come out even, check for directions on how to round your answer. Divide out one more place, then round.

$\dfrac{25.714}{7 \overline{)180.000}}$ ← Divide out to thousandths so you can round to hundredths.

Step 4 Write the solution in the original proportion and check by finding the cross products.

$(12)(15) = 180$ ←

$\dfrac{7}{12} \approx \dfrac{15}{25.71}$ Very close, but *not* equal due to rounding the solution

$(7)(25.71) = 179.97$ ←

The cross products are slightly different because you rounded the value of x. However, they are close enough to see that the problem was done correctly and **25.71** is the approximate solution (**not** 179.97).

···· **Work Problem ④ at the Side.** ▶

---

④ Find the unknown numbers. Round to hundredths when necessary. Check your answers by finding the cross products.

GS (a)

$2 \cdot x$ ←

$\dfrac{1}{2} = \dfrac{x}{12}$ Cross products

$1 \cdot 12$ ←

$2 \cdot x = 12$ Now find the solution. Divide both sides by 2.

(b) $\dfrac{6}{10} = \dfrac{15}{x}$

(c) $\dfrac{28}{x} = \dfrac{21}{9}$

(d) $\dfrac{x}{8} = \dfrac{3}{5}$

(e) $\dfrac{14}{11} = \dfrac{x}{3}$

Answers

4. (a) $\dfrac{\overset{1}{2} \cdot x}{\underset{1}{2}} = \dfrac{12}{2}; x = 6$ **(b)** $x = 25$

(c) $x = 12$ **(d)** $x = 4.8$

(e) $x \approx 3.82$ (rounded to nearest hundredth)

The next example shows how to solve for the unknown number in a proportion with fractions or decimals.

EXAMPLE 5 Solving Proportions with Mixed Numbers and Decimals

Find the unknown number in each proportion.

(a) $\dfrac{2\frac{1}{5}}{6} = \dfrac{x}{10}$

Step 1

$\dfrac{2\frac{1}{5}}{6} = \dfrac{x}{10}$ ⟍⟋ $\begin{array}{l} 6 \cdot x \\ \\ 2\frac{1}{5} \cdot 10 \end{array}$ ← Find the cross products.

Find $2\frac{1}{5} \cdot 10$.

$$2\frac{1}{5} \cdot 10 = \frac{11}{5} \cdot \frac{10}{1} = \frac{11 \cdot 2 \cdot \overset{1}{\cancel{5}}}{\cancel{5} \cdot 1} = \frac{22}{1} = 22$$

Changed to improper fraction

Step 2 $6 \cdot x = 22$ ← Show that cross products are equal.

Step 3 $\dfrac{\overset{1}{\cancel{6}} \cdot x}{\underset{1}{\cancel{6}}} = \dfrac{22}{6}$ ← Divide both sides by 6.

Write the solution as a mixed number in lowest terms.

$$x = \frac{22 \div 2}{6 \div 2} = \frac{11}{3} = 3\frac{2}{3}$$

Step 4 Write the solution in the original proportion and check by finding the cross products.

$$6 \cdot 3\frac{2}{3} = \frac{2 \cdot \overset{1}{\cancel{3}}}{1} \cdot \frac{11}{\underset{1}{\cancel{3}}} = \frac{22}{1} = 22 \leftarrow$$

$\dfrac{2\frac{1}{5}}{6} = \dfrac{3\frac{2}{3}}{10}$ ⟍⟋ Equal

$$2\frac{1}{5} \cdot 10 = \frac{11}{\underset{1}{\cancel{5}}} \cdot \frac{2 \cdot \overset{1}{\cancel{5}}}{1} = \frac{22}{1} = 22 \leftarrow$$

The cross products are equal, so $3\frac{2}{3}$ is the correct solution.

The solution is $3\frac{2}{3}$, **not** 22.

Continued on Next Page

Note

You can use decimal numbers and your calculator to solve **Example 5(a)** on the previous page. $2\frac{1}{5}$ is equivalent to 2.2, so the cross products are

$$6 \cdot x = (2.2)(10)$$

$$\frac{\overset{1}{\cancel{6}} \cdot x}{\cancel{6}} = \frac{22}{6}$$

When you divide 22 by 6 on your calculator, it shows 3.666666667. Write the answer using a bar to show the repeating digit: $3.\overline{6}$. Or round the answer to 3.67 (nearest hundredth).

(b) $\dfrac{1.5}{0.6} = \dfrac{2}{x}$

$(1.5)(x) = (0.6)(2) \leftarrow$ Show that cross products are equal.

$(1.5)(x) = 1.2$

$\dfrac{(\overset{1}{\cancel{1.5}})(x)}{\underset{1}{\cancel{1.5}}} = \dfrac{1.2}{1.5} \longleftarrow$ Divide both sides by 1.5.

$x = \dfrac{1.2}{1.5}$ Complete the division. $1.5\overline{\smash{)}1.20}$ gives $.8$

$x = 0.8$

So the solution is 0.8.

Write the solution in the original equation, and check by finding the cross products.

$$(0.6)(2) = 1.2 \leftarrow$$

$$\frac{\mathbf{1.5}}{\mathbf{0.6}} = \frac{\mathbf{2}}{\mathbf{0.8}} \qquad \text{Equal}$$

$$(1.5)(0.8) = 1.2 \leftarrow$$

The cross products are equal, so **0.8** is the correct solution. ⟵ The solution is 0.8 (not 1.2)

· **Work Problem ⑤ at the Side.** ▶

---

⑤ Find the unknown numbers. Round to hundredths on the decimal problems when necessary. Check your solutions by finding the cross products.

(a) $\dfrac{3\frac{1}{4}}{2} = \dfrac{x}{8}$ $\overset{2 \cdot x}{}$

$$3\frac{1}{4} \cdot 8 = \frac{13}{\underset{1}{\cancel{4}}} \cdot \frac{\overset{2}{\cancel{8}}}{1}$$

$$= \frac{26}{1}$$

$2 \cdot x = 26$ Find the solution.

(b) $\dfrac{x}{3} = \dfrac{1\frac{2}{3}}{5}$

(c) $\dfrac{0.06}{x} = \dfrac{0.3}{0.4}$

(d) $\dfrac{2.2}{5} = \dfrac{13}{x}$

(e) $\dfrac{x}{6} = \dfrac{0.5}{1.2}$

(f) $\dfrac{0}{2} = \dfrac{x}{7.092}$

Answers

5. **(a)** $x = 13$ **(b)** $x = 1$ **(c)** $x = 0.08$
  (d) $x \approx 29.55$ (rounded to nearest hundredth)
  (e) $x = 2.5$ **(f)** $x = 0$

6.3 Exercises

  MyMathLab®

CONCEPT CHECK *Write each proportion.* ***See Example 1.***

1. $9 is to 12 cans as $18 is to 24 cans.

2. 28 people is to 7 cars as 16 people is to 4 cars.

3. 200 adults is to 450 children as 4 adults is to 9 children.

4. 150 trees is to 1 acre as 1500 trees is to 10 acres.

5. 120 feet is to 150 feet as 8 feet is to 10 feet.

6. $6 is to $9 as $10 is to $15.

Determine whether each proportion is true or false by writing the ratios in lowest terms. Show the simplified ratios and then write true *or* false. ***See Example 2.***

7. $\dfrac{6}{10} = \dfrac{3}{5}$

8. $\dfrac{1}{4} = \dfrac{9}{36}$

9. $\dfrac{5}{8} = \dfrac{25}{40}$

10. $\dfrac{2}{3} = \dfrac{20}{27}$

11. $\dfrac{150}{200} = \dfrac{200}{300}$

12. $\dfrac{100}{120} = \dfrac{75}{100}$

13. CONCEPT CHECK What is a proportion? Explain. Then draw arrows on the proportion below and show what numbers to multiply to find the cross products.

$$\frac{30}{6} = \frac{45}{9}$$

14. CONCEPT CHECK Explain how to tell if a proportion is true or false after you have found the cross products.

In Exercises 15–26, use cross products to determine whether each proportion is true or false. Show the cross products and then circle True *or* False. ***See Example 3.***

15. $\dfrac{2}{9} = \dfrac{6}{27}$

True   False

16. $\dfrac{20}{25} = \dfrac{4}{5}$

True   False

17. $\dfrac{20}{28} = \dfrac{12}{16}$

True   False

18. $\dfrac{16}{40} = \dfrac{22}{55}$

True   False

19. $\dfrac{110}{18} = \dfrac{160}{27}$

True   False

20. $\dfrac{600}{420} = \dfrac{20}{14}$

True   False

21. $\dfrac{3.5}{4} = \dfrac{7}{8}$

True   False

22. $\dfrac{36}{23} = \dfrac{9}{5.75}$

True   False

23. $\dfrac{18}{15} = \dfrac{2\frac{5}{6}}{2\frac{1}{2}}$

True   False

24. $\dfrac{1\frac{3}{10}}{3\frac{1}{5}} = \dfrac{4}{9}$

True   False

25. $\dfrac{6}{3\frac{2}{3}} = \dfrac{18}{11}$

True   False

26. $\dfrac{16}{13} = \dfrac{2}{1\frac{5}{8}}$

True   False

27. CONCEPT CHECK Suppose Joe Mauer of the Minnesota Twins had 68 hits in 200 times at bat, and Joey Votto of the Cincinnati Reds was at bat 450 times and got 153 hits. Paula is trying to convince Jamie that the two men hit equally well. Show how you could use a proportion and cross products to see whether Paula is correct.

28. CONCEPT CHECK Jay worked 3.5 hours and packed 91 cartons. Craig packed 126 cartons in 5.25 hours. To see if the men worked equally fast, Barry set up this proportion:

$$\dfrac{3.5}{91} = \dfrac{126}{5.25}$$

Explain what is wrong with Barry's proportion and write a correct one. Is the correct proportion true or false?

Solve each proportion to find the unknown number. Round your answers to hundredths when necessary. Check your answers by finding cross products. **See Examples 4 and 5.**

$3 \cdot x$

29. $\dfrac{1}{3} = \dfrac{x}{12}$

$1 \cdot 12$

$3 \cdot x = \underline{1 \cdot 12}$

$3 \cdot x = \underline{}$

$\dfrac{\overset{1}{\cancel{3}} \cdot x}{\underset{1}{\cancel{3}}} = \dfrac{\underline{}}{3}$

$x = \underline{}$

$6 \cdot 15$

30. $\dfrac{x}{6} = \dfrac{15}{18}$

$x \cdot 18$

$x \cdot 18 = \underline{6 \cdot 15}$

$x \cdot 18 = \underline{}$

$\dfrac{x \cdot \overset{1}{\cancel{18}}}{\underset{1}{\cancel{18}}} = \dfrac{\underline{}}{18}$

$x = \underline{}$

31. $\dfrac{15}{10} = \dfrac{3}{x}$

32. $\dfrac{5}{x} = \dfrac{20}{8}$

33. $\dfrac{x}{11} = \dfrac{32}{4}$

34. $\dfrac{12}{9} = \dfrac{8}{x}$

35. $\dfrac{42}{x} = \dfrac{18}{39}$

36. $\dfrac{49}{x} = \dfrac{14}{18}$

37. $\dfrac{x}{25} = \dfrac{4}{20}$

38. $\dfrac{6}{x} = \dfrac{4}{8}$

39. $\dfrac{8}{x} = \dfrac{24}{30}$

40. $\dfrac{32}{5} = \dfrac{x}{10}$

41. $\dfrac{99}{55} = \dfrac{44}{x}$

42. $\dfrac{x}{12} = \dfrac{101}{147}$

43. $\dfrac{0.7}{9.8} = \dfrac{3.6}{x}$

44. $\dfrac{x}{3.6} = \dfrac{4.5}{6}$

45. $\dfrac{250}{24.8} = \dfrac{x}{1.75}$

46. $\dfrac{4.75}{17} = \dfrac{43}{x}$

*Find the unknown number in each proportion. Write your answers as whole or mixed numbers when possible. **See Example 5.***

47. $\dfrac{15}{1\frac{2}{3}} = \dfrac{9}{x}$

48. $\dfrac{x}{\frac{3}{10}} = \dfrac{2\frac{2}{9}}{1}$

49. $\dfrac{2\frac{1}{3}}{1\frac{1}{2}} = \dfrac{x}{2\frac{1}{4}}$

50. $\dfrac{1\frac{5}{6}}{x} = \dfrac{\frac{3}{14}}{\frac{6}{7}}$

Solve each proportion two different ways. First change all the numbers to decimal form and solve. Then change all the numbers to fraction form and solve; write your answers in lowest terms.

51. $\dfrac{\frac{1}{2}}{x} = \dfrac{2}{0.8}$

52. $\dfrac{\frac{3}{20}}{0.1} = \dfrac{0.03}{x}$

53. $\dfrac{x}{\frac{3}{50}} = \dfrac{0.15}{1\frac{4}{5}}$

54. $\dfrac{8\frac{4}{5}}{1\frac{1}{10}} = \dfrac{x}{0.4}$

Relating Concepts (Exercises 55–56) For Individual or Group Work

Work Exercises 55–56 in order. *First prove that the proportions are **not** true. Then create four true proportions for each exercise by changing only one number at a time.*

55. $\dfrac{10}{4} = \dfrac{5}{3}$

56. $\dfrac{6}{8} = \dfrac{24}{30}$

Summary Exercises *Ratios, Rates, and Proportions*

Use the bar graph of the countries with the most websites to complete Exercises 1–4. Write each ratio as a fraction in lowest terms.

1. Write the ratio of the number of websites in Japan to the number of websites in Germany.

2. What is the ratio of the number of websites in Brazil to the number of websites in Italy?

3. Find the ratio of the number of websites in Italy and Germany compared to the number of websites in Japan.

4. Write the ratio of the number of websites in the USA compared to the total number of websites in all the other countries shown in the graph.

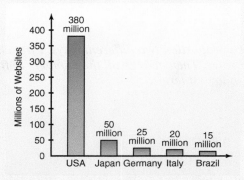

COUNTRIES WITH THE MOST WEBSITES

Number of websites, rounded to the nearest 5 million.

Source: *Scholastic Book of World Records.*

The bar graph shows the number of Americans who play various instruments. Use the graph to complete Exercises 5 and 6. Write each ratio as a fraction in lowest terms.

AMERICANS MAKE MUSIC BY THE MILLIONS

How many people play each type of instrument?

Piano 22 million
Guitar 20 million
Organ 6 million
Clarinet 4 million
Drums 3 million
Violin 2 million

Source: *America by the Numbers.*

5. Write six ratios that compare the least popular instrument to each of the other instruments.

6. Which two instruments give each of these ratios? There may be more than one correct answer.

   (a) $\frac{5}{1}$

   (b) $\frac{2}{1}$

CONCEPT CHECK *The table lists data on the top three individual scoring NBA basketball games of all time. Use the data to answer Exercises 7 and 8. Round answers to the nearest tenth.*

7. What was Wilt Chamberlain's scoring rate in points per minute and in minutes per point?

8. Find Kobe Bryant's scoring rate in points per minute and minutes per point.

Player	Date	Points	Min
Wilt Chamberlain	3/2/62	100	48
Kobe Bryant	1/22/06	81	48
David Thompson	9/4/78	73	43

Source: *sportcity.com*

Wilt Chamberlain (#13)

9. Lucinda's paycheck showed gross pay of $652.80 for 40 hours of work and $195.84 for 8 hours of overtime work. Find her regular hourly pay rate and her overtime rate.

10. Satellite TV service is being offered to new subscribers at $29.99 per month for 150 channels, $34.99 per month for 210 channels, or $39.99 per month for 225 channels. What is the monthly cost per channel under each plan, to the nearest cent? (*Source:* DIRECTV)

11. Find the best buy on gourmet coffee beans. Round to the nearest cent.

11 ounces for $6.79

12 ounces for $7.24

16 ounces for $10.99

(*Source:* Cub Foods.)

12. Which brand of cat food is the best buy? You have a coupon for $2 off on Brand P, and another for $1 off on Brand N.

Brand N is $3.75 for 3.5 pounds

Brand P is $5.99 for 7 pounds

Brand R is $10.79 for 18 pounds

Use either the method of writing in lowest terms or the method of finding cross products to decide whether each proportion is true or false. Show your work and then write true *or* false.

13. $\dfrac{28}{21} = \dfrac{44}{33}$

14. $\dfrac{2.3}{8.05} = \dfrac{0.25}{0.9}$

15. $\dfrac{2\frac{5}{8}}{3\frac{1}{4}} = \dfrac{21}{26}$

Solve each proportion to find the unknown number. Round your answers to hundredths when necessary.

16. $\dfrac{7}{x} = \dfrac{25}{100}$

17. $\dfrac{15}{8} = \dfrac{6}{x}$

18. $\dfrac{x}{84} = \dfrac{78}{36}$

19. $\dfrac{10}{11} = \dfrac{x}{4}$

20. $\dfrac{x}{17} = \dfrac{3}{55}$

21. $\dfrac{2.6}{x} = \dfrac{13}{7.8}$

22. $\dfrac{0.14}{1.8} = \dfrac{x}{0.63}$

23. $\dfrac{\frac{1}{3}}{8} = \dfrac{x}{24}$

24. $\dfrac{6\frac{2}{3}}{4\frac{1}{6}} = \dfrac{6\frac{5}{5}}{x}$

6.4 Problem Solving with Proportions

OBJECTIVE

1 **Use proportions to solve application problems.**

OBJECTIVE 1 **Use proportions to solve application problems.** Proportions can be used to solve a wide variety of problems. Watch for problems in which you are given a ratio or rate and then asked to find part of a corresponding ratio or rate. Remember that a ratio or rate compares two quantities and often includes one of these indicator words.

in   for   on   per   from   to

Use the six problem-solving steps from **Chapter 3.** When setting up the proportion, use a variable to represent the unknown number. We have used the letter x, but you may use any letter you like.

EXAMPLE 1   **Solving a Proportion Application**

Mike's car can travel 163 miles **on** 6.4 gallons of gas. How far can it travel on a full tank of 14 gallons of gas? Round to the nearest mile.

Step 1 **Read** the problem. It is about how far a car can travel on a certain amount of gas.

> Unknown: miles traveled on 14 gallons of gas
> Known: 163 miles traveled on 6.4 gallons of gas

Step 2 **Assign a variable.** There is only one unknown, so let x be the number of miles traveled on 14 gallons.

Step 3 **Write an equation.** The equation is in the form of a proportion. Decide what is being compared. This problem compares miles to gallons. Write the two rates described in the problem. Be sure that *both* rates compare miles to gallons in the same order. In other words, miles is in both numerators and gallons is in both denominators.

Matching units

This rate compares miles to gallons. $\left\{ \dfrac{163 \text{ miles}}{6.4 \text{ gallons}} = \dfrac{x \text{ miles}}{14 \text{ gallons}} \right.$ This rate compares miles to gallons.

Matching units

Step 4 **Solve** the equation. Ignore the units while finding the cross products.

$$\frac{163 \text{ miles}}{6.4 \text{ gallons}} = \frac{x \text{ miles}}{14 \text{ gallons}}$$

$(6.4)(x) = (163)(14)$ Show that cross products are equal.

$(6.4)(x) = 2282$

$$\frac{(6.4)(x)}{6.4} = \frac{2282}{6.4}$$ Divide both sides by 6.4

$x = 356.5625$ Round to 357   Always check the problem for rounding directions.

Step 5 **State the answer.** Mike's car can travel **357 miles,** rounded to the nearest mile, on a full tank of gas.

Continued on Next Page

Step 6 **Check** that the solution is reasonable and fits the facts given in the original statement of the problem. The car traveled 163 miles on 6.4 gallons of gas; 14 gallons is a little more than *twice as much gas*, so the car should travel a little more than *twice as far*.

$$(2)(163 \text{ miles}) = 326 \text{ miles} \leftarrow \text{Estimate}$$

The solution, 357 miles, is a little more than the estimate of 326 miles, so it is reasonable.

> **CAUTION**
>
> When setting up the proportion, do *not* mix up the units in the rates.
>
> $$\left.\begin{array}{c}\text{compares miles}\\\text{to gallons}\end{array}\right\} \quad \dfrac{163 \text{ miles}}{6.4 \text{ gallons}} \neq \dfrac{14 \text{ gallons}}{x \text{ miles}} \quad \left\{\begin{array}{c}\text{compares gallons}\\\text{to miles}\end{array}\right.$$
>
> These rates do *not* compare things in the same order and *cannot* be set up as a proportion.

·········· **Work Problem ❶ at the Side.** ▶

EXAMPLE 2 Solving a Proportion Application

A newspaper report says that 7 out of 10 people surveyed watch the news on TV. At that rate, how many of the 3200 people in town would you expect to watch the news?

Step 1 **Read** the problem. It is about people watching the news on TV.

> Unknown: how many people in town are expected to watch the news on TV
> Known: 7 out of 10 people surveyed watched the news on TV.

Step 2 **Assign a variable.** There is only one unknown, so let x be the number of people in town who watch the news on TV.

Step 3 **Write an equation.** Set up the two rates as a proportion. You are comparing people who watch the news to people surveyed. Write the two rates described in the example. Be sure that both rates make the same comparison. "People who watch the news" is mentioned first, so it should be in the numerator of *both* rates.

$$\begin{array}{c}\text{People who watch the news} \rightarrow \\ \text{Total group} \rightarrow \\ \text{(people surveyed)}\end{array} \dfrac{7}{10} = \dfrac{x}{3200} \begin{array}{c}\leftarrow \text{People who watch the news} \\ \leftarrow \text{Total group} \\ \text{(people in town)}\end{array}$$

Step 4 **Solve** the equation.

$$\frac{7}{10} = \frac{x}{3200}$$

$$(10)(x) = (7)(3200) \quad \text{Show that cross products are equal.}$$

$$(10)(x) = 22{,}400$$

$$\frac{\overset{1}{\cancel{10}}(x)}{\cancel{10}} = \frac{22{,}400}{10} \quad \text{Divide both sides by 10.}$$

$$x = 2240 \quad \boxed{\text{No rounding is needed here.}}$$

··········· **Continued on Next Page**

---

❶ Set up and solve a proportion for each problem using the six problem-solving steps.

(a) If 2 pounds of fertilizer will cover 50 square feet of garden, how many pounds are needed for 225 square feet?

$$\frac{2 \text{ pounds}}{50 \text{ square feet}} = \frac{\_\_\_\_ \text{ pounds}}{\_\_\_\_ \text{ square feet}}$$

(b) A U.S. map has a scale of 1 inch to 75 miles. Lake Superior is 4.75 inches long on the map. What is the lake's actual length, to the nearest whole mile?

(c) Cough syrup should be given at the rate of 30 milliliters for each 100 pounds of body weight. How much should be given to a 34-pound child? Round to the nearest whole milliliter.

Answers

1. (a) $\dfrac{2 \text{ pounds}}{50 \text{ sq. feet}} = \dfrac{x \text{ pounds}}{225 \text{ sq. feet}}$
$x = 9$ pounds

(b) $\dfrac{1 \text{ inch}}{75 \text{ miles}} = \dfrac{4.75 \text{ inches}}{x \text{ miles}}$
$x = 356.25$ miles, rounds to 356 miles

(c) $\dfrac{30 \text{ milliliters}}{100 \text{ pounds}} = \dfrac{x \text{ milliliters}}{34 \text{ pounds}}$
$x \approx 10$ milliliters (rounded)

2 Solve each problem to find a reasonable answer. Then flip one side of your proportion to see what answer you get with an **incorrect** set-up. Explain why the second answer is **unreasonable**.

(a) A survey showed that 2 out of 3 people would like to lose weight. At this rate, how many people in a group of 150 want to lose weight?

$$\left.\begin{matrix}\text{Lose}\\\text{weight}\end{matrix}\right\} \rightarrow \frac{2}{3} = \frac{x}{\underline{\hspace{1cm}}} \left\{\begin{matrix}\text{Lose}\\\text{weight}\end{matrix}\right.$$
$$\left.\begin{matrix}\text{People}\\\text{surveyed}\end{matrix}\right\} \nearrow \qquad \nwarrow \left\{\begin{matrix}\text{People}\\\text{surveyed}\end{matrix}\right.$$

(b) In one state, 3 out of 5 college students receive financial aid. At this rate, how many of the 4500 students at Central Community College receive financial aid?

Step 5 **State the answer.** You would expect **2240 people** in town to watch the news on TV.

> Be sure to write **people** in your answer.

Step 6 **Check** that the solution is reasonable by putting it back into the original statement of the problem.

Notice that 7 out of 10 people is more than half the people, but less than all the people. Half of the 3200 people in town is $3200 \div 2 = 1600$, so between 1600 and 3200 people would be expected to watch the news on TV. The solution, 2240 people, is between 1600 and 3200, so it is reasonable.

CAUTION

Always check that your answer is reasonable. If it isn't, look at the way your proportion is set up. Be sure you have matching units in the numerators and matching units in the denominators.

For example, suppose you set up the last proportion **incorrectly,** as shown below.

$$\frac{7}{10} = \frac{3200}{x} \quad \leftarrow \textbf{Incorrect set-up}$$

$$(7)(x) = (10)(3200)$$

$$\frac{\overset{1}{(7)}(x)}{\underset{1}{7}} = \frac{32{,}000}{7}$$

$$x \approx 4571 \text{ people} \leftarrow \textbf{Unreasonable answer}$$

This answer is **unreasonable** because there are only 3200 people in the town; it is **not** possible for 4571 people to watch the news.

······◀ **Work Problem ② at the Side.**

Answers

2. **(a)** $\frac{2}{3} = \frac{x}{150}$; 100 people (reasonable); incorrect set-up gives 225 people (only 150 people in the group).
(b) 2700 students (reasonable); incorrect set-up gives 7500 students (only 4500 students at the college).

6.4 Exercises

FOR EXTRA HELP

  Download the MyDashBoard App

▶ **MyMathLab®**

CONCEPT CHECK *Complete the proportion for each situation in Exercises 1–2.*
*Do **not** solve the proportion.*

1. When Linda makes potato salad, she uses 6 potatoes and 4 hard-boiled eggs. How many eggs will she need if she uses 12 potatoes? Write the rest of the units in the proportion below.

$$\frac{6 \text{ potatoes}}{4 \text{\_\_\_\_}} = \frac{12 \text{\_\_\_\_}}{x \text{\_\_\_\_}}$$

2. A potato chip bag says that 1 serving is 15 chips. Joe ate 70 chips. How many servings did he eat? Write the rest of the units in the proportion below.

$$\frac{1 \text{\_\_\_\_}}{15 \text{ chips}} = \frac{x \text{\_\_\_\_}}{70 \text{\_\_\_\_}}$$

*Set up and solve a proportion for each application problem. **See Example 1.***

3. Caroline can sketch four cartoon strips in five hours. How long will it take her to sketch 18 strips?

Compares cartoon strips to hours } $\dfrac{4 \text{ strips}}{5 \text{ hours}} = \dfrac{\text{\_\_\_\_strips}}{\text{\_\_\_\_hours}}$

4. The Cosmic Toads recorded eight songs on their first album in 26 hours. At this same rate, how long will it take them to record 14 songs for their second album?

Compares songs to hours } $\dfrac{8 \text{ songs}}{26 \text{ hours}} = \dfrac{\text{\_\_\_\_ songs}}{\text{\_\_\_\_ hours}}$

5. Sixty newspapers cost $27. Find the cost of 16 newspapers.

6. Twenty-two guitar lessons cost $528. Find the cost of 12 lessons.

7. If three pounds of fescue grass seed cover about 350 square feet of ground, how many pounds are needed for 4900 square feet?

8. Anna earns $1242.08 in 14 days. How much does she earn in 260 days?

9. Tom makes $672.80 in five days. How much does he make in three days?

10. If 5 ounces of a medicine must be mixed with 8 ounces of water, how many ounces of medicine would be mixed with 20 ounces of water?

11. The bag of rice noodles shown below makes 7 servings. At that rate, how many ounces of noodles do you need for 12 servings, to the nearest ounce?

12. This can of sweet potatoes is enough for 4 servings. How many ounces are needed for 9 servings, to the nearest ounce?

13. Three quarts of a latex enamel paint will cover about 270 square feet of wall surface. How many quarts will you need to cover 350 square feet of wall surface in your kitchen and 100 square feet of wall surface in your bathroom?

14. One gallon of clear gloss wood finish covers about 550 square feet of surface. If you need to apply three coats of finish to 400 square feet of surface, how many gallons do you need, to the nearest tenth?

Use the floor plan shown to answer Exercises 15–18. On the plan, one inch represents four feet.

15. What is the actual length and width of the kitchen?

16. What is the actual length and width of the family room?

17. What is the actual length and width of the dining area?

18. What is the actual length and width of the entire floor plan?

The table below lists recommended amounts of food to order for 25 party guests. Use the table to answer Exercises 19 and 20. (Source: Cub Foods.)

FOOD FOR 25 GUESTS

Item	Amount
Fried chicken	40 pieces
Lasagna	14 pounds
Deli meats	4.5 pounds
Sliced cheese	$2\frac{1}{3}$ pounds
Bakery buns	3 dozen
Potato salad	6 pounds

19. How much of each food item should Nathan and Amanda order for a graduation party with 60 guests?

20. Taisha is having 20 neighbors over for a Fourth of July picnic. How much food should she buy?

21. CONCEPT CHECK 8 out of 10 students voted to take a fifteen-minute break in the middle of a two-hour class. There are 35 students in the class. How many students voted for the break? Carl set up the proportion below. Explain how to tell if Carl's answer is reasonable or not.

$$\frac{8}{10} = \frac{35}{x} \qquad 8 \cdot x = 350$$

$$\frac{\overset{1}{\cancel{8}} \cdot x}{\cancel{8}_{1}} = \frac{350}{8}$$

$$x \approx 44 \text{ students (rounded)}$$

22. CONCEPT CHECK Many experts recommend 30 minutes of exercise each day. If Vera follows that advice for 60 days, how many minutes of exercise will she get? Vera set up the proportion below. Explain how to tell if Vera's answer is reasonable or not.

$$\frac{1}{30} = \frac{x}{60} \qquad 30 \cdot x = 60$$

$$\frac{\overset{1}{\cancel{30}} \cdot x}{\cancel{30}_{1}} = \frac{60}{30}$$

$$x = 2 \text{ minutes}$$

Set up a proportion to solve each problem. Check to see whether your answer is reasonable. Then flip one side of your proportion to see what answer you get with an incorrect set-up. Explain why the second answer is unreasonable. **See Example 2.**

23. About 7 out of 10 people entering our community college need to take a refresher math course. If we have 2950 entering students, how many will probably need refresher math? (*Source:* Minneapolis Community and Technical College.)

24. In a survey, only 3 out of 100 people like their eggs poached. At that rate, how many of the 60 customers who ordered eggs at Soon-Won's restaurant this morning asked to have them poached? Round to the nearest whole person.

25. About 1 out of 3 people choose vanilla as their favorite ice cream flavor. If 238 people attend an ice cream social, how many would you expect to choose vanilla? Round to the nearest whole person.

26. In a test of 200 sewing machines, only one had a defect. At that rate, how many of the 5600 machines shipped from the factory have defects?

Set up and solve a proportion for each problem.

27. The stock market report says that five stocks went up for every six stocks that went down. If 750 stocks went down yesterday, how many went up?

28. The human body contains 90 pounds of water for every 100 pounds of body weight. How many pounds of water are in a child who weighs 80 pounds?

29. The ratio of the length of an airplane wing to its width is 8 to 1. If the length of a wing is 32.5 meters, how wide must it be? Round to the nearest hundredth.

30. The Rosebud School District wants a student-to-teacher ratio of 19 to 1. How many teachers are needed for 1850 students? Round to the nearest whole number.

31. The number of calories you burn is proportional to your weight. A 150-pound person burns 222 calories during 30 minutes of tennis. How many calories would a 210-pound person burn, to the nearest whole number? (*Source: Wellness Encyclopedia.*)

32. (Complete **Exercise 31** first.) A 150-pound person burns 189 calories during 45 minutes of grocery shopping. How many calories would a 115-pound person burn, to the nearest whole number? (*Source: Wellness Encyclopedia.*)

33. At 3 P.M., Coretta's shadow is 1.05 meters long. Her height is 1.68 meters. At the same time, a tree's shadow is 6.58 meters long. How tall is the tree? Round to the nearest hundredth.

34. (Complete **Exercise 33** first.) Later in the day, Coretta's shadow was 2.95 meters long. How long a shadow did the tree have at that time? Round to the nearest hundredth.

Shadow 1.05 meters

1.68 meters

Shadow 6.58 meters

Shadow 2.95 meters

Shadow ?

35. CONCEPT CHECK Can you set up a proportion to solve this problem? Explain why or why not. Jim is 25 years old and weighs 180 pounds. How much will he weigh when he is 50 years old?

36. CONCEPT CHECK Write your own application problem that can be solved by setting up a proportion. Also show the proportion and the steps needed to solve your problem.

37. A survey of college students shows that 4 out of 5 drink coffee. Of the students who drink coffee, 1 out of 8 adds cream to it. How many of the 56,100 students at Ohio State University would be expected to use cream in their coffee?

38. About 9 out of 10 adults think it is a good idea to exercise regularly. But of the ones who think it is a good idea, only 1 in 6 actually exercises at least three times a week. At this rate, how many of the 300 employees in our company exercise regularly?

39. The nutrition information on a bran cereal box says that a $\frac{1}{3}$ cup serving provides 80 calories and 8 grams of dietary fiber. At that rate, how many calories and grams of fiber are in a $\frac{1}{2}$ cup serving? (*Source:* Kraft Foods, Inc.)

40. A $\frac{3}{4}$ cup serving of whole grain penne pasta has 210 calories and 6 grams of dietary fiber. How many calories and grams of fiber would be in a 1 cup serving? (*Source:* Barilla Pasta.)

Relating Concepts (Exercises 41–42) For Individual or Group Work

A box of instant mashed potatoes has the list of ingredients shown in the table. Use this information to **work Exercises 41–42 in order.**

Ingredient	For 12 Servings
Water	$3\frac{1}{2}$ cups
Margarine	6 tablespoons
Milk	$1\frac{1}{2}$ cups
Potato flakes	4 cups

Source: General Mills.

41. Find the amount of each ingredient needed for six servings. Show *two* different methods for finding the amounts. One method should use proportions.

42. Find the amount of each ingredient needed for 18 servings. Show *two* different methods for finding the amounts, one using proportions and one using your answers from **Exercise 41.**

Chapter 6   *Summary*

Key Terms

6.1

ratio   A ratio compares two quantities that have the same units. For example, the ratio of 6 apples to 11 apples is written in fraction form as $\frac{6}{11}$. The common units (apples) divide out.

6.2

rate   A rate compares two measurements with different units. Examples are 96 dollars for 8 hours, or 450 miles on 18 gallons.

unit rate   A unit rate has 1 in the denominator.

cost per unit   Cost per unit is a rate that tells how much you pay for one item or one unit. The lowest cost per unit is the best buy.

6.3

proportion   A proportion states that two ratios or rates are equal.

cross products   Multiply along one diagonal and then along the other diagonal to find the cross products of a proportion. If the cross products are equal, the proportion is true.

Key Terms

alternate interior angles When two parallel lines are crossed by a transversal, there are two pairs of alternate interior angles and each pair is congruent. They are on opposite sides of the transversal. *Example*: In the figure at the right, line *m* is parallel to line *n*. The pairs of alternate interior angles are ∠3 and ∠5, ∠4 and ∠6.

similar figures Similar figures have the same shape but are different sizes.

congruent triangles Congruent triangles are triangles with the same shape and the same size; corresponding angles measure the same number of degrees and corresponding sides have the same length.

similar triangles Similar triangles are triangles with the same shape but not necessarily the same size; corresponding angles measure the same number of degrees and the *ratios* of the lengths of corresponding sides are equal.

Test Your Word Power

See how well you have learned the vocabulary in this chapter.

1 A **rate**
- **A.** can be written only as a decimal
- **B.** compares two quantities that have the same units
- **C.** compares two quantities that have different units.

2 **Cost per unit** is
- **A.** the best buy
- **B.** a ratio written in lowest terms
- **C.** the price of one item or one unit.

3 A **proportion**
- **A.** shows that two ratios or rates are equal
- **B.** contains only whole numbers or decimals
- **C.** always has one unknown number.

4 An **obtuse angle**
- **A.** is formed by perpendicular lines
- **B.** measures more than 90° but less than 180°
- **C.** measures less than 90°.

5 Two angles that are **complementary**
- **A.** have measures that add up to 180°
- **B.** form a straight angle
- **C.** have measures that add up to 90°.

6 **Perpendicular lines**
- **A.** intersect to form a right angle
- **B.** intersect to form an acute angle
- **C.** never intersect.

Answers to Test Your Word Power

1. C; *Example:* $4.50 for 3 pounds is a rate comparing dollars to pounds.

2. C; *Example:* $1.95 per pound tells the price of one pound (one unit).

3. A; *Example:* The proportion $\frac{5}{6} = \frac{25}{30}$ says that $\frac{5}{6}$ is equal to $\frac{25}{30}$.

4. B; *Examples:* Angles that measure 91°, 120°, and 175° are all obtuse angles.

5. C; *Example:* If ∠1 measures 35° and ∠2 measures 55°, the angles are complementary because 35° + 55° = 90°.

6. A; *Example:* $\overleftrightarrow{EF}$ is perpendicular to $\overleftrightarrow{GH}$.

Quick Review

Concepts	Examples

6.1 Writing a Ratio

A ratio compares two quantities that have the same units. A ratio is usually written as a fraction with the number that is mentioned first in the numerator. The common units divide out and are not written in the answer. Check that the fraction is in lowest terms.

Write this ratio as a fraction in lowest terms.

60 ounces of medicine **to** 160 ounces of water

$$\frac{60 \text{ ounces}}{160 \text{ ounces}} = \frac{60 \div 20}{160 \div 20} = \frac{3}{8} \quad \left\{ \begin{array}{l} \text{Ratio in} \\ \text{lowest terms} \end{array} \right.$$

Divide out common units.

6.1 Using Mixed Numbers in a Ratio

If a ratio has mixed numbers, change the mixed numbers to improper fractions. Rewrite the problem in horizontal form, using the "÷" symbol for division. Finally, multiply by the reciprocal of the divisor.

Write as a ratio of whole numbers in lowest terms.

$$2\frac{1}{2} \quad \text{to} \quad 3\frac{3}{4}$$

$$\frac{2\frac{1}{2}}{3\frac{3}{4}} \quad \text{Ratio with mixed numbers}$$

$$= \frac{\frac{5}{2}}{\frac{15}{4}} \quad \text{Ratio with improper fractions}$$

$$= \frac{5}{2} \div \frac{15}{4} = \frac{5}{2} \cdot \frac{4}{15} = \frac{\overset{1}{5} \cdot \overset{1}{2} \cdot 2}{2 \cdot 3 \cdot \underset{1}{5}} = \frac{2}{3} \left\{ \begin{array}{l} \text{Ratio in} \\ \text{lowest} \\ \text{terms} \end{array} \right.$$

Reciprocals

6.1 Using Measurements in Ratios

When a ratio compares measurements, both measurements must be in the *same* units. It is usually easier to compare the measurements using the smaller unit, for example, inches instead of feet.

Write 8 inches to 6 feet as a ratio in lowest terms.

Compare using the smaller unit, inches. Because 1 foot has 12 inches, 6 feet is

$$6 \cdot 12 \text{ inches} = 72 \text{ inches}$$

The ratio is shown below.

$$\frac{8 \text{ inches}}{6 \text{ feet}} = \frac{8 \text{ inches}}{72 \text{ inches}} = \frac{8 \div 8}{72 \div 8} = \frac{1}{9} \left\{ \begin{array}{l} \text{Ratio in} \\ \text{lowest terms} \end{array} \right.$$

6.2 Writing Rates

A rate compares two measurements with different units. The units do *not* divide out, so you must write them as part of the rate.

Write the rate as a fraction in lowest terms.

475 miles in 10 hours

$$\frac{475 \text{ miles} \div 5}{10 \text{ hours} \div 5} = \frac{95 \text{ miles}}{2 \text{ hours}} \left] \begin{array}{l} \text{Must write units:} \\ \text{miles and hours} \end{array} \right.$$

Concepts	Examples

6.2 Finding a Unit Rate

A unit rate has 1 in the denominator. To find the unit rate, divide the numerator by the denominator. Write unit rates using the word **per** or a / mark.

Write as a unit rate: $1278 in 9 days.

$$\frac{\$1278}{9 \text{ days}} \leftarrow \text{Fraction bar indicates division.}$$

$$9\overline{)1278}^{\,142} \quad \text{so} \quad \frac{\$1278 \div 9}{9 \text{ days} \div 9} = \frac{\$142}{1 \text{ day}}$$

Write the answer as $142 **per** day or $142/day.

6.2 Finding the Best Buy

The best buy is the item with the lowest cost per unit. Divide the price by the number of units. Round to thousandths when necessary. Then compare to find the lowest cost per unit.

Find the best buy on apples.

2 pounds for $2.25

3 pounds for $3.40

Find cost per unit (cost per pound).

$$\frac{\$2.25}{2} = \$1.125 \text{ per pound}$$

$$\frac{\$3.40}{3} \approx \$1.133 \text{ per pound}$$

The lower cost per pound is $1.125, so 2 pounds of apples is the best buy.

6.3 Writing Proportions

A proportion states that two ratios or rates are equal. The proportion "5 is to 6 as 25 is to 30" is written as shown below.

$$\frac{5}{6} = \frac{25}{30}$$

To see whether a proportion is true or false, multiply along one diagonal, then multiply along the other diagonal. If the two cross products are equal, the proportion is true. If the two cross products are unequal, the proportion is false.

Write as a proportion: 8 is to 40 as 32 is to 160

$$\frac{8}{40} = \frac{32}{160}$$

Is this proportion true or false?

$$\frac{6}{8\frac{1}{2}} = \frac{24}{34}$$

Find the cross products.

$$\frac{6}{8\frac{1}{2}} = \frac{24}{34}$$

$$8\frac{1}{2} \cdot 24 = \frac{17}{2} \cdot \frac{\overset{1}{2} \cdot 12}{\underset{1}{1}} = \mathbf{204}$$

$$6 \cdot 34 = \mathbf{204} \leftarrow$$

Equal

The cross products are equal, so the proportion is true.

Concepts	Examples

6.3 Solving Proportions

Solve for an unknown number in a proportion by using these steps.

Find the unknown number.

$$\frac{12}{x} = \frac{6}{8} \;\Big]\; \text{Write } \tfrac{6}{8} \text{ in lowest terms.}$$

$$\frac{12}{x} = \frac{3}{4} \;\Longleftarrow$$

Step 1 Find the cross products. (If desired, you can rewrite the ratios in lowest terms before finding the cross products.)

Step 1 $\dfrac{12}{x} = \dfrac{3}{4}$ $\begin{array}{l} x \cdot 3 \;\Longleftarrow \\ 12 \cdot 4 \;\Longleftarrow \end{array} \Big]\begin{array}{l}\text{Find the cross}\\\text{products.}\end{array}$

Step 2 Show that the cross products are equal.

Step 2 $x \cdot 3 = \underbrace{12 \cdot 4}$ $\begin{array}{l}\text{Show that cross products}\\\text{are equal.}\end{array}$

$x \cdot 3 = \;\;\;48$

Step 3 Divide both sides of the equation by the coefficient of the variable term.

Step 3 $\dfrac{x \cdot \overset{1}{\cancel{3}}}{\underset{1}{\cancel{3}}} = \dfrac{48}{3}$ Divide both sides by 3.

$x = 16$ The solution is 16.

Step 4 Check by writing the solution in the *original* proportion and finding the cross products.

Step 4

$x \text{ is } 16. \rightarrow \dfrac{12}{16} = \dfrac{6}{8}$ $\begin{array}{l}16 \cdot 6 = 96 \;\Longleftarrow \\ 12 \cdot 8 = 96 \;\Longleftarrow\end{array}\Big]\text{Equal}$

The cross products are equal, so **16 is the correct solution** (**not** 96).

6.4 Applications of Proportions

Use the six problem-solving steps from **Chapter 3.**

If 3 pounds of grass seed cover 450 square feet of lawn, how much seed is needed for 1500 square feet of lawn?

Step 1 **Read** the problem.

Step 1 The problem is about the amount of grass seed needed for a lawn.

Unknown: pounds of seed needed for 1500 square feet of lawn

Known: 3 pounds cover 450 square feet of lawn

Step 2 **Assign a variable.**

Step 2 There is only one unknown, so let x be the pounds of seed needed for 1500 square feet of lawn.

Step 3 **Write an equation.**

Step 3 The equation is in the form of a proportion. Be sure that both rates in the proportion compare pounds to square feet in the same order.

Matching units

$$\frac{3 \text{ pounds}}{450 \text{ square feet}} = \frac{x \text{ pounds}}{1500 \text{ square feet}}$$

Matching units

(Continued)

Concepts	Examples

6.4 Applications of Proportions (Continued)

Step 4 **Solve** the equation.

Step 4 Ignore the units while finding the cross products and solving for x.

$$450 \cdot x = 3 \cdot 1500$$
$$450 \cdot x = 4500$$

Show that cross products are equal.

$$\frac{\overset{1}{\cancel{450}} \cdot x}{\underset{1}{\cancel{450}}} = \frac{4500}{450}$$

Divide both sides by 450.

$$x = 10$$

Step 5 **State the answer.**

Step 5 **10 pounds** of grass seed are needed for 1500 square feet of lawn.

Step 6 **Check** that the solution is reasonable by putting it back into the original statement of the problem.

Step 6 450 square feet of lawn needs 3 pounds of seed; 1500 square feet is about *three times as much* lawn, so about *three times as much* seed is needed.

$$(3)(3 \text{ pounds}) = 9 \text{ pounds} \leftarrow \text{Estimate}$$

The solution, 10 pounds, is close to the estimate of 9 pounds, so it is reasonable.

Chapter 6 *Review Exercises*

6.1 *Write each ratio as a fraction in lowest terms. Change to the same units when necessary, using the table of measurement comparisons in the first section of this chapter. Use the information in the graph to answer Exercises 1–3.*

AVERAGE LENGTH OF SHARKS AND WHALES

Great white shark

Orca whale

Whale shark

Blue whale

10 20 30 40 50 60 70 80
ft   ft   ft   ft   ft   ft   ft   ft

Source: Grolier Multimedia Encyclopedia.

1. Orca whale's length to whale shark's length

2. Blue whale's length to great white shark's length

3. Which two animals' lengths give a ratio of $\frac{1}{2}$? There is more than one correct answer.

4. $2.50 to $1.25

5. $0.30 to $0.45

6. $1\frac{2}{3}$ cups to $\frac{2}{3}$ cup

7. $2\frac{3}{4}$ miles to $16\frac{1}{2}$ miles

8. 5 hours to 100 minutes

9. 9 in. to 2 ft

10. 1 ton to 1500 pounds

11. 8 hours to 3 days

12. Jake sold $350 worth of his kachina figures. Ramona sold $500 worth of her pottery. What is the ratio of Ramona's sales to Jake's sales?

13. Ms. Wei's new car gets 35 miles per gallon. Her old car got 25 miles per gallon. Find the ratio of the new car's mileage to the old car's mileage.

14. This fall, 6000 students are taking math courses and 7200 students are taking English courses. Find the ratio of math students to English students.

6.2 *Write each rate as a fraction in lowest terms.*

15. $88 for 8 dozen

16. 96 children in 40 families

17. When entering data into his computer, Patrick can type four pages in 20 minutes. Give his rate in pages per minute and minutes per page.

18. Elena made $60 in three hours. Give her earnings in dollars per hour and hours per dollar.

Find the best buy.

19. Minced onion

      8 ounces for $4.98

      3 ounces for $2.49

      2 ounces for $1.89

20. Dog food; you have a coupon for $1 off on 8 pounds or more.

      35.2 pounds for $36.96

      17.6 pounds for $18.69

      3.5 pounds for $4.25

6.3 *Use either the method of writing in lowest terms or of finding cross products to decide whether each proportion is true or false. Show your work and then write* true *or* false.

21. $\dfrac{6}{10} = \dfrac{9}{15}$

22. $\dfrac{6}{48} = \dfrac{9}{36}$

23. $\dfrac{47}{10} = \dfrac{98}{20}$

24. $\dfrac{1.5}{2.4} = \dfrac{2}{3.2}$

25. $\dfrac{3\frac{1}{2}}{2\frac{1}{3}} = \dfrac{6}{4}$

Find the unknown number in each proportion. Round answers to the nearest hundredth when necessary.

26. $\dfrac{4}{42} = \dfrac{150}{x}$

27. $\dfrac{16}{x} = \dfrac{12}{15}$

28. $\dfrac{100}{14} = \dfrac{x}{56}$

29. $\dfrac{5}{8} = \dfrac{x}{20}$

30. $\dfrac{x}{24} = \dfrac{11}{18}$

31. $\dfrac{7}{x} = \dfrac{18}{21}$

32. $\dfrac{x}{3.6} = \dfrac{9.8}{0.7}$

33. $\dfrac{13.5}{1.7} = \dfrac{4.5}{x}$

34. $\dfrac{0.82}{1.89} = \dfrac{x}{5.7}$

6.4 *Set up and solve a proportion for each application problem.*

35. The ratio of cats to dogs at the animal shelter is 3 to 5. If there are 45 dogs, how many cats are there?

36. Danielle had 8 hits in 28 times at bat during last week's games. If she continues to hit at the same rate, how many hits will she get in 161 times at bat?

37. If 3.5 pounds of ground beef cost $9.77, what will 5.6 pounds cost? Round to the nearest cent.

38. About 4 out of 10 students are expected to vote in campus elections. There are 8247 students. How many are expected to vote? Round to the nearest whole number.

39. The scale on Brian's model railroad is 1 inch to 16 feet. One of the scale model boxcars is 4.25 inches long. What is the length of a real boxcar in feet?

40. Marvette makes necklaces to sell at a local gift shop. She made 2 dozen necklaces in $16\frac{1}{2}$ hours. How long will it take her to make 40 necklaces?

41. A 180-pound person burns 284 calories playing basketball for 25 minutes. At this rate, how many calories would the person burn in 45 minutes, to the nearest whole number? (*Source: Wellness Encyclopedia.*)

42. In the hospital pharmacy, Michiko sees that a medicine is given at the rate of 3.5 milligrams for every 50 pounds of body weight. How much medicine should be given to a patient who weighs 210 pounds?

Mixed Review Exercises

Find the unknown number in each proportion. Round to hundredths when necessary.

63. $\dfrac{x}{45} = \dfrac{70}{30}$

64. $\dfrac{x}{52} = \dfrac{0}{20}$

65. $\dfrac{64}{10} = \dfrac{x}{20}$

66. $\dfrac{15}{x} = \dfrac{65}{100}$

67. $\dfrac{7.8}{3.9} = \dfrac{13}{x}$

68. $\dfrac{34.1}{x} = \dfrac{0.77}{2.65}$

Write each ratio as a fraction in lowest terms. Change to the same units when necessary.

69. 4 dollars to 10 quarters

70. $4\dfrac{1}{8}$ inches to 10 inches

71. 10 yards to 8 feet

72. $3.60 to $0.90

73. 12 eggs to 15 eggs

74. 37 meters to 7 meters

75. 3 pints to 4 quarts

76. 15 minutes to 3 hours

77. $4\dfrac{1}{2}$ miles to $1\dfrac{3}{10}$ miles

Set up and solve a proportion for each application problem.

78. Nearly 7 out of 8 fans buy something to drink at rock concerts. How many of the 28,500 fans at today's concert would be expected to buy a beverage? Round to the nearest hundred fans.

79. Emily spent $150 on car repairs and $400 on car insurance. What is the ratio of the amount spent on insurance to the amount spent on repairs?

80. Antonio is choosing among three packages of plastic wrap. Is the best buy 25 feet for $0.78; 75 feet for $1.99; or 100 feet for $2.59? He has a coupon for 50¢ off that is good for either of the larger two packages.

81. On this scale drawing of a backyard patio, 0.5 inch represents 6 feet. If the patio measures 1.75 inches long and 1.25 inches wide on the drawing, what will be the actual length and width of the patio when it is built?

0.5 in. = 6 ft

82. A vitamin supplement for cats should be given at the rate of 1000 milligrams for a 5-pound cat. (*Source:* St. Jon Pet Care Products.)

(a) How much should be given to a 7-pound cat?

(b) How much should be given to an 8-ounce kitten?

83. Charles made 251 points during 169 minutes of playing time last year. At that same rate, how many points would you expect him to make if he plays 14 minutes in tonight's game? Round to the nearest whole number.

84. An antibiotic should be given at the rate of $1\dfrac{1}{2}$ teaspoons for every 24 pounds of body weight. How much should be given to an infant who weighs 8 pounds?

Label each figure. Choose from these labels: line segment, ray, parallel lines, perpendicular lines, intersecting lines, acute angle, right angle, straight angle, obtuse angle. *Indicate the number of degrees in the right angle and the straight angle.*

85.

86.

87.

88.

89.

90.

91.

92.

93.

94. Explain what is happening in each sentence.

   (a) The road was so slippery that my car did a 360.

   (b) After the election, the governor's view on new taxes took a 180° turn.

95. (a) Can two obtuse angles be supplementary? Explain why or why not.

   (b) Can two acute angles be complementary? Explain why or why not.

96. In the figure below, ∠ 2 measures 45° and ∠ 7 measures 55°. Find the measure of each of the other angles.

97. In the figure below, line *m* is parallel to line *n* and ∠ 5 measures 75°. Find the measures of the other angles.

Write each rate or ratio as a fraction in lowest terms. Change to the same units when necessary.

1. $15 for 75 minutes

2. 3 hours to 40 minutes

3. The little theater at our college has 320 seats. The auditorium has 1200 seats. Find the ratio of auditorium seats to theater seats.

4. Find the best buy on spaghetti sauce. You have a coupon for 75¢ off Brand X and a coupon for 50¢ off Brand Y.

26 ounces of Brand X for $3.89

16 ounces of Brand Y for $1.89

14 ounces of Brand Z for $1.29

Find the unknown number in each proportion. In Problems 5–7, round answers to the nearest hundredth when necessary.

5. $\dfrac{5}{9} = \dfrac{x}{45}$

6. $\dfrac{3}{1} = \dfrac{8}{x}$

7. $\dfrac{x}{20} = \dfrac{6.5}{0.4}$

8. $\dfrac{2\frac{1}{3}}{x} = \dfrac{\frac{8}{9}}{4}$

Set up and solve a proportion for each application problem.

9. Pedro entered 18 orders into his computer in 30 minutes at his job. At that rate, how many orders could he enter in forty minutes?

10. About 2 out of every 15 people are left-handed. How many of the 650 students in our school would you expect to be left-handed? Round to the nearest whole number.

11. A medication is given at the rate of 8.2 grams for every 50 pounds of body weight. How much should be given to a 145-pound person? Round to the nearest tenth of a gram.

12. On a scale model, 1 inch represents 8 feet. If a building in the model is 7.5 inches tall, what is the actual height of the building in feet?

Choose the figure that matches each label. For right and straight angles, indicate the number of degrees in the angle.

(a)   (b)   (c)   (d)   (e)   (f)   (g)

13. Acute angle is figure _____.

14. Right angle is figure _____ and its measure is _____.

15. Ray is figure _____.

16. Straight angle is figure _____ and its measure is _____.

17. Write a definition of parallel lines and a definition of perpendicular lines. Make a sketch to illustrate each definition.

18. Find the complement of an 81° angle.

19. Find the supplement of a 20° angle.

20. In the figure below, ∠ 4 measures 50° and ∠ 6 measures 95°. Find the measures of the other angles.

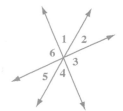

21. In the figure below, line *m* is parallel to line *n* and ∠ 3 measures 65°. Find the measures of the other angles.

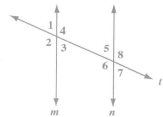

State which method can be used to prove that each pair of triangles is congruent.

22.

23.

24. Find the unknown lengths in these similar triangles.

25. Find the perimeter of each of these similar triangles.

1. Write these numbers in words.

(a) 77,001,000,805

(b) 0.02

2. Write these numbers using digits.

(a) Three and forty thousandths

(b) Five hundred million, thirty-seven thousand

Simplify.

3. $\dfrac{0}{-16}$

4. $|0| + |-6 - 8|$

5. $4\dfrac{3}{4} - 1\dfrac{5}{6}$

6. $\dfrac{h}{5} - \dfrac{3}{10}$

7. $100 - 0.0095$

8. $\dfrac{-4 + 7}{9 - 3^2}$

9. $-6 + 3(0 - 4)$

10. $\dfrac{-8}{\frac{4}{7}}$

11. $\dfrac{5n}{6m^3} \div \dfrac{10}{3m^2}$

12. $(0.06)(-0.007)$

13. $\dfrac{x}{14y} \cdot \dfrac{7}{xy}$

14. $\dfrac{9}{n} + \dfrac{2}{3}$

15. $-40 + 8(-5) + 2^4$

16. $5.8 - (-0.6)^2 \div 0.9$

17. $\left(-\dfrac{1}{2}\right)^3\left(\dfrac{2}{3}\right)^2$

Solve each equation. Show your work.

18. $7y + 5 = -3 - y$

19. $-2 + \dfrac{3}{5}x = 7$

20. $\dfrac{4}{x} = \dfrac{14}{35}$

Solve each application problem using the six problem-solving steps from **Chapter 3.**

21. Tuyen heard on the radio that the temperature had risen 15 degrees by noon, then dropped 23 degrees due to a storm, then risen 5 degrees and was now at 71 degrees. What was the starting temperature?

22. The width of a rectangular swimming pool is 14 ft less than the length. The perimeter of the pool is 100 ft. Find the length and the width.

Find the unknown length, perimeter, area, or volume. When necessary, use 3.14 as the approximate value of π and round answers to the nearest tenth.

23. Find the perimeter and the area.

2.8 km

0.7 km ⬚ 0.7 km

2.8 km

24. Find the diameter, circumference, and area.

8.5 m

25. Find the volume and surface area.

3 ft

12 ft

Solve each application problem. Show your work.

26. The honor society has a goal of collecting 1500 pounds of food to fill Thanksgiving baskets. So far they've collected $\frac{5}{6}$ of their goal. How many more pounds do they need?

27. The directions on a can of plant food call for $\frac{1}{2}$ teaspoon in two quarts of water. How much plant food is needed for five quarts?

28. The distance around Dunning Pond is $1\frac{1}{10}$ miles. Norma ran around the pond four times in the morning and $2\frac{1}{2}$ times in the afternoon. How far did she run in all?

29. Rodney used 40.8 gallons of gas for his car while driving 896.5 miles on a vacation. How many miles per gallon did he get, rounded to the nearest tenth?

Use the information in the table on international long-distance calling card rates to answer Exercises 30–33. Round answers to the nearest whole minute when necessary.

$20 International Phone Cards No Connection Fee!	
Place a call to	**Cost per minute**
Mexico	$0.02
Philippines	$0.084
Japan (to a cell phone)	$0.099
Hong Kong	$0.018
Canada	$0.10
India (to a cell phone)	$0.106
Afghanistan	$0.134

Source: noblecom.com

30. List the per-minute rates from least to greatest.

31. If you buy a $20 calling card, how long a call could you make to a cell phone in Japan?

32. How many $20 cards would you have to buy to make six hours' worth of calls to a cell phone in India?

33. What is the ratio of minutes you can call Mexico for $20 to minutes you can call Canada for $20?

7 Percent

Everyone likes to buy things that are "on sale." It helps if you can estimate the sale price *before* deciding to buy. Most states add on a sales tax, so that is part of your final cost as well. In this chapter you'll learn how to calculate discounts and sales tax, estimate restaurant tips, and calculate the interest on loans.

7.1 The Basics of Percent

OBJECTIVES

1. Learn the meaning of percent.
2. Write percents as decimals.
3. Write decimals as percents.
4. Write percents as fractions.
5. Write fractions as percents.
6. Use 100% and 50%.

1 Write a percent to describe each situation.

(a) You leave a $20 tip for a restaurant bill of $100. What percent tip did you leave?

The tip is $20 per $100

or $\dfrac{\quad}{100}$ or ____%.

(b) The tax on a $100 graphing calculator is $5. What is the tax rate?

(c) You earn 94 points on a 100-point test. What percent of the points did you earn?

OBJECTIVE 1 Learn the meaning of percent. You have probably seen percents frequently in daily life. The symbol for percent is %. For example, during one day you may leave a 15% tip for the server at dinner, pay 7% sales tax on a smartphone, and buy shoes at 25% off the regular price. The next day your score on a math test may be 89% correct.

The Meaning of Percent

A **percent** is a ratio with a denominator of 100. So percent means "per 100" or "how many out of 100." The symbol for percent is %. Read 15% as "fifteen percent."

EXAMPLE 1   Understanding Percent

Write a percent to describe each situation.

(a) If you left a $15 tip when the restaurant bill was $100, then you left $15 per $100 or $\frac{15}{100}$ or 15%.

(b) If you pay $7 in tax on a $100 smartphone, then the tax rate is $7 per $100 or $\frac{7}{100}$ or 7%.

(c) If you earn 89 points on a 100-point math test, then your score is 89 out of 100 or $\frac{89}{100}$ or 89%.

◀ Work Problem 1 at the Side.

OBJECTIVE 2 Write percents as decimals. In order to work with percents, you will need to write them as decimals or as fractions. We'll start by writing percents as equivalent decimal numbers. Twenty-five percent, or 25%, means 25 parts out of 100 parts, or $\frac{25}{100}$. Remember that the fraction bar indicates division. So we can write $\frac{25}{100}$ as $25 \div 100$. When you do the division, $25 \div 100$ is 0.25.

Indicates division ⟶ $\dfrac{25}{100}$ can be written as $25 \div 100 = 0.25$

Indicates division

Another way to remember how to write a percent as a decimal is to use the meaning of the word *percent*. The first part of the word, *per,* is an indicator word for *division*. The last part of the word, *cent,* comes from the Latin word for *hundred*. (Recall that there are 100 *cent*s in a dollar, and 100 years in a *cent*ury.)

25%   is   25 percent

$25 \div 100 = 0.25$

Answers

1. (a) $\frac{20}{100}$; 20% **(b)** 5% **(c)** 94%

Writing a Percent as an Equivalent Decimal

To write a percent as a decimal, drop the % symbol and divide by 100.

| EXAMPLE 2 | Writing Percents as Decimals |

Write each percent as a decimal.

(a) 47%   47% = 47 ÷ 100 = 0.47   Decimal form

(b) 3%   3% =   3 ÷ 100 = 0.03   Decimal form

(c) 28.2%   28.2% = 28.2 ÷ 100 = 0.282   Decimal form

(d) 100%   100% = 100 ÷ 100 = 1.00   Decimal form

(e) 135%   135% = 135 ÷ 100 = 1.35   Decimal form

CAUTION

In **Example 2(d)** above, notice that 100% is 1.00, or 1, which is a whole number. Whenever you have a percent that is *100% or greater*, the equivalent decimal number will be *1 or greater*. Notice in **Example 2(e)** above that 135% is 1.35 (greater than 1).

· Work Problem ❷ at the Side. ▶

In the exercise set on dividing decimal numbers, you discovered a shortcut for *dividing* by 100: Move the decimal point *two* places to the *left*. You can use this shortcut when writing percents as decimals.

| EXAMPLE 3 | Changing Percents to Decimals by Moving the Decimal Point |

Write each percent as a decimal by dropping the percent symbol and moving the decimal point two places to the left.

(a) 17%

              — Decimal point starts at far right side.

17% = 17.%

     .17 ← Percent symbol is dropped.

        — Decimal point is moved
         two places to the *left*.

               Moving the decimal point *two places* to the *left* is a quick way to *divide by 100.*

17% = 0.17

(b) 160%

   160% = 160.% = 1.60 or 1.6   Decimal point starts at far right side.
                          1.60 is equivalent to 1.6

(c) 4.9%

        04.9%   0 is attached so the decimal point can be moved
                two places to the *left*.

   4.9% = 0.049 ← Drop the % symbol.

(d) 0.6%

             Drop the % symbol.

   00.6% = 0.006   0 is attached so the decimal point can be
                  moved *two places* to the *left*.

· **Continued on Next Page**

❷ Write each percent as a decimal.

(GS) (a) 68%

   68% = 68 ÷ _____ = 0.___ ___

(b) 5%

(c) 40.6%

(GS) (d) 200%

   200% = 200 ÷ _____ = _____

(e) 350%

Answers

2. (a) 68 ÷ 100 = 0.68   (b) 0.05   (c) 0.406
   (d) 200 ÷ 100 = 2.00 or 2   (e) 3.50 or 3.5

❸ Write each percent as a decimal by moving the decimal point.

(a) 90%

$$90\% = 90.\% = \underline{\hspace{1cm}}$$

Move the decimal point **two** places to the **left.**

Drop the % symbol.

(b) 9%

(c) 900%

(d) 9.9

$$9.9\% = 09.9\% = \underline{\hspace{1cm}}$$

Drop the % symbol.

(e) 0.9%

Answers

3. (a) 0.90 or 0.9   **(b)** 0.09   **(c)** 9.00 or 9
  (d) 0.099   **(e)** 0.009

Note

In **Example 3(d)** on the previous page, notice that 0.6% is less than 1%. Because 1% is equivalent to 0.01 or $\frac{1}{100}$, any fraction of a percent smaller than 1% is less than 0.01. The decimal equivalent of 0.6% is 0.006, which is less than 0.01.

◀ Work Problem **❸** at the Side.

OBJECTIVE ❸ **Write decimals as percents.** You can write a decimal as a percent. For example, the decimal 0.25 is the same as the fraction $\frac{25}{100}$.

This fraction means 25 out of 100 parts, or 25%. Notice that multiplying 0.25 by 100 gives the same result.

$$(0.25)(100) = 25 \quad \text{so} \quad 0.25 = 25\%$$

This result makes sense because we are doing the reverse of what we did to change a percent to a decimal.

To change a percent to a decimal, we *drop* the % symbol and *divide* by 100. So, to *reverse* the process and change a decimal to a percent, we *multiply* by 100 and *attach* a % symbol.

Writing a Decimal as a Percent

To write a decimal as a percent, multiply by 100 and attach a % symbol.

Note

A quick way to *multiply* a number by 100 is to move the decimal point *two* places to the *right*. Notice that this is the reverse of the shortcut for *dividing* by 100.

Drop % symbol; *divide* by 100.
(Move decimal point two places *left*.)

Decimal

Percent

Multiply by 100; attach % symbol.
(Move decimal point two places *right*.)

EXAMPLE 4 **Changing Decimals to Percents by Moving the Decimal Point**

Write each decimal as a percent.

(a) 0.21

> Moving the decimal point *two places* to the *right* is a quick way to *multiply by 100*.

0.21

0.21 = 21% ⟵ Percent symbol is attached after decimal point is moved.

Decimal point is *not* written with whole number percents.

(b) 0.529 = 52.9% ⟵ Percent symbol is attached after decimal point is moved.

(c) 1.92 = 192% ⟵ Percent symbol is attached after decimal point is moved.

Continued on Next Page

(d) 2.5

2.5<u>0</u>   0 is attached so the decimal point can be moved two places to the right.

2.5 = 250%

(e) 3

3<u>.</u> = 3.<u>00</u>   so   3.<u>00</u> = 300%

> Hint:
> 1 = 100%
> 2 = 200%
> 3 = 300%
> and so on.

CAUTION

In **Examples 4(c), 4(d), and 4(e)** above, notice that 1.92, 2.5, and 3 are greater than 1. Because the number 1 is equivalent to 100%, all *numbers greater than 1* will be equivalent to *percents greater than 100%*.

······· Work Problem **4** at the Side. ▶

OBJECTIVE ▶ **4** **Write percents as fractions.** Percents can also be written as fractions. Recall that a percent is a ratio with a denominator of 100. For example, 89% is $\frac{89}{100}$. Because the fraction bar indicates division, we are dividing by 100, just as we did when writing a percent as a decimal.

Writing a Percent as a Fraction

To write a percent as a fraction, drop the % symbol and write the number over 100. Then write the fraction in lowest terms.

EXAMPLE 5   **Writing Percents as Fractions**

Write each percent as a fraction or mixed number in lowest terms or as a whole number.

(a) 25%   Drop the % symbol and write 25 over 100.

$$25\% = \frac{25}{100} \longleftarrow 25 \text{ per } 100$$

$$= \frac{25 \div 25}{100 \div 25} = \frac{1}{4} \longleftarrow \boxed{\text{Lowest terms}}$$

As a check, write 25% as a decimal.

$$25\% = 25 \div 100 = 0.25 \longleftarrow \text{Percent sign dropped}$$

Recall that 0.25 means 25 hundredths.

$$0.25 = \frac{25}{100} = \frac{25 \div 25}{100 \div 25} = \frac{1}{4} \longleftarrow \text{Same result as above}$$

(b) 76%   Drop the % symbol and write 76 over 100.

This number becomes the numerator.

$$76\% = \frac{76}{100} \longleftarrow \begin{array}{l}\text{The } \textit{denominator} \text{ is always 100 because} \\ \text{percent means } \textit{parts per 100.}\end{array}$$

Write $\frac{76}{100}$ in lowest terms. $\frac{76 \div 4}{100 \div 4} = \frac{19}{25}$ $\longleftarrow$ $\boxed{\text{Lowest terms}}$

······· **Continued on Next Page**

---

4 Write each number as a percent.

GS **(a)** 0.95

0.9<u>5</u> = _____

   Move the   Write the
   decimal point   percent
   two places   symbol.
   to the **right.**

(b) 0.16

(c) 0.09

(d) 0.617

(e) 0.4

(f) 5.34

GS **(g)** 2.8

2.8<u>0</u> = _____

      Write the
      % symbol.

(h) 4

Answers

4. (a) 95% **(b)** 16% **(c)** 9% **(d)** 61.7%
   (e) 40% **(f)** 534% **(g)** 280%
   (h) 400%

5 Write each percent as a fraction or mixed number in lowest terms or as a whole number.

(a) 50%

$$50\% = \frac{50}{100} = \frac{50 \div}{100 \div}$$

$$= \frac{}{} \leftarrow \text{Lowest terms}$$

(b) 19%

(c) 80%

(d) 6%

(e) 125% *Hint:* Your final answer will be a mixed number.

(f) 300% *Hint:* Your final answer will be a whole number.

(c) 150%

$$150\% = \frac{150}{100} = \frac{150 \div 50}{100 \div 50} = \frac{3}{2} = 1\frac{1}{2} \leftarrow \text{Mixed number}$$

(d) $100\% = \frac{100}{100} = 1 \leftarrow \text{Whole number}$

> Always simplify fraction answers.

Note

Remember that percent means *per 100.*

⊲ **Work Problem 5 at the Side.**

Example 6 below shows how to write decimal percents and fraction percents as fractions.

EXAMPLE 6 **Writing Decimal Percents or Fraction Percents as Fractions**

Write each percent as a fraction in lowest terms.

(a) 15.5%

Drop the % symbol and write 15.5 over 100.

$$15.5\% = \frac{15.5}{100}$$

To get a whole number in the numerator, multiply the numerator and denominator by 10. (Multiplying by $\frac{10}{10}$ is the same as multiplying by 1.)

$$\frac{15.5}{100} = \frac{(15.5)(10)}{(100)(10)} = \frac{155}{1000}$$

Write the fraction in lowest terms.

$$\frac{155 \div 5}{1000 \div 5} = \frac{31}{200} \quad \text{Lowest terms}$$

(b) $33\frac{1}{3}\%$

Drop the % symbol and write $33\frac{1}{3}$ over 100.

$$33\frac{1}{3}\% = \frac{33\frac{1}{3}}{100}$$

When there is a mixed number in the numerator, write it as an improper fraction. So $33\frac{1}{3}$ is $\frac{100}{3}$.

> Think:
> 3 · 33 is 99
> and 99 + 1 is 100
> so $33\frac{1}{3}$ is $\frac{100}{3}$

$$\frac{33\frac{1}{3}}{100} = \frac{\frac{100}{3}}{100}$$

⋯⋯⋯⋯⋯ **Continued on Next Page**

Answers

5. (a) $\frac{50 \div 50}{100 \div 50} = \frac{1}{2}$ **(b)** $\frac{19}{100}$ **(c)** $\frac{4}{5}$

(d) $\frac{3}{50}$ **(e)** $1\frac{1}{4}$ **(f)** 3

Now you have a complex fraction (see **Chapter 4**). Rewrite the complex fraction using the $\div$ symbol for division. Then follow the steps for dividing fractions.

$$\frac{\frac{100}{3}}{100} = \frac{100}{3} \div 100 = \frac{100}{3} \div \frac{100}{1} = \frac{100}{3} \cdot \frac{1}{100} = \frac{\overset{1}{100} \cdot 1}{3 \cdot \underset{1}{100}} = \frac{1}{3}$$

Reciprocals

Note

In **Example 6(a)** on the previous page, we could have changed 15.5% to $15\frac{1}{2}\%$ and then written it as the improper fraction $\frac{31}{2}$ over 100. But it is usually easier to work with decimal percents as they are.

·········· Work Problem **6** at the Side. ▶

OBJECTIVE ▶ 5 Write fractions as percents. Recall that to write a percent as a fraction, you *drop* the percent symbol and *divide* by 100. So, to reverse the process and change a fraction to a percent, you *multiply* by 100 and *attach* a percent symbol.

Writing a Fraction as a Percent

To write a fraction as a percent, multiply by 100 and attach a % symbol. This is the same as multiplying by 100%.

Note

Look back at **Example 5(d)** near the top of the previous page to see that 100% = 1. Recall that multiplying a number by 1 does *not* change the value of the number. So multiplying by 100% does not change the value of a number; it just gives us an *equivalent percent*.

EXAMPLE 7   Writing Fractions as Percents

Write each fraction as a percent. Round to the nearest tenth of a percent when necessary.

(a) $\frac{2}{5}$ Multiply $\frac{2}{5}$ by 100%.

$$\frac{2}{5} = \left(\frac{2}{5}\right)(100\%) = \left(\frac{2}{5}\right)\left(\frac{100}{1}\%\right) = \left(\frac{2}{5}\right)\left(\frac{5 \cdot 20}{1}\%\right) = \frac{2 \cdot \overset{1}{5} \cdot 20}{\underset{1}{5} \cdot 1}\%$$

$$= \frac{40}{1}\% = 40\%$$

To check the result, write 40% as $\frac{40}{100}$ and simplify the fraction.

$$40\% = \frac{40}{100} = \frac{40 \div 20}{100 \div 20} = \frac{2}{5} \leftarrow \text{Original fraction}$$

········· **Continued on Next Page**

---

6 Write each percent as a fraction in lowest terms.

GS (a) 18.5%

$$18.5\% = \frac{18.5}{100} = \frac{(18.5)(10)}{(100)(10)}$$

$$= \frac{185}{1000} = \frac{185 \div}{1000 \div} = \underline{\quad\quad}$$

(b) 87.5%

(c) 6.5%

GS (d) $66\frac{2}{3}\%$

$$\frac{66\frac{2}{3}}{100} = \frac{\frac{200}{3}}{100} = \frac{200}{3} \div \frac{100}{1}$$

$$= \frac{\overset{2}{200}}{3} \cdot \frac{1}{\underset{1}{100}} = \underline{\quad\quad}$$

(e) $12\frac{1}{3}\%$

(f) $62\frac{1}{2}\%$

Answers

6. (a) $\frac{185 \div 5}{1000 \div 5} = \frac{37}{200}$ (b) $\frac{7}{8}$ (c) $\frac{13}{200}$
   (d) $\frac{2}{3}$ (e) $\frac{37}{300}$ (f) $\frac{5}{8}$

7 Write each fraction as a percent. If you're using a calculator, first work each one by hand. Then use your calculator and round to the nearest tenth of a percent when necessary.

GS (a) $\dfrac{1}{2}$

$\dfrac{1}{2}(100\%) = \left(\dfrac{1}{2}\right)\left(\dfrac{100}{1}\%\right)$

$= \left(\dfrac{1}{\underset{1}{2}}\right)\left(\dfrac{\overset{1}{2} \cdot 50}{1}\%\right) = \underline{\quad}$

(b) $\dfrac{3}{4}$

(c) $\dfrac{1}{10}$

(d) $\dfrac{7}{8}$

(e) $\dfrac{5}{6}$

(f) $\dfrac{2}{3}$

Answers

7. (a) $\dfrac{50}{1}\% = 50\%$ **(b)** 75%   **(c)** 10%

(d) $87\dfrac{1}{2}\%$ or 87.5% (Both are exact answers.)

(e) exactly $83\dfrac{1}{3}\%$, or 83.3% (rounded)

(f) exactly $66\dfrac{2}{3}\%$, or 66.7% (rounded)

(b) $\dfrac{5}{8}$ Multiply $\frac{5}{8}$ by 100%.

$\dfrac{5}{8} = \left(\dfrac{5}{8}\right)(100\%) = \left(\dfrac{5}{8}\right)\left(\dfrac{100}{1}\%\right) = \left(\dfrac{5}{2 \cdot 4}\right)\left(\dfrac{4 \cdot 25}{1}\%\right) = \dfrac{5 \cdot \overset{1}{4} \cdot 25}{2 \cdot \underset{1}{4} \cdot 1}\%$

$= \dfrac{125}{2}\% = 62\dfrac{1}{2}\%$

You can also do the last step of simplifying $\frac{125}{2}$ on your calculator. Enter $\frac{125}{2}$ as 125 ÷ 2 =. The result is 62.5, so $\frac{5}{8} = 62\frac{1}{2}\%$ or $\frac{5}{8} = 62.5\%$.

(c) $\dfrac{1}{6}$ Multiply $\frac{1}{6}$ by 100%.

$\dfrac{1}{6} = \left(\dfrac{1}{6}\right)(100\%) = \left(\dfrac{1}{6}\right)\left(\dfrac{100}{1}\%\right) = \left(\dfrac{1}{2 \cdot 3}\right)\left(\dfrac{2 \cdot 50}{1}\%\right) = \dfrac{1 \cdot \overset{1}{2} \cdot 50}{\underset{1}{2} \cdot 3 \cdot 1}\%$

$= \dfrac{50}{3}\% = 16\dfrac{2}{3}\%$

To simplify $\frac{50}{3}$ on your calculator, enter 50 ÷ 3 =. The result is 16.66666666, with the 6 continuing to repeat. The directions say to round to the nearest *tenth* of a percent.

Next digit is *5 or more.*

16.66666666%   rounds to   16.7%   ← When the next digit is *5 or more*, round up.

Tenths place

So $\frac{1}{6} = 16\frac{2}{3}\%$ (exact answer)   or $\frac{1}{6} \approx 16.7\%$ (rounded answer).

🖩 **Calculator Tip**

In **Example 7(a)** on the previous page, you can use your calculator to write $\frac{2}{5}$ as a percent.

Step 1   Enter $\frac{2}{5}$ as 2 ÷ 5 =. Your calculator shows   **0.4**

Decimal equivalent of $\dfrac{2}{5}$

Step 2   Change the decimal number 0.4 to a percent by moving the decimal point two places to the right (multiply by 100%).

$0.40 = 40\%$ ← Attach % symbol.

Try this technique on **Examples 7(b) and 7(c)** on this page.

For $\frac{5}{8}$, enter 5 ÷ 8 =. Your calculator shows   **0.625**

Move the decimal point in 0.625 two places to the right.

$0.625 = 62.5\%$ ← Attach % symbol.

⋯⋯⋯ **Continued on Next Page**

For $\frac{1}{6}$, enter 1 ÷ 6 =. Your calculator shows | **0.166666666**

Some calculators show 7 in the last place. ⟶

Move the decimal point two places to the right. Then round to the nearest tenth.

$$0.166666666 = 16.66666666\% \approx 16.7\% \leftarrow \text{Attach } \% \text{ symbol.}$$

With a fraction such as $\frac{1}{6}$, your calculator gives only an *approximate* answer. You can't get the exact answer of $16\frac{2}{3}\%$ by using your calculator.

························· **Work Problem 7 on the Previous Page at the Side.** ▶

OBJECTIVE ▶ 6 Use 100% and 50%. When working with percents, it is helpful to have several reference points. 100% and 50% are two helpful reference points.

100% means 100 parts out of 100 parts. That's *all* of the parts. If you pay 100% of a $245 dentist bill, you pay $245 (*all* of it).

EXAMPLE 8 Finding 100% of a Number

Fill in the blanks.

(a) 100% of $42 is _____.

100% is *all* of the money.

So 100% of $42 is ___$42___.

(b) 100% of 9 miles is _____.

100% is *all* of the miles.

So 100% of 9 miles is ___9 miles___.

························· **Work Problem 8 at the Side.** ▶

50% means 50 parts out of 100 parts, which is *half* of the parts because $\frac{50}{100} = \frac{1}{2}$. So 50% of $12 is $6 (*half* of the money).

EXAMPLE 9 Finding 50% of a Number

Fill in the blanks.

(a) 50% of $42 is _____.

50% is *half* of the money.

So 50% of $42 is ___$21___.

(b) 50% of 9 miles is _____.

50% is *half* of the miles.

So 50% of 9 miles is ___$4\frac{1}{2}$ miles___.

························· **Work Problem 9 at the Side.** ▶

---

8 Fill in the blanks.

GS (a) 100% of $4.60 is _____.

100% is *all* of the money.

(b) 100% of 3000 students is _____.

(c) 100% of 7 pages is _____.

(d) 100% of 272 miles is _____.

(e) 100% of $10\frac{1}{2}$ hours is _____.

9 Fill in the blanks.

GS (a) 50% of $4.60 is _____.

50% is *half* of the money.

(b) 50% of 3000 students is _____.

(c) 50% of 7 pages is _____.

(d) 50% of 272 miles is _____.

(e) 50% of $10\frac{1}{2}$ hours is _____.

Answers

8. (a) $4.60 **(b)** 3000 students **(c)** 7 pages
(d) 272 miles **(e)** $10\frac{1}{2}$ hours

9. (a) $2.30 **(b)** 1500 students
(c) $3\frac{1}{2}$ pages **(d)** 136 miles
(e) $5\frac{1}{4}$ hours

7.1 Exercises

  MyMathLab®

1. CONCEPT CHECK

(a) A shortcut for dividing by 100 is to move the decimal point _____.

(b) Draw arrows to show how to use the shortcut when changing these percents to decimals.

48 % =   120 % =

3 5% =   6 % =

2. CONCEPT CHECK

(a) A shortcut for multiplying by 100 is to move the decimal point _____.

(b) Draw arrows to show how to use the shortcut when changing these decimals to percents.

0.88 =   2.7 =

0.105 =   0.3 =

*Write each percent as a decimal. **See Examples 2 and 3.***

3. 25%

4. 35%

5. 30%

6. 20%

7. 6%
GS $06.\%\ = 0.\_\_\ \_\_$

8. 3%
GS $03.\%\ = 0.\_\_\ \_\_$

9. 140%

10. 250%

11. 7.8%

12. 6.7%

13. 100%

14. 600%

15. 0.5%

16. 0.2%

17. 0.35%

18. 0.076%

*Write each decimal as a percent. **See Example 4.***

19. 0.5

20. 0.6

21. 0.62

22. 0.18

23. 0.03

24. 0.07

25. 0.125

26. 0.875

27. 2

28. 5

29. 2.6

30. 1.8

31. 0.0312

32. 0.0625

*Write each percent as a fraction or mixed number in lowest terms. **See Examples 5 and 6.***

33. 20%
GS $\dfrac{20}{100} = \underline{\quad} \leftarrow \begin{array}{l}\text{Lowest}\\ \text{terms}\end{array}$

34. 40%
$\dfrac{40}{100} = \underline{\quad} \leftarrow \begin{array}{l}\text{Lowest}\\ \text{terms}\end{array}$

35. 50%

36. 75%

37. 55%

38. 35%

39. 37.5%

40. 87.5%

41. 6.25%

42. 43.75%

43. $16\dfrac{2}{3}\%$

44. $83\dfrac{1}{3}\%$

45. 130%

46. 175%

47. 250%

48. 325%

Write each fraction as a percent. If you're using a calculator, first work each one by hand. Then use your calculator and round to the nearest tenth of a percent when necessary. **See Example 7.**

49. $\dfrac{1}{4}$
(GS)

$$\left(\dfrac{1}{4}\right)(100\%) = \left(\dfrac{1}{4}\right)\left(\dfrac{100}{1}\%\right)$$

$$= \left(\dfrac{1}{\overset{1}{\cancel{4}}}\right)\left(\dfrac{\overset{1}{\cancel{4}} \cdot 25}{1}\%\right) =$$

50. $\dfrac{1}{5}$
(GS)

$$\left(\dfrac{1}{5}\right)(100\%) = \left(\dfrac{1}{5}\right)\left(\dfrac{100}{1}\%\right)$$

$$= \left(\dfrac{1}{\overset{1}{\cancel{5}}}\right)\left(\dfrac{\overset{1}{\cancel{5}} \cdot 20}{1}\%\right) =$$

51. $\dfrac{3}{10}$

52. $\dfrac{9}{10}$

53. $\dfrac{3}{5}$

54. $\dfrac{3}{4}$

55. $\dfrac{37}{100}$

56. $\dfrac{63}{100}$

57. $\dfrac{3}{8}$

58. $\dfrac{1}{8}$

59. $\dfrac{1}{20}$

60. $\dfrac{1}{50}$

61. $\dfrac{5}{9}$

62. $\dfrac{7}{9}$

63. $\dfrac{1}{7}$

64. $\dfrac{5}{7}$

In each statement, write percents as decimals and decimals as percents. **See Examples 2–4.**

65. In 1900, only 8% of U.S. homes had a telephone. (*Source: Harper's Index.*)

66. In 1900, only 14% of homes in the United States had a bathtub. (*Source: Harper's Index.*)

67. Tornadoes can occur on any day of the year, but 49% of them appeared in May and June of 2010. (*Source:* ncdc.noaa.gov)

68. Only 2.8% of tornadoes occurred in March 2010, making it the month with the fewest twisters. (*Source:* ncdc.noaa.gov)

69. The property tax rate in Alpine County is 0.035.

70. The average human brain uses 0.2 of the body's oxygen and energy.

71. The number of people taking CPR training this session is 2 times that of the last session.

72. Attendance at this year's company picnic is 3 times last year's attendance.

Write a fraction and a percent for the shaded part of each figure. Then write a fraction and a percent for the unshaded part of each figure.

73.

74.

75.

76.

CONCEPT CHECK *Find three items that are equivalent in each list and circle them.*

77. 50% $\frac{1}{4}$ 1.00 0.5 $\frac{1}{2}$ 5% 1.5

78. $\frac{3}{4}$ 100% 0.25 4% $\frac{1}{4}$ 0.3 25%

Complete this table. Write fractions and mixed numbers in lowest terms.

	Fraction	Decimal	Percent
79.	$\frac{1}{100}$	_____	_____
80.	$\frac{1}{10}$	_____	_____
81.	_____	0.2	_____
82.	_____	0.25	_____
83.	_____	_____	30%
84.	_____	_____	40%
85.	$\frac{1}{2}$	_____	_____
86.	$\frac{3}{4}$	_____	_____
87.	_____	_____	90%
88.	_____	_____	100%
89.	_____	1.5	_____
90.	_____	2.25	_____

The road signs in Exercises 91–92 tell drivers that they are approaching a steep, downward hill. For example, the 8% sign means that for every 100 ft of roadway length, the road will drop a total of 8 ft in elevation.

91. Write the percent on the sign as a decimal and as a fraction in lowest terms.

92. Write the percent on the sign as a decimal and as a fraction in lowest terms.

93. Suppose the roadway dropped 5 ft in elevation for every 100 ft of length. Write a percent, a decimal, and a fraction in lowest terms to describe this situation.

94. Suppose the roadway dropped 7 ft in elevation for every 100 ft of length. Write a percent, a decimal, and a fraction in lowest terms to describe this situation.

The diagram shows the different types of teeth in an adult's mouth. Use the diagram to answer Exercises 95–100. Write each answer in Exercises 95–98 as a fraction in lowest terms, as a decimal, and as a percent.

95. What portion of an adult's teeth are incisors, designed to bite and cut?

96. The pointy canine teeth tear and rip food. They are what portion of an adult's teeth?

97. The molars, which grind up food, are what portion of an adult's teeth?

98. What portion of an adult's teeth are premolars?

99. Some people have four fewer molars than shown in the tooth diagram. For these people, the canines are what portion of their teeth? Write your answer as a fraction in lowest terms and as a percent.

100. For the adults who have four fewer molars than shown, the incisors are what portion of their teeth? Write your answer as a fraction in lowest terms and as a percent.

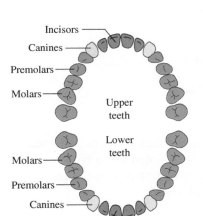

Source: Time-Life *Human Body.*

101. Explain and correct the errors made by students when they used their calculators on these problems.

   (a) Write $\frac{7}{20}$ as a percent.

     Student entered 7 ÷ 20 =, and the result was 0.35, so $\frac{7}{20} = 0.35\%$

   (b) Write $\frac{16}{25}$ as a percent.

     Student entered 25 ÷ 16 =, and the result was 1.5625, so $\frac{16}{25} = 156.25\%$

102. Explain and correct the errors made by students who moved decimal points to solve these problems.

   (a) Write 3.2 as a percent.

     03.2 = 0.032 so 3.2 = 0.032%

   (b) Write 60% as a decimal.

     00.60 = 0.0060 so 60% = 0.0060

Fill in the blanks in Exercises 103–118. Remember that 100% *is* all *of something and* 50% *is* half *of it.* **See Examples 8 and 9.**

103. **(a)** 100% of $78 is _____.

   (b) 50% of $78 is _____.

104. **(a)** 100% of 5 hours is _____.

   (b) 50% of 5 hours is _____.

105. **(a)** 100% of 15 inches is _____.

   (b) 50% of 15 inches is _____.

106. **(a)** 100% of $6000 is _____.

   (b) 50% of $6000 is _____.

107. **(a)** 100% of 2.8 miles is _____.

   (b) 50% of 2.8 miles is _____.

108. **(a)** 100% of $2.50 is _____.

   (b) 50% of $2.50 is _____.

109. There are 20 children in the preschool class. 100% of the children are served breakfast and lunch. How many children are served both meals?

_____

110. The Speedy Delivery company owns 345 vans. 100% of the vans are painted white with blue lettering. How many company vans are painted white with blue lettering?

_____

111. Alyssa needs 120 credits to graduate. She has earned 50% of the credits. How many credits has she earned?

_____

112. Ian has a limit of $1500 on his credit card. He has used 50% of the limit. How many dollars of credit has he used?

_____

113. **(a)** John owes $285 for tuition. Financial aid will pay 50% of the cost. Financial aid will pay

_____.

(b) What *percent* of the tuition will John have to pay?

_____

(c) How much *money* will John have to pay?

_____

114. **(a)** The Animal Humane Society took in 20,000 animals last year. About 50% of them were dogs. The number of dogs taken in was about how many?

_____

(b) What *percent* of the animals were *not* dogs?

_____

(c) How many *animals* were not dogs?

_____

115. **(a)** About 50% of the 8200 students at our college work more than 20 hours per week. How many *students* is this?

_____

(b) What *percent* of the students work 20 hours or less per week?

_____

116. **(a)** Shalayna's cell phone plan includes 1600 minutes of "off-peak" calling time per month. Last month she used 50% of her "off-peak" minutes. How many *minutes* did she use?

_____

(b) What *percent* of her "off-peak" minutes were *not* used?

_____

117. **(a)** Dylan's test score was 100%. How many of the 35 problems did he work correctly?

_____

(b) How many *problems* did Dylan miss?

_____

118. **(a)** Latrell made 100% of his 12 free throws during a practice game today. How many free throws did he make?

_____

(b) How many *free throws* did Latrell miss?

_____

119. Describe a shortcut way to find 50% of a number. Include two examples to illustrate the shortcut.

120. Describe a shortcut way to find 100% of a number. Include two examples to illustrate the shortcut.

7.2 The Percent Proportion

OBJECTIVES

1. Identify the percent, whole, and part.
2. Solve percent problems using the percent proportion.

We will show you two ways to solve percent problems. One is the proportion method, which we discuss in this section. The other is the percent equation method, which we explain in the next section.

OBJECTIVE ▶ 1 Identify the percent, whole, and part. You learned that a statement of two equal ratios is called a proportion (see **Chapter 6**). For example, the fraction $\frac{3}{5}$ is the same as the ratio 3 to 5, and 60% is the ratio 60 to 100. As the figure below shows, these two ratios are equal and make a proportion.

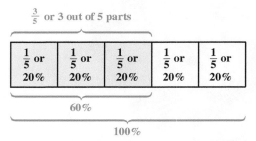

The **percent proportion** can be used to solve percent problems.

The Percent Proportion

Percent is to *100*   as   *part* is to *whole*.

$$\underset{\substack{\text{Always 100} \longrightarrow \\ \text{because } percent \\ \text{means "per 100"}}}{}\quad \frac{\text{percent}}{100} = \frac{\text{part}}{\text{whole}}$$

In some textbooks the percent proportion is written using the words *amount* and *base*.

$$\frac{\text{percent}}{100} = \frac{\text{amount}}{\text{base}}$$

Here is the proportion for the figure at the top of the page.

$$\left.\begin{array}{l}\text{60\% means 60 parts} \\ \text{out of 100 parts.}\end{array}\right\}\quad \frac{60}{100} = \frac{3}{5}\begin{array}{l}\leftarrow \text{Shaded (3 parts)} \\ \leftarrow \text{Whole (5 parts)}\end{array}$$

If we write $\frac{60}{100}$ in lowest terms, it is equal to $\frac{3}{5}$, so the proportion is true.

$$\frac{60}{100} = \frac{60 \div 20}{100 \div 20} = \frac{3}{5} \leftarrow \left\{\begin{array}{l}\text{Matches ratio above on} \\ \text{right side of proportion}\end{array}\right.$$

When using the percent proportion, you must be able to pick out the *percent,* the *whole,* and the *part.* Look for the percent first; it is the easiest to identify.

Identifying the Percent

The **percent** is a ratio of a part to a whole, with 100 as the denominator. In a problem, the percent appears with the word *percent* or with the symbol % after it.

EXAMPLE 1   Identifying the Percent in Percent Problems

Identify the percent in each problem.

(a) 32% of the 900 women were retired. How many were retired?

Percent

The percent is 32. The number 32 appears with the symbol %.

(b) $150 is 25 percent of what number?

Percent

The percent is 25 because 25 appears with the word *percent*.

(c) If 7 students failed, what percent of the 350 students failed?

Percent (unknown)

The word *percent* has no number with it, so the percent is the unknown part of the problem.

·················· **Work Problem ❶ at the Side.** ▶

The second thing to look for is the *whole* (sometimes called the *base*).

> **Identifying the Whole**
>
> The **whole** is the entire quantity. In a problem, the *whole* often appears after the word **of.**

EXAMPLE 2   Identifying the Whole in Percent Problems

These problems are the same as those in **Example 1** above. Now identify the *whole*.

(a) 32% of the 900 women were retired. How many were retired?

Percent   Whole

The whole is 900 women. The number 900 appears after the word *of*.

(b) $150 is 25 percent of what number?

Percent   Whole (unknown; follows *of*)

The whole is unknown.

(c) If 7 students failed, what percent of the 350 students failed?

Percent (unknown)   Whole (follows *of*)

The whole is 350 students. The number 350 appears after the word *of*.

·················· **Work Problem ❷ at the Side.** ▶

The final thing to identify is the *part* (sometimes called the *amount*).

> **Identifying the Part**
>
> The **part** is the number being compared to the whole.

❶ Identify the percent.

(a) 15% of the $2000 was spent on a washing machine.

(b) 60 employees is what percent of 750 employees?

(c) The state sales tax is $6\frac{1}{2}$ percent of the $590 price.

(d) $30 is 48% of what amount of money?

(e) 75 of the 110 rental cars were rented today. What percent were rented?

❷ Identify the whole.

(a) 15% of the $2000 was spent on a washing machine.

(b) 60 employees is what percent of 750 employees?

(c) The state sales tax is $6\frac{1}{2}$ percent of the $590 price.

(d) $30 is 48% of what amount of money?

(e) 75 of the 110 rental cars were rented today. What percent were rented?

Answers

1. (a) 15%   **(b)** unknown   **(c)** $6\frac{1}{2}$ percent
    (d) 48%   **(e)** unknown
2. (a) $2000   **(b)** 750 employees   **(c)** $590
    (d) unknown   **(e)** 110 rental cars

3 Identify the part.

(a) 15% of the $2000 was spent on a washing machine.

(b) 60 employees is what percent of 750 employees?

(c) The state sales tax is $6\frac{1}{2}$ percent of the $590 price.

(d) $30 is 48% of what amount of money?

(e) 75 of the 110 rental cars were rented today. What percent were rented?

> **Note**
>
> If you have trouble identifying the *part,* find the *whole* and the *percent* first. The remaining number is the *part.*

EXAMPLE 3   Identifying the Part in Percent Problems

These problems are the same as those in **Examples 1 and 2** on the previous page. Identify the *part.*

(a)
32% of the 900 women were retired. How many were retired?

Percent   Whole   Part (unknown)

The part of the women who were retired is unknown. In other words, some part of 900 women were retired.

(b) $150 is 25 percent of what number?

Part   Percent   Whole (unknown)

$150 is the remaining number, so $150 is the part.

(c) If 7 students failed, what percent of 350 students failed?

Part   Percent (unknown)   Whole

The part of the students who failed is 7 students.

◀ Work Problem **3** at the Side.

OBJECTIVE **2** Solve percent problems using the percent proportion.

EXAMPLE 4   Using the Percent Proportion to Find the Part

Use the percent proportion to answer this question.

15% of $165 is how much money?

Recall that the percent proportion is $\dfrac{\text{percent}}{100} = \dfrac{\text{part}}{\text{whole}}$. First identify the percent by looking for the % symbol or the word *percent.* Then look for the *whole* (usually follows the word *of*). Finally, identify the *part.*

15% of $165 is how much money?

Percent   Whole   Part (unknown)
          (follows *of*)

Set up the percent proportion. Here we use *n* as the variable representing the unknown part. You may use any letter you like.

Percent → $\dfrac{15}{100} = \dfrac{n}{165}$ ← Part (unknown)
Always 100 →   ← Whole

Recall that the first step in solving a proportion is to find the cross products.

Step 1 $\dfrac{15}{100} = \dfrac{n}{165}$

$100 \cdot n$ ⎫
             ⎬ Find the cross products.
$15 \cdot 165$ ⎭

Continued on Next Page

Step 2 $100 \cdot n = \underline{15 \cdot 165}$ Show that the cross products are equal.

$100 \cdot n = 2475$

Step 3 $\dfrac{\overset{1}{\cancel{100}} \cdot n}{\underset{1}{\cancel{100}}} = \dfrac{2475}{100}$ Divide both sides by 100, the coefficient of the variable term. On the left side, divide out the common factor of 100.

$n = 24.75$ On the right side, $2475 \div 100$ is 24.75

The part is $24.75, so 15% of $165 is **$24.75**.   [Write a **$** in your answer.]

> **CAUTION**
>
> When you use the percent proportion, do **not** move the decimal point in the percent or in the answer.

··········· **Work Problem** ④ **at the Side.** ▶

EXAMPLE 5 **Using the Percent Proportion to Find the Percent**

Use the percent proportion to answer this question.

8 pounds is what percent of 160 pounds?

     ↓   ↓   ↓

  Part   Percent   Whole
        (unknown) (follows of)

The percent proportion is $\dfrac{\text{percent}}{100} = \dfrac{\text{part}}{\text{whole}}$. Set up the proportion using p as the variable representing the unknown percent. Then find the cross products.

Percent (unknown) ⇢ $\dfrac{p}{100} = \dfrac{8}{160}$ ← Part
    Always 100 ⇢   ← Whole

$\dfrac{p}{100} \bowtie \dfrac{8}{160}$
$100 \cdot 8 = 800$
$p \cdot 160$ Cross products

$p \cdot 160 = 800$ Show that the cross products are equal.

$\dfrac{p \cdot \overset{1}{\cancel{160}}}{\underset{1}{\cancel{160}}} = \dfrac{800}{160}$ Divide both sides by 160

$p = 5$ [The *percent* was unknown. Write **%** in your answer.]

The percent is 5%. So 8 pounds is **5%** of 160 pounds.

> **CAUTION**
>
> When you're finding an unknown percent, as in **Example 5** above, be careful to label your answer with the % symbol. Do **not** add a decimal point or move the decimal point in your answer.

··········· **Work Problem** ⑤ **at the Side.** ▶

---

④ Use the percent proportion to answer these questions.

(GS) **(a)** 9% **of** 3250 miles is how many miles?

Percent ⇢ $\dfrac{9}{100} = \dfrac{n}{3250}$ ← Part
Always 100 ⇢   ← Whole

(b) 78% of $5.50 is how much?

(c) What is $12\frac{1}{2}\%$ of 400 homes? (*Hint:* Write $12\frac{1}{2}\%$ as 12.5%.)

⑤ Use the percent proportion to answer these questions.

(GS) **(a)** 1200 books is what percent **of** 5000 books?

Percent ⇢ $\dfrac{p}{100} = \dfrac{1200}{5000}$ ← Part
Always 100 ⇢   ← Whole

(b) What percent of $6.50 is $0.52?

(c) 20 athletes is what percent of 32 athletes?

Answers

4. **(a)** The part is 292.5 miles.
  (b) $\dfrac{78}{100} = \dfrac{n}{5.50}$ The part is $4.29.
  (c) $\dfrac{12.5}{100} = \dfrac{n}{400}$ The part is 50 homes.
5. **(a)** 24%
  (b) $\dfrac{p}{100} = \dfrac{0.52}{6.50}$; 8%
  (c) $\dfrac{p}{100} = \dfrac{20}{32}$; 62.5% or $62\frac{1}{2}\%$

6 Use the percent proportion to answer these questions.

(a) 37 cars is 74% **of** how many cars?

$$\text{Percent} \rightarrow \frac{74}{100} = \frac{37}{n} \begin{matrix} \leftarrow \text{Part} \\ \leftarrow \text{Whole} \end{matrix}$$
$$\text{Always 100} \rightarrow$$

(b) 45% **of** how much money is $139.59?

(c) 1.2 tons is $2\frac{1}{2}$% **of** how many tons?

EXAMPLE 6 **Using the Percent Proportion to Find the Whole**

Use the percent proportion to answer this question.

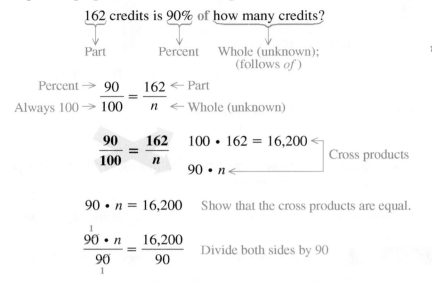

162 credits is 90% **of** how many credits?

Part   Percent   Whole (unknown);
(follows *of*)

$$\text{Percent} \rightarrow \frac{90}{100} = \frac{162}{n} \begin{matrix} \leftarrow \text{Part} \\ \leftarrow \text{Whole (unknown)} \end{matrix}$$
$$\text{Always 100} \rightarrow$$

$$\frac{90}{100} = \frac{162}{n} \qquad 100 \cdot 162 = 16{,}200$$
$$90 \cdot n \qquad\qquad \text{Cross products}$$

$$90 \cdot n = 16{,}200 \qquad \text{Show that the cross products are equal.}$$

$$\frac{\overset{1}{\cancel{90}} \cdot n}{\cancel{90}_{1}} = \frac{16{,}200}{90} \qquad \text{Divide both sides by 90}$$

$$n = 180$$

Write **credits** in your answer.

The whole is **180 credits**. So 162 credits is 90% of **180 credits.**

◀ **Work Problem 6** at the Side.

So far in all the examples, the part has been *less* than the whole. This is because all the percents have been less than 100%. Recall that 100% of something is *all* of it. When the percent is *less* than 100%, you have *less* than all of it.

Now let's look at percents *greater* than 100%. For example,

100% of $20 is all of the money, or $20.

150% of $20 is *greater* than $20.

100%	+	50%	=	150%
of the		of the		of the
money is		money is		money is
$20	+	$10	=	$30

So 150% of $20 is $30.

When the percent is *greater* than 100%, the part is *greater* than the whole, as you'll see in **Example 7** on the next page.

Answers

6. **(a)** 50 cars

(b) $\frac{45}{100} = \frac{139.59}{n}$; $310.20

(c) $\frac{2.5}{100} = \frac{1.2}{n}$;   48 tons

| EXAMPLE 7 | **Working with Percents Greater Than 100%** |

Use the percent proportion to answer each question.

(a) How many students is 210% of 40 students?

Part (unknown)   Percent   Whole (follows *of*)

$$\text{Percent} \rightarrow \frac{210}{100} = \frac{n}{40} \leftarrow \text{Part (unknown)}$$
$$\text{Always } 100 \rightarrow \qquad\qquad \leftarrow \text{Whole}$$

$$\frac{210}{100} \bowtie \frac{n}{40} \qquad \begin{array}{l} 100 \cdot n \leftarrow \\ 210 \cdot 40 = 8400 \leftarrow \end{array} \quad \text{Cross products}$$

$$100 \cdot n = 8400 \qquad \text{Show that the cross products are equal.}$$

$$\frac{\overset{1}{100} \cdot n}{\underset{1}{100}} = \frac{8400}{100} \qquad \text{Divide both sides by 100}$$

$$n = 84$$

The part is **84 students**, which is *greater* than the whole of 40 students. This result makes sense because the percent is 210%. If it was exactly 200%, we would have *2 times the whole,* and 2 times 40 students is 80 students. So 210% should be even a little more than 80 students. Our answer of 84 students is reasonable.

(b) What percent of $50 is $68?

Percent   Whole   Part
(unknown) (follows *of*)

$$\text{Percent (unknown)} \rightarrow \frac{p}{100} = \frac{68}{50} \leftarrow \text{Part}$$
$$\text{Always } 100 \rightarrow \qquad\qquad \leftarrow \text{Whole}$$

$$\frac{p}{100} \bowtie \frac{68}{50} \qquad \begin{array}{l} 100 \cdot 68 = 6800 \leftarrow \\ p \cdot 50 \leftarrow \end{array} \quad \text{Cross products}$$

$$p \cdot 50 = 6800 \qquad \text{Show that the cross products are equal.}$$

$$\frac{p \cdot \overset{1}{50}}{\underset{1}{50}} = \frac{6800}{50} \qquad \text{Divide both sides by 50}$$

$$p = 136$$

Write % in your answer.

The percent is **136%**. This result makes sense because $68 is *greater* than $50, so $68 has to be *greater than 100%* of $50.

· **Work Problem 7 at the Side.** ▶

7 Use the percent proportion to answer each question.

(a) 350% **of** $6 is how much?

$$\text{Percent} \rightarrow \frac{350}{100} = \frac{n}{6} \leftarrow \text{Part}$$
$$\text{Always } 100 \rightarrow \qquad\qquad \leftarrow \text{Whole}$$

(b) 23 hours is what percent of 20 hours?

(c) 225% of what amount is $106.47?

Answers

7. **(a)** $21 **(b)** $\dfrac{p}{100} = \dfrac{23}{20}$; 115%

  (c) $\dfrac{225}{100} = \dfrac{106.47}{n}$; $47.32

7.2 Exercises
FOR EXTRA HELP

Download the MyDashBoard App

MyMathLab®

CONCEPT CHECK *In Exercises 1–6, (**a**) identify the percent; (**b**) identify the whole; (**c**) identify the part; (**d**) write a percent proportion. Do **not** solve the proportion. See Examples 1–6.*

1. What is 10% of 3000 runners?

2. What is 35% of 2340 volunteers?

3. 16 pepperoni pizzas is what percent of 32 pizzas?

4. 35 hours is what percent of 140 hours?

5. 495 successful students is 90% of what number of students?

6. 84 e-mails is 28% of what number of e-mails?

Write a percent proportion and solve it to answer Exercises 7–24. If necessary, round money answers to the nearest cent and percent answers to the nearest tenth of a percent. See Examples 1–7.

7. 4% of 120 feet is how many feet?

$$\text{Percent} \rightarrow \frac{4}{100} = \frac{n}{120} \begin{matrix} \leftarrow \text{Part} \\ \leftarrow \text{Whole} \end{matrix}$$
Always 100

8. 9% of $150 is how much money?

$$\text{Percent} \rightarrow \frac{9}{100} = \frac{n}{150} \begin{matrix} \leftarrow \text{Part} \\ \leftarrow \text{Whole} \end{matrix}$$
Always 100

9. What percent of 200 calories is 16 calories?

10. What percent of 350 parking spaces is 7 accessible parking spaces?

11. $12\frac{1}{2}\%$ of what amount is $3.50?

$$\text{Percent} \rightarrow \frac{12.5}{100} = \frac{3.50}{n} \begin{matrix} \leftarrow \text{Part} \\ \leftarrow \text{Whole} \end{matrix}$$
Always 100

12. $5\frac{1}{2}\%$ of what amount is $17.60?

$$\text{Percent} \rightarrow \frac{5.5}{100} = \frac{17.60}{n} \begin{matrix} \leftarrow \text{Part} \\ \leftarrow \text{Whole} \end{matrix}$$
Always 100

13. 250% of 7 hours is how long?

14. What is 130% of 60 trees?

15. What percent of $172 is $32?

16. $14 is what percent of $398?

17. 748 e-books is 110% of what number of e-books?

18. 145% of what number of inches is 11.6 inches?

19. What is 14.7% of $274?

20. 8.3% of $43 is how much?

21. 105 employees is what percent of 54 employees?

22. What percent of 46 websites is 100 websites?

23. $0.33 is 5% of what amount?

24. 6% of what amount is $0.03?

25. A student turned in the following answers on a test. You can see that *two* of the answers are incorrect *without working the problems*. Find the incorrect answers and explain how you identified them (without actually solving the problems).

50% of $84 is ___$42___   25% of $16 is ___$32___

150% of $30 is ___$20___   100% of $217 is ___$217___

26. Name the three parts in a percent problem. For each of these three parts, write a sentence telling how you identify it.

27. Explain and correct the *two* errors that a student made when solving this problem: $14 is what percent of $8?

$$\frac{p}{100} = \frac{8}{14} \qquad p \cdot 14 = 100 \cdot 8$$

$$\frac{p \cdot \overset{1}{\cancel{14}}}{\underset{1}{\cancel{14}}} = \frac{800}{14}$$

$$p \approx 57.1$$

The answer is 57.1 (rounded).

28. Explain and correct the *two* errors that a student made when solving this problem: 9 children is 30% of what number of children?

$$\frac{30}{100} = \frac{n}{9} \qquad 100 \cdot n = 30 \cdot 9$$

$$\frac{\overset{1}{\cancel{100}} \cdot n}{\underset{1}{\cancel{100}}} = \frac{270}{100}$$

$$n = 2.7$$

The answer is 2.7%.

7.3 The Percent Equation

OBJECTIVES

1. Estimate answers to percent problems involving 25%.

2. Find 10% and 1% of a number by moving the decimal point.

3. Solve basic percent problems using the percent equation.

1 Estimate the answer to each question.

(a) What is 25% of $110.38?

Round $110.38 to $100.
25% is $\frac{1}{4}$ so divide
$100 by 4 to get _____
Estimate —↗

(b) Find 25% of 7.6 hours.

(c) 25% of 34 pounds is how many pounds?

OBJECTIVE **1** **Estimate answers to percent problems involving 25%.** Before showing you the percent equation, we need to do some more estimation. Estimating the answer helps you catch mistakes. Also, when you're out shopping or eating in a restaurant, you can estimate the sales tax, discount, or tip.

Earlier we used shortcuts for 100% of a number (all of the number) and 50% of a number (divide the number by 2). Now we look at a quick way to work with 25%.

25% means 25 parts out of 100 parts, or $\frac{25}{100}$, which is the same as $\frac{1}{4}$

25% of $40 would be $\frac{1}{4}$ of $40, or $10

A quick way to find $\frac{1}{4}$ of a number is to *divide it by 4*. The denominator, 4, tells you that the whole is divided into 4 equal parts.

EXAMPLE 1   Estimating 25% of a Number

Estimate the answer to each question.

(a) What is 25% of $817?
Use front end rounding to round $817 to $800. Then divide $800 by 4. The estimate is **$200**.

> 25% is $\frac{1}{4}$, so to find 25% of a number, divide it by 4.

(b) Find 25% of 19.7 miles.
Use front end rounding to round 19.7 miles to 20 miles. Then divide 20 miles by 4. The estimate is **5 miles**.

(c) 25% of 49 days is how long?
You could round 49 days to 50 days, using front end rounding. Then divide 50 by 4 to get an estimate of **12.5 days**.

However, the division step is simpler if you notice that 48 is a multiple of 4. You can round 49 days to 48 days and divide by 4 to get an estimate of **12 days**. Either way gives you a fairly good idea of the correct answer.

◄ **Work Problem ① at the Side.**

OBJECTIVE **2** **Find 10% and 1% of a number by moving the decimal point.** There are also helpful shortcuts for finding 10% or 1% of a number.

Ten percent, or 10%, means 10 parts out of 100 parts or $\frac{10}{100}$, which is the same as $\frac{1}{10}$. A quick way to find $\frac{1}{10}$ of a number is to *divide it by 10*. The denominator, 10, tells you that the whole is divided into 10 equal parts. The shortcut for dividing by 10 is to move the decimal point *one* place to the *left*.

EXAMPLE 2   Finding 10% of a Number by Moving the Decimal Point

Find the *exact* answer to each question by moving the decimal point.

(a) What is 10% of $817?
To find 10% of $817, divide $817 by 10. Do the division by moving the decimal point *one* place to the *left*. The decimal point starts at the right side of $817.

10% of $817. = $81.70 ← Exact answer

> Do **not** leave it as $81.7

↑
Write this 0 because it's money.

So 10% of $817 is **$81.70**.

Answers

1. **(a)** $25
   (b) 8 hours ÷ 4 gives an estimate of 2 hours.
   (c) 30 pounds ÷ 4 gives an estimate of 7.5 pounds, or 32 pounds ÷ 4 gives an estimate of 8 pounds.

·········· **Continued on Next Page**

(b) Find 10% of 19.7 miles.

To find 10% of 19.7 miles, divide 19.7 by 10.

Move the decimal point *one* place to the *left*.

$$10\% \text{ of } 19.7 \text{ miles} = 1.97 \text{ miles} \leftarrow \text{Exact answer}$$

So 10% of 19.7 miles is **1.97 miles**.

· **Work Problem ② at the Side.** ▶

One percent, or 1%, is 1 part out of 100 parts or $\frac{1}{100}$. This time the denominator of 100 tells you that the whole is divided into 100 parts. Recall that a quick way to divide by 100 is to move the decimal point *two* places to the *left*.

EXAMPLE 3   **Finding 1% of a Number by Moving the Decimal Point**

Find the *exact* answer to each question by moving the decimal point.

(a) What is 1% of $817?

To find 1% of $817, divide $817 by 100. Do the division by moving the decimal point *two* places to the *left*.

$$1\% \text{ of } \$817. = \$8.17 \leftarrow \text{Exact answer}$$

So 1% of $817 is **$8.17**.

(b) Find 1% of 19.7 miles.

To find 1% of 19.7 miles, divide 19.7 by 100.

Move the decimal point *two* places to the *left*.

$$1\% \text{ of } 19.7 \text{ miles} = 0.197 \text{ mile} \leftarrow \text{Exact answer}$$

So 1% of 19.7 miles is **0.197 mile**.

· **Work Problem ③ at the Side.** ▶

Here is a summary of some of the shortcuts you can use with percents.

Percent Shortcuts

200% of a number is 2 times the number; 300% of a number is 3 times the number; and so on.

100% of a number is the entire number.

To find **50% of a number,** divide the number by 2.

To find **25% of a number,** divide the number by 4.

To find **10% of a number,** divide the number by 10. To do the division, move the decimal point in the number *one* place to the *left*.

To find **1% of a number,** divide the number by 100. To do the division, move the decimal point in the number *two* places to the *left*.

---

② Find the *exact* answer to each question by moving the decimal point.

(a) What is 10% of $110.38?

10% of $110.38 = _____
      Exact answer

(b) Find 10% of 7.6 hours.

(c) 10% of 34 pounds is how many pounds?

③ Find the *exact* answer to each question by moving the decimal point.

(a) What is 1% of $110.38?

1% of $110.38 = _____
      Exact answer

(b) Find 1% of 7.6 hours.

(c) 1% of 34 pounds is how many pounds?

Answers

2. (a) $110.38 = $11.038 or $11.04 to the nearest cent
   (b) 7.6 hours = 0.76 hour
   (c) 34. pounds = 3.4 pounds
3. (a) $110.38 = $1.1038 or $1.10 to the nearest cent
   (b) 07.6 hours = 0.076 hour
   (c) 34. pounds = 0.34 pound

OBJECTIVE ▶ ③ **Solve basic percent problems using the percent equation.**
In the previous section you used a proportion to solve percent problems.
Now you will learn how to solve these problems using the percent equation.

Percent Equation

$$\text{percent of whole} = \text{part}$$

The word **of** indicates multiplication, so the **percent equation** becomes

$$\text{percent} \cdot \text{whole} = \text{part}$$

Be sure to write the percent as a decimal or fraction before using the
equation.

The percent equation is just a rearrangement of the percent proportion.
Recall that in the proportion you wrote the percent over 100. Because there
is no 100 in the equation, you have to change the percent to a decimal or
fraction by dividing by 100 *before* using the equation.

Note

Once you have set up a percent equation, we encourage you to use your
calculator to do the multiplying or dividing needed to solve the equation.
For this reason, we will always write the percent as a decimal. If you're
doing the problems by hand, changing the percent to a fraction may be
easier at times. Either method will work.

Examples 4, 5, and 6 below are the same percent questions that were in
the examples in the previous section. There we used a proportion to answer
each question. Now we will use an equation to answer them. You can then
compare the equation method with the proportion method.

EXAMPLE 4   **Using the Percent Equation to Find the Part**

Write and solve a percent equation to answer each question.

(a) 15% of $165 is how much money?

Translate the sentence into an equation. Recall that *of* indicates multiplication and *is* translates to the equal sign. The percent must be written in
decimal form. Use any letter you like to represent the unknown quantity.
(We will use *n* for an unknown number and *p* for an unknown percent.)

Write 15% as
the decimal 0.15

15.% of $165 is how much money?

$$0.15 \quad \cdot \quad 165 \quad = \quad n$$

To solve the equation, simplify the left side, multiplying 0.15 by 165.

$$(0.15)(165) = n$$
$$24.75 = n$$

So 15% of $165 is **$24.75**, which matches the answer obtained using a
proportion (see **Example 4** in the previous section).

· **Continued on Next Page**

CHECK Use estimation to check that the solution is reasonable. First find 10% of $165 by moving the decimal point.

$$10\% \text{ of } 165. \text{ is } \$16.50 \quad \text{and}$$

5% of $165 would be half as much, that is, half of $16.50 or about $8.

So the *estimate* for 15% of $165 is $16.50 + $8 = $24.50. The exact answer of $24.75 is very close to this estimate, so it is reasonable.

(b) How many students is 210% of 40 students?
Translate the sentence into an equation. Write the percent in decimal form.

How many students is 210.% of 40 students?

$$n \qquad = 2.10 \quad \bullet \quad 40$$

> Write 210% as the decimal 2.10

This time the two sides of the percent equation are reversed, so

$$\text{part} = \text{percent} \bullet \text{whole}$$

Recall that the variable may be on either side of the equal sign. To solve the equation, simplify the right side, multiplying 2.10 by 40.

$$n = (2.10)(40)$$
$$n = \quad 84$$

So **84 students** is 210% of 40 students. This matches the answer obtained by using a proportion (see **Example 7(a)** in the previous section).

CHECK Use estimation to check that the solution is reasonable. 210% is close to 200%.

$$200\% \text{ of } 40 \text{ students is } 2 \text{ times } 40 \text{ students} = 80 \text{ students} \longleftarrow \text{Estimate}$$

The exact answer of 84 students is close to the estimate, so it is reasonable.

·········· **Work Problem ④ at the Side.** ▶

EXAMPLE 5 | **Using the Percent Equation to Find the Percent**

Write and solve a percent equation to answer each question.

(a) 8 pounds is what percent of 160 pounds?
Translate the sentence into an equation. This time the percent is unknown. Do *not* move the decimal point in the other numbers.

8 pounds is what percent of 160 pounds?

$$8 \quad = \quad p \quad \bullet \quad 160$$

To solve the equation, divide both sides by 160.

On the left side, divide 8 by 160
$$\frac{8}{160} = \frac{p \bullet \overset{1}{\cancel{160}}}{\underset{1}{\cancel{160}}}$$
On the right side, divide out the common factor of 160

Solution in *decimal* form } $0.05 = p$

> Multiply the solution by 100% to change it from a *decimal* to a *percent.*

$$0.05 = 5\%$$

So 8 pounds is **5%** of 160 pounds. This matches the answer obtained by using a proportion (see **Example 5** in the previous section).

·········· **Continued on Next Page**

---

④ Write and solve an equation to answer each question.

(a) 9% of 3250 miles is how many miles?

$$09.\% \text{ of } 3250 \text{ miles is } \overset{how}{\underset{miles}{many}}$$

$$0.09 \quad \bullet \quad 3250 \quad = \quad n$$

(b) 78% of $5.50 is how much?

(c) What is $12\frac{1}{2}\%$ of 400 homes? (*Hint:* Write $12\frac{1}{2}\%$ as 12.5%. Then move the decimal point two places to the left.)

(d) How much is 350% of $6?

Answers

4. **(a)** 292.5 miles
   (b) $(0.78)(5.50) = n$; $4.29
   (c) $n = (0.125)(400)$;   50 homes
   (d) $n = (3.5)(6)$; $21

5 Write and solve an equation to answer each question.

(GS) (a) 1200 books is what percent of 5000 books?

$$\underbrace{1200}_{\substack{\text{books}}} \quad \underbrace{\text{is}}_{\downarrow} \quad \underbrace{\text{what}}_{\substack{\text{percent}}} \quad \underbrace{\text{of}}_{\downarrow} \quad \underbrace{5000}_{\substack{\text{books}}}$$

$$1200 \;=\; p \;\cdot\; 5000$$

(b) 23 hours is what percent of 20 hours?

(c) What percent of $6.50 is $0.52?

CHECK The solution makes sense because 10% of 160 pounds would be 16 pounds.

$$10\% \text{ of } 160 \text{ pounds is } 16 \text{ pounds} \quad \text{so}$$

5% of 160 pounds is half as much, that is, half of 16 pounds, or 8 pounds.

8 pounds matches the number given in the original problem, so 5% is the correct solution.

(b) What percent of $50 is $68?
 Translate the sentence into an equation and solve it.

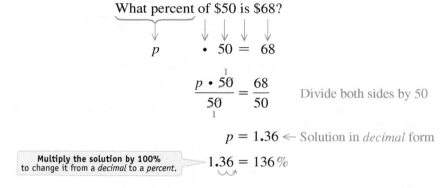

$$\text{What percent of \$50 is \$68?}$$

$$p \;\cdot\; 50 \;=\; 68$$

$$\frac{p \cdot \overset{1}{\cancel{50}}}{\underset{1}{\cancel{50}}} = \frac{68}{50} \qquad \text{Divide both sides by 50}$$

$$p = 1.36 \leftarrow \text{Solution in } \textit{decimal} \text{ form}$$

> **Multiply the solution by 100%** to change it from a *decimal* to a *percent*.

$$1.36 = 136\%$$

So **136%** of $50 is $68. This matches the answer obtained by using a proportion (see **Example 7(b)** in the previous section).

CHECK The solution makes sense because 100% of $50 would be $50 (all of it), and 200% of $50 would be 2 times $50, or $100. So $68 has to be between 100% and 200%.

$$\left.\begin{array}{l}136\% \text{ is between} \\ 100\% \text{ and } 200\%.\end{array}\right\} \rightarrow \begin{array}{l}100\% \text{ of \$50} = \$50 \\ 200\% \text{ of \$50} = \$100\end{array} \leftarrow \left\{\begin{array}{l}\$68 \text{ is between} \\ \$50 \text{ and } \$100\end{array}\right.$$

The solution of 136% fits the conditions.

> **CAUTION**
>
> When you use an equation to solve for an unknown percent, *the solution will be in decimal form*. Remember to **multiply the solution by 100%** to change it from decimal form to a percent. The shortcut is to move the decimal point in the solution *two* places to the *right* and attach the % symbol.
>
> Recall that 100% = 1, and multiplying a number by 1 does *not* change the value of the number; it just gives us an *equivalent percent*.

◀ **Work Problem 5 at the Side.**

Answers

5. **(a)** 0.24 = 24%

 (b) 23 = p • 20; 1.15 = 115%

 (c) p • 6.50 = 0.52; 0.08 = 8%

| EXAMPLE 6 | Using the Percent Equation to Find the Whole |

Write and solve a percent equation to answer each question.

(a) 162 credits is 90% of how many credits?

Translate the sentence into an equation. Write the percent in decimal form.

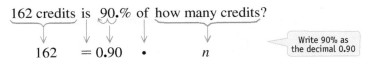

162 credits is 90.% of how many credits?

$$162 = 0.90 \cdot n$$

Write 90% as the decimal 0.90

Recall that 0.90 is equivalent to 0.9, so use 0.9 in the equation.

$$\frac{162}{0.9} = \frac{\overset{1}{(0.\cancel{9})}(n)}{\underset{1}{0.\cancel{9}}}$$ Divide both sides by 0.9

$$180 = n$$

Write **credits** in your answer.

So 162 credits is 90% of **180 credits**. This matches the answer we got using a proportion (see **Example 6** in the previous section.)

CHECK The solution makes sense because 90% of 180 credits should be 10% less than 100% of the credits, and 10% of 180. credits is 18 credits.

| 100% | − | 10% | = | 90% |
| of 180 credits | | of 180. credits | | of 180 credits |

| 180 credits | − | 18 credits | = | 162 credits | ← Matches the number given in the original problem |

(b) 250% of what amount is $75?

Translate the sentence into an equation. Write the percent in decimal form.

250.% of what amount is $75?

Write 250% as the decimal 2.5

$$2.5 \cdot n = 75$$

$$\frac{\overset{1}{(2.\cancel{5})}(n)}{\underset{1}{2.\cancel{5}}} = \frac{75}{2.5}$$ Divide both sides by 2.5

$$n = 30$$

Write a $ in your answer.

So 250% of **$30** is $75.

CHECK The solution makes sense because 200% of $30 is 2 times $30 = $60, and 50% of $30 is $30 ÷ 2 = $15.

| 200% | + | 50% | = | 250% |
| of $30 | | of $30 | | of $30 |

| (2)($30) | | $30 ÷ 2 | | |

| $60 | + | $15 | = | $75 | ← Matches the number given in the original problem |

· **Work Problem** ❻ **at the Side.** ▶

❻ Write and solve an equation to answer each question.

GS **(a)** 74% of how many cars is 37 cars?

| 74.% | of | how many cars | is | 37 cars |
| 0.74 | • | n | = | 37 |

(b) 1.2 tons is $2\frac{1}{2}$% of how many tons?

(c) 216 calculators is 160% of how many calculators?

7.3 Exercises

FOR EXTRA HELP

Download the MyDashBoard App

MyMathLab®

CONCEPT CHECK *In Exercises 1–14, use your estimation skills and the percent shortcuts to select the most reasonable answers. Circle your choices. Do* **not** *write an equation or proportion and solve it.* **See Examples 1–3.**

1. Find 50% of 3000 patients.

150 patients   1500 patients   300 patients

2. What is 50% of 192 Facebook updates?

48 updates   384 updates   96 updates

3. 25% of $60 is how much?

$15 $6 $30

4. Find 25% of $2840.

$28.40 $710 $284

5. What is 10% of 45 pounds?

0.45 pound   22.5 pounds   4.5 pounds

6. 10% of 7 feet is how many feet?

0.7 foot   3.5 feet   14 feet

7. Find 200% of $3.50.

$0.35 $1.75 $7.00

8. What is 300% of $12?

$4 $36 $1.20

9. 1% of 5200 students is how many students?

520 students   52 students   2600 students

10. Find 1% of 460 miles.

0.46 mile   46 miles   4.6 miles

11. Find 10% of 8700 smartphones.

8700 phones   4350 phones   870 phones

12. 25% of 28 video games is how many games?

14 games   7 games   112 games

13. What is 25% of 19 hours?

4.75 hours   1.9 hours   2.5 hours

14. What is 1% of $37?

$370 $3.70 $0.37

15. (a) Describe a shortcut for finding 10% of a number and explain *why* your shortcut works.

16. (a) Describe a shortcut for finding 1% of a number and explain *why* your shortcut works.

(b) Once you know 10% of a certain number, explain how you could use that information to find 20% and 30% of the same number.

(b) Once you know 1% of a certain number, explain how you could use that information to find 2% and 3% of the same number.

Write and solve an equation to answer each question in Exercises 17–48.
See Examples 4–6.

17. 35% of 660 programs is how many programs?

35.%   of   660 programs   is   how many programs

0.35   •   660   =   *n*

18. 55% of 740 students is how many students?

55.%   of   740 students   is   how many students

0.55   •   740   =   *n*

19. 70 coffee mugs is what percent of 140 mugs?

20. 30 fire extinguishers is what percent of 75 extinguishers?

21. 476 circuits is 70% of what number of circuits?

22. 621 tons is 45% of what number of tons?

23. $12\frac{1}{2}\%$ of what number of people is 135 people?

24. $6\frac{1}{2}\%$ of what number of iPads is 130 iPads?

25. What is 65% of 1300 blog posts?

26. What is 75% of 360 dosages?

27. 4% of $520 is how much?

28. 7% of $480 is how much?

29. 38 styles is what percent of 50 styles?

30. 75 offices is what percent of 125 offices?

31. What percent of $264 is $330?

32. What percent of $480 is $696?

33. 141 employees is 3% of what number of employees?

34. 16 e-readers is 8% of what number of e-readers?

35. 32% of 260 quarts is how many quarts?

36. 44% of 430 liters is how many liters?

37. $1.48 is what percent of $74?

38. $0.51 is what percent of $8.50?

39. How many tablets is 140% of 500 tablets?

40. How many patients is 175% of 540 patients?

41. 40% of what number of babies is 130 babies?

42. 75% of what number of pumpkins is 675 pumpkins?

43. What percent of 160 liters is 2.4 liters?

44. What percent of 600 miles is 7.5 miles?

45. 225% of what number of gallons is 11.25 gallons?

225.% of what number of gallons is 11.25 gallons
2.25 • n = 11.25

46. 180% of what number of ounces is 6.3 ounces?

180.% of what number of ounces is 6.3 ounces
1.8 • n = 6.3

47. What is 12.4% of 8300 meters?

48. What is 13.2% of 9400 acres?

In Exercises 49–52, find the error made by a student. Explain the error. Then find the correct answer.

49. 3 hours is what percent of 15 hours?

$$3 = p \cdot 15$$

$$\frac{3}{15} = \frac{p \cdot \cancel{15}^{\,1}}{\cancel{15}_{\,1}}$$

$$0.2 = p$$

The answer is 0.2%.

50. 12 inches is 5% of what number of inches?

$$(12)(0.05) = n$$

$$0.6 = n$$

The answer is 0.6 inch.

51. $50 is what percent of $20?

$$50 \cdot p = 20$$

$$\frac{\cancel{50}^{\,1} \cdot p}{\cancel{50}_{\,1}} = \frac{20}{50}$$

$$p = 0.40 = 40\%$$

The answer is 40%.

52. What is 4% of 30 pounds?

$$n = (4)(30)$$

$$n = 120$$

The answer is 120 pounds.

Relating Concepts (Exercises 53–56)   For Individual or Group Work

*Use your knowledge of percents as you **work Exercises 53–56 in order.***

53. 25% of the 80 children at the day care center are boys. How many boys are there? Show how to use the shortcut for 25% to solve this problem.

54. What percent of the children at the day care center are girls? Explain how you solved this problem.

55. How many girls are at the day care center? Explain **two** different ways to solve this problem *without* setting up an equation or proportion.

56. 10% of the boys at the day care center are left handed. None of the girls are left handed. How many children at the center are left handed? Explain how you can solve this problem *without* setting up an equation or proportion.

Summary Exercises *Percent Computation*

1. Complete this table. Write fractions in lowest terms and as whole or mixed numbers when possible.

	Fraction	Decimal	Percent
(a)	$\frac{3}{100}$		
(b)			30%
(c)		0.375	
(d)			160%
(e)	$\frac{1}{16}$		
(f)			5%
(g)		2.0	
(h)	$\frac{4}{5}$		
(i)		0.072	

2. Use percent shortcuts to answer these questions.

  (a) 10% of 35 ft is _____.

  (b) 100% of 19 miles is _____.

  (c) 50% of 210 cows is _____.

  (d) 1% of $8 is _____.

  (e) 25% of 2000 women is _____.

  (f) 300% of $15 is _____.

  (g) 10% of $875 is _____.

  (h) 25% of 48 pounds is _____.

  (i) 1% of 9500 students is _____.

Use the percent proportion or percent equation to answer each question. If necessary, round money answers to the nearest cent and percent answers to the nearest tenth of a percent.

3. 9 websites is what percent of 72 websites?

4. 30 text messages is 40% of what number of text messages?

5. 6% of $8.79 is how much?

6. 945 students is what percent of 540 students?

7. $3\frac{1}{2}$% of 168 pounds is how much, to the nearest tenth of a pound?

8. 1.25% of what number of hours is 7.5 hours?

9. What percent of 80,000 deer is 40,000 deer?

10. 465 camp sites is 93% of what number of camp sites?

11. What number of golf balls is 280% of 35 golf balls?

12. What percent of $66 is $1.80?

13. 9% of what number of tweets is 207 tweets?

14. What weight is 84% of 0.75 ounce?

15. $1160 is what percent of $800?

16. Find 3.75% of 6500 voters, to the nearest whole number.

17. What is 300% of 0.007 inch?

18. 24 minutes is what percent of 6 minutes?

19. What percent of 60 yards is 4.8 yards?

20. $0.17 is 25% of what amount?

The circle graph shows the average costs for various wedding expenses. Use the graph to answer Exercises 21–24. Round money answers to the nearest cent, if necessary.

WHAT IT COSTS TO RING THE WEDDING BELLS
The average wedding has 178 guests and costs $30,800. Here is how couples are spending the money.

Flowers $6\frac{1}{2}$%
Rings for bride and groom 6.7%
All other expenses 7.4%
Invitations $2\frac{3}{4}$%
Reception 48%
Photography/Videography 12%
Bride's dress/men's formalwear 8.5%
Ceremony $8\frac{1}{5}$%

Percents are rounded.

Source: soundvision.com/info/weddings

21. Which item in the graph is least expensive? On average, how much is spent on that item?

22. What is the average amount spent on the ceremony?

23. Find the cost of photography and videography.

24. What amount is spent on rings for the bride and groom?

25. (a) How much is spent on the reception?

(b) On average, what is the cost for each guest at the reception?

7.4 Problem Solving with Percent

OBJECTIVES

1. Solve percent application problems.

2. Solve problems involving percent of increase or decrease.

1 About 65% of the students at City Center College receive some form of financial aid. How many of the 9280 students enrolled this year are receiving aid?

Let *n* be the number of students receiving aid.

$$0.65 \cdot 9280 = n$$

OBJECTIVE **1** **Solve percent application problems.** Solving percent problems involves identifying three items: the *percent*, the *whole,* and the *part*. Then you can write a percent equation or percent proportion and solve it to answer the question in the problem. Use the six problem-solving steps from **Chapter 3.**

EXAMPLE 1   Finding the Part

A new low-income housing project charges 30% of a family's income as rent. The Smiths' family income is $1260 per month. How much will the Smiths pay for rent each month?

Step 1 **Read the problem.** It is about a family paying part of its income for rent.

>   Unknown: amount of rent

>   Known: 30% of income paid for rent; $1260 monthly income

Step 2 **Assign a variable.** There is only one unknown, so let *n* be the amount paid for rent each month.

Step 3 **Write an equation.** Use the percent equation.

$$\text{percent} \cdot \text{whole} = \text{part}$$

Recall that the *whole* often follows the word *of.*

>   The percent is given in the problem: 30%. The key word *of* appears *right after* 30%, which means that you can use the phrase "30% of a family's income" to help you write one side of the equation.

| Write 30% as the decimal 0.30 | 30.% of a family's income is the rent. |

$$0.30 \cdot \$1260 = n$$

Step 4 **Solve the equation.** Simplify the left side, multiplying 0.30 by 1260.

$$\underbrace{(0.30)(1260)}_{} = n$$
$$378 = n \quad \text{Write a \$ in your answer.}$$

Step 5 **State the answer.** The Smiths will pay **$378** for rent each month.

Step 6 **Check** the solution. The solution of $378 makes sense because 10% of $1260 is $126, so 30% would be 3 times $126, or $378.

Note

You could also use the percent proportion in *Step 3* above.

$$\text{Percent} \longrightarrow \frac{30}{100} = \frac{n}{1260} \begin{array}{l} \longleftarrow \text{Part (unknown)} \\ \longleftarrow \text{Whole} \end{array}$$
$$\text{Always 100} \longrightarrow$$

The answer will be the same, $378.

Throughout the rest of this chapter, we will use the percent equation. You may, if you wish, use the percent proportion instead. The final answers will be the same.

Answer

1. 6032 students receive aid.
    Check. 10% of 9280 students is 928, which rounds to 900 students. So 60% would be 6 times 900 students = 5400 students, and 70% would be 7 • 900 = 6300. The solution falls between 5400 and 6300 students, so it is reasonable.

◀ **Work Problem ❶ at the Side.**

When Britta received her first $180 paycheck as a math tutor, $12\frac{1}{2}\%$ was withheld for federal income tax. How much was withheld?

Step 1 **Read** the problem. It is about part of Britta's pay being withheld for taxes.

   Unknown: amount withheld for taxes

   Known: $12\frac{1}{2}\%$ of earnings withheld; $180 in pay

Step 2 **Assign a variable.** There is only one unknown, so let n be the amount withheld for taxes.

Step 3 **Write an equation.** Use the percent equation. The *percent* is given: $12\frac{1}{2}\%$. Write $12\frac{1}{2}\%$ as 12.5% and then move the decimal point two places to the left. So 12.5% becomes the decimal 0.125.

   The key word *of* doesn't appear after $12\frac{1}{2}\%$. Instead, think about whether you know the *whole* or the *part*. You know Britta's *whole* paycheck is $180, but you do *not* know what *part* of it was withheld.

> **Be careful!**
> $12\frac{1}{2}\%$ is 12.5%, but remember to *move the decimal point two places to the left* to get 0.125

$$\text{percent} \cdot \text{whole} = \text{part}$$
$$12.5\% \cdot \$180 = n$$

Step 4 **Solve.**
$$(0.125)(180) = n$$
$$22.5 = n$$

Step 5 **State the answer.** $22.50 was withheld from Britta's paycheck.

Step 6 **Check the solution.** The solution of $22.50 makes sense because 10% of $180 is $18, so a little more than $18 should be withheld.

··· **Work Problem ② at the Side.** ▶

On a 15-point quiz, Zenitia earned 13 points. What percent correct is this, to the nearest whole percent?

Step 1 **Read** the problem. It is about points earned on a quiz.

   Unknown: percent correct

   Known: earned 13 out of 15 points

Step 2 **Assign a variable.** Let p be the unknown percent.

Step 3 **Write an equation.** Use the percent equation. There is no number with a % symbol in the problem. The question, "What percent is this?" tells you that the *percent* is unknown. The *whole* is all the points on the quiz (15 points), and 13 points is the *part* of the quiz that Zenitia did correctly.

$$\text{percent} \cdot \text{whole} = \text{part}$$
$$p \cdot 15 \text{ points} = 13 \text{ points}$$

··· **Continued on Next Page**

② There were 50 points on the first math test. Hue's score was 83% correct. How many points did Hue earn?

Let n be the points Hue earned. The whole is all the points on the test.

$$\text{percent} \cdot \text{whole} = \text{part}$$
$$83.\% \cdot 50 \text{ points} = n$$

Answer

2. $(0.83)(50) = n$
Hue earned 41.5 points.
Check. 10% of 50 points is 5 points, so 80% would be 8 times 5 points = 40 points. Hue earned a little more than 80%, so 41.5 points is reasonable.

3 The Los Angeles Lakers made 47 of 80 field goal attempts in one game. What percent is this, to the nearest whole percent?

Let p be the unknown percent. The whole is all the field goal attempts.

$$\text{percent} \cdot \text{whole} = \text{part}$$
$$\downarrow \qquad\qquad \downarrow \qquad\qquad \downarrow$$
$$p \quad \cdot \quad 80 \text{ attempts} = 47 \text{ made}$$

4 Valley College predicted that 1200 new students would enroll in the fall. It actually had 1620 new students enroll. The actual enrollment is what percent of the predicted number?

Let p be the unknown percent.

$$\underbrace{\text{actual}}_{\text{enrollment}} \text{ is } \underbrace{\text{percent}}_{\text{what}} \text{ of } \underbrace{\text{predicted}}_{\text{number}}$$
$$\downarrow \qquad \downarrow \qquad \downarrow \qquad \downarrow$$
$$1620 \quad = \quad p \quad \cdot \quad 1200$$

Answers

3. $p = 0.5875$
   $0.5875 = 58.75\% \approx 59\%$
   The Lakers made 59% of their field goals, to the nearest whole percent.
   Check. The Lakers made a little more than half of their field goals. $\frac{1}{2} = 50\%$, so the solution of 59% is reasonable.

4. $1.35 = p$
   $1.35 = 135\%$
   Enrollment is 135% of the predicted number. **Check.** More than 1200 students enrolled (more than 100%), so 1620 students must be more than 100% of the predicted number. The solution of 135% is reasonable.

Step 4   **Solve** the equation.

$$\frac{p \cdot \overset{1}{\cancel{15}}}{\cancel{15}} = \frac{13}{15} \qquad \text{Divide both sides by 15}$$

> CAUTION! **Multiply the solution by 100% to change it from a *decimal* to a *percent*.**

$$p = 0.8\overline{6} \leftarrow \begin{array}{l}\text{The solution is a} \\ \text{repeating decimal.}\end{array}$$

$$0.866666667 = 86.6666667\% \approx 87\% \leftarrow \text{Rounded}$$

Step 5   **State the answer.** Zenitia had 87% correct, rounded to the nearest whole percent.

Step 6   **Check the solution.** The solution of 87% makes sense because she earned most of the possible points, so the percent should be fairly close to 100%.

◀ **Work Problem 3 at the Side.**

EXAMPLE 4   **Finding the Percent**

The rainfall in the Red River Valley was 33 inches this year. The average rainfall is 30 inches. This year's rainfall is what percent of the average rainfall?

Step 1   **Read the problem.** It is about comparing this year's rainfall to the average rainfall.

> **Unknown:** This year's rain is what percent of the average?
> **Known:** 33 inches this year; 30 inches is average

Step 2   **Assign a variable.** Let p be the unknown percent.

Step 3   **Write an equation.** The percent is unknown. The key word *of* appears *right after* the word *percent*, so you can use that sentence to help you write the equation.

$$\underbrace{\text{This year's rainfall}}_{} \text{ is } \underbrace{\text{what percent}}_{} \text{ of } \underbrace{\text{the average rainfall?}}_{}$$
$$\downarrow \qquad\qquad \downarrow \qquad\quad \downarrow \qquad\qquad \downarrow$$
$$33 \text{ inches} \quad = \quad p \quad \cdot \quad 30 \text{ inches}$$

Step 4   **Solve the equation.**

$$33 = p \cdot 30$$

$$\frac{33}{30} = \frac{p \cdot \overset{1}{\cancel{30}}}{\cancel{30}} \qquad \text{Divide both sides by 30}$$

Solution in *decimal* form → $1.1 = p$

> **Multiply the solution by 100% to change it from a *decimal* to a *percent*.**

$$1.10 = 110\%$$

Step 5   **State the answer.** This year's rainfall is 110% of the average rainfall.

Step 6   **Check the solution.** The solution of 110% makes sense because 33 inches is *more* than 30 inches (more than 100% of the average rainfall), so 33 inches must be *more* than 100% of 30 inches.

◀ **Work Problem 4 at the Side.**

EXAMPLE 5	Finding the Whole

A newspaper article stated that 648 pints of blood were donated at the blood bank last month, which was only 72% of the number of pints needed. How many pints of blood were needed?

Step 1   **Read the problem.** It is about blood donations.

>   Unknown: number of pints needed

>   Known: 648 pints were donated;
>   648 pints is 72% of the number needed.

Step 2   **Assign a variable.** Let n be the number of pints needed.

Step 3   **Write an equation.** The percent is given in the problem: 72%. The key word of appears *right after* 72%, so you can use the phrase "72% of the number of pints needed" to help you write one side of the equation.

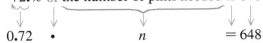

>   72.% of the number of pints needed is 648 pints.
>   0.72   • n = 648

Step 4   **Solve.** $0.72 \cdot n = 648$

$$\frac{(0.\overset{1}{\cancel{72}})(n)}{\underset{1}{\cancel{0.72}}} = \frac{648}{0.72}$$ Divide both sides by 0.72

$$n = 900$$

> Write **pints** in your answer.

Step 5   **State the answer.** 900 pints of blood were needed.

Step 6   **Check the solution.** The solution of 900 pints makes sense because 10% of 900 pints is 90 pints, so 70% would be 7 times 90 pints, or 630 pints, which is close to the number given in the problem (648 pints).

·········· **Work Problem** ❺ **at the Side.** ▶

OBJECTIVE ❷ **Solve problems involving percent of increase or decrease.** We are often interested in looking at increases or decreases in prices, earnings, population, and many other numbers. This type of problem involves finding the percent of change. Use the following steps to find the **percent of increase.**

Finding the Percent of Increase

Step 1   Use subtraction to find the *amount* of increase.

Step 2   Use a form of the percent equation to find the *percent* of increase.

>   percent of   whole   =   part
>   ↓   ↓   ↓   ↓
>   percent of original value = amount of increase

---

❺ **(a)** Ezra did 15 problems correctly on a test, giving him a score of $62\frac{1}{2}\%$. How many problems were on the test?

Let n be number of problems on the test. This is the *whole* test.

The *part* of the problems that Ezra did correctly is 15.

>   percent • whole = part
>   ↓   ↓   ↓
>   62.5% • n =   15

(b) A frozen dinner advertises that only 18% of its calories are from fat. If the dinner contains 55 calories from fat, what is the total number of calories in the dinner? Round to the nearest whole number.

Answers

5. (a) $(0.625)(n) = 15$
   There were 24 problems on the test.
   Check. 50% of 24 problems is
   $24 \div 2 = 12$ problems correct, so
   it is reasonable that $62\frac{1}{2}\%$ would be
   15 problems correct.
(b) Let n be total number of calories.
   $(0.18)(n) = 55$
   There were 306 calories (rounded) in
   the dinner. **Check.** 10% of 306 calories
   is about 30 calories, so 20% would be
   $2 \cdot 30 = 60$ calories, which is close to
   the number given (55 calories).

6 (a) Over the last two years,
Duyen's rent has increased
from $650 per month to
$767. What is the percent
increase?

Let p be the percent of
increase.

$$\$767 - 650 = \$117 \begin{cases} \text{amount of} \\ \text{increase} \end{cases}$$

percent   of   original   =   amount of
                rent   increase
  ↓   ↓   ↓   ↓
  p •   650   =   117

(b) A medical clinic increased
the number of accessible
parking spaces from 8 to 20.
What is the percent increase?

Answers

6. (a) $p = 0.18 = 18\%$
    Duyen's rent increased 18%.
    Check. 10% increase would be
    $650. = \$65$; 20% increase would be
    $2 \cdot \$65 = \$130$; so an 18% increase is
    reasonable.

(b) $20 - 8 = 12$ space increase
    Let p be percent increase.
    $p \cdot 8 = 12$
    $p = 1.50 = 150\%$
    The number of accessible parking spaces
    increased 150%.

    Check. 150% is $1\frac{1}{2}$, and $1\frac{1}{2} \cdot 8 =$
    12 space increase, so it checks.

EXAMPLE 6	Finding the Percent of Increase

Brad's hourly wage as assistant manager of a fast-food restaurant was raised
from $9.40 to $9.87. What was the percent of increase?

Step 1 **Read the problem.** It is about an increase in wages.

> Unknown: percent of increase

> Known: Original hourly wage was $9.40;
>   new hourly wage is $9.87.

Step 2 **Assign a variable.** Let p be the percent of increase.

Step 3 **Write an equation.** First subtract $9.87 − $9.40 to find how much
Brad's wage went up. That is the *amount* of increase. Then write
an equation to find the unknown *percent* of increase. Be sure to use
his *original* wage ($9.40) in the equation because we are looking
for the change from his *original* wage. Do ***not*** use the new wage of
$9.87 in the equation.

$$\$9.87 - 9.40 = \$0.47 \leftarrow \textit{Amount of increase}$$

percent of original wage = amount of increase

   ↓   ↓   ↓
   p • $\$9.40$ = $\$0.47$

> Do **not** use $9.87
> in the equation.
> Use the **original**
> wage of $9.40.

Step 4 **Solve.**
$$\frac{(p)(9.\overset{1}{\cancel{40}})}{9.\underset{1}{\cancel{40}}} = \frac{0.47}{9.40} \quad \begin{array}{l}\text{Divide both sides}\\\text{by 9.40}\end{array}$$

$$p = 0.05 \leftarrow \textit{Solution in decimal form}$$

> Multiply the solution by 100% to
> change it from a *decimal* to a *percent*.

$$0.05 = 5\%$$

Step 5 **State the answer.** Brad's hourly wage increased **5%**.

Step 6 **Check the solution.** 10% of $9.40 would be a $0.94 raise. A raise of
$0.47 is half as much, and half of 10% is 5%, so the solution checks.

CAUTION

When writing the percent equation in *Step 3* above, be sure to multiply
the percent (p) by the ***original*** wage. Do ***not*** use the *new* wage in the
percent equation.

◀ Work Problem **6** at the Side.

Use a similar procedure to find the **percent of decrease**.

Finding the Percent of Decrease

Step 1 Use subtraction to find the *amount* of decrease.

Step 2 Use a form of the percent equation to find the *percent* of
decrease.

percent of   whole   =   part
  ↓   ↓   ↓   ↓

percent of original value = amount of decrease

EXAMPLE 7 Finding the Percent of Decrease

Rozenia trained for six months to run in a marathon. Her weight dropped from 137 pounds to 122 pounds. Find the percent of decrease, to the nearest whole percent.

Step 1 **Read the problem.** It is about a decrease in weight.

Unknown: percent of decrease

Known: Original weight was 137 pounds;
new weight is 122 pounds.

Step 2 **Assign a variable.** Let p be the percent of decrease.

Step 3 **Write an equation.** First subtract 137 pounds − 122 pounds to find how much Rozenia's weight went down. That is the *amount* of decrease. Then write an equation to find the unknown *percent* of decrease. Be sure to use her *original* weight (137 pounds) in the equation because we are looking for the change from her *original* weight. Do *not* use the new weight of 122 pounds in the equation.

137 pounds − 122 pounds = 15 pounds ← *Amount* of decrease

percent of original weight = amount of decrease

$$p \cdot 137 \text{ pounds} = 15 \text{ pounds}$$

Do **not** use 122 pounds in the equation. Use the **original** weight of 137 pounds.

Step 4 **Solve.**

$$\frac{p \cdot \overset{1}{\cancel{137}}}{\underset{1}{\cancel{137}}} = \frac{15}{137} \quad \text{Divide both sides by 137}$$

$$p \approx 0.109489051 \leftarrow \text{Solution in } \textit{decimal} \text{ form}$$

Multiply the solution by 100% to change it from a *decimal* to a *percent*.

$$0.109489051 = 10.9489051\% \approx 11\%$$

Rounded to nearest whole percent

Step 5 **State the answer.** Rozenia's weight decreased approximately 11%.

Step 6 **Check the solution.** A 10% decrease would be 137. = 13.7 pounds, so an 11% decrease is a reasonable solution.

CAUTION

When writing the percent equation in *Step 3* above, be sure to multiply the percent (*p*) by the **original** weight. Do *not* use the *new* weight in the percent equation.

· **Work Problem ❼ at the Side.** ▶

❼ Find each percent of decrease. Round answers to the nearest whole percent.

(a) During a severe winter storm, average daily attendance at an elementary school fell from 425 students to 200 students. What was the percent decrease?

Let *p* be the percent decrease.

425 students − 200 = 225 students

Amount of decrease

percent of original attendance = amount of decrease

$$p \cdot 425 = 225$$

(b) The makers of a brand of spaghetti sauce claim that the number of calories from fat in each serving has been reduced by 20%. Is the claim correct if the number of calories from fat dropped from 70 calories to 60 calories per serving? Explain your answer.

Answers

7. **(a)** $p \approx 0.529 \approx 53\%$ (rounded)
Daily attendance decreased 53%.
Check. A 50% decrease would be $425 \div 2 \approx 212$, so a 53% decrease is reasonable.
(b) 70 − 60 = 10 calorie decrease
Let *p* be percent of decrease.
$$p \cdot 70 = 10$$
$$p \approx 0.143 \approx 14\% \text{ (rounded)}$$
The claim of a 20% decrease is not true; the decrease in calories is about 14%.
Check. A 10% decrease would be 70. = 7 calories; a 20% decrease would be $2 \cdot 7 = 14$ calories, so a 14% decrease is reasonable.

7.4 Exercises

  MyMathLab®

CONCEPT CHECK *Find each percent using the shortcuts for 50%, 25%, 10%, and 1%.*

1. An ATM machine charges $2 for any size cash withdrawal. The $2 fee is what percent of a
   (a) $20 withdrawal
   (b) $40 withdrawal
   (c) $200 withdrawal.

2. An online company charges $8 for shipping and handling on any order of $100 or less. The $8 shipping charge is what percent of a
   (a) $16 order
   (b) $32 order
   (c) $80 order

Use the six problem-solving steps in Exercises 3–22. Round percent answers to the nearest tenth of a percent when necessary. **See Examples 1–5.**

3. Robert Garrett, who works part-time, earns $210 per week and has 18% of this amount withheld for taxes, Social Security, and Medicare. Find the amount withheld.

   Let *n* be the amount withheld.

   18.% of pay is withheld

   0.18 • $210 = *n*

4. Most shampoos contain 75% to 90% water. If a 16-ounce bottle of shampoo contains 78% water, find the number of ounces of water in the bottle, to the nearest tenth. (*Source: Consumer Reports.*)

   Let *n* be the ounces of water.

   78.% of shampoo is water

   0.78 • 16 ounces = *n*

The circle graph below shows, on average, what portion of the human body is made up of water, protein, fat, and so on. Use the graph to answer Exercises 5 and 6. Round answers to the nearest tenth of a pound. (*Source:* fao.org)

Composition of the Human Body

Carbohydrates 1.5%
Minerals 6.1%
Fats 13.8%
Water 61.6%
Proteins 17%

5. If an adult weighs 165 pounds, how much of that weight is
   (a) water
   (b) minerals
   (c) proteins.

6. If a teenager weighs 92 pounds, how much of that weight is
   (a) fat
   (b) carbohydrates
   (c) water.

7. When 480 people were asked what they planned to do with their tax refunds, 283 said they would pay off debt; 317 said they would save or invest the money; and 110 said they would buy something. (People could give more than one answer.) What percent of the people gave each answer? (*Source:* Synovate.)

8. Airline passengers generate 880 million tons of waste each year. Only 176 million tons are being recycled now. It is estimated that 660 million tons could be recycled if the airlines made an effort to do so. What percent of the waste is being recycled now? What percent could be recycled? (*Source: Washington Post.*)

9. The U.S. Census Bureau reported that Americans who are 65 years of age or older made up 13.0% of the total population in 2010. It said that there were 40.3 million Americans in this group. Find the total U.S. population for that year.

10. Julie Ward has 8.5% of her earnings deposited into the credit union. If this amounts to $263.50 per month, find her monthly and annual earnings.

11. The campus honor society hoped to raise $50,000 in donations from businesses for scholarships. It actually raised $69,000. This amount was what percent of the goal?

12. Doug had budgeted $220 for textbooks but ended up spending $316.80. The amount he spent was what percent of his budget?

13. Alfonso earned a score of 85% on his test. He did 34 problems correctly. How many problems were on the test?

14. In an online survey, 182 adults said they order food delivered to their homes on Fridays. This was 36% of the adults in the survey. How many adults were surveyed, to the nearest whole number? (*Source: Technomic Inc.*)

15. During the 2010–2011 NBA season, Kris Humphries made 307 field goals, which was 52.7% of the shots he tried. How many shots did he try, to the nearest whole number? (*Source:* NBA.com)

16. Kevin Durant, who plays basketball in the NBA, attempted 492 free throws during the 2010–2011 season. He made 87.4% of his shots. How many free throws did Durant make, to the nearest whole number? (*Source:* NBA.com)

17. An ad for steel-belted radial tires promises 15% better mileage. If Sheera's SUV has gotten 20.6 miles per gallon in the past, what mileage can she expect after the new tires are installed? (Round to the nearest tenth of a mile.)

18. Annie Leung set the world record for a female playing the video game "Guitar Hero III: Legends of Rock." Annie scored 789,349 points, which is 80.24% of the possible points for a single song on the Expert Level. How many points were possible, to the nearest whole number? (*Source: Guinness Book of World Records.*)

⊞ *The bar graph shows the median weekly earnings for adults with various levels of education. Use the graph to answer Exercises 19–22. Round percent answers to the nearest whole percent.*

Median Weekly Earnings

Master's degree	$1272
Bachelor's degree	$1038
Associate degree	$767
Some college, no degree	$712
High school diploma	$626
Less than a high school diploma	$444

Source: U.S. Bureau of Labor Statistics.

19. The weekly earnings of a person with less than a high school diploma are what percent of the weekly earnings of a person with an associate degree? How much more does the person with the associate degree earn in a year? (Assume the people receive pay for 52 weeks each year.)

20. The weekly earnings of someone with a high school diploma are what percent of the weekly earnings of someone with an associate degree? How much more does the person with the associate degree earn in ten years? (Assume the people receive pay for 52 weeks each year.)

21. What percent are the weekly earnings of a person with a bachelor's degree compared to the weekly earnings of a person with an associate degree?

22. What percent are the weekly earnings of a person with a master's degree compared to the weekly earnings of a person with some college but no degree?

Use the six problem-solving steps to find the percent increase or decrease. Round your answers to the nearest tenth of a percent. **See Examples 6 and 7.**

23. Henry Ford started the Ford Motor Company. The Model T first appeared in 1908 and cost $825. In 1913, Ford started using an assembly line and the price of the Model T dropped to $290. What was the percent of decrease? (*Source:* Kenneth C. Davis.)

First subtract: $825 − $290 = _____

$$\underset{p}{\underset{\downarrow}{\text{percent}}} \quad \underset{}{\underset{\downarrow}{\text{of}}} \quad \underset{\$825}{\underset{\downarrow}{\underbrace{\text{original}\atop\text{cost}}}} \quad = \quad \underset{\_\_\_\_}{\underset{\downarrow}{\underbrace{\text{amount of}\atop\text{decrease}}}}$$

24. In 1914, Henry Ford became a hero to his workers because he doubled the daily minimum wage. He also cut the workday from nine hours to eight hours. Find the percent of decrease in the number of hours in the workday. (*Source:* Kenneth C. Davis.)

First subtract: 9 hours − 8 hours = _____

$$\underset{p}{\underset{\downarrow}{\text{percent}}} \quad \underset{}{\underset{\downarrow}{\text{of}}} \quad \underset{9 \text{ hours}}{\underset{\downarrow}{\underbrace{\text{original}\atop\text{hours}}}} \quad = \quad \underset{\_\_\_\_}{\underset{\downarrow}{\underbrace{\text{amount of}\atop\text{decrease}}}}$$

25. Students at Lane College were charged $1449 as tuition this semester. If the tuition was $1328 last semester, find the percent of increase.

26. Americans are eating more fish. In 2010, the average American ate 16.3 pounds compared to only 11.7 pounds per year in 1970. Find the percent of increase. (*Source:* USDA/Economic Research Service.)

27. Jordan's part-time work schedule was reduced to 18 hours per week. He had been working 30 hours per week. What is the percent decrease?

28. Janis works as a hair stylist. During January, she cut her price on haircuts from $35 to $31.50 to try to get more customers. By what percent did she decrease the price?

29. In 1967 there were 78 animal species listed as threatened with extinction in the United States. In 2011 there were 588 animals on the list. What was the percent increase, to the nearest whole percent? (*Source:* U.S. Fish and Wildlife Service.)

Condor with wing tag

Florida panther

Bighorn sheep

30. The world population was estimated at 6,980,445,600 people in 2011. It is projected to reach 7,892,758,700 people by 2025. By what percent will the world's population increase in those 14 years? (*Source:* United Nations.)

31. CONCEPT CHECK   You can have an *increase* of 150% in the price of something. Could there be a 150% *decrease* in its price? Explain why or why not.

32. CONCEPT CHECK   Show how to use a shortcut to find 25% of $80. Then explain how to use the result to find 75% of $80 and 125% of $80 *without* solving a proportion or equation.

Relating Concepts (Exercises 33–36)   For Individual or Group Work

*As you **work Exercises 33–36 in order,** explain why each solution does **not** make sense. Then find and correct the error.*

33. The recommended maximum daily amount of dietary fat is 65 grams. George ate 78 grams of fat today. He ate what percent of the recommended amount?

$$p \cdot 78 = 65$$
$$\frac{p \cdot \cancel{78}^{1}}{\cancel{78}_{1}} = \frac{65}{78}$$
$$p = 0.833 = 83.3\%$$

34. The Goblers soccer team won 18 of its 25 games this season. What percent did the team win?

$$p \cdot 25 = 18$$
$$\frac{p \cdot \cancel{25}^{1}}{\cancel{25}_{1}} = \frac{18}{25}$$
$$p = 0.72\%$$

35. The human brain is $2\frac{1}{2}\%$ of total body weight. How much would the brain of a 150-pound person weigh?

$$2\frac{1}{2}\% \text{ of } 150 = n$$
$$(2.5)(150) = n$$
$$375 = n$$

36. Yesterday, because of an ice storm, 80% of the students were absent. How many of the 800 students made it to class?

$$80\% \text{ of } 800 = n$$
$$(0.80)(800) = n$$
$$640 = n$$

The answer is 640 students.

Study Skills
PREPARING FOR YOUR FINAL EXAM

Your math final exam is likely to be a **comprehensive exam.** This means that it will cover material from the **entire term.** The end of the term will be less stressful if you **make a plan** for how you will prepare for each of your exams.

First, figure out the **score you need to earn on the final exam** to get the course grade you want. Check your course syllabus for grading policies, or ask your instructor if you are not sure of them. This allows you to set a goal for yourself.

> How many points do you need to earn on your mathematics final exam to get the grade you want? _____
> _____

Create a Plan

Second, create a **final exam week plan for your work and personal life.** If you need to make an adjustment in your work schedule, do it in advance, so you aren't scrambling at the last minute. If you have family members to care for, you might want to enlist some help from others so you can spend extra time studying. Try to plan in advance so you don't create additional stress for yourself. You will have to set some priorities, and studying has to be at the top of the list! Although life doesn't stop for finals, some things can be ignored for a short time. You don't want to "burn out" during final exam week; **get enough sleep and healthy food so you can perform your best.**

> What adjustments in your personal life do you need to make for final exam week? _____
> _____

Study and Review

Third, use the following suggestions to guide your studying and reviewing.

▶ **Know exactly which chapters and sections will be on the final exam.**

▶ **Divide up the chapters,** and decide how much you will review each day.

▶ Begin your reviewing **several days** before the exam.

▶ **Use returned quizzes and tests** to review earlier material (if you have them).

▶ **Practice all types of problems,** but emphasize the types that are most difficult for you. Use the **Cumulative Reviews** that are at the end of each chapter in your textbook.

▶ **Rewrite your notes or make mind maps** to create summaries.

▶ **Make study cards for all types of problems.** Be sure to use the same **direction words** (such as *simplify, solve, estimate*) that your exam will use. Carry the cards with you and review them whenever you have a few spare minutes.

Managing Stress

Of course, a week of final exams produces stress. **Students who develop skills for reducing and managing stress do better on their final exams and are less likely to "bomb" an exam.** You already know the damaging effect of adrenaline on your ability to think clearly. But several days (or weeks) of elevated stress is also harmful to your brain and your body. You will feel better if you make a conscious effort to reduce your stress level. Even if it takes you away from studying for a little while each day, the time will be well spent.

Reducing Physical Stress

Examples of ways to reduce **physical stress** are listed below. Can you add any of your own ideas to the list?

▶ *Laugh until your eyes water.* Watching your favorite funny movie, exchanging a joke with a friend, or viewing a comedy bit on the Internet are all ways to generate a healthy laugh. Laughing raises the level of *calming* chemicals (endorphins) in your brain.

▶ *Exercise for 20 to 30 minutes.* If you normally exercise regularly, do NOT stop during final exam week! Exercising helps relax muscles, diffuses adrenaline, and raises the level of endorphins in your body. If you don't exercise much, get some gentle exercise, such as a daily walk, to help you relax.

▶ *Practice deep breathing.* Several minutes of deep, smooth breathing will calm you. Close your eyes too.

▶ *Visualize a relaxing scene.* Choose something that you find peaceful and picture it. Imagine what it feels like and sounds like. Try to put yourself in the picture.

▶ If you feel stress in your muscles, such as in your shoulders or back, *slowly squeeze the muscles as much as you can, and then release them.* Sometimes we don't realize we are clenching our teeth or holding tension in our shoulders until we consciously work with them. Try to notice what it feels like when they are relaxed and loose. Squeezing and then releasing muscles is also something you can do during an exam if you feel yourself tightening up.

Reducing Mental Stress

Mental stress reduction is also a powerful tool both before and during an exam. In addition to these suggestions, do you have any of your own techniques?

▶ *Talk positively to yourself.* Tell yourself you will get through it.

▶ *Reward yourself.* Give yourself small breaks, a little treat—something that makes you happy—every day of final exam week.

▶ *Make a list of things to do* and feel the sense of accomplishment when you cross each item off.

▶ When you take time to relax or exercise, *make sure you are relaxing your mind too.* Use your mind for something *completely* different from the kind of thinking you do when you study. Plan your garden, play your favorite music, walk your dog, read a good book.

▶ *Visualize.* Picture yourself completing exams and projects successfully. Picture yourself taking the test calmly and confidently.

Which techniques will you try?

_____
_____
_____

Which techniques will you try?

_____
_____
_____

Chapter 7   *Summary*

Key Terms

7.1

percent Percent means "per one hundred." A percent is a ratio with a denominator of 100.

7.2

percent proportion The proportion used to solve percent problems is: $\dfrac{\text{percent}}{100} = \dfrac{\text{part}}{\text{whole}}$

whole The *whole* in a percent problem is the entire quantity or the total. It is sometimes called the *base*.

part The *part* in a percent problem is the number being compared to the *whole*.

7.3

percent equation The percent equation is: percent • whole = part. The equation can be used instead of the percent proportion to solve percent problems.

7.4

percent of increase or decrease Percent of increase or decrease is the amount of change (increase or decrease) expressed as a percent of the original value.

New Symbols

%   percent symbol (meaning "per 100")

Test Your Word Power

See how well you have learned the vocabulary in this chapter.

1 **Percent** means
   A. per one thousand
   B. a ratio with 10 in the denominator
   C. per one hundred.

2 The **whole** in a percent problem is
   A. the entire quantity or total
   B. a ratio with a denominator of 100
   C. always 100.

3 When calculating sales tax, the **rate** is
   A. the whole
   B. the total cost
   C. the percent.

4 The **interest formula** is
A. $I = prt$
B. percent • whole = part
C. $\dfrac{\text{percent}}{100} = \dfrac{\text{part}}{\text{whole}}$.

6 The **percent of increase or decrease** compares the amount of change to
A. 100
B. the original value before the change
C. the new value after the change.

8 A **discount** is
A. added to the original price
B. divided by 100
C. subtracted from the original price.

5 When calculating interest on a loan, the **principal** is the
A. amount of money borrowed
B. total amount due
C. rate charged for borrowing money.

7 The **percent equation** is
A. $I = prt$
B. percent • whole = part
C. $\dfrac{\text{percent}}{100} = \dfrac{\text{part}}{\text{whole}}$.

Answers to Test Your Word Power

1. C; *Example:* 7% means 7 per 100, or 7 out of 100.

2. A; *Example:* In the problem "15 computers is what percent of 75 computers," the whole is 75 computers, which is the total group of computers.

3. C; *Example:* In 2012, Houston had a sales tax rate of 8.25%; Minneapolis had a sales tax rate of 7.775%.

4. A; *Example:* The interest formula is: Interest = principal • rate • time. If you borrow $4000 for 2 years at a rate of 9%, then
$I = (4000)(0.09)(2) = \$720$.

5. A; *Example:* If you borrow $4000 for 2 years at a rate of 9%, the principal is $4000.

6. B; *Example:* If your rent increased from $800 to $850, the *percent of increase* compares the amount of change ($50) to the *original* rent ($800).

7. B; *Example:* To answer the question, "What percent of 40 calculators is 12 calculators," let p be the unknown percent and write the equation as: $p \cdot 40 = 12$.

8. C; *Example:* If sunglasses are on sale at 10% off, then a pair of sunglasses regularly priced at $25 will have a discount of $2.50 subtracted from the price; you will pay $22.50. To find the amount of discount, multiply $(0.10)(\$25)$ to get $2.50.

Quick Review

Concepts	Examples

7.1 Basics of Percent

Writing a Percent as a Decimal
To write a percent as a decimal, move the decimal point *two* places to the *left* and drop the % sign.

$50\% = 50.\% = 0.50 \text{ or } 0.5$

$3\% = 03.\% = 0.03$

Writing a Decimal as a Percent
To write a decimal as a percent, move the decimal point *two* places to the *right* and attach a % sign.

$0.75 = 0.75 = 75\%$

$3.6 = 3.60 = 360\%$

Writing a Percent as a Fraction
To write a percent as a fraction, drop the % symbol and write the number over 100. Then write the fraction in lowest terms.

$35\% = \dfrac{35}{100} = \dfrac{35 \div 5}{100 \div 5} = \dfrac{7}{20} \leftarrow \text{Lowest terms}$

$125\% = \dfrac{125}{100} = \dfrac{125 \div 25}{100 \div 25} = \dfrac{5}{4} = 1\dfrac{1}{4}$

Writing a Fraction as a Percent
To write a fraction as a percent, multiply by 100 and attach a % symbol. This is the same as multiplying by 100%.

$\dfrac{3}{5} = \left(\dfrac{3}{5}\right)\left(\dfrac{100}{1}\%\right) = \dfrac{3 \cdot \overset{1}{\cancel{5}} \cdot 20}{\underset{1}{\cancel{5}} \cdot 1}\% = \dfrac{60}{1}\% = 60\%$

$\dfrac{7}{8} = \left(\dfrac{7}{8}\right)\left(\dfrac{100}{1}\%\right) = \dfrac{7 \cdot \overset{1}{\cancel{4}} \cdot 25}{2 \cdot \underset{1}{\cancel{4}} \cdot 1}\% = \dfrac{175}{2}\%$

$= 87\dfrac{1}{2}\% \quad \text{or} \quad 87.5\%$

Concepts	Examples

7.2 Using the Percent Proportion

The percent proportion is shown below.

$$\text{Always 100} \rightarrow \frac{\text{percent}}{100} = \frac{\text{part}}{\text{whole}}$$

Identify the percent first. It appears with the word *percent* or the % symbol.

The *whole* is the entire quantity or total. It often appears after the word **of**.

The *part* is the number being compared to the whole.

30 children is what percent of 75 children?

$$\text{Percent (unknown)} \rightarrow \frac{p}{100} = \frac{30}{75} \begin{array}{l}\leftarrow \text{Part}\\ \leftarrow \text{Whole (follows } of)\end{array}$$
Always 100 →

To solve the proportion, find the cross products.

$$\frac{P}{100} = \frac{30}{75} \qquad \begin{array}{l} 100 \cdot 30 = 3000 \leftarrow \\ p \cdot 75 \leftarrow \end{array} \Big] \text{Cross products}$$

$$p \cdot 75 = 3000 \qquad \begin{array}{l}\text{Show that the cross}\\ \text{products are equal.}\end{array}$$

$$\frac{p \cdot \overset{1}{\cancel{75}}}{\underset{1}{\cancel{75}}} = \frac{3000}{75} \qquad \text{Divide both sides by 75}$$

$$p = 40$$

30 children is **40**% of 75 children.

7.3 Percent Shortcuts

200% of a number is 2 times the number.

100% of a number is the entire number.

To find 50% of a number, divide the number by 2.

To find 25% of a number, divide the number by 4.

To find 10% of a number, move the decimal point *one* place to the *left*.

To find 1% of a number, move the decimal point *two* places to the *left*.

200% of $35 is 2 times $35 = $70.

100% of 600 women is *all* the women (600 women).

50% of $8000 is $8000 ÷ 2 = $4000.

25% of 40 pens is 40 ÷ 4 = 10 pens.

10% of $92.40 is $9.24.

1% of 62. miles is 0.62 mile.

7.3–7.4 Using the Percent Equation

Use the six problem-solving steps from **Chapter 3**.

Step 1   **Read** the problem.

Todd's regular pay is $540 per week but $43.20 is taken out of each paycheck for medical insurance. What percent is that?

Step 1   The problem asks for the percent of Todd's pay that is taken out for insurance.

      Unknown: percent taken out

      Known: Whole paycheck is $540; $43.20 taken out.

Step 2   **Assign a variable.**

Step 2   Let *p* be the unknown percent.

Step 3   **Write an equation.**

Step 3   Use the percent equation. The *whole* is Todd's entire pay of $540 and the *part* is $43.20 (the part taken out of his paycheck).

$$\text{percent} \cdot \text{whole} = \text{part}$$
$$p \quad \cdot \quad 540 = 43.20$$

(Continued)

Concepts	Examples

7.3–7.4 **Using the Percent Equation** *(Continued)*

Step 4 **Solve the equation.**

Step 5 **State the answer.**

Step 6 **Check** the solution.

Step 4

$$\frac{p \cdot \overset{1}{\underset{1}{540}}}{540} = \frac{43.20}{540} \quad \text{Divide both sides by 540}$$

$$p = 0.08 \leftarrow \text{Decimal form}$$

Multiply 0.08 by 100% so that $0.08 = 8\%$.

Step 5 8% of Todd's pay is taken out for medical insurance.

Step 6 Use estimation. If 10% of Todd's pay were withheld, then 10% of $540 = $54, which is a little more than the $43.20 actually withheld. So 8% is a reasonable solution.

7.4 **Finding Percent of Increase or Decrease**

Use subtraction to find the *amount* of increase or decrease. When writing the equation, be careful to use the *original* value as the whole.

Enrollment rose from 3820 students to 5157 students. Find the percent of increase.

$$5157 \text{ students} - 3820 \text{ students} = 1337 \text{ students}$$
$$\uparrow$$
$$\text{Amount of increase}$$

$$\text{percent } \underbrace{\text{of}}\ \underbrace{\text{original value}} = \underbrace{\text{amount of increase}}$$
$$\quad\ \downarrow \quad\ \downarrow$$
$$\quad\ p \quad \cdot \quad 3820 \quad = \quad 1337$$

$$p \cdot 3820 = 1337$$

$$\frac{p \cdot \overset{1}{\underset{1}{3820}}}{3820} = \frac{1337}{3820} \quad \text{Divide both sides by 3820}$$

$$p = 0.35 \leftarrow \text{Decimal form}$$

$$0.35 = 35\% \leftarrow \text{Percent increase}$$

The enrollment increased **35%**.

Chapter 7 Review Exercises

7.1 *Write each percent as a decimal and each decimal as a percent.*

1. 25%

2. 180%

3. 12.5%

4. 7%

5. 2.65

6. 0.02

7. 0.3

8. 0.002

Write each percent as a fraction or mixed number in lowest terms. Write each fraction as a percent.

9. 12%

10. 37.5%

11. 250%

12. 5%

13. $\frac{3}{4}$

14. $\frac{5}{8}$

15. $3\frac{1}{4}$

16. $\frac{3}{50}$

Complete this table.

Fraction	Decimal	Percent
$\frac{1}{8}$	**17.** _____	**18.** _____
19. _____	0.15	**20.** _____
21. _____	**22.** _____	180%

Use percent shortcuts to fill in the blanks.

23. 100% of $46 is _____.

24. 50% of $46 is _____.

25. 100% of 9 hours is _____.

26. 50% of 9 hours is _____.

7.2 *Use a percent proportion to answer each question. If necessary, round percent answers to the nearest tenth of a percent.*

27. 338.8 meters is 140% of what number of meters?

28. 2.5% of what number of cases is 425 cases?

29. What is 6% of 450 smartphones?

30. 60% of 1450 math books is how many books?

31. What percent of 380 pairs is 36 pairs?

32. 1440 cans is what percent of 640 cans?

7.3 *Use the percent equation to answer each question. Round money answers to the nearest cent, if necessary.*

33. 11% of $23.60 is how much?

34. What is 125% of 64 days?

35. 1.28 ounces is what percent of 32 ounces?

36. $46 is 8% of what number of dollars?

37. 8 people is 40% of what number of people?

38. What percent of 174 ft is 304.5 ft?

7.4 *Use the six problem-solving steps to answer each question. If necessary, round percent answers to the nearest tenth of a percent.*

39. (a) A medical clinic found that 16.8% of the patients were late for their appointments in January. The number of patients who were late was 504. Find the total number of patients in January.

(b) In February, only 345 patients were late. Find the percent of decrease in late patients from January to February.

40. (a) Coreen budgeted $280 for food on her vacation. She actually spent 130% of that amount. How much did she spend on food?

(b) Coreen's vacation budget included $50 for gifts and souvenirs, but she spent $112. What percent of the budgeted amount did she spend?

41. (a) In the first part of a tree-planting project, 640 of the 800 trees planted were still living one year later. What percent of the trees planted were still living?

(b) In the second part of the project, 850 trees were planted. What was the percent of increase in trees planted?

42. New types of radar help weather forecasters warn people sooner about tornadoes. The average lead time for tornado warnings was 7 minutes in 1975, and 13 minutes in 2010. What is the percent of increase in the lead time? (*Source:* National Weather Service.)

Mixed Review Exercises

The bar graph shows the types of electronic/computer games that adults like to play.
Use the information in the graph to answer Exercises 51–54.

CARE FOR A GAME OF CARDS?
One out of three adults say they play electronic or computer games. Types of games they play:

Cards 68%

Sports/driving 46%

Action/combat 43%

Board 39%

Sci-fi/simulation 37%

Note: People may play more than one type of game, so the percents add up to more than 100%.

Source: Cable & Telecommunications Association for Marketing.

51. Write the portion of adults who like to play electronic/computer games as a fraction and as a percent.

52. What type of game is most popular? Write the portion of players who picked this type as a percent, a decimal, and a fraction in lowest terms.

53. If 830 adults were surveyed, how many of them play electronic/computer games, to the nearest whole number?

54. Using your answer from **Exercise 53,** how many of the playing adults in the survey chose the most popular and least popular types of game?

The table shows the number of animals received during the first six months of 2011 by the Minneapolis/St. Paul Animal Humane Society, and the number placed in new homes. Use the table to answer Exercises 55–60. Round percent answers to the nearest tenth of a percent.

Animals Received	Placed in New Homes
4629 dogs	3440 dogs
6230 cats	3891 cats
944 other*	852 other*

*"Other" includes birds, rabbits, guinea pigs, gerbils, etc.
Source: Animalhumanesociety.org

55. What percent of the dogs were placed in new homes?

56. The number of dogs received during the first six months was 81% of the total number expected for the year. How many dogs were expected, to the nearest whole number?

57. What percent of the cats were placed in new homes?

58. During the first six months of the previous year, 8748 cats were received. What is the percent decrease in cats received?

59. What percent of all the animals received were placed in new homes?

60. The Society's goal was to place 70% of all animals received into new homes. So far they have missed their goal by how many animals? Round to the nearest whole number.

Write each percent as a decimal and each decimal as a percent.

1. 75%

2. 0.6

3. 1.8

4. 0.075

5. 300%

6. 2%

Write each percent as a fraction or mixed number in lowest terms.

7. 62.5%

8. 240%

Write each fraction or mixed number as a percent.

9. $\dfrac{1}{20}$

10. $\dfrac{7}{8}$

11. $1\dfrac{3}{4}$

Write and solve a proportion or an equation to answer Problems 12–17. Show your work.

12. 16 laptops is 5% of what number of laptops?

13. $192 is what percent of $48?

14. Erica Green has saved 75% of the amount needed for a down payment on a condominium. If she has saved $14,625, find the total down payment needed.

15. The price of a used car is $7950 plus sales tax of $6\frac{1}{2}\%$. Find the total cost of the car including sales tax.

16. Enrollment in mathematics courses increased from 1440 students last semester to 1925 students this semester. Find the percent of increase, to the nearest whole percent.

17. Explain a shortcut for finding 50% of a number and a shortcut for finding 25% of a number. Show an example of how to use each shortcut.

18. Explain how you would *estimate* a 15% tip on a restaurant bill of $31.94. Then explain how you would *estimate* a 20% tip on the same bill.

19. Find the exact 15% tip, to the nearest cent, for the restaurant bill in **Problem 18.** If you and two friends are sharing the bill and the exact tip, how much will each person pay?

Find the amount of discount and the sale price of each item in Problems 20 and 21.
Round answers to the nearest cent when necessary. Show your work.

20. Jeremy plans to use his 8% employee discount to buy a $48 clock radio so he can get to work on time.

21. A Sony 3-D Blu-ray player regularly priced at $229.95 is on sale at 18% off.

22. Jamal found a $1089 computer on sale at 30% off because it was a "discontinued" model. The store will let him pay for it over 6 months with no interest charge. How much will each monthly payment need to be to cover the discounted price plus 7% sales tax?

23. What is the simple interest and total amount due on a four-year loan of $5000 at $8\frac{1}{4}\%$?

24. Kendra borrowed $860 to pay medical expenses. The loan is for 6 months at 12% simple interest. Find the simple interest and total amount due on the loan.

Chapters 1–7 *Cumulative Review Exercises*

1. Write these numbers in words.
   (a) 90.105

   (b) 125,000,670

2. Write these numbers in digits.
   (a) Thirty billion, five million

   (b) Seventy-eight ten-thousandths

3. Find the mean and median for these rent prices:
   $810, $880, $750, $885, $1225, $795, $840, $785.

4. Find the best buy on cereal.
   17 ounces of Brand A for $2.89
   21 ounces of Brand B for $3.59
   15 ounces of Brand C for $2.79

Simplify.

5. $50 - 1.099$

6. $(-3)^2 + 2^3$

7. $\dfrac{3b}{10a} \cdot \dfrac{15ab}{4}$

8. $3\dfrac{3}{10} - 2\dfrac{4}{5}$

9. $3 + 2(-6 + 1)$

10. $\dfrac{4}{5} + \dfrac{x}{4}$

11. $(-0.5)(0.002)$

12. $\dfrac{-16 + 2^4}{-3 - 2}$

13. $\dfrac{7}{8} - \dfrac{2}{m}$

14. $\dfrac{4.8}{-0.16}$

15. $\dfrac{8}{9} \div 2n$

16. $1\dfrac{5}{6} + 1\dfrac{2}{3}$

Evaluate each expression when w is −4, x is −2, and y is 3.

17. $-6w - 5$

18. $5x + 3y$

19. x^3y

20. $-5w^2x$

Solve each equation. Show your work.

21. $12 - h = -3h$

22. $5a - 0.6 = 10.4$

23. $2(x + 3) = -4x + 18 + 2x$

24. Translate into an equation and solve. The sum of a number and 31 is three times the number plus 1. Find the number.

25. Use the six problem-solving steps from **Chapter 3.** Susanna and Neoka are splitting $1620 for painting a house. Neoka worked twice as many hours, so she should earn twice as much. How much should each woman receive?

Find the unknown length, perimeter, circumference, or area. When necessary, use 3.14 as the approximate value of π and round answers to the nearest tenth.

26. Find the perimeter and the area.

27. Find the circumference and the area.

28. Find the unknown length and the area of the figure.

Solve each application problem. Show your work.

29. A survey of the 5600 students on our campus found that $\frac{3}{8}$ of the students work 20 hours or more per week. How many students is that?

30. The Americans With Disabilities Act provides the single parking space design below. Find the perimeter and area of this parking space, including the accessible aisle.

31. The Jackson family is making three kinds of holiday cookies that require brown sugar. The recipes call for $2\frac{1}{4}$ cups, $1\frac{1}{2}$ cups, and $\frac{3}{4}$ cup, respectively. They bought two packages of brown sugar, each holding $2\frac{1}{3}$ cups. The amount bought is how much more or less than the amount needed?

32. Leather jackets are on sale at 30% off the regular price. Tracy likes a jacket with a regular price of $189. Find the amount of discount and the sale price she will pay.

33. On the Illinois map, one centimeter represents 12 kilometers. The center of Springfield is 7.8 cm from the center of Bloomington on the map. What is the actual distance in kilometers?

34. On a 35-problem math test, Juana solved 31 problems correctly. What percent of the problems were correct? Round to the nearest tenth of a percent.

35. Daniel uses an online company to make prints from his digital camera. He ordered 18 prints at $0.12 per print plus $1.97 for shipping. What is the cost per print, including shipping, to the nearest cent? (*Source:* snapfish.com)

9

Graphs and Graphing

Information can be represented visually with tables and a variety of graphs. In this chapter you'll learn how to interpret and make graphs.

9.1 Problem Solving with Tables and Pictographs

9.2 Reading and Constructing Circle Graphs

9.3 Bar Graphs and Line Graphs

9.4 The Rectangular Coordinate System

9.5 Introduction to Graphing Linear Equations

	07-12	07-13
	$150	$148
	$100	$0
	$150	$160
	$3,000	$7,300
	$3,000	$58
	$10,000	$13,400
	$0	$0
	$0	$3,750
	200	$0
	,000	$0
	0	$0
	600	$24,816
	47	$16,044
	55	$19,268
	4	$22,491

Sales

MAY 8.74%
JUN 8.36%
JUL 10.17%
APR 9.35%
MAR 7.39%
FEB 7.80%
JAN

9.1 Problem Solving with Tables and Pictographs

OBJECTIVES

1 Read and interpret data presented in a table.

2 Read and interpret data from a pictograph.

VOCABULARY TIP

Rows and Columns **Rows** are read across from left to right. **Columns** are read from top to bottom. Pay attention to the labels on rows and columns.

So far, you've used numbers, expressions, formulas, and equations to communicate information. Now you'll see how *tables, pictographs, circle graphs, bar graphs,* and *line graphs* are also used to communicate information.

OBJECTIVE ▶ 1 Read and interpret data presented in a table. A **table** presents data organized into rows and columns. The advantage of a table is that you can find very specific, exact values. The disadvantages are that you may have to spend some time searching through the table to find what you want, and it may not be easy to see trends or patterns.

The table below shows information about the performance of eight U.S. airlines during the year 2011 (January–December).

PERFORMANCE DATA FOR SELECTED U.S. AIRLINES JANUARY–DECEMBER 2011

Airline	On-Time Performance	Luggage Handling*
American	78%	3.6
Atlantic Southeast	75%	5.5
Continental	77%	3.4
Delta	82%	2.7
Hawaiian	93%	2.6
JetBlue	73%	2.2
Southwest	81%	3.7
United	80%	3.7

*Luggage problems per 1000 passengers.
Source: Department of Transportation Air Travel Consumer Report.

For example, by reading from left to right along the row marked United, you first see that 80% of United's flights were on time during 2011. The next number is 3.7 and the heading at the top of that column is *Luggage Handling**. The little star (asterisk) tells you to look below the table for more information. Next to the asterisk below the table it says "Luggage problems per 1000 passengers." So, almost 4 passengers out of every 1000 passengers on United flights had some sort of problem with their luggage.

EXAMPLE 1 Reading and Interpreting Data from a Table

Use the table above on airline performance to answer these questions.

(a) What percent of JetBlue's flights were on time?

Look across the row labeled JetBlue. 73% of its flights were on time.

(b) Which airline had the worst luggage handling record?

Look down the column headed Luggage Handling. To find the *worst* record, look for the *highest* number, which is 5.5. Then look to the left to find the airline, which is Atlantic Southeast.

(c) What was the average percent of on-time flights for the three airlines with the best performance, to the nearest whole percent?

Look down the column headed On-Time Performance to find the three highest numbers: 93%, 82%, and 81%. To find the average, add the values and divide by 3.

Continued on Next Page

$$\frac{93 + 82 + 81}{3} = \frac{256}{3} \approx 85 \text{ (rounded)}$$

The average on-time performance for the three best airlines was about 85%.

················· **Work Problem ❶ at the Side.** ▶

EXAMPLE 2 **Interpreting Data from a Table**

The table below shows the maximum cab fares in five different cities in 2011. The "flag drop" charge is made when the driver starts the meter. "Wait time" is the charge for having to wait in the middle of a ride.

MAXIMUM TAXICAB FARES ALLOWED IN SELECTED CITIES IN 2011

City	Flag Drop	Price per Mile	Wait Time (per Hour)
Chicago	$2.25	$1.80	$20
Denver	$2.50	$2.25	$24
Miami	$2.50	$2.40	$24
New York	$2.50	$2	$24
San Francisco	$3.50	$2.75	$27

Source: taxifarefinder.com

Use the table to answer these questions.

(a) What is the maximum fare for a 9-mile ride in New York that includes having the cab wait 15 minutes while you pick up a package at a store?

The price per mile in New York is $2, so the cost for 9 miles is $9(\$2) = \$18$. Then, add the flag drop charge of $2.50. Finally, figure out the cost of the wait time. One way to do that is to set up a proportion. Recall that 1 hour is 60 minutes, so each side of the proportion compares the cost to the number of minutes of wait time.

$$\text{Cost} \rightarrow \frac{\$24}{60 \text{ min}} = \frac{\$x}{15 \text{ min}} \leftarrow \text{Cost}$$
$$\text{Wait time} \rightarrow \qquad \leftarrow \text{Wait time}$$

Show that cross products are equal. $\quad 60 \cdot x = 24 \cdot 15$

$$\frac{\overset{1}{\cancel{60}}x}{\cancel{60}_{1}} = \frac{360}{60} \qquad \text{Divide both sides by 60.}$$

$$x = \$6 \longleftarrow \text{Charge for waiting 15 minutes}$$

Total fare $= \$18 + \$2.50 + \$6 = \$26.50$

(b) It is customary to give the cab driver a tip. Find the total cost of the cab ride in part (a) above if the passenger added a 15% tip, rounded to the nearest quarter (nearest $0.25).

Use the percent equation to find the exact tip.

$$\text{percent} \cdot \text{whole} = \text{part} \qquad \text{Percent equation}$$
$$(15.\%)(\$26.50) = n \qquad \text{Write 15\% as a decimal.}$$

Write 15% as 0.15

$$(0.15)(\$26.50) = n$$
$$\$3.975 = n \qquad \text{Round to \$4 (nearest \$0.25).}$$

The total cost of the cab ride is $26.50 + $4 tip = $30.50.

················· **Work Problem ❷ at the Side.** ▶

---

❶ Use the table of airline performance on the previous page to answer these questions.

(a) Which airline had the best on-time performance?

(b) Which airline had the best record for luggage handling? (*Hint*: Look for the *lowest* number of luggage problems.)

(c) Which airline(s) had 3 or fewer luggage handling problems per 1000 passengers?

(d) What was the average number of luggage problems for all eight airlines, to the nearest tenth?

❷ Use the table of cab fares on this page to answer these questions.

GS (a) What is the difference in the maximum fare for a cab ride of 6.5 miles in Chicago compared to San Francisco? Assume there is no wait time.

Chicago fare
$= 6.5(\$1.80) + \$2.25 = \underline{\quad}$

San Francisco fare
$= 6.5(\$2.75) + \$3.50 = \underline{\quad}$

(b) Find the total cost for a cab ride of 4.5 miles in Denver, including 30 minutes of wait time and a 15% tip. Round the tip to the nearest $0.25.

Answers

1. **(a)** Hawaiian **(b)** JetBlue
   (c) Delta, Hawaiian, JetBlue
   (d) $27.4 \div 8 \approx 3.4$ (rounded)
2. **(a)** Chicago $13.95;
   San Francisco $21.38 (rounded);
   San Francisco fare is $7.43 higher.
   (b) $24.63 + $3.75 tip = $28.38

3 Use the pictograph in **Example 3** to answer these questions.

(a) What is the approximate population of Chicago?

How many whole symbols are shown for Chicago? _____

Each whole symbol represents _____ people.

Multiply to find that the approximate population of Chicago is _____.

(b) What is the approximate population of Atlanta?

(c) Approximately how much less is the population of Los Angeles than that of New York?

(d) The population of Dallas is approximately how much greater than that of Atlanta?

Answers

3. **(a)** 5 symbols; 2 million, or, 2,000,000; 10 million people (or 10,000,000)
(b) 5 million people (or 5,000,000)
(c) 6 million people (or 6,000,000)
(d) 1 million people (or 1,000,000)

OBJECTIVE ▶ **2** **Read and interpret data from a pictograph.** Tables show numbers in rows and columns. Graphs, on the other hand, are a *visual* way to communicate data; that is, they show a *picture* of the information rather than a list of numbers. In this section you'll work with one type of graph, *pictographs,* and in the next two sections you'll learn about circle graphs, bar graphs, and line graphs.

The advantage of a graph is that you can easily make comparisons or see trends just by looking. The disadvantage is that the graph may not give you the specific, more exact numbers you need in some situations.

EXAMPLE 3 **Reading and Interpreting a Pictograph**

A **pictograph** uses symbols or pictures to represent various amounts. The pictograph below shows the population of five U.S. metropolitan areas (cities with their surrounding suburbs) in 2010. The *key* at the bottom of the graph tells you that each symbol of a person represents 2 million people. Half of a symbol represents half of 2 million people, or 1 million people.

Source: U.S. Census Bureau, U.S. Department of Commerce.

Use the pictograph to answer these questions.

(a) What is the approximate population of Los Angeles?

The population of Los Angeles is represented by 6 whole symbols (6 • 2 million = 12 million) plus half of a symbol ($\frac{1}{2}$ of 2 million is 1 million) for a total of 13 million people.

Because 2 million can be written as 2,000,000, another way to get the answer is to multiply 6.5 (the number of symbols) times 2,000,000 people for a total of 13,000,000 people.

(b) How much greater is the population of New York than that of Atlanta?

New York shows $9\frac{1}{2}$ symbols and Atlanta shows $2\frac{1}{2}$ symbols. So New York has 7 more symbols than Atlanta, and 7 • 2 million = 14 million. Thus, New York has about 14 million (or 14,000,000) more people than Atlanta.

Note

One disadvantage of a pictograph is that you often have to round numbers a great deal; in this case, to the nearest *million* people. The actual population of the Dallas area is 6,448,000 but the graph shows 3 symbols (6,000,000 people) so it is off by about 448,000 people.

◀ **Work Problem 3** at the Side.

9.1 Exercises

FOR
EXTRA
HELP

 Download the MyDashBoard App

 ▶ MyMathLab®

CONCEPT CHECK *Circle the letter of the correct answer to complete each statement.*

1. A table presents data organized into:
   (a) a circle graph   (b) rows and columns

2. An advantage of a table of data is that you can:
   (a) find exact values   (b) see trends and patterns

3. An advantage of a pictograph is that you can:
   (a) find exact values
   (b) easily make comparisons

4. In a pictograph, the *key* tells you:
   (a) what the graph is about
   (b) what each symbol represents

This table lists the basketball players in the NBA with the all-time highest number of points scored (at the time the 2010–2011 season ended). Use the table to answer Exercises 5–12. **See Examples 1 and 2.**

**ALL-TIME NBA STATISTICAL LEADERS—POINTS SCORED
(AT THE TIME THE 2010–2011 SEASON ENDED)**

Player	Games	Points	Average Points Per Game
Kareem Abdul-Jabbar	1560	38,387	24.6
Karl Malone	1476	36,928	25.0
Michael Jordan	1072	32,292	30.1
Wilt Chamberlain	1045	31,419	30.1
Shaquille O'Neal	1207	28,596	
Kobe Bryant	1117	28,316	

Source: National Basketball Association.

5. (a) How many points did Wilt Chamberlain score during his NBA career?

   (b) Which player(s) scored more points than Chamberlain?

6. (a) How many games did Karl Malone play in during his career in the NBA?

   (b) Which player is closest to Malone in number of games?

7. (a) Which player has been in the greatest number of games?

   (b) Which player has been in the fewest number of games?

8. Find the total number of points scored by the top three players in the table.

9. What is the difference in points scored between the player with the greatest number of points and the player with the least number of points?

10. How many more games has Shaquille O'Neal played in than Michael Jordan?

11. Complete the table by finding the average number of points scored per game by Shaquille O'Neal and Kobe Bryant. Look at the other averages in the table to decide how to round your answers.

For Shaquille: Total points $\rightarrow$ $\dfrac{28{,}596}{1207}$
Total games $\rightarrow$

$28{,}596 \div 1207 =$ _____   Show hundredths so you can round to tenths.

Now round to the nearest tenth. _____ points per game

12. Find the overall scoring average (points per game) for all six players listed in the table. Use the numbers in the *Games* column and the *Points* column to calculate your answer.

Total points for all six players $\rightarrow$ _____
Total games for all six players $\rightarrow$ 7477

Divide. Show the digits in the tenths and hundredths places. Then round to the nearest tenth.

_____ $\div$ 7477 $\approx$ _____ $\approx$ _____ points per game

This table shows the number of calories burned during 30 minutes of various types of exercise. The table also shows how the number of calories burned varies according to the weight of the person doing the exercise. Use the table to answer Exercises 13–22.
See Examples 1 and 2.

CALORIES BURNED DURING 30 MINUTES OF EXERCISE BY PEOPLE OF DIFFERENT WEIGHTS

Activity	Calories Burned in 30 Minutes		
	110 Pounds	140 Pounds	170 Pounds
Moderate jogging	322	410	495
Moderate walking	110	140	170
Moderate bicycling	140	180	220
Aerobic dance	200	255	310
Racquetball	210	268	325
Tennis	160	205	250

Source: Fairview Health Services.

13. A person weighing 140 pounds is looking at the table.

(a) How many calories are burned during 30 minutes of aerobic dance?

(b) Which activity burns the most calories?

14. A person weighing 170 pounds is looking at the table.

(a) How many calories are burned during 30 minutes of tennis?

(b) Which activity burns the fewest calories?

15. (a) Which activities can a 110-pound person do to burn at least 200 calories in 30 minutes?

(b) Which activities can a 170-pound person do to burn at least 200 calories in 30 minutes?

16. (a) Which activities burn fewer than 200 calories in 30 minutes for a 140-pound person?

(b) Which activities burn fewer than 300 calories in 30 minutes for a 170-pound person?

17. How many total calories will a 140-pound person burn during 15 minutes of moderate bicycling and 60 minutes of moderate walking?

18. How many total calories will a 110-pound person burn during 90 minutes of tennis and 15 minutes of aerobic dance?

Set up and solve proportions to answer Exercises 19–22.

19. How many calories would you expect a 125-pound person to burn

(a) during 30 minutes of moderate jogging?

From the table, a 110-pound person burns 322 calories during 30 minutes of moderate jogging.

Set up a proportion and find the cross products.

$$\frac{322 \text{ calories}}{110\text{-pound person}} = \frac{x \text{ calories}}{125\text{-pound person}}$$

$$(110)(x) = (322)(125) \quad \text{Now divide both sides by 110.}$$

(b) during 30 minutes of racquetball? Round to the nearest whole number.

20. How many calories would you expect a 185-pound person to burn

(a) during 30 minutes of moderate walking?

From the table, a 170-pound person burns 170 calories during 30 minutes of moderate walking.

Set up a proportion and find the cross products.

$$\frac{170 \text{ calories}}{170\text{-pound person}} = \frac{x \text{ calories}}{185\text{-pound person}}$$

$$(170)(x) = (170)(185) \quad \text{Now divide both sides by 170.}$$

(b) during 30 minutes of moderate bicycling? Round to the nearest ten.

21. How many more calories would a 158-pound person burn during 15 minutes of aerobic dance than during 20 minutes of moderate walking? Round to the nearest whole number.

22. How many fewer calories would a 196-pound person burn during 25 minutes of moderate walking than during 20 minutes of tennis? Round to the nearest whole number.

This pictograph shows the approximate number of passenger arrivals and departures at selected U.S. airports in 2010. Use the pictograph to answer Exercises 23–30.
See Example 3.

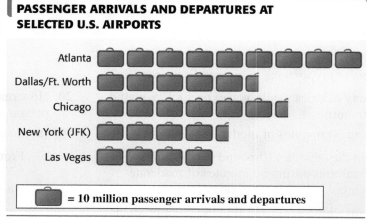

PASSENGER ARRIVALS AND DEPARTURES AT SELECTED U.S. AIRPORTS

Atlanta

Dallas/Ft. Worth

Chicago

New York (JFK)

Las Vegas

= 10 million passenger arrivals and departures

Source: Airports Council International—North America.

23. Approximately how many passenger arrivals and departures took place at the

   (a) Atlanta airport?

   (b) New York's JFK airport?

24. Approximately how many passenger arrivals and departures took place at the

   (a) Las Vegas airport?

   (b) Dallas airport?

25. What is the approximate total number of arrivals and departures at the two busiest airports?

26. What is the difference in the number of arrivals and departures at the busiest airport and the least busy airport?

27. How many fewer arrivals and departures did the Las Vegas airport have compared to New York's JFK airport?

28. Find the approximate total number of arrivals and departures for the three least busy airports.

29. What is the approximate total number of arrivals and departures for all five airports?

30. Find the average number of arrivals and departures for the five airports.

9.2 Reading and Constructing Circle Graphs

A *circle graph* is another way to show a *picture* of a set of data. This picture can often be understood faster and more easily than a formula or a list of numbers.

OBJECTIVE ▶ **1** **Read a circle graph.** A **circle graph** is used to show how a total amount is divided into parts. The circle graph below shows you how 24 hours in the life of a college student are divided among different activities.

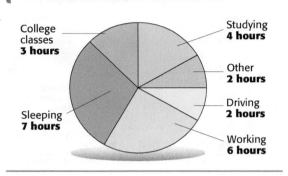

THE DAY OF A COLLEGE STUDENT

College classes **3 hours**

Sleeping **7 hours**

Studying **4 hours**

Other **2 hours**

Driving **2 hours**

Working **6 hours**

Work Problem **1** at the Side. ▶

OBJECTIVE ▶ **2** **Use a circle graph.** The circle graph above uses pie-shaped pieces called *sectors* to show the amount of time spent on each activity (the total must be 24 hours). The circle graph can therefore be used to compare the time spent on one activity to the total number of hours in the day.

EXAMPLE 1 Using a Circle Graph

Find the ratio of time spent in college classes to the total number of hours in a day. Write the ratio as a fraction in lowest terms.

The circle graph shows that 3 of the 24 hours in a day are spent in class. The ratio of class time to the hours in a day is shown below.

$$\frac{3 \text{ hours (college classes)}}{24 \text{ hours (whole day)}} = \frac{3 \text{ hours}}{24 \text{ hours}} = \frac{\overset{1}{\cancel{3}}}{\underset{1}{\cancel{3}} \cdot 8} = \frac{1}{8} \leftarrow \begin{cases} \text{Ratio in} \\ \text{lowest terms} \end{cases}$$

Work Problem **2** at the Side. ▶

The circle graph above can also be used to find the ratio of the time spent on one activity to the time spent on any other activity. See the next example.

EXAMPLE 2 Finding a Ratio from a Circle Graph

Find the ratio of working time to class time.

The circle graph shows 6 hours spent working and 3 hours spent in class.

$$\frac{6 \text{ hours (working)}}{3 \text{ hours (class)}} = \frac{6 \text{ hours}}{3 \text{ hours}} = \frac{\overset{1}{\cancel{3}} \cdot 2}{\underset{1}{\cancel{3}}} = \frac{2}{1} \leftarrow \text{Ratio in lowest terms}$$

So the ratio is 2 hours spent working for every 1 hour in class.

Work Problem **3** at the Side. ▶

OBJECTIVES

1 Read a circle graph.

2 Use a circle graph.

3 Use a protractor to draw a circle graph.

VOCABULARY TIP

Data means "information." It may be pronounced "**day**-tuh" or "**dad**-uh."

1 Use the circle graph on this page to answer each question.

(a) The greatest number of hours is spent in which activity? How many hours is that?

(b) Find the total number of hours spent studying, working, and attending classes.

2 Use the circle graph to find each ratio. Write the ratios as fractions in lowest terms.

GS **(a)** Hours spent driving to whole day

driving ⟶ $\dfrac{2 \text{ hours}}{24 \text{ hours}}$ = _____
whole day →

(b) Hours spent studying to whole day

3 Use the circle graph to find each ratio. Write the ratios as fractions in lowest terms.

(a) Hours spent studying to hours spent working

(b) Hours spent studying to hours spent driving

Answers

1. **(a)** sleeping; 7 hours **(b)** 13 hours

2. **(a)** $\dfrac{1}{12}$ **(b)** $\dfrac{1}{6}$

3. **(a)** $\dfrac{2}{3}$ **(b)** $\dfrac{2}{1}$

4 Use the circle graph on the oil spill to find the amount of oil still at sea, skimmed, evaporated, or dispersed.

GS **(a)** Still at sea or on shores

percent • whole = part
↓ ↓ ↓
26.% • 5,000,000 barrels = n

(b) Skimmed

(c) Evaporated or dissolved

(d) Chemically dispersed

A circle graph often shows data as percents. For example, the Deepwater Horizon oil well that exploded in the Gulf of Mexico in 2010 leaked a total of 5 million barrels of oil into the water. The circle graph shows where the oil ended up. The entire circle represents 5 million barrels of oil. Each sector represents the amount of oil that was removed from the Gulf, was dispersed in various ways, or still remains in the Gulf. The sector amounts are shown as a percent of the total oil spill. The total in a circle graph must be 100%, though it may be slightly more or less due to rounding the percent for each sector.

WHERE DID THE OIL GO?

The Deepwater Horizon oil well leaked 5 million barrels of oil into the Gulf of Mexico. The percent of the oil that was removed, was dispersed in various ways, or still remains in the Gulf, is rounded to the nearest whole percent.

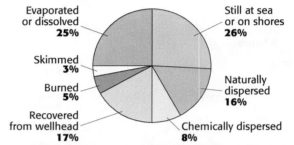

Evaporated or dissolved **25%**
Skimmed **3%**
Burned **5%**
Recovered from wellhead **17%**
Still at sea or on shores **26%**
Naturally dispersed **16%**
Chemically dispersed **8%**

Source: National Oceanic and Atmospheric Administration (NOAA).

EXAMPLE 3 **Calculating an Amount Using a Circle Graph**

Use the circle graph above on the Deepwater Horizon oil spill to find the amount of oil that was burned.

Use the percent equation: percent • whole = part

The percent of oil burned was 5%. Rewrite 5% as the decimal 0.05. The *whole* is the total oil spill of 5 million barrels (the entire circle).

percent • whole = part
↓ ↓ ↓
05.% • 5 million barrels = n

> Write 5% as 0.05

(0.05)(5,000,000 barrels) = n

> Write 5 million barrels as 5,000,000 barrels.

250,000 barrels = n

The amount of oil burned was 250,000 barrels.

◄ Work Problem **4** at the Side.

OBJECTIVE **3** **Use a protractor to draw a circle graph.** The coordinator of the Fair Oaks Youth Soccer League organizes teams in five age groups. She counts the number of registered players in each age group as shown in the table on the next page. Then she calculates what percent of the total each group represents. For example, there are 59 players in the "Under 8" group, out of 298 total players.

percent • whole = part

p • 298 = 59

$$\frac{p \cdot 298}{298} = \frac{59}{298}$$

> Multiply the decimal answer by 100% to get the percent.

$p \approx 0.198 \approx 19.8\%$ rounds to 20%

Answers
4. **(a)** $(0.26)(500,000,000) = n$;
   $1,300,000 = n$; 1,300,000 barrels
   (b) 150,000 barrels   **(c)** 1,250,000 barrels
   (d) 400,000 barrels

FAIR OAKS YOUTH SOCCER LEAGUE

Age Group	Number of Players	Percent of Total (rounded to nearest whole percent)
Under 8 years	59	20% ← 59 players ≈ 20% of 298
Ages 8–9	46	15%
Ages 10–11	75	25%
Ages 12–13	74	25%
Ages 14–15	44	15%
Total	**298**	**100%**

You can show these percents in a circle graph. A circle has 360 degrees (written 360°). The 360° represents the entire league, or 100% of the players.

EXAMPLE 4   **Drawing a Circle Graph**

Using the data on *age groups,* find the number of degrees in the sector that would represent the "Under 8" group, and begin constructing a circle graph.

A complete circle has 360°. Because the "Under 8" group makes up 20% of the total number of players, the number of degrees needed for the "Under 8" sector of the circle graph is 20% of 360°.

$$20.\% \text{ of } 360° = n$$

Write 20% as 0.20 ⟶ $(0.20)(360°) = n$

$$72° = n$$

Use the circle drawn below and a tool called a **protractor** to make a circle graph. First, using a ruler or straightedge, draw a line from the center of the circle to the left edge. Place the hole in the protractor over the center of the circle, making sure that the 0 mark and the black line on the protractor are right over the line you drew. Find 72° and make a mark as shown in the illustration. Then remove the protractor and use the straightedge to draw a line from the 72° mark to the center of the circle. This sector is 72° and represents the "Under 8" group.

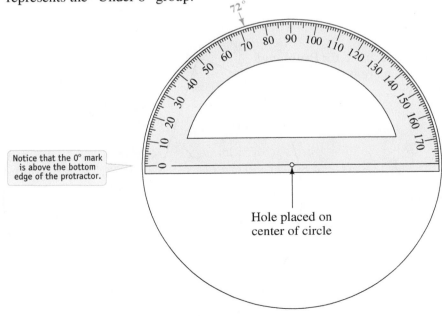

Notice that the 0° mark is above the bottom edge of the protractor.

Hole placed on center of circle

Continued on Next Page

5 Using the information on the soccer age groups in the table on the previous page, find the number of degrees needed for each sector. Then complete the circle graph at the bottom right on this page.

(a) "Ages 10–11" sector

"Ages 10–11" makes up 25% of the total number of players, so that sector needs 25% of the circle or 25% of 360°.

$$25.\% \text{ of } 360° = n$$
$$(0.25)(360°) = n$$
$$\underline{} = n$$

(b) "Ages 12–13" sector

(c) "Ages 14–15" sector

To draw the "Ages 8–9" sector, begin by finding the number of degrees in the sector, which is 15% of the total circle, or 15% of 360°.

$$15.\% \text{ of } 360° = n$$

Write 15% as 0.15 → $(0.15)(360°) = n$

$$54° = n$$

Again, place the hole of the protractor over the center of the circle, but this time align 0 with the previous 72° mark. Make a mark at 54° and draw a line from the mark to the center of the circle. This sector represents the "Ages 8–9" group.

Line up 0 with previous 72° mark.

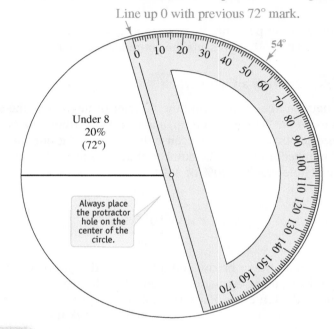

Under 8
20%
(72°)

Always place the protractor hole on the center of the circle.

CAUTION

You must be certain that the hole in the protractor is placed on the exact center of the circle each time you measure the size of a sector.

◀ **Work Problem 5 at the Side.**

Use this circle for **Problem 5** in the margin.

Ages 8–9
15%
(54°)

Under 8
20%
(72°)

Answers

5. **(a)** 90° = n; 90° for "Ages 10–11" sector
   (b) 90°   **(c)** 54°

9.2 Exercises

 FOR EXTRA HELP

 Download the MyDashBoard App

▶ MyMathLab®

CONCEPT CHECK *Circle the letter of the correct answer to complete each statement.*

1. A circle graph shows:
   (a) a trend or pattern
   (b) how a total is divided into parts
   (c) symbols to represent amounts

2. The pie-shaped pieces in a circle graph are called:
   (a) bars
   (b) lines
   (c) sectors

3. The tool used to draw circle graphs is called a
   (a) calculator
   (b) compass
   (c) protractor

4. When making a circle graph, remember that a circle has
   (a) 360°
   (b) 180°
   (c) 90°

This circle graph shows the results of an online survey. Adults were asked on which day of the week they were most likely to order food delivered to their homes. Use the graph to answer Exercises 5–14. Write ratios as fractions in lowest terms.
See Examples 1 and 2.

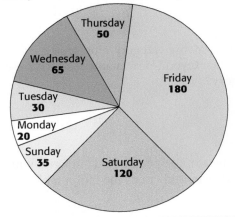

NO COOKING TONIGHT!

Number of American adults who picked the day of the week they were most likely to order food for delivery:

- Thursday 50
- Wednesday 65
- Tuesday 30
- Monday 20
- Sunday 35
- Friday 180
- Saturday 120

Source: Technomic, Inc.

5. Find the total number of people in the survey.

6. Which day is the second most popular, and how many people picked it?

7. What is the most popular day of the week to order food, and how many people picked it?

8. Which day is the least popular day of the week to order food?

9. Find the ratio of the people who picked Thursday to
GS the total people in the survey.

$$\text{Picked Thursday} \to \frac{50}{500} = \frac{50 \div 50}{500 \div 50} = \underline{\quad}$$
$$\text{Total people} \to$$

10. What is the ratio of the people who picked Friday to
GS the total people in the survey?

$$\text{Picked Friday} \to \frac{180}{500} = \frac{180 \div 20}{500 \div 20} = \underline{\quad}$$
$$\text{Total people} \to$$

11. What is the ratio of the people who picked Friday to the people who picked Saturday?

12. Find the ratio of the people who picked Wednesday to the people who picked Tuesday.

13. What is the ratio of people who picked Friday or Saturday to the people who picked Monday?

14. What is the ratio of the people who picked Thursday to the people who picked Monday or Tuesday?

This circle graph shows the results of an online survey of 400 people who have a cat as a pet. They answered the question, "How does your cat react when you entertain?" The responses are expressed as percents of the 400 people in the survey. Use the graph to answer Exercises 15–20. **See Example 3.**

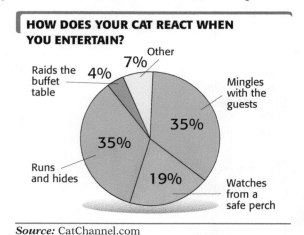

HOW DOES YOUR CAT REACT WHEN YOU ENTERTAIN?

Other 7%
Raids the buffet table 4%
Mingles with the guests 35%
Runs and hides 35%
Watches from a safe perch 19%

Source: CatChannel.com

15. How many people said their cat mingles with the guests?

$$35.\% \text{ of } 400 \text{ people} = n$$

16. How many cat owners said their cats watch from a safe perch?

$$19.\% \text{ of } 400 \text{ people} = n$$

17. Which response was given least often and by how many people?

18. Which response category represented 7% of the people surveyed? How many people were in this category?

19. How many fewer people said "watches from a safe perch" than said "runs and hides"?

20. How many more people said "mingles with the guests" than said "raids the buffet table"?

This circle graph shows the results of a survey on favorite hot dog toppings in the United States. Each topping is expressed as a percent of the 3200 people in the survey. Use the graph to find the number of people favoring each of the toppings in Exercises 21–26.

21. Onions

22. Sauerkraut

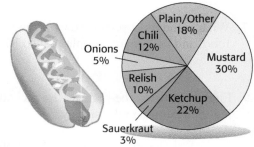

FAVORITE HOT DOG TOPPINGS

Plain/Other 18%
Chili 12%
Onions 5%
Mustard 30%
Relish 10%
Ketchup 22%
Sauerkraut 3%

Source: National Hot Dog and Sausage Council.

23. The most popular topping

24. The second-most-popular topping

25. How many more people chose chili than chose relish?

26. How many fewer people chose onions than chose mustard?

27. Describe the steps for calculating the size of the sector for each item in a circle graph.

28. A protractor is the tool used to draw a circle graph. Give a brief explanation of what the protractor does and how you would use it to measure and draw each sector in the circle graph.

29. The grades in an algebra course are based on the number of points a student earns. The total number of points in the course is 800. The number of points that can be earned for various class activities is shown in the table below. Find all the missing numbers in the table. Then use the information to draw a circle graph.
See Example 4.

Item	Number of Points	Percent of Total	Degrees of a Circle
(a) Chapter tests	400 points	50%	_____
(b) Final exam	160 points	_____	_____
(c) Homework	40 points	_____	_____
(d) Quizzes	120 points	_____	_____
(e) Project	80 points	_____	_____

(f) Draw a circle graph using the information from the table. Label each sector with the item and the percent of total for that item.

30. The Pathfinder Research Group asked 4488 Americans how they fall
asleep. The results are shown in the figure on the right.

Use this information to complete the table. Round to the nearest whole
percent and to the nearest degree.

	Sleeping Position	Number of Americans	Percent of Total	Number of Degrees
(a)	Side			
(b)	Back			
(c)	Stomach			
(d)	Varies			
(e)	Not sure			

SET TO SLEEP

Number of Americans surveyed who fall
asleep on their:

Source: Pathfinder Research Group.

(f) Add up the percents. Is the total 100%? Explain why or why not.

(g) Add up the degrees. Is the total 360°? Explain why or why not.

(h) Draw a circle graph using the information from the table above.
Label each sector with the sleeping position and the percent of total
for that position.

31. White Water Rafting Company divides its annual sales into five categories as shown in the table below.

Category	Annual Sales	Percent of Total
Adventure classes	$12,500	
Grocery/provision sales	$40,000	
Equipment rentals	$60,000	
Rafting tours	$50,000	
Equipment sales	$37,500	

(a) Find the total sales for the year.

(b) Find the percent of the total for each category and write it in the table.

(c) Find the number of degrees in a circle graph for each item.

(d) Make a circle graph showing the sales information. Label each sector with the category and the percent of total for that category.

32. A book publisher had 25% of total sales in mysteries, 10% in biographies, 15% in cookbooks, 15% in romance novels, 20% in science, and the rest in travel books.

(a) Find the number of degrees in a circle graph for each type of book.

(b) Draw a circle graph, using the information given. Label each sector with the type of book and the percent of total for that type.

9.3 Bar Graphs and Line Graphs

1 Use the bar graph to find the number of K–12 students in the school district for each of these years.

(a) 2011

The bar for 2011 rises to 30. Multiply 30 by _____ to get _____ students.

(b) 2009

(c) 2008

(d) 2012

OBJECTIVE 1 **Read and understand a bar graph.** A **bar graph** is useful for showing comparisons. For example, the bar graph below compares the number of K–12 students in a city school district during each of five years.

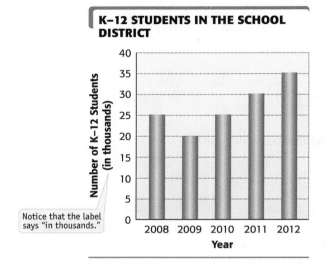

K–12 STUDENTS IN THE SCHOOL DISTRICT

Notice that the label says "in thousands."

EXAMPLE 1 **Using a Bar Graph**

How many K–12 students were in the district in 2010?

The bar for 2010 rises to 25. Notice the label along the left side of the graph that says "Number of K–12 Students (in thousands)." The phrase *in thousands* means you have to **multiply 25 by 1000** to get 25,000. So there were 25,000 (**not** 25) students in the district in 2010.

◀ **Work Problem** 1 **at the Side.**

OBJECTIVE 2 **Read and understand a double-bar graph.** A **double-bar graph** can be used to compare two sets of data. The graph below shows the number of new high-speed Internet connections in each quarter for two different years.

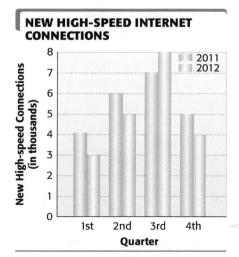

NEW HIGH-SPEED INTERNET CONNECTIONS

1st quarter = Jan., Feb., Mar.
2nd quarter = Apr., May, June
3rd quarter = July, Aug., Sept.
4th quarter = Oct., Nov., Dec.

Answers

1. (a) 1000; 30,000 students
(b) 20,000 students **(c)** 25,000 students
(d) 35,000 students

EXAMPLE 2 **Reading a Double-Bar Graph**

Use the double-bar graph on the previous page to find the following.

(a) The number of new high-speed connections in the second quarter of 2011.

There are two bars for the second quarter. The color code in the upper right-hand corner of the graph tells you that the red bars represent 2011. So the red bar on the *left* is for the 2nd quarter of 2011. It rises to 6.

Now multiply 6 by 1000 because the label on the left side of the graph says *in thousands*. There were 6000 new high-speed connections in the second quarter of 2011.

(b) The number of new high-speed connections in the second quarter of 2012.

The green bar for the second quarter rises to 5 and 5 times 1000 is 5000. So, in the second quarter of 2012, there were 5000 new high-speed connections.

······································· **Work Problem ❷ at the Side.** ▶

OBJECTIVE ▶ ❸ **Read and understand a line graph.** A **line graph** is often useful for showing a trend. The line graph below shows the number of trout stocked in the Feather River during five months. Each dot indicates the number of trout stocked during the month directly below that dot.

TROUT STOCKED IN FEATHER RIVER

Use a ruler to line up each dot with the numbers along the left side.

EXAMPLE 3 **Understanding a Line Graph**

Use the line graph above to answer each question.

(a) In which month were the least number of trout stocked?

The lowest point on the graph is the dot directly above August, so the least number of trout were stocked in August.

(b) How many trout were stocked in August?

Use a ruler or straightedge to line up the August dot with the numbers along the left edge of the graph. (See the red dashed line on the graph.)

The August dot is halfway between the 2 and 3. Notice that the label on the left side says *in ten-thousands*. So the August dot is halfway between (2 • 10,000) and (3 • 10,000). It is halfway between 20,000 and 30,000. That means 25,000 trout were stocked in August.

······································· **Work Problem ❸ at the Side.** ▶

---

❷ Use the double-bar graph on the previous page to find the number of new high-speed connections in 2011 and 2012 for each quarter.

GS **(a)** 1st quarter.

The red bar represents 2011. It rises to 4, and 4 times

_____ is _____ new connections.

The green bar represents 2012. It rises to _____, and _____ times _____ is _____ new connections.

(b) 3rd quarter

(c) 4th quarter

Vocabulary Tip

Trend A **trend** is a pattern of change that happens over time.

❸ Use the line graph on trout to answer these questions.

(a) How many trout were stocked in June?

(b) How many fewer trout were stocked in May than in April?

(c) Find the total number of trout stocked during the five months.

(d) In which month were the most trout stocked? How many were stocked?

Answers

2. (a) 1000; 4000;
    3; 3 times 1000; 3000
  (b) 7000; 8000 connections
  (c) 5000; 4000 connections
3. (a) 55,000 trout **(b)** 10,000 fewer trout
  (c) 210,000 trout **(d)** July; 60,000 trout

4 Use the comparison line graph on car and truck sales to find the following.

(a) The number of cars sold in 2007, 2009, 2010, and 2011.

The dot on the blue line above 2007 lines up with 14 on the left edge. Then multiply 14 by _____ to get sales of _____ cars.

Cars sold in 2009 = _____

Cars sold in 2010 = _____

Cars sold in 2011 = _____

(b) The number of pickup trucks sold in 2007, 2008, 2009, and 2011

(c) In which year were the sales of pickup trucks unchanged from the previous year?

(d) The amount of increase and percent of increase in car sales from 2009 to 2010

OBJECTIVE ▸ 4 Read and understand a comparison line graph. Two sets of data can also be compared by drawing two line graphs together as a **comparison line graph.** For example, the line graph below compares the number of cars sold and the number of pickup trucks sold during each of five years.

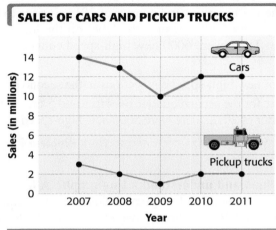

SALES OF CARS AND PICKUP TRUCKS

Source: pickuptrucks.com; evsroll.com

EXAMPLE 4 **Interpreting a Comparison Line Graph**

Use the comparison line graph above to find the following.

(a) The number of cars sold in 2008

Find the dot on the **blue line** above 2008. Use a ruler or straightedge to line up the dot with the numbers along the left edge. The dot is halfway between 12 and 14, which is 13. Then, 13 times 1,000,000 is 13,000,000 cars sold in 2008.

(b) The number of pickup trucks sold in 2010

The **red line** on the graph shows that 2,000,000 trucks were sold in 2010.

(c) The amount of decrease and the percent of decrease in car sales from 2008 to 2009. Round to the nearest whole percent.

Use subtraction to find the *amount* of decrease.

$$\begin{array}{ccccc} \text{car} & & \text{car} & & \text{amount} \\ \text{sales in 2008} & - & \text{sales in 2009} & = & \text{of decrease} \\ 13{,}000{,}000 & - & 10{,}000{,}000 & = & 3{,}000{,}000 \end{array}$$

Now use the percent equation to find the *percent* of decrease.

$$\text{percent of original sales} = \text{amount of decrease}$$

$$p \cdot 13{,}000{,}000 = 3{,}000{,}000$$

$$\frac{p \cdot 13{,}000{,}000}{13{,}000{,}000} = \frac{3{,}000{,}000}{13{,}000{,}000} \quad \text{Divide both sides by 13,000,000}$$

Multiply by 100% to change the decimal to a percent.

$$p \approx 0.231 \quad \leftarrow \text{Solution in } decimal \text{ form}$$

$$p \approx 0.231 = 23.1\% \approx 23\% \text{ to nearest whole percent}$$

The *amount* of decrease is 3,000,000 cars.
The **percent** of decrease is 23% (rounded).

◀ Work Problem 4 at the Side.

Answers

4. (a) 1,000,000; 14,000,000; 2009 is 10,000,000; both 2010 and 2011 are 12,000,000 cars
   (b) 3,000,000; 2,000,000; 1,000,000; 2,000,000 pickup trucks
   (c) 2011
   (d) increase of 2,000,000 cars; 20% increase

9.3 Exercises

CONCEPT CHECK *Circle the letter of the correct answer to complete each statement.*

1. A comparison of two sets of data can be easily shown in a:
   (a) circle graph
   (b) pictograph
   (c) double-bar graph

2. A line graph is often useful for showing
   (a) trends or patterns
   (b) how a whole is divided into parts
   (c) specific, exact values

3. If a dot on a line graph lines up with "3" on the left side, and the label on the left side says, "in ten-thousands," then the dot represents
   (a) 3000
   (b) 30,000
   (c) 300,000

4. If the top of a bar on a bar graph lines up with "5" on the left side, and the label on the left side says, "in millions," then the bar represents
   (a) 50,000
   (b) 5,000,000
   (c) 5000

For each category of purchases, this bar graph shows what percent of the total purchases were made online. The rest of the purchases were made in stores. Use the graph to answer Exercises 5–10. **See Example 1.**

What Are People Buying Online?

Music and videos	74%
Electronics	74%
Clothing	66%
Toys and games	61%
Sporting goods	58%
Computer products	48%
Drugs/health aids	9%

Source: U.S. Census Bureau.

5. People buy the highest percent of what category of purchases online? What percent is this?

6. What category has the lowest percent of total purchases online? What percent is this?

7. People spent a total of $4.4 billion buying toys and games. Find the portion of the total that was spent online. Round to the nearest tenth of a billion.

   $$61.\% \cdot \$4.4 \text{ billion} = n$$

8. Total sales for electronics online and in stores were $11.3 billion. What amount did people spend online for electronics? Round to the nearest tenth of a billion.

   $$74.\% \cdot \$11.3 \text{ billion} = n$$

9. Which category had about $\frac{2}{3}$ of its total sales online?

10. Which category had about $\frac{1}{10}$ of its total sales online?

This double-bar graph shows the number of workers who were unemployed in Detroit during the last six months of 2010 and 2011. Use this graph to answer Exercises 11–16. Round percent answers to the nearest whole percent. **See Example 2.**

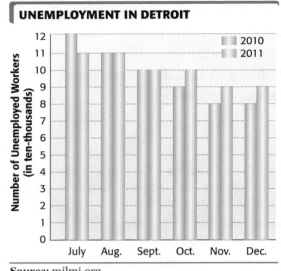

Source: milmi.org

11. In the last half of 2010, which month had the greatest number of unemployed workers? What was the total number unemployed in that month?

12. How many workers were unemployed in October of 2011?

13. How many more workers were unemployed in December of 2011 than in December of 2010?

14. How many fewer workers were unemployed in July of 2011 than in July of 2010?

15. Find the amount of decrease and the percent of decrease in the number of unemployed workers from July 2010 to December 2010.

$$120,000 - \underline{\hspace{1.2cm}} = \underline{\hspace{1.2cm}} \left\{ \begin{array}{l} \text{amount of} \\ \text{decrease} \end{array} \right.$$

16. Find the amount of decrease and the percent of decrease in the number of unemployed workers from July 2011 to November 2011.

$$110,000 - \underline{\hspace{1.2cm}} = \underline{\hspace{1.2cm}} \left\{ \begin{array}{l} \text{amount of} \\ \text{decrease} \end{array} \right.$$

This double-bar graph shows the percent of employers in a survey who expected to hire more new college graduates, or to hire fewer new college graduates. The percents are given for four different academic years and are rounded to the nearest 5%. Use the graph to answer Exercises 17–22.

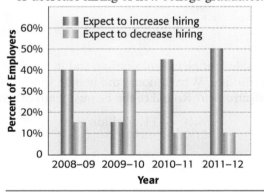

Source: National Association of Colleges and Employers.

17. What percent of employers expected to hire more graduates in 2009–10?

18. What percent of employers expected to hire fewer graduates in 2008–09?

19. Which year had the greatest difference between the percent of employers expecting to hire more graduates and the percent expecting to hire fewer graduates?

20. The percent of employers expecting to hire more graduates increased the most between which two consecutive years?

21. There were 172 employers in the survey. How many of them expected to hire fewer graduates in 2011–12? Round your answer to the nearest whole number.

$$10\% \cdot 172 \text{ employers} = n$$

22. Of the 172 employers in the survey, how many expected to hire more graduates in 2010–11? Round your answer to the nearest whole number.

$$45\% \cdot 172 \text{ employers} = n$$

This line graph shows how sales of personal computers (PCs) have increased since they became widely available in 1985. Use the line graph to answer Exercises 23–28. Round percents to the nearest whole percent. **See Example 3.**

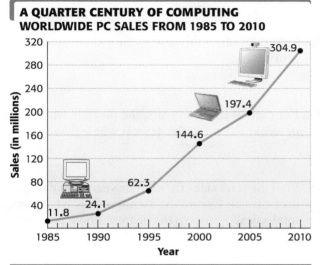

A QUARTER CENTURY OF COMPUTING
WORLDWIDE PC SALES FROM 1985 TO 2010

Source: Gartner Dataquest, ARS Technica, and Canalys.

23. How many PCs were sold in 1990?

24. What number of PCs were sold in 2010?

25. How many more PCs were sold in 2005 than in 1985?

26. Place a ruler or straightedge on the graph to find the year in which PC sales reached
  (a) 40 million.
  (b) 120 million.

27. Find the amount of increase in sales from 1995 to 2000. What was the percent of increase, to the nearest whole percent?

28. What was the amount of increase and the percent of increase in PC sales from 2000 to 2010?

This comparison line graph shows the number of DVDs sold by two different chain stores during each of five years. Use this graph to find the annual number of DVDs sold in each year listed in Exercises 29–32 and to answer Exercises 33–34. **See Example 4.**

DVD SALES

29. (a) Chain Store A in 2008
  (b) Chain Store B in 2008

30. (a) Chain Store A in 2009
  (b) Chain Store B in 2009

31. (a) Chain Store A in 2011
  (b) Chain Store A in 2012

32. (a) Chain Store B in 2010
  (b) Chain Store B in 2011

33. Describe the pattern(s) or trend(s) you see in the graph.

34. Store B used to have lower sales than Store A. What might have happened to cause this change? Give four possible explanations.

This comparison line graph shows the sales and profits of Tacos-To-Go for each of four years. Use the graph to answer Exercises 35–40.

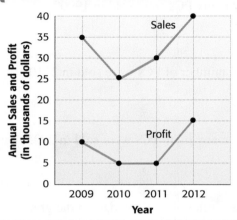

TACOS-TO-GO ANNUAL SALES

35. Find the year of lowest sales and the amount of sales.

36. Find the year of greatest profit and the amount of profit.

37. For each of the four years, the profit is what percent of sales? Round to the nearest whole percent.

38. Find the total sales for all four years and the total profit for all four years. Total profit is what percent of total sales? Round to the nearest whole percent.

39. Give two possible explanations for the decrease in sales from 2009 to 2010 and two possible explanations for the increase in sales from 2010 to 2012.

40. *Based on the graph,* what conclusion can you make about the relationship between sales and profits for Tacos-To-Go?

Relating Concepts (Exercises 41–46) For Individual or Group Work

Use the line graph of Worldwide PC Sales on the previous page as you work Exercises 41–46 in order. Round percent answers to the nearest whole percent.

41. What overall trend do you see in the line graph on worldwide sales of personal computers (PCs)?

42. Give at least two possible explanations for the increase in PC sales.

43. Look back at your earlier answers or find the percent of increase in PC sales from

(a) 1985 to 1990

(b) 1990 to 1995

(c) 1995 to 2000 (see **Exercise 27**)

(d) 2000 to 2005

(e) 2005 to 2010.

44. Look at the percents of increase in **Exercise 43**. What trend do you see?

45. What future events could cause a decrease in PC sales?

46. Can you accurately predict future PC sales from the line graph? Why or why not?

9.4 The Rectangular Coordinate System

1 **Plot a point, given the coordinates, and find the coordinates, given a point.** A bar graph or line graph shows the relationship between two things. The line graph below is from **Example 3** in the previous section. It shows the relationship between the month of the year and the number of trout stocked in the Feather River.

TROUT STOCKED IN FEATHER RIVER

Each black dot on the graph represents a particular month paired with a particular number of trout. This is an example of **paired data.** We write each pair inside parentheses, with a comma separating the two items. To be consistent, we always list the item on the *horizontal axis* first. In this case, the months are shown on the **horizontal axis** (the line that goes "left and right"), and the number of trout is shown along the **vertical axis** (the line that goes "up and down").

Paired Data from Line Graph on Trout Stocked in Feather River

(Apr, 40,000) (May, 30,000) (June, 55,000) (July, 60,000) (Aug, 25,000)

Each data pair gives you the location of a particular spot on the graph, and that spot is marked with a dot. This idea of paired data can be used to locate particular places on any flat surface.

Think of a small town laid out in a grid of square blocks, as shown below. To tell a taxi driver where to go, you could say, "the corner of 4th Avenue and 2nd Street" or just "4th and 2nd." As an *ordered pair,* it would be (4, 2). Of course, both you and the taxi driver need to know that the avenue is mentioned first (the number on the horizontal axis) and that the street is mentioned second (the number on the vertical axis). If the driver goes to (2, 4) instead, you'll be at the wrong corner.

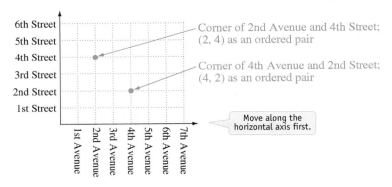

1 Plot each point on the grid. Write the ordered pair next to each point.

GS **(a)** $(1, 4)$

Start at 0.

Move to the right until you reach 1.

Then move up _____ units and make a dot.

Write (_____, _____) next to the dot.

(b) $(5, 2)$

(c) $(4, 1)$

Careful! This is **not** the same point as $(1, 4)$.

(d) $(3, 3)$

EXAMPLE 1 **Plotting Points on a Grid**

Use the grid at the right to plot each point.

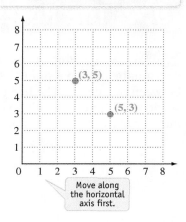

(a) $(3, 5)$

Start at 0. Move *to the right* along the horizontal axis until you reach 3. Then move *up* 5 units so that you are aligned with 5 on the vertical axis. Make a dot. This is the plot, or graph, of the point $(3, 5)$.

(b) $(5, 3)$

Start at 0. Move *to the right* along the horizontal axis until you reach 5. Then move *up* 3 units so that you are aligned with 3 on the vertical axis. Make a dot. This is the plot, or graph, of the point $(5, 3)$.

CAUTION

In **Example 1,** notice that the points $(3, 5)$ and $(5, 3)$ are **not** the same. The "address" of a point is called an **ordered pair** because the *order* within the pair is important. Always move along the horizontal axis first.

◀ Work Problem **1** at the Side.

You have used both positive and negative numbers throughout this book. We can extend our grid system to include negative numbers, as shown below. The horizontal axis is now a number line with 0 at the center, positive numbers extending to the right and negative numbers to the left. This horizontal number line is called the *x*-**axis.**

The vertical axis is also a number line, with positive numbers extending upward from 0 and negative numbers extending downward from 0. The vertical axis is called the *y*-**axis.** Together, the *x*-axis and the *y*-axis form a rectangular **coordinate system.** The point $(0, 0)$ is where the *x*-axis crosses the *y*-axis; it is called the **origin.**

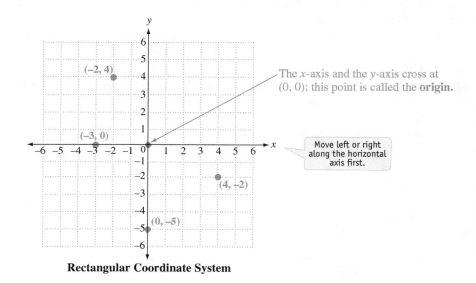

The *x*-axis and the *y*-axis cross at $(0, 0)$; this point is called the **origin.**

Move left or right along the horizontal axis first.

Rectangular Coordinate System

Answers

1. **(a)** move up 4 units; write $(1, 4)$ next to the dot.
   (b)–(d) See points on the grid below.

EXAMPLE 2 Plotting Points on a Rectangular Coordinate System

Plot each point on the rectangular coordinate system shown at the bottom of the previous page.

(a) $(4, -2)$

Start at 0. Then move left or right along the horizontal x-axis first.

Because 4 is *positive,* move *to the right* until you reach 4. Now, because the 2 is *negative,* move *down* 2 units so that you are aligned with -2 on the y-axis. Make a dot and label it $(4, -2)$.

(b) $(-2, 4)$

Starting at 0, move left or right along the horizontal x-axis first. In this case, move *to the left* until you reach -2. Then move *up* 4 units. Make a dot and label it $(-2, 4)$. Notice that $(-2, 4)$ is *not* the same as $(4, -2)$.

(c) $(0, -5)$

Start at 0. Move left or right along the horizontal x-axis first. However, because the first number is 0, do *not* move left or right. Then move *down* 5 units. Make a dot and label it $(0, -5)$.

(d) $(-3, 0)$

Starting at 0, move *to the left* along the horizontal x-axis to -3. Then, because the second number is 0, stay on -3. Do *not* move up or down. Make a dot and label it $(-3, 0)$.

Note

When the *first* number in an ordered pair is 0, the point is on the y-axis, as in **Example 2(c)** above. When the *second* number in an ordered pair is 0, the point is on the x-axis, as in **Example 2(d)** above.

Work Problem **2** at the Side. ▶

A coordinate system and an ordered pair can show the location of any point. The numbers in the ordered pair are called the **coordinates** of the point.

EXAMPLE 3 Finding the Coordinates of Points

Find the coordinates of points A, B, C, and D.

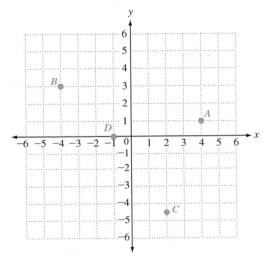

To reach point A from the origin, move 4 units *to the right;* then move *up* 1 unit. The coordinates are $(4, 1)$.

Continued on Next Page

---

2 Plot each point on the coordinate system below. Write the ordered pair next to each point.

(a) $(5, -3)$ Start at 0.

Move to the _____

until you reach ____.

Then move _____ 3 units.

Make a dot and label it

$(\underline{}, \underline{})$.

(b) $(-5, 3)$

(c) $(0, 3)$ Start at 0.

Do *not* move left or right.

Move _____ 3 units.

Make a dot and label it

$(\underline{}, \underline{})$.

This point is on the ____-axis.

(d) $(-4, -4)$

(e) $(-2, 0)$ Start at 0.

Move to the _____ until

you reach ____.

Do *not* move up or down.

This point is on the ____-axis.

Answers

2. (a) right, 5; down; $(5, -3)$
   (b) See the point labeled $(-5, 3)$ below.

(c) up; $(0, 3)$; y-axis
(d) See the point labeled $(-4, -4)$ on the grid.
(e) left, -2; x-axis

3 Find the coordinates of points *A*, *B*, *C*, *D*, and *E*.

To reach point *B* from the origin, move 4 units *to the left;* then move *up* 3 units. The coordinates are $(-4, 3)$.

To reach point *C* from the origin, move 2 units *to the right;* then move *down* approximately $4\frac{1}{2}$ units. The approximate coordinates are $\left(2, -4\frac{1}{2}\right)$.

To reach point *D* from the origin, move 1 unit *to the left;* then do *not* move either up or down. The coordinates are $(-1, 0)$.

> **Note**
>
> If a point is between the lines on the coordinate system, you can use fractions to give the approximate coordinates. For example, the approximate coordinates of point *C* above are $\left(2, -4\frac{1}{2}\right)$.

◄ **Work Problem 3** at the Side.

OBJECTIVE ▶ 2 Identify the four quadrants and determine which points lie within each one. The *x*-axis and *y*-axis divide the coordinate system into four regions, called **quadrants.** These quadrants are numbered with Roman numerals, as shown below. Points on the *x*-axis or *y*-axis are **not in any quadrant.**

4 (a) All points in the fourth quadrant are similar in what way? Give two examples of points in the fourth quadrant.

Hint: Look at the grid in the text and find the part that is labeled Quadrant IV. (In Roman numerals, IV represents "4.")

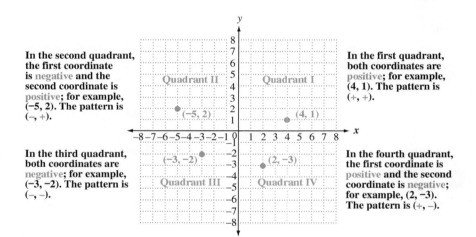

In the second quadrant, the first coordinate is negative and the second coordinate is positive; for example, $(-5, 2)$. The pattern is $(-, +)$.

In the first quadrant, both coordinates are positive; for example, $(4, 1)$. The pattern is $(+, +)$.

In the third quadrant, both coordinates are negative; for example, $(-3, -2)$. The pattern is $(-, -)$.

In the fourth quadrant, the first coordinate is positive and the second coordinate is negative; for example, $(2, -3)$. The pattern is $(+, -)$.

(b) In which quadrant is each point located: $(-2, -6)$; $(0, 5)$; $(-3, 1)$; $(4, -1)$?

EXAMPLE 4   **Working with Quadrants**

(a) All points in the third quadrant are similar in what way? Give two examples of points in the third quadrant.

For all points in Quadrant III, both coordinates are negative. The pattern is $(-, -)$. There are many possible examples, such as $(-2, -5)$ and $(-4, -4)$. Just be sure that both numbers are negative.

(b) In which quadrant is each point located: $(3, 5)$; $(1, -6)$; $(-4, 0)$?

For $(3, 5)$ the pattern is $(+, +)$, so the point is in **Quadrant I.**

For $(1, -6)$ the pattern is $(+, -)$, so the point is in **Quadrant IV.**

The point corresponding to $(-4, 0)$ is on the *x*-axis, so it isn't in any quadrant.

> When one of the numbers is 0, the point is on an axis line.

Answers

3. *A* is $(-4, -1)$; *B* is $(3, -3)$; *C* is $(5, 0)$; *D* is $(0, -2)$; *E* is approximately $\left(-1\frac{1}{2}, 5\right)$.

4. (a) The pattern for all points in Quadrant IV is $(+, -)$. Examples will vary; just be sure that they fit the $(+, -)$ pattern.
(b) III; no quadrant; II; IV

◄ **Work Problem 4** at the Side.

9.4 Exercises

 FOR EXTRA HELP

 Download the MyDashBoard App

▶ MyMathLab®

CONCEPT CHECK *A rectangular coordinate system is shown here.*

1. **(a)** Make a dot at the origin of the coordinate system.

   (b) Label the *x*-axis and the *y*-axis on the coordinate system.

2. **(a)** Write the Roman numerals for 1, 2, 3, and 4.

   (b) Use the Roman numerals to label the four quadrants on the coordinate system.

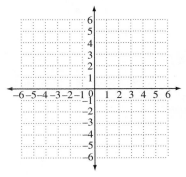

Plot each point on the rectangular coordinate system. Label each point with its coordinates. ***See Examples 1 and 2.***

3. $(3, 5)$ $(-2, 2)$ $(-3, -5)$ $(2, -2)$
   $(0, 6)$ $(6, 0)$ $(0, -4)$ $(-4, 0)$

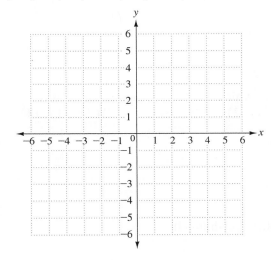

4. $(5, 2)$ $(-3, -3)$ $(4, -1)$ $(-4, 1)$
   $(-1, 0)$ $(0, 3)$ $(2, 0)$ $(0, -5)$

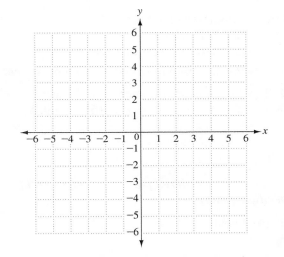

5. $(-5, 3)$ $(4, 4)$ $\left(-2\frac{1}{2}, 0\right)$ $(3, -5)$
   ▶ $(0, 0)$ $\left(2, \frac{1}{2}\right)$ $(-3, -3)$ $(-1, -6)$

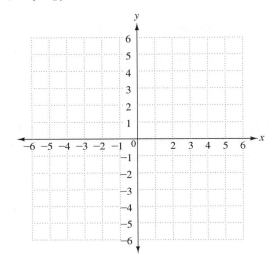

6. $(1, 5)$ $\left(0, 3\frac{1}{2}\right)$ $(-5, -1)$ $(6, -2)$
   $(-2, 6)$ $(0, 0)$ $(-3, 3)$ $\left(-\frac{1}{2}, -2\right)$

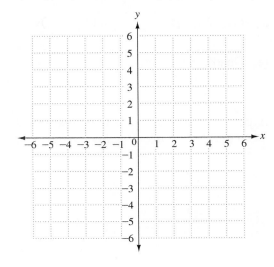

Give the coordinates of each point. ***See Example 3.***

7.

8.
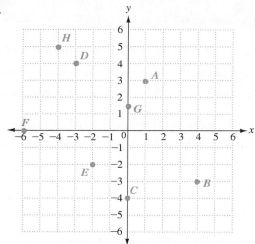

Identify the quadrant in which each point is located. ***See Example 4.***

9. In which quadrant is each point located?

$(-3, -7)$ $(0, 4)$ $(10, -16)$ $(-9, 5)$

10. In which quadrant is each point located?
$(1, 12)$ $(20, -8)$ $(-5, 0)$ $(-14, 14)$

Complete each ordered pair with a number that will make the point fall in the specified quadrant.

11. (a) Quadrant II $(-4, \underline{\hspace{0.4in}})$

   (b) Quadrant IV $(7, \underline{\hspace{0.4in}})$

   (c) No quadrant $(\underline{\hspace{0.4in}}, -2)$

   (d) Quadrant III $(\underline{\hspace{0.4in}}, -1\frac{1}{2})$

   (e) Quadrant I $(3\frac{1}{4}, \underline{\hspace{0.4in}})$

12. (a) Quadrant III $(-5, \underline{\hspace{0.4in}})$

   (b) Quadrant I $(\underline{\hspace{0.4in}}, 3)$

   (c) Quadrant IV $(\underline{\hspace{0.4in}}, -\frac{1}{2})$

   (d) No quadrant $(6, \underline{\hspace{0.4in}})$

   (e) Quadrant II $(\underline{\hspace{0.4in}}, 1\frac{3}{4})$

13. Explain how to graph the ordered pair (a, b), where a and b are positive or negative integers.

14. Explain how to graph the ordered pair (a, b) where a is 0 and b is an integer. Explain how to graph (a, b) where a is an integer and b is 0.

9.5 Introduction to Graphing Linear Equations

OBJECTIVES

1. Graph linear equations in two variables.

2. Identify the slope of a line as positive or negative.

In earlier chapters you solved equations that had only one variable, such as $2n - 3 = 7$ or $\frac{1}{3}x = 10$. Each of these equations had exactly one solution; n is 5 in the first equation, and x is 30 in the second equation. In other words, there was only *one* number that could replace the variable and make the equation balance. As you take more algebra courses, you will work with equations that have two variables and many different numbers that will make the equation balance. This section will get you started.

OBJECTIVE ▶ 1 Graph linear equations in two variables. Suppose that you have 6 hours of study time available during a weekend. You plan to study math and psychology. For example, you could spend 4 hours on math and 2 hours on psychology, for a total of 6 hours. Or you could spend $1\frac{1}{2}$ hours on math and $4\frac{1}{2}$ hours on psychology, for a total of 6 hours. Here is a list of *some* of the possible combinations.

Hours on Math	+	Hours on Psychology	=	Total Hours Studying
0	+	6	=	6
1	+	5	=	6
$1\frac{1}{2}$	+	$4\frac{1}{2}$	=	6
3	+	3	=	6
4	+	2	=	6
$5\frac{1}{2}$	+	$\frac{1}{2}$	=	6
6	+	0	=	6

We can write an equation to represent this situation.

$$\begin{array}{ccccc} \text{hours studying} & & \text{hours studying} & & \text{total of} \\ \text{math} & + & \text{psychology} & = & \text{6 hours} \\ m & + & p & = & 6 \end{array}$$

This equation, $m + p = 6$, has *two* variables. The hours spent on math (m) can vary, and the hours spent on psychology (p) can vary.

As you can see, there is more than one solution for this equation. We can list possible solutions as *ordered pairs*. The first number in the pair is the value of m (hours studying math), and the second number in the pair is the corresponding value of p (hours studying psychology).

$$\begin{array}{ccccccc} (m,p) & (m,p) & (m,p) & (m,p) & (m,p) & (m,p) & (m,p) \\ \downarrow\downarrow & \downarrow\downarrow & \downarrow\downarrow & \downarrow\downarrow & \downarrow\downarrow & \downarrow\downarrow & \downarrow\downarrow \\ (0,6) & (1,5) & \left(1\frac{1}{2},4\frac{1}{2}\right) & (3,3) & (4,2) & \left(5\frac{1}{2},\frac{1}{2}\right) & (6,0) \end{array}$$

Another way to show the solutions is to plot the ordered pairs, as you learned to do in the previous section. This method gives us a "picture" of the solutions that we listed on the previous page.

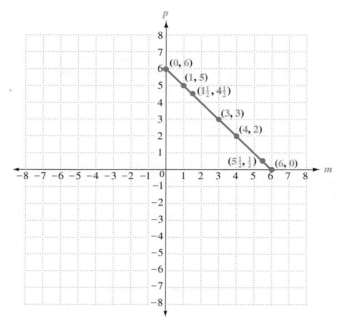

$m + p = 6$

The variables m and p represent hours, and hours can be 0 or positive numbers, but *not* negative numbers.

Notice that all the solutions (all the ordered pairs) lie on a straight line. When you draw a line connecting the ordered pairs, you have graphed the solutions. **Every point on the line is a solution.** You can use the line to find additional solutions besides the ones that we listed. For example, the point $(5, 1)$ is on the line. This point tells you that another solution is 5 hours on math and 1 hour on psychology. The fact that the line is a *straight* line tells you that $m + p = 6$ is a *linear equation.* (The word *line* is part of the word *line*ar.) Later on in algebra you will work with equations whose solutions form a curve rather than a straight line when you graph them.

To draw the line for $m + p = 6$, we really needed only two solutions (two ordered pairs). But it's a good idea to use a third ordered pair as a check. If the three ordered pairs are *not* in a straight line, there is an error in your work.

VOCABULARY TIP

Linear means "like a straight line."

> **Graphing a Linear Equation**
>
> To **graph a linear equation,** find at least three ordered pairs that satisfy the equation. Then plot the ordered pairs on a coordinate system and connect them with a straight line. *Every* point on the line is a solution of the equation.

EXAMPLE 1   Graphing a Linear Equation

Graph $x + y = 3$ by finding three solutions and plotting the ordered pairs. Then use the graph to find a fourth solution of the equation.

There are many possible solutions. Start by picking three different values for x. You can choose any numbers you like, but 0 and small numbers usually are easy to use. Then find the value of y that will make the sum equal to 3. Set up a table to organize the information.

·········· Continued on Next Page

x	y	Check that $x + y = 3$	Ordered Pair (x, y)
0	3	$0 + 3 = 3$	$(0, 3)$
1	2	$1 + 2 = 3$	$(1, 2)$
2	1	$2 + 1 = 3$	$(2, 1)$

Start by picking easy numbers for x.

Plot the ordered pairs and draw a line through the points, extending it in both directions as shown below.

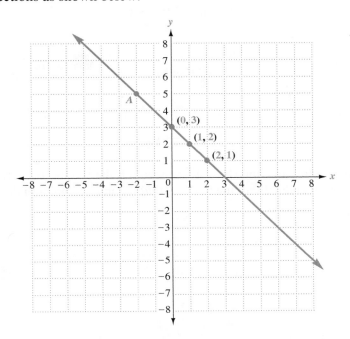

Now you can use the graph to find more solutions of $x + y = 3$. ***Every point on the line is a solution.*** Suppose that you pick **point A**. The coordinates are $(-2, 5)$.

To check that $(-2, 5)$ is a solution, substitute -2 for x and 5 for y in the original equation.

$$x + y = 3 \quad \text{Original equation}$$
$$-2 + 5 = 3$$
$$3 = 3 \checkmark \quad \text{Balances}$$

$(-2, 5)$ is a solution, **not** 3.

The equation balances, so $(-2, 5)$ is another solution of $x + y = 3$.

Note

The line in **Example 1** above was extended in both directions because *every* point on the line is a solution of $x + y = 3$. However, when we graphed the line for the hours spent studying, $m + p = 6$, we did *not* extend the line. That is because the variables m and p represented hours, and hours can only be 0 or positive numbers; all the solutions had to be in the first quadrant.

Work Problem **1** at the Side. ▶

1 Graph $x + y = 5$ by finding three solutions and plotting the ordered pairs. Then use the graph to find *two* other solutions of the equation.

x	y	Check that $x + y = 5$	Ordered Pair (x, y)
0	5	$0 + 5 = \_\_$	$(0, \_\_)$
1	4	$1 + 4 = \_\_$	$(\_\_, \_\_)$
2	__	$2 + \_\_ = \_\_$	$(\_\_, \_\_)$

Two other solutions are $(\_\_, \_\_)$ and $(\_\_, \_\_)$.

Answers

1. First row of table: $0 + 5 = 5$; $(0, 5)$; second row: $1 + 4 = 5$; $(1, 4)$; third row: 3; $2 + 3 = 5$; $(2, 3)$.

Plot $(0, 5)$, $(1, 4)$, and $(2, 3)$.

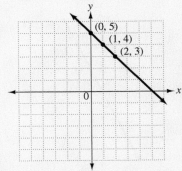

There are many other solutions. Some possibilities are $(-1, 6)$; $(3, 2)$; $(4, 1)$; $(5, 0)$; $(6, -1)$.

2 Graph $y = 2x$ by finding three solutions and plotting the ordered pairs. Then use the graph to find *two* other solutions of the equation.

x	$y = 2 \cdot x$	Ordered Pair (x, y)
0	$2 \cdot 0$ is 0	$(0, \underline{})$
1	$2 \cdot 1$ is $\underline{}$	$(1, \underline{})$
2	$2 \cdot \underline{}$ is $\underline{}$	$(\underline{}, \underline{})$

Two other solutions are $(\underline{}, \underline{})$ and $(\underline{}, \underline{})$.

Answers

2. First row of table: $(0, 0)$; second row: $2 \cdot 1$ is 2; $(1, 2)$; third row: $2 \cdot 2$ is 4; $(2, 4)$

Plot $(0, 0)$, $(1, 2)$, and $(2, 4)$.

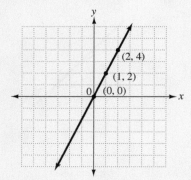

There are many other solutions. Some possibilities are $(3, 6)$; $(-1, -2)$; $(-2, -4)$; $(-3, -6)$.

EXAMPLE 2 **Graphing a Linear Equation**

Graph $y = -3x$ by finding three solutions and plotting the ordered pairs. Then use the graph to find a fourth solution of the equation.

You can choose any three values for x, but small numbers such as 0, 1, and 2 are easy to use. Then $y = -3x$ tells you that y is -3 times the value of x.

$$y = -3x$$
$$y \text{ is } -3 \text{ times } x$$

First set up a table.

Start by picking easy numbers for x.

x	$y = -3 \cdot x$	Ordered Pair (x, y)
0	$-3 \cdot 0$ is 0	$(0, 0)$
1	$-3 \cdot 1$ is -3	$(1, -3)$
2	$-3 \cdot 2$ is -6	$(2, -6)$

Plot the ordered pairs and draw a line through the points. Be sure to draw arrows on both ends of the line to show that it continues in both directions.

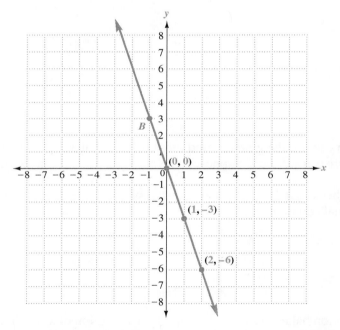

Now use the graph to find more solutions. *Every* point on the line is a solution.

Suppose that you pick **point B**. The coordinates are $(-1, 3)$. To check that $(-1, 3)$ is a solution, substitute -1 for x and 3 for y in the original equation.

$$y = -3x \qquad \text{Original equation}$$
$$3 = -3(-1)$$
$$3 = 3 \checkmark \qquad \text{Balances}$$

The equation balances, so $(-1, 3)$ is another solution of $y = -3x$.

◀ **Work Problem 2** at the Side.

EXAMPLE 3 **Graphing a Linear Equation**

Graph $y = \dfrac{1}{2}x$ by finding three solutions and plotting the ordered pairs. Then use the graph to find a fourth solution of the equation.

Complete the table. The coefficient of x is $\frac{1}{2}$, so choose even numbers like 2, 4, and 6 as values for x because they are easy to divide in half. The equation $y = \frac{1}{2}x$ tells you that y is $\frac{1}{2}$ *times* the value of x.

Pick *even* numbers for x; they are easy to multiply by $\frac{1}{2}$

x	$y = \frac{1}{2} \cdot x$	Ordered Pair (x, y)
2	$\frac{1}{2} \cdot 2$ is 1	$(2, 1)$
4	$\frac{1}{2} \cdot 4$ is 2	$(4, 2)$
6	$\frac{1}{2} \cdot 6$ is 3	$(6, 3)$

Plot the ordered pairs and draw a line through the points.

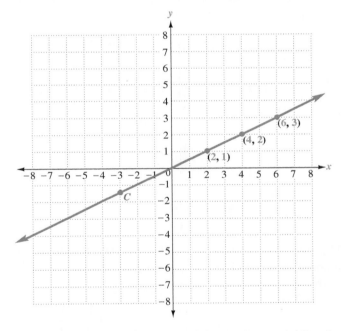

Now use the graph to find more solutions. *Every* point on the line is a solution.

Suppose that you pick **point C**. The coordinates are $\left(-3, -1\frac{1}{2}\right)$. Check that $\left(-3, -1\frac{1}{2}\right)$ is a solution by substituting -3 for x and $-1\frac{1}{2}$ for y.

$$y = \frac{1}{2}x \quad \text{Original equation}$$

$$-1\frac{1}{2} = \frac{1}{2}(-3)$$

$$-1\frac{1}{2} = -\frac{3}{2} \checkmark \quad \text{Balances}$$

$-1\frac{1}{2}$ is equivalent to $-\frac{3}{2}$.

The equation balances, so $\left(-3, -1\frac{1}{2}\right)$ is another solution of $y = \frac{1}{2}x$.

❸ Graph $y = -\frac{1}{2}x$ by finding
GS three solutions and plotting the ordered pairs. Then use the graph to find *two* more solutions.

x	$y = -\frac{1}{2} \cdot x$	Ordered Pair (x, y)
2	$-\frac{1}{2} \cdot 2$ is -1	$(2, \_\_)$
4	$-\frac{1}{2} \cdot 4$ is $\_\_$	$(4, \_\_)$
6	$-\frac{1}{2} \cdot \_\_$ is $\_\_$	$(\_\_, \_\_)$

Two other solutions are $(\_\_, \_\_)$ and $(\_\_, \_\_)$.

Answers

3. First row of table: $(2, -1)$;
   second row: $-\frac{1}{2} \cdot 4$ is -2; $(4, -2)$;
   third row: $-\frac{1}{2} \cdot 6$ is -3; $(6, -3)$

   Plot $(2, -1)$, $(4, -2)$, and $(6, -3)$.

There are many other solutions. Some possibilities are $(0, 0)$; $(-2, 1)$; $(-4, 2)$;

$(-6, 3)$; $\left(1, -\frac{1}{2}\right)$; $\left(3, -1\frac{1}{2}\right)$; $\left(5, -2\frac{1}{2}\right)$.

Work Problem **❸** at the Side. ▶

4 Graph the equation $y = x - 5$ by finding three solutions and plotting the ordered pairs. Then use the graph to find *two* more solutions.

x	$y = x - 5$	Ordered Pair (x, y)
1	1 − 5 is −4	(1, __)
2	2 − 5 is __	(2, __)
3	__ − 5 is __	(__, __)

Two other solutions are (__, __) and (__, __).

Answers

4. First row of table: $(1, -4)$;
second row: 2 − 5 is −3; $(2, -3)$;
third row: 3 − 5 is −2; $(3, -2)$

Plot $(1, -4)$, $(2, -3)$, and $(3, -2)$.

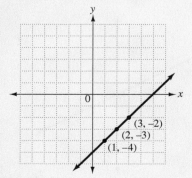

There are many other solutions. Some possibilities are $(-1, -6)$; $(0, -5)$; $\left(4\frac{1}{2}, -\frac{1}{2}\right)$; $(5, 0)$; $\left(5\frac{1}{2}, \frac{1}{2}\right)$.

EXAMPLE 4 **Graphing a Linear Equation**

Graph the equation $y = x + 4$ by finding three solutions and plotting the ordered pairs. Then use the graph to find two more solutions of the equation.

First set up a table. The equation $y = x + 4$ tells you that y must be 4 more than the value of x.

x	$y = x + 4$	Ordered Pair (x, y)
0	0 + 4 is 4	$(0, 4)$
1	1 + 4 is 5	$(1, 5)$
2	2 + 4 is 6	$(2, 6)$

Plot the ordered pairs and draw a line through the points.

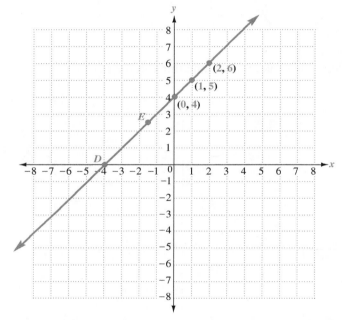

Now use the graph to find two more solutions. *Every* point on the line is a solution. Suppose that you pick **point D** at $(-4, 0)$ and **point E** at $\left(-1\frac{1}{2}, 2\frac{1}{2}\right)$. Check that both ordered pairs are solutions.

CHECK $(-4, 0)$

$$y = x + 4$$
$$0 = -4 + 4$$
$$0 = 0 \checkmark \text{ Balances}$$

$(-4, 0)$ is a solution, **not** 0.

CHECK $\left(-1\frac{1}{2}, 2\frac{1}{2}\right)$

$$y = x + 4$$
$$2\frac{1}{2} = -1\frac{1}{2} + 4$$
$$\frac{5}{2} = -\frac{3}{2} + \frac{8}{2}$$
$$\frac{5}{2} = \frac{5}{2} \checkmark \text{ Balances}$$

$2\frac{1}{2}$ can be written as $\frac{5}{2}$ and $-1\frac{1}{2}$ can be written as $\frac{3}{2}$.

Both equations balance, so $(-4, 0)$ and $\left(-1\frac{1}{2}, 2\frac{1}{2}\right)$ are also solutions of $y = x + 4$.

◄ **Work Problem** **4** **at the Side.**

OBJECTIVE ❷ Identify the slope of a line as positive or negative.
Let's look again at some of the lines that we graphed for various equations.
All are straight lines, but some are almost flat and some tilt steeply upward
or downward. The **slope** of a line is how much tilt it has.

Graph from **Example 1:** $x + y = 3$

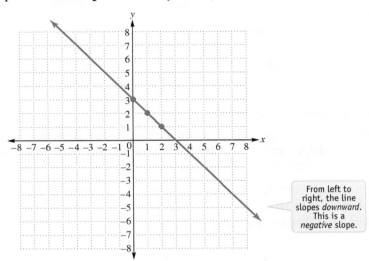

From left to
right, the line
slopes *downward*.
This is a
negative slope.

As you move from *left to right*, the line slopes downward, as if you were walking down a hill. When a line tilts downward, we say that it has a **negative slope.**
    Now look at the table of solutions we used to draw the line.

The value of
x is *increasing*
from 0 to 1 to 2

x	y
0	3
1	2
2	1

The value of
y is *decreasing*
from 3 to 2 to 1

As the value of *x increases,* the value of *y* does the *opposite*—it *decreases.*
Whenever one variable increases while the other variable decreases, the line
will have a negative slope.

Graph from **Example 3:** $y = \dfrac{1}{2}x$

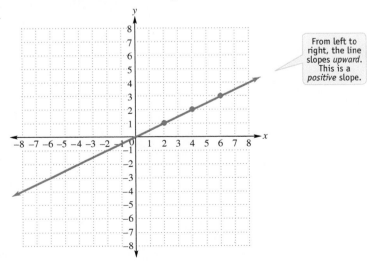

From left to
right, the line
slopes *upward*.
This is a
positive slope.

As you move from *left to right,* this line slopes upward, as if you were walking
up a hill. When a line tilts upward, we say that it has a **positive slope.**

5 Look back at the graphs in **Margin Problems 2 and 3.** Then complete these sentences.

(a) The graph of $y = 2x$ has a _____ slope. As the value of x increases, the value of y _____.

Now look at the table of solutions we used to draw the line.

The value of x is *increasing* from 2 to 4 to 6

x	y
2	1
4	2
6	3

The value of y is *increasing* from 1 to 2 to 3

As the value of x *increases,* the value of y does the *same* thing—it also *increases*. Whenever both variables do the same thing (both increase or both decrease), the line will have a positive slope.

Positive and Negative Slopes

As you move from left to right, a line with a *positive* slope tilts *upward* or rises. As the value of one variable increases, the value of the other variable also increases (does the same).

As you move from left to right, a line with a *negative* slope tilts *downward* or falls. As the value of one variable increases, the value of the other variable decreases (does the opposite).

EXAMPLE 5 **Identifying Positive or Negative Slope in a Line**

Look back at the graph of $y = -3x$ in **Example 2.** Then complete these sentences.

The graph of $y = -3x$ has a _____ slope.

As the value of x increases, the value of y _____.

(b) The graph of $y = -\frac{1}{2}x$ has a _____ slope. As the value of x increases, the value of y _____.

The graph of $y = -3x$ has a <u>negative</u> slope (because it tilts downward).

As the value of x increases, the value of y <u>decreases</u> (does the opposite).

◀ **Work Problem 5** **at the Side.**

9.5 Exercises   MyMathLab®

Download the
MyDashBoard App

CONCEPT CHECK *Circle the letter of the correct answer to complete each statement.*

1. The graph of a linear equation is a
   (a) curved line
   (b) circle
   (c) straight line

2. When you draw the graph of a linear equation
   (a) three of the points on the line are solutions
   (b) every point on the line is a solution
   (c) none of the solutions are on the line

Graph each equation by completing the table to find three solutions and plotting the ordered pairs. Then use the graph to find two *other solutions. **See Example 1.***

3. $x + y = 4$

x	y	Ordered Pair (x, y)
0	4	(0, 4)
1	3	(1, ____)
2		(2, ____)

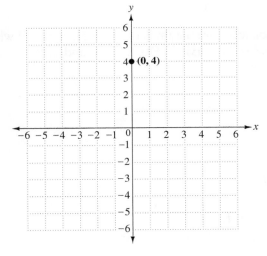

Two other solutions are (____, ____) and (____, ____).

4. $x + y = -4$

x	y	Ordered Pair (x, y)
0	-4	(0, -4)
1	-5	(1, ____)
2		(2, ____)

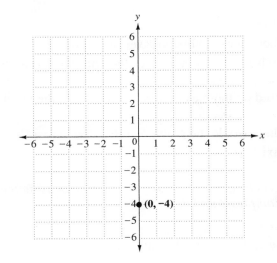

Two other solutions are (____, ____) and (____, ____).

5. $x + y = -1$

x	y	Ordered Pair (x, y)
0		
1		
2		

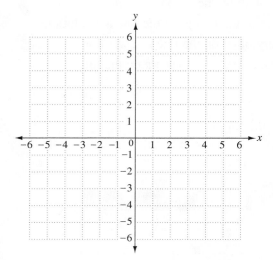

Two other solutions are (____, ____) and (____, ____).

6. $x + y = 1$

x	y	Ordered Pair (x, y)
0		
1		
2		

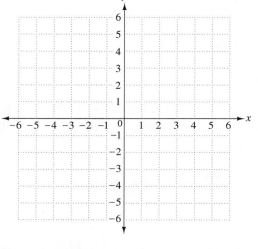

Two other solutions are (____, ____) and (____, ____).

7. Where does the line in **Exercise 3** cross the y-axis? ____ Where does the line in **Exercise 5** cross the y-axis? ____
Based on these examples, where would the graph of $x + y = -6$ cross the y-axis? ____
Where would the graph of $x + y = 99$ cross the y-axis? ____

8. Look at where the line crosses the x-axis and where it crosses the y-axis in **Exercises 4 and 6.** What pattern do you see?

Graph each equation. Make your own table using the listed values of x.
See Examples 2 and 4.

9. $y = x - 2$
Use 1, 2, and 3 as the values of x.

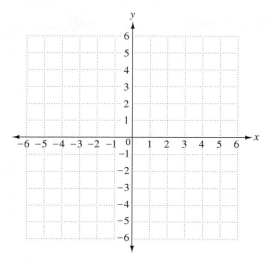

10. $y = x + 1$
Use 1, 2, and 3 as the values of x.

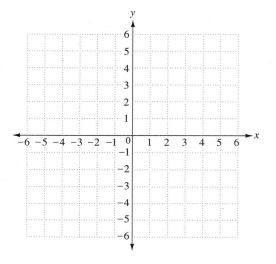

11. $y = x + 2$

Use 0, −1, and −2 as the values of x.

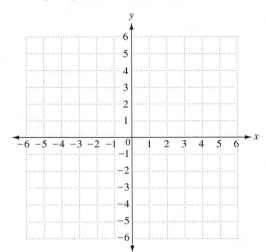

12. $y = x - 1$

Use 0, −1, and −2 as the values of x.

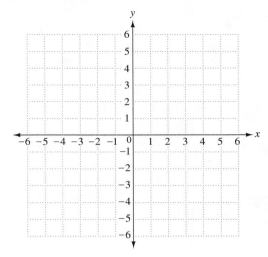

13. $y = -3x$

Use 0, 1, and 2 as the values of x.

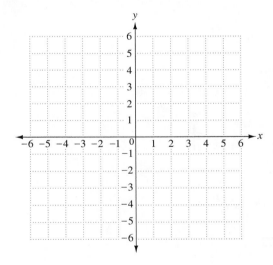

14. $y = -2x$

Use 0, 1, and 2 as the values of x.

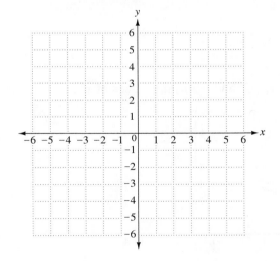

15. Look back at the graphs in **Exercises 3, 5, 9, 11, and 13.** Which lines have a positive slope? Which lines have a negative slope?

16. Look back at the graphs in **Exercises 4, 6, 10, 12, and 14.** Which lines have a positive slope? Which lines have a negative slope?

Graph each equation. Make your own table using the listed values of x.
See Examples 1–4.

17. $y = \frac{1}{3}x$

Use 0, 3, and 6 as the values of x.

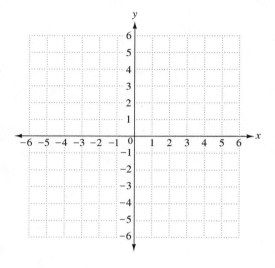

18. $y = \frac{1}{2}x$

Use 0, 2, and 4 as the values of x.

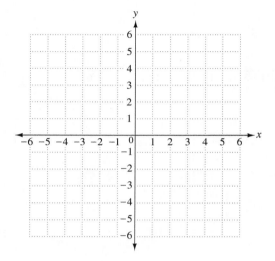

19. $y = x$

Use -1, -2, and -3 as the values of x.

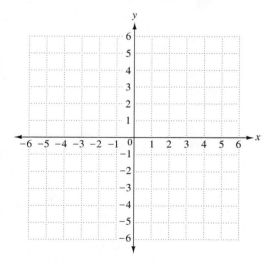

20. $x + y = 0$

Use 1, 2, and 3 as the values of x.

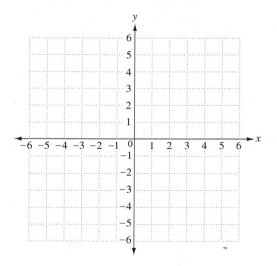

21. $y = -2x + 3$

Use 0, 1, and 2 as the values of x.

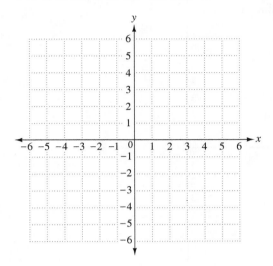

22. $y = 3x - 4$

Use 0, 1, and 2 as the values of x.

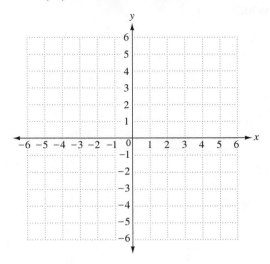

Graph each equation. Choose three values for x. Make a table showing your x values and the corresponding y values. After graphing the equation, state whether the line has a positive or negative slope. ***See Examples 1–5.***

23. $x + y = -3$

24. $x + y = 2$

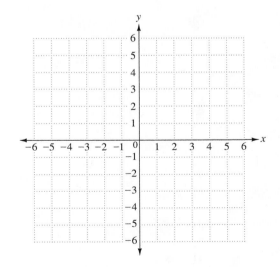

25. $y = \dfrac{1}{4}x$ (*Hint:* Try using 0 and multiples of 4 as the values of x.)

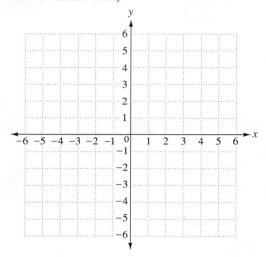

26. $y = -\dfrac{1}{3}x$ (*Hint:* Try using 0 and multiples of 3 as the values of x.)

27. $y = x - 5$

28. $y = x + 4$

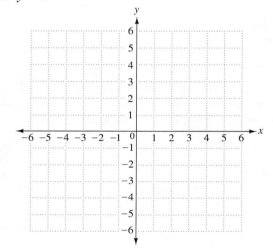

29. $y = -3x + 1$

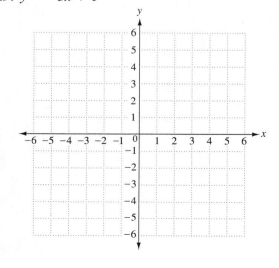

30. $y = 2x - 2$

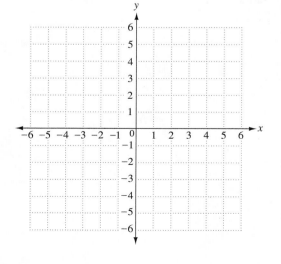

Chapter 9   *Summary*

Key Terms

9.1

table A table presents data organized into rows and columns.

pictograph A pictograph uses symbols or pictures to represent various amounts.

9.2

circle graph A circle graph shows how a total amount is divided into parts or sectors. It is based on percents of $360°$.

protractor A protractor is a tool (usually in the shape of a half-circle) used to measure the number of degrees in an angle or part of a circle.

9.3

bar graph A bar graph uses bars of various heights to show quantity or frequency.

double-bar graph A double-bar graph compares two sets of data by showing two sets of bars.

line graph A line graph uses dots connected by line segments to show trends.

comparison line graph A comparison line graph shows how two or more sets of data relate to each other by showing a line graph for each set of data.

9.4

paired data When each number in a set of data is matched with another number by some rule of association, we call it paired data.

horizontal axis The horizontal axis is the number line in a coordinate system that goes "left and right."

vertical axis The vertical axis is the number line in a coordinate system that goes "up and down."

ordered pair An ordered pair is the "address" of a point in a coordinate system. The *order* of the numbers is important. The first number tells how far to move left or right from 0 along the horizontal axis. The second number tells how far to move up or down from 0 along the vertical axis.

x-axis The horizontal axis is called the x-axis.

y-axis The vertical axis is called the y-axis.

coordinate system Together, the x-axis and the y-axis form a rectangular coordinate system. *Example:* See figure below.

origin The x-axis and the y-axis in a rectangular coordinate system cross at $(0, 0)$; this point is called the origin. *Example:* See black dot marking $(0, 0)$ in figure below.

coordinates Coordinates are the numbers in the ordered pair that specify the location of a point on a rectangular coordinate system. *Example:* See the point $(-4, 2)$ in the figure below.

quadrants The x-axis and the y-axis divide the coordinate system into four regions called quadrants; they are designated with Roman numerals. *Example:* The point $(-4, 2)$ below is in Quadrant II.

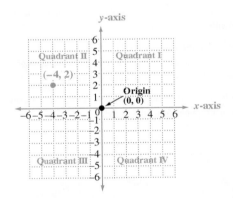

9.5

graph a linear equation All the solutions of a linear equation (all the ordered pairs that satisfy the equation) lie along a straight line. When you draw the line, you have graphed the equation.

slope The slope of a line is how much tilt the line has. As you move from left to right, an upward tilting line has a positive slope. A downward tilting line has a negative slope.

New Symbols

(x, y) ordered pair

Test Your Word Power

See how well you have learned the vocabulary in this chapter.

① A **circle graph**
 A. uses symbols to represent various amounts
 B. is useful for showing trends
 C. shows how a total amount is divided into parts.

② A **line graph**
 A. uses symbols to represent various amounts
 B. is useful for showing trends
 C. shows how a total amount is divided into parts.

③ A **protractor** is used to
 A. measure degrees in an angle
 B. draw circles of various sizes
 C. measure lengths.

④ Two sets of data can be compared using a
 A. circle graph
 B. pictograph
 C. double-bar graph.

⑤ The **x-axis** in a rectangular coordinate system is the
 A. number line that goes "up and down"
 B. number line that goes "left and right"
 C. center point of the grid.

⑥ **Quadrants** are the
 A. numbers in an ordered pair
 B. four regions in a coordinate system
 C. paired data shown on a graph.

⑦ **Coordinates** are
 A. points in a straight line on a coordinate system
 B. designated with Roman numerals
 C. numbers used to locate a point in a coordinate system.

⑧ A **rectangular coordinate system**
 A. is formed by the *x*-axis and *y*-axis
 B. is divided into eight quadrants
 C. has only positive numbers.

Answers To Test Your Word Power

1. C; *Example:* A circle graph can show how a 24-hour day is divided among various activities.

2. B; *Example:* A line graph can show changes in the amount of sales over several months or several years.

3. A; *Example:* A protractor is a tool, usually in the shape of a half-circle, used to measure or draw angles of a certain number of degrees. A tool called a compass is used to draw circles of various sizes.

4. C; *Example:* Two sets of bars in different colors can compare monthly unemployment figures for two different years.

5. B; *Example:* The x-axis is the horizontal number line with 0 at the center, negative numbers extending to the left, and positive numbers extending to the right.

6. B; *Example:* The x-axis and the y-axis divide the coordinate system into four regions; each region is designated by a Roman numeral.

7. C; *Example:* To locate the point $(2, -3)$, start at the origin and move 2 units to the right along the x-axis, then move down 3 units.

8. A; *Example:* Together, a horizontal number line (x-axis) and a vertical number line (y-axis) form a rectangular coordinate system.

Quick Review

Concepts	Examples

9.1 Reading a Table

The data in a table is organized into rows and columns. As you read from left to right along each row, check the heading at the top of each column.

Use the table below to answer the question.

PER CAPITA CONSUMPTION OF SELECTED BEVERAGES IN GALLONS

	1995	2000	2005	2010
Milk	23.9	22.5	21.0	20.6
Coffee	20.2	26.3	24.3	23.3
Bottled water	11.6	16.7	23.2	28.3
Soft drinks	50.6	53.2	52.3	46.0

Source: U.S. Dept. of Agriculture Economic Research Service.

In which year was the consumption of milk greater than the consumption of coffee?

Read across the rows labeled "milk" and "coffee" from left to right, comparing the numbers in each column. In 1995 the figure for milk (23.9 gallons) is greater than for coffee (20.2 gallons).

Concepts	Examples

9.1 Reading a Pictograph

A pictograph uses symbols or pictures to represent various amounts. The *key* tells you how much each symbol represents. A fractional part of a symbol represents a fractional part of the symbol's value.

Use the pictograph to answer these questions.

SALES OF FOOD AND DRINK AT U.S. RESTAURANTS

1980 [symbol]

1990 [symbol][symbol][symbol]

2000 [symbol][symbol][symbol][symbol]

2010 [symbol][symbol][symbol][symbol][symbol][symbol]

[symbol] = $100 billion

Source: National Restaurant Association.

(a) How much was spent at U.S. restaurants in 1990?

Sales for 1990 are represented by 2 whole symbols (2 • $100 billion = $200 billion) plus half of a symbol $\left(\frac{1}{2}$ of $100 billion = $50 billion$\right)$ for a total of $250 billion.

(b) How much did restaurant expenditures increase from 2000 to 2010?

The year 2010 shows two more symbols than 2000, so the increase is 2 • $100 billion = $200 billion.

9.2 Constructing a Circle Graph

Step 1 Determine the percent of the total for each item.

Step 2 Find the number of degrees out of 360° that each percent represents.

Step 3 Use a protractor to measure the number of degrees for each item in the circle.

Step 4 Label each sector in the circle with the item name and percent of total for that item.

Construct a circle graph for these expenses from a business trip.

Item	Amount
Transportation	$350
Lodging	$300
Food	$250
Other	$100
Total	$1000

(Continued)

Concepts		Examples

9.2 Constructing a Circle Graph (*Continued*)

Item	Amount	Percent of Total		Sector Size
Transportation	$350	$\dfrac{\$350}{\$1000} = \dfrac{7}{20} = 35\%$	so $\quad$ 35% of 360° $= (0.35)(360)$	$= 126°$
Lodging	$300	$\dfrac{\$300}{\$1000} = \dfrac{3}{10} = 30\%$	so $\quad$ 30% of 360° $= (0.30)(360)$	$= 108°$
Food	$250	$\dfrac{\$250}{\$1000} = \dfrac{1}{4} = 25\%$	so $\quad$ 25% of 360° $= (0.25)(360)$	$= 90°$
Other	$100	$\dfrac{\$100}{\$1000} = \dfrac{1}{10} = 10\%$	so $\quad$ 10% of 360° $= (0.10)(360)$	$= 36°$

BUSINESS TRIP EXPENSES

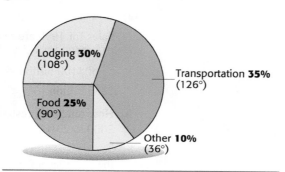

Lodging **30%** (108°)

Transportation **35%** (126°)

Food **25%** (90°)

Other **10%** (36°)

9.3 Reading a Bar Graph

The height of the bar is used to show the quantity or frequency (number) in a specific category. If necessary, use a ruler or straightedge to line up the top of each bar with the numbers on the left side of the graph.

Use the bar graph below to determine the number of students who earned each letter grade.

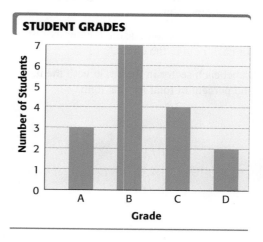

The number of students earning each letter grade were A: 3 students; B: 7 students; C: 4 students; D: 2 students.

Concepts	Examples

9.3 Reading a Line Graph

A dot is used to show the number or quantity in a specific class. The dots are connected with line segments. This kind of graph is used to show a trend.

The line graph below shows the annual sales for the Fabric Supply Center for each of four years.

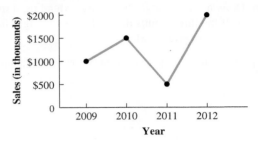

Which year had the lowest sales? What was the amount of sales that year?

2011; sales were $500 · 1000 = $500,000

9.4 Plotting Points

Start at the center of the coordinate system (the origin). The first number in an ordered pair tells you how far to move *left* or *right* along the horizontal axis; *positive* numbers are to the *right*, and *negative* numbers are to the *left*. The second number in an ordered pair tells you how far to move *up* or *down; positive* numbers are *up*, and *negative* numbers are *down*.

To plot $(3, -2)$, start at 0, move to the *right* 3 units, and then move *down* 2 units.

To plot $(-2, 3)$, start at 0, move to the *left* 2 units, and then move *up* 3 units.

9.4 Identifying Quadrants

The *x*-axis and *y*-axis divide the coordinate system into four regions called quadrants. The quadrants are designated with Roman numerals.

Points in the first quadrant fit the pattern $(+, +)$.

Points in the second quadrant fit the pattern $(-, +)$.

Points in the third quadrant fit the pattern $(-, -)$.

Points in the fourth quadrant fit the pattern $(+, -)$.

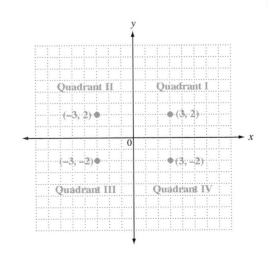

Concepts

9.5 Graphing Linear Equations

Choose any three values for *x*. Then find the corresponding values of *y*. Plot the three ordered pairs on a coordinate system. Draw a line through the points, extending it in both directions. If the three points do *not* lie on a straight line, there is an error in your work.

Every point on the line is a solution of the given equation.

Graph $y = -2x$. Then use the graph to find *two* other solutions.

x	y = −2 · x	Ordered Pair (x, y)
1	−2 · 1 is −2	(1, −2)
2	−2 · 2 is −4	(2, −4)
3	−2 · 3 is −6	(3, −6)

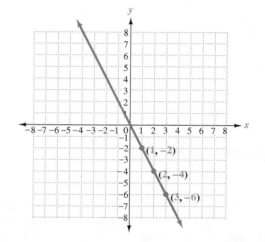

Every point on the line is a solution. Some of the other solutions are $(0, 0)$; $(-1, 2)$; $(-2, 4)$; and $\left(-2\frac{1}{2}, 5\right)$.

Chapter 9 *Review Exercises*

9.1 *Use the table at the right to answer Exercises 1–4.*

1. Which sport had the
   (a) fewest men's teams?

   (b) second-greatest number
       of women's teams?

2. Which sport had
   (a) about 16,000 female athletes?

   (b) about 14,000 male athletes?

PARTICIPATION IN SELECTED NCAA SPORTS 2010–2011

Sport	Males			Females		
	Teams	Athletes	Average Squad	Teams	Athletes	Average Squad
Basketball	1051	17,500	16.7	1072	15,708	14.7
Cross country	952	13,976	14.7	1026	15,319	14.9
Golf	811	8436	10.4	575	4565	7.9
Gymnastics	17	318	18.7	83	1463	17.6
Volleyball	95	1456		1039	15,597	

Source: The National Collegiate Athletic Association (NCAA).

3. (a) How many more men participated in basketball
       than cross country?

   (b) How many fewer women participated in
       gymnastics than volleyball?

4. Find the average squad size for men's and women's
   volleyball teams and complete the table. Round to the
   nearest tenth.

Use the pictograph on average yearly snowfall to answer Exercises 5–8.

5. What is the average yearly snowfall in
   (a) Juneau?

   (b) Washington, D.C.?

6. What is the average yearly snowfall in
   (a) Minneapolis?

   (b) Cleveland?

7. Find the difference in the average yearly snowfall
   between
   (a) Buffalo and Cleveland.

   (b) Memphis and Minneapolis.

8. Find the difference in the average yearly snowfall
   between the city with the greatest amount and the city
   with the least amount.

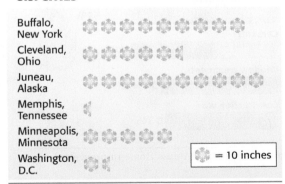

AVERAGE YEARLY SNOWFALL IN SELECTED U.S. CITIES

Source: National Climatic Data Center.

9.2 *Use this circle graph for Exercises 9–13.*

9. (a) What was the largest single expense of the vacation? How much was that item?

(b) What was the second-most-expensive item? How much was that item?

(c) What was the total cost of the vacation?

COST OF A FAMILY VACATION

Use the family vacation circle graph above to find each ratio. Write the ratios as fractions in lowest terms.

10. Cost of lodging to the cost of food

11. Cost of gasoline to the total cost of the vacation

12. Cost of sightseeing to the total cost of the vacation

13. Cost of gasoline to the cost of the Other category

9.3 *This bar graph shows the top six home improvement projects that people do themselves. Use the graph to answer Exercises 14–19. Multiple responses were allowed.*

CAN YOU FIX IT?

Projects homeowners take on themselves according to a recent survey:

Painting, wallpapering — 63%
Landscaping, gardening — 54%
Interior decorating — 51%
Carpentry — 43%
Window treatments — 34%
Construction work — 33%

Source: American Express Home Improvement.

14. What is the most popular project? What percent of the homeowners in the survey gave that answer?

15. Which project was selected the least? What percent of the homeowners in the survey gave that answer?

16. What percent of the homeowners in the survey selected carpentry projects? There were 341 people surveyed. How many of them selected carpentry, to the nearest whole number?

17. Of the 341 homeowners surveyed, how many selected landscaping or gardening projects? Round to the nearest whole number.

18. Name the project(s) selected by about
  (a) $\frac{1}{2}$ of the homeowners.

  (b) $\frac{1}{3}$ of the homeowners.

19. Give two reasons why painting and wallpapering might be selected so much more than construction work.

This double-bar graph shows the number of acre-feet of water in the Lake Natoma reservoir for each of the first six months of 2011 and 2012. Use this graph to answer Exercises 20–25.

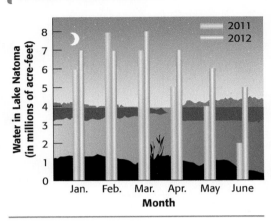

WATER IN LAKE NATOMA

20. From January through June 2012, which month had the greatest amount of water in the lake? How much was there?

21. During which month in the first half of 2011 was the least amount of water in the lake? How much was there?

22. How many acre-feet of water were in the lake in June of 2012?

23. How many acre-feet of water were in the lake in January of 2011?

24. Find the amount of decrease and the percent of decrease in the acre-feet of water in the lake from March 2012 to June 2012.

25. Find the amount of decrease and the percent of decrease in the acre-feet of water in the lake from April 2011 to June 2011.

This comparison line graph shows the annual floor-covering sales of two different home improvement centers during each of five years. Use this graph to find the amount of sales in each year listed in Exercises 26–29 and to answer Exercises 30 and 31.

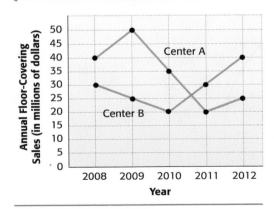

ANNUAL FLOOR-COVERING SALES

26. Center A in 2009

27. Center A in 2011

28. Center B in 2010

29. Center B in 2012

30. What trend do you see in Center A's sales from 2009 to 2012? Why might this have happened?

31. What trend do you see in Center B's sales starting in 2010? Why might this have happened?

9.2 *The Broadway Hair Salon spent a total of* $22,400 *to remodel their salon.*
The breakdown of the cost for various items is shown. Find all the missing
numbers in Exercises 32–36.

Item	Dollar Amount	Percent of Total	Degrees of Circle
32. Plumbing and electrical changes	$2240	10%	_____
33. Work stations	$7840	_____	_____
34. Small appliances	$4480	_____	_____
35. Interior decoration	$5600	_____	_____
36. Supplies	_____	_____	36°

37. Draw a circle graph using the information in **Exercises 32–36.** Label each sector
with the item and the percent of total for that item.

9.4 *In Exercise 38, plot each point on the rectangular coordinate system and label it with its coordinates. In Exercise 39, give the coordinates of each point.*

38. $(1, 7)$ $\left(-1\frac{1}{2}, 0\right)$ $(-4, -2)$ $(0, 3)$ $\left(2, -\frac{1}{2}\right)$ **39.**

$(-7, 1)$ $(5, -5)$ $(0, -4)$

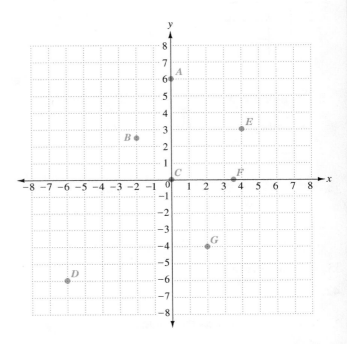

9.5 *Graph each equation. Complete the table using the listed values of x. State whether each line has a positive or negative slope. Use the graph to find two other solutions of the equation.*

40. $x + y = -2$

Use 0, 1, and 2 as the values of x.

x	y	(x, y)

The graph of $x + y = -2$ has a _____ slope.

Two other solutions of $x + y = -2$ are

(____ , ____) and (____ , ____).

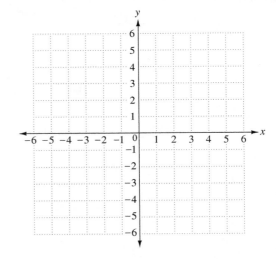

41. $y = x + 3$

Use 0, 1, and 2 as the values of x.

x	y	(x, y)

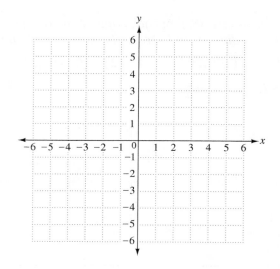

The graph of $y = x + 3$ has a _____ slope.

Two other solutions for $y = x + 3$ are
(___, ___)   and   (___, ___).

42. $y = -4x$

Use -1, 0, and 1 as the values of x.

x	y	(x, y)

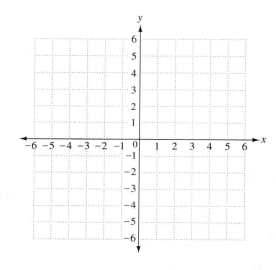

The graph of $y = -4x$ has a _____ slope.

Two other solutions of $y = -4x$ are
(___, ___)   and   (___, ___).

Chapter 9 Test

The Chapter Test Prep Videos with test solutions are available on DVD, in MyMathLab, and on YouTube — search "LialPrealgebra" and click on "Channels."

Use this table to answer Problems 1–3.

1. Which food has
   (a) the greatest amount of calcium in one serving?

   (b) the least amount of calcium in one serving?

AMOUNT OF CALCIUM IN SELECTED FOODS

Food	Serving size	Calories	Calcium (mg)
Swiss cheese	1 oz	95	219
Cream cheese	1 oz	100	23
Yogurt, fruit flavor	8 oz	230	345
Skim milk	1 cup	85	302
Sardines	3 oz	175	371

Source: U.S. Department of Agriculture.

2. A packet of Swiss cheese contains 1.75 oz. How many calories are in that amount of Swiss cheese? Round to the nearest whole number.

3. Find the amount of calcium in a 6 oz container of fruit-flavored yogurt. Round to the nearest whole number.

Use this pictograph to answer Problems 4–6.

4. (a) Which group (or groups) has the greatest number of endangered species?

   (b) How many endangered species are in the top group(s)?

5. How many more species of mammals are endangered than reptiles?

6. What is the total number of endangered species shown in the pictograph?

This circle graph shows the advertising budget for Lakeland Amusement Park. Find the dollar amount budgeted for each category listed in Problems 7–10. The total advertising budget is $2,800,000.

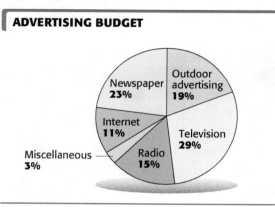

ADVERTISING BUDGET

7. Which form of advertising has the largest budget? What amount is this?

8. Which form of advertising has the smallest budget? How much is this?

9. How much is budgeted for Internet advertising?

10. How much is budgeted for newspaper ads?

This graph shows one student's income and expenses for four years.

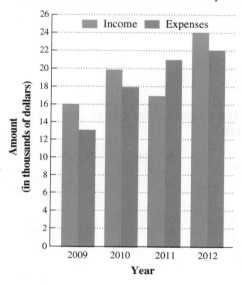

11. In what year did the student's expenses exceed income? By how much?

12. Find the amount of increase and the percent of increase in the student's expenses from 2009 to 2010. Round to the nearest whole percent.

13. In what year did the student's income decline? Give two possible explanations for the decline.

This graph shows enrollment at two community colleges.

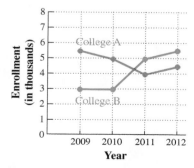

14. What was College A's enrollment in 2009? What was College B's enrollment in 2010?

15. Which college had higher enrollment in 2012? How much higher?

16. Give two possible explanations for the fact that College B's enrollment passed College A's.

During a one-year period, Oak Mill Furniture Sales had a total of $480,000 in expenses. Find all the numbers missing from the table.

Item	Dollar Amount	Percent of Total	Degrees of a Circle
17. Salaries	$168,000	_____	_____
18. Delivery expense	$24,000	_____	_____
19. Advertising	$96,000	_____	_____
20. Rent	$144,000	_____	_____
21. Other	_____	_____	36°

22. Draw a circle graph using a protractor and the information in **Problems 17–21.** Label each sector with the item and the percent of total for that item.

Plot each point on the coordinate system below. Label each point with its coordinates.

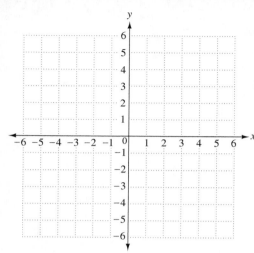

23. $(-5, 3)$

24. $(1, -4)$

25. $(0, 6)$

26. $(2, 0)$

Give the coordinates of each lettered point shown below, and state which quadrant the point is in.

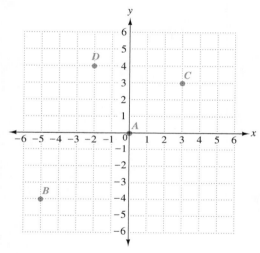

27. Point A

28. Point B

29. Point C

30. Point D

31. Graph $y = x - 4$ on the coordinate system below. Make your own table using 0, 1, and 2 as the values of x.

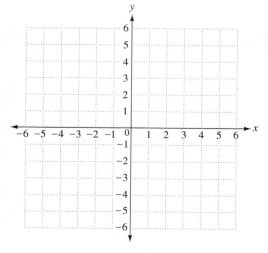

32. (a) Use the graph in **Problem 31** to find *two* other solutions of $y = x - 4$.

(b) State whether the graph of $y = x - 4$ has a positive or negative slope.

Chapters 1–9 *Cumulative Review Exercises*

Simplify.

1. $\dfrac{4}{5} + 2\dfrac{1}{3}$

2. $\dfrac{0.8}{-3.2}$

3. $5^2 + (-4)^3$

4. $(0.002)(-0.05)$

5. $\dfrac{4a}{9} \cdot \dfrac{6b}{2a^3}$

6. $1\dfrac{1}{4} - 3\dfrac{5}{6}$

7. $-13 + 2.993$

8. $\dfrac{2}{7} - \dfrac{8}{x}$

9. $-3 - 33$

10. $\dfrac{10m}{3n^2} \div \dfrac{2m^2}{5n}$

11. $\dfrac{-3}{-\dfrac{9}{10}}$

12. $\dfrac{3(-7)}{2^4 - 16}$

13. $10 - 2\dfrac{5}{8}$

14. $\dfrac{3}{w} + \dfrac{x}{6}$

15. $8 + 4(2 - 5)$

16. $\dfrac{7}{8}$ of 960

17. $\dfrac{(-4)^2 + 8(0 - 2)}{8 \div 2(-3 + 5) - 10}$

18. $0.5 - 0.25(3.2)^2$

19. $6\left(-\dfrac{1}{2}\right)^3 + \dfrac{2}{3}\left(\dfrac{3}{5}\right)$

Solve each equation. Show your work.

20. $-12 = 3(y + 2)$

21. $6x = 14 - x$

22. $-8 = \dfrac{2}{3}m + 2$

23. $3.4x - 6 = 8 + 1.4x$

24. $2(h - 1) = -3(h + 12) - 11$

25. Translate this sentence into an equation and solve it. If five times a number is subtracted from 12, the result is the number. Find the number.

26. Solve using the six problem-solving steps. An $1800 scholarship is to be split between two people so that one person gets $500 more than the other. How much will each person receive?

Find the unknown length, perimeter, circumference, area, or volume. Use 3.14 as the approximate value of π, and round answers to the nearest tenth when necessary.

27. Find the perimeter and area.

28. A circular hot tub has a diameter of 6 ft. Find its circumference and the area of the tub's floor.

29. Find the unknown length, the perimeter, and the area.

Solve each application problem.

30. A survey found that 19 out of 25 adults are nonsmokers. If Mathtronic has 732 employees, how many would be expected to be nonsmokers? Round to the nearest whole number.

31. Esther bought a smartphone at a 15% discount. The regular price was $129. She also paid $6\frac{1}{2}$% sales tax. What was her total cost for the phone, to the nearest cent?

32. Abiola earned 167 points out of 180 on the prealgebra final exam. What percent of the points did she earn, to the nearest tenth?

33. Wayne bought $2\frac{1}{4}$ pounds of lunch meat. He used $\frac{1}{6}$ pound of meat on each of five sandwiches. How much meat is left?

34. Plot the following points and label each one with its coordinates. Which of the points are in Quadrant II? Which are in the Quadrant III?

$(3, -5)$ $(0, -4)$ $\left(-2, 3\frac{1}{2}\right)$ $(1, 0)$ $(4, 2)$

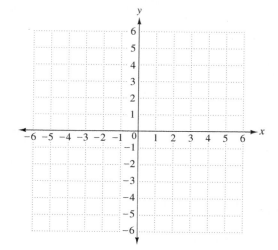

35. Graph $y = x + 6$. Use $0, -1$, and -2 as the values of x. After graphing the equation, state whether the line has a positive or negative slope, and find two other solutions of $y = x + 6$.

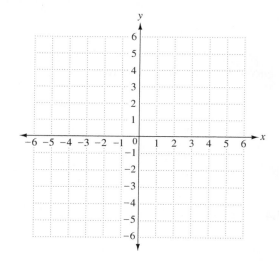

Whole Numbers Computation: Pretest

This test will check your skills in doing whole numbers computation, using paper and pencil. Each part of the test is keyed to a section in the Review Chapter, which follows this test. Based on your test results, work the appropriate section(s) in the Review Chapter *before you start Chapter 1.*

Adding Whole Numbers   *(Do not use a calculator.)*

| 1. | 368
 + 22 | 2. | 7093
 + 6073 | 3. | 85
 + 2968 | 4. | 57,208
 915
 + 59,387 |

5. $714 + 3728 + 9 + 683{,}775$

Subtracting Whole Numbers   *(Do not use a calculator.)*

| 1. | 426
 − 76 | 2. | 3358
 − 2729 | 3. | 30,602
 − 5 708 |

4. $4006 - 97$ **5.** $679{,}420 - 88{,}033$

Multiplying Whole Numbers   *(Do not use a calculator.)*

1. $3 \times 3 \times 0 \times 6$ **2.** 3841×7 **3.** $(520)(3000)$

(Continued)

Multiplying Whole Numbers   *(Continued)*
Do not use a calculator; show your work.

4.   71
$\times\ 26$

5. Multiply 359 and 48.

6. 853×609

Dividing Whole Numbers   *(Do not use a calculator; show your work.)*

1. $3\overline{)69}$

2. $12 \div 0$

3. $\dfrac{25{,}036}{4}$

4. $7\overline{)5655}$

5. $52\overline{)1768}$

6. $45{,}000 \div 900$

7. $38\overline{)2300}$

8. $83\overline{)44{,}799}$

Now check your answers on page A–32 in the Answers section at the back of the book. Record the number of problems you worked correctly in each part of the test.

Adding Whole Numbers: _____ correct out of 5.

   If you got 0, 1, or 2 correct, work **Section R.1** in the Review Chapter.

Subtracting Whole Numbers: _____ correct out of 5.

   If you got 0, 1, or 2 correct, work **Section R.2** in the Review Chapter.

Multiplying Whole Numbers: _____ correct out of 6.

   If you got 0, 1, 2, or 3 correct, work **Section R.3** in the Review Chapter.

Dividing Whole Numbers: _____ correct out of 8.

   If you got 0, 1, or 2 correct, work **Sections R.4** and **R.5** in the Review Chapter.

   If you got 3 or 4 correct, work **Section R.5** in the Review Chapter.

Whole Numbers Review

Note

Use the **Whole Numbers Computation: Pretest** on the previous two pages to decide which sections you need to work in this chapter.

R.1 Adding Whole Numbers

There are 4 triangles on the left and 2 triangles on the right. In all, there are 6 triangles.

The process of finding the total is called *addition*. Here 4 and 2 are added to get 6. Addition is written with a $+$ symbol, as shown below.

$$4 + 2 = 6$$

OBJECTIVES

1. Add two or three single-digit numbers.
2. Add more than two numbers.
3. Add when regrouping is not required.
4. Add with regrouping.
5. Use addition to solve application problems.
6. Check the sum in addition.

OBJECTIVE ▶ ① **Add two or three single-digit numbers.** In addition problems, the numbers being added are called **addends,** and the answer is called the **sum** or **total.**

$$\begin{array}{r} 4 \; \longleftarrow \text{Addend} \\ + \, 2 \; \longleftarrow \text{Addend} \\ \hline 6 \; \longleftarrow \text{Sum (answer)} \end{array}$$

Addition problems can also be written horizontally as shown below.

$$\underset{\underset{\text{Addend}}{\uparrow}}{4} \quad + \quad \underset{\underset{\text{Addend}}{\uparrow}}{2} \quad = \quad \underset{\underset{\text{Sum}}{\uparrow}}{6}$$

1 Add. Then use the commutative property to write another addition problem and find the sum.

(a) 3 + 4

(b) 9 + 9

(c) 7 + 8

(d) 6 + 9

2 Find each sum.

(a) 5
     4
     6
     9
   + 2

(b) 7
     5
     1
     2
   + 6

(c) 9
     2
     1
     3
   + 4

(d) 3
     8
     6
     4
   + 8

Commutative Property of Addition

The **commutative property of addition** states that changing the *order* of two addends in an addition problem does *not* change the sum.

For example, the sum of 4 + 2 is the same as the sum of 2 + 4. Both sums are 6. This allows the addition of the same numbers in a different order.

EXAMPLE 1   Adding Two Single-Digit Numbers

Add. Then use the commutative property to write another addition problem and find the sum.

(a) 6 + 2 = **8**   and   2 + 6 = **8**   (b) 5 + 9 = **14**   and   9 + 5 = **14**

(c) 8 + 8 = **16**   (No change occurs when commutative property is used.)

◀ **Work Problem 1** at the Side.

OBJECTIVE 2   Add more than two numbers. Some additions involve more than two addends.

Associative Property of Addition

By the **associative property of addition,** changing the *grouping* of addends does *not* change the sum.

For example, find the sum of 3 + 5 + 6.

$(3 + 5) + 6 = 8 + 6 = \mathbf{14}$ Parentheses tell you to add 3 + 5 first.

$3 + (5 + 6) = 3 + 11 = \mathbf{14}$ Parentheses tell you to add 5 + 6 first.

By the associative property, either grouping gives a sum of 14.

To add four or more numbers, first write them in a column. Add the first number to the second. Add this sum to the third number and so on.

EXAMPLE 2   Adding More Than Two Numbers

Find the sum of 2, 5, 6, 1, and 4.

    2 ⎤ 2 + 5 = 7
    5 ⎦
         7 + 6 = 13
    ⑥
    ①   13 + 1 = 14
  + ④   14 + 4 = 18
   ─────
    18 ← Sum

Note

You may also add numbers by starting at the bottom of a column. Adding down from the top or adding up from the bottom will give the same sum.

◀ **Work Problem 2** at the Side.

OBJECTIVE 3   Add when regrouping is not required. If numbers have two or more digits, arrange the numbers in columns so that the ones digits are in the same column, tens are in the same column, hundreds are in the same column, and so on. Then add column by column, starting with the ones column.

EXAMPLE 3 Adding without Regrouping

Add: 511 + 23 + 154 + 10

First line up the numbers in columns, with the ones column at the right.

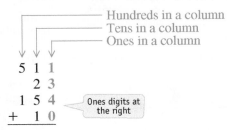

Now start at the right and add the ones digits. Add the tens digits next, and finally, add the hundreds digits.

```
        5 1 1
          2 3
        1 5 4
      +   1 0
        6 9 8
        ↑ ↑ ↑
            └──── Sum of ones
          └────── Sum of tens
        └──────── Sum of hundreds
```

The sum of the four numbers is 698.

··· **Work Problem ❸ at the Side.** ▶

OBJECTIVE ❹ Add with Regrouping. If the sum of the digits in a column is more than 9, use **regrouping** (sometimes called *carrying*).

EXAMPLE 4 Adding with Regrouping

Find the sum of 47 and 29.

Add the digits in the ones column.

```
    47
  + 29
    ↑
    └── 7 ones + 9 ones = 16 ones
```

Regroup 16 ones as 1 ten and 6 ones. Write 6 ones in the ones column and write 1 ten in the tens column.

Write 1 ten in the tens column.
```
    1 ◄
    47
  + 29     7 ones + 9 ones = 16 ones  ◄── Regroup 16 ones as
    6 ◄                                    1 ten and 6 ones.
```
Write 6 ones in the ones column.

Add the digits in the tens column, including the regrouped 1.

```
    1
    47      Remember
  + 29      to add the 1
    76      regrouped ten.
    ↑
    └──── 1 ten + 4 tens + 2 tens = 7 tens
```

·· **Work Problem ❹ at the Side.** ▶

---

❸ Add.

(a)
```
    25
  + 73
```

(b)
```
   364
 + 532
```

(c)
```
   42,305
 + 11,563
```

❹ Find each sum using regrouping.

(a)
```
    69
  + 26
```

(b)
```
    76
  + 18
```

(c)
```
    56
  + 37
```

(d)
```
    34
  + 49
```

Answers

3. (a) 98 **(b)** 896 **(c)** 53,868
4. (a) 95 **(b)** 94 **(c)** 93 **(d)** 83

5 Find each sum, regrouping when necessary.

(a)
```
   481
    79
    38
 + 395
```

(b)
```
  4271
   372
  8976
 + 162
```

(c)
```
    57
     4
   392
   804
    51
 +  27
```

(d)
```
  7821
   435
    72
   305
 + 1693
```

(e)
```
  15,829
     765
      78
      15
       9
       7
 + 13,179
```

EXAMPLE 5 **Adding with Regrouping**

Add: $324 + 7855 + 23 + 7 + 86$

Step 1 Add the digits in the ones column.

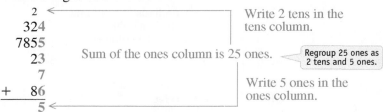

Step 2 Add the digits in the tens column, including the regrouped 2.

Step 3 Add the hundreds column, including the regrouped 1.

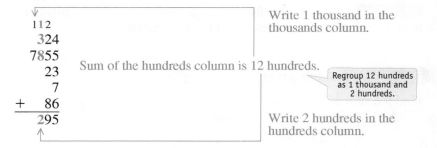

Step 4 Add the thousands column, including the regrouped 1.

```
  112
   324
  7855
    23     Sum of the thousands
     7     column is 8 thousands.
 +  86
  8295
```

Thus, $324 + 7855 + 23 + 7 + 86 = 8295$.

◀ **Work Problem** **5** **at the Side.**

Answers

5. **(a)** 993 **(b)** 13,781 **(c)** 1335
  (d) 10,326 **(e)** 29,882

OBJECTIVE ⑤ **Use addition to solve application problems.**

EXAMPLE 6 Applying Addition Skills

On this map, the distance in miles from one town to another is written alongside the road. Find the shortest route from Altamonte Springs to Clear Lake.

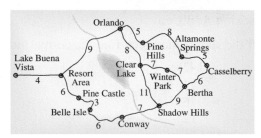

Approach Add the mileage along various routes from Altamonte Springs to Clear Lake. Then select the shortest route.

Solution One way from Altamonte Springs to Clear Lake is through Orlando. Add the mileage numbers along this route.

$$
\begin{array}{rl}
8 & \text{Altamonte Springs to Pine Hills} \\
5 & \text{Pine Hills to Orlando} \\
+\ 8 & \text{Orlando to Clear Lake} \\
\hline
21 & \rightarrow \text{miles from Altamonte Springs to Clear Lake,} \\
& \quad \text{going through Orlando}
\end{array}
$$

Another way is through Casselberry, Bertha, and Winter Park. Add the mileage numbers along this route.

$$
\begin{array}{rl}
5 & \text{Altamonte Springs to Casselberry} \\
6 & \text{Casselberry to Bertha} \\
7 & \text{Bertha to Winter Park} \\
+\ 7 & \text{Winter Park to Clear Lake} \\
\hline
25 & \rightarrow \text{miles from Altamonte Springs to Clear Lake} \\
& \quad \text{through Casselberry, Bertha, and Winter Park}
\end{array}
$$

The shortest route from Altamonte Springs to Clear Lake is 21 miles through Orlando.

···················· **Work Problem ⑥ at the Side.** ▶

EXAMPLE 7 Applying Addition Skills

Using the map in **Example 6** above, find the total mileage from Shadow Hills to Casselberry to Orlando and back to Shadow Hills through Clear Lake.

Solution Add the mileage numbers from the map.

$$
\begin{array}{rl}
9 & \text{Shadow Hills to Bertha} \\
6 & \text{Bertha to Casselberry} \\
5 & \text{Casselberry to Altamonte Springs} \\
8 & \text{Altamonte Springs to Pine Hills} \\
5 & \text{Pine Hills to Orlando} \\
8 & \text{Orlando to Clear Lake} \\
+\ 11 & \text{Clear Lake to Shadow Hills} \\
\hline
52 & \rightarrow \text{miles from Shadow Hills to Casselberry to} \\
& \quad \text{Orlando and back to Shadow Hills}
\end{array}
$$

···················· **Work Problem ⑦ at the Side.** ▶

⑥ Use the map on this page to find the shortest route from Conway to Pine Hills.

⑦ The road is closed between Orlando and Clear Lake, so this route cannot be used. Find the next shortest route from Orlando to Clear Lake.

Answers

6. 29 miles through Belle Isle

7.
$$
\begin{array}{lr}
\text{Orlando to Pine Hills} & 5 \\
\text{Pine Hills to Altamonte Springs} & 8 \\
\text{Altamonte Springs to Casselberry} & 5 \\
\text{Casselberry to Bertha} & 6 \\
\text{Bertha to Winter Park} & 7 \\
\text{Winter Park to Clear Lake} & +\ 7 \\
\hline
 & 38 \text{ miles}
\end{array}
$$

8 Check each addition. If the sum is incorrect, find the correct sum.

(a)
```
    32
     8
     5
 + 14
    59
```

(b)
```
   872
   539
    46
 + 152
  1609
```

(c)
```
    79
   218
     7
 + 639
   953
```

(d)
```
  21,892
  11,746
+ 43,925
  79,563
```

OBJECTIVE ▶ 6 **Check the sum in addition.** Checking the answer is an important part of problem solving. A common method for checking addition is to re-add from the bottom to the top. This is an application of the commutative and associative properties of addition.

EXAMPLE 8 **Checking Addition**

Check each sum. If the sum is incorrect, find the correct sum.

(a)   Add down.
```
     1428  ↑
      738
       63
      125
       17
   + 485      └─ To check, add up.
     1428
```

Adding down and adding up should give the same sum. In this case, the answers agree, so the sum is probably correct.

(b)
```
            1033  ↑   Correct, because both
   785      785        answers are the same
    63       63
 + 185    + 185      └─ To check, add up.
  1033     1033
```

(c)
```
            2454  ↑   Error, because answers
   635      635        are different
    73       73
   831      831
 + 915    + 915      └─ To check, add up.
  2444     2444
```

Re-add to find that the correct sum is 2454.

◀ **Work Problem 8 at the Side.**

R.1 Exercises

   Download the MyDashBoard App MyMathLab®

Add. See Examples 2 and 3.

1. (a)   5   (b)   9   2. (a)   2   (b)   3
       7   2   9   8
       6   1   5   6
   + 5   3   + 1   4
                  + 4   + 8

3. (a) 3213 + 5715   4. (a) 6344 + 1655

   (b) 38,204 + 21,020   (b) 63,251 + 36,305

*Find each sum, regrouping when necessary. **See Examples 4 and 5.***

5.   67   6.   78   7.   746   8.   621   9.   798
   + 83   + 36   + 905   +359   + 206

10.   172   11.   7968   12.   1768   13.   7896   14.   9382
    + 156   + 1285   + 8275   + 3728   + 7586

15.   3705   16.   6629   17.   32   18.   402   19.   3077
    3916   6076   + 4977   + 9938   8
  + 9037   + 8218   + 421

20.   56   21.   9056   22.   4022   23.   18   24.   1708
   7721   78   709   708   321
 + 172   6089   8621   9286   61
             + 731   +   37   +   636   + 8926

*Check each sum by adding from bottom to top. If an answer is incorrect, find the correct sum. **See Example 8.***

25. ____   26. ____   27. ____   28. ____
   179   17   4713   6 215
   214   296   28   744
 + 376   713   615   36
   759   +   94   +   64   + 4 284
            1220   5420   11,279

Using the map below, find the shortest route between each pair of cities.
See Examples 6 and 7.

29. Southtown and Rena

30. Elk Hill and Oakton

31. Thomasville and Murphy

32. Austin and Wilson

Solve each application problem.

33. The sale price for a basic auto tune-up is $159, a tire rotation is $24, and an oil change is $29. Find the total cost for all the services.

34. Jane Lim bought an 11-piece set of golf clubs for $249, a dozen golf balls for $12, golf shoes for $109, and a golf glove for $20. How much did she spend in all? (*Source:* Golfsmith.)

35. There are 413 women and 286 men on the sales staff. How many people are on the sales staff?

36. One department in an office building has 283 employees while another department has 218 employees. How many employees are in the two departments?

37. According to the 2010 census, the two states with the highest populations are California with 37,253,956 people and Texas with 25,145,561 people. How many people live in those two states? (*Source:* U.S. Census Bureau.)

38. The two states with the smallest populations are Wyoming with 563,626 people and Vermont with 625,741 people. What is the total population of the two states? (*Source:* U.S. Census Bureau.)

Find the perimeter of each figure. Perimeter is the total distance around the outside edges of a flat shape.

39.

98 inches
49 inches
49 inches
98 inches

40.

65 meters
73 meters
73 meters
98 meters

41.

286 feet
114 feet
308 feet

42.

206 yards 197 yards
109 yards
109 yards
327 yards

R.2 Subtracting Whole Numbers

Suppose you have $18, and you spend $15 for food. You then have $3 left. There are two different ways of looking at these numbers.

As an addition problem:

$$\$15 \;+\; \$3 \;=\; \$18$$

Amount spent   Amount left   Original amount

As a subtraction problem:

$$\$18 \;-\; \$15 \;=\; \$3$$

Original amount   Subtraction symbol   Amount spent   Amount left

OBJECTIVES

1 Change addition problems to subtraction problems or the reverse.

2 Identify the minuend, subtrahend, and difference.

3 Subtract when no regrouping is needed.

4 Use addition to check subtraction answers.

5 Subtract with regrouping.

6 Use subtraction to solve application problems.

OBJECTIVE ▸ 1 **Change addition problems to subtraction problems or the reverse.** As this example shows, an addition problem can be changed to a subtraction problem and a subtraction problem can be changed to an addition problem.

EXAMPLE 1 Changing Addition Problems to Subtraction

Change each addition problem to a subtraction problem.

(a) $4 + 1 = 5$

Two subtraction problems are possible, as shown below.

$$5 - 1 = 4 \quad \text{or} \quad 5 - 4 = 1$$

These figures show each subtraction problem.

$$5 - 1 = 4 \qquad\qquad 5 - 4 = 1$$

(b) $10 + 17 = 27$

$$27 - 17 = 10 \quad \text{or} \quad 27 - 10 = 17$$

⋯⋯⋯⋯⋯⋯⋯⋯⋯⋯⋯⋯⋯⋯⋯⋯ **Work Problem 1 at the Side.** ▶

EXAMPLE 2 Changing Subtraction Problems to Addition

Change each subtraction problem to an addition problem.

(a) $8 - 3 = 5$

$$8 = 3 + 5$$

It is also correct to write $8 = 5 + 3$ (using the commutative property).

⋯⋯⋯⋯⋯⋯⋯⋯⋯⋯⋯⋯⋯⋯⋯⋯⋯ **Continued on Next Page**

1 Write two subtraction problems for each addition problem.

(a) $4 + 3 = 7$

(b) $6 + 5 = 11$

(c) $150 + 220 = 370$

(d) $623 + 55 = 678$

Answers

1. **(a)** $7 - 3 = 4$ or $7 - 4 = 3$
   (b) $11 - 5 = 6$ or $11 - 6 = 5$
   (c) $370 - 220 = 150$ or $370 - 150 = 220$
   (d) $678 - 55 = 623$ or $678 - 623 = 55$

2 Write an addition problem for each subtraction problem.

(a) $5 - 3 = 2$

(b) $8 - 3 = 5$

(c) $21 - 15 = 6$

(d) $58 - 42 = 16$

3 Subtract.

(a) $\begin{array}{r} 56 \\ -31 \end{array}$

(b) $\begin{array}{r} 38 \\ -14 \end{array}$

(c) $\begin{array}{r} 378 \\ -235 \end{array}$

(d) $\begin{array}{r} 3927 \\ -2614 \end{array}$

(e) $\begin{array}{r} 5464 \\ -324 \end{array}$

Answers

2. (a) $5 = 3 + 2$ (b) $8 = 3 + 5$
(c) $21 = 15 + 6$ (d) $58 = 42 + 16$
3. (a) 25 (b) 24 (c) 143 (d) 1313
(e) 5140

(b) $19 - 14 = 5$
$19 = 14 + 5$

(c) $290 - 130 = 160$
$290 = 130 + 160$

◀ **Work Problem 2 at the Side.**

OBJECTIVE ▶ 2 Identify the minuend, subtrahend, and difference. In subtraction, as in addition, the numbers in a problem have names. For example, in the problem $8 - 5 = 3$, the number 8 is the **minuend,** 5 is the **subtrahend,** and 3 is the **difference** or answer.

$$8 \quad - \quad 5 \quad = 3 \leftarrow \text{Difference (answer)}$$
$$\underset{\text{Minuend}}{\uparrow} \qquad \underset{\text{Subtrahend}}{\uparrow}$$

$\begin{array}{r} 8 \leftarrow \text{Minuend} \\ -5 \leftarrow \text{Subtrahend} \\ \hline 3 \leftarrow \text{Difference} \end{array}$

OBJECTIVE ▶ 3 Subtract when no regrouping is needed. Subtract two numbers by lining up the numbers in columns so that the digits in the ones place are in the same column, tens are in the same column, and so on. Then, subtract by columns, starting at the right with the ones column.

EXAMPLE 3 Subtracting Two Numbers without Regrouping

Ones digits are lined up in the same column.

(a) $\begin{array}{r} 53 \\ -21 \\ \hline 32 \end{array}$ Subtract in the ones column first.

3 ones − 1 one = 2 ones
5 tens − 2 tens = 3 tens

Ones digits are lined up.

(b) $\begin{array}{r} 385 \\ -165 \\ \hline 220 \end{array}$ ← 5 ones − 5 ones = 0 ones

8 tens − 6 tens = 2 tens
3 hundreds − 1 hundred = 2 hundreds

(c) $\begin{array}{r} 9837 \\ -\ 210 \\ \hline 9627 \end{array}$ ← 7 ones − 0 ones = 7 ones

3 tens − 1 ten = 2 tens
8 hundreds − 2 hundreds = 6 hundreds
9 thousands − 0 thousands = 9 thousands

◀ **Work Problem 3 at the Side.**

OBJECTIVE ▶ 4 Use addition to check subtraction answers. You can check $8 - 3 = 5$ by *adding* 3 and 5.

$$3 + 5 = 8 \quad \text{so} \quad 8 - 3 = 5 \quad \text{is correct.}$$

EXAMPLE 4 Checking Subtraction

Use addition to check each answer. If incorrect, find the correct answer.

(a)   89
    − 47
    ⎯⎯
    42

Rewrite as an addition problem.

Subtraction problem
{
   89
   − 47
   ⎯⎯
   42
   ⎯⎯
   89
}
Addition problem
   47
   + 42
   ⎯⎯
   89

Because 47 + 42 = 89, the subtraction was done correctly.

(b) 72 − 41 = 21

Rewrite as an addition problem.

Does   72 = 41 + 21? ◁ 41 + 21 = 62, *not* 72, so there is an error!

But, 41 + 21 = 62, *not* 72, so the subtraction was done *incorrectly*. Rework the original subtraction to get the correct answer of 31. Then, 41 + 31 = 72.

(c)   374 ◁⎯ Match ⎯┐
    − 141 }141 + 233 = 374   The answer checks.
    ⎯⎯
    233

··········· **Work Problem ④ at the Side.** ▶

OBJECTIVE ▶ ⑤ Subtract with regrouping. If a digit in the minuend is *less* than the one directly below it, **regrouping** is necessary (sometimes called *borrowing*).

EXAMPLE 5 Subtracting with Regrouping

Subtract 19 from 57.

Watch the wording! Subtract 19 **from** 57 is
57 / −19 **not** −57 / 19

Rewrite the problem in vertical format.

   5 7
   −1 9

In the ones column, 7 is *less* than 9, so, in order to subtract, you must regroup 1 ten as 10 ones.

5 tens − 1 ten = 4 tens ⟶ 4 17 ← 1 ten = 10 ones,
                            5̸ 7   and 10 ones + 7 ones = 17 ones
                            −1 9

Now subtract 17 ones minus 9 ones in the ones column. Then subtract 4 tens minus 1 ten in the tens column.

                 4 17
                 5̸ 7
                 −1 9
4 tens − 1 ten = 3 tens → 3 8 ← 17 ones − 9 ones = 8 ones

Thus, 57 − 19 = 38. Check by adding 19 and 38. You should get 57.

··········· **Work Problem ⑤ at the Side.** ▶

④ Use addition to check each answer. If incorrect, find the correct answer.

(a)   65   CHECK
    − 23
    ⎯⎯
    42

(b)   46   CHECK
    − 32
    ⎯⎯
    24

(c)   374   CHECK
    − 251
    ⎯⎯
    113

(d)   7531   CHECK
    − 4301
    ⎯⎯
    3230

⑤ Find each difference.

(a)   67
    − 38

(b)   97
    − 29

(c)   31
    − 17

(d)   863
    − 47

(e)   762
    − 157

Answers

4. (a) 23 + 42 = 65; correct
   (b) 32 + 24 ≠ 46; incorrect; should be 14
   (c) 251 + 113 ≠ 374; incorrect; should be 123
   (d) 4301 + 3230 = 7531; correct
5. (a) 29 (b) 68 (c) 14 (d) 816 (e) 605

6 Subtract.

(a) $\begin{array}{r} 354 \\ -\ 82 \\ \hline \end{array}$

(b) $\begin{array}{r} 457 \\ -\ 68 \\ \hline \end{array}$

(c) $\begin{array}{r} 874 \\ -\ 486 \\ \hline \end{array}$

(d) $\begin{array}{r} 1437 \\ -\ 988 \\ \hline \end{array}$

(e) $\begin{array}{r} 8739 \\ -\ 3892 \\ \hline \end{array}$

Answers

6. (a) 272 **(b)** 389 **(c)** 388 **(d)** 449
   (e) 4847

| EXAMPLE 6 | Subtracting with Regrouping |

Subtract, regrouping when necessary.

(a) $\begin{array}{r} 7856 \\ -\ 137 \\ \hline \end{array}$

Regroup 1 ten as 10 ones.

10 ones + 6 ones = 16 ones

$\begin{array}{r} \overset{4\ 16}{7\ 8\ \cancel{5}\ \cancel{6}} \\ -\ 1\ 3\ 7 \\ \hline 7\ 7\ 1\ 9 \end{array}$ ← Difference

(b) $\begin{array}{r} 635 \\ -\ 546 \\ \hline \end{array}$

Regroup 1 ten as 10 ones.

10 ones + 5 ones = 15 ones

$\begin{array}{r} \overset{2\ 15}{6\ \cancel{3}\ \cancel{5}} \\ -\ 5\ 4\ 6 \\ \hline 9 \end{array}$

Need to regroup further because 2 is less than 4 in tens column.

Regroup 1 hundred as 10 tens.

10 tens + 2 tens = 12 tens

$\begin{array}{r} \overset{5\ 12\ 15}{\cancel{6}\ \cancel{3}\ \cancel{5}} \\ -\ 5\ 4\ 6 \\ \hline 8\ 9 \end{array}$ ← Difference

(c) $\begin{array}{r} 412 \\ -\ 225 \\ \hline \end{array}$

$\begin{array}{r} \overset{0\ 12}{4\ \cancel{1}\ \cancel{2}} \\ -\ 2\ 2\ 5 \\ \hline 7 \end{array}$

Need to regroup further because 0 is less than 2 in tens column.

$\begin{array}{r} \overset{3\ 10\ 12}{\cancel{4}\ \cancel{1}\ \cancel{2}} \\ -\ 2\ 2\ 5 \\ \hline 1\ 8\ 7 \end{array}$ ← Difference

◀ **Work Problem 6 at the Side.**

Sometimes a minuend has zeros in some of the positions. In such cases, regrouping may be a little more complicated than what we have shown so far.

| EXAMPLE 7 | Regrouping with Zeros |

Subtract.

$$\begin{array}{r} 4607 \\ -\ 3168 \\ \hline \end{array}$$

There are no tens that can be regrouped into ones. So you must first regroup 1 hundred as 10 tens.

Regroup 1 hundred as 10 tens.

Write 10 tens.

$\begin{array}{r} \overset{5\ 10}{4\ \cancel{6}\ \cancel{0}\ 7} \\ -\ 3\ 1\ 6\ 8 \\ \hline \end{array}$

Now regroup 1 ten as 10 ones.

Regroup 1 ten as 10 ones;
10 tens − 1 ten = 9 tens
10 ones + 7 ones = 17 ones

$\begin{array}{r} \overset{5\ \overset{9}{10}\ 17}{4\ \cancel{6}\ \cancel{0}\ \cancel{7}} \\ -\ 3\ 1\ 6\ 8 \\ \hline 9 \end{array}$

-- **Continued on Next Page**

Complete the problem.

$$
\begin{array}{r}
\overset{9}{} \\
\overset{5\ \ 10\ 17}{} \\
4\ 6\ 0\ 7 \\
-3\ 1\ 6\ 8 \\
\hline
1\ 4\ 3\ 9
\end{array}
\leftarrow \text{Difference}
$$

Check by adding 1439 and 3168; you should get 4607.

··· **Work Problem 7 at the Side.** ▶

EXAMPLE 8 Regrouping with Zeros

Find each difference.

(a) $\begin{array}{r} 708 \\ -\ 149 \\ \hline \end{array}$

Write 10 tens. ─────────╮   ┌───── Regroup 1 ten as 10 ones.

Regroup 1 hundred ───→ $\overset{9}{6}\ \overset{}{10}\ \overset{}{18}$ ◄─── 10 ones + 8 ones = 18 ones
as 10 tens.

$$
\begin{array}{r}
7\ \cancel{0}\ 8 \\
-1\ 4\ 9 \\
\hline
5\ 5\ 9
\end{array}
$$

(b) $\begin{array}{r} 380 \\ -\ 276 \\ \hline \end{array}$

Regroup 1 ten ─────────╮   ┌───── Write 10 ones.
as 10 ones.

$$
\begin{array}{r}
7\ 10 \\
3\ 8\ \cancel{0} \\
-2\ 7\ 6 \\
\hline
1\ 0\ 4
\end{array}
$$

(c) $\begin{array}{r} 9000 \\ -\ 6999 \\ \hline \end{array}$

$$
\begin{array}{r}
9\ \ \ 9 \\
8\ 10\ 10\ 10 \\
9\ \cancel{0}\ \cancel{0}\ \cancel{0} \\
-6\ 9\ 9\ 9 \\
\hline
2\ 0\ 0\ 1
\end{array}
$$

······················ **Work Problem 8 at the Side.** ▶

Recall that an answer to a subtraction problem can be checked by adding.

EXAMPLE 9 Checking Subtraction

Use addition to check each answer.

                                CHECK

(a) $\begin{array}{r} 613 \\ -\ 275 \\ \hline 338 \end{array}$ ◄─── *Matches* *Correct* $\begin{array}{r} 275 \\ +\ 338 \\ \hline 613 \end{array}$

··· **Continued on Next Page** ▶

---

7 Find each difference.

(a) $\begin{array}{r} 308 \\ -\ 285 \\ \hline \end{array}$

(b) $\begin{array}{r} 206 \\ -\ 148 \\ \hline \end{array}$

(c) $\begin{array}{r} 5073 \\ -\ 1632 \\ \hline \end{array}$

8 Find each difference.

(a) $\begin{array}{r} 405 \\ -\ 267 \\ \hline \end{array}$

(b) $\begin{array}{r} 370 \\ -\ 163 \\ \hline \end{array}$

(c) $\begin{array}{r} 1570 \\ -\ 983 \\ \hline \end{array}$

(d) $\begin{array}{r} 7001 \\ -\ 5193 \\ \hline \end{array}$

(e) $\begin{array}{r} 4000 \\ -\ 1782 \\ \hline \end{array}$

Answers

7. (a) 23 **(b)** 58 **(c)** 3441
8. (a) 138 **(b)** 207 **(c)** 587 **(d)** 1808
   (e) 2218

9 Use addition to check each answer. If an answer is incorrect, find the correct answer.

(a)
```
    425        CHECK
  − 368
    ----
     57
```

(b)
```
    670        CHECK
  − 439
    ----
    241
```

(c)
```
  14,726       CHECK
  − 8 839
   ------
    5 887
```

CHECK

(b)
```
    1915  ←              1635
  − 1635     Matches   + 280
    ----     Correct     ----
     280  →            → 1915
```

CHECK

(c)
```
  15,803  ←                 7 325
  − 7 325    Does not match  + 8 578
   ------     Error           ------
    8 578  →               → 15,903
```

Rework the original problem to get the correct answer, 8478. Then, 7325 + 8478 *does* equal 15,803.

◄ **Work Problem 9** at the Side.

OBJECTIVE ➤ **6** **Use subtraction to solve application problems.**

EXAMPLE 10 **Applying Subtraction Skills**

Diana Lopez drives a delivery truck. Using the table below, decide how many more deliveries were made by Ms. Lopez on Monday than on Thursday.

10 Use the table from **Example 10** at the right.

(a) How many fewer deliveries did Ms. Lopez make on Tuesday than on Friday?

(b) What was the difference in the number of deliveries on Tuesday from the number on Wednesday?

(c) How many more deliveries did she make on Thursday than on Saturday?

PACKAGE DELIVERY (LOPEZ)

Day	Number of Deliveries
Monday	137
Tuesday	126
Wednesday	119
Thursday	89
Friday	147
Saturday	0

Ms. Lopez made 137 deliveries on Monday, but had only 89 deliveries on Thursday. Find how many more deliveries were made on Monday than on Thursday by subtracting 89 from 137.

```
   137  ← Deliveries on Monday
 −  89  ← Deliveries on Thursday
   ----
    48  ← More deliveries on Monday
```

Ms. Lopez made 48 more deliveries on Monday than she made on Thursday.

◄ **Work Problem 10** at the Side.

Answers

9. (a) 368 + 57 = 425; correct
(b) 439 + 241 ≠ 670; incorrect; should be 231
(c) 8839 + 5887 = 14,726; correct
10. (a) 21 fewer deliveries
(b) 7 fewer deliveries on Wednesday
(c) 89 more deliveries

R.2 Exercises

FOR EXTRA HELP

 Download the MyDashBoard App

 MyMathLab®

Use addition to check each subtraction. If an answer is incorrect, find the correct answer. **See Examples 3 and 4.**

1. 89
    − 27
    ‾‾‾‾
    63

2. 47
    − 35
    ‾‾‾‾
    13

3. 382
    − 261
    ‾‾‾‾
    131

4. 838
    − 516
    ‾‾‾‾
    322

Find each difference, regrouping when necessary. **See Examples 5–8.**

5. 36
    − 28

6. 97
    − 39

7. 83
    − 58

8. 65
    − 28

9. 45
    − 29

10. 93
    − 37

11. 719
    − 658

12. 916
    − 618

13. 771
    − 252

14. 973
    − 788

15. 9861
    − 684

16. 6171
    − 1182

17. 9988
    − 2399

18. 3576
    − 1658

19. 38,335
    − 29,476

20. 61,278
    − 3 559

21. 40
    − 37

22. 80
    − 73

23. 60
    − 37

24. 70
    − 27

25. 6020
    − 4078

26. 7050
    − 6045

27. 8503
    − 2816

28. 16,004
    − 5 087

29. 80,705
    − 61,667

30. 72,000
    − 44,234

31. 66,000
    −   444

32. 77,000
    −   308

33. 20,080
    −   96

34. 80,056
    −   69

Use addition to check each subtraction. If an answer is incorrect, find the correct answer. **See Example 9.**

35. 3070
    − 576
    ‾‾‾‾
    2596

36. 1439
    − 1169
    ‾‾‾‾
    270

37. 27,600
    −   807
    ‾‾‾‾‾‾
    26,793

38. 34,021
    − 33,708
    ‾‾‾‾‾‾
    727

Solve each application problem. ***See Example 10.***

39. Swimming laps burns 255 calories in 30 minutes. Hiking burns 185 calories in 30 minutes. How many fewer calories are burned in 30 minutes by hiking than by swimming?

40. Lynn Couch had $553 in her bank account. She paid $308 for school fees. How much is left in her account?

41. An airplane was carrying 254 passengers. When it landed in Atlanta, 183 passengers got off and 109 passengers got on. How many passengers were on the plane then?

42. On Tuesday, 5822 people went to a soccer game, and on Friday, 7994 people went to a soccer game. How many more people went to the game on Friday? What was the total attendance at the two games?

This table shows the median yearly earnings for various occupations. Use the table to answer Exercises 43 and 44.

ALL WALKS OF LIFE

Median yearly earnings for selected occupations; starting salaries are lower

Accountant (CPA)	$61,690
Auto mechanic	$35,790
Computer programmer	$74,900
Licensed practical nurse (LPN)	$41,365
Medical secretary	$31,820
Registered nurse (RN)	$67,720
State police officer	$55,620
Elementary school teacher	$54,330

Source: U.S. Department of Labor *Occupational Outlook Handbook.*

43. **(a)** Identify the occupations with the highest and lowest earnings.

(b) What is the difference in the yearly earnings for these two occupations?

44. **(a)** How much less are the yearly earnings of an auto mechanic than a state police officer?

(b) How much more are the yearly earnings of a registered nurse than a licensed practical nurse?

45. Downtown Toronto's skyline is dominated by the CN Tower, which rises 1815 feet. The Willis Tower in Chicago is 1451 feet high. Find the difference in height between the two structures. (*Source: World Almanac and Book of Facts.*)

CN Tower Willis Tower

46. The fastest animal in the world, the peregrine falcon, dives at 242 miles per hour. A Boeing 747 cruises at 560 miles per hour. How much faster does the plane cruise than the falcon dives? (*Source: Audubon magazine.*)

Diving peregrine **242 mph**   Boeing 747 **560 mph**

R.3 Multiplying Whole Numbers

Suppose we want to know the total number of computers in a computer lab. The computers are arranged in three rows with four computers in each row. Adding the number 4 a total of 3 times gives 12.

$$4 + 4 + 4 = 12$$

This result is illustrated below. There are 4 computers in each row.

4

4

+ 4
―――
12

3 rows

OBJECTIVE ▶ **1** **Identify the parts of a multiplication problem.** Multiplication is a shortcut for repeated addition. The numbers being multiplied are called **factors.** The answer is called the **product.** The product of 3 and 4 can be written with the symbol $\times$, a raised dot, parentheses, or, in computer work, an asterisk.

$3 \leftarrow$ Factor (also called *multiplicand*)
$\underline{\times\ 4} \leftarrow$ Factor (also called *multiplier*)
$12 \leftarrow$ Product (answer)

$3 \times 4 = 12 \quad 3 \cdot 4 = 12 \quad (3)(4) = 12 \quad 3 * 4 = 12$

Raised dot   In computer work

Work Problem ❶ at the Side. ▶

Commutative Property of Multiplication

By the **commutative property of multiplication,** changing the *order* of two factors does *not* change the product.

For example: $3 \times 5 = 15$ and $5 \times 3 = 15$ Both products are 15.

CAUTION

Remember, addition also has a commutative property. For example, $4 + 2$ has the same sum as $2 + 4$. Subtraction, however, is ***not*** commutative.

EXAMPLE 1   Multiplying Two Numbers

Multiply. (Remember, a raised dot means to multiply.) Do the work mentally.

(a) $3 \times 4 = 12$ By the commutative property, $4 \times 3 = 12$ also.

(b) $6 \cdot 0 = 0$ The product of any number and 0 is 0; if you give no money to each of 6 relatives, you give no money.

(c) $(4)(8) = 32$ By the commutative property, $(8)(4) = 32$ also.

Work Problem ❷ at the Side. ▶

OBJECTIVES

1 Identify the parts of a multiplication problem.

2 Do chain multiplications.

3 Multiply by single-digit numbers.

4 Multiply quickly by numbers ending in zeros.

5 Multiply by numbers having more than one digit.

6 Use multiplication to solve application problems.

---

❶ Identify the factors and the product in each multiplication problem.

(a) $3 \times 6 = 18$

(b) $32 = 8 \times 4$

(c) $5 \cdot 7 = 35$

(d) $(3)(9) = 27$

❷ Multiply. Do the work mentally. Then use the commutative property to write another multiplication problem and find the product.

(a) 4×7

(b) 0×9

(c) $8 \cdot 6$

(d) $5 \cdot 5$

(e) $(3)(8)$

Answers

1. **(a)** factors: 3, 6; product: 18
   (b) factors: 8, 4; product: 32
   (c) factors: 5, 7; product: 35
   (d) factors: 3, 9; product: 27
2. **(a)** 28; $7 \times 4 = 28$ **(b)** 0; $9 \times 0 = 0$
   (c) 48; $6 \cdot 8 = 48$ **(d)** 25; no change
   (e) 24; $(8)(3) = 24$

3 Find each product.

(a) $2 \times 3 \times 4$

(b) $6 \cdot 1 \cdot 5$

(c) $(8)(3)(0)$

(d) $3 \times 3 \times 7$

(e) $4 \cdot 2 \cdot 8$

(f) $(2)(2)(9)$

OBJECTIVE **2** **Do chain multiplications.** Some multiplications involve more than two factors.

> **Associative Property of Multiplication**
>
> By the **associative property of multiplication**, changing the *grouping* of factors does *not* change the product.

EXAMPLE 2 **Multiplying Three Numbers**

Multiply $2 \times 3 \times 5$.

$(2 \times 3) \times 5 = 6 \times 5 \ = 30$ Parentheses tell you to multiply 2×3 first.

$2 \times (3 \times 5) = 2 \times 15 = 30$ Parentheses tell you to multiply 3×5 first.

By the associative property, either grouping results in the same product.

> **Calculator Tip**
>
> The calculator approach to **Example 2** above uses chain calculations. Notice that you can enter *all* the factors before pressing the ⊜ key.
>
> 2 ⊗ 3 ⊗ 5 ⊜ 30

◀ **Work Problem** **3** **at the Side.**

OBJECTIVE **3** **Multiply by single-digit numbers.** Regrouping may be needed in multiplication problems with larger factors.

EXAMPLE 3 **Regrouping with Multiplication**

Find each product.

(a) $\begin{array}{r} 53 \\ \times\ 4 \end{array}$

Start by multiplying in the ones column. Multiply 4 times 3 ones.

$\begin{array}{r} 1 \\ 53 \\ \times\ 4 \\ \hline 2 \end{array}$ Write 1 ten in the tens column.

4×3 ones = 12 ones

Write 2 ones in the ones column.

Next, multiply 4 times 5 tens.

$\begin{array}{r} 1 \\ 53 \\ \times\ 4 \\ \hline 2 \end{array}$ 4×5 tens = 20 tens

$\begin{array}{r} 1 \\ 53 \\ \times\ 4 \\ \hline 212 \end{array}$ Add the 1 ten that was written at the top of the tens column.

20 tens + 1 ten = **21** tens

Continued on Next Page

(b) 724
× 5

Work as shown below.

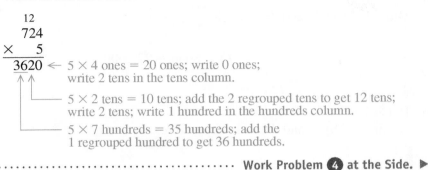

12
724
× 5
3620 ← 5 × 4 ones = 20 ones; write 0 ones;
write 2 tens in the tens column.

5 × 2 tens = 10 tens; add the 2 regrouped tens to get 12 tens;
write 2 tens; write 1 hundred in the hundreds column.

5 × 7 hundreds = 35 hundreds; add the
1 regrouped hundred to get 36 hundreds.

··· Work Problem **4** at the Side. ▶

OBJECTIVE **4** **Multiply quickly by numbers ending in zeros.** The product of two whole number factors is also called a **multiple** of either factor. For example, since 4 • 2 = 8, the number 8 is a multiple of 4, and 8 is also a multiple of 2. Multiples of 10 are very useful when multiplying. A *multiple of 10* is a whole number that ends in 0, such as 10, 20, or 30; 100, 200, or 300; 1000, 2000, or 3000; and so on. There is a quick way to multiply by multiples of 10. Look at the following examples.

$$26 \times 1 = 26$$
$$26 \times 10 = 260$$
$$26 \times 100 = 2600$$
$$26 \times 1000 = 26{,}000$$

Do you see a pattern in the multiplications? These examples suggest the following rule.

Multiplying by Multiples of 10

To multiply a whole number by 10, by 100, or by 1000, attach one, two, or three zeros to the right of the whole number.

EXAMPLE 4   **Multiplying by Multiples of 10**

Multiply.

(a) 59 × 10 = 590
└──── Attach 0

(b) 100 × 74 = 7400
└──── Attach 00

(c) 803 × 1000 = 803,000
└──── Attach 000

··· Work Problem **5** at the Side. ▶

You can also find the product of other multiples of ten by attaching zeros.

---

4 Find each product.

(a) 52
× 5

(b) 79
× 0

(c) 862
× 9

(d) 2831
× 7

(e) 4714
× 8

5 Multiply by attaching zeros.

(a) 45 × 10

(b) 102 × 100

(c) 1000 × 571

(d) 100 × 3625

(e) 69 × 1000

Answers

4. **(a)** 260 **(b)** 0 **(c)** 7758 **(d)** 19,817
(e) 37,712
5. **(a)** 450 **(b)** 10,200 **(c)** 571,000
(d) 362,500 **(e)** 69,000

6 Find each product by attaching zeros.

(a) 14×50

(b) $(68)(400)$

(c) $\begin{array}{r} 180 \\ \times\ 30 \\ \hline \end{array}$

(d) $\begin{array}{r} 6100 \\ \times\ \ \ 90 \\ \hline \end{array}$

(e) $\begin{array}{r} 800 \\ \times\ 200 \\ \hline \end{array}$

(f) $(5000)(700)$

(g) $(9)(20,000)$

Answers

6. (a) 700 (b) 27,200 (c) 5400
   (d) 549,000 (e) 160,000 (f) 3,500,000
   (g) 180,000

EXAMPLE 5 **Multiplying with Other Multiples of 10**

Find each product.

(a) 75×3000

Multiply 75 by 3, and then attach three zeros.

$$\begin{array}{r} 75 \\ \times\ \ 3 \\ \hline 225 \end{array} \qquad 75 \times 3000 = 225{,}000$$

(b) 150×70

Multiply 15 by 7, and then attach two zeros.

$$\begin{array}{r} 15 \\ \times\ \ 7 \\ \hline 105 \end{array} \qquad 150 \times 70 = 10{,}500$$

◀ Work Problem **6** at the Side.

OBJECTIVE 5 Multiply by numbers having more than one digit. The next example shows multiplication when both factors have more than one digit.

EXAMPLE 6 **Multiply by Numbers with More Than One Digit**

Multiply.

(a) $(46)(23)$

Rewrite the problem in vertical format. Then start by multiplying 46 by 3.

$$\begin{array}{r} 1 \\ 46 \\ \times\ \ 3 \\ \hline 138 \end{array} \leftarrow 46 \times 3 = 138$$

Next, multiply 46 by 20.

$$\begin{array}{r} 1 \\ 46 \\ \times\ 20 \\ \hline 138 \\ 920 \end{array} \leftarrow 46 \times 20 = 920$$

Add the results.

$$\begin{array}{r} 46 \\ \times\ 23 \\ \hline 138 \leftarrow 46 \times 3 \\ +\ 920 \leftarrow 46 \times 20 \\ \hline 1058 \leftarrow \text{Add to find the product.} \end{array}$$

Both 138 and 920 are called *partial products*.
To save time, the 0 in 920 is usually not written.

$$\begin{array}{r} 46 \\ \times\ 23 \\ \hline 138 \\ 92 \\ \hline 1058 \end{array}$$

0 not written. Be very careful to place the 2 in the tens column.

Continued on Next Page

(b)
```
      233
  ×   132
      466
      699    Tens lined up
      233    Hundreds lined up
   30,756 ← Product
```

(c)
```
   538
  × 46
```

First multiply by 6.

```
     24     ⟵ Regrouping is needed here.
    538
  ×  46
   3228
```

Now multiply by 4, being careful to line up the tens.

```
     13
     24
    538
  ×  46
   3228  ┐— Add the partial products.
   2152  ┘
  24,748
```

······················ **Work Problem 7 at the Side.** ▶

When 0 appears in the multiplier, be sure to move the partial product to the left to account for the position held by the 0.

EXAMPLE 7   Multiplication with Zeros

Find each product.

(a)
```
     137
  ×  306
     822
     000    Tens lined up
     411    Hundreds lined up
   41,922
```

(b)
```
      1406              1406
    ×2001            ×2001
      1406              1406
    0000 ← 0 to line up tens
    0000 ← 0 to line up hundreds    281200
   2812                          
  2,813,406             2,813,406
```

Zeros are written so that you start writing the partial product 2812 in the *thousands* column.

CAUTION

In **Example 7(b)** above, in the solution on the right, be careful to insert zeros so that thousands are lined up in the thousands column.

···················· **Continued on Next Page**

7 Find each product.

(a)
```
    38
  × 15
```

(b)
```
    31
  × 43
```

(c)
```
    67
  × 59
```

(d)
```
   234
  × 73
```

(e)
```
   835
  × 189
```

Answers

7. (a) 570 **(b)** 1333 **(c)** 3953
(d) 17,082 **(e)** 157,815

8 Find each product.

(a) 28
 × 60

(b) 817
 × 30

(c) 481
 × 206

(d) 3526
 × 6002

9 Find the total cost of these items.

(a) 36 months of cable TV costing $79 each month

(b) 15 laptop computers priced at $1090 each

(c) 60 months of car payments at $389 per month

········◀ **Work Problem 8 at the Side.**

OBJECTIVE **6** Use multiplication to solve application problems.

EXAMPLE 8 **Applying Multiplication Skills**

Find the total cost of 24 months of Internet service at $59 per month.

Approach To find the total cost, multiply the cost for one month of service ($59) by the number of months (24).

Solution Multiply $59 by 24.

$$\begin{array}{r} 59 \\ \times\ 24 \\ \hline 236 \\ 118\ \ \\ \hline 1416 \end{array}$$

The total cost of 24 months of Internet service is $1416.

Calculator Tip

If you are using a calculator for **Example 8** above, press the following keys.

59 ⊗ 24 ⊜ **1416**

········◀ **Work Problem 9 at the Side.**

Answers

8. (a) 1680 (b) 24,510 (c) 99,086
 (d) 21,163,052
9. (a) $2844 (b) $16,350 (c) $23,340

R.3 Exercises

  MyMathLab®

Find each product. Try to do the work mentally. **See Examples 1 and 2.**

1. $3 \times 1 \times 3$

2. $2 \times 8 \times 2$

3. $9 \times 1 \times 7$

4. $2 \times 4 \times 5$

5. $9 \cdot 5 \cdot 0$

6. $6 \cdot 0 \cdot 8$

7. $(4)(1)(6)$

8. $(1)(5)(7)$

9. $(2)(3)(6)$

10. $(4)(1)(9)$

Find each product. **See Examples 3–7.**

11. $\begin{array}{r} 35 \\ \times\ 7 \\ \hline \end{array}$

12. $\begin{array}{r} 76 \\ \times\ 9 \\ \hline \end{array}$

13. $\begin{array}{r} 28 \\ \times\ 6 \\ \hline \end{array}$

14. $\begin{array}{r} 83 \\ \times\ 5 \\ \hline \end{array}$

15. $\begin{array}{r} 3182 \\ \times\ \ \ 6 \\ \hline \end{array}$

16. $\begin{array}{r} 7326 \\ \times\ \ \ 5 \\ \hline \end{array}$

17. $\begin{array}{r} 36{,}921 \\ \times\ \ \ \ \ 7 \\ \hline \end{array}$

18. $\begin{array}{r} 28{,}116 \\ \times\ \ \ \ \ 4 \\ \hline \end{array}$

19. $\begin{array}{r} 125 \\ \times\ 100 \\ \hline \end{array}$

20. $\begin{array}{r} 246 \\ \times\ 100 \\ \hline \end{array}$

21. $\begin{array}{r} 1485 \\ \times\ \ \ 30 \\ \hline \end{array}$

22. $\begin{array}{r} 8522 \\ \times\ \ \ 50 \\ \hline \end{array}$

23. $\begin{array}{r} 900 \\ \times\ 300 \\ \hline \end{array}$

24. $\begin{array}{r} 400 \\ \times\ 700 \\ \hline \end{array}$

25. $\begin{array}{r} 43{,}000 \\ \times\ \ \ 2000 \\ \hline \end{array}$

26. $\begin{array}{r} 11{,}000 \\ \times\ \ \ 9000 \\ \hline \end{array}$

27. $\begin{array}{r} 68 \\ \times\ 22 \\ \hline \end{array}$

28. $\begin{array}{r} 82 \\ \times\ 32 \\ \hline \end{array}$

29. $(83)(45)$

30. $(43)(27)$

31. $(32)(475)$

32. $(67)(218)$

33. $(729)(45)$

34. $(681)(47)$

35. $\begin{array}{r} 538 \\ \times\ 342 \\ \hline \end{array}$

36. $\begin{array}{r} 3228 \\ \times\ \ \ 751 \\ \hline \end{array}$

37. $\begin{array}{r} 8162 \\ \times\ \ \ 407 \\ \hline \end{array}$

38. $\begin{array}{r} 528 \\ \times\ 106 \\ \hline \end{array}$

39. $\begin{array}{r} 6310 \\ \times\ \ 3008 \\ \hline \end{array}$

40. $\begin{array}{r} 3533 \\ \times\ \ 5001 \\ \hline \end{array}$

Solve each application problem. ***See Example 8.***

41. Giant kelp plants in the ocean can grow 18 inches each day. How much could kelp grow in two weeks? How much could it grow in a 30-day month? (*Source:* Natural Bridges State Park, CA.)

42. A hospital has 20 bottles of thyroid medication, with each bottle containing 2500 tablets. How many of these tablets does the hospital have in all?

43. There are 12 tomato plants to a flat. If a garden center has 48 flats, find the total number of tomato plants.

44. A hummingbird's wings beat about 65 times per second, a chickadee's wings about 27 times per second. How many times does each bird's wings beat in one minute? (*Source: Birder's Handbook.*)

45. A new Prius hybrid automobile gets 48 miles per gallon on the highway. How many highway miles can it travel on 11 gallons of gas?

46. Find the total cost of 16 gallons of paint at $36 per gallon.

Ruby-throated hummingbird
65 wing beats per second

Use addition, subtraction, or multiplication to solve each problem.

47. The distance from Reno, Nevada, to the Atlantic Ocean is 2695 miles, while the distance from Reno to the Pacific Ocean is 255 miles. How much farther is it to the Atlantic Ocean than it is to the Pacific Ocean? If you make three round trips from Reno to the Atlantic Ocean, how many frequent flier miles will you earn?

48. The largest living land mammal is the African elephant, and the largest mammal of all time is the blue whale. An African bull elephant may weigh 15,225 pounds and a blue whale may weigh 12 to 25 times that amount. Find the range of weights for the blue whale and the difference between the lightest and heaviest. (*Source: Big Book of Knowledge.*)

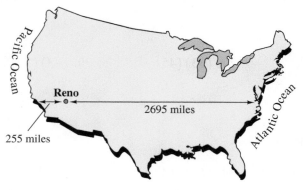

49. A high-fat meal contains 1406 calories, while a low-fat meal contains 348 calories. How many more calories are in seven high-fat meals than in seven low-fat meals?

50. Dannie Sanchez bought four tires at $110 each, two seat covers at $49 each, and a set of socket wrenches for $20. Sales tax was $43. Find the total amount that he spent.

R.4 Dividing Whole Numbers

$12 is divided equally among 3 children. Each child gets $4, as shown here.

$12 total   3 equal parts
$4 in each part

OBJECTIVES

1. Write division problems in three ways.
2. Identify the parts of a division problem.
3. Divide 0 by a number.
4. Recognize that division by 0 is undefined.
5. Divide a number by itself.
6. Use short division.
7. Use multiplication to check quotients.
8. Use tests for divisibility.

OBJECTIVE 1 Write division problems in three ways. Recall that $3 \cdot 4$, 3×4, and $(3)(4)$ are different ways to write the *multiplication* of 3 and 4. There are several ways to write 12 *divided* by 3.

Being divided   Divided by   Being divided   Being divided
    ↓   ↓ 4   ↓   ↓
$12 \div 3 = 4$ $3\overline{)12}$ $\dfrac{12}{3} = 4$ $12\,/\,3 = 4$
    ↑   ↑   ↑
Divided by   Being divided   Divided by

                                             ↑
                                        Divided by

We will use three division symbols: $\div$, $\overline{)}$, and —. In algebra the bar, —, is frequently used. In computer science a slash, /, is used.

EXAMPLE 1   Using Division Symbols

Rewrite each division using two other symbols.

(a) $20 \div 4 = 5$ can also be written $4\overline{)20}^{\,5}$ or $\dfrac{20}{4} = 5$

(b) $\dfrac{18}{6} = 3$ can also be written $18 \div 6 = 3$ or $6\overline{)18}^{\,3}$

(c) $5\overline{)40}^{\,8}$ can also be written $40 \div 5 = 8$ or $\dfrac{40}{5} = 8$

·········· **Work Problem ❶ at the Side.** ▶

OBJECTIVE 2 Identify the parts of a division problem. In division, the number being divided is the **dividend,** the number you are dividing by is the **divisor,** and the answer is the **quotient.**

$$\text{dividend} \div \text{divisor} = \text{quotient}$$

$$\text{divisor}\overline{)\text{dividend}}^{\,\text{quotient}} \qquad \dfrac{\text{dividend}}{\text{divisor}} = \text{quotient}$$

EXAMPLE 2   Identifying the Parts in a Division Problem

Identify the dividend, divisor, and quotient.

(a) $35 \div 7 = 5$

$$35 \div 7 = 5 \leftarrow \text{Quotient}$$
Dividend   Divisor

·········· **Continued on Next Page**

1. Rewrite each division using two other symbols.

(a) $48 \div 6 = 8$

(b) $24 \div 6 = 4$

(c) $9\overline{)36}^{\,4}$

(d) $\dfrac{42}{6} = 7$

Answers

1. **(a)** $6\overline{)48}^{\,8}$ and $\dfrac{48}{6} = 8$

   (b) $6\overline{)24}^{\,4}$ and $\dfrac{24}{6} = 4$

   (c) $36 \div 9 = 4$ and $\dfrac{36}{9} = 4$

   (d) $6\overline{)42}^{\,7}$ and $42 \div 6 = 7$

2 Identify the dividend, divisor, and quotient.

(a) $10 \div 2 = 5$

(b) $6 = 30 \div 5$

(c) $\dfrac{28}{7} = 4$

(d) $2\overline{)36}$ (with 18 above)

3 Divide.

(a) $0 \div 9$

(b) $\dfrac{0}{36}$

(c) $57\overline{)0}$

4 Write each division problem as a multiplication problem.

(a) $6\overline{)18}$ (with 3 above)

(b) $\dfrac{28}{4} = 7$

(c) $48 \div 8 = 6$

Answers

2. (a) dividend: 10; divisor: 2; quotient: 5
   (b) dividend: 30; divisor: 5; quotient: 6
   (c) dividend: 28; divisor: 7; quotient: 4
   (d) dividend: 36; divisor: 2; quotient: 18
3. all 0
4. (a) $6 \cdot 3 = 18$ (b) $4 \cdot 7 = 28$
   (c) $8 \cdot 6 = 48$

(b) $\dfrac{100}{20} = 5$

Dividend

$\dfrac{100}{20} = 5 \leftarrow$ Quotient

↑ Divisor

(c) $12\overline{)72}$ (with 6 above)

$6 \leftarrow$ Quotient

$12\overline{)72} \leftarrow$ Dividend

↑ Divisor

◀ **Work Problem 2 at the Side.**

OBJECTIVE **3** **Divide 0 by a number.** If no money, or $0, is divided equally among five people, each person gets $0. There is a general rule for dividing 0.

Dividing 0	
When 0 is divided by any other number (except 0), the quotient is 0.	

EXAMPLE 3 **Dividing 0 by a Number**

Divide.

(a) $0 \div 12 = 0$

(b) $0 \div 1728 = 0$

(c) $\dfrac{0}{375} = 0$

(d) $129\overline{)0}$ (with 0 above)

◀ **Work Problem 3 at the Side.**

Recall that a subtraction such as $8 - 3 = 5$ can be written as the addition $8 = 3 + 5$. In a similar way, any division can be written as a multiplication. For example, $12 \div 3 = 4$ can be written as

$$3 \times 4 = 12 \quad \text{or, by the commutative property,} \quad 4 \times 3 = 12$$

EXAMPLE 4 **Changing Division to Multiplication**

Change each division to multiplication.

(a) $\dfrac{20}{4} = 5$ becomes $4 \cdot 5 = 20$

(b) $8\overline{)48}$ (with 6 above) becomes $8 \cdot 6 = 48$

(c) $72 \div 9 = 8$ becomes $9 \cdot 8 = 72$

◀ **Work Problem 4 at the Side.**

OBJECTIVE ▶ 4 Recognize that division by 0 is undefined. Division by 0 cannot be done. To see why, try to find the answer to this division.

$$9 \div 0 = ?$$

Remember, any division problem can be changed to a multiplication problem.

$$\text{divisor} \cdot \text{quotient} = \text{dividend}$$

If you convert the problem $9 \div 0 = ?$ to its multiplication counterpart, it reads as follows.

$$0 \cdot ? = 9$$

You already know that 0 times any number must always equal 0. Try any number you like to replace the ? and you'll always get 0 instead of 9. Therefore, the division problem $9 \div 0$ *cannot* be done. Mathematicians say it is *undefined* and have agreed never to divide by 0. However, $0 \div 9$ *can* be done. Check by rewriting it as a multiplication problem.

$$0 \div 9 = 0 \quad \text{because} \quad 9 \cdot 0 = 0 \text{ is true.}$$

Dividing by 0

Dividing by 0 cannot be done. We say that *division by 0 is undefined.* It is impossible to calculate an answer.

EXAMPLE 5   **Dividing by 0 Is Undefined**

All of these divisions are *undefined*.

(a) $\dfrac{6}{0}$ is undefined.

> It is **not possible** to divide by 0. Write *undefined* as the answer (**not** 0).

(b) $0\overline{)8}$ is undefined.

(c) $18 \div 0$ is undefined.

Division Involving 0

$$\dfrac{0}{\text{nonzero number}} = 0 \quad \textbf{but} \quad \dfrac{\text{number}}{0} \text{ is } \textit{undefined.}$$

CAUTION

When 0 is the divisor in a problem, write *undefined.*
Never divide by 0.

·········· **Work Problem 5 at the Side.** ▶

🖩 Calculator Tip

Try these two problems on your calculator. Jot down your answers.

$$9 \div 0 = _____ \qquad 0 \div 9 = _____$$

When you try to divide by 0, the calculator cannot do it, so it shows the word "Error" in the display, or the letters "ERR" or "E" (for "error").

---

5 Find the quotient whenever possible.

(a) $\dfrac{8}{0}$

(b) $\dfrac{0}{8}$

(c) $0\overline{)32}$

(d) $32\overline{)0}$

(e) $100 \div 0$

(f) $0 \div 100$

Answers

5. (a) undefined (b) 0 (c) undefined
(d) 0 (e) undefined (f) 0

6 Divide.

(a) $5 \div 5$

(b) $14\overline{)14}$

(c) $\dfrac{37}{37}$

7 Divide using short division.

(a) $2\overline{)18}$

(b) $3\overline{)39}$

(c) $4\overline{)88}$

(d) $2\overline{)462}$

OBJECTIVE ▶ **5** **Divide a number by itself.** What happens when a number is divided by itself? For example, $4 \div 4$ or $97 \div 97$?

> **Dividing a Number by Itself**
>
> When a nonzero number is divided by itself, the quotient is 1.

EXAMPLE 6 **Dividing a Nonzero Number by Itself**

Divide.

(a) $16 \div 16 = 1$

(b) $32\overset{1}{\overline{)32}}$

(c) $\dfrac{57}{57} = 1$

◀ **Work Problem** **6** at the Side.

OBJECTIVE ▶ **6** **Use short division.** **Short division** is a quick method of dividing a number by a one-digit divisor.

EXAMPLE 7 **Using Short Division**

Divide $2\overline{)86}$.

First, divide 8 by 2.

$$2\overset{4}{\overline{)86}} \qquad \frac{8}{2} = 4$$

Next, divide 6 by 2.

$$2\overset{43}{\overline{)86}} \qquad \frac{6}{2} = 3$$

The quotient is 43.

◀ **Work Problem** **7** at the Side.

When two numbers do *not* divide evenly, the leftover portion is called the **remainder.** The remainder is always *less* than the divisor.

EXAMPLE 8 **Using Short Division with a Remainder**

Divide 147 by 4.

Rewrite the problem. $\qquad 4\overline{)147}$

Because 1 cannot be divided by 4, divide 14 by 4.

$$4\overset{3}{\overline{)14^27}} \qquad \frac{14}{4} = 3 \text{ with 2 left over}$$

········ **Continued on Next Page**

Next, divide 27 by 4. The final number left over is the remainder. Write the remainder to the side. "R" stands for remainder.

$$3\ 6\ \textbf{R}3 \qquad \frac{27}{4} = 6 \text{ with 3 left over}$$
$$4\overline{)14^27}$$

The quotient is 36 **R**3.

·· **Work Problem 8** at the Side. ▶

EXAMPLE 9   **Writing Zeros in the Quotient**

Divide 1439 by 7.

Rewrite the problem. Then, divide 14 by 7.

$$2 \qquad \frac{14}{7} = 2 \text{ with 0 left over}$$
$$7\overline{)1439}$$
└── No need to write 0 ──┘

Next, divide 3 by 7. But 7 will not go into 3 even one time, so write a 0 in the quotient.

Be sure to write the 0 in the quotient.
$$20 \qquad \frac{3}{7} = 0 \text{ with 3 left over}$$
$$7\overline{)143^39}$$

Finally, divide 39 by 7.

$$20\ 5\ \textbf{R}4 \qquad \frac{39}{7} = 5 \text{ with 4 left over}$$
$$7\overline{)143^39}$$

The quotient is 205 **R**4.

·· **Work Problem 9** at the Side. ▶

OBJECTIVE ▶ 7 Use multiplication to check quotients.

Checking Division

(divisor × quotient) + remainder = dividend

Parentheses tell you what to do first. In this case, multiply the divisor by the quotient first and then add the remainder.

EXAMPLE 10   **Using Multiplication to Check Division**

Check each quotient.

(a) $5\overline{)458}$ 91 **R**3

(divisor × quotient) + remainder = dividend
↓   ↓   ↓
(5 × 91) + 3
↓
455 + 3 = **458** ← Matches original dividend so the quotient is correct.

·· **Continued on Next Page**

---

8 Divide.

(a) $2\overline{)225}$

(b) $3\overline{)275}$

(c) $4\overline{)538}$

(d) $\dfrac{819}{5}$

9 Divide.

(a) $4\overline{)837}$

(b) $\dfrac{747}{7}$

(c) $5\overline{)4538}$

(d) $8\overline{)2440}$

Answers

8. (a) 112 **R**1   (b) 91 **R**2   (c) 134 **R**2
(d) 163 **R**4
9. (a) 209 **R**1   (b) 106 **R**5   (c) 907 **R**3
(d) 305

10 Check each division. If a quotient is incorrect, find the correct quotient.

(a) $3\overline{)115}$ 38 **R**1

(b) $8\overline{)743}$ 92 **R**2

(c) $4\overline{)1312}$ 328

(d) $5\overline{)2033}$ 46 **R**3

(b) $6\overline{)1258}$ 29 **R**4

(divisor $\times$ quotient) $+$ remainder $=$ dividend

$$(6 \quad \times \quad 29) \quad + \quad 4$$

$$174 \quad + \quad 4 = 178$$

Does **not** match original dividend of 1258

The quotient does *not* check. Rework the original problem to get the correct quotient, 209 **R**4. Then, to check, $(6 \times 209) + 4 = 1254 + 4 = 1258$, the original dividend.

CAUTION

A common error is forgetting to add the remainder. Be sure to add any remainder when checking a division problem.

◄ **Work Problem 10 at the Side.**

OBJECTIVE **8** **Use tests for divisibility.** It is often important to know whether a number is divisible by another number. You will find this useful when working with fractions.

Divisibility

A whole number is *divisible* by another whole number if the remainder is 0.

There are some quick tests you can use to decide whether one number is divisible by another.

Tests for Divisibility

A number is divisible by

2	if it ends in 0, 2, 4, 6, or 8.
3	if the sum of its digits is divisible by 3.
4	if the last two digits make a number that is divisible by 4.
5	if it ends in 0 or 5.
6	if it is divisible by both 2 and 3.
8	if the last three digits make a number that is divisible by 8.
9	if the sum of its digits is divisible by 9.
10	if it ends in 0.

The most commonly used divisibility tests are those for 2, 3, 5, and 10.

Answers

10. (a) correct
   (b) incorrect; should be 92 **R**7
   (c) correct
   (d) incorrect; should be 406 **R**3

Divisibility by 2
A number is divisible by **2** if the number ends in 0, 2, 4, 6, or 8.

EXAMPLE 11 Testing for Divisibility by 2

Which numbers are divisible by 2?

(a) 986

⎵——— Ends in 6

Because the number ends in 6, which is in the list (0, 2, 4, 6, or 8), the number 986 is divisible by 2.

(b) 3255 is *not* divisible by 2.

⎵—— Ends in 5, and *not* in 0, 2, 4, 6, or 8

········ **Work Problem 11 at the Side.** ▶

Divisibility by 3
A number is divisible by **3** if the sum of its digits is divisible by **3.**

EXAMPLE 12 Testing for Divisibility by 3

Which numbers are divisible by 3?

(a) 4251

Add the digits.

4 2 5 1

$4 + 2 + 5 + 1 = 12$

Is 12 divisible by 3? Yes. So the *original* number of 4251 is *also* divisible by 3.

Because 12 is divisible by 3, the number 4251 is divisible by 3.

(b) 29,806

Add the digits.

2 9 8 0 6

$2 + 9 + 8 + 0 + 6 = 25$

Is 25 divisible by 3? No. So the original number of 29,806 is *not* divisible by 3.

Because 25 is *not* divisible by 3, the number 29,806 is *not* divisible by 3.

CAUTION

Be careful when testing for divisibility by *adding the digits*. This method works only when testing for divisibility by 3 or by 9.

········ **Work Problem 12 at the Side.** ▶

11 Which numbers are divisible by 2?

(a) 612

(b) 315

(c) 2714

(d) 36,000

12 Which numbers are divisible by 3?

(a) 836

(b) 7005

(c) 242,913

(d) 102,484

Answers
11. (a), (c), (d)
12. (b) and (c)

13 Which numbers are divisible by 5?

(a) 160

(b) 635

(c) 3381

(d) 108,605

14 Which numbers are divisible by 10?

(a) 290

(b) 218

(c) 2020

(d) 11,670

Divisibility by 5 and by 10

A number is divisible by **5** if it ends in 0 or 5.

A number is divisible by **10** if it ends in 0.

EXAMPLE 13 Determining Divisibility by 5

Which numbers are divisible by 5?

(a) 12,900   ends in 0, so it is divisible by 5.

(b) 4325   ends in 5, so it is divisible by 5.

(c) 592   ends in 2, so it is *not* divisible by 5.

◀ Work Problem **13** at the Side.

EXAMPLE 14 Determining Divisibility by 10

Which numbers are divisible by 10?

(a) 700 and 9140   end in 0, so both numbers are divisible by 10.

(b) 355 and 18,043   do *not* end in 0, so these numbers are *not* divisible by 10.

◀ Work Problem **14** at the Side.

Answers

13. (a), (b), (d)
14. (a), (c), (d)

R.4 Exercises

Download the MyDashBoard App

MyMathLab®

Divide. Then rewrite each division using two other division symbols.
See Examples 1, 3, 5, and 6.

1. $\dfrac{12}{12}$

2. $\dfrac{9}{0}$

3. $24 \div 0$

4. $4 \div 4$

5. $\dfrac{0}{4}$

6. $0 \div 8$

7. $0 \div 12$

8. $\dfrac{0}{7}$

9. $0\overline{)21}$

10. $2 \div 0$

Find each quotient using short division. **See Examples 7–9.** *Also, in Exercises 11–14, identify the dividend, the divisor, and the quotient.* **See Example 2.**

11. $4\overline{)84}$

12. $2\overline{)66}$

13. $9\overline{)324}$

14. $8\overline{)176}$

15. $6\overline{)9125}$

16. $9\overline{)8371}$

17. $6\overline{)1854}$

18. $8\overline{)856}$

19. $4024 \div 4$

20. $16,024 \div 8$

21. $15,019 \div 3$

22. $32,013 \div 8$

23. $\dfrac{26,684}{4}$

24. $\dfrac{16,398}{9}$

25. $\dfrac{74,751}{6}$

26. $\dfrac{72,543}{5}$

27. $\dfrac{71,776}{7}$

28. $\dfrac{77,621}{3}$

29. $\dfrac{128,645}{7}$

30. $\dfrac{172,255}{4}$

Check each quotient. If a quotient is incorrect, find the correct quotient. **See Example 10.**

31. $7\overline{)4692}$ 67 **R**2

32. $9\overline{)5974}$ 663 **R**5

33. $6\overline{)21,409}$ 3 568 **R**5

34. $4\overline{)103,516}$ 25,879

35. $6\overline{)18,023}$ 3 003 **R**5

36. $8\overline{)33,664}$ 4 208

37. $6\overline{)69,140}$ 11,523 **R**2

38. $3\overline{)82,510}$ 2 753 **R**1

Solve each application problem.

39. Kaci Salmon, a supervisor at Albany Electric, earns $184 for an 8-hour shift. The workers she supervises each earn $112 or $152 for an 8-hour shift. What are the hourly wages for Kaci and for her workers?

40. In a hospital weight loss program, Patient A lost 72 pounds in six months, Patient B lost 81 pounds in nine months, and Patient C lost 91 pounds in seven months. On average, how much did each patient lose each month?

41. Six identical delivery vans for Rosita's Bakery cost a total of $111,600. Find the cost of each van.

42. Ted Slauson, the local coordinator of Books for Africa, has collected 2628 donated textbooks. If his group sends an equal number of books to four schools, how many books will each school receive?

A college theater group is looking at two different budgets to cover the cost of props, costumes, and programs for the spring play. They are not sure whether to charge $5, $7, or $9 per ticket. The play's director organized the information in the table at the right. Use the table for Exercises 43–46.

Budget Amount	Number of $5 Tickets	Number of $7 Tickets	Number of $9 Tickets
$1890			
$2205			

43. For the $1890 budget, find the number of tickets that would need to be sold at $5 each; at $7 each; at $9 each. Write your answers in the table above.

44. For the $2205 budget, find the number of tickets that would need to be sold at $5 each; at $7 each; at $9 each. Write your answers in the table above.

45. If the director thinks that 300 tickets can be sold, which ticket price ($5, $7, or $9) is the lowest price that will cover the $1890 budget? How much extra money will there be?

46. If the director thinks that 300 tickets can be sold, which ticket price will cover the $2205 budget? How much money will be left over?

47. Circle the numbers that are

    (a) divisible by 2

       358   2047   190   85

    (b) divisible by 3

       736   10,404   5603   78

    (c) divisible by 5.

       53   13,740   985   5506

48. Circle the numbers that are

    (a) divisible by 2

       443   3500   256   74

    (b) divisible by 3

       26,001   9316   92   840

    (c) divisible by 5.

       5051   95   30,652   710

*Put a ✓ mark in the blank if the number at the left is divisible by the number at the top of each column. Use the divisibility tests from **Examples 11–14.***

	2	3	5	10
49. 30	____	____	____	____
51. 184	____	____	____	____
53. 445	____	____	____	____
55. 903	____	____	____	____
57. 5166	____	____	____	____
59. 21,763	____	____	____	____

	2	3	5	10
50. 25	____	____	____	____
52. 192	____	____	____	____
54. 897	____	____	____	____
56. 500	____	____	____	____
58. 8302	____	____	____	____
60. 32,472	____	____	____	____

R.5 Long Division

Long division is used to divide by a number with more than one digit.

OBJECTIVE ▶ 1 Use long division. In long division, estimate the various numbers by using a *trial divisor* to get a *trial quotient*.

EXAMPLE 1 Using a Trial Divisor and a Trial Quotient

Divide: $42\overline{)3066}$

Because 42 is closer to 40 than to 50, use 4 as a trial divisor.

$$42$$
⤒ Trial divisor is 4.

Try to divide the first digit of the dividend by 4. Because 3 cannot be divided by 4, use the first *two* digits, 30.

$$\frac{30}{4} = 7 \text{ with remainder 2}$$

$$7 \leftarrow \text{Trial quotient is 7.}$$
$$42\overline{)3066}$$

> Be careful to write the 7 over the 6, because $\frac{306}{42}$ is about 7.

Multiply 7 and 42 to get 294; then subtract 294 from 306.

$$
\begin{array}{r}
7 \\
42\overline{)3066} \\
294 \leftarrow 7 \times 42 = 294 \\
\hline
12 \leftarrow 306 - 294 = 12
\end{array}
$$

Bring down the 6 at the right.

$$
\begin{array}{r}
7 \\
42\overline{)3066} \\
294\!\downarrow \\
\hline
126 \leftarrow 6 \text{ brought down}
\end{array}
$$

Use the trial divisor, 4.

$$
\begin{array}{r}
73 \leftarrow \\
42\overline{)3066} \\
294 \\
\hline
126 \leftarrow \text{First two digits of 126} \rightarrow \frac{12}{4} = 3 \\
126 \leftarrow 3 \times 42 = 126 \\
\hline
0
\end{array}
$$

Check the quotient by multiplying 42 and 73. The product should be 3066, which matches the original dividend.

CAUTION

The first digit in the answer in long division must be placed in the proper position over the dividend.

···· **Work Problem ❶ at the Side.** ▶

OBJECTIVES

1. Use long division.
2. Divide by multiples of 10.
3. Use multiplication to check quotients.

---

❶ Divide.

(a) $64\overline{)4608}$ *Hint:* 64 is closer to 60 than 70, so use 6 as the trial divisor.

(b) $32\overline{)1792}$ Use _____ as the trial divisor.

(c) $51\overline{)2295}$ Use _____ as the trial divisor.

(d) $\dfrac{6391}{83}$ Use _____ as the trial divisor.

Answers

1. (a) 72 **(b)** Use 3; 56 **(c)** Use 5; 45
(d) Use 8; 77

2 Divide.

(a) $56\overline{)2352}$

(b) $38\overline{)1599}$

(c) $65\overline{)5416}$

(d) $89\overline{)6649}$

EXAMPLE 2 **Dividing to Find a Trial Quotient**

Divide: $58\overline{)2730}$

Use 6 as a trial divisor, because 58 is closer to 60 than to 50.

First two digits → $\dfrac{27}{6} = 4$ with remainder 3
of dividend

Be careful to write the 4 over the 3.

$$
\begin{array}{r}
4 \leftarrow \text{Trial quotient is 4.}\\
58\overline{)2730}\\
232 \leftarrow 4 \times 58 = 232\\
\hline
41 \leftarrow 273 - 232 = 41 \text{ (smaller than 58,}\\
\text{the divisor)}
\end{array}
$$

Bring down the 0.

$$
\begin{array}{r}
4\\
58\overline{)2730}\\
232\downarrow\\
\hline
410 \leftarrow \quad 0 \text{ brought down}
\end{array}
$$

$$
\begin{array}{r}
46\\
58\overline{)2730}\\
232\\
\hline
410\\
348 \leftarrow 6 \times 58 = 348\\
\hline
62 \leftarrow \textbf{Greater than 58}
\end{array}
$$

First two digits of 410

$\dfrac{41}{6} = 6$ with remainder 5

The remainder, 62, is *greater than the divisor*, 58, so **7** should be used in the quotient instead of **6**.

$$
\begin{array}{r}
47 \ \textbf{R}4 \leftarrow\\
58\overline{)2730}\\
232\\
\hline
410\\
406 \leftarrow 7 \times 58 = 406\\
\hline
4 \leftarrow 410 - 406 = 4
\end{array}
$$

◀ **Work Problem 2 at the Side.**

Sometimes it is necessary to write a 0 in the quotient.

EXAMPLE 3 **Writing Zeros in the Quotient**

Divide: $42\overline{)8734}$

Start as in **Example 2** above.

$$
\begin{array}{r}
2\\
42\overline{)8734}\\
84 \leftarrow 2 \times 42 = 84\\
\hline
3 \leftarrow 87 - 84 = 3
\end{array}
$$

Bring down the 3.

$$
\begin{array}{r}
2\\
42\overline{)8734}\\
84\downarrow\\
\hline
33 \leftarrow 3 \text{ brought down}
\end{array}
$$

Continued on Next Page

Since 33 *cannot* be divided by 42, write a 0 in the quotient as a placeholder.

$$\begin{array}{r} 20 \\ 42\overline{)8734} \\ \underline{84} \\ 33 \end{array}$$

Write a 0 in the quotient.

Bring down the final digit, the 4.

$$\begin{array}{r} 20 \\ 42\overline{)8734} \\ \underline{84}\downarrow \\ 334 \end{array}$$ $\leftarrow$ 4 brought down

Complete the problem.

$$\begin{array}{r} 207\ \mathbf{R}40 \\ 42\overline{)8734} \\ \underline{84} \\ 334 \\ \underline{294} \\ 40 \end{array}$$
$\leftarrow 7 \times 42 = 294$
$\leftarrow 334 - 294 = 40$

The quotient is 207 **R**40.

> **CAUTION**
> There must be a digit in the quotient (answer) above *every* digit in the dividend *once the answer has begun*. Notice that in **Example 3** above, a 0 was used to assure an answer digit above every digit in the dividend.

·········· **Work Problem ❸ at the Side.** ▶

OBJECTIVE ❷ **Divide by multiples of 10.** When the divisor and dividend both contain zeros at the far right, recall that these numbers are multiples of 10. There is a short way to divide multiples of 10. Look at the following examples.

$$26{,}000 \div 1 = 26{,}000$$
$$26{,}000 \div 10 = 2600$$
$$26{,}000 \div 100 = 260$$
$$26{,}000 \div 1000 = 26$$

Do you see a pattern in these divisions using multiples of 10? These examples suggest the following rule.

> **Dividing by Multiples of 10**
> When a whole number has zeros at the far right, divide the number by 10, by 100, or by 1000 by dropping one, two, or three zeros from the whole number.

EXAMPLE 4 Dividing by Multiples of 10

Divide.

$\rule{0pt}{0pt}$ —— 0 in divisor

(a) $60 \div 1\mathbf{0} = 6$

—— Drop 0 from dividend to get the quotient.

··········· **Continued on Next Page**

❸ Divide.

(a) $24\overline{)3127}$

(b) $52\overline{)10{,}660}$

(c) $39\overline{)15{,}933}$

(d) $78\overline{)23{,}462}$

Answers
3. (a) 130 **R**7 **(b)** 205 **(c)** 408 **R**21
  (d) 300 **R**62

4 Divide by dropping zeros.

(a) $50 \div 10$

(b) $1800 \div 100$

(c) $305,000 \div 1000$

(d) $67,000 \div 100$

5 Drop zeros and then divide.

(a) $60\overline{)7200}$

(b) $130\overline{)131,040}$

(c) $2600\overline{)195,000}$

6 Check each division. If the quotient is incorrect, find the correct quotient.

(a) $18\overline{)774}$
$\underline{72}$
54
$\underline{54}$
0

quotient 43

(b) $426\overline{)19,170}$
$\underline{1\ 704}$
$1\ 130$
$\underline{952}$
178

quotient 42 **R**178

Answers

4. (a) 5   (b) 18   (c) 305   (d) 670

5. (a) 120   (b) 1008   (c) 75

6. (a) correct   (b) incorrect; should be 45

---

00 in divisor

(b) $3500 \div 100 = 35$

Drop 00 from dividend to get the quotient.

000 in divisor

(c) $915,000 \div 1000 = 915$

Drop 000 from dividend to get the quotient.

◀ **Work Problem 4 at the Side.**

EXAMPLE 5   **Dividing by Multiples of 10**

Divide by using the shortcut of dropping zeros.

(a) $40\overline{)11,000}$ Drop 0 from the divisor and the dividend.

$4\overline{)1100}$ quotient 275   *Be sure to drop the same number of zeros from both the divisor and dividend.*
$\underline{8}$
30
$\underline{28}$
20
$\underline{20}$
0

(b) $3500\overline{)31,500}$ Drop two zeros from the divisor and the dividend.

$35\overline{)315}$ quotient 9
$\underline{315}$
0

◀ **Work Problem 5 at the Side.**

OBJECTIVE ➌ Use multiplication to check quotients. Quotients in long division can be checked just as quotients in short division were checked. Multiply the quotient and divisor, then add any remainder. The result should match the original dividend.

EXAMPLE 6   **Checking Division**

Check the quotient.

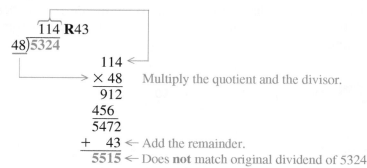

$48\overline{)5324}$ quotient 114 **R**43

114
$\underline{\times\ 48}$ Multiply the quotient and the divisor.
912
$\underline{456}$
5472
$\underline{+\quad 43}$ ← Add the remainder.
5515 ← Does **not** match original dividend of 5324

The quotient does *not* check. Rework the original problem to get 110 **R**44.

◀ **Work Problem 6 at the Side.**

MyMathLab®

*First, indicate what number to use as the trial divisor. Then use the trial divisor to find the first digit in the quotient and write it in the correct position. Do **not** finish the division.*

1. 24)768

Use ____ as the trial divisor.

2. 35)805

Use ____ as the trial divisor.

3. 18)4500

Use ____ as the trial divisor.

4. 28)3500

Use ____ as the trial divisor.

5. 86)10,327

Use ____ as the trial divisor.

6. 51)24,026

Use ____ as the trial divisor.

7. 52)38,025

Use ____ as the trial divisor.

8. 63)34,400

Use ____ as the trial divisor.

9. 77)249,826

Use ____ as the trial divisor.

10. 92)247,892

Use ____ as the trial divisor.

11. 420)470,800

Use ____ as the trial divisor.

12. 190)901,050

Use ____ as the trial divisor.

*Find each quotient by using long division. **See Examples 1–3.** In Exercises 21–24, drop zeros before dividing. **See Examples 4 and 5.***

13. 29)1859

14. 58)2204

15. 47)11,121

16. 83)39,692

17. 26)62,583

18. 28)84,249

19. 63)78,072

20. 55)43,223

21. 150)499,760

22. 720)52,560

23. 400)340,000

24. 900)153,000

Check each division. If a quotient is incorrect, find the correct quotient. **See Example 6.**

25. $\overset{106\ \mathbf{R}17}{56\overline{)5943}}$

26. $\overset{37\ \mathbf{R}37}{87\overline{)3254}}$

27. $\overset{658\ \mathbf{R}9}{600\overline{)394,800}}$

28. $\overset{463\ \mathbf{R}200}{300\overline{)139,100}}$

29. $\overset{62\ \mathbf{R}3}{410\overline{)25,420}}$

30. $\overset{174\ \mathbf{R}360}{760\overline{)132,600}}$

31. $\overset{450\ \mathbf{R}65}{72\overline{)32,465}}$

32. $\overset{23\ \mathbf{R}29}{47\overline{)9570}}$

Solve each application problem by using addition, subtraction, multiplication, or division.

33. In 1900, the average workweek was 59 hours. In 2011, it was 34 hours. How many more hours were worked each year in 1900 than today? Assume 50 weeks of work per year. (*Source:* Statista.com.)

34. In the United States, 45,000,000 tons of paper are recycled each year. What is the average amount of paper recycled on each of 250 work days in one year?

35. While planning a vacation, a travel agent found hotel prices ranging from $69 per night to $475 per night. What is the difference in cost between the most expensive and least expensive rooms for a five-night stay?

36. Two divorced parents share their child's education costs, which amount to $3718 per year. If one parent pays $1880 each year, find the amount paid by the other parent over five years.

37. Judy Martinez has a 36-month loan. The total debt, including interest, is $11,088. What is her monthly payment?

38. A consultant charged $41,140 for studying the environmental impact of a new shopping mall. If the consultant worked 220 hours, find the rate charged per hour.

39. Clarence Hanks can assemble 42 circuits in one hour. How many circuits can he assemble in a 5-day workweek of 8 hours per day?

40. Tuition at the community college is $151 per credit. There is also a $10 per credit technology fee, a $2 per credit student health fee, and a one-time application fee of $20. How much will Stephanie, a new student, pay to register for 14 credits?

41. The elementary school PTA brought in $7588 from a fund-raising project. Expenses of $838 were paid first. The balance of the money was divided evenly among 18 classrooms. How much did each classroom receive?

42. Feather Farms Egg Ranch collected 3545 eggs in the morning and 2575 eggs in the afternoon. If the eggs are packed in flats containing 30 eggs each, find the number of flats needed for packing.

Appendix: Inductive and Deductive Reasoning

Inductive and Deductive Reasoning

OBJECTIVES

1. Use inductive reasoning to analyze patterns.
2. Use deductive reasoning to analyze arguments.
3. Use deductive reasoning to solve problems.

OBJECTIVE 1 **Use inductive reasoning to analyze patterns.** In many scientific experiments, conclusions are drawn from specific outcomes. After many repetitions and similar outcomes, the findings are generalized into statements that appear to be true. When general conclusions are drawn from specific observations, we are using a type of reasoning called **inductive reasoning.** The next examples illustrate this type of reasoning.

EXAMPLE 1 Using Inductive Reasoning

Find the next number in the sequence 3, 7, 11, 15, ...

To discover a pattern, calculate the difference between each pair of successive numbers.

$$7 - 3 = 4$$
$$11 - 7 = 4$$
$$15 - 11 = 4$$

Notice that the difference is always 4. Each number is 4 greater than the previous one. Thus, the next number in the pattern is $15 + 4$, or 19.

······· **Work Problem 1 at the Side.** ▶

1 Find the next number in the sequence 2, 8, 14, 20, ... Describe the pattern.

EXAMPLE 2 Using Inductive Reasoning

Find the next number in this sequence.

$$7, 11, 8, 12, 9, 13, ...$$

The pattern in this example involves addition and subtraction.

$$7 + 4 = 11$$
$$11 - 3 = 8$$
$$8 + 4 = 12$$
$$12 - 3 = 9$$
$$9 + 4 = 13$$

To get the second number, we add 4 to the first number. To get the third number, we subtract 3 from the second number. To obtain subsequent numbers, we continue the pattern. The next number is $13 - 3 = 10$.

······· **Work Problem 2 at the Side.** ▶

2 Find the next number in the sequence 6, 11, 7, 12, 8, 13, ... Describe the pattern.

Answers

1. 26; add 6 each time.
2. 9; add 5, subtract 4.

3 Find the next number in the sequence 2, 6, 18, 54, ... Describe the pattern.

EXAMPLE 3 **Using Inductive Reasoning**

Find the next number in the sequence 1, 2, 4, 8, 16, ...

    Each number after the first is obtained by multiplying the previous number by 2. So the next number would be 16 • 2 = 32.

◄ **Work Problem 3 at the Side.**

EXAMPLE 4 **Using Inductive Reasoning**

(a) Find the next geometric shape in this sequence.

    The figures alternate between a blue circle and a red triangle. Also, the number of dots increases by 1 in each subsequent figure. Thus, the next figure should be a blue circle with five dots inside it.

4 Find the next shape in this sequence.

(b) Find the next geometric shape in this sequence.

    The first two shapes consist of vertical lines with horizontal lines at the bottom extending first *left* and then *right*. The third shape is a vertical line with a horizontal line at the top extending to the *left*. Therefore, the next shape should be a vertical line with a horizontal line at the top extending to the *right*.

◄ **Work Problem 4 at the Side.**

OBJECTIVE 2 Use deductive reasoning to analyze arguments. In the previous discussion, specific cases were used to find patterns and predict the next event. There is another type of reasoning called **deductive reasoning,** which moves from general cases to specific conclusions.

EXAMPLE 5 **Using Deductive Reasoning**

Does the conclusion follow from the premises in this argument?

        All Hondas are automobiles. ← Premise

        All automobiles have horns. ← Premise

      ∴   All Hondas have horns. ← Conclusion

    In this example, the first two statements are called *premises* and the third statement (below the line) is called a *conclusion*. The symbol ∴ is a mathematical symbol meaning "**therefore**." The entire set of statements is called an *argument*.

Answers

3. 162; multiply by 3.

4.

················· **Continued on Next Page**

The focus of deductive reasoning is to determine whether the conclusion follows (is valid) from the premises. A set of circles called **Euler circles** is used to analyze the argument.

In **Example 5,** the statement "All Hondas are automobiles" can be represented by two circles, one for Hondas and one for automobiles. Note that the circle representing Hondas is totally inside the circle representing automobiles because the first premise states that *all* Hondas are automobiles.

Now, a circle is added to represent the second statement, vehicles with horns. This circle must completely surround the circle representing automobiles because the second premise states that *all* automobiles have horns.

To analyze the conclusion, notice that the circle representing Hondas is *completely* inside the circle representing vehicles with horns. Therefore, it must follow that all Hondas have horns. ***The conclusion is valid.***

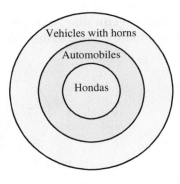

·········· **Work Problem ⑤ at the Side.** ▶

EXAMPLE 6   Using Deductive Reasoning

Does the conclusion follow from the premises in this argument?

All tables are round.

All glasses are round.
———————————————
∴   All glasses are tables.

Use Euler circles. Draw a circle representing tables *inside* a circle representing round objects, because the first premise states that *all* tables are round.

The second statement requires that a circle representing glasses must now be drawn inside the circle representing round objects, but not necessarily inside the circle representing tables. Therefore, the conclusion does ***not*** follow from the premises. This means that ***the conclusion is invalid.***

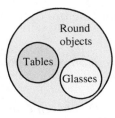

·········· **Work Problem ⑥ at the Side.** ▶

---

⑤ Does the conclusion follow from the premises in the following argument?

All cars have four wheels.

All Fords are cars.
———————————————
∴ All Fords have four wheels.

⑥ Does each conclusion follow from the premises?

(a) All animals are wild.

All cats are animals.
———————————————
∴ All cats are wild.

(b) All students use math.

All adults use math.
———————————————
∴ All adults are students.

Answers

5. The conclusion follows from the premises; it is valid.
6. **(a)** The conclusion follows from the premises; it is valid.
   (b) The conclusion does *not* follow from the premises; it is invalid.

7 In a college class of 100 students, 35 take both math and history, 50 take history, and 40 take math. How many take neither math nor history? Draw a Venn diagram.

8 A Chevy, BMW, Cadillac, and Ford are parked side by side. The known facts are:

(a) The Ford is on the right end.

(b) The BMW is next to the Cadillac.

(c) The Chevy is between the Ford and the Cadillac.

Which car is parked on the left end?

Answers

7.

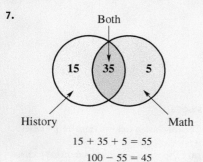

$15 + 35 + 5 = 55$

$100 - 55 = 45$

45 students take neither math nor history.

8. BMW

OBJECTIVE ▶ 3 Use deductive reasoning to solve problems. Another type of deductive reasoning problem occurs when a set of facts is given in a problem and a conclusion must be drawn using these facts.

EXAMPLE 7 Using Deductive Reasoning

There were 25 students enrolled in a ceramics class. During the class, 10 of the students made a bowl and 8 students made a birdbath. Three students made both a bowl and a birdbath. How many students did not make either a bowl or a birdbath?

This type of problem is best solved by organizing the data using a drawing called a **Venn diagram.** Two overlapping circles are drawn, with each circle representing one item made by the students, as shown below.

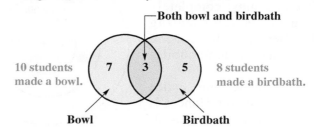

In the region where the circles overlap, write the number of students who made *both* items, namely, 3. In the remaining portion of the birdbath circle, write the number 5, which when added to 3 will give the total number of students who made a birdbath, namely, 8. In a similar manner, write 7 in the remaining portion of the bowl circle, since $7 + 3 = 10$, the total number of students who made a bowl. The total of all three numbers written in the circles is 15. Since there were 25 students in the class, this means $25 - 15$ or 10 students did not make either a birdbath or a bowl.

◀ Work Problem **7** at the Side.

EXAMPLE 8 Using Deductive Reasoning

Four cars in a race finish first, second, third, and fourth. The following facts are known.

(a) Car A beat Car C.

(b) Car D finished between Cars C and B.

(c) Car C beat Car B.

In which order did the cars finish?

To solve this type of problem, it is helpful to use a line diagram.

1. *Write A before C,* because Car A beat Car C (fact **a**).

A   C

2. *Write B after C,* because Car C beat Car B (fact **c**).

A   C   B

3. *Write D between C and B,* because Car D finished between Car C and Car B (fact **b**).

The correct order of finish is shown below.

A   C   D   B

◀ Work Problem **8** at the Side.

Appendix Exercises

FOR EXTRA HELP

 Download the MyDashBoard App

MyMathLab®

Find the next number in each sequence. Describe the pattern in each sequence.
See Examples 1–3.

1. 2, 9, 16, 23, 30, …

2. 5, 8, 11, 14, 17, …

3. 0, 10, 8, 18, 16, …

4. 3, 9, 7, 13, 11, …

5. 1, 2, 4, 8, …

6. 1, 4, 16, 64, …

7. 1, 3, 9, 27, 81, …

8. 3, 6, 12, 24, 48, …

9. 1, 4, 9, 16, 25, …

10. 6, 7, 9, 12, 16, …

Find the next shape in each sequence. ***See Example 4.***

11.

12.

13.

14.

For each argument, draw Euler circles and then state whether or not the conclusion follows from the premises. **See Examples 5 and 6.**

15. All animals are wild.
All lions are animals.
∴ All lions are wild.

16. All students are hard workers.
All business majors are students.
∴ All business majors are hard workers.

17. All teachers are serious.
All mathematicians are serious.
∴ All mathematicians are teachers.

18. All boys ride bikes.
All Americans ride bikes.
∴ All Americans are boys.

Solve each application problem. **See Examples 7 and 8.**

19. In a given 30-day period, a husband watched television 20 days and his wife watched television 25 days. If they watched television together 18 days, how many days did neither watch television? Draw a Venn diagram.

20. In a class of 40 students, 21 students take both calculus and physics. If 30 students take calculus and 25 students take physics, how many do not take either calculus or physics? Draw a Venn diagram.

21. Tom, Dick, Mary, and Joan all work for the same company. One is a secretary, one is a computer operator, one is a receptionist, and one is a mail clerk.

 (a) Tom and Joan eat dinner with the computer operator.

 (b) Dick and Mary carpool with the secretary.

 (c) Mary works on the same floor as the computer operator and the mail clerk.

 Who is the computer operator?

22. Four cars—a Ford, a Buick, a Mercedes, and an Audi—are parked in a garage in four spaces.

 (a) The Ford is in the last space.

 (b) The Buick and Mercedes are next to each other.

 (c) The Audi is next to the Ford but not next to the Buick.

 Which car is in the first space?

Answers to Selected Exercises

SECTION 1.1 (pages 7–10)

1. false; we can also use the digit 0. **2.** true **3.** true **4.** false; the left-most 7 has a value of 7 ten-thousands; the right-most 7 has a value of 7 tens. **5.** 15; 0; 83,001 **7.** 7; 362,049 **9.** hundreds **11.** hundred-thousands **13.** ten-millions **15.** hundred-billions **17.** ten-trillions, hundred-billions, millions, hundred-thousands, ones **18.** trillions, ten-billions, hundred millions, ten-thousands, hundreds **19.** eight thousand, four hundred twenty-one **21.** forty-six thousand, two hundred five **23.** three million, sixty-four thousand, eight hundred one **25.** eight hundred forty million, one hundred eleven thousand, three **27.** fifty-one billion, six million, eight hundred eighty-eight thousand, three hundred twenty-one **29.** three trillion, seven hundred twelve million **31.** 46,805 **33.** 5,600,082 **35.** 271,900,000 **37.** 12,417,625,310 **39.** 600,000,071,000,400 **41.** six thousand, forty-one **43.** 760,309,000 **45.** one billion, fifty-six million, seven hundred twenty thousand **47.** the year two thousand; 141,000,700 **49.** six million, four hundred thousand every day; two billion, three hundred thirty-six million in one year **51.** 4,200,000,000 **53.** largest: 97,651,100; ninety-seven million, six hundred fifty-one thousand, one hundred; smallest: 10,015,679; ten million, fifteen thousand, six hundred seventy-nine **54.** Answers will vary. **55.** sixty-fours; thirty-twos; sixteens; eights **(a)** 101 **(b)** 1010 **(c)** 1111 **56. (a)** Answers will vary but should mention that the location or place in which a digit is written gives it a different value. **(b)** $8 =$ VIII; $38 =$ XXXVIII; $275 =$ CCLXXV; $3322 =$ MMMCCCXXII **(c)** The Roman system is *not* a place value system because no matter what place it's in, M = 1000, C = 100, etc. One disadvantage is that it takes much more space to write many large numbers; another is that there is no symbol for zero.

SECTION 1.2 (pages 17–18)

1. +29,035 feet or 29,035 feet **2.** −5314 feet **3.** −128.6 degrees **4.** +98.6 degrees or 98.6 degrees **5.** −18 yards **6.** +25 yards or 25 yards **7.** +$100 or $100 **8.** −$37 **9.** $-6\frac{1}{2}$ pounds **10.** $+2\frac{1}{2}$ ounces or $2\frac{1}{2}$ ounces

11.
$$-5\ -4\ -3\ -2\ -1\ \ 0\ \ 1\ \ 2\ \ 3\ \ 4\ \ 5$$

13.
$$-5\ -4\ -3\ -2\ -1\ \ 0\ \ 1\ \ 2\ \ 3\ \ 4\ \ 5$$

15. (a) Zero is less than five, or, zero is less than positive five. **(b)** Negative ten is greater than negative seventeen. **16. (a)** Three is greater than negative seven, or, positive three is greater than negative seven. **(b)** Twelve is less than twenty-two, or, positive twelve is less than positive twenty-two. **17.** > **19.** < **21.** < **23.** > **25.** < **27.** > **29.** > **31.** < **33.** 15 **35.** 3 **37.** 0 **39.** 200 **41.** 75 **43.** 8042

45.
$$\begin{array}{cccc} A & C & D & B \\ \end{array}$$
$$-2 \quad -1 \quad 0 \quad 1$$

46. −1.5, −1, 0, 0.5 **47.** A: may be at risk; B: above normal; C: normal; D: normal **48. (a)** The patient would think the interpretation was "above normal" and wouldn't get treatment. **(b)** Patient D's score of 0; zero is neither positive nor negative.

SECTION 1.3 (pages 26–29)

1. 3
$$-7\ -6\ -5\ -4\ -3\ -2\ -1\ \ 0\ \ 1\ \ 2\ \ 3$$

3. −7
$$-7\ -6\ -5\ -4\ -3\ -2\ -1\ \ 0\ \ 1\ \ 2\ \ 3$$

5. −1
$$-7\ -6\ -5\ -4\ -3\ -2\ -1\ \ 0\ \ 1\ \ 2\ \ 3$$

7. (a) −10 **(b)** 10 **9. (a)** 12 **(b)** −12 **11. (a)** −50 **(b)** 50 **13. (a)** 158 **(b)** −158 **15.** The absolute values are the same in each pair of answers, so the only difference in the sums is the common sign. **16.** Add the absolute values and use the common sign as the sign of the sum. **17. (a)** 2 **(b)** −2 **19. (a)** −7 **(b)** 7 **21. (a)** −5 **(b)** 5 **23. (a)** 150 **(b)** −150 **25.** Each pair of answers differs only in the sign of the answer. This occurs because the signs of the addends are reversed. **26.** Subtract the lesser absolute value from the greater absolute value. Use the sign of the number with the greater absolute value as the sign of the sum. **27.** −3 **29.** 7 **31.** −7 **33.** 1 **35.** −8 **37.** −20 **39.** −17 **41.** −22 **43.** −19 **45.** 6 **47.** −5 **49.** 0 **51.** 5 **53.** −32 **55.** $13 + (-17) = -4$ yards **57.** $-62 + 50 = -$12$ **59.** $-88 + 35 = -$53$ **61.** Jeff: $-20 + 75 + (-55) = 0$ points; Terry: $42 + (-15) + 20 = 47$ points **63.** −2 **65.** 2 **67.** $-5 + (-18); -23$ **69.** $15 + (-4); 11$ **71.** $6 + (-14 + 14);$ $6 + 0 = 6$ **73.** $(14 + 6) + (-7); 20 + (-7) = 13$ **75.** Answers will vary. Some possibilities are: $-6 + 0 = -6$; $10 + 0 = 10; 0 + 3 = 3$ **76.** Answers will vary. Some possibilities are: $(1 + 2) + 3 = 1 + (2 + 3)$ Both sums are 6; $(-5 + 0) + 4 = -5 + (0 + 4)$ Both sums are −1; $(-15 + 6) + 9 = -15 + (6 + 9)$ Both sums are −0. **77.** −4116 **79.** 8686 **81.** −96,077

SECTION 1.4 (pages 32–33)

1. $-6; 6 + (-6) = 0$ **3.** $13; -13 + 13 = 0$ **5.** The student forgot to change 6 to its opposite, −6. It should be $-6 + (-6) = -12$. **6.** The student changed the sign of the first number, which is the error.

It should be $-7 + (-5) = -12$. **7.** 14 **9.** -2 **11.** -12 **13.** -25
15. -23 **17.** 8; 5 **19.** 20 **21.** 11 **23.** -60 **25.** 0 **27.** 0 **29.** -6
31. (a) 8 **(b)** -2 **(c)** 2 **(d)** -8 **33. (a)** -3 **(b)** 11 **(c)** -11
(d) 3 **35.** -6 **37.** -5 **39.** 3 **41.** -10 **43.** 12 **45.** -5
47. (a) 21 °F; $30 - 21 = 9$ degrees difference **(b)** 0 °F; $15 - 0 = 15$
degrees difference **(c)** -17 °F; $5 - (-17) = 22$ degrees difference
(d) -41 °F; $-10 - (-41) = 31$ degrees difference **49.** -11 **51.** -5
53. -10 **55.** Answers on left: -8; 8. On right: -1; 1 Subtraction is *not*
commutative; the absolute value of the answer is the same, but the sign
changes. **56.** Subtracting 0 from a number does *not* change the number.
For example, $-5 - 0 = -5$. But subtracting a number from 0 *does* change
the number to its opposite. For example, $0 - (-5) = 5$.

SECTION 1.5 (pages 40–43)

1. (a)

3702 Next digit is 4 or less, so leave
0 as 0 in the tens place.
Tens place

(b)

908,546 Next digit is 5 or more, so change
8 to 9 in the thousands place.
Thousands place

2. (a)

65,081 Next digit is 5 or more, so change 0
to 1 in the hundreds place.
Hundreds place

(b)

723,900 Next digit is 4 or less, so leave
2 as 2 in the ten-thousands place.
Ten-thousands place

3. 630 **5.** -1080 **7.** 7900 **9.** $-86,800$ **11.** 42,500 **13.** -6000
15. $-78,000$ **17.** 6000 **19.** 600,000 **21.** $-9,000,000$
23. 140,000,000 **25.** 20,000,000,000 **27.** 9,000,000,000

29. Answers will vary but should mention looking only at the second digit,
rounding first digit up when second digit is 5 or more, leaving first digit
unchanged when second digit is 4 or less. Examples will vary.
30. Examples will vary. Some possibilities are: rounded numbers are
used when budgeting or talking about driving distances; exact numbers
are important for paychecks and medications. **31.** 30,000 miles
33. -60 degrees **35.** $10,000 **37.** 50,000,000,000 minutes
39. 700,000 people in Alaska; 40,000,000 people in California
41. *Estimate:* $-40 + 90 = 50$; *Exact:* $-42 + 89 = 47$
42. *Estimate:* $-70 + 30 = -40$; *Exact:* $-66 + 25 = -41$
43. *Estimate:* $20 + (-100) = -80$; *Exact:* $16 + (-97) = -81$
45. *Estimate:* $-300 + (-400) = -700$; *Exact:* $-273 + (-399) = -672$
47. *Estimate:* $3000 + 7000 = 10,000$; *Exact:* $3081 + 6826 = 9907$
49. *Estimate:* $20 + (-80) = -60$; *Exact:* $23 - 81 = 23 + (-81) = -58$
51. *Estimate:* $-40 + (-40) = -80$; *Exact:* $-39 - 39 =$
$-39 + (-39) = -78$ **53.** *Estimate:* $-100 + 30 + (+70) = 0$;
Exact: $-106 + 34 - (-72) = -106 + 34 + (+72) = 0$ **55.** *Estimate:*
$80,000 - 50,000 = \$30,000$; *Exact:* $78,650 - 52,882 = \$25,768$
57. *Estimate:* $2000 - 800 - 300 - 400 - 200 - 200 = \$100$;
Exact: $2120 - 845 - 325 - 365 - 182 - 240 = \$163$
59. *Estimate:* $-100 + 40 + 50 = -10$ degrees; *Exact:*
$-102 + 37 + 52 = -13$ degrees **61.** *Estimate:* $400 + 100 = 500$
doors and windows; *Exact:* $412 + 147 = 559$ doors and windows

SECTION 1.6 (pages 50–53)

1. (a) 63 **(b)** 63 **(c)** -63 **(d)** -63 **2. (a)** -54 **(b)** -54 **(c)** 54
(d) 54 **3. (a)** -56 **(b)** -56 **(c)** 56 **(d)** 56 **4. (a)** 48 **(b)** 48
(c) -48 **(d)** -48 **5.** -35 **7.** -45 **9.** -18 **11.** -50 **13.** -40
15. -56 **17.** 32 **19.** 77 **21.** 0 **23.** 133 **25.** 13 **27.** 0 **29.** 48
31. -56 **33.** -160 **35.** 5 **37.** -3 **39.** -1 **41.** 0 **43.** 5
45. -4 **47.** Commutative property: changing the *order* of the factors
does not change the product. Associative property: changing the *grouping*
of the factors does not change the product. Examples will vary. **48.** No.
Work with two factors at a time. The final result is -27.

$$\underbrace{(-3) \cdot (-3)}_{\underbrace{9 \cdot (-3)}_{-27}} \cdot (-3)$$

49. $= 9 \cdot (-3) + 9 \cdot 5$ Both results are 18. **51.** $= 8 \cdot 25$ Both
products are 200. **53.** $= (-3 \cdot 2) \cdot 5$ Both products are -30.
55. *Estimate:* $300 \cdot 50 = \$15,000$; *Exact:* $324 \cdot 52 = \$16,848$
57. *Estimate:* $-10,000 \cdot 10 = -\$100,000$; *Exact:* $-9950 \cdot 12 = -\$119,400$
59. *Estimate:* $200 \cdot 10 = \$2000$; *Exact:* $182 \cdot 13 = \$2366$
61. *Estimate:* $20 \cdot 400 = 8000$ hours; *Exact:* $24 \cdot 365 = 8760$ hours
63. -512 **65.** 0 **67.** $-355,299$ **69.** \$247 **71.** -22 degrees
73. 772 points **75.** Examples will vary. Some possibilities are:
(a) $6 \cdot (-1) = -6$; $2 \cdot (-1) = -2$; $15 \cdot (-1) = -15$
(b) $-6 \cdot (-1) = 6$; $-2 \cdot (-1) = 2$; $-15 \cdot (-1) = 15$ The result of
multiplying any nonzero number times -1 is the number with the opposite sign.
76. The products are 4, -8, 16, -32. The absolute value doubles each
time and the sign changes. The next three products are 64, -128, and 256.

SECTION 1.7 (pages 59–62)

1. (a) 7 **(b)** 7 **(c)** -7 **(d)** -7 **2. (a)** 6 **(b)** 6 **(c)** -6 **(d)** -6
3. (a) -7 **(b)** 7 **(c)** -7 **(d)** 7 **4. (a)** 9 **(b)** -9 **(c)** 9 **(d)** -9
5. (a) 1 **(b)** 35 **(c)** -13 **(d)** 1 **7. (a)** 0 **(b)** undefined
(c) undefined **(d)** 0 **9.** -4 **11.** -3 **13.** 6 **15.** -11
17. undefined **19.** -14 **21.** 10 **23.** 4 **25.** -1 **27.** 0 **29.** 191
31. -499 **33.** 2 **35.** -4 **37.** 40 **39.** -48 **41.** 5 **43.** 0
45. $2 \div 1 = 2$ but $1 \div 2 = 0.5$, so division is not commutative.
46. $(12 \div 6) \div 2 = 2 \div 2 = 1$; $12 \div (6 \div 2) = 12 \div 3 = 4$; different
quotients. Division is not associative. **47.** Similar: If the signs match, the
result is positive. If the signs are different, the result is negative. Different:
Multiplication is commutative, division is not. You can multiply by 0, but
dividing by 0 is undefined. **48.** Examples will vary. The properties are: Any
nonzero number divided by itself is 1. Any number divided by 1 is the number.
Division by 0 is undefined. Zero divided by any other number (except 0) is 0.
49. (a) $\dfrac{-6}{-1} = 6$; $\dfrac{-2}{-1} = 2$; $\dfrac{-15}{-1} = 15$
(b) $\dfrac{6}{-1} = -6$; $\dfrac{2}{-1} = -2$; $\dfrac{15}{-1} = -15$ When dividing by -1, change the
sign of the dividend to its opposite to get the quotient.
50. Division is not commutative. $\dfrac{0}{-3} = 0$ because $0 \cdot -3 = 0$. But $\dfrac{-3}{0}$
is undefined because when $\dfrac{-3}{0} = ?$ is rewritten as $? \cdot 0 = -3$, no
number can replace ? and make a true statement. **51.** *Estimate:*
$-40,000 \div 20 = -2000$ feet; *Exact:* $-35,836 \div 17 = -2108$ feet
53. *Estimate:* $-200 + 500 = \$300$; *Exact:* $-238 + 450 = \$212$
55. *Estimate:* $400 - 100 = 300$ days; *Exact:* $365 - 106 = 259$ days
57. *Estimate:* $-700 \cdot 40 = -28,000$ feet; *Exact:* $-730 \cdot 37 = -27,010$ feet

59. *Estimate:* 300 ÷ 5 = 60 miles; *Exact:* 315 ÷ 5 = 63 miles
61. Average score of 168   **63.** The back shows 520 grams, which is 10 grams more than the front.   **65.** −$15   **67.** 16 hours, with 40 minutes left over   **69.** 33 rooms, with space for 2 people unused.
71. −10   **73.** undefined   **75.** 31.70979198 rounds to 32 years.

SUMMARY EXERCISES Operations with Integers (pages 63–64)

1. −6   **2.** 0   **3.** −7   **4.** −7   **5.** 63   **6.** −1   **7.** −56   **8.** −22
9. 12   **10.** 8   **11.** −13   **12.** 0   **13.** 0   **14.** −17   **15.** −48   **16.** −10
17. −50   **18.** undefined   **19.** −14   **20.** −6   **21.** 0   **22.** 16   **23.** −30
24. undefined   **25.** 48   **26.** −19   **27.** 2   **28.** −20   **29.** 0   **30.** 16
31. −3   **32.** −36   **33.** 6   **34.** −7   **35.** −5   **36.** −31   **37.** −2
38. −32   **39.** −5   **40.** −4   **41.** −9732   **42.** 100   **43.** 4   **44.** −343
45. 5   **46.** −6   **47.** −10   **48.** −5   **49. (a)** The quotient is 0.
(b) The product is 0.   **(c)** The quotient is 1.   **50. (a)** The quotient is −1.
Adding 15 + (−15) would give a *sum* of 0.   **(b)** Dividing by zero cannot be done; the correct answer is "undefined."   **(c)** Work with two numbers at a time: −10 ÷ (−2) is 5; then 5 ÷ (−5) is −1, *not* positive 1.

SECTION 1.8 (pages 73–76)

1. 4 • 4 • 4; 4 cubed or 4 to the third power   **2.** 10 • 10; 10 squared or 10 to the second power   **3.** 2^7; 128; 2 to the seventh power   **4.** 3^5; 243; 3 to the fifth power   **5.** 5^4; 625; 5 to the fourth power   **6.** 2^6; 64; 2 to the sixth power   **7.** 7^2; 7 • 7; 49   **8.** 6^3; 6 • 6 • 6; 216   **9.** 10^1; 10; 10
10. 4^4; 4 • 4 • 4 • 4; 256   **11. (a)** 10   **(b)** 100   **(c)** 1000   **(d)** 10,000
13. (a) 4   **(b)** 16   **(c)** 64   **(d)** 256   **15.** 9,765,625   **17.** 4096   **19.** 4
21. 25   **23.** −64   **25.** 81   **27.** −1000   **29.** 1   **31.** 108   **33.** 200
35. −750   **37.** −32   **39. (a)** The answers are 4, −8, 16, −32, 64, −128, 256, −512. When a negative number is raised to an even power, the answer is positive; when raised to an odd power, the answer is negative.
(b) negative; positive   **40.** We need rules so everyone will work problems the same way and get the same answers. We probably want to work from left to right because in many languages we read from left to right.
41. −6   **43.** 0   **45.** −39   **47.** 16   **49.** 23   **51.** −43   **53.** 7   **55.** −3
57. 0   **59.** −38   **61.** 41   **63.** −2   **65.** 13   **67.** 126   **69.** 8
71. $\dfrac{27}{-3} = -9$ **73.** $\dfrac{-48}{-4} = 12$ **75.** $\dfrac{-60}{-1} = 60$ **77.** −4050   **79.** 7
81. $\dfrac{27}{0}$ is undefined.

Chapter 1 REVIEW EXERCISES (pages 85–88)

1. 86, 0, 35,600   **2.** eight hundred six   **3.** three hundred nineteen thousand, twelve   **4.** sixty million, three thousand, two hundred
5. fifteen trillion, seven hundred forty-nine billion, six   **6.** 504,100
7. 620,080,000   **8.** 99,007,000,356
9.
10. >   **11.** <   **12.** >   **13.** <   **14.** 5   **15.** 9   **16.** 0   **17.** 125
18. −1   **19.** −13   **20.** −3   **21.** 0   **22.** 1   **23.** −24   **24.** −7   **25.** 3
26. 0   **27.** −17   **28.** 5; −5 + 5 = 0   **29.** −18; 18 + (−18) = 0
30. −7   **31.** 17   **32.** −16   **33.** 13   **34.** 18   **35.** −22   **36.** 0
37. −20   **38.** −1   **39.** −3   **40.** 14   **41.** 15   **42.** −16   **43.** 3
44. −8   **45.** 0   **46.** 210   **47.** 59,000   **48.** 85,000,000   **49.** −3000
50. −7,060,000   **51.** 400,000   **52.** −200 pounds   **53.** −1000 feet

54. 2,000,000,000 Internet users   **55.** 10,000,000,000 people   **56.** −54
57. 56   **58.** −100   **59.** 0   **60.** 24   **61.** 17   **62.** −48   **63.** 125
64. −36   **65.** 50   **66.** −72   **67.** 9   **68.** −7   **69.** undefined   **70.** 5
71. −18   **72.** 0   **73.** 15   **74.** −1   **75.** −5   **76.** 18   **77.** 0
78. 156 days and 2 extra hours   **79.** 10,000   **80.** 32   **81.** 27   **82.** 16
83. −125   **84.** 8   **85.** 324   **86.** −200   **87.** −25   **88.** −2
89. 10   **90.** −28   **91.** $\dfrac{8}{-8} = -1$ **92.** $\dfrac{11}{0}$ is undefined.
93. associative property of addition   **94.** commutative property of multiplication   **95.** addition property of 0   **96.** multiplication property of 0   **97.** distributive property   **98.** associative property of multiplication   **99.** *Estimate:* $10,000 • 200 = $2,000,000; *Exact:* $11,900 • 192 = $2,284,800   **100.** *Estimate:* $200 + $400 − $700 = −$100; *Exact:* $185 + $428 − $706 = −$93
101. *Estimate:* 900 ÷ 20 = 45 miles; *Exact:* 880 ÷ 22 = 40 miles
102. *Estimate:* ($40 • 20) + ($90 • 10) = $1700; *Exact:* ($39 • 19) + ($85 • 12) = $1761   **103.** −$700, −$100, $700, $900, $0, $700
104. January; April   **105.** $2100   **106.** −$1850

Chapter 1 TEST (pages 89–90)

1. twenty million, eight thousand, three hundred seven   **2.** 30,000,700,005
3.
4. >; <   **5.** 10; 14   **6.** −6   **7.** −5   **8.** 7   **9.** −40   **10.** 10
11. 64   **12.** −50   **13.** undefined   **14.** −60   **15.** −5   **16.** −45
17. 6   **18.** 25   **19.** 0   **20.** 9   **21.** 128   **22.** −2   **23.** 8   **24.** −36
25. An exponent shows how many times to use a factor in repeated multiplication. Examples will vary. Some possibilities are $(2)^4 = 2 • 2 • 2 • 2 = 16$ and $(−3)^2 = (−3)(−3) = 9$.
26. Commutative property: changing the *order* of addends does not change the sum. Associative property: changing the *grouping* of addends does not change the sum. Examples will vary.   **27.** 900
28. 36,420,000,000   **29.** 350,000   **30.** *Estimate:* $200 + $300 + (−$500) = $0; *Exact:* $184 + $293 + (−$506) = −$29
31. *Estimate:* −1000 ÷ 20 = −50 pounds; *Exact:* −1144 ÷ 22 = −52 pounds   **32.** *Estimate:* 30 (200 − 100) = 3000 calories; *Exact:* 31 (220 − 110) = 3410 calories   **33.** −10 − (−100) = −10 + (+100) = 90 degrees difference   **34.** 27 cartons because 26 cartons would leave 28 books unpacked

CHAPTER 2 Understanding Variables and Solving Equations

SECTION 2.1 (pages 101–104)

1. constant.   **2.** *d*   **3.** *m* is the variable; −3 is the constant.   **4.** *n* is the variable; −4 is the constant.   **5.** *h* is the variable; 5 is the coefficient.
6. *s* is the variable; 3 is the coefficient.   **7.** *c* is the variable; 2 is the coefficient; 10 is the constant.   **8.** *b* is the variable; 6 is the coefficient; 1 is the constant.   **9.** *x* and *y* are variables.   **10.** *x* and *y* are variables.
11. *g* is the variable; −6 is the coefficient; 9 is the constant.
12. *k* is the variable; −10 is the coefficient; 15 is the constant.
13. (a) 664 robes.   **(b)** 208 + 10 is 218 robes.   **(c)** 95 + 10 is 105 robes.
15. (a) 3 • 11 inches is 33 inches.   **(b)** 3 • 3 feet is 9 feet.

17. (a) $3 \cdot 12 - 5$ is 31 brushes.   **(b)** $3 \cdot 16 - 5$ is 43 brushes.

19. (a) $\dfrac{332}{4}$ is 83 points.   **(b)** $\dfrac{637}{7}$ is 91 points.   **21.** $12 + 12 + 12 + 12$ is 48, $4 \cdot 12$ is 48; $0 + 0 + 0 + 0$ is 0, $4 \cdot 0$ is 0; $(-5) + (-5) + (-5) + (-5)$ is -20, $4 \cdot -5$ is -20 **23.** $-2(-4) + 5$ is $8 + 5$, or 13; $-2(-6) + (-2)$ is $12 + (-2)$, or 10; $-2(0) + (-8)$ is $0 + (-8)$, or -8

25. A variable is a letter that represents the part of a rule that varies or changes depending on the situation. An expression expresses, or tells, the rule for doing something. For example, $c + 5$ is an expression, and c is the variable.

26. The number part in a multiplication expression is the coefficient. For example, 4 is the coefficient in $4s$. A constant is a number that is added or subtracted in an expression. It does not vary. For example, 5 is the constant in $c + 5$.   **27.** $b \cdot 1 = b$ or $1 \cdot b = b$ **29.** $\dfrac{b}{0}$ is undefined or $b \div 0$ is undefined.   **31.** $c \cdot c \cdot c \cdot c \cdot c \cdot c$ **33.** $x \cdot x \cdot x \cdot x \cdot y \cdot y \cdot y$

35. $-3 \cdot a \cdot a \cdot a \cdot b$ **37.** $9 \cdot x \cdot y \cdot y$ **39.** $-2 \cdot c \cdot c \cdot c \cdot c \cdot c \cdot d$

41. $a \cdot a \cdot a \cdot b \cdot c \cdot c$ **43.** 16   **45.** -24 **47.** -18 **49.** -128

51. $-18,432$ **53.** $311,040$ **55.** 56   **57.** $\dfrac{36}{0}$ is undefined.

59. (a) 3 miles   **(b)** 2 miles   **(c)** 1 mile   **60. (a)** $\dfrac{1}{2}$ mile; take half of the distance for 5 seconds   **(b)** $7\dfrac{1}{2}$ seconds; find the number halfway between 5 seconds and 10 seconds   **(c)** $12\dfrac{1}{2}$ seconds; find the number halfway between 10 seconds and 15 seconds

SECTION 2.2 (pages 114–117)

1. The like terms are $2b^2$ and b^2; the coefficients are 2 and 1.   **2.** The like terms are x^3 and $2x^3$; the coefficients are 1 and 2.   **3.** The like terms are $-xy$ and $2xy$; the coefficients are -1 and 2.   **4.** The like terms are $-a^2b$ and $-3a^2b$; the coefficients are -1 and -3.   **5.** The like terms are 7, 3, and -4; they are constants.   **6.** The like terms are -5, 1, and 4; they are constants.   **7.** $12r$ **9.** $6x^2$ **11.** $-4p$ **13.** $-3a^3$ **15.** 0   **17.** xy

19. $6t^4$ **21.** $4y^2$ **23.** $-8x$ **25.** $12a + 4b$ **27.** $7rs + 14$

29. $a + 2ab^2$ **31.** $-2x + 2y$ **33.** $7b^2$ **35.** cannot be simplified.

37. $-15r + 5s + t$ **39.** $30a$ **41.** $-8x^2$ **43.** $-20y^3$ **45.** $18cd$

47. $21a^2bc$ **49.** $12w$ **51.** $6b + 36$ **53.** $7x - 7$ **55.** $21t + 3$

57. $-10r - 6$ **59.** $-9k - 36$ **61.** $50m - 300$ **63.** $8y + 16$

65. $6a^2 + 3$ **67.** $9m - 34$ **69.** -25 **71.** $24x$ **73.** $5n + 13$

75. $11p - 1$ **77.** A simplified expression usually still has variables, but it is written in a simpler way. When evaluating an expression, the variables are all replaced by specific numbers and the final result is a numerical answer.

78. The answers are $15x + 10$ and $10 + 15x$. They are equivalent because of the commutative property of addition.   **79.** Like terms have matching variable parts, that is, matching letters and exponents. The coefficients do not have to match. Examples will vary.   **80.** Add the coefficients of like terms. If no coefficient is shown, it is assumed to be 1. Keep the variable part the same. Examples will vary.   **81.** Keep the variable part unchanged when combining like terms. The correct answer is $5x + 8$.

82. In the last step, do not change the sign of the first term. The correct answer is $-4a - 5$.   **83.** $-2y + 9$ **85.** 0   **87.** $-9x$

SUMMARY EXERCISES Variables and Expressions (pages 120–121)

1. m is the variable; -1 is the coefficient; -10 is the constant.   **2.** c and d are the variables; -8 is the coefficient.   **3.** x is the variable; 4 is the coefficient; 6 is the constant.   **4. (a)** 32 yards   **(b)** 120 inches

5. (a) \$13,080   **(b)** \$22,342   **6.** $a \cdot d \cdot d \cdot d \cdot d$ **7.** $b \cdot b \cdot b \cdot c \cdot d$

8. $-7 \cdot a \cdot b \cdot b \cdot b \cdot b \cdot c \cdot c$ **9.** 625   **10.** 0   **11.** 0

12. 60   **13.** -8 **14.** 120   **15.** -216 **16.** -800 **17.** 120,960

18. $24b$ **19.** $7x + 7$ **20.** $-8c - 32$ **21.** 0   **22.** $12c^2d$ **23.** $-6f$

24. $6w + 8$ **25.** $-2a - 6b$ **26.** $50x^3y^2$ **27.** $10r^3$ **28.** $7h^2$

29. -9 **30.** $-32y + 25$ **31.** $36x - 10$ **32.** $19n + 1$ **33. (a)** Forgot to multiply $6 \cdot 2$; correct answer is $6n + 12$.   **(b)** Two negative factors give a *positive* product; correct answer is $20a$.   **(c)** Keep the variable part unchanged; correct answer is $5y - 10$.   **34.** In the last step, do not change the sign of the first term; keep $-7x$ as $-7x$. The correct answer is $-7x - 9$.

SECTION 2.3 (pages 128–133)

1. 58 is the solution.   **2.** 25 is the solution.   **3.** -16 is the solution.

4. -17 is the solution.   **5. (a)** Add 8 to both sides because $-8 + 8$ gives $m + 0$ on the left side.   **(b)** Add -5 to both sides because $5 + (-5)$ gives $w + 0$ on the right side.   **6. (a)** Add -2 to both sides because $2 + (-2)$ gives $n + 0$ on the left side.   **(b)** Add 6 to both sides because $-6 + 6$ gives $b + 0$ on the right side.

7. $p = 4$ CHECK $\underbrace{4 + 5}_{9} = 9$
$9 = 9$ ✓

9. $r = 10$ CHECK $8 = \underbrace{10 - 2}_{8}$
$8 = 8$ ✓

11. $n = -8$ CHECK $-5 = n + 3$
$-5 = \underbrace{-8 + 3}_{-5}$
$-5 = -5$ ✓

13. $k = 18$ CHECK $-4 + k = 14$
$\underbrace{-4 + 18}_{14} = 14$
$14 = 14$ ✓

15. $y = 6$ CHECK $y - 6 = 0$
$\underbrace{6 - 6}_{0} = 0$
$0 = 0$ ✓

17. $r = -6$ CHECK $7 = r + 13$
$7 = \underbrace{-6 + 13}_{7}$
$7 = 7$ ✓

19. $x = 0$ CHECK $x - 12 = -12$
$\underbrace{0 + (-12)}_{-12} = -12$
$-12 = -12$ ✓

21. $t = -3$ CHECK $-5 = -2 + t$
$-5 = \underbrace{-2 + (-3)}_{-5}$
$-5 = -5$ ✓

23.
Does not balance $\dfrac{-2 + (-5)}{-7} = 3$ $-7 \neq 3$
The correct solution is 8. $\underbrace{8 - 5}_{3} = 3$
Balances $3 = 3$ ✓

25.
$7 + x = -11$
$\underbrace{7 + (-18)}_{-11} = -11$
Balances $-11 = -11$ ✓
-18 is the correct solution.

27.

$$-10 = -10 + b$$
$$\downarrow$$
$$-10 = \underline{-10 + 10}$$

Does not balance $\quad -10 \neq \quad 0$

The correct solution is 0. $\quad -10 = \underline{-10 + 0}$

Balances $\quad -10 = \quad -10 \checkmark$

29. $c = 6$; see *Student's Solutions Manual* for **Checks** of odd-numbered Exercises 29–37; Exercise 39 is in the Solutions section in the back of this book. **31.** $y = 5$ **33.** $b = -30$ **35.** $t = 0$ **37.** $z = -7$
39. $w = 3$ **41.** $x = -10$ **43.** $a = 0$ **45.** $y = -25$ **47.** $x = 15$
49. $k = 113$ **51.** $b = 18$ **53.** $r = -5$ **55.** $n = -105$ **57.** $h = -5$
59. No, the solution is -14, the number used to replace x in the original equation. **60.** To correct the errors, change $-3 - 6$ to $-3 + (-6)$. Then, add 5 to both sides, not -5. The correct solution is -4. **61.** $g = 295$ graduates **63.** $c = 55$ chirps **65.** $p = \$110$ per month in winter
67. $m = -19$ **69.** $x = 2$ **71. (a)** Equations will vary. Some possibilities are $n - 1 = -3$ and $8 = x + 10$. **(b)** Equations will vary. Some possibilities are $y + 6 = 6$ and $-5 = -5 + b$. **72. (a)** $x = \dfrac{1}{2}$ **(b)** $y = \dfrac{5}{4}$
(c) $n = \$0.85$ **(d)** Equations will vary.

SECTION 2.4 (pages 138–141)

1. 6; $\dfrac{6z}{6} = \dfrac{12}{6}$; $z = 2$ $\quad$ CHECK $12 = 12 \checkmark$

2. 8; $\dfrac{8k}{8} = \dfrac{24}{8}$; $k = 3$ $\quad$ CHECK $24 = 24 \checkmark$

3. $r = 4$ $\quad$ CHECK $48 = 12r$
$$48 = 12 \cdot 4$$
$$48 = \quad 48 \checkmark$$

4. $m = 9$ $\quad$ CHECK $99 = 11m$
$$99 = 11 \cdot 9$$
$$99 = \quad 99 \checkmark$$

5. $y = 0$ $\quad$ CHECK $\quad 3y = 0$
$$3 \cdot 0 = 0$$
$$0 \ = 0 \checkmark$$

6. $a = 0$ $\quad$ CHECK $\quad 5a = 0$
$$5 \cdot 0 = 0$$
$$0 \ = 0 \checkmark$$

7. $k = -10$ **9.** $r = 6$ **11.** $b = -5$

13. $r = 3$ $\quad$ CHECK $2 \cdot 3 = 6$
$$6 \ = 6 \checkmark$$

15. $p = -3$ $\quad$ CHECK $-12 = 5p - p$
$$-12 = 5 \cdot (-3) - (-3)$$
$$-12 = \quad (-15) + (+3)$$
$$-12 = \quad -12 \checkmark$$

17. $a = -5$ **19.** $x = -10$ **21.** $w = 0$ **23.** $t = 3$ **25.** $t = 0$
27. $m = 9$ **29.** $y = -1$ **31.** $z = -5$ **33.** $p = -2$ **35.** $k = 7$
37. $b = -3$ **39.** $x = -32$ **41.** $w = 2$ **43.** $n = 50$ **45.** $p = -10$
47. Each solution is the opposite of the number in the equation. So the rule is: When you change the sign of the variable from negative to positive, then change the number in the equation to its opposite. In $-x = 5$, the opposite

of 5 is -5, so $x = -5$. **49.** Divide by the coefficient of x, which is 3, *not* by the opposite of 3. The correct solution is 5. **50.** You can divide both sides of an equation by the same nonzero number and keep the balance.
51. $s = 15$ ft **53.** $s = 24$ meters **55.** $y = 27$ **57.** $x = 1$

SECTION 2.5 (pages 146–151)

1. $p = 1$ $\quad$ CHECK $12 = 12 \checkmark$

2. $k = 2$ $\quad$ CHECK $15 = 15 \checkmark$

3. $1 = y$, or $y = 1$ $\quad$ CHECK $2 = 8y - 6$
$$2 = 8(1) - 6$$
$$2 = \underline{8} - 6$$
$$2 = \quad 2 \checkmark$$

4. $p = 2$ $\quad$ CHECK $10 = 11p - 12$
$$10 = 11(2) - 12$$
$$10 = \underline{22} - 12$$
$$10 = \quad 10 \checkmark$$

5. $a = -2$ $\quad$ CHECK $28 = -9a + 10$
$$28 = -9(-2) + 10$$
$$28 = \underline{18} + 10$$
$$28 = \quad 28 \checkmark$$

6. $k = 0$ $\quad$ CHECK $-4k + 5 = 5$
$$-4(0) + 5 = 5$$
$$\underline{0} + 5 = 5$$
$$5 \ = 5 \checkmark$$

7. $m = 0$ **9.** $x = -4$

11. $p = 4; 4 = p$ $\quad$ CHECK $6(4) - 2 = 4(4) + 6$
$$\underline{24} - 2 = \underline{16} + 6$$
$$22 \ = \quad 22 \checkmark$$

13. $k = -2; -2 = k$ $\quad$ CHECK $-2k - 6 = 6k + 10$
$$-2(-2) - 6 = 6(-2) + 10$$
$$\underline{4} + (-6) = \underline{-12} + 10$$
$$-2 \ = \quad -2 \checkmark$$

15. $a = 5; 5 = a$ **17.** $t = 0$ **19.** $b = -8$ **21.** $w = 6$ **23.** $y = -9$
25. $t = -5$ **27.** $x = 0$ **29.** $h = 1$ **31.** $y = -2$ **33.** $m = -3$
35. $w = 2$ **37.** $x = 5$ **39.** $a = 3$ **41.** $b = -3$ **43.** $k = 4$ **45.** $c = 0$
47. $y = -5$ **49.** $n = 21$ **51.** $c = 30$ **53.** $p = -2$ **55.** $b = 0$
57. The series of steps may vary. One possibility is:

$$-2t - 10 = 3t + 5 \quad \text{Change subtraction to adding the opposite.}$$

$$\dfrac{-2t + (-10)}{2t} = \dfrac{3t + 5}{2t} \quad \text{Add } 2t \text{ to both sides (addition property).}$$

$$\dfrac{0 + (-10)}{-5} = \dfrac{5t + 5}{-5} \quad \text{Add } -5 \text{ to both sides (addition property).}$$

$$\dfrac{-15}{5} = \dfrac{5t}{5} \quad \text{Divide both sides by 5 (division property).}$$

$$-3 = t$$

58. Multiplication distributes over both addition and subtraction. Examples will vary. Some possibilities are $3(2y + 6)$ is $6y + 18$ and $5(x - 3)$ is $5x - 15$.

59. CHECK $-8 + \underbrace{4(3)}_{} = \underbrace{2(3)}_{} + 2$

$\underbrace{-8 + 12}_{4} = \underbrace{6}_{} + 2$

$4 \ne 8$ false

The check does not balance, so 3 is not the correct solution. The student added $-2a$ to -8 on the left side, instead of adding $-2a$ to $4a$. The correct solution is 5.

60. CHECK $2\underbrace{(-10 + 4)}_{} = -16$

$\underbrace{2(-6)}_{-12} = -16$

$-12 \ne -16$ false

The check does not balance, so -10 is not the correct solution. In the first step on the left side, $2(x + 4)$ is $2x + 8$. The student forgot to multiply $2(4)$. The correct solution is -12.   **61. (a)** It must be negative.
(b) The sum of x and a positive number is negative, so x must be negative.
62. (a) It must be positive.   **(b)** The sum of d and a negative number is positive, so d must be positive.   **63. (a)** It must be positive; when the signs are different, the product is negative.   **(b)** The product of n and a negative number is negative, so n must be positive.   **64. (a)** It must be negative also; when the signs match, the product is positive.   **(b)** The product of y and a negative number is positive, so y must be negative.

Chapter 2 REVIEW EXERCISES (pages 159–160)

1. (a) Variable is k; coefficient is 4; constant is -3.   **(b)** $-9y + 20$
2. (a) 70 test tubes   **(b)** 106 test tubes   **3. (a)** $x \cdot x \cdot y \cdot y \cdot y \cdot y$
(b) $5 \cdot a \cdot b \cdot b \cdot b$ **4. (a)** 9   **(b)** -27 **(c)** -128 **(d)** 720
5. $ab^2 + 3ab$ **6.** $-4x + 2y - 7$ **7.** $16g^3$ **8.** $12r^2t$ **9.** $5k + 10$
10. $-6b - 8$ **11.** $6y$ **12.** $20x + 2$ **13.** Expressions will vary.
One possibility is $6a^3 + a^2 + 3a - 6$.

14. $n = -11$ CHECK $16 + \quad n = 5$

$\underbrace{16 + -11}_{5} = 5$

$5 = 5$ ✓

15. $a = 4$ CHECK $-4 + 2 = 2a \quad - 6 - a$

$\underbrace{-4 + 2}_{-2} = \underbrace{2(4)}_{} - 6 - 4$

$-2 = \underbrace{8 + (-6) + (-4)}_{-2}$

$-2 = -2$ ✓

16. $m = -8$ **17.** $k = 10$ **18.** $t = 0$ **19.** $p = -6$ **20.** $r = 2$
21. $h = -12$ **22.** $w = 4$ **23.** $c = -2$ **24.** $n = 15$ employees
25. $a = -5$ **26.** $p = 10$ **27.** $y = 5$ **28.** $m = 3$ **29.** $x = 9$
30. $b = 7$ **31.** $z = -3$ **32.** $n = 4$ **33.** $t = 0$ **34.** $d = 5$
35. $b = -2$

Chapter 2 TEST (pages 161–162)

1. -7 is the coefficient; w is the variable; 6 is the constant.
2. Buy 177 hot dogs.   **3.** $x \cdot x \cdot x \cdot x \cdot x \cdot y \cdot y \cdot y$
4. $4 \cdot a \cdot b \cdot b \cdot b \cdot b$ **5.** -200 **6.** $-4w^3$ **7.** 0   **8.** c
9. cannot be simplified   **10.** $-40b^2$ **11.** $15k$ **12.** $21t + 28$
13. $-4a - 24$ **14.** $6x - 15$ **15.** $-9b + c + 6$

16. $x = 5$ CHECK $-4 = x - 9$

$-4 = \underbrace{5 - 9}_{}$

$-4 = -4$ ✓

17. $w = -11$ CHECK $\qquad -7w = 77$

$\underbrace{-7(-11)}_{77} = 77$

$77 = 77$ ✓

18. $p = -14$ CHECK $\qquad -p = 14$

$\underbrace{-1(-14)}_{14} = 14$

$14 = 14$ ✓

19. $a = 3$ CHECK $-15 = -3(a + 2)$

$-15 = -3(3 + 2)$

$-15 = -3(5)$

$-15 = -15$ ✓

20. $n = -8$ **21.** $m = 15$ **22.** $x = -1$ **23.** $m = 2$ **24.** $b = 54$
25. $c = 0$ **26.** Equations will vary. Two possibilities are $x - 5 = -9$
and $-24 = 6y$.

Chapters 1–2 CUMULATIVE REVIEW EXERCISES (pages 163–164)

1. three hundred six billion, four thousand, two hundred ten
2. 800,066,000   **3. (a)** $>$ **(b)** $<$ **4. (a)** commutative property of addition   **(b)** multiplication property of 0   **(c)** distributive property
5. (a) 9000   **(b)** 290,000   **6.** -8 **7.** 10   **8.** 30   **9.** 25   **10.** 7
11. 0   **12.** -64 **13.** undefined   **14.** -60 **15.** -40 **16.** -9
17. -25 **18.** -28 **19.** $\dfrac{11}{-11} = -1$ **20.** *Estimate:* $600 \div 20 =$
30 miles; *Exact:* $616 \div 22 = 28$ miles   **21.** *Estimate:* $-50 + 20 =$
-30 degrees; *Exact:* $-48 + 23 = -25$ degrees   **22.** *Estimate:*
$\$2000 - (50 \cdot 8) = \$1600$; *Exact:* $\$2132 - (52 \cdot 8) = \$1716$
23. *Estimate:* $10(800 + 50) = \$8500$; *Exact:* $12(758 + 45) = \$9636$
24. $-4 \cdot a \cdot b \cdot b \cdot b \cdot c \cdot c$ **25.** 120   **26.** h **27.** 0
28. $5n^2 - 4n - 2$ **29.** $-30b^2$ **30.** $28p - 28$ **31.** $-9w^2 - 12$

32. $x = -4$ CHECK $\underbrace{3(-4)}_{-12} = \underbrace{-4 - 8}_{-12}$

$-12 = -12$ ✓

33. $y = -6$ CHECK $-44 = -2 + 7(-6)$

$-44 = \underbrace{-2 + (-42)}_{}$

$-44 = -44$ ✓

34. $k = 7$ CHECK $2(7) - 5(7) = -21$

$\underbrace{14 - 35}_{-21} = -21$

$-21 = -21$ ✓

35. $m = 4$ CHECK $\underbrace{4 - 6}_{} = \underbrace{-2(4) + 6}_{}$

$-2 = \underbrace{-8 + 6}_{-2}$

$-2 = -2$ ✓

36. $x = -1$ **37.** $r = -18$ **38.** $b = -5$ **39.** $t = 1$ **40.** $y = -12$

CHAPTER 3 Solving Application Problems

SECTION 3.1 (pages 171–174)

1. A square has four right angles, and all four sides have the same length. Drawings will vary, but should have the same measurement for every side.
2. $P = 4s$; P stands for perimeter; s stands for side (the length of one side).
3. $P = 4 \cdot 9$ cm; $P = 36$ cm   **5.** $P = 100$ in.   **7.** $P = 4$ miles
9. $P = 88$ mm   **11.** 30 ft $= s$ **13.** $s = 23$ yards   **15.** $s = 2$ ft
17. A rectangle is a figure with four sides that meet to form four right angles. Each set of opposite sides is parallel and has the same length. Drawings will vary, but the two longer sides should have the same measurement and the two shorter sides should have the same measurement.

18. $P = 2l + 2w$; P stands for perimeter; l stands for length; w stands for width. **19.** $P = 16$ yd $+ 12$ yd; $P = 28$ yd **21.** $P = 70$ cm **23.** $P = 72$ ft **25.** $P = 26$ in. **27.** $l = 9$ cm CHECK 9 cm + 9 cm + 6 cm + 6 cm = 30 cm **29.** $w = 1$ mile CHECK 4 mi + 4 mi + 1 mi + 1 mi = 10 mi **31.** $w = 2$ ft CHECK 6 ft + 6 ft + 2 ft + 2 ft = 16 ft **33.** $l = 2$ m CHECK 2 m + 2 m + 1 m + 1 m = 6 m **35.** $P = 320$ ft **37.** $P = 54$ mm **39.** $P = 48$ ft **41.** $P = 78$ in. **43.** $P = 125$ m **45.** $? = 40$ cm **47.** $? = 12$ in. **49. (a)** Sketches will vary. **(b)** Formula for perimeter of an equilateral triangle is $P = 3s$, where s is the length of one side. **(c)** The formula will *not* work for other kinds of triangles because the sides will have different lengths. **50. (a)** $P = 5s$ **(b)** $P = 6s$ **(c)** $P = 10s$ **(d)** $P = ns$ **51. (a)** 140 miles **(b)** 350 miles **(c)** 560 miles **52. (a)** 70 miles **(b)** 175 miles **(c)** 280 miles **(d)** The rate is half of 70 miles per hour, so the distance will be half as far; divide each result in **Exercise 51** by 2. **53. (a)** 50 hours **(b)** 60 hours **(c)** 150 hours **54. (a)** 61 miles per hour **(b)** 57 miles per hour **(c)** 65 miles per hour

SECTION 3.2 (pages 181–184)

1. $A = s^2$ or $A = s \cdot s$; A stands for area; s stands for side (the length of one side). **2.** $A = l \cdot w$; A stands for Area; l stands for length; w stands for width. **3. (a)** 100 **(b)** 20 **(c)** 625 **(d)** 50 **4. (a)** 64 **(b)** 16 **(c)** 900 **(d)** 60 **5.** $A = 77$ ft^2 **7.** $A = 6$ in. $\cdot$ 6 in.; $A = 36$ in.^{2} **9.** $A = 775$ mm^2 **11.** $A = 105$ cm^2 **13.** $A = 72$ ft^2 **15.** $A = 625$ mi^2 **17.** $l = 6$ ft CHECK $A = 6$ ft $\cdot$ 3 ft; $A = 18$ ft^2 **19.** $w = 80$ yd CHECK $A = 90$ yd $\cdot$ 80 yd; $A = 7200$ yd^2 **21.** $l = 14$ in. CHECK $A = 14$ in. $\cdot$ 11 in.; $A = 154$ in.^{2} **23.** 6; $s = 6$ m **25.** $s = 2$ ft **27.** $h = 20$ cm CHECK $A = 25$ cm $\cdot$ 20 cm; $A = 500$ cm^2 **29.** $b = 17$ in. CHECK $A = 17$ in. $\cdot$ 13 in.; $A = 221$ in.^{2} **31.** $h = 1$ m CHECK $A = 9$ m $\cdot$ 1 m; $A = 9$ m^2 **33.** Height is not part of perimeter. Square units are used for area, not perimeter. $P = 25$ cm + 25 cm + 25 cm + 25 cm; $P = 100$ cm **34.** To find s^2, multiply 7 ft $\cdot$ 7 ft. Area is measured in square units. $A = 7$ ft $\cdot$ 7 ft; $A = 49$ ft^2 **35.** Square; $P = 180$ in; $A = 2025$ in.^{2} **37.** Parallelogram; $P = 60$ cm; $A = 180$ cm^2 **39.** $P = 48$ m; $A = 144$ m^2 **41.** \$108 **43.** \$725 **45.** 53 yd **47.** $P = 52$ ft; $A = 169$ ft^2; 21 ft^2 for each camper (rounded)

49.

50. (a) 5 ft by 1 ft has area of 5 ft^2; 4 ft by 2 ft has area of 8 ft^2; 3 ft by 3 ft has area of 9 ft^2 **(b)** The square plot 3 ft by 3 ft has the greatest area.

51.

52. (a) 7 ft^2, 12 ft^2, 15 ft^2, 16 ft^2 **(b)** Square plots have the greatest area.

SUMMARY EXERCISES Perimeter and Area (pages 185–186)

1. Rectangle; $P = 32$ m; $A = 39$ m^2 **2.** Square; $P = 104$ ft; $A = 676$ ft^2 **3.** Parallelogram; $P = 34$ yd; $A = 56$ yd^2 **4.** Rectangle; $P = 36$ cm; $A = 80$ cm^2 **5.** Square; $P = 36$ in.; $A = 81$ in.^{2} **6.** Parallelogram; $P = 30$ m; $A = 45$ m^2 **7.** Rectangle; $P = 26$ ft; $A = 36$ ft^2 **8.** Parallelogram; $P = 188$ ft; $A = 2100$ ft^2

9. $w = 1$ ft

CHECK 7 ft + 7 ft + 1 ft + 1 ft = 16 ft

10. $b = 5$ yd

CHECK $A = 5$ yd $\cdot$ 1 yd
$A = 5$ yd^2

11. $s = 6$ in.

CHECK $A = 6$ in. $\cdot$ 6 in.
$A = 36$ in.^{2}

12. $w = 2$ m

CHECK $A = 42$ m $\cdot$ 2 m
$A = 84$ m^2

13. $s = 16$ cm

CHECK $P = 16$ cm + 16 cm + 16 cm + 16 cm
$P = 64$ cm

14. $l = 15$ ft

CHECK $P = 15$ ft + 15 ft + 9 ft + 9 ft
$P = 48$ ft

15. 504 meters of fencing **16.** 9600 yd^2 − 5000 yd^2 = 4600 yd^2 **17.** 9 inches **18.** 176 cm of braid **19.** $7(15$ ft$^2) = 105$ ft^2 of fabric; $7(16$ ft$) = 112$ ft of binding **20.** 48 ft

SECTION 3.3 (pages 192–195)

1. (a) false; a number subtracted from 14, or, 14 minus a number. **(b)** true **(c)** false; the quotient of −20 and a number, or, −20 divided by a number. **2. (a)** true **(b)** false; the product of 18 and a number, or, 18 times a number **(c)** false; the quotient of a number and 42, or, a number divided by 42. **3.** $14 + x$ or $x + 14$ **5.** $-5 + x$ or $x + (-5)$ **7.** $20 - x$ **9.** $x - 9$ **11.** $-6x$ **13.** $2x$ **15.** $\frac{x}{2}$ **17.** $2x + 8$ or $8 + 2x$ **19.** $7x - 10$ **21.** $2x + x$ or $x + 2x$

23. $n = 7$ CHECK $\underbrace{4 \cdot 7}_{28} - 2$ does equal 26
$\underbrace{28 - 2}_{26}$

25. $2n + n = -15$ or $n + 2n = -15$; $n = -5$ CHECK $\underbrace{2 \cdot (-5)}_{-10} + (-5)$ does equal -15
$\underbrace{-10 + (-5)}_{-15}$

27. $5n + 12 = 7n$; $n = 6$ CHECK $\underbrace{5 \cdot 6}_{30} + 12 = \underbrace{7 \cdot 6}_{42}$
$\underbrace{30 + 12}_{42} = 42$

29. $30 - 3n = 2 + n$; $n = 7$ CHECK $30 - \underbrace{3 \cdot 7}_{21} = \underbrace{2 + 7}_{9}$
$\underbrace{30 - 21}_{9} = 9$

31. $w + 15 - 28 + 5 = 177$. He weighed 185 pounds originally. **33.** Let c be the number of cookies the children ate. $18 - c + 36 = 49$. Her children ate 5 cookies. **35.** Let p be the number of pens in each box.

$6p - 32 - 35 = 5$. There were 12 pens in each box. **37.** Let d be each member's dues. $14d + 340 - 575 = -25$. Each member paid $15. **39.** $4a - 75 = a$. Tamu is 25 years old. **41.** Let m be the amount Brenda spent. $2m - 3 = 81$. Brenda spent $42. **43.** Let b be the number of pieces in each bag. $5b - 3 \cdot 48 = b$. There were 36 pieces of candy in each bag. **45.** Let d be the daily amount for a young child. $4d + 8 = 60$. A young child should receive 13 mg of vitamin C.

SECTION 3.4 (pages 200–201)

1. (a) known parts; unknown parts **(b)** least **2. (a)** label; or, include the units **(b)** all the facts in the original problem **3.** $a + a + 9 = 51$. I am 21; my sister is 30. **5.** m is husband's earnings; $m + 1500$ is Lien's. $m + m + 1500 = 37,500$. Husband earned $18,000; Lien earned $19,500. **7.** m is printer's cost; $8m$ is computer's cost. $m + 8m = 396$; printer cost $44; computer cost $352. **9.** Shorter piece is x; longer piece is $x + 10$. So, $x + x + 10 = 78$. Shorter piece is 34 cm; longer piece is 44 cm. **11.** Longer piece is x; shorter piece is $x - 7$ So, $x + x - 7 = 31$. Longer piece is 19 ft; shorter piece is 12 ft. **13.** s is number of Senators; $5s - 65$ is number of Representatives. $s + 5s - 65 = 535$. 100 Senators; 435 Representatives **15.** First part is x; second part is x; third part is $x + 25$. So, $x + x + x + 25 = 706$. First part is 227 m; second part is 227 m; third part is 252 m. **17.** Length is 19 yd. **19.** Length is 12 ft; width is 6 ft. **21.** Length is 13 in.; width is 5 in. **23.** $P = 52$ in.; $A = 168$ in.^{2}

Chapter 3 REVIEW EXERCISES (pages 210–211)

1. Square; $P = 112$ cm **2.** Rectangle; $P = 22$ mi **3.** Parallelogram; $P = 42$ yd **4.** $P = 140$ m **5.** 12 ft $= 4s$; $s = 3$ ft **6.** 128 yd $= 2l + 2(31$ yd$)$; $l = 33$ yd **7.** 72 in. $= 2(21$ in.$) + 2w$; $w = 15$ in. **8.** $A = 40$ ft^2 **9.** $A = 625$ m^2 **10.** $A = 208$ yd^2 **11.** 126 ft$^2 = 14$ ft $\cdot$ w; $w = 9$ ft **12.** 88 cm$^2 = 11$ cm $\cdot$ h; $h = 8$ cm **13.** 100 mi$^2 = s \cdot s$; $s = 10$ mi **14.** $57 - x$ **15.** $15 + 2x$ or $2x + 15$ **16.** $-9x$ **17.** $4n + 6 = -30$; $n = -9$ **18.** $10 - 2n = 4 + n$; $n = 2$ **19.** m is money originally in account. $m - 600 + 750 + 75 = 309$. $84 was originally in Grace's account. **20.** c is number of candles in each box. $4c - 25 = 23$. There were 12 candles in each box. **21.** p is Reggie's prize money; $p + 300$ is Donald's prize money. $p + p + 300 = 1000$. Reggie gets $350; Donald gets $650. **22.** w is the width; $2w$ is the length. $84 = 2(2w) + 2(w)$. The width is 14 cm; the length is 28 cm. **23. (a)** 36 ft $= 4s$; $s = 9$ ft **(b)** $A = 9$ ft $\cdot$ 9 ft; $A = 81$ ft^2 **24.** Rectangles will vary. Two possibilities are: $A = 7$ ft $\cdot$ 3 ft, $A = 21$ ft^2; $A = 6$ ft $\cdot$ 4 ft, $A = 24$ ft^2 **25.** Let f be the fencing for the garden. $36 - f + 20 = 41$. 15 ft of fencing was used on the garden. **26.** w is the width; $w + 2$ is the length. $36 = 2(w + 2) + 2 \cdot w$. Width is 8 ft; length is 10 ft.

Chapter 3 TEST (pages 212–213)

1. $P = 262$ m **2.** $P = 40$ in. **3.** $P = 12$ miles **4.** $P = 12$ ft **5.** $P = 110$ cm **6.** $A = 486$ mm^2 **7.** $A = 140$ cm^2 **8.** $A = 3740$ mi^2 **9.** $A = 36$ m^2 **10.** 12 ft $= 4s$; $s = 3$ ft **11.** 34 ft $= 2l + 2(6$ ft$)$; $l = 11$ ft **12.** 65 in.$^2 = 13$ in. $\cdot$ h; $h = 5$ in. **13.** 12 cm$^2 = 4$ cm $\cdot$ w; $w = 3$ cm **14.** 16 ft$^2 = s^2$; $s = 4$ ft **15.** Answers will vary; one possibility: Linear units like ft are used to measure length, width, height, and perimeter. Area is measured in square units like ft^2 (squares that measure 1 ft on each side). **16.** $4n + 40 = 0$; $n = -10$ **17.** $7n - 23 = n + 7$; $n = 5$ **18.** Let m represent money spent on groceries. $43 - m + 16 = 44$. Son spent $15.

19. Let d represent daughter's age. $39 = 5d + 4$. Daughter is 7 years old. **20.** Let p be length of one piece; $p + 4$ be length of second piece. $p + p + 4 = 118$. One piece is 57 cm; second piece is 61 cm. **21.** Let w be width; $4w$ be length. $420 = 2(4w) + 2(w)$. Sketches may vary; length is 168 ft; width is 42 ft. **22.** Let h be Marcella's hours; $h - 3$ be Tim's hours. $h + h - 3 = 19$. Marcella worked 11 hours; Tim worked 8 hours.

Chapters 1–3 CUMULATIVE REVIEW EXERCISES (pages 214–215)

1. four billion, two hundred six thousand, three hundred **2.** 70,005,489 **3.** $<$ $>$ **4. (a)** multiplication property of 1 **(b)** addition property of 0 **(c)** associative property of multiplication **5. (a)** 3800 **(b)** 490,000 **6.** -24 **7.** 27 **8.** -3 **9.** -100 **10.** 5 **11.** 0 **12.** -13 **13.** 25 **14.** -32 **15.** $\dfrac{27}{0}$ is undefined. **16.** $10 \cdot w \cdot w \cdot x \cdot y \cdot y \cdot y \cdot y$ **17.** 240 **18.** $2k$ **19.** $3m^2 + 2m$ **20.** 0 **21.** $-20a$ **22.** $-2x^2 - 3$ **23.** $-12n + 1$ **24.** $x = 2$ CHECK $\underbrace{6 - 20}_{-14} = \underbrace{2(2) - 9(2)}_{\underset{-14}{4 - 18}}$ ✓

25. $y = -1$ CHECK $\underbrace{-5(-1)}_{5} = \underbrace{-1 + 6}_{5}$ ✓

26. $b = 4$ **27.** $h = -2$ **28.** $x = 0$ **29.** $a = -3$ **30.** $P = 60$ in.; $A = 198$ in.^{2} **31.** $P = 60$ m; $A = 225$ m^2 **32.** $P = 24$ ft; $A = 32$ ft^2 **33.** $5n + (-50) = 0$; $n = 10$ **34.** $10 - 3n = 2n$; $n = 2$ **35.** Let p be number of people originally. $p - 3 + 6 - 2 = 5$. There were 4 people in line. **36.** Let m be amount paid by each player. $12m - 2200 = -40$. Each player paid $180. **37.** Let g be one group; $3g$ the other. $g + 3g = 192$. 48 students in one group; 144 in the other. **38.** Let w be the width; $w + 14$ be the length. $92 = 2(w + 14) + 2(w)$. Width is 16 ft; length is 30 ft.

CHAPTER 4 Rational Numbers: Positive and Negative Fraction

SECTION 4.1 (pages 225–228)

1. (a) parts of equal size. **(b)** denominator **2. (a)** numerator **(b)** a fraction bar **3.** $\dfrac{\text{shaded parts} \to 5}{\text{number of equal parts} \to 8}$; $\dfrac{3}{8}$ unshaded **5.** $\dfrac{2}{3}$; $\dfrac{1}{3}$ **7.** $\dfrac{3}{2}$; $\dfrac{1}{2}$ **9.** $\dfrac{11}{6}$; $\dfrac{1}{6}$ **11.** $\dfrac{2}{11}$; $\dfrac{3}{11}$; $\dfrac{4}{11}$ **13. (a)** $\dfrac{6}{20}$; **(b)** $\dfrac{19}{20}$ **15.** N: 3; D: 4; 4 equal parts **17.** N: 12; D: 7; 7 equal parts **19.** Proper: $\dfrac{1}{3}, \dfrac{5}{8}, \dfrac{7}{16}$; Improper: $\dfrac{8}{5}, \dfrac{6}{6}, \dfrac{12}{2}$

21.

23.

25.

27. $-\dfrac{3}{4}$ pound **28.** $\dfrac{1}{3}$ cup

29. $\frac{3}{10}$ mile   **30.** $-\frac{1}{2}$ quart   **31.** $\frac{2}{5}$ **33.** 0   **35. (a)** 2 times 12; $\frac{12}{24}$
(b) $\frac{8}{24}$ **(c)** $\frac{16}{24}$ **(d)** $\frac{6}{24}$ **(e)** $\frac{18}{24}$ **(f)** $\frac{4}{24}$ **(g)** $\frac{20}{24}$ **(h)** $\frac{3}{24}$ **(i)** $\frac{9}{24}$
(j) $\frac{15}{24}$ **37. (a)** $-\frac{1}{3}$ **(b)** $-\frac{2}{3}$ **(c)** $-\frac{2}{3}$ **(d)** $-\frac{1}{3}$ **(e)** $-\frac{2}{3}$ **(f)** Some

possibilities are: $-\frac{4}{12} = -\frac{1}{3}$; $-\frac{8}{24} = -\frac{1}{3}$; $-\frac{20}{30} = -\frac{2}{3}$; $-\frac{24}{36} = -\frac{2}{3}$.

39. You cannot do it if you want the numerator to be a whole number, because 5 does not divide into 18 evenly. You could use multiples of 5 as the denominator, such as 10, 15, 20, etc.   **40.** No, a fraction cannot have a denominator of 0, because division by 0 is not allowed.   **41.** 10   **43.** -1 **45.** -6 **47.** 3
49. 2   **51.** -9 **53.** 1   **55.** -8 **57.** $\frac{2}{5}$ is unshaded.   **59.** $\frac{5}{8}$ is unshaded.
61. One possibility is shown. ○□□□□□□□△△△

63. One possibility is shown. ⊙‼ ! ! ! , . . . ? ? ?   **65. (a)** $\frac{1467}{3912}$ **(b)** Divide

3912 by 8 to get 489; multiply 3 by 489 to get 1467.   **66. (a)** $\frac{4256}{5472}$

(b) Divide 5472 by 9 to get 608; multiply 7 by 608 to get 4256.

67. (a) $-\frac{1}{5}$ **(b)** Divide 3485 by 2, by 3, and by 5 to see that dividing

by 5 gives 697. Or divide 3485 by 697 to get 5.   **68. (a)** $-\frac{1}{6}$

(b) Divide 4902 by 4, by 6, and by 8 to see that dividing by 6 gives 817. Or divide 4902 by 817 to get 6.

SECTION 4.2 (pages 237–240)

1. (a) yes   **(b)** No, 5 is a common factor.   **(c)** yes   **(d)** yes   **(e)** No, 3 is a common factor.   **(f)** No, 7 is a common factor.   **2. (a)** No, 2 is a common factor.   **(b)** No, 3 is a common factor   **(c)** yes   **(d)** No, 11 is a common factor.   **(e)** yes   **(f)** yes   **3. (a)** $\frac{2}{3}$ **(b)** $\frac{2}{3}$ **(c)** $-\frac{1}{4}$ **(d)** $-\frac{1}{2}$
(e) $\frac{8}{9}$ **(f)** $-\frac{2}{5}$ **5.** comp., prime, comp., neither, prime, prime, comp., comp.
6. comp., prime, prime, comp., neither, comp., prime, comp.
7. $6 = 2 \cdot 3$

② ③

9. $2 \cdot 2 \cdot 5$ **11.** $5 \cdot 5$ **13.** $2 \cdot 2 \cdot 3 \cdot 3$ **15. (a)** $2 \cdot 2 \cdot 11$
(b) $2 \cdot 2 \cdot 2 \cdot 11$ **17. (a)** $3 \cdot 5 \cdot 5$ **(b)** $2 \cdot 2 \cdot 17$ **(c)** $3 \cdot 3 \cdot 3 \cdot 7$
19. $\frac{\cancel{2} \cdot \cancel{2} \cdot \cancel{2}}{\cancel{2} \cdot \cancel{2} \cdot \cancel{2} \cdot 2} = \frac{1}{2}$ **21.** $\frac{\cancel{2} \cdot \cancel{2} \cdot \cancel{2} \cdot \cancel{2} \cdot 2}{\cancel{2} \cdot \cancel{2} \cdot \cancel{2} \cdot \cancel{2} \cdot 3} = \frac{2}{3}$ **23.** $\frac{2 \cdot \cancel{7}}{3 \cdot \cancel{7}} = \frac{2}{3}$
25. $\frac{\cancel{2} \cdot 2 \cdot \cancel{3} \cdot 3}{\cancel{2} \cdot \cancel{3} \cdot 7} = \frac{6}{7}$ **27.** $\frac{2 \cdot 5 \cdot 5}{3 \cdot 3 \cdot 7}$ already in lowest terms
29. $\frac{\cancel{3} \cdot \cancel{3} \cdot 3}{\cancel{3} \cdot \cancel{3} \cdot 5} = \frac{3}{5}$ **31.** $\frac{\cancel{2} \cdot 2 \cdot \cancel{3}}{\cancel{2} \cdot \cancel{3} \cdot 3} = \frac{2}{3}$ **33.** $\frac{\cancel{5} \cdot 7}{2 \cdot 2 \cdot 2 \cdot \cancel{5}} = \frac{7}{8}$
35. $\frac{\cancel{2} \cdot \cancel{3} \cdot \cancel{3} \cdot \cancel{5}}{\cancel{2} \cdot 2 \cdot \cancel{3} \cdot \cancel{3} \cdot \cancel{5}} = \frac{1}{2}$ **37.** $\frac{2 \cdot \cancel{3} \cdot \cancel{5} \cdot \cancel{7}}{3 \cdot \cancel{3} \cdot \cancel{5} \cdot \cancel{7}} = \frac{2}{3}$
39. $\frac{\cancel{3} \cdot \cancel{11} \cdot 13}{\cancel{3} \cdot 3 \cdot 5 \cdot \cancel{11}} = \frac{13}{15}$ **41. (a)** $\frac{1}{4}$ **(b)** $\frac{1}{2}$ **(c)** $\frac{1}{10}$ **(d)** $\frac{60}{60} = 1$
43. (a) $\frac{1}{3}$ **(b)** $\frac{1}{6}$ **(c)** $\frac{1}{2}$ **45.** Men, $\frac{2}{5}$; Women, $\frac{3}{5}$ **47.** The result of dividing 3 by 3 is 1, so 1 should be written above and below all the slashes.

The numerator is $1 \cdot 1$, so the correct answer is $\frac{1}{4}$.   **48.** You must divide numerator and denominator by the *same* number. The fraction is already in lowest terms because 9 and 16 have no common factor besides 1.
49. $\frac{2c}{5}$ **51.** $\frac{4}{7}$ **53.** $\frac{6r}{5s}$ **55.** $\frac{1}{7n^2}$ **57.** already in lowest terms
59. $\frac{7}{9y}$ **61.** $\frac{7k}{2}$ **63.** $\frac{1}{3}$ **65.** $\frac{c}{d}$ **67.** $\frac{6ab}{c}$ **69.** already in lowest terms   **71.** $3eg^2$

SECTION 4.3 (pages 249–252)

1. multiply; denominators   **2.** positive; negative   **3.** $-\frac{3}{16}$ **5.** $\frac{9}{10}$
7. $\frac{1}{2}$ **9.** -6 **11.** 36   **13.** $\frac{15}{4y}$ **15.** $\frac{1}{2}$ **17.** $\frac{6}{5}$ **19.** -9 **21.** $-\frac{1}{6}$
23. $\frac{11}{15d}$ **25.** b **27. (a)** Forgot to write 1s in numerator when dividing out common factors. Answer is $\frac{1}{6}$.   **(b)** Used reciprocal of $\frac{2}{3}$ in multiplication, but the reciprocal is used only in division. Correct answer is $\frac{16}{3}$.
28. (a) Answer is not in lowest terms; should be $\frac{2}{3}$.   **(b)** Error made when dividing out common factor; correct answer is $\frac{3}{20}$.   **29. (a)** Forgot to use reciprocal of $\frac{4}{1}$; correct answer is $\frac{1}{6}$.   **(b)** Used reciprocal of $\frac{5}{6}$ instead of reciprocal of $\frac{10}{9}$; correct answer is $\frac{3}{4}$.   **30. (a)** Division by 0 is undefined; there is no answer.   **(b)** Forgot to use reciprocal of $\frac{1}{3}$; correct answer is $\frac{9}{10}$.
31. $\frac{4}{15}$ **33.** $-\frac{9}{32}$ **35.** 21   **37.** 15   **39.** undefined   **41.** $-\frac{55}{12}$ **43.** $8b$
45. $\frac{3}{5d}$ **47.** $\frac{2x^2}{w}$ **49.** $\frac{3}{10}$ yd^2 **51.** 80 dispensers   **53.** earn \$9300; borrow \$3100   **55.** About 75 infield players   **57.** 9 trips   **59.** 3200 times
61. $\frac{3}{20}$ of $1600 = 240$ students   **63.** $160 - 64 = 96$ students
65. 7 million horses   **67.** 154 million dogs and cats   **69.** Rewrite division as multiplication. Leave the first number (dividend) the same. Change the second number (divisor) to its reciprocal by "flipping" it. Then multiply.
70. $\frac{3}{?} \div \frac{4}{5} = \frac{3}{?} \cdot \frac{5}{4} = \frac{3 \cdot \cancel{5}}{? \cdot 4} = \frac{3}{4}$, so ? must be 5 in order to divide out as a common factor.

SECTION 4.4 (pages 260–263)

1. (a) like fractions   **(b)** add them   **2. (a)** different denominators
(b) add only the numerators   **3.** $\frac{7}{8}$ **5.** $-\frac{1}{2}$ **7.** $\frac{1}{2}$ **9.** $-\frac{9}{40}$ **11.** $-\frac{13}{24}$
13. $-\frac{3}{5}$ **15.** $-\frac{7}{18}$ **17.** $\frac{8}{7}$ **19.** $-\frac{3}{8}$ **21.** $\frac{3 + 5c}{15}$ **23.** $\frac{10 - m}{2m}$
25. $\frac{8}{b^2}$ **27.** $\frac{bc + 21}{7b}$ **29.** $\frac{-4 - cd}{c^2}$ **31.** $-\frac{44}{105}$ **33.** $\frac{a^2b + 12}{3a^2}$
35. $\frac{-w^3 + 50}{10w^2}$ **37.** $\frac{m^4}{n^2}$ **39. (a)** $\frac{15}{20} + \frac{8}{20} = \frac{23}{20}$ Cannot add fractions with unlike denominators; use 20 as the LCD.   **(b)** When rewriting fractions with 18 as the denominator, you must multiply denominator and numerator by the same number. The correct answer is $\frac{15}{18} - \frac{8}{18} = \frac{7}{18}$.
40. (a) Answer must be written in lowest terms.   **(b)** Cannot subtract fractions with unlike denominators; use 20 as the LCD.
41. $\frac{47}{60}$ in.   **43.** $\frac{23}{24}$ cup   **45.** $\frac{3}{4}$ acre   **47.** $\frac{23}{50}$ of workers   **49.** $\frac{4}{25}$ of workers   **51.** $\frac{5}{16}$ inch   **53.** $\frac{1}{12}$ mile   **55. (a)** $\frac{1}{12}$; $\frac{1}{12}$; addition is commutative.   **(b)** $\frac{1}{3}$; $-\frac{1}{3}$; subtraction is *not* commutative.
(c) $-\frac{3}{5}$; $-\frac{3}{5}$; multiplication is commutative.

(d) $6; \frac{1}{6}$; division is *not* commutative. **56. (a)** 0; 0; the sum of a number and its opposite is 0. **(b)** 1; 1; when a nonzero number is divided by itself, the quotient is 1. **(c)** $\frac{5}{6}; -\frac{17}{20}$; multiplying by 1 leaves a number unchanged. **(d)** 1; 1; a number times its reciprocal is 1.

SECTION 4.5 (pages 275–278)

1.

Shade $2\frac{1}{3}$ of the circles.

2.

Shade $1\frac{3}{4}$ of the rectangles.

3.

Shade $\frac{3}{2}$ of the squares.

4.

Shade $\frac{11}{3}$ of the circles.

5. $\frac{9}{2}$ **7.** $-\frac{8}{5}$ **9.** $\frac{19}{8}$ **11.** $-\frac{57}{10}$ **13.** $\frac{161}{15}$ **15.** $4\frac{1}{3}$ **17.** $-2\frac{1}{2}$

19. $3\frac{2}{3}$ **21.** $-5\frac{2}{3}$ **23.** $11\frac{3}{4}$ **25.** $\frac{63}{8} = 7\frac{7}{8}$; $2 \cdot 4 = 8$

27. $1\frac{5}{21}$; $3 \div 3 = 1$ **29.** $5\frac{1}{2}$; $4 + 2 = 6$ **31.** $3\frac{2}{3}$; $4 - 1 = 3$

33. $\frac{17}{18}$; $6 \div 6 = 1$ **35.** $6\frac{1}{5}$; $8 - 2 = 6$ **37.** $P = 7$ in.; $A = 3\frac{1}{16}$ in.^{2}

39. $P = 19\frac{1}{2}$ yd; $A = 21\frac{1}{8}$ yd^2 **41.** $P = 11\frac{5}{6}$ ft; $A = 6\frac{1}{2}$ ft^2

43. $13 + 9 = 22$ ft; $21\frac{1}{6}$ ft **45.** $2 \cdot 6 = 12$ ounces; $9\frac{5}{8}$ ounces

47. $4 - 2 = 2$ miles; $2\frac{3}{10}$ miles **49.** $4 \cdot 5 = 20$ yd; $18\frac{3}{4}$ yd **51.** $\frac{5}{8}$ mile;

53. $6\frac{3}{8}$ miles **55.** $21\frac{3}{8}$ in. **57.** $24 + 35 + 24 + 35 = 118$ in.;

$116\frac{1}{2}$ in. **59.** $126 \div 2 = 63$ loads; 84 loads

61. $(4 \cdot 22) + (5 \cdot 23) + (3 \cdot 24) + (12 \cdot 1) = 287$ in.; $280\frac{1}{8}$ in.

SUMMARY EXERCISES Computation with Fractions (pages 279–280)

1. (a) $\frac{3}{8}; \frac{5}{8}$ **(b)** $\frac{4}{5}; \frac{1}{5}$ **2.**

3. (a) 24 **(b)** 4 **4. (a)** 1 **(b)** -4 **(c)** 9 **5. (a)** $2 \cdot 2 \cdot 2 \cdot 3 \cdot 3$
(b) $3 \cdot 5 \cdot 7$ **6. (a)** $\frac{4}{5}$ **(b)** $\frac{7}{8}$ **7.** $\frac{1}{2}$ **8.** $-\frac{5}{24}$ **9.** $\frac{17}{16}$ **10.** $\frac{5}{6}$

11. $-\frac{2}{15}$ **12.** $-\frac{3}{8}$ **13.** 56 **14.** $\frac{11}{24}$ **15.** $-\frac{7}{6}$ **16.** $-\frac{19}{12}$ **17.** $\frac{25}{12}$

18. 35 **19.** $7\frac{7}{12}$; $5 + 3 = 8$ **20.** $11\frac{3}{7}$; $2 \cdot 5 = 10$ **21.** $3\frac{3}{10}$;

$6 - 3 = 3$ **22.** $\frac{16}{35}$; $2 \div 4 = \frac{2}{4}$ or $\frac{1}{2}$ **23.** 4; $5 \div 1 = 5$ **24.** $2\frac{2}{3}$;

$3 - 1 = 2$ **25. (a)** $2\frac{1}{16}$ in. **(b)** $\frac{5}{16}$ in. **26.** $P = 3\frac{1}{2}$ in.; $A = \frac{49}{64}$ in.^{2}

27. 12 batches **28.** 6¢ **29.** Not sure, 225 adults; Real, 675 adults; Imaginary, 600 adults **30.** diameter $= \frac{1}{4}$ in.; $P = 4\frac{1}{2}$ in.

31. 46 bottles **32.** $P = 6$ in.; $A = 2\frac{1}{4}$ in.^{2}

SECTION 4.6 (pages 284–287)

1. (a) $-\frac{3}{8}$ **(b)** exponent **(c)** $\left(-\frac{3}{8}\right)\left(-\frac{3}{8}\right)$ **2. (a)** positive

(b) $5\left(-\frac{3}{10}\right)$ and $\left(-\frac{5}{6}\right)\left(\frac{3}{5}\right)$ **3.** $\frac{9}{16}$ **5.** $\frac{8}{125}$ **7.** $-\frac{1}{27}$ **9.** $\frac{1}{32}$

11. $\frac{49}{100}$ **13.** $\frac{36}{25}$ or $1\frac{11}{25}$ **15.** $\frac{12}{25}$ **17.** $\frac{1}{100}$ **19.** $-\frac{3}{2}$ or $-1\frac{1}{2}$

21. (a) The answers are $\frac{1}{4}, -\frac{1}{8}, \frac{1}{16}, -\frac{1}{32}, \frac{1}{64}, -\frac{1}{128}, \frac{1}{256}, -\frac{1}{512}$.
(b) When a negative number is raised to an even power, the answer is positive. When a negative number is raised to an odd power, the answer is negative.
22. (a) Ask yourself, "What number, times itself, is 4?" This is the numerator. Then ask, "What number, times itself, is 9?" This is the denominator. The number under the ketchup is either $\frac{2}{3}$ or $-\frac{2}{3}$.

(b) The number under the ketchup is $-\frac{1}{3}$ because
$\left(-\frac{1}{3}\right)\left(-\frac{1}{3}\right)\left(-\frac{1}{3}\right) = -\frac{1}{27}$. **(c)** Either $\frac{1}{2}$ or $-\frac{1}{2}$.

23. $\frac{1}{5} - \frac{42}{10}; \frac{2 - 42}{10} = -\frac{40}{10} = -4$ **25.** $\frac{5}{16}$ **27.** $\frac{1}{3}$ **29.** $\frac{1}{6}$ **31.** $-\frac{17}{24}$

33. $-\frac{4}{27}$ **35.** $\frac{1}{36}$ **37.** $\frac{9}{64}$ in.^{2} **39.** $\frac{19}{10}$ or $1\frac{9}{10}$ miles **41.** 4

43. $-\frac{25}{2}$ or $-12\frac{1}{2}$ **45.** $\frac{1}{14}$ **47.** $\frac{5}{18}$ **49.** -8 **51.** $\frac{9}{100}$

SECTION 4.7 (pages 293–296)

1. (a) $\frac{5}{2}$ **(b)** $\frac{5}{2}$ is the reciprocal of $\frac{2}{5}$. Multiplying $\frac{\overset{1}{\cancel{5}}}{\cancel{2}}\left(\frac{\cancel{2}}{\cancel{5}}c\right)$

gives $1c$, or just c, on the left side of the equal sign. **2. (a)** $\frac{4}{1}$

(b) $\frac{4}{1}$ is the reciprocal of $\frac{1}{4}$. Multiplying $\frac{\overset{1}{\cancel{4}}}{1}\left(\frac{1}{\cancel{4}}x\right)$ gives $1x$, or just x,

on the right side of the equal sign.

3. $a = 30$ CHECK $\frac{1}{3}(30) = 10$

$10 = 10$ ✓

5. $b = -24$ CHECK $-20 = \frac{5}{6}(-24)$

$-20 = -20$ ✓

7. $c = 6$ CHECK $-\frac{7}{2}(6) = -21$

$-21 = -21$ ✓

9. $d = -\frac{6}{5}$ CHECK $\frac{3}{10} = -\frac{1}{4}\left(-\frac{6}{5}\right)$

$\frac{3}{10} = \frac{3}{10}$ ✓

11. $n = 12$ CHECK $\frac{1}{6}(12) + 7 = 9$

$2 + 7 = 9$

$9 = 9$ ✓

13. $r = -9$ CHECK $-10 = \frac{5}{3}(-9) + 5$

$-10 = -15 + 5$

$-10 = -10$ ✓

15. $x = 24$ CHECK $\frac{3}{8}(24) - 9 = 0$

$9 - 9 = 0$

$0 = 0$ ✓

17. 5; $y = 45$ **19.** $n = -18$ **21.** $x = \frac{1}{12}$ **23.** $b = -\frac{1}{8}$ **25.** $n = 0$

27. (a) $\frac{1}{6}(18) + 1 = -2$

$3 + 1 = -2$

$4 \ne -2$

Does *not* balance; correct solution is -18.

(b) $-\frac{3}{2} = \frac{9}{4}\left(-\frac{2}{3}\right)$

$-\frac{3}{2} = -\frac{3}{2}$ ✓

Balances, so $-\frac{2}{3}$ is correct solution.

28. (a) $-\frac{3}{4}\left(\frac{5}{6}\right) = -\frac{5}{8}$

$-\frac{5}{8} = -\frac{5}{8}$ ✓

Balances, so $\frac{5}{6}$ is correct solution.

(b) $16 = -\frac{7}{3}(6) + 2$

$16 = -14 + 2$

$16 \ne -12$

Does not balance; correct solution is -6.

29. Let a be the man's age.

$109 = 100 + \frac{a}{2}$

The man is 18 years old.

31. Let a be the woman's age.

$122 = 100 + \frac{a}{2}$

The woman is 44 years old.

33. Let a be the woman's age.

$128 = 100 + \frac{a}{2}$

The woman is 56 years old.

35. Let p be the penny size. $\frac{p}{4} + \frac{1}{2} = 3$. The penny size is 10.

37. Let p be the penny size. $\frac{p}{4} + \frac{1}{2} = \frac{5}{2}$. The penny size is 8.

39. Some possibilities are: $\frac{1}{2}x = 4$; $-\frac{1}{4}a = -2$; $\frac{3}{4}b = 6$.

40. Some possibilities are: $\frac{1}{2}y = -6$; $w = -8$; $-\frac{1}{12}d = 1$

SECTION 4.8 (pages 302–304)

1. Multiply $\frac{1}{2}$ times 58 m times 66 m; the units in the answer will be m².
2. Add 58 m plus 72 m plus 72 m; the units in the answer will be m.

3. $P = 202$ m; $A = 1914$ m²   **5.** $P = 5$ ft; $A = \frac{27}{32}$ ft²

7. $P = 26\frac{1}{4}$ yd; $A = 30\frac{3}{4}$ yd²   **9.** $P = \frac{454}{15}$ yd or $30\frac{4}{15}$ yd;

$A = \frac{115}{3}$ yd² or $38\frac{1}{3}$ yd²   **11.** $A = 52$ m • 37 m; $A = 1924$ m²;

$A = 1924$ m² $- 208$ m²; $A = 1716$ m²   **13.** $A = \frac{63}{8}$ ft² or $7\frac{7}{8}$ ft²

15. 132 m of curbing; 726 m² of sod   **17.** Rectangular solid;

$V = 528$ cm³   **19.** Rectangular solid or cube; $V = 15\frac{5}{8}$ in.³

21. Pyramid; $V = 800$ cm³   **23.** $V = 106\frac{2}{3}$ ft³   **25.** $V = 18$ in.³

27. $V = 651{,}775$ m³

Chapter 4 REVIEW EXERCISES (pages 315–316)

1. $\frac{2}{5}; \frac{1}{5}$ **2.** $\frac{3}{10}; \frac{7}{10}$ **3.**

4. (a) -4 **(b)** 8   **(c)** -1 **5.** $\frac{7}{8}$ **6.** $\frac{3}{5}$ **7.** already in lowest terms

8. $\frac{3x}{8}$ **9.** $\frac{1}{5b}$ **10.** $\frac{4n}{7m^2}$ **11.** $\frac{1}{16}$ **12.** -12 **13.** $\frac{8}{27}$ **14.** $\frac{1}{6x}$

15. $2a^2$ **16.** $\frac{6}{7k}$ **17.** $\frac{5}{24}$ **18.** $-\frac{2}{15}$ **19.** $\frac{19}{6}$ or $3\frac{1}{6}$ **20.** $\frac{3}{2}$ or $1\frac{1}{2}$

21. $\frac{4n+15}{20}$ **22.** $\frac{3y-70}{10y}$ **23.** $1\frac{5}{13}$; $2 \div 2 = 1$ **24.** $2\frac{1}{2}$; $7 - 5 = 2$

25. $4\frac{1}{20}$; $2 + 2 = 4$ **26.** $-\frac{27}{64}$ **27.** $\frac{1}{36}$ **28.** $-\frac{4}{5}$ **29.** $\frac{7}{6}$ or $1\frac{1}{6}$

30. 10   **31.** $-\frac{4}{27}$ **32.** $w = 20$ **33.** $r = -15$ **34.** $x = \frac{1}{2}$

35. $A = 14$ ft²   **36.** Rectangular solid; $V = 32\frac{1}{2}$ in.³

37. Pyramid; $V = 93\frac{1}{3}$ yd³   **38.** $\frac{1}{4}$ pound; $7\frac{1}{2}$ pounds

39. $\frac{5}{6}$ hour; $10\frac{11}{12}$ hours   **40.** 12 preschoolers, 40 toddlers, 8 infants

41. $P = 2\frac{1}{10}$ miles; $A = \frac{9}{40}$ mi²

Chapter 4 TEST (pages 317–318)

1. $\frac{5}{6}; \frac{1}{6}$ **2.**

3. $\frac{1}{4}$ **4.** already in lowest terms **5.** $\frac{2a^2}{3b}$ **6.** $\frac{13}{15}$ **7.** -2 **8.** $-\frac{7}{40}$

9. 14 **10.** $-\frac{2}{27}$ **11.** $\frac{25}{8}$ or $3\frac{1}{8}$ **12.** $\frac{4}{9}$ **13.** $\frac{9}{16}$ **14.** $\frac{4}{7y}$

15. $\frac{24-n}{4n}$ **16.** $\frac{10+3a}{15}$ **17.** $\frac{1}{18b}$ **18.** $-\frac{1}{18}$ **19.** $-\frac{31}{30}$ or $-1\frac{1}{30}$

20. $5 \div 1 = 5; \frac{64}{15}$ or $4\frac{4}{15}$ **21.** $3 - 2 = 1; \frac{3}{2}$ or $1\frac{1}{2}$ **22.** $d = 35$

23. $t = -\frac{15}{7}$ or $-2\frac{1}{7}$ **24.** $b = 8$ **25.** $x = -15$ **26.** $A = 52$ m^2

27. $A = \frac{117}{2}$ yd^2 or $58\frac{1}{2}$ yd^2 **28.** Rectangular solid; $V = 6480$ m^3

29. Pyramid; $V = 16$ yd^3 **30.** $14\frac{3}{4}$ hours; $1\frac{5}{6}$ hours

31. $\frac{7}{2}$ days or $3\frac{1}{2}$ days **32.** 7392 students work

Chapters 1–4 CUMULATIVE REVIEW EXERCISES (pages 319–320)

1. five hundred five million, eight thousand, two hundred thirty-eight **2.** 35,600,000,916 **3. (a)** 60,700 **(b)** 100,000 **(c)** 3210 **4. (a)** commutative property of multiplication **(b)** associative property of addition **(c)** distributive property **5.** -54 **6.** -20 **7.** undefined **8.** 81 **9.** 10 **10.** 4 **11.** -16 **12.** $\frac{27}{27} = 1$ **13.** -8 **14.** 35

15. $\frac{15a}{2}$ **16.** $\frac{3}{xy^2}$ **17.** $-\frac{8}{15}$ **18.** $\frac{5}{16}$ **19.** $\frac{14-3b}{21}$ **20.** $\frac{8n+15}{5n}$

21. $\frac{13}{9}$ or $1\frac{4}{9}$ **22.** $\frac{13}{20}$ **23.** -1 **24.** $-\frac{5}{8}$ **25.** $a = 1$ **26.** $y = -5$

27. $k = -36$ **28.** $x = -4$ **29.** $m = 2$ **30.** Square; $P = 18$ in.; $A = 20\frac{1}{4}$ in.^{2} **31.** Triangle; $P = 20$ yd; $A = 18\frac{3}{4}$ yd^2 **32.** Parallelogram; $P = 78$ mm; $A = 288$ mm^2 **33.** Let b be the original weight of each bag. $3b - 16 - 25 = 79$; there were 40 pounds in each bag. **34.** Let w be the width; $2w$ is the length. $2(2w) + 2(w) = 102$; width is 17 yd; length is 34 yd.

CHAPTER 5 Rational Numbers: Positive and Negative Decimals

SECTION 5.1 (pages 327–330)

1. 3 **2.** 4 **3.** 8 tenths **4.** 3 thousandths **5.** 7; 0; 4 **7.** 4; 7; 8 **9.** 1; 8; 9 **11.** 6; 2; 1 **13.** 410.25 **15.** 6.5432 **17.** 5406.045

19. $\frac{7}{10}$ **21.** $13\frac{2}{5}$ **23.** $\frac{7}{20}$ **25.** $\frac{33}{50}$ **27.** $10\frac{17}{100}$ **29.** $\frac{3}{50}$ **31.** $\frac{41}{200}$

33. $5\frac{1}{500}$ **35.** $\frac{343}{500}$ **37.** five tenths **39.** seventy-eight hundredths **41.** one hundred five thousandths **43.** twelve and four hundredths **45.** one and seventy-five thousandths **47.** 6.7 **49.** 0.32 **51.** 420.008 **53.** 0.0703 **55.** 75.030 **57.** Anne should not say "and" because that denotes a decimal point. **58.** Jerry used "and" twice; only the first "and" is correct. **59.** ten thousandths inch; $\frac{10}{1000} = \frac{1}{100}$ inch **61.** 12 pounds **63.** 3-C **64.** 4-C **65.** 4-A **66.** 3-B **67.** one and six hundred two thousandths centimeters **68.** One and twenty-six thousandths centimeters **69.** millionths, ten-millionths, hundred-millionths, billionths; these match the words on the left side of the place value chart in Chapter 1, with "ths" attached. **70.** First place to the left of the decimal point is ones. "Oneths" would mean a fraction with a denominator of 1, which would equal 1 or

more. Anything that is 1 or more is to the *left* of the decimal point. **71.** seventy-two million four hundred thirty-six thousand nine hundred fifty-five hundred-millionths **72.** six hundred seventy-eight thousand five hundred fifty-four billionths **73.** eight thousand six and five hundred thousand one millionths **74.** twenty thousand sixty and five hundred five millionths **75.** 0.0302040 **76.** 9,876,543,210.100200300

SECTION 5.2 (pages 336–337)

1. 0 **2.** 9 **3.** Look only at the 6, which is **5 or more**. Round up by adding 1 thousandth to 5.709 to get 5.710. **4.** Look only at the 2, which is **4 or less**. So the part you are keeping, 10.0, stays the same. **5.** 16.9 **7.** 0.956 **9.** 0.80 **11.** 3.661 **13.** 794.0 **15.** 0.0980 **17.** 9.09 **19.** 82.0002 **21.** $0.82 **23.** $1.22 **25.** $0.70 **27.** $48,650 **29.** $840 **31.** $500 **33.** $1.00 **35.** $1000 **37. (a)** 253 miles per hour **(b)** 135 miles per hour **39. (a)** 186.0 miles per hour **(b)** 763.0 miles per hour **41.** Rounds to $0 (zero dollars) because $0.499 is closer to $0 than to $1. **42.** Rounding $0.499 to the nearest cent to get $0.50 is more helpful. Guideline: Round amounts less than $1.00 to the nearest cent instead of the nearest dollar. **43.** Rounds to $0.00 (zero cents) because $0.0015 is closer to $0.00 than to $0.01. **44.** Both round to $0.60. Rounding to the nearest thousandth (tenth of a cent) would allow you to identify $0.597 as less than $0.601.

SECTION 5.3 (pages 344–347)

1. $\begin{array}{r} 6.420 \\ +10.163 \end{array}$ **2.** $\begin{array}{r} 7.000 \\ +9.204 \end{array}$ **3.** $\begin{array}{r} 20.0000 \\ +9.1263 \end{array}$ **4.** $\begin{array}{r} 137.06 \\ -12.00 \end{array}$

5. 17.72 **7.** 11.98 **9.** 115.861 **11.** 59.323 **13.** 6 should be written 6.00; sum is 46.22 **14.** 65 should be written 65.00; sum is 85.36 **15.** 0.3000 written as a fraction in lowest terms is $\frac{3}{10}$, which is equivalent to 0.3 or $0.3000 = \frac{3000 \div 1000}{10,000 \div 1000} = \frac{3}{10} = 0.3$ **16.** Write 7.0 and 0.7 in fraction form to see the difference. 7.0 is $7\frac{0}{10}$ but 0.7 is $\frac{7}{10}$. **17.** 89.7 **19.** 0.109 **21.** 0.91 **23.** 6.661 **25.** The student subtracted in the wrong order; 15.32 should be on top; correct answer is 7.87 **26.** The two problems are done in a different order: $8 - 2.9$ is not the same as $2.9 - 8$ because subtraction is not commutative. **27. (a)** 24.75 in. **(b)** 3.95 in. **29. (a)** 62.27 in. **(b)** 0.39 in. **31.** 23.013 **33.** -45.75 **35.** -6.69 **37.** -6.99 **39.** -4.279 **41.** -0.0035 **43.** 5.37 **45.** *Exact:* 6.275 **47.** *Estimate:* $-7 + 1 = -6$; *Exact:* -5.8 **49.** *Estimate:* $-1 + (-9) = -10$; *Exact:* -9.671 **51.** *Estimate:* $8 + (+50) = 58$; *Exact:* 59.23 **53.** *Estimate:* $80 - 30 = 50$ million people; *Exact:* 50.4 million people **55.** *Estimate:* $400 + 200 + 100 + 80 + 40 + 30 + 30 = 880$ million people *Exact:* 940.82 million people **57.** *Estimate:* $2 + 2 + 2 = 6$ m *Exact:* 6.19 m, which is 0.21 m less than the rhino's height. **59.** *Estimate:* $20 - 9 = 11$; *Exact:* $10.88 **61.** *Estimate:* $5 - 5 = $0; *Exact:* $0.30 **63.** *Estimate:* $19 + 2 + 2 + 10 + 2 = $35; *Exact:* $35.25 **65.** 2059.36 **67.** 103.97 **69.** $b = 1.39$ cm **71.** $q = 7.943$ ft

SECTION 5.4 (pages 351–354)

1. 3 **2.** 5 **3.** 2 **4.** 4 **5.** 0.1344 **7.** -159.10 **9.** 15.444 **11.** $34,500.20 **13.** -43.2 **14.** -43.2 **15.** 0.432 **16.** 0.432 **17.** 0.0432 **18.** 0.0432 **19.** 0.0000312 **21.** 0.000009 **23.** *Exact:* 190.08 **25.** *Estimate:* $40 \times 40 = 1600$; *Exact:* 1558.2

27. *Estimate:* $7 \times 5 = 35$; *Exact:* 30.038   **29.** *Estimate:* $3 \times 7 = 21$; *Exact:* 19.24165   **31.** unreasonable; $289.00   **33.** reasonable
35. unreasonable; $4.19   **37.** unreasonable; 9.5 pounds   **39.** $945.87 (rounded)   **41.** $2.45 (rounded)   **43.** $77.10 (rounded)   **45.** $20,265
47. (a) Area before 1929 $\approx$ 23.2 in.^{2}; Area today $\approx$ 16.0 in.^{2}
(b) 7.2 in.^{2} **49. (a)** 0.43 inch   **(b)** 4.3 inches   **51.** $1264.04; $2723.72
53. $4.09 (rounded)   **55. (a)** $72.05   **(b)** $27.80   **57.** 59.6; 4.76; 7226; 32; 803.5; 9. Multiplying by 10, decimal point moves one place to the right; by 100, two places to the right; by 1000, three places to the right.   **58.** 5.96; 0.0476; 6.5; 0.32; 8.035; 52.3. Multiplying by 0.1, decimal point moves one place to the left; by 0.01, two places to the left; by 0.001, three places to the left.

SECTION 5.5 (pages 362–365)

1. $25.5 \div 5$; $5\overline{)25.5}$ **2.** $42.3 \div 7$; $7\overline{)42.3}$ **3.** $2.2\overline{)8.24}$ **4.** $5.1\overline{)10.5}$
5. -3.9 **7.** 0.47   **9.** 400.2   **11.** 36   **13.** 0.06   **14.** 0.6   **15.** 6000
16. 6   **17.** 60   **18.** 600   **19.** 0.0006   **20.** 0.006   **21.** 25.3   **23.** 516.67 (rounded)   **25.** -26.756 (rounded)   **27.** 10,082.647 (rounded)
29. unreasonable; *Estimate:* $40 \div 8 = 5$; $8\overline{)37.8}$ = 4.725   **31.** reasonable; *Estimate:* $50 \div 50 = 1$ **33.** unreasonable; *Estimate:* $300 \div 5 = 60$; $5.1\overline{)307.02}$ = 60.2   **35.** $4.00 (rounded)   **37.** $67.08   **39.** $11.92 per hour
41. 28.0 miles per gallon (rounded)   **43.** $0.03 (rounded)   **45.** 7.37 meters (rounded)   **47.** 0.08 meter   **49.** 22.49 meters   **51.** First: Work inside parentheses; subtract $9.5 - 3.1$ to get 6.4   Second: Apply the exponent; multiply $(2.2)(2.2)$ to get 4.84   Third: Add 4.84 plus 6.4 to get 11.24   **52.** First: Work inside parentheses; add $0.4 + 5.07$ to get 5.47   Second: Multiply 5.47 times 3 to get 16.41   Third: Subtract $60.41 - 16.41$ to get 44   **53.** 14.25   **55.** 3.8   **57.** -16.155 **59.** 3.714
61. (a) 1,083,333 pieces (rounded)   **(b)** 18,056 pieces (rounded)
(c) 301 pieces (rounded)   **63.** 100,000 box tops   **65.** 2632 box tops (rounded)   **67.** 0.377; 0.0886; 40.65; 0.91; 3.019; 662.57 **(a)** Dividing by 10, decimal point moves one place to the left; by 100, two places to the left; by 1000, three places to the left.   **(b)** The decimal point moved to the *right* when multiplying by 10, by 100, or by 1000; here it moves to the *left* when dividing by 10, by 100, or by 1000.   **68.** 402; 3.39; 460; 71; 157.7; 8730 **(a)** Dividing by 0.1, decimal point moves one place to the right; by 0.01, two places to the right; by 0.001, three places to the right.
(b) The decimal point moved to the *left* when multiplying by 0.1, 0.01, or 0.001; here it moves to the *right* when dividing by 0.1, 0.01, or 0.001.

SUMMARY EXERCISES Computation with Decimal Numbers (pages 366–367)

1. $\frac{4}{5}$ **2.** $6\frac{1}{250}$ **3.** $\frac{7}{20}$ **4.** ninety-four and five tenths
5. two and three ten-thousandths   **6.** seven hundred six thousandths
7. 0.05   **8.** 0.0309   **9.** 10.7   **10.** 6.19   **11.** 1.0   **12.** 0.420
13. $0.89   **14.** $3.00   **15.** $100   **16.** -0.945 **17.** 49.6199
18. -50 **19.** 15.03   **20.** 0.00488   **21.** -2.15 **22.** 9.055
23. 18.4009   **24.** -6.995 **25.** -808.9 **26.** 2.12   **27.** 0.04
28. $P = 52.1$ in.   **29.** $P = 9.735$ meters   **30.** $1.80   **31.** $91.28
32. (a) 169 ft^2 **(b)** $0.75 (rounded)   **33.** 144 ft^2; $0.69 (rounded)
34. (a) 9 days (rounded)   **(b)** 15.6 pounds (rounded)   **35.** Average weight of food eaten by bee is 0.32 ounce.   **36.** 0.112 ounce

SECTION 5.6 (pages 372–375)

1. (a) Not correct; $5\overline{)2}$ **(b)** $7\overline{)1}$ **(c)** $8\overline{)3}$ **2. (a)** $9\overline{)4}$
(b) Not correct; $3\overline{)1}$ **(c)** $6\overline{)5}$ **3.** $4\overline{)3.}$ To continue dividing, write zeros in the dividend.   **4.** $8\overline{)1.}$ To continue dividing, write zeros in the dividend.
5. (a) less than   **(b)** greater than   **(c)** less than   **6. (a)** less than
(b) greater than   **(c)** greater than   **7.** 0.5   **9.** 0.75   **11.** 0.3
13. 0.9   **15.** 0.6   **17.** 0.875   **19.** 2.25   **21.** 14.7   **23.** 3.625
25. 6.333 (rounded)   **27.** 0.833 (rounded)   **29.** 1.889 (rounded)
31. $\frac{2}{5}$ **33.** $\frac{5}{8}$ **35.** $\frac{7}{20}$ **37.** 0.35   **39.** $\frac{1}{25}$ **41.** 0.2   **43.** $\frac{9}{100}$
45. shorter; 0.72 inch   **47.** more; 0.05 inch   **49.** too much; 0.005 gram
51. 0.9991 cm, 1.0007 cm   **53. (a)** $<$ **(b)** $=$ **(c)** $>$ **(d)** $<$
55. 0.5399, 0.54, 0.5455   **57.** 5.0079, 5.79, 5.8, 5.804   **59.** 0.6009, 0.609, 0.628, 0.62812   **61.** 2.8902, 3.88, 4.876, 5.8751   **63.** 0.006, 0.043, $\frac{1}{20}$, 0.051   **65.** 0.37, $\frac{3}{8}$, $\frac{2}{5}$, 0.4001   **67. (a)** red box; green box
(b) 0.01 inch   **68. (a)** green box   **(b)** no difference; they are equivalent.   **69.** 1.4 in. (rounded)   **71.** 0.3 in. (rounded)   **73.** 0.4 in. (rounded)   **75. (a)** A proper fraction like $\frac{5}{9}$ is less than 1, so $\frac{5}{9}$ cannot be equivalent to a decimal number that is greater than 1.   **(b)** $\frac{5}{9}$ means $5 \div 9$ or $9\overline{)5}$ so correct answer is 0.556 (rounded). This makes sense because both the fraction and decimal are less than 1.
76. (a) $2.035 = 2\frac{35}{1000} = 2\frac{7}{200}$, not $2\frac{7}{20}$ **(b)** Adding the whole number part gives $2 + 0.35$, which is 2.35 not 2.035. To check, $2.35 = 2\frac{35}{100} = 2\frac{7}{20}$ but $2.035 = 2\frac{35}{1000} = 2\frac{7}{200}$ **77.** Just add the whole number part to 0.375. So $1\frac{3}{8} = 1.375$; $3\frac{3}{8} = 3.375$; $295\frac{3}{8} = 295.375$ **78.** It works only when the fraction part has a one-digit numerator and a denominator of 10, or a two-digit numerator and a denominator of 100, and so on.

SECTION 5.7 (pages 380–382)

1. (a) average   **(b)** the number of values   **2. (a)** the number of times it occurs (frequency)   **(b)** grade point average (GPA)   **3.** 8; $\frac{588}{8} \approx 69.8$ (rounded)   **5.** $39,622   **7.** 6.1 (rounded)   **9.** 2.60   **11. (a)** 2.8
(b) 2.93 (rounded)   **(c)** 3.13 (rounded)   **13.** 15 texts   **15.** 516 students
17. 48.5 pounds of shrimp   **19.** 4296 miles (rounded)   **21.** 2754.5 miles
23. 8 samples   **25.** 68 and 74 years (bimodal)   **27.** no mode
29. -10 degrees; 4 degrees; 14 degrees warmer

SECTION 5.8 (pages 387–390)

1. 4   **3.** 8   **5.** 3.317 (rounded)   **7.** 2.236 (rounded)   **9.** 8.544 (rounded)   **11.** 10.050 (rounded)   **13.** 19   **15.** 31.623 (rounded)
17. 30 is about halfway between 25 and 36, so $\sqrt{30}$ should be about halfway between 5 and 6, or about 5.5. Using a calculator, $\sqrt{30} \approx 5.477$ Similarly, $\sqrt{26}$ should be a little more than $\sqrt{25}$; by calculator $\sqrt{26} \approx 5.099$ And $\sqrt{35}$ should be a little less than $\sqrt{36}$; by calculator $\sqrt{35} \approx 5.916$ **18.** Squaring a number is multiplying the number times itself. Finding the square root "undoes" squaring. It is asking what number was multiplied by itself. Examples will vary.   **19.** $\sqrt{1521} = 39$ ft
21. $\sqrt{289} = 17$ in.   **23.** $\sqrt{144} = 12$ mm   **25.** $\sqrt{73} \approx 8.5$ in.
27. $\sqrt{65} \approx 8.1$ yd   **29.** $\sqrt{195} \approx 14.0$ cm   **31.** $\sqrt{7.94} \approx 2.8$ m

33. $\sqrt{65.01} \approx 8.1$ cm   **35.** $\sqrt{292.32} \approx 17.1$ km   **37.** The student used the formula for finding the hypotenuse but the unknown side is a leg, so use leg $= \sqrt{(20)^2 - (13)^2}$. Also, the final answer should be m, not m². Correct answer is $\sqrt{231} \approx 15.2$ m.   **38.** The student did not square the numbers correctly: 9^2 is 81 and 7^2 is 49. Also, the final answer was rounded to the nearest thousandth instead of tenth. Correct answer is $\sqrt{130} \approx 11.4$ in.   **39.** hypotenuse $= \sqrt{65} \approx 8.1$ ft
41. leg $= \sqrt{360,000} = 600$ m   **43.** hypotenuse $= \sqrt{48.5} \approx 7.0$ ft
45. leg $= \sqrt{135} \approx 11.6$ ft.   **47.** $\sqrt{16,200} \approx 127.3$ ft
48. (a)   **(b)** $\sqrt{7200} \approx 84.9$ ft

49. The distance from third to first is the same as the distance from home to second because the baseball diamond is a square.   **50. (a)** The side length is less than 60 ft.   **(b)** $80^2 = 6400$; $6400 \div 2 = 3200$; $\sqrt{3200} \approx 56.6$ ft

SECTION 5.9 (pages 395–396)

Please see *Solutions* section for sample *checks* of some odd-numbered exercises.   **1.** Add 6.2 to both sides because $-6.2 + 6.2$ gives $x + 0$ on the right side.   **2.** Divide both sides by -4.5 because $\dfrac{-4.5y}{-4.5}$ gives y on the left side.   **3.** -1.4, $n = -1.4$ **5.** $b = 0.008$ **7.** $a = 0.29$
9. $p = -120$ **11.** $t = 0.7$ **13.** $x = -0.82$ **15.** $z = 0$ **17.** $h = 110$
19. $c = 0.45$ **21.** $w = 28$ **23.** $p = -40.5$ **25.** Let d be the adult dose. $0.3d = 9$; The adult dose is 30 milligrams.   **27.** Let d be the number of days. $65.95d + 12 = 275.80$; The saw was rented for 4 days.
29. $0.7(220 - a) = 140$; The person is 20 years old.
30. $0.7(220 - a) = 126$; The person is 40 years old.
31. $0.7(220 - a) = 134$; $a \approx 28.57$, which rounds to 29. The person is about 29 years old.   **32.** $0.7(220 - a) = 117$; $a \approx 52.86$, which rounds to 53. The person is about 53 years old.

SECTION 5.10 (pages 405–408)

1. perimeter; ft   **2.** radius; divide by 2   **3.** $d = 18$ mm
5. $r = 0.35$ km   **7.** $C \approx 69.1$ ft; $A \approx 379.9$ ft²   **9.** $C \approx 8.2$ m;
$A \approx 5.3$ m²   **11.** $C \approx 47.1$ cm; $A \approx 176.6$ cm²   **13.** $C \approx 23.6$ ft;
$A \approx 44.2$ ft²   **15.** $A \approx 76.9$ in.²   **17.** $A \approx 57$ cm²   **19.** $A \approx 7850$ yd²
21. $C \approx 91.4$ in.; Bonus: 693 revolutions/mile (rounded)
23. $A \approx 70,650$ mi²   **25.** watch: $C \approx 3.1$ in.; $A \approx 0.8$ in.²; wall clock: $C \approx 18.8$ in.; $A \approx 28.3$ in.²

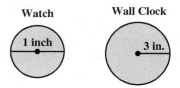

27. $A \approx 78.5$ mi² $- 12.6$ mi²; difference ≈ 65.9 mi²

29. (a) $d \approx 45.9$ cm   **(b)** Divide the circumference by π
(144 cm $\div$ 3.14).   **31.** $C \approx 14.6$ ft   **33.** $A \approx 197.8$ cm²
35. $V \approx 471$ ft³; $S \approx 345.4$ ft²   **37.** $V = 1617$ m³; $S \approx 849.4$ m²
39. $V \approx 763.0$ in.³ (rounded); $S \approx 678.2$ in.² (rounded)
41. $V = 5550$ mm³; $S = 2150$ mm²   **43.** Student should use radius of 3.5 cm instead of diameter of 7 cm in the formula; units for volume are cm³, not cm². Correct answer is $V \approx 192.3$ cm³   **44. (a)** Length, width, and height are all the same.   **(b)** Multiply the side measurement times itself to get the area of one face of the cube, then multiply by 6 to find the total surface area. $S = 6s^2$, where s is the length of one edge of the cube.
45. $V \approx 3925$ ft³   **47.** $S \approx 163.6$ in.²

Chapter 5 REVIEW EXERCISES (pages 417–422)

1. 0; 5   **2.** 0; 6   **3.** 8; 9   **4.** 5; 9   **5.** 7; 6   **6.** $\dfrac{1}{2}$ **7.** $\dfrac{3}{4}$ **8.** $4\dfrac{1}{20}$
9. $\dfrac{7}{8}$ **10.** $\dfrac{27}{1000}$ **11.** $27\dfrac{4}{5}$ **12.** eight tenths   **13.** four hundred and twenty-nine hundredths   **14.** twelve and seven thousandths
15. three hundred six ten-thousandths   **16.** 8.3   **17.** 0.205
18. 70.0066   **19.** 0.30   **20.** 275.6   **21.** 72.79   **22.** 0.160
23. 0.091   **24.** 1.0   **25.** $15.83   **26.** $0.70   **27.** $17,625.79
28. $350   **29.** $130   **30.** $100   **31.** $29   **32.** -5.67
33. -0.03 **34.** 5.879   **35.** -6.435 **36.** *Estimate:*
100 million $-$ 40 million $=$ 60 million; *Exact:* 51.1 million people
37. *Estimate:* $400 $-$ $300 $-$ $70 = $30; *Exact:* $15.80
38. *Estimate:* $2 + $5 + $20 = $27; $30 $-$ $27 = $3; *Exact:* $4.14
39. *Estimate:* $2 + 4 + 5 = 11$ kilometers; *Exact:* 11.55 kilometers
40. *Estimate:* $6 \times 4 = 24$; *Exact:* 22.7106   **41.** *Estimate:* $40 \times 3 = 120$; *Exact:* 141.57   **42.** 0.0112   **43.** -0.000355 **44.** reasonable; *Estimate:* $700 \div 10 = 70$ **45.** unreasonable; *Estimate:* $30 \div 3 = 10$; $2.8)\overline{26.6}^{\,9.5}$
46. 14.467 (rounded)   **47.** 1200   **48.** -0.4 **49.** $708 (rounded)
50. $4.99 (rounded)   **51.** 133 shares (rounded)   **52.** $8.02 (rounded)
53. -4.715 **54.** 10.15   **55.** 3.8   **56.** 0.64   **57.** 1.875   **58.** 0.111
(rounded)   **59.** 3.6008, 3.68, 3.806   **60.** 0.209, 0.2102, 0.215, 0.22
61. $\dfrac{1}{8}, \dfrac{3}{20}$, 0.159, 0.17   **62.** mean: 28.5 phones; median: 19.5 phones
63. mean: 44 loans; median: 39 loans   **64.** $51.05   **65.** Store J: $107 and $160 (bimodal); Store K: $119   **66.** $\sqrt{289} = 17$ in.   **67.** $\sqrt{49} = 7$ cm
68. $\sqrt{104} \approx 10.2$ cm (rounded)   **69.** $\sqrt{52} \approx 7.2$ in. (rounded)
70. $\sqrt{6.53} \approx 2.6$ m (rounded)   **71.** $\sqrt{71.75} \approx 8.5$ km (rounded)
72. $b = 0.25$ **73.** $x = 0$ **74.** $n = -13$ **75.** $a = -1.5$
76. $y = -16.2$ **77.** $d = 137.8$ m   **78.** $r = 1\dfrac{1}{2}$ in. or 1.5 in.
79. $C \approx 6.3$ cm (rounded); $A \approx 3.1$ cm² (rounded)   **80.** $C \approx 109.3$ m (rounded); $A \approx 950.7$ m² (rounded)   **81.** $C \approx 37.7$ in. (rounded); $A \approx 113.0$ in.² (rounded)   **82.** $V \approx 549.5$ cm³; $S \approx 376.8$ cm²
83. $V = 1808.6$ m³ (rounded); $S \approx 1205.8$ m² (rounded)
84. $V \approx 7.9$ ft³ (rounded); $S = 25.5$ ft²   **85.** 404.865   **86.** -254.8
87. 3583.261 (rounded)   **88.** 29.0898   **89.** 0.03066   **90.** 9.4
91. -15.065 **92.** -9.04 **93.** -15.74 **94.** 8.19   **95.** 0.928
96. 35   **97.** -41.859 **98.** 0.3   **99.** $3.00 (rounded)   **100.** $2.17
(rounded)   **101.** $35.96   **102.** $199.71   **103.** $78.50
104. $y = -0.7$ **105.** $x = 30$ **106.** 15.7 ft long rubber strip;
$A \approx 19.6$ ft² (rounded)   **107.** mean is 67.6; median is 82
108. 20 miles   **109.** $V \approx 49.5$ in.³ (rounded)

Chapter 5 TEST (pages 423–424)

1. $18\frac{2}{5}$ **2.** $\frac{3}{40}$ **3.** sixty and seven thousandths   **4.** two hundred eight ten-thousandths   **5.** *Estimate:* $8 + 80 + 40 = 128$; *Exact:* 129.2028
6. *Estimate:* $-6(1) = -6$; *Exact:* -6.948 **7.** *Estimate:* $-80 - 4 = -84$; *Exact:* -82.702 **8.** *Estimate:* $-20 \div (-5) = 4$; *Exact:* 4.175
9. 669.004 **10.** 480 **11.** 0.000042 **12.** $\$3.79$ per foot (rounded)
13. Davida, by 0.441 minute   **14.** $\$5.35$ (rounded)   **15.** $y = -6.15$
16. $x = -0.35$ **17.** $a = 10.9$ **18.** $n = 2.85$ **19.** $0.44, \frac{9}{20}, 0.4506,$
0.451 **20.** 32.09 **21.** 75 books   **22.** $103°$ and $104°$ (bimodal)
23. $\$11.25$ **24.** $\$50.55$ **25.** $\sqrt{85} \approx 9.2$ cm (rounded)
26. $\sqrt{279} \approx 16.7$ ft (rounded)   **27.** $r = 12.5$ in.   **28.** $C \approx 5.7$ km (rounded)   **29.** $A \approx 206.0$ cm^2 (rounded)   **30.** $V \approx 5086.8$ ft^3
31. $S \approx 2599.9$ ft^2 (rounded)

Chapters 1–5 CUMULATIVE REVIEW EXERCISES (pages 425–426)

1. (a) forty-five and two hundred three ten-thousandths   **(b)** thirty billion, six hundred fifty thousand, eight   **2. (a)** $160,000,500$ **(b)** 0.075
3. $46,900$ **4.** 6.20 **5.** 0.661 **6.** $10,000$ **7.** -13 **8.** -0.00006
9. undefined   **10.** 44 **11.** 18 **12.** -6 **13.** 56.621 **14.** $\frac{3}{2}$
or $1\frac{1}{2}$ **15.** $\frac{3}{8b}$ **16.** 11.147 **17.** $-\frac{9}{20}$ **18.** $-\frac{1}{32}$ **19.** 1.3 (rounded)
20. $\frac{5x + 6}{10}$ **21.** -8 **22.** -32 **23.** $\frac{18}{18} = 1$ **24.** -5.76
25. $\frac{55}{24}$ or $2\frac{7}{24}$ **26.** 24.2 years (rounded)   **27.** 23.5 years
28. 20 and 26 years (bimodal)   **29.** $h = -4$ **30.** $x = 5$
31. $r = 10.9$ **32.** $y = -2$ **33.** $n = 4$ **34.** $P = 54$ ft; $A = 140$ ft^2
35. $C \approx 40.8$ m (rounded); $A \approx 132.7$ m^2 (rounded)   **36.** $x \approx 12.6$ km (rounded); $A \approx 37.8$ km^2 **37.** $V \approx 3.4$ in.^{3} (rounded); $S \approx 13.5$ in.^{2}
38. *Estimate:* $\$60 - \$50 - \$1 = \$9$; *Exact:* $\$11.17$
39. *Estimate:* $2 + 4 = 6$ yards; *Exact:* $6\frac{5}{24}$ yards   **40.** *Estimate:* $\$6 \div 3 = \$2$ per pound; *Exact:* $\$2.29$ per pound (rounded)
41. *Estimate:* $\$80,000 \div 100 = \$800$; *Exact:* $\$729$ (rounded)
42. Let x be first student's money and $3x$ be second student's money. $x + 3x = 30,000$; one student receives $\$7500$; the other receives $\$22,500$.
43. Let w be the width and $w + 4$ be the length. $2(w + 4) + 2w = 48$; The width is 10 in. and the length is 14 in.

CHAPTER 6 Ratio, Proportion, and Line/Angle/Triangle Relationships

SECTION 6.1 (pages 433–434)

1. Answers will vary. One possibility is: A ratio compares two quantities with the same units. Examples will vary.   **2.** You can divide out the common units.   **3.** $20; \frac{4}{1}$ **4.** $5; \frac{4}{15}$ **5.** $\frac{8}{9}$ **7.** $\frac{2}{1}$ **9.** $\frac{1}{3}$ **11.** $\frac{9}{7}$
13. $\frac{5}{6}$ **15.** ounces; takes fewer steps to solve and you do not have to work with a mixed number.   **16.** hours; takes fewer steps to solve and you do not have to work with a mixed number.   **17.** 48 in.; $\frac{8}{5}$ **19.** $\frac{1}{12}$
21. $\frac{4}{1}$ **23.** $\frac{1}{6}$ **25.** $\frac{15}{1}$ **27.** *White Christmas* to *It's Now or Never;*

White Christmas to *I Will Always Love You; Candle in the Wind* to *I Want to Hold Your Hand*   **29.** $\frac{6}{1}$ **31.** $\frac{38}{17}$ **33.** $\frac{1}{4}$ **35.** $\frac{34}{35}$

SECTION 6.2 (pages 439–442)

1. $\frac{3 \text{ feet}}{7 \text{ seconds}}$ **3.** $\frac{5 \text{ letters}}{1 \text{ minute}}$ **5.** $\frac{18 \text{ miles}}{1 \text{ gallon}}$ **7.** Divide; correct set-up is $\frac{\$5.85}{3 \text{ boxes}}$ or $3\overline{)5.85}$ **8.** 5 rooms for 1 nurse   **9.** $\$12$ per hour or $\$12$/hour
11. 1.25 pounds/person   **13.** $\$103.30$/day   **15.** $325.9; 21.0$ (rounded)
17. $338.6; 20.9$ (rounded)   **19.** 4 ounces for $\$3.65$, about $\$0.913$/ounce
21. 14 ounces for $\$2.89$, about $\$0.206$/ounce   **23.** 18 ounces for $\$1.79$, about $\$0.099$/ounce   **25.** Answers will vary. For example, you might choose Brand B because you like more chicken, so the cost per chicken chunk may actually be the same as or less than Brand A.   **26.** Answers will vary. For example, if you use only half of the larger bag, you really pay $\$0.30$ per pound, so the smaller bag is the best buy.   **27.** 1.75 pounds/week
29. $\$12.26$/hour   **31. (a)** Penny Saver, $\$0.415$; Most Minutes, $\$0.503$ (rounded); USA card, $\$0.30$ **(b)** Penny Saver, $\$0.083$/min; Most Minutes, $\$0.101$/min (rounded); USA card, $\$0.06$/min; USA card is the best buy.   **33.** Penny Saver total $\$0.54$, $\$0.018$/min; Most Minutes total $\$0.565$, $\$0.019$/min (rounded); USA Card total $\$0.55$, $\$0.018$/min (rounded); all three unit rates are very similar.   **35.** One battery for $\$1.79$; like getting 3 batteries so $\$1.79 \div 3 \approx \$0.597$ per battery   **37.** Brand P with the $50¢$ coupon is the best buy. $(\$3.39 - \$0.50 = \$2.89,$ $\$2.89 \div 16.5$ ounces $\approx \$0.175$ per ounce$)$ **39.** Plan A: $\$0.09$/min; Plan B: $\$0.07$/min; Plan B is the better buy.   **40. (a)** 15 min/day
(b) 30 min/day   **41.** $(60$ extra min$)$ $(\$0.45) = \$27$ overage; $\$39.95 + \$27$ overage $= \$66.95$
$$\frac{\$66.95}{450 \text{ min} + 60 \text{ min}} = \frac{\$66.95}{510 \text{ min}} \approx \$0.13/\text{min}$$
42. $(90$ extra min$)$ $(\$0.40) = \$36$ overage; $\$59.95 + \$36$ overage $= \$95.95$;
$$\frac{\$95.95}{900 \text{ min} + 90 \text{ min}} = \frac{\$95.95}{990 \text{ min}} \approx \$0.10/\text{min}$$
43. From Exercise 41: $\dfrac{\$69.95}{510 \text{ min}} \approx \$0.14/\text{min}$

From Exercise 42: $\dfrac{\$69.95}{990 \text{ min}} \approx \$0.07/\text{min}$

SECTION 6.3 (pages 450–453)

1. $\dfrac{\$9}{12 \text{ cans}} = \dfrac{\$18}{24 \text{ cans}}$ **2.** $\dfrac{28 \text{ people}}{7 \text{ cars}} = \dfrac{16 \text{ people}}{4 \text{ cars}}$
3. $\dfrac{200 \text{ adults}}{450 \text{ children}} = \dfrac{4 \text{ adults}}{9 \text{ children}}$ **4.** $\dfrac{150 \text{ trees}}{1 \text{ acre}} = \dfrac{1500 \text{ trees}}{10 \text{ acres}}$
5. $\dfrac{120}{150} = \dfrac{8}{10}$ **6.** $\dfrac{6}{9} = \dfrac{10}{15}$ **7.** $\dfrac{3}{5} = \dfrac{3}{5}$; true   **9.** $\dfrac{5}{8} = \dfrac{5}{8}$; true
11. $\dfrac{3}{4} \neq \dfrac{2}{3}$; false   **13.** Wording may vary slightly. A proportion shows that two ratios are equal. The multiplication on the proportion should show $6 \cdot 45 = 270$ and $30 \cdot 9 = 270$.   **14.** Wording may vary slightly. If the cross products are equal, the proportion is true. If the cross products are not equal, the proportion is false.
15. $54 = 54$; true   **17.** $336 \neq 320$; false   **19.** $2880 \neq 2970$; false
21. $28 = 28$; true   **23.** $42\frac{1}{2} \neq 45$; false   **25.** $66 = 66$; true

27. $\dfrac{68 \text{ hits}}{200 \text{ at bats}} = \dfrac{153 \text{ hits}}{450 \text{ at bats}}$ $\begin{array}{l}200 \cdot 153 = 30{,}600 \\ 68 \cdot 450 = 30{,}600\end{array}$ Cross products are equal so the proportion is *true*; they hit equally well.   **28.** Left-hand ratio compares hours to cartons but right-hand ratio compares cartons to hours. Correct proportion is: $\dfrac{3.5 \text{ hours}}{91 \text{ cartons}} = \dfrac{5.25 \text{ hours}}{126 \text{ cartons}}$ $\begin{array}{l}(91)(5.25) = 477.75 \\ (3.5)(126) = 441\end{array}$ Cross products are *not* equal, so the proportion is *false*; they did not work equally fast.

29. $3 \cdot x = 1 \cdot 12$

$\qquad 3 \cdot x = 12$

$\qquad \dfrac{\overset{1}{\cancel{3}} \cdot x}{\underset{1}{\cancel{3}}} = \dfrac{12}{3}$

$\qquad\qquad x = 4$

31. $x = 2$ **33.** $x = 88$ **35.** $x = 91$ **37.** $x = 5$ **39.** $x = 10$
41. $x \approx 24.44$ (rounded)   **43.** $x = 50.4$ **45.** $x \approx 17.64$ (rounded)
47. $x = 1$ **49.** $x = 3\frac{1}{2}$ **51.** $x = 0.2$ or $x = \frac{1}{5}$ **53.** $x = 0.005$
or $x = \dfrac{1}{200}$ **55.** Find the cross products: $20 \neq 30$, so the proportion

is false. $\dfrac{6\frac{2}{3}}{4} = \dfrac{5}{3}$ or $\dfrac{10}{6} = \dfrac{5}{3}$ or $\dfrac{10}{4} = \dfrac{7.5}{3}$ or $\dfrac{10}{4} = \dfrac{5}{2}$

56. Find the cross products: $192 \neq 180$, so the proportion is false.

$\dfrac{6.4}{8} = \dfrac{24}{30}$ or $\dfrac{6}{7.5} = \dfrac{24}{30}$ or $\dfrac{6}{8} = \dfrac{22.5}{30}$ or $\dfrac{6}{8} = \dfrac{24}{32}$

SUMMARY EXERCISES Ratios, Rates, and Proportions (pages 454–455)

1. $\dfrac{50 \text{ million}}{25 \text{ million}} = \dfrac{2}{1}$ **2.** $\dfrac{15 \text{ million}}{20 \text{ million}} = \dfrac{3}{4}$ **3.** $\dfrac{20 \text{ million} + 25 \text{ million}}{50 \text{ million}} = \dfrac{9}{10}$

4. $\dfrac{380 \text{ million}}{110 \text{ million}} = \dfrac{38}{11}$ **5.** Comparing the violin to piano, guitar, organ,

clarinet and drums gives ratios of $\dfrac{1}{11}, \dfrac{1}{10}, \dfrac{1}{3}, \dfrac{1}{2},$ and $\dfrac{2}{3}$, respectively.
6. (a) guitar to clarinet   **(b)** organ to drums, or clarinet to violin
7. 2.1 points/min; 0.5 min/point (both rounded)   **8.** 1.7 points/min; 0.6 min/point (both rounded)   **9.** $16.32/hour; $24.48/hour for overtime
10. $0.20/channel; $0.17/channel; $0.18/channel (all answers rounded)
11. 12 ounces for $7.24, about $0.60 per ounce (rounded)
12. Brand P with the $2 coupon is the best buy at $0.57 per pound.
13. $\dfrac{4}{3} = \dfrac{4}{3}$ or $924 = 924$; true   **14.** $2.0125 \neq 2.07$; false
15. $68\frac{1}{4} = 68\frac{1}{4}$; true   **16.** $x = 28$ **17.** $x = 3.2$ **18.** $x = 182$
19. $x \approx 3.64$ (rounded)   **20.** $x \approx 0.93$ (rounded)   **21.** $x = 1.56$
22. $x \approx 0.05$ (rounded)   **23.** $x = 1$ **24.** $x = \dfrac{3}{4}$

SECTION 6.4 (pages 459–462)

1. $\dfrac{6 \text{ potatoes}}{4 \text{ eggs}} = \dfrac{12 \text{ potatoes}}{x \text{ eggs}}$ **2.** $\dfrac{1 \text{ serving}}{15 \text{ chips}} = \dfrac{x \text{ servings}}{70 \text{ chips}}$ **3.** $\dfrac{18}{x}$; 22.5 hours
5. $7.20   **7.** 42 pounds   **9.** $403.68   **11.** 10 ounces (rounded)
13. 5 quarts   **15.** 14 ft, 10 ft   **17.** 14 ft, 8 ft   **19.** 96 pieces of chicken;
33.6 pounds lasagna; 10.8 pounds deli meats; $5\frac{3}{5}$ pounds cheese;
7.2 dozen (about 86) buns; 14.4 pounds potato salad.   **21.** 44 students is
an unreasonable answer because there are only 35 students in the class.

22. 2 minutes is an unreasonable answer because it is less than the
30 minutes she gets in just one day.   **23.** 2065 students (reasonable);
about 4214 students with incorrect set-up (only 2950 students in the group)
25. about 79 people (reasonable); about 714 people with incorrect
set-up (only 238 people attended)   **27.** 625 stocks   **29.** 4.06 meters
(rounded)   **31.** 311 calories (rounded)   **33.** 10.53 meters (rounded)
35. You cannot solve this problem using a proportion because the ratio
of age to weight is not constant. As Jim's age increases, his weight may
decrease, stay the same, or increase.   **36.** Answers will vary.
Exercises 3–34 are all examples of application problems.
37. 5610 students use cream.   **39.** 120 calories and 12 grams of fiber
41. $1\frac{3}{4}$ cups water, 3 tablespoons margarine, $\frac{3}{4}$ cup milk, 2 cups flakes
42. $5\frac{1}{4}$ cups water, 9 tablespoons margarine, $2\frac{1}{4}$ cups milk, 6 cups flakes

SECTION 6.5 (pages 473–476)

1. Wording may vary slightly. A **line** is a row of points continuing in both
directions forever; the drawing should have arrows on both ends. A **line
segment** is a piece of a line; the drawing should have an endpoint (dot) on
each end. A **ray** has one endpoint and goes on forever in one direction; the
drawing should have one endpoint (dot) and an arrowhead on the other end.
2. Wording may vary slightly. An **acute angle** measures less than 90°;
a **right angle** measures exactly 90° and forms a "square corner"; an **obtuse
angle** measures more than 90° but less than 180°; a **straight angle**
measures exactly 180° and forms a straight line. Drawings of an acute
and obtuse angle may vary.   **3.** line named $\overleftrightarrow{CD}$ or $\overleftrightarrow{DC}$ **5.** line segment
named $\overline{GF}$ or $\overline{FG}$ **7.** ray named $\overrightarrow{PQ}$ **9.** perpendicular   **11.** parallel
13. intersecting   **15.** $\angle AOS$ or $\angle SOA$ **17.** $\angle AQC$ or $\angle CQA$
19. right (90°)   **21.** acute   **23.** straight (180°)   **25.** $\angle EOD$ and
$\angle COD$; $\angle AOB$ and $\angle BOC$ **27.** $\angle HNE$ and $\angle ENF$; $\angle ACB$ and $\angle KOL$
29. 50°   **31.** 4°   **33.** 50°   **35.** 90°   **37.** $\angle SON \cong \angle TOM$;
$\angle TOS \cong \angle MON$ **39.** $\angle GOH$ measures 63°; $\angle EOF$ measures 37°;
$\angle AOC$ and $\angle GOF$ both measure 80°.   **41.** True, because $\overleftrightarrow{UQ}$ is
perpendicular to $\overleftrightarrow{ST}$.   **42.** True, because they form a 90° angle, as indicated by the small red square   **43.** False; the angles have the same mea-
sure (both are 180°).   **44.** False; $\overleftrightarrow{ST}$ and $\overleftrightarrow{PR}$ are parallel.   **45.** False; $\overleftrightarrow{QU}$
and $\overleftrightarrow{TS}$ are perpendicular.   **46.** True, because both angles are formed by
perpendicular lines, so they both measure 90°   **47.** corresponding angles;
$\angle 1$ and $\angle 8$, $\angle 2$ and $\angle 5$, $\angle 3$ and $\angle 6$, $\angle 4$ and $\angle 7$; alternate interior angles;
$\angle 4$ and $\angle 5$, $\angle 3$ and $\angle 8$.   **49.** $\angle 2, \angle 4, \angle 6, \angle 8$ all measure 130°; $\angle 1$,
$\angle 3, \angle 5, \angle 7$ all measure 50°.   **51.** $\angle 6, \angle 1, \angle 3, \angle 8$ all measure 47°;
$\angle 5, \angle 2, \angle 7, \angle 4$ all measure 133°.   **53.** $\angle 6, \angle 8, \angle 4, \angle 2$ all measure
114°; $\angle 7, \angle 5, \angle 3, \angle 1$ all measure 66°.   **55.** $\angle 1 \cong \angle 3$, both are 138°;
$\angle 2 \cong \angle ABC$, both are 42°.

SECTION 6.6 (pages 483–486)

1. One dictionary definition is "conforming; agreeing." Examples of
congruent objects include two matching chairs and two pieces of paper
from the same notebook.   **2.** One dictionary definition is "resembling,
but not identical." Examples of similar objects are sets of different size
pots or measuring cups; small and large size cans of beans.   **3.** $\angle 1$ and
$\angle 4$; $\angle 2$ and $\angle 5$; $\angle 3$ and $\angle 6$; $\overline{AB}$ and $\overline{DE}$; $\overline{BC}$ and $\overline{EF}$; $\overline{AC}$ and $\overline{DF}$.
5. $\angle 1$ and $\angle 6$; $\angle 2$ and $\angle 4$; $\angle 3$ and $\angle 5$; $\overline{ST}$ and $\overline{YW}$; $\overline{TU}$ and $\overline{WX}$;

$\overline{SU}$ and $\overline{YX}$ **7.** $\angle 1$ and $\angle 6$; $\angle 2$ and $\angle 5$; $\angle 3$ and $\angle 4$; $\overline{LM}$ and $\overline{TS}$; $\overline{LN}$ and $\overline{TR}$; $\overline{MN}$ and $\overline{SR}$ **9.** SAS **11.** SSS **13.** ASA **15.** use SAS: $BC = CE$, $\angle ABC \cong \angle DCE$, $BA = CD$ **17.** use SAS: $PS = RS$, $m\angle QSP = m\angle QSR = 90°$, $QS = QS$ (common side) **19.** $a = 6$ cm; $\dfrac{7.5}{b} = \dfrac{6}{12}$; $b = 15$ cm **21.** $a = 5$ mm; $b = 3$ mm **23.** $a = 24$ in.; $b = 20$ in. **25.** $x = 24.8$ m; Perimeter $= 72.8$ m; $y = 15$ m; Perimeter $= 54.6$ m **27.** Perimeter $= 8$ cm $+ 8$ cm $+ 8$ cm $= 24$ cm; Area $\approx (0.5)(8 \text{ cm})(6.9 \text{ cm}) \approx 27.6 \text{ cm}^2$; The area is approximate because the height was rounded to the nearest tenth. **29.** $h = 24$ ft **31.** $x = 50$ m **33.** $n = 110$ m

Chapter 6 REVIEW EXERCISES (pages 495–500)

1. $\dfrac{3}{4}$ **2.** $\dfrac{4}{1}$ **3.** great white shark to whale shark; whale shark to blue whale **4.** $\dfrac{2}{1}$ **5.** $\dfrac{2}{3}$ **6.** $\dfrac{5}{2}$ **7.** $\dfrac{1}{6}$ **8.** $\dfrac{3}{1}$ **9.** $\dfrac{3}{8}$ **10.** $\dfrac{4}{3}$ **11.** $\dfrac{1}{9}$ **12.** $\dfrac{10}{7}$ **13.** $\dfrac{7}{5}$ **14.** $\dfrac{5}{6}$ **15.** $\dfrac{\$11}{1 \text{ dozen}}$ **16.** $\dfrac{12 \text{ children}}{5 \text{ families}}$ **17.** 0.2 page/minute or $\dfrac{1}{5}$ page/minute; 5 minutes/page **18.** \$20/hour; 0.05 hour/dollar or $\dfrac{1}{20}$ hour/dollar **19.** 8 ounces for \$4.98, about \$0.623/ounce **20.** 17.6 pounds for \$18.69 $-$ \$1 coupon, about \$1.005/pound **21.** $\dfrac{3}{5} = \dfrac{3}{5}$ or $90 = 90$; true **22.** $\dfrac{1}{8} \neq \dfrac{1}{4}$ or $432 \neq 216$; false **23.** $\dfrac{47}{10} \neq \dfrac{49}{10}$ or $980 \neq 940$; false **24.** $4.8 = 4.8$; true **25.** $14 = 14$; true **26.** $x = 1575$ **27.** $x = 20$ **28.** $x = 400$ **29.** $x = 12.5$ **30.** $x \approx 14.67$ (rounded) **31.** $x \approx 8.17$ (rounded) **32.** $x = 50.4$ **33.** $x \approx 0.57$ (rounded) **34.** $x \approx 2.47$ (rounded) **35.** 27 cats **36.** 46 hits **37.** \$15.63 (rounded) **38.** 3299 students (rounded) **39.** 68 ft **40.** $27\dfrac{1}{2}$ hours or 27.5 hours **41.** 511 calories (rounded) **42.** 14.7 milligrams **43.** line segment named $\overline{AB}$ or $\overline{BA}$ **44.** line named $\overleftrightarrow{CD}$ or $\overleftrightarrow{DC}$ **45.** ray named $\overrightarrow{OP}$ **46.** parallel **47.** perpendicular **48.** intersecting **49.** acute **50.** obtuse **51.** straight; 180° **52.** right; 90° **53.** (a) 10° (b) 45° (c) 83° **54.** (a) 25° (b) 90° (c) 147° **55.** $\angle 1$ and $\angle 4$ measure 30°; $\angle 3$ and $\angle 6$ measure 90°; $\angle 5$ measures 60° **56.** $\angle 8$, $\angle 3$, $\angle 6$, $\angle 1$ all measure 160°; $\angle 4$, $\angle 7$, $\angle 2$, $\angle 5$ all measure 20° **57.** SSS **58.** SAS **59.** ASA **60.** $y = 30$ ft; $x = 34$ ft; $P = 104$ ft **61.** $y = 7.5$ m; $x = 9$ m; $P = 22.5$ m **62.** $x = 12$ mm; $y = 7.5$ mm; $P = 38$ mm **63.** $x = 105$ **64.** $x = 0$ **65.** $x = 128$ **66.** $x \approx 23.08$ (rounded) **67.** $x = 6.5$ **68.** $x \approx 117.36$ (rounded) **69.** $\dfrac{8}{5}$ **70.** $\dfrac{33}{80}$ **71.** $\dfrac{15}{4}$ **72.** $\dfrac{4}{1}$ **73.** $\dfrac{4}{5}$ **74.** $\dfrac{37}{7}$ **75.** $\dfrac{3}{8}$ **76.** $\dfrac{1}{12}$ **77.** $\dfrac{45}{13}$ **78.** 24,900 fans (rounded) **79.** $\dfrac{8}{3}$ **80.** 75 ft for \$1.99 $-$ \$0.50 coupon, about \$0.020/ft **81.** 21 ft long; 15 ft wide **82.** (a) 1400 milligrams (b) 100 milligrams **83.** 21 points (rounded) **84.** $\dfrac{1}{2}$ or 0.5 teaspoon **85.** parallel lines **86.** line segment **87.** acute angle **88.** intersecting lines **89.** right angle; 90° **90.** ray **91.** straight angle; 180° **92.** obtuse angle **93.** perpendicular lines **94.** (a) The car turned around in a complete circle. (b) The governor took the opposite view, for example, having once opposed taxes but now supporting them. **95.** (a) No; because obtuse angles are $> 90°$, their sum would be $> 180°$. (b) Yes; because acute angles are $< 90°$, their sum could equal 90°. **96.** $\angle 1$ measures 45°; $\angle 3$ and $\angle 6$ measure 35°; $\angle 4$ measures 55°; $\angle 5$ measures 90° **97.** $\angle 5$, $\angle 2$, $\angle 7$, $\angle 4$ all measure 75°; $\angle 6$, $\angle 1$, $\angle 8$, $\angle 3$ all measure 105°.

Chapter 6 TEST (pages 501–502)

1. $\dfrac{\$1}{5 \text{ minutes}}$ **2.** $\dfrac{9}{2}$ **3.** $\dfrac{15}{4}$ **4.** 16 ounces for \$1.89 $-$ \$0.50 coupon, about \$0.087/ounce **5.** $x = 25$ **6.** $x \approx 2.67$ (rounded) **7.** $x = 325$ **8.** $x = 10\dfrac{1}{2}$ **9.** 24 orders **10.** 87 students (rounded) **11.** 23.8 grams (rounded) **12.** 60 feet **13.** (e) **14.** (a); 90° **15.** (d) **16.** (g); 180° **17.** Parallel lines are lines in the same plane that never intersect. Perpendicular lines intersect to form a right angle. Sketches will vary. **18.** 9° **19.** 160° **20.** $m\angle 1 = 50°$, $m\angle 2 = 35°$, $m\angle 3 = 95°$, $m\angle 5 = 35°$ **21.** Measures of $\angle 1$, $\angle 3$, $\angle 5$, and $\angle 7$ are all 65°; measures of $\angle 2$, $\angle 4$, $\angle 6$, and $\angle 8$ are all 115°. **22.** ASA (Angle–Side–Angle) **23.** SAS (Side–Angle–Side) **24.** $y = 12$ cm; $z = 6$ cm **25.** In the larger triangle, $x = 12$ mm, $P = 46.8$ mm; in the smaller triangle, $y = 14$ mm, $P = 39$ mm

Chapters 1–6 CUMULATIVE REVIEW EXERCISES (pages 503–504)

1. (a) seventy-seven billion, one million, eight hundred five (b) two hundredths **2.** (a) 3.040 (b) 500,037,000 **3.** 0 **4.** 14 **5.** $2\dfrac{11}{12}$ **6.** $\dfrac{2h - 3}{10}$ **7.** 99.9905 **8.** $\dfrac{3}{0}$ is undefined. **9.** -18 **10.** -14 **11.** $\dfrac{n}{4m}$ **12.** -0.00042 **13.** $\dfrac{1}{2y^2}$ **14.** $\dfrac{27 + 2n}{3n}$ **15.** -64 **16.** 5.4 **17.** $-\dfrac{1}{18}$ **18.** $y = -1$ **19.** $x = 15$ **20.** $x = 10$ **21.** Let t be the starting temperature. $t + 15 - 23 + 5 = 71$. The starting temperature was 74 degrees. **22.** Let l be the length; $l - 14$ is the width. $2(l) + 2(l - 14) = 100$. Length is 32 ft; width is 18 ft. **23.** $P = 7$ km; $A \approx 2.0$ km^2 (rounded) **24.** $d = 17$ m; $C \approx 53.4$ m (rounded); $A \approx 226.9$ m^2 (rounded) **25.** $V \approx 339.1$ ft^3 (rounded); $S \approx 282.6$ ft^2 **26.** 250 pounds **27.** $1\dfrac{1}{4}$ teaspoons **28.** $7\dfrac{3}{20}$ miles **29.** 22.0 miles per gallon (rounded) **30.** \$0.018, \$0.02, \$0.084, \$0.099, \$0.10, \$0.106, \$0.134 **31.** 202 minutes (rounded) **32.** 189 minutes (rounded) per \$20 card, so buy 2 cards to cover 360 minutes (6 hours). **33.** $\dfrac{1000}{200} = \dfrac{5}{1}$

CHAPTER 7 Percent

SECTION 7.1 (pages 514–519)

1. (a) 2 places to the left (b) $48.\% = 0.48$; $120.\% = 1.20$ or 1.2; $03.5\% = 0.035$ **2.** (a) 2 places to the right (b) $0.88 = 88\%$; $2.70 = 270\%$; $0.105 = 10.5\%$ **3.** 0.25 **5.** 0.30 or 0.3 **7.** 0.06 **9.** 1.40 or 1.4 **11.** 0.078 **13.** 1.00 or 1 **15.** 0.005 **17.** 0.0035 **19.** 50% **21.** 62% **23.** 3% **25.** 12.5% **27.** 200% **29.** 260% **31.** 3.12% **33.** $\dfrac{1}{5}$ **35.** $\dfrac{1}{2}$ **37.** $\dfrac{11}{20}$ **39.** $\dfrac{3}{8}$ **41.** $\dfrac{1}{16}$ **43.** $\dfrac{1}{6}$ **45.** $1\dfrac{3}{10}$ **47.** $2\dfrac{1}{2}$ **49.** 25% **51.** 30% **53.** 60% **55.** 37% **57.** $37\dfrac{1}{2}\%$ or 37.5%

59. 5%   **61.** exactly $55\frac{5}{9}$%, or 55.6% (rounded)   **63.** exactly $14\frac{2}{7}$%, or 14.3% (rounded)   **65.** 0.08   **67.** 0.49   **69.** 3.5%   **71.** 200%

73. $\frac{95}{100}$ or 95% shaded; $\frac{5}{100}$ or 5% unshaded   **75.** $\frac{3}{4}$ or 75% shaded; $\frac{1}{4}$ or 25% unshaded   **77.** 50%; 0.5; $\frac{1}{2}$ **78.** 0.25; $\frac{1}{4}$; 25%   **79.** 0.01; 1%

81. $\frac{1}{5}$; 20%   **83.** $\frac{3}{10}$; 0.3   **85.** 0.5; 50%   **87.** $\frac{9}{10}$; 0.9   **89.** $1\frac{1}{2}$; 150%

91. 0.08; $\frac{2}{25}$ **93.** 5%; 0.05; $\frac{1}{20}$ **95.** $\frac{1}{4}$; 0.25; 25%   **97.** $\frac{3}{8}$; 0.375; 37.5%

99. $\frac{1}{7}$; exactly $14\frac{2}{7}$%, or 14.3%(rounded)   **101. (a)** The student forgot to move the decimal point in 0.35 two places to the right. So $\frac{7}{20} = 35\%$.

(b) The student did the division in the wrong order. Enter $16 \div 25$ to get 0.64 and then move the decimal point two places to the right. So $\frac{16}{25} = 0.64 = 64\%$.   **102. (a)** The student should move the decimal point two places to the *right*. So $3.2 = 320\%$.   **(b)** The decimal point starts at the far *right* side of 60. So $60\% = 0.60$.   **103. (a)** $78   **(b)** $39

105. (a) 15 inches   **(b)** $7\frac{1}{2}$ inches   **107. (a)** 2.8 miles   **(b)** 1.4 miles
109. 20 children   **111.** 60 credits   **113. (a)** $142.50   **(b)** 50%
(c) $142.50   **115. (a)** 4100 students   **(b)** 50%   **117. (a)** 35 problems
(b) 0 problems   **119.** 50% means 50 out of 100 parts. That's half of the number. A shortcut for finding 50% of a number is to divide the number by 2. Examples will vary.   **120.** Since 100% means 100 parts out of 100 parts, 100% is all of the number. Examples will vary.

SECTION 7.2 (pages 526–527)

1. (a) 10%   **(b)** 3000 runners   **(c)** unknown   **(d)** $\frac{10}{100} = \frac{n}{3000}$

2. (a) 35%   **(b)** 2340 volunteers   **(c)** unknown   **(d)** $\frac{35}{100} = \frac{n}{2340}$

3. (a) unknown   **(b)** 32 pizzas   **(c)** 16 pizzas   **(d)** $\frac{p}{100} = \frac{16}{32}$

4. (a) unknown   **(b)** 140 hours   **(c)** 35 hours   **(d)** $\frac{p}{100} = \frac{35}{140}$

5. (a) 90%   **(b)** unknown   **(c)** 495 students   **(d)** $\frac{90}{100} = \frac{495}{n}$

6. (a) 28%   **(b)** unknown   **(c)** 84 e-mails   **(d)** $\frac{28}{100} = \frac{84}{n}$

7. 4.8 feet   **9.** $\frac{p}{100} = \frac{16}{200}$; 8%   **11.** $28   **13.** $\frac{250}{100} = \frac{n}{7}$; 17.5 hours

15. $\frac{p}{100} = \frac{32}{172}$; 18.6% (rounded)   **17.** $\frac{110}{100} = \frac{748}{n}$; 680 e-books

19. $\frac{14.7}{100} = \frac{n}{274}$; $40.28 (rounded)   **21.** $\frac{p}{100} = \frac{105}{54}$; 194.4% (rounded)

23. $\frac{5}{100} = \frac{0.33}{n}$; $6.60   **25.** 150% of $30 cannot be *less* than $30; 25% of $16 cannot be *greater than* $16.   **26.** The *percent* is the ratio of the part to the whole. It appears with the word *percent* or % after it. The *whole* is the entire quantity. It often appears after the word *of*. The *part* is the number being compared to the whole.   **27.** The correct proportion is $\frac{p}{100} = \frac{14}{8}$. The answer should be labeled with the % symbol. Correct answer is 175%.

28. The correct proportion is $\frac{30}{100} = \frac{9}{n}$. The answer is *not* a percent; it is the number of children. Correct answer is 30 children.

SECTION 7.3 (pages 534–537)

1. 1500 patients   **2.** 96 updates   **3.** $15   **4.** $710   **5.** 4.5 pounds
6. 0.7 foot   **7.** $7.00   **8.** $36   **9.** 52 students   **10.** 4.6 miles
11. 870 phones   **12.** 7 games   **13.** 4.75 hours   **14.** $0.37
15. (a) 10% means $\frac{10}{100}$ or $\frac{1}{10}$. The denominator tells you to divide the whole by 10. The shortcut for dividing by 10 is to move the decimal point one place to the left.   **(b)** Once you find 10% of a number, multiply the result by 2 for 20% and by 3 for 30%.   **16. (a)** 1% means $\frac{1}{100}$ and the denominator of 100 tells you to divide the whole by 100. The shortcut is to move the decimal point two places to the left.   **(b)** Once you find 1% of a number, multiply the result by 2 for 2% and by 3 for 3%.   **17.** 231 programs   **19.** 50%   **21.** 680 circuits   **23.** 1080 people   **25.** 845 posts
27. $20.80   **29.** 76%   **31.** 125%   **33.** 4700 employees   **35.** 83.2 quarts   **37.** 2%   **39.** 700 tablets   **41.** 325 babies   **43.** 1.5%
45. 5 gallons   **47.** 1029.2 meters   **49.** Multiply 0.2 by 100% to change it from a decimal to a percent. So, $0.20 = 20\%$.   **50.** The correct equation is $12 = (0.05)(n)$, so the solution is 240 inches.   **51.** The correct equation is $50 = p \cdot 20$, so the solution is 250%.   **52.** The percent must be changed to a decimal. The correct equation is $n = (0.04)(30)$, and the solution is 1.2 pounds.   **53.** Shortcut for 25%: Divide 80 by 4 to get 20. There are 20 boys.   **54.** 100% is all the children, so $100\% - 25\%$ who are boys = 75% who are girls.   **55.** Method 1: 80 children − 20 boys = 60 girls. Method 2: From Exercise 53, 25% of the children is 20 boys. So 75% is 3 times 20 = 60 girls.   **56.** There are 20 boys (from Exercise 53). The shortcut for finding 10% is dividing by 10, or moving the decimal point one place to the left. 10% of 20. is 2 boys who are left handed. There are no left-handed girls, so the total for left-handed children is 2.

SUMMARY EXERCISES Percent (pages 538–539)

1. (a) 0.03; 3%   **(b)** $\frac{3}{10}$; 0.3   **(c)** $\frac{3}{8}$; 37.5%   **(d)** $1\frac{3}{5}$; 1.6

(e) 0.0625; 6.25%   **(f)** $\frac{1}{20}$; 0.05   **(g)** 2; 200%   **(h)** 0.8; 80%

(i) $\frac{9}{125}$; 7.2%   **2. (a)** 3.5 ft   **(b)** 19 miles   **(c)** 105 cows   **(d)** $0.08

(e) 500 women   **(f)** $45   **(g)** $87.50   **(h)** 12 pounds   **(i)** 95 students

3. $12\frac{1}{2}$% or 12.5%   **4.** 75 messages   **5.** $0.53 (rounded)   **6.** 175%

7. 5.9 pounds (rounded)   **8.** 600 hours   **9.** 50%   **10.** 500 camp sites
11. 98 golf balls   **12.** 2.7% (rounded)   **13.** 2300 tweets
14. 0.63 ounce   **15.** 145%   **16.** 244 voters (rounded)   **17.** 0.021 inch
18. 400%   **19.** 8%   **20.** $0.68   **21.** Invitations; $847   **22.** $2525.60
23. $3696   **24.** $2063.60   **25. (a)** $14,784   **(b)** $83.06 (rounded)

SECTION 7.4 (pages 546–549)

1. (a) 10%   **(b)** 5%   **(c)** 1%   **2. (a)** 50%   **(b)** 25%   **(c)** 10%
3. $37.80   **5. (a)** 101.6 pounds (rounded)   **(b)** 10.1 pounds (rounded)
(c) 28.1 pounds (rounded)   **7.** Pay off debt, 59.0%; save or invest, 66.0%; buy something, 22.9% (all rounded).   **9.** 310 million people   **11.** 138%
13. 40 problems   **15.** 583 shots (rounded)   **17.** 23.7 miles per gallon (rounded)   **19.** 58% (rounded); $16,796   **21.** 135% (rounded)
23. $535; $535; 64.8% (rounded)   **25.** 9.1% (rounded)   **27.** 40%

29. 654% (rounded)   **31.** No. 100% is the entire price, so a decrease of 100% would take the price down to 0. Therefore, 100% is the maximum possible decrease in the price of something.   **32.** 25% of $80 is $80 ÷ 4 = $20; 75% would be 3 times $20 = $60; 125% would be $80 + $20 = $100   **33.** George ate more than 65 grams, so the percent must be >100%. Use $p \cdot 65 = 78$ to get 120%.   **34.** The team won more than half the games, so the percent must be > 50%. Correct solution is $0.72 = 72\%$.   **35.** The brain could not weigh 375 pounds, which is more than the person weighs. $2\frac{1}{2}\% = 2.5\% = 0.025$, so $(0.025)(150) = n$ and $n = 3.75$ pounds   **36.** If 80% were absent, then only 20% made it to class. $800 - 640 = 160$ students, or use $(0.20)(800) = n$.

SECTION 7.5 (pages 556–561)

1. (a) 0.065   **(b)** 0.0125   **(c)** 0.1025   **(d)** 0.0575   **2. (a)** 0.75 year **(b)** 11.5 years   **(c)** 4.25 years   **(d)** 8.75 years   **3.** $29.28 (rounded); $395.26   **5.** 3%; $70.04   **7.** $0.12 (rounded); $2.22   **9.** $4\frac{1}{2}\%$; $13,167 **11.** $3 + $1.50 = $4.50; $4.83 (rounded); 2($3) = $6; $6.43 (rounded) **13.** $8 + $4 = $12; $11.75 (rounded); 2($8) = $16; $15.67 (rounded) **15.** $1 + $0.50 = $1.50; $1.43 (rounded); 2($1) = $2; $1.91 **17.** $15; $85   **19.** 30%; $126   **21.** $4.38 (rounded); $13.12 **23.** $3.79 (rounded); $34.09   **25.** $42; $342   **27.** $33.30; $773.30 **29.** $56.25; $1556.25   **31.** $919.67 (rounded); $18,719.67   **33.** $1170 **35.** $7978.13 (rounded)   **37.** $26.61 (rounded)   **39.** 8%   **41.** $74.25 **43.** $25.13   **45.** $395.67; $803.33   **47.** $2016.38 (rounded) **49.** $21 (rounded)   **51.** $92.38   **53.** $230.12   **55. (a)** $15,000 **(b)** $1289 more   **56. (a)** $34,000   **(b)** $66,627 more   **57. (a)** $60,000; $1,113,909 more   **(b)** 19 times greater (rounded)

Chapter 7 REVIEW EXERCISES (pages 569–572)

1. 0.25   **2.** 1.8   **3.** 0.125   **4.** 0.07   **5.** 265%   **6.** 2%   **7.** 30% **8.** 0.2%   **9.** $\frac{3}{25}$ **10.** $\frac{3}{8}$ **11.** $2\frac{1}{2}$ **12.** $\frac{1}{20}$ **13.** 75%   **14.** 62.5% or $62\frac{1}{2}\%$ **15.** 325%   **16.** 6%   **17.** 0.125   **18.** 12.5%   **19.** $\frac{3}{20}$ **20.** 15%   **21.** $1\frac{4}{5}$ **22.** 1.8   **23.** $46   **24.** $23   **25.** 9 hours **26.** $4\frac{1}{2}$ hours   **27.** 242 meters   **28.** 17,000 cases   **29.** 27 smartphones **30.** 870 math books   **31.** 9.5% (rounded)   **32.** 225%   **33.** $2.60 (rounded)   **34.** 80 days   **35.** 4%   **36.** $575   **37.** 20 people **38.** 175%   **39. (a)** 3000 patients   **(b)** 31.5% decrease (rounded) **40. (a)** $364   **(b)** 224%   **41. (a)** 80%   **(b)** 6.3% increase (rounded) **42.** 85.7% (rounded)   **43.** $0.11 (rounded); $2.90   **44.** $7\frac{1}{2}\%$; $838.50   **45.** $4 + $2 = $6; $6.41 (rounded); 2($4) = $8; $8.55 (rounded)   **46.** $0.80 + $0.40 = $1.20; $1.21 (rounded); 2($0.80) = $1.60; $1.61   **47.** $3.75; $33.75   **48.** 25%; $189 **49.** $34.13 (rounded); $384.13   **50.** $183.60; $1713.60   **51.** $\frac{1}{3}$; $33\frac{1}{3}\%$ (exact) or 33.3% (rounded)   **52.** cards; 68%; 0.68; $\frac{17}{25}$ **53.** 277 adults (rounded)   **54.** cards, 188 adults (rounded); sci-fi/simulation, 102 adults (rounded)   **55.** 74.3% (rounded)   **56.** 5715 dogs (rounded) **57.** 62.5% (rounded)   **58.** 28.8% decrease (rounded) **59.** 69.3% (rounded)   **60.** 79 animals (rounded)

Chapter 7 TEST (pages 573–574)

1. 0.75   **2.** 60%   **3.** 180%   **4.** 7.5% or $7\frac{1}{2}\%$ **5.** 3.00 or 3   **6.** 0.02 **7.** $\frac{5}{8}$ **8.** $2\frac{2}{5}$ **9.** 5%   **10.** 87.5% or $87\frac{1}{2}\%$ **11.** 175%   **12.** 320 laptops **13.** 400%   **14.** $19,500   **15.** $8466.75   **16.** 34% increase (rounded) **17.** To find 50% of a number, divide the number by 2. To find 25% of a number, divide the number by 4. Examples will vary.   **18.** Round $31.94 to $30. Then 10% of $30. is $3 and 5% of $30 is half of $3 or $1.50, so a 15% tip estimate is $3 + $1.50 = $4.50. A 20% tip estimate is 2($3) = $6. **19.** Exact tip is $4.79 (rounded). Each person pays $12.24 (rounded). **20.** $3.84; $44.16   **21.** $41.39 (rounded); $188.56 **22.** $815.66 ÷ 6 ≈ $135.94   **23.** $1650; $6650   **24.** $51.60; $911.60

Chapters 1–7 CUMULATIVE REVIEW EXERCISES (pages 575–576)

1. (a) ninety and one hundred five thousandths   **(b)** one hundred twenty-five million, six hundred seventy   **2. (a)** 30,005,000,000   **(b)** 0.0078 **3.** Mean is $871.25; median is $825.   **4.** 17 ounces for $2.89, which is $0.17/ounce   **5.** 48.901   **6.** 17   **7.** $\frac{9b^2}{8}$ **8.** $\frac{1}{2}$ **9.** -7 **10.** $\frac{16 + 5x}{20}$ **11.** -0.001 **12.** 0   **13.** $\frac{7m - 16}{8m}$ **14.** -30 **15.** $\frac{4}{9n}$ **16.** $3\frac{1}{2}$ **17.** 19   **18.** -1 **19.** -24 **20.** 160   **21.** $h = -6$ **22.** $a = 2.2$ **23.** $x = 3$ **24.** $n + 31 = 3n + 1$; $n = 15$ **25.** Let p be Susanna's pay. Let $2p$ be Neoka's pay. $p + 2p = 1620$. Susanna receives $540; Neoka receives $1080.   **26.** $P = 50$ yd; $A = 143.5$ yd²   **27.** $C \approx 31.4$ ft; $A \approx 78.5$ ft²   **28.** $y \approx 24.2$ mm (rounded); $A = 142.5$ mm²   **29.** 2100 students   **30.** $P = 64$ ft; $A = 252$ ft²   **31.** $\frac{1}{6}$ cup more than the amount needed   **32.** $56.70; $132.30   **33.** 93.6 km   **34.** 88.6% (rounded)   **35.** $0.23 (rounded)

CHAPTER 8 Measurement

SECTION 8.1 (pages 584–587)

1. (a) inch, foot, yard, mile   **(b)** fluid ounce, cup, pint, quart, gallon **2. (a)** ounce, pound, ton   **(b)** second, minute, hour, day, week   **3. (a)** 3 **(b)** 12   **5. (a)** 8   **(b)** 2   **7. (a)** 2000   **(b)** 16   **9. (a)** 60   **(b)** 60 **11. (a)** 2   **(b)** 240   **13. (a)** $\frac{1}{2}$ or 0.5   **(b)** 78   **15.** 14,000 to 16,000 lb **17.** $\frac{3 \text{ ft}}{1 \text{ yd}}$; 27 ft   **19.** 112   **21.** 10   **23.** $1\frac{1}{2}$ or 1.5   **25.** $\frac{1}{4}$ or 0.25 **27.** $1\frac{1}{2}$ or 1.5   **29.** $2\frac{1}{2}$ or 2.5   **31.** snowmobile/ATV; person walking **33.** 5000   **35.** 17   **37.** 4 to 8 in.   **39.** 216   **41.** 28   **43.** 518,400 **45.** 48,000   **47. (a)** pound/ounces   **(b)** quarts/pints or pints/cups **(c)** minutes/hours or seconds/minutes   **(d)** feet/inches   **(e)** pounds/tons **(f)** days/weeks   **48.** Feet and inches both measure length, so you can add them once you've changed 12 inches into 1 ft. But pounds measure weight and cannot be added to a length measurement.   **49.** 174,240 **51.** 800   **53.** 0.75 or $\frac{3}{4}$ **55.** $1.83 (rounded)   **57.** $140 **59. (a)** 1056 sec   **(b)** 17.6 min   **61. (a)** $12\frac{1}{2}$ qt   **(b)** 4 containers, because you can't buy part of a container   **63. (a)** 0.8 mi (rounded) **(b)** 13,031 ft   **(c)** 2.5 mi (rounded)   **64. (a)** 183 yd (rounded)

(b) 6600 in. **(c)** 0.1 mi (rounded) **(d)** 9 ft (rounded)

65. (a) $1\frac{1}{2}$ to $2\frac{1}{2}$ ft, or 1.5 to 2.5 ft **(b)** 8400 months **(c)** 140 more years, for a total of 840 years in all **66. (a)** 283 mi (rounded) **(b)** 377 mi (rounded)

SECTION 8.2 (pages 593–594)

1. 1000 **2.** 10 **3.** $\frac{1}{1000}$ or 0.001; $\frac{1}{1000}$ or 0.001
4. $\frac{1}{10}$ or 0.1; $\frac{1}{10}$ or 0.1 **5.** $\frac{1}{100}$ or 0.01; $\frac{1}{100}$ or 0.01 **6.** 100; 100
7. (a) cm **(b)** mm **(c)** cm **8. (a)** km **(b)** cm **(c)** km
9. Answers will vary; about 8 to 10 cm. **11.** Answers will vary; about 20 to 25 mm. **13.** cm **15.** m **17.** km **19.** mm **21.** cm **23.** m
25. 700 cm **27.** 0.040 m or 0.04 m **29.** 9400 m **31.** 5.09 m
33. 40 cm **35.** 910 mm **37.** less; 18 cm or 0.18 m **38.** greater; 22 m or 0.022 km

39. ↓ 5 mm = 0.5 cm
← 1 mm = 0.1 cm

41. 0.061 km **43.** 164 cm; 1640 mm **45.** 0.0000056 km

SECTION 8.3 (pages 601–604)

1. (a) milliliters **(b)** liters **(c)** milligrams **(d)** kilograms
2. (a) grams **(b)** liters **(c)** milliliters **(d)** milligrams **3.** mL
5. L **7.** kg **9.** g **11.** mL **13.** mg **15.** L **17.** kg
19. unreasonable; too much **20.** reasonable **21.** unreasonable; too much
22. unreasonable; too much **23.** reasonable **24.** reasonable
25. reasonable **26.** unreasonable; too little **27.** Unit for your answer (g) is in numerator; unit being changed (kg) is in denominator so it will divide out. The unit fraction is $\frac{1000\ g}{1\ kg}$. **28.** From mg to g is three places to the left on the metric conversion line, so move the decimal point three places to the left. 020. mg = 0.02 g **29.** three; right; 15,000 mL **31.** 3 L **33.** 0.925 L **35.** 0.008 L **37.** 4150 mL
39. 8 kg **41.** 5200 g **43.** 850 mg **45.** 30 g **47.** 0.598 g
49. 0.06 L **51.** 0.003 kg **53.** 990 mL **55.** mm **57.** mL **59.** cm
61. mg **63.** 0.3 L **65.** 1340 g; 5000 g **67.** 0.9 L **69.** 3 kg to 4 kg
71. greater; 5 mg or 0.005 g **72.** less; 10 mL or 0.01 L **73.** 200 nickels
75. (a) 1,000,000 **(b)** $\frac{3.5\ \text{Mm}}{1} \cdot \frac{1,000,000\ \text{m}}{1\ \text{Mm}} = 3,500,000$ m
76. (a) 1,000,000,000 **(b)** $\frac{2500\ \text{m}}{1} \cdot \frac{1\ \text{Gm}}{1,000,000,000\ \text{m}} = 0.0000025$ Gm
77. (a) 1,000,000,000,000 **(b)** 1000; 1,000,000
78. 1,000,000; 1,000,000,000; $2^{20} = 1,048,576$; $2^{30} = 1,073,741,824$

SUMMARY EXERCISES U.S. and Metric Measurement Units (pages 605–606)

1. Length: inch (in.), foot (ft), yard (yd), mile (mi)
Weight: ounce (oz), pound (lb), ton (ton)
Capacity: fluid ounce (fl oz), cup (c), pint (pt), quart (qt), gallon (gal)
2. Length: millimeter (mm), centimeter (cm), meter (m), kilometer (km)
Weight: milligram (mg), gram (g), kilogram (kg)
Capacity: milliliter (mL), liter (L)
3. (a) ft **(b)** yd **(c)** 5280 **4. (a)** min **(b)** 60 **(c)** 24 **5. (a)** 8 **(b)** gal **(c)** 2 **6. (a)** lb **(b)** 2000 **(c)** 16 **7.** mL **8.** m **9.** kg
10. mg **11.** cm **12.** mm **13.** L **14.** g **15.** 0.45 m **16.** 45 sec

17. 600 mL **18.** 8000 mg **19.** 30 cm **20.** $3\frac{3}{4}$ or 3.75 ft
21. 0.050 or 0.05 L **22.** $4\frac{1}{2}$ or 4.5 gal **23.** 7280 g **24.** 36 oz
25. 0.009 kg **26.** 180 in. **27.** 272 cm; 2720 mm **28.** 2.64 m; 0.00264 km **29.** 0.04 m; 4 cm; 40 mm **30.** 24 cm; 0.24 m; 240 mm
31. $5.19 (rounded) **32.** 9.3 ft (rounded)

SECTION 8.4 (pages 609–610)

1. c **2.** b **3.** kg; kg; $0.83 (rounded) **5.** 89.5 kg **7.** 71 beats (rounded)
9. 180 cm; $0.02/cm (rounded) **11.** 5.03 m **13.** 4 bottles; 175 mL or 0.175 L **15.** 1.89 g **17. (a)** 1.54 m **(b)** 308 cm **19.** 215 g; 4.3 g; 4300 mg **20.** 330 g; 0.33 g; 330 mg **21.** 1550 g; 1500 g; 3 g **22.** 55 g; 50 g; 0.5 g

SECTION 8.5 (pages 615–618)

1. (a) $\frac{1\ kg}{2.20\ lb}$; $\frac{2.20\ lb}{1\ kg}$ **(b)** kg; denominator **2. (a)** $\frac{1\ qt}{0.95\ L}$; $\frac{0.95\ L}{1\ qt}$
(b) qt; denominator **3.** 21.8 yd **5.** 262.4 ft **7.** 4.8 m **9.** 5.3 oz
11. 111.6 kg **13.** 30.3 qt **15. (a)** 0.2 oz (rounded) **(b)** probably not
17. 31.8 L (rounded) **19.** 1.3 cm (rounded) **21.** $-8\,°C$ **22.** $80\,°C$
23. $40\,°C$ **24.** $25\,°C$ **25.** $150\,°C$ **26.** $10\,°C$ **27.** $16\,°C$ (rounded)
29. $-20\,°C$ **31.** $46\,°F$ (rounded) **33.** $23\,°F$ **35.** $58\,°C$ (rounded); $-89\,°C$ (rounded) **37. (a)** pleasant weather, above freezing but not hot
(b) $75\,°F$ to $39\,°F$ (rounded) **(c)** Answers will vary. In Minnesota, it's $0\,°C$ to $-40\,°C$; in California, $24\,°C$ to $0\,°C$. **39.** $50\,°F$; $104\,°F$
41. 1.8 m (rounded) **42.** 5.0 kg (rounded) **43.** 3040.2 km (rounded)
44. 38 hr 23 min **45.** 300 m (rounded) **46.** less than 3790 mL
47. 59.4 mL (rounded) **48.** about 1.6% (rounded)

Chapter 8 REVIEW EXERCISES (pages 625–628)

1. 16 **2.** 3 **3.** 2000 **4.** 4 **5.** 60 **6.** 8 **7.** 60 **8.** 5280
9. 12 **10.** 48 **11.** 3 **12.** 4 **13.** $\frac{3}{4}$ or 0.75 **14.** $2\frac{1}{2}$ or 2.5
15. 28 **16.** 78 **17.** 112 **18.** 345,600
19. (a) $4153\frac{1}{3}$ yd (exact) or 4153.3 yd (rounded) **(b)** 2.4 mi (rounded)
20. $2465.20 **21.** mm **22.** cm **23.** km **24.** m **25.** cm
26. mm **27.** 500 cm **28.** 8500 m **29.** 8.5 cm **30.** 3.7 m
31. 0.07 km **32.** 930 mm **33.** mL **34.** L **35.** g **36.** kg **37.** L
38. mL **39.** mg **40.** g **41.** 5 L **42.** 8000 mL **43.** 4580 mg
44. 700 g **45.** 0.006 g **46.** 0.035 L **47.** 31.5 L
48. 357 g (rounded) **49.** 87.25 kg **50.** $1.42 (rounded)
51. 6.5 yd (rounded) **52.** 11.7 in. (rounded) **53.** 67.0 mi (rounded)
54. 1288 km **55.** 21.9 L (rounded) **56.** 44.0 qt (rounded) **57.** $0\,°C$
58. $100\,°C$ **59.** $37\,°C$ **60.** $20\,°C$ **61.** $25\,°C$ **62.** $-15\,°C$
63. $28\,°F$ (rounded) **64.** $120\,°F$ (rounded) **65.** L **66.** kg **67.** cm
68. mL **69.** mm **70.** km **71.** g **72.** m **73.** mL **74.** g
75. mg **76.** L **77.** 105 mm **78.** $\frac{3}{4}$ hr or 0.75 hr **79.** $7\frac{1}{2}$ ft or 7.5 ft
80. 130 cm **81.** $77\,°F$ **82.** 14 qt **83.** 0.7 g **84.** 810 mL
85. 80 oz **86.** 60,000 g **87.** 1800 mL **88.** $30\,°C$ **89.** 36 cm
90. 0.055 L **91.** 1.26 m **92.** 18 tons **93.** 113 g; $177\,°C$ (both rounded) **94.** 178.0 lb; 6.0 ft (both rounded) **95.** 13.2 m **96.** 22.0 ft
97. 3.6 m **98.** 39.8 in. **99.** 484,000 lb **100.** 19.0 to 22.7 L
101. (a) 242 tons **(b)** 144 in. **102. (a)** 1.02 m **(b)** 670 cm

Chapter 8 TEST (pages 629–630)

1. 36 qt   **2.** 15 yd   **3.** 2.25 hr or $2\frac{1}{4}$ hr   **4.** 0.75 ft or $\frac{3}{4}$ ft

5. 56 oz   **6.** 7200 min   **7.** kg   **8.** km   **9.** mL   **10.** g   **11.** cm

12. mm   **13.** L   **14.** cm   **15.** 2.5 m   **16.** 4600 m   **17.** 0.5 cm

18. 0.325 g   **19.** 16,000 mL   **20.** 400 g   **21.** 1055 cm   **22.** 0.095 L

23. 3.2 ft (rounded)   **24. (a)** 1390 mg   **(b)** 200 mg or 0.2 g more

25. 95 °C   **26.** 0 °C   **27.** 1.8 m   **28.** 56.3 kg (rounded)   **29.** 13 gal

30. 5.0 mi (rounded)   **31.** 23 °C (rounded)   **32.** 10 °F (rounded)

33. 6 m ≈ 6.54 yd; $26.03 (rounded)   **34.** Possible answers: Use same system as rest of the world; easier system for children to learn; less use of fractional numbers; compete internationally.

Chapters 1–8 CUMULATIVE REVIEW EXERCISES (pages 631–632)

1. $\frac{3}{4xy}$ **2.** $\frac{18-5c}{6c}$ **3.** undefined   **4.** $-\frac{5}{12}$ **5.** $\frac{27xy}{4}$ **6.** $\frac{2m+3n}{3m}$

7. $2\frac{5}{6}$ **8.** $-\frac{7}{45}$ **9.** 2   **10.** −3.2   **11.** 0   **12.** $n = 2$ **13.** $x = 0.4$

14. $w = 20$ **15.** $y = -5$ **16.** $2n - 8 = n + 7$; $n = 15$ **17.** Let p be the longer piece; $p - 6$ the shorter piece. $p + p - 6 = 90$ The pieces are 48 ft and 42 ft long.   **18.** $P = 9$ ft; $A = 5\frac{1}{16}$ ft^2 or 5.1 ft^2 (rounded)

19. $C \approx 28.3$ mm (rounded); $A \approx 63.6$ mm^2 (rounded)   **20.** $y = 12$ yd; $A = 96$ yd^2 **21.** $V = 96$ cm^3; $S = 128$ cm^2 **22.** 54 in.   **23.** 3 days

24. 3700 g   **25.** 0.6 m   **26.** 58% (rounded)   **27.** Brand T at 15.5 oz for $2.99 − $0.30 coupon, about $0.174/ounce   **28. (a)** 93.6 km

(b) 58.0 mi (rounded)   **29.** 5.97 kg   **30.** $1\frac{1}{12}$ yards

31. $9.74 (rounded)   **32.** $18.99 (rounded); $170.95   **33.** 120 rows

34. $2821.88 (rounded); $21,571.88   **35.** 23 blankets; $9 left over

36. $0.15/application   **37.** 37.5% decrease

CHAPTER 9 Graphs

SECTION 9.1 (pages 637–640)

1. b   **2.** a   **3.** b   **4.** b   **5. (a)** 31,419 points   **(b)** Michael Jordan, Karl Malone, and Kareem Abdul-Jabbar   **7. (a)** Kareem Abdul-Jabbar   **(b)** Wilt Chamberlain   **9.** 10,071 points   **11.** For Shaquille: 23.69 ≈ 23.7 points per game; for Kobe: 28,316 ÷ 1117 ≈ 25.4 points per game   **13. (a)** 255 calories   **(b)** moderate jogging   **15. (a)** moderate jogging, aerobic dance, racquetball   **(b)** moderate jogging, moderate bicycling, aerobic dance, racquetball, tennis   **17.** 370 calories   **19. (a)** 366 calories (rounded)   **(b)** 239 calories (rounded)   **21.** about 39 calories   **23. (a)** 90 million or 90,000,000   **(b)** 45 million or 45,000,000   **25.** 155 million or 155,000,000   **27.** 5 million or 5,000,000   **29.** 295 million or 295,000,000

SECTION 9.2 (pages 645–649)

1. b   **2.** c   **3.** c   **4.** a   **5.** 500 people   **7.** Friday; 180 people   **9.** $\frac{1}{10}$ **11.** $\frac{180}{120} = \frac{3}{2}$ **13.** $\frac{300}{20} = \frac{15}{1}$ **15.** $(0.35)(400) = 140$ people   **17.** raids the buffet table; 16 people   **19.** 64 fewer people   **21.** 160 people   **23.** mustard; 960 people   **25.** 64 more people   **27.** First, find the percent of the total that is represented by each item. Next, multiply the percent by 360° to find the size of each sector. Finally, use a protractor to draw each sector.   **28.** A protractor is used to measure the number of degrees in a sector. First, you draw a

line from the center of the circle to the left edge. Next, place the hole of the protractor at the center of the circle, making sure that the 0 on the protractor is on the line. Finally, make a mark at the desired number of degrees. This gives you the size of the sector.   **29. (a)** 180°   **(b)** 20%; 72°   **(c)** 5%; 18°   **(d)** 15%; 54°   **(e)** 10%; 36°   **(f)** See circle graph below.

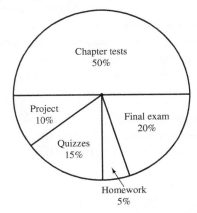

31. (a) $200,000   **(b)** 6.25%; 20%; 30%; 25%; 18.75%   **(c)** 22.5°; 72°; 108°; 90°; 67.5°   **(d)** See circle graph below.

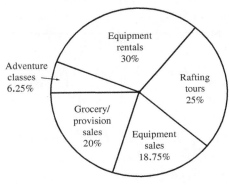

SECTION 9.3 (pages 653–656)

1. c   **2.** a   **3.** b   **4.** b   **5.** Music and video is tied with electronics for highest percent; 74%   **7.** $(0.61)($4.4 billion) ≈ $2.7 billion (rounded)   **9.** clothing   **11.** July; 120,000 unemployed   **13.** 10,000 more workers   **15.** 120,000 − 80,000 = 40,000 fewer workers; 33% decrease (rounded)   **17.** 15%   **19.** 2011–12   **21.** $(0.10)(172) ≈ 17$ employers (rounded)   **23.** 24.1 million or 24,100,000 PCs   **25.** 185.6 million or 185,600,000 more PCs   **27.** 82.3 million or 82,300,000 PCs; 132% increase (rounded)   **29. (a)** 3,000,000 DVDs   **(b)** 1,500,000 DVDs   **31. (a)** 2,500,000 DVDs   **(b)** 3,000,000 DVDs   **33.** Answers will vary. Possibilities include: Both stores had decreased sales from 2008 to 2009 and increased sales from 2010 to 2011; Store B had lower sales than Store A in 2008–09 but higher sales than Store A in 2010–2012.   **34.** Answers will vary. Some possibilities are that Store B may have started to do more advertising, keep longer store hours, train their staff, employ more help, or give better service than Store A   **35.** 2010; $25,000   **37.** 2009, 29% (rounded); 2010, 20%; 2011, 17% (rounded); 2012, 38% (rounded)   **39.** Answers will vary. Possibilities include: The decrease in sales may have resulted from poor service or greater competition; the increase in sales may have been a result of more advertising or better service.   **40.** Most of the time, as sales increase or decrease, so do profits

41. Sales have increased at a rapid rate since 1985. **42.** Answers will vary. Some possibilities are lower prices; more uses and applications for students, home use, and businesses; improved technology. **43. (a)** 104% (rounded) **(b)** 159% (rounded) **(c)** 132% (rounded) **(d)** 37% (rounded) **(e)** 54% (rounded) **44.** Since 2000, the percent of increase for each 5-year period has been much lower than in earlier periods. **45.** Answers will vary. One possibility is that people will buy new devices such as smartphones and tablets instead of PCs. **46.** No. The line graph shows the amount of sales in previous years but cannot accurately predict future sales; we can only make a guess based on the trend in the graph.

SECTION 9.4 (pages 661–662)

1. (a) See dot at center of coordinate grid below. **(b)** See x-axis and y-axis labels on grid below. **2. (a)** I, II, III, IV **(b)** See coordinate grid below.

3.

5.

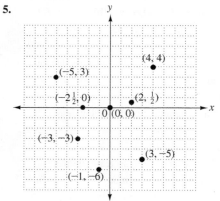

7. A is $(3, 4)$; B is $(5, -5)$; C is $(-4, -2)$; D is approximately $\left(4, \frac{1}{2}\right)$; E is $(0, -6)$; F is $(-5, 5)$; G is $(-2, 0)$; H is $(0, 0)$. **9.** III, none, IV, II
11. (a) any positive number **(b)** any negative number **(c)** 0 **(d)** any negative number **(e)** any positive number **13.** Starting at the origin, move left or right along the x-axis to the number a; then move up if b is positive or move down if b is negative. **14.** When a is 0, the point is on the y-axis. When b is 0, the point is on the x-axis.

SECTION 9.5 (pages 671–676)

1. c **2.** b **3.** $(1, 3)$; 2; $(2, 2)$;
All points on the line are solutions.

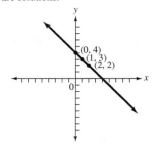

5. -1; $(0, -1)$; -2; $(1, -2)$; -3; $(2, -3)$;
All points on the line are solutions.

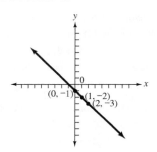

7. 4; -1; -6; 99 **8.** The line in Exercise 4 crosses both the x-axis and y-axis at -4; the sum of $x + y$ is -4 in the equation. Similarly, in Exercise 6, the line crosses both the x-axis and y-axis at 1; the sum of $x + y$ is 1 in the equation.

9.

x	y	(x, y)
1	-1	$(1, -1)$
2	0	$(2, 0)$
3	1	$(3, 1)$

See graph at the right.

11.

x	y	(x, y)
0	2	$(0, 2)$
-1	1	$(-1, 1)$
-2	0	$(-2, 0)$

See graph at the right.

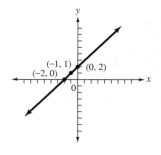

13.

x	y	(x, y)
0	0	(0, 0)
1	−3	(1, −3)
2	−6	(2, −6)

See graph at the right.

15. The lines in Exercises 9 and 11 have a positive slope. The lines in Exercises 3, 5, and 13 have a negative slope.

17.

x	y	(x, y)
0	0	(0, 0)
3	1	(3, 1)
6	2	(6, 2)

See graph at the right.

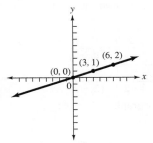

19.

x	y	(x, y)
−1	−1	(−1, −1)
−2	−2	(−2, −2)
−3	−3	(−3, −3)

See graph at the right.

21.

x	y	(x, y)
0	3	(0, 3)
1	1	(1, 1)
2	−1	(2, −1)

See graph at the right.

23.

negative slope

25.

positive slope

27.

positive slope

29.

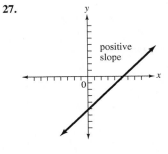

negative slope

Chapter 9 REVIEW EXERCISES (pages 683–688)

1. (a) gymnastics **(b)** volleyball **2. (a)** basketball **(b)** cross country **3. (a)** 3524 men **(b)** 14,134 women **4.** men's, 15.3 (rounded); women's, 15.0 (rounded) **5. (a)** 100 inches **(b)** 15 inches **6. (a)** 50 inches **(b)** 55 inches **7. (a)** 35 inches **(b)** 45 inches **8.** 95 inches difference between Juneau and Memphis **9. (a)** lodging; $560 **(b)** food; $400 **(c)** $1700 **10.** $\frac{560}{400} = \frac{7}{5}$ **11.** $\frac{300}{1700} = \frac{3}{17}$ **12.** $\frac{280}{1700} = \frac{14}{85}$ **13.** $\frac{300}{160} = \frac{15}{8}$ **14.** painting and wall papering; 63% **15.** construction work; 33% **16.** 43%; 147 homeowners (rounded) **17.** 184 homeowners (rounded) **18. (a)** interior decorating and landscaping/gardening **(b)** construction work and window treatments **19.** Answers will vary. Possibilities include: painting and wall papering are easier to do, take less time, or cost less than construction work. **20.** March; 8,000,000 acre-feet **21.** June; 2,000,000 acre-feet **22.** 5,000,000 acre-feet **23.** 6,000,000 acre-feet **24.** 3,000,000 acre-feet; 37.5% decrease **25.** 3,000,000 acre-feet; 60% decrease **26.** $50,000,000 **27.** $20,000,000 **28.** $20,000,000 **29.** $40,000,000 **30.** Sales decreased for two years and then moved up slightly. Answers will vary. Perhaps there is less new construction, remodeling, and home improvement in the area near Center A. Or, better product selection and service may have reversed the decline in sales. **31.** Sales are increasing. Answers will vary. New construction may have increased in the area near Center B, or greater advertising may attract more attention. **32.** 36° **33.** 35%; 126° **34.** 20%; 72° **35.** 25%; 90° **36.** $2240; 10% **37.** See graph below.

38.

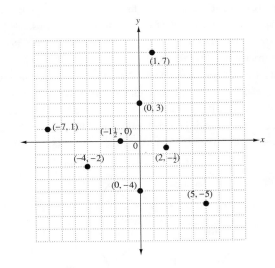

39. A is $(0, 6)$; B is approximately $\left(-2, 2\frac{1}{2}\right)$; C is $(0, 0)$; D is $(-6, -6)$;

E is $(4, 3)$; F is approximately $\left(3\frac{1}{2}, 0\right)$; G is $(2, -4)$.

40.

x	y	(x, y)
0	−2	(0, −2)
1	−3	(1, −3)
2	−4	(2, −4)

The graph of $x + y = -2$ has a *negative* slope.

There are many other solutions because all points on the line are solutions. Some possibilities are $(-1, -1)$ and $(-2, 0)$.

41.

x	y	(x, y)
0	3	(0, 3)
1	4	(1, 4)
2	5	(2, 5)

See graph below.

All points on the line are solutions. Some possibilities are $(-1, 2)$ and $(-2, 1)$.

42.

x	y	(x, y)
−1	4	(−1, 4)
0	0	(0, 0)
1	−4	(1, −4)

See graph below.

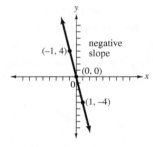

All points on the line are solutions. Some possibilities are $\left(-\frac{1}{2}, 2\right)$ and $\left(\frac{1}{2}, -2\right)$.

Chapter 9 TEST (pages 689–692)

1. (a) sardines   **(b)** cream cheese   **2.** 166 calories (rounded)
3. 259 mg (rounded)   **4. (a)** birds and fish are tied for the greatest number   **(b)** 75 bird species and 75 fish species   **5.** 55 species
6. 270 species   **7.** television; $812,000   **8.** miscellaneous; $84,000
9. $308,000   **10.** $644,000   **11.** 2011; $4000   **12.** $5000; 38% increase (rounded)   **13.** 2011; explanations will vary. Some possibilities are: laid off from work, changed jobs, was ill, cut down on hours worked.
14. 5500 students; 3000 students   **15.** College B; 1000 students
16. Explanations will vary. For example, College B may have added new courses or lowered tuition or added child care.   **17.** 35%; 126°
18. 5%; 18°   **19.** 20%; 72°   **20.** 30%; 108°   **21.** $48,000; 10%
22.

23–26.

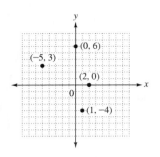

27. $(0, 0)$; no quadrant   **28.** $(-5, -4)$; Quadrant III
29. $(3, 3)$; Quadrant I   **30.** $(-2, 4)$; Quadrant II
31.

x	y	(x, y)
0	−4	(0, −4)
1	−3	(1, −3)
2	−2	(2, −2)

See graph at the right.

32. (a) Answers will vary; all points on the line are solutions. Some possibilities are $(3, -1)$ and $(4, 0)$.   **(b)** Positive slope

Chapters 1–9 CUMULATIVE REVIEW EXERCISES (page 693–694)

1. $3\frac{2}{15}$ **2.** -0.25 **3.** -39 **4.** -0.00010 or -0.0001 **5.** $\frac{4b}{3a^2}$

6. $-2\frac{7}{12}$ **7.** -10.007 **8.** $\frac{2x - 56}{7x}$ **9.** -36 **10.** $\frac{25}{3mn}$ **11.** $3\frac{1}{3}$

12. undefined   **13.** $7\frac{3}{8}$ **14.** $\frac{18 + wx}{6w}$ **15.** -4 **16.** 840

17. $\frac{0}{-2} = 0$ **18.** -2.06 **19.** $-\frac{7}{20}$ **20.** $y = -6$ **21.** $x = 2$

22. $m = -15$ **23.** $x = 7$ **24.** $h = -9$ **25.** $12 - 5n = n$; $n = 2$
26. Let m be the smaller amount; $m + 500$ the larger amount.
$m + m + 500 = 1800$. The two amounts are $650 and $1150.
27. $P = 36$ ft; $A = 70$ ft^2 **28.** $C \approx 18.8$ ft rounded; $A \approx 28.3$ ft^2
(rounded)   **29.** $x = 25$ mi; $P = 56$ mi; $A = 84$ mi^2 **30.** 556 nonsmoking employees (rounded)   **31.** $116.78 (rounded)   **32.** 92.8% (rounded)

33. $1\frac{5}{12}$ pounds

34.

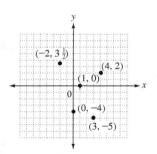

$\left(-2, 3\frac{1}{2}\right)$ is in Quadrant II; no points in Quadrant III.

35.

x	y	(x, y)
0	6	(0, 6)
−1	5	(−1, 5)
−2	4	(−2, 4)

See graph at the right.

Positive slope; all points on the line are solutions, so there are many possibilities such as $(-3, 3)$ and $(-4, 2)$.

CHAPTER 10 Exponents and Polynomials

SECTION 10.1 (pages 701–702)

1. 1   **2.** three squared; five cubed; seven to the fourth power   **3.** false; $3^3 = 3 \cdot 3 \cdot 3 = 27$ **4.** false; $2^4 + 2^3 = 16 + 8 = 24$ **5.** false; $(a^2)^3 = a^{2 \cdot 3} = a^6$ **6.** false; $4^5 \cdot 4^3 = 4^8$ **7.** $(-2)^5$ **9.** $\left(\dfrac{1}{2}\right)^6$
11. $(-8p)^2$ **13.** The expression $(-3)^4 = (-3)(-3)(-3)(-3) = 81$, while $-3^4 = -(3 \cdot 3 \cdot 3 \cdot 3) = -81$.   **14.** The expression $(5x)^3 = (5x)(5x)(5x) = 125x^3$, but $5x^3 = 5 \cdot x \cdot x \cdot x$ **15.** Base is 3; exponent is 5; 243   **17.** Base is -3; exponent is 5; -243 **19.** Base is $-6x$; exponent is 4   **21.** Base is x; exponent is 4   **23.** The product rule does not apply to $5^2 + 5^3$ because it is a *sum*, not a product. $5^2 + 5^3 = 25 + 125 = 150$ **24.** The product rule applies only to exponential expressions with the same base. $3^2 \cdot 4^3 = 9 \cdot 64 = 576$ **25.** $5^{2+6} = 5^8$ **27.** 4^{12} **29.** $(-7)^9$ **31.** t^{17} **33.** $-56r^7$ **35.** $42p^{10}$ **37.** $5x^4 + 9x^4 = 14x^4$; $(5x^4)(9x^4) = 45x^8$ **39.** $-7a^2 + 2a^2 + 10a^2 = 5a^2$; $(-7a^2)(2a^2)(10a^2) = -140a^6$ **41.** 4^6 **43.** t^{20} **45.** $7^3 r^3$ **47.** $5^5 x^5 y^5$ **49.** $8q^3 r^3$ **51.** $\dfrac{1^3}{2^3}$ **53.** $\dfrac{a^3}{b^3}$ **55.** $\dfrac{9^8}{5^8}$ **57.** $(-2)^3 x^6 y^3$ **59.** $3^2 a^6 b^4$ **61.** $A = (4x^3)(3x^2) = 12x^5$

SECTION 10.2 (pages 707–708)

1. negative   **2.** positive   **3.** negative   **4.** negative   **5.** positive
6. negative   **7.** 1   **9.** -1 **11.** 0   **13.** 0   **15.** 2   **17.** $\dfrac{1}{32}$ **19.** 0
21. $\dfrac{1}{64}$ **23.** $\dfrac{8}{15}$ **25.** $-\dfrac{1}{8}$ **27.** 6^5 **29.** 10^3 **31.** $\dfrac{1}{y^4}$ **33.** c^1 or c
35. $\dfrac{1}{5^4}$ **37.** $\dfrac{1}{m^1}$ or $\dfrac{1}{m}$ **39.** 3^4 **41.** a^3 **43.** $\dfrac{1}{2^8}$ **45.** $\dfrac{1}{r^4}$ **47.** 10^{10}
49. $\dfrac{1}{10^5}$ **51.** 10^{11} **53.** $\dfrac{1}{10^8}$ **55.** 10^4 **57.** $\dfrac{1}{a^1}$ or $\dfrac{1}{a}$ **59.** $\dfrac{1}{2^8}$ **61.** $\dfrac{1}{x^{11}}$
63. 10^2 **65.** $\dfrac{1}{y^2}$ **67.** m^9 **69.** $\dfrac{1}{10^6}$

SUMMARY EXERCISES Using Exponent Rules (pages 709–710)

1. 9   **2.** 150   **3.** 1   **4.** $-\dfrac{4}{45}$ **5.** 1   **6.** $\dfrac{1}{64}$ **7.** -9 **8.** 72   **9.** -8
10. -1 **11.** $\dfrac{5}{12}$ **12.** 9   **13.** $\dfrac{1}{32}$ **14.** 1   **15.** -8 **16.** 1   **17.** 6^8
18. $\dfrac{1}{x^7}$ **19.** $\dfrac{1}{10^8}$ **20.** 2^9 **21.** $y^0 = 1$ **22.** $2^5 m^{10} n^5$ **23.** $(-5)^{10}$
24. w^3 **25.** m^{24} **26.** $\dfrac{1}{n^2}$ **27.** $\dfrac{1}{10^6}$ **28.** d^9 **29.** $16x^8$ **30.** $\dfrac{1}{c^1}$ or $\dfrac{1}{c}$

31. 10^8 **32.** 4^5 **33.** $\dfrac{x^6}{y^6}$ **34.** 3^{11} **35.** 7^1 or 7   **36.** h^1 or h **37.** $-16a^4$
38. $\dfrac{1^4}{2^4}$ **39.** $5^3 x^3 y^3$ **40.** m^5 **41.** $\dfrac{1}{10^7}$ **42.** $\dfrac{1}{b^1}$ or $\dfrac{1}{b}$ **43.** b^{15} **44.** $\dfrac{1}{5^7}$
45. $\dfrac{1}{10^3}$ **46.** $21y^8$ **47.** 10^{13} **48.** $\dfrac{1}{k^8}$ **49.** $10a^4 b^4$ **50.** $\dfrac{1}{x^9}$

SECTION 10.3 (pages 715–716)

1. in scientific notation   **2.** in scientific notation   **3.** not in scientific notation   **4.** not in scientific notation   **5.** not in scientific notation   **6.** not in scientific notation   **7.** not in scientific notation   **8.** not in scientific notation   **9.** in scientific notation   **10.** in scientific notation
11. 5.53×10^{-2}; 3.1783×10^2 **13.** 1.5×10^9; 1.425×10^9
15. 5.876×10^9 **17.** 8.235×10^4 **19.** 7×10^{-6} **21.** 2.03×10^{-3}
23. 750,000   **25.** 5,677,000,000,000   **27.** 6.21   **29.** 0.00078
31. 0.000000005134   **33.** 6×10^{11}; 600,000,000,000   **35.** 1.5×10^7; 15,000,000   **37.** 6.426×10^4; 64,260   **39.** 3×10^{-4}; 0.0003
41. 4×10^1; 40   **43.** 2.6×10^{-3}; 0.0026   **45.** 3.64×10^2 (rounded) or 364 people per square mile   **47.** (a) 1×10^{-4} or 0.0001 meter
(b) 1×10^{-1} or 0.1 meter   **49.** 5.77×10^2 (rounded) or about 577 items

SECTION 10.4 (pages 721–724)

1. one term; 6; monomial   **2.** one term; -9; monomial   **3.** one term; 1; monomial   **4.** one term; 1; monomial   **5.** two terms; -19, -1; binomial   **6.** two terms; 2, -1; binomial   **7.** three terms; 1, 8, -8; trinomial   **8.** three terms; 1, -2, 2; trinomial   **9.** $-3mn$; mn; $9mn$
10. $4x^2$; $-x^2$ **11.** no like terms   **12.** $-2ab^2$; ab^2 **13.** 16; -1
14. no like terms   **15.** $2m^5$ **17.** $-r^5$ **19.** cannot be simplified; already written with descending power   **21.** $-5x^5$ **23.** $5p^9 + 4p^7$ **25.** $-2y^2$
27. already simplified and written in descending powers; degree 4; binomial   **29.** already simplified; write in descending powers as $6m^5 + 5m^4 - 7m^3 - 3m^2$; degree 5; none of these   **31.** $x^4 + \dfrac{1}{3}x^2 - 4$; degree 4; trinomial   **33.** $7x$; degree 1; monomial   **35.** (a) -1 (b) 5
37. (a) 19   (b) -2 **39.** (a) 36   (b) -12 **41.** (a) -124 (b) 5
43. $5m^2 + 3m$ **45.** $-6x^3 + x + 6$ **47.** $3w^3 + 5$ **49.** $4x^4 - 4x^2$
51. $8r^2 + 5r - 12$ **53.** $5m^2 - 14m + 6$ **55.** $4x^3 + 2x^2 + 5x$
57. $12m^3 - 13m^2 + 6m + 11$ **59.** $-11x^2 - 3x - 3$ **61.** $8x^2 + 8x + 6$
63. $8t^2 + 8t + 13$ **65.** $D = 100 - 13$; $D = 87$ ft   **66.** 0, (0, 0); 47, (0.5, 47); 121, (1.5, 121); 148, (2, 148); 169, (2.5, 169); 183, (3, 183); 191, (3.5, 191)
67.

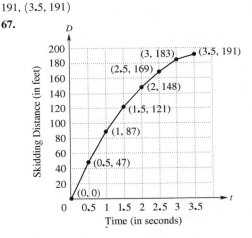

68. Answers will vary. This graph is a curve instead of the straight lines graphed for linear equations. Also, the rate of change in the distance is not consistent. From 0.5 sec to 1 sec, the distance increases 40 ft, but from 3 sec to 3.5 sec, the distance only increases 8 ft.

SECTION 10.5 (pages 727–728)

1. (a) 7; 1 **(b)** −1; 4 **2. (a)** two **(b)** three **3. (a)** binomial **(b)** monomial **4.** multiplication; multiplication; addition
5. (a) $(9 + 3)b^4 = 12b^4$ **(b)** $(9 \cdot 3)b^{4+4} = 27b^8$
6. (a) $(1 + 5)y^3 = 6y^3$ **(b)** $(1 \cdot 5)y^{3+3} = 5y^6$ **7.** $40y^3 + 15y$
9. $-6m^2 - 4m$ **11.** $24x^4 - 12x^3 + 8x^2$ **13.** $-6k^6 + 9k^5 + 3k^4 - 3k^3$
15. $n^2 + 1n - 6$ **17.** $8r^2 - 10r - 3$ **19.** $12x^3 + 26x^2 + 10x + 1$
21. $20m^4 - m^3 - 8m^2 - 17m - 15$ **23.** $5x^4 - 13x^3 + 20x^2 + 7x + 5$
25. $x^2 + 7x + 12$ **27.** $2x^3 + 7x^2 + 3x$ **29.** D; B; A; C
31. The answers are $x^2 - 16$, $y^2 - 9$, and $r^2 - 49$. Each answer is the difference of the squares of the first terms and the squares of the last terms from the binomials.

Chapter 10 REVIEW EXERCISES (pages 731–732)

1. $(-5)^{11}$ **2.** $-72x^7$ **3.** $10x^{14}$ **4.** 19^5x^5 **5.** $5p^4t^4$ **6.** $\dfrac{7^6}{5^6}$
7. $3^3x^6y^9$ **8.** Does not apply because it is the *sum* of 7^2 and 7^4, not their *product* **9.** 2 **10.** $\dfrac{1}{32}$ **11.** 10 **12.** $\dfrac{5}{16}$ **13.** $\dfrac{1}{p^{12}}$ **14.** r^4
15. $\dfrac{1}{5^1}$ or $\dfrac{1}{5}$ **16.** $\dfrac{1}{10^7}$ **17.** $\dfrac{1}{n^3}$ **18.** 10^3 **19.** $\dfrac{1}{2^8}$ **20.** x^6
21. 4.8×10^7 **22.** 8.24×10^{-8} **23.** 24,000 **24.** 0.00000000000995
25. 8×10^2; 800 **26.** 3×10^{-5}; 0.00003 **27.** 1×10^{-2}; 0.01
28. 8.8×10^1 (rounded) or about 88 people per square mile **29.** 1.08×10^7 or 10,800,000 kilometers **30.** $22m^2$; degree 2; monomial
31. $-8y^5 - 7y^4 + 9y$; degree 5; trinomial **32.** $-5a^3 + 4a^2$
33. $11y^2 - 10y + 9$ **34.** $4y^3 - 5y^2 - 4y + 26$ **35.** $7r^4 - 4r^3 - 1$
36. $10x^2 + 70x$ **37.** $-6p^5 + 15p^4$ **38.** $6r^3 + 8r^2 - 17r + 6$
39. $6k^2 - 9k - 6$ **40.** $12p^2 - 48pq + 21q^2$
41. $2m^4 + 5m^3 - 16m^2 - 28m + 9$ **42.** 0 **43.** 3^4p^4 **44.** $\dfrac{1}{7^2}$
45. $-8m^7 - 10m^6 - 6m^5$ **46.** $\dfrac{1}{2} + \dfrac{1}{4} = \dfrac{3}{4}$ **47.** $a^3 - 2a^2 - 7a + 2$
48. $8y^3 - 9y^2 + 5$ **49.** $P = 6x - 2$; $A = 2x^2 + x - 6$

Chapter 10 TEST (pages 733–734)

1. $\dfrac{1}{625}$ **2.** 2 **3.** $\dfrac{7}{12}$ **4.** 6^1 or 6 **5.** $12x^3y^3$ **6.** $\dfrac{1}{10^4}$ **7.** $\dfrac{1}{r^5}$
8. $-21x^7$ **9.** m^3 **10.** $3^2a^8b^2$ or $9a^8b^2$ **11.** Cannot use product rule; $81 + 9 = 90$ **12.** 3.0×10^{11} **13.** 5.57×10^{-6} **14.** 29,000,000
15. 0.0000000607 **16.** 1.97×10^{30} kg (rounded) **17.** $-7x^2 + 8x$; degree 2; binomial **18.** $4n^4 + 13n^3 - 10n^2$; degree 4; trinomial
19. $4t^4 - 2t^2$ **20.** $2y^4 - 3y^2 - 6y$ **21.** $-12t^2 + 8$ **22.** $-12x^5 + 20x^4$
23. $3y^2 + 5y - 2$ **24.** $2r^3 + r^2 - 16r + 15$ **25.** $P = 12x + 36$; $A = 9x^2 + 54x + 81$

Chapters 1–10 CUMULATIVE REVIEW EXERCISES (pages 735–736)

1. (a) ten and thirty-five thousandths **(b)** four hundred ten billion, three hundred fifty-one thousand, one hundred nine **2. (a)** 300,006,080 **(b)** 0.0055 **3. (a)** 0.80 **(b)** 341,000,000 **(c)** 15.0 **4.** Mean is

$52.70; median is $44.50; mode is $41. **5.** -4.171 **6.** -18
7. $2\dfrac{4}{15}$ **8.** $\dfrac{0}{-14} = 0$ **9.** $\dfrac{16w}{3x}$ **10.** -0.125 **11.** $\dfrac{1}{10}$ **12.** $-\dfrac{7}{12}$
13. 28 **14.** $-12y^7$ **15.** $\dfrac{25}{3ab}$ **16.** $\dfrac{rt + 48}{8t}$ **17.** undefined
18. 750 **19.** -0.00012 **20.** $2^4a^{12}b^8$ or $16a^{12}b^8$ **21.** $\dfrac{4m - 54}{9m}$
22. $\dfrac{1}{t^1}$ or $\dfrac{1}{t}$ **23.** $\dfrac{5}{32}$ **24.** $4\dfrac{1}{16}$ **25.** n^1 or n **26.** -96 **27.** $1\dfrac{1}{2}$
28. $1\dfrac{1}{5}$ **29.** 12 **30.** -3 **31.** 30 **32.** $h = 5$ **33.** $x = -7.9$
34. $a = 6$ **35.** $20 - 3n = 2n$; $n = 4$ **36.** Let b be number of elephant breaths; $16b$ the number of mouse breaths; $b + 16b = 170$; $b = 10$. Elephant takes 10 breaths; mouse takes 160. **37.** 3 runs **38.** 145%
39. $4.87 (rounded); $69.82 **40.** 1.61×10^{10} (rounded) or 16,100,000,000 miles **41. (a)** $5\dfrac{1}{8}$ in. **(b)** size 7 **(c)** $\dfrac{5}{16}$ in.
42. $P = 23.8$ m; $A = 30.6$ m^2 **43.** $C \approx 28.3$ cm (rounded); $A \approx 63.6$ cm^2 (rounded)

Whole Numbers Computation: Pretest

PRETEST (pages 737–738)

Adding Whole Numbers

1. 390 **2.** 13,166 **3.** 3053 **4.** 117,510 **5.** 688,226

Subtracting Whole Numbers

1. 350 **2.** 629 **3.** 24,894 **4.** 3909 **5.** 591,387

Multiplying Whole Numbers

1. 0 **2.** 26,887 **3.** 1,560,000 **4.** 1846 **5.** 17,232 **6.** 519,477

Dividing Whole Numbers

1. 23 **2.** undefined **3.** 6259 **4.** 807 **R**6 **5.** 34 **6.** 50
7. 60 **R**20 **8.** 539 **R**62

CHAPTER R Whole Numbers Review

SECTION R.1 (pages 745–746)

1. (a) 23 **(b)** 19 **3. (a)** 8928 **(b)** 59,224 **5.** 150 **7.** 1651
9. 1004 **11.** 9253 **13.** 11,624 **15.** 16,658 **17.** 5009 **19.** 3506
21. 15,954 **23.** 10,648 **25.** incorrect; should be 769 **27.** correct
29. 33 miles **31.** 38 miles **33.** $212 **35.** 699 people
37. 62,399,517 people **39.** 294 inches **41.** 708 feet

SECTION R.2 (pages 753–754)

1. incorrect; should be 62 **3.** incorrect; should be 121 **5.** 8 **7.** 25
9. 16 **11.** 61 **13.** 519 **15.** 9177 **17.** 7589 **19.** 8859 **21.** 3
23. 23 **25.** 1942 **27.** 5687 **29.** 19,038 **31.** 65,556 **33.** 19,984
35. incorrect; should be 2494 **37.** correct **39.** 70 calories
41. 180 passengers **43. (a)** Highest is computer programmer; lowest is medical secretary. **(b)** $43,080 **45.** 364 feet

SECTION R.3 (pages 761–762)

1. 9 **3.** 63 **5.** 0 **7.** 24 **9.** 36 **11.** 245 **13.** 168 **15.** 19,092
17. 258,447 **19.** 12,500 **21.** 44,550 **23.** 270,000 **25.** 86,000,000

27. 1496   **29.** 3735   **31.** 15,200   **33.** 32,805   **35.** 183,996
37. 3,321,934   **39.** 18,980,480   **41.** 252 inches; 540 inches
43. 576 plants   **45.** 528 miles   **47.** 2440 miles; 16,170 miles
49. 7406 calories

SECTION R.4 (pages 771–772)

1. 1; $12\overline{)12}$; $12 \div 12$ **3.** undefined; $\dfrac{24}{0}$; $0\overline{)24}$ **5.** 0; $4\overline{)0}$; $0 \div 4$

7. 0; $\dfrac{0}{12}$; $12\overline{)0}$ **9.** undefined; $\dfrac{21}{0}$; $21 \div 0$ **11.** 21; dividend: 84;
divisor: 4; quotient: 21.   **13.** 36; dividend: 324; divisor: 9; quotient: 36
15. 1520 **R**5   **17.** 309   **19.** 1006   **21.** 5006 **R**1   **23.** 6671
25. 12,458 **R**3   **27.** 10,253 **R**5   **29.** 18,377 **R**6   **31.** incorrect; should
be 670 **R**2   **33.** incorrect; should be 3568 **R**1   **35.** correct   **37.** correct
39. $23; $14; $19   **41.** $18,600   **43.** 378 for $5 tickets; 270 for
$7 tickets; 210 for $9 tickets   **45.** $7; $210   **47.** **(a)** 358; 190
(b) 10,404; 78   **(c)** 13,740; 985   **49.** 2, 3, 5, 10   **51.** 2   **53.** 5
55. 3   **57.** 2, 3   **59.** none of the above

SECTION R.5 (pages 777–778)

1. $24\overline{)768}$ $\overset{3}{}$ Use 2 as the trial divisor.   **3.** $18\overline{)4500}$ $\overset{2}{}$ Use 2 as the trial divisor.

5. $86\overline{)10,327}$ $\overset{1}{}$ Use 9 as the trial divisor.   **7.** $52\overline{)38,025}$ $\overset{7}{}$ Use 5 as the trial divisor.

9. $77\overline{)249,826}$ $\overset{3}{}$ Use 8 as the trial divisor.   **11.** $420\overline{)470,800}$ $\overset{1}{}$ Use 4 as the trial divisor.   **13.** 64 **R**3

15. 236 **R**29   **17.** 2407 **R**1   **19.** 1239 **R**15   **21.** 3331 **R**110   **23.** 850
25. incorrect; should be 106 **R**7   **27.** incorrect; should be 658
29. incorrect; should be 62   **31.** correct   **33.** 1250 hours   **35.** $2030
37. $308   **39.** 1680 circuits   **41.** $375

Appendix

(pages A-5–A-6)

1. 37; add 7   **3.** 26; add 10, subtract 2   **5.** 16; multiply by 2
7. 243; multiply by 3   **9.** 36; add 3, add 5, add 7, etc.; or 1^2, 2^2, 3^2, etc.
11. ⌐   **13.** ⟍

15. Conclusion follows.

17. Conclusion does not follow.

$2 + 18 + 7 = 27$
$30 - 27 = 3$

19.

Neither watched TV on 3 days.
21. Dick is the computer operator.

Solutions to Selected Exercises

SECTION 1.1 (pages 7–10)

23. To write 3,064,801 in words start at the left: three million, sixty-four thousand, eight hundred one. Do **not** write "eight hundred *and* one" at the end. Use "and" when there is a decimal point in the number.

39. Six hundred *trillion,* seventy-one million, four hundred

The first group name is *trillion,* so you need to fill *five groups* of three digits: trillions, billions, millions, thousands, and ones.

$\underline{6\,0\,0},\underline{0\,0\,0},\underline{0\,7\,1},\underline{0\,0\,0},\underline{4\,0\,0}$

There are no billions or thousands, so fill these groups with zeros.

47. One hundred forty-one *million,* seven hundred

The first group name is *million,* so you need to fill *three groups* of three digits: millions, thousands, and ones.

$\underline{1\,4\,1},\underline{0\,0\,0},\underline{7\,0\,0}$

There are no thousands, so fill the thousands group with zeros.
The number is: 141,000,700

SECTION 1.2 (pages 17–18)

23. -3 is to the *right* of -6 on the number line, so -3 is *greater than* -6. Write $-3 > -6$.

25. -10 is to the *left* of -2 on the number line, so -10 is *less than* -2. Write $-10 < -2$.

41. $|-75| = 75$ because the distance between 0 and -75 on the number line is 75 spaces.

SECTION 1.3 (pages 26–29)

39. $-17 + 0 = -17$
Adding zero to any number leaves the number unchanged.

49. Add from left to right.

$-3 + (-11) + 14$ — First add $-3 + (-11)$.

$= -14 + 14$ — Add $-14 + 14$.

$= 0$

---

53. Add from left to right.

$-7 + 28 + (-56) + 3$ — First add $-7 + 28$.

$= 21 + (-56) + 3$ — Add $21 + (-56)$.

$= -35 + 3$ — Add $-35 + 3$.

$= -32$

61. First write Jeff's scores as a sum of integers. Then add from left to right.

$-20 + 75 + (-55)$ — First add $-20 + 75$.

$= 55 + (-55)$ — Add $55 + (-55)$.

$= 0$ points

First write Terry's scores as a sum of integers. Then add from left to right.

$42 + (-15) + 20$ — First add $42 + (-15)$.

$= 27 + 20$ — Add $27 + 20$.

$= 47$ points

81. When entering $-99,000$ on your calculator, be sure to use the *negative* key as opposed to the *subtraction* key.
$86 + (-99,000) + 0 + 2837 = -96,077$

SECTION 1.4 (pages 32–33)

11. $7 - 19$ — Change subtraction to addition. Change 19 to -19.

$= 7 + (-19)$

$= -12$

17. $-3 - (-8)$ — Change subtraction to addition. Change -8 to $+8$.

$= -3 + (+8)$

$= 5$

23. $-30 - 30$ — Change subtraction to addition. Change 30 to -30.

$= -30 + (-30)$

$= -60$

39. $3 - (-3) - 10 - (-7)$ — Change all subtractions to additions.

Change -3 to $+3$, 10 to -10, and -7 to $+7$.

$= 3 + (+3) + (-10) + (+7)$ — Add from left to right. First add $3 + 3$.

$= 6 + (-10) + (+7)$ — Then add $6 + (-10)$.

$= -4 + (+7)$ — Finally, add $-4 + 7$.

$= 3$

51. $0 - |-7 + 2|$ — Simplify the sum inside the absolute value bars first: $-7 + 2$ is -5.

$= 0 - |-5|$ — $|-5|$ is 5 because the distance from 0 to -5 on the number line is 5 spaces.

$= 0 - 5$ — Change subtraction to addition. Change 5 to -5.

$= 0 + (-5)$ — Add.

$= -5$

SECTION 1.5 (pages 40–43)

15. $-7\underline{8},499 \approx -78,000$ (nearest thousand)
The next digit is 4 or less, so the thousands place remains 8. Change 4, 9, and 9 to 0.

25. $19,\underline{9}51,880,500 \approx 20,000,000,000$ (nearest hundred-million)
The next digit is 5 or more, so the hundred-millions place changes from 9 to 10. Write 0 and regroup 1 to billions place. In the billions place, $9 +$ regrouped 1 is 10. Write the 0 and regroup 1 to ten-billions.

35. $\$9942 \approx \$10,000$
Round to the nearest thousand since the leftmost digit is in the thousands place. Next digit is 5 or more, so the thousands place changes from 9 to 10. Write 0 and regroup 1 to the ten-thousands place. Change 9, 4, and 2 to 0. $\$9942$ is closer to $\$10,000$ than to $\$9000$.

43. $16 + (-97)$
Because the leftmost digit is in the tens place, round 16 and -97 to the nearest ten.
$\underline{1}6$ is closer to 20 than 10.
$-\underline{9}7$ is closer to -100 than -90.
Estimate: $20 + (-100) = -80$
Exact: $16 + (-97) = -81$

53. $-106 + 34 - (-72)$ Change $34 - (-72)$ to adding the opposite: $34 + (+72)$.

$-106 + 34 + (+72)$

Because the leftmost digit is in the hundreds place, round -106 to the nearest hundred.

$-106 \approx -100$

Because the leftmost digit is in the tens place, round 34 and 72 to the nearest ten.

$34 \approx 30$ and $72 \approx 70$

Estimate: $-100 + 30 + (+70) = 0$

Exact: $-106 + 34 - (-72)$

$= -106 + 34 + (+72) = 0$

SECTION 1.6 (pages 50–53)

3. (a) $7(-8) = -56$ Factors have *different* signs, so the product is *negative.*

(b) $-7(8) = -56$ Factors have *different* signs, so the product is *negative.*

(c) $7(8) = 56$ Factors have the *same* sign, so the product is *positive.*

(d) $-7(-8) = 56$ Factors have the *same* sign, so the product is *positive.*

27. $(0)(-25) = 0$ Use the multiplication property of 0, which says that multiplying any number by 0 gives a product of 0.

31. Multiply from left to right.

$(-4)(-2)(-7)$ Multiply $(-4)(-2)$ first. The factors have the *same* sign, so the product is *positive.*

$= 8(-7)$ Then multiply $8(-7)$. The factors have *different* signs, so the product is *negative.*

$= -56$

39. Because -17 is a *negative* product, the factors must have *different* signs.

$-17 = 17(-1)$

45. Because -5 and -2 have the same sign, their product of 10 is positive. The final product of -40 is negative, so the missing factor must be negative.

$(-4)(-5)(-2) = -40$

$(-4)(10) = -40$

---

49. $9(-3 + 5)$ rewritten using the distributive property is

$9 \cdot (-3) + 9 \cdot 5$

To check:

$9(-3 + 5) = 9 \cdot (-3) + 9 \cdot 5$

$9(2) = -27 + 45$

$18 = 18$

67. $|6 - 7| \cdot (-355{,}299)$ Work inside the absolute value bars first.

$= |6 + (-7)| \cdot -355{,}299$ Change subtraction to addition; change 7 to -7. Then add $6 + (-7)$ to get -1.

$= |-1| \cdot (-355{,}299)$ $|-1|$ is 1.

$= 1 \cdot (-355{,}299)$ Multiplication property of 1

$= -355{,}299$

71. The temperature drops 3 degrees $(-3$ degrees) for every 1000 feet climbed into the air. An altitude of 24,000 feet would require 24 increases of 1000 feet each.

$-3 \cdot 24 = -72$ degrees

To find the temperature at an altitude of 24,000 feet, add the change in temperature (-72) to the temperature on the ground (50). The temperature at 24,000 feet is $50 + (-72) = -22$ degrees.

SECTION 1.7 (pages 59–62)

1. (a) $14 \div 2 = 7$

(Same signs, quotient is *positive)*

(b) $-14 \div (-2) = 7$

(Same signs, quotient is *positive)*

(c) $14 \div (-2) = -7$

(Different signs, quotient is *negative)*

(d) $-14 \div 2 = -7$

(Different signs, quotient is *negative)*

7. (a) $\dfrac{0}{50} = 0$; zero divided by any nonzero number is 0.

(b) $\dfrac{50}{0}$ is undefined; division by zero is undefined.

(c) $\dfrac{-11}{0}$ is undefined; division by zero is undefined.

(d) $\dfrac{0}{-11} = 0$; zero divided by any nonzero number is 0.

25. $\dfrac{-18}{18} = -1$ *(Different* signs, quotient is *negative)*

---

29. $\dfrac{-573}{-3} = 191$ *(Same* signs, quotient is *positive)*

35. $-64 \div (-8) \div (-2)$ No, work inside parentheses so start at left: $-64 \div (-8)$ is 8. The signs are the *same* so the quotient is *positive.*

$= 8 \div (-2)$ $8 \div (-2)$ is -4. The signs are *different* so the quotient is *negative.*

$= -4$

41. $-5 \div (-5)(-10) \div (-2)$ Start at left; $-5 \div (-5)$ is 1. The signs are the *same* so the quotient is *positive.*

$= 1(-10) \div (-2)$ Next, $1(-10)$ is -10. The signs are *different* so the product is *negative.*

$= -10 \div (-2)$ Finally, $-10 \div (-2)$ is 5. The signs are the *same* so the quotient is *positive.*

$= 5$

57. Descending implies a negative, -730 feet each minute. Use front end rounding: -730 rounds to -700 and 37 rounds to 40. Use multiplication to find how far the plane descended.

Estimate: $-700 \cdot 40 = -28{,}000$ feet

Exact: $-730 \cdot 37 = -27{,}010$ feet

The exact answer of $-27{,}010$ feet is close to the estimate of $-28{,}000$ feet.

69. Use division to find the number of rooms.

$$\dfrac{163 \text{ people}}{5 \text{ people per room}}$$

$$
\begin{array}{r}
3\,2 \\
5\overline{)1\,6\,3} \\
1\,5 \\
\hline
1\,3 \\
1\,0 \\
\hline
3
\end{array}
$$

32 rooms will be full, and that leaves 3 people. So 33 rooms are needed. One room will have only 3 people in it.

73. $-6(-8) \div \underbrace{(-5 + 5)}$ Work inside parentheses.

$= -6(-8) \div \quad 0$ Add $-5 + 5$ to get 0.

Multiply $-6(-8)$ to get 48.

$= 48 \div 0$ Division by zero is undefined.

Undefined

SECTION 1.8 (pages 73–76)

13. **(a)** $4^1 = 4$

(b) $4^2 = 4 \cdot 4 = 16$

(c) $4^3 = 4 \cdot 4 \cdot 4$

$= 16 \cdot 4$

$= 64$

(d) $4^4 = 4 \cdot 4 \cdot 4 \cdot 4$ Multiply two factors at a time.

$= 16 \cdot 4 \cdot 4$

$= 64 \cdot 4$

$= 256$

21. $(-5)^2 = (-5)(-5)$ *Same* signs

$= 25$ Product is *positive*.

27. $(-10)^3 = (-10)(-10)(-10)$

$= 100(-10)$ Multiply two factors at a time.

$= -1000$

35. $6^1(-5)^3$ Apply the exponents first. 6^1 is 6 and $(-5)^3$ is $(-5)(-5)(-5)$ or -125.

$= 6(-125)$

$= -750$

51. $-7 + 6(8 - 14)$ Work inside parentheses first. Change subtraction to adding the opposite, so $8 + (-14)$ is -6.

$= -7 + 6(-6)$ Multiply $6(-6)$ to get -36.

$= -7 + (-36)$ Add last.

$= -43$

59. $2 - (-5)(-2)^3$ Apply the exponent: $(-2)^3$ is -8.

$= 2 - (-5)(-8)$ Multiply $(-5)(-8)$ to get 40.

$= 2 - 40$ Change $2 - 40$ to $2 + (-40)$.

$= 2 + (-40)$ Add last.

$= -38$

67. $4(3^2) + 7(3 + 9) - (-6)$ Work inside parentheses: $3 + 9$ is 12.

$= 4(3^2) + 7(12) - (-6)$ Apply exponent: 3^2 is 9.

$= 4(9) + 7(12) - (-6)$ Multiply $4(9)$ to get 36.

$= 36 + 7(12) - (-6)$ Multiply $7(12)$ to get 84.

$= 36 + 84 - (-6)$ Change $84 - (-6)$ to $84 + (+6)$.

$= 36 + 84 + 6$ Add $36 + 84$.

$= 120 + 6$ Add $120 + 6$.

$= 126$

75. $\dfrac{2^3 \cdot (-2 - 5) + 4(-1)}{4 + 5(-6 \cdot 2) + (5 \cdot 11)}$

First do the work in the numerator.

$2^3 \cdot (-2 - 5) + 4(-1)$ Work inside parentheses: Change $-2 - 5$ to $-2 + (-5)$ to get -7.

$= 2^3 \cdot (-7) + 4(-1)$ Apply the exponent: 2^3 is 8.

$= 8 \cdot (-7) + 4(-1)$ Multiply $8(-7)$ to get -56.

$= -56 + 4(-1)$ Multiply $4(-1)$ to get -4.

$= -56 + (-4)$ Add last.

$= -60$

Next, do the work in the denominator.

$4 + 5(-6 \cdot 2) + (5 \cdot 11)$ Work inside parentheses: $-6 \cdot 2$ is -12.

$= 4 + 5(-12) + (5 \cdot 11)$ Work inside parentheses: $5 \cdot 11$ is 55.

$= 4 + 5(-12) + 55$ Multiply $5(-12)$ to get -60.

$= 4 + (-60) + 55$ Add from left to right.

$= -56 + 55$

$= -1$

The last step is the division:

$\dfrac{-60}{-1} = 60$

CHAPTER 2 Understanding Variables and Solving Equations

SECTION 2.1 (pages 101–104)

17. Expression (rule) for ordering brushes:

$3c - 5$

(a) Evaluate the expression when c, the class size, is 12.

$3c - 5$ Replace c with 12.

$\underbrace{3 \cdot 12} - 5$ Multiply before subtracting.

$\underbrace{36 - 5}$

31 brushes must be ordered.

(b) Evaluate the expression when c, the class size, is 16.

$3c - 5$ Replace c with 16.

$\underbrace{3 \cdot 16} - 5$ Multiply before subtracting.

$\underbrace{48 - 5}$

43 brushes must be ordered.

37. $9xy^2$ can be written as $9 \cdot x \cdot y \cdot y$. The exponent 2 applies only to the base y and means that y is used as a factor two times.

51. Evaluate $r^2 s^5 t^3$ when r is -3, s is 2, and t is -4, using a calculator.

$r^2 s^5 t^3$ Replace r with -3, s with 2, and t with -4.

$(-3)^2(2)^5(-4)^3$ Use the y^x key (or $\wedge$ key) for each exponent.

$(9)(32)(-64)$ Multiply from left to right.

$\dfrac{(288)(-64)}{-18,432}$

57. Evaluate $\dfrac{z^2}{-3y + z}$ when y is -2 and z is -6.

$\dfrac{z^2}{-3y + z}$ Replace z with -6 and y with -2.

$\dfrac{(-6)^2}{-3(-2) + (-6)}$ Follow the order of operations.

$\dfrac{36}{0}$ Numerator: $(-6)^2$ is $(-6)(-6)$ or 36. Denominator: $-3(-2) + (-6)$ is $6 + (-6)$ or 0.

Undefined   Division by 0 is undefined.

SECTION 2.2 (pages 114–117)

15. $\dfrac{c - c}{0}$ Any number minus itself is 0.

23. $-x - 6x - x$ These are like terms. Rewrite $-x$ as $-1x$ and x as $1x$.

$-1x - 6x - 1x$ Change both subtractions to adding the opposite.

$-1x + (-6x) + (-1x)$ Add the coefficients.

$\underbrace{[-1 + (-6) + (-1)]}x$

$-8x$ The variable part, x, stays the same.

35. $-x^3 + 3x - 3x^2 + 2$

There are no like terms. The expression cannot be simplified.

57. $-2(5r + 3)$ — Use the distributive property.

$\underbrace{-2 \cdot 5r} + (-2) \cdot 3$

$-10r + \underbrace{(-2) \cdot 3}$

$-10r + \underbrace{(-6)}$ — Change addition to subtracting the opposite.

$-10r - 6$

69. $-5(k + 5) + 5k$ — Use the distributive property.

$\underbrace{-5 \cdot k} + (-5) \cdot 5 + 5k$

$-5k + \underbrace{(-5) \cdot 5} + 5k$ — Multiply $-5 \cdot 5$ to get -25.

$-5k + (-25) + 5k$

$-5k + 5k + (-25)$ — Rewrite using the commutative property.

$\underbrace{(-5 + 5)}k + (-25)$ — Add the coefficients of like terms.

$\qquad 0k \quad + (-25)$ — Zero times any number is 0.

$\qquad \underbrace{0 \quad + (-25)}$ — Zero added to any number is the number.

$\qquad\qquad -25$

73. $5 + 2(3n + 4) - n$ — Use the distributive property.

$5 + 2 \cdot 3n + 2 \cdot 4 - n$

$5 + \underbrace{2 \cdot 3n} + 2 \cdot 4 - 1n$ — Rewrite n as $1n$. Multiply $2 \cdot 3n$ to get $6n$.

$5 + 6n + \underbrace{2 \cdot 4} - 1n$ — Multiply $2 \cdot 4$ to get 8.

$5 + 6n + 8 - 1n$ — Change subtraction to adding the opposite.

$5 + 6n + 8 + (-1n)$

$\underbrace{6n + (-1n)} + 5 + 8$ — Rewrite using the commutative property.

$5n + \underbrace{5 + 8}$ — Add the coefficients of like terms; $6 + (-1)$ is 5.

$5n + 13$ — Add $5 + 8$ to get 13.

85. $-10 + 4(-3b + 3) + 2(6b - 1)$

Use the distributive property.

$-10 + 4 \cdot (-3b) + 4 \cdot 3 + 2 \cdot 6b - 2 \cdot 1$

Do all the multiplication.

$-10 + (-12b) + 12 + 12b - 2$

Change subtraction to adding the opposite.

$-10 + (-12b) + 12 + 12b + (-2)$

Group like terms and add the coefficients.

$\underbrace{-12b + 12b} + \underbrace{(-10) + 12 + (-2)}$

$\qquad 0b \qquad + \qquad 0$

Any number times 0 is 0, so $0b$ is 0.

Simplified expression: 0

SECTION 2.3 (pages 128–133)

21. To solve $-5 = -2 + t$, we want to get the variable, t, by itself on the right side of the equal sign. To do that, we add the opposite of -2, which is 2. Then $-2 + 2$ will be 0.

$-5 = -2 + t$ — Add the opposite of -2, which is 2, to both sides.

$\dfrac{2 \qquad 2}{-3 = 0 + t}$ — Adding 0 to t leaves t unchanged.

$-3 = t$ — The solution is -3.

CHECK $-5 = -2 + t$ — Replace t with -3.

$-5 = -2 + (-3)$

$-5 = -5$ ✓ — Balances

27. The given solution is 10.

CHECK $-10 = -10 + b$ — Replace b with 10.

$-10 = -10 + 10$

$-10 \neq 0$ — Does **not** balance; 10 is **not** the correct solution.

Find the correct solution.

$-10 = -10 + b$ — Add the opposite of -10, which is 10, to both sides. Then $-10 + 10$ is 0.

$\dfrac{10 = \quad 10}{0 = 0 + b}$ — Adding 0 to b leaves b unchanged.

$0 = b$ — The solution is 0.

CHECK $-10 = -10 + b$ — Replace b with 0.

$-10 = -10 + 0$

$-10 = -10$ ✓ — Balances

The correct solution is 0.

39. $-5w + 2 + 6w = -4 + 9$ — Rearrange and combine like terms.

$\underbrace{-5w + 6w} + 2 = \underbrace{-4 + 9}$ — On the left side, combine $-5w + 6w$. On the right side, add $-4 + 9$.

$1w + 2 = 5$

$\dfrac{-2 \quad -2}{1w + 0 = 3}$ — Add -2 to both sides.

$1w + 0 = 3$ — $1w$ is equivalent to w.

$w = 3$ — The solution is 3.

CHECK

$-5w + 2 + 6w = -4 + 9$ — Replace w with 3.

$-5 \cdot 3 + 2 + 6 \cdot 3 = -4 + 9$ — Multiply.

$-15 + 2 + 18 = -4 + 9$ — Add.

$5 = 5$ ✓ — Balances

57. $-9 + 9 = 5 + h$ — Combine like terms.

$0 = 5 + h$

$\dfrac{-5 \quad -5}{-5 = 0 + h}$ — Add -5 to both sides.

$-5 = h$ — The solution is -5.

69. $-6x + 2x + 6 + 5x$

$\qquad = |0 - 9| - |-6 + 5|$

On the left side, rearrange the terms and add like terms.

$-6x + 2x + 5x + 6 = |0 - 9| - |-6 + 5|$

$x + 6 = |0 - 9| - |-6 + 5|$

On the right side, work inside each set of absolute value bars:

$|0 - 9|$ is $|0 + (-9)|$ or $|-9|$ or 9

$|-6 + 5|$ is $|-1|$ or 1

So the equation becomes:

$x + 6 = 9 - 1$

Change subtraction to adding the opposite.

$x + 6 = 9 + (-1)$ — Add $9 + (-1)$ to get 8.

$x + 6 = 8$

$\dfrac{-6 \quad -6}{x + 0 = 2}$ — Add -6 to both sides.

$x = 2$ — The solution is 2.

SECTION 2.4 (pages 138–141)

15. $-12 = 5p - p$ — Change subtraction to adding the opposite.

$-12 = 5p + (-p)$ — Rewrite $-p$ as $-1p$.

$-12 = 5p + (-1p)$ — Combine like terms.

$-12 = 4p$

$\dfrac{-12}{4} = \dfrac{4p}{4}$ — Divide *both* sides by 4.

$-3 = p$ — The solution is -3.

CHECK

$-12 = 5p - p$ — Replace p with -3.

$-12 = 5 \cdot (-3) - (-3)$ — Multiply.

$-12 = -15 - (-3)$ — Change subtraction to adding the opposite.

$-12 = -15 + (3)$

$-12 = -12$ ✓ — Balances

29. $100 - 96 = 31y - 35y$ — Change subtractions to adding the opposite.

$100 + (-96) = 31y + (-35y)$

$4 = -4y$ — Combine like terms.

$\dfrac{4}{-4} = \dfrac{-4y}{-4}$ — Divide *both* sides by -4.

$-1 = y$ — The solution is -1.

35. $-2(-4k) = 56$ — Use the associative property.

$(-2)(-4) \cdot k = 56$

$8k = 56$ — Multiply $(-2)(-4)$ to get 8.

$\dfrac{8k}{8} = \dfrac{56}{8}$ — Divide *both* sides by 8.

$k = 7$ — The solution is 7.

43. $-n = -50$ Rewrite $-n$ as $-1n$.

$-1n = -50$

$\dfrac{-1n}{-1} = \dfrac{-50}{-1}$ Divide *both* sides by -1.

$n = 50$ The solution is 50.

57. $-37(14x) + 28(21x)$

$= |72 - 72| + |-166 + 96|$

On the right side, simplify within the absolute value bars.

$-37(14x) + 28(21x) = |0| + |-70|$

Find the absolute values.

$-37(14x) + 28(21x) = 0 + 70$

Use the associative property to multiply on the left side.

$(-37 \cdot 14) \cdot x + (28 \cdot 21) \cdot x = 0 + 70$

$-518x + 588x = 0 + 70$

$-518x + 588x = 70$

Combine like terms.

$70x = 70$

Divide both sides by the coefficient, 70, to get x by itself.

$\dfrac{70x}{70} = \dfrac{70}{70}$

$x = 1$

The solution is 1.

SECTION 2.5 (pages 146–151)

5. $28 = -9a + 10$ To get $-9a$ by itself, add -10 to *both* sides.

$\dfrac{-10 \qquad\quad -10}{18 = -9a + 0}$

$18 = -9a$

$\dfrac{18}{-9} = \dfrac{-9a}{-9}$ Divide *both* sides by -9.

$-2 = a$ The solution is -2.

CHECK $28 = -9a + 10$ Use the *original* equation and replace a with -2.

$28 = -9(-2) + 10$

$28 = 18 + 10$

$28 = 28$ ✓   Balances

15. $-18 + 7a = 2a + 3 + 4$ Simplify right side.

$-18 + 7a = 2a + 7$

$\dfrac{-2a \quad -2a}{-18 + 5a = 0 + 7}$ Add $-2a$ to both sides.

$-18 + 5a = 7$

$\dfrac{18 \qquad\qquad 18}{0 + 5a = 25}$ Add 18 to both sides.

$5a = 25$

$\dfrac{5a}{5} = \dfrac{25}{5}$ Divide *both* sides by 5.

$a = 5$ The solution is 5.

---

31. $0 = -2(y + 2)$ Use the distributive property.

$0 = -2y + (-4)$

$\dfrac{4 \qquad\qquad 4}{4 = -2y + 0}$ Add 4 to both sides.

$4 = -2y$

$\dfrac{4}{-2} = \dfrac{-2y}{-2}$ Divide *both* sides by -2.

$-2 = y$ The solution is -2.

41. $7 - 5b = 28 + 2b$ Change subtraction to adding the opposite.

$7 + (-5b) = 28 + 2b$

$\dfrac{5b \qquad\qquad 5b}{7 + 0 = 28 + 7b}$ Add $5b$ to both sides.

$7 = 28 + 7b$

$\dfrac{-28 \quad -28}{-21 = 0 + 7b}$ Add -28 to both sides.

$-21 = 7b$

$\dfrac{-21}{7} = \dfrac{7b}{7}$ Divide *both* sides by 7.

$-3 = b$ The solution is -3.

45. $10(c - 6) + 4 = 2 + c - 58$

Use the distributive property.

$10c - 60 + 4 = 2 + c - 58$

Rewrite subtractions as adding the opposite.

$10c + (-60) + 4 = 2 + c + (-58)$

Combine like terms.

$10c + (-56) = 1c + (-56)$

$\dfrac{-1c \qquad\qquad -1c}{9c + (-56) = 0 + (-56)}$ Add $-1c$ to both sides.

$9c + (-56) = -56$

$\dfrac{56 \qquad\quad 56}{9c + 0 = 0}$ Add 56 to *both* sides.

$\dfrac{9c}{9} = \dfrac{0}{9}$ Divide *both* sides by 9.

$c = 0$ The solution is 0.

53. $-5(2p + 2) - 7 = 3(2p + 5)$

Use the distributive property on both sides.

$-10p + (-10) - 7 = 6p + 15$

Write subtraction as adding the opposite.

$-10p + (-10) + (-7) = 6p + 15$

Combine like terms.

$-10p + (-17) = 6p + 15$

$\dfrac{-6p \qquad\qquad -6p}{-16p + (-17) = 0 + 15}$ Add $-6p$ to both sides.

$-16p + (-17) = 15$

$\dfrac{17 \qquad\qquad 17}{-16p + 0 = 32}$ Add 17 to both sides.

$-16p = 32$

$\dfrac{-16p}{-16} = \dfrac{32}{-16}$ Divide both sides by -16.

$p = -2$ The solution is -2.

CHAPTER 3 Solving Application Problems

SECTION 3.1 (pages 171–174)

13. The perimeter of a square parking lot is 92 yards (yd). Use the formula for perimeter of a square, $P = 4s$.

$P = 4s$

$92 \text{ yd} = 4s$ Replace P with 92 yd.

$\dfrac{92 \text{ yd}}{4} = \dfrac{4s}{4}$ Divide both sides by 4.

$23 \text{ yd} = s$

The length of one side of the parking lot is 23 yards.

27. Use the formula for the perimeter of a rectangle, $P = 2l + 2w$. The value of P is 30 cm, and the value of w is 6 cm.

$P = 2l + 2w$ Replace P with 30 cm and w with 6 cm.

$30 \text{ cm} = 2l + \underline{2 \cdot 6 \text{ cm}}$ Multiply on the right side.

$30 \text{ cm} = 2l + 12 \text{ cm}$

$\dfrac{-12 \text{ cm} \qquad -12 \text{ cm}}{18 \text{ cm} = 2l + 0}$ Add -12 cm to both sides.

$\dfrac{18 \text{ cm}}{2} = \dfrac{2l}{2}$ Divide both sides by 2.

$9 \text{ cm} = l$

The length is 9 cm.

CHECK

$P = 9 \text{ cm} + 9 \text{ cm} + 6 \text{ cm} + 6 \text{ cm}$

$P = 30 \text{ cm}$

30 cm matches the original perimeter, so 9 cm is the correct length.

35. Add all four sides to find the perimeter. Because the figure is a parallelogram, opposite sides have the same length.

$P = 100 \text{ ft} + 60 \text{ ft} + 100 \text{ ft} + 60 \text{ ft}$

$P = 320 \text{ ft}$

The perimeter is 320 ft.

45. $P = 10\,\text{cm} + 10\,\text{cm} + 30\,\text{cm}$
$\qquad + 25\,\text{cm} + ?$

$P = 75\,\text{cm} + ?$

Because the perimeter is 115 cm, replace P with 115 cm.

$$115\,\text{cm} = 75\,\text{cm} + ?$$

$$\frac{-75\,\text{cm} \quad -75\,\text{cm}}{40\,\text{cm} \;=\; 0 \quad + ?}$$ Add -75 cm to both sides.

$$40\,\text{cm} = ?$$

The length of the unknown side is 40 cm.

SECTION 3.2 (pages 181–184)

9. The figure is a parallelogram.

Use the formula $A = bh$.

Turn your book sideways to identify that the height is 25 mm and the base is 31 mm. Replace b with 31 mm and h with 25 mm in the formula.

$A = 31\,\text{mm} \cdot 25\,\text{mm}$

$A = 775\,\text{mm}^2$

The area is 775 mm²

Be careful to use mm² in your answer (**not** mm) because this is *area*.

21. Use the formula for the area of a rectangle, $A = lw$. The value of A is 154 in.² and the value of w is 11 in.

$A = l \cdot w$ \qquad Replace A with 154 in.² and w with 11 in.

$154\,\text{in.}^2 = l \cdot 11\,\text{in.}$

$$\frac{154\,\text{in.} \cdot \text{in.}}{11\,\text{in.}} = \frac{l \cdot 11\,\text{in.}}{11\,\text{in.}}$$ Divide both sides by 11 in.

$14\,\text{in.} = l$

The length of the photo is 14 in.

CHECK

$\quad$ 14 in.

11 in. | Photo $A = 154\,\text{in.}^2$ | 11 in.

$\quad$ 14 in.

$A = l \cdot w$

$A = 14\,\text{in.} \cdot 11\,\text{in.}$

$A = 154\,\text{in.}^2$ \qquad Matches area given in the problem

29. Use the area formula for the area of a parallelogram, $A = bh$. Replace A with 221 in.² and h with 13 in.

$A = b \cdot h$

$221\,\text{in.}^2 = b \cdot 13\,\text{in.}$

$$\frac{221\,\text{in.} \cdot \text{in.}}{13\,\text{in.}} = \frac{b \cdot 13\,\text{in.}}{13\,\text{in.}}$$ Divide both sides by 13 in.

$17\,\text{in.} = b$

The base is 17 in.

CHECK

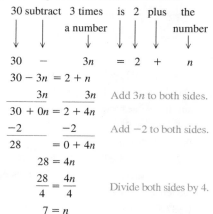
$\qquad$ 13 in.
$\mid\!\!\leftarrow\!\!-17\,\text{in.}\!\!-\!\!\rightarrow\!\!\mid$

$A = b \cdot h$

$A = 17\,\text{in.} \cdot 13\,\text{in.}$

$A = 221\,\text{in.}^2 \leftarrow$ Matches

41.

 $\quad$ 4 m

$\quad$ 5 m

Tyra is decorating the top edges of her walls, so find the *perimeter* of her ceiling.

$P = 2 \cdot l + 2 \cdot w$ \qquad Perimeter of a rectangle

$P = 2 \cdot 5\,\text{m} + 2 \cdot 4\,\text{m}$ \qquad Replace l with 5 m and w with 4 m.

$P = 10\,\text{m} + 8\text{m}$

$P = 18\,\text{m}$

The strip costs $6 per meter. To find the cost of 18 meters, multiply $6(18) to get $108.

To have the top edges of her walls decorated, Tyra will spend $108.

47. The floor of the Coleman tent is a square.

$\quad$ 13 ft

| | 13 ft

To find the perimeter, use the formula for the perimeter of a square, $P = 4s$.

$P = 4s$ \qquad Formula for perimeter of a square

$P = 4 \cdot 13\,\text{ft}$ \qquad Substitute 13 ft for s.

$P = 52\,\text{ft}$

The perimeter of the tent is 52 ft.

To find the area, use the formula for the area of a square, $A = s^2$.

$A = s^2$ \qquad Formula for area of a square

$A = s \cdot s$

$A = 13\,\text{ft} \cdot 13\,\text{ft}$ \qquad Multiply $13 \cdot 13$ to get 169.

$A = 169\,\text{ft}^2$ \qquad Multiply ft · ft to get ft².

The area of the tent is 169 ft².

Because the tent sleeps 8 campers, divide the area of the floor, 169 ft², by 8.

$$\frac{169\,\text{ft}^2}{8} \approx 21\,\text{ft}^2 \text{ (rounded)}$$

There is about 21 ft² of floor space for each camper.

SECTION 3.3 (pages 192–195)

29. Let n represent the unknown number.

30 subtract $\;$ 3 times $\;$ is $\;$ 2 plus $\;$ the
$\qquad\qquad$ a number $\qquad\qquad\quad$ number

$30 \quad - \quad 3n \quad = \quad 2 \quad + \quad n$

$30 - 3n = 2 + n$

$$\frac{3n \qquad\qquad 3n}{30 + 0n = 2 + 4n}$$ Add $3n$ to both sides.

$$\frac{-2 \qquad\qquad -2}{28 \qquad = 0 + 4n}$$ Add -2 to both sides.

$28 = 4n$

$$\frac{28}{4} = \frac{4n}{4}$$ Divide both sides by 4.

$7 = n$

The number is 7.

CHECK Three times 7 is 21. When 21 is subtracted from 30, the result is 9; 2 plus 7 is also 9. *True*

33. *Step 1*

The problem is about the number of cookies in the cookie jar.

Unknown: number of cookies the children ate

Known: 18 cookies at the start, three dozen cookies put in the jar, 49 cookies at the end

Step 2(a)

Let c represent the number of cookies the children ate.

Step 3

Cookies at the start	−	Cookies eaten	+	Cookies added	=	Ended up with 49 cookies
18	−	c	+	36	=	49

Step 4

$18 - c + 36 = 49$ \qquad Write the understood $1c$. Change subtraction to adding the opposite.

$54 + (-1c) = 49$

$$\frac{-54 \qquad\qquad -54}{0 + (-1c) = -5}$$ Add -54 to both sides.

$$\frac{-1c}{-1} = \frac{-5}{-1}$$ Divide both sides by -1.

$c = 5$

Step 5 The children ate 5 cookies.

Step 6

There were 18 cookies at the start. The children ate 5 cookies, so $18 - 5 = 13$ cookies in the jar.

Three dozen cookies were added. There are 12 cookies in a dozen, so 36 cookies were added. $13 + 36 = 49$ cookies, which matches the original problem.

The correct answer is 5 cookies.

37. *Step 1*

The problem is about the bank account of a music club.

Unknown: the dues paid by each member

Known: 14 members, earned \$340, spent \$575, and account is overdrawn by \$25

Step 2(a)

Let d represent the dues paid by each member.

Step 3

Total dues paid	Earned	Spent	Overdrawn
$+$ \$340	$-$ \$575	$=$	bank account
$\downarrow$	$\downarrow$	$\downarrow$	$\downarrow$
$14 \cdot d$ $+$ 340	$-$ 575 $=$		-25

Step 4

$$14d + 340 - 575 = -25$$

$14d + 340 + (-575) = -25$ Add on the left.

$14d + (-235) = -25$

$$\underline{235 \qquad\quad 235}$$ Add 235 to both sides.

$14d + 0 = 210$

$$\dfrac{14d}{14} = \dfrac{210}{14}$$ Divide by 14.

$d = 15$

Step 5   Each member paid \$15 in dues.

Step 6

14 members paid dues of \$15 each.

$14(\$15) = \$210$ in the bank account.

Earned \$340, so

$\$210 + \$340 = \$550$ in the account.

Spent \$575, so

$\$550 - \$575 = \$550 + (-\$575) = -\$25$ in the account.

The account was overdrawn by \$25, which matches the original problem.

The correct answer is \$15 dues.

41. *Step 1*

The problem is about spending money for clothes.

Unknown: amount spent by Brenda

Known: Consuelo spent \$3 less than twice the amount that Brenda spent, Consuelo spent \$81.

Step 2(a)

Let m represent the amount of money that Brenda spent.

Step 3

Consuelo spent	$=$	\$3 less than twice the amount that Brenda spent
$\downarrow$		$\downarrow$
81	$=$	$2m - 3$

Step 4

$81 = 2m - 3$ Change subtraction to adding the opposite.

$81 = 2m + (-3)$

$$\underline{3 \qquad\qquad 3}$$ Add 3 to both sides.

$84 = 2m + 0$

$$\dfrac{84}{2} = \dfrac{2m}{2}$$ Divide both sides by 2.

$42 = m$

Step 5   Brenda spent \$42 on clothes.

Step 6

Consuelo spent \$3 less than twice the amount that Brenda spent, or

$2 \cdot \$42 + (-\$3) = \$84 - (\$3) = \$81$, which matches the original problem.

The correct answer is \$42.

SECTION 3.4 (pages 200–201)

7. *Step 1*

The problem is about the price of a computer and the price of a printer.

Unknowns: the computer's price; the printer's price

Known: The computer's price is eight times the printer's price. The total paid for both items is \$396.

Step 2(b)

You know the least about the printer's price, so let m represent the printer's price. The price of the computer is 8 times as much, so it can be represented by $8 \cdot m$, or $8m$.

Step 3

The total price for both items is \$396.

Printer price	$+$	Computer price	$=$	Total price
$\downarrow$		$\downarrow$		$\downarrow$
m	$+$	$8m$	$=$	396

Step 4

$m + 8m = 396$ Combine like terms.

$$\dfrac{9m}{9} = \dfrac{396}{9}$$ Divide both sides by 9.

$m = 44$

Step 5

The printer's price is m, so the printer cost \$44. The computer's price is $8m$, so the computer cost $8 \cdot \$44 = \$352$.

Step 6

Eight times \$44 is \$352 and the sum of \$44 and \$352 is \$396, so the solution checks.

15. *Step 1*

The problem is about cutting a fence into three parts.

Unknowns: Length of first part; length of second part; length of third part

Known: Two parts are of equal length. The third part is 25 m longer than each of the other parts. The entire fence is 706 m long.

Step 2(b)

Let x represent the length of the first part. Because the second part is the same length as the first, use another x for the second part. Then the third part is 25 m longer, so its length is $x + 25$.

Step 3

The lengths of the three parts add up to 706.

$x + x + (x + 25) = 706$

Step 4

$x + x + x + 25 = 706$ Combine like terms.

$3x + 25 = 706$

$$\underline{-25 \qquad -25}$$ Add -25 to both sides.

$3x + 0 = 681$

$$\dfrac{3x}{3} = \dfrac{681}{3}$$ Divide both sides by 3.

$x = 227$

Step 5

x is the length of the first part and the second part, so each of those parts is 227 m long. The third part is $x + 25$ or $227 + 25 = 252$ m in length.

The three parts are 227 m, 227 m, and 252 m.

Step 6

Since $252 - 227 = 25$ and $227 + 227 + 252 = 706$, the solution checks.

21. *Step 1*

The problem is about the length and the width of a jewelry box.

Unknowns: The length of the box; width of the box

Known: The length is 3 in. more than twice the width. The perimeter is 36 in.

(Continued)

Step 2(b)

You know the least about the width, so let w represent the width. The length is 3 in. more than twice the width, so $2w + 3$ represents the length.

$$2w + 3$$
$$w \quad\quad\quad w$$
$$2w + 3$$

Step 3

Use the formula for the perimeter of a rectangle, $P = 2l + 2w$, or $2l + 2w = P$.

$2 \cdot (2w + 3) + 2 \cdot w = 36$

Step 4

$2(2w + 3) + 2w = 36$ Use the distributive property.

$4w + 6 + 2w = 36$ Combine like terms.

$6w + 6 = 36$
$\underline{\quad -6 \quad -6 \quad}$ Add -6 to both sides.

$\dfrac{6w}{6} = \dfrac{30}{6}$ Divide both sides by 6.

$w = 5$

Step 5

w is the width, so the width is 5 in. The length is $2w + 5$, or $2(5) + 3 = 13$ in.

Step 6

The length of 13 in. is 3 in. longer than twice the width of 5 in.

$P = 2l + 2w$
$P = 2 \cdot 13 + 2 \cdot 5$
$P = 26 + 10$
$P = 36$ in. $\rightarrow$ Matches perimeter given in the problem

CHAPTER 4 Rational Numbers: Positive and Negative Fractions

SECTION 4.1 (pages 225–228)

9. An area equal to 11 of the $\frac{1}{6}$ parts is shaded: $\frac{11}{6}$

An area equal to 1 of the $\frac{1}{6}$ parts is unshaded: $\frac{1}{6}$

13. **(a)** Under the circle, it says, "out of every 20 women surveyed." In the circle, it shows 6 women choosing "at work." So 6 out of every 20 women would like flowers delivered at work. The fraction is $\frac{6}{20}$.

(b) $13 + 6 = 19$ out of every 20 women would like flowers delivered either at home or at work: $\frac{19}{20}$

37. **(a)** $-\dfrac{2}{6} = -\dfrac{2 \div 2}{6 \div 2} = -\dfrac{1}{3}$

(b) $-\dfrac{4}{6} = -\dfrac{4 \div 2}{6 \div 2} = -\dfrac{2}{3}$

(c) $-\dfrac{12}{18} = -\dfrac{12 \div 6}{18 \div 6} = -\dfrac{2}{3}$

(d) $-\dfrac{6}{18} = -\dfrac{6 \div 6}{18 \div 6} = -\dfrac{1}{3}$

(e) $-\dfrac{200}{300} = -\dfrac{200 \div 100}{300 \div 100} = -\dfrac{2}{3}$

(f) Some possibilities are:

$-\dfrac{1}{3} = -\dfrac{1 \cdot 4}{3 \cdot 4} = -\dfrac{4}{12};$

$-\dfrac{1}{3} = -\dfrac{1 \cdot 8}{3 \cdot 8} = -\dfrac{8}{24};$

$-\dfrac{2}{3} = -\dfrac{2 \cdot 10}{3 \cdot 10} = -\dfrac{20}{30};$

$-\dfrac{2}{3} = -\dfrac{2 \cdot 12}{3 \cdot 12} = -\dfrac{24}{36}.$

53. $\dfrac{150}{150} = 150 \div 150 = 1$

55. $-\dfrac{32}{4} = -32 \div 4 = -8$

SECTION 4.2 (pages 237–240)

17. **(a)**

$$75$$
$$3 \quad\quad 25$$
$$\quad\quad 5 \quad 5$$

The prime factorization of 75 is $3 \cdot 5 \cdot 5$.

(b)

$$68$$
$$2 \quad\quad 34$$
$$\quad\quad 2 \quad 17$$

The prime factorization of 68 is $2 \cdot 2 \cdot 17$.

(c)

$$189$$
$$3 \quad\quad 63$$
$$\quad 3 \quad\quad 21$$
$$\quad\quad\quad 3 \quad 7$$

The prime factorization of 189 is $3 \cdot 3 \cdot 3 \cdot 7$.

35. The prime factorization of 90 is $2 \cdot 3 \cdot 3 \cdot 5$. The prime factorization of 180 is $2 \cdot 2 \cdot 3 \cdot 3 \cdot 5$.

$\dfrac{90}{180} = \dfrac{\overset{1}{\cancel{2}} \cdot \overset{1}{\cancel{3}} \cdot \overset{1}{\cancel{3}} \cdot \overset{1}{\cancel{5}}}{\underset{1}{\cancel{2}} \cdot 2 \cdot \underset{1}{\cancel{3}} \cdot \underset{1}{\cancel{3}} \cdot \underset{1}{\cancel{5}}} = \dfrac{1}{2}$

41. 60 minutes in an hour means 60 parts in the whole.

(a) $\dfrac{15}{60} = \dfrac{\overset{1}{\cancel{3}} \cdot \overset{1}{\cancel{5}}}{2 \cdot 2 \cdot \underset{1}{\cancel{3}} \cdot \underset{1}{\cancel{5}}} = \dfrac{1}{4}$ of an hour

(b) $\dfrac{30}{60} = \dfrac{\overset{1}{\cancel{2}} \cdot \overset{1}{\cancel{3}} \cdot \overset{1}{\cancel{5}}}{2 \cdot 2 \cdot \underset{1}{\cancel{3}} \cdot \underset{1}{\cancel{5}}} = \dfrac{1}{2}$ of an hour

(c) $\dfrac{6}{60} = \dfrac{\overset{1}{\cancel{2}} \cdot \overset{1}{\cancel{3}}}{\underset{1}{\cancel{2}} \cdot 2 \cdot \underset{1}{\cancel{3}} \cdot 5} = \dfrac{1}{10}$ of an hour

(d) $\dfrac{60}{60} = 60 \div 60 = 1$ hour

57. $\dfrac{9x^2}{16y^2} = \dfrac{3 \cdot 3 \cdot x \cdot x}{2 \cdot 2 \cdot 2 \cdot 2 \cdot y \cdot y}$

There are no common factors, so the fraction is already in lowest terms.

67. $\dfrac{210ab^3c}{35b^2c^2}$

$= \dfrac{2 \cdot 3 \cdot \overset{1}{\cancel{5}} \cdot \overset{1}{\cancel{7}} \cdot a \cdot \overset{1}{\cancel{b}} \cdot \overset{1}{\cancel{b}} \cdot b \cdot \overset{1}{\cancel{c}}}{\underset{1}{\cancel{5}} \cdot \underset{1}{\cancel{7}} \cdot \underset{1}{\cancel{b}} \cdot \underset{1}{\cancel{b}} \cdot \underset{1}{\cancel{c}} \cdot c}$

$= \dfrac{6ab}{c}$

SECTION 4.3 (pages 249–252)

11. $\dfrac{4}{9}$ of $81 = \dfrac{4}{9} \cdot \dfrac{81}{1} = \dfrac{4 \cdot \overset{9}{\cancel{81}} \cdot 9}{\underset{1}{\cancel{9}} \cdot 1} = \dfrac{36}{1} = 36$

13. $\left(\dfrac{3x}{4}\right)\left(\dfrac{5}{xy}\right) = \dfrac{3 \cdot x \cdot 5}{2 \cdot 2 \cdot x \cdot y}$

$3x$ means $3 \cdot x$

4 means $2 \cdot 2$

$= \dfrac{3 \cdot \overset{1}{\cancel{x}} \cdot 5}{2 \cdot 2 \cdot \underset{1}{\cancel{x}} \cdot y} = \dfrac{15}{4y}$

21. Signs do not match, so the quotient will be negative.

$-\dfrac{2}{3} \div 4 = -\dfrac{2}{3} \div \dfrac{4}{1} = -\dfrac{2}{3} \cdot \dfrac{1}{4}$

Reciprocals

$= -\dfrac{\overset{1}{\cancel{2}} \cdot 1}{3 \cdot \underset{1}{\cancel{2}} \cdot 2} = -\dfrac{1}{6}$

25. $\dfrac{ab^2}{c} \div \dfrac{ab}{c} = \dfrac{ab^2}{c} \cdot \dfrac{c}{ab} = \dfrac{\overset{1}{\cancel{a}} \cdot \overset{1}{\cancel{b}} \cdot b \cdot \overset{1}{\cancel{c}}}{\underset{1}{\cancel{c}} \cdot \underset{1}{\cancel{a}} \cdot \underset{1}{\cancel{b}}}$

Reciprocals

$= \dfrac{b}{1} = b$

37. Signs match, so the quotient will be positive.

$-9 \div \left(-\dfrac{3}{5}\right) = -\dfrac{9}{1} \cdot \left(-\dfrac{5}{3}\right)$

Reciprocals

$\dfrac{\overset{1}{\cancel{3}} \cdot 3 \cdot 5}{1 \cdot \underset{1}{\cancel{3}}} = \dfrac{15}{1} = 15$

43. $\frac{4}{7}$ of $14b = \frac{4}{7} \cdot 14b = \frac{4}{7} \cdot \frac{14b}{1}$

$= \frac{2 \cdot 2 \cdot 2 \cdot \overset{1}{\cancel{7}} \cdot b}{\underset{1}{\cancel{7}} \cdot 1} = \frac{8b}{1} = 8b$

53. Todd must earn $\frac{3}{4}$ of the \$12,400 cost.

$\frac{3}{4} \cdot 12{,}400 = \frac{3}{4} \cdot \frac{12{,}400}{1} = \frac{3 \cdot \overset{1}{\cancel{4}} \cdot 3100}{\underset{1}{\cancel{4}} \cdot 1}$

$= \frac{9300}{1} = \$9300 \text{ earned}$

Todd must borrow the rest:
\$12,400 − \$9300 = \$3100

67. Dogs: $175 \cdot \frac{2}{5} = \frac{175}{1} \cdot \frac{2}{5}$

$= \frac{\overset{1}{\cancel{5}} \cdot 35 \cdot 2}{1 \cdot \underset{1}{\cancel{5}}} = 70$

Cats: $175 \cdot \frac{12}{25} = \frac{175}{1} \cdot \frac{12}{25}$

$= \frac{7 \cdot \overset{1}{\cancel{25}} \cdot 12}{\underset{1}{\cancel{25}}}$

$= 84$

$70 + 84 = 154$ million U.S. pets that are dogs or cats.

SECTION 4.4 (pages 260–263)

9. $\frac{3}{8} - \frac{3}{5}$

Step 1 The LCD is $8 \cdot 5 = 40$.

Step 2

$\frac{3}{8} = \frac{3 \cdot 5}{8 \cdot 5} = \frac{15}{40}$ and $\frac{3}{5} = \frac{3 \cdot 8}{5 \cdot 8} = \frac{24}{40}$

Step 3 Subtract the numerators. Write the difference over the common denominator.

$\frac{3}{8} - \frac{3}{5} = \frac{15}{40} - \frac{24}{40}$

$15 + (-24)$ is -9

$= \frac{15 - 24}{40} = \frac{-9}{40}$ or $-\frac{9}{40}$

Step 4 $-\frac{9}{40}$ is already in lowest terms.

17. $2 - \frac{6}{7} = \frac{2}{1} - \frac{6}{7}$

Step 1 The LCD is 7.

Step 2

$2 = \frac{2 \cdot 7}{1 \cdot 7} = \frac{14}{7}$ and $\frac{6}{7}$ has the LCD.

Step 3

$\frac{2}{1} - \frac{6}{7} = \frac{14}{7} - \frac{6}{7} = \frac{14 - 6}{7} = \frac{8}{7}$

Step 4 $\frac{8}{7}$ is already in lowest terms.

23. $\frac{5}{m} - \frac{1}{2}$

Step 1 The LCD is $2 \cdot m$ or $2m$.

Step 2

$\frac{5}{m} = \frac{5 \cdot 2}{m \cdot 2} = \frac{10}{2m}; \frac{1}{2} = \frac{1 \cdot m}{2 \cdot m} = \frac{1m}{2m}$

Step 3

$\frac{5}{m} - \frac{1}{2} = \frac{10}{2m} - \frac{1m}{2m}$

$= \frac{10 - 1m}{2m}$ or $\frac{10 - m}{2m}$

Step 4 Already in lowest terms.

29. $-\frac{4}{c^2} - \frac{d}{c}$

Step 1 The LCD is c^2.

Step 2

$-\frac{4}{c^2}$ has the LCD and $\frac{d}{c} = \frac{d \cdot c}{c \cdot c} = \frac{cd}{c^2}$

Step 3

$-\frac{4}{c^2} - \frac{d}{c} = -\frac{4}{c^2} - \frac{cd}{c^2} = \frac{-4 - cd}{c^2}$

Step 4 Already in lowest terms.

53. If the total perimeter is $\frac{7}{8}$ mile, use subtraction to find the length of the fourth side. The LCD of the fractions is 24.

Length of fourth side

$= \frac{7}{8} - \frac{1}{4} - \frac{1}{6} - \frac{3}{8}$

Change subtractions to adding the opposite.

$= \frac{7}{8} + \left(-\frac{1}{4}\right) + \left(-\frac{1}{6}\right) + \left(-\frac{3}{8}\right)$

$= \frac{21}{24} + \left(-\frac{6}{24}\right) + \left(-\frac{4}{24}\right) + \left(-\frac{9}{24}\right)$

$= \frac{21 + (-6) + (-4) + (-9)}{24}$

Add in the numerator, keep the common denominator.

$= \frac{2}{24} = \frac{1}{12}$ mile

The fourth side is $\frac{1}{12}$ mile long.

SECTION 4.5 (pages 275–278)

13. $10\frac{11}{15}$

Step 1

$15 \cdot 10 = 150; \quad 150 + 11 = 161$

Step 2 $10\frac{11}{15} = \frac{161}{15}$ Keep the same denominator.

21. Divide 51 by 9.

$9\overline{)51} \\ \frac{45}{6} \\ 5$

Keep the negative sign.

so $-\frac{51}{9} = -5\frac{6}{9} = -5\frac{2}{3} \leftarrow$ Lowest terms

29. $3\frac{2}{3}$ rounds to 4   and $1\frac{5}{6}$ rounds to 2.

Estimate: $4 + 2 = 6$

To find the exact answer first rewrite each mixed number as an equivalent improper fraction: $3\frac{2}{3}$ is $\frac{11}{3}$ and $1\frac{5}{6}$ is $\frac{11}{6}$. The LCD for $\frac{11}{3}$ and $\frac{11}{6}$ is 6, so rewrite $\frac{11}{3}$ as an equivalent fraction with a denominator of 6.

Exact: $3\frac{2}{3} + 1\frac{5}{6} = \frac{11}{3} + \frac{11}{6} = \frac{22}{6} + \frac{11}{6}$

$= \frac{22 + 11}{6} = \frac{33}{6}$

$= 5\frac{3}{6} = 5\frac{1}{2} \leftarrow$ Lowest terms

33. $5\frac{2}{3}$ rounds to 6. *Estimate:* $6 \div 6 = 1$

To find the exact answer, first rewrite the mixed number and the whole number as improper fractions: $5\frac{2}{3}$ is $\frac{17}{3}$ and 6 is $\frac{6}{1}$. Then rewrite the division problem as multiplying by the reciprocal of $\frac{6}{1}$.

Exact:

$5\frac{2}{3} \div 6 = \frac{17}{3} \div \frac{6}{1} = \frac{17}{3} \cdot \frac{1}{6} = \frac{17}{18}$

Reciprocals

35. $1\frac{4}{5}$ rounds to 2. *Estimate:* $8 - 2 = 6$

To find the exact answer, first rewrite 8 as $\frac{8}{1}$ and $1\frac{4}{5}$ as the improper fraction $\frac{9}{5}$. The LCD for $\frac{8}{1}$ and $\frac{9}{5}$ is 5, so rewrite $\frac{8}{1}$ as an equivalent fraction with a denominator of 5.

Exact: $8 - 1\frac{4}{5} = \frac{8}{1} - \frac{9}{5} = \frac{40}{5} - \frac{9}{5}$

$= \frac{40 - 9}{5} = \frac{31}{5} = 6\frac{1}{5}$

37. The figure is a square.

$P = 4s = 4 \cdot 1\frac{3}{4} = \frac{4}{1} \cdot \frac{7}{4} = \frac{\overset{1}{\cancel{4}} \cdot 7}{1 \cdot \underset{1}{\cancel{4}}}$

$= \frac{7}{1} = 7$ in.

$A = s \cdot s = 1\frac{3}{4} \cdot 1\frac{3}{4} = \frac{7}{4} \cdot \frac{7}{4} = \frac{49}{16}$

$= 3\frac{1}{16}$ in.^{2}

SOLUTIONS

SECTION 4.6 (pages 284–287)

19. $\left(-\dfrac{3}{2}\right)^3\left(-\dfrac{2}{3}\right)^2$ — Three factors of $-\dfrac{3}{2}$

$= \left(-\dfrac{3}{2}\right)\left(-\dfrac{3}{2}\right)\left(-\dfrac{3}{2}\right)\left(-\dfrac{2}{3}\right)\left(-\dfrac{2}{3}\right)$

Two factors of $-\dfrac{2}{3}$

$= -\dfrac{\cancel{3}\cdot\cancel{3}\cdot 3 \cdot \cancel{2}\cdot\cancel{2}}{\cancel{2}\cdot\cancel{2}\cdot 2\cdot\cancel{3}\cdot\cancel{3}}$ — Divide out all common factors.

$= -\dfrac{3}{2}$ or $-1\dfrac{1}{2}$

23. $\dfrac{1}{5} - 6\left(\dfrac{7}{10}\right)$

There is no work to be done inside the parentheses. There are no exponents, so after rewriting 6 as $\dfrac{6}{1}$, start with Step 3, multiplying and dividing.

$= \dfrac{1}{5} - \dfrac{6}{1}\left(\dfrac{7}{10}\right)$ — Multiply.

$= \dfrac{1}{5} - \dfrac{42}{10}$ — Subtract; LCD is 10.

$= \dfrac{2}{10} - \dfrac{42}{10}$

$= \dfrac{2 - 42}{10}$

$= \dfrac{-40}{10}$ — Write $-\dfrac{40}{10}$ in lowest terms:

$\dfrac{-4\cdot\cancel{10}}{\cancel{10}} = \dfrac{-4}{1} = -4$

$= -4$ — Lowest terms

27. $-\dfrac{3}{10} \div \dfrac{3}{5}\left(-\dfrac{2}{3}\right)$

There is no work to be done inside the parentheses. There are no exponents, so start with Step 3, multiplying and dividing. Change division to multiplying by the reciprocal.

$= -\dfrac{3}{10} \cdot \dfrac{5}{3}\left(-\dfrac{2}{3}\right)$ — Divide out common factors and then multiply.

$= -\dfrac{\cancel{3}\cdot\cancel{5}}{2\cdot\cancel{5}\cdot\cancel{3}}\left(-\dfrac{2}{3}\right)$

$= -\dfrac{1}{2}\left(-\dfrac{2}{3}\right)$ — Multiply; matching signs so the product is positive.

$= \dfrac{1\cdot\cancel{2}}{\cancel{2}\cdot 3}$

$= \dfrac{1}{3}$

41. $\dfrac{-\dfrac{7}{9}}{-\dfrac{7}{36}}$ — Rewrite using the ÷ symbol for division.

$= -\dfrac{7}{9} \div \left(-\dfrac{7}{36}\right) = -\dfrac{7}{9}\cdot\left(-\dfrac{36}{7}\right)$

Reciprocals

$= \dfrac{\cancel{7}\cdot\cancel{9}\cdot 4}{\cancel{9}\cdot\cancel{7}}$ — Divide out common factors.

$= \dfrac{4}{1} = 4$ — Matching signs so answer is positive.

SECTION 4.7 (pages 293–296)

15. $\dfrac{3}{8}x - 9 = 0$ — Add 9 to both sides to get the variable term by itself.

$\dfrac{9 \quad\quad 9}{\dfrac{3}{8}x + 0 = 9}$

Multiply both sides by $\dfrac{8}{3}$ (the reciprocal of $\dfrac{3}{8}$.)

$\dfrac{\cancel{8}}{\cancel{3}}\cdot\dfrac{\cancel{3}}{\cancel{8}}x = \dfrac{8}{\cancel{3}}\cdot\dfrac{\cancel{9}}{1}$

$x = 24$

CHECK $\dfrac{3}{8}(24) - 9 = 0$

The solution is 24. Replace x with 24 in the original equation.

$9 - 9 = 0$

$0 = 0$ ✓ Balances

When x is 24, the equation balances, so 24 is the correct solution (**not** 0).

23. $\dfrac{3}{10} = -4b - \dfrac{1}{5}$

$\dfrac{\dfrac{1}{5} \quad\quad\quad \dfrac{1}{5}}{\dfrac{3}{10} + \dfrac{1}{5} = -4b + 0}$ — Add $\dfrac{1}{5}$ to both sides.

Rewrite $\dfrac{1}{5}$ as an equivalent fraction with a denominator of 10, the LCD for $\dfrac{3}{10}$ and $\dfrac{1}{5}$.

$\dfrac{3}{10} + \dfrac{2}{10} = -4b$ — Add on the left side.

$\dfrac{5}{10} = -4b$

$-\dfrac{1}{4}\cdot\dfrac{5}{10} = -\dfrac{1}{4}(-4b)$ — Multiply both sides by $-\dfrac{1}{4}$, the reciprocal of -4.

$-\dfrac{5}{40} = b$

$-\dfrac{\cancel{5}}{\cancel{5}\cdot 8} = b$ — Write the fraction in lowest terms.

$-\dfrac{1}{8} = b$

37. Let p be the penny size.

$\dfrac{p}{4} + \dfrac{1}{2} = \dfrac{5}{2}$

$\dfrac{-\dfrac{1}{2} \quad\quad -\dfrac{1}{2}}{\dfrac{p}{4} + 0 = 2}$ — Add $-\dfrac{1}{2}$ to both sides. Rewrite $\dfrac{p}{4}$ as $\dfrac{1}{4}p$.

$\dfrac{1}{4}p = 2$

$\dfrac{\cancel{4}}{1}\left(\dfrac{1}{\cancel{4}}p\right) = \dfrac{4}{1}(2)$ — Multiply both sides by $\dfrac{4}{1}$, the reciprocal of $\dfrac{1}{4}$.

$p = 8$

The penny size is 8.

SECTION 4.8 (pages 302–304)

9. $P = 12\dfrac{3}{5}$ yd $+ 7\dfrac{2}{3}$ yd $+ 10$ yd

Write mixed numbers as improper fractions.

$P = \dfrac{63}{5}$ yd $+ \dfrac{23}{3}$ yd $+ 10$ yd

Rewrite fractions as equivalent fractions with a denominator of 15, the LCD

$P = \dfrac{189}{15}$ yd $+ \dfrac{115}{15}$ yd $+ \dfrac{150}{15}$ yd — Add.

$P = \dfrac{454}{15}$ yd or $30\dfrac{4}{15}$ yd

$A = \dfrac{1}{2}bh$ — Replace b with 10 yd and h with $7\dfrac{2}{3}$ yd.

$A = \dfrac{1}{2}(10\text{ yd})\left(7\dfrac{2}{3}\text{ yd}\right)$

Multiply $\dfrac{1}{2}(10$ yd$)$ to get 5 yd.

$A = (5\text{ yd})\left(7\dfrac{2}{3}\text{ yd}\right)$

$A = \dfrac{5\text{ yd}}{1}\cdot\dfrac{23\text{ yd}}{3}$

$A = \dfrac{5\text{ yd}\cdot 23\text{ yd}}{3}$

$A = \dfrac{115}{3}$ yd² or $38\dfrac{1}{3}$ yd²

11. The *entire* figure is a rectangle.

$A = lw$

$A = 37\text{ m}\cdot 52\text{ m} = 1924\text{ m}^2$

The unshaded portion is a triangle.

$A = \dfrac{1}{2}bh$

$A = \dfrac{1}{2}\cdot\dfrac{52\text{ m}}{1}\cdot\dfrac{8\text{ m}}{1}$

$A = \dfrac{1\cdot\cancel{2}\cdot 26\text{ m}\cdot 8\text{ m}}{\cancel{2}\cdot 1\cdot 1}$

$A = 208\text{ m}^2$

Subtract to find the area of the shaded portion.

$A = 1924\text{ m}^2 - 208\text{ m}^2$

$= 1716\text{ m}^2$

The shaded area is 1716 m².

15. Amount of curbing to go "around" the space implies perimeter.

$P = 33\text{ m} + 55\text{ m} + 44\text{ m}$

$P = 132\text{ m}$

132 m of curbing is needed.

Amount of sod to "cover" the space implies area.

The figure is a triangle.

$A = \dfrac{1}{2} bh$

$A = \dfrac{1}{2} \cdot 44 \text{ m} \cdot 33 \text{ m}$

$A = \dfrac{1}{2} \cdot \dfrac{44 \text{ m}}{1} \cdot \dfrac{33 \text{ m}}{1}$

$A = \dfrac{1 \cdot \overset{1}{\cancel{2}} \cdot 22 \text{ m} \cdot 33 \text{ m}}{\underset{1}{\cancel{2}} \cdot 1 \cdot 1}$

$A = 726 \text{ m}^2$

726 m² of sod is needed.

21. The figure is a pyramid.

First find the area of the rectangular base.

$B = l \cdot w$

$= 8 \text{ cm} \cdot 15 \text{ cm}$

$= 120 \text{ cm}^2$

Now find the volume of the pyramid.

$V = \dfrac{B \cdot h}{3}$

$= \dfrac{\overset{40}{\cancel{120}} \text{ cm}^2 \cdot 20 \text{ cm}}{\underset{1}{\cancel{3}}}$

$= \dfrac{800 \text{ cm}^3}{1} = 800 \text{ cm}^3$

CHAPTER 5 Rational Numbers: Positive and Negative Decimals

SECTION 5.1 (pages 327–330)

5. 7 0.4 8 9

tens · ones · tenths — hundredths — thousandths

17. 5 4 0 6.0 4 5

thousands · hundreds · tens · ones · tenths · hundredths · thousandths

31. $0.205 = \dfrac{205}{1000} = \dfrac{205 \div 5}{1000 \div 5} = \dfrac{41}{200}$

45. 1.075 is one and seventy-five thousandths.

5 is in thousandths place

1.075

one and seventy-five **thousandths**

53. Seven hundred three ten-thousandths: fill *four* decimal places for ten-thousandths.

$\dfrac{703}{10,000} = 0.0703$

ten-thousandths place

59. 8-pound test line has a diameter of 0.010 inch, which is read "ten thousandths inch."

$0.010 = \dfrac{10}{1000} = \dfrac{10 \div 10}{1000 \div 10} = \dfrac{1}{100} \text{ inch}$

SECTION 5.2 (pages 336–337)

13. 793.988 to the nearest tenth

Draw a cut-off line after the tenths place:

793.9 | 88

The first digit cut is 8, which is *5 or more,* so round up by adding 1 tenth to the part you are keeping.

$\begin{array}{r} 793.9 \\ + 0.1 \\ \hline 794.0 \end{array}$

$793.988 \approx 794.0$

You must write the zero in the tenths place to show that the number was rounded to the nearest tenth.

17. Round 9.0906 to the nearest hundredth.

Draw a cut-off line: 9.09 | 06. The first digit cut is 0, which is *4 or less.* The part you keep stays the same.

$9.0906 \approx 9.09$

35. $999.73 to the nearest dollar

Draw a cut-off line: $999 | .73

The first digit cut is 7, which is *5 or more,* so round up by adding $1.

$\begin{array}{r} \$999 \\ + 1 \\ \hline \$1000 \end{array}$

Answer: $999.73 rounded to the nearest dollar is $1000

SECTION 5.3 (pages 344–347)

23. Rewrite 8.339 from 15 in vertical format.

Watch the *order* of the numbers.

Line up decimal points.

$\begin{array}{r} 15.000 \\ -8.339 \\ \hline 6.661 \end{array}$ ← Write a decimal point and three zeros.
← Subtract as usual.

41. $-1.7035 - (5 - 6.7)$

Work inside parentheses first. Rewrite the subtraction as adding the opposite.

$5 - 6.7 = 5 + (-6.7) = -1.7$

Now the problem becomes:

$-1.7035 - (-1.7)$

Rewrite subtraction as adding the opposite. Because -1.7035 has the larger absolute value and is negative, the answer will be negative.

$= -1.7035 + 1.7$

$= -0.0035$

47. Using front end rounding, we can estimate $-6.5 + 0.7$ as $-7 + 1 = -6$, so -5.8 is the most reasonable answer.

57. Add the heights of the three basketball players.

Estimate:		Exact:
2	Rounds to	2.13
2	Rounds to	1.98
+ 2	Rounds to	+ 2.08
6 meters		6.19 meters

To find the difference, subtract 6.19 meters from the rhino's height of 6.4 meters.

$\begin{array}{r} 6.40 \\ -6.19 \\ \hline 0.21 \end{array}$

The basketball players' combined height of 6.19 meters is 0.21 meter less than the rhino's height of 6.4 meters.

SECTION 5.4 (pages 351–354)

15. $(7.2)(0.06) = 0.432$

The factors have the *same* sign, so the product is *positive*.

7.2 has *1 decimal place.* ⎱ Product has
0.06 has *2 decimal places.* ⎰ *3 decimal places.*

21. $(-0.003)^2$ means $(-0.003)(-0.003)$

$\begin{array}{r} 0.003 \\ \times 0.003 \\ \hline 0.000009 \end{array}$ ← *3 decimal places*
← *3 decimal places*
← *6 decimal places*

Write five zeros so you can count over 6 decimal places in the answer. The factors have the *same* sign, so the product is *positive*.

35. A gallon of milk for $419 is *unreasonable;* it is too much. Write a decimal point in $419 to get a reasonable answer of $4.19

43. Multiply the number of gallons that Michelle pumped into her SUV by the price per gallon, using a calculator.

$\begin{array}{r} 20.510 \\ \times \$3.759 \\ \hline \$77.09709 \end{array}$

Round $77.09709 to the nearest cent (nearest hundredth). Michelle paid $77.10 for the gas.

47. **(a)** To find the area of the bill before 1929, multiply length by width. Use a calculator.

$(7.4218)(3.125) = 23.193125$

Rounding to the nearest tenth gives an area of 23.2 in.²

To find the area from 1929 on, multiply length by width. $(6.14)(2.61) = 16.0254$

Rounding to the nearest tenth gives an area of 16.0 in.²

(b) Subtract to find the difference in the areas. $23.2 - 16.0 = 7.2$

The difference in the rounded areas is 7.2 in.²

SOLUTIONS

55. (a) Multiply to find the cost for 3 short-sleeved, solid-color shirts. Each shirt is $14.75.

$$\begin{array}{r} \$14.75 \\ \times\ \ \ 3 \\ \hline \$44.25 \end{array}$$

Based on this subtotal, shipping is $7.95. Next, multiply to find the cost of 3 monograms.

$$\begin{array}{r} \$4.95 \\ \times\ \ \ 3 \\ \hline \$14.85 \end{array}$$

Add these amounts, plus $5.00 for a gift box.

$44.25 ← Shirts
   7.95 ← Shipping
 14.85 ← Monograms
+5.00 ← Gift box
$72.05

The total cost is $72.05.

(b) Subtract the cost of the shirts to find the difference.

$$\begin{array}{r} \$72.05 \\ -\ 44.25 \\ \hline \$27.80 \end{array}$$

The monograms, gift box, and shipping added $27.80 to the cost of the gift.

SECTION 5.5 (pages 362–365)

11. The numbers have the same sign, so the quotient is positive.

$$1.5\,\overline{)\,5\,4.0}$$

$3\,6.$

Move decimal point in divisor and dividend 1 place; write one 0 in the dividend. Then line up the decimal point in the quotient.

$$\begin{array}{r} 4\,5 \\ \hline 9\,0 \\ 9\,0 \\ \hline 0 \end{array}$$

25. First consider $240.8 \div 9$. Write extra zeros in the dividend so that you can continue dividing.

$$9\,\overline{)\,2\,4\,0.8\,0\,0\,0}$$

$2\,6.7\,5\,5\,5$

$$\begin{array}{r} 1\,8 \\ \hline 6\,0 \\ 5\,4 \\ \hline 6\,8 \\ 6\,3 \\ \hline 5\,0 \\ 4\,5 \\ \hline 5\,0 \\ 4\,5 \\ \hline 5\,0 \\ 4\,5 \\ \hline 5 \end{array}$$

Rounding the quotient to the nearest thousandth gives 26.756. The quotient is *negative* because the divisor and the dividend have *different* signs.

$-240.8 \div 9 \approx -26.756$

33. Does $307.02 \div 5.1 = 6.2$?

Estimate: $300 \div 5 = 60$

A quotient of 6.2 is *unreasonable;* it is too small compared to an estimate of 60.

$$5.1\,\overline{)\,3\,0\,7.0\,2}$$

$6\,0.2$

$$\begin{array}{r} 3\,0\,6 \\ \hline 1\,0 \\ 0 \\ \hline 1\,0\,2 \\ 1\,0\,2 \\ \hline 0 \end{array}$$

The correct quotient is 60.2, which is close to the estimate of 60.

57.
$$\begin{aligned} & -8.68 - \underline{4.6(10.4)} \div 6.4 \qquad \text{Multiply.} \\ &= -8.68 - \underline{47.84 \div 6.4} \qquad \text{Divide.} \\ &= \underline{-8.68 - \qquad 7.475} \qquad \text{Subtract.} \\ &= \qquad -16.155 \end{aligned}$$

65. Divide 100,000 box tops (the answer from Exercise 63) by 38 weeks.

$$38\,\overline{)\,1\,0\,0,0\,0\,0.0}$$

$2\ 6\,3\,1.5$

$$\begin{array}{r} 7\,6 \\ \hline 2\,4\,0 \\ 2\,2\,8 \\ \hline 1\,2\,0 \\ 1\,1\,4 \\ \hline 6\,0 \\ 3\,8 \\ \hline 2\,2\,0 \\ 1\,9\,0 \\ \hline 3\,0 \end{array}$$

2631.5 rounds to 2632

The school needs to collect 2632 box tops (rounded) during each of the 38 weeks.

SECTION 5.6 (pages 372–375)

23. $3\dfrac{5}{8} = \dfrac{29}{8}$

Divide 29 by 8.

$$8\,\overline{)\,2\,9.0\,0\,0}$$

$3.6\,2\,5$

$$\begin{array}{r} 2\,4 \\ \hline 5\,0 \\ 4\,8 \\ \hline 2\,0 \\ 1\,6 \\ \hline 4\,0 \\ 4\,0 \\ \hline 0 \end{array}$$

$3\dfrac{5}{8} = 3.625$

35. $0.35 = \dfrac{35}{100} = \dfrac{35 \div 5}{100 \div 5} = \dfrac{7}{20}$

51. Write zeros so that all the numbers have four decimal places.

1.0100 > 1.0020 *unacceptable*

0.9991 > 0.9980   and
0.9991 < 1.0020 *acceptable*

1.0007 > 0.9980   and
1.0007 < 1.0020 *acceptable*

0.9900 < 0.9980 *unacceptable*

The lengths of 0.9991 cm and 1.0007 cm are acceptable.

65. First write $\dfrac{3}{8}$ and $\dfrac{2}{5}$ as decimals.

$$8\,\overline{)\,3.0\,0\,0}$$

$0.3\,7\,5$

$$\begin{array}{r} 2\,4 \\ \hline 6\,0 \\ 5\,6 \\ \hline 4\,0 \\ 4\,0 \\ \hline 0 \end{array}$$

$$5\,\overline{)\,2.0}$$

0.4

$$\begin{array}{r} 2\,0 \\ \hline 0 \end{array}$$

So, $\dfrac{3}{8} = 0.375$ and $\dfrac{2}{5} = 0.4$. Now write zeros so that all the numbers have four decimal places.

$\dfrac{3}{8} = 0.3750$

$\dfrac{2}{5} = 0.4000$ ← second greatest

$0.37 = 0.3700$ ← least
$0.4001 = 0.4001$ ← greatest

From least to greatest: $0.37, \dfrac{3}{8}, \dfrac{2}{5}, 0.4001$

SECTION 5.7 (pages 380–382)

3. mean

$$\begin{aligned} &= \frac{\text{sum of all values}}{\text{number of values}} \\ &= \frac{92 + 51 + 59 + 86 + 68 + 73 + 49 + 80}{8} \\ &= \frac{558}{8} = 69.75 \quad \text{(rounds to 69.8)} \end{aligned}$$

The mean (average) final exam score was 69.8 (rounded).

7.

Quiz Score	Frequency	Product
3	4	$3 \cdot 4 = 12$
5	2	$5 \cdot 2 = 10$
6	5	$6 \cdot 5 = 30$
8	5	$8 \cdot 5 = 40$
9	2	$9 \cdot 2 = 18$
Totals	18	110

$$\text{weighted mean} = \frac{\text{sum of products}}{\text{total number of quizzes}}$$

$$= \frac{110}{18} = 6.\overline{1} \ \text{(rounds to 6.1)}$$

The mean (average) quiz score was 6.1 (rounded).

9.

Course	Credits	Grade	Product (Credits · Grade)
Biology	4	B (=3)	$4 \cdot 3 = 12$
Biology Lab	2	A (=4)	$2 \cdot 4 = 8$
Mathematics	5	C (=2)	$5 \cdot 2 = 10$
Health	1	F (=0)	$1 \cdot 0 = 0$
Psychology	3	B (=3)	$3 \cdot 3 = 9$
Totals	15		39

$$\text{GPA} = \frac{\text{sum of products}}{\text{total number of credits}}$$

$$= \frac{39}{15} = 2.60$$

SOLUTIONS

17. First, arrange the numbers in order from least to greatest.

34, 40, 40, 47, 48, 49, 51, 56, 95, 96
                     └─ Middle two numbers ─┘

The list has 10 numbers so there is no single middle number. The middle *two* numbers are 48 and 49, so the median is the average of those two numbers.

$$\frac{48 + 49}{2} = 48.5 \text{ pounds of shrimp}$$

25. 74, 68, 68, 68, 75, 75, 74, 74, 70, 77

Both 68 years and 74 years occur three times, which is more often than any of the other values, so each is a mode. This list is *bimodal* (has two modes).

29. For Barrow, Alaska
mean

$$= \frac{-2 + (-11) + (-13) + (-18) + (-15) + (-2)}{6}$$

$$= \frac{-61}{6} \approx -10°F$$

For Fairbanks, Alaska
mean

$$= \frac{3 + (-7) + (-10) + (-4) + 11 + 31}{6}$$

$$= \frac{24}{6} = 4°F$$

Find the difference:

$4 - (-10) = 4 + (+10) = 14$

Fairbanks' mean is 14 degrees warmer than Barrow's mean.

SECTION 5.8 (pages 387–390)

25. The unknown length is the side opposite the right angle, which is the hypotenuse. Use the formula for finding the hypotenuse. The legs are 8 in. and 3 in.

$$\text{hypotenuse} = \sqrt{(\text{leg})^2 + (\text{leg})^2}$$
Legs are 8 and 3.

$$= \sqrt{(8)^2 + (3)^2}$$
(8)(8) is 64 and (3)(3) is 9.

$$= \sqrt{64 + 9}$$
Use a calculator to find $\sqrt{73}$.

$$= \sqrt{73}$$
Round to the nearest tenth.

$$\approx 8.5 \text{ in.}$$

The hypotenuse is approximately 8.5 in. long.

35. The hypotenuse is 21.6 km long. One leg is 13.2 km long.

$$\text{leg} = \sqrt{(\text{hypotenuse})^2 - (\text{leg})^2}$$
Hypotenuse is 21.6; one leg is 13.2.

$$= \sqrt{(21.6)^2 - (13.2)^2}$$
(21.6)(21.6) is 466.56 and (13.2)(13.2) is 174.24

$$= \sqrt{466.56 - 174.24}$$
Use a calculator to find $\sqrt{292.32}$

$$= \sqrt{292.32}$$
Round to the nearest tenth.

$$\approx 17.1 \text{ km}$$

The length of the leg is approximately 17.1 km.

43. The diagonal brace is the hypotenuse of a right triangle with legs that have lengths of 6.5 ft and 2.5 ft.

$$\text{hypotenuse} = \sqrt{(\text{leg})^2 + (\text{leg})^2}$$
Legs are 6.5 and 2.5

$$= \sqrt{(6.5)^2 + (2.5)^2}$$
(6.5)(6.5) is 42.25 and
(2.5)(2.5) is 6.25

$$= \sqrt{42.25 + 6.25}$$
Use a calculator to find $\sqrt{48.5}$

$$= \sqrt{48.5}$$
Round to the nearest tenth.

$$\approx 7.0 \text{ ft}$$

The diagonal brace is about 7.0 ft long.

45.

The length of the ladder is the hypotenuse (12 ft) and the length of one leg is (3 ft). Find the length of the other leg.

$$\text{leg} = \sqrt{(\text{hypotenuse})^2 - (\text{leg})^2}$$
Hypotenuse is 12; one leg is 3.

$$= \sqrt{(12)^2 - (3)^2}$$
(12)(12) is 144 and (3)(3) is 9.

$$= \sqrt{144 - 9}$$
Use a calculator to find $\sqrt{135}$.

$$= \sqrt{135}$$
Round to the nearest tenth.

$$\approx 11.6 \text{ ft}$$

The ladder will reach about 11.6 ft high on the building.

SECTION 5.9 (pages 395–396)

3. $-20.6 + n = -22$ Add 20.6 to both sides.
$+20.6 = +20.6$
$0 + n = -1.4$
$n = -1.4$

CHECK
$-20.6 + n = -22$
$\downarrow$ Original equation
$-20.6 + (-1.4) = -22$
${.}4)$ Replace *n* with -1.4
$-22 = -22$
 Balances

When *n* is replaced with -1.4, the equation balances, so -1.4 is the correct solution (**not** -22).

11. $-3.3t = -2.31$
$$\frac{-3.3t}{-3.3} = \frac{-2.31}{-3.3}$$
Divide both sides by -3.3

On the left side, divide out the common factor of -3.3

$$\frac{\cancel{-3.3}t}{\cancel{-3.3}} = 0.7$$
On the right side, $-2.31 \div -3.3$ is 0.7

$$t = 0.7$$

CHECK $-3.3t = -2.31$
$\downarrow$ Original equation
$-3.3(0.7) = -2.31$
 Replace *t* with 0.7
$-2.31 = -2.31$
Balances, so 0.7 is the correct solution.

21. $0.8w - 0.4 = -6 + w$ Add 0.4 to
$+ 0.4 +0.4$ both sides.
$\overline{0.8w + 0 = -5.6 + w}$ Write *w* as 1*w*.
$0.8w = -5.6 + 1w$
$0.8w = -5.6 + 1w$ Add -1*w*
$-1.0w -1w$ to both sides.
$\overline{-0.2w = -5.6 + 0}$
$$\frac{\cancel{-0.2}w}{\cancel{-0.2}} = \frac{-5.6}{-0.2}$$ Divide both sides by -0.2
$$w = 28$$

25. *Step 1*

The problem is about doses of a medication.
Unknown: the adult dose
Known: child's dose is 0.3 times the adult dose; child's dose is 9 mg

Step 2   Let *d* be the adult dose.

Step 3

adult dose multiplied by 0.3	is	child's dose
↓	↓	↓
0.3d	=	9

Step 4

$0.3d = 9$

$$\frac{\cancel{0.3}d}{\cancel{0.3}} = \frac{9}{0.3}$$ Divide both sides by 0.3

$$d = 30$$

Step 5   The adult dose is 30 milligrams.

Step 6

0.3(30 milligrams) = 9 milligrams
(Matches amount given in problem.)

SECTION 5.10 (pages 405–408)

13. First, find the circumference.

The diameter is $7\frac{1}{2}$ ft, so use the formula with *d* in it. Write $7\frac{1}{2}$ ft in decimal form as 7.5 ft.

$$C = \pi \cdot d$$
$$\approx 3.14 \cdot 7.5 \text{ ft}$$
$$\approx 23.6 \text{ ft}   \text{(rounded)}$$

(Continued)

To find the area, first find the radius by dividing the diameter by 2.

$$r = \frac{7.5 \text{ ft}}{2} = 3.75 \text{ ft}$$

$$A = \pi \cdot r \cdot r$$
$$\approx 3.14 \cdot 3.75 \text{ ft} \cdot 3.75 \text{ ft}$$
$$\approx 44.2 \text{ ft}^2 \quad \text{(rounded)}$$

17. First, find the area of a whole circle with a radius of 10 ft.

$$A = \pi \cdot r \cdot r$$
$$\approx 3.14 \cdot 10 \text{ cm} \cdot 10 \text{ cm}$$
$$\approx 314 \text{ cm}^2$$

Divide the area of the whole circle by 2 to find the area of the semicircle.

$$\frac{314 \text{ cm}^2}{2} = 157 \text{ cm}^2$$

Then find the area of the triangle.

$$A = \frac{1}{2} \cdot b \cdot h$$
$$= \frac{1}{2} \cdot 20 \text{ cm} \cdot 10 \text{ cm}$$
$$= 100 \text{ cm}^2$$

Finally, subtract the area of the triangle from the area of the semicircle. The shaded area is about

$$157 \text{ cm}^2 - 100 \text{ cm}^2 = 57 \text{ cm}^2$$

21. The distance that a point on the tire tread moves in one complete turn is the same as the circumference of the tire.

$$C = \pi \cdot d$$
$$\approx 3.14 \cdot 29.10 \text{ in.}$$
$$\approx 91.4 \text{ in.}$$

Bonus question:

$$\frac{1 \text{ revolution}}{91.4 \text{ inches}} \cdot \frac{12 \text{ inches}}{1 \text{ foot}} \cdot \frac{5280 \text{ feet}}{1 \text{ mile}}$$
$$\approx 693 \text{ revolutions/mile}$$

23. If the station can be heard for 150 miles in all directions, its signal covers a circular area with a radius of 150 miles.

$$A = \pi \cdot r \cdot r$$
$$\approx 3.14 \cdot 150 \text{ mi} \cdot 150 \text{ mi}$$
$$= 70,650 \text{ mi}^2$$

There are about 70,650 mi² in the broadcast area.

29. (a)
$$C = 144 \text{ cm}$$
$$C = \pi \cdot d$$
$$144 \text{ cm} = \pi \cdot d \quad \text{Replace } C \text{ with 144 cm.}$$
$$144 \text{ cm} \approx 3.14 \cdot d \quad \text{Replace } \pi \text{ with 3.14.}$$
$$\frac{144 \text{ cm}}{3.14} \approx \frac{3.14 \cdot d}{3.14} \quad \text{Divide both sides by 3.14.}$$
$$45.9 \approx d$$

The diameter is about 45.9 cm.

(b) Divide the circumference by π (144 cm ÷ 3.14).

39. First, find the radius of the cylinder.

$$r = \frac{d}{2} = \frac{18 \text{ in.}}{2} = 9 \text{ in.}$$

Then find the volume.

$$V = \pi \cdot r \cdot r \cdot h$$
$$\approx 3.14 \cdot 9 \text{ in.} \cdot 9 \text{ in.} \cdot 3 \text{ in.}$$
$$\approx 763.0 \text{ in.}^3 \quad \text{(rounded)}$$

Now find the surface area

$$S = (2 \cdot \pi \cdot r \cdot h)$$
$$+ (2 \cdot \pi \cdot r \cdot r)$$
$$\approx (2 \cdot 3.14 \cdot 9 \text{ in.} \cdot 3 \text{ in.})$$
$$+ (2 \cdot 3.14 \cdot 9 \text{ in.} \cdot 9 \text{ in.})$$
$$\approx 169.56 + 508.68$$
$$\approx 678.2 \text{ in.}^2 \quad \text{(rounded)}$$

47. Use the formula for the surface area of a rectangular solid.

$$S = 2lw + 2lh + 2wh$$
$$= (2 \cdot 5.5 \text{ in.} \cdot 2.8 \text{ in.})$$
$$+ (2 \cdot 5.5 \text{ in.} \cdot 8 \text{ in.})$$
$$+ (2 \cdot 2.8 \text{ in.} \cdot 8 \text{ in.})$$
$$= 30.8 + 88 + 44.8$$
$$= 163.6 \text{ in.}^2$$

The amount of cardboard needed is 163.6 in.²

CHAPTER 6 Ratio, Proportion, and Line/Angle/Triangle Relationships

SECTION 6.1 (pages 433–434)

7. $100 to $50

The ratio is $\frac{100}{50}$. The common units, $, divide out and are not written. Write this ratio in lowest terms by dividing the numerator and the denominator by 50.

$$\frac{\$100}{\$50} = \frac{100}{50} = \frac{100 \div 50}{50 \div 50} = \frac{2}{1}$$

13. $1\frac{1}{4}$ to $1\frac{1}{2}$

Write the ratio as $\dfrac{1\frac{1}{4}}{1\frac{1}{2}}$. Then write $1\frac{1}{4}$ and $1\frac{1}{2}$ as improper fractions. Rewrite as a division problem in horizontal format using the ÷ symbol. Then multiply by the reciprocal of the divisor.

$$\frac{1\frac{1}{4}}{1\frac{1}{2}} = \frac{\frac{5}{4}}{\frac{3}{2}} = \frac{5}{4} \div \frac{3}{2} = \frac{5}{\overset{2}{\cancel{4}}} \cdot \frac{\overset{1}{\cancel{2}}}{3} = \frac{5}{6}$$

29.
$$\frac{\text{longest side}}{\text{shortest side}} = \frac{1.8 \text{ meters}}{0.3 \text{ meters}} = \frac{1.8}{0.3}$$
$$= \frac{(1.8)(10)}{(0.3)(10)} = \frac{18}{3}$$
$$= \frac{18 \div 3}{3 \div 3} = \frac{6}{1}$$

The ratio of the length of the longest side to the length of the shortest side is $\frac{6}{1}$.

33. Subtract to find the increase in price.

$$\$12.50 - \$10 = \$2.50$$

Increase in price → $\dfrac{\$2.50}{\$10} = \dfrac{2.50}{10}$
Original price →

$$= \frac{(2.50)(10)}{(10)(10)} = \frac{25}{100}$$
$$= \frac{25 \div 25}{100 \div 25} = \frac{1}{4}$$

The ratio of the increase in price to the original price is $\frac{1}{4}$.

SECTION 6.2 (pages 439–442)

11. Write the rate as a fraction: $\dfrac{7.5 \text{ pounds}}{6 \text{ people}}$

Then divide 7.5 by 6 to find the unit rate.

$$6\overline{)7.5} \to 1.25$$

$$\frac{7.5 \text{ pounds} \div 6}{6 \text{ people} \div 6} = \frac{1.25 \text{ pounds}}{1 \text{ person}}$$

The unit rate is 1.25 pounds/person.

17. Subtract to find the miles traveled.

$$28,396.7 - 28,058.1 = 338.6$$

Then set up the rate. Divide to find the unit rate and round to the nearest tenth.

$$\frac{\text{miles} \to}{\text{per} \to} \frac{338.6 \text{ miles}}{16.2 \text{ gallons}} \approx 20.901 \approx 20.9 \text{ miles per gallon}$$

21.

Size	Cost per Unit	
12 ounces	$\dfrac{\$2.49}{12 \text{ ounces}}$	$\approx \$0.208$
14 ounces	$\dfrac{\$2.89}{14 \text{ ounces}}$	$\approx \$0.206$
18 ounces	$\dfrac{\$3.96}{18 \text{ ounces}}$	$= \$0.22$

The lowest cost per ounce is $0.206, so the best buy is 14 ounces for $2.89.

35. One battery for $1.79 that lasts 3 times longer is like getting 3 batteries for $1.79. So $1.79 ÷ 3 ≈ $0.597 per battery. An eight-pack of AA batteries for $4.99 is $4.99 ÷ 8 ≈ $0.624 per battery. The better buy is the one battery package.

SECTION 6.3 (pages 450–453)

11. $\dfrac{150}{200} = \dfrac{200}{300}$

Write each ratio in lowest terms.

$\dfrac{150 \div 50}{200 \div 50} = \dfrac{3}{4}$ and $\dfrac{200 \div 100}{300 \div 100} = \dfrac{2}{3}$

Because $\dfrac{3}{4}$ is *not* equal to $\dfrac{2}{3}$, the proportion is *false*.

23. $\dfrac{18}{15} = \dfrac{2\frac{5}{6}}{2\frac{1}{2}}$

Cross products:

$15 \cdot 2\frac{5}{6} = \dfrac{\overset{5}{\cancel{15}}}{1} \cdot \dfrac{17}{\underset{2}{\cancel{6}}} = \dfrac{85}{2} = 42\frac{1}{2}$

$18 \cdot 2\frac{1}{2} = \dfrac{\overset{9}{\cancel{18}}}{1} \cdot \dfrac{5}{\underset{1}{\cancel{2}}} = \dfrac{45}{1} = 45$

The cross products are *unequal*, so the proportion is *false*.

35. $\begin{aligned} x \cdot 18 &\leftarrow \\ 42 \cdot 39 &\leftarrow \end{aligned}$ — Cross products

$x \cdot 18 = 42 \cdot 39$ — Show that cross products are equal.

$\dfrac{x \cdot \overset{1}{\cancel{18}}}{\underset{1}{\cancel{18}}} = \dfrac{1638}{18}$ — Divide both sides by 18.

$x = 91$

CHECK

$42 \cdot 39 = 1638$ and $91 \cdot 18 = 1638$

Cross products are equal, so 91 is the correct solution (*not* 1638).

41. $\dfrac{99}{55} = \dfrac{44}{x}$ or $\dfrac{9}{5} = \dfrac{44}{x}$ — Write $\frac{99}{55}$ in lowest terms as $\frac{9}{5}$.

$9 \cdot x = 5 \cdot 44$ — Show that cross products are equal.

$\dfrac{\overset{1}{\cancel{9}} \cdot x}{\underset{1}{\cancel{9}}} = \dfrac{220}{9}$ — Divide both sides by 9.

$x = \dfrac{220}{9}$

$x \approx 24.44$ — Round to the nearest hundredth.

CHECK

$9 \cdot 24.44 = 219.96$ and $5 \cdot 44 = 220$

The cross products are slightly different because you rounded the value of x. However, they are close enough to see that the problem was done correctly and 24.44 is the approximate solution.

49. $\dfrac{2\frac{1}{3}}{1\frac{1}{2}} = \dfrac{x}{2\frac{1}{4}}$

$1\frac{1}{2} \cdot x = 2\frac{1}{3} \cdot 2\frac{1}{4}$ — Show that cross products are equal.

$\dfrac{3}{2} \cdot x = \dfrac{7}{\underset{1}{\cancel{3}}} \cdot \dfrac{\overset{3}{\cancel{9}}}{4}$ — Write mixed numbers as improper fractions.

$\dfrac{3}{2} \cdot x = \dfrac{21}{4}$

$\dfrac{\frac{\cancel{3}}{\cancel{2}} \cdot x}{\frac{\cancel{3}}{\cancel{2}}} = \dfrac{\frac{21}{4}}{\frac{3}{2}}$ — Divide both sides by $\frac{3}{2}$.

$x = \dfrac{21}{4} \div \dfrac{3}{2} = \dfrac{\overset{7}{\cancel{21}}}{\underset{2}{\cancel{4}}} \cdot \dfrac{\overset{1}{\cancel{2}}}{\underset{1}{\cancel{3}}} = \dfrac{7}{2} = 3\frac{1}{2}$

53. $\dfrac{x}{\frac{3}{50}} = \dfrac{0.15}{1\frac{4}{5}}$

Change to decimals: $\dfrac{3}{50}$ is $3 \div 50 = 0.06$

and $1\frac{4}{5}$ is $\dfrac{9}{5}$ or $9 \div 5 = 1.8$

$\dfrac{x}{0.06} = \dfrac{0.15}{1.8}$

$(x)(1.8) = (0.06)(0.15)$ — Show that cross products are equal.

$\dfrac{(x)(\overset{1}{\cancel{1.8}})}{\underset{1}{\cancel{1.8}}} = \dfrac{0.009}{1.8}$ — Divide both sides by 1.8

$x = 0.005$

Change to fractions: 0.15 is $\dfrac{15}{100}$ or

$\dfrac{15 \div 5}{100 \div 5} = \dfrac{3}{20}$

$\dfrac{x}{\frac{3}{50}} = \dfrac{\frac{3}{20}}{1\frac{4}{5}}$

$x \cdot 1\frac{4}{5} = \dfrac{3}{50} \cdot \dfrac{3}{20}$ — Show that cross products are equal.

$\dfrac{x \cdot \overset{1}{\cancel{1\frac{4}{5}}}}{\underset{1}{\cancel{1\frac{4}{5}}}} = \dfrac{\frac{9}{1000}}{1\frac{4}{5}}$ — Divide both sides by $1\frac{4}{5}$.

$x = \dfrac{9}{1000} \div 1\frac{4}{5} = \dfrac{\overset{1}{\cancel{9}}}{\underset{200}{\cancel{1000}}} \cdot \dfrac{\overset{1}{\cancel{5}}}{\underset{1}{\cancel{9}}} = \dfrac{1}{200}$

CHECK

$0.005 = \dfrac{5}{1000}$ or $\dfrac{5 \div 5}{1000 \div 5}$

$= \dfrac{1}{200}$ ← Matches

The two answers are equivalent.

SECTION 6.4 (pages 459–462)

11. *Step 1* The problem is about how many ounces of rice noodles are needed for a given number of servings.

Unknown: ounces needed for 12 servings

Known: 6 ounces needed for 7 servings

Step 2 Let x be the number of ounces needed for 12 servings.

Step 3

$\dfrac{6 \text{ ounces}}{7 \text{ servings}} = \dfrac{x \text{ ounces}}{12 \text{ servings}}$

Step 4

$7 \cdot x = 6 \cdot 12$ — Cross products

$\dfrac{\overset{1}{\cancel{7}} \cdot x}{\underset{1}{\cancel{7}}} = \dfrac{72}{7}$ — Divide both sides by 7.

$x = 10\frac{2}{7} \approx 10$ (rounded)

Step 5 You need about 10 ounces for 12 servings.

Step 6 You are making 12 servings, a little less than twice 7 servings. So you need a little less than twice 6 ounces of noodles; an exact answer of 10 ounces is reasonable.

17. The length of the dining area is the same as the length of the kitchen, which you found to be 14 feet in Exercise 15.

Find the width of the dining area. First find its width on the floor plan.

$4.5 - 2.5$ inches $= 2$ inches on the floor plan

$\dfrac{1 \text{ inch}}{4 \text{ feet}} = \dfrac{2 \text{ inches}}{x \text{ feet}}$

$1 \cdot x = 4 \cdot 2$

$x = 8$

The dining area is 8 feet wide.

23. *Step 1* The problem is about the number of students who will need to take a refresher math course.

Unknown: how many entering students need to take a refresher math course.

Known: 7 out of 10 entering students need to take a refresher math course; 2950 entering students

Step 2 Let x be the number of entering students who need to take a refresher math course.

Step 3

$\dfrac{7 \text{ need refresher}}{10 \text{ entering}} = \dfrac{x \text{ need refresher}}{2950 \text{ entering}}$

Step 4

$\dfrac{7}{10} = \dfrac{x}{2950}$

$10 \cdot x = 7 \cdot 2950$ — Cross products

$\dfrac{\overset{1}{\cancel{10}} \cdot x}{\underset{1}{\cancel{10}}} = \dfrac{20{,}650}{10}$ — Divide both sides by 10.

$x = 2065$

(Continued)

Step 5 2065 entering students will probably need a refresher math course.

Step 6 This is a reasonable answer because it's more than half the students, but not all the students.

Incorrect set-up

$$\frac{10 \text{ entering}}{7 \text{ need refresher}} = \frac{x \text{ need refresher}}{2950 \text{ entering}}$$

$$7 \cdot x = 10 \cdot 2950$$

$$\frac{\overset{1}{\cancel{7}} \cdot x}{\cancel{7}_{1}} = \frac{29{,}500}{7}$$

$$x \approx 4214$$

The *incorrect* set-up gives an *unreasonable* estimate of 4214 entering students; there are only 2950 entering students.

33. Coretta's shadow → $\dfrac{1.05 \text{ meters}}{1.68 \text{ meters}}$
Coretta's height →

$= \dfrac{6.58 \text{ meters}}{x}$ ← tree shadow
← tree height

$(1.05)(x) = (1.68)(6.58)$ Cross products.

$\dfrac{\overset{1}{\cancel{(1.05)}}(x)}{\cancel{1.05}_{1}} = \dfrac{11.0544}{1.05}$ Divide both sides by 1.05

$x = 10.528 \approx 10.53$ Round to hundredths.

The height of the tree is about 10.53 meters.

39. First find the number of calories in a $\frac{1}{2}$-cup serving of bran cereal.

$$\frac{\frac{1}{3} \text{ cup}}{80 \text{ calories}} = \frac{\frac{1}{2} \text{ cup}}{x \text{ calories}}$$

$$\frac{1}{3} \cdot x = 80 \cdot \frac{1}{2}$$ Cross products

$$\frac{\frac{1}{\cancel{3}} \cdot x}{\frac{1}{\cancel{3}}_{1}} = \frac{40}{\frac{1}{3}}$$ Divide both sides by $\frac{1}{3}$.

$$x = 40 \div \frac{1}{3} \text{ or } \frac{40}{1} \cdot \frac{3}{1}$$

$$x = 120 \text{ calories}$$

Then find the number of grams of fiber in a $\frac{1}{2}$-cup serving of bran cereal.

$$\frac{\frac{1}{3} \text{ cup}}{8 \text{ grams of fiber}} = \frac{\frac{1}{2} \text{ cup}}{x \text{ grams of fiber}}$$

$$\frac{1}{3} \cdot x = 8 \cdot \frac{1}{2}$$ Cross products

$$\frac{\frac{1}{\cancel{3}} \cdot x}{\frac{1}{\cancel{3}}_{1}} = \frac{4}{\frac{1}{3}}$$ Divide both sides by $\frac{1}{3}$.

$$x = 4 \div \frac{1}{3} \text{ or } \frac{4}{1} \cdot \frac{3}{1}$$

$$x = 12 \text{ grams of fiber}$$

A $\frac{1}{2}$-cup serving of bran cereal provides 120 calories and 12 grams of fiber.

SECTION 6.5 (pages 473–476)

7. The figure starts at point P and goes on forever in one direction, so it is a ray named $\overrightarrow{PQ}$.

9. The lines are *perpendicular* because they intersect at right angles. The small red square indicates the right angle (90°).

23. Two rays in a straight line pointing in opposite directions measure 180°. An angle that measures 180° is called a *straight angle*.

31. Find the complement of 86° by subtracting. 90° − 86° = 4° ← Complement

35. Find the supplement of 90° by subtracting. 180° − 90° = 90° ← Supplement

37. $\angle SON \cong \angle TOM$ because they are vertical angles.
$\angle TOS \cong \angle MON$ because they are vertical angles.

39. Because $\angle COE$ and $\angle GOH$ are vertical angles, they are also congruent. This means they have the same measure. $\angle COE$ measures 63°, so $\angle GOH$ also measures 63°.
The sum of the measures of $\angle COE$, $\angle AOC$, and $\angle AOH$ equals 180°. Therefore, $\angle AOC$ measures 180° − (63° + 37°) = 180° − 100° = 80°. Since $\angle AOC$ and $\angle GOF$ are vertical angles, they are congruent, so $\angle GOF$ also measures 80°. Since $\angle AOH$ and $\angle EOF$ are vertical angles, they are congruent, so $\angle EOF$ measures 37°.

51. $\angle 6 \cong \angle 1$ (vertical angles), so the measure of $\angle 1$ is also 47°.
$\angle 6 \cong \angle 8$ (corresponding angles), so the measure of $\angle 8$ is also 47°.
$\angle 6 \cong \angle 3$ (alternate interior angles), so the measure of $\angle 3$ is also 47°.
Notice that the exterior sides of $\angle 6$ and $\angle 5$ form a straight angle of 180°. Therefore, $\angle 6$ and $\angle 5$ are supplementary angles and the sum of their measures is 180°. If $\angle 6$ is 47° then $\angle 5$ must be 133° because 180° − 47° = 133°. So the measure of $\angle 5$ is 133°.

$\angle 5 \cong \angle 2$ (vertical angles), so the measure of $\angle 2$ is also 133°.
$\angle 5 \cong \angle 7$ (corresponding angles), so the measure of $\angle 7$ is also 133°.
$\angle 7 \cong \angle 4$ (vertical angles), so the measure of $\angle 4$ is also 133°.

SECTION 6.6 (pages 483–486)

5. Notice that *rotating* $\triangle STU$ makes it possible to slide it on top of $\triangle WXY$ so the triangles match.
The corresponding angles are:
$\angle 1$ and $\angle 6$; $\angle 2$ and $\angle 4$; $\angle 3$ and $\angle 5$
The corresponding sides are:
$\overline{ST}$ and $\overline{YW}$; $\overline{TU}$ and $\overline{WX}$; $\overline{SU}$ and $\overline{YX}$

13. On both triangles, two corresponding angles and the side that connects them measure the same, so the Angle–Side–Angle (ASA) method can be used to prove that the triangles are congruent.

21. You want to find the values of a and b in the smaller triangle. Notice that the side that is 6 mm long in the smaller triangle corresponds to the side that is 12 mm long in the larger triangle.
Set up a ratio of corresponding sides.
$$\frac{6 \text{ mm}}{12 \text{ mm}} = \frac{6}{12} = \frac{1}{2} \text{ in lowest terms}$$

Write a proportion to find a.
$$\frac{a}{10} = \frac{1}{2}$$
$$a \cdot 2 = 10 \cdot 1$$ Cross products are equal.
$$\frac{a \cdot \overset{1}{\cancel{2}}}{\cancel{2}_{1}} = \frac{10}{2}$$ Divide both sides by 2.
$$a = 5 \text{ mm}$$

Write a proportion to find b.
$$\frac{b}{6} = \frac{1}{2}$$
$$b \cdot 2 = 6 \cdot 1$$ Cross products are equal.
$$\frac{b \cdot \overset{1}{\cancel{2}}}{\cancel{2}_{1}} = \frac{6}{2}$$ Divide both sides by 2.
$$b = 3 \text{ mm}$$

27. Since triangles CDE and FGH are similar and all of the sides of CDE are the same length, all the sides of FGH are also the same length. Therefore, each missing side of triangle FGH is 8 cm.
Now add the lengths of all three sides to find the perimeter of triangle FGH.
$$P = 8 \text{ cm} + 8 \text{ cm} + 8 \text{ cm}$$
$$P = 24 \text{ cm}$$

SOLUTIONS

Set up a ratio of corresponding sides to find the height (h) of triangle FGH.

$$\frac{10.4}{12} = \frac{h}{8}$$

$(12)(h) = (10.4)(8)$ Cross products are equal.

$\dfrac{(\cancel{12})(h)}{\cancel{12}} = \dfrac{83.2}{12}$ Divide both sides by 12.

$h \approx 6.9$ cm   Rounded

Area of triangle FGH

$= 0.5 \cdot b \cdot h$

$\approx (0.5)(8 \text{ cm})(6.9 \text{ cm})$

$\approx 27.6 \text{ cm}^2$ Approximate area because height was rounded.

33. The side 50 m long in the smaller triangle corresponds to the side with length n in the larger triangle.

Write a proportion to find n.

$$\frac{50}{n} = \frac{100}{100 + 120} = \frac{100}{220}$$

Write $\dfrac{100}{220}$ in lowest terms as $\dfrac{5}{11}$.

$$\frac{50}{n} = \frac{5}{11}$$

$5 \cdot n = 50 \cdot 11$ Cross products

$\dfrac{\cancel{5} \cdot n}{\cancel{5}} = \dfrac{550}{5}$ Divide both sides by 5.

$n = 110$ m

The length of the lake is 110 m.

CHAPTER 7 Percent

SECTION 7.1 (pages 514–519)

9. $140\% = 140.\% = 1.40$ or 1.4

Drop the percent symbol and move the decimal point two places to the left.

15. $0.5\% = 00.5\% = 0.005$

0 is attached so the decimal point can be moved two places to the left. Drop the percent symbol.

19. $0.5 = 0.50 = 50\%$

— Decimal point *not* written with whole number percents

0 is attached so the decimal point can be moved two places to the right. Attach a percent symbol.

27. $2 = 2.00 = 200\%$

Two zeros are attached so the decimal point can be moved two places to the right. Attach a percent symbol.

---

41. $6.25\% = \dfrac{6.25}{100} = \dfrac{(6.25)(100)}{(100)(100)}$

$\qquad = \dfrac{625 \div 625}{10,000 \div 625} = \dfrac{1}{16}$

Drop the % symbol, and write 6.25 over 100. Multiply the numerator and denominator by 100 to get whole numbers. Then write the fraction in lowest terms.

43. $16\dfrac{2}{3}\% = \dfrac{16\frac{2}{3}}{100} = \dfrac{\frac{50}{3}}{100}$

$\qquad = \dfrac{50}{3} \div \dfrac{100}{1} = \dfrac{\cancel{50}}{3} \cdot \dfrac{1}{\cancel{100}} = \dfrac{1}{6}$

Drop the % symbol and write $16\dfrac{2}{3}$ over 100. Rewrite $16\dfrac{2}{3}$ as the improper fraction $\dfrac{50}{3}$. Rewrite the complex fraction using the $\div$ symbol for division. Then follow the steps for dividing fractions.

57. Multiply $\dfrac{3}{8}$ by 100%.

$\left(\dfrac{3}{8}\right)(100\%) = \left(\dfrac{3}{8}\right)\left(\dfrac{100}{1}\%\right)$

$\qquad = \dfrac{3 \cdot \cancel{4} \cdot 25}{2 \cdot \cancel{4} \cdot 1}\% = \dfrac{75}{2}\%$

$\qquad = 37\dfrac{1}{2}\%$ or 37.5%

61. Multiply $\dfrac{5}{9}$ by 100%.

$\left(\dfrac{5}{9}\right)(100\%) = \left(\dfrac{5}{9}\right)\left(\dfrac{100}{1}\%\right) = \dfrac{500}{9}\%$

$\qquad = 55\dfrac{5}{9}\%$ (exactly), or

$\qquad\qquad\qquad 55.6\%$ (rounded)

89. $1.5 = \dfrac{150}{100} = \dfrac{150 \div 50}{100 \div 50}$

$\qquad = \dfrac{3}{2} = 1\dfrac{1}{2}$ ← Mixed number

$1.50 = 150\%$ ← Percent

99. There are 4 canines and 28 total teeth.

$\dfrac{4}{28} = \dfrac{4 \div 4}{28 \div 4} = \dfrac{1}{7}$ ← Fraction

$\dfrac{1}{7} = \left(\dfrac{1}{7}\right)(100\%) = \dfrac{100}{7}\%$

$\qquad = 14\dfrac{2}{7}\%$ (exactly), or 14.3% (rounded)

113. (a) 50% of $285 is half of $285 or $285 \div 2 = \$142.50$

(b) John will have to pay the remaining 50% of the tuition $(100\% - 50\% = 50\%)$.

(c) Since John has to pay 50% (half) of the tuition, he will pay $\$285 \div 2 = \$142.50$

SECTION 7.2 (pages 526–527)

13. $\underset{\text{Percent}}{\underline{250\%}}$ of $\underset{\substack{\text{Whole} \\ \text{(follows } of\,)}}{\underline{7 \text{ hours}}}$ is $\underset{\substack{\text{Part} \\ \text{(unknown)}}}{\underline{\text{how long?}}}$

Percent $\rightarrow \dfrac{250}{100} = \dfrac{n}{7} \leftarrow$ Part (unknown)
Always 100 $\rightarrow \qquad\qquad \leftarrow$ Whole

Step 1 $\quad \dfrac{250}{100} = \dfrac{n}{7}$

Step 2 $\quad 100 \cdot n = 250 \cdot 7$

$\qquad\qquad 100 \cdot n = 1750$

Step 3 $\quad \dfrac{\cancel{100} \cdot n}{\cancel{100}} = \dfrac{1750}{100}$

$\qquad\qquad\qquad n = 17.5$

250% of 7 hours is 17.5 hours.

21. $\underset{\text{Part}}{\underline{105 \text{ employees}}}$ is $\underset{\substack{\text{Percent} \\ \text{(unknown)}}}{\underline{\text{what percent}}}$ of $\underset{\substack{\text{Whole} \\ \text{(follows } of\,)}}{\underline{54 \text{ employees?}}}$

Percent (unknown) $\rightarrow \dfrac{p}{100} = \dfrac{105}{54} \leftarrow$ Part
Always 100 $\rightarrow \qquad\qquad\qquad \leftarrow$ Whole

Step 1 $\quad \dfrac{p}{100} = \dfrac{105}{54}$

Step 2 $\quad p \cdot 54 = 100 \cdot 105$

$\qquad\qquad p \cdot 54 = 10,500$

Step 3 $\quad \dfrac{p \cdot \cancel{54}}{\cancel{54}} = \dfrac{10,500}{54}$

$\qquad\qquad\qquad p \approx 194.4$ Round to nearest tenth.

105 employees is 194.4% (rounded) of 54 employees.

23. $\underset{\text{Part}}{\underline{\$0.33}}$ is $\underset{\text{Percent}}{\underline{5\%}}$ of $\underset{\substack{\text{Whole (unknown);} \\ \text{(follows } of\,)}}{\underline{\text{what amount?}}}$

Percent $\rightarrow \dfrac{5}{100} = \dfrac{0.33}{n} \leftarrow$ Part
Always 100 $\rightarrow \qquad\qquad\qquad \leftarrow$ Whole (unknown)

Step 1 $\quad \dfrac{5}{100} = \dfrac{0.33}{n}$

Step 2 $\quad 5 \cdot n = 100 \cdot 0.33$

$\qquad\qquad 5 \cdot n = 33$

Step 3 $\quad \dfrac{\cancel{5} \cdot n}{\cancel{5}} = \dfrac{33}{5}$

$\qquad\qquad\qquad n = 6.6$

$0.33 is 5% of $6.60.

SECTION 7.3 (pages 534–537)

5. To find 10% of 45 pounds, divide 45 by 10. To divide by 10, move the decimal point one place to the left.

10% of $45. = 4.5$ pounds.

Choose 4.5 pounds.

23. Write $12\frac{1}{2}\%$ as 12.5%. Then move the decimal point two places to the left.

12.5%	of	what number of people	is	135 people
0.125	•	n	=	135

$$\frac{(0.125)(n)}{0.125} = \frac{135}{0.125}$$

$$n = 1080$$

$12\frac{1}{2}\%$ of 1080 people is 135 people.

31.

What percent	of	$264	is	$330?
p	•	264	=	330

$$\frac{p \cdot 264}{264} = \frac{330}{264}$$

$$p = 1.25 = 125\%$$

125% of $264 is $330.

37.

$1.48	is	what percent	of	$74?
1.48	=	p	•	74

$$\frac{1.48}{74} = \frac{(p)(74)}{74}$$

$$0.02 = p$$

$$2\% = p$$

$1.48 is 2% of $74.

45.

225.%	of	what number of gallons	is	11.25 gallons?
2.25	•	n	=	11.25

$$\frac{(2.25)(n)}{2.25} = \frac{11.25}{2.25}$$

$$n = 5$$

225% of 5 gallons is 11.25 gallons.

SECTION 7.4 (pages 546–549)

11. *Step 1* The problem is about raising money for scholarships.

Unknown: the percent of goal raised
Known: the goal was $50,000; $69,000 was actually raised.

Step 2 Let p be the percent of the goal that was raised.

Step 3 Use the percent equation.

percent • whole = part

$$p \cdot 50{,}000 = 69{,}000$$

Step 4

$$\frac{p \cdot 50{,}000}{50{,}000} = \frac{69{,}000}{50{,}000} \quad \text{Divide both sides by 50,000.}$$

$$p = 1.38$$

Multiply the solution by 100% to change it from a decimal to a percent.

$$1.38 = 138\%$$

Step 5 The society raised 138% of their goal.

Step 6 The solution 138% makes sense because the amount raised was *greater* than the goal, so the percent should be *greater* than 100%.

15. *Step 1* The problem is about shots tried by a basketball player.

Unknown: the number of shots tried
Known: 307 shots were made; 307 is 52.7% of the shots tried

Step 2 Let n be the number of shots tried.

Step 3 The percent is given in the problem: 52.7%. The key word "of" appears right after 52.7%, so you can use the phrase "52.7% *of* the shots he tried" to help you write one side of the equation.

52.7%	of	the shots he tried
0.527	•	$n = 307$

Step 4

$$\frac{(0.527)(n)}{0.527} = \frac{307}{0.527} \quad \text{Divide both sides by 0.527}$$

$$n \approx 583$$

Step 5 He tried 583 shots (rounded).

Step 6 The solution of 583 shots tried makes sense because 50% of 583 shots is about 292 shots, which is close to the number given in the problem (307 shots).

17. *Step 1* This problem is about mileage an SUV gets with new tires.

Unknown: the amount of increase in mileage
Known: supposed to get 15% better mileage than old mileage of 20.6 mpg

Step 2 Let n be the amount of increase in mileage with the new tires.

Step 3 Write 15% as 0.15 in decimal form.

Percent	•	Original mileage	=	Amount of increase
0.15	•	20.6	=	n
		3.09	=	n

Step 4 The new tires should increase her mileage by 3.09 miles per gallon.

Step 5 Her new mileage should be

$$20.6 + 3.09 = 23.69 \approx 23.7 \text{ miles per}$$
gallon (rounded)

Step 6 The solution of 23.7 miles per gallon is reasonable because $23.7 - 20.6 = 3.1$, which is about 15% of 20.6 (3 is 15% of 20).

23. *Step 1* This problem is about finding the percent decrease in the cost of a Model T car.

Unknown: the percent of decrease
Known: $825 was the original cost; $290 was the new cost

Step 2 Let p be the percent decrease.

Step 3 First subtract to find the *amount* of decrease. Then write an equation.

Amount
of decrease = $825 − $290 = $535

percent	of	original cost	=	amount of decrease
p	•	$825	=	$535

Step 4

$$\frac{p \cdot 825}{825} = \frac{535}{825} \quad \text{Divide both sides by 825.}$$

$$p \approx 0.648 = 64.8\%$$

Step 5 The percent of decrease was 64.8% (rounded).

Step 6 The solution of 64.8% is reasonable because the amount of decrease was greater than half the original value and less than three-quarters of the original value. So, the percent should be between 50% and 75%.

29. *Step 1* This problem is about the percent increase in the number of species threatened with extinction in the United States.

Unknown: the percent of increase
Known: there were 78 species on the list in 1967; there were 588 species on the list in 2011

Step 2 Let p be the percent of increase

Step 3 First subtract to find the *amount* of increase. $588 - 78 = 510$

percent	of	original number	=	amount of increase
p	•	78	=	510

Step 4

$$\frac{p \cdot 78}{78} = \frac{510}{78} \quad \text{Divide both sides by 78.}$$

$$p \approx 6.54 = 654\%$$

Step 5 The percent of increase is 654% (rounded).

Step 6 The solution of 654% is reasonable because the amount of increase is more than six times as much as the original number (6 times is 600%).

SECTION 7.5 (pages 556–561)

9. Cost of item is \$12,600

Tax rate is unknown (p)

Sales tax is \$567

tax rate	•	cost of item	=	sales tax
↓		↓		↓
p	•	12,600	=	567

$$\frac{(p)(12,600)}{12,600} = \frac{567}{12,600} \quad \text{Divide both sides by 12,600.}$$

$$p = 0.045 = 4.5\%$$

The tax rate is 4.5% or $4\frac{1}{2}\%$.

Total cost = \$12,600 + \$567 = \$13,167

11. The bill of \$32.17 rounds to \$30.

Estimate of 15% tip:

10% of \$30. is \$3 and 5% of \$30 is half of \$3, or \$1.50. An estimate is \$3 + \$1.50 = \$4.50.

Exact 15% tip:

Percent • whole = part

$(0.15)(\$32.17) = \$4.8255 \approx \$4.83$ (rounded)

Estimate of 20% tip:

10% of \$30. is \$3 and 20% is 2 times \$3, or \$6. An estimate is \$6.

Exact 20% tip:

Percent • whole = part

$(0.20)(\$32.17) = \$6.434 \approx \$6.43$ (rounded)

21. Original price is \$17.50

Rate of discount is 25.% = 0.25

rate of discount • original price = amount of discount

$(0.25)(17.50) = n$

$\$4.375 = n$

The amount of discount is \$4.375 $\approx$ \$4.38. Then, original price − amount of discount = sale price

\$17.50 − \$4.38 = \$13.12

The sale price is \$13.12.

31. \$17,800 at $7\frac{3}{4}\%$ for 8 months

The principal is \$17,800. The rate is $7\frac{3}{4}\%$ or 7.75%. Then 07.75% = 0.0775 as a decimal.

The time is 8 months, which is $\frac{8}{12}$ of a year. Use the formula $I = prt$.

$$I = p \cdot r \cdot t$$

$$= (17{,}800)(0.0775)\left(\frac{8}{12}\right)$$

$$= (1379.5) \quad \left(\frac{8}{12}\right)$$

$$= \left(\frac{1379.5}{1}\right)\left(\frac{8}{12}\right)$$

$$= \frac{11{,}036}{12} \approx 919.67 \text{ (rounded)}$$

The interest is \$919.67.

amount due = principal + interest

$\qquad = \$17{,}800 + \$919.67$

$\qquad = \$18{,}719.67$

The total amount due is \$18,719.67.

37. Cost of item is \$24.99

Tax rate is $6\frac{1}{2}\%$ or 06.5% = 0.065

tax rate • cost of item = sales tax

$0.065 \cdot 24.99 = n$

$(0.065)(24.99) = n$

$1.62 \approx n$

The sales tax (rounded) is \$1.62.

Total cost = \$24.99 + \$1.62 = \$26.61

The total cost of the headset is \$26.61.

53. Camcorder: original price of \$287.95; 65% off

Write 65.% as 0.65 in decimal form.

amount of discount = $(0.65)(\$287.95) \approx \$187.17$

sale price = \$287.95 − \$187.17 = \$100.78

sales tax = 0.06(\$100.78) $\approx$ \$6.05

Total = \$100.78 + \$6.05 = \$106.83

Jeans: 2 pairs at \$48 each; 45% off; write 45.% as 0.45

amount of discount = $(0.45)(\$48) = \$21.60$

sale price = \$48 − \$21.60 = \$26.40

sales tax: no tax on clothing

Total for 2 pairs = 2(\$26.40) = \$52.80

Ring: original price of \$95; 30% off; write 30.% as 0.30

amount of discount = $(0.30)(\$95) = \$28.50$

sale price = \$95 − \$28.50 = \$66.50

sales tax = $(0.06)(\$66.50) = \$3.99$

Total = \$66.50 + \$3.99 = \$70.49

Total Bill = \$106.83 + \$52.80 + \$70.49 = \$230.12

CHAPTER 8 Measurement

SECTION 8.1 (pages 584–587)

25. 3 in. to feet

$$\frac{\overset{1}{\cancel{3} \text{ in.}}}{1} \cdot \frac{1 \text{ ft}}{\underset{4}{\cancel{12} \text{ in.}}} = \frac{1}{4} \text{ ft or } 1 \div 4 = 0.25 \text{ ft}$$

35. $4\frac{1}{4}$ gal to quarts

$$\frac{4\frac{1}{4} \text{ gal}}{1} \cdot \frac{4 \text{ qt}}{1 \text{ gal}} = \frac{17}{\cancel{4}} \cdot \frac{\overset{1}{\cancel{4}}}{1} \text{ qt} = 17 \text{ qt}$$

43. 6 days to seconds

$$\frac{6 \text{ days}}{1} \cdot \frac{24 \text{ hr}}{1 \text{ day}} \cdot \frac{60 \text{ min}}{1 \text{ hr}} \cdot \frac{60 \text{ sec}}{1 \text{ min}}$$

$$= 6 \cdot 24 \cdot 60 \cdot 60 \text{ sec}$$

$$= 518{,}400 \text{ sec}$$

55. Step 1

The problem asks for the price per pound of strawberries.

Step 2

Convert ounces to pounds. Then divide the cost by the number of pounds.

Step 3

To estimate, round \$2.29 to \$2. Then, there are 16 oz in a pound, so 20 oz is a little more than 1 lb. Thus, \$2 ÷ 1 = \$2 per pound is our estimate.

Step 4

Use a unit fraction to convert 20 oz to pounds.

$$\frac{\overset{5}{\cancel{20} \text{ oz}}}{1} \cdot \frac{1 \text{ lb}}{\underset{4}{\cancel{16} \text{ oz}}} = \frac{5}{4} \text{ lb} = 1.25 \text{ lb}$$

$$\begin{matrix} \text{Cost} \Rightarrow \\ \text{per} \Rightarrow \\ \text{pound} \Rightarrow \end{matrix} \frac{\$2.29}{1.25 \text{ lb}} = 1.832 \approx 1.83$$

Step 5

The strawberries are \$1.83 per pound (to the nearest cent).

Step 6

The exact answer, \$1.83, is close to our estimate of \$2.

61. (a) Find the total number of cups per week. Then convert cups to quarts.

$$\frac{2}{3} \cdot 15 \cdot 5 = \frac{2}{\cancel{3}} \cdot \frac{\overset{5}{\cancel{15}}}{1} \cdot \frac{5}{1} = 50 \text{ cups}$$

$$\frac{\overset{25}{\cancel{50} \text{ cups}}}{1} \cdot \frac{1 \text{ pt}}{\underset{1}{\cancel{2} \text{ cups}}} \cdot \frac{1 \text{ qt}}{2 \text{ pt}} = \frac{25}{2} \text{ qt}$$

$$= 12\frac{1}{2} \text{ qt}$$

The center needs $12\frac{1}{2}$ qt of milk per week.

(Continued)

(b) Convert quarts to gallons.

$$\frac{12\frac{1}{2}\text{ qt}}{1} \cdot \frac{1\text{ gal}}{4\text{ qt}}$$

$$= \frac{25}{2} \cdot \frac{1}{4}\text{ gal} = 3.125\text{ gal}$$

The center should order 4 gallon containers, because you can't buy part of a container.

SECTION 8.2 (pages 593–594)

21. A paper clip is about 3 cm long. Both meters and kilometers would be much too long, and 3 mm is a very tiny length. (see ruler in this section).

25. 7 m to cm using a unit fraction:

$$\frac{7\text{ m}}{1} \cdot \frac{100\text{ cm}}{1\text{ m}} = 7 \cdot 100\text{ cm} = 700\text{ cm}$$

33. 400 mm to cm using the conversion line:
From mm to cm is *one* place to the *left* on the conversion line, so move the decimal point *one* place to the *left* also.
400. mm = 40.0 cm   or   40 cm

37. 82 cm to m
From cm to m is *two* places to the *left* on the conversion line, so move the decimal point *two* places to the *left* also.
82. cm = 0.82 m
0.82 m is less than 1 m, so 82 cm is **less than** 1 m. The difference in length is 1 m − 0.82 m = 0.18 m or 100 cm − 82 cm = 18 cm

45. 5.6 mm to km

$$\frac{5.6\text{ mm}}{1} \cdot \frac{1\text{ m}}{1000\text{ mm}} \cdot \frac{1\text{ km}}{1000\text{ m}}$$

$$= \frac{5.6}{1,000,000}\text{ km}$$

$$= 0.0000056\text{ km}$$

SECTION 8.3 (pages 601–604)

9. Lori caught a small sunfish weighing 150 g. Weight is measured in mg, g, or kg. 150 mg is less than the weight of a dollar bill, and 150 kg would be more than 300 pounds. So 150 g is correct.

35. 8 mL to L using a unit fraction:

$$\frac{8\text{ mL}}{1} \cdot \frac{1\text{ L}}{1000\text{ mL}} = \frac{8}{1000}\text{ L} = 0.008\text{ L}$$

41. 5.2 kg to g using the conversion line:
From kg to g is *three* places to the *right* on the conversion line.
5.200 kg = 5200. g   or   5200 g

67. Convert 900 mL to L.

$$\frac{900\text{ mL}}{1} \cdot \frac{1\text{ L}}{1000\text{ mL}} = \frac{900}{1000}\text{ L} = 0.9\text{ L}$$

On average, we breathe in and out roughly 0.9 L of air every 10 seconds.

73. Convert 1 kg to g.

$$\frac{1\text{ kg}}{1} \cdot \frac{1000\text{ g}}{1\text{ kg}} = 1000\text{ g}$$

Divide the 1000 g by the weight of 1 nickel.

$$\frac{1000\text{ g}}{5\text{ g}} = 200$$

There are 200 nickels in 1 kg of nickels.

SECTION 8.4 (pages 609–610)

9. Multiply to find the total length of pencil lead in mm, then convert mm to cm.
60 mm • 30 = 1800 mm of pencil lead

$$\frac{\overset{180}{1800}\text{ mm}}{1} \cdot \frac{1\text{ cm}}{\underset{1}{10}\text{ mm}} = 180\text{ cm}$$

The total length of pencil lead is 180 cm. Divide to find the cost per cm.

$$\frac{\$3.29}{180\text{ cm}} \approx \$0.0183/\text{cm} \approx \$0.02/\text{cm}$$

The cost is $0.02/cm (rounded).

15. Three cups a day for one week is 3 • 7 = 21 cups in one week.

$$\frac{21\text{ cups}}{1} \cdot \frac{90\text{ mg}}{1\text{ cup}} = 1890\text{ mg}$$

Convert 1890 mg to g.

$$\frac{1890\text{ mg}}{1} \cdot \frac{1\text{ g}}{1000\text{ mg}} = 1.89\text{ g}$$

Agnete consumes 1.89 g of caffeine in one week.

SECTION 8.5 (pages 615–618)

5. 80 m to feet

$$\frac{80\text{ m}}{1} \cdot \frac{3.28\text{ ft}}{1\text{ m}} \approx 262.4\text{ ft}$$

19. Convert 0.5 in. to centimeters.

$$\frac{0.5\text{ in.}}{1} \cdot \frac{2.54\text{ cm}}{1\text{ in.}} = 1.27\text{ cm} \approx 1.3\text{ cm}$$
$$\text{(rounded)}$$

The dwarf gobie is about 1.3 cm long.

29. −4 °F

$$C = \frac{5(-4 - 32)}{9} = \frac{5(-36)}{9}$$

$$= \frac{-180}{9} = -20$$

−4 °F = −20 °C

37. (a) Since the comfort range of the boots is from 24 °C to 4 °C, you would wear

these boots in pleasant weather—above freezing, but not hot.

(b) Change 24 °C to Fahrenheit.

$$F = \frac{9C}{5} + 32 = \frac{9(24)}{5} + 32$$

$$= \frac{216}{5} + 32$$

$$= 43.2 + 32 = 75.2$$

Thus, 24 °C ≈ 75 °F (rounded).

Change 4 °C to Fahrenheit.

$$F = \frac{9C}{5} + 32 = \frac{9(4)}{5} + 32$$

$$= \frac{36}{5} + 32$$

$$= 7.2 + 32 = 39.2$$

Thus, 4 °C ≈ 39 °F (rounded).
The boots are designed for Fahrenheit temperatures of about 75 °F to about 39 °F.

(c) The range of metric temperatures in January would depend on where you live. In Minnesota, it's 0 °C to −40 °C, and in California it's 24 °C to 0 °C.

47. Fuel left after landing

$$\frac{2\text{ fl oz}}{1} \cdot \frac{1\text{ qt}}{32\text{ fl oz}} \cdot \frac{0.95\text{ L}}{1\text{ qt}} \cdot \frac{1000\text{ mL}}{1\text{ L}}$$

$$= \frac{1900}{32}\text{ mL} = 59.375\text{ mL} \approx 59.4\text{ mL}$$

CHAPTER 9 Graphs

SECTION 9.1 (pages 637–640)

11. To find the average number of points scored per game, divide the number in the points column by the number in the games column for each player.
Round answers to the nearest tenth to match other numbers in that column in the table.

Shaquille O'Neal: $\dfrac{28,596}{1207} \approx 23.7$

Kobe Bryant: $\dfrac{28,316}{1117} \approx 25.4$

19. (a) $\dfrac{322\text{ calories}}{110\text{ pounds}} = \dfrac{x\text{ calories}}{125\text{ pounds}}$

Find the cross products.
$$(110)(x) = (322)(125)$$
Divide both sides by 110.

$$\frac{\overset{1}{110}x}{\underset{1}{110}} = \frac{40,250}{110}$$

$$x \approx 366\text{ (rounded)}$$

The person would burn approximately 366 calories.

(b) $\dfrac{210 \text{ calories}}{110 \text{ pounds}} = \dfrac{x \text{ calories}}{125 \text{ pounds}}$

Find the cross products.

$$(110)(x) = (210)(125)$$

Divide both sides by 110.

$$\dfrac{\overset{1}{\cancel{110}}x}{\underset{1}{\cancel{110}}} = \dfrac{26{,}250}{110}$$

$$x \approx 239 \text{ (rounded)}$$

The person would burn approximately 239 calories.

29. There are 29.5 symbols in all.

29.5 (10 million) = 295 million

The total number is 295 million or 295,000,000 arrivals and departures.

SECTION 9.2 (pages 645–649)

13. Picked Friday or Saturday $\rightarrow$ $\dfrac{180 + 120}{20}$
Picked Monday $\rightarrow$

$$= \dfrac{300}{20} = \dfrac{300 \div 20}{20 \div 20} = \dfrac{15}{1}$$

19. The percent for "runs and hides" is 35%.

percent $\cdot$ whole = part

35% $\cdot$ 400 = n

(0.35) (400) = n

140 = n

The number of people who said "runs and hides" is 140.

The number of people who said "watches from a safe perch" is 76 (from Exercise 16). $140 - 76 = 64$ so 64 fewer people said "watches from a safe perch" than said "runs and hides."

31. (a) Total sales = \$12,500 + \$40,000 + \$60,000 + \$50,000 + \$37,500 = \$200,000

(b) Adventure classes = \$12,500

percent of total = $\dfrac{12{,}500}{200{,}000} = 0.0625$

$= 6.25\%$

Grocery/provision sales = \$40,000

percent of total = $\dfrac{40{,}000}{200{,}000} = 0.2 = 20\%$

Equipment rentals = \$60,000

percent of total = $\dfrac{60{,}000}{200{,}000} = 0.3 = 30\%$

Rafting tours = \$50,000

percent of total = $\dfrac{50{,}000}{200{,}000} = 0.25 = 25\%$

Equipment sales = \$37,500

percent of total = $\dfrac{37{,}500}{200{,}000} = 0.1875$

$= 18.75\%$

(c) Adventure classes:

number of degrees = $(0.0625)(360°)$
$= 22.5°$

Grocery/provision sales:

number of degrees = $(0.2)(360°) = 72°$

Equipment rentals:

number of degrees = $(0.3)(360°) = 108°$

Rafting tours:

number of degrees = $(0.25)(360°) = 90°$

Equipment sales:

number of degrees = $(0.1875)(360°)$
$= 67.5°$

(d)

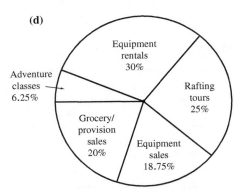

SECTION 9.3 (pages 653–656)

7. 61% of the total sales of \$4.4 billion for toys and games was spent online.

percent $\cdot$ whole = part

61% $\cdot$ \$4.4 billion = n

(0.61) (\$4.4 billion) = n

\$2.684 billion = n

\$2.7 billion, rounded to the nearest tenth, was spent online.

15. The number of unemployed workers decreased from 120,000 in July 2010 to 80,000 in December 2010. The amount of decrease was 40,000 workers.

percent of July 2010 = Amount
unemployed workers of decrease

p $\cdot$ 120,000 = 40,000

$$\dfrac{p \cdot \overset{1}{\cancel{120{,}000}}}{\underset{1}{\cancel{120{,}000}}} = \dfrac{40{,}000}{120{,}000}$$

$$p = \dfrac{4}{12}$$

$$p \approx 0.333 \approx 33\%$$

The percent of decrease was 33% (rounded).

27. The amount of increase in sales from 1995 to 2000 was 144.6 million − 62.3 million = 82.3 million or 82,300,000 PCs.

percent of 1995 = amount
sales of increase

p $\cdot$ 62.3 = 82.3

$$\dfrac{p \cdot \overset{1}{\cancel{62.3}}}{\underset{1}{\cancel{62.3}}} = \dfrac{82.3}{62.3}$$

$$p \approx 1.32 = 132\%$$

The percent of increase was 132% (rounded).

37. For 2009: Profit is \$10,000; sales are \$35,000

profit is what percent of sales

10,000 = p $\cdot$ 35,000

$$\dfrac{10{,}000}{35{,}000} = \dfrac{p \cdot \overset{1}{\cancel{35{,}000}}}{\underset{1}{\cancel{35{,}000}}}$$

$$p \approx 0.286 \approx 29\% \text{ (rounded)}$$

For 2010: Profit is \$5,000; sales are \$25,000

$$\dfrac{\$5{,}000}{\$25{,}000} = p$$

$$p = 0.20 = 20\%$$

For 2011: Profit is \$5,000; sales are \$30,000

$$\dfrac{\$5{,}000}{\$30{,}000} = p$$

$$p \approx 0.166 \approx 17\% \text{ (rounded)}$$

For 2012: Profit is \$15,000; sales are \$40,000

$$\dfrac{\$15{,}000}{\$40{,}000} = p$$

$$p \approx 0.375 \approx 38\% \text{ (rounded)}$$

SECTION 9.4 (pages 661–662)

9. For $(-3, -7)$ the pattern is $(-, -)$, so the point is in Quadrant III.

The point corresponding to $(0, 4)$ is on the y-axis, so it is not in any quadrant.

For $(10, -16)$ the pattern is $(+, -)$, so the point is in Quadrant IV.

For $(-9, 5)$ the pattern is $(-, +)$, so the point is in Quadrant II.

11. (a) Any *positive* number, because points in Quadrant II have the pattern $(-, +)$.

(b) Any *negative* number, because points in Quadrant IV have the pattern $(+, -)$.

(c) 0, because points that are not in any quadrant have a zero as one of the numbers in the ordered pair.

(d) Any *negative* number, because points in Quadrant III have the pattern $(-, -)$.

(e) Any *positive* number, because points in Quadrant I have the pattern $(+, +)$.

SECTION 9.5 (pages 671–676)

5. $x + y = -1$

To complete the table, replace x in the equation with each value listed for x.

When x is 0: $0 + y = -1$ so y must be -1.

This gives the ordered pair $(0, -1)$.

When x is 1: $1 + y = -1$ so y must be -2.

This gives the ordered pair $(1, -2)$.

When x is 2: $2 + y = -1$ so y must be -3.

This gives the ordered pair $(2, -3)$.

x	y	Ordered Pair (x, y)
0	-1	$(0, -1)$
1	-2	$(1, -2)$
2	-3	$(2, -3)$

Plot $(0, -1)$ and $(1, -2)$ and $(2, -3)$ on the grid. Draw a line connecting the points and extend it in both directions.

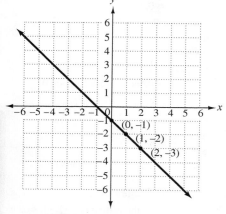

All points on the line are solutions so there are many possibilities for solutions.

Two other possible solutions are $(-1, 0)$ and $(-2, 1)$.

To check that $(-1, 0)$ and $(-2, 1)$ are solutions, substitute into the original equation.

21. $y = -2x + 3$

x	$y = -2 \cdot x + 3$	(x, y)
0	$-2(0) + 3$ is 3	$(0, 3)$
1	$-2(1) + 3$ is 1	$(1, 1)$
2	$-2(2) + 3$ is -1	$(2, -1)$

See graph at top of next column.

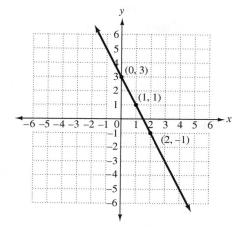

25. $y = \dfrac{1}{4}x$

One possible table that uses 0 and multiples of 4 as values of x is shown.

x	$y = \dfrac{1}{4} \cdot x$	(x, y)
0	$\dfrac{1}{4}(0)$ is 0	$(0, 0)$
4	$\dfrac{1}{4}(4)$ is 1	$(4, 1)$
-4	$\dfrac{1}{4}(-4)$ is -1	$(-4, -1)$

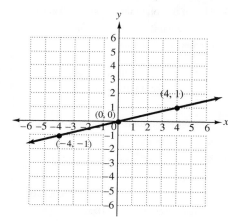

The line has a positive slope (it rises from left to right).

CHAPTER 10 Exponents and Polynomials

SECTION 10.1 (pages 701–702)

7. Since (-2) occurs as a factor five times, the base is (-2) and the exponent is 5. Make sure to *write* -2 *in parentheses* in the exponential expression.

$$\underbrace{(-2)(-2)(-2)(-2)(-2)}_{5 \text{ factors of } (-2)} = (-2)^5$$

35. Recall that $-6p^5$ means $-6 \cdot p^5$ and $-7p^5$ means $-7 \cdot p^5$. Now use the associative and commutative properties and the product rule.

$$(-6p^5)(-7p^5) = (-6)(-7) \cdot (p^5 \cdot p^5)$$
$$= 42p^{5+5}$$
$$= 42p^{10}$$

57. $(-2x^2y)^3 = (-2)^3(x^2)^3(y^1)^3$ Power rule (b)

$$= (-2)^3 x^{2\cdot3} y^{1\cdot3}$$ Power rule (a)

$$= (-2)^3 x^6 y^3$$

61. Use the formula for the area of a rectangle, $A = lw$, where l is $4x^3$ and w is $3x^2$.

$$A = (4x^3)(3x^2)$$
$$= 4 \cdot 3 \cdot x^3 \cdot x^2$$
$$= 12x^{3+2} = 12x^5$$

SECTION 10.2 (pages 707–708)

9. $-9^0 = -(9^0) = -(1) = -1$

23. $5^{-1} + 3^{-1} = \dfrac{1}{5} + \dfrac{1}{3}$ Definition of negative exponent

$$= \dfrac{3}{15} + \dfrac{5}{15} = \dfrac{8}{15}$$ Use the LCD of 15.

37. $\dfrac{m^7}{m^8} = m^{7-8} = m^{7+(-8)} = m^{-1}$

$$= \dfrac{1}{m^1} \quad \text{or} \quad \dfrac{1}{m}$$

43. $\dfrac{2^{-10}}{2^{-2}} = 2^{-10-(-2)} = 2^{-10+2} = 2^{-8} = \dfrac{1}{2^8}$

47. $\dfrac{10^6}{10^{-4}} = 10^{6-(-4)} = 10^{6+4} = 10^{10}$

65. Using the product rule, add the exponents.

$$(y^{-3})(y^5)(y^{-4}) = y^{-3+5+(-4)} = y^{-2} = \dfrac{1}{y^2}$$

SECTION 10.3 (pages 715–716)

19. 0.000007

Move the decimal point to the right of the first nonzero digit. Count the number of places moved.

$$0.0\,0\,0\,0\,0\,7 \qquad \text{Moved 6 places}$$

So the absolute value of the exponent on 10 will be 6. The original number is "small" (between 0 and 1) so the exponent is *negative*.

$$0.000007 = 7 \times 10^{-6}$$

25. 5.677×10^{12}

Since the exponent is positive, make 5.677 larger by moving the decimal point 12 places to the right. We need to write in nine zeros.

$$5.677 \times 10^{12} = 5.677000000000$$
$$= 5,677,000,000,000$$

35. $(5 \times 10^4)(3 \times 10^2)$

$= (5 \times 3)(10^4 \times 10^2)$ Commutative and associative properties.

$= 15 \times 10^{4+2}$

$= 15 \times 10^6$ Product rule for exponents

$= 1.5 \times 10^7$ Scientific notation

$= 15,000,000$ Write without exponents.

45. Write 3,700,000 square miles as 3.7×10^6 square miles

$$\frac{1.347 \times 10^9 \text{ people}}{3.7 \times 10^6 \text{ sq miles}} = \frac{1.347}{3.7} \times \frac{10^9}{10^6}$$

$$\approx 0.364 \times 10^3$$

$$= 0.364 \times 10^{3-1}$$

$$= 3.64 \times 10^2$$
$$\text{(rounded)}$$

$$= 364 \text{ people per square mile}$$

SECTION 10.4 (pages 721–724)

31. $\dfrac{5}{3}x^4 - \dfrac{2}{3}x^4 + \dfrac{1}{3}x^2 - 4$

$= \left(\dfrac{5}{3} - \dfrac{2}{3}\right)x^4 + \dfrac{1}{3}x^2 - 4$

$= \dfrac{3}{3}x^4 + \dfrac{1}{3}x^2 - 4$

$= 1x^4 + \dfrac{1}{3}x^2 - 4$

$= x^4 + \dfrac{1}{3}x^2 - 4$

The resulting polynomial is a *trinomial* (three terms) of degree 4 (because the term x^4 has the greatest sum of exponents).

41. (a) $-4x^5 + x^2$

$= -4(2)^5 + (2)^2$ Replace x with 2.

$= -4(32) + 4$ Apply the exponents.

$= -128 + 4$ Multiply.

$= -124$ Add.

(b) $-4x^5 + x^2$

$= -4(-1)^5 + (-1)^2$ Replace x with -1.

$= -4(-1) + 1$ Apply the exponents; $(-1)^5$ is -1 and $(-1)^2$ is 1.

$= 4 + 1$ Multiply.

$= 5$ Add.

47.
$$3w^3 - 2w^2 + 8w$$
$$\underline{ 2w^2 - 8w + 5}$$
$$3w^3 + 0w^2 + 0w + 5$$

$= 3w^3 + 5$ Change subtraction to addition.

57. $(12m^3 - 8m^2 + 6m + 7) - (5m^2 - 4)$

Change *every* sign in the second polynomial to its opposite.

$= (12m^3 - 8m^2 + 6m + 7)$
$\quad + (-5m^2 + 4)$

$= 12m^3 + (-8m^2 - 5m^2) + 6m$
$\quad + (7 + 4)$ Combine like terms.

$= 12m^3 - 13m^2 + 6m + 11$

SECTION 10.5 (pages 727–728)

13. $-3k^3(2k^3 - 3k^2 - k + 1)$

$= -3k^3(2k^3) + (-3k^3)(-3k^2)$
$\quad + (-3k^3)(-k) + (-3k^3)(1)$
   Distributive property

$= -6k^6 + 9k^5 + 3k^4 - 3k^3$
   Multiply monomials

17. Multiply each term of the second polynomial by each term of the first. Then combine like terms.

$(4r + 1)(2r - 3)$

$= 4r(2r) + 4r(-3) + 1(2r) + 1(-3)$

$= 8r^2 + (-12r) + 2r + (-3)$

$= 8r^2 - 10r - 3$

25. $(-x - 3)(-x - 4)$ Multiply vertically.

$$-x - 3$$
$$\underline{ -x - 4}$$
$$ 4x + 12 \leftarrow -4(-x - 3)$$
$$\underline{x^2 + 3x \leftarrow -x(-x - 3)}$$
$$x^2 + 7x + 12 \leftarrow \text{Add like terms.}$$

Photo Credits

Index

Study Skills

Are you feeling a little uncertain of your ability to learn and remember mathematics? You'll find the help you need on special study skills pages in this book. At the beginning of Chapter 1, read "Your Brain *Can* Learn Mathematics" to find out how your brain learns and remembers best. Then, throughout the rest of Chapters 1–4, watch for special activities to learn brain-friendly ways to use your textbook, take lecture notes, do homework, make study cards, prepare for and take math tests, and much more. It's your ticket to success in mathematics! (See the Table of Contents in the front of the book for study skills titles and locations.)

Formulas

(*See next page for geometry formulas.*)

Percent proportion: $\dfrac{percent}{100} = \dfrac{part}{whole}$

Percent equation: percent • whole = part

Simple interest: Interest = principal • rate • time

Converting from Celsius to Fahrenheit: $F = \dfrac{9C}{5} + 32$

Converting from Fahrenheit to Celsius: $C = \dfrac{5(F - 32)}{9}$

Mean $= \dfrac{\text{sum of all values}}{\text{number of values}}$

Order of Operations

1. Do all operations inside *parentheses* or *other grouping symbols.*
2. Simplify any expressions with *exponents* and find any *square roots.*
3. Do the remaining *multiplications* and *divisions* as they occur from left to right.
4. Do the remaining *additions* and *subtractions* as they occur from left to right.

Example 1

$6^2 - 8 \div 2 + (7 + 3)$ Work inside parentheses.

$6^2 - 8 \div 2 + \quad 10$ Simplify exponents.

$36 - 8 \div 2 + \quad 10$ Divide.

$36 - \quad 4 \quad + \quad 10$ Add and subtract from left to right.

$32 \quad + \quad 10$

42

Example 2

$4 + 10 \div 2\,(6) - 3\,(8 \div 4)$ Work inside parentheses.

$4 + 10 \div 2\,(6) - \quad 3\,(2)$ Multiply and divide from left to right.

$4 + \quad 5\,(6) - \quad 3\,(2)$

$4 + \quad 30 \quad - \quad 3\,(2)$

$4 + \quad 30 \quad - \quad 6$ Add and subtract from left to right.

$34 \quad - \quad 6$

28

A phrase to help you remember the order of operations:

Please	**Excuse**	**My**	**Dear**	**Aunt**	**Sally**
Parentheses;	**E**xponents;	**M**ultiply and **D**ivide;	**A**dd and **S**ubtract		

Fraction-Decimal-Percent Equivalents

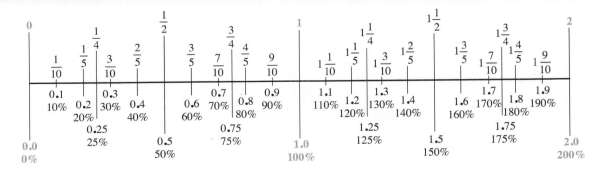

Geometry Formulas

Rectangle

Perimeter: $P = 2l + 2w$

Area: $A = lw$

Square

Perimeter: $P = 4s$

Area: $A = s^2$, which means $s \cdot s$

Parallelogram

Perimeter: Add the lengths of the sides.

Area: $A = bh$

Triangle

Perimeter: Add the lengths of the sides.

Area: $A = \dfrac{1}{2} bh$

or $A = 0.5bh$

Circle

diameter: $d = 2r$

radius: $r = \dfrac{d}{2}$

Circumference: $C = \pi d$

or $C = 2\pi r$

Area: $A = \pi r^2$, which means $\pi \cdot r \cdot r$

Use 3.14 as the approximate value of π.

Right Triangle (one 90° angle)

hypotenuse $= \sqrt{(\text{leg})^2 + (\text{leg})^2}$

leg $= \sqrt{(\text{hypotenuse})^2 - (\text{leg})^2}$

Rectangular Solid

Volume: $V = lwh$

Surface area:
$S = 2lw + 2lh + 2wh$

Right Circular Cylinder

Volume: $V = \pi r^2 h$

Surface area: $S = 2\pi rh + 2\pi r^2$

Use 3.14 as the approximate value of π.

Pyramid

Volume: $V = \dfrac{1}{3}Bh$

or $V = \dfrac{Bh}{3}$

B is area of the base.

Classifying Angles: Four Types of Angles

Acute angles measure less than 90°.

Right angles measure *exactly* 90°.

Obtuse angles measure more than 90° but less than 180°.

Straight angles measure *exactly* 180°.